THE SEARCH FOR THE MODERN WORLD

THE SEARCH FOR THE MODERN WORLD

Edited by

LUDWIG F. SCHAEFER
Carnegie-Mellon University

DANIEL P. RESNICK
Carnegie-Mellon University

GEORGE L. NETTERVILLE, III
Southern University

THE DRYDEN PRESS
Hinsdale, Illinois

Copyright Acknowledgments

**Text Design and Maps
by Plasencia Design
Associates, Inc.**

COVER left to right: Radio Times Hulton Picture Library; *Diderot Pictorial Encyclopedia of Trades and Industry,* Dover Publications, Inc., New York, 1959, vol. II, plate 471; Historical Pictures Service, Chicago; Japan Information Service, Consulate General of Japan; United Nations (India). INSIDE FRONT COVER left to right: first row: French Embassy Press & Information Division; Japan Information Service, Consulate General of Japan; Eastfoto (Czechoslovakia); second row: French Embassy Press and Information Division; Regional Information Service, Kaduna, Northern Nigeria; German Information Center; Eastfoto (Poland); third row: British Tourist Authority; Nigerian Consulate General; British Tourist Authority. INSIDE BACK COVER left to right: first row: FPG/Gordon Alexander (United States); United Nations (Greece); UPI (Nuremberg, West Germany, 1969); second row: Information Bureau, Government of India; UPI (Paris, 1968); French Government Tourist Office; third row: UPI (student poster, Macao); Japan Information Service, Consulate General of Japan; Radio Times Hulton Picture Library (Korea). FRONTISPIECE: UPI. p. 7: The New York Public Library; p. 9: Bulloz; p. 10: Courtesy of the Trustees of the British Museum; p. 14: Metropolitan Museum of Art; p. 20: Musée du Louvre (Alinari); p. 21: Courtesy of the Trustees of the British Museum; p. 23: Herzog Anton Ulrich Museum, Braunschweig; p. 24: The New York Public Library; pp. 38 and 42: Alinari; p. 44: Libreria Piccolomini Duomo, Siena (Alinari); p. 45: Vatican Museum (Alinari); pp. 46 and 49: Alinari; p. 53, left: Staatsbibliothek, Berlin, right: Metropolitan Museum of Art; p. 54: Rare Book Division, The New York Public Library; p. 60: 1. National Gallery of Art, Kress Collection, 2. and 3. Alinari; p. 61: 4. and 5. Alinari; pp. 64 and 65, Alinari; p. 75: Alinari; p. 81: Roland Bainton (American Heritage); p. 87, left: Alte Pinakothek, Munich, right: Metropolitan Museum of Art; p. 88: Culver Pictures; p. 95: Bibliotheque Publique et Universitaire, Geneva; p. 98: The New York Public Library; p. 112: Bibliothèque Nationale; following p. 116 "The Expansion of the West"—first page: Rare Book Division, The New York Public Library. Second page: Rijksmusem, Amsterdam. Third page, left: The Brooklyn Museum, right: (detail) Musée Guimet, Paris. Fourth page: left and center, Rare Book Division, The New York Public Library, right, The New York Public Library. Fifth page: Schoenfeld Collection, Three Lions, Inc., The New York Public Library. Sixth page: Victoria and Albert Museum, London. Crown Copyright. p. 122: Rare Book Division, The New York Public Library; p. 123: The New York Public Library; p. 126: Bibliothèque

Nationale; p. 127: Victoria and Albert Museum; p. 128: The New York Public Library; p. 130: Giraudon; p. 132, top: Ohio State University, bottom: The New York Public Library; p. 149: Prints Division, The New York Public Library; p. 151: Hale Observatories; p. 155: Rare Book Division, The New York Public Library; p. 159: Mauritshuis, The Hague; p. 162: 1. The Bettmann Archive, 2. and 3. Historical Pictures Service, Chicago, 4. UPI; p. 163: 5. Historical Pictures Service, Chicago, 6. The Bettmann Archive, 7. and 8. Culver Pictures; p. 164: 9. Private Collection (Lomeo), 10. Swiss National Tourist Office, 11. The New York Public Library, 12. Courtesy Ludwig Schaefer, 13. Private Collection (Lomeo), 14. British Tourist Authority; following p. 176: "Science and Technology in the Traditional World"—first page: Chart amplified from *A History of Technology,* edited by Singer, Holmyard, Hall, and Williams, vol. 2, 1956, by permission of The Clarendon Press, Oxford. Second page, above left: The New York Public Library, left: The Bettmann Archive, astrolabe: The Metropolitan Museum of Art. Third page, upper right: The New York Public Library, left: The Bettmann Archive, lower right: The Granger Collection. Fourth page, upper right: The New York Public Library, lower right: The Bettmann Archive, left: The Bettmann Archive, lower left: The Bettmann Archive. Fifth page, upper left: The Granger Collection, lower left and right: The Bettmann Archive. Sixth page: Historical Pictures Service, Chicago. p. 201: Radio Times Hulton Picture Library; pp. 225 and 226: Musée du Château de Versailles; p. 231: Culver Pictures; following p. 235 "Majesty of State"—first page, right: Turkish Tourism and Information Office, bottom: Casa de Portugal. Second page, left: Ewing Galloway, right: Tourist Organization of Thailand. Third page, left: Turkish Tourism and Information Office, center: Ewing Galloway, right: Schloss Schönbrunn, Grosse Galerie, lower right: Metropolitan Museum of Art. Fourth page: Metropolitan Museum of Art. Fifth page, left: Giraudon, right: The Bettmann Archive. Sixth page, left: Metropolitan Museum of Art, right: Historical Pictures Service, Chicago. Seventh page, upper left: Swedish Information Service, upper right: The New York Public Library, lower left: Charles Phelps Cushing, lower right: The New York Public Library. Eighth page, upper left: Ewing Galloway, upper right: The New York Public Library, lower left: Swedish Information Service, far right: The New York Public Library. p. 237: The Bettmann Archive; p. 239: Historical Pictures Service, Chicago; p. 240: The Royal Library, Windsor, copyright reserved; p. 246: Trustees of The British Museum; pp. 251 and 252: The Bettmann Archive; p. 265: The

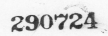

Preface

Three years have elapsed since the publication of our two-volume text, *The Shaping of Western Civilization*. To meet the widely stated demand for a more comprehensive work, we have now prepared a one-volume complement to our original effort. The present study focuses on the process of modernization which began in medieval Europe and today continues to spread over the globe. Substantial new material has been added and chapters from the preceding volumes regrouped in a way that calls forth our new title, *The Search for the Modern World*.

The contours of contemporary history are never certain but recent experience has made imperative a historical explanation of changing relations with Asia and a closer look at the nature and limits of Western influence in the world. Readers will find new topics on China and Japan, a pictorial introduction of India's steps to independence, and six new portfolios on subjects of common concern to East and West.

Our narrative opens with the brash but naive civilization of cities and villages in the late Middle Ages, hesitatingly mercantile in a Christian and traditional world, but soon to sail forth beyond the Mediterranean to explore the cultures of a distant Asia, Africa and the Americas. Our closing chapters represent no terminus to this saga, for they explore the extent to which the values and achievements of Western society have become the common property of developing and developed nations, each with its own separate traditions and cultures. Despite our recognition of forces at work that threaten older forms of European influence outside the West, the world in which we live is one unmistakably shaped by the forces of technology, commerce and nationhood generated in the West.

The editors have attempted to examine the varieties and tensions of man's experience through the eyes of laymen and scholars, contemporary participants and historians who demonstrate the relevance of the past. The result is a set of considered arguments about man's myths, traditions, ideals and achievements. It is our hope that we have brought some critical perspective to these developments and will have helped Westerners to understand better the threat and promise of the modernizing process.

The text is divided into chapters and topics. Each topic includes an introductory narrative, primary sources and interpretive selections. Each topic has been designed as a single assignment—its unifying theme briefly stated in an introduction. Appropriate study questions conclude the topic. Although designed as an integral text, the volume may also serve as a book of readings or provide issues for class discussions. The readings can easily be reordered to meet individual needs.

The initial readings were the product of an experimental course designed, under a grant from the Carnegie Corporation of New York, to develop more effective approaches to the teaching of history. Without this assistance the project would scarcely have been possible. Those who have collaborated with us in a Cooperative Program in History include representatives from Catholic colleges, community colleges, predominantly Black colleges of the South, and other private and state-related institutions. Numerous suggestions from faculty and students of these institutions have enriched this work, in particular those of Pearle Mankins, Benjamin Moskowitz, and James and Virginia Welch.

Mary Zarroli typed much of the original manuscript; Helen Prine performed the innumerable duties connected with providing material for a thousand students scattered from Vermont to Texas; Judith Sichel and Thomas Delare are responsible for many research details. Finally, a pioneering effort of this sort requires creative backing from its publishers. To Enid Klass and Susan Fletcher we are indebted for imaginative photo research; to Milton Mautner and Raymond Gill for conscientious and concerned editing; to Clifford Snyder for his vision and support; and to William Knowles for continuing direction. To them and others we are properly grateful.

Ludwig F. Schaefer
Daniel P. Resnick
George L. Netterville, III

Carnegie-Mellon University
Southern University
January 1973

Contents

Chapter 5 THE EVOLUTION OF NATIONALISM 1789–1918

Chapter 6   ACCELERATION IN HISTORY: THE TWENTIETH CENTURY   595

THE SEARCH FOR THE MODERN WORLD

Chapter 1

The Brink of the Modern World

With the waning of the Middle Ages came the breakdown of traditional Latin Christendom, tied to the soil, locked in European frontiers, united in a common faith, and organized in a single Church. Beyond the specific breakdown of medieval values, however, the period of the thirteenth through sixteenth centuries witnessed a great onslaught upon the structure of traditional society itself.

It was not a period that can be neatly labelled. "Commercial Revolution," "Renaissance," and "Reformation" touch upon its perimeter but do not catch the spirit of the whole. It was a time of bridging between what had been and what was to come, as is true in a sense of all historical time, but, in this case, what had been was the traditional world and what was to come, the modern.

As such, it was an age of marked contradictions. Towns grew up and capitalism developed, but the vast masses of society remained in rural isolation. Vestiges of feudalism contrasted with the efforts of kings to extend royal authority. Popes upheld the universality of the Church, while religious dissidents multiplied. On the one hand there was a marked striving for a renewal of religious values and a return to an earlier sense of community; on the other, materialism and individualism, grown from the affluence of the commercial revival and the subsequent loosening of traditional ties, had ever growing impact.

Capitalism, the growth of national states, the recoupling of links with ancient civilization, the "discovery" of man, and the rise of religious questioning are all hallmarks of these years, as well as that strong urge to exploit the non-Western world for the benefit of European interests, which we call the "Age of Discovery." Western man was thus developing an awareness of how he might move beyond the traditional Christian society but was still restrained by the limitations of the old world-view. He had been brought in his consciousness to the brink of the modern world.

1271–1295	Marco Polo's trip to Orient
1302	Papal bull, *Unam Sanctam*
1304–1374	Petrarch
1305	Avignon becomes seat of Papacy
c. 1328–1384	John Wyclif
1337–1453	Hundred Years' War
1358	Jacquerie (peasant uprising) in France
c. 1369–1415	John Huss
1378	Schism in Church—election of two popes
1378	Ciompi uprising
1381	English Peasants' Revolt
1394–1460	Prince Henry the Navigator
1401–1407	First public banks of deposit (Italy)
1404–1472	Leon Battista Alberti
1414	Council of Constance
1451	Joan of Arc burned
1452–1519	Leonardo da Vinci
1453	Constantinople falls to Ottoman Turks
1455	Gutenberg Bible
1471–1484	Renaissance popes: Sixtus IV
1484–1492	Innocent VIII
1492–1503	Alexander VI
1503–1513	Julius II
1484–1492	Granada retaken by Christians
1487	Dias rounds Cape of Good Hope
1492	Columbus discovers America
1492	Jews expelled from Spain
1494	First French invasion of Italy
1498	Vasco da Gama lands in Calicut
1389–1464	Medici dynasty, Florence: Cosimo
1449–1492	Lorenzo
1452–1498	Girolamo Savonarola
1501	First cargo of African slaves carried to New World
1509	Erasmus, *The Praise of Folly*
1509–1547	Tudor Monarchs: Henry VIII
1547–1553	Edward VI
1553–1558	Mary I
1558–1603	Elizabeth I
1510–1525	Height of Fugger fortune, Augsburg
1513	Machiavelli, *The Prince*
1517	Luther, *95 Theses*
1518	Cortez conquers Aztec Empire
1519–1556	Emperor Charles V

1521	Luther excommunicated: Diet of Worms
1524–1525	Peasants' Rebellion, Germany
1534	Founding of Society of Jesus
1536	Calvin, *Institutes of the Christian Religion*
1542	Inquisition begins
1545–1563	Council of Trent
1553	Michael Servetus burned for heresy, Geneva
1555	Peace of Augsburg
1560	Knox's Articles of the Presbyterian Church
1564	Tridentine Profession of Faith
1564–1616	William Shakespeare

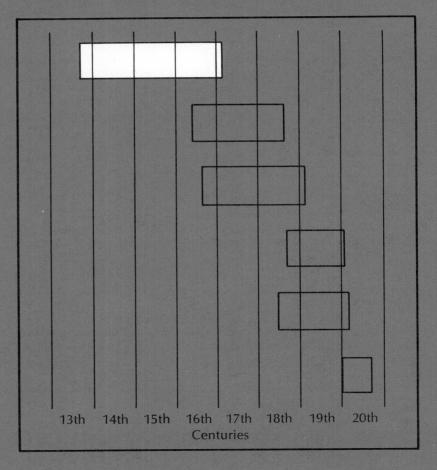

13th 14th 15th 16th 17th 18th 19th 20th
Centuries

TOPIC 1

THE REEMERGENCE OF COMMERCE AND TOWNS

The first great crack in the wall of medieval traditionalism had been the revival of urban living in the eleventh and twelfth centuries. Fortified areas and trading centers multiplied, older Roman cities were revitalized, and many new towns were laid out, challenging the rigid social division of the feudal system. The serfs who fled their servile status and other persons who migrated to the towns expected to be treated as free men and resented existing feudal restraints on their movement and livelihood. That they were still without an acknowledged place in the social order was particularly galling to the growing number of merchants, whose material affluence often exceeded that of nobles dependent on the manorial economy. The readings trace the growth of the merchant class, the development of towns, and the aspirations for self-rule on the part of their inhabitants. The final readings shift to China, where, in the reportage of Marco Polo, a man typical of the traders who restlessly pushed out beyond the bounds of the known world, a glimpse is caught of the attraction to wealth and power that motivated the new class.

Henri Pirenne: The Origins of the Merchant Class

Henri Pirenne (1862–1935), pioneering Belgian medieval historian, emphasized in his writing the historical role of the capitalist class. His theme is apparent in this reading which concerns the emergence of the medieval merchants and their efforts to win status within the feudal order. From *Medieval Cities* by Henri Pirenne (Copyright 1925, 1952 Princeton University Press; Princeton Paperback, 1969). Reprinted by permission of Princeton University Press.

I

In certain countries, trade appears as an original and spontaneous phenomenon. This was the case, for example, at the dawn of history in Greece and Scandinavia. There, navigation was at least as old as agriculture. Everything led men to engage in it: the deep conformation of the coast-lines, the abundance of harbors, and the subtle attraction of those islands and low-lying shores which were visible on the horizon and which made a sea-faring life seem the more tempting because there was so little to be hoped for from a soil as barren as was that of the homeland. The proximity of older and poorly defended civilizations held out, in addition, the lure of rich plunder. Piracy was the initiator of maritime trade among the Greeks of the Homeric era, as among the Norse vikings; for a long time the two vocations developed in concert.

Nothing of the sort, however, was to be found in the Middle Ages. There was no sign of that heroic and barbarian occupation. The Germanic tribes that invaded the Roman provinces in the fifth century were complete strangers to a maritime life. They contented themselves with appropriating the soil, and the shipping of the Mediterranean continued, as in the past, to fill the peaceful role which had fallen to it under the Empire.

The Moslem invasion which caused its ruin and closed the sea provoked no reaction. The situation was taken for granted, and the continent of Europe, deprived of its traditional markets, remained an essentially rural civilization. The sporadic trade which Jews, peddlers and occasional merchants still carried on during the Carolingian era was too feeble and was too effectively discouraged by the invasions of the Norsemen and Saracens to lend support to the belief that it was the precursor of the commercial revival whose first symptoms were visible in the tenth century.

It would seem natural to suppose, at first glance, that a merchant class grew up little by little in the midst of the agricultural masses. Nothing, however, gives credence to that theory. In the social organization of the late Middle Ages, where each family from father to son was bound to the soil, it is hard to see what possibly could have induced men to exchange, for a livelihood made sure by the possession of the soil, the precarious livelihood of the trader. The love of gain and the desire to ameliorate one's condition must have carried, at best, very little weight with a population accustomed to a traditional way of living, having no contact with the outside world, in which no novelty, no curiosity stirred the imagination, and in which the spirit of initiative was probably completely lacking. Though they frequented the small local markets the peasants never made enough money out of them to be inspired with the desire for, or even to be inclined to envisage the possibility of, a manner of life based on trade. Theirs must have seemed to them merely a normal and customary occupation. The idea of selling one's land in order to procure liquid assets certainly did not occur to any of them. The state of society and the general outlook on life was entirely opposed to it. . . .

It was in the course of the tenth century that there reappeared in continental Europe a class of professional merchants whose progress, very slow at first, gathered speed as the following century moved forward. The increase in population, which began to be manifest at the same era, is certainly in direct relation to this phenomenon. It had as a result the detaching from the land an increasingly important number of individuals and committing them to that roving and hazardous existence which, in every agricultural civilization, is the lot of those who no longer find themselves with their roots in the soil. It multiplied the crowd of vagabonds drifting about all through society, living from day to day by alms from the monasteries, hiring themselves out at harvest-time, enlisting in the armies in time of war and holding back from neither rapine nor pillage when occasion presented. It is among this crowd of foot-loose adventurers that the first adepts of trade must, without any doubt, be looked for.

Their manner of life naturally drove them towards all those localities where the affluence of the inhabitants gave them the hope of gain or offered some fortunate opening. If they assiduously took part in pilgrimages, they were certainly no less drawn by the ports, the markets, and the fairs. There they hired themselves out as sailors, as boatmen, as stevedores or porters. Energetic characters, tempered by the experience of a life full of the unexpected, must have abounded among them. Many knew foreign languages and were conversant with the customs and needs of divers lands. Let a lucky chance present itself—and heaven knows that chances are numerous in the life of a vagabond—they were remarkably well equipped to profit thereby. And a small profit, with skill and intelligence, can always be turned into a big profit. This must have been particularly true in an era when the insufficiency of communications and the relative rarity of merchandise offered for sale must have naturally kept prices at a very high level. Famines were multiplied throughout Europe, sometimes in one province and sometimes in another, by that inadequate system of communications, and increased still more the opportunities, for those who knew how to make use of them, of getting rich. A few timely sacks of wheat, transported to the right spot, sufficed for the realizing of huge profits. For a man, adroit and sparing no pains, Fortune then held out the prospect of fruitful operations. . . .

The nobility never had anything but disdain for these upstarts come from no one knew where, and whose insolent good fortune they could not bear. They were infuriated to see them better supplied with money than themselves; they were humiliated by being obliged to have recourse, in time of trouble, to the purse of these newly rich. Save in Italy, where aristocratic families did not hesitate to augment their fortunes by having an interest in commercial operations in the capacity of money-lender, the prejudice that it was degrading to engage in business remained deep-rooted in the heart of the feudal caste up to the time of the French Revolution.

As to the clergy, their attitude in regard to merchants was still more unfavorable. In the eyes of the Church, commercial life was dangerous to the safety of the soul. "The merchant," says a text attributed to St. Jerome, "can please God only with difficulty." Trade seemed to the canonists to be a form of usury. They condemned profit-seeking, which they confounded with avarice. . . . Every form of speculation seemed to them a sin. And this severity was not entirely caused by the strict interpretation of Christian morality. Very likely, it should also be attributed to the conditions under which the Church existed. The subsistence of the Church, in fact, depended exclusively on that [manorial] organization which, as has been seen above, was so foreign to the idea of enterprise and profit. If to this be added the ideal of poverty which Clunisian mysticism gave to religious fervor, it can be readily understood why the Church took a defiant and hostile attitude toward the commercial revival which must, from the very first, have seemed to it a thing of shame and a cause of anxiety.

We must admit, however, that this attitude was not without its benefits. It certainly resulted in preventing the passion for gain from spreading without limit; it protected, in a certain measure, the poor from the rich, debtors from creditors. The scourge of debts, which in Greek and Roman antiquity so sorely afflicted the people, was spared the social order of the Middle Ages, and it may well be that the Church contributed largely to that happy result. The universal prestige it enjoyed served as a moral check-rein. If it was not strong enough to subject the traders to the doctrine of "fair price," it was strong enough to restrain them from giving way entirely to greediness for profits. They were certainly very uneasy over the peril to which their way of living exposed their eternal salvation. The fear of the future life tormented their conscience. Many there were who, on their death beds, founded by their wills charitable institutions or appropriated a part of their wealth to reimburse sums unjustly acquired. . . .

II

The legal status of the merchants eventually gave them a thoroughly singular place in that society which they astonished in so many respects. By virtue of the wandering existence they led, they were everywhere regarded as foreigners. No one knew the origins of these eternal travellers. Certainly the majority among them were born of non-free parents, from whom they had early taken leave in order to launch upon adventures. But serfdom was not to be presumed: it had to be proven. The law necessarily treated as a free man one who could not be ascribed to a master. It therefore came about that it was necessary to treat the merchants, most of whom were without doubt the sons of serfs, as if they had always enjoyed freedom. In detaching themselves from their natal soil they had freed themselves in fact. In the midst of a social organization where the populace was attached to the land and where everyone was dependent upon a liege lord, they presented the strange picture of circulating everywhere without being claimed by anyone. They did not demand freedom; it was conceded to them because no one could prove that they did not already enjoy it. They acquired it, so to speak, by usage and limitation. In short, just as agrarian civilization had made of the peasant a man whose normal state was servitude, trade made of the merchant a man whose normal condition was liberty. From that time on, in place of being subject to seignorial and demesnial jurisdiction, he was answerable only to public jurisdiction. Alone competent to try him were the tribunals which still kept, above the multitude of private courts, the old framework of the judicial constitution of the Frankish State.

Public authority at the same time took him under its protection. The local princes whose task it was to preserve, in their territories, peace and public order—to which pertained the policing of the highways and the safe-guarding of travellers—extended their tutelage over the merchants. In doing so they did nothing more than to continue the tradition of the State, the powers of which they had usurped. In that agricultural empire of his, Charlemagne himself had given careful attention to the maintenance of the freedom of circulation. He had issued edicts in favor of pilgrims and traders, Jew or Christian, and the capitularies of his successors attest to the fact that they remained faithful to that policy. The emperors of the House of Saxony followed suit in Germany, and the kings of France, after they came into power, did likewise. The princes had, furthermore, every interest in attracting numerous merchants to their countries, whither they brought a new animation and where they augmented bountifully the revenues from the market-tolls. The counts early took active measures against highwaymen, watching over the good conduct of the fairs and the security of the routes of communication. In the eleventh century great progress had been made and the chroniclers state that there were regions where one could travel with a sack full of gold without running the risk of being despoiled. On its part, the Church punished highwaymen with excommunication, and the Truces of God, in which it took the initiative in the tenth century, protected the merchants in particular.

But it was not enough that merchants be placed under the safeguard and the jurisdiction of the public authority. The novelty of their profession had further consequences. It forced a law, made for a civilization based on agriculture, to become more flexible and to adapt itself to the fundamental needs which this novelty imposed upon it. Judicial procedure, with its rigid and traditional formalism, with its delays, with its methods of proof as primitive as the duel, with its abuse of the absolutory oath, with its "ordeals" which left to chance the outcome of a trial, was for the merchants a perpetual nuisance. They needed a simpler legal system, more expeditious and more equitable. At the fairs and markets they elaborated among themselves a commercial code (*jus mercatorum*) of which the oldest traces may be noted by the beginning of the eleventh century. Most probably it was introduced very early into the legal practice, at least for suits between merchants. It must have constituted for them a sort of personal law, the benefits of which the judges had no motive for refusing them. The contemporary texts which make allusion to it unfortunately do not make clear its terms. There is, however, no doubt but that it was a collection of usages born of business experience and which spread from place to place commensurately with the spread of trade itself. The great fairs whither came, periodically, merchants from divers countries and which had a special tribunal charged with the rendering of speedy justice, must have seen from the very first the elaboration of a sort of commercial jurisprudence, the same everywhere despite the differences in country, language, and national laws.

The merchant thus seems to have been not only a free man but a privileged man to boot. Like the cleric and the noble, he enjoyed a law of exception. Like them, he escaped the demesnial and seignorial authority which continued to bear down upon the peasants.

The Rise of Towns

From *Economic History of Europe,* 3d ed., by S. B. Clough & C. W. Cole. Copyright ©, 1952, by D. C. Heath & Co., a Division of Raytheon Education Co., Boston, Mass.

It was indeed in the Italian towns that the commerce of medieval western Europe came to life, and it was a commerce born of, based on, and carried on by towns. In every country the rise of towns and cities was one of the most important phenomena of the middle ages. It can be explained only by the fact that the rebirth of commerce, local and distant, necessitated the creation of trade centers and gave them the opportunity to engage in industrial production for a market which slowly grew larger and larger.

In Italy many of the Roman towns never disappeared, and it required only the stimulus of the increasing trade to reawaken them into vigorous life. Rome, Naples, Ravenna, Florence, Milan, Verona, Lucca, Pisa, Genoa, among others, enjoyed some sort of continuous existence from Roman times on into the middle ages. Venice, probably no more than a fishing village in Roman days, was gradually peopled after the fifth century by refugees who fled from the mainland during the invasions. In other lands, too, Roman cities, towns, villages, and camps, and even the early non-Roman towns of the Germans, were inhabited continuously, and were ready to grow and flourish when opportunity offered.

THE BURG

Outside of Italy many towns owed their origin not to Roman survivals but to medieval conditions. During the troublous times of local wars and invasion by Saracens or Norsemen, some kind of fortified retreat was almost essential for a locality. A stockade with a moat around it and a fortified tower inside was a crude but effective safeguard against marauding bands. Such a place was most often called a *burgus,* and in one form or another the word has survived in many modern town names (Edinburgh, Hamburg, Peterborough, Luxembourg, Bourg-en-Bresse, etc.). Often such a burg would be the home of a bishop or a count or a prince. Gradually from his needs, his tax collections, trade sprang up and the burg might become a market center to which the neighborhood sent its surplus produce. Indeed, the needs of trade and the needs of defense were the twin origins of many towns. A town might grow up under the wing of a castle or a monastery that offered some protection, but it might also rise at the crossing of two roads or trade routes, at the head of navigation on a stream, at the junction of two rivers, or on a good harbor. There were thousands of burgs or villages clustered beside strongholds. Those that grew to be important usually had some advantage of site or general location. . . .

The process by which a burg, castle, monastery, shrine, or church grew into a town was varied. Often the presence of a lord or church-

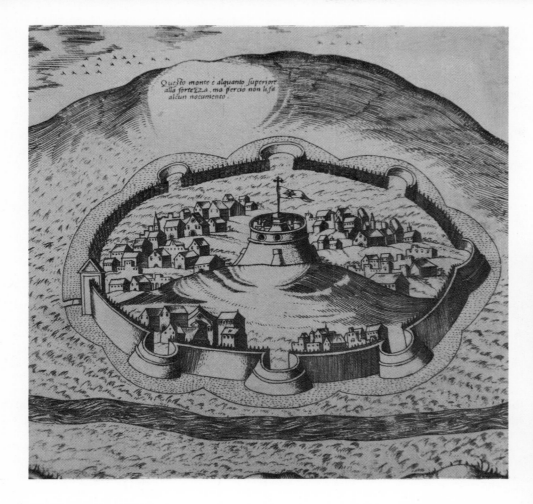

The fortified town of Agria in Hungary (1368) provides a good example of a medieval burg. Moat and wall surround a central tower on a hill about which the houses cluster.

Medieval streets are still found in the old quarters of European cities today.

men encouraged the creation of a small but regular market, or perhaps merely stimulated a little local market which had had some sort of existence for centuries. Slowly traders gathered and built their huts in the shadow of the wall while the lord smiled on them, for from them he collected tolls and dues. The presence of traders, even though some of them might be peddlers who returned only from time to time, attracted other residents—people to supply them with food and clothing, drink and lodging. . . .

Because most medieval towns were within walls—first of palisades and earthwork, later of stone—they were crowded, huddled together as if they remembered, in fear, the times of invasion and war. The streets were narrow, often only six or eight feet wide. To gain more floor space, the upper stories of the houses projected over the street until they nearly met in the middle. Pigs ran in the streets and were the chief means of garbage disposal. There were no street lights. There were only open sewers (if any) awaiting the next rainfall for a flushing. Cows and horses were stabled in sheds built into or on to the houses. Stores opened directly on the streets, each with a wooden window of which half was raised to make a canopy, and half was lowered to make a counter. The population was often as dense as in a modern city with much taller buildings. The medieval town was a hustling, lusty, dirty, crowded place. Some chroniclers report that such a town could be smelled from more than a mile away.

From a modern point of view, medieval towns and cities were never very large in population. In the fourteenth century it is likely that only Paris, Palermo, Venice, and Florence had as many as 100,000 inhabitants. A few more, such as London and Milan, had about 50,000. But a town of 20,000 was considered good-sized, and many important centers were much smaller.

Despite its walls, the medieval town was not cut off so distinctly from the surrounding countryside as is a twentieth century city. As a town grew, peasants from round about moved in for protection and for social life, but continued to cultivate their fields. Towns that grew out of villages retained their old common fields and pastures, and some of the townsmen would fare forth each day to work in them. Villagers from neighboring manors brought their produce into the town once a week to sell in the market, and stayed a while to gossip, drink a cup of wine, or buy some needed article. It is easy to forget this rural side of town life, but it was important. Cambridge was still girt about by common fields in the seventeenth century. At Norwich, in the sixteenth century, the weavers had to stop work each year to help with the harvest. Even in London the Husting Court was suspended in harvest time. One of the chief thoroughfares in Ghent is still called Field Street.

Yet in the feudal countryside the slowly growing towns were in some ways alien. In the earlier stages, the feudal lords tended to treat them like overgrown manors. They taxed them, subjected them to the feudal courts, and preserved the banalities, endeavoring on the one hand to fit them into the existing order of things, and on the other to get as much revenue from them as possible. Indeed, a town was so profitable to its lord that many a noble and churchman encouraged the founding of new towns (villes neuves, etc.) on his lands. In the course of time, however, as the towns grew in size and strength the feudal bonds irked them more and more. Gradually they shook themselves loose from the more burdensome forms of control. In some areas, especially in England and France, towns developing on royal lands gained considerable freedom early, for the kings saw in these rising centers a power which could be set against the overweening authority of the great nobles; but for most towns the acquisition of freedom was the fruit of a long, hard struggle.

From early days, most of the merchants were freemen; even if serfs by birth, since they traveled far from home, they were not likely to be recaptured by their lords. But the artisans, laborers, and other workers who came in from the neighborhood were usually serfs still within reach of their lords. Furthermore, the children of a free merchant and a serf wife were apt to be considered serfs. What the towns wanted was, first, personal freedom for the inhabitants, second, their own court which would enforce town, merchant law, not feudal land law; and third, exemption from the feudal dues, taxes, and restrictions. In the eleventh century the towns began to be strong enough to gain their demands, though the merchants of Venice won power even earlier (976). The Italian cities led the way. Milan revolted against its lord, the archbishop, in 1057 and eventually secured the right to have its own magistrates, who were called consuls. Lucca had a city court by 1068. Before many years Cremona, Bologna, Florence, Genoa, Pavia, and other towns had gained some degree of self-government.

From Italy the movement spread northward. Marseilles had consuls by 1128, as did Nimes and Arles shortly after. In Flanders the movement was almost contemporaneous with that in Italy. Cambrai revolted against its bishop in 1077 and formed a *commune* or municipal government, and before the middle of the twelfth century other cities of the Low Countries and northern France had followed suit. Many towns, especially in England, bought their way to freedom. For the varied feudal dues they were able to substitute a single payment (*firma burgi*) which they raised themselves by municipal taxes, thus excluding the tax agents of the lord. Many a noble anxious to raise money for a crusade sold municipal rights or privileges to a town on his land for a lump sum and annual payments thereafter. In other instances, from Italy to Germany, the winning of town freedom was the result of a long and often bloody struggle between the commune desirous of the new freedom and the lord anxious to maintain his old rights. By the thirteenth century many towns had won from their overlords charters granting them the right to have their own institutions, and it was generally conceded that the town air made men free. A serf who stayed in a town for a year and a day without being reclaimed by his lord was considered a freeman. The towns were largely self-governing even though they might give dues or allegiance to king or noble; and the burgher owed his first loyalty, his patriotism, to his town. It was his home, his country. The townsman was free. He was to a large degree outside the feudal system. He belonged to a new and growing class—the middle class, the burghers, the *bourgeoisie,* which was to increase in importance until at last it overthrew the old feudal system. . . .

To protect their interests and preserve their local monopoly the merchants and tradesmen of a town from the early days joined together in an organization usually called a gild merchant or merchant gild. This gild was often older than the town charter. In fact, it was frequently the merchant gild which waged the fight or raised the funds that secured a charter from the overlord. The gild did not include all townsmen but was composed rather of the merchants and tradesmen to the exclusion of nobles, serfs, ecclesiastics, and ordinary workmen. In Saint-Omer there was a merchant gild by 1050, with a head to enforce discipline, with regular meetings for eating, drinking, and deliberation, with funds for community purposes and the assistance of sick members, and with a gildhall in which to meet. Other towns of Flanders probably had similar organizations, and during the next century and a half merchant gilds were organized in most of the important towns of France, Flanders, England, and Germany.

Because a gild merchant included all the important businessmen of a town, it was able to maintain a real monopoly which it relaxed only on the occasions of markets and fairs. Ordinarily only a gildsman could buy, sell, or manufacture goods in a town. An outsider could do business only with gildsmen. Certain goods could be exported only by gild members. A foreigner passing through might be forced to sell his wares to gildsmen. The merchant gilds negotiated with the overlord on behalf of the town. They dominated the town government. In England, for example, the municipal government and the merchant gild became so interlocked that it was sometimes

Gildsmen in their shops in a late fourteenth-century town scene. From left to right are tailors, furriers, a barber, and a druggist.

One of the primary functions of the gild was to maintain standards. Here a regal figure, symbolic of the spirit of the gild, oversees the work of a stone-mason chiseling a capital for a column, perhaps intended for a church, and of a carpenter drilling with an auger.

clined in importance after the thirteenth century, the merchant gild functioned as the organization that took care of all the interests of the businessmen of the town.

Helmar Krueger: Impact of the Crusades on Commerce

Helmar Krueger (1904–   ), specialist in medieval economic history, here points out the role played by Italian townsmen and merchants in exploiting the commercial possibilities of a Mediterranean reopened in the wake of the Crusades. From Helmar C. Krueger, "Economic Aspects of Expanding Europe" in *Twelfth-Century Europe and the Foundations of Modern Society*, ed. Marshall Clagett, Gaines Post, and Robert Reynolds (Madison, Wis.: University of Wisconsin Press, 1961), pp. 71–73.

To the Italian merchants the Crusades always appeared to be extraordinary economic opportunities. From the very start the Italians gained financial rewards. Their ships carried the crusaders and their equipment, even their horses, to the Holy Land, and then supplied

impossible to distinguish between them. The merchant gild carried on negotiations and made treaties with towns near-by and in distant countries, often getting special and important privileges. If a member got into trouble on his travels, the gild paid his fine, or bargained for his release, or paid his debts. If a town treated visiting merchants unfairly, their home gilds retaliated by seizing merchants or goods from the offending place. The gild had a chapel in the local church and took part in religious ceremonies. It provided impressive funerals for its deceased members and took care of their widows. It supervised the regulations for markets, business, weights, measures, and quality. In short, until it de-the Crusaders with food, drink, and, on occasion, with timber, manpower, and siege machinery. Genoa and Pisa commandeered all possible ships in their domains for transport purposes and ordered the construction of more and larger vessels. The transport services were a source of immediate income for the communes, merchants, and shipowners. . . .

In at least a dozen coastal towns of the Levant the Italians possessed throughout most of the twelfth century residential and commercial quarters, from which they gained an income from rentals, leases, harbor dues, and court fines. In these centers the Italian merchants carried on their trade with the European colonists and feudal residents, with Arab traders, and with their associates and agents who worked in the area. The Italian quarters of the Levant became the centers of exchange for Oriental and European goods and markets for the western imports that increased as the century wore on. The Oriental trade was highly profitable and another source of capital in the new money economy of the period. The Crusades were the strongest influence on the development of medieval trade and industry.

Something needs to be said about the Crusades and the general structure of medieval business and capitalism. First of all, the Crusades created a situation in which capital appeared and circulated. Feudal, clerical, and royal participants mortgaged and sold their holdings to obtain money to buy equipment, hire soldiers, and pay for passage. In some instances they melted down their plate and jewelry. . . . Guibert de Nogent wrote: "As everyone hastened to take the road of God, each hurried to change into money everything that was not of use for the journey, and the price was fixed not by the seller, but by the buyer." Generally, as already indicated, this capital went to the Italian merchants and shippers for transportation or other services connected with the venture. Eventually, numerous other people received jobs and wages, including armorers, shipbuilders, ropemakers, and vintners. Obviously, much of the capital paid to the Italians covered the cost of materials and labor, but a considerable part was profit and gain. In turn, much of the profit was reinvested in the Levantine trade, which also was extremely lucrative. The Crusades had promoted the capitalistic cycle of capital, investment, profit, and reinvestment of profit for further profit and capital. The Crusades, cities, and commerce initiated a money economy which threatened and certainly modified the older land economy of western Europe.

Another capitalistic instrument given impetus by the Crusades was credit. Credit, after all, was based on the expectancy of income and profit by the borrower. Many participants in the Crusades bought their equipment or obtained loans on credit, expecting to profit from the material rewards which Urban had promised. In the Holy Land many again resorted to loans from the Templars and Hospitallers, hoping to repay from their ventures in the Near East or from their properties in western Europe. The rulers of course, could expect to pay their loans from tax receipts or new crusade aids. . . .

Similarly, the Crusades gave to commerce an international aspect. They again opened up the entire Mediterranean Sea to Christian ships and trade and provided an entry into the trade with the Near and Far East. The crusaders' acquaintance with Arab and Moslem customs created a demand for Oriental goods in Christian Europe, so that dyes, spices, pearls, and alum became regular western imports from the Italian quarters in the East. Henry of Champagne acknowledged some gifts of Saladin with: "You know that your robes and turbans are far from being held in scorn among us. I will certainly wear your gifts." At the same time the growing industries of the West gave the Italian merchants the chance to carry western goods, especially cloths, eastward to exchange them for the Levantine goods, and the continued residence of westerners in the East created a demand for those western wares. . . .

List of Rules for the Spurriers' Gild (1345)

This list of rules for the London craftsmen who made spurs for horsemen is typical of medieval gild regulations. From James H. Robinson, *Readings in European History* (Boston, 1904), Vol. I, pp. 409–411.

Be it remembered, that on Tuesday, the morrow of St. Peter's bonds, in the nineteenth year of the reign of King Edward III, the articles underwritten were read before John Hammond, mayor, Roger de Depham, recorder, and the other aldermen; and seeing that the same were deemed befitting, they were accepted and enrolled in these words.

In the first place, that no one of the trade of spurriers shall work longer than from the beginning of the day until curfew rings out at the church of St. Sepulcher, without Newgate; by reason that no man can work so neatly by night as by day. And many persons of the said trade, who compass how to practice deception in their work, desire to work by night rather than by day; and then they introduce false iron, and iron that has been cracked, for tin, and also they put gilt on false copper, and cracked.

And further, many of the said trade are wandering about all day, without working at all at their trade; and then, when they have become drunk and frantic, they take to their work, to the annoyance of the sick, and all their neighborhood as well, by reason of the broils that arise between them and the strange folk who are dwelling among them. And then they blow up their fires so vigorously, that their forges begin all at once to blaze, to the great peril of themselves and of all the neighborhood around. And then, too, all the neighbors are much in dread of the sparks, which so vigorously issue forth in all directions from the mouths of the chimneys in their forges.

By reason thereof it seems unto them that working by night should be put an end to, in order to avoid such false work and such perils; and therefore the mayor and the aldermen do will, by the assent of the good folk of the said trade and for the common profit, that from henceforth such time for working, and such false work made in the trade, shall be forbidden. And if any person shall be found in the said trade to do the contrary hereof, let him be amerced [fined], the first time in forty pence, one half to go to the use of the Chamber of the Guildhall of London, and the other half to the use of the said trade; the second time, in half a mark; and the third time, in ten shillings, to the use of the same Chamber and trade; and the fourth time, let him forswear the trade forever.

Also that no one of the said trade shall hang his spurs out on Sundays, or on any other days that are double feasts; but only a sign indicating his business; and such spurs as they shall so sell, they are to show and sell within their shops, without exposing them without or opening the doors or windows of their shops, on the pain aforesaid.

Also, that no one of the said trade shall keep a house or shop to carry on his business, unless he is free of the city; and that no one shall cause to be sold, or exposed for sale, any manner of old spurs for new ones, or shall garnish them or change them for new ones.

Also, that no one of the said trade shall take an apprentice for a less term than seven years, and such apprentice shall be enrolled according to the usages of the said city. . . .

Also, that no alien of another country, or foreigner of this country, shall follow or use the said trade, unless he is enfranchised before the mayor, aldermen, and chamberlain; and that, by witness and surety of the good folk of the said trade, who will go surety for him, as to his loyalty and his good behavior.

Also, that no one of the said trade shall work on Saturdays, after *nones* has been rung out in the city; and not from that hour until the Monday morning following.

Merchants Riot in Cologne (1074)

The rebellion described in this reading is an example of the reaction to the pretensions of the lords that usually led to the gaining of self-government for the cities. Such rebellions frequently began with merchant discontent. Cologne was one of the three major episcopal cities in Germany and an important Rhine shipping center. The reference to Worms at the end of the reading concerns a similar uprising in a neighboring episcopal city. From the *Annals of Lambert of Hersfeld,* V, pp. 211 ff. in Oliver Thatcher & E. H. McNeal, *A Source Book for Medieval History* (New York, 1905), pp. 585–586.

The archbishop spent Easter in Cologne with his friend, the bishop of Münster, whom he had invited to celebrate this festival with him. When the bishop was ready to go home, the archbishop ordered his servants to get a suitable boat ready for him. They looked all about, and finally found a good boat which belonged to a rich merchant of the city, and demanded it for the archbishop's use. They ordered it to be got ready at once and threw out all the merchandise with which it was loaded. The merchant's servants, who had charge of the boat, resisted, but the archbishop's men threatened them with violence unless they immediately obeyed. The merchant's servants hastily ran to their lord and told him what had happened to the boat, and asked him what they should do. The merchant had a son who was both bold and strong. He was related to the great families of the city, and, because of his character, very popular. He hastily collected his servants and as many of the young men of the city as he could, rushed to the boat, ordered the servants of the archbishop to get out of it, and violently ejected them from it. The advocate of the city was called in, but his arrival only increased the tumult, and the merchant's son drove him off and put him to flight. The friends of both parties seized their arms and came to their aid, and it looked as if there were going to be a great battle fought in the city. The news of the struggle was carried to the archbishop, who immediately sent men to quell the riot, and being very angry, he threatened the rebellious young men with dire punishment in the next session of court. Now the archbishop was endowed with all virtues, and his uprightness in all matters, both of the state and of the church, had often been proved. But he had one vice. When he became angry, he could not control his tongue, but overwhelmed everybody, without distinction, with bitter upbraidings and violent vituperation. When his anger had passed, he regretted his fault and reproached himself for it. The riot in the city was finally quieted a little, but the young man, who was very angry as well as elated over his first success, kept on making all the disturbance he could. He went about the city making speeches to the people about the harsh government of the archbishop, and accused him of laying unjust burdens on the people, of depriving innocent persons of their property, and of insulting honorable citizens with his violent and offensive words. . . . It was not difficult for him to raise a mob. . . . Besides, they all regarded it as a great and glorious deed on the part of the people of Worms that they had driven out their bishop because he was governing them too rigidly. And since they were more numerous and wealthy than the people of Worms, and had arms, they disliked to have it thought that they were not equal to the people of Worms in courage, and it seemed to them a disgrace to submit like women to the rule of the archbishop, who was governing them in a tyrannical manner. . . .

Marco Polo Tells Tales of Cathay

Marco Polo (1254–1324) was born in Venice and in 1271 accompanied his merchant father and uncle to the vast Asian empire of the Mongol conqueror Kublai Khan. There the Polos stayed for twenty-four years and rose high in the esteem of the emperor whom they served on various public missions that carried them across China. Finally they returned in 1295 to Venice (after traveling for three years), where they amazed their skeptical friends and relatives with sumptuous silks and precious stones carried back with them to Europe. Even more amazing were the fanciful tales of fabulous Cathay (as China then was called) which Marco Polo told. When a few years later he was captured in a naval battle between Venice and Genoa and imprisoned for several months, he utilized the opportunity to write down his adventures, excerpts from which form this reading. The account of the riches to be had in far-away places served as a spur to generations of adventurers and businessmen who dreamed of excitement and easy wealth. For did not Polo himself on his deathbed, when begged to retract some of his more extreme descriptions, sigh, "I have not told half of what I saw." From *The Book of Ser Marco Polo the Venetian concerning the Kingdoms and Marvels of the East,* trans. and ed. Henry Yule (London, 1875).

I

You must know that for three months of the year, to wit December, January, and February, the Great Khan resides in the capital city of Cathay, which is called Cambaluc and which is at the north-eastern extremity of the country. In that city stands his great palace, and now I will tell you what it is like. . . .

The hall of the palace is so large that it could easily dine 6000 people; and it is quite a marvel to see how many rooms there are besides. The building is altogether so vast, so rich, and so beautiful, that no man on earth could design anything superior to it. The outside of the roof also is all coloured with vermilion and yellow and green and blue and other hues, which are fixed with a varnish so fine and exquisite that they shine like crystal, and lend a resplendent lustre to the palace as seen for a great way round. This roof is made, too, with such strength and solidity that it is fit to last for ever.

On the interior side of the palace are large buildings with halls and chambers, where the Emperor's private property is placed, such as his treasures of gold, silver, gems, pearls, and gold plate, and in which reside the ladies and concubines. There he occupies himself at his own convenience, and no one else has access. . . .

You must know that the City of Cambaluc hath such a multitude of houses, and such a vast population inside the walls and outside, that it seems quite past all possibility. There is a suburb outside each of the gates, which are twelve in number; and these suburbs are so great that they contain more people than the city itself, for the suburb of one gate spreads in width till it meets the suburb of the next, whilst they extend in length some three or four miles. In those suburbs lodge the foreign merchants and travellers, of whom there are always great numbers who have come to bring presents to the Emperor, or to sell articles at Court, or because the city affords so good a mart to attract traders. There

are in each of the suburbs, to a distance of a mile from the city, numerous fine hostelries for the lodgment of merchants from different parts of the world, and a special hostelry is assigned to each description of people, as if we should say there is one for the Lombards, another for the Germans, and a third for the Frenchmen. And thus there are as many good houses outside of the city as inside, without

The wealth and magnificence of China during the Western Middle Ages can be seen in these two works of art. The thirteenth-century ink drawing depicts the imperial palace at Loyang. The procession of courtiers at a New Year's reception was painted in the eleventh century.

counting those that belong to the great lords and barons, which are very numerous.

You must know that it is forbidden to bury any dead body inside the city. If the body be that of an Idolater it is carried out beyond the city and suburbs to a remote place assigned for the purpose, to be burnt. And if it be of one belonging to a religion the custom of which is to bury, such as the Christian, the Saracen, or what not, it is also carried out beyond the suburbs to a distant place assigned for the purpose. And thus the city is preserved in a better and more healthy state.

Moreover, no public woman resides inside the city, but all such abide outside in the suburbs. And 'tis wonderful what a vast number of these there are for the foreigners; it is a certain fact that there are more than twenty thousand of them living by prostitution. And that so many can live in this way will show you how vast is the population.

Guards patrol the city every night in parties of thirty or forty, looking out for any persons who may be abroad at unseasonable hours, i.e. after the great bell hath stricken thrice. If they find any such person he is immediately taken to prison, and examined next morning by the proper officers. If these find him guilty of any misdemeanour they order him a proportionate beating with the stick. Under this punishment people sometimes die; but they adopt it in order to eschew bloodshed; for their Bacsis say that it is an evil thing to shed man's blood.

To this city also are brought articles of greater cost and rarity and in greater abundance of all kinds than to any other city in the world. For people of every description and from every region bring things (including all the costly wares of India, as well as the fine and precious goods of Cathay itself with its provinces), some for the sovereign, some for the court, some for the city which is so great, some for the crowds of barons and knights, some for the great hosts of the Emperor which are quartered round about; and thus between court and city the quantity brought in is endless.

As a sample, I tell you, no day in the year passes that there do not enter the city a thousand cart-loads of silk alone, from which are made quantities of cloth of silk and gold, and of other goods. And this is not to be wondered at; for in all the countries round about there is no flax, so that everything has to be made of silk. It is true, indeed, that in some parts of the country there is cotton and hemp, but not sufficient for their wants. This, however, is not of much consequence, because silk is so abundant and cheap, and is a more valuable substance than either flax or cotton.

Round about this great city of Cambaluc there are some two hundred other cities at various distances, from which traders come to sell their goods and buy others for their lords; and all find means to make their sales and purchases, so that the traffic of the city is passing great. . . .

II

All merchants arriving from India or other countries, and bringing with them gold or silver or gems and pearls, are prohibited from selling to anyone but the Emperor. He has twelve experts chosen for this business, men of shrewdness and experience in such affairs; these appraise the articles, and the Emperor then pays a liberal price for them in those pieces of paper. The merchants accept his price readily, for in the first place they would not get so good an one from anybody else, and secondly they are paid without any delay. And with this paper-money they can buy what they like anywhere over the Empire, whilst it is also vastly lighter to carry about on their journeys. And it is a truth that the merchants will several times in the year bring wares to the amount of 400,000 bezants, and the Grand Sire pays for all in that paper. So he buys such a quantity of those precious things every year that his treasure is endless, whilst all the time the money he pays away costs him nothing at all. Moreover several times in the year proclamation is made through the city that any one who may have gold or silver or gems or pearls, by taking them to the Mint shall get a handsome price for them. And the owners are glad to do this, because they would find no other purchaser to give so large a price. Thus the quantity they bring in is marvellous, though those who do not choose to do so may let it alone. Still, in this way, nearly all the valuables in the country come into the Khan's possession.

When any of those pieces of paper are spoilt—not that they are so very flimsy neither—the owner carries them to the Mint, and by paying three per cent on the value he gets new pieces in exchange. And if any baron, or any one else soever, hath need of gold or silver or gems or pearls in order to make plate or girdles or the like, he goes to the Mint and buys as much as he list, paying in this paper-money. . . .

It is a fact that all over the country of Cathay there is a kind of black stones existing in beds in the mountains, which they dig out and burn like firewood. If you supply the fire with them at night, and see that they are well kindled, you will find them still alight in the morning; and they make such capital fuel that no other is used throughout the country. It is true that they have plenty of wood also, but they do not burn it, because those stones burn better and cost less.

Moreover with that vast number of people, and the number of hot-baths that they maintain—for every one has such a bath at least three times a week, and in winter if possible every day, whilst every nobleman and man of wealth has a private bath for his own use—the wood would not suffice for the purpose.

You must know that when the Emperor sees that corn is cheap and abundant, he buys up large quantities, and has it stored in all his provinces in great granaries, where it is so well looked after that it will keep for three or four years.

And this applies, let me tell you, to all kinds of corn, whether wheat, barley, millet, rice, panic, or what not, and when there is any scarcity of a particular kind of corn he causes that to be issued. And if the price of the corn is at one bezant the measure, he lets them have it at a bezant for four measures, or at whatever price will produce general cheapness; and every one can have food in this way. And by this providence of the Emperor's, his people can never suffer from dearth. He does the same over his whole Empire; causing these supplies to be stored everywhere according to calculation of the wants and necessities of the people.

Nathaniel Peffer: The West Reestablishes Contact with the East

Professor Peffer holds that history is a study in comparative culture of the relationship between one form of life and another. Here he describes the sparse and intermittent interrelations between the Western world and the Far East to the end of the Middle Ages, a time when Chinese civilization was vastly superior to that in the West. From Nathaniel Peffer, *The Far East: A Modern History* (Ann Arbor, Mich.: The University of Michigan Press, 1958), pp. 42–44.

Eastern Asia and Europe were first joined, literally, by a silken thread. It used to be written with poetic flourish that the togas of the Caesars were woven with silk spun from worms that fed on the mulberry trees of China. This is true as well as poetic. Both by caravan, on the land route from the China coast across Central Asia to Eastern Europe—called the Silk Road to this day—and by ship, along the coast of Asia through the South China Sea, Indian Ocean, Persian Gulf, Red Sea, and Mediterranean, Chinese silk was borne to Rome. The lure of the luxuries and riches of the East, it will be seen, began to exercise its pull early in European history. Its attraction has grown with the centuries.

There was trade, too, with the Arabs very early, a colony of Arab traders having settled in Canton in the fourth century. Also the first Christians began to arrive as early as the seventh century, when the Nestorians made their way from Persia. They were hospitably received and for at least two hundred years well treated. Likewise small companies of Jews arrived, though exactly when is not certain. They, too, were well treated and have been entirely absorbed by the Chinese, now being indistinguishable from Chinese although until after the beginning of the present century they were conscious of themselves as a different people and the last synagogue was still standing in Kaifeng, in Central China. It is interesting to observe, in parenthesis, that the Chinese are the only people to have fully absorbed the Jews. They are also the only people to have treated them without discrimination. There may or may not be a cause and effect relation here. It may be that the physical and cultural vitality of the Chinese gives them greater assimilative power than other peoples or it may be that the Jews were willing to assimilate when well treated. In any case the fact is worth noting.

Beyond this, however, there was little intercourse between East and West until the Middle Ages. About the thirteenth century Europe began to take a more active interest in the East, perhaps as a by-product of the Crusades. A number of travelers, emissaries either of the Church or of European monarchies, attempted the perilous journey across Asia, not all of them getting as far as China. But they learned enough about the mighty Asian empire to whet Europe's interest. So in the same way did another historic travel exploit, though one of another order and not exactly representing East-West intercourse. This was the prodigious sweep of the Mongol hordes across the Eurasian continent from the shores of the Pacific to the Hungarian plains, first under Genghis Khan and then under his grandson Kublai Khan, who brought China under his sway in the thirteenth century and established the Yuan dynasty, destined to last a hundred years. By making a kind of bridge between East and West, though a bridge of corpses and ruins, the Mongols added to Europe's awareness of the East, especially China.

In the thirteenth century also came the most famous visitation of all, that which was really to open Europe's eyes to China and help to generate the eagerness and curiosity that produced the great explorers who opened the unknown world. This was the legendary journey of Marco Polo, who came to China, traveled all over the country, and became an official under Kublai Khan. After a second journey to China he went back to Europe and wrote his famous book reporting on his experiences—probably the most remarkable travel book in history. Marco Polo made an immeasurable and lasting impression on the Western world in his time and after. His book is a glowing account of wonders to behold. He came, it must be remembered, from Venice when Venice was at its height and exemplified what was best in European culture at the time. And coming from Venice he was astounded by the marvels that he found in China—cities of unparalleled magnificence, impressive public works, law and order, efficient government, lavish wealth, luxury, an atmosphere of culture and refinement, elegance in houses and private grounds, in costume and manners. He might well have been. Compared with Hangchow, Soochow, and Canton, the cities of Europe were provincial, if not backward. The Europeans were somewhat incredulous but also dazzled and, still more, tempted.

It is in the light of this attitude of Europe that one must try to understand China's state of mind and actions later. The comparison was one of which the Chinese, too, became conscious, and if later they were to manifest airs of superiority to the West, manifest them openly and even with contempt, it was not only out of conceit and arrogance. There was arrogance no doubt, but it also had some basis. When East and West first came together, the East really was superior in all the things by which excellence is measured—culture, wealth, refinement, efficiency, public order, good government, technological grasp. Unfortunately the Chinese assumed that the world was static and immutable and were so indurated in certitude and complacency that 500 years later they could not perceive that the balance had shifted, and they still bore themselves to the white man as if Europe were still the Europe of the thirteenth century. . . .

STUDY QUESTIONS

1. How, according to Pirenne, did the merchant class develop in the Middle Ages? Why didn't it fit into the feudal social order?

2. How did towns develop? What were they like? Why were townsmen so uncomfortable with feudal practices?

3. What role did the gilds play in commercial and daily town life?

4. How did the Crusades influence the development and spread of commerce?

5. In what way did gild regulations limit the freedom of London's spur-makers? How did the spurriers benefit from these regulations? How were others in the community affected by the rules?

6. What does the riot in Cologne reveal about the attitudes of lords and townspeople toward one another?

7. How do you think you would have been affected by Marco Polo's description of China, had you been a fourteenth-century Venetian?

8. What does Peffer mean in implying that contact with the West in the Middle Ages ultimately had an unfortunate effect on China?

The Beginnings of Capitalism

From *Economic History of Europe,* 3d ed., by S. B. Clough & C. W. Cole. Copyright ©, 1952, by D. C. Heath & Co., a Division of Raytheon Education Co., Boston, Mass.

I

Money-Making in Medieval Society

Many people talk about capitalism, but nobody seems to know exactly what it is. . . . To talk intelligently about capitalism and its development, however, we must have a . . . definite notion as to its chief characteristics, which are many. . . . But for the sake of simplicity we can focus our attention, in describing the rise of capitalism, on three main features: (1) the growth of the capitalist spirit—that is, the desire for profits as a dominating motive in life; (2) the accumulation of capital—that is, the heaping up of money which is then used in business for the purpose of making profits (more money); (3) the development of capitalist techniques—that is, methods by which capital can be built up, handled, transferred, and used in business so as to make profits. . . . It is evident that the early middle ages were not capitalistic. In the twelfth century, for example, the desire for profits was not the most powerful or even an important motive in men's lives. There were no large accumulations of capital. Capital was not generally used in any fashion to make profits. . . .

The medieval thinker had a functional idea of society. To him, society was an organic whole. Each man belonged to a class. Each class had its function. The priests, monks, and nuns were to pray. The nobles were to fight and protect. The rest were to work. Each was doing his bit not for himself but for all men. The monk's prayers, the knight's battles, the peasant's plowing, represented a contribution to the welfare of everybody. Each person was expected to try to do the work appropriate to his station in life. He was born to a station and he should remain in it, contentedly doing his part and thinking of his reward in heaven. For a man to want to raise himself to a higher class betokened selfishness of some sort.

It was therefore wrong for a man to try to earn more than was necessary to keep him comfortably in the station of life to which he was born. The peasant should live like a peasant, the artisan like an artisan, the merchant like a merchant. To try to climb the economic or social ladder was wrong, and the worst way to rise was by heaping up wealth. The middle ages distrusted wealth. Jesus had told the rich man to take all that he had and give it to the poor, and He had indicated that it would be difficult if not impossible for a rich man to get into heaven. If a man got rich, it was suspected that he had obtained his wealth at the expense of his fellows. Certainly he had not given enough to charity or he would not be rich. . . .

Of the ways of making money, that of the merchant or trader was to the middle ages particularly dangerous and suspect. If the merchant worked on the goods he sold and took a fair reward for his labors, or even if he was content to earn by his efforts just

---

TOPIC 2

THE NEW WORLD OF BUSINESS

By the thirteenth and fourteenth century ways of conducting business had developed that can be called capitalistic. Merchants accumulated and reinvested capital, organized business partnerships, and introduced sophisticated methods of financial exchange and bookkeeping. The need for money and credit called into being an intricate banking system, far removed from the ancient services of money changers and money lenders. Merchants and bankers made and lost fortunes that outdid the incomes of kings. The Church raised moral objections to the new emphasis on profit-making but was itself too involved in business enterprise to combat consistently the trend of the times. The readings describe the new men and business techniques which were challenging the structure of feudal society.

enough to keep him comfortably in his station of life, his activities could be justified. But the trader was tempted to cheat and to seek profits. He risked his immortal soul in every transaction, for he might give way to avarice or greed. To the strictest view, any profits from pure trade were wrong. Gratian, an Italian monk of the twelfth century, wrote:

> Whosoever buys a thing, not that he may sell it whole and unchanged, but that it may be material for fashioning something, he is no merchant. But the man who buys it in order that he may gain by selling it again unchanged and as he bought it, that man is of the buyers and sellers who are cast forth from God's temple.

Thomas Aquinas, the greatest of the medieval philosophers, showed how strongly ethics influenced his views on trade when he insisted that a person knowingly selling an article with a defect in it was committing a sin and was morally bound to make restitution. It was a sin not to tell a buyer of a concealed defect in the goods. It was even a sin, according to Thomas, to trade with gain as the primary object, though it was legitimate for the merchant to seek moderate gains with which to support his family or to aid charity.

The medieval point of view is clearly seen in two economic doctrines on which there was substantial agreement—that of the *just price* and that of the *prohibition of usury*. The idea underlying the just price was that it was wrong to sell a thing for more than it was worth. What it was worth could be determined roughly in several ways. First, it was worth just enough to give to each person who helped to produce it a sum sufficient to reward him for his labor and keep him in his station in life. Second, it was worth what "common estimation" held it to be worth—that is, what well-informed people would say it was worth if they were consulted. Finally, it might be worth what the city, or state, or Church said it was worth in an ordinance or law issued to protect the consumer. Thomas Aquinas held that, "to sell dearer or buy cheaper than a thing is worth is in itself unjust and unlawful," though he admitted that, since "the just price of things is not absolutely definite but depends rather upon a kind of estimate," slight variations from the just price could be permitted.

The prohibition of usury was more complicated. Usury to the middle ages meant any charge purely for the use of money loaned or advanced. What we should call interest on borrowed money would then have been called usury. The belief that usury was wrong was based partly on a number of passages in the Bible which forbade taking it . . . .

> If thou lend to any of my people that is poor by thee, thou shalt not be to him as a usurer, neither shalt thou lay upon him usury. [Exodus, 22:25.]

> Take thou no usury of him or increase. [Leviticus, 25:36.]

> Lend hoping for nothing again. [Luke, 6:35.]

Aside from the Biblical injunctions, there was a general feeling that money was sterile. If you lent a man a field, he could raise crops on it. If you lent him a horse, he could ride it. If you lent him a house, he could live in it. But if you lent him money, he could only spend it. Money could not breed money. Aristotle, the most respected of the ancient philosophers, had been of this opinion. . . .

In the world of business between 1300 and 1500, many ways were evolved by which a loan at interest could be made to look like something else—a sale, a lease, an exchange transaction, a partnership. High profits might be immoral, but it seems that many a medieval merchant sought them with the utmost avidity. In the realm of ideas, the same period saw a weakening of the moral stand of the earlier day. Teachers, preachers, and writers began to justify usury and profits, from a dozen different angles. It was early held that if the lender suffered a loss by lending he might charge interest as compensation. Before long some people were maintaining that if by lending money a man missed a chance to make profits, it was proper to take interest. Gradually the very word *usury* took on its modern meaning of excessive charges for loans, while *interest* or some other pleasing word was used for moderate charges. The same gradual weakening took place in regard to the doctrine of the just price. By the fifteenth century a churchman so holy that he was later made a saint (Saint Antoninus, 1389–1459) was arguing that it was sometimes permissible for a seller to charge as much as 50 per cent more than the fixed price.

The development can be summed up briefly. In the centuries following the twelfth, with the rise of commerce and business, there grew up a class of merchants, traders, and financiers who sought profits and in many cases took usury as a normal part of their business life. As they became more and more important and as the Church, itself wealthy, became involved in the financial and business mechanisms of the times, the ideas of the Church and the public slowly readjusted themselves toward the acceptance of the capitalist spirit. The process was not complete

cloth, and wine. They financed ships and trading voyages. They transferred money from city to city. They loaned money to needy rulers and ambitious merchants alike.

Two factors that helped the Italian banking firms to become important were the kings and the papacy. The kings of France, England, and Castile were gradually consolidating their territories and slowly organizing them into more unified states. Continually involved in wars, they needed money to pay for troops, supplies, and fortifications, to bribe their enemies, or to keep up a kingly luxury. When they had used up all the income from taxes and feudal dues, they frequently had to resort to borrowing, paying the bankers who could supply the cash they needed handsome rates of interest that ranged from 10 per cent to 40 per cent or more.

The papacy was even more important. It collected taxes, dues, fees, Peter's pence, or the like, from almost every land in Europe. These moneys had to be collected. They had to be sent to Rome or elsewhere. They had to be held till they were needed. Sometimes, despite its wealth, the papacy had to borrow money to meet a temporary need. All the financial machinery thus required was gradually converted into a highly organized working system during the course of the thirteenth century. In this process the Italian bankers played a great part as fiscal agents, collectors, lenders, transferrers, and holders of deposits.

The towns and cities were also active in financial affairs. They borrowed money to build walls, wage wars, make public improvements, or buy grain in famine times. It was in connection with municipal debts and financial

by 1500, since more than a century later usury was still being denounced by churchmen, rulers, and publicists; but by the end of the middle ages the change was well under way. . . .

II

The New Bankers in Italy

During the thirteenth century a new kind of banking was built up by a series of Italian firms, usually partnerships of the family type.

These new bankers were no mere pawnbrokers sitting behind tables and making small loans in the Lombard Street of some European city. They were wealthy financiers who participated in trade and moneylending on a big scale. Such Italian bankers were loaning money to German churchmen at the fairs of Champagne as early as 1213. In 1233 bankers from Siena were acting as financial agents of the papacy. These bankers sought out profit in any line of work that seemed to promise it. They dealt in wheat, spices, transactions that the first public banks of deposit were founded—in Barcelona in 1401, in Valencia in 1407, and in Genoa (Bank of St. George, which carried on deposit banking from 1407 to 1445 and again after 1586). These banks were created and controlled by the cities to facilitate the handling of their debts and money affairs. But many towns with large debts were dependent on private bankers, often the big Italian firms. . . .

The Bardi, one of the most successful of the Florentine houses, may serve as an example. Their prosperity began in 1294 when they began to deal with the King of Naples, who was also Count of Provence (in southern France). They lent him money to finance his wars and in return got the exclusive right to control the exports of grain, fruit, and dairy products from Apulia (southern Italy) and grain from Provence. Later they traded extensively in French textiles and scarlet cloth from Ypres. In 1303 they became one of the firms active in banking for the pope, and in his behalf they transferred funds in Europe, to Cyprus, and even as far as Armenia. They helped to collect Peter's pence in England for the pope, and used the proceeds to buy wool which they sent to Florence to be manufactured into fine cloth. By 1310 the Bardi had surpassed their chief rivals, the Acciaiuoli and Peruzzi. Already in 1300 their interests in northern Europe were so extensive that none of the fifteen partners was residing in Florence. In 1320 the capital of the firm was

The offices of a Genoese banker in the late fourteenth century: at top, the bankers are counting coins and taking money from a strong box; at bottom, customers await service while the bankers refer to their account book.

149,796 livres of Paris. From 1310 to 1330 its annual profits averaged about 20 percent. But troubles lay ahead. Joanna of Naples repudiated half the debt owed to the Bardi by her kingdom. English mobs rioted against the foreign usurers. Finally in 1345–1346 Edward III of England was unable to pay the huge sums he had borrowed from the Bardi. This catastrophe threw the Bardi into bankruptcy and they paid their creditors only "forty-eight cents on the dollar." It was probably little comfort to them that the Peruzzi were involved in the same crisis and likewise went bankrupt.

A number of firms survived the crash of the mid-fourteenth century, but the financial leadership in Florence in the fifteenth century went to a relatively new family, the Medici, whose coat of arms (red balls on a gold field) gave rise to the modern pawnbroker's sign. In the early fifteenth century, the Medici banking firm had branches in Paris, London, Bruges, Lyons, Venice, Rome, Genoa, Naples, and eight other cities as well as the home office in Florence. Mixing politics with finance, the Medici made themselves actual rulers of the city-state of Florence. They used their great fortune for diplomatic as well as business ends, and also beautified Florence with churches, paintings, and sculpture. Cosimo de' Medici (1389–1464) spent more than $10,000,000 (1940 dollars) on such patronage of art and religion. At the time of his death, the income of his family was more than $3,000,000 a year. The most famous of the Medici, Lorenzo the Magnificent, ruled Florence in splendor from 1469 to 1492. Though the political power of the family waned after the end of the middle ages, they remained important. They gave the Church a number of cardinals and two popes, and France two queens (Catherine and Marie). Branches of

the family were princes and dukes down into the eighteenth century. . . .

An important point to notice in connection with most of these early capitalists is the combination of commercial and financial activities, of trade and banking. The type of capitalism which was growing up in Europe in the middle ages and was well established by 1500 was predominantly of this sort. There were examples of purely financial capitalism in the early Jewish or Lombard money-lenders, and there were rich merchants who did little banking and much trade. But as wealth accumulated and the capitalist's desire for profits grew, it was normal for a firm to use its money in the way that seemed to promise the quickest, surest, and largest return, whether that involved investing in shipping, loaning money to merchants, churchmen, and rulers, or dealing directly in goods. For the most part the production of goods was still carried on in a small way, on the basis of handicraft work. . . .

III

The Fuggers of Germany

Though there were many family firms of bankers in the sixteenth century, none achieved quite the position of the Fuggers. A brief account of their history will serve to illustrate many things—the accumulation of capital, the connection between banking and commerce, the relationship between state finance and the rise of capitalists, the organization of a family partnership, the power of the capitalist. The first Fugger known to history is Hans, a weaver by trade, who came to Augsburg in southern Germany from the village of Graben about 1380. In his new home he built up a considerable business. He made and sold fustians (a fabric made of linen and cotton). He imported cotton from Venice, for himself

and probably for his fellow weavers as well. He may have dealt in other goods. At his death he left a small fortune of 3,000 gold gulden (the equivalent of something like $100,000 today).

The business passed to his son Jacob I, who, before his death in 1469, increased the family fortune from the cloth trade. Jacob's widow managed the business for a while, then passed it on to her oldest sons, Ulrich and George. They dealt in silks, damasks, and brocades as well as woolens, linens, and fustians; and in spices, fruit, saffron, and jewels as well as textiles. They established commercial connections with Italy, the Netherlands, Silesia, Poland, and Hungary. In 1473 the Fugger brothers began selling textiles to the Habsburgs, the ruling house of Austria, and about the same time they began to do financial work for the pope, transferring money for him from Scandinavia to Rome. The main interests of the Fuggers were still commercial, the wholesale and retail trade in textiles and other goods, but they were commencing to lend money and deal in bills of exchange. Before long they were loaning money to the Habsburgs as well as selling them goods.

Ulrich and George Fugger had a younger brother named Jacob II (1459–1525), later called Jacob the Rich. He had intended to enter the priesthood but in 1478 he gave up that idea, went into the business, and spent some time in Venice studying bookkeeping and business methods. Back in Augsburg he quickly became the most active member of the firm. Even before the death of his brothers (1506 and 1510) he was the dominant figure in it, and from 1510 to 1525 he shaped all its policies. This family enterprise was organized and reorganized several times, but the articles of agreement of 1502 were typical. They provided that only Fuggers in the direct line should be members of the firm. No outsiders, not even relatives by marriage, were to be admitted. The brothers were to run the business until only one was left alive. The survivor was to train up a son or nephew to succeed him as head of the firm. The bulk of the capital was to be left in the business, and the part called the "preferred share" was never to be taken out of it.

Jacob II was shrewd, fearless, able, a business genius typical of the new capitalism. One of his favorite sayings was "Business is business." On one occasion, when he was urged to abandon a risky mining venture, he sounded the keynote of the new capitalist age by replying, "I am of quite a different point of view and wish to continue making a profit as long as I can." Jacob brought to the firm the best business methods of the day. He built up an elaborate news service by which agents in every port and city kept him informed of each turn of the markets, of wars, piracy, and political rumors. He used the most up-to-date bookkeeping techniques. He got security for every loan, took his profits while he still had them, and skillfully cut his losses when they were unavoidable. He had branches, agencies, or agents for trade and banking operations in almost every important commercial city of Europe.

Under Jacob II the Fuggers' old cloth and merchandise business became secondary. On the one hand, he engaged heavily in mining ventures. He lent money to the Habsburgs on the security of the royalties coming to them from the copper and silver mines of the Tyrol and after 1522 rapidly acquired extensive holdings there for his firm. In alliance with a family of mine experts and managers named Thurzo he came to control the copper, silver, and lead mines of Hungary. By 1525 the Fuggers

had made 1,500,000 gold gulden out of Hungarian minerals. At one point they controlled so much copper that they joined with some other firms in an unsuccessful attempt to corner the market and raise the price.

On the other hand, Jacob II engaged in finance. The greatest private banker of his time, he transferred money for kings, popes, and merchants. He accepted deposits and bought, sold, and issued bills of exchange and letters of credit. At some periods business preferred bills on the Fuggers to gold coin. Most important, he loaned money, financing merchants, bishops, cities, and kings. Especially close were his relations with the Habsburgs. Charles V won his election as Holy Roman Emperor through bribes financed by Jacob Fugger. Jacob the Rich had his finger in almost every financial pie in Europe. Luther's great revolt against the Church was initiated in part as a protest against the high pressure salesmanship of a certain indulgence hawker named Tetzel. On his travels, Tetzel was accompanied by a Fugger agent, who took charge of all the money collected, of which part went to pay debts owed to the Fuggers.

Jacob II was popular in Augsburg. He gave plays, dances, and skating parties, and lived in splendor. For the poor of the city he built a walled garden suburb called the Fuggerei, where rents were very low. But many people in Germany denounced him as a usurer, a grasping monopolist, a ruthless seeker after wealth. Indeed, so strong was the feeling that Fugger became a term of abuse. The capital of the Fugger firm had been 54,385 gold gulden in 1494. At Jacob's death in 1525 it amounted to about 2,000,000 gold gulden, probably the largest sum that had ever up till then been under the control of a single business firm. . . .

Jacob Fugger (seated) discusses business with his chief bookkeeper Matthäus Schwartz, who painted this watercolor sketch (1516). The drawers in the background designate branch offices of the Fugger bank—Rome, Venice, Cracow, Lisbon, etc.

The Merchant of Prato, a Fourteenth-Century Man of Wealth

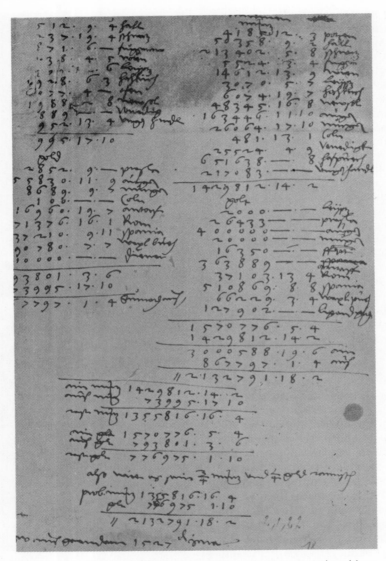

An idea of the Fugger riches can be gained from this page reproduced from their account books of 1527, two years after Jacob Fugger's death. The balance 2,132,791.18 gulden is equivalent to well over $50,000,000 today.

In her biography of Francesco di Marco Datini, the Italian historian Iris Origo explored the mind and accomplishments of a successful fourteenth-century international merchant. Like all good biography, the account of the merchant of Prato brings the reader closer both to the man and to the world of his experience. From *The Merchant of Prato,* by Iris Origo. © Copyright 1957 by Iris Origo. Reprinted by permission of Alfred A. Knopf, Inc. This is published in Canada by Jonathan Cape Limited.

In the square of the busy little city of Prato, beneath the faded brick walls of the Palazzo Comunale in which he sat as a councillor, stands the statue of a merchant. Clothed in the round biretta and sweeping robes of the fourteenth century, he holds in his hand a sheaf of bills of exchange. This is the man to whom Prato owes the foundation of her riches: Francesco di Marco Datini [1335–1410].

The story of the rise of his trading-houses in Avignon, Prato and Florence, in Pisa and Genoa, in Spain and Majorca, is as remarkable as the success-story of a modern millionaire, and quite as fully recorded. His fellow citizens to this day pride themselves on it and dwell, above all, on the charity which bequeathed to the poor of Prato not only his whole fortune of 70,000 gold florins, but the very house in which he lived, and in it, his greatest gift to posterity, his papers. During his lifetime he himself collected every letter and business document he received, telling the managers of all his branches to do the same, and in his will he left instructions for all these papers to be collected and preserved in his own house in Prato.

These instructions were carried out somewhat carelessly, for although there is a record in 1560 that Francesco di Marco's ledgers and papers had been carefully put away in cupboards in his own house, they were found three hundred years later in sacks in a dusty recess under the stairs. But in the long run this neglect may not prove to have been entirely unfortunate. *"Bene qui latuit, bene vixit."* A few of these pages were nibbled by mice or worms; but at least thieves and fools remained unaware of their existence—and when in 1870 some learned citizens of Prato brought them to light, an astonishing number still remained: some 150,000 letters, over 500 account-books and ledgers, 300 deeds of partnership (some of the other small companies connected with his own), 400 insurance policies, and several thousand bills of lading, letters of advice, bills of exchange, and cheques. Thus has been preserved, in the very house of the man whose life-work it represented, an invaluable and indeed, in its fullness and homogeneity, a unique record of medieval trade.

The picture of commercial activity which these letters present is very remarkable. When Datini returned to Italy from Avignon in 1382, his branch in that city (entrusted to two Tuscan partners) continued to be as active as before; and he at once opened a central house in Prato, as well as branches in Florence, Pisa, and Genoa, in Barcelona and Valencia, and finally in Majorca and Ibiza, all managed by his own partners or *fattori* on the spot but controlled by his own untiring pen.

Between these *fondachi* sailed the ships which carried his wares: lead and alum and pilgrims' robes from Roumania, slaves and spices from the Black Sea, English wool from London and Southampton and African or Spanish wool from Majorca and Spain, salt from Ibiza, silk from Venice, leather from Cordoba and Tunis, wheat from Sardinia and Sicily, oranges and dates and bark and wine from Catalonia. . . . Small wonder that Francesco's fellow citizens gaped as the great bales came pouring in, and whispered that he was "the greatest merchant who ever came out of Prato!" . . .

Francesco's own character is very sharply etched. It is impossible to imagine a more completely Tuscan figure. Intensely individualistic, he owed his success entirely to his own personal enterprise, to an audacity always tempered at just the right moment by shrewdness and mistrust of his neighbour. A hard businessman, he gathered his golden florins wherever he could find them: he traded in armour, wool, metals, and wheat; he made cloth and bought slaves; he opened (though this laid him open to the accusation of being a usurer) a bank. But he also never failed to conform to the conventions of pious practice: he neglected no fast-days, assigned a due proportion of his profits to alms and charity, built chapels and adorned churches. Self-indulgent during his prosperous years in Avignon—"keeping women and living on partridges," and begetting several little bastards—he was also capable, in the pursuit of his business, of a life as industrious and exacting as a monk's. . . .

Francesco's outstanding trait as a merchant is the variety of his activities. First an armourer and then a mercer in Avignon, he had become a cloth-maker in Prato and was now again a

shopkeeper in Florence; next he founded a flourishing import-and-export business, and became the chief partner of a number of different trading-companies: he dealt in wool, cloth, veils, wheat, metals, and hides, in spices and pictures and jewels. In 1404 he joined yet another guild—that of the cloth-finishers, the *Arte di Calimala*. He even took over, for a short time, the city tolls for meat and wine in Prato; he did some under-writing; and finally (against the advice of all his friends) he set up a bank.

Such varied ventures were entirely characteristic of his time, when the fundamental distinction between the international merchant and the "little man" did not consist in whether his trade was wholesale or retail, or even in the quantity of his merchandise, but rather in the outlook of two different kinds of men. The local merchant was still, in his way of life, his lack of enterprise, and his parsimony, a man with the outlook of a craftsman—trading with a number of familiar clients, strictly subservient to the rules of his guild, taking small risks and expecting small profits. The international trader—whether he was the chief partner of a great company like the Alberti's, or a small one like Datini's—still retained something of the enterprise and audacity of his ancestor, the travelling peddler; he was prepared to take great risks, but diminished them by spreading them over the widest possible field; he acquainted himself with foreign languages and foreign ways, adapted himself to the needs of foreign markets, was both merchant and banker, dealt simultaneously in both wholesale and retail trade. As the Bardi had continued to run a draper's shop in Via di Calimala even while they were exporting enough wheat from Puglie to feed a whole city and financing the

English campaigns in France, so Datini, even at the time of his most successful foreign ventures, never closed his little mercer's shop in Por S. Maria.

But to his timid Florentine partners the variety of his enterprises was most alarming; they could not forget how many other great trading-houses, in recent years, had ended in bankruptcy. The following letter from Domenico di Cambio is typical of their warnings:

> Francesco, I have heard you would embark on a new enterprise. Before God, I beseech you, open your eyes wide and look well to what you do! You are rich and at ease, and not a boy any more, that you should need to undertake so much—and bethink you how we are mortal, and the man who does many things will assuredly meet with disaster. . . . Bethink you how Donato Dini must feel, who is now over seventy, and because he has tried to do too much is bankrupt, and gets only five *soldi* in the *lira!*

But Francesco did not heed. The opening of his new branches followed each other swiftly; first the Pisan *fondaco* in 1382, the Florentine in 1386, and the Genoese in 1388. Then came new branches in Spain and in the Balearic Islands in 1393 and 1394, while at the same time the company in Avignon prospered and trade with both the Black Sea and the Balkans increased. . . .

It is after the opening of the Spanish and Genoese branches, too, that we find reference to yet another line—the slave trade, of which the Balearic Islands were then the chief centre in the western Mediterranean. This trade was, of course, nothing new. In the eleventh and twelfth centuries Spain had been the great slave-market of western Europe, and as early as 1128 traders from Barcelona were selling Moslem slaves in the markets of Genoa. But it was the labour shortage after the Black Death of 1348 that suddenly caused a demand for domestic slaves to revive, and brought them to Italy not only from Spain and Africa, but from the Balkans, Constantinople, Cyprus and Crete, and, above all, from the shores of the Black Sea. In Florence a decree of the *Signoria,* issued in 1336, officially authorized their importation—provided only that they were infidels, not Christians, and they were also soon to be found in most prosperous Genoese and Venetian households. Many of them mere children of nine or ten, they belonged to a great variety of different races: yellow-skinned, slanting-eyed Tartars, handsome fair Circassians, Greeks, Russians, Georgians, Alans, and Lesghians. Sold by their parents for a crust of bread, or kidnapped by Tartar raiders and Italian sailors, they were brought from the slave-markets of Tana and Caffa, of Constantinople, Cyprus, and Crete to the Venetian and Genoese quays, where they were bought by dealers and forwarded to customers inland. By the end of the fourteenth century there was hardly a well-to-do household in Tuscany without at least one slave: brides brought them as part of their dowry, doctors accepted them from their patients in lieu of fees—and it was not unusual to find them even in the service of a priest. They were employed, too (as we shall see), in Francesco's own household, and he would sometimes oblige Tuscan friends by selecting one for them through his agents in Genoa or Venice; but the most active part in this trade was taken by his branches in Majorca and Ibiza, where both African slaves bound for Italy and eastern slaves bound for Spain were collected and sold.

Many letters in these files bear witness to these transactions, though they did not take place on any large scale; the most frequent entries refer rather to a few slaves included in a shipment of other assorted wares. The bill of lading, for instance, of a ship arriving in Genoa from Roumania on May 21, 1396, listed "17 bales of pilgrims' robes, 191 pieces of lead and 80 slaves." Another ship, sailing from Syracuse to Majorca, carried 1,547 leather hides and 10 slaves, and one sailing from Venice to Ibiza "128 sacks of woad, 55 bales of brass, 15 sacks of raw cotton, 5 sacks of cotton yarn, 4 bales of paper, 3 barrels of gallnuts, and 9 Turkish heads." The "9 heads" were then forwarded to Valencia to be sold, with a letter stating that one of them was a woman who could "sew and do everything," and who was therefore, in the writer's opinion, "too good for the people of Ibiza"—"for they are like dogs." "Your money," he added, "will be well placed in her." . . .

At the turn of the century Francesco—who had reached his sixty-fifth year—appears to us in a new aspect: wearing the garb of a penitent and a pilgrim. Clad in a long robe of coarse white cloth, with a cowl on his head, a friar's cord about his waist, and a lighted candle in his hand, he set forth barefoot, in a company of several thousand men, for a nine-day pilgrimage.

To none of Francesco's contemporaries did it seem strange to see him thus: the performance, in calamitous times, of such acts of devotion and self-abasement was part of an accepted pattern of life. The Datini papers, indeed, bring fresh confirmation of the extent to which a life of Christian conformity was led even by men (like Francesco himself) whose natural temperament was far from pious. Just as many of the laws they obeyed were still largely founded upon usage—*consuetudo*—so their devotional life rested upon a series of unquestioned, familiar acts, from the cradle to the grave. Hard-headed merchants not only gave lipservice to Christian doctrine, but paid tribute to it in their daily practice: they led their whole lives within an intricate framework of pious observance. During his whole youth and prime Francesco was not, and did not consider himself, a virtuous man; but he never questioned the necessity or the efficacy of these devout customs. His business contracts, like his private letters, began and ended with a pious formula; the Ten Commandments stood at the head of his ledgers; a fresco of St. Christopher guarded his front door. In Lent and on other fast-days both he and his wife fasted so strictly that Domenico di Cambio said his health would not permit to come and stay with them, and if he sometimes worked on a Sunday, he blamed himself most severely in the year in which he had attended only *six* Lenten sermons! Though he often scoffed at priests and monks, he went regularly to confession, and, in sickness, called five Franciscans to his bedside; though ungenerous by nature, he gave alms freely, paid his tithes regularly, built shrines and chapels. There was hardly a rich man of his time who did not do the same, and the few who failed to fulfill these duties were considered wicked men.

Many of these acts, of course, had a strong propitiatory character; it was through them that men hoped to receive protection from the terrors and mysteries of life in this world, as well as God's mercy in the next. Man is at all times a fear-ridden animal; and certainly many Tuscans of the *trecento* had good rea-son to dread a sudden death. The persistence of the tradition of vengeance by bloodshed—still considered not only a sacred duty but a pleasure—the permanent sense of insecurity produced by party strife and civil war, the frequent recurrence of famine, and, above all, the constant, haunting menace of the Black Death—this was the dark background of their lives. . . .

Raymond de Roover: The Doctrine of Usury and Renaissance Business

The intensive examination of the organization and operations of the Medici Bank from which this reading is taken is the result of years of research in the Florentine archives by Professor de Roover, Belgian-born American economic historian. Here the author considers the impact of the Church's position on usury upon economic growth. Reprinted by permission of the publishers from Raymond de Roover, *The Rise and Decline of the Medici Bank, 1397–1494,* Cambridge, Mass.: Harvard University Press, Copyright 1963 by the President and Fellows of Harvard College, pp. 10–13.

Medieval banking cannot be understood without keeping in mind the usury doctrine of the Church. Since the bankers, in this regard, tried as much as possible to comply with religious precepts, they had to operate with-out incurring the censure of the theologians. As a result banking in the Middle Ages and even much later—on the Continent until far into the eighteenth century—was quite different from what it is today. It would be erroneous to believe that the usury doctrine was simply disregarded and had scarcely any effect on banking practices: on the contrary, as the available evidence proves, it exerted an enormous influence. First of all, the need for evading the usury prohibition, by legitimate means if possible, affected the entire structure of medieval banking. Second, it determined how the banks operated. And third, the usury doctrine, by recognizing certain transactions as licit and declaring others to be illicit, influenced business ethics and public opinion. . . .

The ban against usury did not halt the growth of banking, but recent research has shown that it certainly diverted the course of this development. Since the taking of interest was ruled out, the bankers had to find other ways of lending at a profit. The favorite method was by means of exchange by bills (*cambium per litteras*). It did not consist in discounting as practiced today, but in the negotiation of bills payable in another place and usually in another currency. Interest, of course, was included in the price of the bill which was fittingly called a "bill of exchange." Although the presence of concealed interest is undeniable, the merchants argued—and most of the theologians accepted these views —that an exchange transaction was not a loan (*cambium non est mutuum*) but either a commutation of moneys (*permutatio*) or a buying and selling of foreign currency (*emptio venditio*). In other words, the exchange transaction was used to justify the credit transaction, and speculative profits on

27

exchange served as a cloak to cover interest charges. Nevertheless, it was argued that cambium was not usurious, since there could be no usury where there was no loan.

The practical consequence was to tie banking to exchange, be it manual exchange or exchange by bills. It is perhaps significant that the bankers' gild of Florence was called the Arte del Cambio, or the Moneychanger's Gild. In the account books of the Italian merchant-bankers, including those of the Medici, one rarely, if ever, finds traces of discount, but there are thousands and thousands of entries relating to exchange transactions. There is no account for interest income, but an account entitled *Pro e danno di cambio* (Profit and Loss on Exchange). . . .

It is untrue that the bankers openly disregarded the teachings of the Church. To be sure, they were not always consistent and often violated the precept against usury in private contracts. It does not follow, however, that there were many who pertinaciously questioned a doctrine erected into a dogma by the Church. On the contrary, many a banker had an uneasy conscience about his unholy deals. Overwhelming evidence is given in the numerous medieval testaments in which the testator ordered restitution of all usury and ill-gotten gains. True, such clauses became scarcer after 1350 because the merchant-bankers, while still continuing to make bequests to the Church for the salvation of their souls, were less and less eager to be branded as self-confessed usurers by referring specifically to restitution in their wills.

Moreover, they contended, with a semblance of truth, that they were engaged in legitimate business and not in usurious activities. In fact, they did shun illicit contracts as much as possible. Even the Pratese merchant-banker, Francesco di Marco Datini (1335–1410), although ruthless and grasping, boasted in letters to his wife that he had never made illicit profits. When his branch manager in Barcelona became involved in questionable exchange dealings, he was promptly rebuked by an irate master and told to desist. . . . In the partnership agreements of the Medici, illicit exchange was as a rule expressly forbidden, although this provision was not always carried out, as account books and other records prove. It is, therefore, understandable that Cosimo de' Medici himself was troubled by qualms about ill-acquired wealth and secured a papal bull which allowed him to atone for his covetousness by endowing the monastery of San Marco in Florence. . . .

If it had not been for the usury doctrine, why would the merchants have adopted a cumbersome procedure when simpler methods were available? It is far easier to discount instruments of debt than to work with bills of exchange payable abroad in foreign currencies. First of all, this procedure complicates bookkeeping. Next, it requires the bankers to operate with a network of correspondents in other places. Another drawback is that lenders, as well as borrowers, have to speculate and to run the risks of adverse exchange fluctuations. Moreover, the purchaser of a bill is exposed to loss not only through the insolvency of his debtor, but also through the failure of the correspondent to whom he sends a remittance. This is perhaps why the big bankers preferred to operate with their own branches. As for the borrower, if he had no funds standing to his credit in another place, he had to find some one willing to accept his drafts and to pay them when due. The drawee or payer would then have to recover his outlay at his own risk. The use of the bill of exchange thus increased both trouble and expense, so that the practical result of the usury prohibition, intended to protect the borrower, was to raise the cost of borrowing. To this extent the Church's legislation on usury may have retarded economic growth. . . .

The Church as a Business Organization

Medieval Churchmen may have considered profit seductive and interest sinful, but efficient administration of the Church's income from her vast properties and the Christian congregation required efficient business organization. The papal camera (office of fiscal administration) seems to date from the Cluniac reform period of the mid-eleventh century. One of its major tasks was to oversee the collecting and transferring of Church income to Rome. Such income came from many sources: rents (census) for Church property, feudal dues (tribute), membership contributions (Peter's Pence), income taxes, a proportion of the annual income of bishops, abbots, etc. (common services), and others. The first reading describes the use made by the camera of available Italian merchants. The second consists of documents illustrating that relationship. From William E. Lunt, *Papal Revenues in the Middle Ages* (New York: Columbia University Press, 1934), I, pp. 51–53, 55–56, 301–302, 323–324, 338–340; II, 300–302.

I

Merchants as Agents of Church Finance

As early as the second half of the twelfth century the papacy was using agents outside the camera [Papal department of fiscal administration] for the deposit, transport and exchange of money, and for the contract of loans. At first the Templars performed these functions, and throughout the major portion of the thirteenth century the houses of the Templars continued to serve as places of deposit. . . . When the rising Italian capitalists began to establish agencies in the various commercial centers of Europe, they offered better facilities for the transaction of the growing fiscal business of the papacy. In the early years of the thirteenth century the papacy began to use Italian merchants concurrently with the Templars for the deposit and transportation of funds. By the time of Gregory IX (1227–1241), Italian merchants had become the principal bankers of the camera. For the remainder of the middle ages firms of bankers, which were for the most part Italian, took a large part in handling the finances of the papacy. . . .

The bankers supplied a variety of services. Their agents received deposits from the collectors, either for safe-keeping or for transportation to the camera. For these sums they gave receipts in which they promised to restore the amounts in full in any designated place on the demand of the collector or of an accredited agent of the pope. They took all risks such as those of fire, robbery and shipwreck, and pledged the possessions of the whole firm as a guarantee of repayment. The deposits might sometimes be kept for a long period, during which the merchants could use the money profitably in their own

enterprises. In the fourteenth century, however, it became customary to require delivery of money assigned to them within a stated interval. Long before the close of the thirteenth century the bankers had become the principal agents for the conveyance of funds to the camera. . . . The cameral merchants might transport the actual specie, or make the transfer by order on the representative of the firm at the papal court or by bill of exchange. For this service they received a portion of the money transferred, and they might also charge for the exchange of the money from the currency of the country in which it was received into the money current at the papal court.

The papal bankers might be empowered to receive from the payers revenues that were owed to the papacy. Payments of census and services occasionally reached the camera in that manner throughout the period. The use of cameral merchants as collectors, however, was of comparatively rare occurrence.

The papal merchants were constantly called upon to lend money to the camera. Often the loans anticipated the receipt of taxes, which were pledged to the merchants for repayment. . . .

The patronage and protection of the papacy aided the cameral merchants greatly in the development of their banking operations. The numerous ecclesiastics, who, on coming to Rome, were obliged to borrow in order to meet papal charges, turned naturally to the bankers standing in relations with the curia [papal government]. Such loans were ordinarily made only with the permission of the pope, who gave the creditor special rights of recovering from the debtor. The latter was compelled to pledge as security not only his own property but also that of his church. If

the debt was not paid within a month of the time specified, the creditor could obtain a special executory process for speedy recovery to be carried out by officials appointed at the papal court and enforced by ecclesiastical censures. If clergy outside the curia needed money to meet papal taxation or other expenses, they also were likely to place business with the accredited agents of the holy see. Some of these debts bore interest, of which the popes were sometimes aware, though they seem seldom to have taken official cognizance of the fact. The bankers were privileged to employ the ecclesiastical courts to enforce the payment of such debts, and might require the borrower to agree to submit to the jurisdiction of the auditor of the camera. The cameral merchants were accredited to sovereigns by the papacy, and, when occasion demanded, papal diplomacy was used in their behalf, not only with prelates and clergy but also with rulers and peoples. The prominent position held by the Italian bankers in European financial affairs must be attributed in no small degree to the business and the protection of the papacy. . . .

II

1. Early Instance of the Association of Merchants with a Papal Collector (1229)

Moreover, the same Master Stephen [i.e., the papal collector] had with him certain most wicked usurers, who called themselves merchants, cloaking usury under the name of the business of banking, who offered money to those who were poor and vexed with exactions; and the said Stephen urging, many were forced under the severest penalty to accept a loan, who afterward fell into their snares, incurring irreparable damages.

2. Papal Order to a Collector To Deliver His Receipts to Specified Cameral Merchants (1262)

To the beloved son, brother John of Kent, of the order of Friars Minors, greeting, etc.

By the authority of the present we command that whatever you may receive or have received from the census of our dearest son in Christ, the illustrious king of the English, or from Peter's pence, which we have committed to you to be collected through our other letters, you assign with due caution to Deutaviva Guidi and Rayner Bonaccursi, merchants of Siena, as we have ordered you by those letters, but with the knowledge of the beloved son, Master Leonard, cantor of Messina, our chaplain, whom we are sending into England on certain business.

Given at Viterbo, II nones February, in the first year.

3. Papal Order for the Sequestration of the Goods of a Deceased Cameral Merchant Who Was Indebted to the Roman Church (1300)

Boniface, bishop, servant of the servants of God, to the venerable brother, the bishop of Lucca, greeting and apostolic benediction.

Recently it has come to our hearing that the late Labrus Vulpelli, of the society of Riczardi of Lucca, closed his last day. Therefore, since the said Labrus and the aforesaid society were and are debtors to us and the Roman church in large sums of money, we command your fraternity by apostolic writing, ordering you strictly in virtue of your obedience, that on the receipt of the present, without the obstacle of difficulty and delay, by you and others, you take care to take, receive, hold and keep by our authority, . . .

all and each of the movable and immovable goods, with whomever they may be, which you are able to learn about and discover, invoking the aid of the secular arm for this, if need should be, . . . notwithstanding . . . if the aforesaid goods or any of them should be obligated in any way to another or others, by whom we do [not] wish [them] to be carried away against this our mandate, without our special knowledge.

Do you write back to us faithfully by your letters containing the sequence of these whatever you do and find about this.

Given at the Lateran, II kalends December, in the sixth year of our pontificate.

4. Action Taken by the Papacy To Secure the Release of Cameral Merchants from Prison (1251)

To . . . archbishop of Besançon and . . . the elect of Lyons.

Since on Holy Thursday at Lyons we caused Ponzardus de Duno to be cited by a formal proclamation that before the festival of the apostles Peter and Paul last past he should return to the command of the church prepared to give full satisfaction concerning the wrongs, excesses and enormous offenses, on account of which he was held bound by the chain of excommunication, or else we should proceed against him more severely, because he neither returns to the devotion of the church, nor comes to us, nor sends sufficient or suitable answer, but, raging into greater offense and adding enormities upon enormities, taking Hugolinus Belmontis, Orlando Bartholomei, Theobald Thebalducii and Rainer Tetii, merchants of Siena, whom we sent for the affairs of the church, he holds them in captivity to the offense of the apostolic see, we, not being able to tolerate further in pa-

tience his bold presumption and hardened iniquity, command that each of you, laying all of the land of [Ponzardus] under ecclesiastical interdict, do not permit baptisms, the eucharist, or any other ecclesiastical sacraments to be administered to any in that land. . . . Furthermore, do you place under ecclesiastical interdict any cities, towns, villas and places to which [Ponzardus] may happen to come, in which divine services may not afterward be celebrated in any wise without the special license of the apostolic see.

Given at Milan, VIII kalends September, in the ninth year.

5. Papal Intercession with the King of France in Behalf of Cameral Merchants (1291)

To the dearest son in Christ, Philip, illustrious king of France.

. . . Whereas you are said to have caused the Italian merchants staying in your said kingdom to be arrested, we ask and earnestly exhort your royal serenity that those merchants, and particularly those of the societies of the sons of Bonsignoris of Siena, of Thomas Spiliati and Lapus Hugonis, of the Spina, of the Pulici and Rimbertini and of the Lambertinii of the Friscobaldis of Florence, of the Riczardi of Lucca and of the Clarentini of Pistoia, who and the colleagues of whom are special merchants of our camera and have long served the Roman church advantageously, . . . you free from the restraint of this arrest and from any burden imposed on them anywhere, and restore to them their rightful liberty. When goods have been restored to them in full, do you, from the royal clemency, allow them to sojourn freely in the parts of the said kingdom, to be free to carry on legal commerce, and hold them committed favorably to your care in their opportunities. . . .

Given at Orvieto, V kalends June, in the fourth year of our pontificate.

6. A Pledge by the Camera of Church Income as Security for a Loan from the Fuggers (1501)

To the most admirable men, Ulrich Fucher [Fuggers] and Brothers, German merchants following the Roman court, greeting in the Lord.

You have lent to our most holy lord, for the necessities of him, the see and the apostolic camera, 6,000 gold ducats; and his holiness wished and ordered to be given to you as a gift 400 of the same: which sum, including in all 6,400 gold ducats, our same most holy lord wished, promised and ordered to be restored to you, namely, one-half at the end of two and one-half months and the other half at the end of five months to be calculated from the twentieth day of the pres-

ent month of December, with authority and license, in the event that satisfaction should not be given to you . . . [the Fuggers served as transferers of Papal funds] of removing from the account and retaining for yourselves from the common services of the churches and monasteries, which may happen to be expedited by your hands from Germany and Hungary and Poland only, until you have been fully satisfied for the said 6,400 ducats. . . .

Given at Rome in the apostolic camera, on the last day of December entering January 1502, in the tenth year of the pontificate of our aforesaid most holy lord. . . .

Marginal Notes Made by Official of Papal Camera

For the loan made to our most holy lord.

Assignment of 6,400 gold ducats of the camera for Ulric Fucher and Brothers, German merchants.

In deduction. Note that by mandate by receipt and issue, under the day 15 April 1502, they had 247½ ducats.

Item by another mandate, under the day 15 July 1502, they had 700 ducats 10 s. 8 d. of gold of the camera.

Item, in another mandate, under the day 6 August 1502, for the common service of the pope of the church of Schleswig 427½ ducats.

Item, in another mandate, under the day 27 December 1503 (sic), for common service of the church of Hildesheim 475 ducats.

Item, in another mandate, under the day 22 March 1503, for the common service of the church of Basel 475 ducats.

Item, in another mandate, under the day 24 June 1503, 902½ ducats for the common service of the churches of Verden and Transylvania.

From Lord John Conarii for the common service of the church of Cracow 1272 florins.

From Lord John Turzo for the common service of the church of Breslau 1,900 florins.

Constituting in all the sum of 6,400 ducats, in which he [Fugger] was creditor by the force of these patents, which is acknowledged by the lord's depositaries, and here accounted formally.

STUDY QUESTIONS

1. What was the medieval attitude toward money-making and the occupation of merchant? How did the Church's position on usury affect this attitude? Why did the position change?

2. What explains the rise of banking on a large scale in the thirteenth and fourteenth centuries? Why did merchants often turn to banking? Why was early business so full of risks?

3. Apply the tests of capitalism to the Fuggers. How would the existence of a wealthy middle class affect the existing social order?

4. In what business activities did Francesco Datini engage? Do you think that his attitude toward these activities reflects the "capitalist spirit" mentioned in the preceding reading? In what ways was he still a medieval man?

5. What are bills of exchange and why were they frequently used in the period? Why does de

Roover argue that the Church's views on usury may have retarded economic growth?

6. How did the Papacy make use of Italian merchants? What did the merchants gain in return for their services? How might such collaboration with merchants have affected the Church's views on money-making?

7. What do the documents concerning the merchants who served as agents for the Church tell us about the Church as a business organization?

The City-States of Italy

TOPIC 3

THE NEW POLITICS

The appearance of a money economy strengthened the reassertions of central political authority that had begun in the late Middle Ages. Kings in France, England, and Spain pushed forward their efforts to uproot feudalism and establish national monarchies. In Italy, by contrast, where the commercial revolution had first developed, the city-state in the fourteenth and fifteenth centuries once again became the dominant political form. For two centuries Italy was free from foreign invasion while other sections of Europe were preoccupied with their own affairs. At the same time, the ties of traditional society and the medieval Church were steadily loosening. Without these restraints, the values of the new capitalist spirit—competition, enterprise, and success—openly governed Italian political life and fashioned an approach to government that served as a model for later state systems. The readings are thus concerned with the transfer of these values to political organization.

From *The Renaissance* by Wallace K. Ferguson. Copyright 1940 by Holt, Rinehart and Winston, Inc. Copyright © 1968 by Wallace K. Ferguson. Reprinted by permission of Holt, Rinehart and Winston, Inc.

I

At the end of the thirteenth century the urban classes were still a minority in European society, and would long remain so. Even in Northern Italy and the Netherlands, the cities contained only a relatively small proportion of the total population. Yet the burghers had already exerted an influence out of all proportion to their numerical strength, and the future was theirs. . . .

The most obvious and the most immediately significant aspect of the transformation [that followed] was the change that took place in political organization. The expansion of money economy enabled the feudal monarchs of the West to assert their authority effectively and to transform amorphous feudal kingdoms into strongly centralized territorial states. And this new political organization, in turn, exercised an ever increasing influence on social and economic life. By the end of the fifteenth century the monarchs of England, France and the kingdoms of the Spanish peninsula had succeeded in destroying all but the last vestiges of political feudalism, while a similar result was accomplished in the Netherlands by the Dukes of Burgundy. The collapse of the Holy Roman Empire in the thirteenth century paralyzed central government in both Germany and Italy and prevented the rise of a national state in either country. . . . Yet even in Germany feudal chaos was mitigated by the consolidation of central government in the larger fiefs, which transformed them for all practical purposes into territorial principalities. . . .

The dynamic forces which transformed and finally destroyed medieval civilization began to operate first in Italy and developed there much more rapidly and intensively than in the northern countries. Before the end of the thirteenth century, feudalism had disappeared in central and northern Italy, giving place to a vigorous urban society in politically independent city-states. . . .

Italy owed her wealth and the early rise of her cities in the first place to her geographical position, which made her the natural entrepôt between the East and the West. From the beginning of the commercial revival in the eleventh century, it was the international trade of Italy that formed the basis for her extraordinary economic activity and kept for her the undisputed economic hegemony of Europe, until the explorations of the late fifteenth century and the growth of commerce and industry in the northern and western states combined to shift the centre of European commerce from the Mediterranean to the Atlantic coast. Moreover, it was the unique preponderance of foreign over domestic trade in Italy, the wide geographical scope of her commercial enterprises, and the unusual opportunities for profit arising from the luxury trade with the East that enabled

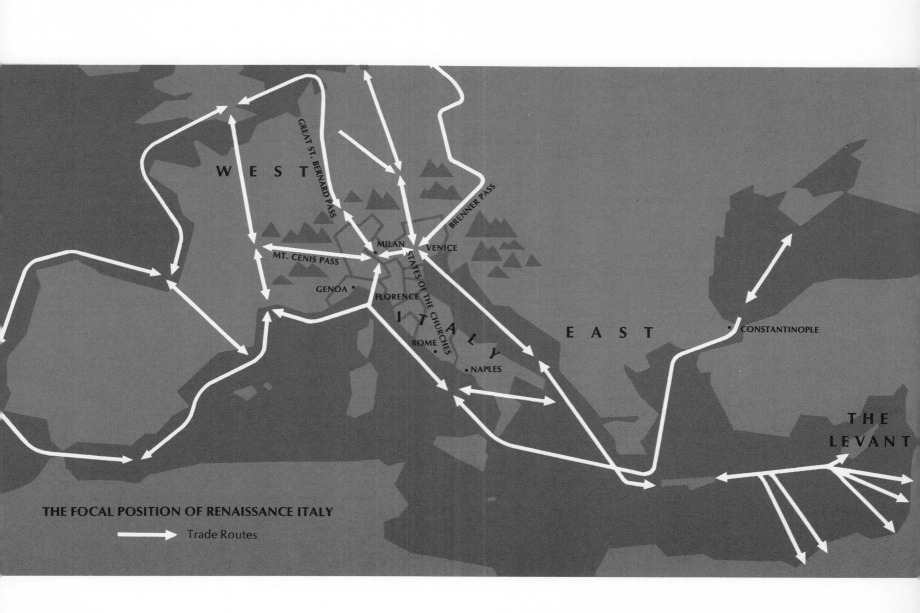

WEST

GREAT ST. BERNARD PASS

BRENNER PASS

MT. CENIS PASS

MILAN

VENICE

STATES OF THE CHURCHES

GENOA

FLORENCE

ITALY

ROME

NAPLES

EAST

CONSTANTINOPLE

THE LEVANT

THE FOCAL POSITION OF RENAISSANCE ITALY

Trade Routes

the Italian merchants to accumulate fortunes of unprecedented size, and to work out techniques for handling capital and credit far in advance of their northern neighbors. The concentration of wealth, which resulted from this early evolution of Italian capitalism, exercised a profound influence on the formation of Renaissance society and culture. . . .

The Political Evolution of the Italian States

The political like the economic evolution of Italy was in many respects exceptional, though the same forces were at work there that transformed the feudal states beyond the Alps. But, whereas in the North the rise of money economy and city life led to the growth of central government and to the creation of great territorial or national states, in Italy the cities helped to destroy what central government there was. By the end of the High Middle Ages, each city, save in the southern Kingdom of Naples, had become the center of a separate little territorial state. . . .

Another factor in the exceptional character of Italy's political evolution was the early destruction of feudalism. Everywhere the rise of the cities and of money economy brought about the eventual decline of the nobility, but in Italy the influence of the cities was direct and overwhelming. By the twelfth century, the cities dominated the Italian scene and the feudal nobles were drawn into them by the irresistible attraction of their wealth and political power. The nobles combined with the rich merchants to form a patrician ruling class, contributing their military skill to the struggle for independence. Many of the nobles intermarried with the wealthy burgher families, engaged in trade, and gradually abandoned

their feudal way of life. Those of the old nobility, indeed, who could not adjust themselves to urban economy did not survive. Their lands passed into the hands of the merchants and money-lenders, for land alone, when cultivated without capital and in the customary feudal fashion, could not produce enough money to meet the rising standard of living set by the rich urban classes. The ownership of land was thus concentrated in the cities, either by the migration of the old landholders or by purchase. A natural corollary of this was the extension not only of the city's economic control but also of its political authority over the surrounding country districts. No similar extension of the political power of the cities occurred in other parts of Europe, for elsewhere the feudal nobles kept to the land and retained their jurisdiction over it until the growth of central government vested all political power in the state. In Italy there was neither a bellicose landed nobility nor a strong central government to prevent the communes from acquiring full political rights over the surrounding countryside. The rural population, thus subjected to the rule of the cities, received no political rights and played no active part in the political life of the state.

Since every city was an independent city-state with its own tumultuous history of party strife and war with its neighbors, the political history of Italy during the early Renaissance is a bewildering story. Later, the confusion became somewhat less confounded as Venice, Milan and Florence expanded their subject territory and between them conquered nearly all of Lombardy and Tuscany. Toward the end of the Renaissance, too, the popes finally succeeded in restoring their authority over the Papal States and so destroyed the inde-

pendence of the numerous little city-states which had sprung up in central Italy. Even then, the story is still too complex for brief summary. Nevertheless, some common characteristics may be observed and one may hazard certain generalizations regarding the course of political development in all the states. In the first place, the political evolution of each state was determined, more or less, by the nature of the city's economic life and by the conflicting interests of the various classes. And secondly, in nearly every state republican government broke down, to be replaced by the rule of a despot.

The Italian communes began their career as urban republics. In the early period of their existence they were in theory burgher democracies, but in almost every instance they were actually ruled by a patriciate of rich merchants and nobles. These old wealthy families, who were referred to indiscriminately as *grandi,* nobles or magnates, enjoyed the prestige of having led the cities triumphantly through the struggle for independence. With greater security, however, their government became increasingly selfish, and during the thirteenth century their domination was challenged by a rising class of new rich—merchants, industrial capitalists and bankers—who felt that their wealth entitled them to political influence and who were eager to direct state policy in accordance with their own economic interests. In Florence, these latter were aptly named the *popolo grasso,* the fat people. Below them were the middle class of small burghers—guild masters, shop-keepers and professional men. These were the *popolo.* Their interests centred about local trade and they were generally opposed to the economic imperialism of the great merchants, which so often involved the city-states in expensive wars. On the whole, however, they were in closer sympathy with the new rich who had arisen from their midst than with the aristocratic *grandi* on the one hand, or the propertyless industrial proletariat on the other. These last were the *popolo minuto,* the little people, strong in numbers but usually devoid of political rights. As the cities grew in population and wealth, the relative importance of the long-established patrician families declined, and each of the classes strove, singly or in combination with others, to seize control of the government.

The purely mercantile patriciate of Venice, where commerce was all important, formed the outstanding exception. There, the old merchant families succeeded in maintaining a rigid control of both the economic and political life of the city for centuries, so that Venice remained throughout the Renaissance a republic ruled by an aristocratic merchant oligarchy. The *grandi* of Florence were less fortunate. The industrial and commercial growth of the Tuscan city in the thirteenth century produced an exceptionally powerful class of new capitalists, who by 1293 were strong enough to exclude the *grandi* from office. This new oligarchy kept up the forms of democracy by admitting the *popolo* of the lesser guilds to a minor share in the government, but they excluded the growing class of proletarian workers who were the employees of the industrial capitalists. A successful rising of the weavers and other workers (the Ciompi) in 1378 gave them a brief political power, but in 1382 the *popolo grasso* regained control and kept it until 1434, when Cosimo de' Medici gathered the strings of the republican machine into his own capable hands. . . .

In most of the Italian cities, wealth was not so largely concentrated in the hands of one class as in Venice and Florence. As the political importance of the *grandi* began to decline, therefore, a fairly even balance of classes produced an unstable state of equilibrium in which no one class could dominate. Short-sighted selfishness and family pride prevented the old patrician families from sharing their traditional political privileges with the new rich, so that the wealthy classes remained divided and lost the opportunity to establish a secure plutocracy. . . . Security and internal peace are necessary to the welfare of a business community, and these the old republican administrations seemed unable to provide. Nor, while weakened by internal strife, could they give the strong leadership needed by cities perennially at war with one another in a struggle for more land, for control of trade routes or merely to ruin economic competitors.

Before the end of the thirteenth century there was a growing conviction that the only solution to this troubled situation was the rule of one man, who could suppress factional strife and give consistent direction to state policy. . . .

Despots rose to power in a variety of ways, and the legal foundation of their authority was often a rather feeble structure. Yet they all owed their power, in a sense, to the popular will, and they could continue to rule only with the tacit consent of the citizens. They could not, however, depend upon a long tradition of loyalty as could the northern monarchs. There was always danger of revolution or of assassination at the hands of some eager aspirant to the despot's office, often enough a member of his own family. Ruling an Italian state was a hazardous occupation, and the

mortality rate among despots was high. On the other hand, the despotic princes were not hampered by feudal traditions and laws, nor had they to meet the problems involved in the transformation of a feudal régime into a centralized state. They took over states in which the government was already centralized. In these urban states money had long been the instrument of power and there was a long-established tradition of taxation. The Italian despots had merely to take over personal control of a going concern. They were the practically minded products of a business community and, if they were not all the self-made supermen of popular conception, most of them were intelligent enough to realize that their own prosperity depended on the prosperity of their subjects. The final justification of their government was that they fostered business, kept order and gave the states greater stability than had the old faction-torn republics. And they expended their wealth freely in the patronage of arts and letters. The concentration of wealth allied with political power in the princely courts was a very significant factor in the cultural and social development of the Renaissance.

II

The government of the Italian states was in many respects more rational than that of the northern monarchies that were just emerging from feudalism. The despots grew up in a society that had lost the personal loyalties of the feudal régime and had abandoned many of the moral conceptions of the Middle Ages regarding the conduct of business and politics. They were inclined to regard any means as justifiable that led to the ultimate end of increasing the power of the state, which was embodied in themselves. The conception of the state as a law unto itself and of public morality as something entirely distinct from private morality appeared earlier and in more complete form in Italy than in the rest of Europe. Long before Machiavelli wrote *The Prince,* the despots were working on the conviction that an act of clemency or the keeping of a promise that might harm the state was little short of silly. In both government and diplomacy the calculated subordination of means to ends gave to the Italian states an air of practical efficiency that was in part an illusion, for there were disadvantages in this uninhibited virtuosity. Intricate diplomacy based on treachery often defeated its own ends, and the ruthless government of the despots failed to build up public spirit among the citizens of the state.

One of the most unfortunate results of this, as Machiavelli pointed out, was that the Italian states were forced to depend exclusively upon mercenary soldiers for defence or aggression. Neither the despots nor the oligarchies dared arm their subjects, nor would even the most loyal citizens be willing to fight for a government which they accepted, but for which they felt no active responsibility. The government had no choice but to bargain with one of the professional condottieri to supply it with an army. This was a straight business transaction. The condottieri were in reality military entrepreneurs, the capitalists of warfare. Many of them were skilled strategists, but they owed no real loyalty to the state they fought for and they usually preferred not to risk decisive battles, since in that event either a defeat or a victory meant the termination of a lucrative contract. The most successful condottieri were not the best generals but the best businessmen. However effective they might appear in action against one another, they proved quite incapable of defending the Italian states against the great national armies of France and Spain, when the foreign invasions began at the end of the fifteenth century.

Italy had escaped invasion, during the period when she was least united and therefore most helpless, largely because the great northern and western states were otherwise engaged. Until the latter part of the fifteenth century, France was involved in the Hundred Years' War and the struggle with Burgundy, and Spain was divided among five separate kingdoms. Meanwhile the expansion of the richest Italian states had restored a certain degree of unity to Italy. At the time of the first French invasion in 1494, five large states, Venice, Milan, Florence, the Papal States, and the Kingdom of Naples occupied most of the peninsula. . . . For half a century these states had kept a reasonable degree of peace through maintaining a balance of power. But they all regarded one another with suspicion and never dreamt of uniting, even when threatened by foreign conquest. The lack of Italian national patriotism and the selfish policy of states and princes sealed the doom of Italy in the following century.

Alfred von Martin: The Dynamic Spirit of Capitalism

Alfred von Martin (1882–   ), German sociologist, is the author of numerous sociological interpretations of historical periods. In this reading he discusses the impact of a money economy on politics in the Renaissance. Of importance is his observation that here for the first time one meets the modern concept that time is money. From Alfred von Martin, *Sociology of the Renaissance* (Oxford University Press, 1944), pp. 1–3, 15–16.

The centre of gravity of medieval society was the land, was the soil. With the Renaissance the economic and thus the social emphasis moves into the town: from the conservative to the liberal, for the town is a changeable and changing element. . . . As the burghers became a power with the rise of a money economy, as the small artisan became the great merchant, we find a gradual emancipation from the traditional forms of society and the mediaeval outlook: there was a revolt against those sections of society which were most dependent upon this structure and upon these ways of thought, by virtue of which they exercised their authority. We find arising against the privileged clergy and the feudal nobility the bourgeoisie, which was throwing off their tutelage and emerging on the twin props of money and intellect as a bourgeoisie of "liberal" character. By revolting against the old domination they also freed themselves from the old community ties which had been interlinked with it. Blood, tradition and group feeling had been the basis of the community relationships as well as of the old domination. The democratic and urban spirit was destroying the old social forms and the "natural" and accepted divine order. It thus became necessary to order the world starting from the individual and to shape it, as it were, like a work of art. The guiding rules in this task accorded with those liberal aims set by the constructive will of the bourgeoisie.

Life in a primary community is apt to produce a conservative type of thought, a religious way of thought which orders the world in an authoritarian manner. Everything temporal is to it no more than a parable, a symbol of the metaphysical, and nature is but a reflection of the transcendental. But the bourgeois world as seen from the coolly calculating, realist point of view of the city-state is a world that has lost its magic. The liberal mode of thought of the emancipated individual attempts to control the outside world more and more consciously. Thus community becomes society, and thus arises the new domination by a new oligarchy, the capitalist domination by the moneyed great bourgeoisie, which exploits those "democratic" tendencies which had destroyed feudalism, as the best way to ensure its own domination. In the Middle Ages political power with religious sanction had prevailed: now comes the era of an intellectually supported economic power. Religion as well as politics becomes a means, just as previously commerce and secular culture had been no more than the means to an end.

The Middle Ages in their social structure as well as in their thought had a rigidly graduated system. There was a pyramid of Estates as well as a pyramid of values. Now these pyramids are about to be destroyed, and "free competition" is proclaimed as the law of nature. God and blood, the traditional powers, are deposed, and though they maintain some of their importance their dominance is shattered.

The spirit of capitalism which begins to rule the modern world with the Renaissance deprives the world of the divine element in order to make it more real. But the spirit of early capitalism did not as yet dehumanize it. Reason was not as yet rated above humanity; it was not yet the be-all and end-all of all action. Riches were, as yet, no more than a means to independence, respect and fame. . . .

NEW MODES OF THOUGHT

Money capital and mobile property naturally linked up with the kindred power of time for, seen from that particular point of view, time is money. Time is a great "liberal" power as opposed to the "conservative" power of space, the immobile soil. In the Middle Ages power belonged to him who owned the soil, the feudal lord; but now Alberti could say that he who knew how to exploit money and time fully could make himself the master of all things: such are the new means to power of the bourgeois. . . . Money, because it circulates, as landed property cannot, shows how everything became more mobile. Money which can change one thing into another brought a tremendous amount of unrest into the world. The tempo of life was increased. Only now was formulated the new interpretation of time which saw it as a value, as something of utility. It was felt to be slipping away continuously—after the fourteenth century the clocks in the Italian cities struck all the twenty-four hours of the day. It was realized that time was always short and hence valuable, that one had to husband it and use it economically if one wanted to become the "master of all things." Such an attitude had been unknown to the Middle Ages; to them time was plentiful and there was no need to look upon it as something precious. It became so only when regarded from the point of view of the individual who could think in terms of the time measured out to him. . . .

Cosimo de Medici Rules Florence

The best example of the relation between wealth and political power at this time is found in the Medici family of Florence. The Medici had accumulated a large fortune from trade and moneylending in the fourteenth century. Members of the family had long played an active political role in the city, but in 1434 their then head, Cosimo (1389–1464), gained permanent control of the city by astutely playing rival political factions against one another. Not holding office himself, Cosimo ran the city in the manner of a modern political boss, rewarding his supporters with political appointments and money gifts, while lavishly patronizing religion and art and turning a ready ear to popular demands. This account of the life of the great merchant prince is found in Niccolo Machiavelli's history of Florence, a work which marks the beginning of modern critical historical scholarship. The section on Cosimo is, nonetheless, a eulogy of one man who fit Machiavelli's standard for effective political leadership. From Niccolo Machiavelli, *History of Florence and of the Affairs of Italy* (New York, 1901), pp. 314–319.

Of all who have left memorials behind them, and who were not of the military profession, Cosimo was the most illustrious and the most renowned. He not only surpassed all his contemporaries in wealth and authority, but also in generosity and prudence; and among the qualities which contributed to make him prince in his own country, was his surpassing all others in magnificence and

Palazzo Riccardi, built in 1430, was one of several Medici townhouses in Florence. Note the fortress-like nature of the lower story to guard against popular riots.

This Medici country villa in Poggio a Caiano was built for Lorenzo the Magnificent, grandson of Cosimo.

generosity. His liberality became more obvious after his death, when to Piero, his son, wishing to know what he possessed, it appeared there was no citizen of any consequence to whom Cosimo had not lent a large sum of money. . . . His magnificence is evident from the number of public edifices he erected; for in Florence are the convents and churches of St. Marco and St. Lorenzo, and the monastery of Santa Verdiana; in the mountains of Fiesole, the church and abbey of St. Girolamo; and in the Mugello, he not only restored, but rebuilt from its foundation, a monastery of the Frati Minori, or Minims. . . . To these sacred edifices are to be added his private dwellings, one in Florence, of extent and elegance adapted to so great a citizen, and four others . . . each, for size and grandeur, equal to royal palaces. And, as if it were not sufficient to be distinguished for magnificence of buildings in Italy alone, he erected an hospital at Jerusalem, for the reception of poor and infirm pilgrims. Although his habitations, like all his other works and actions, were quite of a regal character, and he alone was prince in Florence, still everything was so tempered with his prudence, that he never transgressed the decent moderation of civil life; in his conversation, his servants, his traveling, his mode of living, and the relationships he formed, the modest demeanor of the citizen was always evident; for he was aware that a constant exhibition of pomp brings more envy upon its possessor than greater realities borne without ostentation. . . .

No one of his time possessed such an intimate knowledge of government and state affairs as himself; and hence amid such a variety of fortune, in a city so given to change, and among a people of such extreme inconstancy, he retained possession of the government thirty-one years; for being endowed with the utmost prudence, he foresaw evils at a distance, and therefore had an opportunity either of averting them, or preventing their injurious results. He thus not only vanquished domestic and civil ambition, but humbled the pride of many princes with so much fidelity and address, that whatever powers were in league with himself and his country, either overcame their adversaries, or remained uninjured by his alliance; and whoever were opposed to him, lost either their time, money, or territory. . . .

After the age of forty, he enjoyed the greatest felicity; and not only those who assisted him in public business, but his agents who conducted his commercial speculations throughout Europe, participated in his prosperity. Hence many enormous fortunes took their origin in different families of Florence, as in that of the Tornabuoni, the Benci, the Portinari, and the Sassetti. Besides these, all who depended upon his advice and patronage became rich; and, though he was constantly expending money in building churches, and in charitable purposes, he sometimes complained to his friends that he had never been able to lay out so much in the service of God as to find the balance in

his own favor, intimating that all he had done or could do, was still unequal to what the Almighty had done for him. He was of middle stature, olive complexion, and venerable aspect; not learned but exceedingly eloquent, endowed with great natural capacity, generous to his friends, kind to the poor, comprehensive in discourse, cautious in advising, and in his speeches and replies, grave and witty. . . . Some [opponents] gave him to understand they were "not dreaming." He said, "he believed it, for he had robbed them of their sleep." When Pope Pius was endeavoring to induce the different governments to join in an expedition against the Turks he said, "he was an old man, and had undertaken the enterprise of a young one." . . . A few hours before his death, his wife asked him why he kept his eyes shut, and he said, "to get them in the way of it." Some citizens saying to him, after his return from exile, that he injured the city, and that it was offensive to God to drive so many religious persons out of it; he replied, that, "it was better to injure the city, than to ruin it; that two yards of rose-colored cloth would make a gentleman, and that it required something more to direct a government than to play with a string of beads." These words gave occasion to his enemies to slander him, as a man who loved himself more than his country, and was more attached to this world than to the next. . . . He died, however, at the zenith of his glory and in the enjoyment of the highest renown. The city, and all the Christian princes, condoled with his son Piero for his loss. His funeral was conducted with the utmost pomp and solemnity, the whole city following his corpse to the tomb in the church of St. Lorenzo, on which, by public decree, he was inscribed, "FATHER OF HIS COUNTRY." . . .

Machiavelli Advises Princes How To Govern (1513)

Niccolo Machiavelli (1469–1527), Renaissance writer and statesman, is best known for his little book of advice for princes, in which Renaissance reliance on individualism is translated into practical examples of conduct for those in authority. The term "machiavellian" has come to describe one who is crafty or deceitful. From *The Prince* by Niccolo Machiavelli. Translated by W. K. Marriott. Everyman's Library Edition. Reprinted by permission of E. P. Dutton & Co., Inc. This is published in Canada by J. M. Dent & Sons Ltd.

I. CONCERNING CRUELTY AND CLEMENCY, AND WHETHER IT IS BETTER TO BE LOVED THAN FEARED

I say that every prince ought to desire to be considered clement and not cruel. Nevertheless he ought to take care not to misuse this clemency. . . . A prince, so long as he keeps his subjects united and loyal, ought not to mind the reproach of cruelty; because with a few examples he will be more merciful than those who, through too much mercy, allow disorders to arise, from which follow murder or robbery; for these are wont to injure the whole people, whilst those executions which originate with a prince offend the individual only.

And of all princes, it is impossible for the new prince to avoid the imputation of cruelty, owing to new states being full of dangers. . . . Nevertheless he ought to be slow to believe and to act, nor should he himself show fear, but proceed in a temperate manner with prudence and humanity, so that too much confidence may not make him incautious and too much distrust render him intolerable.

Upon this a question arises: whether it be better to be loved than feared or feared than loved? It may be answered that one should wish to be both, but, because it is difficult to unite them in one person, it is much safer to be feared than loved, when, of the two, either must be dispensed with. Because this is to be asserted in general of men, that they are ungrateful, fickle, false, cowards, covetous, and as long as you succeed they are yours entirely; they will offer you their blood, property, life, and children, as is said above, when the need is far distant; but when it approaches they turn against you. And that prince who, relying entirely on their promises, has neglected other precautions, is ruined; because friendships that are obtained by payments, and not by greatness or nobility of mind, may indeed be earned, but they are not secured, and in time of need cannot be relied upon; and men have less scruple in offending one who is beloved than one who is feared, for love is preserved by the link of obligation which, owing to the baseness of men, is broken at every opportunity for their advantage; but fear preserves you by a dread of punishment which never fails.

Nevertheless a prince ought to inspire fear in such a way that, if he does not win love, he avoids hatred; because he can endure very well being feared whilst he is not hated, which will always be as long as he abstains from the property of his citizens and subjects and from their women. But when it is necessary for him to proceed against the life of some one, he must do it on proper justification and for manifest cause, but above all things he must keep his hands off the prop-erty of others, because men more quickly forget the death of their father than the loss of their patrimony. Besides, pretexts for taking away the property are never wanting; for he who has once begun to live by robbery will always find pretexts for seizing what belongs to others; but reasons for taking life, on the contrary, are more difficult to find and sooner lapse. But when a prince is with his army, and has under control a multitude of soldiers, then it is quite necessary for him to disregard the reputation of cruelty, for without it he would never hold his army united or disposed to its duties. . . .

Returning to the question of being feared or loved, I come to the conclusion that, men loving according to their own will and fearing according to that of the prince, a wise prince should establish himself on that which is in his own control and not in that of others; he must endeavour only to avoid hatred, as is noted.

II. CONCERNING THE WAY IN WHICH PRINCES SHOULD KEEP FAITH

Every one admits how praiseworthy it is in a prince to keep faith, and to live with integrity and not with craft. Nevertheless our experience has been that those princes who have done great things have held good faith of little account, and have known how to circumvent the intellect of men by craft, and in the end have overcome those who have relied on their word. You must know there are two ways of contesting, the one by the law, the other by force; the first method is proper to men, the second to beasts; but because the first is frequently not sufficient, it is necessary to have recourse to the second. Therefore it is necessary for a prince to understand how to avail himself of the beast and the man. This has been figuratively taught to princes by ancient writers, who describe how Achilles and many other princes of old were given to the Centaur Chiron to nurse, who brought them up in his discipline; which means solely that, as they had for a teacher one who was half beast and half man, so it is necessary for a prince to know how to make use of both natures, and that one without the other is not durable. A prince, therefore, being compelled knowingly to adopt the beast, ought to choose the fox and the lion; because the lion cannot defend himself against snares and the fox cannot defend himself against wolves. Therefore, it is necessary to be a fox to discover the snares and a lion to terrify the wolves. Those who rely simply on the lion do not understand what they are about. Therefore a wise lord cannot, nor ought he to, keep faith when such observance may be turned against him, and when the reasons that caused him to pledge it exist no longer. If men are entirely good this precept would not hold, but because they are bad, and will not keep faith with you, you too are not bound to observe it with them. Nor will there ever be wanting to a prince legitimate reasons to excuse this non-observance. Of this endless modern examples could be given, showing how many treaties and engagements have been made void and of no effect through the faithlessness of princes; and he who has known best how to employ the fox has succeeded best.

But it is necessary to know well how to disguise this characteristic, and to be a great pretender and dissembler; and men are so simple, and so subject to present necessities, that he who seeks to deceive will always find some one who will allow himself to be deceived. One recent example I cannot pass over in silence. [Pope] Alexander the Sixth did nothing else but deceive men, nor ever thought of doing otherwise, and he always found victims; for there never was a man who had greater power in asserting, or who with greater oaths would affirm a thing, yet would observe it less; nevertheless his deceits always succeeded according to his wishes, because he well understood this side of mankind.

Therefore it is unnecessary for a prince to have all the good qualities I have enumerated, but is very necessary to appear to have them. And I shall dare to say this also, that to have them and always to observe them is injurious, and that to appear to have them is useful; to appear merciful, faithful, humane, religious, upright, and to be so, but with a mind so framed that should you require not to be so, you may be able and know how to change to the opposite.

And you have to understand this, that a prince, especially a new one, cannot observe all those things for which men are esteemed, being often forced, in order to maintain the state, to act contrary to fidelity, friendship, humanity, and religion. Therefore it is necessary for him to have a mind ready to turn itself accordingly as the winds and variations of fortune force it, yet, as I have said above, not to diverge from the good if he can avoid doing so, but, if compelled, then to know how to set about it.

The Venetians Turn down a Crusade

In the fourteenth century a new menace from the East, the Ottoman Turks, began the gradual conquest of the Byzantine Empire that culminated in the fall of Constantinople in 1453. Pope Pius II (1458–1464), a brilliant writer and orator, called a congress in Mantua in 1459 at which he hoped to repeat the success of Pope Urban in organizing a crusade against the infidel. Essential to his efforts was the cooperation of the rich mercantile city-state of Venice that had extensive commercial interests in the eastern Mediterranean. Venetian hesitation to associate themselves in hostilities against the Turks unless they were assured of united action on the part of the Western nations doomed the papal efforts. In 1463 Pius dramatically took the Cross himself but died before he could set off on his crusade. This reading consists of comments on the congress dictated by the Pope himself. Reprinted by permission of G. P. Putnam's Sons from *Memoirs of a Renaissance Pope: The Commentaries of Pius II,* translated by Florence Gragg, edited by Leona C. Gabel. Copyright © 1959 by Florence A. Gragg.

We wish at this point to speak more fully of the Venetians, since they are today the most powerful state on both land and sea and seem not unfitted for the larger empire to which they aspire. . . .

Venetia originally occupied almost all the islands between Grado and Loredo which constituted one body politic composed of a number of towns. Today the buildings are continuous, forming one city divided by canals flooded with salt water which serve as streets. The large canals are broad enough to permit a galley to be rowed in them. There are paths paved with brick for pedestrians. Merchandise is shipped here from almost the entire world and there is no more famous trading center in all Europe. Merchants from all over the West bring their wares here and carry away the wares of the East. They have an armory and a magnificent dockyard called the Arsenal protected by all sorts of engines where they are ceaselessly building galleys and other craft. It is thought that at a moment's notice they could at pleasure equip 100 galleys and as a matter of fact they have sometimes done so.

The entire city is constructed of brick, but if their empire continues to flourish, it will soon be of marble, and indeed at the present time the palaces of the nobles are veneered with marble and glitter with gold. The celebrated church of St. Mark the Evangelist is constructed of eastern marble, its many gilded domes adorned with the work called mosaic. They say that in this church there is a treasury which surpasses the wealth of kings, containing rubies, diamonds, and all kinds of precious stones. . . .

So much for the Venetians. Though they long refused to send their ambassadors to the Congress of Mantua, finally on learning that the Duke of Clèves had arrived, that the French envoys were expected soon, that Francesco Sforza, Duke of Milan, himself was present, and that they alone of all Italy were missing, fearing public infamy they sent two envoys with a picked company of young nobles, accompanied as a mark of honor by some 500 knights. Francesco Sforza out of respect to the city of Venice met them outside the walls and entered the city riding between the two envoys. One of them, Lodovico, delivered a brilliant speech in a public consistory, for he was not only a jurist but an eloquent orator. The purport of the speech was as follows: The Venetians execrated the insolence of the Turks in invading the lands of others, but they accused the Christians of cowardice in not defending their own possessions or daring to take arms for their religion. They had only praise for the Pope, who in his anxiety for the common weal had come to

Several of the principal buildings of St. Mark's Square seen from the vantage point of the Grand Canal. The gilded palace of the Doge faces the canal to the right; behind it are the domes of St. Mark's Cathedral. To the left the *campanile* (bell tower) soars above the square. Painting by Giovanni Antonio Canaletto (1697–1768).

Mantua at the cost of toil and money. They urged a crusade against the Turks if it could be undertaken by the united forces of all Christians and they promised to do great things to bring that about.

In answer Pius, after some preliminary words about the origin of the Venetians and their glorious history, praised their offers in defense of religion even though they were made on a condition very difficult to fulfill. He rebuked the lateness of the ambassadors, who had been the last to arrive though they were nearest the place of the Congress. He recalled the great affection of Pope Alexander III for the Venetians and assured them that he himself would hold them in no less regard if they stoutly did their part, as they should, to defend the Faith. . . .

The following day all the ambassadors and princes from Italy who were present were summoned before the Pope. The Genoese were not as yet officially present but had secretly promised their aid. The cardinals sat to the right and left of the Pope; the princes and the ambassadors were seated by districts. When they were ready to listen, the Pope said, "My sons, on your advice we have determined to declare war against the Turks and we have no doubt that if Christians come to the defense of their own salvation there will be horses, men, ships, and money in abundance. Now we must consider whether we are to attack the enemy by land or sea or both together; how large a fleet and land army is needed; from what nations soldiers are to be levied: whether we desire to aid the Hungarians with money or with men. Take counsel for the good of all and state openly what help you can promise."

After this there was a long argument with the Venetian ambassadors, whose words were very different from their feelings. They favored the war against the Turks with their lips but condemned it in their hearts. They are not people who embrace splendid projects. They are mostly merchants whose nature, intent on gain, usually shrinks from noble aims which cannot be achieved without expense. The Venetians thought that if war were declared against the Turks, all their trade with the East, on which their livelihood depended, would cease and that after Greece was freed the western princes would not allow the Venetian republic to have sovereignty in Dalmatia and the East. They feared too that while they were occupied with a war with the Turks, the Duke of Milan would attack them; for men always suspect others of their own designs. They had therefore instructed their ambassadors to prolong the discussion and hold out fair hopes, but to promise nothing definite or binding. When however they were pressed more insistently they said that the Venetians would join in the war only on condition that they be allowed the sole conduct of naval matters; that they should have the spoils taken from the enemy; that a large fleet be raised; that an army of 50,000 cavalry and 20,000 infantry should march from Hungary against the Turks. They said a fleet of sixty galleys and twenty saette was needed and 8,000 soldiers besides rowers and other sailors to man them though before they had said that a much smaller number would suffice. They promised only that they would furnish the ships themselves and their equipment. For everything else they expected pay and for this purpose they demanded the tenths, twentieths, and thirtieths raised within their jurisdiction, which they thought would amount to 150,000 ducats. Not satisfied even with this they demanded from the general treasury 1,500,000 more. Such was the liberality of the Venetians.

The Pope answered them as follows: "Ambassadors of the Venetians, we see that it is not your purpose to defend religion, since you ask an almost impossible price. It is a matter for sorrow that your state has so degenerated that she who in the past has gladly armed great fleets for the defense of the Faith is now unwilling, if we take everything into account, to arm even a single ship. Against the Pisans and the Genoese, against kings and emperors you have often waged great wars at your own expense in behalf of your allies and subjects. You now demand a price to fight for Christ against the impious Turks, but even if it were given you you would not arm. Alas! Venetian race, how much of your ancient character have you lost! Too much intercourse with the Turks has made you the friends of the Mohammedans and you care no more for religion."

Much was said to this same effect and often more severely. The envoys being cautious made answers more specious than true. Nothing on their lips matched what was in their hearts.

They opened one line of argument after another, exaggerating the strength of the enemy and belittling ours and trying to take up time till the Congress should be dissolved. Nor did they come to the palace except by appointment. Their bearing was full of pomp and pride. They knelt reluctantly in the Pope's presence and though they saw the ambassadors of kings and of the Emperor himself and mighty princes lie prostrate long after kissing the Pope's feet, they themselves, either from their inveterate pride or the rudeness inherited from their fishermen ancestors, rose immediately. If they were kept waiting a sin-

Despite the hesitation of the Venetians, Pius determined to carry out his crusade. Here the pope (in a sedan chair) arrives at the seaport of Ancona where he died suddenly of fever in August 1464.

gle minute in the Pope's anteroom they at once complained as if insulted and wrote to their senate that they were no more honored by the Pope than if they had been ambassadors from Ancona [a small town]. . . . But as a matter of fact he was excessive and lavish in the honors shown the Venetians rather than remiss. They made these and countless other misrepresentations, in order to pile trouble on trouble. . . .

Worldliness of the Renaissance Papacy

From pp. 30–33, 161–163 *The World of Humanism 1453–1517* by Myron P. Gilmore. Copyright 1952 by Harper & Row, Publishers, Incorporated. By permission of Harper & Row, Publishers.

The economic and political changes . . . produced serious strains in that most comprehensive of all governmental systems, the Christian church. The growing powers of secular states made compromises inevitable. Economic pressures and an expanding standard of wealth accelerated the scramble for the accumulation of benefices. The resulting decline in moral and institutional standards was felt in all parts of the great ecclesiastical organization, but was most dramatically apparent at the apex of the system in the papacy itself. To the long history of opposition to Roman financial exactions and papal control of appointments was now added an increasing lack of respect for the head of the church and his immediate court. Never had the gap appeared so wide between the pretensions of the incumbents of the see of Peter and their actual performance.

The two humanist popes of the mid-fifteenth century, Nicholas V and Pius II, had maintained a high sense of the responsibilities of their position, and if their patronage of the new learning had created precedents that in the long run might be dangerous, yet their pontificates had been free from serious scandals. Beginning, however, with the pontificate of Sixtus IV in 1471, the decline was rapid.

Sixtus IV, born Francesco della Rovere, was the son of a poor and large family. He had distinguished himself in the Franciscan order and in theological disputes on the currently debated doctrine of the Immaculate Conception. Strong, intelligent, ambitious, he embarked on a career of political activity motivated in part by the desire to provide in a suitably splendid way for his eleven nephews and two nieces. Melozzo da Forlì's celebrated picture of the pope receiving Platina, the papal librarian, shows us, symbolically enough, Sixtus attended by his favorite nephews, whose faces reveal their greed, complacency, and ruthlessness. It was a family which had "arrived." During this pontificate significant steps were taken toward enlarging

Pope Sixtus IV (right) receives Platina (kneeling). The pope's nephews are in the background.

TEMPLA DOMVM EXPOSITIS:VICOS FORA MOENIA PONTES:
VIRGINEAM TRIVII QVOD REPARARIS AQVAM.
PRISCA LICET NAVTIS STATVAS DARE COMMODA PORTVS:
ET VATICANVM CINGERE SIXTE IVGVM:
PLVS TAMEN VRBS DEBET:NAM QVAE SQVALORE LATEBAT:
CERNITVR IN CELEBRI BIBLIOTHECA LOCO.

Michelangelo spent four and a half years (1508–1512) lying on his back on scaffolding, to complete the magnificent ceiling of the Sistine Chapel, commissioned by Pope Julius II. The painting retells the story of Genesis from the Creation to the Flood and contains hundreds of massive figures. On the end wall of the chapel is the dramatic "Last Judgment" painted by the artist between 1534 and 1541.

the papal control of the Romagna, where lordships were created for the various nephews . . . and when he died in 1484 he left the inheritance of a papacy increasingly dedicated to its position as a princely power in Italy. The tone of his court had become more and more magnificent and an extravagant luxury the common order of high ecclesiastical life in Rome.

His successor, Giovanni Cibo, who took the title of Innocent VIII, was elected at a conclave distinguished for the openly political struggle between the rival candidates. He was weak, compliant, undistinguished, and dominated by the influence of Giuliano della Rovere [nephew of Pope Sixtus IV], who was considered pope in all but name. Innocent's pontificate was notable because of the extent to which the pope's own children were avowed and openly provided for. His death in 1492 fell at a critical turning point in Italian political history, but it can hardly be supposed that if he had continued to live he would have had a very great influence on the evolution of the system of alliances.

Roderigo Borgia came to the throne in 1492 and took the name of Alexander VI. He reigned for eleven years. Although many of the famous scandals associated with his name and pontificate are highly colored versions of the truth, yet he has long since ceased to have any serious defenders. One of the most ambitious and aggressive of all the popes, he centered his hopes on the position of his family rather than on the institution which he presumably served. For over a decade his maneuvers, bargains and shifts of alliance occupied the center of the stage of European diplomacy, but in the end his favorite son, Caesar, failed to hold the position it had cost so much to win. This disastrous pontificate marked the lowest point of corruption and immorality in the Vatican itself.

After the short reign of Pius III, who died less than four weeks after his election, Giuliano della Rovere at last came to the papal throne as Julius II. The most famous of Renaissance popes, the "papa terribile" devoted himself to the enlargement of the states of the church on lines laid down by his predecessors. By a tremendous effort of energy and will triumphed over a series of crises and lived to see the defeat of the French and the failure of the attempted council of Pisa. He had in a sense delivered the church, but at the price of opening the way to the Spanish domination of the Italian peninsula. One of the greatest patrons in the whole history of the arts, Julius commissioned the work of Michelangelo, Bramante and Raphael. Indeed, the sudden flowering of the style of the High Renaissance in Rome has been attributed to his personal inspiration. It has been suggested that this style was the appropriate expression of the pontiff's religious ideals, the product of a sincere conversion. Whatever the personal religious beliefs of Julius II and their relationship to the artistic achievements of his age, there were many contemporaries who considered the pope's career and ambitions far removed from Christian example. Perhaps no document better illustrates this aspect of contemporary opinion than the satire, *Julius Exclusus,* attributed to Erasmus. . . . Although the satire was not published until 1514 and was always denied by its author, it had a rapid circulation and must have made a profound impression on all who read it. It is cast in the form of a dialogue between Julius II and Saint Peter, in which the former, contrary to his expectation, finds himself excluded from Heaven. Every resource of the author's irony is directed to making manifest the incompatibility between the aims and achievements of this greatest of Renaissance popes and the ideals of the founder of Christianity. Julius finds that he is equipped only with the keys of his money box and of his political power, not with those of the Kingdom of Heaven. Saint Peter refuses to recognize in the warlike figure with his magnificent tiara and pallium the representative of the apostolic succession he had established. The success of this satire, and of others like it, is an indication of the degree to which the prestige of the papacy was declining among the intellectuals. . . .

STUDY QUESTIONS

1. How did the commercial revival affect the medieval approach to government? Why were city-states developed in Italy? Who controlled the government in these states? Why did most of them end up under the rule of despots?

2. What were the major shortcomings of the Italian system?

3. How, according to von Martin, did reliance on a money economy help to liberate men from the limits of traditional society?

4. How does the career of Cosimo de Medici illustrate the connection between wealth and political power?

5. Compare Machiavelli's advice on how to govern with the Christian tradition of kingship. What kind of moral rules did he urge princes to follow? What seems to be his view of what men are like? Why do you think "princes" in Italy have to be so concerned with their public image?

6. Given the time and the circumstances, do you think that the Venetian position on the Turkish crusade was unreasonable? Why was the pope unsuccessful in organizing a crusade?

7. How can you explain the actions of the Renaissance popes?

The Rise of Humanism

From *The Western Heritage,* Second Edition, by Stewart C. Easton. Copyright © 1961, 1966 by Holt, Rinehart and Winston, Inc. Reprinted by permission of Holt, Rinehart and Winston, Inc.

Although there is division of opinion among historians on almost everything else concerned with the Renaissance, including the question of whether there was a Renaissance at all, there is consensus that it started in Italy. . . . There is also no doubt that the Renaissance was most exclusively an urban phenomenon. The medieval nobility had chivalry as its ideal; its pastimes were rudely physical, not to say rustic. Its primary interest was in fighting, not in books. The medieval noble, even in Italy, was rarely literate; even if he lived in a city he was likely to retain his feudal tastes. Most of the Renaissance leaders sprang from a bourgeois background, and had made enough money to be able to afford a life of some leisure and to indulge their taste for literature and the arts. . . .

Italy had never experienced the full pressure of the barbarian invasions at the end of the Roman Empire. Though Ostrogoths and Lombards ruled much of Italy, Italians—descended directly from the Romans—remained in the majority. So the Renaissance Italians believed themselves to be the direct inheritors of the Romans. Their language was the nearest of the European languages to Latin. It was not difficult for them to learn it, and many of the Latin classics were still easily available, even before the humanists began their search for manuscripts. Moreover, there were far more Roman remains in Italy than elsewhere. Thus it was that the Italians, seeking for new ideals suitable to the new situation, had no further to look for examples of secular living than their own Roman ancestors; and it is not surprising that the first stirrings of the Renaissance spirit found expression in the search for ancient manuscripts and the accumulation of libraries of works in the Latin language—not, of course, medieval Latin, which to a true humanist was a barbarous Germanized hodge-podge, but the stately periods of Cicero and the works of the Augustan age.

The consistent ideal of the Renaissance was humanism, which in its widest sense meant the cultivation of the human personality, the regarding of man as the earthly creature he apparently is, and not exclusively as a candidate for salvation. The Greeks in this sense were humanists, as were some of the better-educated Romans, such as Cicero, who had been permeated by Greek culture. It was, however, not unnatural for the men of the Renaissance to give humanism a more restricted meaning. They used it to mean especially the cultivation of the classics, or what are called the humanities. When one speaks therefore of the humanists as a class at this period, the reference is particularly to the scholars who cultivated the use of classical Latin and Greek, and sought for ancient manuscripts in these languages.

Probably the earliest example of this type of humanist was Francesco Petrarca (usually

---

THE CLASSICAL REVIVAL

The literal meaning of Renaissance is "rebirth" and the most unifying feature of the period known as the Renaissance was the revival of interest in Greek and Roman literature and art. Italian writers of the fourteenth and fifteenth centuries viewed the medieval past as a thousand years of cultural obscurity and ignorance and were convinced that their own age was heir to the greatness of antiquity, that had been interrupted by barbarian invasion and the subsequent loss of ancient learning. The readings examine the relationship of this classical revival to the scholarly, artistic, and Christian life.

called Petrarch, 1304–1374), a man of varied talents and complex character, who, without being a great genius, was to set the fashion for generations of later humanists, some of whom surpassed him in talent. He wrote some of the best love lyrics in the Italian tongue, but valued far more highly his often pedantic and uninspired Latin epics, because Latin was the language of his beloved Cicero. He was worried in later life about the salvation of his soul because he had loved Laura and addressed to her his exquisite lyrics. He searched for manuscripts, found one of Homer and adored it, but could not bring himself to learn Greek in order to read it. He climbed a minor mountain for the purpose of enjoying nature in the raw and himself expatiating upon that pleasure. He allowed himself to be crowned with laurel as a poet, and accepted with due humility this uncontested title given to him by a self-appointed group of unauthorized donors. But when all this is admitted, the Italian lyrics and odes remain; the self-advertisement did advertise to all that the profession of letters could lead to fame and was thus worthy of pursuit by others; he did initiate the search for manuscripts, and they were safer in the hands of humanists than in fourteenth-century monasteries. Moreover, there can be little doubt that the humanists appreciated them more than did the monks, and they made them available to others who would likewise appreciate them. . . .

THE IDEAL OF THE "UNIVERSAL MAN"

Ultimately more important than the much publicized recovery of antiquity was the idea of the *uomo universale*, or universal man—the man of versatility who was learned and

Petrarch, crowned with a laurel wreath in emulation of the Roman poets of the Classical past. Detail in Palazzo Vecchio, Florence.

skilled in all things to which he set his hand. Such a man was Leonardo da Vinci, painter, scientist, and inventor; or Lorenzo the Magnificent, the Medici prince of Florence, poet and literary artist, munificent patron of the arts, soldier, administrator, and businessman. In the great period of the Italian Renaissance few aspired to be specialists, with only one skill highly developed and the remainder left unused. The ideal expressed by a young noble, Pico della Mirandola who, if he had lived to maturity, might well have been among the great universal men of the Renaissance—was

the ideal of all. In his *Oration on the Dignity of Man* he gave fine expression to the ideal of man's latent powers to create of himself what he would: "Restrained by no narrow bonds, according to thy own free will . . . thou, thy own free maker and molder, mayest fashion thyself in whatever manner thou likest best." . . .

Unquestionably this was a reaction against the medieval and Christian ideal—the monk whose task was to work and pray, the scholastic philosopher who concentrated his thought on a limited field of knowledge and added little to it from his experience, the feudal noble with his martial ideals and activities, and his total ignorance of almost everything that lay beyond them. . . .

Paul Kristeller: The Renaissance Study of the Humanities

Reprinted by permission of the publishers from Paul O. Kristeller, *The Classics and Renaissance Thought,* Cambridge, Mass.: Harvard University Press, Copyright 1955 by the Board of Trustees of Oberlin College. Pp. 9–13, 18–21, 25, 27–28, 30–34.

The term *humanista,* coined at the height of the Renaissance period, was in turn derived from an older term, that is, from the "humanities" or *studia humanitatis.* This term was apparently used in the general sense of a liberal or literary education by such ancient

Roman authors as Cicero and Gellius, and this use was resumed by the Italian scholars of the late fourteenth century. By the first half of the fifteenth century, the *studia humanitatis* came to stand for a clearly defined cycle of scholarly disciplines, namely grammar, rhetoric, history, poetry, and moral philosophy, and the study of each of these subjects was understood to include the reading and interpretation of its standard ancient writers in Latin and, to a lesser extent, in Greek. This meaning of the *studia humanitatis,* remained in general use through the sixteenth century and later, and we may still find an echo of it in our use of the term "humanities." Thus Renaissance humanism was not as such a philosophical tendency or system, but rather a cultural and educational program which emphasized and developed an important but limited area of studies. This area had for its center a group of subjects that was concerned essentially neither with the classics nor with philosophy, but might be roughly described as literature. . . .

The central importance of literary preoccupations in Renaissance humanism might be illustrated by the professional status of the humanists, most of whom were active either as teachers of the humanities in secondary schools or universities, or as secretaries to princes or cities, and by the bulk of their extant writings, which consist of orations, letters, poems, and historical works and which are in part still unpublished or even unsifted. It cannot be our task . . . to give an account of these professional activities of the humanists, or of their contributions to Neolatin literature and to the various vernacular literatures. I merely want to point out that Renaissance humanism must be understood as a characteristic phase in what may be called the rhetorical tradition in Western culture. This tradition is as old as the Greek Sophists, and it is very much alive in our own day, although the word "rhetoric" has become distasteful to many people. For the studies of speech and composition, of English and creative writing, of advertisement and business correspondence are nothing but modern varieties of the age old rhetorical enterprise that tries to teach oral and written expression by means of rules and models. . . . It was the novel contribution of the humanists to add the firm belief that in order to write and to speak well it was necessary to study and to imitate the ancients. Thus we can understand why classical studies in the Renaissance were rarely, if ever, separated from the literary and practical aim of the rhetorician to write and to speak well. This practical and professional connection provided a strong incentive towards classical studies and helped to supply for them the necessary manpower for their proper development. For I cannot help feeling that the achievements of a given nation or period in particular branches of culture depend not only on individual talents, but also on the available professional channels and tasks into which these talents can be drawn and for which they are trained. . . .

The humanist treatises are important in many ways and deserve a more thorough study than they have received. They please through the elegance and clarity of their style and their vivid personal and historical flavor as well as through their well-selected and mellowed classical wisdom. They also air or express interesting opinions on matters that occupied the heart and thought of the authors and their contemporaries. They derive added importance from the fact that some of the genuine and more concrete problems of moral philosophy were apparently neglected by the professional philosophers of the time, and thus the humanists prepared the ground for a more systematic treatment of the same problems by later philosophers. This seems to be the function of poets, writers, and amateur thinkers at any time when the professional philosophers are absorbed in technicalities and refuse to discuss certain basic problems.

If we remember the range and extent of humanist scholarship and literature, we shall not be surprised to learn that Isocrates, Plutarch, and Lucian were among their favorite authors, but that the ancient writer who earned their highest admiration was Cicero. Renaissance humanism was an age of Ciceronianism in which the study and imitation of Cicero was a widespread concern, although the exaggeration of this tendency also found its critics. Cicero's influence in the Renaissance has been the subject of more than one study, and we can merely try to state in a few words some of the main features of this influence. Above all, Cicero's rhetorical works provided the theory, and his orations, letters, and dialogues the concrete models for the main branches of prose literature, whereas the structure of his well-cadenced sentences was imitated in all kinds of literary compositions. Through his philosophical writings, he served as a source of information for several schools of Greek philosophy and also as a model of that eclectic type of thinking which was prepared to take its crumbs of knowledge wherever it could find them, and which also characterizes many of the humanist treatises. Finally, the synthesis of philosophy and rhetoric in his work provided the humanists with a favorite ideal, namely the combination of eloquence and wisdom, an ideal which pervades so much of Renaissance literature. . . .

After the middle of the fifteenth century, the influence of humanistic learning spread outside the limits of the *studia humanitatis* into all areas of Renaissance culture, including philosophy and the various sciences. This was due not only to the fashionable prestige of the humanities, but also the fact that practically every scholar received a humanistic training in secondary school before he acquired a professional training in any of the other disciplines at the university. On the other hand, some of the humanists also began to realize that a thorough study of philosophy should be added to the *studia humanitatis.* Consequently, we find a number of important thinkers in the fifteenth century, such as Cusanus, Ficino, and Pico, and many more in the sixteenth, who combined a more or less thorough-going humanist background with solid philosophical achievements which were derived from different origins. I believe that the discussion of Renaissance humanism in its original meaning has been confused by the attempts to claim these philosophers as an integral part of it, and thus to identify humanism with all or most of Renaissance philosophy. On the other hand, these thinkers should be taken into account if we wish to understand the indirect influence of humanism on Renaissance thought, an influence which in many ways was even more important than its direct contribution.

The pervasive influence of humanism on all aspects of Renaissance culture and especially on its philosophical thought is a vast subject of which we can mention only a few major points. Some influential aspects of Renaissance humanism are characteristic of the age, and not necessarily due to classical influences. There is the emphasis on man, on his dignity and privileged place in the universe, which was forcefully expressed by Petrarch, Manetti, and other humanists, and later elaborated or criticized by many philosophers. This idea was undoubtedly implied in, and connected with, the concept and program of the *studia humanitatis,* and it has provided the opening entry for many modern interpretations of humanism, whenever the specific content of the humanities was left out of account. Another characteristic feature is the tendency to express, and to consider worth expressing, the concrete uniqueness of one's feelings, opinions, experiences, and surroundings, a tendency which appears in the biographical and descriptive literature of the time as well as in its portrait painting, which is present in all the writings of the humanists, and which finds its fullest philosophical expression in Montaigne, who claims that his own self is the main subject matter of his philosophy. This tendency has been adequately described by Burckhardt, who called it "individualism," and those who have debated the individualism of the Renaissance have missed this point entirely when they understand by individualism merely the existence of great individuals. . . .

The Spread of Learning

The enthusiasm of the humanists for classical learning is shown in a letter of Petrarch (1304–1374) to a friend who had lent him a copy of Cicero. In the days before the printing press, books had to be copied by hand. The second selection describes the founding of the Vatican Library by Pope Nicholas V (1447–1455). From J. H. Robinson, *Readings in European History* (Boston, 1904), I, pp. 527–530.

I. PETRARCH ON CICERO (14TH CENTURY)

Your copy of Cicero has been in my possession four years and more. There is a good reason, though, for so long a delay; namely, the great scarcity of copyists who understand such work. It is a state of affairs that has resulted in an incredible loss to scholarship. . . . But I must return to your Cicero. I could not do without it, and the incompetence of the copyists would not let me possess it. What was left for me but to rely upon my own resources, and press these weary fingers and this worn and ragged pen into the service? The plan that I followed was this. I want you to know it, in case you should ever have to grapple with a similar task. Not a single word did I read except as I wrote. But how is that, I hear some one say; did you write without knowing what it was that you were writing? Ah! but from the very first it was enough for me to know that it was a work of Tullius [Cicero], and an extremely rare one too. And then as soon as I was fairly started, I found at every step so much sweetness and charm, and felt so strong a desire to advance, that the only difficulty which I experienced in reading and writing at the same time came from the fact that my pen could not cover the ground so rapidly as I wanted it to, whereas my expectation had been rather that it would outstrip my eyes, and that my ardor for writing would be chilled by the slowness of my reading.

So the pen held back the eye, and the eye drove on the pen, and I covered page after page, delighting in my task, and committing many and many a passage to memory as I wrote. For just in proportion as the writing is slower than the reading does the passage make a deep impression and cling to the mind.

.

II. POPE NICHOLAS V FOUNDS THE VATICAN LIBRARY (15TH CENTURY)

Owing to the jubilee of 1450 a great quantity of money came in by this means to the apostolic see, and with this the pope commenced building in many places, and sent for Greek and Latin books, wherever he was able to find them, without regard to price. He gathered together a large band of writers, the best that he could find, and kept them in constant employment. He also summoned a number of learned men, both for the purpose of composing new works and of translating such existing works as were not already translated, giving them most abundant provision for their needs meanwhile; and when the works were translated and brought to him, he gave them large sums of money, in order that they should do more willingly that which they undertook to do.

He made great provision for the needs of learned men. He gathered together great numbers of books upon every subject, both Greek and Latin, to the number of five thousand volumes. So at his death it was found by inventory that never since the time of Ptolemy had half that number of books of every kind been brought together. All books he caused to be copied, without regard to what it cost him, and there were few places where his Holiness had not copiers at work.

When he could not procure a book for himself in any way, he had it copied.

After he had assembled at Rome, as I said above, many learned men at large salaries, he wrote to Florence to Messer Giannozzo Manetti . . . urging him to attempt the translation of the books of the Bible and of Aristotle, and to complete the book already commenced by him, *Contra Judoeos et gentes*; a wonderful work, if it had been completed, but he carried it only to the tenth book. . . .

It was Pope Nicholas' intention to found a library in St. Peter's, for the general use of the whole Roman curia, which would have been an admirable thing indeed, if he had been able to carry it out, but death prevented his bringing it to completion. He illumined the Holy Scriptures through innumerable books, which he caused to be translated; and in the same way with the works of the pagans, including certain works upon grammar, of use in learning Latin,—the *Orthography* of Messer Giovanni Tortelle, who was of his Holiness' household and worked upon the library, a worthy book and useful to grammarians; the *Iliad* of Homer; Strabo's *De situ orbis* he caused to be translated by Guerrino, and gave him five hundred florins for each part,—that is to say, Asia, Africa, and Europe; that was in all fifteen hundred florins. Herodotus and Thucydides he had translated by Lorenzo Valla, and rewarded him liberally. . . .

The Invention of Printing

From Sir George Clark, *Early Modern Europe from About 1450 to About 1720* (New York, 1960: Oxford University Press), pp. 52–60.

I

In the year after the fall of Constantinople [1454] Pope Nicholas V proclaimed an indulgence, a remission of spiritual penalties for their sins, for all who would contribute money to the defence of Cyprus against the Turks. It happens that the announcement of this indulgence is the earliest piece of paper printed from movable type in Europe to which we can assign a definite date. We have no reason to suppose that anyone foresaw the full significance of this new technological contrivance. Certainly Mahomet II [the Turkish conqueror], if he ever heard of it, did not infer that the west had new reserves of strength and inventiveness which in time would reverse its relations with the east. . . .

We cannot be certain whether the Europeans learnt printing directly or indirectly from the Chinese or found it out for themselves. We do not even know exactly when or where it was first practised in Europe, but our ignorance of these matters reinforces the knowledge that the new art was not brought full-grown from outside to a western civilization wholly unprepared for it, as the telephone was brought to nineteenth-century Africa. There had been a series of preparatory stages on the technical side. As early as the thirteenth, or even the twelfth, century designs had been printed on textile fabrics from wood blocks cut in relief. Until the beginning of the fifteenth century writing had to be done on parchment and similar materials made from skins, of which the quantity was necessarily limited and the price comparatively high. From that time, however, there were ample supplies of rag-paper, and these made it possible for book-production and writing in general to expand indefinitely. Block-printing on paper came in: there were woodcut pictures of saints, and playing-cards.

The laborious and time-consuming task of writing a manuscript by hand was greatly simplified by the invention of the printing press. Left, a medieval German scholar; right, a scene from a printer's shop in Amsterdam about 1600.

Then only a few adaptations of presses and block-making were necessary to perfect the art, and the final steps were taken most likely in Mainz, a rich trading town and a cultivated ecclesiastical capital. . . .

Works of art became familiar which were not unique, or approximately like their originals, as hand-drawn copies may be, but so nearly identical that for ordinary purposes there was no difference. Many people could possess the same picture. That was a very great change, but there were others. By constantly seeing woodcuts and other engravings, people acquired a new habit or power of seeing not in colour but in black and white, which in some ways enriched and in other ways impoverished their mode of seeing. The world of sight and imagination altered. . . .

No sooner was printing discovered than a great demand for printed books and papers made itself effective throughout all the Latin area. Within a generation there were presses at work in France, Italy, Spain, the Netherlands, England, and Denmark. Before the end of the century Portugal and Sweden had them, and even Montenegro, the Balkan outpost. Books, of course, could be exported to countries where there was no printing; in the sixteenth century a well-organized international book-trade grew up, serving most of the western countries. . . .

Books could now be produced far more quickly, far more cheaply, and in far greater

Facsimile page from the Gutenberg Bible, 1454. Note that although the work was printed with movable type, the pages are illuminated in order to imitate a handcopied manuscript.

numbers. This was a revolution, a revolution continuing until, in our own time, the new inventions for reproducing sound have ended the age in which the printed word has been the main vehicle for spreading knowledge, information, ideas, and even emotions abroad. Beneath all the events of these centuries there has gone on the change from the first printers, who could put out a few hundred copies of a book in a few weeks, to the modern printers who can make a million copies of a newspaper in a few hours. The world has been filled with these uncountable printed sheets and volumes, large and small, cheap or costly, rare or universally familiar, durable or ephemeral, treasured or neglected, commonplace or exquisitely beautiful. Every one of them has left some result behind it, and the sum of these results is far beyond calculation.

It is easy to see that printing made the spread of literacy much easier; and the power to read and write is an instrument of authority if it belongs to a few, but a stepping-stone to equality if it belongs to many. As the number of readers increased, the influence of writers grew with it. In universities, in public affairs, and among general readers there were more books to be had, and so the more personal influence of the teacher or expositor gave way before the might of the book, of the unseen author. Literary reputations could be made and spread as quickly as ships and horses could carry packages of books. Erasmus had a European reputation, and every book he published was known from one end of the continent to the other as soon as it was ready. Every man who could read or be read to was accessible to persuasions, propaganda, from far and near, perhaps authorized, perhaps directed against established ideas and institutions. Governments and the Church, trying, in accordance with their traditions, to keep their control of men's minds, made rules of censorship and new institutions for enforcing them; but the simple machinery of government . . . was often unable to dam the rising streams. From clandestine presses, through secret channels of distribution, writers could still appeal to their readers against the established order. . . .

II

Perhaps the greatest changes which printing brought with it were not these social changes, but the changes in language and literature themselves. Printed books set the standards of uniformity for languages, and so the multiplicity of dialects began to give way before a few great standard literary languages, centred on the political or academic or trading capitals. All Englishmen came to write the language of London; all Frenchmen that of Paris; most of the Spaniards that of Castile. This took time, and it happened more or less quickly according to circumstances. . . . Wherever it did emerge the metropolitan language had a binding and inspiring force of its own, and strengthened the national feeling that was already growing.

In literature the changes were subtle, but radical. It was much easier than before to bring together many books in one place, and so masses of information could be assembled quickly, and the apparatus of learning was transformed. Great books of reference, dictionaries, encyclopaedias, histories, and collections of texts, put at the disposal of every student knowledge which once could not have been gathered in a lifetime. Knowledge of the present was deepened, but also complicated and hindered, by an ever-present consciousness of the past. At the same time standards of correctness became more exacting. With so many identical copies of books before them, not varied by the little touches of individuality which scribes and copyists always introduced intentionally or by accident, readers learnt a new strictness in verbal accuracy and grammatical correctness. The individual work of an author was distinguished more sharply from the inherited or borrowed elements. Copyright became a legal fact, while authorship and plagiarism, as literary and ethical conceptions, were more clearly defined. The Renaissance was helped on not only as an intellectual movement but as a movement in the art of letters as well.

The commonest way of enjoying poetry had been to hear it recited; the commonest way of using a book had been to read it aloud. Now there was so much reading that more and more people read silently to themselves, and books came to be written so that they could best be taken in by the eye and not the ear. Prose gained at the expense of verse; sense gained at the expense of sound. Memory lost some of its value. The story that can be followed without a teller has to be told in a special way: the words themselves, without a voice to clothe them in expression, without accent or intonation, must create their own illusion. So printing set new problems for literature, and as skilful writers devised means of solving them, the range of literature increased until it became, for millions of human beings, almost a substitute for thought and imagination. In the beginning of pre-history speech had given the power of communicating experience, of imagining oneself as a different being, in another time or place. Long afterwards writing had made imagination fixed and lasting and able to add one fancy to another beyond the range of memory, far away from the personal present. Printing set the works of imagination, along with those of thought and emotion, still more securely outside the chances of the present time and place.

Petrarch Is Torn between the Spirit and the World

Francesco Petrarch (1304–1374), one of the greatest humanists, wrote extensively in both Latin and Italian and was one of the first to realize the potential of classical literature in providing men with a new cultural framework. Nonetheless, born in the High Middle Ages, he was torn by the conflict of spiritual and secular values which he reveals in this imaginary conversation between himself and St. Augustine. From Francesco Petrarch, *The Secret, or the Soul's Conflict with Passion,* trans. by William H. Draper. (London, 1911), pp. 175–192.

[St. Augustine] . . . But let us take for granted (what is quite impossible) that the duration of life will be long and assured: still, do you not find it is the height of madness to squander the best years and the best parts of your existence on pleasing only the eyes of others and tickling other men's ears, and to keep the last and worst—the years that are almost good for nothing—that bring nothing but distaste for life and then its end—to keep these, I say, for God and yourself, as though the welfare of your soul were the last thing you cared for?

Even supposing the time were certain, is it not reversing the true order to put off the best to the last?

[Petrarch] I do not think my way of looking at it is so unreasonable as you imagine. My principle is that, as concerning the glory which we may hope for here below, it is right for us to seek while we are here below. One may expect to enjoy that other more radiant glory in heaven, when we shall have there arrived, and when one will have no more care or wish for the glory of earth. Therefore, as I think, it is in the true order that mortal men should first care for mortal things; and that to things transitory things eternal should succeed; because to pass from those to these is to go forward in most certain accordance with what is ordained for us, although no way is open for us to pass back again from eternity to time.

[St. Augustine] O man, little in yourself, and of little wisdom! Do you, then, dream that you shall enjoy every pleasure in heaven and earth, and everything will turn out fortunate and prosperous for you always and everywhere? But that delusion has betrayed thousands of men thousands of times, and has sunk into hell a countless host of souls. Thinking to have one foot on earth and one in heaven, they could neither stand here below nor mount on high. Therefore they fell miserably, and the moving breeze swept them suddenly away, some in the flower of their age, and some when they were in midst of their years and all their business. . . .

[Petrarch] What must I do, then? Abandon my unfinished works? Or would it be better to hasten them on, and, if God gives me grace, put the finishing touches to them? If I were once rid of these cares I would go forward, with a mind more free, to greater things; for hardly could I bear the thought of leaving half completed a work so fine and rich in promise of success.

[St. Augustine] Which foot you mean to hobble on, I do not know. You seem inclined to leave yourself derelict, rather than your books.

As for me, I shall do my duty, with what success depends on you; but at least I shall have satisfied my conscience. Throw to the winds these great loads of histories; the deeds of the Romans have been celebrated quite enough by others, and are known by their own fame. Get out of Africa* and leave it to its possessors. You will add nothing to the glory of your Scipio [Roman leader] or to your own. He can be exalted to no higher pinnacle, but you may bring down his reputation, and with it your own. Therefore leave all this on one side, and now at length take possession of yourself; and to come back to our starting point, let me urge you to enter upon the meditation of your last end, which comes on step by step without your being aware. . . .

When your eyes behold some ancient building, let your first thought be, Where are those who wrought it with their hands? and when you see new ones, ask, Where, soon, the builders of them will be also? If you chance to see the trees of some orchard, remember how often it falls out that one plants it and another plucks the fruit; for many a time the saying of the *Georgics* comes to pass—

> "One plants the tree, but ah, the slow-grown shade
> His grandchild will enjoy."

*Petrarch was writing a history of the war between Rome and Carthage.

And when you look with pleased wonder at some swiftly flowing stream, then, that I bring no other poet's thought, keep ever in mind this one of your own—

> "No river hurries with more rapid flight
> Than Life's swift current." . . .

[Petrarch] Ah! would that you had told me all this before I had surrendered myself over to these studies! . . .

I will be true to myself, so far as in me lies. I will pull myself together and collect my scattered wits, and make a great endeavour to possess my soul in patience. But even while we speak, a crowd of important affairs, though only of the world, is waiting my attention.

[St. Augustine] For the common herd of men these may be what to them seem more important; but in reality there is nothing of more importance, and nothing ought to be esteemed of so much worth. For, of other trains of thought, you may reckon them to be not essential for the soul, but the end of life will prove that these we have been engaged in are of eternal necessity.

[Petrarch] I confess they are so. And I now return to attend to those other concerns only in order that, when they are discharged, I may come back to these.

I am not ignorant that, as you said a few minutes before, it would be much safer for me to attend only to the care of my soul, to relinquish altogether every by-path and follow the straight path of the way of salvation. But I have not strength to resist that old bent for study altogether. . . .

Pico Della Mirandola Extols the Uniqueness of Man (1486)

Giovanni Pico Della Mirandola (1463–1494), a brilliant young Italian philosopher, wrote this praise of man at the age of twenty-four. The "Oration on the Dignity of Man" introduced 900 theses in which Pico tried to reconcile Greek and Christian thought, a daring attempt which led to trouble with the Church. From G. Pico Della Mirandola, *Oration on the Dignity of Man,* trans. A. R. Caponigri (Chicago: Gateway, 1956), pp. 1–5.

Most esteemed Fathers, I have read in the ancient writings of the Arabians that Abdala the Saracen on being asked what, on this stage, so to say, of the world, seemed to him most evocative of wonder, replied that there was nothing to be seen more marvelous than man. And that celebrated exclamation of Hermes Trismegistus, "What a great miracle is man, Asclepius," confirms this opinion.

And still, as I reflected upon the basis assigned for these estimations, I was not fully persuaded by the diverse reasons advanced by a variety of persons for the preeminence of human nature; for example: that man is the intermediary between creatures, that he is the familiar of the gods above him as he is lord of the beings beneath him; that, by the acuteness of his senses, the inquiry of his reason and the light of his intelligence, he is the interpreter of nature, set midway between the timeless unchanging and the flux of time; the living union (as the Persians say), the very marriage hymn of the world, and, by

David's testimony but little lower than the angels. Their reasons are all, without question, of great weight; nevertheless, they do not touch the principal reasons, those, that is to say, which justify man's unique right to such unbounded admiration. Why, I asked, should we not admire the angels themselves and the beatific choirs more: At long last, however, I feel that I have come to some understanding of why man is the most fortunate of living things and, consequently, deserving of all admiration; of what may be the conditions in the hierarchy of beings assigned to him, which draws upon him the envy, not of the brutes alone, but of the astral beings and of the very intelligences which dwell beyond the confines of the world. A thing surpassing belief and smiting the soul with wonder. Still, how could it be otherwise? For it is on this ground that man is, with complete justice, considered and called a great miracle and a being worthy of all admiration.

Hear then, oh Fathers, precisely what this condition of man is; and in the name of your humanity, grant me your benign audition as I pursue this theme.

God the Father, the Mightiest Architect, had already raised, according to the precepts of His hidden wisdom, this world we see, the cosmic dwelling of divinity, a temple most august. He had already adorned the supercelestial region with Intelligences, infused the heavenly globes with the life of immortal souls and set the fermenting dung-heap of the inferior world teeming with every form of animal life. But when this work was done, the Divine Artificer still longed for some creature which might comprehend the meaning of so vast an achievement, which might be moved with love at its beauty and smitten

with awe at its grandeur. When, consequently, all else had been completed (as both Moses and Timaeus testify), in the very last place, He bethought Himself of bringing forth man. Truth was, however, that there remained no archetype according to which He might fashion a new offspring, nor in His treasure-houses the wherewithal to endow a new son with a fitting inheritance, nor any place, among the seats of the universe, where this new creature might dispose himself to contemplate the world. All space was already filled; all things had been distributed in the highest, the middle and the lowest orders. Still, it was not in the nature of the power of the Father to fail . . . nor was it in the nature of that supreme Wisdom to hesitate through lack of counsel in so crucial a matter; nor, finally, in the nature of His beneficent love to compel the creature destined to praise the divine generosity in all other things to find it wanting in himself.

At last, the Supreme Maker decreed that this creature, to whom He could give nothing wholly his own, should have a share in the particular endowment of every other creature. Taking man, therefore, this creature of indeterminate image, He set him in the middle of the world and thus spoke to him:

"We have given you, Oh Adam, no visage proper to yourself, nor any endowment properly your own, in order that whatever place, whatever form, whatever gifts you may, with premeditation, select, these same you may have and possess through your own judgment and decision. The nature of all other creatures is defined and restricted within laws which We have laid down; you, by contrast, impeded by no such restrictions, may, by your own free will, to whose custody We have assigned you, trace for yourself the lineaments of your own nature. I have placed you at the very center of the world, so that from that vantage point you may with greater ease glance round about you on all that the world contains. We have made you a creature neither of heaven nor of earth, neither mortal nor immortal, in order that you may, as the free and proud shaper of your own being, fashion yourself in the form you may prefer. It will be in your power to descend to the lower, brutish forms of life; you will be able, through your own decision, to rise again to the superior orders whose life is divine.

Oh unsurpassed generosity of God the Father, Oh wondrous and unsurpassable felicity of man, to whom it is granted to have what he chooses, to be what he wills to be! The brutes, from the moment of their birth, bring with them, as Lucilius says, "from their mother's womb" all that they will ever possess. The highest spiritual beings were, from the very moment of creation, or soon thereafter, fixed in the mode of being which would be theirs through measureless eternities. But upon man, at the moment of his creation, God bestowed seeds pregnant with all possibilities, the germs of every form of life. Whichever of these a man shall cultivate, the same will mature and bear fruit in him. If vegetative, he will become a plant; if sensual, he will become brutish; if rational, he will reveal himself a heavenly being; if intellectual, he will be an angel and the son of God. And if, dissatisfied with the lot of all creatures, he should recollect himself into the center of his own unity, he will there, become one spirit with God, in the solitary darkness of the Father, Who is set above all things, himself transcends all creatures. . . .

Jacob Burckhardt: Leon Battista Alberti

The classic interpretation of the Italian Renaissance was formulated by the Swiss cultural historian Jacob Burckhardt (1818–1897) in *The Civilization of the Renaissance in Italy* (1860). Burckhardt believed that each time period has its own pattern of culture, and he felt that the fourteenth and fifteenth centuries in Italy marked the beginning of the modern world. For him the new era was characterized most notably by man's rediscovery of the world about him and his reassessment of his own potential. In the reading Burckhardt describes the varied capabilities of one such Renaissance man. From Jacob Burckhardt, *The Civilization of the Renaissance in Italy,* trans. S. Middlemore (London: Phaidon Press Ltd., 1951), pp. 85–87.

The fifteenth century is, above all, that of the many-sided man. . . . But among these many-sided men, some, who may truly be called all-sided, tower above the rest. Before analysing the general phases of life and culture of this period, we may here, on the threshold of the fifteenth century, consider for a moment the figure of one of these giants— Leon Battista Alberti (b. 1404, d. 1472). His biography, which is only a fragment, speaks of him but little as an artist, and makes no mention at all of his great significance in the history of architecture. We shall now see what he was, apart from these special claims to distinction.

In all by which praise is won, Leon Battista was from his childhood the first. Of his various gymnastic feats and exercises we read with astonishment how, with his feet together, he could spring over a man's head; how, in the cathedral, he threw a coin in the air till it was heard to ring against the distant roof; how the wildest horses trembled under him. In three things he desired to appear faultless to others, in walking, in riding, and in speaking. He learned music without a master, and yet his compositions were admired by professional judges. Under the pressure of poverty, he studied both civil and canonical law for many years, till exhaustion brought on a severe illness. In his twenty-fourth year, finding his memory for words weakened, but his sense of facts unimpaired, he set to work at physics and mathematics. And all the while he acquired every sort of accomplishment and dexterity, cross-examining artists, scholars and artisans of all descriptions, down to the cobblers, about the secrets and peculiarities of their craft. Painting and modelling he practised by the way, and especially excelled in admirable likenesses from memory. Great admiration was excited by his mysterious 'camera obscura', in which he showed at one time the stars and the moon rising over rocky hills, at another wide landscapes with mountains and gulfs receding into dim perspective, and with fleets advancing on the waters in shade or sunshine. And that which others created he welcomed joyfully, and held every human achievement which followed the laws of beauty for something almost divine. To all this must be added his literary works, first of all those on art, which are landmarks and authorities of the first order for the Renaissance of Form, especially in architecture; then his Latin prose writings—novels and other works—of which some have been taken for productions of

1.

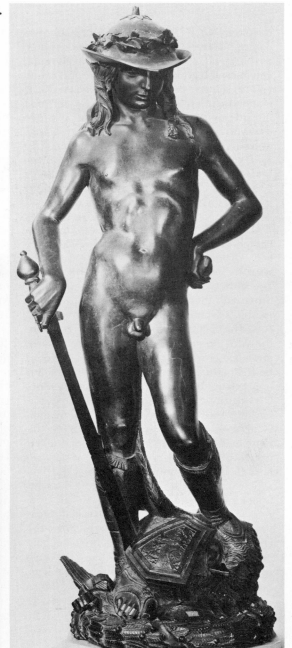

2.

3.

4.

1. "Bindo Altoviti" by Raphael, about 1515.

2. "David" by Donatello, about 1453. This is the first nude statue since Roman times.

3. "Adoration of the Magi" by Boticelli, completed in 1478. Piero, Cosimo and Giovanni di Medici appear in the painting as the Three Wise Men.

4. "Birth of Saint John the Baptist" by Ghirlandaio, completed about 1490. The ladies in the painting are members of the Tornabuoni family which commissioned the painting.

5. "The Descent From the Cross" by Pontormo, c.1526–28. Later Renaissance art called Mannerism.

5.

antiquity; his elegies, eclogues, and humorous dinner-speeches. He also wrote an Italian treatise on domestic life in four books; and even a funeral oration on his dog. His serious and witty sayings were thought worth collecting, and specimens of them, many columns long, are quoted in his biography. And all that he had and knew he imparted, as rich natures always do, without the least reserve, giving away his chief discoveries for nothing. But the deepest spring of his nature has yet to be spoken of—the sympathetic intensity with which he entered into the whole life around him. At the sight of noble trees and waving cornfields he shed tears; handsome and dignified old men he honoured as 'a delight of nature', and could never look at them enough. Perfectly formed animals won his goodwill as being specially favoured by nature; and more than once, when he was ill, the sight of a beautiful landscape cured him. No wonder that those who saw him in this close and mysterious communion with the world ascribed to him the gift of prophecy. He was said to have foretold a bloody catastrophe in the family of Este, the fate of Florence and that of the Popes many years beforehand, and to be able to read in the countenances and the hearts of men. It need not be added that an iron will pervaded and sustained his whole personality; like all the great men of the Renaissance, he said, 'Men can do all things if they will'. . . .

Alberti Praises His Fellow Artists

Leon Battista Alberti (1404–1472) wrote the letter from which the following excerpts are taken to another renowned architect, Filippo

Brunelleschi (1377–1446), designer of the famous dome of the Cathedral of Florence. From *Literary Source of Art History: An Anthology of Texts from Theophilus to Goethe,* ed. by Elizabeth Holt (Copyright 1947 by Princeton University Press), pp. 109–110. Reprinted by permission of Princeton University Press.

I used to be at once amazed and grieved that so many fine and godly arts and sciences, which we know, from their works and histories, flourished in those most virtuous ancients of old, are now lacking and almost entirely lost: painters, sculptors, architects, musicians, geometricians, rhetoricians, soothsayers, and similar most noble and wonderful minds are very rare and of little account. Hence I believed that it was as many people told me, that nature, the mistress of things, had now indeed grown old and weary, and, just as she no longer brought forth giants, so with talents, which in her younger and more glorious times, so to speak, she brought forth plentifully and wonderfully.

But after I was brought back here to this city of ours, adorned above all others, from the long exile in which we Alberti have grown old, I realized that in many, but especially in you, Filippo, and in our dear friend Donato the sculptor, and in those others, Nencio, Luca, and Masaccio, there was talent for every noble thing not to be ranked below any who was ancient and famous in these arts. Therefore I perceived that the power to gain praise consists in our industry and diligence no less than in the benefit of nature and the times. And I reveal to you, that if it was less difficult for the ancients, having as they had so very many to learn from and imitate, to rise to a knowledge of those supreme arts that are so toilsome for us today, then so much the more

our fame should be greater if we, without teachers or any model, find arts and sciences unheard of and never seen. Who is so stubborn or so envious that he would not praise Pippo the architect, when he sees such a big building here, set aloft above the heavens, ample to cover all the peoples of Tuscany with its shade, made without any aid from scaffolding or quantity of timber?—a skillful construction which, if my opinion is right, as in our times it was unbelievable that it could be done, so among the ancients it was perhaps not known or known about.

J. H. Randall: The Humanistic Spirit

In *The Making of the Modern Mind,* John Herman Randall (1899–   ) tried to "make the thought of the present more intelligible by entering sympathetically into the spirit of the past." In this reading Randall comments on the gradual growth of the humanistic spirit that underlay the Renaissance. *The Making of the Modern Mind.* Copyright renewed, 1954, by John Herman Randall, Jr. Reprinted by permission of the publisher, Houghton Mifflin Company.

It is, of course, impossible to speak of *the* Renaissance, as though it were a single age or a single force, and had a definite date, like the French Revolution. Moreover, dramatic and painfully beautiful as were the life and the products of the Italy of the fifteenth and sixteenth centuries, the age of the humanists and of the noontide of Italian art does not mark one of the major intellectual events of the Western peoples. The earlier renaissance of the twelfth and thirteenth centuries was a much more unmistakable rebirth of the mind, while the forces at work in the Middle Ages, which in the sixteenth century were clearly revealed as disruptive of the old order, did not produce their fundamental revolution in men's ways of thinking until the seventeenth and eighteenth. Nevertheless, though the old forms and the old beliefs persisted relatively unchanged, that period which we loosely call the Renaissance was marked by the increasing prevalence of attitudes and interests that had hitherto played but a minor role in the life of Western Europe. These growing interests burst the bonds of the narrow if intricately carved medieval world and left men toying with the fragments. . . .

If, then, the central feature of the period of the Renaissance is an outgrowing, a freeing from ties that have proved to be bonds, it is evident that we have to do with new forces arising within an old order, with stresses and strains, with unstable attempts to effect some kind of adjustment between traditional allegiances and modern appeals. The age of the Renaissance and the Reformation was above all others an age of compromise. If in the joy of widened vistas many were intoxicated by the beauty and the lusts of life at its richest, many more were caught half-hesitant, reluctant, like Bruno, both to leave the Father's house, and not to venture into the glorious world. What was best in Renaissance and Reformation could not last; it was the noble enthusiasm of youth, and what was needed was the hard and painful work of maturity. Nor could what was worst endure; it was the incongruous compromise between elements neither of which was clearly understood, the Christian tradition and the natural, pagan, view of man's life and its scene. The Western

peoples were leaving the old world; eagerly they snatched at the treasures of Greece and Rome as they moved onward to the new. But not till the turn of the seventeenth century did any man realize the nature of that new world, and not till the nineteenth did its features impress the average man. . . .

This rapid growth involved fundamental readjustments in every institution of society; it also demanded thoroughgoing intellectual reconstruction. The changes that came over the mind of Europe during this period, its new knowledge and new ideals, were conditioned by a multitude of other factors, but every new belief, every changed view of man and his destiny, was worked out by men living in such a society and powerfully influenced at every turn by the forces of this society. Only against this background is it possible to understand the new aspirations of the European nations, their achievements and their errors. But if the roots of the new world of the Renaissance are to be sought in economic conditions, its justification and its meaning are to be found in the new spirit and knowledge, that destroyed monasticism and Aristotelian science as capitalism was destroying feudalism and the guilds.

This new spirit consisted at bottom in an increasing interest in human life as it can be lived upon earth, within the bourne of time and space, and without necessary reference to any other destiny in the beyond or the hereafter. It meant the decay of that Oriental dualism in which the flesh for so many long years had lusted against the spirit, and the growth in its stead of the conviction that the life of flesh and spirit merged into one living man is not evil, but good. It meant that when society offered more than a rude mining-camp existence of blood and toil, the monastic temper declined, and gave way to a new

and vital perception of the dignity of man, of the sweetness and glory of being a rational animal.

It happened that those who felt the call of human experience had a great literature to which they could turn, a literature written by peoples who had been stirred by the same passion for the free life of man in its natural setting. The frenzied zeal with which they did find in this literature a confirmation of their own inward stirrings in the face of a rich urban society, has left an indelible impress on the form taken by this interest in the natural man. But if the manuscripts of Greece and Rome had perished every one beneath the monk's missal, the outcome would not have been essentially different. Men would still have turned to man and nature, and if the modern world might not so soon have come into being, it is quite possible that men would not have wandered down so many blind alleys. Of a truth the Renaissance discovered the humanities, but it found them in Florence or Augsburg or Paris, not in ancient books. The books had always been there; they were discovered when men had grown fit to appreciate them. The polished and urbane Cicero, he who had taken the intellectual world of Greece and translated it from the idiom of free and heaven-questioning Athens into the Roman tongue of the market-place and the law-court, he who had dropped from the already fundamentally anthropomorphic wisdom of Hellas all that led the mind away from the passions and the will of the moral life of man, became naturally the idol of those whose days were passed in palace or piazza; and his conception of culture as essentially *Studia humanitatis ac litterarum*, the study of humanity and letters, was acclaimed by those dissatisfied with Acquinas' "truths of God."

STUDY QUESTIONS

1. What is humanism? Why did it originate in Italy? Why were men attracted in the fourteenth and fifteenth centuries to the ideal of the universal man?

2. What, according to Kristeller, did the humanists hope to gain from reading the works of Greek and Roman writers? What was a humanities program like in fifteenth-century Italy?

3. Why did Petrarch hold Cicero in such esteem? Why would he be willing to read him only in the course of recopying the book? How did one build up a library in Petrarch's and Pope Nicholas' time? What do the books collected by the pope tell about Renaissance interests?

4. How has the development of printing changed the lives of men? How did it specifically affect Renaissance society?

5. Why do you think Petrarch made up an imaginary dialogue with St. Augustine? Who, in your opinion, "won" the debate? What does this dialogue tell you about Renaissance values?

6. How did Pico explain the creation of man? How much freedom did man have to become what he willed?

7. Why did Alberti seem to Burckhardt the "ideal" Renaissance man?

8. On what basis did Alberti arrive at his conclusions about the quality of Renaissance art?

9. What, in Randall's view, was the "new spirit" of the Renaissance?

The Renaissance Concept of Female Beauty

The humanistic spirit that inspired the Renaissance was vividly reflected in the favorite subject of its artists, the Virgin Mary, to whom the painters gave the handsome features of contemporary Italian beauties. The four heads on the opposite page range from the sweetly devout face of Alesso Baldovinetti's Virgin and the wholesome peasant look of Andrea Mantegna's (upper left and right) to the mature femininity of Fra Lippo Lippi's and the pensive sophistication of Botticelli's (lower left and right). The sorrowing mother in Michelangelo's Pietà (in St. Peter's in Rome) similarly projects a graceful, ageless beauty.

Struggle for Reform in the Church

From *A History of the Modern World*, by Robert R. Palmer and Joel Colton. Copyright 1950, © 1956, 1965 by Alfred A. Knopf, Inc. Reprinted by permission of the publisher.

TOPIC 5

THE CURRENT OF CHRISTIAN REFORM

The striving of the late medieval Church for wealth and power produced a counter-current of reformist agitation. At issue was the very definition of the Christian Church and its relationship to the values of an increasingly commercial world. The Reformers drew inspiration from the ideals of the early Church, the popular desire for direct communication with God, and growing national feelings. The leaders of the reform movement wanted to change the Church from within, but the nature of their quest threatened, against their own will, to split the Church before they could change it. The readings describe the conditions that weakened the authority of the Church and introduce the programs of reform.

In the light of world history, as we see it today, one of the most momentous experiences that can befall any civilization is for it to break loose from its religious base. . . . It is not, in most cases, that peoples reject their ancestral religion. On the contrary, they often reaffirm it; but they try also to modernize it, to adapt it, to make room for new and nonreligious interests, to bring it about that religion instead of being the womb or matrix from which all else comes, shall be one interest among many.

Latin Christendom was the first modern society to embark on the momentous, troublesome, and long drawn out process of "secularization." In 1300 Europe was still primarily a religious community. The clergy were the prestige-enjoying class. All else was somehow oriented to or pervaded by religious belief. Three centuries later religion was one interest among many. The church itself was divided. The Christian faith still stood; indeed it was purified and reaffirmed both by . . . Protestant and . . . Catholic. But other interests made equal claims upon men's attention. Government, law, philosophy, science, the arts, material and economic activities were pursued without regard to Christian values. Power, order, beauty, wealth, knowledge, control of nature were all accepted as desirable in themselves. . . .

THE DECLINE OF THE CHURCH

At the close of the thirteenth century the church of the High Middle Ages, centralized in the papacy, stood at its zenith. But the church (as good Catholics always remind us) was staffed by mortal men who were no different from others. The church faced the danger that besets every successful institution—a form of government, an army or navy, a business corporation, a labor union, a university, to choose modern examples—the danger of believing that the institution exists for the benefit of those who conduct its affairs. The papacy, being at the top, was the most liable to this danger. The papacy became "corrupt," set in its ways, absorbed by the possession of wealth and authority, afflicted by a self-perpetuating bureaucracy, out of touch with public opinion, more concerned with maintaining papal grandeur than with spiritual religion, unable to reform itself, and unwilling to let anyone else reform it. At the same time, forces quite outside the papacy or the church, forces which had been growing up for generations before 1300, became too strong after 1300 to be held in the old containers, asserted themselves with ever more insistence, and clashed with the official clergy of the international church. Such forces, especially, were the new national monarchies and the commercial classes in the towns.

The decline of the papacy can be readily dated, from the time when Pope Boniface VIII ran into trouble with the kings of England and of France. These two kings, needing money for war, undertook to tax the clergy in their respective kingdoms, in both of which the clergy were substantial owners of land. Boniface prohibited the taxation of clergy by the civil ruler. In the ensuing altercation, in 1302, he issued the famous bull *Unam Sanctam*, the most extreme of all assertions of papal supremacy, declaring that outside the Roman church there was no salvation, and that "every human creature" was "subject to the Roman pontiff." The French king, Philip the Fair, retorted by sending soldiers to arrest Boniface, who soon died. French influence in the college of cardinals brought about the election of a pope who was subservient to Philip, and who took up his residence, with his court and officials, at Avignon on the lower Rhone river, on the then borders of France. Thus began the "Babylonian Captivity" of the church. The rest of Europe regarded the popes at Avignon throughout the century as tools of France. The prestige of the papacy as a universal institution was badly dimmed.

Attempts to correct the situation made matters worse. In 1378 the college of cardinals, torn by French and anti-French factions within it, elected two popes. Both were equally legitimate, being chosen by the cardinals, but one lived at Rome, one at Avignon, and neither would resign. The French and their supporters recognized the Avignon pope, England and most of Germany, the Roman. For forty years both lines were perpetuated. There were now two papacies, estranged by the Great Schism of the West, and it seemed as if the schism might become permanent, as the earlier schism between Rome and Constantinople had proved to be. All agreed that the situation was scandalous and must be ended, but no one in an influential position would make the sacrifice necessary to put it to an end.

Never had the papacy been so externally magnificent as in the days of the Captivity and the Schism. The papal court at Avignon surpassed the courts of kings in splendor. The papal officialdom grew in numbers, ignoring the deeper problems while busily transacting each day's business. Papal revenues mounted, and new papal taxes were devised, for example the "annates," by which every bishop or abbot in Christendom had to transmit to Rome most of the first year's income of his office. In the continuing movement of funds from all over Europe to the papal court, from the thirteenth century on, a new class of international bankers rose and prospered.

But the papacy, never so sumptuous, had never since the tenth century rested on such shaky foundations. People pay willingly for institutions in which they believe, and admire magnificence in leaders whom they respect. But before 1378, with the pope submissive to France, and after 1378, with two popes and two papacies to support, there was growing complaint at the extravagance and worldliness of papal rule. The most pious Christians were the most shocked. To them the behavior of the cardinals was disgraceful. Earnest souls were worried in conscience. To obtain God's grace was to them of all things the most vital, but with two churches under two popes, each claiming to hold the keys of Peter, how could anyone be certain that his church gave him true salvation? In a society that was still primarily a religious community, this sense of religious insecurity was a source of unutterable uneasiness and dread.

It was widely agreed, in this afflicted society, that the true church must be restored in its purity. Led by men like the Italian Marsiglio of Padua, or the Englishmen Ockham and Wycliff, reformers declared that the church consisted in the whole body of the faithful, not merely or even primarily in the clergy. If the clergy, they said, were not performing their spiritual duties to the laity, then either a secular ruler or a general council representing the whole church might enforce reform upon the clergy, and even upon the pope. John Wycliff went even further. He taught, about 1380, that no visible church was needful for salvation, that ordinary persons might obtain divine grace by reading the Bible, without the ministrations of any clergy whatsoever. This doctrine, which, if pursued far enough, would explode any church as an authoritative institution, was promptly branded as heresy. Wycliff nevertheless won many adherents. In England itself they were mostly "poor men," called Lollards, who sought escape from all forms of established authority. In Bohemia, John Huss took up Wycliff's ideas, and here the doctrine became a national movement. The Hussites were both a religious party and at the same time a Slavic or Czech party protesting against the supremacy of the Germans who lived in Bohemia. The Hussite wars ravaged central Europe for decades in the early part of the fifteenth century.

THE CONCILIAR MOVEMENT AND ITS FAILURE

Settled, influential, educated, and established persons did not turn to heresy, nor yet to witchcraft or flagellation. Their answer to the needs of the day was the conciliar movement. Professors at the universities, advisers to kings, enlightened bishops, thoughtful burghers, about 1400, believed the pope (or rather, popes) to be incapable of reforming existing abuses. They demanded a great Europe-wide council of the entire church at

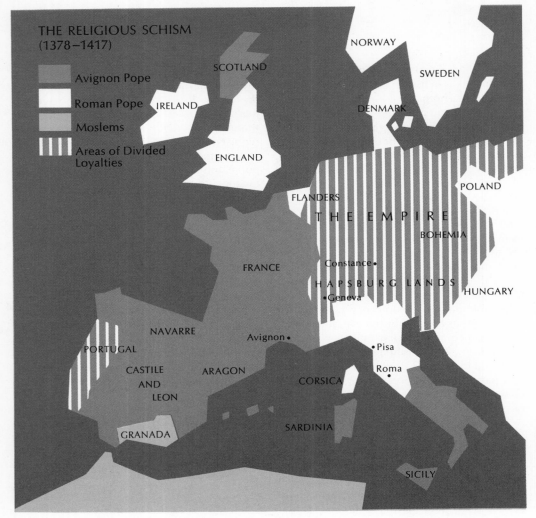

THE RELIGIOUS SCHISM
(1378–1417)

- Avignon Pope
- Roman Pope
- Moslems
- Areas of Divided Loyalties

NORWAY
SCOTLAND
SWEDEN
IRELAND
DENMARK
ENGLAND
POLAND
FLANDERS
THE EMPIRE
BOHEMIA
FRANCE
Constance •
HAPSBURG LANDS
• Geneva
HUNGARY
NAVARRE
Avignon •
• Pisa
PORTUGAL
Roma
CASTILE AND LEON
ARAGON
CORSICA
GRANADA
SARDINIA
SICILY

which all the gravest matters that were troubling Christendom might be discussed and decided. They would introduce into the church, that is to say, the type of parliamentary institutions which at this time were functioning in the civil affairs of almost all countries.

In 1409 such a church council met at Pisa. All parts of the Latin West were represented. The council declared both reigning popes deposed, and obtained the due election of another, but since the first two refused to resign there were now three. In 1414 an even greater and more fully attended council met

at Constance. Its aims were three: to end the now threefold schism, to extirpate heresy, and to reform the church "in head and members," from top to bottom. Not much was accomplished in reform. To discourage heresy, John Huss was interrogated, condemned, and burned at the stake. The schism was ended. All three popes were at last persuaded or compelled to withdraw, and another, Martin V, was elected. The unity of the church, under the papacy, was at last restored.

The majority at the Council of Constance wished to make general councils part of the permanent apparatus of the church for all time in the future. They regarded the pope as, so to speak, a constitutional monarch, and the general body of the faithful as self-governing in religious matters. In its decree *Sacrosancta,* the Council solemnly declared that a council was superior to a pope, and, in the decree *Frequens,* that councils should be assembled every ten years in the future.

Martin V, however, no sooner elected pope, reaffirmed the prerogatives of the papal office. He dissolved the Council of Constance, and repudiated its decrees. The next thirty years saw a continuing tug of war between successive popes and successive councils. On the one hand, with the pope, stood the papal court and central bureaucracy, supported by the monastic orders, and by scattered individuals for various reasons. On the other, with the councils, stood most Catholic bishops from all countries (outside of Italy), together with representatives of the Emperor and the kings. Popes argued that theirs was the true apostolic authority derived from Peter, and that in any case to entrust power to the territorial bishops, exposed as they were to local pressure from kings and princes, would endanger the unity and independence of the church. Councils argued that the bishop of Rome was fundamentally only a bishop like any other; that the authority of Christ was vested in the whole church as a collective body, over which the pope was no more than a symbolic or merely administrative head.

In this acrimonious battle for jurisdiction few reforms could be adopted, and fewer still enforced. Increasingly the life of the church was corrupted by money. No one believed in bribery; but everyone knew that many high churchmen (like many high civil officials of the day) could be bribed. To buy or sell a church office was a crime in the canon law, known as "simony"; but it was a crime which in the fifteenth century could not be suppressed. For churchmen to live with mistresses was considered understandable, if unseemly; the standards of laymen in such matters were not high; but for a bishop or other ecclesiastic to give lucrative church positions to his own children (or other relatives) was the abuse known as nepotism, and it, too, could not be eradicated. To sell divine grace, for money, all agreed, was not only wrong but impossible. In 1300 Boniface VIII had given encouragement to the practice of "indulgences." A person, if properly confessed, absolved, and truly repentant, might, by obtaining an indulgence, be spared certain of the temporal punishments of purgatory. One obtained such an indulgence, almost always, in return for a donation of money. Indulgences were never "sold", but many unenlightened persons thought they were; and a protest arose all over Europe, among both laity and clergy, that the abuse of indulgences was discrediting the sacraments and undermining common morals. But to raise money in this way was fatally easy, and this practice, too, could not be stopped.

The councils insisted that such conditions be reformed, to which popes replied, while agreeing in principle, that the papal authority must be upheld first. Gradually the popes prevailed. The conciliar movement, for Christendom as a whole, was greatly weakened when the powerful French element secured its aims by a local national arrangement. In the Pragmatic Sanction of Bourges, in 1438, the Gallican (or French) church affirmed the supremacy of councils over popes, declared its administrative independence from the Holy See, suppressed the payment of annates to Rome, and forbade papal intervention in the appointment of French prelates. The papacy thus lost influence in France, but the conciliarists themselves were divided. In 1449, with the dissolution of the Council of Basel, the conciliar movement came to an end. In 1450 a great Jubilee was held to celebrate the papal triumph.

The papacy, its prestige and freedom of action thus secured, now passed into the hands of a series of cultivated gentlemen, men of the world, men of "modern" outlook in tune with their times—famous popes of the Renaissance. Some, like Nicholas V (1447–55) or Pius II (1458–64) were accomplished scholars and connoisseurs of books. Some were like Innocent VIII (l484–92), a pleasant man who was the first pope to dine in public with ladies. Alexander VI (1492–1503) exploited his office in the vain attempt to gratify his avaricious relatives who swarmed from Spain. He schemed also to make his son Caesar Borgia the ruler of all Italy. Julius II (1503–13) was a capable general, and Leo X (1513–21) a superb patron of the arts. . . .

Wyclif Explains His Position to the Pope (1384)

John Wyclif (1320–1384) was educated and taught at Oxford during the period of the Avignonese Papacy. He criticized not only the wealth of the clergy, but also the character of the sacraments and the authority assumed by the priesthood. The simplicity of his preaching and its clear appeal to the poor gave his followers, known as Lollards, an important role in the peasant uprising of 1381. When Wyclif was summoned to Rome on charges of heresy in 1384, the last year of his life, he wrote the following letter to Pope Urban VI. From Guy Carleton Lee, *Source Book of English History* (New York, 1900).

I have joyfully to tell what I hold, to all true men that believe, and especially to the pope; for I suppose that if my faith be rightful and given of God, the pope will gladly confirm it; and if my faith be error, the pope will wisely amend it.

I suppose over this that the gospel of Christ be heart of the corps [body] of God's law; for I believe that Jesus Christ, that gave in His own person this gospel, is very God and very man, and by this heart passes all other laws.

I suppose over this that the pope be most obliged to the keeping of the gospel among all men that live here; for the pope is highest vicar that Christ has here in earth. For moreness of Christ's vicar is not measured by worldly moreness, but by this, that this vicar follows more Christ by virtuous living; for thus teacheth the gospel, that this is the sentence of Christ.

And of this gospel I take as believe, that Christ for time that He walked here, was most poor man of all, both in spirit and in having [possessions]; for Christ says that He was made needy for our love. And more poor might no man be, neither bodily nor in spirit. And thus Christ put from Him all manner of worldly lordship. For the gospel of John telleth that when they would have made Christ king, He fled and hid Him from them, for He would none such worldly highness.

And over this I take it as believe, that no man should follow the pope, nor no saint that now is in heaven, but in as much as he [the pope] follows Christ. For John and James erred when they coveted worldly highness; and Peter and Paul sinned also when they denied and blasphemed in Christ; but men should not follow them in this, for then they went from Jesus Christ. And this I take as wholesome counsel, that the pope leave his worldly lordship to worldly lords, as Christ gave them—and more speedily all his clerks [clergy] to do so. For thus did Christ, and taught thus His disciples, till the fiend [Satan] had blinded this world. And it seems to some men that clerks that dwell lastingly in this error against God's law, and flee to follow Christ in this, [are] open heretics, and their fautors [supporters] been partners. . . .

John Huss Attacks the Papacy

Wyclif's doctrines had far-reaching consequences in their influence on John Huss (c.1369–1415), a scholar at the University of Prague in Bohemia. Huss made so funda-mental a criticism of the worldliness of the Papacy that the authority of the existing Church was brought into question. The theological arguments in his treatise, *The Church*, furnished the grounds for which he was condemned and burned as a heretic at the Council of Constance. Some of his arguments became important to the Lutheran movement a century later. Reprinted with the permission of Charles Scribner's Sons from *The Church: A Treatise* by John Huss, pages 143–149, by David S. Schaff. Copyright 1915 Charles Scribner's Sons.

From these and other sayings it is evident that no pope is the manifest and true successor of Peter, the prince of the apostles, if in morals he lives at variance with the principles of Peter; and, if he is avaricious, then is he the vicar of Judas, who loved the reward of iniquity and sold Jesus Christ. And by the same kind of proof the cardinals are not the manifest and true successors of the college of Christ's other apostles unless the cardinals live after the manner of the apostles and keep the commands and counsels of our Lord Jesus Christ. For, if they climb up by another way than by the door of our Lord Jesus Christ, then are they thieves and robbers. . . .

Hence, if the cardinals heap up to themselves ecclesiastical livings and barter with them and take money for their sale either themselves or through others, and so devour and consume in luxurious living the goods of the poor, and if they do not do miracles or preach the Word of God to the people or pray sincerely or fill the place of deacons . . . in how far, I ask, are they the vicars of the apostles? [Not when] in the morning they come into the pope's presence clad in the most splendid apparel, and attended with the most sumptuous retinue of horsemen—thus attended, not on account of the distance of place or difficulty of the journey but to show their magnificence to the world and their contrariety to Christ and his apostles, who went about the towns, cities, and castles clad in humble garb, on foot, preaching the kingdom of God.

Nor in this are they the true and manifest vicars of Christ that they permit themselves to be adored of men on bended knee or that they surround the pope with visitors from abroad, that while he sits on high, splendidly apparelled even down to his feet, yea and far beyond his chair, they with bended knee humbly seek the kisses of his blessed feet, as if the sanctity of this father, the pope, would descend even to the place where his foot is planted. . . .

It is said goodness in a pope is like salt for all, and badness in him inures to the damnation of persons without number. If, therefore, the pope and the cardinals by pompous equipages, resplendence of dress, exquisite and wonderful furnishings, by excessive anxiety to heap up benefices or money, and by the manifest ambition for honour in greater measure than secular laymen—if they offend those who believe in Christ—how is it that they always and necessarily continue to be essential "for the government of the universal church as manifest and true successors in the office of Peter and Christ's other apostles?" Never was the office of the apostles other than one of following Christ in good living and in teaching the church, baptizing men, healing the sick, casting out devils, offering up the sacrifice of Christ's body and everywhere exercising the power connected with their office for the perfecting of the church. If therefore, the pope and his cardinals exercise that office, then the pope holds the Office of Peter. But, if he with the cardinals falls away from it, who doubts that he falls away from the true vicariate of Christ and his apostles?

Should the Councils or the Pope Have Greater Authority?

When Nicholas of Cusa (1401–1464), a German churchman and humanist reformer, later Roman cardinal, wrote *De Concordantia Catholica,* from which the first selection is taken, the Council of Basel (1431–1438) was still in session. The goal of Church reform was not attained, however, at either the Council of Basel or its continuation at Florence (1438–1458), and Pope Pius II, who had been a supporter of the conciliar movement at Basel, dealt it a heavy blow in the Bull, "Execrablis," part of which is excerpted in the second selection. I. From *De Concordantia Catholica,* trans. F. W. Coker, in *Readings in Political Philosophy* (New York, 1938), pp. 261–263. Reprinted by permission of Macmillan Company. II. From Henry Bettenson, ed., *Documents of the Christian Church* (New York: Oxford University Press, 1947), pp. 193–194.

I. NICHOLAS OF CUSA: ON THE SUPREMACY OF THE GENERAL COUNCILS (1433)

We know that Peter received from Christ no more authority than the other apostles; for nothing was said to Peter that was not also said to the others. Is it not true that just as it was said to Peter, "Whatsoever thou shalt bind upon the earth," it was also said to the others, "Whomsoever ye shall bind?" And although it was said to Peter, "Thou art Peter and upon this Rock" nevertheless by rock we understand Christ, whom Peter confessed. And if by *petra* ("rock"), Peter is to be understood as the foundation stone of the church, then, according to St. Jerome, all the other apostles were similarly foundation stones of the church (concerning which there is a discussion in next to the last chapter of the Apocalypse, wherein by the twelve foundation stones of the city of Jerusalem—that is the holy Church—no one doubts that the apostles are meant). If it was said to Peter, "Feed the sheep," it is nevertheless clear that this feeding is by word and example. So also, according to St. Augustine in his gloss upon the same passage, the same command was given for all. In the verse—"Go ye into all the world" (Matthew and Mark, at the end), it does not appear that anything was said to Peter that implied any supremacy. Therefore, we rightly say that all the apostles are equal in authority with Peter. It should also be remembered that at the beginning of the Church there was only one general episcopate, diffused throughout the whole world, without division into dioceses. . . .

Therefore, since the power of binding and loosing, on which all ecclesiastical jurisdiction is founded, is immediately from Christ, and since from this power comes the power of divine jurisdiction, it is evident that all bishops, and perhaps even presbyters, are of equal authority in respect to jurisdiction, although not in respect to the execution, which is confined within certain positive limits. . . .

Every constitution is founded on natural law (*jure naturali*), and if it contradicts this it cannot be valid. Wherefore, since natural law exists by nature in reason, every law (*lex*) is basically congenital with man. Accordingly, those who are wiser and more excellent than others are chosen as rulers, in order that, endowed with a naturally clear reason and with wisdom and prudence, they may choose just laws and by these govern others and hear cases, so as to preserve the peace; such are the judgments of the wise. . . .

Since by nature all men are free, all government—whether based on written law or on law embodied in a ruler through whose government the subjects are restrained from evil deeds and their liberty regulated, for a good end, by fear of punishment—arises solely from agreement and consent of the subjects. For if men are by nature powerful and equally free, a valid and ordained authority of any one person, whose power by nature is like that of the rest, cannot be created save by election and consent of the others, just as law is established by consent. . . .

Wherefore we see that in councils, canons issue from agreement, acceptance, consent, and approval; and that decretals or judicial decisions of the Roman pontiffs, or of contested incumbents in emergencies, have received the strength of stability and justness, not from a merely powerful will, but from the fact that in accordance with the canons it was right that those decisions should be made. . . .

II. PIUS II: AN EXECRABLE ABUSE (1460)

There has sprung up in our time an execrable abuse, unheard of in earlier ages, namely that some men, imbued with the spirit of rebellion, presume to appeal to a future council from the Roman pontiff, the vicar of

Jesus Christ, to whom in the person of blessed Peter it was said, 'Feed my sheep' and 'Whatsoever thou shalt bind on earth shall be bound in heaven'; and that not from a desire for a sounder judgment but to escape the penalties of their misdeeds. Anyone who is not wholly ignorant of the laws can see how this contravenes the sacred canons and how detrimental it is to Christendom. And is it not plainly absurd to appeal to what does not now exist and the date of whose future existence is unknown? Wishing therefore to cast out from the Church of God this pestilent poison and to take measures for the safety of the sheep committed to our care, and to ward off from the sheepfold of our Saviour all that may offend. . . . We condemn appeals of this kind and denounce them as erroneous and detestable. . . .

Thomas à Kempis Advises Christians To Imitate Christ (c. 1427)

The Imitation of Christ, written by a German monk, Thomas à Kempis (1379–1471), has probably been the second most widely read book in the Christian world (after the Bible). For fifteenth-century Christians it counselled a mystical devotion to Christ as the most important effective way of obtaining salvation. From *The Imitation of Christ,* in J. Scott, A. Hyma, A. Noyes, *Readings in Medieval History* (New York: Appleton-Century-Crofts Division of Meredith Publishing Company, 1933), pp. 548–549.

"The Kingdom of God is within you," says the Lord.

Turn yourself with your whole heart to the Lord, and forsake this wretched world; and your soul will find rest.

Learn to despise outward things and to give yourself to things within; and you will see the Kingdom of God coming within you.

For the Kingdom of God is peace and joy in the Holy Ghost, which is not given to the wicked.

Christ will come to you and will show you this consolation, if you prepare for him a worthy mansion within you.

All his glory and beauty is from within, and there is his delight.

He frequently visits the inner man; sweet discourse, pleasant solace, much peace, familiarity exceedingly wonderful.

Go to, faithful soul, make ready your heart for this Bridegroom, that he may vouchsafe to come to you and dwell in you.

For thus he says: "If any man love me, he will keep my Commandments; and my Father will love him, and we will come to him and make our abode with him."

Make therefore room for Christ, and deny entrance to all others.

When you have Christ, you are rich, and you have enough.

He will be your provider and faithful watchman in all things, so that it will not be necessary to trust in men.

For men soon change, and swiftly pass away, but Christ remains forever, and stands firmly by us till the end. . . .

Christ was also . . . despised of men, and when in greatest need, forsaken by friends and acquaintances, in the midst of slander.

Christ was willing to suffer and be despised; and dare you complain of any man?

Christ had adversaries and backbiters, and do you wish all men as your friends and benefactors?

Whence will your patience get its crown if no adversity befall you?

If you wish to suffer nothing, how will you be the friend of Christ?

Suffer with Christ and for Christ, if you desire to reign with Christ. . . .

A lover of Jesus, and inwardly true, and free from inordinate affections, can freely turn himself to God, and lift himself above himself in spirit, and rest fruitfully.

He who judges things as they are, not as they are said or esteemed to be, is truly wise, and taught more by God than by men.

He who knows how to walk, and to set little value upon outward things, neither requires places nor expects times for the performing of religious exercises. . . .

Savonarola Suffers for Attacking Renaissance Worldliness

What could happen to the religious reformer is seen in the case of Girolamo Savonarola (1452–1498). Savonarola entered a Dominican monastery in 1475, explaining that "the reasons which drove me to become a religious are the miserable conditions of the world and the evils of which men are guilty such as rape, immorality, robbery, pride, idolatry, cursing, all in so grave measure that almost no one can be found who has any regard for what is good."

In Florence, after 1481, he found himself in a position to do something about the evils of mankind. With the French invasion of Italy in 1494 and the exile of the Medici family, Savonarola became the spiritual ruler of Florence. Horrified by the scandalous Roman court of Pope Alexander VI, the friar sided with the French invaders against the pope. A fiery, effective preacher, he pressed moral reform in Florence itself and organized gangs of children to spy out and report on the sins of their elders. For a while the city government was under his thumb. The readings describe Savonarola's approach to reform and the terrible final consequences. The first reading is taken from a biography of the friar which contains many quotations from his sermons to the excitable Florentine masses. The second reading consists of excerpts from the diary of a contemporary Florentine druggist. I. From *The Life of Girolamo Savonarola*, by Roberto Ridolfi, trans. by Cecil Grayson. © Copyright 1959 by Routledge & Kegan Paul. Reprinted by permission of Alfred A. Knopf. II. From *Luca Landucci. A Florentine Diary from 1450 to 1516*, ed. Iodoco del Badia, trans. Alice Jervis (London: J. M. Dent & Sons Ltd., 1927), pp. 122–123, 138, 139, 142–143.

I. SAVONAROLA PUSHES REFORM IN FLORENCE (1497)

For the time being, the Friar triumphed, and his name stood above all things. Some part of the reform of women and children was approved after great difficulty, but it remained a dead letter. Gambling and sodomy were pursued with terrible laws. That these were not issued merely 'for show' . . . is shown by the effects which this chronicler himself has to record a few pages later. . . .

Then came the Christian festivities of the Savonarolan Carnival and the first 'burning of the vanities', celebrated in the Piazza de' Signori on the 7th of February, 1497. There had been erected a wooden construction in the shape of a pyramid with eight sides rising in steps, on which were displayed the 'anathema' that the Friar's lads had gone from house to house collecting: obscene books and pictures, lutes, women's false hair, cosmetics, perfumes, mirrors, dolls, playing-cards, dice, gaming-tables. A Venetian merchant tried to buy up all these beautiful things for 20,000 ducats, but all he achieved was that a fine picture of himself was put on the top of the edifice to share with the effigy of Carnival the rule of the vanities.

The procession of boys formed at San Marco (the Dominican convent) and came down to the square, each quarter of the city represented by a group with its own banner. They took up their positions on the steps and in the loggia of the Signori, singing *laudi* (hymns) in the vulgar tongue recently composed in praise of Jesus Christ and against Carnival. Finally they set fire to the wooden structure, which was full of brushwood, straw, and gunpowder, and with a joyful mingling of the music of the fifes and trumpets of the Signoria, the ringing of bells, the crackle of the flames, and the songs of the children, the burning was celebrated amid the great enthusiasm of the entire population. This has sometimes been exaggeratedly represented as the symbol of iconoclastic barbarism; it appears rather to us to symbolize the triumph of Savonarola and of his civil and religious reforms in the city of the Medici. . . .

During Lent Savonarola ['s] . . . criticisms of prelates and the Court of Rome became more frequent, his expression harsher. After

the just but hard punishment he gave them in the sermons of the 13th, 14th, 21st, and 22nd of February and others, came the more violent scourges of the 4th of March: 'There is a proverb among friars: "He comes from Rome, don't trust him." . . . O wicked Church, listen to me! In the courts men are always dying [spiritually], they are all finished. Wretched people! I do not say this is true for everyone, but few remain good. When you see that they gladly stay on in Rome, you say they are cooked. He's cooked. You understand me.' I believe that when he passes from the plural to the singular, and particularly with his pointed 'you understand me', he was alluding to the Pope. If I am wrong, then I think that many of the Friar's audience that morning made the same mistake, even though the preacher added at once: 'I am not speaking of anyone in particular.'

He went on: 'You, harlot Church, you used to be ashamed of pride and lasciviousness. Now you are ashamed no longer. See how once the priests called their children "nephews"; now they are called sons, not nephews: sons everywhere.' This is the infamy that attaches to Borgia, the first of Roman Pontiffs to do such a thing. In that very year 1497, or at the end of 1496, the last son of Alexander VI was born, and it is likely that Savonarola, always well informed, knew something about it. . . .

Over and above the petty jealousies and mediocre monastic differences, Fra Girolamo appealed in [another] sermon to monks of all Orders to unite with him in the great work of reform. . . .

Come, for Christ wishes to revive His Church. Come, I call on you, but I will cry in a loud voice and name no names.

O priests, *Magister adest*—the Master is at hand, He is come, and He calls and desires you to reform His Church. He calls you to prayer, for the axe is laid to the root. O monks, black, white, or brown, all of whatever colour: the Orders have been abased. *Magister adest*, the Master is here, and calls for reform. O mendicant friars, the Lord wishes to renovate His Church: *Magister adest*, the Master is here. O nuns, *Magister adest*. You who cannot believe, pray, for the Master is here and will renew all things. Go to all the priests, monks, and nuns, and speak in their ear this good news: soon there will be reform, and they must pray. . . .

The body of the Church was rotten, but he had courage enough to revive it:

You who are in France, in Germany, who have friends in those parts, send letters everywhere, write that they should go to their churchmen and say: 'That Friar says that he bids you on behalf of God to turn to the Lord and pray, for the Lord is coming.' Come, send off messengers, for this dead body cannot be revived otherwise! . . . Many of you say that there will be excommunications. . . ; do you not know who they are that seek them? Last year it did not succeed. Did I not tell you that, though it may come, those who do this, seek to do worse harm than merely excommunicate? I pray God it may come soon. 'Are you not afraid?' Not I, for they would excommunicate me because I do no evil. Bear it upon a lance, open the gates to it. And I will answer it; and if I do not astonish you, then say what you

will. I will cause so many faces there and here to turn pale that you will be well pleased, and we shall utter a great cry, like that of Lazarus, and you will see the whole body tremble. . . . Lord, cause me to be persecuted: I ask Thee this favour—that I may not die in my bed, but that I may shed my blood for Thee, as Thou has done for me. . . .

II. THE EXCOMMUNICATION AND EXECUTION OF FRA GIROLAMO (1497–1498)

1497 18th June   An excommunication came from the Pope excommunicating Fra Girolamo, which was published this morning in Santo Spirito, in Santa Maria Novella, in Santa Croce, in the Badia, and at the Servi. I heard it read and proclaimed in Santo Spirito, in the chancel, between two lighted tapers, and amidst a number of friars. It was read and proclaimed by Fra Leonardo, their preacher, and the adversary of Fra Girolamo. It declared that the said *Frate* [monk] had not obeyed a certain Brief which had been sent as far back as the November of 1496, summoning him on his vow of obedience to go to the Pope; and if he did not choose to obey the excommunication, no one was to give him aid or support, and no one must go and hear him, nor go to any place where he was, on pain of excommunication. . . .

1498 11th February   Fra Girolamo began to preach in *Santa Maria del Fiore*, and the stands (for the boys) were made as before. Many people went there, and it was much talked of, on account of his excommunication; and many did not go, for fear of being excommunicated. . . . I was one of those who did not go. . . .

1498 10th April   At 9 in the evening (5 p.m.) the *Frate* was carried to the Bargello by two men on their crossed hands, because his feet and hands were in irons, and Fra Domenico also; and they seized them and put Fra Girolamo to the rack three times and Fra Domenico four times; and Fra Girolamo said: "Take me down, and I will write you my whole life." You may imagine that it was not without tears that right-minded men who had faith in him, heard that he had been tortured; he who had taught this prayer, *Fac bene bonis et rectis corde*. No, it was not without tears and grief, and urgent prayers to God. . . .

19th April   The protocol of Fra Girolamo, written by his own hand, was read in Council, in the Great Hall; he whom we had held to be a prophet, confessed that he was no prophet, and had not received from God the things which he preached; and he confessed that many things which had occurred during the course of his preaching were contrary to what he had given us to understand. I was present when this protocol was read, and I marvelled, feeling utterly dumbfounded with surprise. My heart was grieved to see such an edifice fall to the ground on account of having been founded on a lie. Florence had been expecting a new Jerusalem, from which would issue just laws and splendour and an example of righteous life, and to see the renovation of the Church, the conversion of unbelievers, and the consolation of the righteous; and I felt that everything was exactly contrary, and had to resign myself with the thought: *In voluntate tua Domine omnia sunt posita*. . . .

22nd May (Wednesday morning)   The sacrifice of the three *Frati* was made. They took them out of the Palagio and brought them on to the Square, where were assembled the

In this early painting Savanarola and his companions are shown hanging and being burned in the main square of Florence. Unknown Florentine, sixteenth century.

"Eight" and the *Collegi,* the papal envoy, the General of the Dominicans, and many canons, priests and monks of divers Orders, and the Bishop . . . who was deputed to degrade the three monks; and here on the Square the said ceremony was to be performed. They were robed in all their vestments, which were taken off one by one, with the appropriate words for the degradation, it being constantly affirmed that Fra Girolamo was a heretic and schismatic, and on this account condemned to be burnt; then their faces and hands were shaved, as is customary in this ceremony.

When this was completed, they left the *Frati* in the hands of the "Eight", who immediately made the decision that they should be hung and burnt; and they were led straight on to the platform at the foot of the cross. . . . This all happened without a word from one of them, which was considered extraordinary, especially by good and thoughtful people, who were much disappointed, as everyone had been expecting some signs, and desired the glory of God, the beginning of righteous life, the renovation of the Church, and the conversion of unbelievers; hence they were not without bitterness and not one of them made an excuse. Many, in fact, fell from their faith. When all three were hung, Fra Girolamo being in the middle, facing the *Palagio,* the scaffold was separated from the Square, and a fire was made on the circular platform round the cross, upon which gunpowder was put and set alight, so that the said fire burst out with a noise of rockets and cracking. In a few hours they were burnt, their legs and arms gradually dropping off; part of their bodies remaining hanging to the chains, a quantity of stones were thrown to make them fall, as there was a fear of the people getting hold of them; and then the hangman and those whose business it was, hacked down the post and burnt it on the ground, bringing a lot of brushwood, and stirring the fire up over the dead bodies, so that the very least piece was consumed. Then they fetched carts, and accompanied by the mace-bearers, carried the last bit of dust to the Arno, by the Ponte Vecchio, in order that no remains should be found. Nevertheless, a few good men had so much faith that they gathered some of the floating ashes together, in fear and secrecy, because it was as much as one's life was worth to say a word, so anxious were the authorities to destroy every relic. . . .

Erasmus Satirizes the Practice of Religion in the Renaissance

One of the most slashing attacks on popular Christianity and the clergy of his day was made by the Dutch scholar Desiderius Erasmus (1466–1536). Known to his peers as the prince of humanists, Erasmus was not only a lover of the Greek and Roman classics but also a noted Biblical scholar and translator. His writing style, the biting wit of his pen, and the solid content of his essays made him the most famous publicist of his day and the favored guest of princes and other pillars of society. *The Praise of Folly,* from which this reading is drawn, was written in 1509. Its popularity was such that the first printed version appeared in the following year. Erasmus took the precaution of not signing his name to the work, although the authorship was widely known. No action against him was taken by the Church authorities, and he remained a loyal Catholic amidst the uproar of the religious revolt that broke out only a few years later. From *The Praise of Folly,* by Desiderius Erasmus, trans. by Hoyt Hopewell Hudson (Princeton University Press, 1941). Reprinted by permission of Princeton University Press.

[20] Next come the folk who have arrived at the foolish but gratifying belief that if they gaze on a picture of Polyphemus-Christopher they will not die that day, or that whoever salutes in certain prescribed words an image of Barbara will come through a battle unharmed, or that by making application to [St.] Erasmus on certain days, using a certain kind of candles and certain prayers, one will shortly become rich. . . . Then what shall I say of the people who so happily fool themselves with forged pardons for sins, measuring out time to be spent in purgatory as if with an hour-glass, and figuring its centuries, years, months, days, and hours as if from a mathematical table, beyond possibility of error? Or I might speak of those who will promise themselves any and every thing, relying upon certain charms or prayers devised by some pious impostor either for his soul's sake or for money, to bring them wealth, reputation, pleasure, plenty, good health, long life, and a green old age, and at last a seat next to Christ's in heaven—but they do not wish to get it too soon. That is to say, when the pleasures of this life have finally failed them, willy-nilly, though they struggled tooth and nail to hold on to them, then it is time for the bliss of heaven to arrive.

I fancy that I see some merchant or soldier or judge laying down one small coin from his extensive booty and expecting that the whole cesspool of his life will be at once purified. He conceives that just so many perjuries, so many lustful acts, so many debauches, so many fights, murders, frauds, lies, and so many breaches of faith, are bought off as by contract; and so bought off that with a clean slate he may start from scratch upon a new round of sins. . . . And is it not almost as bad when the several countries each lay claim to a particular saint of their own, and then assign particular powers respectively to the various saints and observe for each one his own peculiar rites of worship? One saint assists in time of toothache, another is propitious to women in travail, another recovers stolen goods, a fourth stands by with help in a shipwreck, and still another keeps the sheep in good repair; and so the rest, though it would take too long to specify all of them. Some of them are good for a number of purposes, particularly the Virgin Mother, to whom the common people tend to attribute more than to the Son. . . .

[33] Our popes, cardinals, and bishops for some time now have earnestly copied the state and practice of princes, and come near to beating them at their own game. Let a bishop but consider what his alb, the white emblem of sincerity, should teach him, namely, a life in every way blameless; and what is signified on his part by the two-horned miter, the two peaks bound by the same knot—I suppose it is a perfect knowledge of the Old and New Testaments; what is meant by covering his hands with gloves, a clean administration of the sacrament and one unsullied by any taint of human concerns; what the crozier symbolizes, most watchful care of the flock put under his charge; what is indicated by the cross that is carried before him, to wit, a victory over all carnal affections. If he would contemplate these and other lessons of the sort, I say, would he not lead a sad and troubled life? . . .

As to these Supreme Pontiffs who take the place of Christ, if they tried to emulate His life, I mean His poverty, labors, teaching, cross, and contempt for safety, if even they thought upon the title of Pope—that is, Father—or the addition "Most Holy," who on earth would be more afflicted? Who would purchase that seat at the price of every resource and effort? Or who defend it, when purchased, by the sword, by poison, or by anything else? Were wisdom to descend upon them, how it would inconvenience them! Wisdom did I say? Nay, even a grain of salt would do it—a grain of that salt which is spoken of by Christ. It would lose them all that wealth and honor, all those possessions, triumphal progresses, offices, dispensations, tributes, and indulgences; it would lose them so many horses, mules and retainers; so many pleasures. . . . In place of these it would bring vigils, fasts, tears, prayers, sermons, studies, sighs, and a thousand troublesome tasks of the sort. Nor should we pass over the circumstance that all those copyists and notaries would be in want, as would all those lawyers, promoters, secretaries, muleteers, grooms, bankers, and pimps—I was about to add something more tender, though rougher, I am afraid, on the ears. In short, that great host of men which burdens—I beg your pardon, I mean adorns—the Roman See would beg for their bread. . . .

As it is now, what labor turns up to be done they hand over to Peter and Paul, who have leisure for it. But the splendor and the pleasure they take care of personally. And so it comes about . . . that scarcely any kind of men live more softly or less oppressed with care; believing that they are amply acceptable to Christ if with a mystical and almost theatrical finery, with ceremonies, and with those titles of Beatitude and Reverence and Holiness, along with blessing and cursing, they perform the office of bishops. To work miracles is primitive and old-fashioned, hardly suited to our times; to instruct the people is irksome; to interpret the Holy Scriptures is pedantry; to pray is otiose; to shed tears is distressing and womanish; to live in poverty is sordid; to be beaten in war is dishonorable and less than worthy of one who will hardly admit kings, however great, to kiss his sacred foot; and finally, to die is unpleasant, to die on the cross a disgrace. . . .

Norman Cantor: Why the Reformation Did Not Occur Earlier

Reprinted with permission of The Macmillan Company from *Medieval History, The Life and Death of a Civilization* by Norman F. Cantor. Copyright © by The Macmillan Company, 1968.

There is nothing, or almost nothing, in the writings of Martin Luther or of any of the Protestant reformers of the sixteenth century that cannot be found in fourteenth-century literature. The question is not why the Protestant Revolt and schism came in the sixteenth century, but why it did not come a hundred or a hundred and fifty years before. This is perhaps the most important question which can be asked with regard to the later middle ages. Five reasons can be given for the failure of the heretical movement of the fourteenth century to produce a schism in Christendom. In the first place, the fourteenth century did not have the printing press, which did not come into use until just before 1500. It was very hard for the heretical theorists to disseminate their doctrines. In the early sixteenth century the same ideas spread like wildfire across Europe. Wyclif's doctrines were carried into Bohemia, presumably as the result of a dynastic marriage and consequent relations between England and that distant country, but he did not gain disciples in France and Germany. Second, the long depression of the later middle ages, while it produced discontent, sapped men's energy and distracted their interests, making them unlikely to get involved in a major struggle with ecclesiastical authority. Third, there is the paradoxical fact that the papacy was so weak in the fourteenth century that it did very little to combat the heretical movements. By not forcing the issue, the papacy allowed the new wave of heresy to run its course.

The last two reasons are undoubtedly the most important. The wealthier classes in Europe were frightened by the apparent social implications of heresy. It seemed to foment social revolt, and this led them around 1400 to turn against the heretical movements. The fourteenth century was the era of the first social revolts in medieval Europe. The industrial proletariat spawned by the textile industry in Flanders and Florence engaged in bitter, and ultimately unsuccessful, struggles against the oligarchies who dominated urban life. Even the peasant, whose economic position had been ameliorated in many parts of Europe because of a labor shortage, lifted up his head for the first time. Wherever the hitherto docile and mute peasant thought he was being ill-treated or the new freedom which seemed to be coming his way impeded by desperate landlords, he resorted to savage rebellion—the Jacquerie in France, the Peasants' Revolt in England. The English peasant uprising certainly was encouraged, and perhaps even led, by itinerant heretical preachers, and this caused the English government and nobility to turn against Wyclif's disciples. Similarly, the proto-Protestants of Bohemia made their doctrines into a national religion, raised armies, and terrified Germany. Even after the heretical leader John Huss had been burned by order of the Council of Constance, his disciples continued to harass southern Germany. What happened, then, was that the heretical movements unleashed feelings of social discontent and national hatred, as they were to do in the sixteenth century. But there was no Luther in the late middle ages to stem the tide of reaction and dissociate the religious radicalism from social and political extremism. Antisacerdotal doctrines did not entirely disappear in the fifteenth century, but they had been discredited by such terrifying events as the Peasants' Revolt and the Hussite wars, and they were driven underground for another century.

The final reason why the Reformation did not occur in the fourteenth or early fifteenth century is that the royal governments were so inept and distracted by other problems that they failed to take advantage of the religious situation as many sixteenth-century kings were to do. In the first decade of the fourteenth century the national monarchies of France and England appeared destined for continual and unlimited accretion of power, but the next one hundred and fifty years turned out to be disastrous for the royal governments in both countries. Europe had to wait until the late fifteenth century for the territorial sovereign state to secure its position of leadership in European society. In the interval the aristocracy was given a final chance to dominate the governments of the two most centralized states; but the great lords exhibited only greed and laziness in their role as the dominant force in the fourteenth- and fifteenth-century political life. The result was a degree of social disorder not experienced in Europe since the tenth century. . . .

STUDY QUESTIONS

1. What conditions weakened Church authority over faithful Christians in the fourteenth and fifteenth centuries?

2. How did Wyclif's attitude toward poverty and the Gospel affect his view of papal and priestly authority?

3. On what grounds did Huss criticize the Church?

4. How, in Nicholas of Cusa's view, did both scriptural and natural law support the assumption by Church councils of powers exercised by the pope? On what grounds did Pope Pius condemn the conciliar movement?

5. What kind of relationship to God did Thomas à Kempis counsel men to seek? How might this strengthen religious practice? Weaken the authority of the Church?

6. What vision of society did Savonarola have? What factors seem responsible for his death?

7. On what grounds did Erasmus criticize popular Christianity and Church leadership? Compare his criticism with that of John Huss. Why, in your opinion, wasn't Erasmus tried for heresy?

8. Compare the objectives of these reformers and the ways they attempted to realize these objectives. In what ways were they similar, or dissimilar?

Luther's Revolt

TOPIC 6

THE LUTHERAN PROTEST

The movement for reform, contained for more than two hundred years within the Roman Church, splintered Latin Christendom in the sixteenth century. No single figure assumes more responsibility for this than the stocky Augustinian monk from Wittenberg, Martin Luther. Echoing charges made by many reformers before him, Luther also gave expression to fresh and raw feelings of public anger at a foreign-dominated, wealthy, and corrupt Church. From the depth of his own religious conviction, Luther appealed for support to all elements of German society. Powerful forces of political and social unrest, shored up by strong religious feeling, produced a series of civil wars and compelled a realignment of the religious and political map of Central Europe. The readings trace the lines of Luther's attack and his response to those who found in a renewed religion the grounds for a general assault on the order of late medieval society.

From Crane Brinton, John B. Christopher and Robert Lee Wolff, *Civilization in the West,* © 1964. Reprinted by permission of Prentice-Hall, Inc., Englewood Cliffs, New Jersey.

Though all aspects of the past arouse our emotions to some extent at least, most of us can remain relatively detached until we come to the issues that engage us in this chapter. Here even the terms in common use betray involvement: the Protestant refers to the Protestant *"Reformation,"* the Catholic to the Protestant *"Revolt."* Even the secularist or skeptic can hardly claim to be impartial, for he inevitably feels that Protestantism, if only because it did shatter the unity and conformity of mediaeval Catholicism, prepared the way for such as him to exist. Old exaggerations, old slanders from the partisan struggle of the times are still bandied about: that Luther led a revolt against the Church so that he, a monk, could marry; that the Catholic clergy sold salvation; that Henry VIII broke with the Pope so that he might marry; and many more.

On October 31, 1517, Martin Luther (1483–1546) nailed his 95 Theses to the door of the court church at Wittenberg in Saxony. The action touched off what proved to be a major social, economic, and intellectual revolution. Neither Luther nor other later major leaders like Calvin intended such a revolution. They conceived of themselves not as starting *new* churches but as going back to the true old church, as reformers. Again and again, as we know, the Catholic church had faced reform movements like the Cluniac, the Cistercian, the Franciscan, and had absorbed them. In the fourteenth and fifteenth centuries Wyclif and Hus had almost created separate, or schismatic churches. The Conciliar movement, in the early fifteenth century, had challenged papal authority, though it had failed to subordinate the pope to the views of a general council.

This time, however, Luther's action led to the organization of a separate church outside the Catholic communion. Within a generation after 1517, dozens of sects or denominations in addition to the Lutheran came into existence: Anglican, Calvinist, Anabaptist, and many others. We take this multiplicity so much for granted today that it is worth emphasizing how great a departure this was in the sixteenth century, what a real revolution from mediaeval religious unity.

Son of a German peasant who became a miner and eventually a prosperous investor in mining enterprises, Luther studied law in his youth; then in 1505, at the age of 22, he had a shattering experience. Caught in a severe thunderstorm and greatly frightened, he prayed to St. Anne for help, and pledged himself to become a monk. Once in the monastery, however, he underwent a major personal crisis: He was sure he was a lost soul without hope of salvation. Though he submitted to the monastic discipline of his order and made a pilgrimage to Rome in 1510, none of the good works he did could free him from the fear that he could not attain God's grace and so was destined for hell. It was only when his confessor told him to study the Bible that Luther, from his readings in the Epistles of St. Paul and in St. Augustine, found an answer to his anxiety: He must have faith in God, faith in the possibility of his own salvation. The Roman Church had of course always taught this. What was new about Luther was his emphasis on *faith alone, to the exclusion of works.* The promise that faith alone might mean salvation had a particular attraction in an age of doubt and gloom rather like the era when men had first turned to Christianity.

Luther then began to question certain practices which in his view were abuses tending to corrupt or weaken faith. He cast his questions in the form of the 95 Theses, written in Latin and in the manner of the mediaeval scholastics as a challenge to debate. The specific abuse that he attacked he called the "sale" of "indulgences," particularly the activities of Tetzel, a Dominican, who, with papal authorization, was conducting a "drive" for contributions to rebuild St. Peter's in Rome.

The theory of indulgences concerned the remission of the punishment for sins: Since only God can forgive a sin, no indulgence can assure such forgiveness. A repentant sinner has to undergo punishment on earth in the form of penance and after death in purgatory, where he atones by temporary but painful punishment and is prepared for heaven. The Church claimed that Christ, the Virgin, and the Saints had performed so many good works that the surplus constituted a Treasury of Merit. A priest could secure for a layman a draft, as it were, on this heavenly treasury. This was an indulgence and could remit penance and part or all of the punishment in purgatory. According to Catholic theory, an indulgence was "granted" by the priest, and

any monetary contribution thereupon made by the recipient was a free-will offering. Luther called Tetzel's activity the sale of indulgences.

The doctrine of indulgences was too complex for the ordinary layman to grasp completely. To the man in the street in sympathy with the reformers, it seemed as though a sinner could obtain *not only* remission of punishment *but also* forgiveness of sin, *if only* he secured enough indulgences, and that this depended on his money-gifts to Tetzel. In the 95 Theses Luther objected vehemently both to Tetzel's perversion of indulgences and to the whole doctrine behind them. He thus minimized the importance of good works at a moment when many ordinary believers were trying to increase their stock of such works by drawing on the Treasury of Merit. Christian theory usually insists on the need for *both* faith and good works. Luther's emphasis on faith drove his papal opponents into a corresponding extreme emphasis on works, and this in turn drove him, in moments of excitement, to deny the uses of works and to insist on faith alone. Since "works" include all earthly ecclesiastical organization and the priestly way of doing things, Luther before long was denying that priests are necessary. He had enunciated the doctrine of the priesthood of all believers, in popular terms, "every man his own priest."

In 1518, Luther defied a papal emissary, and refused to recant some of his propositions on indulgences. In 1519, at Leipzig, in debate with a learned theologian, John Eck, who accused him of disobeying the authority of the popes and church councils, Luther said that popes and councils were not necessarily authoritative. He said he accepted certain views of Hus, which the Council of Constance

had declared heretical. In 1520, in his *Appeal to the Christian Nobility of the German Nation,* Luther called the term "spiritual estate," as used to describe the clergy, a "lie," and declared that "all Christians are truly of the spiritual estate, and there is no difference among them save the office." When Pope Leo X issued a bull condemning Luther's teaching, Luther burnt it. In 1521 he was excommunicated, and the Emperor Charles V and the imperial diet solemnly declared him an outlaw at Worms. Once again he was asked whether he would recant. His reply contained his most famous words:

> Your Imperial Majesty and Your Lordships demand a simple answer. Here it is, plain and unvarnished. Unless I am convicted of error by the testimony of Scripture or (since I put not trust in the unsupported authority of Pope or of councils, since it is plain that they have often erred and often contradicted themselves) by manifest reasoning I stand convicted by the Scriptures to which I have appealed, and my conscience is taken captive by God's word. I cannot and will not recant anything, for to act against our conscience is neither safe for us, nor open to us.
>
> *Hier stehe ich. Ich kann nicht anders. Gott helff mir. Amen.* (On this I take my stand. I can do no other. God help me. Amen.)

The empire and the papacy took their drastic actions in vain, for Luther was already gathering a substantial following and becoming a national hero. He had the protection of the ruler of his own German state, the Elector Frederick the Wise of Saxony, and was soon to secure the backing of other princes.

In the next few years he translated the Bible into vigorous and effective German, and remodeled the church in Saxony according to his own views. His revolt was a success.

THE REASONS FOR LUTHER'S SUCCESS

More than theology was at issue in Luther's revolt. The Catholic Church that Luther attacked was, as many Catholic historians grant, at the time in one of its more worldly periods. Especially in its center at Rome, it had come under the influence of the new wealth of the Renaissance and the new fashions of good living. The papacy, triumphant over the councils, had been drawn into Italian politics, and the Rome Luther visited in his younger days was a shocking spectacle of intrigue, display, and corruption. Some part of Luther's success lay in the fact that he was attacking practices revolting to decent men, and reasserting the primacy of the spirit over materialism.

There was a second great reason for his success: In the name of good Germans he was attacking the practices of Italians and Italianate Germans. In the eyes of Luther and his followers Tetzel was not only extending an abuse theologically and morally outrageous; he was raising money to enrich Italy. . . . What Luther started, a good many German princes soon took out of his hands. They stood to gain, not only by cutting off the flow of German money to Italy, but by confiscating Catholic property, especially monastic property, which was not needed for the Lutheran church. Moreover, Luther gave them a new weapon in the eternal struggle against their feudal overlord, the emperor. The princes were also moved by Luther's German patriotism; some, like Frederick the Wise of Saxony, sympathized with many of his ideas.

Luther preaches from the Bible while his congregation receives both bread and wine. In the right foreground, other members of the clergy, including the Pope, are swallowed up in the mouth of hell. Woodcut by Cranach, sixteenth century.

Luther's personal energy, courage, and intelligence were also of major importance. He wrote the pamphlets that did for this revolution what Tom Paine and the Declaration of Independence did for the American. He put his *Appeal to the Christian Nobility of the German Nation* in the vernacular German, not the academic Latin, so that it became a "best-seller." Luther's translation of the Bible made that book a part of German life, and made Luther's language one of the bases of modern literary German. His marriage to a former nun and his raising of a large family dramatized the break with Rome. And behind all this was his passionate conviction that he was doing what he had to do. . . .

The forces that opposed Luther were relatively weak. Clerical opposition centered in the top levels of the Catholic bureaucracy: Pope Leo X was only its willing instrument. Moderate Catholics, anxious to compromise and avert a schism, existed. Had there been at the head of the Catholic Church a pope willing to reform and to make concessions not harmful to the Church's basic position as God's chosen instrument on earth, even Luther might perhaps have been reconciled. Yet, as in all the great modern revolutions, the moderates—gifted, numerous, and active though they were—could not hold up against the extremists. Once Leo X had excommunicated Luther in 1521, the way to compromise was probably blocked, for Luther's associates could have been won away from him only by concessions too great for a Catholic to make.

Politically, the opposition in these critical years centered in the young Emperor Charles V (reigned 1519–1556). . . . Together with the Habsburgs' lands in Austria and elsewhere and their claim to the title of Emperor he inherited the Low Countries, Spain and the Spanish lands overseas, and parts of Italy. This was the nearest approach to a European superstate since Charlemagne, and Charles V wanted to make it a reality. The activities of Luther's princely German supporters threatened his hold over Germany; moreover, Charles, though by no means a mere papal instrument, was Catholic. He decided to fight.

WAR AND REBELLION
IN THE 1520'S

Charles V entrusted the government of the Germans to his younger brother Ferdinand, who formed alliances with Bavaria and other Catholic German states to oppose the Lutheran states. Thus began a long series of combinations, the fruits of which were the religious wars of the next few generations, and the enduring territorial division of Germany into, roughly, a Protestant north and east and a Catholic south and west. But the imperial Habsburg power also had to fight against the French, and so could not steadily concentrate on defeating the Lutherans in Germany. In 1529 the Lutheran princes protested against the sudden new imperial severity against them. It is from this protest that the term "Protestant" arose.

In Germany, below the level of the princes, the knights espoused Luther's cause. Some of them held castles and small estates direct from the Emperor and were in theory just as "independent" as a greater prince. Others were vassals of some greater lord; some were younger sons, who were feeling the decline of their status caused by changing economic and social conditions. Under the leadership of Ulrich von Hutten and Franz von Sickingen they rose in 1522, in what is called the "Knights' War." Troops of the western German archbishoprics put them down, but their struggle added to the confusion of the period.

Worse still was the Peasants' Rebellion of 1524–1525, not unlike the French Jacquerie of 1358 or the English Peasants' Revolt of 1381: like them directed against the remaining burdens of the manorial system, like them without competent military commanders, and like them ruthlessly suppressed. It centered, not in the eastern German regions where serfdom had been completely enforced, but in the southwest, where the peasants had begun to emancipate themselves and wanted to finish the process. Much as Wyclif and the Lollards had influenced the English peasants, Luther's preaching stirred those in Germany. More than their English counterparts of the fourteenth century, the German peasants had educated leaders, who had a revolutionary program of their own, which they embodied in the "Twelve Articles." Couched in Biblical language, the articles seem moderate enough today: each parish should choose its own priest; tithes and taxes should be cut; the peasants should have the right to take game and firewood from the forests; and so on.

LUTHERAN CONSERVATISM

Horrified at the peasants' interpretation of the Bible that he had translated into German for them, Luther denounced the rebels in unbridled terms. He intended his church to be respectful of established political authority. . . . This conservatism is quite consistent with Luther's fundamental spiritual position. If the visible external world is subordinate to the invisible spiritual world, the best one can hope for here on earth is that good order be maintained. Kings, princes, authority, custom, law: All existing institutions are preferable to discussion and dissension.

The princes of northern Germany and the Scandinavian kingdoms reciprocated. They superintended and hastened the process of converting the willing to Lutheranism and evicting the unwilling. By the mid-sixteenth century Lutheranism had become the state religion of these regions, and as such, it was often the docile instrument of political rulers.

In organizing his own church, Luther showed the same conservatism. After all, the logical extreme of the priesthood of all believers is no church at all, or as many churches as there are individual human beings; in Saxony reformers influenced by Luther tried out these anarchical concepts before Luther and the moderates intervened. The new

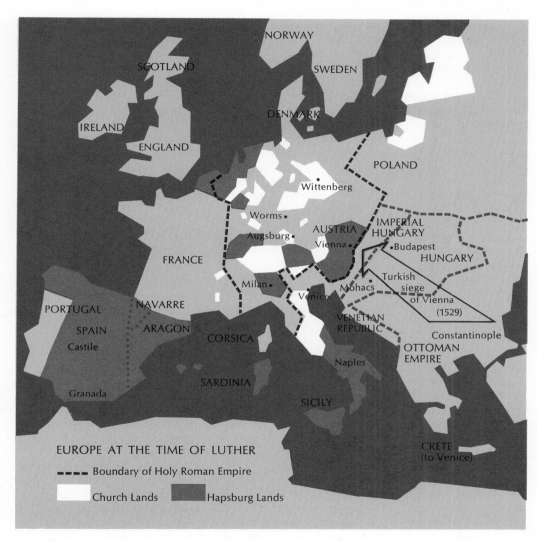

EUROPE AT THE TIME OF LUTHER

- - - - Boundary of Holy Roman Empire

☐ Church Lands ■ Hapsburg Lands

lous quality. Veneration of saints and relics, fasts, pilgrimages, monastic orders all vanished. Though the changes were great, the forms of worship retained much that had been traditional. To Luther this new church was not merely an alternative to the Church of Rome, it was the *one true church,* a return to early Christianity before Rome had corrupted it.

Martin Luther Attacks the Papacy

Martin Luther was a master of the written word. The two works drawn on in part in this reading, set in print and read by tens of thousands of Germans and other dissatisfied Europeans, had a mjaor impact on the Protestant revolt. In the *Ninety-Five Theses* Luther attacked certain practices of the Church. In the *Address to the German Nobility,* he sought, as the title implies, the support of the secular powers in Germany for his definition of the Christian Church. I. From Henry Bettenson, ed., *Documents of the Christian Church* (New York: Oxford University Press, 1947), pp. 263, 267, 270–271. II. From J. H. Robinson, *Readings in European History* (Boston, 1906), II, pp. 75–80.

I. THE NINETY-FIVE THESES (1517)

A disputation of Master Martin Luther, Theologian, for the elucidation of the virtue of Indulgences.

From a zealous desire to bring to light the truth, the following theses will be maintained at Wittenberg, under the presidency of the

church Luther established, often by simply taking over the existing church buildings, did have priests; but they were free to marry, a sign that they had no more sacramental powers than other men. The Lutherans retained two of the sacraments: baptism and the Eucharist, both specifically mentioned in the Bible, but deprived them of their miracu-

Rvd. Fr. Martin Luther, Master of Arts, Master of Sacred Theology and official Reader therein. He therefore asks that all who are unable to be present and dispute with him verbally will do so in writing. In the name of our Lord Jesus Christ, Amen. . . .

43. Christians are to be taught that to give to the poor or to lend to the needy is a better work than the purchase of pardons.

44. And that because through a work of charity, charity is increased and a man advances in goodness; whereas through pardons there is no advance in goodness but merely an increased freedom from penalty.

45. Christians are to be taught that a man who sees a brother in need and passes him by to give his money for the purchase of pardon wins for himself not the indulgences of the pope but the indignation of God. . . .

48. Christians are to be taught that in dispensing pardons the pope has more desire (as he has more need) for devout prayer on his behalf than of ready money.

49. Christians are to be taught that the pope's pardons are useful if they do not put their trust in them, but most harmful if through them they lose the fear of God.

50. Christians must be taught that if the pope knew the exactions of the preachers of indulgences he would rather have S. Peter's basilica reduced to ashes than built with the skin, flesh and bones of his sheep.

51. Christians are to be taught that the pope (as is his duty) would desire to give of his own substance to those poor men from many of whom certain sellers of pardons are extracting money; that to this end he would even, if need be, sell the basilica of Saint Peter.

52. Confidence in salvation through letters of indulgence is vain; and that even if the commissary, nay, even if the pope himself, should pledge his soul as a guarantee. . . .

81. This wanton preaching of pardons makes it hard even for learned men to defend the honor of the pope against calumny, or at least against the shrewd questions of the laity.

82. They ask: Why does not the pope empty purgatory on account of most holy charity and the great need of souls, the most righteous of causes, seeing that he redeems an infinite number of souls on account of sordid money, given for the erection of a basilica, which is a most trivial cause? . . .

86. The pope's riches at this day far exceed the wealth of the richest millionaires, cannot he therefore build one single basilica of S. Peter out of his own money, rather than out of the money of the faithful poor?

87. What does the pope remit or dispense to those who through perfect contrition have the right to plenary remission and dispensation?

88. What greater good would be gained by the Church if the pope were to do a hundred times a day what he does once a day; i.e. distribute these remissions and dispensations to any of the faithful?

89. If the pope by means of his pardons now seeks the salvation of souls rather than payment, why does he suspend letters and pardons formerly granted, since they are equally efficacious?

90. To suppress these careful arguments of the laity merely by papal authority, instead of clearing them up by a reasoned reply, is to expose the Church and the pope to the ridicule of the enemy and to render Christians unhappy.

91. Now if pardons were preached according to the spirit and mind of the pope all these questions would easily be disposed of; nay, they would not arise.

92. And so let all those prophets depart who say to Christ's people 'Peace, peace' and there is no peace.

93. And farewell to all those prophets who say to Christ's people 'the cross, the cross' and there is no cross.

94. Christians are to be exhorted to endeavor to follow Christ, their head, through pains, deaths, and hells.

95. And so let them trust to enter heaven rather through many tribulations than through the false confidence of peace. . . .

II. ADDRESS TO THE GERMAN NOBILITY (1520)

The Romanists have with great dexterity built themselves about with three walls, which hitherto have protected them against reform; and thereby is Christianity fearfully fallen.

In the first place, when the temporal power has pressed them hard, they have affirmed and maintained that the *temporal power has no jurisdiction over them,—that, on the contrary, the spiritual is above the temporal.*

Secondly, when it was proposed to admonish them from the Holy Scriptures they said, *"It beseems no one but the pope to interpret the Scriptures."*

And thirdly, when they were threatened with a council, they invented the idea that *no one but the pope can call a council.* . . .

And whenever they have been compelled to call a council, they have made it of no avail, by binding the princes beforehand with an oath to let them alone. Besides this they have given the pope full power over the ordering of the council, so that it is all one, whether we have many councils or no councils, for in any case they deceive us with pretenses and false tricks, so grievously do the Romanists tremble for their skins before a true, free council; and thus they have overawed kings and princes, so that these believe that they would be offending God if they refused to believe in all their knavish tricks.

Now may God help us, and give us one of those trumpets that overthrew the walls of Jericho, so that we may also blow down these walls of straw and paper, and that we may regain possession of our Christian rods for the chastisement of sin, and expose the craft and deceit of the devil; thus may we amend ourselves by punishment and again obtain God's favor.

Let us, in the first place, attack the first wall.

It has been discovered that the pope, bishops, priests, and monks should be called the "spiritual estate," while princes, lords, artisans, and peasants form the "temporal estate,"—a very fine hypocritical invention. But let no one be made afraid by it; and that for this reason: All Christians are truly of the spiritual estate, and there is no difference among us, save of office alone. As St. Paul says (1 Cor. xii), we are all one body, though each member has its own work to do, whereby it may serve the others. This is because we have one baptism, one gospel, one faith, and are all Christians alike; for baptism, gospel, and faith, these alone make spiritual and Christian folk. . . .

We see then that those we call churchmen, be they priests, bishops, or popes, are not set apart from or above other Christians, except in so far as they have to do with the word of God and the sacraments, for that is their calling and office. And moreover the temporal authorities wield the sword and the rod to chastise the wicked and protect the good. A cobbler, a smith, a peasant—every man has his own calling and office, just like the consecrated priests and bishops: and every one in his office or calling must help and serve the rest, so that all may work together for the common good, as the various members of the body all serve each other. . . .

The second wall is even more flimsy and tottering than the first,—namely, the claim that they alone are masters of the Scriptures. . . . But that we fight not with our own words, let us bring forth the Scriptures. St. Paul says: "If any thing be revealed to another that sitteth by, let the first hold his peace" (I Cor. xiv. 30). What would be the use of this commandment if we were to believe him alone who speaks first or sits in the highest seat? Christ himself says that all Christians shall be taught of God (John vi. 45). . . .

The third wall falls of itself as soon as the first two have fallen; for if the pope acts contrary to the Scriptures, we are bound to stand by the Scriptures and to punish and restrain him, in accordance with Christ's commandment (Matt. xviii. 15). . . . Moreover there is nothing in the Scriptures to show that the pope has the sole right to summon and confirm a council; the Romanists have nothing but their own laws, and these hold good only so long as they are not opposed to Christianity and the laws of God; but when the pope deserves punishment these laws cease to exist, since Christianity would suffer if he were not punished by means of a council. . . .

What is the use in Christendom of those who are called "cardinals"? I will tell you. In Italy and Germany there are many rich convents, endowments, holdings, and benefices; and as the best way of getting these into the hands of Rome they created cardinals, and gave to them the bishoprics, convents, and prelacies, and thus destroyed the service of God. . . .

Now that Italy is sucked dry, they come to Germany and begin very quietly but we shall soon see Germany brought into the same state as Italy. We have a few cardinals already. What the Romanists really mean to do, the "drunken Germans" are not to see until they have lost everything. . . .

Social Consequences of the German Reformation: The Peasant Uprising (1524-1525)

Luther's successful break with the Church encouraged others to take similar steps. The peasantry in southern Germany, in the name of religion, demanded an end to serfdom and economic repression. The following selections contain: I. some of the Articles expressing the position of the peasants, II. Luther's reaction to the Articles, III. some excerpts from a contemporary diary describing the peasant uprising, and IV. Luther's final statement on civil uprising. In James H. Robinson, *Readings in European History* (Boston: Ginn & Co., 1906), Vol. II, pp. 94–108.

I. THE ARTICLES OF THE PEASANTS (1524)

There are many evil writings put forth of late which take occasion, on account of the assembling of the peasants, to cast scorn upon the gospel, saying, "Is this the fruit of the new teaching, that no one should obey but that all should everywhere rise in revolt, and rush together to reform, or perhaps destroy altogether, the authorities, both ecclesiastic and lay?" The articles below shall answer these godless and criminal faultfinders, and serve, in the first place, to remove the reproach from the word of God and, in the second place, to give a Christian excuse for the disobedience or even the revolt of the entire peasantry.

In the first place, the gospel is not the cause of revolt and disorder, since it is the message of Christ, the promised Messiah; the word of life, teaching only love, peace, patience, and concord. Thus all who believe in Christ should learn to be loving, peaceful, long-suffering, and harmonious. This is the foundation of all the articles of the peasants (as will be seen), who accept the gospel and live according to it.

The Third Article. It has been the custom hitherto for men to hold us as their own property, which is pitiable enough, considering that Christ has delivered and redeemed us all, without exception, by the shedding of his precious blood, the lowly as well as the great. Accordingly it is consistent with Scripture that we should be free and should wish to be so. Not that we would wish to be absolutely free and under no authority. God does not teach us that we should lead a disorderly life in the lusts of the flesh, but that we should love the Lord our God and our neighbor. We would gladly observe all this as God has commanded us in the celebration of the communion. He has not commanded us not to obey the authorities, but rather that we should be humble, not only towards those in authority, but towards every one. We are thus ready to yield obedience according to God's law to our elected and regular authorities in all proper things becoming to a Christian. We therefore take it for granted that you will release us from serfdom as true Christians, unless it should be shown us from the gospel that we are serfs. . . .

The Sixth Article. Our sixth complaint is in regard to the excessive services which are demanded of us and which are increased from day to day. We ask that this matter be properly looked into, so that we shall not continue to be oppressed in this way, but that some gracious consideration be given us, since our forefathers were required only to serve according to the word of God.

The Seventh Article. Seventh, we will not hereafter allow ourselves to be farther oppressed by our lords, but will let them demand only what is just and proper according to the word of the agreement between the lord and the peasant. The lord should no longer try to force more services or other dues from the peasant without payment, but permit the peasant to enjoy his holding in peace and quiet. The peasant should, however, help the lord when it is necessary, and at proper times, when it will not be disadvantageous to the peasant, and for a suitable payment. . . .

II. LUTHER'S COMMENTS ON THE PEASANT ARTICLES (1525)

There should be no serfs, because Christ has freed us all! What is that we hear? That is to make Christian freedom wholly bodily. Did not Abraham and the other patriarchs and prophets have serfs? Read what St. Paul says of servants, who in all times have been serfs. So this article is straight against the gospel, and moreover it is robbery, since each man would take his person from his lord to whom it belongs. A serf can be a good Christian and enjoy Christian liberty, just as a prisoner or a sick man may be a Christian although he is not free. This article would make all men equal and convert the spiritual kingdom of Christ into an external worldly one; but that is impossible, for a worldly realm cannot stand where there is no inequality; some must be free, others bond; some rulers, others subjects. . . .

My counsel would be that a few counts and lords should be chosen from the nobles, and from the towns a few councilors, who should settle the matter peacefully. You lords should unbend your stiff minds a bit,—for you will have to do that sooner or later whether you will or no,—and give up a little of your oppression and tyranny, so that the poor man can have a little space and air. On the other hand, the peasants will have to let a few of their articles go, which are screwed up too high. In this way the matter, even if it cannot be treated in a Christian spirit, can at least be adjusted according to human laws and agreements. . . .

III. A DESCRIPTION OF THE PEASANT UPRISING IN ROTHENBURG (SPRING, 1525)

On March 21, a Tuesday, thirty or forty peasants got together in a mob in Rothenburg, bought a kettledrum, and marched about the town, a part going to Pretheim and a part toward Orenbach. They got together again on Thursday and on Friday, as many as four hundred.

The working classes in the town now begin to revolt. They cease to obey the authorities and form a committee of thirty-six to manage affairs. Cunz Eberhardt and George Bermeter are meanwhile dispatched to learn what the peasants are doing; but the peasants will give

The gulf in life-style between noble and peasant is evident in this portrait of Margrave Joachim of Brandenburg (1499–1535) by Lucas Cranach and in the scene of peasants harvesting grain by Pieter Bruegel.

no reply, for they say that they have not all got together yet. A letter is received from Margrave Casimir [of Brandenburg]. This is read to the community. He offers to aid the town authorities and if necessary come in person to reëstablish peace and harmony. The community and their committee of thirty-six treat this scornfully and do not accept the offer.

March 24. This evening . . . some one knocked off the head of Christ's image on a crucifix and struck off the arms.

March 25. The town councils are in great danger and anxiety, for they are oppressed by the community and its committee of thirty-six.

March 27. The councilors are forced to pledge their obedience to the community, for they are taken out one by one, guarded by members of the committee of thirty-six. Each thought he was going to be killed, but after taking the pledge he was secretly sent home without his companions' knowledge.

March 26. Chrischainz, the baker, knocked the missal out of the priest's hand in the chapel of our Lady and drove away the priest from mass. To-day the peasants let themselves be seen in the field outside the Galgenthor [city-gate]. . . .

On [March 31] all the artisans were to lay all their complaints and demands before a committee. The taxes, wages, and methods of weighing were discussed. The peasants encamped near Santhof. Friday, April 7, Kueplein, during the sermon, threw the lighted oil lamps about the church. Some of the peasants came into Rothenburg and the neighboring towns, everywhere plundering cupboards and cellars.

On Good Friday all services were suspended in the churches of Rothenburg, for there was neither chanting nor preaching except that Dr. John Teuschel preached against emperor, kings, princes, and lords, ecclesiastical and lay, with foul abuse and slander, on the ground that they were hindering God's word. . . .

Friday. All priests are forced to become citizens, otherwise whey would have lost all their goods. They are to take their share of guard duty and work on the fortifications.

On Wednesday [April 26] Lorenz Knobloch was hewn to pieces by the peasants at Ostheim; and then they pelted one another with the fragments. They said he was a traitor and that he wanted to mislead them. . . .

April 30. The monastery of Anhausen was plundered and burned in the night, also that near Dinkelsbühl. The peasants also attacked

Peasants prepare to murder a knight in this scene from the peasant war. On the raised banner is a peasant's ungainly shoe, symbol of the revolt.

the monastery of Schwarzach, and the castle of Reichelsberg was burned.

May 6. Early in the morning the great bell rang three times, summoning the people to hear a message from Margrave Casimir, brought by three noblemen, and inviting all to take refuge in Rothenburg under his protection. The greater part refused, and some were noted by the Margrave's representative, and afterward lost their heads.

Monday. The peasants approach Neuhaus, and next day plunder and burn. . . .

On the next Monday Margrave Casimir proceeds with his forces to subdue and punish the peasants. Hans Krelein the older, priest at Wernitz, was beheaded, with four peasants,

at Leutershausen. Seven have their fingers cut off. Likewise at Neuenstat eighteen burghers and peasants are beheaded. At Kitzingen fifty-eight have their eyes put out and are forbidden to enter the town again.

On Friday before Whitsuntide the forces of the Swabian League slay four thousand peasants at Königshofen. . . .

On June 6 messengers are sent from Rothenburg to Casimir to ask for pardon. Next day others are sent to the League, but they are told that they must surrender unconditionally.

On Thursday following, after the League had retaken the town of Würzburg, they beheaded sixty-two.

On Friday after Corpus Christi, mass was once more chanted in Rothenburg, as formerly. . . .

On the eve of Peter and Paul's day Margrave Casimir rides into Rothenburg with four hundred horsemen, a thousand footmen, and two hundred wagons full of arms and equipments. . . .

IV. LUTHER URGES THE ANNIHILATION OF REBELS

In my preceding pamphlet [on the "Twelve Articles"] I had no occasion to condemn the peasants, because they promised to yield to law and better instruction, as Christ also demands.

But before I can turn around, they go out and appeal to force, in spite of their promises, and rob and pillage and act like mad dogs. From this it is quite apparent what they had in their false minds, and that what they put forth under the name of the gospel in the "Twelve Articles" was all vain pretense. . . .

Since, therefore, those peasants and miserable wretches allow themselves to be led astray and act differently from what they declared, I likewise must write differently concerning them; and first bring their sins before their eyes, as God commands, whether perchance some of them may come to their senses; and, further, I would instruct those in authority how to conduct themselves in this matter. . . .

. . . They cause uproar and sacrilegiously rob and pillage monasteries and castles that do not belong to them, for which, like public highwaymen and murderers, they deserve the twofold death of body and soul. It is right and lawful to slay at the first opportunity a rebellious person, who is known as such, for he is already under God's and the emperor's ban. Every man is at once judge and executioner of a public rebel; just as, when a fire starts, he who can extinguish it first is the best fellow. Rebellion is not simply vile murder, but is like a great fire that kindles and devastates a country; it fills the land with murder and bloodshed, makes widows and orphans, and destroys everything, like the greatest calamity.

. . . They cloak their frightful and revolting sins with the gospel, call themselves Christian brethren, swear allegiance, and compel people to join them in such abominations. Thereby they become the greatest blasphemers and violators of God's holy name, and serve and honor the devil under the semblance of the gospel, so that they have ten times deserved death of body and soul, for never have I heard of uglier sins. . . .

Carl Gustavson: The Causes of the Reformation

In *A Preface to History* Carl Gustavson (1915–   ) of Ohio University sought to present college freshmen with "an outline of the nature of historical-mindedness." Each chapter dealt with an aspect of historical reasoning; his chapter on causation focused on the Reformation. Gustavson wanted his readers to recognize that no single cause "ever adequately explains a historical episode." From *A Preface to History* by Carl G. Gustavson. (Copyright 1955 McGraw-Hill.) Used with permission of McGraw-Hill Book Company. Pp. 56–62.

Quite obviously the immediate cause for the Reformation is to be found in the activity of Luther between 1517 and 1521, although the selection of a specific event may bring differences of opinion; the most likely choices would be the nailing of the ninety-five theses, the Diet of Worms, or the famous disputation with Eck, in which Luther first clearly crossed the line between Catholicism and heresy. Identifying the initial spark, however, by no means explains the enormous extent of the conflagration which followed.

Luther's ninety-five theses immediately became the best seller of that day. Great crowds gathered to applaud him as he went to the Diet of Worms. If we can decide why he suddenly experienced this popularity, we may also gain some idea of the reason for his success. . . . Luther had been denouncing the outrageous methods used in the sale of indulgences, an issue everyone could understand far better than discussions of abstruse theology. He was hitting out at unpopular figures, always a good way to attract a following. The friar of Wittenberg was a German, a son of the people, courageously talking up to pope and emperor, speaking for the common people and expressing what many of them felt. . . .

The career of John Hus of Prague is apt to come to mind. His life story bears several marked resemblances to that of Luther, and his proposals were very similar to those of his successors; there was a major difference however—he was burned for his temerity. A whole century before the Lutheran Reformation some of its principles were already widely approved, as witness the obstinate refusal of the Bohemians to give up the reforms of Hus. (Note, also, that Bohemia borders on Saxony, Luther's home district.)

Other reformers had also preceded Luther: Peter Waldo, Wyclif, Savonarola, to mention the most prominent. Nor should the criticism of the Church by such writers as Erasmus and Valla be forgotten. Evidences of Protestant ideas appear everywhere in Western Europe during the preceding century. . . .

One point to note is that the criticism of the Church usually did not carry with it a threat to leave the institution. It was criticized, its officials castigated, its practices and policies assailed in the same spirit in which Americans treat their governmental institutions. The object was reform, not separation, the attacks representing no more a desire to destroy the Church than we expect to abolish Congress. Some people might dislike papal authority in much the same way as some Americans suspect the power of a strong President. When Luther appeared at Worms, he had no expectation of founding a separate church, and in fact he may have gone to the diet with the lurking hope of converting Charles V to his own viewpoint. Had this happened, a sweeping reform within the Church could have resulted and the universal Church remained united at least for a longer time. Even after the break had occurred, the Lutheran and Anglican churches insisted that it was the Roman Catholics who had abandoned the original idea of the Church, while they themselves were simply purifying it of impure accretions.

Only a rugged, roughhewn, obstinate man could have shouldered his way to success in the circumstances—the looming figure of Luther makes the personal factor important in the causation of the Reformation. Unless the odds are too great, the victory is likely to go to the side inspired by genuine zeal for a cause. Historical movements, however much they are impelled by economic and social factors, after all are carried through by men. Their states of mind are important. Even Luther, however, could have accomplished little more than propagate his ideas if he had not found many others in the same mood. Had Luther alone, or a small circle of disciples only, held Protestant ideas, no social force of sufficient magnitude to create historical events would have existed. When tens of thousands, however, were possessed of the same general outlook, the scene was set for action, and it took only Luther's words and actions to precipitate the formation of a spiritual force of enormous extent and potency. . . .

The circumstances were ready for the man, and his religious zeal furnished a focal point for the hitherto diffused causes for the Reformation. One may legitimately question if any one single force, albeit as powerful as this one, could in itself have altered the course of history. From our perspective . . . a number of social forces seem to converge upon the . . . events and carry them forward.

We have seen gunpowder and the better ocean-going vessels make possible the expansion of the European into other parts of the world. The printing press, another technological advance, served as a tool of incalculable importance in the Reformation. Someone might argue very plausibly that no Reformation could have occurred had it not been for the invention of the printing press. Without this method of spreading ideas, the Lutheran doctrines could not have been disseminated so rapidly, and, if support had not quickly manifested itself, the emperor and Church might have succeeded in suppressing the movement. The press also aided the reformers by undermining the claim of the Church to pose as the custodian of final truth, since it was now becoming possible for more persons to acquire a copy of the Bible.

Social forces emerging from economic motives, powerful as they were, must have exercised an important influence on these events. The kind of merchant that we encountered in Florence or in sixteenth-century England, and who was also active in Germany, would deplore the constant flow of money to Rome. Most people, indeed, would feel indignation at this continual drain on the national wealth, and any rebel against papal authority would find useful ammunition here. The incessant sniping at the wealth of the bishops and the monasteries was partly due to the unfortunate contrast with the early ideal of the Church, but the criticisms were also likely to remind people that their contributions were not always usefully applied. Especially would the growing middle class deplore the drag on productivity caused by the clerical possession of land, the numerous church festivals, and the presumed idleness of the monks. With their ideals of thrift and industry, the middle class found many church habits irritating. Luther appealed to these feelings, with violent and exaggerated words, in his *Address to the Christian Nobility of the German Nation:* "What has brought us Germans to such a pass that we have to suffer this robbery and this destruction of our property by the pope?. . . Do we still wonder why princes, cities, foundations, convents, and people grow poor? We should rather wonder that we have anything left to eat."

We know that the nobles were always eager to expand their holdings. They had long eyed the lands of the Church, and the Reformation, with its expropriation of clerical wealth, offered the awaited opportunity. Many of

England's noble families had their origin in grants of this kind, and these were likely to remain Protestant, since any reversion to the old order would jeopardize their new acquisitions. The princes of Germany likewise benefited in this fashion. . . .

Why did Luther "get away with it" when others before him had failed? The truth is that Charles V was in a dilemma. New on the throne, he was uncertain of his support and would hesitate before alienating his German subjects. Luther's own prince, the Elector of Saxony, was friendly to the reformers and possessed the force and prestige to raise a rebellion. The loud acclaim of the friar must have alarmed Charles and dissuaded him from a highly unpopular move. He undoubtedly underestimated the potentialities of the movement, the more so since he had grave political problems to grapple with elsewhere. The Ottoman Turks were approaching the far-flung borders of his realm, and Charles needed German unity in order to meet this threat. All in all, "the king *was* weak," not so much because of his own personality as in his inheritance of an enfeebled government from his predecessors.

The Crown was one of the institutions which should have suppressed the rebellion. The other was the Church itself. After many centuries as the universal Church of Western Europe, it had undergone both a loss of positive vitality and a diminishing strength in comparison with new emerging forces. It had failed to suppress the Hussite heretics. The internecine struggle between two organs of the Church, the papacy and the council, in the conciliar movement might be seen as a portent of disruption. Perhaps most significant of all, the Renaissance was having a debilitating spiritual effect upon the papacy; popes who were using spiritual resources for temporal ends were blunting their own swords. . . . By making the papacy synonymous with the Church, they drew upon the Church itself a shower of invective. The fact that many believed the Church to be corrupt shook the all-important allegiance of the great masses of the people.

The Church no longer possessed as much power, proportionately, either. New forces were rising which had long challenged the Church and which now overwhelmed it. One of these was the national state. . . .

During the fourteenth and fifteenth centuries, national kings continued to add to their power, and in France, England, and Spain these rulers arrogated to themselves increasing control over the national churches. Seen in the light of later events, the rivalry of nations during the Avignon period, the schism, and the conciliar movement betoken a growing national feeling which would burst asunder the ancient bonds. The Catholic Church was faced with its perennial problem, how to keep its international character although threatened by national feelings and provincial attachments. The Church, after all, was essentially an institution of the southland. From thence it had come, there it had matured and built up its customs and symbols. At one time, the cultural inferiority of the north caused these peoples to accept southern leadership as natural; as the northern peoples developed, however, the subservience to the south began to rankle.

In the northern countries, a sense of nationalism was a strong factor in the break with Rome. In Germany, where other national aspirations went unsatisfied, this was particularly true. The Reformation passed into effect in Sweden coincident with the overthrow of Danish rule. The English struggle against Spain would tend to associate the state church with national existence in that country. The native language was substituted for Latin in the churches of these regions. In nearly all instances, the advent of the Reformation brought added power and wealth to the kings or territorial princes. The institutional factor is a powerful one in the causation of the Reformation; one institution, the Church, was losing ground to another institution, the national monarchy, and the spiritual crisis precipitated by Luther offered the territorial princes of Germany and the kings of northern Europe a splendid opportunity to establish state control over the Church.

STUDY QUESTIONS

1. With what contemporary religious practices did Luther take issue? Why?

2. Why was the Lutheran revolt successful? In what ways was it more than just a religious revolt? What was Luther's goal?

3. How are the 95 Theses like earlier religious reform programs? What were the three walls that Luther claimed the "Romanists" had falsely constructed? How did he demolish the walls?

4. To what extent were the demands of the South German peasantry based on the Gospel? On Luther's example? On other factors?

5. Why was the peasant uprising so harshly suppressed? Who supported it in Rothenburg and who suppressed it?

6. How did Luther define freedom? What explains the contrast between his earlier counsel and his position after the uprising was in full swing?

7. To what causes does Gustavson attribute the outbreak and success of the Lutheran revolt?

Calvinism in Theory and Practice

From *Civilization Past and Present* by T. Walter Wallbank, Alastair M. Taylor, Nels M. Bailkey, Copyright © 1965 by Scott, Foresman and Company. Pp. 298–299, 300.

The most famous sixteenth-century Protestant leader after Luther was John Calvin (1509–1564). A Frenchman of the middle class, Calvin studied theology and law at Paris, where he became interested in Luther's teachings. About 1533 he had what he called a "conversion," whereby he abandoned Catholicism. When Francis I began to persecute heretics, Calvin fled to Switzerland and settled first at Basel, a Protestant city. There he published in 1536 the first edition of his great work the *Institutes of the Christian Religion,* unquestionably one of the most significant books of systematic theology ever written. His capacity for creative thinking was overshadowed by his ability as an organizer and synthesist. Influenced by his legal training as well as by humanistic scholarship and the doctrines of Luther, Calvin set forth a system that was a masterpiece of logical reasoning.

Whereas Luther's central doctrine was justification by faith, Calvin's was the sovereignty of God. "The great text for Luther was 'Thy sins are forgiven,' but for Calvin it was 'If God is for us who can be against us?' Both Calvin and Luther had an overwhelming sense of the majesty of God, but whereas for Luther this served to point up the miracle of forgiveness, for Calvin it gave rather the assurance of the impregnability of God's purpose." God was omnipotent and for His own purposes had created the world and also man in His image. Since Adam and Eve had fallen from a state of sinlessness, man was utterly depraved and lost.

Carrying these doctrines to their logical conclusions, Calvin defined man's relations to God in his famous doctrine of predestination. Since God is omniscient, He knows the past, present, and future. Consequently, He must always know which men are to be saved by Him and which men are to be damned eternally. Man's purpose in life, then, is not to try to work out his salvation—for this has already been determined—but to honor God. While Calvin did not profess to know absolutely who among men were to be God's chosen—the elect—he believed that the following three tests constituted a good yardstick by which to judge who might be saved: participation in the two sacraments—Baptism and the Lord's Supper; an upright moral life; and a public profession of the faith.

It was the duty of the living members of the church to glorify God by establishing a theocracy that would be governed according to scriptural precept. The Bible was the supreme authority, and the community should discipline or remove any found guilty of blasphemy or unseemly behavior. . . .

Pains were taken to provide instruction in the fundamentals of faith, to prepare the young for useful Christian citizenship, to safeguard the purity of the faith, to extirpate any remnant of Catholicism. Although the regime was high-minded, it carried its zeal to ridiculous lengths. Penalties were inflicted for

---

TOPIC 7

CALVIN'S CITY OF GOD

In the wake of the Lutheran protest, Protestant reform movements mushroomed. Of the ideas at work in these movements, the doctrines of the brilliant but stern Frenchman, John Calvin, had the greatest impact on the future development of Western civilization. Calvin went far beyond Luther, who was some thirty years his senior, in establishing the rule of religion in everyday life. In Geneva, the Swiss community he dominated, laymen played an important role in enforcing a strict code of personal behavior. Tolerance found no new defenders in the closed climate of Geneva, but where Calvinists were in a minority their own self-interest made them defenders of religious, and hence often political freedom. In the world of commerce, Calvinist thinking seemed at home with the new affluence and social mobility bred by economic opportunity. The readings examine the relevance of Calvinism to the great religious, economic, social, and political questions of the day.

being absent from sermons or laughing during the church service, for wearing bright colors, for swearing or dancing, for inability to recite prayers, for playing cards, or for having one's fortune told by gypsies. Such regulations had also existed in medieval times, but in Calvin's Geneva they were energetically enforced.

In regard to more serious offenses, especially in the religious sphere, Calvin and his associates acted with the utmost severity. Torture was used to obtain some confessions, and citizens of Geneva were banished for heresy, blasphemy, witchcraft, and adultery. When Servetus, a scholarly anti-Trinitarian, appeared in Geneva, Calvin prosecuted him for heresy, saying that his defense was:

> . . . no better than the braying of an ass, and that the prisoner was like a villainous cur wiping his muzzle.

THE SPREAD OF CALVINISM

From Geneva, Calvinism spread far and wide, imbued with its founder's austerity of spirit, power of mind, and high purpose. Much of this influence stemmed from the Academy (today the University of Geneva), which trained students from other countries in Calvin's theology. In France, Calvinism made influential converts among both the bourgeoisie and the nobility. . . .

Carried down the Rhine River to the northern Netherlands, Calvin's teachings formed the basis for the Dutch Reformed religion. In the latter half of the sixteenth century and the first half of the seventeenth, the Dutch struggle for independence against a Catholic king of Spain strengthened Protestantism in their country. And in Scotland the authority of the Roman Church was challenged by John Knox. . . .

PRESBYTERIANISM IN SCOTLAND

The religious revolt in Scotland was largely the work of the zealous reformer John Knox (1505?–1572), who had become acquainted with Calvin in Geneva and frequently consulted him concerning church doctrine and civil authority. After returning to his native Scotland in about 1559, Knox became leader of the Lords of the Congregation, a group of Protestant nobles who wished to overthrow the jurisdiction of the Roman Catholic Church in their land. In 1560 Knox drew up the Articles of the Presbyterian Church, which abolished the authority of the pope and condemned the creeds and practices of the old Church. With the help of English troops, he effected a religious revolution.

One year later, the beautiful but ill-fated Mary Stuart returned from France to find her bleak kingdom alienated from her own Catholic views. From his pulpit and in his debates with Mary about questions of theology and the loyalty owed by a subject to his monarch, Knox defied the queen's authority and thundered against her religious principles. Although Mary showed amazing skill and logic in her arguments with him, the fiery reformer gained the support of the Scottish people in his denunciation of the queen. By the time Mary had been executed by Elizabeth [of England] in 1587, Scotland had been won over to Calvinistic Presbyterianism.

Calvin Explains God's Will

The key to Calvin's beliefs is found in the *Institutes of the Christian Religion,* published in 1536 when he was twenty-seven. Extracts in this reading present Calvin's views on predestination and on what he called man's calling. (I) From the *Institutes of the Christian Religion* in *Documents of the Christian Church,* Henry Bettenson, ed. (New York, 1947), p. 302. Reprinted by permission of the Oxford University Press. (II) From *Institutes of the Christian Religion,* John Calvin, Vol. I, translated by John Allen, edited by Benjamin B. Warfield. Published 1936 by the Presbyterian Board of Christian Education, Philadelphia, U.S.A. Pp. 789–791.

I. PREDESTINATION

No one who wishes to be thought religious dares outright to deny predestination, by which God chooses some for the hope of life, and condemns others to eternal death. But men entangle it with captious quibbles; and especially those who make foreknowledge the ground of it. We indeed attribute to God both predestination and foreknowledge; but we call it absurd to subordinate one to the other. When we attribute foreknowledge to God we mean that all things have ever been, and eternally remain, before his eyes; so that to his knowledge nothing is future or past, but all things are present; and present not in the sense that they are reproduced in imagination (as we are aware of past events which are retained in our memory), but present in the sense that he really sees and observes them placed, as it were, before his eyes. And this foreknowledge extends over the whole universe and over every creature. By predestination we mean the eternal decree of God, by which he has decided . . . what he wishes to happen in the case of each individual. For all men are not created on an equal footing, but for some eternal life is pre-ordained, for others eternal damnation. . . .

II. MAN'S PLACE IN LIFE

The Scripture has . . . a third rule, by which it regulates the use of earthly things; of which something was said, when we treated of the precepts of charity. For it states, that while all these things are given to us by the Divine goodness, and appointed for our benefit, they are, as it were, deposits intrusted to our care, of which we must one day give an account. We ought, therefore, to manage them in such a manner that this alarm may be incessantly sounding in our ears, "Give an account of thy stewardship." Let it also be remembered by whom this account is demanded; that it is by him who has so highly recommended abstinence, sobriety, frugality, and modesty; who abhors profusion, pride, ostentation, and vanity; who approves of no other management of his blessings, than such as is connected with charity; who has with his own mouth already condemned all those pleasures which seduce the heart from chastity and purity, or tend to impair the understanding.

Lastly, it is to be remarked, that the Lord commands every one of us, in all the actions of life, to regard his vocation. For He knows with what great inquietude the human mind is inflamed, with what desultory levity it is hurried hither and thither, and how insatiable is its ambition to grasp different things at once. Therefore, to prevent universal confusion being produced by our folly and temerity, He has appointed to all their particular duties in different spheres of life. And that no one might rashly transgress the limits prescribed, He has styled such spheres of life *vocations*, or *callings*. Every individual's line of life, therefore, is as it were, a post assigned him by the Lord, that he may not wander about in uncertainty all his days. And so

necessary is this distinction, that in His sight all our actions are estimated according to it, and often very differently from the sentence of human reason and philosophy.

There is no exploit esteemed more honorable, even among philosophers, than to deliver our country from tyranny; but the voice of the celestial Judge openly condemns the private man who lays violent hands on a tyrant. It is not my design, however, to stay to enumerate examples. It is sufficient if we know that the principle and foundation of right conduct in every case is the vocation of the Lord, and that he who disregards it will never keep the right way in the duties of his station. He may sometimes, perhaps, achieve something apparently laudable; but however it may appear in the eyes of men, it will be rejected at the throne of God; besides which, there will be no consistency between the various parts of his life.

Our life, therefore, will then be best regulated, when it is directed to this mark; since no one will be impelled by his own temerity to attempt more than is compatible with his calling, because he will know that it is unlawful to transgress the bounds assigned to him. He that is in obscurity will lead a private life without discontent, so as not to desert the station in which God has placed him. It will also be no small alleviation of his cares, labors, troubles, and other burdens, when a man knows that in all these things he has God for his guide. The magistrate will execute his office with greater pleasure, the father of a family will confine himself to his duty with more satisfaction, and all, in their respective spheres of life, will bear and surmount the inconveniences, cares, disappointments, and anxieties which befall them, when

they shall be persuaded that every individual has his burden laid upon him by God. Hence also will arise peculiar consolation since there will be no employment so mean and sordid (provided we follow our vocation) as not to appear truly respectable, and be deemed highly important in the sight of God.

The Lives of the Genevans Are Regulated (1547)

Some idea of what life in Calvin's heavenly city was like can be gained by reading the city ordinances to which all inhabitants of Geneva had to conform. In *Translations and Reprints from the Original Source of European History,* Merrick Whitcomb, ed. (Philadelphia, n.d.), III, No. 3, pp. 10–11.

CONCERNING THE TIME OF ASSEMBLING AT CHURCH

That the temples be closed for the rest of the time, in order that no one shall enter therein out of hours, impelled thereto by superstition; and if any one be found engaged in any special act of devotion therein or near by he shall be admonished for it: if it be found to be of a superstitious nature for which simple correction is inadequate, then he shall be chastised.

BLASPHEMY

Whoever shall have blasphemed, swearing by the body or by the blood of our Lord, or in similar manner, he shall be made to kiss the earth for the first offence; for the second to pay 5 sous, and for the third 5 sous, and for the last offence be put in the pillory for one hour.

DRUNKENNESS

1. That no one shall invite another to drink under penalty of 3 sous.

2. That taverns shall be closed during the sermon, under penalty that the tavern-keeper shall pay 3 sous, and whoever may be found therein shall pay the same amount.

3. If any one be found intoxicated he shall pay for the first offence 3 sous and shall be remanded to the consistory, for the second offence he shall be held to pay the sum of 6 sous, and for the third 10 sous and be put in prison. . . .

SONGS AND DANCES

If any one sing immoral, dissolute or outrageous songs, or dance the *virollet* or other dance, he shall be put in prison for three days and then sent to the consistory.

USURY

That no one shall take upon interest or profit more than five per cent, upon penalty of confiscation of the principal and of being condemned to make restitution as the case may demand.

GAMES

That no one shall play at any dissolute game or at any game whatsoever it may be, neither for gold nor silver nor for any excessive stake, upon penalty of 5 sous and forfeiture of stake played for.

A Calvinist church in Lyons, France, in the sixteenth century. The building and the clothing of the congregation reflect the simplicity and severity of this Protestant creed.

Protestants Persecute a Heretic: Michael Servetus' Sentence (1553)

Miguel Serveto (1511–1553), or as he latinized his name, Michael Servetus, a frequent practice among Renaissance scholars, was a Spanish physician who, while living in France, wrote a book attacking the Trinity and the belief that Jesus had existed from eternity. Arrested, Servetus escaped to Geneva but there Calvin found his theological views as abhorrent as the Catholics had. Servetus was tried as a heretic. The sentence of the Calvinist judges contains a statement of the case against him, a statement that in most particulars could have been written five centuries earlier. From R. H. Bainton, trans., *Hunted Heretic: The Life and Death of Michael Servetus* (Boston: Beacon Press, 1953), pp. 207–209.

This is the sentence pronounced against Michel Servet de Villeneufve of the Kingdom of Aragon in Spain who some twenty-three or twenty-four years ago printed a book at Hagenau in Germany against the Holy Trinity containing many great blasphemies to the scandal of the said churches of Germany, the which book he freely confesses to have printed in the teeth of the remonstrances made to him by the learned and evangelical doctors of Germany. In consequence he became a fugitive from Germany. Nevertheless, he continued in his errors and, in order the more to spread the venom of his heresy, he printed secretly a book in Vienne of Dauphiny [France] full of the said heresies and horrible, execrable blasphemies against the Holy Trinity, against the Son of God, against the baptism of infants and the foundations of the Christian religion. He confesses that in this book he called believers in the Trinity Trinitarians and atheists. He calls this Trinity a diabolical monster with three heads. He blasphemes detestably against the Son of God, saying that Jesus Christ is not the Son of God from eternity. He calls infant baptism an invention of the devil and sorcery. His execrable blasphemies are scandalous against the majesty of God, the Son of God and the Holy Spirit. This entails the murder and ruin of many souls. Moreover he wrote a letter to one of our ministers in which, along with other numerous blasphemies, he declared our holy evangelical religion to be without faith and without God and that in place of God we have a three-headed Cerberus. He confesses that because of this abominable book he was made a prisoner at Vienne and perfidiously escaped. He has been burned there in effigy together with five bales of his books. Nevertheless, having been in prison in our city, he persists maliciously in his detestable errors and calumniates true Christians and faithful followers of the immaculate Christian tradition.

Wherefore we Syndics, judges of criminal cases in this city, having witnessed the trial conducted before us . . . and having seen your voluntary and repeated confessions and your books, judge that you, Servetus, have for a long time promulgated false and thoroughly heretical doctrine, despising all remonstrances and corrections and that you have with malicious and perverse obstinacy sown and divulged even in printed books opinions against God the Father, the Son and the Holy Spirit, in a word against the fundamentals of the Christian religion, and that you have tried to make a schism and trouble the Church of God by which many souls may have been ruined and lost, a thing horrible, shocking, scandalous and infectious. And you have had neither shame nor horror of setting yourself against the divine Majesty and the Holy Trinity, and so you have obstinately tried to infect the world with your stinking heretical poison. . . . For these and other reasons, desiring to purge the Church of God of such infection and cut off the rotten member, having taken counsel with our citizens and having invoked the name of God to give just judgment . . . having God and the Holy Scriptures before our eyes, speaking in the name of the Father, Son and Holy Spirit, we now in writing give final sentence and condemn you, Michael Servetus, to be bound and taken to Champel and there attached to a stake and burned with your book to ashes. And so you shall finish your days and give an example to others who would commit the like.

A Witch Is Tracked down in Germany (1628)

Religious division among Christians reinforced men's resolves to be on their guard against the machinations of the Devil. A side effect of these fears was the increase in persecution of persons suspected of witchcraft. The reading presents one such case, that of the Burgomaster (Mayor) of Bamberg in southeastern Germany, Johannes Junius. The minutes of the trial are followed by a letter of Junius to his daughter. The bracketed commentary to this letter was written by the editor of the English translation. From *Translations and Reprints from the Original Sources of European History*, George Burr, ed. (Philadelphia: University of Pennsylvania, n.d.) Vol. III, No. 4, pp. 23–24, 25–28.

I. MINUTES OF THE WITCH TRIAL OF JOHANNES JUNIUS

. . . On Wednesday, June 28, 1628, was examined without torture Johannes Junius, Burgomaster at Bamberg, on the charge of witchcraft: how and in what fashion he had fallen into that vice. Is fifty-five years old, and was born at Niederwaysich in the Wetterau. Says he is wholly innocent, knows nothing of the crime, has never in his life renounced God; says that he is wronged before God and the world, would like to hear of a single human being who has seen him at such gatherings [as the witch-sabbaths].

Confrontation of Dr. Georg Adam Haan. Tells him to his face he will stake his life on it, that he saw him, Junius, a year and a half ago at a witch-gathering in the electoral council-room, where they ate and drank. Accused denies the same wholly.

Confronted with Hopffens Elsse. Tells him likewise that he was on Hauptsmoor at a witch-dance; but first the holy wafer was desecrated. Junius denies. Hereupon he was told that his accomplices had confessed against him and was given time for thought.

On Friday, June 30, 1628, the aforesaid Junius was again without torture exhorted to confess, but again confessed nothing, whereupon, . . . since he would confess nothing, he was put to the torture, and first the

Thumb-screws were applied. Says he has never denied God his Saviour nor suffered himself to be otherwise baptized; will again stake his life on it; feels no pain in the thumb-screws.

Leg-screws. Will confess absolutely nothing; knows nothing about it. He has never renounced God; will never do such a thing; has never been guilty of this vice; feels likewise no pain.

Is stripped and examined; on his right side is found a bluish mark, like a clover leaf, is thrice pricked therein, but feels no pain and no blood flows out.

Strappado. He has never renounced God; God will not forsake him; if he were such a wretch he would not let himself be so tortured; God must show some token of his innocence. He knows nothing about witchcraft. . . .

On July 5, the above named Junius is without torture, but with urgent persuasions, exhorted to confess, and at last begins and confesses:

When in the year 1624 his law-suit at Rothweil cost him some six hundred florins, he had gone out, in the month of August, into his orchard at Friedrichsbronn; and, as he sat there in thought, there had come to him a woman like a grass-maid, who had asked him why he sat there so sorrowful; he had answered that he was not despondent, but she had led him by seductive speeches to yield him to her will. . . . And thereafter this wench had changed into the form of a goat, which bleated and said, "Now you see with whom you have had to do. You must be mine or I will forthwith break your neck." Thereupon he had been frightened, and trembled all over for fear. Then the transformed spirit had seized him by the throat and demanded that

he should renounce God Almighty, whereupon Junius said, "God forbid," and thereupon the spirit vanished through the power of these words. Yet it came straightway back, brought more people with it, and persistently demanded of him that he renounce God in Heaven and all the heavenly host, by which terrible threatening he was obliged to speak this formula: "I renounce God in Heaven and all the heavenly host, and will henceforward recognize the Devil as my God." . . .

Of crimes. His paramour [female witch] had immediately after his seduction demanded that he should make away with his younger son Hans Georg, and had given him for this purpose a gray powder; this, however, being too hard for him, he had made away with his horse, a brown, instead.

His paramour had also often spurred him on to kill his daughter, . . . and because he would not do this he had been maltreated with blows by the evil spirit.

Once at the suggestion of his paramour he had taken the holy wafer out of his mouth and given it to her. . . .

A week before his arrest as he was going to St. Martin's church the Devil met him on the way, in the form of a goat, and told him that he would soon be imprisoned, but that he should not trouble himself—he would soon set him free. Besides this, by his soul's salvation, he knew nothing further; but what he had spoken was the pure truth; on that he would stake his life. On August 6, 1628, there was read to the aforesaid Junius this his confession, which he then wholly ratified and confirmed, and was willing to stake his life upon it. And afterward he voluntarily confirmed the same before the court.

A late seventeenth-century torture chamber of the Inquisition. The hanging figure at the left is in strappado.

II. JUNIUS WRITES THE TRUE FACTS TO HIS DAUGHTER

[So ended the trial of Junius, and he was accordingly burned at the stake. But it so happens that there is also preserved in Bamberg a letter, in quivering hand, secretly written by him to his daughter while in the midst of his trial (July 24, 1628):]

Many hundred thousand good-nights, dearly beloved daughter Veronica. Innocent have I come into prison, innocent have I been tortured, innocent must I die. For whoever comes into the witch prison must become a witch or be tortured until he invents something out of his head and—God pity him—bethinks him of something. I will tell you how it has gone with me. When I was the first time put to the torture, Dr. Braun, Dr. Kötzendörffer, and two strange doctors were there. Then Dr. Braun asks me, "Kinsman, how come you here?" I answer, "Through false-hood, through misfortune." "Hear, you," he says, "you are a witch; will you confess it voluntarily? If not, we'll bring in witnesses and the executioner for you." I said "I am no witch, I have a pure conscience in the matter; if there are a thousand witnesses, I am not anxious, but I'll gladly hear the witnesses." Now the chancellor's son was set before me . . . and afterward Hoppfens Elsse. She had seen me dance on Haupts-moor. . . . I answered: "I have never renounced God, and will never do it—God graciously keep me from it. I'll rather bear whatever I must." And then came also—God in the highest Heaven have mercy—the executioner, and put the thumb-screws on me, both hands bound together, so that the blood ran out at the nails and everywhere, so that for four weeks I could not use my hands, as you can see from the writing. . . . Thereafter they first stripped me, bound my hands behind me, and drew me up in the torture.* Then I thought heaven and earth were at an end; eight times did they draw me up and let me fall again, so that I suffered terrible agony. . . .

And this happened on Friday, June 30, and with God's help I had to bear the torture. . . . When at last the executioner led me back into the prison, he said to me: "Sir, I beg you, for God's sake confess something, whether it be true or not. Invent something, for you cannot endure the torture which you will be put to; and, even if you bear it all, yet you will not

*This torture of the strappado, which was that in most common use by the courts, consisted of a rope, attached to the hands of the prisoner (bound behind his back) and carried over a pulley at the ceiling. By this he was drawn up and left hanging. To increase the pain, weights were attached to his feet or he was suddenly jerked up and let drop.

escape, not even if you were an earl, but one torture will follow after another until you say you are a witch. Not before that," he said, "Will they let you go, as you may see by all their trials, for one is just like another." . . .

And so I begged, since I was in wretched plight, to be given one day for thought and a priest. The priest was refused me, but the time for thought was given. Now, my dear child, see in what hazard I stood and still stand. I must say that I am a witch, though I am not,—must now renounce God, though I have never done it before. Day and night I was deeply troubled, but at last there came to me a new idea. I would not be anxious, but, since I had been given no priest with whom I could take counsel, I would myself think of something and say it. It were surely better that I just say it with mouth and words, even though I had not really done it; and afterwards I would confess it to the priest, and let those answer for it who compel me to do it. . . . And so I made my confession as follows; but it was all a lie.

Now follows, dear child, what I confessed in order to escape the great anguish and bitter torture, which it was impossible for me longer to bear.

[Here follows his confession, substantially as it is given in the minutes of his trial. But he adds:]

Then I had to tell what people I had seen [at the witch-sabbath]. I said that I had not recognized them. "You old rascal, I must set the executioner at you. Say—was not the Chancellor there?" So I said yes. "Who besides?" I had not recognized anybody. So he said: "Take one street after another; begin at the market, go out on one street and back on the next." I had to name several persons there. Then came the long street. I knew

nobody. Had to name eight persons there. Then the Zinkenwere—one person more. Then over the upper bridge to the Georgthor, on both sides. Knew nobody again. Did I know nobody in the castle—whoever it might be, I should speak without fear. And thus continuously they asked me on all the streets, though I could not and would not say more. So they gave me to the executioner, told him to strip me, shave me all over, and put me to the torture. "The rascal knows one on the market-place, is with him daily, and yet won't name him." By that they meant Dietmeyer: so I had to name him too.

Then I had to tell what crimes I had committed. I said nothing. . . . "Draw the rascal up!" So I said that I was to kill my children, but I had killed a horse instead. It did not help. I had also taken a sacred wafer, and had desecrated it. When I had said this, they left me in peace.

Now, dear child, here you have all my confession, for which I must die. And they are sheer lies and made-up things, so help me God. For all this I was forced to say through fear of the torture which was threatened beyond what I had already endured. For they never leave off with the torture till one confesses something; be he never so good, he must be a witch. Nobody escapes, though he were an earl. . . .

Dear child, keep this letter secret so that people do not find it, else I shall be tortured most piteously and the jailers will be beheaded. So strictly is it forbidden. . . . Dear child, pay this man a dollar. . . . I have taken several days to write this: my hands are both lame. I am in a sad plight. . . .

Good night, for your father Johannes Junius will never see you more. July 24, l628.

[And on the margin of the letter he adds:]

Dear child, six have confessed against me at once; the Chancellor, his son, Neudecker, Zaner, Hoffmaisters Ursel, and Hoppfens Elsse—all false, through compulsion, as they have all told me, and begged my forgiveness in God's name before they were executed. . . . They know nothing but good of me. They were forced to say it. . . .

John Knox Debates Religion with Queen Mary of Scots (c. 1562)

The teachings of Calvin, spread by his disciple John Knox (1505–1572), were soon adopted by the majority of the hard-working inhabitants of the poor northern kingdom of Scotland. The return of the Scottish queen, Mary (1542–1587), in 1561 after the death of her husband, the king of France, initiated a hard-hitting debate between the twenty-one-year-old Catholic queen and the dour Calvinist minister. At issue was the question of ultimate authority. Although this account of the debate was written by Knox himself, the exchange of opinion accurately reflects the difference between the lay and spiritual positions. From John Knox, *The History of the Reformation in Scotland,* ed. W. M'Gavin (Glasgow, 1832), pp. 250, 252–253.

Whether it was by counsel of others, or the queen's own desire, we know not; but the queen spake with John Knox, and had long reasoning with him, none being present, except the lord James—two gentlemen stood in the other end of the house. The sum of their reasoning was this. . . .

"But yet," said she, "ye have taught the people to receive another religion, than their princes can allow: and how can that doctrine be of God, seeing, that God commands subjects to obey their princes?"

"Madam," said he, "as that right religion takes neither origin or authority from worldly princes, but from the eternal God alone, so are not subjects bound to frame their religion according to the appetite of their princes; for oft it is, that princes are the most ignorant of all others in God's true religion, as we may read as well in the histories before the death of Christ Jesus, as after. If all the seed of Abraham should have been of the religion of Pharaoh, to whom they were long subjects, I pray you, madam, what religion should there have been in the world? For, if all men, in the days of the apostles, should have been of the religion of the Roman emperors, what religion should have been upon the face of the earth? Daniel and his fellows were subjects to Nebuchadnezzar, and unto Darius, and yet, madam, they would not be of their religion, neither of the one nor of the other: for the three children said, 'We make it known unto thee, O king, that we will not worship thy gods.' And Daniel did pray publicly unto his God, against the express commandment of the king. And so, madam, ye may perceive, that subjects are not bound to the religion of their princes, albeit they are commanded to give them obedience."

"Yea," said she, "none of those men raised the sword against their princes." "Yet, madam," said he, "ye cannot deny but that they resisted: for these that obey not the commandments that are given, in some sort

they resist." "But yet," said she, "they resisted not by the sword." "God," said he, "madam, had not given unto them the power and the means." "Think ye," said she, "that subjects having power may resist their princes?" "If their princes exceed their bounds," said he, "madam, and do against that wherefore they should be obeyed, it is no doubt but they may be resisted, even by power." . . .

At these words, the queen stood as it were amazed, more than a quarter of an hour; her countenance altered, so that lord James began to entreat her, and to demand, "What has offended you, madam?" At length, she said, "Well, then, I perceive, that my subjects shall obey you, and not me; and shall do what they list, and not what I command: and so must I be subject to them, and not they to me." "God forbid," answered he, "that ever I take upon me to command any to obey me, or yet to set subjects at liberty to do what pleases them. But my travail is, that both princes and subjects obey God. And think not," said he, "madam, that wrong is done unto you, when you are willed to be subject unto God: for, it is He that subjects the people under princes, and causes obedience to be given unto them; yea, God craves of kings, 'That they be, as it were, foster-fathers to His kirk, and commands queens to be nurses unto His people.' And this subjection, madam, unto God, and unto His troubled kirk, is the greatest dignity that flesh can get upon the face of the earth, for it shall carry them to everlasting glory."

"Yea," said she, "but ye are not the kirk that I will nurse. I will defend the kirk of Rome, for it is, I think, the true kirk of God."

"Your will," said he, "madam, is no reason; neither doth your thought make that Roman

harlot to be the true and immaculate spouse of Jesus Christ. And wonder not, madam, that I call Rome a harlot; for that kirk is altogether polluted with all kind of spiritual fornication, as well in doctrine as in manners. Yea, madam, I offer myself farther to prove, that the kirk of the Jews, that crucified Christ Jesus, when that they manifestly denied the Son of God, was not so far degenerated from the ordinances and statutes which God gave by Moses and Aaron unto His people, as that the kirk of Rome is declined, and more than five hundred years hath declined from the purity of that religion, which the apostles taught and planted."

"My conscience," said she, "is not so." "Conscience, madam," said he, "requires knowledge; and I fear that right knowledge you have none." "But," said she, "I have both heard and read." "So, madam," said he, "did the Jews who crucified Christ Jesus, read both the law and the prophets, and heard the same interpreted after their manner. Have ye heard," said he, "any teach, but such as the pope and the cardinals have allowed? And ye may be assured, that such will speak nothing to offend their own estate." "Ye interpret the scriptures," said she, "in one manner, and they in another; whom shall I believe, and who shall be judge?" "You shall believe God," said he, "that plainly speaketh in His word: and farther than the word teacheth you, you neither shall believe the one nor the other. The word of God is plain in the self; and if there appear any obscurity in any place, the Holy Ghost, who is never contrarious to Himself, explains the same more clearly in other places: so that there can remain no doubt, but unto such as will remain obstinately ignorant."

Erich Fromm: The Theology of Anxiety

Erich Fromm (1900–   ), a social philosopher and psychoanalyst, left his native Germany in protest against the Nazi take-over. His best-selling *Escape From Freedom* (1941) applied the techniques of psychoanalysis to the social process. In this reading Fromm seeks the psychological motivations for religious change. He explores these motivations in their social and economic context and, in his book, sees parallels between the sixteenth and twentieth centuries. From *Escape from Freedom* by Erich Fromm. Copyright 1941, © 1949 by Erich Fromm. Reprinted by permission of Holt, Rinehart & Winston, Inc., pp. 39, 79–81, 90–93.

I. THE LUTHERAN CONCEPT OF FREEDOM

Ideological similarity is not the only one that makes the study of the fifteenth and sixteenth centuries a particularly fruitful starting point for the understanding of the present scene. There is also a fundamental likeness in the social situation. I shall try to show how this likeness is responsible for the ideological and psychological similarity. Then as now a vast sector of the population was threatened in its traditional way of life by revolutionary changes in the economic and social organization; especially was the middle class, as today, threatened by the power of monopolies and the superior strength of capital, and this threat had an important effect on the spirit and the ideology of the threatened sector of society by enhancing the individual's feeling of aloneness and insignificance. . . .

What is the connection of Luther's doctrines with the psychological situation of all but the rich and powerful toward the end of the Middle Ages? As we have seen, the old order was breaking down. The individual had lost the security of certainty and was threatened by new economic forces, by capitalists and monopolies; the corporative principle was being replaced by competition; the lower classes felt the pressure of growing exploitation. The appeal of Lutheranism to the lower classes differed from its appeal to the middle class. The poor in the cities, and even more the peasants, were in a desperate situation. They were ruthlessly exploited and deprived of traditional rights and privileges. They were in a revolutionary mood which found expression in peasant uprisings and in revolutionary movements in the cities. The Gospel articulated their hopes and expectations as it had done for the slaves and laborers of early Christianity, and led the poor to seek for freedom and justice. In so far as Luther attacked authority and made the word of the Gospel the center of his teachings, he appealed to these restive masses as other religious movements of an evangelical character had done before him.

Although Luther accepted their allegiance to him and supported them, he could do so only up to a certain point; he had to break the alliance when the peasants went further than attacking the authority of the Church and merely making minor demands for the betterment of their lot. They proceeded to become a revolutionary class which threatened to overthrow all authority and to destroy the foundations of a social order in whose maintenance the middle class was vitally interested. For, . . . the middle class, even its

lower stratum, had privileges to defend against the demands of the poor; and therefore it was intensely hostile to revolutionary movements which aimed to destroy not only the privileges of the aristocracy, the Church, and the monopolies, but their own privileges as well.

The position of the middle class between the very rich and the very poor made its reaction complex and in many ways contradictory. They wanted to uphold law and order, and yet they were themselves vitally threatened by rising capitalism. Even the more successful members of the middle class were not wealthy and powerful as the small group of big capitalists was. They had to fight hard to survive and make progress. The luxury of the moneyed class increased their feeling of smallness and filled them with envy and indignation. As a whole, the middle class was more endangered by the collapse of the feudal order and by rising capitalism than they were helped.

Luther's picture of man mirrored just this dilemma. Man is free from all ties binding him to spiritual authorities, but this very freedom leaves him alone and anxious, overwhelms him with a feeling of his own individual insignificance and powerlessness. This free, isolated individual is crushed by the experience of his individual insignificance. Luther's theology gives expression to this feeling of helplessness and doubt. The picture of man which he draws in religious terms describes the situation of the individual as it was brought about by the current social and economic evolution. The member of the middle class was as helpless in face of the new economic forces as Luther described man to be in his relationship to God.

But Luther did more than bring out the feeling of insignificance which already pervaded the social classes to whom he preached—he offered them a solution. By not only accepting his own insignificance but by humiliating himself to the utmost, by giving up every vestige of individual will, by renouncing and denouncing his individual strength, the individual could hope to be acceptable to God. Luther's relationship to God was one of complete submission. In psychological terms his concept of faith means: if you completely submit, if you accept your individual insignificance, then the all-powerful God may be willing to love you and save you. If you get rid of your individual self with all its shortcomings and doubts by utmost self-effacement, you free yourself from the feeling of your own nothingness and can participate in God's glory. Thus, while Luther freed people from the authority of the Church, he made them submit to a much more tyrannical authority, that of a God who insisted on complete submission of man and annihilation of the individual self as the essential condition to his salvation. . . .

II. CALVIN AND THE COMPULSION TO WORK

. . . The particular emphasis on a virtuous life which was characteristic for Calvinism had also a particular psychological significance. Calvinism emphasized the necessity of unceasing human effort. Man must constantly try to live according to God's word and never lapse in his effort to do so. This doctrine appears to be a contradiction of the doctrine that human effort is of no avail with regard to man's salvation. The fatalistic attitude of not making any effort might seem like a much more appropriate response. Some psychological considerations, however, show that this is not so. The state of anxiety, the feeling of powerlessness and insignificance, and especially the doubt concerning one's future after death, represent a state of mind which is practically unbearable for anybody. Almost no one stricken with this fear would be able to relax, enjoy life, and be indifferent as to what happened afterwards. One possible way to escape this unbearable state of uncertainty and the paralyzing feeling of one's own insignificance is the very trait which became so prominent in Calvinism: the development of a frantic activity and a striving to do something. Activity in this sense assumes a compulsory quality: the individual has to be active in order to overcome his feeling of doubt and powerlessness. This kind of effort and activity is not the result of inner strength and self-confidence; it is a desperate escape from anxiety.

This mechanism can be easily observed in attacks of anxiety panic in individuals. A man who expects to receive within a few hours the doctor's diagnosis of his illness—which may be fatal—quite naturally is in a state of anxiety. Usually he will not sit down quietly and wait. Most frequently his anxiety, if it does not paralyze him, will drive him to some sort of more or less frantic activity. He may pace up and down the floor, start asking questions and talk to everybody he can get hold of, clean up his desk, write letters. He may continue his usual kind of work but with added activity and more feverishly. Whatever form his effort assumes it is prompted by anxiety and tends to overcome the feeling of powerlessness by frantic activity.

Effort in the Calvinist doctrine had still another psychological meaning. The fact that one did not tire in that unceasing effort and that one succeeded in one's moral as well as one's secular work was a more or less distinct sign of being one of the chosen ones. The irrationality of such compulsive effort is that the activity is not meant to create a desired end but serves to indicate whether or not something will occur which has been determined beforehand, independent of one's own activity or control. This mechanism is a well-known feature of compulsive neurotics. Such persons when afraid of the outcome of an important undertaking may, while awaiting an answer, count the windows of houses or trees on the street. If the number is even, a person feels that things will be all right; if it is uneven, it is a sign that he will fail. Frequently this doubt does not refer to a specific instance but to a person's whole life, and the compulsion to look for "signs" will pervade it accordingly. Often the connection between counting stones, playing solitaire, gambling, and so on, and anxiety and doubt, is not conscious. A person may play solitaire out of a vague feeling of restlessness and only an analysis might uncover the hidden function of his activity: to reveal the future.

In Calvinism this meaning of effort was part of the religious doctrine. Originally it referred essentially to moral effort, but later on the emphasis was more and more on effort in one's occupation and on the results of this effort, that is, success or failure in business. Success became the sign of God's grace; failure, the sign of damnation.

These considerations show that the compulsion to unceasing effort and work was far from being in contradiction to a basic conviction of man's powerlessness; rather was it the psychological result. Effort and work in this sense assumed an entirely irrational character. They were not to change fate since this was predetermined by God, regardless of any effort on the part of the individual. They served only as a means of forecasting the predetermined fate; while at the same time the frantic effort was a reassurance against an otherwise unbearable feeling of powerlessness.

This new attitude towards effort and work as an aim in itself may be assumed to be the most important psychological change which has happened to man since the end of the Middle Ages. In every society man has to work if he wants to live. Many societies solved the problem by having the work done by slaves, thus allowing the free man to devote himself to "nobler" occupations. In such societies, work was not worthy of a free man. In medieval society, too, the burden of work was unequally distributed among the different classes in the social hierarchy, and there was a good deal of crude exploitation. But the attitude toward work was different from that which developed subsequently in the modern era. Work did not have the abstract character of producing some commodity which might be profitably sold on the market. One worked in response to a concrete demand and with a concrete aim: to earn one's livelihood. There was, as Max Weber particularly has shown, no urge to work more than was necessary to maintain the traditional standard of living. It seems that for some groups of medieval society work was enjoyed as a realization of productive ability; that many others worked because they had to and felt this necessity was conditioned by pressure from the outside. What was new in modern society was that men came to be driven to work not so much by external pressure but by an internal compulsion, which made them work as only a very strict master could have made people do in other societies. . . .

STUDY QUESTIONS

1. What were Calvin's main religious views? What kinship do they have to Luther's? In what way were they incompatible with those of the Catholic Church? What kind of religious community did Calvin set up in Geneva?

2. What did Calvin mean by predestination? Why did he assume that men were not created equal? What is man's *vocation* or *calling,* as Calvin describes it? Do you think that Calvin was opposed to social mobility?

3. What kinds of human behavior did the Genevan magistrates try to restrict? By what means? Why?

4. On what theological grounds was Michael Servetus condemned as a heretic? Why did Calvin wish to see him burn at the stake? Why were the Genevans so intolerant?

5. Was Johannes Junius, in 1628, tried as a heretic? What is the difference between a suspected heretic and a suspected witch? Why did Junius' torturers insist on a confession of guilt?

6. About what matters did John Knox and Mary Queen of Scots disagree? Whom do you think had the better of the argument?

7. How, according to Fromm, did reformers, like Luther or Calvin, satisfy the psychological needs of the people of their time? Can you think of other reasons, besides the doctrine of predestination, that might explain the modern devotion to work?

The Persistence of Reform

From *Civilization Past and Present* by T. Walter Wallbank, Alastair M. Taylor, Nels M. Bailkey. Copyright © 1965 by Scott, Foresman and Company. Pp. 302–306.

TOPIC 8

THE CATHOLIC REFORMATION

The search for religious renewal tore at the sinews of the Roman Church, dividing families and nations as it pulled at the European conscience. The reflex of the papacy, weakened by the seditious example of northern reformers and the amputation of large territories from its religious control, was to place its own house in order, while closing its doors to dissent and reaffirming its legitimacy and authority. New agencies were created to meet the menace of Protestantism and these helped the Church to slow the advance of its Christian rival, contain it, and even recover lost territories. But its answer to the challenge marked the Church with the stamp of conservatism. The Church remained responsive to the religious needs of the members, but not until the middle of the twentieth century would the institution be open to currents of radical change. The readings examine the movement for Catholic reform.

The Catholic Reformation should not be viewed as only a retaliatory movement or a series of measures taken to stem the rising tide of Protestantism. The Roman Church had always retained latent forces of recuperation and strength which were drawn upon in challenging times. Before Luther had nailed his ninety-five theses to the church door at Wittenberg, renewed vitality and internal reform were apparent in the Roman Church.

One of the prime examples of this resurgence occurred in Spain, where humanistic energies were expended in the fields of religion and government. In this passionately orthodox country, royalty enlisted the services of the humanist Cardinal Ximenes de Cisneros (1436?–1517). At once a hairshirted Franciscan friar, a reformer of lax clergymen, the grand inquisitor, and the chancellor of the realm, Cardinal Ximenes was also a Renaissance scholar who founded the University of Alcala, where humanistic studies were pursued. The melding of his humanistic and religious interests is revealed in the careful scholarship involved in new translations of the Bible. Under the supervision and financial support of Ximenes, the famous Polyglot Bible was prepared. In what was the most scientific study of the Scriptures in the sixteenth century, the Polyglot Bible reproduced in its six large volumes all the original texts together with the Vulgate.

In a unique category of his own was Savonarola (1452–1498), a Dominican preacher and reformer in the city of Florence. A persuasive speaker, he induced the wealthy and pleasure-loving Florentines to make bonfires of their luxuries. When the discredited Medici fled before the invasion of Charles VIII of France, Savonarola organized Florence as a republic and managed to keep the French from sacking the city. He also attacked the iniquities of the Borgia pope, Alexander VI. But despite the fact that he was later hailed by Luther and the Protestants as a forerunner of their movement, Savonarola was actually attempting to return the papacy to its tradition of simple living and dedicated service. By this means he hoped to avert a real revolt against the Church. Unfortunately Savonarola did not possess the power to enforce his dictates. Publicly humiliated by having his Dominican garb torn from him in the great square of Florence, Savonarola was hanged and burned, a victim of political intrigue.

In Italy other forces were also at work to revitalize and purify the Church. In the same year that Luther issued his ninety-five theses, a group of clerics and laymen in Rome founded the Oratory of Divine Love. Its purpose was to use prayer, sermons, and good works to create a strong personal religious consciousness but at the same time to retain the traditional Catholic framework and the leadership of the papacy. Other oratories were founded in Italy, but their work was relatively short-lived.

By the middle of the sixteenth century, the inroads of Protestantism were apparent, and in retaliation the Church rallied its forces and prepared a powerful offensive. This renewal of strength is known as the Catholic Reformation. As we shall see, the reforming spirit penetrated almost all areas of the Church. New monastic orders infused with crusading zeal were organized, and a resurgence of mysticism occurred. The pope himself adopted a program of vigorous reform. Climaxing the whole movement was the Council of Trent, where the Church boldly reaffirmed its traditional doctrines and flatly refused to compromise in any way with the Protestants.

REFORMING ORDERS

Reverting to methods which it had almost perfected during medieval eras of reform, the Church instituted new monastic orders. Springing up in the sixteenth century, several new orders performed useful work in a variety of fields—charitable works, education, and conversion.

In 1524, the order of the Theatines was founded in Italy by a member of the Oratory of Divine Love. By preaching and exemplary conduct, the Theatines undertook to check the spread of heresy. They also performed such good works as supporting hospitals and orphanages. The number of Theatines was small but their work proved highly influential.

Among other orders established at this time were the Capuchins, an offshoot of the Franciscan order. Seeking to return to the original Rule and spirit of St. Francis, they became notable for their preaching and for their care

of the poor and sick. Still another successful movement was that of the Ursulines, founded in 1535 to educate girls.

A Spanish ex-soldier, Ignatius Loyola (1491–1556), founded in 1534 the Society of Jesus, better known as the Jesuit order, which played a vital role in the Catholic Reformation. In addition to the three vows of chastity, obedience, and poverty, the Jesuits took a special vow of allegiance to the pope. By means of preaching and education, this order intended to win back converts to the Roman Church. They succeeded remarkably well, recovering most of Poland and maintaining Catholicism in Bavaria, the southern Netherlands (now Belgium), Austria, and Ireland. Owing to their efforts and to the weight always lent by tradition, Italy, Spain, and Portugal remained loyally Catholic, while France saw Protestantism checked. In addition, the Jesuits performed excellent missionary work in North and South America, China, and India. . . .

PAPAL REFORM: PAUL III

A new era was at hand for the Church when Paul III, who reigned from 1534 to 1549, ascended the papal throne. He chose outstanding men as cardinals and appointed a commission to look into the need for reform. Their report listed the evils requiring correction, including the appointment of worldly bishops and priests; the traffic in benefices, in indulgences, and other financial abuses; the venality of some cardinals; and the absence of others from the papal court. There was considerable opposition from various quarters to Paul's decision to begin acting upon this report. He persisted, however, and among other reforms improved the papal

administrative machinery. Again ignoring the opposition of high churchmen who feared for their positions and incomes, Paul made plans to reform the entire Church organization of a general council.

THE COUNCIL OF TRENT: CLIMAX OF THE CATHOLIC REFORMATION

Reviving the device of a Church council, so useful at the time of the Great Schism, the Catholic Reformation came to a climax in the Council of Trent (1545–1563). There, a clear enunciation of Catholic doctrines was set forth. In no point of dogma did the Catholic Church compromise with the Protestants. The successors of St. Thomas Aquinas, who had done so much to shape the dogmas of the medieval Church, reaffirmed the doctrines of the Church as the basis of Christianity and the role of the Church as the only interpreter of these vital elements. As proof of the fact that the Catholic Church in no wise departed from its age-old body of beliefs, the following statement reiterates the validity of the sacramental system:

> If any one saith that the sacraments of the new lay were not all instituted by Jesus Christ, our Lord; or that they are more or less than seven . . . or even that any one of these seven is not truly and properly a sacrament; let him be anathema.

At the same time, drastic reforms were made in Church discipline and administration. Such evils as simony, absenteeism, and secular pursuits on the part of the clergy were strictly forbidden. The Council forbade prelates and other holders of ecclesiastical offices to aid their kinsmen at the expense of the Church:

It [the Council] strictly forbids them . . . to strive to enrich their own kindred or domestics out of the revenues of the Church; seeing that even the canons of the apostles forbid them to give to their kindred the property of the Church, which belongs to God . . . yea, this holy Council, with the utmost earnestness, admonishes them completely to lay aside all this human and carnal affection towards brothers, nephews, and kindred, which is the seed plot of many evils in the Church.

EFFECTS OF THE RELIGIOUS UPHEAVAL

Prior to 1517 there had been two religious divisions of Christendom—Greek Orthodox and Roman Catholic. By 1550 Christendom was composed of three divisions—Orthodox, Catholic, and Protestant. Protestantism had become uppermost in northern Europe, while Catholicism held sway in the south. This great religious division had struck a mortal blow at the medieval unity of Europe. The Catholics placed their faith in the infallibility of the pope and the need for a mediatory priesthood. The Protestants placed their faith in the infallibility of the Bible and individual interpretation of it; furthermore, every Christian could win salvation without priestly mediation. The Protestants differed among themselves in their interpretation of the Bible and the methods of church organization; in time hundreds of Protestant sects arose, many claiming to possess the one and only true interpretation and logical administration.

Although the religious upheaval irreparably split the unity of Christendom and in so doing fostered the religious diversity of modern times, it also represented in some aspects a return to medievalism. It was a great religious revival, a renewal of faith. After the Renaissance era of free and secular thought, of individualism and humanism, men's thoughts were turned again to salvation and the life hereafter. Free thought gave way again to authority—for Protestants it was the Bible; for Catholics, the Church. The Renaissance movement, having fostered doubt and criticism of medieval values, was now engulfed in a return to some of those values. Free thinkers were persecuted by both sides, and talented writers and thinkers who in Renaissance times might have followed the prevailing pattern of individualism and secularism now devoted their abilities to arguing one side or another of the burning conflict of the day. Thus, temporarily at least, the Renaissance spirit was stifled. But it was to prove stronger than this intense religious revival and in the end was to profit from the passing of the single religious authority of the universal Church.

In addition to renewing the surge of faith, the religious upheaval brought about a great deal of genuine religious reform. Protestant service of worship was simplified in an effort to return to the purity of early Christian times. Strict attention was given to conduct and morals. Within the Catholic Church a reform movement also took place in answer to the Protestant challenge, beginning, as we have seen, with the accession of Pope Paul III and culminating in the decrees of the Council of Trent. This movement changed neither doctrine nor organization but aimed at clarifying and reaffirming doctrine and purifying and strengthening discipline among the clergy and laity alike. . . .

While religious developments fostered a return to medieval attitudes in many ways, in the economic sphere the opposite was true. The Renaissance encouraged a new individualism in economic matters, which contributed to a breakdown of the guild system and to the rise of the individual entrepreneur. Protestantism did away with the old concept of the "just price" and the ban against receiving interest on money loaned (usury). Investment of capital and loaning of money became respectable. Calvinism especially encouraged enterprise; some Calvinists regarded prosperity as a sign of election to grace and poverty as evidence of damnation. The confiscation of monastic lands in Protestant countries also stimulated economic development. England in particular benefited from the use of former monastic lands. We have noted earlier that the business classes were among those that encouraged the revolt from Rome. We can now see that they were also among those that most benefited by it.

In many cases the religious division of Europe followed political lines. Just as the English king bound the national church and the national state together under his own leadership, so in Germany the Peace of Augsburg gave the ruler of each state the right to decide the faith of his subjects, thus controlling the church in his realm. Similarly, rulers of other countries, both Catholic and Protestant, developed national churches, so that Europe was divided religiously into an Anglican Church, a Dutch Church, a Swedish Church, and so on.

In many countries one effect of such division was to strengthen the hand of the king in building a unified state. The authority and prestige of the Protestant monarch was increased as he became the spiritual as well as the political ruler of his subjects. Even in Catholic countries, though the pope remained the spiritual ruler, the Church became

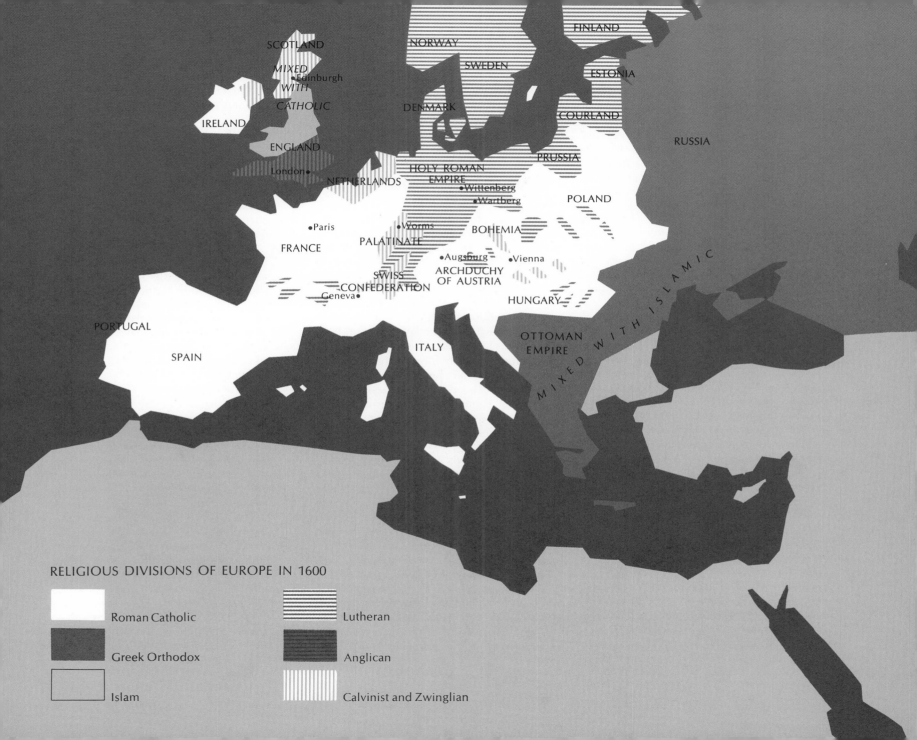

SCOTLAND

MIXED WITH CATHOLIC

•Edinburgh

IRELAND

ENGLAND

London•

NETHERLANDS

NORWAY

SWEDEN

FINLAND

ESTONIA

DENMARK

COURLAND

RUSSIA

HOLY ROMAN EMPIRE

PRUSSIA

•Wittenberg

•Wartberg

POLAND

•Paris

FRANCE

•Worms

PALATINATE

BOHEMIA

•Augsburg

•Vienna

SWISS CONFEDERATION

ARCHDUCHY OF AUSTRIA

Geneva•

HUNGARY

PORTUGAL

SPAIN

ITALY

OTTOMAN EMPIRE

MIXED WITH ISLAMIC

RELIGIOUS DIVISIONS OF EUROPE IN 1600

Roman Catholic

Lutheran

Greek Orthodox

Anglican

Islam

Calvinist and Zwinglian

national in sentiment, and it was the king rather than the pope who enforced religious conformity among his subjects. Conversely, in countries where the split between Protestants and Catholics was deep, as in the Holy Roman Empire, the power of the central ruler was limited and national unity impeded.

Freedom of religion was still far from a reality. Protestants were persecuted in Catholic countries and Catholics in Protestant states, partly because of the intolerance engendered by the clash between faiths but even more because religious uniformity was the ideal of the rulers of the rising national states. Just as he sought to create a uniform system of law and justice throughout his realm, so the strong monarch endeavored to establish a single faith to which his subjects owed complete obedience. An incidental result of this policy was the emigration of religious minorities to areas where they could worship freely, as in the New World. . . .

The Society of Jesus Seeks Converts to Catholicism (16th Century)

These documents illustrate two aspects of the Jesuit order: first, the complete obedience of its members to the wishes of the Pope, and second, its educational role in recovering Christians for the Catholic Church. The second selection is taken from the *Ratio Studiorum* which set forth methods of instruction for Jesuit professors. I. From Henry Bettenson, ed., *Documents of the Christian Church* (New York: Oxford University Press, 1947), p. 366. II. *St. Ignatius and the Ratio Studiorum,* ed. Edward Fitzgerald (New York: McGraw-Hill, Inc., 1933), pp. 280–282.

I. JESUIT RULE OF OBEDIENCE (1539)

Let us with the utmost pains strain every nerve of our strength to exhibit this virtue of obedience, firstly to the Highest Pontiff [Pope], then to the Superiors of the Society; so that in all things, to which obedience can be extended with charity, we may be most ready to obey his voice, just as if it issued from Christ our Lord. . . , leaving any work, even a letter, that we have begun and have not yet finished; by directing to this goal all our strength and intention in the Lord, that holy obedience may be made perfect in us in every respect, in performance, in will, in intellect; by submitting to whatever may be enjoined on us with great readiness, with spiritual joy and perseverance; by persuading ourselves that all things [commanded] are just; by rejecting with a kind of blind obedience all opposing opinion or judgment of our own; and that in all things which are ordained by the Superior where it cannot be clearly held that any kind of sin intervenes. And let each one persuade himself that they that live under obedience ought to allow themselves to be borne and ruled by divine providence working through their Superiors exactly as if they were a corpse which suffers itself to be borne and handled in any way whatsoever; or just as an old man's stick which serves him who holds it in his hand wherever and for whatever purpose he wishes to use it. . . .

II. REGULATIONS FOR JESUIT INSTRUCTION (1599)

Rules of the Professor of Scholastic Theology

1. *Duty.* He shall realize that it is his duty to join a well-founded subtlety in disputation with an orthodox faith and devotion in such a way that the former shall especially serve the latter.

2. *Following St. Thomas.* All members of our Order shall follow the teaching of St. Thomas in scholastic theology, and consider him as their special teacher; they shall center all their efforts in him so that their pupils may esteem him as highly as possible. However, they should realize that they are not confined to him so closely that they are never permitted to depart from him in any matter, since even those who especially profess to be Thomists occasionally depart from him, and it would not befit the members of our Order to be bound to St. Thomas more tightly than the Thomists themselves.

3. *With Some Exceptions.* Therefore, in regard to the conception of Blessed Mary, and in regard to the solemnity of vows, let them follow the opinion which is more common at this time, and more generally received among theologians, and in questions merely philosophical and also in those which belong to Scripture and Canon Law, he will be allowed to follow other authorities also who have treated those subjects *ex professo.*

4. *Choice of Opinions on Doubtful Questions.* On those questions in which the

opinion of St. Thomas is not clear, or which he does not treat, if Catholic scholars do not agree, he may hold either side of the question, as provided in the Common Rules, Rule 5.

5. *Regard for Faith and Devotion.* In teaching, he shall first have regard for strengthening faith and fostering devotion. Wherefore, in those questions which St. Thomas does not explicitly treat, no one shall teach anything which does not accord with the interpretation of the Church and with her traditions, or which tends to weaken the foundation of true devotion. Whence it comes that they are not to reject the accepted arguments, even though they are only probable, by which matters of faith are accustomed to be proved; nor shall any form new opinions hastily, unless from firmly established principles.

6. *Not to Assert Views Which Offend Catholics.* If any opinions, regardless of authority, are known to be seriously offensive to the Catholics of any province or school, he shall not teach them or defend them there. When no doctrine of faith or uprightness of morals is involved, charitable prudence requires that the members of the Order accommodate their actions to those with whom they are dealing.

Rules for the Professor of Philosophy

1. *Purpose.* Since the arts and the natural sciences prepare the mind for theology and help to a perfect knowledge and use of it and of themselves aid in reaching this end, the instructor, seeking in all things sincerely the honor and glory of God, shall so treat them as to prepare his hearers and especially ours for theology and stir them up greatly to the knowledge of their Creator.

2. *How Far Aristotle Is to Be Followed.* In matters of any importance let him not depart from Aristotle unless something occurs which is foreign to the doctrine which academies everywhere approve of; much more if it is opposed to the orthodox faith, and if there are any arguments of this or any other philosopher against the faith, he will endeavor earnestly to refute them according to the Lateran Council.

3. *Authors Hostile to Christianity.* He shall not read without careful selection or bring into class interpreters of Aristotle who are out of harmony with the Christian religion and he will take care that his students do not become influenced by them. . . .

A Jesuit Explains His Motives (1580)

Robert Persons became disillusioned with English Protestantism while a student at Oxford. Crossing to the continent, he entered the Catholic Church and later joined the Society of Jesus. In 1580 Persons returned secretly to England to help English Catholics in their efforts to hold out against the Protestant current. The reading contains an excerpt from the confession of faith prepared by the Jesuit in anticipation of possible detection while on his dangerous mission. From *Letters and Memorials of Father Robert Persons, S.J.,* ed. L. Hicks, S.J. (London: Catholic Record Society, 1942), pp. 36–38.

With regard to my faith and considered religious principles, although the description of "Catholic" has adequately indicated them, yet I desire to explain them more clearly, if possible. Let Your Worships then know that *as a young man I had for long been led hither and thither by the misleading utterances of false preachers,* and this was accentuated after I had come to the University. There for many years I desired to accept the attitude newly adopted by my country [Protestantism] and by degrees to reconcile my conscience which was very opposed to it; for I perceived that all promotion in the service of the kingdom had been made to depend on this. I have to thank God, however, that He never allowed my wavering soul, though I was daily listening to and reading the new teachers, to adhere to them so obstinately as to be infected with this plague which it was God's will to keep from me. Yet the more I kept reading, ever the more uncertain and restless I seemed to become. But after I had begun to peruse the sacred writings of the Fathers, I perceived that everything they contained was so repugnant to this new doctrine that I was ashamed any longer to tempt God and do violence to my own convictions. . . .

And so be it known to you that I firmly believe all that which the Catholic Church of Christ in any way proposes for belief. And I mean by this that church which has always been acknowledged as the visible church of Christ on earth. Of this I hold the Roman church is to be the most honoured part, and

I hold the holy Bishop of that See to have been constituted by God, next after Himself, as the universal Pastor and supreme Governor of the whole of it; and all heretics, both ancient and modern, who have left the Church or shall leave it in the time to come, inventing some new form of belief, I hate to the death, and especially the heresiarchs of our day, *Luther, Zwingli, Calvin, Béza,* and men of the same kidney . . . for I am firmly convinced that there can no more be a new faith or religion than there can be some new God, or a Christ other than Him in whom we conscientiously believe.

And now I will set down openly and truthfully what has been the motive of my coming to these parts at this time. It is not unknown to you, I imagine, that there is a certain Society called, from its imitating in a special way the life of our Saviour, the Society of Jesus; and you have heard perhaps that by its profession it incurs the liability of being sent to any part of the whole world to preach the gospel of Christ, without taking any account of danger. It is with this end in view that so many men in these last few years have flocked to it through the various Colleges in which they arm themselves with the weapons necessary for so great a conflict. Here they spend their time partly in giving earnest attention to letters, partly also in taking stock of the strength for so great a labour as this; thereby fulfilling the counsel of Christ, who exhorts him who will build a tower to reckon the expense necessary for it, and so, too, him who is entering on a battle, especially when it is a most bloody one, to hold an inspection of his forces. And when this has been done and they perceive that they have laid aside all sensual love and have won a complete victory over themselves, so as to be resolved to de-spise for Christ's sake even the greatest advancement in this world, and to give up their own liberty and yield themselves wholly to the disposition of their superiors, holding no danger to be an excuse from carrying out their commands, then at length, when they have put off all earthly affections, whatever mission may be assigned to them, they welcome it invariably for the honour of God (always after the customary outpouring of prayer) without any dread at all, nay more, subjugating to the service of Christ their intellects and all their inclinations, and promising themselves the favour and help of Him for whose sake they are undertaking this enterprise. And that God has not failed them up to now, the many glorious deeds they have done in nearly all parts of the world bear witness. . . .

Catholics Persecute Heretics: Sacred Procession in Paris (1535)

Protestantism spread rapidly in the decades after Luther's revolt. As in Germany, men dissatisfied with social, economic, and political, as well as religious, conditions were converted. Such religious rebels posed a threat to the stability of the state, especially in a country like France which had freed itself from papal administrative and financial control as early as 1438 (Pragmatic Sanction of Bourges). The reading describes how Francis I (reigned 1515–1547) dealt with this threat. From Roland H. Bainton, *The Age of the Reformation* (Princeton, N.J.: G. Van Nostrand Reinhold Company, 1956), pp. 180–181.

The most Christian king, our sovereign lord [Francis I], knowing that certain damnable heresies and blasphemies swarmed in his kingdom and desiring with the aid of God to extirpate the same decreed that a sacred procession should be held in this city of Paris on the twenty-first day of January 1535. The streets were adorned with gorgeous tapestries and the crowds held in order by archers in uniform. First came the crosses and banners of the Diocese of Paris followed by citizens and merchants carrying torches, then the four monastic orders with relics, next priests and canons of the parochial churches with relics, and the monks of Saint Martin with the head of that saint. Another carried the head of Saint Philip, one of the most precious relics in Paris. The body of Madame Saincte Genevieve was borne by six citizens in their shirts. Then followed the Canons of Notre Dame, the Rector of the University, and the Swiss Guard with their band of violins, trumpets, and cornets. Among the relics were the true cross of Christ and the crown of thorns and the lance that pierced his side. Then came a great number of the archbishops and bishops with the blood of our Saviour, the rod of Moses, and the head of John the Baptist. Next the cardinals. The precious body of our Lord was carried by archdeacons on a velvet cushion of violet adorned with *fleurs de lys.* Following the Holy Sacrament came the King alone with bare head carrying a lighted taper. After him marched Monseigneur the Cardinal of Lorraine, then all the princes and knights and members of the *Parlement,* etc. The Holy Sacrament was taken to the church of Notre Dame and there deposited with great reverence by the Bishop of Paris. Then the King and his children, the Queen and her attendants and many notables had dinner with the Bishop of Paris. After dinner the King made a speech against the execrable and damnable opinions dispersed throughout his kingdom. While the King, the Queen, and their court were with the Bishop of Paris, into their presence we brought six of the said heretics, and in front of the church of Notre Dame they were burned alive. A number of other heretics went to the stake during the days following so that all over Paris one saw gibbets by which the people were filled with terror.

Catholics Combat Heresy with the Inquisition

The reforming Pope Paul III (1534–1549) sought to reverse the spread of Protestantism by correcting abuses within the Church and by combatting heresy. One instrument in the latter effort was the new Jesuit Order. Another was the creation of the Inquisition. The first reading, taken from the Pope's decree establishing the Inquisition, describes its functions. The second reading provides an example of the campaign against heresy in Spain, where the Inquisition was under the control of the king and was used to exterminate opposition to both papal and royal authority. I. From Roland H. Bainton, *The Age of the Reformation* (Princeton, N.J.: G. Van Nostrand Reinhold Company, 1956), p. 155. II. From Charles Lea, *A History of the Inquisition of Spain* (New York, 1906), III, pp. 437–442.

I. THE ESTABLISHMENT OF THE ROMAN INQUISITION (1542)

Although from the beginning of our Pontificate we have been concerned for the flourishing of the Catholic faith and the expurgation of heresy that those seduced by diabolical wiles might return to the fold and unity of the Church and that those who persist in their damnable course should be removed and their punishment might serve as an example to others, nevertheless hoping that the mercy of God, the prayers of the faithful and the preaching of the learned would cause them to recognize their errors and come back to the Holy Catholic Church, and if any delayed they would be induced by the authority of the sacred, ecumenical and general council, which we hope speedily to convene, therefore we deferred the establishment of the Inquisition of heretical Pravity, but now, since for a variety of reasons, the council has not met and the enemy of the human race has disseminated even more heresy among the faithful and the robe of Christ is further rent, consequently, lest pending a council things grow worse, we have appointed our beloved sons, Giovanni Caraffa [*and five others*], Inquisitors General with jurisdiction throughout Christendom including Italy and the Roman Curia. They are to investigate by way of inquisition all and single who wander from the way of the Lord and the Catholic faith, as well as those suspected of heresy, together with their followers and abettors, public or private, direct or indirect. The guilty and the suspects are to be imprisoned and proceeded against up to the final sentence. Those adjudged guilty are to be punished in accord with canonical penalties. After the infliction of death goods may be put up for sale.

The aid of the civil arm may be invoked to implement whatever measures the above named deem needful. Any who impede will incur the indignation of Almighty God and of the blessed Apostles, Peter and Paul.

II. INQUISITION IN SPAIN: AUTO-DA-FÉ OF 1559

Nothing was spared to enhance the effect of the auto-da-fé of Trinity Sunday, May 21, 1559, in which the first portion of the Valladolid [northern Spanish city] prisoners were to suffer. It was solemnly proclaimed fifteen days in advance, during which the buildings of the Inquisition were incessantly patrolled, day and night, by a hundred armed men, and guards were stationed at the stagings in the Plaza Mayor, for there were rumors that the prison was to be blown up and that the stagings were to be fired. Along the line of the procession palings were set in the middle of the street, forming an unobstructed path for three to march abreast. . . . Every house-front along the line and around the plaza had its stagings; people flocked in from thirty and forty leagues around and encamped in the fields. . . .

The procession was headed by the effigy of Leonor de Vivero, who had died during trial, clad in widow's weeds and bearing a mitre with flames and appropriate inscriptions, and followed by a coffin containing her remains to be duly burnt. Those who were to be relaxed in person numbered fourteen, of whom one, Gonzalo Baez, was a Portuguese convicted of Judaism. Those admitted to reconciliation, with penance more or less severe, were sixteen in number, including an Englishman variously styled Anthony Graso or Bagor—probably Baker—punished for Protestantism, like all the rest, excepting Baez.

Actus fidei prout in Hispania celebratur.

A seventeenth-century auto-da-fé in Spain. In the foreground convicted heretics are herded from the tribunal, where their cases have been judged, to their fiery death (left).

When the procession reached the plaza, Austin Cozalla was placed in the highest seat, as the conspicuous chief of the heresy, and next to him his brother, Francisco de Vivero. Melchor Cano at once commenced the sermon, which occupied an hour, and then Valdés and the bishops approached the Princess Juana and Prince Carlos, who were present, and administered to them the oath to protect and aid the Inquisition, to which the multitude responded in a mighty roar, "To the death!" Cozalla, his brother and Alonso Pérez, who were in orders, were duly degraded from the priesthood, the sentences were read, those admitted to reconciliation made the necessary adjurations and those condemned to relaxation were handed over to the secular arm. Mounted on asses, they were carried to the Plaza de la Puerta de Campo, where the requisite stakes had been erected, and there they met their end. . . .

Of these there were only two or three who merit special consideration. Cozalla, on his trial, had at first equivocated and denied that he had dogmatized, asserting that he had only spoken of these matters to those already converted. As a rule, all the prisoners eagerly denounced their associates; he may have been more reticent at first, for he was sentenced to torture . . . but when stripped he promised to inform against them fully, which he did, including Carranza among those who had misled him as to purgatory. He recanted, professed conversion and eagerly sought reconciliation. . . . He declared that, when opportunity offered in the auto, he would curse and detest Lutheranism and persuade everyone to do the same, with which purpose he took his place in the procession.

So great was his emotional exaltation that he fulfilled this promise with such exuberance during the auto that he had to be checked. . . . On the way to the brasero he continued to exhort the people and directed his efforts especially to the heroic Herrezuelo, who had steadfastly refused to abandon his faith and was to be burnt alive. . . .

It was otherwise with Herrezuelo, the only martyr in the group. He avowed his faith and resolutely adhered to it, in spite of all effort to convert him and of the dreadful fate in store for him. On their way to the brasero, Cozalla wasted on him all his eloquence. He was gagged and could not reply, but his stoical endurance showed his unyielding pertinacity. When chained to the stake, a stone thrown at him struck him in the forehead, covering his face with blood but, as we are told, it did him no good. Then he was thrust through the belly by a pious halberdier, but this moved him not and, when the fire was set, he bore his agony without flinching and, to the general surprise, he thus ended diabolically. Illescas, who stood so near that he could watch every expression, reports that he seemed as impassive as flint but, though he uttered no complaint and manifested no regret, yet he died with the strangest sadness in his face, so that it was dreadful to look upon him as on one who in a brief moment would be in hell with his comrade and master, Luther. . . .

The remainder of the Valladolid reformers were reserved for another celebration, October 8th, honored with the presence of [King] Philip II, who obediently took the customary oath, with bared head and ungloved hand. It was, if possible, an occasion of greater solemnity than the previous one. A Flemish official, who was present, estimates the number of spectators at two hundred thousand and, though he must have been hardened to such scenes at home, he could not repress an expression of sympathy with the sufferers. Besides a Morisco who was relaxed, a Judaizer reconciled and two penitents for other offences, there were twenty-six Protestants. The lesson was the same as in the previous auto, that few had the ardor of martyrdom. Thirteen had made their peace in time to secure reconciliation or penance. Even Juana Sánchez, who had managed to bring with her a pair of scissors and had cut her throat, recanted before death, but her confession was considered imperfect and she was burnt in effigy. . . . Only in two cases did this withstand the test of fire. Carlos de Seso was unyielding to the end and, when we are told that he had to be supported by two familiars to enable him to stand when hearing his sentence, we can guess the severity of the torture endured by him. Juan Sánchez was likewise pertinacious; when the fire was set it burnt the cord fastening him to the stake; he leaped down and ran in flames; it was thought that he wanted to confess but, when a confessor was brought, he refused to listen to him; one account says that the guards thrust him back into the flames, another, that he looked up and saw Carlos de Seso calmly burning and himself leaped back into the blazing pile. . . . Thus was exterminated the nascent Protestantism of Valladolid. . . .

Religion and Life in the 16th Century: Letters of the Fugger Banking House

The Fuggers were the most important European banking house in the sixteenth century. Loyal Catholic subjects of the Hapsburgs, this family made use of its house as the principal financier of Hapsburg ventures. Its enterprises extended, however, throughout the known world and its agents were encouraged to solicit and report back to the main office the news and rumor of the day. Some dispatches of the 1580s and 1590s are printed below. Reprinted by permission of G. P. Putnam's Sons from *News and Rumor in Renaissance Europe: The Fugger Newsletters*, edited by George T. Mathews. Copyright © 1959, by G. P. Putnam's Sons, pp. 84, 157–159, 190–191, 202–203.

I. PERSECUTION OF JESUITS IN ENGLAND

From Antwerp, the 16th day of September, 1581

Several English Jesuits, who had come from Rouen to London, and, at the behest of the Pope, were trying to convert the people to their Faith, were taken prisoner in London. Three were hanged and two were quartered. They are said to have committed all manner of treachery and to have denounced the Queen shamefully.

II. DISTURBANCES IN PRAGUE

From Prague, the 24th day of December, 1590

During the past day a clamour was raised here that the Jesuits and the priests of the Pope are minded to take by force several churches of the Hussites on Christmas Eve, and retain them for the purpose of holding their services therein. It was also rumoured that the Jesuits have received outfits for war for some hundred men and have hidden them in their College. This alarm was raised by a monk, who said that he was awarded by the late Pope the privilege of obtaining possession of the monastery and church of St. Emaus, together with its revenue and appurtenances. This outcry came to the ears of His Imperial Majesty, who ordered inquiries to be made with reference to the matter. It has transpired that several artisans had spoken thus during a carousal. At the order of His Majesty they were examined by the councillors of the city of Prague. They were sent to court and questioned from whom they held such information. It resulted in a tanner being charged with spreading the rumour. He was put in prison in the Altstadt where he was questioned in kindly manner, but later

put to the rack, as to where he had first heard these tales. But he pleaded ignorance. His journeymen were called and testified that he voiced such opinions before even they had partaken any wine. The aldermen condemned him to be executed with the sword. They submitted the sentence to the Emperor and asked him whether they should carry it out.

His Majesty issued a proclamation in the Bohemian language which was exhibited in all public places and, to some extent, has pacified the people, who were in an ugly temper. At first they had armed for resistance, although they had no grounds for so doing. In all parts of Prague there broke out disturbances. It has been ordered that a number of burgesses hold night-watch in all the suburbs of Prague. Likewise, a house-to-house visitation was carried out in order to ascertain how many strange guests there be with each citizen, how named, from whence, and of what nature their business. This had to be reported to His Majesty. Moreover, it was ordained that whosoever should know or hear of any danger should give tidings thereof to His Majesty or the Council. This scheme may lead to great bloodshed, theft and pillaging, if by chance a daring murderer or robber make use of this rumour to start an outcry and raise disorder in the town of Prague.

III. BIRTH OF ANTICHRIST

From Venice, the 14th day of April, 1592

This week a News-letter has been circulated here which is said to have been written by the Grand Master of Malta and divers other Christian princes. This News-letter reports that in a certain province of Babylon there has been born to a woman of evil repute a child whose father is unknown. The child is

reported to be covered with cat's hair and to be a dreadful sight. It began to talk eight days after its birth and to walk after a month. It is said to have intimated that it is the Son of God. At its birth the sun grew dark at midday and on the previous night a mighty flame of fire appeared above its house. Many mountains opened, and in one of these there was seen a column covered with Hebrew script reading: "This is the hour of my birth!" On the next day there fell from Heaven a goodly quantity of manna and precious stones; at other places, howsoever, snakes and other horrible creatures. When the child was questioned as to the meaning of this, it made answer: that the precious stones stand for the supreme delight of those who will keep his commandments, the snakes for the martyrdom and castigation of the disobedient. Adoration of this infant has already begun because it has performed great miracles, awakening the dead and making the blind to see and the lame to walk. The populace is being encouraged by a bare-footed friar, who alleges that this is the true Son of God. For the sake of brevity I must omit further reports which do not sound very credible. It is said that the Rabbis have come to the conclusion that this is the Child of Perdition, the Antichrist.

IV. PERSECUTION OF PROTESTANTS IN SALZBURG

Copy of the Princely Mandate of Salzburg concerning the exercise of the Religion, on the 3rd day of September 1588

We, Wolf Dietrich, Archbishop of Salzburg by the Grace of God, Legate of the Holy

Roman See, hereby declare and make known: In our Capital of Salzburg, we have found several of our citizens and inhabitants opposed to our old and true Catholic Faith, who after loyal and fatherly exhortation, information and instruction, in spite of the several weeks' respite granted, have stubbornly persisted in their pre-conceived and antagonistic opinions. On this account we bid them to leave the town and the Archbishopric, for the sake of preventing further trouble and embarrassment. So that they may know how it stands with their real and movable property and their merchandise, we have publicly announced the following articles:

Firstly: It is our earnest will that those who leave our town of Salzburg make a statement of all their real estate and property before their departure and omit nothing nor leave it unregistered. This also applies to those who have already left. This statement is to be handed to us in writing. Should any one show disobedience herein or hide anything, his property is to become forfeit to us as fiscal property and subject to our domain. So that those who are no longer here should not remain in ignorance, they are to be advised of this by our Civic Authorities, through their tenants, or their own messengers, otherwise we shall proceed against the recalcitrant with heavy fines.

Secondly: They are to sell their houses and property, in and around our town, within one month, to such persons as shall find favour in our eyes, or, after this time has lapsed, make them over to them for a reasonable sum until the latter can dispose of them. Since we shall not permit that the houses be closed or that we see bad servants and citizens within them, we shall let such houses and gardens through our Civic Authorities to others for a low rent. For as Prince and Ruler of these lands we are not willing to have our capital stand partly empty, but wish that it should be fully inhabited.

Thirdly: Those who leave this town for the sake of their faith are not to hold any civic rights or honours in our Archbishopric. They are to be treated here as foreigners and strangers, but if any one of them should again return to the Catholic Faith, and tender the customary allegiance, we will reinstate him fully in all things. In the meantime, however, they are to be allowed to take their goods and chattels through our Archbishopric, unhampered, as do other strangers and foreigners.

Fourthly: They are not to venture to trade in the outer town of Salzburg or any other town in our Archbishopric. But should they resort to smuggling or carry on their calling with their own servants or other citizens and inhabitants of this town in any other name, their wares are to be considered our fiscal property.

Fifthly: They are to be permitted, as need arises, to travel through our Archbishopric. But they must not cause any offence and must frequent only the open inns. Neither are they allowed to sojourn longer than three days without our Councillor's knowledge, especially within our town of Salzburg.

Sixthly: Whatever they have need to transact in our Archbishopric, this may they do, but only through Catholic proxies, and not through sectarian servants.

Seventhly: Those who hold guardianships and have foster-children are to make over their trust-moneys and render proper account of them. In their place are to be appointed Catholic guardians who will bring up the wards in the Catholic Faith.

Eighthly: Wards, who are not here, but live in sectarian places are to be cited and brought hither by our Town Council. They are to be sent to strange places only with our foreknowledge.

Ninthly: All those who have already put their property in order or do not hold any and are ready to depart, are to leave our town of Salzburg and our Archbishopric within fourteen days of this date and see to it that they are not encountered here any more.

All this is our Will, Wish and Command.

In true Testimony of this our Mandate we have signed and written it by our own hand.

Issued in our town of Salzburg on the 3rd day of September in the year 1588 after Christ our Lord and Redeemer's birth.

Wolf Dietrich m.p.

The Tridentine Profession of Faith (1564)

A most important result of the Catholic reform movement was this clear statement on matters of faith. With slight modification it has remained the basic statement of Catholic doctrine to the present. From Henry Bettenson, ed., *Documents of the Christian Church* (New York, Oxford University Press, 1947), pp. 374–375.

I [Name] with steadfast faith believe and profess each and all the things contained in the symbol of faith which the Holy Roman Church uses, namely 'I believe in One God, etc. [The Nicene Creed.]

I most firmly acknowledge and embrace the Apostolical and ecclesiastical traditions and other observances and constitutions of the same Church. I acknowledge the sacred Scripture according to that sense which Holy Mother Church has held and holds, to whom it belongs to decide upon the true sense and interpretation of the holy Scriptures, nor will I ever receive and interpret the Scripture except according to the unanimous consent of the Fathers.

I profess also that there are seven sacraments. . . . I embrace and receive each and all of the definitions and declarations of the sacred Council of Trent on Original Sin and Justification.

I profess likewise that true God is offered in the Mass, a proper and propitiatory sacrifice for the living and the dead, and that in the most Holy Eucharist there are truly, really and substantially the body and blood, together with the soul and divinity of Our Lord Jesus Christ, and that a conversion is made of the whole substance of bread into his body and of the whole substance of wine into his blood, which conversion the Catholic Church calls transubstantiation. I also confess that the whole and entire Christ and the true sacrament is taken under the one species alone.

I hold unswervingly that there is a purgatory and that the souls there detained are helped by the intercessions of the faithful; likewise also that the Saints who reign with Christ are to be venerated and invoked; that they offer prayers to God for us and that their relics are to be venerated. I firmly assert that the images of Christ and of the ever-Virgin Mother of God, as also those of other Saints, are to be kept and retained, and that due honor and veneration is to be accorded them; and I affirm that the power of indulgences has been left by Christ in the Church, and that their use is very salutary for Christian people.

I recognize the Holy Catholic and Apostolic Roman Church as the mother and mistress of all churches; and I vow and swear true obedience to the Roman Pontiff, the successor of blessed Peter, the chief of the Apostles and the representative [*vicarius*] of Jesus Christ.

I accept and profess, without doubting, the traditions, definitions and declarations of the sacred Canons and Oecumenical Councils and especially those of the holy Council of Trent, and at the same time I condemn, reject and anathematize all things contrary thereto, and all heresies condemned rejected and anathematized by the Church. This true Catholic Faith (without which no one can be in a state of salvation), which at this time I of my own will profess and truly hold, I, *N*, vow and swear, God helping me, most constantly to keep and confess entire and undefiled to my life's last breath, and that I will endeavor, as far as in me shall lie, that it be held, taught and preached by my subordinates or by those who shall be placed under my care: so help me God and these Holy Gospels of God.

STUDY QUESTIONS

1. What kinds of reforms were enacted within the Catholic Church? To what extent does their timing suggest they are a response to the challenge of a Protestant revolt?

2. In what sense did the sixteenth century represent "a return to medievalism?" In what sense did it signal a new vision of the Christian life?

3. How did the Jesuit rule of obedience lend support to the Catholic reformation in Europe? How did the society view the purpose of education? How did their orthodoxy affect their freedom as teachers?

4. What were Father Persons' motives in returning to England?

5. How did the convocation of a religious procession in 1535 help the French King to wipe out heresy?

6. Why did Pope Paul establish the Inquisition? What effect was it likely to have on the discussion of religious ideas within the Church? What did the Spanish king hope to achieve by persecution of nonconformists?

7. What place did national feeling have in the disturbances in Prague? What does the circulation of the story of an Antichrist in the Fugger dispatches indicate about the religious temper of the times? What was the Catholic solution to religious differences in Salzburg?

8. In what areas of doctrine does the Tridentine Profession of Faith set Catholics and Protestants apart? To what extent does this document seem a response to the reform movement within and without the Church?

Labels within image: B, E, C, K, H, I, Gelderlant, Dordreche, Medemblick, Gelderlant, Medemblick, West Frislant, Amsterdam, S, West Frislant, Dordrecht, Amsterdam, AA

1   Tidore, valued for its cloves, was the site of the first Spanish garrison in the Spice Islands. Control of this important island was assumed by the Portuguese in 1529, and the Dutch tried to wrest it from them at the turn of the century. This etching by the Flemish artist De Bry offers a contemporary view of a Dutch attack on the garrison.

The Expansion of the West

It is a vanity of Europeans in their Age of Exploration that they took to themselves responsibility for the "discovery" of already inhabited lands. This was no innocent conceit, however, for their pride in discovery reflected a sense of legitimate possession and a determination to assert title to territory. Two centuries of piracy and colonial warfare did not terminate the struggle among Western powers for the lands revealed to Europeans in the first voyages to Asia, Africa, and the New World. The voyages were explosive and productive, bringing to the parochial consciousness of Western Europeans a knowledge of tastes and life styles largely denied them since the end of the West's earlier outpouring in the Crusades. At the same time they established a world-wide colonial economy in service to the needs of a European market. Its effects would take centuries to measure. The collision of cultures has been recorded in the pictorial archives of the mother country as well as in the art of the native, silent witness to an alien encounter. From this mirror of exploration come a few shocks of recognition and a sense of participation in the creation of a more universal history.

1 A sober but satisfied Dutch trader points with a malacca cane to the ships of the Dutch East India Company in the harbor of Batavia (now Djakarta). By the middle of the seventeenth century, when this picture was painted, one hundred vessels in regular commerce linked Holland with the spice depots in the East Indies. A native servant shields the couple from the sun with a parasol.

2 Europeans in the developed civilizations of China and Japan in the seventeenth and eighteenth centuries were tolerated at the pleasure of the native rulers. As a class of missionaries, Jesuit priests from Portugal had reason to recognize the tenuousness of their position. Identified in the eyes of the rulers with the Portuguese traders, they were harassed, mistreated, and finally expelled from Japan in 1641. This detail from a Japanese screen revives the memory of the Portuguese in curiosity rather than rancor. For the Japanese, they belonged to the world of the exotic, just as the Oriental did for the European. Jesuit priests (left) are visited by a group of Portuguese merchants. The latter enter with dogs, and African servants. The native artist portrays the Portuguese as he perceived them, with big noses and billowy pantaloons.

1 The passage of the martial European is clearly marked in native art. This sixteenth-century bronze plaque from Benin, West Africa, shows a Portuguese soldier with a mace raised in his right hand and a sword across his waist. The native artist has tried to capture faithfully the alien westerner in dress and facial detail.

1 Macao in the late sixteenth century was the main port for the European trade with China until the opening of Hong Kong in the mid-nineteenth century. The six square mile enclave is still under Portuguese control, though under Chinese suffrance with a predominantly Asian population. In De Bry's somewhat fanciful etching, European merchants adapt to their new circumstances. Note the parasols and sedan chairs, and also the church bells and the cross.

2 Chinese mandarin carried in a sedan chair from De Bry's collection. The chair is still used for transportation in portions of mainland China.

3 This early eighteenth-century etching opposite places an Indian next to a tobacco plant. Tobacco, an exotic crop of the New World, was used by the aborigines of America long before the arrival of Europeans. Natives smoking rolled leaves of the plant were seen by the crew of Christopher Columbus in a stopover in Cuba in 1492. Tobacco smoking spread to Europe in the sixteenth and seventeenth centuries and from there to Africa and Asia. The plant was used for a variety of purposes in early European medicine, largely because of its characteristics as a narcotic. By the beginning of the eighteenth century, however, it was being taken largely for pleasure. Some opposition to the use of the plant on moral and medical grounds followed closely upon its introduction to Europe. By 1828 nicotine had been isolated as a poisonous alkaloid.

Tobacco, in Europe, occasionally produced its own cult and rituals. Frederick William I of Prussia created his own somewhat notorious "tobacco parliment," shown in this painting by a contemporary artist. Foreign ambassadors were compelled to state their business before this gathering, and one of the king's chief delights was to sicken his guests with tobacco smoke. Frederick William sits at the table facing two of the younger princes who have entered the room to say good night. The fourteen-year-old Crown Prince, later known as Frederick the Great, sits at his right. (4) Coffee as a drink, made from roasted and ground beans, originated in Arabia in the fifteenth century and spread around the world. Recognized as a stimulant, and opposed initially by both Mohammedans and Catholics, it gained widespread acceptance in Europe by the mid-seventeenth century. The brew was first drunk outside the home in the coffeehouse, pictured below right, seed-bed of literary imagination, radicalism, and community in the seventeenth and eighteenth centuries. This etching of an eighteenth-century coffeehouse crowd, made from an old drawing, conveys a sense of the strong tempers, seditious literature, and leisurely routines that mixed at the tables. (5)

4

3

5

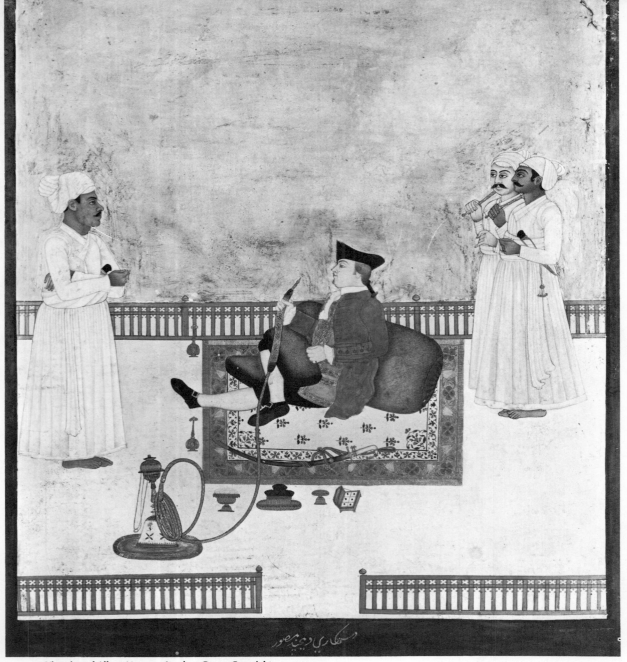

مصور ده ديو مصكاري

Victoria and Albert Museum, London. Crown Copyright.

1 In India, by contrast, the British reached a dominant position during the eighteenth century. The entire administration of Bengal lay in the hands of the British East India Company. The miniature shown here, by the Indian artist Dip Chand, is believed to be a portrait of the Scottish surgeon with the East India Company, Dr. William Fullerton. Here he reclines on stuffed cushions, draws on his hookah, and almost fades into the Oriental scene. The portrait was executed in Bengal in 1760.

European Expansion in the Perspective of World History

TOPIC 9

AGE OF DISCOVERY

The fifteenth century witnessed both the contraction and the expansion of the European world. In 1453 Constantinople fell to the Ottoman Turks and a thousand years of Byzantine history came to an end. At almost the same time a sea captain in the service of the Portuguese reached the most western point of the African continent. By the end of the century Vasco da Gama had found the sea way to India and Columbus had landed in the Western Hemisphere. Europeans could never thereafter remain isolated from the world, for the voyages of discovery set Europe on a course that led to empire and the global dispersion of Western culture. The readings examine why and how this expansion began and what some of its consequences were.

From pp. 30–33, 161–163 *The World of Humanism 1453–1517* by Myron P. Gilmore. Copyright 1952 by Harper & Row, Publishers, Incorporated. By permission of Harper & Row, Publishers.

Seen in the perspective of world history, Latin Christendom occupied in the fifteenth century a territory relatively small and insignificant in comparison with the habitable areas of the earth's surface. It amounted in fact to no more than a western peninsula jutting out from the great Asiatic land mass. From time to time, and especially in the thirteenth and early fourteenth centuries, vistas had been opened toward the east. These vistas provided glimpses of societies whose territorial extent, population, material wealth, and political stability were superior to anything in recent European experience, and whose achievements in arts and letters bore at the very least a favorable comparison with the Latin west. This knowledge had never been shared by many and was now in the fifteenth century blurred and overlaid with a mass of legend. The most optimistic calculation taken in the middle of that century might have concluded that a society that had occupied western Europe for so long a time, with occasional if ephemeral bursts of outward expansion, might continue to survive and hold its own.

No one, however, in this general situation could have foreseen that before the fifteenth century was finished western Europeans would have discovered the vast lands of the western hemisphere that now lay open to exploitation, or would have established the new sea routes to the civilizations of the east, which this time were to be regular and permanent. By 1500 the greatest steps in this unique and dramatic expansion had been taken, and within two more decades—by the time the religious revolution was beginning in Germany—the Portuguese Empire had been established in India and southeast Asia; European Christians traded in Malacca and Canton, and in the New World the Aztec Empire was about to fall to a small band of Spanish adventurers. A man who remembered the fall of Constantinople as a boy could easily have lived to hear the news of the circumnavigation of the globe. Within the space of hardly more than a generation the horizon of Latin Christendom had lifted; Europe was in a position to take a view of the world, and this perspective was not again to be closed.

It is natural that history would have endowed the men and events associated with this achievement with a transcendent significance. Adam Smith in the eighteenth century declared that the discovery of America and of a passage to the East Indies by the Cape of Good Hope were the two greatest and most important events recorded in the history of mankind, and at least half of this judgment is enshrined in the memory of every American schoolboy. Succeeding generations, recalling these names and dates, have celebrated not only the triumphs of individual genius and persistence; they have also and more importantly registered a conviction that here began a new epoch in the history of Europe and the world. We are dealing here with the kind of events that become symbolic of dramatic and revolutionary change. What is often minimized or forgotten is the extent to which the voyages of Columbus and Da Gama rested upon the labors of countless predecessors in the European past, but what is never forgotten is the fact that they were succeeded by increasing numbers of followers who finally carried the civilization of Europe to the remotest parts of the earth. In this sense their historical significance depends upon the belief that they mark the beginning of a continuous process. It may seem unnecessarily obvious to suggest that if Columbus had returned from his first voyage and reported his results to a society absolutely indifferent whether the east was reached or not—if in other words there had been no encouragement, no response, no imitation—then the date 1492 would hardly occupy its present sacred place in the historical calendar. When we celebrate this date the emotional focus is on Columbus with all the drama justified by history and enriched by legend. We forget the extent to which we presuppose or imply the existence in fifteenth-century Europe of a society ready and eager to follow the paths which had been opened. So strongly do we feel that it was natural, indeed inevitable, to seize all the advantages that followed from the great voyages of the fifteenth century that we cannot imagine a condition of affairs in which the achievements of a Columbus or a Da Gama would have remained without consequences. Yet there have been other societies and other times in the history of Europe itself in which comparable achievements appear as isolated phenomena, irrelevant happenings, promising beginnings that led to nothing. The voyages of the Norsemen to North America left no perceptible mark except in literature either on the lands which they reached or on the society from which they came. The successes of the Polos inaugurated no permanent routes between Europe and the east.

If examples from the history of Europe are not convincing on this point, consider the case of China. The same fifteenth century in which the eastern Europeans began their successful expansion by sea to the east was the century in which the tribute fleets of the Chinese emperors accomplished their most remarkable voyages in the south and west. In the years between 1405 and 1433 seven great expeditions ordered by the Ming emperors sailed to the western seas under the command of the eunuch, Cheng Ho. Their purpose seems to have been the establishment of diplomatic relations and the collection of tribute from the barbarian kingdoms. They were official undertakings of formidable size. Typically each expedition consisted of over 27,000 men embarked in fifty or more huge ocean-going junks. These great fleets visited the East Indies, Malacca, Siam, Ceylon, India, Ormuz in the Persian Gulf, the Red Sea and the eastern coast of Africa. Aden and other Red Sea ports were reached several times and a delegation from at least one of the expeditions was sent to Mecca. The fleets touched at various places on the African coast at least as far south as Melinda and perhaps beyond.

During the years when the China Sea, the Indian Ocean, the Red Sea and the Persian Gulf were thus being swept by Chinese fleets, the Portuguese were inching along the western coast of Africa and, in 1434, the year after the last great recorded expedition of the Ming, Gil Eannes in the service of Prince Henry rounded Cape Bojeador, only a little more than eight hundred miles from Lisbon.

In the long history of the relations between east and west there are few contrasts more dramatic than that presented by these two voyages, the Portuguese with its *barca* of twenty-five tons carrying a handful of men, and the Chinese fleet manned by thousands. Yet the Chinese voyages had no revolutionary consequences in the society from which they came, and in the end it was the west that conquered. Cheng Ho's ships visited over twenty countries and brought back many rare and costly things, but these results failed to stimulate in China the same aggressive impulse to expansion that was produced in the west by a handful of gold dust and a few slaves brought back from the Guinea coast.

The contrast between the achievements and attitudes of the Chinese and those of the Europeans in the fifteenth century is one of the striking coincidences of history, but the Chinese were of course not alone in failing to exploit possibilities of cultural and commercial expansion in the way that became characteristic of Europeans after the fifteenth century. Throughout the medieval and early modern period the civilization of Islam was in some ways in a uniquely favored position to undertake a program of further military, political or cultural conquests until its influence should circle the globe. The far-flung commerce of the Arabs stretched from China to western Europe. Their geographers knew more about the world than those of any other society. Their merchants were in direct contact with the greatest number and variety of religious and political systems. Yet with all this the Arab civilization failed to produce the same kind of thinking and action that developed in Europe. So it has been with others. The expansion of Latin Christendom, with all its fateful consequences, has been a unique phenomenon in the history of the world. . . .

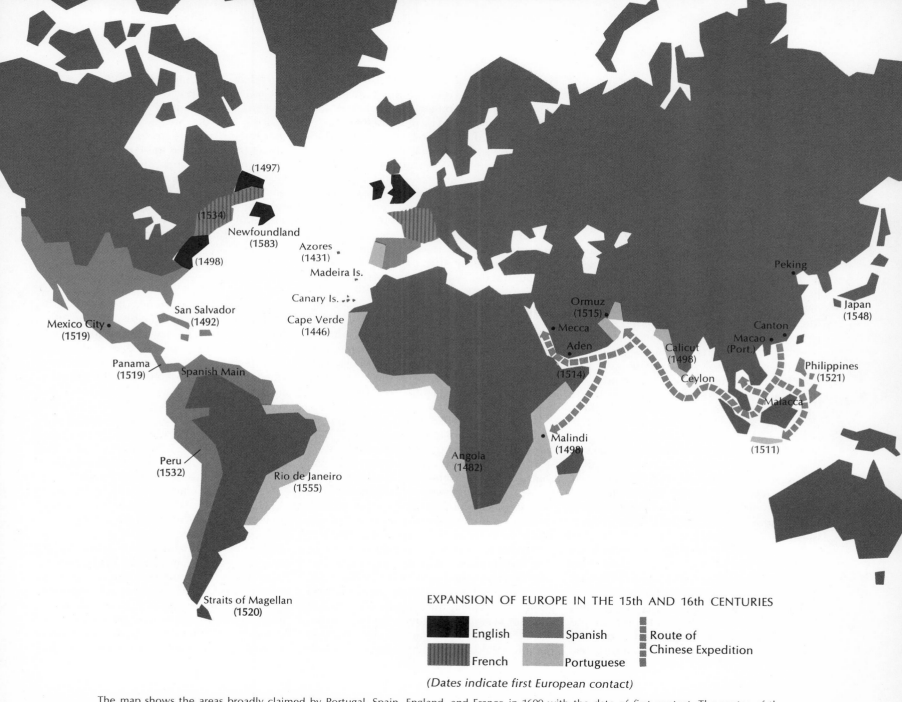

(1497)

(1534)

Newfoundland
(1583)

Azores
(1431)

Madeira Is.

Canary Is.

Cape Verde
(1446)

San Salvador
(1492)

Mexico City
(1519)

Panama
(1519)

Spanish Main

Peru
(1532)

Rio de Janeiro
(1555)

(1498)

Straits of Magellan
(1520)

Mecca

Aden

Ormuz
(1515)

(1514)

Calicut
(1498)

Ceylon

Malindi
(1498)

Angola
(1482)

Peking

Japan
(1548)

Canton

Macao
(Port.)

Philippines
(1521)

Malacca

(1511)

EXPANSION OF EUROPE IN THE 15th AND 16th CENTURIES

█ English

░ French

▓ Spanish

▒ Portuguese

▪ Route of
Chinese Expedition

(Dates indicate first European contact)

The map shows the areas broadly claimed by Portugal, Spain, England, and France in 1600 with the date of first contact. The routes of the seven great Chinese expeditions between 1405 and 1433 are also indicated.

The Course of Expansion

L. S. Stavrianos, *The World Since 1500: A Global History,* © 1966. Reprinted by permission of Prentice-Hall, Inc., Englewood Cliffs, New Jersey.

I. ROOTS OF SPANISH AND PORTUGUESE EXPANSIONISM

Religion was an important factor in European overseas expansion, but nowhere was it so important as in the Iberian Peninsula. Both the Spaniards and the Portuguese were impelled by memories of their long anti-Moslem crusade. To other peoples of Europe, Islam was a distant menace, but for the Iberians it represented a traditional and ever present enemy. Most of the peninsula at one time had been under Moslem rule, and now, in the fifteenth century, Granada in the south still remained a Moslem stronghold. Furthermore, the Moslems were in control of the nearby North African coast, while the growing Turkish seapower was making itself felt throughout the Mediterranean. Other Europeans were crusaders by fits and starts, but for the devout and patriotic Iberian, the struggle against Islam was a stern imperative—a combination of religious duty and patriotic necessity.

Prince Henry (1394–1460), called the Navigator, was a prime force in expanding the geographic bounds of the European world. Younger son of the King of Portugal, he was inspired by the stories of captured Arabs about the riches of the land south of the Sahara Desert to devote his life to exploring the sea routes around the west coast of Africa.

From the observatory he established at the southern tip of Portugal, the Prince, surrounded by a new breed of map-makers and ship-designers, sent expedition after expedition into the Atlantic and laid the foundation for the onward movement of discovery.

Prince Henry the Navigator first won fame in 1415 for his gallant role in the capture of the town and fortress of Ceuta across the Straits of Gibraltar. Likewise Queen Isabella [of Spain], moved by intense religious conviction, was determined to wipe out Moslem Granada and to carry the war into the enemy's territory in North Africa, as the Portuguese had done at Ceuta. Isabella began her crusade against Granada in 1482, and pressed on, village by village, until final victory in 1492. Immediately thereafter, the Spaniards crossed the Straits and captured the city of Melilla. In this same year, 1492, a royal decree required all Jews in Spain to accept the Catholic faith or leave the realm. Ten years later a similar decree was issued against the Moslems remaining in Castile. . . .

The Iberians were lured overseas also by four groups of islands—the Canaries, the Madeira, the Azores, and the Cape Verde—stretching westward across the Atlantic and southward down the coast of Africa. These were highly attractive, partly because they were fertile and productive, but also because they provided strategic bases and ports of call. When the Portuguese began settling Madeira in 1420, they first obtained high quality timber; next they produced sugar very profitably, and, when this was undercut by Brazilian sugar, they introduced from Crete the Malvoisie grape, from which the characteristic dessert wines of Madeira are made to the present day.

In contrast to Madeira, which was indisputably Portuguese, the Canaries were claimed by both Spain and Portugal. After appeals to the Pope and savage local fighting, the Portuguese dropped their claim to the Canaries, and the Spaniards conceded the other three island groups to the Portuguese. This settlement forced the Portuguese to sail far out into the Atlantic on their way south, to avoid Spanish privateers based on the Canaries. Their first port of call, therefore, was the Azores, which they explored systematically, until by the mid-fifteenth century they had reached the westernmost islands, about a quarter of the way across the Atlantic.

Throughout the fifteenth century, then, sailors had been discovering islands located far out into the ocean. It was natural that they should assume the existence of more islands awaiting discovery and exploitation. Atlantic charts were peppered with such imaginary islands, providing stepping stones to the East. The agreement that Columbus reached with Isabella in 1492 provided that he should head an expedition "to discover and acquire islands and mainland in the Ocean Sea."

It was Portugal, however, rather than Spain, that took the lead in overseas enterprise during the fifteenth century. Spain moved belatedly, and usually in reaction to Portuguese initiative. There were two reasons for Portugal's head start. One was its small size and its location on the Atlantic coast, surrounded on three sides by Spanish territory. This effectively safeguarded the Portuguese from temptation to squander their resources in European wars. Thanks to the leadership of Prince Henry, they turned instead to oceanic projects. The other was Portugal's superior knowledge of navigation, gained primarily from the Italians. Lisbon was on the route of Genoese and Venetian sea traffic with Flanders through the Straits of Gibraltar; and the

THE WORLD ACCORDING TO BEHAIM IN 1492

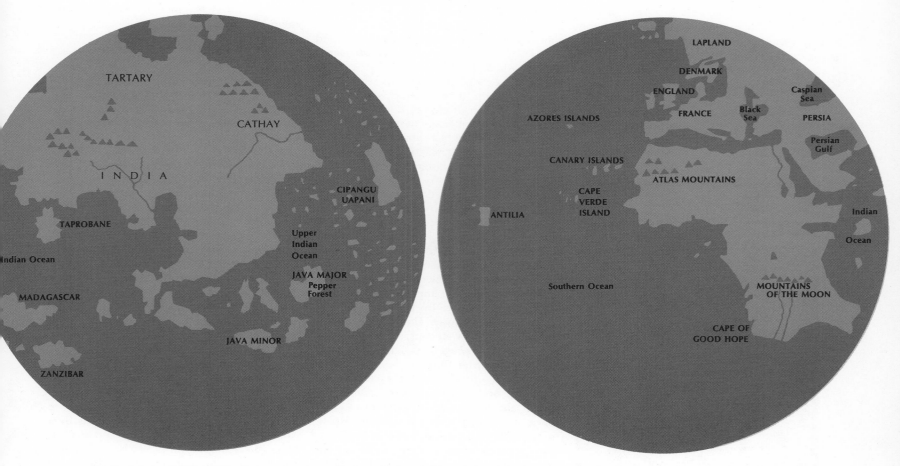

TARTARY

CATHAY

I N D I A

TAPROBANE

Indian Ocean

MADAGASCAR

ZANZIBAR

JAVA MINOR

CIPANGU
UAPANI

Upper
Indian
Ocean

JAVA MAJOR
Pepper
Forest

LAPLAND

DENMARK

ENGLAND

AZORES ISLANDS

FRANCE

Caspian
Sea

Black
Sea

PERSIA

Persian
Gulf

CANARY ISLANDS

ATLAS MOUNTAINS

ANTILIA

CAPE
VERDE
ISLAND

Indian

Ocean

Southern Ocean

MOUNTAINS
OF THE MOON

CAPE OF
GOOD HOPE

Martin Behaim (1459?–1506?), German traveler and cosmographer, fashioned this globe in 1492 and gave it to his native city of Nuremberg. It was such a view of the world that motivated Columbus to consider the Atlantic the shortest route to Asia.

Portuguese took advantage of this, by employing Italian captains and pilots in the royal navy. Prince Henry followed up by assembling a galaxy of talented seamen, including Italians, Catalans, and even a Dane. Furthermore, Henry's work was continued by the crown following his death, so that the Portuguese became the most knowledgeable of all Europeans in seamanship and geography. It was this steady and consistent government direction and support that gave the Portuguese a decisive advantage over their Spanish neighbors and rivals.

Portugal's interest in exploration quickened following the capture of Ceuta in 1415. Moslem prisoners divulged information concerning the ancient and profitable trade across the Sahara with the Negro kingdoms of the Sudan. For centuries the latter had provided ivory, slaves, and gold in return for various manufactured goods and salt. Since Western Europe in general and Portugal in particular were then suffering from a serious shortage of bullion, Prince Henry was intrigued by the possibility of tapping this gold trade. . . .

One of Columbus' ships on his voyage of discovery. Woodcut published in Basel in 1496.

A major step forward in early Portuguese exploration was taken when Prince Henry's captains passed the desert coast in 1445 and found below it a verdant new land "covered with palms and other green and beautiful trees, and it was even so with the plains thereof." By the time of Henry's death, the coast had been explored down to Sierra Leone, and a number of coastal stations had been established which enabled the Portuguese to attract at least a part of the caravan trade that they were after. Later on, in 1487, they established a factory at Wadan, an inland entrepôt, which enabled them to obtain a larger share of the north-south caravan traffic.

Meanwhile, even before Henry's death, Portuguese aspirations had come to encompass India as well as Africa. Because Europe at this time was blocked from access to the East by the Moslem power that controlled all of North Africa and the Middle East, the Mediterranean was for the Europeans a prison rather than a highway. Therefore, with the exception of the Venetians, who profited as middlemen, they eagerly sought a new route "to the Indies where the spices grow." Prince Henry had not thought of India when he first began his operations, but as his ships crept further and further down the African coast, it was natural that his horizon should expand from the African caravan trade to the Indies spice trade. From then on, the discovery and the domination of the spice route was the prime objective of Portuguese policy. It is significant that when Albuquerque urged his followers before Malacca to "quench the fire of the sect of Mahamede," he also emphasized the prospects for material gain. "I hold it certain that if we take this trade of Malacca away from them (the Moors) Cairo and Mecca will be entirely ruined and Venice receive no spiceries unless her merchants go and buy them in Portugal."

II. COLUMBUS DISCOVERS AMERICA

In view of Portugal's pioneering work in the theory and practice of oceanic navigation, it is paradoxical that the first great discovery—that of the New World—was effected under Spanish auspices. It is even more paradoxical that the reason for this outcome is that the Portuguese were more advanced in their geographical knowledge than the Spaniards and figured correctly that Columbus was wrong in his calculations. It was common knowledge among informed people by the fifteenth century that the world was round. The question was not the shape of the world but its size, and the relationship of the continents to the oceans. By combining Marco Polo's estimate of the east-west extent of Asia, which was an overestimate, the same traveler's report of the distance of Japan from the Asian mainland—1,500 miles—an extreme overestimate, and Ptolemy's estimate of the circumference of the globe, which was an underestimate, Columbus concluded that less than 3,000 miles of ocean separated Europe from Japan. Accordingly, he believed that the shortest and easiest route to Asia was by a short voyage across the Atlantic, and this was the project that he proposed before various courts. The Portuguese, thanks to Prince Henry, had more practical experience and were better informed of the most advanced knowledge of the day. They were convinced that the globe was larger than Columbus held, that the oceans were wider, and that the shortest route to the Orient was around Africa rather than across the Atlantic. For this reason the Portuguese king turned Columbus down when he applied for financial assistance in 1484. Two years later Columbus was at the Spanish court where, after a preliminary rejection, he finally won the support of Queen Isabella.

On August 2, 1492, Columbus set sail from Palos with three small ships manned by reliable crews with capable and seasoned officers. By September 6 the expedition had left the Canary Islands behind and sailed into the open ocean. Luckily there was a fair wind all the way out, but as the days and weeks went by, the men became restless. To calm their apprehension, Columbus gave out false information about the distances covered. Birds were sighted on October 7, but still no land appeared on the horizon. Even Columbus became worried, for he had now sailed so far west that, according to his calculations, he should have sighted Japan. On October 9 he promised to turn back in three days if land were not found. Just before time ran out, the lookout sighted one of the Bahaman Islands, which Columbus named San Salvador. It was an hour fraught with destiny for all of mankind.

One of the supreme ironies of world history is that Columbus was convinced until the end of his life that he had reached Asia. He was certain that San Salvador was very near to where Japan ought to be, and the next step was to find Japan itself. When he sailed southwest to the mainland of the New World, he believed that he was somewhere near the Malacca Straits. The fact that Columbus persisted in his delusion had momentous consequences: it spurred on further exploration of the Americas until the great prizes in Mexico and Peru were discovered. But if the Spaniards had realized from the outset that they had merely chanced upon a New World

Poma de Ayala (1535–1616), who traveled with the Spanish forces, sketched scenes of the Spanish conquest of the Incas. At left, Atahualpa and his retinue receive the Spaniards; at right, Atahualpa is held prisoner and in chains by one of Pizarro's band.

far away from the Continent of Asia, they might very well have turned away from what appeared at first to be an unattractive and unprofitable wilderness. In that case, the New World might have been ignored for many decades, particularly because Portugal's Vasco da Gama had in the meantime opened the extremely profitable Cape route to India.

The Spanish monarchs loyally supported Columbus and invested large sums in outfitting him for three additional expeditions. But not till 1518 did the Spaniards stumble upon the rich Aztec Empire in Mexico. During the quarter century between this windfall and Columbus' first expedition, disappointment followed disappointment as the Spaniards explored the innumerable and unpromising islands of the West Indies. . . .

III. PORTUGAL IN ASIA

The Portuguese in the meantime had been making considerable profit from their trade along the African Guinea Coast. Coarse pepper, gold, ivory, cotton, sugar, and slaves now entered European commerce through Portugal. The slave trade alone supported fifty to sixty merchants in Lisbon. It is significant that when the conquistador Bernal Díaz observed the sale of slaves in the Aztec capital, he was moved to remark, "This slave market was upon as great a scale as the Portuguese market for negro slaves at Guinea."

Prince Henry's successors continued his work of opening up the West African coast. A breakthrough occurred in 1487 when Bartholomeu Dias, while probing along the coast, was caught by a gale that blew his ships south for thirteen days out of sight of land. When the wind moderated, Dias steered for the West African coast but discovered that he had already passed the Cape without knowing it. He landed at Mossel Bay on the Indian Ocean, and wished to explore further, but his weary and frightened men forced him to return. On the homeward passage he first sighted the great cape, and named it the Cape of Storms. It was the Portuguese king who, upon Dias' return, renamed it the Cape of Good Hope. . . .

These expeditions, and several others by both land and sea, made the Portuguese the best informed in Europe on global geography and trade routes. But they failed to follow up on Dias' rounding of the Cape because of political and financial complications. The result, as noted, was that Columbus was the first to reach the New World, which he persisted in claiming to be the Orient. The more knowledgeable Portuguese were dubious from the beginning, but they now hastened to open and secure the Cape route to India. On July 8, 1497, Vasco da Gama sailed from Portugal with four ships, and at the end of May, 1498, he entered Calicut harbor. This was not so great a feat of navigation as that of Columbus. Da Gama had been able to stop at various Portuguese stations on the way south, and he knew from various sources of the Arab cities on the East African coast. . . .

Da Gama did not receive a warm welcome in Calicut. The resident Arab merchants were naturally alarmed by this threat to their traditional monopoly and did their best to throw obstacles in the way of European intruders. Furthermore, the Portuguese trade goods—mostly trinkets and woolen cloth—were unsuitable for the Indian market. The fact is that the Portuguese had completely underestimated the level and sophistication of Indian civilization. This is evident in the nature of the presents that da Gama offered to the ruler of Calicut—woolen cloth, hats, strings of coral beads, washbasins, and jars of oil and honey—which definitely did not make a favorable impression. . . .

With much effort da Gama collected a cargo of pepper and cinnamon and cleared for home, arriving in September, 1499. The cargo proved to be worth sixty times the cost of the entire expedition. Dazzling horizons opened up before the delighted Portuguese, and King Manuel assumed the titles "Lord of the Conquest, Navigation, and Commerce of Ethiopia, Arabia, Persia, and India." These titles were taken quite seriously. The Portuguese were determined to monopolize the trade along the new route and to exclude, not only other Europeans, but also the Arabs and other Eastern peoples who had traded in the Indian Ocean for centuries. To enforce their claims, the Portuguese resorted to ruthless terrorism, particularly when they encountered the hated Moslems. Da Gama, on a later voyage, found some unarmed vessels returning from Mecca. He captured the vessels and, in the words of a fellow Portuguese, "after making the ships empty of goods, prohibited anyone from taking out of it any Moor and then ordered them to set fire to it." Another contemporary Portuguese declared,

It is true that there does exist a common right to all to navigate the seas and in Europe we recognize the rights which others hold against us; but the right does not extend beyond Europe and therefore the Portuguese as Lords of the Sea are justified in confiscating the goods of all those who navigate the seas without their permission.

Such was the nature of the epochal meeting of two Eurasian cultures brought face to face for the first time after millennia of regional isolation. The Europeans were the aggressive intruders. They were the ones who seized the initiative and retained it until gradually, but inexorably, they emerged the masters in every quarter of the globe. . . .

An Arab Traveler Reports on Africa

The Portuguese learned about the land in Africa south of Sahara from the stories of Arab merchants and travelers and the tales told by mariners. In addition to wealth, legend had it that beyond the recesses of the Saharan desert lay Prester John's Christian kingdom. These expectations spurred the exploration of Africa's western coast and permitted the discovery of a sea route to India. Ibn Battúta (1304–c.1368) from whose *Travels in Asia and Africa* this reading is taken was a widely traveled North African Moslem. His first-hand report of life in West Africa added substance to the dreams of gold, and remains an important source for our knowledge of the West African empires before the European organization of the slave trade. Ibn Battúta, *Travels in Asia and Africa, 1325–1354,* trans. H. A. R. Gibb (London: Routledge & Keagan Paul Ltd., 1929), pp. 317–318, 324, 326–330.

I

From Marrákush I travelled with the suite of our master [the Sultan] to Fez, where I took leave of our master and set out for the Negrolands. . . . At Sijilmása I bought camels and a four months' supply of forage for them. Thereupon I set out on the 1st Muharram of the year [seven hundred and] fifty-three [18th February 1352] with a caravan including, amongst others, a number of the merchants of Sijilmása. After twenty-five days we reached Tagházá. . . . No one lives at Tagházá except the slaves of the Massúfa tribe, who dig for the salt; they subsist on dates imported from Dar'a and Sijilmása, camels' flesh, and millet imported from the Negrolands. The negroes come up from their country and take away the salt from there. At Iwálátan a load of salt brings eight to ten *mithqáls;* in the town of Mállí it sells for twenty to thirty, and sometimes as much as forty. The negroes use salt as a medium of exchange, just as gold and silver is used [elsewhere]; they cut it up into pieces and buy and sell with it. The business done at Tagházá, for all its meanness, amounts to an enormous figure in terms of hundredweights of golddust. . . .

II

The sultan of Mállí is Mansá Sulaymán, *mansá* meaning [in Mande] sultan, and Sulaymán being his proper name. . . . On certain days the sultan holds audiences in the palace yard, where there is a platform under a tree, with three steps; this they call the *pempi.* It is carpeted with silk and has cushions placed on it. [Over it] is raised the umbrella, which is a sort of pavilion made of silk, surmounted by a bird in gold, about the size of a falcon. The sultan comes out of a door in a corner of the palace, carrying a bow in his hand and a quiver on his back. On his head he has a golden skull-cap, bound with a gold band which has narrow ends shaped like knives, more than a span in length. His usual dress is a velvety red tunic, made of the European fabrics called *mutanfas.* The sultan is preceded by his musicians, who carry gold and silver guimbris [two-stringed guitars], and behind him come three hundred armed slaves. He walks in a leisurely fashion, affecting a very slow movement, and even stops from time to time. On reaching the *pempi* [a richly carpeted platform] he stops and looks round the assembly, then ascends it in the sedate manner of a preacher ascending a mosque-pulpit. As he takes his seat the drums, trumpets, and bugles are sounded. Three slaves go out at a run to summon the sovereign's deputy and the military commanders, who enter and sit down. Two saddled and bridled horses are brought, along with two goats, which they hold to serve as a protection against the evil eye. . . .

III

I was at Mállí during the two festivals of the sacrifice and the fast-breaking. On these days the sultan takes his seat on the *pempi* after the midafternoon prayer. The armour-bearers bring in magnificent arms—quivers of gold and silver, swords ornamented with gold and with golden scabbards, gold and silver lances, and crystal maces. At his head stand four amirs driving off the flies, having in their hands silver ornaments resembling saddle-stirrups. The commanders, qádí, and preacher sit in their usual places. The interpreter Dúghá comes with his four wives and his slave-girls, who are about a hundred in number. They are wearing beautiful robes, and on their heads they have gold and silver fillets, with gold and silver balls attached. A chair is placed for Dúghá to sit on. He plays on an instrument made of reeds, with some small calabashes at its lower end, and chants a poem in praise of the sultan, recalling his battles and deeds of valour. The women and girls sing along with him and play with bows. Accompanying them are about thirty youths, wearing red woollen tunics and white skull-caps; each of them has his drum slung from his shoulder and beats it. Afterwards come his boy pupils who play and turn wheels in the air, like the natives of Sind. They show a marvellous nimbleness and agility in these exercises and play most cleverly with swords. Dúghá also makes a fine play with the sword. Thereupon the sultan orders a gift to be presented to Dúghá and he is given a purse containing two hundred *mithqáls* of gold dust, and is informed of the contents of the purse before all the people. . . .

The negroes dislike Mansá Sulaymán because of his avarice. His predecessor was Mansá Maghá, and before him reigned Mansá Músá, a generous and virtuous prince, who loved the whites and made gifts to them. It was he who gave Abú Isháq as-Sáhílí four thousand *mithqáls* in the course of a single day. I heard from a trustworthy source that he gave three thousand *mithqáls* on one day to Mudrik ibn Faqqús, by whose grandfather his own grandfather, Sáraq Játa, had been converted to Islám.

The negroes possess some admirable qualities. They are seldom unjust, and have a greater abhorrence of injustice than any other people. Their sultan shows no mercy to anyone who is guilty of the least act of it. There is complete security in their country. Neither traveller nor inhabitant in it has anything to fear from robbers or men of violence. They do not confiscate the property of any white man who dies in their country, even if it be uncounted wealth. On the contrary, they give it into the charge of some trustworthy person among the whites, until the rightful heir takes possession of it. They are careful to observe the hours of prayer, and assiduous in attending them in congregations, and in bringing up their children to them. On Fridays, if a man does not go early to the mosque, he cannot find a corner to pray in, on account of the crowd. . . .

Another of their good qualities is their habit of wearing clean white garments on Fridays. Even if a man has nothing but an old worn shirt, he washes it and cleans it, and wears it to the Friday service. Yet another is their zeal for learning the Koran by heart. They put their children in chains if they show any backwardness in memorizing it, and they are not set free until they have it by heart. I visited the qádí in his house on the day of the festival. His children were chained up, so I said to him "Will you not let them loose?" He replied "I shall not do so until they learn the Koran by heart." . . .

Vasco da Gama as Viceroy of India. From a Portuguese manuscript c.1524.

Vasco da Gama Sails around Africa to India

(1498)

This account of da Gama's visit to Calicut on his epic voyage around Africa is by an unknown member of the expedition. From *A Journal of the First Voyage of Vasco da Gama, 1497–1499*, ed. and trans. E. G. Ravenstein (London, 1898).

When we arrived at Calicut [May 1498] the king was fifteen leagues away. The captain-major sent two men to him with a message, informing him that an ambassador had arrived from the King of Portugal with letters, and that if he desired it he would take them to where the king then was. . . .

The king was in a small court, reclining upon a couch covered with a cloth of green velvet, above which was a good mattress, and upon this again a sheet of cotton stuff, very white and fine, more so than any linen. The cushions were after the same fashion. In his left hand the king held a very large golden cup [spittoon], having a capacity of half an almude [8 pints]. At its mouth this cup was two palmas [16 inches] wide, and apparently it was massive. Into this cup the king threw the husks of a certain herb which is chewed by the people of this country because of its soothing effects, and which they call *atambor* [betel nut]. On the right side of the king stood a basin of gold, so large that a man might just encircle it with his arms; this contained the herbs. There were likewise many silver jugs. The canopy above the couch was all gilt. . . .

And the captain told him he was the ambassador of a King of Portugal, who was Lord of many countries and the possessor of great wealth of every description, exceeding that of any king of these parts; that for a period of sixty years his ancestors had annually sent out vessels to make discoveries in the direction of India, as they knew that there were Christian kings there like themselves. This, he said, was the reason which induced them to order this country to be discovered, not because they sought for gold or silver, for of this they had such abundance that they needed not what was to be found in this country. He further stated that the captains sent out travelled for a year or two, until their provisions were exhausted, and then returned to Portugal, without having succeeded in making the desired discovery. There reigned a king now whose name was Dom Manuel, who had ordered him to build three vessels,

Babar the Tiger, Mongul emperor of India (1483–1530), receives visitors.

of which he had been appointed captain-major, and who had ordered him not to return to Portugal until he should have discovered this King of the Christians, on pain of having his head cut off. . . .

On Tuesday [May 29] the captain got ready the following things to be sent to the king, viz., twelve pieces of *lambel* [striped cloth], four scarlet hoods, six hats, four strings of coral, a case containing six wash-hand basins, a case of sugar, two casks of oil, and two of honey. And as it is the custom not to send anything to the king without the knowledge of the Moor, his factor, and of the *bale* [Governor] the captain informed them of his intention. They came, and when they saw the present they laughed at it, saying that it was not a thing to offer to a king, that the poorest merchant from Mecca, or any other part of India, gave more, and that if he wanted to make a present it should be in gold, as the king would not accept such things. When the captain heard this he grew sad, and said that he had brought no gold, that, moreover, he was no merchant, but an ambassador; that he gave of that which he had, which was his own [private gift] and not the king's; that if the King of Portugal ordered him to return he would intrust him with far richer presents. . . .

On Wednesday morning the Moors returned, and took the captain to the palace, and us others with him. The palace was crowded with armed men. Our captain was kept waiting with his conductors for fully four long hours, outside a door, which was only opened when the king sent word to admit him. . . . The king then said that he had told him that he came from a very rich kingdom, and yet had brought him nothing. . . .

The king then asked what kind of merchandise was to be found in his country. The captain said there was much corn, cloth, iron, bronze, and many other things. The king asked whether he had any merchandise with him. The captain replied that he had a little of each sort, as samples, and that if permitted to return to the ships he would order it to be landed, and that meantime four or five men would remain at the lodgings assigned them. The king said no! He might take all his people with him, securely moor his ships, land his merchandise, and sell it to the best advantage. Having taken leave of the king the captain returned to his lodgings, and we with him. . . .

Columbus Discovers India in the Atlantic (1492)

Columbus wrote the following letter to a Spanish official in 1493 upon his return from the Western hemisphere. From *Select Letters of Christopher Columbus,* ed. R. H. Major (London, 1870), pp. 1–18.

As I know that it will afford you pleasure that I have brought my undertaking to a successful result, I have determined to write you this letter to inform you of everything that has been done and discovered in this voyage of mine.

This woodcut appeared in the first published edition (1496) of Columbus' letter to Sanchez, a Spanish official. The scene is Columbus' landing on the island (now known as Santo Domingo).

On the thirty-third day after leaving Cadiz I came into the Indian Sea, where I discovered many islands inhabited by numerous people. I took possession of all of them for our most fortunate King by making public proclamation and unfurling his standard, no one making any resistance. To the first of them I have given the name of our blessed Saviour, trusting in whose aid I had reached this and all the rest; but the Indians call it Guanahani. To each of the others also I gave a new name, ordering one to be called Sancta Maria de Concepcion, another Fernandina, another Hysabella, another Johana; and so with all the rest. . . . From there I saw another island to the eastwards, distant 54 miles from this Johana, which I named Hispana, and proceeded to it. . . .

In the island, which I have said before was called Hispana, there are very lofty and beautiful mountains, great farms, groves and fields, most fertile for cultivation and for pasturage, and well adapted for constructing buildings. The convenience of the harbors in this island, and the excellence of the rivers, in volume and salubrity, surpass human belief, unless one should see them. In it the trees, pasturelands, and fruits differ much from those of Johana. Besides, this Hispana abounds in various kinds of spices, gold, and metals. The inhabitants of both sexes of this and of all the other islands I have seen, or of which I have any knowledge, always go as naked as they came into the world, except that some of the women cover parts of their bodies with leaves or branches, or a veil of cotton, which they prepare themselves for this purpose. They are all, as I said before, unprovided with any sort of iron, and they are destitute of arms, which are entirely unknown to them, and for which they are not adapted; not on account of any bodily deformity, for they are well made, but because they are timid and full of terror. They carry, however, canes dried in the sun in place of weapons, upon whose roots they fix a wooden shaft, dried and sharpened to a point. But they never dare to make use of these, for it has often happened, when I have sent two or three of my men to some of their villages to speak with the inhabitants, that a crowd of Indians has sallied forth; but, when they saw our men approaching, they speedily took to flight, parents abandoning their children, and children their parents. This happened not because any loss or injury had been inflicted upon any of them. On the contrary, I gave whatever I had, cloth and many other things, to whomsoever I approached, or with whom I could get speech, without any return being made to me; but they are by nature fearful and timid. . . .

I was informed that there is another island larger than the aforesaid Hispana, whose inhabitants have no hair; and that there is a greater abundance of gold in it than in any of the others. Some of the inhabitants of these islands and of the others I have seen I am bringing over with me to bear testimony to what I have reported. Finally, to sum up in a few words the chief results and advantages of our departure and speedy return, I make this promise to our most invincible Sovereigns, that, if I am supported by some little assistance from them, I will give them as much gold as they have need of, and in addition spices, cotton, and mastic, which is found only in Chios, and as much aloeswood, and as many heathen slaves as their Majesties may choose to demand. . . .

Therefore let King and Queen and Princes, and their most fortunate realms, and all other Christian provinces, let us all return thanks to our Lord and Saviour Jesus Christ, who has bestowed so great a victory and reward upon us; let there be processions and solemn sacrifices prepared; let the churches be decked with festal boughs; let Christ rejoice upon earth as he rejoices in Heaven, as he foresees that so many souls of so many people heretofore lost are to be saved; and let us be glad not only for the exaltation of our faith, but also for the increase of temporal prosperity, in which not only Spain, but all Christendom is about to share. . . .

The Spaniards Exploit the West Indians

Columbus' discovery of the Indies was followed by a rush to the New World of adventurers and others eager to gain quick profit. Finding the natives unwilling to work for them, the first settlers persuaded Queen Isabella to issue a decree commanding forced labor from the Indians. Isabella's decree is the first selection; the second contains excerpts from a sermon by Bishop Bartholomew de Las Casas (1474–1566), who was known as the "Apostle of the Indians," and who devoted his life, in vain, to winning more humane treatment for them. I. From Lesley Simpson, *The Encomienda in New Spain: Forced Native Labor in the Spanish Colonies, 1492–1550* (Berkeley: University of California Press, 1929). Reprinted by permission of The Regents of the University of California, pp. 30–31. II. From Francis A. MacNutt, *Bartholomew de Las Casas: His Life, His Apostolate, and His Writings* (New York, 1909), pp. 314–318.

I. A ROYAL DECREE (1503)

Medina del Campo, Dec. 20, 1503. Isabella, by the Grace of God, Queen of Castile, etc. In as much as the King, my Lord, and I, in the instruction we commanded given to Don Fray Nicolás de Ovando, [Governor of Espanola] at the time when he went to the islands and mainland of the Ocean Sea, decreed that the Indian inhabitants and residents of the island of Espanola, are free and not subject . . . and as now we are informed that because of the excessive liberty enjoyed by the said Indians they avoid contact and community with the Spaniards to such an extent that they will not even work for wages, but wander about idle, and cannot be had by the Christians to convert to the Holy Catholic Faith; and in order that the Christians of the said island . . . may not lack people to work their holdings for their maintenance, and may be able to take out what gold there is on the island . . . and because we desire that the said Indians be converted to our Holy Catholic Faith and taught in its doctrines; and because this can better be done by having the Indians living in community with the Christians of the island, and by having them go among them and associate with them, by which means they will help each other to cultivate and settle and increase the fruits of the island and take the gold which may be there and bring profit to my kingdom and subjects:

I have commanded this my letter to be issued on the matter, in which I command you, our said Governor, that beginning from the day you receive my letter you will compel and force the said Indians to associate with the Christians of the island and to work on their buildings, and to gather and mine the

After the decimation of the Indian population, slaves from Africa were brought in for the gold mines of Santo Domingo. Here Spaniards supervise the mining operations. Etching, seventeenth century.

gold and other metals, and to till the fields and produce food for the Christian inhabitants and dwellers of the said island; and you are to have each one paid on the day he works the wage and maintenance which you think he should have . . . and you are to order each cacique to take charge of a certain number of the said Indians so that you may make them work wherever necessary, and so

that on feast days and such days as you think proper they may be gathered together to hear and be taught in matters of the Faith. . . .

II. A BISHOP CHARGES GENOCIDE (1552)

The Indies were discovered in the year fourteen hundred and ninety-two. The year following, Spanish Christians went to inhabit them, so that it is since forty-nine years that numbers of Spaniards have gone there: and the first land, that they invaded to inhabit, was the large and most delightful Isle of Hispaniola, which has a circumference of six hundred leagues. . . .

Among these gentle sheep, gifted by their Maker with the above qualities, the Spaniards entered, as soon as they knew them, like wolves, tigers, and lions which had been starving for many days, and since forty years they have done nothing else; nor do they otherwise at the present day, than outrage, slay, afflict, torment, and destroy them with strange and new, and divers kinds of cruelty, never before seen, nor heard of, nor read of, of which some few will be told below: to such extremes has this gone that, whereas there were more than three million souls, whom we saw in Hispaniola, there are today, not two hundred of the native population left.

The island of Cuba is almost as long as the distance from Valladolid to Rome; it is now almost entirely deserted. The islands of San Juan [Puerto Rico], and Jamaica, very large and happy and pleasing islands, are both desolate. The Lucaya Isles lie near Hispaniola and Cuba to the north and number more than sixty, including those that are called the Giants, and other large and small Islands; the poorest of these, which is more fertile, and pleasing than the King's garden in Seville, is the healthiest country in the world, and contained more than five hundred thousand souls, but to-day there remains not even a single creature. All were killed in transporting them, to Hispaniola, because it was seen that the native population there was disappearing. . . .

The reason why the Christians have killed and destroyed such infinite numbers of souls, is solely because they have made gold their ultimate aim, seeking to load themselves with riches in the shortest time and to mount by high steps, disproportioned to their condition: namely by their insatiable avarice and ambition, the greatest, that could be on the earth. These lands, being so happy and so rich, and the people so humble, so patient, and so easily subjugated, they have had no more respect, nor consideration nor have they taken more account of them (I speak with truth of what I have seen during all the aforementioned time) than—I will not say of animals, for would to God they had considered and treated them as animals—but as even less than the dung in the streets.

In this way have they cared for their lives—and for their souls: and therefore, all the millions above mentioned have died without faith, and without sacraments. And it is a publicly known truth, admitted, and confessed by all, even by the tyrants and homicides themselves, that the Indians throughout the Indies never did any harm to the Christians: they even esteemed them as coming from heaven, until they and their neighbours had suffered the same many evils, thefts, deaths, violence and visitations at their hands.

Hawkins Brings Slaves to the New World (1568)

John Hawkins (1532–1595) made a reputation as one of the dogged English sailors who defeated the mighty Spanish Armada in 1587. Earlier, he made a fortune as one of the many slave traders who purchased (or seized) Africans and sold them to the Spaniards in the Caribbean to take the place of the native peoples. This reading is taken from Hawkins' own account of a trip made in 1567–1568. From *Voyages of the Elizabethan Seamen*, ed. E. J. Payne (London, 1880), pp. 52–53.

The Third troublesome Voyage made with the *Jesus of Lubeck,* the *Minion,* and four other ships, to the parts of Guinea and the West Indies, in the years 1567 and 1568, by Master John Hawkins.

The ships departed from Plymouth, the 2nd day of October, Anno 1567, . . . and arrived at Cape Verde on the 18th day of November: where we landed 150 men, hoping to obtain some negroes, where we got but few, and those with great hurt and damage to our men, which chiefly proceeded of their envenomed arrows. And although in the beginning they seemed to be but small hurts, yet there hardly escaped any that had blood drawn of them, but died in strange sort, with their mouths shut some ten days before they died, and after their wounds were whole; where I myself had one of the greatest wounds, yet, thanks be to God, escaped. From thence we passed the time upon the coast of Guinea, searching with all diligence the rivers from Rio Grande unto Sierra Leone, till the 12th of January, in which time we had not gotten together a hundred and fifty negroes. . . . But even in that present instant, there came to us a negro, sent from a king, oppressed by other kings his neighbours, desiring our aid, with promise that as many negroes as by these wars might be obtained, as well of his part as of ours, should be at our pleasure. Whereupon we concluded to give aid, and sent 120 of our men, which on the 15th of January assaulted a town of the negroes of our ally's adversaries, which had in it 8,000 inhabitants, being very

Europeans constructed strongholds along the West African coast to serve as trading posts and slave warehouses. This sketch by a Dutch officer of El Mina Castle and its attached settlement has a very European appearance.

This sketch of a cross-section of a slave ship was made during a parliamentary investigation of the slave trade in England in 1788. English law permitted a ship of 320 tons to carry 454 persons. Inspection of an actual 320-ton ship, the BROOKES (sketch), demonstrated that in fact only 451 persons could be crammed aboard. The viewer should draw his own conclusions about the conditions of transport.

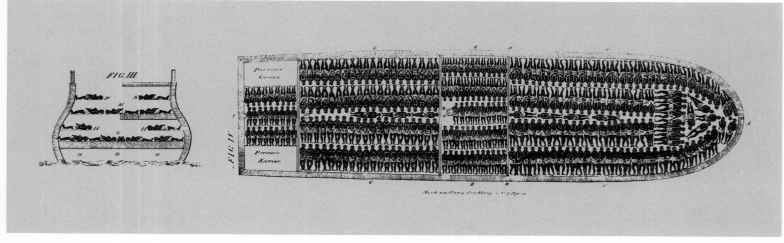

strongly impaled and fenced after their manner. But it was so well defended, that our men prevailed not, but lost six men and forty hurt: so that our men sent forthwith to me for more help. Whereupon, considering that the good success of this enterprise might highly further the commodity of our voyage, I went myself, and with the help of the king of our side, assaulted the town, both by land and by sea and very hardly with fire (their houses being covered with dry palm leaves) obtained the town and put the inhabitants to flight, where we took 250 persons, men, women, and children, and by our friend the king of our side, there were taken 600 prisoners, whereof we hoped to have our choice. But the negro (in which nation is seldom or never found truth) meant nothing less: for that night he removed his camp and prisoners, so that we were fain to content us with those few which we had gotten ourselves.

Now had we obtained between four and five hundred negroes, wherewith we thought it somewhat reasonable to seek the coast of the West Indies; and there, for our negroes, and our other merchandise, we hoped to obtain whereof to countervail our charges with some gains. Whereunto we proceeded with all diligence, furnished our watering, took fuel, and departed the coast of Guinea on the 3d of February, continuing at the sea with a passage more hard than before hath been accustomed till the 27th day of March, which day we had sight of an island, called Dominica, upon the coast of the West Indies, in fourteen degrees. From thence we coasted from place to place, making our traffic with the Spaniards as we might, somewhat hardly, because the king had straitly commanded all his governors in those parts by no means to suffer any trade to be made with us. Notwithstanding, we had reasonable trade, and courteous entertainment, from the Isle of Margarita unto Cartagena, without anything greatly worth the noting, saving at Capo de la Vela, in a town called Rio de la Hacha, from whence come all the pearls. The treasurer, who had the charge there, would by no means agree to any trade, or suffer us to take water. He had fortified his town with divers bulwarks in all places where it might be entered, and furnished himself with an hundred arquebusiers, so that he thought by famine to have enforced us to have put on land our negroes. Of which purpose he had not greatly failed, unless we had by force entered the town; which (after we could by no means obtain his favour) we were enforced to do, and so with two hundred men brake in upon their bulwarks, and entered the town with the loss only of two men of our part, and no hurt done to the Spaniards, because after their volley of shot discharged, they all fled. Thus having the town with some circumstance, as partly by the Spaniards' desire of negroes, and partly by friendship of the treasurer, we obtained a secret trade: whereupon the Spaniards resorted to us by night, and bought of us to the number of 200 negroes. In all other places where we traded the Spanish inhabitants were glad of us and traded willingly.

STUDY QUESTIONS

1. What factors made geographic expansion appeal to fifteenth-century Europeans?

2. Why did Portugal and Spain take the lead in European expansion? What were Prince Henry's objectives? How did it happen that a Spanish expedition discovered America? What effect did this have on the Portuguese?

3. What was African society like according to Ibn Battúta? What conclusions might Europeans draw from accounts such as his?

4. Why did Vasco da Gama go to India? Why did the society he discovered pose more serious obstacles to European control than that discovered by Columbus?

5. What were Columbus' objectives? In what way are they reflected in his promise to the king and queen?

6. Can you make a defense of Isabella's Decree of 1503? What causes underlay the decline of the native Caribbean population?

7. How were Africans obtained by slave traders? Why were the Africans taken to the West Indies? Why do you think the Spanish settlers were forbidden to trade with foreigners?

Chapter 2

The Impact of the Scientific Revolution

None of the revolutions that undermined the established authority of the traditional world was more radical and seminal than that of early modern science. In the receptive environment of the seventeenth and eighteenth centuries, prepared by earlier divisions over religious commitment and by the new secular interests shaped in Europe's urban and overseas expansion, science mounted an assault on both the physics of Aristotle and the theology of medieval Christianity. Conclusions drawn from fresh observation, careful experimentation, and ambitious theorizing displaced the earth as the center of the known universe and increased man's power over nature.

The scientific world view gave man a new sense of mastery through the habits of mind and belief it encouraged, and through the knowledge it provided. This knowledge promised to change the social as well as the natural order, for in its name the intellectuals of the Enlightenment carried on the war of reason against prejudice and injustice. Out of the attempt to establish the laws by which nature was governed came the desire to impose a rational order on society itself and to design a world of justice responsive to the reasonable men who had created it.

1543	Copernicus, *On the Revolutions of the Heavenly Orbs*
1543	Vesalius, *De Fabrica Humani in Corporis*
1546–1601	Tycho Brahe
1610	Galileo observes the satellites of Jupiter
1620	Francis Bacon, *New Organon*
1622–1673	Molière
1623–1662	Blaise Pascal
1628	William Harvey discovers how blood circulates
1632–1723	Anton van Leeuwenhoek, inventor of microscope
1633	Galileo's trial. Forced to deny publicly that the earth moves around the sun.
1637	Descartes, *Discourse on Method*
1644	Descartes, *Principles of Philosophy*
1660	Royal Society founded in England
1667	French Académie des Sciences
1687	Newton, *Mathematical Principles of Natural Philosophy*
1690	John Locke, *Essay on Human Understanding*
1692	Salem witchcraft trials
1694–1778	Voltaire
1700	Leibnitz founds Academy of Sciences, Berlin
1703–1791	John Wesley
1704	Newton, *Optics*
1724–1804	Immanuel Kant
1726	J. Swift, *Gulliver's Travels*
1748	Montesquieu, *The Spirit of Laws*
1751–1772	The *Grand Encyclopèdie*
1754	*Candide*
1762	Rousseau, *Emile, Social Contract*
1762	Calas Case
1764	Beccaria, *Essay on Crimes and Punishment*

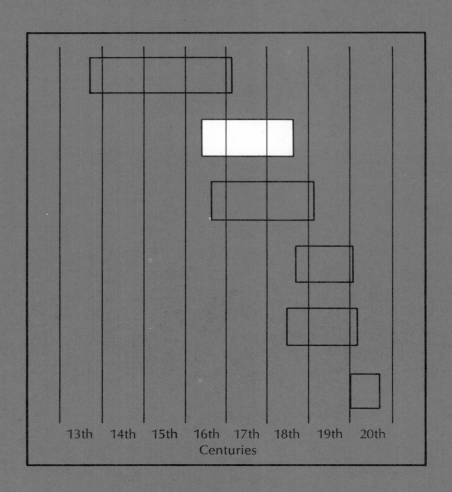

13th   14th   15th   16th   17th   18th   19th   20th
Centuries

TOPIC 10

Nicolaus Copernicus:
On the Revolutions of the Heavenly Orbs.
Preface and Dedication to Pope Paul III (1543)

A NEW UNIVERSE

The reexamination of man and the world that had its start in the fifteenth and sixteenth centuries was climaxed by a fresh view of the universe, based neither on theology nor Aristotelian logic. The publication in 1543 of Nicolaus Copernicus' mathematical proof of the heliocentric theory set the stage for a scientific explosion that revolutionized society. The readings express the Copernican challenge to the still widely held medieval Christian world view.

Nicolaus Copernicus (1473–1543) was born in Thorn in northern Poland. This was an area inhabited by Poles and Germans and his family's origin is not certain. One of his uncles was a bishop and young Copernicus was educated at Polish and then at several Italian universities. Most of his life was spent as a canon (a master of church law) at Frauenburg Cathedral in Prussia. Copernicus lived at the height of the Renaissance and was in many ways a typical figure of the period. Besides being a lawyer and a minor church official, he was a doctor, a painter, a mathematician, and an astronomer. He became interested in astronomy as a student in Italy and spent much of his life studying the heavens. Copernicus first hinted at his revolutionary views on the position of the earth within the universe in 1530 in a slim pamphlet that he passed around among his friends. He hesitated to publish his theories, however, and his famous book *On the Revolutions of the Heavenly Orbs* (the preface to which follows) only appeared in 1543, shortly before his death. Copernicus was not only a man of the Renaissance; his life spanned the beginnings of the Protestant Reformation which spread rapidly across northern Europe after 1517. From Nicolaus Copernicus, *De Revolutionibus Coelestium Orbium.* Simplified by L. F. Schaefer.

I can recognize easily enough, Most Holy Father, that as soon as certain people learn that I claim in this book . . . that our globe undergoes certain movements, these people will immediately shout to have me and my opinion hooted off the stage. For I am not so pleased by my own works that I do not care what others will say about them. Although I do believe that the conclusions of a philosopher should not be influenced by the way other people think, since it is his loving duty to seek out the truth in all things, even philosophers should avoid coming to conclusions that are utterly wrong. I have had to consider how absurd my conclusion that the Earth moves will be held by those who know that learned men in the past have proved that the Earth rests immovable in the middle of the heavens as the center of the universe. For a long time, therefore, I hesitated whether I should publish my comments written to demonstrate the Earth's movement . . . and the scorn which I had to fear on account of the newness and absurdity of my opinion almost drove me to abandon the work I had done.

But my friends made me change my course in spite of my long-continued hesitation and even resistance. First among them was Nicholas Schonberg, Cardinal of Capua, a man distinguished in all branches of learning. Next to him was my devoted friend Tiedemann Giese, Bishop of Kulm, a man filled with the greatest love of the divine and liberal arts: for he in particular urged me frequently and even spurred me on by scolding into publishing this book and letting come to light a work I had kept hidden among my things for not merely nine years, but almost four times nine years. Quite a few other learned and distinguished men demanded the same thing of me, urging me to refuse no longer—on account of the fear which I felt—to add my work for the benefit of those men who are really interested in mathematics (science). They said that even if my teaching about the movement of the Earth now seems absurd to a lot of people, these same people will greet it with wonder and thanksgiving when, once the book is published, they see the fog of absurdity driven away by my clear explanations. I was led by such persuasion, and by the hope which they expressed, to permit my friends to make arrangements for publication.

But perhaps Your Holiness will not be so surprised by the fact that I have finally published my findings—especially after having taken such care in working them out that I did not hesitate to put down in writing my concept of the movement of the Earth—as you would like to know how it happened that I dared imagine the Earth moved, since this conclusion goes against the opinions of most mathematicians and almost goes against common sense. And so I do not want to hide the reason for my interest from Your Holiness. It was the fact that mathematicians have not agreed with one another in their research that moved me to think of a different scheme for drawing up the movements of the spheres of the world. . . .

Accordingly, when I thought about the lack of certainty in traditional mathematics concerning the movements of the spheres of the world, I began to be annoyed that those philosophers, who in other respects had very carefully studied the tiniest details of the world in which we live, had discovered no sure explanation for the movements of the machinery of a world built for us by the Best and Most Orderly Workman of all, I, therefore, took the trouble to reread all the books by philosophers that I could get hold of, to see if any of them even made a guess that the movements of the spheres of the world were different from those taught by the professors of mathematics in the universities. And, as a matter of fact, I did find . . . that some ancient writers thought the Earth moved. . . .

This discovery moved me to think about the mobility of the Earth. And, although it seemed at first absurd, nonetheless because I knew that other men before me had been allowed to draft unusual formulae to prove heavenly phenomena, I thought that I too had the right to test whether or not, by assuming that the Earth had some movement, I could not find proofs for the revolutions of the heavenly bodies less shaky than those of my predecessors.

And so, after much long observation I discovered that if the movements of the other wandering stars are correlated with the circular movement of the Earth, and if the movements are computed in accordance with the revolution of each planet, not only do all the other facts about them follow from this but this correlation binds the order and magnitudes of the planets, the spheres in which they orbit, and the heavens themselves so closely together that nothing can be shifted around in any part of them without disrupting

the remaining parts and the universe as a whole. . . .

I have no doubt that talented and learned mathematicians will agree with me, if they are willing to give deep thought and effort to what I bring forward in this book in explaining these things. But in order that the unlearned as well as the learned may see that I am not trying to escape anyone's judgment of what I have said, I preferred to dedicate these results of my study to Your Holiness rather than to anyone else. Even in this far off corner of the earth where I live, you are highly respected for your personal dignity, your love of learning, and even your knowledge of mathematics. Your judgment, therefore, provides a guard against the bites of those who may want to do me wrong. . . .

But, if by chance, there are certain "idle talkers" who take it upon themselves to make judgments, even though they are wholly ignorant of mathematics, and if these persons dare to attack my work by shamelessly distorting the sense of some passage from the Holy Bible to suit their purpose, let me say that such fellows worry me not one bit. Thus Lactantius, who is a distinguished writer but hardly a mathematician, speaks in an utterly childish fashion about the shape of the Earth. He laughs at those who say that it has the shape of a globe. Serious people should not be surprised that people like that will laugh at us. Mathematics is written for mathematicians. Among them, if I am not mistaken, my work will be recognized as a contribution to the Christian community of which Your Holiness is head. For not many years ago, under Pope Leo X when the Lateran Council was considering the question of reforming the calendar, no decision could be reached because the length of the year and of the months and the movements of the sun and moon had not yet been measured with sufficient accuracy. From that time on I gave attention to making more accurate observation of these things. . . . What I have accomplished I leave to the judgment of Your Holiness in particular and to that of all other learned mathematicians. . . .

Early Science

Reprinted from *A Short History of Science and Scientific Thought* by F. Sherwood Taylor. By permission of W. W. Norton & Company, Inc. Copyright 1949 by W. W. Norton & Company, Inc. This is published in Canada by Heinemann Educational Books Ltd.

THE BEGINNINGS OF SCIENCE

The history of science . . . must begin with the history of crafts, for these are the foundation and necessary fore-runners of true science. Before architects and engineers came carpenters and smiths, and before these the simple unspecialized Man.

The making of flint tools is the first known craft, which was discovered by creatures of a different species from ourselves, a million or so years ago, more or less. These early man-like creatures made rough flint weapons and worked bone and horn, but we know almost nothing as to their mentality. Our own species, *homo sapiens,* appeared perhaps some fifty thousand years ago, and from the first showed evidence of high intelligence. The first men had almost everything to learn: we do not even know if they had words by which

to name and so to classify what they saw and handled. They improved the making of flint weapons; invented and brought to great perfection pictorial art. No one has drawn bison better than it was drawn in the Altamira caves at the very beginning of the human story. Such drawings imply close observation, the making or collection of pigments, and also the use of fire and of lamps to see by, for they are depicted on the walls of dark caves.

As time went on men began to build huts and to make crude pottery. Such cultures have existed in many different ages and parts of the world, but that which developed into civilization and gave rise to science was in Egypt, where, perhaps about 5000 B.C. or even earlier, there dwelt the most cultured men of that distant age. They had learnt to domesticate animals and plants, and so were able to provide a securer supply of food and settle down in small communities. Dogs, cattle, goats, sheep and pigs were domesticated at least as early as the neolithic period immediately preceding civilization in the near East: the ass probably somewhat later and the horse later still. Agriculture dates from a period at least as early, for wheat grains of a type showing much advance over the wild forms have been found in tombs and settlements dating from c. 3500 B.C. These men rapidly increased in skill. The flint-work was such as no one could imitate today: they made stone vessels by grinding them out with emery; and although they had not the potter's wheel, yet they made sound and shapely pottery ornamented in black and red and white. They had learnt to make cloth and mats and baskets, they built simple huts to dwell in and travelled in boats with oars and sails: they even carved spirited representations of hunting and crude statues of their gods.

They lacked however three very important things, metal, writing, and a national organization; and from the discovery of these we may date civilization.

The very early history of civilization is still largely unknown, but at the present it appears that in the earliest times there were at least three contemporary civilizations. First that of the Nile Valley—the Egyptian; secondly, that of the Sumerians, who transmitted their culture to the Babylonians in Mesopotamia and thence to the Assyrians; thirdly, a civilization in the Indus valley, of which as yet we know comparatively little. All three civilizations seem to have developed about 4000–3400 B.C. and to have had a similar level of culture.

Material culture and scientific study did not continue steadily to advance throughout the thirty centuries in which the Egyptian and Assyrian cultures continued to flourish. It seems, on the contrary, that the first centuries of these civilizations were the greatest: that their art and learning reached the highest point before 2400 B.C. and thereafter were transmitted with no more than minor alterations, not always for the better. The products of the Old Kingdom of Egypt, made in the years following 3000 B.C., are artistically and technically equal or superior to later ones.

What did these early civilizations contribute to science?

1. The necessary means for discovering and recording scientific fact; e.g. tools; vessels; materials of all kinds, and especially the metals; writing, and writing materials.
2. Beginnings of medicine and surgery.
3. Beginnings of astronomy, and a fairly satisfactory calendar.
4. Beginnings of mathematics.

This may not sound a great achievement for three thousand years of civilization, but we have to remember, first, that beginnings are very hard to make, and that each advance in thought makes the next advance easier; secondly, that these peoples very soon found a way of living which was reasonably satisfactory to themselves, or at least to the learned caste, and that there was therefore little incentive to discovery. . . .

THE GREEKS AND SCIENCE:
THE SPIRIT OF INQUIRY

The contribution of the Greeks was nothing less than the creation of the very idea of science as we know it. As far as we know, the Egyptians and earlier Babylonians recorded and studied only those facts about the material world that were of immediate practical use, whereas the Greeks introduced what is still the chief motive of science, the desire to make a mental model of the whole working of the universe. Practical use they despised, and they desired the knowledge of things as a means of understanding and realizing the harmony and order of the world. It is one thing to desire knowledge: another to find the right way to achieve it, and the first requisite for obtaining accurate knowledge about the world, namely the making of great numbers of accurately recorded observations and experiments, was not to the taste of the Greeks. They were full of curiosity: they had great artistic ability: but they always preferred the discussion of abstract principles to those practical measurements and weighings and prosaic descriptions of things that are the material of science. Simple experiments with tools and vessels and mechanical contrivances they felt to be slavish and degrading, so

naturally they did not go far with physics and chemistry. Certain manual operations, it is true, had an honourable origin and tradition: the healing art, and to a less extent the study of animals and plants, was not unworthy of a philosopher, while astronomy, the study of the eternal mathematical harmony of the universe, was nobler still. But the greatest success of the Greeks was in geometry, for which little or no observation or experiment was required, but simply the exercise of pure reason. . . .

THE DECLINE OF SCIENCE

The Greeks were great logicians and geometers, and fair astronomers; they made a beginning in many other sciences, but no more than a beginning. They were the originators of the scientific spirit and of almost all the science of classical times; for in this the Romans were only their followers. Their best work was finished by 150 B.C. After that we have plenty of encyclopaedists who compile long books from the works of others and may or may not add something themselves. Pliny's *Natural History,* though containing masses of information, is poor uncritical stuff. Only Galen the physician and Ptolemy the astronomer, who date from the second century A.D., are anything more than mere compilers. After about A.D. 300 interest in natural science almost ceases: Christianity, new and living, was giving men what they had always been seeking, and in that new world of inspiration and love, nothing seemed important except to live well and know the Divine truth. So science almost disappears and for centuries the learned world is busy confuting heresies and defining exactly what a Christian can believe without fear of error. . . .

THE REVIVAL OF LEARNING
IN THE WEST

From the time of Charlemagne (c. A.D. 800) we must think of the great nations of Europe taking shape gradually and acquiring more stable government and structure. More and more religious houses were founded, and as there came to be more learned men and more contact between them, so enthusiasm for learning grew. The first centres of learning were the monasteries; but the true function of a monk is not to teach but to pray, and a great step towards universal knowledge was taken when the first Western universities were founded, from about A.D. 1000. Much the earliest was the medical school of Salerno in Italy, but the most influential was the University of Paris, which began near 1100 as a school of logic and was recognized as a University about 1150–70. Oxford dates from before 1200 and Cambridge from a little after.

The twelfth and thirteenth centuries saw a great revival of learning and produced some of the world's greatest men and books. Its strength was in philosophy rather than in science, but even here a level was reached which was not surpassed in seven centuries before then or centuries after.

The keynote of the revival was the rediscovery of some part of Greek learning, most of which had long been unknown to the Western World. The European scholars came to know that the Arabs possessed these treasures. At places where the Arab, Greek, Jewish and Latin culture met, e.g. in Sicily and Spain, Latin translations of Greek texts, some directly from Greek but more from Arabic versions, began to be made in the twelfth century; and early in the thirteenth century Europe possessed a great part of Greek learning in a form somewhat ruffled by translation from Greek to Syriac, and thence to Arabic and Latin (sometimes perhaps with Spanish as a further intermediary). There were very few Western Europeans who knew Greek, but by these a small number of translations were made from Byzantine MSS, direct into Latin. The most important things that were recovered were the works of Aristotle [Greek philosopher, 384–322 B.C.] of which but a fragment was previously known. Here was a wonderful philosophy and system of knowledge; and at the same time Christianity provided a perfect system of doctrine. It was the task of the thirteenth century, especially of St. Albert (Albertus Magnus) and St. Thomas Aquinas his pupil, to harmonize them into a noble system of Christian philosophy.

Not only the philosophical, but also the scientific works of Aristotle were studied, as were those of Ptolemy, Galen, Euclid, and the great Arabs such as Avicenna; none the less the men of the age were not really interested in practical science. A good start towards discovering new facts was made in the thirteenth century by three original geniuses, St. Albert, Peter Peregrine, and Roger Bacon, but the men of the later Middle Ages preferred to study what the earlier authors had said rather than to use their own hands and eyes. . . .

St. Albert and St. Thomas Aquinas made it clear that learning about other than directly spiritual matters was desirable. Earlier Saints and theologians had been doubtful of this, for they had considered that the only knowledge worth having was that which showed the way to heaven; but the great men of the thirteenth century saw that *knowledge was a whole* and that all of it tended to the glory and knowledge of God. It is an illusion to suppose that the Church opposed science in the Middle Ages, for almost all the men of science were clerics. The truth is that but very few of the men of the time were interested in science, and that nearly all were extremely concerned with religion, which was the centre of their lives. The only sciences that they felt they needed were medicine and astronomy. Even medicine was not very important to them, because they believed that to die well was better than to live badly; and the chief interest of astronomy was its relation to astrology—always in favour when life, limb and fortune were uncertain.

Roger Bacon was very far from being as great in the human sense as St. Albert or St. Thomas. He had an unfortunate boastful and abusive manner that made him enemies, but he seems to have come very near to being an experimental scientist of the modern type. He evidently had a laboratory at Oxford and studied lenses and mirrors with great care. There are indications (though no proof) that he had a telescope. There is a tradition that he had a telescope and a burning-glass in his study, and that the University ordered them to be destroyed because the students wasted their time in looking through the telescope, and lighting candles with the burning-glass. In any event, he lays the strongest emphasis on the need to perform experiments, and on the value of mathematics in interpreting nature—ideas that did not come into their own until more than three centuries had gone by.

There were other experimentalists in this age. Peter Peregrine, a Picard who flourished about 1270, wrote a remarkable little treatise on the magnet and compass, but little else has survived.

THE MEDIAEVAL VIEW OF THE WORLD

The general scheme of the world in the years 1200–1500 was based on that of Aristotle. The universe was a sphere within which revolved invisible spheres carrying the stars, sun, moon and planets. These were the changeless heavens; within the sphere of the moon was the terrestrial and corruptible region. The earth was a globe motionless at the centre of the spherical universe. Some, such as Roger Bacon, realized that this spherical earth could be circumnavigated. Asia, Europe, some of Africa had been mapped; but America, the Pacific and Australia were unknown.

Everything was made up of matter and form. The simplest kinds of stuff were earth, air, fire and water, which could be transformed one into another, but had as a basis a simple prime matter which could never be obtained from them. Every kind of matter, if it could be transformed into this prime matter, could be made into any other kind of matter, but in practice this could not be done or only in a few cases. . . .

A notion, really fundamental to the mediaeval world, but less important in that of the earlier Greeks, was the idea of *influences*. God exerted a continuous influence upon his creatures on earth, sometimes directly, but chiefly through the heavenly bodies, and above all the sun. Every stone, plant, animal, organ, human being, or nation, was linked with various heavenly bodies and subject to continuous influence from them. As these heavenly bodies moved through the sky these influences were modified. Plagues and pestilences were caused by these influences—hence our word *influenza*. Man was subject to these influences, but not fatalistically bound by them. He made his life through his own free-will, but he had to cope with the evil influences of the planets as best he could, just as he had to cope with drought and heat and cold and rain. This general system of the world suffered singularly little change or serious dispute before the early sixteenth century.

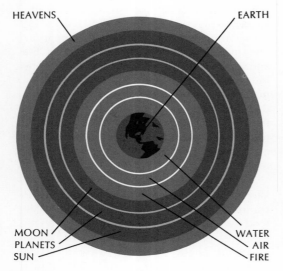

HEAVENS

EARTH

MOON
PLANETS
SUN

WATER
AIR
FIRE

The Aristotelian scheme of the universe, as portrayed in the middle ages. From within, outward, the sphere of earth, water, air, and fire: these compose the terrestrial region; the planetary spheres: the moon, Mercury, Venus, the sun, Mars, Jupiter, Saturn, and the fixed stars. Then come the habitation of God and the saints.

Michael Postan: Why Was Science Backward in the Middle Ages?

Michael Postan (1899–   ), English economic historian, here advances a thesis on why scientific achievement was limited in the Middle Ages. From Michael Postan, "Why Was Science Backward in the Middle Ages?" in *A Short History of Science: Origins and Results of the Scientific Revolution*. (London: Routledge & Kegan Paul Ltd.), pp. 10–17.

It is generally agreed that the Middle Ages preserved for the use of later times the science of the ancients. Therein lies both the scientific achievement and the scientific failure of the medieval civilization. The achievement was all the greater for being indirect. Men in the Dark Ages did not find in the parts of the Western Empire which they occupied a scientific tradition as rich as that which the Arabs inherited in the eastern provinces. Scientific learning came to them later, mostly in the twelfth and thirteenth centuries, from the Arabs and the Jews. To have borrowed and absorbed a scientific culture from peoples which were at that time so distant and so alien was indeed a great achievement. It was all that great, but no greater. What the Middle Ages took over they did not very much enrich. Indeed so small was their own contribution that historians of science are apt to regard the Middle Ages as something of a pause.

Needless to say, the pause was not undisturbed or unbroken. In the course of centuries medieval men improved somewhat their practical arts and added a little to their understanding of nature: and in some periods, such

as the turn of the twelfth and thirteenth centuries, their own advances were sufficiently great to make it possible for us to speak of the scientific renaissance, or revival, in the Middle Ages. As a result of the revival, scientific knowledge became much richer than it had once been. As late as the early eleventh century medieval mathematics were still confined to simple computations, to an elementary theory of simple numbers, to some rudimentary propositions of pre-Pythagorean geometry, the use of the counting frame (the abacus), and perhaps to decimal fractions. But by the end of the thirteenth century mathematicians were tackling advanced problems of the geometry of Pythagoras, approaching the solution of cubic equations by the intersection of cones, discussing spherical trigonometry, and indeed approaching the very verge of differential calculus. In the same period the astrologists had not only absorbed the Ptolemaic astronomy of the ancients, but had also got to know the map of the skies and the courses of stars and planets, and had thereby prepared the great Copernican revolution in astronomy. Similarly the medieval alchemists had stumbled across some new facts about the properties of metals and gases, while the compilers of medieval lapidaries or lists of magic stones, of medieval herbals and of the medieval bestiaries, paved the way for the great scientific classifications of the sixteenth and seventeenth centuries. Some curious and learned men went even further than that. We have all heard about Frederick II's dissection of animals, but he was apparently not alone in this kind of investigation, for by the end of the Middle Ages dissectors and surgeons had accumulated a certain amount of new anatomical knowledge as well as a few rudimentary facts of human physiology. Now and again we find men engaging in practical tests which look like primitive experiments.

On the more practical plane we find here and there instances of great technical progress. Thus at the beginning of the medieval epoch, in the Dark Ages, the tillers of the soil were sufficiently enterprising to invent, or at least to adopt, what was at that time a brand-new system of agricultural technique—the rotation of crops by a two- or three-field system, the use of the heavy wheeled plough, and above all the modern system of harnessing animals from the shoulder, none of which had been known to the Romans or, if known, used extensively by them. During the same period the large water-mill, sometimes equipped with the overshot wheel and geared transmission, replaced in many parts of Europe the small horizontal water-mill of the so-called Irish or Norse type. It is also probable that, during the period of active land reclamation in Flanders during the tenth and eleventh, and in eastern Germany in the twelfth and thirteenth centuries, peasants adopted a more efficient lay-out of villages, an improved method of drainage, and possibly even more intensive forms of agriculture. We also find great technical ingenuity in mining and in the construction and improvements of implements of war, especially of machines for siege. Above all there was continuous technical progress in the greatest of medieval practical arts, in that of building. In the interval between the tenth and thirteenth centuries the technique of building developed much faster and went much further than during those four or five centuries of renaissance architecture which were to come between medieval buildings and the ferroconcrete structures of our own day.

Thus some advance on planes both purely intellectual and technical there was; yet taken together and placed against the vast panorama of medieval life, or indeed against the achievements of Greek and Hellenistic science in the fourth century B.C., or with the scientific activity of the seventeenth century, all these achievements are bound to appear very poor. Why then this poverty?

To this question many answers can be and have been given. But what most of them boil down to is the absence in medieval life of what I should be inclined to call scientific incentives. Students of science sometimes differ about the true inspiration of scientific progress. Some seek and find it in man's intellectual curiosity, in his desire to understand the workings of nature. Others believe that scientific knowledge grew and still grows out of man's attempts to improve his tools and his methods of production; that, in short, scientific truth is a by-product of technical progress. I do not want here to take sides in this particular controversy; what I want to suggest is that the Middle Ages were doubly unfortunate in that both the inspirations, the intellectual as well as the practical, failed more or less.

The easiest to account for is the intellectual. The Middle Ages were the age of faith, and to that extent they were unfavourable to scientific speculation. It is not that scientists as such were proscribed. For on the whole the persecution of men for their scientific ideas was very rare: rare because men with dangerous ideas, or indeed with any scientific ideas at all, were themselves very rare; and it is indeed surprising that there were any at all. This does not mean that there were no intellectual giants. All it means is that in an age which was one of faith, men of intellect

and spirit found the calls of faith itself—its elucidation, its controversies, and its conquests—a task sufficient to absorb them. To put it simply, they had no time for occupations like science.

In fact they had neither the time nor the inclination. For even if there had been enough men to engage in activities as mundane as science, there would still be very little reason for them to do so. In times when medieval religious dogma stood whole and unshaken the intellectual objects and the methods of science were, to say the least, superfluous. The purpose of scientific enquiry is to build up piecemeal a unified theory of the universe, of its origin and of its working. But in the Middle Ages was that process really necessary? Did not medieval man already possess in God, in the story of Creation and in the doctrine of Omnipotent Will, a complete explanation of how the world came about and of how, by what means and to what purpose, it was being conducted? Why build up in laborious and painstaking mosaic a design which was already there from the outset, clear and visible to all?

So much for intellectual incentive. The practical incentive was almost equally feeble. Greater understanding of nature could not come from technical improvements, chiefly because technical improvements were so few. Medieval occupations continued for centuries without appreciable change of method. After the great period of initial development, i.e. after the late eleventh century, the routine of medieval farming in the greater part of Europe became as fixed as the landscape itself. In the history of the smithies, the weaving shops, or the potteries, there were occasional periods of innovation, but taking the Middle Ages as a whole technical improvement was very rare and very slow.

For this medieval economic policy was largely to blame. In the course of centuries, economic activities got surrounded with a vast structure of bye-laws and regulations. In the villages regulations were necessary in order to guarantee to the landlords that their tenants would be able to pay or to work off their dues, but also in order to secure the rights and obligations of individual members of a village community. In most towns of the later Middle Ages there were regulations to secure fair prices, to maintain wages, to lay down standards of quality, and above all, to protect individual masters from competition. But, however necessary or commendable these objects may have been, they made technical improvement very difficult. For bye-laws were as a rule based on the technical methods in existence when they were framed; and once framed they were to stand in the way of all subsequent change.

What is more, so deeply ingrained was the spirit of protection that in every local trade the technical methods were treated as a secret. The medieval craft guild described itself as a 'mystery' and often was one. To take an example, the prosperity of the Bologna silk industry, famous all over Europe, was in its early stages due to many new processes and labour-saving devices. But it is characteristic of medieval technology that the machine for throwing silk which was invented in 1272 by Borghesano of Bologna (and was certainly employed in the Bolognese silk industry in the later Middle Ages) was not to be known outside Bologna until 1538, and was not effectively imitated until a traveling Englishman obtained its designs by ruse in the seventeenth century. Much of the specialized local skill of certain areas of medieval Europe was rooted in knowledge carefully guarded from outsiders. It is for that reason that industries with advanced techniques, e.g. mining or cloth finishing, seldom spread to new areas except by mass migration and resettlement of the men who practised them.

It is thus no wonder that knowledge painfully acquired in industrial practice so seldom percolated into the realm of science, while the scientific knowledge of the scholars so seldom influenced the industrial technique. Thus the main qualities of iron had been discovered and its resilience known at the very dawn of the Middle Ages and before, but we have no record of the leaf spring until the seventeenth century or of the spiral spring until the fifteenth. For several hundred years after the appearance in Europe of Arab numerals, and for at least a hundred and fifty years after the earlier western treatises explaining their use in computation, commercial and state accountancy still employed the awkward Roman numerals. On the other hand, for centuries after the pump, especially in its simpler syringe form, was employed in industry, the development of theoretical mechanics floundered in error through the failure to employ the concept of vacuum. None of the experience accumulated and utilized in the construction of appliances, mostly military, employing the pressure of water and air, or the expansion of heated air and steam, was capable of affecting the official theory of hydrostatics or of suggesting a theory of the expansion of gases or of atmospheric pressure. And although levers, both curved and straight, had been employed in construction since time immemorial, mechanics did not arrive at the concept of 'moment of force' until about the end of the thirteenth century. The practical knowledge of the medieval farmers and stockbreeders remained virtually without effect on biological theory, the experience of the dyers and the fullers remained without effect on the chemical theories. Medieval technology and medieval science each kept to their carefully circumscribed spheres.

Indeed, nothing exemplifies this general condition of technical stagnation better than the exceptions I have already mentioned. The great agricultural innovations of the early Middle Ages took place at the time when medieval population was still, so to speak, on the move, and when the medieval economic organization and its laws had not yet taken shape. Agricultural innovations of a later age, such as the Flemish and German of the twelfth and thirteenth centuries, were part and parcel of the colonization movement, i.e. were only possible because society was again on the move. The great technical discoveries in industrial occupations took place only when and where the industry happened to be beyond the reach of local authority. The technology of war was in the service of princes, and princes were not bound by the social aims or economic objectives of medieval guilds. The great technical changes in the English cloth industry in the fourteenth century were made possible only by the flight of industry from the towns to the villages over which the authority of municipalities did not extend. Above all, medieval building was in the hands of masons who were 'free', free in the sense that they were migratory labourers seldom subject to supervision and technical control by town governments.

In spheres more purely intellectual, the quickening of scientific activity in the late twelfth and thirteenth centuries, the so-called medieval renaissance, was also in some respects exceptional. It will be a mistake to put it down solely to the influx of translations. The translations, far from explaining the scientific activity, themselves require an explanation. For at least three hundred years the Arabs had been there with their versions of ancient philosophy, while the contacts with them were not necessarily closer in 1250 than they had been, say, in 850. Yet neither in the early centuries of the Middle Ages nor in its closing centuries was there a comparable flow of translations.

How are we then to account for the spate in the thirteenth century? Certainly not by the Italian trade in the Levant or by the Crusades. Few of the translations came from the Levant; hardly any were the work of Crusaders or of the Italian merchants or of anybody in their service. A cause more fundamental and more directly intellectual was obviously at work. For, unless I am mistaken, the intellectual climate in the middle centuries of the Middle Ages had changed. It is even possible that, for the time being, faith itself did not wholly absorb the interests of men. Mundane and secular preoccupations, both literary and philosophical, suddenly appeared amidst a culture still mainly religious. Within religion itself minority movements of every kind, including those of the early friars, disturbed more than ever before the uniformity of ideas. Disagreements appeared at the very centres of medieval learning, philosophical controversies seemed to shake the very foundations of dogma, and behind some of the milder manifestations of dissent lurked the possibilities of the profoundest scepticism and doubt. No wonder a Frenchman, Taine, described the whole period as an epoch tormented by doubt. And from the doubts of the thirteenth

century, as from similar doubts in later ages, there was bound to issue a current of intellectual curiosity, a willingness to re-open questions which hitherto appeared closed, and to seek answers from every source capable of giving them. Hence the revived interest in the philosophical and scientific doctrines of antiquity; hence the eagerness to learn from the Greeks and Arabs; hence also the translations.

In this way the very achievement of the late twelfth and thirteenth centuries merely underlines the verdict about the Middle Ages as a whole. The men of the Middle Ages were unable to do more than they did because they were lacking in scientific incentive. What they achieved in advancing the practical arts of humanity or in preserving and transmitting ancient learning, they did in so far and as long as they were not typically medieval.

Edwin Burtt: The Problem of the New Astronomy

In his introduction to the book from which this reading is taken, American philosopher Edwin A. Burtt (1892–   ) writes of the way in which modern men think about the world. "The cosmology underlying our mental processes is but three centuries old—a mere infant in the history of thought—and yet we cling to it with . . . zeal . . . take it piously to be ours and allow it . . . unhindered control over our thinking." What is true of us is even more relevant when applied to the ancient cosmology attacked by Copernicus. The reading

supplies evidence of why men were ready for the acceptance of a new view of the universe. From E. A. Burtt, *The Metaphysical Foundations of Modern Physical Science* (London: Routledge & Kegan Paul Ltd, 1932), pp. 23–25, 27–28, 37–40.

Why did Copernicus . . . in advance of any empirical confirmation of the new hypothesis that the earth is a planet revolving on its axis and circling round the sun, while the fixed stars remain at rest, believe it to be a true picture of the astronomical universe? This is historically the most convenient question with which to open our attack.

By way of preparing an answer to this question let us ask another, namely what ground a sane, representative thinker, contemporary to Copernicus, would have for rejecting this new hypothesis as a piece of rash and quite unjustified apriorism? We are so accustomed to think of the opposition to the great astronomer as being founded primarily on theological considerations (which was, of course, largely true at the time) that we are apt to forget the solid scientific objections that could have been, and were, urged against it.

First of all, there were no known celestial phenomena which were not accounted for by the Ptolemaic method with as great accuracy as could be expected without more modern instruments. Predictions of astronomical events were made which varied no more from the actual occurrence than did predictions made by a Copernican. And in astronomy, as elsewhere, possession is nine-tenths of the law. No sensible thinker would have abandoned a hoary, time-tested theory of the universe in favour of a new fangled scheme unless there were important advantages to be gained, and in this case there was distinctly no gain in accuracy. The motions of the heavenly bodies could be charted according to Ptolemy just as correctly as according to Copernicus.

In the second place, the testimony of the senses appeared to be perfectly plain on the matter. It was before the days when one could actually see by the aid of a telescope the spots on the sun, the phases of Venus, the rough surface of the moon—could discover, in a word, fairly convincing proof that these bodies were made of essentially the same material as the earth, and could determine how vast their actual distances were. To the senses it must have appeared incontestable that the earth was a solid, immovable substance, while the light ether and the bits of starry flame at its not too distant limit floated easily around it day by day. The earth is to the senses the massive, stable thing; the heavens are by comparison, as revealed in every passing breeze and every flickering fire, the tenuous, the unresisting, the mobile thing.

In the third place, there had been built up on the basis of this supposedly unshakeable testimony of the senses a natural philosophy of the universe which furnished a fairly complete and satisfactory background for man's thinking. The four elements of earth, water, air, fire, in their ascending scale not only as to actual spatial relations, but also in dignity and value, were the categories in which men's thinking about the inanimate realm had become accustomed to proceed. There was necessarily involved in this mode of thinking the assumption that the heavenly bodies were more noble in quality and more mobile in fact than the earth, and when these prepossessions were added to the other fundamentals of the Aristotelian metaphysics, which brought this astronomical conception into general harmony with the totality of human experience to date, the suggestion of a widely different theory in astronomy would inevitably appear in the light of a contradiction of every important item of knowledge man had gained about his world. . . .

The new astronomy involved . . . the assertion that the correct point of reference in astronomy was not the earth, as had been taken for granted hitherto by all but a handful of ancient speculators, but the fixed stars and the sun. That such a tremendous shift in the point of reference could be legitimate was a suggestion quite beyond the grasp of people trained for centuries to think in terms of a homocentric philosophy and a geocentric physics. No one whatsoever could be expected even to entertain such a notion a hundred years prior to Copernicus, save an occasional astronomer skilled in the lore of his science and able to realize that at least there was some recompense in the form of greater simplicity for considering the possibilities of a solar-centric system. But certain things had happened during these hundred years that made it not quite so impossible to persuade people who could appreciate the advantages of a new point of reference to give it some scope in their minds. The Renaissance had happened, namely the shifting of man's centre of interest in literature from the present to the golden age of antiquity. The Commerical Revolution had begun, with its long voyages and exciting discoveries of previously unknown continents and unstudied civilizations; the business leaders of Europe and the champions of colonialism were turning their attention from petty local fairs to the great untapped centres of trade in Asia and the Americas. The realm of man's previous ac-quaintance seemed suddenly small and meagre; men's thoughts were becoming accustomed to a widening horizon. The earth was circumnavigated, which proved in more popular fashion its rotundity. The antipodes were found to be quite inhabited. It seemed a possible corollary that the centre of importance in the universe was perhaps not even in Europe. Further, the unprecedented religious upheaval of the times had contributed powerfully to loosen men's thinking. Rome had been taken for granted as the religious centre of the world for well over a thousand years; now there appeared a number of distinct centres of religious life besides Rome. The rise of vernacular literatures and the appearance of distinctly national tendencies in art added their bit to the same unsettlement; there was a renouncement, in all these respects, of man's former centres of interest and a fixation on something new. In this ferment of strange and radical ideas, widely disseminated by the recent invention of printing, it was not so difficult for Copernicus to consider seriously for himself and suggest persuasively to others that a still greater shift than any of these must now be made, a shift of the centre of reference in astronomy from the earth to the sun. . . .

The particular event which led Copernicus to consider a new point of reference in astronomy was his discovery that the ancients had disagreed about the matter. Ptolemy's system had not been the only theory advanced.

When, therefore, I had long considered this uncertainty of traditional mathematics, it began to weary me that no more definite explanation of the movement of the world-machine established in our behalf by the best and most systematic builder of all, existed among the philosophers who had studied so exactly in other respects the minutest details in regard to the sphere. Wherefore I took upon myself the task of rereading the books of all the philosophers which I could obtain, to seek out whether anyone had ever conjectured that the motions of the spheres of the universe were other than they supposed who taught mathematics in the schools. And I found first, that, according to Cicero, Nicetas had thought the earth was moved. Then later I discovered, according to Plutarch, that certain others had held the same opinion. . . .

Likewise in the brief *Commentariolus,* written about 1530, after describing his dissatisfaction with the ancient astronomers for their inability to get a consistent geometry of the heavens that should not violate the postulate of uniform velocity, he proceeds:

Hence this kind of theory did not seem sufficiently certain, nor sufficiently in accord with reason. So when I had noted these things, I often considered if perchance a more rational system of circles might be discovered, on which all the apparent diversity might depend,

and in such a manner that each of the planets would be uniformly moved, as the principle of absolute motion requires. Attacking a problem obviously difficult and almost inexplicable, at length I hit upon a solution whereby this could be reached by fewer and much more convenient constructions than had been handed down of old, if certain assumptions, which are called axioms, be granted me. . . .

Accorded then these premises, I shall attempt to show briefly how simply the uniformity of motion can be saved. . . .

These passages show clearly that to Copernicus' mind the question was not one of truth or falsity, not, does the earth move? He simply included the earth in the question which Ptolemy had asked with reference to the celestial bodies alone; what motions should we attribute to the earth in order to obtain the simplest and most harmonious geometry of the heavens that will accord with the facts? That Copernicus was able to put the question in this form is ample proof of the continuity of his thought with the mathematical developments just recounted, and this is why he constantly appealed to mathematicians as those alone able to judge the new theory fairly. He was quite confident that they, at least, would appreciate and accept his view. . . .

But now, of course, the question which Copernicus has thus easily answered carries with it a tremendous metaphysical assumption. Nor were people slow to see it and bring it to the forefront of discussion. *Is it legitimate to take any other point of reference in astronomy than the earth?* Mathematicians who were themselves subject to all the influences working in Copernicus' mind, would, so he hoped, be apt to say yes. But of course the whole Aristotelian and empirical philosophy of the age rose up and said no. For the question went pretty deep, it meant not only, is the astronomical realm fundamentally geometrical, which almost any one would grant, *but is the universe as a whole, including our earth, fundamentally mathematical in its structure?* Just because this shift of the point of reference gives a simpler geometrical expression for the facts, is it legitimate to make it? To admit this point is to overthrow the whole Aristotelian physics and cosmology. Even many mathematicians and astronomers might not be willing to follow the tendencies of their science to this extreme; the current of their general thinking flowed on another bed. To follow Ptolemy in ancient times meant merely to reject the cumbrous crystalline spheres. To follow Copernicus was a far more radical step, it meant to reject the whole prevailing conception of the universe. . . .

STUDY QUESTIONS

1. What was the subject of Copernicus' book? What reasons did he give for writing it? Why did he wait thirty years before publishing the book and then dedicate it to the pope?

2. What did early man contribute to the advance of science? What was the Greek contribution?

3. What was the weakness of Greek science? What caused the decline of science and its revival in the late Middle Ages?

4. What was the medieval view of the universe? How did Copernicus' thesis differ? Does one of these views make more sense to you than the other?

5. Do you agree with Postan's answer to the questions he raises in Reading 213? Are deep religious convictions unfavorable to scientific incentive?

6. Why, according to Burtt, was it possible to persuade sixteenth-century men to accept a shift of the center of reference in astronomy from the earth to the sun?

The Founders of Modern Science

Reprinted from *A Short History of Science and Scientific Thought* by F. Sherwood Taylor. By permission of W. W. Norton & Company, Inc. Copyright 1949 by W. W. Norton & Company, Inc. This is published in Canada by Heinemann Educational Books Ltd.

TOPIC 11

METHODS AND GOALS OF EARLY MODERN SCIENCE

The sixteenth and seventeenth centuries posed a sharp challenge to medieval beliefs through the phenomenon known as the scientific revolution. The following readings seek to explain why this revolution occurred and how it developed in its early stages. The readings focus particularly on the scientific achievements of Galileo Galilei and the predicament in which he found himself.

SCIENCE REVIVES

Science has had its periods of advance and regress, yet since the middle of the fifteenth century it has been in continuous advance. There have been, it is true, some false trails and blind alleys, but work has never slackened nor interest declined. The Middle Ages were not so barren of scientific achievement as is generally thought, yet it is obvious that between 1450 and 1500, there was a rapid intensification of scientific interest. The scholastic philosophy had shown the men of the Middle Ages the world under the guise of purpose, but had done very little to describe it in terms of number, weight and measure. The desire for more knowledge of the world came from three chief sources: first, a new study of the learning of Greece; secondly, a growing dissatisfaction with the inaccuracy and small extent of man's knowledge of the world; lastly, from the growing interest which attached to industry, as its products became socially more important. . . .

ASTRONOMY— THE COPERNICAN THEORY

Nicholas Copernicus made it his life's work to put forward and support the view, which he had derived from certain of the Greeks, that—

1. the sun and stars were motionless at the centre and circumference of the universe respectively,
2. that the earth rotated on its axis in 24 hours,
3. that the earth and the planets revolved about the sun, while the moon revolved about the earth. . . .

His great book *On the Revolution of the Celestial Spheres* was published in 1543. It excited much interest, but there adhered to his views only a small proportion of astronomers, and scarcely any of the general learned public. Copernicus had presented an attractive hypothesis but had given very little evidence in its favour. Such evidence was provided by Kepler and Galileo in the opening years of the next century; and it was only then that most of the learned world was convinced of the truth of the Copernican theory.

Copernicus was followed by a great observer, Tycho Brahe (1546–1601), who built a magnificent observatory and installed the first large and accurately constructed instruments. . . . He did not agree with the views of Copernicus but suggested that the earth was stationary, that the sun revolved about it, while the other planets revolved about the sun. His system found little favour, but his observations provided a basis of accurate measurements which enabled Kepler to discover the simple and beautiful laws that express the planetary motions. In these astronomers of the fifteenth and sixteenth centuries we see three of the characteristics of true scientists:

1. they *observe for themselves,* seeking ever higher accuracy:
2. they *abandon preconceptions* about the nature of the universe:
3. they keep accurate records of their work and publish them to all.

THE BIOLOGICAL SCIENCES— ANDREAS VESALIUS

The only sciences which in this period made progress at all comparable with astronomy are the biological, especially human anatomy. Rather perfunctory anatomical demonstrations had continued throughout the Middle Ages, but in the early sixteenth century a few men began to observe exactly and draw accurately. Several artists of the fifteenth and sixteenth centuries made dissections in order to study artistic anatomy. Leonardo da Vinci, artist and scientist, dissected some thirty bodies and left note-books containing wonderful anatomical drawings; but as these were not published they had no general effect. The influential anatomist was Andreas Vesalius, who in 1543 published his chief work, "De Fabrica Humani in Corporis", *On the Fabric of the Human Body.* This is a completely new departure. The tone is that of modern science: change but a few terms and long passages could appear without strangeness in a modern scientific journal. He is not concerned to *prove* any general theories, simply to find out and record the structure of the body. He even carries out physiological experiments. . . . The illustrations are superb, and indeed the noble wood-cuts and engravings of the sixteenth century were a great contribution to scientific record. Vesalius and other great anatomists of the time cleared up and recorded the main points of gross anatomy that could be seen with the

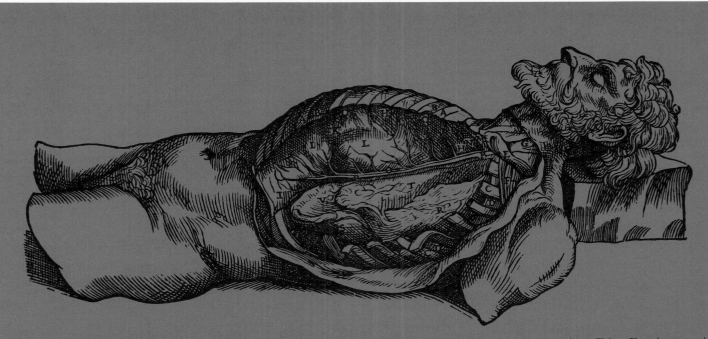

This is a plate from *De Fabrica,* the woodblock for which was made in the workshop of the famous Renaissance painter Titian. The plate reveals the great importance assigned to careful observation and detailed description of the body's structure.

naked eye; for there were as yet no micro-scopes, by which the fine structures could be elucidated. . . .

SCIENCE IN THE
SIXTEENTH CENTURY

Summing up the century and a half from 1450 to 1600, we see practical improvements and expansion of knowledge in almost every science. But there is little attempt to assess the value of evidence or to put knowledge into system and order, and theory—except in astronomy—lags vastly behind fact. The ancients were no longer considered as reliable authorities, yet nobody laid down what was to be believed as scientific fact and what was not; nor did anyone propose any *method* of going about scientific problems. Credulity remained gigantic. All sorts of magical sympathies and antipathies still ranked among natural laws: the most unlikely travellers' tales and traditional lore still gained credence; and it was common enough to find men who practised or at least treated of magic and science together: Paracelsus, Dr. John Dee and Baptista della Porta afford us examples. Science needed to sort out its valuables and set them in order—and this was one of the many achievements of the seventeenth century.

THE SEVENTEENTH CENTURY:
THE EXPERIMENTAL METHOD

The first requirement of natural science is the harvesting of reliable facts. We have seen that in the fifteenth and sixteenth centuries the astronomers endeavoured to make more and more accurate observations; the biologists and anatomists began to see for themselves, and very occasionally men of the calibre of Andreas Vesalius began to do things

in order to see what would happen. This last step takes us from the realm of *observation*—natural history—into that of *experimental science*. . . .

Galileo Galilei (1564–1642) was the first to employ the modern scientific method in its fullness. His work was in two fields, physics and astronomy. Galileo was an enthusiastic and versatile man, skillful with his hands, a fine writer and an able mathematician. His main achievement in physics was the founding of the science of mechanics. Aristotle's ideas on motion had been occasionally questioned, but still reigned supreme. A 2 lb. weight, other things being equal, was believed to fall twice as fast as a 1 lb. weight. Bodies of a given weight falling through a given medium were supposed to have a fixed and more or less constant speed which was supposed to be inversely proportional to the resistance of that medium; but how that resistance was to be defined did not appear. Nobody had tried to measure the velocities of such bodies, let alone the forces that impelled them. Such terms as motion, force, movement were used almost interchangeably.

In setting up a science of mechanics, Galileo had first to confute the Aristotelean views. In the year 1586 Simon Stevin had published (in Dutch) an experiment which confuted Aristotle's notion that the speed of falling bodies was proportional to their weight, but his work was little known. Galileo did many similar experiments, though he does not record the exact circumstances:* but the

*The story of his experiment of dropping weights from the Leaning Tower of Pisa may be true, but rests on slender evidence. There is no doubt, however, that he frequently dropped different weights from various eminences and observed that they struck the ground almost simultaneously.

great advance he made was to put forward a theory that bodies fell with an accelerated motion which could be expressed by a mathematical formula. There were as yet no devices suitable for timing falling bodies, so he tried out his theory on bodies rolling on an inclined plane: this is one of the earliest examples of a quantitative experiment, carefully checked and controlled. Moreover, he saw that a smooth ball rolling on a smooth rising slope must slow down, and on a descending slope must speed up: this led him to the very important conclusion that a body in uniform motion on a flat level surface without friction, would so continue until some agency caused it to stop, whereas physicists had formerly considered with Aristotle, that some agency must continually act on a body in order to keep it in motion. Later in his life he combined these conclusions; he saw that a projectile, e.g. a cannon-ball fired over a cliff must continue to move horizontally at a uniform pace, and must also fall with an acceleration. He then calculated mathematically that the path of a body which moved with these simultaneous motions was a parabola. . . . Here is a man of science experimenting, deducing laws, and building on these again. . . .

Galileo and the Telescope

Galileo Galilei (1564–1642) was one of the most important early supporters of the Copernican theory. Galileo was born in Pisa, Italy. His father wanted him to study medicine, but he turned instead to mathematics and became a teacher at the University of Pisa in his early twenties. Later, he was professor of mathematics at the nearby University of Padua for many years. Galileo was a keen observer of the world around him. It is said that he discovered the law of the pendulum by noticing a heavy lamp swinging back and forth on a chain attached to the ceiling of the cathedral at Pisa. The conclusions he drew from his discoveries with the telescope got him into difficulties with the Roman Church. His writings were placed on the Index of Prohibited Books which Roman Catholics were not permitted to read and he was forced in 1633 to deny publicly that the earth moved around the sun. His last years were spent in semi-imprisonment. Reprinted by permission of the publishers from Harlow Shapley and Helen E. Howarth, eds., *A Source Book in Astronomy*, Cambridge, Mass.: Harvard University Press, Copyright 1929 by McGraw-Hill Book Company, Inc.; 1957 by Harlow Shapley and Helen Howarth Lewis. pp. 41–46.

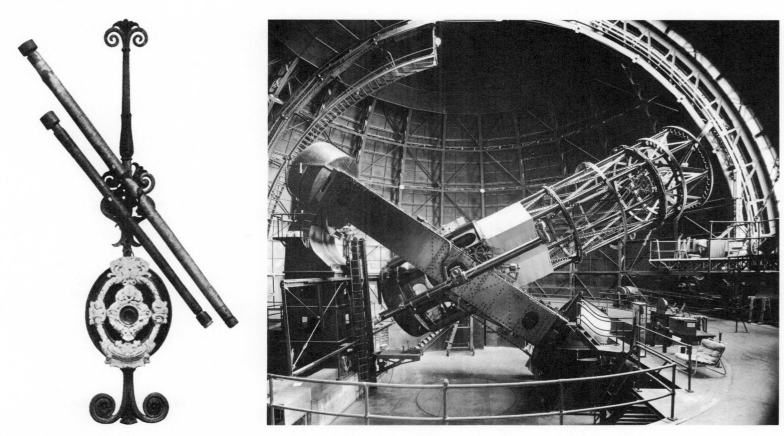

Two of Galileo's simple telescopes preserved in the Tribuna di Galileo in Florence contrast sharply with the complex instruments of today. The modern telescope with its 100-inch mirror is at the Hale Observatories on Mount Wilson in California.

I

In the present small treatise I set forth some matters of great interest for all observers of natural phenomena to look at and consider. They are of great interest, I think, first, from their intrinsic excellence; secondly, from their absolute novelty; and lastly, also on account of the instrument by the aid of which they have been presented to my apprehension.

The number of fixed Stars which observers have been able to see without artificial powers of sight up to this day can be counted. It is therefore decidedly a great feat to add to their number, and to set distinctly before the eyes other stars in myriads, which have never been seen before, and which surpass the old, previously known, stars in number more than ten times.

Again, it is a more beautiful and delightful sight to behold the body of the Moon, which is distant from nearly sixty semidiameters of the Earth, as near as it was at a distance of only two of the same measures; so that the diameter of this same Moon appears about thirty times, and its solid mass nearly 27,000 times larger than when it is viewed only with the naked eye: and consequently any one may know with certainty that is due to the use of our senses, that the Moon certainly does not possess a smooth and polished surface, but one rough and uneven, and, just like the face of the Earth itself, is everywhere full of vast protuberances, deep chasms, and sinuosities.

Then to have got rid of disputes about the Galaxy or Milky Way, and to have made its nature clear to the very senses, not to say to the understanding, seems by no means a matter which ought to be considered of slight importance. In addition to this, to point out, as with one's finger, the nature of those stars which every one of the astronomers up to this time has called *nebulous,* and to demonstrate that it is very different from what has hitherto been believed, will be pleasant, and very fine. But that which will excite the greatest astonishment by far, and which indeed especially moved me to call to the attention of all astronomers and philosophers; is this, namely, that I have discovered four planets, neither known nor observed by any one of the astronomers before my time, which have their orbits round a certain bright star, one of those previously known, like Venus and Mercury around the Sun, and are sometimes in front of it, sometimes behind it, though they never depart from it beyond certain limits. All which facts were discovered and observed a few days ago by the help of a telescope devised by me, through God's grace first enlightening my mind.

Perchance, other discoveries still more excellent will be made from time to time by me or by other observers, with the assistance of a similar instrument, so I will first briefly record its shape and preparation, as well as the occasion of its being devised, and then I will give an account of the observations made by me.

About ten months ago a report reached my ears that a Dutchman had constructed a telescope, by the aid of which visible objects, although at a great distance from the eye of the observer, were seen distinctly as if near; and some proofs of its most wonderful performances were reported, which some gave credence to, but others contradicted. A few days after, I received confirmation of the report in a letter written from Paris by a noble Frenchman, Jacques Badovere, which finally determined me to give myself up first to inquire into the principle of the telescope, and then to consider the means by which I might compass the invention of a similar instrument, which after a little while I succeeded in doing, through deep study of the theory of Refraction and I prepared a tube, at first of lead, in the ends of which I fitted two glass lenses, both plane on one side, but on the other side one spherically convex, and the other concave. Then bringing my eye to the concave lens I saw objects satisfactorily large and near, for they appeared one-third of the distance off and nine times larger than when they are seen with the natural eye alone. I shortly afterwards constructed another telescope with more nicety, which magnified objects more than sixty times. At length, by sparing neither labour nor expense, I succeeded in constructing for myself an instrument so superior that objects seen through it appear magnified nearly a thousand times, and more than thirty times nearer than if viewed by the natural powers of sight alone.

It would be altogether a waste of time to. enumerate the number and importance of the benefits which this instrument may be expected to confer, when used by land or sea. But without paying attention to its use for terrestrial objects, I betook myself to observations of the heavenly bodies; and first of all, I viewed the Moon as near as if it was scarcely two semi-diameters of the Earth distant. After the Moon, I frequently observed other heavenly bodies, both fixed stars and planets, with incredible delight. . . .

II

Discovery of Jupiter's Satellites

There remains the matter, which seems to me to deserve to be considered the most important in this work, namely, that I should disclose and publish to the world the occasion of discovering and observing four planets never seen from the very beginning of the world up to our own times, their positions, and the observations made during the last two months about their movements and their changes of magnitude. . . .

On the 7th day of January in the present year, 1610, in the first hour of the following night, when I was viewing the constellations of the heavens through a telescope, the planet Jupiter presented itself to my view, and as I had prepared for myself a very excellent instrument, I noticed a circumstance which I had never been able to notice before, owing to want of power in my other telescope, namely, that three little stars, small but very bright, were near the planet; and although I believed them to belong to the number of the fixed stars, yet they made me somewhat wonder, because they seemed to be arranged exactly in a straight line, parallel to the ecliptic, and to be brighter than the rest of the stars, equal to them in magnitude. The position of them with reference to one another and to Jupiter was as follows:

On the east side there were two stars, and a single one towards the west. The star which was farthest towards the east, and the western star, appeared rather larger than the third.

I scarcely troubled at all about the distance between them and Jupiter, for, as I have already said, at first I believed them to be fixed stars; but when on January 8th, led by some fatality, I turned again to look at the same part of the heavens, I found a very different state of things, for there were three little stars all west of Jupiter, and nearer together than on the previous night, and they were separated from one another by equal intervals, as the accompanying figure shows.

At this point, although I had not turned my thoughts at all upon the approximation of the stars to one another, yet my surprise began to be excited, how Jupiter could one day be found to the east of all the aforesaid fixed stars when the day before it had been west of two of them; and forthwith I became afraid lest the planet might have moved differently from the calculation of astronomers, and so had passed those stars by its own proper motion. I, therefore, waited for the next night with the most intense longing, but I was disappointed of my hope, for the sky was covered with clouds in every direction.

But on January 10th the stars appeared in the following position with regard to Jupiter, the third, as I thought being hidden by the planet. They were situated as before, exactly in the same straight line with Jupiter, and along the Zodiac.

When I had seen these phenomena, as I knew that corresponding changes of position could not by any means belong to Jupiter, and as, moreover, I perceived that the stars which I saw had always been the same, for there were no others either in front or behind, within a great distance, along the Zodiac—at length, changing from doubt into surprise, I discovered that the interchange of positions which I saw belonged not to Jupiter, but to the stars to which my attention had been drawn, and I thought therefore that they ought to be observed henceforward with more attention and precision.

Accordingly, on January 11th I saw an arrangement of the following kind:

namely, only two stars to the east of Jupiter, the nearer of which was distant from Jupiter three times as far as from the star further to the east; and the star furthest to the east was nearly twice as large as the other one; whereas on the previous night they had appeared nearly of equal magnitude. I, therefore, concluded, and decided unhesitatingly, that there are three stars in the heavens moving about Jupiter, as Venus and Mercury around the Sun; which at length was established as clear as daylight by numerous other subsequent observations. These observations also established that there are not only three, but four, erratic sidereal bodies performing their revolutions round Jupiter. . . .

These are my observations upon the four Medicean planets, recently discovered for the first time by me; and although it is not yet permitted me to deduce by calculation from these observations the orbits of these bodies, yet I may be allowed to make some statements, based upon them, well worthy of attention. . . .

An Exchange of Correspondence between Kepler and Galileo (1610)

The publication of *The Starry Messenger* made Galileo's methods the center of heated controversy. Many scientists, like the famous Johannes Kepler (1571–1630) of Germany, quickly recognized the tremendous possibilities of his discoveries; others, chiefly the college professors who taught Aristotelian theory, saw their view of the world threatened and ridiculed his efforts. Both positions are illuminated in the following excerpts from an exchange of correspondence between Kepler and Galileo in 1610. From Carola Baumgardt, *Johannes Kepler: His Life and Letters* (New York: The Philosophical Library, 1951), pp. 84–86. Reprinted by permission.

KEPLER TO GALILEO, AUGUST 9, 1610

I have received your observations on the Medicean stars from the Ambassador of his Highness the Grand Duke of Tuscany. You have aroused in me a passionate desire to see your instruments, so that at last, I, like you, might enjoy the great performance in the sky. Of the [telescopes] which we have here the best has a tenfold enlargement, the others hardly a threefold; the only one which I have gives a twenty-fold enlargement, but the light is very weak. . . .

You, my Galileo, have opened the holy of the holiest of the skies. What else can you do but despise the noise which has been created. . . . The crown takes vengeance on itself by remaining in eternal ignorance in consequence of its contempt for philosophy [science]. . . .

GALILEO TO KEPLER, AUGUST 19, 1610

What is to be done now? Shall we follow Democritus or Heraclitus? [i.e., laugh or cry; Democritus was said to be the laughing philosopher and Heraclitus the weeping one.] We will laugh at the extraordinary stupidity of the crowd, my Kepler. What do you say to the main philosophers of our school, who, with the stubbornness of vipers, never wanted to see the planets, the moon, or the telescope although I offered a thousand times to show them the planets and the moon. Really, as some have shut their ears, these have shut their eyes toward the light of truth. This is an awful thing, but it does not astonish me. This sort of person thinks that philosophy [science] is a book like the Aeneid or Odyssey and that one has not to search for truth in the world of nature, but in the comparisons of texts (to use their own words). . . .

Galileo Refutes Aristotle

(1632)

The Aristotelian professors and conservative church officials who feared the consequences of Galileo's discoveries managed to have the Copernican Theory declared "false and erroneous" and Copernicus' book banned in 1616. After this, Galileo spent his time in private study for many years. In 1632, however, he published the *Dialogue on the Two Chief World Systems* in which a neutral friend (Sagredus) listens to the points of view of an Aristotelian (Simplicius) and a Copernican (Salviatus). Galileo ended the *Dialogue* with the statement that God, being omnipotent, could create any kind of world and the way it worked need not be understandable to mortal men. It was clear, however, where Galileo's sympathies lay. From Galileo Galilei, *Dialogue on the Great World Systems in the Salusbury Translation* (Chicago: University of Chicago Press, 1953), pp. 56, 137, 238, 335, 340. Copyright 1953 by the University of Chicago.

[Sagredus] Resolve, Simplicius, to produce all the detailed reasons, experiments, and observations, natural as well as astronomical, that may serve to persuade us that the Earth differs from the celestial bodies in that it is immovable, and situated in the centre of the universe, and, whatever else, is prevented from moving like the rest of the planets, say, Jupiter or the Moon. And let Salviatus be pleased to answer to them one by one. . . .

The dedication page of Galileo's *Dialogue* has Aristotle (left) exchanging views with Copernicus (right) and Ptolemy (center) in this edition of 1632.

[Simplicius] I, for my part, have not made either such long or such exact observations as to enable me to boast myself master of the *quod est* of this matter; but I will . . . observe for my own satisfaction whether I can reconcile that which experience shows us with what Aristotle teaches us; for it is a certain maxim that two truths cannot be contrary to one another. . . .

[Salviatus] We may discourse of celestial matters much better than Aristotle; because he confesses their knowledge to be difficult to him by reason of their remoteness from the senses; he thereby acknowledges that one to whom the senses can better represent them may philosophize upon them with more certainty. Now we, by help of the telescope, are brought thirty or forty times nearer to the heavens than Aristotle ever came; so that we may discover in them a hundred things which he could not see, and, among the rest, these spots in the Sun, which were to him absolutely invisible; therefore, we may discourse of the heavens and the Sun with more certainty than Aristotle.

[Simplicius] . . . The Copernican hypothesis would make great confusion and perturbation in the system of the Universe and among its parts. . . .

[Salviatus] It is true that the Copernican system introduces distraction in the Universe of Aristotle, but we are speaking of our Universe, the true and real one.

[Simplicius] . . . From whence do you argue that not the Earth but the Sun is in the centre of the planetary revolutions?

[Salviatus] I infer the same from most evident and therefore necessarily conclusive observations, of which the most potent to exclude the earth from the said centre, and to place the Sun therein, are that we see all the planets sometimes nearer and sometimes farther off from the Earth, with so great differences, that, for example, Venus when it is at the farthest is six times more remote from us than when it is nearest, and Mars rises almost eight times as high at one time as at another. See therefore whether Aristotle was not somewhat mistaken in thinking that it was at all times equidistant from us. . . .

It remains now for us to remove that which seemed a great inconvenience in the motion of the Earth, namely, that, while all the planets move about the Sun, it alone should move round the Sun not solitary, as the rest, but in company with the Moon . . . and that the Moon withal should move every month about the Earth. Here it is necessary once again to exclaim and extol the admirable perspicacity of Copernicus and withal to lament his misfortune in that he is not now alive in our days, when, for removing the seeming absurdity of the Earth and Moon's motion in consort, we see Jupiter, as if it were another Earth, not in consort with the Moon but accompanied by four moons, revolve about the Sun in twelve years together. . . .

The Trial of Galileo (1633)

Galileo had published his *Dialogue* in the vain belief that it was acceptable to the Pope. Instead he was accused of circumventing the ban against teaching the Copernican Theory which had been issued in 1616 and was summoned for trial for heresy before the Inquisition in 1633. Condemned to perpetual house arrest, Galileo spent the last nine years of his life on his farm outside Florence. Legend has it that, having made his forced recantation, he still muttered under his breath in the presence of his persecutors, "And yet it does move." The story typifies the spirit of the scientific revolution. From Giorgio de Santillana, *The Crime of Galileo,* (Chicago: University of Chicago Press, 1955), pp. 306–308, 310, 312. Copyright 1955 by the University of Chicago. Published 1955.

A. THE SENTENCE

Whereas you, Galileo, son of the late Vincenzo Galilei, Florentine, aged seventy years, were in the year 1615 denounced to this Holy Office for holding as true the false doctrine taught by some that the Sun is the center of the world and immovable and that the Earth moves, and also with a diurnal motion; for having disciples to whom you taught the same doctrine; for holding correspondence with certain mathematicians of Germany concerning the same; for having printed certain letters, entitled "On the Sunspots," wherein you developed the same doctrine as true; and for replying to the objections from the Holy Scriptures, which from time to time were urged against it, by glossing the said Scriptures according to your own meaning: and whereas there was thereupon produced the copy of a document in the form of a letter, purporting to be written by you to one formerly your disciple, and in this divers propositions are set forth, following the position of Copernicus, which are contrary to the true sense and authority of Holy Scripture. . . .

And whereas a book appeared here recently, printed last year at Florence, the title of which shows that you were the author, this title being: "Dialogue of Galileo Galilei on the Great World Systems"; and whereas the Holy Congregation was afterward informed that through the publication of the said book the false opinion of the motion of the Earth and the stability of the Sun was daily gaining ground, the said book was taken into careful consideration, and in it there was discovered a patent violation of the . . . injunction that had been imposed upon you, for in this book you have defended the said opinion previously condemned and to your face declared to be so, although in the said book you strive by various devices to produce the impression that you leave it undecided and in express terms as probable: which, however, is a most grievous error, as an opinion can in no wise be probable which has been declared and defined to be contrary to divine Scripture. . . .

We say, pronounce, sentence, and declare that you, the said Galileo, by reason of the matters adduced in trial, and by you confessed as above, have rendered yourself in the judgment of this Holy Office vehemently suspected of heresy, namely, of having believed and held the doctrine—which is false and contrary to the sacred and divine Scripture—that the Sun is the center of the world and does not move from east to west and that the Earth moves and is not the center of the world; and that an opinion may be held and defended as probable after it has been declared and defined to be contrary to the Holy Scriptures; and that consequently you have incurred all the censures and penalties imposed and promulgated in the sacred canons and other constitutions, general and particular, against such delinquents. From which we are content that you be absolved, provided that, first, with a sincere heart and unfeigned faith, you abjure, curse and detest before us the aforesaid errors and heresies and every other error and heresy contrary to the Catholic and Apostolic Roman Church in the form to be prescribed by us for you.

And, in order that this your grave and pernicious error and transgression may not remain altogether unpunished and that you may be more cautious in the future and an example to others that they may abstain from similar delinquencies, we ordain that the book of the "Dialogue of Galileo Galilei" be prohibited by public edict.

We condemn you to the formal prison of this Holy Office during our pleasure, and by way of salutary penance we enjoin that for three years to come you repeat once a week the seven penitential Psalms. . . .

B. THE RECANTATION

I, Galileo, desiring to remove from the minds of your Eminences, and of all faithful Christians, this vehement suspicion justly conceived against me, with sincere heart and unfeigned faith I abjure, curse and detest the aforesaid errors and heresies and generally every other error, heresy, and sect whatsoever contrary to the Holy Church, and I swear that in future I will never again say or assert, verbally or in writing anything that might furnish occasion for a similar suspicion regarding me; but, should I know any heretic or person suspected of heresy, I will denounce him to this Holy Office or to the Inquisitor or Ordinary of the place where I may be. Furthermore, I swear and promise to fulfil and observe in their integrity all penances that have been, or that shall be, imposed upon me by this Holy Office. And, in the event of my contravening (which God forbid!) any of these promises and oaths, I submit myself to all the pains and penalties imposed and promulgated in the sacred canons and other constitutions, general and particular, against such delinquents. So help me God and these His Holy Gospels which I touch with my hands.

William Harvey Discovers How Blood Circulates (1628)

William Harvey (1578–1657) was an English doctor who studied medicine at the University of Padua while Galileo was teaching there. At twenty-six he became a member of the Royal College of Physicians, numbering among his patients Francis Bacon and King James I. Later, he became royal physician to King Charles I whose cause he supported loyally during the English Civil Wars. Harvey was a brilliant lecturer and surgeon, and his classes, in which he dissected animals and gave practical demonstrations on anatomy, were extremely popular. Harvey was a short, dark man with a violent temper who liked to argue and who wore a dagger which he frequently waved in the noses of those who disagreed with him. He was totally involved in his work: there is a fine description of him during a battle in the middle of the Civil Wars—"he withdrew under a hedge and took out of his pocket a book and read." From William Harvey, *An Anatomical Disquisition on the Motion of the Heart and Blood in Animals,* trans. Robert Willis (London, 1847).

I

To His Very Dear Friend, Doctor Argent, the Excellent and Accomplished President of the Royal College of Physicians, and to Other Learned Physicians, His Most Esteemed Colleagues.

I have already and repeatedly presented you, my learned friends, with my new views of the motion and function of the heart, in my anatomical lectures; but having now for nine years and more confirmed these views by multiplied demonstrations in your presence, illustrated them by arguments, and freed them from the objections of the most learned and skillful anatomists, I at length yield to the requests, I might say entreaties, of many, and here present them for general consideration in this treatise. . . .

My dear colleagues, I had no purpose to swell this treatise into a large volume by quoting the names and writings of anatomists, or to make a parade of the strength of my memory, the extent of my reading, and the amount of my pains; because I profess both to learn and to teach anatomy, not from books but from dissections; not from the positions of philosophers but from the fabric of nature. . . .

Chapter 2. Of the Motions of the Heart, as Seen in the Dissection of Living Animals

In the first place, then, when the chest of a living animal is laid open and the capsule that immediately surrounds the heart is slit up or removed, the organ is seen now to move, now to be at rest; there is a time when it moves, and a time when it is motionless.

These things are more obvious in the colder animals, such as toads, frogs, serpents, small fishes, crabs, shrimps, snails and shell-fish. They also become more distinct in warm-blooded animals, such as the dog and hog, if they be attentively noted when the heart begins to flag, to move more slowly, and, as it were, to die; the movements then become slower and rarer, the pauses longer, by which it is made much more easy to perceive and unravel what the motions really are, and how they are performed. In the pause, as in death, the heart is soft, flaccid, exhausted, lying, as it were, at rest. . . .

Chapter 5. Of the Motion, Action, and Office of the Heart

From these and other observations of the like kind, I am persuaded it will be found that the motion of the heart is as follows:

First of all, the auricle contracts, and in the course of its contraction throws the blood (which it contains in ample quantity as the head of the veins, the storehouse and cistern of the blood) into the ventricle, which being filled, the heart raises itself straightway, makes all its fibres tense, contracts the ventricles, and performs a beat, by which beat it immediately sends the blood supplied to it by the auricle into the arteries; the right ventricle sending its charge into the lungs by the vessel which is called the vena arteriosa, but which, in structure and function, and all things else, is an artery; the left ventricle sending its charge into the aorta, and through this by the arteries to the body at large.

These two motions, one of the ventricles, another of the auricles, take place consecutively, but in such a manner that there is a kind of harmony or rhythm preserved between them, the two concurring in such wise that but one motion is apparent especially in the warmer blooded animals, in which the movements of the left ventricle into the arteries was distributed to the body at large, and its several parts, in the same manner as it is sent through the lungs, impelled by the right ventricle into the pulmonary artery, and that it then passed through the veins and along the vena cava, and so round to the left ventricle in the manner already indicated. . . .

Nor is this for any reason other than it is in a piece of machinery, in which though one wheel gives motion to another, yet all the wheels seem to move simultaneously; or in that mechanical contrivance which is adapted to firearms, where the trigger being touched, down comes the flint, strikes against the steel, elicits a spark, which falling among the powder, it is ignited, upon which the flame extends, enters the barrel, causes the explosion, propels the ball, and the mark is attained—all of which incidents, by reason of the celerity with which they happen, seem to take place in the twinkling of an eye. . . .

■

Chapter 8. Of the Quantity of Blood Passing through the Heart from the Veins to the Arteries: and of the Circular Motion of the Blood

Thus far I have spoken of the passage of the blood from the veins into the arteries, and of the manner in which it is transmitted and distributed by the action of the heart; points to which some, moved either by the authority

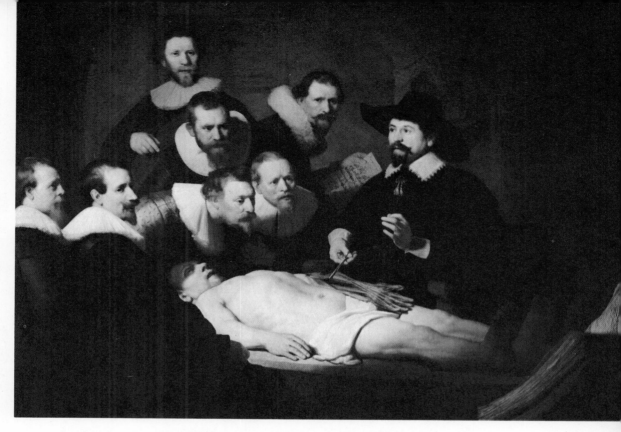

Rembrandt's "The Anatomy Lesson of Dr. Tulp" was commissioned as a portrait of the members of the Gild of Surgeon-Anatomists of Amsterdam in 1632. It reveals the pride in craft and the social standing of the medical profession and the new emphasis on learning through observation and experience.

of Galen or Columbus, or the reasoning of others, will give in their adhesion. But what remains to be said upon the quantity and source of the blood which thus passes is of so novel and unheard-of character, that I not only fear injury to myself from the envy of a few, but I tremble lest I have mankind at large for my enemies, so much doth wont and custom, that become as another nature, and doctrine once sown and that hath struck deep root, and respect for antiquity influence all

men: still the die is cast, and my trust is in my love of truth, and the candour that inheres in cultivated minds. And sooth to say, when I surveyed my mass of evidence, whether derived from vivisections, and my various reflections on them, or from the ventricles of the heart and the vessels that enter into and issue from them, the symmetry and size of these conduits—for nature doing nothing in vain, would never have given them so large a relative size without a purpose—or from the arrangement and intimate structure of the valves in particular, and of the other parts of the heart in general with many things besides, I frequently and seriously bethought me, and long revolved in my mind, what might be the quantity of blood which was transmitted, in how short a time its passage might be effected, and the like; and not finding it possible that this could be supplied by the juices of the ingested aliment without the veins on the one hand becoming drained, and the arteries on the other getting ruptured through the excessive charge of blood, unless the blood should somehow find its way from the arteries into the veins, and so return to the right side of the heart; I began to think where there might not be a *MOTION, AS IT WERE, IN A CIRCLE.* Now this I afterwards found to be true; and I finally saw that the blood, forced by the action of the left ventricle into the arteries, was distributed to the body at large, and its several parts, in the same manner as it is sent through the lungs, impelled by the right ventricle into the pulmonary artery, and that it then passed through the veins and along the vena cava, and so round to the left ventricle in the manner already indicated. . . .

Sir George Clark: The Desire To Know

Sir George Clark, well-known English historian, comments on the beginning of the scientific way of looking at things. From *Early Modern Europe* by Sir George Clark, published by the Oxford University Press. Pp. 164–168, 171–173. Reprinted by permission.

There were an infinite number of motives which led men to engage in scientific work and to clear the scientific point of view from encumbrances; but we may group together some of the most important under general headings, always remembering that in actual life each of them was compounded with the others. There were economic motives. The Portuguese explorers wanted their new instrument for navigation; the German mineowners asked questions about metallurgy and about machines for lifting and carrying heavy loads; Italian engineers improved their canals and locks and harbours by applying the principles of hydrostatics; English trading companies employed experts who used new methods of drawing charts.

Not far removed from the economic motives were those of the physicians and surgeons, who revolutionized anatomy and physiology, and did much more good than harm with their new medicines and new operations, though some of them now seem absurd. Like the doctors, the soldiers called science to their aid in designing and aiming artillery or in planning fortifications. But there were other motives far removed from the economic sphere. Jewellers learnt much about precious and semi-precious stones, but so did magicians. Musicians learnt the mathematics of harmony; painters and architects studied light and colour, substances and proportions, not only as craftsmen but as artists. For a number of reasons religion impelled men to scientific study. The most definite and old-established was the desire to reach absolute correctness in calculating the dates for the annual fixed and movable festivals of the Church: it was a pope who presided over the astronomical researches by which the calendar was reformed in the sixteenth century.

Deeper and stronger was the desire to study the wonders of science, and the order which it unravelled in the universe, as manifestations of the Creator's will. This was closer than any of the other motives to the central impulse which actuated them all, the disinterested desire to know.

Well before the end of the seventeenth century natural science had made such advances in positive achievement, in practical applications, in organization, and in public repute that many able men esteemed it more highly than any other branch of knowledge. There was a definite movement for promoting 'the new philosophy.' Its chief seats were some of the universities: Padua, Leiden, Oxford, and Cambridge housed and fed and applauded some of the greatest experimenters and thinkers; but it also had other means of propagation which sprang from the new conditions of the time. It was helped by improvements of printing, transport, and postal services as Europe grew in prosperity. Its special vehicle of diffusion was not the book but the scientific periodical, which carried the news of the latest experiments and calculations, with tables and diagrams, to a new international public. It also had a new form of organization in the scientific academies, the best of which published their own periodicals. Of these the Royal Society of London, chartered in 1662, may serve as archetype. The main body of its most active and useful members were, from the first, men trained in the universities, and a number of them made their careers in universities; but the Royal Society was unlike a university in two ways. It had nothing to do with teaching, and in it the scientists were associated with men of action and men in power. These men, some of whom were themselves more than mere amateurs, kept the scientists in touch with the needs of government, agriculture, transport, and industry, and in return they provided prizes for inventors, a few paid posts for research workers, honours and rewards for intellectual eminence.

This movement, together with the work of scattered scientists who were more or less independent of it, brought about a great positive advance in practically every branch of science. The greatest triumphs were in astronomy. With the telescope men literally saw new worlds. The work of Copernicus was completed and his hypothesis won general acceptance. A steady advance of mathematics culminated in the comprehensive explanation of the mechanism of the heavens by Sir Isaac Newton, of Cambridge, in the light of his principle of gravitation. This surpassed anything that had ever been done before in any field to bring together a multiplicity of facts as manifestations of a single law. It was however, only the supreme example of a process which was at work in every branch of physics. Outside that realm there was nothing that appealed so forcibly to the contemporary imagination; but chemistry and its allied sciences were set on sound foundations; in anatomy and physiology a new era began with research into the circulation of the blood and the detection by the microscope of living organisms so small that their existence had been unknown. In botany, zoology, and geology there were no revolutions yet, but there was steady preparatory work, and there were puzzling new questions.

As population, wealth, and enterprise grew, and as the scale of economic organization grew with them, there were many opportunities for applying the new knowledge in practice, and it was associated with many im-provements in technology. Technology gained most where it could make use of the new dynamics. Clocks were greatly improved. The introduction of the pendulum into clocks in the late seventeenth century is the first important example of an industrial invention made not by a craftsman, or a person directly concerned with manufacture, but by a scientist whose interest was primarily not practical at all. Pocket watches which kept tolerably good time were made possible in the same generation and soon became common. Before the end of the seventeenth century the results of a long series of investigations into atmospheric pressure, carried on over a long period of time in various European countries were brought together in the first steam-engine. For many years steam-engines were few in number; there were none outside England, and they were not used for any purpose except pumping the water out of mines. But in due course steam-power was to become the great instrument of transforming economic life. It was the greatest single product of a general improvement in technology. Not only were quicker, cheaper, and more effective practices devised for agriculture and many industries. So much was done to provide instruction by textbooks and articles in periodicals that the general level of efficiency was slowly raised. . . .

When we consider the wider consequences of the intellectual movement, we see that the influence of science in any narrow sense cannot be disentangled from other influences which worked through all the studies of the history, languages, beliefs, and social life of mankind. The classical scholars went forward from the printing of texts to a general study of ancient times, and in this they applied a new and specialized technique of chronology which involved an understanding of the astronomical basis of reckoning time. There were other ways besides this in which historical and social studies become more 'scientific'. Nevertheless the most important fact about the intellectual life of the seventeenth century is a fact about natural science, a main fact so well established, indeed so obvious, that it is often forgotten because it has become too familiar to be noticed. The main fact about this intellectual movement is not that it led to improvements in technology, and so assisted the rise of capitalism and the wealth of nations; or even that it made the first great strategic advances in man's conquest of nature. It is a fact on a different plane from these, on the plane of thought and not on the plane where thought and action interpenetrate. . . .

This central reality is that the scientific movement was a great illumination of the human mind. Knowledge is a good, and ignorance is an evil. There is, of course, a great deal to be said about the relation of knowledge to other values; not all knowledge is equally good, and so on. But, whatever our scale of values may be, it must give knowledge its due place, and it must accord to natural science the full value which belongs to knowledge as such. Among the nine muses of the ancients there was one, Urania, like the others a daughter of Zeus and Memory, whose special province was astronomy and who had mathematical instruments among her symbols. In the sixteenth and seventeenth centuries she widened her domain. After a long interruption there were now leaders of thought who felt, if we may adapt a telling phrase which has been used of another kind of study: 'There is poetry in science; its poetry consists in being true.' . . .

1. What were such sixteenth-century scientists as Copernicus, Brahe, and Vesalius trying to do? How did they go about it?

2. How did the work of seventeenth-century scientists differ from that of earlier scientists? What did they have in common? Compare Galileo and Harvey with Copernicus.

3. Why was Galileo so excited about the telescope? Can one make great discoveries today with the aid of a simple instrument?

4. What was significant about the discovery of Jupiter's satellites? Why did some people refuse even to look through the telescope?

5. How did Galileo refute the Aristotelian position? On what basis was he condemned by the Church? What effect on the tempo of change might such a trial have?

6. How did Harvey approach learning about the circulation of the blood? What was the importance of his discovery? How do you think most seventeenth-century men reacted to his comparison of the heart to a piece of machinery?

7. What motivated men to engage in scientific work? How does what Clark considers the central reality of the scientific movement differ from the motivating force in the ancient world?

Clocks Were Greatly Improved: Sir George Clark

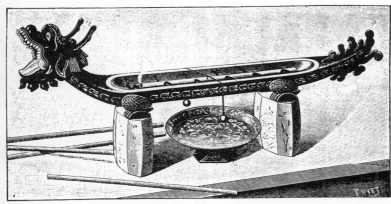

Man early discovered ways of marking the passage of time, such as (**1**) this Chinese dragon in which a bamboo rod was burned to measure an interval of time (the metal balls which fell into the dish when the cord was severed served as a gong), (**2**) the commonly used hour or sandglass, or (**3**) the Indian water bowl which had a hole in its base and sank to the bottom of the basin in 24 minutes or $\frac{1}{60}$ of a day. The first system devised by man that indicated the time of day, however, was the sundial. The Babylonians may have invented it in the seventh century B.C. Illustration (**4**) shows an ancient sundial in a monastery in Manchuria.

Although the sundial was adapted into the compact version shown (**5**) in this German pen drawing by Urs Graf in 1504, its obvious disadvantages caused it to be rapidly superseded when Peter Henlein of Nuremberg invented the mainspring in the sixteenth century. Pocket watches that kept reasonably good time were soon the prized possessions of the rich. (**6**) illustrates a large metal watch with intricate silver work, (**7**) a German calendar watch of 1690, and (**8**) a seventeenth-century chiming watch with African figures.

5

6

7

8

9

10

Unlike watches, clocks seem to have existed as early as the thirteenth century when they were used in monasteries to mark the times of services. In the fourteenth century, as men began to grasp that "time meant money," large clocks were mounted in public buildings in Europe, sometimes with moving figures attached. In the seventeenth century elaborate automaton clocks became a household vogue. The lion on this German clock (13⅜ inches high) (**9**) opens its mouth to roar and waves its tail when the clock strikes. The Swiss eighteenth-century clock (**10**) features a girl musician who announces the hours by playing the flute.

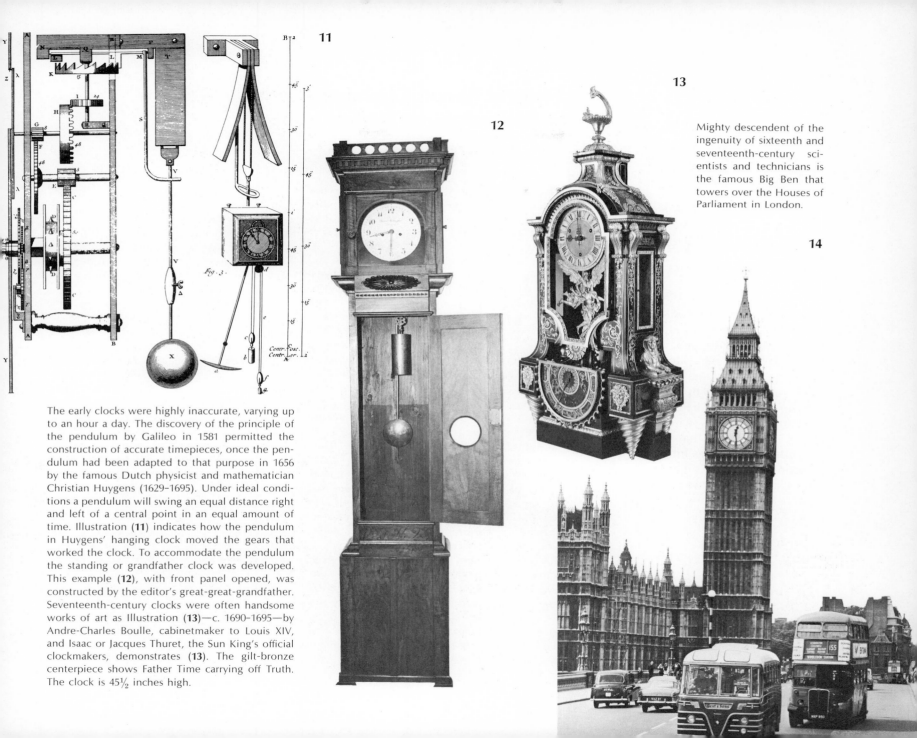

11

12

13

Mighty descendent of the ingenuity of sixteenth and seventeenth-century scientists and technicians is the famous Big Ben that towers over the Houses of Parliament in London.

14

The early clocks were highly inaccurate, varying up to an hour a day. The discovery of the principle of the pendulum by Galileo in 1581 permitted the construction of accurate timepieces, once the pendulum had been adapted to that purpose in 1656 by the famous Dutch physicist and mathematician Christian Huygens (1629–1695). Under ideal conditions a pendulum will swing an equal distance right and left of a central point in an equal amount of time. Illustration (**11**) indicates how the pendulum in Huygens' hanging clock moved the gears that worked the clock. To accommodate the pendulum the standing or grandfather clock was developed. This example (**12**), with front panel opened, was constructed by the editor's great-great-grandfather. Seventeenth-century clocks were often handsome works of art as Illustration (**13**)—c. 1690–1695—by Andre-Charles Boulle, cabinetmaker to Louis XIV, and Isaac or Jacques Thuret, the Sun King's official clockmakers, demonstrates (**13**). The gilt-bronze centerpiece shows Father Time carrying off Truth. The clock is 45½ inches high.

Francis Bacon Champions a New Way of Investigating Nature (1620)

TOPIC 12

THE SEARCH FOR CERTAINTY

The results of the observation and experimentation practiced by men like Galileo and Harvey reinforced the efforts of others to find a new systematic approach capable of unlocking the secrets of the material universe. In the seventeenth century three great names were particularly attached to this search for and application of a method that would lead men to truth. The readings introduce the contributions of Francis Bacon, René Descartes, and Isaac Newton to the development of modern science.

The family of Francis Bacon (1561–1626) was related to some of the most famous of the English nobility, and he himself was made a knight and then a baron. A high official under James I, he was convicted of accepting bribes from people who wanted favors from the government. This ended his political career in 1621, but Lord Bacon was more than a politician. He was a philosopher, an historian, and the master of a literary style which has led some people to claim that he, and not his contemporary, William Shakespeare, wrote the famous plays. He died in March 1626 of a curious cause. While he was driving in a snowstorm, he began to wonder whether the cold snow could slow down the spoilage of food. He bought a chicken from a butcher and then hopped into a snowbank to stuff it with snow and caught bronchitis from which he died.

Bacon was convinced that man's ignorance of nature could be rectified if he would use a correct method of investigation and not base his conclusions on his prejudices or on what ancient authorities said. Fundamental to this method was a process called "induction." Bacon's argument was stated in the *New Organon*, published in 1620, excerpts from which make up this reading. "New organon" means "new instrument" as contrasted to the "old instrument," the methodology and body of knowledge based on Aristotle. From *The Works of Francis Bacon*, trans. J. Spedding, R. Ellis, and D. Heath (Boston, 1863), Vol. VIII.

I

1. Man, being the servant and interpreter of Nature, can do and understand so much and so much only as he has observed in fact or in thought of the course of nature. Beyond this he neither knows anything nor can do anything.

8. Moreover, the works already known are due to chance and experiment rather than to sciences; for the sciences we now possess are merely systems for the nice ordering and setting forth of things already invented, not methods of invention or directions for new works.

19. There are and can be only two ways of searching into and discovering truth. The one flies from the senses and particulars to the most general axioms, and from these principles, the truth of which it takes for settled and immovable, proceeds to judgment and to the discovery of middle axioms [deductions]. And this way is now in fashion. The other derives axioms from the senses and particulars, rising by a gradual and unbroken ascent, so that it arrives at the most general axioms last of all [induction]. This is the true way, but as yet untried.

22. Both ways set out from the senses and particulars, and rest in the highest generalities; but the difference between them is infinite. For the one just glances at experiment and particulars in passing, the other dwells duly and orderly among them. . . .

31. It is idle to expect any great advancement in science from the superinducing and engrafting of new things upon old. We must begin anew from the very foundations, unless we would revolve forever in a circle with mean and contemptible progress.

36. One method of delivery alone remains to us which is simply this: we must lead men to the particulars themselves, and their series and order; while men on their side must force themselves for a while to lay their notions by and begin to familiarize themselves with facts.

II

95. These who have handled sciences have been either men of experiment or men of dogma. The men of experiment are like the ant, they only collect and use; the reasoners resemble spiders, who make cobwebs out of their own substance. But the bee takes a middle course: it gathers its material from the flowers of the garden and of the field, but transforms and digests it by a power of its own. Not unlike this is the true business of philosophy [science]; for it neither relies solely or chiefly on the powers of the mind, nor does it take the matter which it gathers from natural history and mechanical experiments and lay it up in the memory whole, as it finds it, but lays it up in the understanding altered and digested. Therefore from a closer and purer league between these two faculties, the experimental and the rational (such as has never yet been made), much may be hoped.

97. No one has yet been found so firm of mind and purpose as resolutely to compel himself to sweep away all theories and common notions, and to apply the understanding,

thus made fair and even, to a fresh examination of particulars. Thus it happens that human knowledge, as we have it, is a mere medley and ill-digested mass, made up of much credulity and much accident, and also of the childish notions which we at first imbibed. . . .

108. So much then for the removing of despair and the raising of hope through the dismissal or rectification of the errors of past time. We must now see what else there is to ground hope upon. And this consideration occurs at once—that if many useful discoveries have been made by accident or upon occasion, when men were not seeking for them but were busy about other things, no one can doubt but that when they apply themselves to seek and make this their business, and that too by method and in order and not by desultory impulses, they will discover far more. . . .

109. Another argument of hope may be drawn from this—that some of the inventions already known are such as before they were discovered it could hardly have entered any man's head to think of; they would have been simply set aside as impossible. For, in conjecturing what may be, men set before them the example of what has been, and divine of the new with an imagination pre-occupied and colored by the old; which way of forming opinions is very fallacious, for streams that are drawn from the springheads of nature do not always run in the old channels.

If, for instance, before the invention of [the cannon], a man had described the thing by its effects, and said that there was a new invention by means of which the strongest towers and walls could be shaken and thrown down at a great distance, men would doubtless have begun to think over all the ways

of multiplying the force of catapults and mechanical engines by weights and wheels and such machinery for ramming and projecting; but the notion of a fiery blast suddenly and violently expanding and exploding would hardly have entered into any man's imagination or fancy, being a thing to which nothing immediately analogous had been seen, except perhaps in an earthquake or in lightning, which as *magnalia* or marvels of nature, and by man not imitable, would have been immediately rejected.

In the same way, if, before the discovery of silk, anyone had said that there was a kind of thread discovered for the purposes of dress and furniture which far surpassed the thread of linen or of wool in fineness and at the same time in strength, and also in beauty and softness, men would have begun immediately to think of some silky kind of vegetable, or of the finer hair of some animal, or of the feathers and down of birds; but a web woven by a tiny worm, and that in such abundance, and renewing itself yearly, they would assuredly never have thought. Nay, if anyone had said anything about a worm, he would no doubt have been laughed at as dreaming of a new kind of cobwebs. . . .

There is therefore much ground for hoping that there are still laid up in the womb of nature many secrets of excellent use, having no affinity or parallelism with anything that is now known, but lying entirely out of the beat of the imagination, which have not yet been found out. They too no doubt will some time or other, in the course and revolution of many ages, come to light of themselves, just as the others did; only by the method of which we are now treating they can be speedily and suddenly and simultaneously presented and anticipated.

René Descartes Finds a Way To Distinguish the True from the False

René Descartes (1596–1650) was a member of a prosperous, middle-class French family. Well educated, mathematics became his favorite subject. At twenty-two, weary of study and wanting to see the world, he joined the forces fighting in the first phase of the Thirty Years' War as a military engineer. It was in this capacity, in Germany in 1619, that he made the "wonderful discovery" described in his *Discourse on Method*. For the next ten years he traveled in Europe, making experiments, measuring the heights of mountains, and studying such natural phenomena as glaciers. In 1629 he settled in Holland where he lived quietly for the next two decades. Holland was at that time one of the most tolerant nations of Europe, and men who held views in opposition to those commonly accepted enjoyed a greater degree of intellectual freedom there than elsewhere. Nonetheless the *Discourse on Method,* appearing a few years after the condemnation of Galileo in 1633, caused bitter controversy, and Descartes was careful to emphasize in his writing that it was in no way in disharmony with Christian doctrine. Invited to Sweden in 1649 as instructor to the fascinating Queen Christina, who believed in starting lessons at five o'clock in the morning, Descartes caught cold on one of these early morning trips to the palace and died in February 1650. The first reading contains excerpts from the *Discourse on Method,* the second a few of the articles from the *Principles of Philosophy.* In *The Method, Meditations and Philosophy of Descartes,* trans. John Veitch (New York, 1901).

I. DISCOURSE ON METHOD (1637)

From my childhood, I have been familiar with letters; and as I was given to believe that by their help a clear and certain knowledge of all that is useful in life might be acquired, I was ardently desirous for instruction. But as soon as I had finished the entire course of study, at the close of which it is customary to be admitted into the order of the learned, I completely changed my opinion. For I found myself involved in so many doubts and errors, that I was convinced I had advanced no farther in all my attempts at learning, than to discover my own ignorance at every turn. And yet I was studying in one of the most celebrated schools in Europe, in which I thought there must be learned men, if such were anywhere to be found. . . .

For these reasons, as soon as my age permitted me to pass from under the control of my instructors, I entirely abandoned the study of letters, and resolved no longer to seek any other science than the knowledge of myself, or of the great book of the world. I spent the remainder of my youth in traveling, in visiting courts and armies, in holding intercourse with men of different dispositions and callings, in collecting varied experience, in proving myself in the different situations into which fortune threw me, and, above all, in making such reflection on my experiences as could profit me . . . [for] I had always a most earnest desire to know how to distinguish the true from the false, in order that I might be able clearly to discriminate the right path in life, and proceed in it with confidence. . . .

I was then in Germany [1619], attracted thither by the wars in that country, which have not yet been brought to an end. As I was returning to the army from the coronation of the Emperor, the setting in of winter de-tained me in a locality where, as I found no society to interest me, and was besides fortunately undisturbed by any cares or passions, I remained the whole day shut up alone in a stove-heated room, with full opportunity to occupy my attention with my own thoughts. . . .

I am in doubt whether I should tell of my first meditations, in the place above mentioned; for these are so metaphysical, and so unusual, that they may not, perhaps, be acceptable to everyone. And yet, that it may be determined whether the foundations that I have laid are sufficiently secure, I find myself compelled to speak of them. I had long noted that it is sometimes necessary to adopt, as if above doubt, opinions which we feel to be highly uncertain, but as I then desired to give my attention solely to the search after truth, I thought that a procedure exactly the opposite was called for, and that I ought to reject as absolutely false all opinions in regard to which I could suppose the least ground for doubt, in order to ascertain whether after that there remained anything in my belief that was wholly indubitable. Accordingly, seeing that our senses sometimes deceive us, I was willing to suppose that there existed nothing really such as they presented to us. . . . I supposed that all the objects that had ever entered into my mind when awake, had in them no more truth than the illusions of my dreams. But immediately upon this I observed that, whilst I thus wished to think that all was false, it was absolutely necessary that I, who thus thought, should be somewhat; and as I observed that this truth, *I think, therefore I am,* was so certain and of such evidence, that no ground of doubt, however extravagant, capable of shaking it could be alleged by sceptics, I concluded that I might without scruple accept it as the first principle of the Philosophy for which I was searching. . . .

In the next place, reflecting on the circumstance that I doubted and that consequently my being was not wholly perfect (for I clearly saw that it was a greater perfection to know than to doubt), I was led to inquire whence I had learned to think of something more perfect than myself; and I clearly recognized that I must hold this notion from some Nature which was indeed more perfect . . . , that is to say, to put it in a single word, which is God. . . .

II. PRINCIPLES OF PHILOSOPHY (1644)

Part One: Of the Principles of Human Knowledge

I. That in order to seek truth, it is necessary once in the course of our life to doubt, as far as possible, of all things. . . .

VII. That we cannot doubt of our existence while we doubt, and that this is the first knowledge we acquire when we philosophise in order.

While we thus reject all of which we can entertain the smallest doubt, and even imagine that it is false, we easily indeed suppose that there is neither God, nor sky, nor bodies, and that we ourselves even have neither hands nor feet, nor finally, a body; but we cannot in the same way suppose that we are not while we doubt of the truth of these things; for there is a contradiction in conceiving that what thinks does not exist at the very time when it thinks. Accordingly, the knowledge, *I think, therefore I am,* is the first and most certain that occurs to one who philosphises orderly.

XXIX. That God is not the cause of our errors.

The first attribute of God which here falls to be considered, is that he is absolutely veracious and the source of all light, so that it is plainly repugnant for him to deceive us, or to be properly and positively the cause of the errors to which we are consciously subject. . . .

Part Two: Of The Principles of Material Things

I. The grounds on which the existence of material things may be known with certainty.

Although we are all sufficiently persuaded of the existence of material things, yet, since this was before called in question by us, and since we reckoned the persuasion of their existence as among the prejudices of our childhood, it is now necessary for us to investigate the grounds on which this truth may be known with certainty. In the first place, then, it cannot be doubted that every perception we have comes to us from some object outside our mind. . . . Because we perceive, or rather, stimulated by sense, clearly and distinctly apprehend, certain matter extended in length, breadth, and thickness, the various parts of which have different figures and motions, and give rise to the sensations we have of colours, smells, pain, etc., God would, without question, deserve to be regarded as a deceiver, if he directly and of himself presented to us by some object which possessed neither extension, figure, nor motion. . . . But since God cannot deceive us, for this is foreign to his nature, as has been already remarked, we must unhesitatingly conclude that there exists a certain object extended in length, breadth, and thickness, and possessing all those properties which we clearly apprehend to belong to what is extended. And this extended substance is what we call body or matter.

XXII. It also follows that the matter of the heavens and earth is the same, and that there cannot be a plurality of worlds.

And it may also be easily inferred from all this that the earth and heavens are made of the same matter; and that even although there were an infinity of worlds, they would all be composed of this matter. . . .

Isaac Newton Discovers the Laws of Nature (1687)

Sir Isaac Newton (1642–1727) laid the foundations for his famous discoveries in mathematics and physical science before he was twenty-five. In 1667, because of the epidemic known as the Great Plague that swept London, Newton moved to the country where it is quite possible that he observed an apple falling in an orchard. That apple is said to have been the basis for his discovery of the Law of Gravitation. The ideas which make up the content of Newton's famous *Mathematical Principles of Natural Philosophy* were first evolved in the 1660s, but he waited until 1687 to publish them in order to prove them so convincingly that he could avoid the controversy that had surrounded the publications of Copernicus, Galileo, and Descartes. The last forty years of his life were filled with honors (he was knighted by Queen Anne in 1705) and the respect of the learned world. The first reading provides several contemporary views of Newton; the second is an account of what he accomplished. I. "Newtoniana" from *The New Treasury of Science* (1965) edited by Harlow Shapley, Samuel Rapport, and Helen Wright. By permission of Harper & Row, Publishers. II. From Chester Starr, Charles Nowell, Bryce Lyon, Raymond Stearns, Theodore Hamerow, *A History of the World* (Chicago: Rand McNally & Company, 1960), II, pp. 200–202.

I. CONTEMPORARY VIEWS OF SIR ISAAC NEWTON

1. "He always kept close to his studies, very rarely went visiting and had few visitors. I never knew him to take any recreation or pastime either in riding out to take the air, walking, bowling, or any other exercise whatever, thinking all hours lost that were not spent in his studies, to which he kept so close that he seldom left his chamber. . . . So intent, so serious upon his studies, that he ate very sparingly, nay, ofttimes he has forgot to eat at all, so that, going into his chamber, I have found his mess untouched, of which, when I have reminded him, he would reply— 'Have I?' and then making to the table would eat a bite or two standing, for I cannot say I ever saw him sit at table by himself. He very rarely went to bed till two or three of the clock, sometimes not until five or six, lying about four or five hours, especially at spring and fall of the leaf, at which times he used to employ about six weeks in his laboratory, the fires scarcely going out either day or night; he sitting up one night and I another till he had finished his chemical experiments, in the performance of which he was the most accurate, strict, exact. What his aim might be I was not able to penetrate into, but his pains, his diligence at these set times made me think he aimed at something beyond the reach of human art and industry. . . . He has sometimes taken a turn or two, has made a sudden stand, turn'd himself about, run up the stairs like another Archimedes, with an Eureka fall to write on his desk standing without giving himself the leisure to draw a chair to sit down on. He would with great acuteness answer a question, but would very seldom start one. Dr. Boerhave, in some of his writings, speaking of Sir Isaac: 'That man,' says he, 'comprehends as much as all mankind besides.' "—Humphrey Newton

2. "On the day of Cromwell's death, when Newton was sixteen, a great storm raged all over England. He used to say, in his old age, that on that day he made his first purely scientific experiment. To ascertain the force of the wind, he first jumped with the wind and then against it, and by comparing these distances with the extent of his own jump on a calm day, he was enabled to compute the force of the storm. When the wind blew thereafter, he used to say it was so many feet strong."—James Parton

3. "I do not know what I may appear to the world, but to myself I seem to have been only like a boy playing on the seashore, and diverting myself in now and then finding a smoother pebble and a prettier shell than ordinary, whilst the great ocean of truth lay all undiscovered before me."—Sir Isaac Newton

II. THE WORK OF ISAAC NEWTON

Isaac Newton became the most famous scientist of the time, although, inevitably, some of his work was built upon that of his predecessors. This was especially true with regard to Galileo's contributions on the laws of motion. By his studies of pendulums, projectiles, falling bodies, and balls rolled on inclined planes, Galileo went far toward perfecting present-day ideas of acceleration; and he disproved the Aristotelian theory that objects fall with velocities proportional to their weights. Newton carried on from Galileo's beginning to formulate the three classical laws of motion. . . .

Beyond these, however, Newton set forth a great theoretical account of the universe based upon the laws of gravitation, which he also described with mathematical precision. All this appeared in his *Philosophiae Naturalis Principia Mathematica* (*Mathematical Principles of Natural Philosophy,* commonly called Newton's *Principia*), published in 1687 by the Royal Society of London. Work on it started at least as early as 1666, when Newton began studies on the force of gravity, traditionally after an apple fell on his head from a tree under which he was sitting. The problem was to explain, not why planets continue to move, but why they move in closed ellipses instead of traveling in straight lines into outer space. Newton found the answer by bringing together Kepler's laws of planetary motion and Galileo's laws of terrestrial motion and showing that they were two aspects of the same laws. Thus Newton enunciated the laws of universal gravitation. The sun, the planets, and their satellites are held in their orbits by the forces of mutual attraction or gravitation. This force of gravitation, according to Newton, is proportional to the product of the masses of two bodies attracted to one another, and inversely proportional to the squares of the distance between them. Thus the whole physical universe is subject to the same laws of gravitation and to the same laws of motion that we experience on earth, and all physical objects in one part of the universe

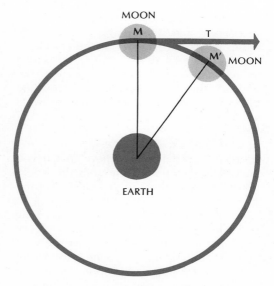

MOON

M

T

M' MOON

EARTH

THE PULL OF GRAVITY ON THE MOON

The moon would travel in a straight line M-T, if it were not for gravitation. Instead the moon moves about the Earth and will fall the distance T-M' by the time it reaches M. T-M' represents the force of gravitation exerted by the Earth.

exercise some influence upon all others. All things in the universe form a cosmic system of interconnected parts which operate upon one another by mechanical laws. In a sense, then, the universe operates like a vast cosmic machine.

Newton's work showed that all motion, whether on the earth or in the solar system, could be described by the same mathematical formulas (if they were timed and measured accurately). All matter moved in accordance with the universal law of gravitation. What the *force* of gravitation was in itself, Newton could not explain. But the knowledge of the

"natural laws" by which it operated enabled men to predict tides, improve navigation, discover longitude at sea, improve map making, and estimate more accurately the trajectory of artillery shells, whereby to improve the firepower of European armed forces. For more than two hundred years Newton's laws were unshaken. Only in the infinitesimal world of the atom or in the vast regions of outer space have they been found wanting—and the limitations in these areas have been recognized only within the present century.

Although Newton did not claim to be a philosopher, his works had an immediate and profound effect upon both philosophy and metaphysics. Further, Newton enunciated "Four Rules of Reasoning in Philosophy" in his *Principia*. In essence, these provided that:

(1) the laws governing the physical world are simple; (2) they are consistent; (3) they are absolute, applicable both to the bodies within reach of our experiment and to all others in the universe beyond our immediate powers to submit to direct experiment; and (4) they can be established by combining inductive and deductive methods of reasoning, that is, by reasoning from observable particular instances to a general rule and then by applying this rule to other instances not observable at first hand. Newton assumed that the entire universe can be explained by his methods. . . . Thus Newton, a devoutly religious man, advocated "Rules of Reasoning in Philosophy" which denounced religious explanations of natural phenomena. These rules separated physics from metaphysics and constructed a materialistic outlook which exhibited nature as a great machine wholly explicable by physical and mathematical laws.

Herbert Butterfield: Newton and His Universe

Herbert Butterfield (1900–   ), British historian of science, argues that the scientific revolution so changed the character of thought and "the very texture of human life" itself, that it is the real origin both of the modern world and of the modern mentality. In this reading he describes the process by which Newton fits together the various theories prevailing in the seventeenth century to produce a new automatic concept of the universe. From Herbert Butterfield, "Newton and His Universe" in *A Short History of Science: Origins and Results of the Scientific Revolution* (London: Routledge and Kegan Paul Ltd, 1959), pp. 51–59.

Various aspects of the Scientific Revolution have now been illustrated and we have examined the changes that were taking place both in scientific method and in modes of thought in the seventeenth century. The climax of the story comes with Sir Isaac Newton in the last quarter of that century. In this period the new methods really come to prevail, and a completely different scheme or diagram of the universe is achieved. . . .

To understand the situation it is necessary that we should cast our eyes over the period of almost exactly a century that led up to Sir Isaac Newton, and we must note certain developments taking place in that period—developments which form the main ribs in the framework of the Scientific Revolution itself. It is useful to remember that Sir Isaac Newton comes to crown a great process of scientific development, and gathers up the achievements of many predecessors, though he combines them into something entirely new. We must note in the first place that Copernicus himself did not produce a satisfactory picture or explanation of what was happening in the skies, and did not scientifically establish his case. The controversy concerning the rotation of the earth did not become even very intense until the close of the sixteenth century, nearly sixty years after his death. Even then the thing which greatly agitated the world was not Copernicus's theory itself but a number of disturbing new discoveries that were made in the sky in that period. The first occurred in 1572, and it was the appearance of a new star—one which shone with particular brightness and then disappeared two years later—a thing which ought to have been impossible, since the skies and the heavenly bodies were supposed to be incapable of change, incapable of either generation or corruption. Then in 1577 a new comet appeared, and as methods of observation had been much improved even since the time of Copernicus, it became impossible to go on believing the old theory that comets existed only under the moon—because this comet was seen to range through the higher skies and actually cut a path through that series of crystal spheres which had been supposed to be impenetrable.

Before this time men had gone on believing that comets were really terrestrial things—exhalations or fumes from the earth which became ignited in the upper atmosphere. Now, however, the comet was proved to be a celestial phenomenon, and it showed that strange irregularities were liable to occur in the skies. Even men who could not swallow the Copernican theory began to believe that the older theory of the universe must have

been wrong, at any rate in parts; and some of them, even though they were conservative-minded, began to realise that the crystal spheres, one above the other, could not exist in reality, and that the sun, the stars and the planets must be floating, unattached to anything, in a wilderness of empty space. There was a demand for a general 'renovation of astronomy' as it was called, a fresh overhauling of the whole matter. This general spring-cleaning in astronomy was a work that depended on revising and correcting one's observation of the skies, and in this it differed from the Copernican attempt to form a system—much of it was due in fact to a Danish astronomer, Tycho Brahe, who did not believe in the Copernican theory at all, but who brought the careful observation of the skies to perhaps the greatest perfection possible before the invention of the telescope. He put forward a compromise theory, halfway between the Copernican and the more ancient one, and in the seventeenth century this theory became somewhat fashionable in its various modified forms. According to this view some of the planets did go round the sun, as Copernicus had said, but still the sun and this miniature solar system revolved with the rest of the planets around the motionless earth.

All the same, if the heavenly bodies were rolling round in the ocean of empty space, it was difficult to imagine what could keep them in position and hold them to their appointed course; and some people inclined to the view of an interesting English experimenter, William Gilbert, who thought that the earth was a species of magnet, and that magnetism held the heavenly bodies in their places, so that the idea of 'attraction' was introduced into the argument. More intellectual disturbance was caused by Galileo,

who with his telescope discovered the spots on the sun and showed that the heavenly bodies could not be made of pure and immaculate material after all. But when Galileo argued that the tides were a proof of the motion of the earth—that the oceans rose and fell because of the shaking of the vessel which held them—he did not convince the world. . . .

Somewhat unconsciously, men were developing a tendency to believe that if you could explain motion on the earth, this would help to explain also the movements in the sky. In other words, they were tending to depart from the older view that everything in the heavens was composed of a special kind of matter subject to its own peculiar laws. The foundation of the new science of dynamics, therefore, was bound to be of importance for the development of the new astronomy. This was realised by Galileo, who tried to dovetail these two sciences into one another—he tried to explain earthly movements and heavenly movements by the same laws.

While these things were happening, further developments were taking place in quite a different branch of scientific thought, though people did not realise the importance that this was going to have in future for the explanation of the problem of the skies. The field in question related to the problem of gravitation; and it will be remembered that on the other theory, which went back to Aristotle, things had weight and tended to fall because they aspired to rush to the centre of the earth. On this view, if you were to take a handful of mud on to the planet Mars, it would tend to fall to the earth, the heavenly bodies being composed of material without weight or gravity. Such a view could not be held any longer if the earth moved round the sun—because the earth would no longer be the centre of the universe, and gravity was supposed to be the tendency to move to the centre of the universe. We find the view being put forward, therefore, at one moment that the sun and the moon, as well as the earth, are able to exert gravity, each acting as an independent centre. Copernicus said that things would be drawn to the sun or the moon or the earth because in everything there was the tendency for matter to assemble into spheres. Early in the seventeenth century gravity was held to be something like a case of magnetic attraction, the greater mass attracting the smaller with a power which was thought to vary in some degree according to distance. Later again, we find the view being put forward that gravity varied inversely as the square of the distance, though this discovery was not widely accepted or even widely known for some time. Somebody also put forward the view that gravity did not merely operate in the sun or the moon or the earth, but was a relationship existing between all particles of matter, an attraction that the various parts of matter exerted on one another. It will be noticed that instead of regarding the apple as having a disposition which induced it to yearn to be at the centre of the earth, men are now beginning to reverse the picture and say that it is the earth which exerts a pull on the apple; all of which makes it clear that a different attitude was being adopted to the problem of gravitation. Somebody suggested—a very modern view —that the moon would fly off at a tangent, right away from the earth, if it was not kept in place by the pull of the earth's gravity upon it.

So there were various theories put forward in the seventeenth century, first of all concerning the motion of the heavenly bodies, and secondly concerning the motion of terrestrial bodies, and thirdly concerning the principle of gravitation. One set of views existed in one man's head, another in another man's head, and the person who had hit on the truth about gravitation would have a false idea of the principles of motion, and nobody had picked out the right theory from all of the sets of ideas. Nobody had realised that when the correct ones had been adopted in each case they might be neatly dovetailed into one another to form a coherent system. . . .

Sir Isaac Newton was a young man and had hardly ceased to be an undergraduate when, in 1665–66, he had the brilliant idea of selecting the right conjecture in the case of each of the problems I have mentioned, and then dovetailing them together to show that they fitted into one another. He accepted the view that the heavenly bodies were floating in space, and that both they and all other particles of matter exerted an attraction on one another, an attraction dependent on their relative mass, and varying inversely with the square of the distance between them. He accepted the modern principle of inertia, and applied it to the planets which tended to maintain their existing motion in a straight line, but which were held in by the pull of gravity so that they were curved round into their elliptical orbits, just as a cannon ball fired into the air is pulled in a curve back to the earth by the effect of its own gravity. He imagined that the moon was like a stone in a sling, tending to fly off at a tangent, but held in by the force of gravity; and he worked out that the 'pull' which was necessary to hold the moon in its course was the equivalent of gravitation—mathematically equivalent to the force which actually draws the apple to the ground. In fact, the same force was tugging at the moon—taking due account of relative weights and distances—as drew the apple down from the branch of a tree.

Newton showed mathematically that if the forces operated in the way that I have said, the planets would describe just the kind of ellipse round the sun which Kepler had shown that they actually followed. For various reasons he was not satisfied with his original calculations, however, and kept them for twenty years, until he had settled certain doubts. By this time, moreover, new observations had rectified certain measurements in the earth and the sky. Newton's results were finally published in the *Principia* in 1687, and they formed the climax of the Scientific Revolution, at a time when, as we have already seen, so many scientists were doing brilliant things in London and in Paris. . . .

Thomas Huxley: Scientific Method Equals Everyday Method

Thomas Huxley (1825–1895), nineteenth-century English biologist, wrote this lucid description of what the scientific method was— to counteract those pseudo-intellectuals who attempted to make it appear impossibly complex and beyond the grasp of nonscientists. Huxley began by disagreeing with those who argued that Francis Bacon (or René Descartes) had originated something novel in human experience. From Thomas H. Huxley, *Darwinian Essays* (London: D. Appleton and Co., 1893), pp. 362–368.

Lord Bacon was undoubtedly a very great man, . . . but notwithstanding all that he did for philosophy, it would be entirely wrong to suppose that the methods of modern scientific inquiry originated with him, or with his age; they originated with the first man, whoever he was; and indeed existed long before him, for many of the essential processes of reasoning are exerted by the higher order of [animals] as completely and effectively as by ourselves. . . .

The method of scientific investigation is nothing but the expression of the necessary mode of working of the human mind. It is simply the mode [by] which all phenomena are reasoned about, rendered precise and exact. There is no more difference, but there is just the same kind of difference, between the mental operations of a man of science and those of an ordinary person, as there is between the operations and methods of a baker or of a butcher weighing out his goods in common scales, and the operations of a chemist in performing a difficult and complex analysis by means of his balance and finely-graduated weights. It is not that the action of the scales in the one case, and the balance in the other differ in the principles of their construction or manner of working; but the beam of one is set on an infinitely finer axis than the other, and of course turns by the addition of a much smaller weight.

You will understand this better, perhaps, if I give you some familiar example. You have all heard it repeated, I dare say, that men of science work by means of induction and deduction, and that by the help of these operations, they, in a sort of sense, wring from Nature certain other things, which are called natural laws, and causes, and that out of

these, by some cunning skill of their own, they build up hypotheses and theories. And it is imagined by many, that the operations of the common mind can be by no means compared with these processes, and that they have to be acquired by a sort of special apprenticeship to the craft. To hear all these large words, you would think that the mind of men of science must be constituted differently from that of his fellow men; but if you will not be frightened by terms, you will discover that you are quite wrong, and that all these terrible apparatus are being used by yourselves every day and every hour of your lives.

A very trivial circumstance will serve to exemplify this. Suppose you go into a [grocery] shop, wanting an apple,—you take up one, and, on biting it, you find it is sour; you look at it, and see that it is hard and green. You take up another one, and that too is hard, green, and sour. The shopman offers you a third; but, before biting it, you examine it, and find that it is hard and green, and you immediately say that you will not have it, as it must be sour, like those that you have already tried.

Nothing can be more simple than that, you think; but if you will take the trouble to analyse and trace out into its logical elements what has been done by the mind, you will be greatly surprised. In the first place, you have performed the operation of induction. You found that, in two experiences, hardness and greenness in apples went together with sourness. It was so in the first case, and it was confirmed by the second. True, it is a very small basis, but still it is enough to make an induction from; you generalize the facts, and you expect to find sourness in apples where you get hardness and greenness. You found

upon that a general law, that all hard and green apples are sour; and, that, so far as it goes, is a perfect induction. Well, having got your natural law in this way, when you are offered another apple which you find is hard and green, you say, "All hard and green apples are sour; this apple is hard and green, therefore this apple is sour." That train of reasoning is what logicians call a syllogism, and has all its various parts and terms,—its major premise, its minor premise, and its conclusion. And, by the help of further reasoning, which, if drawn out, would have to be exhibited in two or three other syllogisms, you arrive at your final determination, "I will not have that apple." So that, you see, you have, in the first place, established a law by induction, and upon that you have founded a deduction, and reasoned out the special conclusion of the particular case.

Well now, suppose, having got your law, that at some time afterwards, you are discussing the qualities with a friend: you will say to him, "It is a very curious thing,—but I find that all hard and green apples are sour!" Your friend says to you, "But how do you know that?" You at once reply, "Oh, because I have tried them over and over again, and have always found them to be so." Well if we were talking science instead of common sense, we should call that an experimental verification. And, if still opposed, you go further, and say, "I have heard from the people in Somersetshire and Devonshire, where a large number of apples are grown, that they have observed the same thing. It is also found to be the case in Normandy, and in North America. In short, I find it to be the universal experience of mankind wherever attention has been directed to the subject." Whereupon, your friend, unless he is a very unreasonable man, agrees with you, and is convinced that you are quite right in the conclusion you have drawn. He believes, although perhaps he does not know he believes it, that the more extensive verifications are,—that the more frequently experiments have been made, and results of the same kind arrived at,—that the more varied the conditions under which the same results are attained, the more certain is the ultimate conclusion, and he disputes the question no further. He sees that the experiment has been tried under all sorts of conditions, as to time, place, and people, and with the same result; and he says with you therefore, that the law you have laid down must be a good one, and he must believe it.

In science we do the same thing;—the philosopher exercises precisely the same faculties, though in a much more delicate manner. In scientific inquiry it becomes a matter of duty to expose a supposed law to every possible kind of verification, and to take care, moreover, that this is done intentionally, and not left to a mere accident, as in the case of the apples. And in science, as in common life, our confidence in a law is in exact proportion to the absence of variation in the result of our experimental verifications. For instance, if you let go your grasp of an article you may have in your hand, it will immediately fall to the ground. That is a very common verification of one of the best established laws of nature—that of gravitation. The method by which men of science establish the existence of that law is exactly the same as that by which we have established the trivial proposition about the sourness of hard and green apples. But we believe it in such an extensive, thorough, and unhesitating manner because the universal experience of mankind verifies it; and we can verify it ourselves at any time;

and that is the strongest possible foundation on which any natural law can rest.

So much, then, by way of proof that the method of establishing laws in science is exactly the same as that pursued in common life. . . .

The English Found a Society To Improve Natural Knowledge (1667)

In 1660 a group of English intellectuals founded a Royal Society to promote "Physico-Mathematicall Experimentall Learning." Here, encouraged by King Charles II, who had a little laboratory of his own, men gathered who were interested in the new scientific approach. Many famous scientists have been members of the Society in its three hundred years of existence. Newton, himself, was president for the last twenty-four years of his life. Similar societies were established in other countries at about the same time, notably the *Academie des Sciences* in France. From Thomas Sprat, *The History of the Royal Society of London for Improving of Natural Knowledge* (London, 1667), ed. J. I. Cope and H. W. Jones (St. Louis: Washington University Press, 1958). pp. 53, 56–57, 61–63.

It was some space after the end of the Civil Wars at Oxford, in Dr. Wilkins' lodgings in Wadham College, which was then the place of resort for virtuous and learned men, that the first meetings were made which laid the foundation of all this that followed. The University had, at that time, many members

of its own who had begun a free way of reasoning; and was also frequented by some gentlemen of philosophical minds whom the misfortunes of the kingdom and the security and ease of retirement amongst gown-men had drawn thither. Their first purpose was no more than only the satisfaction of breathing a freer air, and of conversing in quiet one with another, without being engaged in the passions and madness of that dismal age. . . .

Their meetings were as frequent as their affairs permitted; their proceedings rather by action than discourse, chiefly attending some particular trials in chemistry or mechanics; they had no rules nor method fixed; their intention was more to communicate to each other their discoveries which they could make in so narrow a compass, than a united, constant, or regular inquisition. And methinks their constitution did bear some resemblance to the academy lately begun at Paris, where they have at last turned their thoughts from words to experimental philosophy, and perhaps in imitation of the Royal Society. Their manner likewise is to assemble in a private house to reason freely upon the works of nature, to pass conjectures, and propose problems on any mathematical or philosophical matter which comes in their way. And this is an omen on which I will build some hope, that as they agree with us in what was done at Oxford, so they go on farther, and come by the same degrees to erect another Royal Society in France. I promise for these gentlemen here (so well I know the generosity of their design) that they will be most ready to accept their assistance. To them and to all the learned world besides, they call for aid. No difference of country, interest, or profession of religion will make them backward from taking or affording help in this enterprise. . . .

I will here, in the first place, contract into few words the whole sum of their resolutions, which I shall often have occasion to touch upon in parcels. Their purpose is, in short, to make faithful records of all the works of nature, or art, which can come within their reach; that so the present age, and posterity, may be able to put a mark on the errors which have been strengthened by long prescription; to restore the truths that have lain neglected; to push on those which are already known to more various uses; and to make the way more passable to what remains unrevealed. This is the compass of their design. And to accomplish this, they have endeavored to separate the knowledge of nature from the colors of rhetoric, the devices of fancy, or the delightful deceit of fables. . . . They have studied to make it, not only an enterprise of one season, or of some lucky opportunity, but a business of time; a steady, a lasting, a popular, an uninterrupted work. They have attempted to free it from the artifice and humors and passions of sects, to render it an instrument whereby mankind may obtain a dominion over things, and not only over one another's judgments. And lastly, they have begun to establish these reformations in philosophy, not so much by any solemnity of laws or ostentation of ceremonies, as by solid practice and examples; not by a glorious pomp of words, but by the silent, effectual, and unanswerable arguments of real productions. . . .

As for what belongs to the members themselves that are to constitute the Society: it is to be noted that they have freely admitted men of different religions, countries, and professions of life. This they were obliged to do, or else they would come far short of the largeness of their own declarations. For they openly profess not to lay the foundation of an English, Scotch, Irish, popish, or Protestant philosophy, but a philosophy of mankind. . . .

STUDY QUESTIONS

1. How does man learn according to Bacon? What did he think was wrong with the way people were taught to learn in the past? What "new" method did he propose?

2. How does man learn according to Descartes? What method in learning did he follow? Why has his conclusion that "I think, therefore, I am" been so important in the development of modern civilization?

3. How did Descartes prove the existence of matter?

4. Why was Newton such a significant figure in history? What did he do?

5. What is the scientific method and why is it important?

6. What were the goals of the Royal Society? What impact might such an organization have?

7. How might the theories and discoveries of Bacon, Descartes, and Newton have affected man's conception of himself, his capabilities, and his position in the universe?

Transmission of Certain Techniques From China to the West[1]

The chart provides statistics for the time lag of technical development between East and West that many of the following pictures illustrate.

INVENTION OR DISCOVERY	CHINA		EUROPE		APPROXIMATE MINIMUM TIME-LAG, IN CENTURIES
	PERIOD OF EXPERIMENT	FIRST PRECISE DATE	PERIOD OF EXPERIMENT	FIRST PRECISE DATE	
1 Rotary fan for ventilation		180	15th century?	1556	12
2 Blowing-engines for furnaces and forges, with water-power	2nd to 1st century B.C.	31		13th century	11
3 Piston-bellows, for continuous blast		4th century B.C.	15th century?	16th century	14
4 Silk-working machinery	Before 100 B.C.	1st century B.C.		introduced late 13th century	3–13
5 Wheel-barrow	1st century	231		Ca 1200	9–10
6 Sailing-carriage (first high land speeds)		552		1600	11
7 Efficient draught-harness for horses:					
breast-strap	4th century B.C.	2nd century B.C.	6th century?	Ca 1130	8
collar		3rd to 7th century	9th century?	Ca 920	6
8 Cross-bow (individual weapon)		3rd century B.C.	Known in Roman period not widely used before the Middle Ages	11th century	13
9 Kite		Ca 400 B.C.		1589	12
10 Helicopter top (spun by cord)		320		18th century	14
11 Deep drilling (for water, brine, and natural gas)	2nd century B.C.	1st century		1126	11
12 Iron casting	4th century B.C.	2nd century B.C.	Cast iron yielded only by accident in ancient and medieval times	13th century	10–12
13 Gimbals	First century B.C.	180		Ca 1200	8–9
14 Iron chain suspension-bridges		580	Proposed 1595	1741	10–13
15 Canals and rivers controlled by series of gates		3rd century B.C.		1220	17
16 Ship-building:					
stern-post rudder		8th century		1180	3
water-tight compartments		5th century		1790	12
17 Gunpowder:	8th century	Ca 850		13th century	4
as an igniter for an incendiary weapon		919	(Greek Fire used in 7th century)		
rockets and fire-lances		Ca 1100	Described Ca 1300	15th century	3–4
projectile artillery, explosive grenades and bombs		Ca 1200		Ca 1320	1
		Ca 1000		16th century	4–5
18 Magnetism:					
lodestone spoon rotating on bronze plate	1st century B.C.	83			
floating magnet	1st century A.D.	1020		1190	4
compass used for navigation	11th century	1117		Ca 1350	2
19 Paper:		105		1150	10
printing with wood or metal blocks	6th century	740		Ca 1400	6
printing with movable type		1045 (earthenware) 1314 wood			
printing with movable metal type	Ca 1340	1392 (Korea)		Ca 1440	1
20 Porcelain	1st century	3rd to 7th century		18th century	11–13

NOTES: 1. The table is reproduced from *A History of Technology*, by Charles Singer, E. J. Holmyard, A. R. Hall, and T. I. Williams, vol. 2, (1956), pp. 770–771, which in turn was amplified from table 8 (p. 242) in *Science and Civilization in China*, vol. I (1954), by Joseph Needham with the research assistance of Wang Ling. All dates are A.D. except where otherwise indicated. The periods in Column IV attempt to allow for considerable doubt and obscurity, and therefore are frequently less than the number obtained by subtracting the date in Column II from that in Column III.

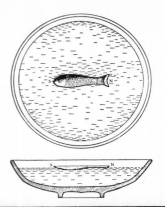

In the first century A.D., a thousand years before the compass was used in Europe, the Chinese had developed the floating magnet (above, left). The iron fish floated on water and pointed south, which the Chinese considered the primary pole. Left, a medieval seaman navigates in the Indian Ocean with the aid of a compass (Miniature from the *Travels of Jean de Mandeville,* ca. 1390). A similar non-Western aid to navigation was the astrolabe, an instrument used to find the altitudes of stars and since replaced by the sextant. The illustration above is of a finely worked late thirteenth-century Yemenite example. The woodcut below from Macrobius' *In Somnium Scipionis* (Venice, 1513) shows Arabian astronomers scanning the heavens.

One of the more complicated Chinese scientific creations, this astronomical observatory dated from about 1090 and used a water-powered clock to rotate the instruments in time with the motion of the stars.

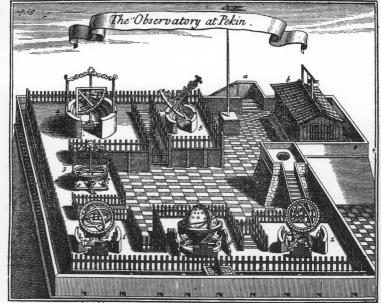

The Observatory at Pekin.

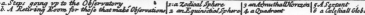

a. Steps going vp to the Observatory   1: a Zodical Sphere   3 an Azimuthall Horezion   5 A Sextant
b. A Retiring Room, for those that make Observations   2 an Equinoctial Sphere   4. a Quadrant   6 a Celestiall Globe

The comparative state of astronomical development in China and Europe in the seventeenth century can be seen in these two illustrations: above the observatory in Peking (reproduced from Le Comte's *Voyage to China*, 1698) and right the observing room at Greenwich, England, late in the century. The three men constituted the entire staff of the Royal Observatory.

CAMERAM STELLATAM.

In the West the horse collar that permitted animals to pull efficiently and made it possible to accumulate the food surplus that underlay the transition to the modern world was not introduced until the tenth century. This Chinese drawing shows that it existed in the East by the fifth century at the latest.

Another means of transportation developed by the Chinese was the wheelbarrow. Practical in the narrow streets of Oriental cities, it was used as a twosome, above left, because the load had to be balanced for the pushing coolie. Wheelbarrows were, of course, also used to carry loads and sometimes had reed sails attached to make them go faster (above). Legend has it that tenth-century Emperor Wan-hoo had a flying chair (left), propelled by 47 rockets.

ΤΟΝ ΤΩΝ ΙΕΗ ΑΗΤΙΘΟΛΟΝ

The Chinese invented gunpowder in the ninth century A.D. but the Byzantines had Greek fire as early as the seventh century, a mixture of quicklime, petroleum and sulphur that burst into flame when the lime came into contact with the water. This is an illustration from the Skylitzes Codex, thirteenth-fourteenth century.

The discovery of gunpowder in Europe is disputed between the adherents of the English and German monks, Roger Bacon and Berthold Schwarz. The latter, who experimented with alchemy, was held by his superstitious contemporaries to have made a pact with the devil (above). At any rate the oldest pictorial representation of a hand mortar used for mixing gunpowder is in the Codex Germanicus, ca. 1350 (right).

PRUNAIRE.

The first guns using powder as a propellant were developed in the fourteenth century. These primitive small arms (top) consisted of a brass or bronze tube about a foot long and closed at one end with a hole bored in the top through which a red-hot wire, or later a match, ignited the powder. The closed end of the tube was attached to a wooden shaft five to eight feet long in order to protect the shooter and control the recoil. The care involved in firing the gun made it impossible to aim. Early guns achieved their greatest effect in frightening horses or scattering groups of men (above). Eventually they grew in size and accuracy but the simple form of early cannon is evident in this fifteenth-century siege scene (right).

TOPIC 13

THE WORLD AS A MACHINE

Newton's synthesis of the scientific theories put forth in the sixteenth and seventeenth centuries provided men with a coherent system of the universe. This system was frequently referred to in terms of a gigantic clock whose supernatural maker, having created a perfect instrument, set it in motion and then ceased to interfere with its operation. What made the clock tick was a problem human beings could solve through the proper application of reason and science. Wide acceptance of the mechanical approach to understanding the universe led to increased probing into the nature of the human mind, but it also led some men to question overreliance on the potentials of reason and to seek instead a balance between it and a more traditional faith. The readings present both the rationalist world view of the seventeenth century and the questions that acceptance of that view raised among contemporaries.

Reading 77

Isaac Newton Fathers the World Machine

Newton's vision of the world is well expressed in this reading taken from his *Optics,* first published in 1704. From Sir Isaac Newton, *Optics, or a Treatise of the Reflections, Refractions, Inflections and Colours of Light,* 4th ed. (London, 1730).

All these things considered, it seems probable to me, that God in the beginning formed matter in solid, massy, hard, impenetrable, moveable particles [atoms], of such sizes and figures, and with such other properties, and in such proportion to space, as most conduced to the end for which he formed them; and that these primitive particles, being solids, are incomparably harder than any porous bodies compounded of them; even so very hard, as never to wear or break in pieces; no ordinary power being able to divide what God himself made one in the first creation. . . .

Now by the help of these principles, all material things seem to have been composed of the hard and solid particles above-mentioned, variously associated in the first creation by the counsel of an intelligent agent. For it became him who created them to set them in order. And if he did so, it's unphilosophical to seek for any other origin of the world or to pretend that it might arise out of a chaos by the mere laws of nature; though being once formed, it may continue by those laws for many ages. . . .

Reading 78

Crane Brinton: The Rationalist World-View of the Seventeenth Century

From Crane Brinton, *Ideas and Men: The Story of Western Thought,* © 1963. Reprinted by permission of Prentice-Hall, Inc., Englewood Cliffs, N.J.

I

Rationalism—A Broad Definition

Once more we confront a big word—*rationalism.* Like most such words, this one can be defined in a variety of ways. We shall here define it very broadly as a cluster of ideas that add up to the belief that the universe works the way a man's mind works when he thinks logically and objectively; that therefore man can ultimately understand everything in his experience as he understands, for instance, a simple arithmetical or mechanical problem. The same wits that showed him how to make, use, and keep in repair any household contrivance will ultimately, the rationalist hopes, show him all about everything.

The foregoing is a rather informal illustration of rationalism, but it should bring home the extent to which the complete rationalist departs from Christian belief, even from such forms of Christian belief as Scholasticism with its emphasis on the ability of the human mind to understand at least in part God's plan for the universe. There are, of course, all sorts of compromises between rationalism and Christianity . . . but the push of rationalist belief is away from Christianity. The rationalist tends to the position that the reasonable is the natural and that *there is no supernatural.* At most there is for him the unknown, which should someday be the known. . . .

Rationalism tends then to banish God and the supernatural from the universe. It has left only the natural, which the rationalist holds to be ultimately understandable, almost always by what most of us know as the methods of scientific investigation. Historically, the growth of scientific knowledge, the ever more skillful use of scientific methods, is closely tied with the growth of the rationalist attitude toward the universe, with the rationalist cosmology. For most rationalists have indeed a complete world-view, a way of life tied up with their belief in reason. Many practicing scientists have been rationalists; any scientist who holds that we have no other true knowledge except knowledge arrived at by the use of the scientific method is logically either a rationalist or a skeptic. But—and this is a very important point—science and rationalism, though historically intertwined, are not by any means the same thing.

Science, both in the sense of a body of accumulated scientific knowledge and in the sense of a way of going to work on problems (that is, scientific method), is not concerned with metaphysics. . . . Science *as science* makes no attempt to answer—does not even ask—the Big Questions of human destiny, of God's ways to man, of Right and Wrong and Good and Bad. Some scientists as individuals come near not asking any of the Big Questions, come near guiding themselves in daily life by custom and authority, as do most of us most of the time. . . . As soon as the scientist asks and tries to answer any of the Big Questions, however, he is ceasing to behave as a scientist. He is at the very least doing something *additional;* he is probably doing something *different.* . . .

The rationalist, on the other hand, has usually a full set of answers for the Big Questions, or at any rate is confident that time and diligence on the part of right-thinking men will produce answers, *correct* answers, not just widely accepted answers. Rationalism as it grew up in the sixteenth and seventeenth centuries in the West is in fact a complete metaphysical system; more than that, it served for a minority, and continues so to serve, as a substitute for religion. . . .

Natural Science

By 1700 most of what we call the natural sciences—then, with the exception of mathematics, known as "natural philosophy"—had reached a stage that made the great synthesis of Newton possible. In the two previous centuries most of the separate disciplines of science, and in particular physics, astronomy, and physiology, had become mature— although not, of course, finished—sciences. There was once more on earth what there had been in Hellenistic Alexandria two thousand years before, a body of researchers and teachers, laboratories, collections, means of exchange of information and ideas—in short, a social and intellectual environment suitable to the advancement of science. The earlier generation of humanists had been no more favorable to natural science than had their medieval scholastic predecessors, but as the sixteenth century wore on scientists like Galileo flourished in the midst of the artists of the Renaissance; and the seventeenth century is not only the century of genius, of men like Newton, Harvey, Descartes, Pascal, it is also the century of the founding of the great scientific societies, such as the British Royal Society (1660), and the French *Académie des Sciences* (1666), the century when, with hundreds of active workers tied together by societies, their publications, and an extraordinary system of private correspondence, science as a social activity came of age. . . .

Someone, finally, comes to bring together all this work into a major scientific generalization, a law or uniformity that—still within the limits of natural science—simplifies and explains, coordinates many separate laws or uniformities into one general law that sums up millions of manhours of investigation. The new law is not (still within the limits of science) a final, unalterable, perfect law. It will almost certainly be modified or even, conceivably, shown to be in some sense wrong, given time and long further investigation. But still it is *relatively* permanent, a plateau, a temporary resting place. Galileo almost made this achievement, and a dozen other major figures such as Kepler made essential contributions to the big generalization. It was Newton, however, who drew everything together into that grand mechanical conception which has been called the "Newtonian world-machine." . . .

Now any such big generalization as that achieved by Newton seems inevitably to influence human thought in many ways, to have its repercussions in fields outside science, in philosophy, in theology, in morals, even in art and literature. Science, we must repeat, does not *as science* provide a cosmology, does not answer, does not indeed *ask,* what in this book we have called the Big Questions. But scientific achievements, at least in the modern world, have been translated into metaphysics. The scientists of these two centuries were a most varied lot, with varied religions and varied [views of the world].

Some could not resist the temptation—indeed they could hardly have thought a temptation was involved—to see God as the master mechanic, or to hold that their mathematics were a clue to all life and death, or to hunt in the laboratory for some kind of absolute truth. Some, indeed, like the pious Robert Boyle, kept their science and their religion pretty well in separate compartments, an achievement many scientists can bring off happily even today.

The increasing body of scientific knowledge was chiefly, however, translated into the attitude toward the universe we have here called rationalism. The scientists of the early modern world had shown how great a degree of orderliness underlay many different physical phenomena, how notions natural enough to common sense, like that of the rising and the setting of the sun, were not accurate descriptions of what really went on. Appearance and reality were in their work sharply contrasted. Indeed, their work suggested that the great order of the universe was not altogether what Aristotle and the Christian Fathers had said it was, that this order could not be apprehended by faith, or by reasoning according to a received word, but could be apprehended by rigorous re-examination of everything in the human cultural tradition—a re-examination to be conducted by that deceptive and well-known faculty, reason. . . .

II

Making the Modern World—A Summary

Between the fifteenth and the eighteenth centuries the modern culture of Western society was formed. By the eighteenth century educated men and women, and we may be-lieve many of the uneducated, had come to hold certain beliefs about themselves, about the universe, about what was worth doing on earth, about what could be done on earth, beliefs that their ancestors of the Middle Ages had not held. They lived in a world that seemed to them new, since their ideas about it were new. They were not, of course, totally new; most of Western society was Christian in 1700, as it had been in 1400. It is a central thesis of this book that much of what men and women of the eighteenth and later centuries believed was incompatible with some very important parts of traditional Christian belief; or less ponderously, that the Enlightenment *radically altered* Christian belief. Still it is clear that a very great deal of Christianity has remained—and not merely the formal organization of the churches.

Yet one very simple and unambiguous change is there for all to see. In the thirteenth century there was but one organized ecclesiastical body in the West, the Roman Catholic Church; in the eighteenth there were already several hundred sects in the whole of Western society. Even in such countries as France where on the surface the Catholic Church was still supreme, there were several hundred thousand Protestants and an unknown number of deists, atheists, and skeptics, all pretty open about their beliefs or lack of belief, and very few exposed to any serious danger of the medieval punishment of their kind. Voltaire's pamphlets against the executions of Calas and de la Barre by Catholics must not mislead us; theirs were the *rare* case, at least in the West. The working unity of Christianity had been broken, and already by 1700 there was a body of writings that defended the notion that religious differences *ought* to be tolerated, that Church and State are rightfully separable, that the individual should make up his own mind in matters of religious belief. Indeed, the way was clear for such eighteenth-century ideas as the notion that there is *some* truth in all religions—even in non-Christian religions.

To Americans today such notions are so common that it is difficult to realize how very new they are, how sharply contrasted with what men and women of only a few centuries ago assumed with equal confidence to be true. They are notions that imply a new criterion of truth—metaphysical and theological truth—rather than the abandonment of the search for this sort of truth. In the Middle Ages these truths were held to be revealed, and perfect in their revelation; men might lose sight of them, might even as heirs of Adam's sin go against them; but no one could be *right*, no one could know the truth, and be against them. In the light of these medieval notions, the burning of heretics was understandable. They were rotten fruit, and if left alone they might corrupt the sound fruit; moreover, they were damned, and to cut them off from actual living was doing them no real harm—they had done that to themselves already. In short, if you know you are right, anyone who differs from you must be wrong. People should be right, and not wrong. You cannot let wrong notions spread without doing very great harm.

Now although the rationalizations or justifications of religious toleration are only beginning to spread and develop in the early eighteenth century, the main lines of defense are clear. Though they vary in detail, they add up to one of three propositions: that there is a new truth, deeper than that of traditional Christianity, which will if tolerated ultimately supplant or thoroughly modify it; that truth is not revealed perfect and complete to men, but must be discovered progressively by trial and error, by investigation, by human effort; or to the proposition, *little held in these early days*, that there is no such thing as truth or certainty in such matters, that all truth is "relative," that neither revelation nor thinking and studying will arrive at absolutes. But all these propositions agree in rejecting at least something in the Christian heritage from the Middle Ages; they all claim to lead to something new and something better.

The change in fundamentals is neatly pointed up at the turn of the seventeenth into the eighteenth century by an apparently insignificant debate among men of letters in France and in England, a debate usually called by its French name *la quérelle des anciens et des modernes*—the quarrel between the ancients and the moderns. One of the memorials of its English phase is Swift's amusing *Battle of the Books*. Briefly, one side maintained that the Greeks and the Romans had achieved a culture in general and in detail unsurpassable; they were the giants who staked out the fields of human culture and set examples we can but imitate from afar. Classical culture was to these people a kind of lay or humanist Eden; it was blasphemy to suppose that the like could ever again appear on earth. The other side maintained that, although the achievements of the Greeks and Romans were very great indeed, they were, so to speak, records that modern Europeans had the chance to break; modern culture could be as good, or better, in every field; there was no use in holding the men of old to be inevitably our superiors, for we could benefit by their works, we could stand on their shoulders and reach all the higher.

The position of the moderns in this quarrel is one of the first forms of the very important doctrine of progress so familiar to all Americans today, the idea that novelty is neither a delusion nor a falling off, but the natural working out of some kind of universal plan. We do not know how this basic, revolutionary change in outlook came about. We do know that it was a very complex and relatively slow process, in which we can discern three main intellectual constituents.

First came a great series of changes in the practices and ideals of Christianity under the name of Protestantism. The Protestant movement had its full share of human heroism and human weakness, of struggle and accident and strange ends. Its narrative history, over which in a book of this sort we have to pass wholly, is a fascinating record. But for the intellectual historian it is probable that the chief importance of Protestantism is as a *dissolvent*—the strongest at work in these years—of medieval authority. The Protestant movement broke through the formal unity Western Christendom had preserved for a millennium and a half, and set up a dozen major and hundreds of minor groups or sects in the position of claiming full religious authority in their fields. Protestantism, by the fact that it split into sects and subsects, prepared the way for religious skepticism. For to a mind at all inclined to doubt, or addicted to logic, the spectacle of a great number of contradictory and antithetical beliefs—each claiming monopoly of truth—could be taken as evidence that there existed no truth to be monopolized. More positively, Protestantism, especially in its Anglican and Lutheran forms, worked as a buttress to strengthen the patriotic sentiments of members of the new territorial national states. God was still—to put it otherwise would have been to leave Christianity wholly behind—a God of all the human race: but in a sense he played favorites, treated the English or the Prussians or the Danes as his preferred children. In the practice and administration of day-to-day religious life these new national churches had no share in an international and cosmopolitan life of the kind the old medieval church had possessed. Calvinist Protestantism in particular encouraged among its faithful a paradoxical mixture of other-worldly longing for union with God, a longing that stands out in all Puritan living, and a very this-worldly respect for the man who worked hard and prospered materially. But the first Protestants made no new universe; they believed in original sin, in the inspiration of the Bible, in an authority not, to be sure, invested in the pope of Rome, but still an authority above the trial-and-error processes of ordinary living. The Protestants believed in an immanent God not at all like the laws of mathematics. They believed in hell-fire and, for the elect, in heavenly bliss.

Humanism, the second force making for change, was much more than the application of some vague Protestant or libertarian spirit to the secular life. It had in common with Protestantism a corrosive effect on what was left of medieval standards. It questioned the authority of immediate custom and of established scholastic philosophy. It was an active rebellion of artists and scholars. Some of its artists mastered their media magnificently (with the help of methods worked out by generations who had been trained in medieval methods) and produced very great art. Many of them were adventurous, free-living, romantic, and exciting people who helped set our modern standards of the artist and writer as necessarily unconventional, impractical, selfish, but rather winning. Its *virtù* was in no clear sense a very Christian ideal, but rather the ideal of a handsome, athletic, though also intellectual, man. Humanism, like Calvinism, had its own deep-seated paradox. The humanists rebelled against clerical authority and the weight of tradition; they seem at least in their practice to hold the modern notion that men *make* their standards, *make* their truth, and do not merely discover it. Yet as a group they fell into a most pious attitude of respect for the masters of antiquity, whom they set up as authorities quite as absolute as any the Middle Ages worshiped. They had little awareness of the coming spread of ideas and aspirations to the masses; they were a privileged group of educated men, rather inclined to aristocratic and monarchical ideals, in no sense democrats. They did not think the world could be a very much better place, except perhaps for themselves.

Rationalism, the third force, was also an agent of destruction, less obvious and less powerful in the early years of the modern age than Protestantism or humanism, in the long run more important and more powerful. The rationalist threw overboard far more of traditional Catholic Christianity than did the Protestant or the humanist. He not merely banished the supernatural from his universe; he was prepared to place man himself wholly within the framework of nature or the "material universe." He thought indeed that man had to guide himself by standards of right and wrong. The rationalists of the earlier centuries of our modern era thought these standards were fixed and certain, and that men *found* rather than made them. But where the medieval Christian found these standards in custom, in authority, in what had been so time out of mind, the rationalist sought to find them beneath appearances, custom, and apparent diversities, and to find them by a patient investigation in which the rational mind found the mathematical reality behind the vulgarly varied and colored appearance. Rationalism has none of the obvious paradoxes of Protestantism and humanism—unless, indeed, you are so far a real skeptic as to hold that it is a paradox to try to think any kind of orderly system into human experience of this world. Rationalism even in these years owed much of its slowly growing prestige to the achievements of natural science. Finally, when with Newton science succeeded in attaining to a marvelously complete scheme of the universe, one that could be tested mathematically and that worked in the sense that it enabled successful prediction, the stage was set for the new rationalist worldview, for a cosmology as different from that of St. Augustine or St. Thomas Aquinas as theirs was from that of a Greek of the fifth century B.C.

Blaise Pascal Debates the Role of Faith and Reason (1658)

Blaise Pascal (1623–1662), a noted French mathematician, scientist, and philosopher, was remarkable even in an age when quite young men made many significant scientific discoveries. At the age of eleven he wrote an essay on the stopping of sounds in vibrating bodies when they are touched. At nineteen he invented a machine for arithmetical calculations from which today's computors trace their development. At twenty-one he invented the barometer. By the time he was twenty-five he had worked out the principles for the modern science of pneumatics and had determined a law of pressure which is still called Pascal's Law. He was, in short, a scientific giant. At the same time, however, he was a man of deep religious convictions. Pascal belonged to a puritanical movement within Roman Catholicism known as Jansenism. After 1654 Pascal virtually retired from the world by entering a Jansenist community. In general ill health since childhood, he died at the age of thirty-nine. Throughout his life he jotted down the random thoughts that came to him. The selections which follow from *Thoughts on Religion* are concerned with the place of reason in an infinite and unknowable universe. From *Pensées* by Blaise Pascal. Translated by W. F. Trotter. Dutton Paperback Edition. Reprinted by permission of E. P. Dutton & Co., Inc. The Canadian publisher is J. M. Dent & Sons Ltd.

I. THOUGHT CONSTITUTES THE GREATNESS OF MAN

I can well conceive a man without hands, feet, head (for it is only experience which teaches us that the head is more necessary than feet). But I cannot conceive man without thought; he would be a stone or a brute.

Man is but a reed, the most feeble thing in nature; but he is a thinking reed. The entire universe need not arm itself to crush him. A vapour, a drop of water suffices to kill him. But, if the universe were to crush him, man would still be more noble than that which killed him, because he knows that he dies and the advantage which the universe has over him; the universe knows nothing of this.

All our dignity consists, then, in thought. By it we must elevate ourselves, and not by space and time which we cannot fill. Let us endeavour, then, to think well; this is the principle of morality.

II. MAN'S DISPROPORTION

A

. . . Let man . . . contemplate the whole of nature in her full and grand majesty, and turn his vision from the low objects which surround him. Let him gaze on that brilliant light, set like an eternal lamp to illumine the universe; let the earth appear to him a point in comparison with the vast circle described by the sun; and let him wonder at the fact that this vast circle is itself but a very fine point in comparison with that described by the stars in their revolution round the firmament. But if our view be arrested there, let our imagination pass beyond; it will sooner exhaust the power of conception than nature that of supplying material for conception. The whole visible world is only an imperceptible atom in the ample bosom of nature. No idea approaches it. We may enlarge our conceptions beyond all imaginable space; we only produce atoms in comparison with the reality of things. It is an infinite sphere, the centre of which is everywhere, the circumference nowhere. In short it is the greatest sensible mark of the almighty power of God, that imagination loses itself in that thought.

Returning to himself, let man consider what he is in comparison with all existence; let him regard himself as lost in this remote corner of nature; and from the little cell in which he finds himself lodged, I mean the universe, let him estimate at their true value the earth, kingdoms, cities, and himself. What is a man in the Infinite?

But to show him another prodigy equally astonishing, let him examine the most delicate things he knows. Let a mite be given him, with its minute body and parts incomparably more minute, limbs with their joints, veins in the limbs, blood in the veins, humours in the blood, drops in the humours, vapours in the drops. Dividing these last things again, let him exhaust his powers of conception, and let the last object at which he can arrive be now that of our discourse. Perhaps he will think that here is the smallest point in nature. I will let him see therein a new abyss. I will paint for him not only the visible universe, but all that he can conceive of nature's immensity in the womb of this abridged atom. Let him see therein an infinity of universes, each of which has its firmament, its planets, its earth, in the same proportion as in the visible world; in each earth animals, and in the last mites, in which he will find again all that the first had, finding still in these others the same thing without end and without cessation. Let him lose himself in wonders as amazing in their littleness as the others in their vastness. For who will not be astounded at the fact that our body, which a little while ago was imperceptible in the universe, itself imperceptible in the bosom of the whole, is now a colossus, a world, or rather a whole, in respect of the nothingness which we cannot reach? He who regards himself in this light will be afraid of himself, and observing himself sustained in the body given him by nature between those two and I think that, as his curiosity changes into admiration, he will be more disposed to contemplate them in silence than to examine them with presumption.

For in fact what is man in nature? A Nothing in comparison with the Infinite, an All in comparison with the Nothing, a mean between nothing and everything. Since he is infinitely removed from comprehending the extremes, the end of things and their beginning are hopelessly hidden from him in an impenetrable secret; he is equally incapable of seeing the Nothing from which he was made, and the Infinite in which he is swallowed up.

What will he do then, but perceive the appearance of the middle of things, in an eternal despair of knowing either their beginning or their end. All things proceed from the Nothing, and are borne towards the Infinite. Who will follow these marvellous processes? The Author of these wonders understands them. None other can do so.

B

Let us then take our compass; we are something, and we are not everything. The nature of our existence hides from us the knowledge of first beginnings which are born of the Nothing; and the littleness of our being conceals from us the sight of the Infinite.

Our intellect holds the same position in the world of thought as our body occupies in the expanse of nature.

Limited as we are in every way; this state which holds the mean between two extremes is present in all our impotence. Our senses perceive no extreme. Too much sound deafens us; too much light dazzles us; too great distance or proximity hinders our view. Too great length and too great brevity of discourse tend to obscurity; too much truth is paralyzing (I know some who cannot understand that to take four from nothing leaves nothing). First principles are too self-evident for us; too much pleasure disagrees with us. Too many concords are annoying in music; too many benefits irritate us; we wish to have the wherewithal to overpay our debts. . . . We feel neither extreme heat nor extreme cold. Excessive qualities are prejudicial to us and not perceptible by the senses; we do not feel but suffer them. Extreme youth and extreme age hinder the mind, as also too much and too little education. In short, extremes are for us as though they were not, and we are not within their notice. They escape us, or we them.

This is our true state; this is what makes us incapable of certain knowledge and of absolute ignorance. We sail within a vast sphere, ever drifting in uncertainty, driven from end to end. When we think to attach ourselves to any point and to fasten to it, it wavers and leaves us; and if we follow it, it eludes our grasp, slips past us, and vanishes for ever. Nothing stays for us. This is our natural condition, and yet most contrary to our inclination; we burn with desire to find solid ground and an ultimate sure foundation whereon to build a tower reaching to the Infinite. But our whole groundwork cracks, and the earth opens to abysses.

Let us therefore not look for certainty and stability. Our reason is always deceived by fickle shadows; nothing can fix the finite between the two Infinites, which both enclose and fly from it. . . .

If man made himself the first object of study, he would see how incapable he is of going further. How can a part know the whole? But he may perhaps aspire to know at least the parts to which he bears some proportion. But the parts of the world are all so related and linked to one another, that I believe it impossible to know one without the other and without the whole.

Man, for instance, is related to all he knows. He needs a place wherein to abide, time through which to live, motion in order to live, elements to compose him, warmth and food to nourish him, air to breathe. He sees light; he feels bodies; in short, he is in a dependent alliance with everything. To know

man, then, it is necessary to know how it happens that he needs air to live, and, to know the air, we must know how it is thus related to the life of man, etc. Flame cannot exist without air; therefore to understand the one, we must understand the other.

Since everything then is cause and effect, dependent and supporting, mediate and immediate, and all is held together by a natural though imperceptible chain, which binds together things most distant and most different, I hold it equally impossible to know the parts without knowing the whole, and to know the whole without knowing the parts in detail.

III. DESCARTES

I cannot forgive Descartes. In all his philosophy he would have been quite willing to dispense with God. But he had to make Him give a fillip [stimulus] to set the world in motion; beyond this, he has no further need of God.

IV. THE HEART HAS ITS REASONS WHICH REASON DOES NOT KNOW

We know truth, not only by the reason, but also by the heart, and it is in this last way that we know first principles; and reason, which has no part in it, tries in vain to impugn them. The sceptics, who have only this for their object, labour to no purpose. We know that we do not dream, and however impossible it is for us to prove it by reason, this inability demonstrates only the weakness of our reason, but not, as they affirm, the uncertainty of all our knowledge. For the knowledge of first principles, as space, time, motion, number, is as sure as any of those which we get from reasoning. . . . And it is useless and

absurd for reason to demand from the heart proofs of her first principles, before admitting them, as it would be for the heart to demand from reason an intuition of all demonstrated propositions before accepting them.

This inability ought, then, to serve only to humble reason, which would judge all, but not to impugn our certainty, as if only reason were capable of instructing us. Would to God, on the contrary, that we had never need of it, and that we knew everything by instinct and intuition! But nature has refused us this boon. On the contrary, she has given us but very little knowledge of this kind; and all the rest can be acquired only by reasoning.

"Therefore, those to whom God has imparted religion by intuition are very fortunate, and justly convinced. But to those who do not have it, we can give it only by reasoning, waiting for God to give them spiritual insight, without which faith is only human, and useless for salvation.

John Locke Examines the Nature of the Human Mind (1690)

John Locke (1632–1704) was an English philosopher whose writings have had a tremendous impact on the development of Western thought. He wrote essays on constitutional government, on justice, on religious toleration, and on the way human beings learn. Locke usually was motivated by very practical considerations. *An Essay Concerning Human Understanding*, for instance, grew out of a discussion with friends in which no common meeting point could be reached. Locke was moved to try to understand the limits of the human mind. Similarly his *Two Treatises on Government* were closely related to the Glorious Revolution of 1688 in which King James II was overthrown. From John Locke, *An Essay Concerning Human Understanding* (Oxford, 1894), pp. 28, 37–38, 121–122, 387, 412–416, 420–421, 425–426.

I

It is an established opinion amongst some men, that there are in the understanding certain *innate principles*; some primary notions, characters, as it were stamped upon the mind of man; which the soul receives in its very first being, and brings into the world with it. It would be sufficient to convince unprejudiced readers of the falseness of this supposition, if I should only show (as I hope I shall in the following parts of this Discourse) how men, barely by the use of their natural faculties, may attain to all the knowledge they have, without the help of any innate impressions; and may arrive at certainty, without any such original notions or principles.

Of Ideals in General, and Their Origin

Every man being conscious to himself that he thinks, and that which his mind is applied about, whilst thinking, being the ideas that are there, it is past doubt, that men have in their minds several ideas, such as those expressed by the words, Whiteness, Hardness, Sweetness, Thinking, Motion, Man, Elephant, Army, Drunkenness, and others. It is in the first place then to be inquired, how he comes by them. I know it is a received doctrine, that men have native ideas, and original characters, stamped upon their minds, in their very first being. This opinion I have, at large, examined already; and, I suppose, what I have said, in the foregoing book, will be much

more easily admitted, when I have shown, whence the understanding may get all the ideas it has, and by what ways and degrees they may come into the mind; for which I shall appeal to every one's own observation and experience.

Let us then suppose the mind to be, as we say, white paper, void of all characters, without any ideas:—How comes it to be furnished? Whence comes it by that vast store which the busy and foundless fancy of man has painted on it with an almost endless variety? Whence has it all the *materials* of reason and knowledge? To this I answer, in one word, from EXPERIENCE. In that all our knowledge is founded; and from that it ultimately derives itself. Our observation employed either about external sensible objects, or about the internal operations of our minds perceived and reflected on by ourselves, is that which supplies our understandings with all the *materials* of thinking. These two are the fountains of knowledge, from whence all the ideas we have, or can naturally have, do spring. . . .

Sense and intuition reach but a very little way. The greatest part of our knowledge depends upon deductions and intermediate ideas: and in those cases where we are fain to substitute assent instead of knowledge, and take propositions for true, without being certain they are so, we have need to find out, examine, and compare the grounds of their probability. In both these cases, the faculty which finds out the means, and rightly applies them, to discover certainty in the one, and probability in the other, is that which we call *reason*. . . .

II

Assent to supposed innate truths depends on having clear and distinct ideas of what

their terms mean, and not on their innateness. A child knows not that three and four are equal to seven, till he comes to be able to count seven, and has got the name and idea of equality; and then, upon explaining those words, he presently assents to, or rather perceives the truth of that proposition. But neither does he then readily assent because it is an innate truth, nor was his assent wanting till then because he wanted the use of reason; but the truth of it appears to him as soon as he has settled in his mind the clear and distinct ideas that these names stand for. And then he knows the truth of that proposition upon the same grounds and by the same means that he knew before that a rod and a cherry are not the same thing; and upon the same grounds also that he may come to know afterwards "That it is impossible for the same thing to be and not to be," as shall be more fully shown hereafter. So that the later it is before any one comes to have those general ideas about which those maxims are; or to know the signification of those general terms that stand for them; or to put together in his mind the ideas they stand for; the later also will it be before he comes to assent to those maxims;—whose terms, with the ideas they stand for, being no more innate than those of a cat or a weasel, he must stay till time and observation have acquainted him with them; and then he will be in a capacity to know the truth of these maxims, upon the first occasion that shall make him put together those ideas in his mind, and observe whether they agree or disagree, according as is expressed in those propositions. And therefore it is that a man knows that eighteen and nineteen are equal to thirty-seven, by the same self-evidence that he knows one and two to be equal to three: yet a child knows this not so soon as the other; not for want of the use of reason, but because the ideas the words eighteen, nineteen, and thirty-seven stand for, are not so soon got, as those which are signified by one, two, and three.

III

Faith and Reason

By what has been before said of reason, we may be able to make some guess at the distinction of things, into those that are according to, above, and contrary to reason. 1. *According to reason* are such propositions whose truth we can discover by examining and tracing those ideas we have from sensation and reflection; and by natural deduction find to be true or probable. 2. *Above reason* are such propositions whose truth or probability we cannot by reason derive from those principles. 3. *Contrary to reason* are such propositions as are inconsistent with or irreconcilable to our clear and distinct ideas. Thus the existence of one God is according to reason; the existence of more than one God, contrary to reason; the resurrection of the dead, above reason. . . .

From these things thus premised, I think we may come to lay down *the measures and boundaries between faith and reason:* the want whereof may possibly have been the cause, if not of great disorders, yet at least of great disputes, and perhaps mistakes in the world. For till it be resolved how far we are to be guided by reason, and how far by faith, we shall in vain dispute, and endeavour to convince one another in matters of religion. . . .

Reason, therefore, here, as contradistinguished to *faith,* I take to be the discovery of the certainty or probability of such propositions or truths, which the mind arrives at by deduction made from such ideas, which it has got by the use of its natural faculties: viz. by sensation or reflection.

Faith, on the other side, is the assent to any proposition, not thus made out by the deductions of reason, but upon the credit of the proposer, as coming from God, in some extraordinary way of communication. This way of discovering truths to men, we call *revelation.* . . .

But yet nothing, I think, can, under that title, [revelation] shake or overrule plain knowledge; or rationally prevail with any man to admit it for true, in a direct contradiction to the clear evidence of his own understanding. . . . And therefore *no proposition can be received for divine revelation . . . if it be contradictory to our clear intuitive knowledge.* Because this would be to subvert the principles and foundations of all knowledge, evidence, and assent whatsoever: and there would be left no difference between truth and falsehood, no measures of credible and incredible in the world, if doubtful propositions shall take place before self-evident; and what we certainly know give way to what we may possibly be mistaken in. In propositions therefore contrary to the clear perception of the agreement or disagreement of any of our ideas, it will be in vain to urge them as matters of faith. They cannot move our assent under that or any other title whatsoever. For faith can never convince us of anything that contradicts our knowledge. . . .

Thus far the dominion of faith reaches, and that without any violence or hindrance to reason; which is not injured or disturbed, but assisted and improved by new discoveries of truth, coming from the eternal fountain of all knowledge. Whatever God hath revealed is certainly true; no doubt can be made of it. This is the proper object of faith: but whether it be a *divine* revelation or no, reason must judge; which can never permit the mind to reject a greater evidence to embrace what is less evident, nor allow it to entertain probability in opposition to knowledge and certainty. There can be no evidence that any traditional revelation is of divine origin, in the words we receive it, and in the sense we understand it, so clear and so certain as that of the principles of reason: and therefore *Nothing that is contrary to, and inconsistent with, the clear and self-evident dictates of reason, has a right to be urged or assented to as a matter of faith, wherein reason hath nothing to do.* . . .

STUDY QUESTIONS

1. What role did God play in Newton's concept of the universe?

2. What is rationalism? How does it depart from Christian belief? Why was it strengthened by the idea of the world-machine?

3. What does Brinton consider the major elements of change that formed modern culture?

4. What did Pascal think about the potentials of human reasoning? What did he mean by "man's disproportion?"

5. What kind of a man do you think Pascal was? Why did he attack Descartes? Who strikes you as more modern, Pascal or Newton? Why?

6. According to Locke, how does man learn? What did he mean by "experience"? How might theories such as Locke's on the nature of human understanding affect society—think of its effect on respect for authority or on existing religious beliefs?

7. How did Locke and Pascal differ on the relative positions of faith and reason?

The Age of Reason

TOPIC 14

ENLIGHTENMENT AND PROGRESS

The achievements of early modern science built up great confidence in the power of men to reshape their universe along lines dictated by reason and natural law. The eighteenth century, known variously as the Age of Reason or the Enlightenment, consequently witnessed the steady spread of efforts to reform European society by the application of the methods that had proved so successful in scientific endeavors. Convinced that the proper use of reason would improve the conditions of human existence generation after generation, reformers gathered forces to put their new knowledge to practical use in ending prevailing injustices in government, jurisprudence, education, economic affairs, social life, and a host of other fields. Against a background of Enlightenment belief, the readings provide examples of such reformist practices.

Isaac Newton (1642–1727) had synthesized the heritage of the sixteenth and seventeenth centuries in physics, astronomy, mathematics, and mechanics, and had added them to his own epoch-making discoveries. The whole formed a compact body of laws explaining the physical universe which was more convincing than any previous scientific synthesis attempted by man. Not many Europeans were erudite enough to comprehend his *Philosophiae Naturalis Principia Mathematica* (1687) in the original Latin, but in a popularized form this vision of the world had a tremendous impact upon men's minds in the succeeding centuries. The vogue for simplified expositions even called forth a special *Newtonism for the Ladies* in Italian.

The reading public of Europe lost interest in theological disputations about religious dogma as they became absorbed in contemplation of Newton's world-machine, whose rules of motion were translated into mathematical formulae. It was amazing to realize that the whole universe was subject to identical physical laws and that these laws could be expressed in mathematical symbols which no one could deny or about which there could be no substantial difference of opinion. Even the skeptical David Hume (1711–1776) expressed his wonderment at the perfect functioning of this world-machine, subdivided into an infinite number of lesser machines: "All these various machines, and even the most minute parts, are adjusted to each other with an accuracy which ravishes into admiration all men who have ever contemplated them. . . ."

SCIENTIFIC METHOD APPLIED TO RELIGION

While scientists in their laboratories and mathematicians in their studies did not engage in open warfare with revealed religion, in eighteenth-century France there arose a group of popular philosophers who took it upon themselves to do battle with the church and to proclaim the conflict between science and religion in a truculent manner. With a few exceptions, these *philosophes* were not scientists themselves. They were rather popularizers and transmitters to the literate public of Europe of the scientific ideas of the seventeenth century, primarily those of Isaac Newton, René Descartes (1596–1650), John Locke (1632–1704), and Francis Bacon (1561–1626). Voltaire was the most brilliant wit in the group, and Denis Diderot the man with the greatest capacity to co-ordinate and simplify for a vast body of readers the scientific knowledge of the age. The *Grand Encyclopedie,* edited by Diderot and Jean d'Alembert (1717–1783) and published from 1751 to 1772, was the great common enterprise in which, despite individual differences, all the philosophers cooperated to present Europe with a unified body of knowledge in the new spirit.

These *philosophes* set up criteria for determining truth which by the end of the century were generally accepted by men outside the church. They allowed as truth only those facts and theories which could be arrived at by the employment of a strict rationalist or scientific method. Their basic principles they adopted from two thinkers of the previous age, Descartes and Bacon, both of whom they assimilated despite fundamental divergences between them. The *philosophes* had an oversimplified formulation of the method of science, one hardly adequate in our own day, but it served their purpose.

Descartes had taught them to reason, to deduce knowledge by logical steps from clear and distinct ideas, the best example of which was mathematics. If in any field of knowledge a man could reason from one axiom to another with the certainty of a mathematical demonstration, he was on absolutely secure ground and nobody could doubt his assertions. His original axioms naturally had to be as well founded as his later deductions. "We think," explained Diderot, "that the greatest service to be done to men is to teach them to use their reason, only to hold for truth what they have verified and proved. . . ."

Even more destructive of accepted religious doctrine was the inductive method which the French *philosophes* acknowledged they learned from the Elizabethan Francis Bacon. . . . The Baconian emphasis on the experimental method led the *philosophes* to discredit anything which was not in conformity with normal everyday experience and which could not be examined for truth or falsehood by experience. For them the only kind of reality was objective and scientific, the only phenomena allowable those which could be apprehended by the senses. Miracles failed

to meet the crucial test. They were strange effects which could not be accounted for by direct natural causes. The religious explanation of their origin was not in conformity with the facts of experience and the workings of natural law in a world which was rational. Diderot argued:

> You see, once one sets foot in this realm of the super-natural, there are no bounds, one doesn't know where one is going nor what one may meet. Someone affirms that five thousand persons have been fed with five small loaves; this is fine! But tomorrow another will assure you that he fed five thousand people with one small loaf, and the following day a third will have fed five thousand with the wind.

At a time when the churches of Europe recognized the existence of angels and devils the *philosophes* demanded that these beliefs submit themselves to the canons of experience. Since no one could prove their existence from experience, they insisted that they were only figments of the imagination, or fabrications of priests who imposed untruths upon mankind.

There was a third set of propositions which fortified the polemics of the French intellectuals against revealed religion, and this was the doctrine of John Locke set forth in the *Essay Concerning Human Understanding* (1690). Along with Newton and Bacon he is one of the seminal thinkers whose writings the *philosophes* imported from England and disseminated throughout Europe. Locke taught that there was nothing in the intellect which had not previously been in the senses, and that the senses received their impressions directly from nature, from the external world.

This thesis, in its simplified form, was as revolutionary a doctrine for the study of man as Newton's world-machine had been for a comprehension of the physical universe. The Christian view of the world had posited an immortal soul which was given and taken away by God and was the center of conflict between good and evil. . . . If all knowledge and the reasoning power itself originated in sensations which were mere reflections of the external world, if they were not God-given, then the absolutes upon which the state and society were presumably based would crumble. Ideas of God, the divine right of kings, immortality, and state authority derived from mere sensory perceptions, nothing more. They were not unalterable. Man-made, they could be modified or abandoned. Though Locke himself never ventured that far, his theory of the source of knowledge led men to question every basic premise of society, to try to find out how many of these ideas, no longer revered as religious absolutes, were actually based on falsehoods inculcated into man and written upon the *tabula rasa*, the clean slate of his mind, after birth. . . .

The vast increase in factual knowledge about the physical universe gave men a tremendous sense of power, a feeling that with this newly acquired knowledge they could dominate nature. This new consciousness of power justified abandonment of the vain search for first principles and primary causes. If man could manipulate matter and conform it to his will, what difference did it make what matter was? The mediaeval conception of human impotence gave way to a marvelous surge of self-confidence, a buoyancy, an optimism which, though at times it was diluted by grave misgivings and doubts, remained overwhelmingly the spirit of the age.

While the mediaeval philosophers had been absorbed with beautitude, and Protestantism had brought turmoil into the breasts of true believers over whether or not they had grace and could be saved, the eighteenth-century man of letters set the problem of terrestrial happiness at the dead center of morals. The primary question was whether man could be happy on earth. Christian moralists had taught that man was born to toil, to suffer, and to lament, for he carried the weight of the Biblical curse and of Adam's original sin. As a response to the same problem, dominant eighteenth-century opinion was convinced that man was capable of great happiness now and in this world, irrespective of any future drama which might be enacted in heaven or hell. Concentration upon the "pursuit of happiness" in this world is magnificently expressed in the language of the American Declaration of Independence, composed by revolutionaries who had been profoundly influenced by the *philosophes*. . . .

THE LAWS OF NATURE

Idealization of the state of nature took on characteristics of a cult, retaining the angels and devils of Christianity in a different guise. Before man was misled from the path of nature, he had absolute liberty and life was blissful. But alas! humanity had been perverted by the impositions of despots and priests, who were the Lucifer and cohorts of the natural order. These wicked ones introduced strange objects and manners into nature which warped its perfection. Whenever man galls or is pushed from nature, whenever he violates the true laws of universal conduct by following petty conventionalities, he suffers the worldly punishment of the new deity—he is unhappy. Thus all the ills of existing

society and the wretchedness of man are to be understood as the inevitable result of deviation from the prescribed laws of man's instinctive being. The eighteenth-century *philosophe* entreated man to forsake his artificial ways, to live according to the laws of the *Systeme de la nature*, and thus to recapture the happiness from which Christian civilization had long barred him.

For the intellectuals were firmly convinced that there were laws governing man's actions in society—laws which could be discovered in precisely the same manner that natural scientists had reached their conclusions. . . . Once the immutable laws of society were made known men would be molded in accordance with their dictates, and greater happiness for all mankind would ensue. . . .

The Idea of Progress and the Philosophes

From *A History of the Modern World,* by Robert R. Palmer and Joel Colton. Copyright 1950, © 1956, 1965 by Alfred A. Knopf, Inc. Reprinted by permission of the publisher.

The idea of progress is often said to be the dominant or characteristic idea of European civilization from the seventeenth century to the twentieth. It is a belief, a kind of nonreligious faith, that the conditions of human life become better as time goes on, that in general each generation is better off than its predecessors and will contribute by its labors to an even better life for generations to come, and that in the long run all mankind will share in the same advance. All the elements of this

belief had been present by 1700. It was after 1700, however, that the idea of progress became explicit. In the seventeenth century it had shown itself in a more rudimentary way, in a sporadic dispute, among men of letters in England and France, known, as the quarrel of Ancients and Moderns. The Ancients held that the works of the Greeks and Romans had never been surpassed. The Moderns, pointing to science, art, literature, and invention, declared that their own time was the best, that it was natural for men of their time to do better than the ancients because they came later and built upon their predecessors' achievements. The quarrel was never exactly settled, but a great many people in 1700 were Moderns. Europeans had always felt themselves better off than the ancients in being Christians where the ancients were pagans. Now, for the first time in the history of Europe, a great many Europeans felt that in purely worldly ways they had outdone the noble Greeks and Romans. And many felt that this progress need never cease.

Far-reaching also was the faith of the age in the natural faculties of the human mind. Pure skepticism, the negation of reason, was overcome. Nor were the educated, after 1700, likely to be superstitious, terrified by the unknown, or addicted to magic. The witchcraft mania abruptly died. Indeed all sense of the supernatural became dim. "Modern" people not only ceased to fear the devil; they ceased also to fear God. They thought of God less as a Father than as a First Cause of the physical universe. There was less sense of a personal God, or of the inscrutable imminence of divine Providence, or of man's need for saving grace. God was less the God of Love; He was the inconceivably intelligent being who had made the amazing universe now discovered by man's reason. The great symbol of the Christian God was the Cross, on which a divine being had suffered in human form. The symbol which occurred to people of scientific view was the Watchmaker. The intricacies of the physical universe were compared to the intricacies of a watch, and it was argued that just as a watch could not exist without a watchmaker, so the universe as discovered by Newton could not exist without a God who created it and set it moving by its mathematical law. . . .

The thought of the Enlightenment was completely secular. The church was considered, at most, a socially useful institution. To the more militant it was a survival of barbarism. . . . By intellectual leaders all churches were pushed aside. Toleration in religion, or even indifference, became the mark of progress. The older Christian view seemed no longer to be necessary. Thinkers provided theories of society, world history, human destiny, and of the nature of good and evil in which Christian explanations had no part. Old Christian virtues, such as humility, chastity, or the patient bearing of pain and sorrow, ceased to be regarded as significant (except in some ways by Rousseau). Christian love was transformed and secularized into humanitarian good will. The most important virtue was to be socially useful. The progress of society, from generation to generation, toward a more comfortable and decent life on earth, became the dominant idea that gave meaning to the history and destiny of mankind. . . .

THE PHILOSOPHES

It was through the *philosophes* that the ideas of the Enlightenment were spread. The *philosophes* were not essentially philosophers in the usual sense of the word. They were rather popularizers or publicists. They read the great books which most people did not read and reworded the ideas in such a way as to hold the interest of the average reader. They were primarily "men of letters". Formerly authors had generally been gentlemen of leisure, or talented protégés of aristocratic or royal patrons, or professors or clerics supported by the income from religious foundations. In the Age of Enlightenment a great many were free-lancers, grub-streeters, or journalists. They wrote for "the publick."

The reading public had greatly expanded. The educated middle class, commercial and professional, was much larger than ever before. Country gentlemen were putting off their rustic habits and even noblemen wished to keep informed. Newspapers and magazines multiplied, and people who could not read them organized for that purpose. There was a great demand also for dictionaries, encyclopedias, and surveys of all fields of knowledge. The new readers wanted matters made interesting and clear. They appreciated wit and lightness of touch. From such a public, literature itself greatly benefited. The style of the eighteenth century became admirably fluent, clear, and exact, neither ponderous on the one hand nor frothy on the other. And from writings of this kind the readers benefited also, from the interior of Europe to the America of Benjamin Franklin. The bourgeois middle class was becoming not only educated but thoughtful. But the movement was not a class movement only.

There was another way in which writings of the day were affected by social conditions. They were all written under censorship. The theory of censorship was to protect people from harmful ideas as they were protected from shoddy merchandise or dishonest weights and measures. In England the censorship was so mild as to have little effect. Other countries, such as Spain, had a powerful censorship but few original writers. France, the center of the Enlightenment, had both a complicated censorship and a large reading and writing public. The church, the Parliament of Paris, the royal officials, and the printers' guilds all had a hand in the censoring of books. French censorship, however, was very loosely administered, and after 1750 writers were disturbed by it very little. It cannot be compared to censorship in some countries in the twentieth century. Yet in one way it had an unfavorable effect on French thought and letters. It discouraged writers from addressing themselves, in a common-sense way, to a serious consideration of concrete public questions. Legally forbidden to criticize church or state, they threw their criticisms on an abstract level. Debarred from attacking things in particular, they tended to attack things in general. Or they talked of the customs of the Persians and the Iroquois but not the French. Their works became full of double meaning, sly digs, innuendoes, and jokes, by which an author, if questioned, could declare that he did not mean what all the world knew he did mean. As for the readers, they developed a taste for forbidden books, which were always easy enough to obtain through illicit channels. No one wanted to read merely authorized literature, and Parisians who heard that a book was frowned upon by the archbishop or the Parliament could hardly wait to read it and talk about it. Ideas were prized because they were daring, or even merely naughty. French thought was made more radical by the halfway measures used to control it.

Paris was the heart of the movement. There ladies in their *salons* held evening parties at which wits, men of letters, and people of society talked brilliantly on many topics. In Paris, too, was published the most serious of all *philosophe* enterprises, the *Encyclopédie*, edited by Denis Diderot in seventeen large volumes and completed over the years 1751 to 1772. It was a great compendium of scientific, technical, and historical knowledge, carrying a strong undertone of criticism of existing society and institutions, and epitomizing the skeptical, rational, and scientific spirit of the age. It was not the first encyclopedia, but it was the first to have a distinguished list of contributors or to be conceived as a positive force for social progress. Virtually all the French *philosophes* contributed—Voltaire, Montesquieu, Rousseau, d'Alembert (who assisted in the editing), Buffon, Turgot, Quesnay, and many others, all sometimes collectively called the Encyclopedists. . . .

Immanuel Kant Defines Enlightenment (1784)

Immanuel Kant (1724–1804), German philosopher and one of the most important thinkers in modern times, spent most of his life as professor at the University of Königsberg, an isolated city in the easternmost part of Prussia. Like Pascal, Kant questioned whether experience and human reason were sufficient sources for knowledge, feeling that there was more to the world than could be explained by reason. He had, nonetheless, great confidence in man's power to create a better civilization. Kant was a small, slight man (five feet tall) who lived by a strict schedule. Every day, rain or shine, he went for a walk at a certain hour and it is said that the residents of Königsberg set their watches as the philosopher passed by, so regular was his schedule. In this reading Kant, after defining what enlightenment means, seeks to determine how enlightened his age is. From Lewis W. Beck, ed., *Foundations of the Metaphysics of Morals, What is Enlightenment?* (Chicago: University of Chicago Press, 1950) Copyright © 1950 by the University of Chicago Press.

Enlightenment is man's release from his self-incurred tutelage. Tutelage is man's inability to make use of his understanding without direction from another. Self-incurred is this tutelage when its cause lies not in lack of reason but in lack of resolution and courage to use it without direction from another. *Sapere aude*! [Dare to know!] "Have courage to use your own reason!"—that is the motto of the enlightenment.

Laziness and cowardice are the reasons why so great a portion of mankind, after nature has long since discharged them from external direction, nevertheless remains under lifelong tutelage, and why it is so easy for others to set themselves up as their guardians. It is so easy not to be of age. If I have a book which understands for me, a pastor who has a conscience for me, a physician who decides my diet, if I can only pay—others will readily undertake the irksome work for me. . . .

For any single individual to work himself out of the life under tutelage which has become almost his nature is very difficult. He has come to be fond of this state, and he is for the present really incapable of making use of his reason, for no one has ever let him try it out. Statutes and formulas, those mechanical tools of the rational employment or rather misemployment of his natural gifts, are the fetters of an everlasting tutelage. Whoever throws them off makes only an uncertain leap over the narrowest ditch because he is not accustomed to that kind of free motion. Therefore, there are only few who have succeeded by their own exercise of mind both in freeing themselves from incompetence and in achieving a steady pace. . . .

If we are asked, "Do we now live in an *enlightened age?*" the answer is "No", but we do live in an *age of enlightenment*. As things now stand, much is lacking which prevents men from being, or easily becoming, capable of correctly using their own reason in religious matters with assurance and free from outside direction. But, on the other hand, we have clear indications that the field has now been opened wherein men may freely deal with these things and that the obstacles to general enlightenment or the release from self-imposed tutelage are gradually being reduced. In this respect, this is the age of enlightenment. . . .

Marquis Beccaria Attacks Prevailing Views on Punishment (1764)

The Marquis Cesare di Beccaria (1735–1794) exemplifies the reforming spirit of the *philosophes*. Like his colleagues he subscribed to the sentiment expressed in a famous Enlightenment poem by Alexander Pope.

Know then thyself, presume not God to scan,
The proper study of mankind is Man.

For Beccaria, an Italian lawyer, the study of man meant reform of law and of the brutal methods of punishment left over from the Middle Ages and Renaissance. He had great faith in education as a means of preventing crime and his ideas had extensive influence on the reform of prison practices. From Cesare Beccaria: *On Crimes and Punishments,* translated by Henry Paolucci, copyright © 1963 by The Bobbs-Merrill Company, Inc., reprinted by permission of the publisher.

A. CRIMES AND PUNISHMENTS

To examine and distinguish all the different sorts of crimes and the manner of punishing them would not be our natural task, were it not that their nature, which varies with the different circumstances of times and places, would compel us to enter upon too vast and wearisome a mass of detail. But it will suffice to indicate the most general principles and the most pernicious and common errors, in order to undeceive no less those who, from a mistaken love of liberty, would introduce anarchy, than those who would be glad to reduce their fellow men to the uniform regularity of a convent.

What will be the penalty suitable for such and such crimes?

Is death a penalty really *useful and necessary* for the security and good order of society?

Are torture and torments *just,* and do they attain the *end* which the law aims at?

What is the best way of preventing crimes?

Are the same penalties equally useful in all times?

What influence have they on customs?

These problems deserve to be solved with such geometrical precision as shall suffice to prevail over the clouds of sophistication, over seductive eloquence, or timid doubt. Had I no other merit than that of having been the first to make clearer to Italy that which other nations have dared to write and are beginning to practise, I should deem myself fortunate; but if, in maintaining the rights of men and of invincible truth, I should contribute to rescue from the spasms and agonies of death any unfortunate victim of tyranny or ignorance, both so equally fatal, the blessings and tears of a single innocent man in the transports of his joy would console me for the contempt of mankind. . . .

B. TORTURE

The torture of a criminal during the course of his trial is a cruelty consecrated by custom in most nations. It is used with an intent either to make him confess his crime, or to explain some contradictions into which he had been led during his examination, or discover his accomplices, or for some kind of metaphysical and incomprehensible purgation of infamy, or, finally, in order to discover other crimes of which he is not accused, but of which he may be guilty.

No man can be judged a criminal until he be found guilty; nor can society take from him the public protection until it has been proved that he has violated the conditions on which it was granted. What right, then, but that of power, can authorize the punishment of a citizen so long as there remains any doubt of his guilt? This dilemma is frequent. Either he is guilty, or not guilty. If guilty, he should only suffer the punishment ordained by the laws, and torture becomes useless, as his confession is unnecessary. If he be innocent his crime has not been proved. Besides, it is confounding all relations to expect that a man should be both the accuser and accused; and that pain should be the test of truth, as if truth resided in the muscles and fibres of a wretch in torture. By this method the robust will escape, and the feeble be condemned. . . .

William Pitt Urges the Abolition of the Slave Trade (1792)

William Pitt (1759–1806) was thirty-three years old when he made his famous speech urging abolition of the slave trade which was particularly rampant in the West Indies. Pitt had been British prime minister for eight years, the youngest man in history to serve in that office. He was a practical politician and not a philosopher, but he was a reformer and humanitarian as well, and one of his close friends was William Wilberforce, leader of the antislavery forces in England. Unfortunately, in spite of the fact that the bill passed Parliament in 1792, the war with France and legal complications prevented it from being fully effective until 1807. The practice of slavery itself, as contrasted to the slave trade, was not ended in the British colonies until 1833. From *The Speech of the Right Hon. William Pitt on a Motion for the Abolition of the Slave Trade in the House of Commons on Monday the Second of April, 1792* (London: Phillips, 1792).

I. . . . congratulate this House, the country, and the world, that this great point has been gained; that we may now consider this [slave] trade as having received its condemnation; that this curse of mankind is seen by the House in its true light; that this stigma on our national character is about to be removed; and that mankind are likely to be delivered from the greatest practical evil that ever afflicted the human race—from the severest and most extensive calamity recorded in the history of the world. . . .

Why ought the slave trade to be abolished? Because it is incurable injustice. . . . Men have been led to place it among the rank of those necessary evils which are supposed to be the lot of human creatures, and to be permitted to fall upon some countries or individuals, rather than upon others, by that Being whose ways are inscrutable to us, and whose dispensations, it is conceived, we ought not to look into. The origin of evil is indeed a subject beyond the reach of human understandings: and the permission of it by the Supreme Being is a subject into which it belongs not to us to inquire. But where the evil in question is a moral evil which a man can scrutinise, and where the moral evil has its origin with ourselves, let us not imagine that we can clear our consciences by this general, not to say irreligious and impious, way of laying aside the question. . . . I know of no evil that ever has existed, nor can imagine any evil to exist, worse than the tearing of seventy or eighty thousand persons annually from their native land, by a combination of the most civilized nations inhabiting the most enlightened part of the globe, but more especially under the sanction of the laws of that nation which calls herself the most free and the most happy of them all. Even if these miserable beings were proved guilty of every crime before you take them off, ought we to take upon ourselves the office of executioners? And even if we condescend so far, still can we be justified in taking them, unless we have clear proof that they are criminals?—But, if we go much further—if we ourselves tempt them to sell their fellow-creatures to us,—we may rest assured that they will take care to provide by every possible method a supply of victims increasing in proportion to our demand. Can we, then hesitate in deciding whether the wars in Africa are their wars or ours? It was our arms in the river Cameroon, put into the hands of the trader, that furnished him with the means of pushing his trade; and I have no more doubt that they are British arms, put into the hands of Africans, which promote universal war and desolation, than I can doubt their having done so in that individual instance. . . .

. . . [Africa], it is said, has been in some degree civilized, and civilized by us. It is said they have gained some knowledge of the principles of justice. Yes, we give them enough of our intercourse to convey to them the means, and to initiate them in the study of mutual destruction. . . . Shall we pretend that we can thus acquire an honest right to exact the labour of these people? Can we pretend that we have a right to carry away to distant regions men of whom we know nothing by authentic inquiry, and of whom there is every reasonable presumption to think that those who sell them to us have no right to do so? But the evil does not stop here. Do you think nothing of the ruin and the miseries in which so many other individuals, still remaining in Africa, are involved in consequence of carrying off so many myriads of people? Do you think nothing of their families left behind? of the connections broken? of the friendships, attachments, and relationships that are burst asunder? Do you think nothing of the miseries in consequence that are felt from generation to generation? of the privation of that happiness which might be communicated to them by an introduction of civilization, and of mental and moral improvement?—a happiness which you withold from them so long as you permit the slave trade to continue.

Thus, Sir, has the perversion of British commerce carried misery instead of happiness to one whole quarter of the globe. False to the very principles of trade, misguided in our policy, and unmindful of our duty, what astonishing mischief have we brought upon that continent! If, knowing the miseries we have caused, we refuse to put a stop to them, how greatly aggravated will be the guilt of this country! Shall we then delay rendering this justice to Africa? I am sure the immediate abolition of the slave trade is the first, the principal, the most indispensable act of policy, of duty, and of justice, that the legislature of this country has to take. . . .

David B. Davis: The Age of Reason Finds Slavery Unreasonable

Reprinted from David B. Davis: *The Problem of Slavery in Western Culture.* Copyright © 1966 by Cornell University. Used by permission of Cornell University Press.

The Age of Reason was also an age of compassion for afflicted humanity. Diderot, who had written a French translation of Shaftesbury, could weep over the relatively minor sufferings of Pamela and Clarissa. Candide shed tears as he entered Surinam, for he had just conversed with a young Negro who, in accordance with the custom of the country, had had an arm and leg cut off, and who had shattered Candide's philosophic optimism by saying that this was the price for the sugar Europeans enjoyed. The hero of *La nouvelle Héloïse* had a similar encounter with slaves. In eighteenth-century literature, a feeling of shock and indignation at the physical cruelties of Negro slavery increasingly became a test of sensibility, just as the cruelties themselves became a symbol of man's inhumanity to man.

But an even more significant source of the new interest in individual happiness was the Lockean belief that society is composed of discrete, self-governing individuals, whose true humanity lies in their proprietorship of their own persons. The disciples of Locke found moral freedom not in self-denial and transcendence of worldly condition, but in a lack of dependence upon the will of others, in the natural exercise of the human faculties, and in the unfettered pursuit of enlightened self-interest. Instead of assuming that this kind of freedom would lead to total anarchy, they held that nature and society could be made compatible only if individuals retained a certain inviolable core of autonomy and self-direction. These ideas, which did so much to shape subsequent political and economic thought, were obviously of the highest importance in discrediting the traditional view of slavery. For in the Lockean philosophy a slave, so long as he is deemed to be human, must either be classed as a criminal who is beyond the pale of the social contract, or be considered a freeman who has been forcefully and unnaturally suppressed. . . .

Rousseau was interested in larger issues than Negro slavery, but because slavery had conventionally been linked with justifications for the existing social order, he saw that an attack on the principle of involuntary servitude might unravel the network of sanctions for every species of injustice. Hence he repeated Montesquieu's arguments on the invalidity of any contract for self-sale, and on the discrepancy between the lawful objectives of war and the enslavement of captives. But Rousseau went on to a far more radical set of conclusions. Men were born free and equal; the renunciation of liberty meant the renunciation of being a man. Since slavery always rested on brute force, which was but thinly disguised by meaningless conventions, bondsmen had no duties or obligations to their masters. The words "slave" and "right" were contradictory and mutually exclusive. . . .

In 1755, the year of Rousseau's *Discours sur l'inégalité,* the death of Montesquieu evoked an introductory eulogy in Volume V of the *Encyclopédie.* The great jurist was specifically credited with having exposed the illegality of human bondage; and in a long article on "Esclavage," which fell within the alphabetical range of the same volume, the Chevalier de Jaucourt developed and strengthened Montesquieu's antislavery arguments. Next to *L'Esprit des lois,* the *Encyclopédie* was without doubt the most important agent in making antislavery a part of the Enlightenment's overriding concern for the happiness and well-being of mankind. It was not until 1765, however, when the editors arrived at "Traite des Nègres," that de Jaucourt's conclusions carried a note of extraordinary simplicity and directness:

Thus there is not a single one of these hapless souls—who, we maintain, are but slaves—who does not have the right to be declared free, since he has never lost his freedom; since it was impossible for him to lose it; and since neither his ruler nor his father nor anyone else had the right to dispose of his freedom; consequently, the sale of his person is null and void in and of itself: this Negro does not divest himself, indeed cannot under any condition divest himself of his natural rights; he carries them everywhere with him, and he has the right to demand that others allow him to enjoy those rights. Therefore, it is a clear case of inhumanity on the part of the judges in those free countries to which the slave is shipped, not to free the slave instantly by legal declaration, since he is their brother, having a soul like theirs.

This passage has seemed worth quoting at some length, since it is one of the earliest and most lucid applications to slavery of the natural rights philosophy, and succeeds in stating a basic principle which was to guide the more radical abolitionists of the nineteenth century. . . .

Locke and Rousseau Differ on Education of the Young

John Locke (1632–1704) and Jean-Jacques Rousseau (1712–1778), famous representatives of enlightened thought, were men of very different temperament. Locke was reserved and a sturdy apologist for the English middle class; Rousseau might be called an eighteenth-century beatnik. Born in Switzerland, Rousseau wandered about France, working at a variety of jobs, until he won first prize in 1749 in a competition for an essay on the influence of civilization and the arts on man. He became a loudly emotional spokesman for all sorts of reform—perhaps most influentially in government and education. In his last years he suffered from growing feelings of persecution, became ever more peculiar, and ended his life more or less insane. The reading presents Locke's and Rousseau's stand on educating children, written seventy-five years and educational centuries apart. I. From John Locke, *Some Thoughts Concerning Education* (London, 1712). II. From Jean-Jacques Rousseau, *Emile,* trans. E. Worthington (Boston, 1883).

I. JOHN LOCKE (1693)

Keep them [children] from vice and vicious dispositions, and such a kind of behavior in general will come with every degree of their age, as is suitable to that age and the company they ordinarily converse with; and as they grow in years, they will grow in attention and application. But that your words may always carry weight and authority with them, if it shall happen upon any occasion that you bid them leave off the doing of any even childish things, you must be sure to carry the point, and not let him have the mastery. But yet, I say, I would have the father seldom interpose his authority and command in these cases, or in any other, but such as have a tendency to vicious habits. I think there are better ways of prevailing with them: and a gentle persuasion in reasoning when the first point of submission to your will is got, will most times do much better.

It will perhaps be wondered that I mention *reasoning* with children; and yet I cannot but think that the true way of dealing with them. They understand it as early as they do language; and, if I misobserve not, they love to be treated as rational creatures sooner than is imagined. 'Tis pride should be cherished in them, and, as much as can be, made the greatest instrument to turn them by.

But when I talk of reasoning, I do not intend any other but such as is suited to the child's capacity and apprehension. Nobody can think a boy of three or seven years old should be argued with as a grown man. Long discourses and philosophical reasonings, at best, amaze and confound but do not instruct children. When I say, therefore, that they must be *treated as rational creatures,* I mean that you should make them sensible, by the mildness of your carriage, and the composure even in your correction of them, that what you do is reasonable in you, and useful and necessary for them; and that it is not out of *capriccio,* passion, or fancy that you command or forbid them anything. This they are capable of understanding; and there is no virtue they should be excited to nor fault they should be kept from which I do not think they may be convinced of; but it must be by such reasons as their age and understandings are capable of, and those proposed always in very few and plain words. . . .

II. JEAN-JACQUES ROUSSEAU (1762)

Reasoning should not begin too soon— Locke's great maxim was that we ought to reason with children, and just now this maxim is much in fashion. I think, however, that its success does not warrant its reputation, and I find nothing more stupid than children who

have been so much reasoned with. Reason, apparently a compound of all other faculties, the one latest developed, and with most difficulty, is the one proposed as agent in unfolding the faculties earliest used! The noblest work of education is to make a reasoning man, and we expect to train a young child by making him reason! This is beginning at the end; this is making an instrument of a result. If children understood how to reason they would not need to be educated. But by addressing them from their tenderest years in a language they cannot understand you accustom them to be satisfied with words, to find fault with whatever is said to them, to think themselves as wise as their teachers, to wrangle and rebel. And what we mean they shall do from reasonable motives we are forced to obtain from them by adding the motive of avarice, or of fear, or of vanity.

Nature intends that children shall be children before they are men. If we insist on reversing this order we shall have fruit early indeed, but unripe and tasteless, and liable to early decay; we shall have young savants and old children. Childhood has its own methods of seeing, thinking, and feeling. Nothing shows less sense than to try to substitute our own methods for these. . . .

In attempting to persuade your pupils to obedience you add to this alleged persuasion force and threats, or worse still, flattery and promises. Bought over in this way by interest, or constrained force, they pretend to be convinced by reason. They see plainly that as soon as you discover obedience or disobedience in their conduct, the former is an advantage and the latter a disadvantage to them. . . . You think you have convinced them, when you have only wearied them out or intimidated them.

What results from this? First of all, that by imposing upon them a duty they do not feel, you set them against your tyranny, and dissuade them from loving you; you teach them to be dissemblers, deceitful, wilfully untrue, for the sake of extorting rewards or of escaping punishments. Finally, by habituating them to cover a secret motive by an apparent motive, you give them the means to constantly mislead you, of concealing their true character from you, and of satisfying yourself and others with empty words when their occasion demands. You may say that the law, although binding on the conscience, uses constraint in dealing with grown men. I grant it; but what are these men but children spoiled by their education? This is precisely what ought to be prevented. With children use force, with men reason; such is the natural order of things. The wise man requires no laws.

STUDY QUESTIONS

1. Why was the eighteenth century known as the Age of Reason? How did achievements in science affect the attitude toward other sectors of society?

2. What was meant by the idea of progress? Why is this a modern idea?

3. Who were the *philosophes?* What did they find wrong with society and how did they try to reach their objectives? How did censorship affect the movement?

4. What solution did the *philosophes* offer to cure the ills of society? Why did they attack the church so violently?

5. How did Kant define "enlightenment"? What did he mean by saying that his contemporaries lived in an age of enlightenment but not in an enlightened age?

6. How should punishment be determined according to Beccaria? On what grounds did Pitt argue that slavery should be abolished?

7. In what ways was the concept of slavery in general contrary to the beliefs of the Enlightenment?

8. How did Locke and Rousseau differ on educating children? In what way were both men products of the Age of Reason?

9. On the basis of today's readings to what conclusions can you come about the goals of the Enlightenment and the ways men tried to reach those goals?

Voltaire: Candide, or The Optimist (1759)

TOPIC 15

VOLTAIRE: A PHILOSOPHER IN ACTION

Among the *philosophes* of the eighteenth century Voltaire was without peer as a literary critic, crusader, satirist, and master of the printed word. His championship of the cause of toleration and the protection of the innocent doggedly challenged the moral values of his day, and his attack on prejudice, clerical power, and feudal privilege helped alter the social and political climate of prerevolutionary France. His stubborn independence, critical intelligence, and social concern have made him a model for the role the intellectual can play in modern society. The samples of his writings that follow and the scholarly comment present Voltaire in such a role by examining his impatience with myths and false ideals and his concern with serving the cause of a higher justice.

François Arouet (1694–1778), better known as Voltaire, was the most famous of the eighteenth-century *philosophes,* writing an endless number of plays, histories, novels, and philosophical essays. His ability and, even more, his biting wit first made him a favorite at the French court and later got him into frequent difficulties. Imprisoned for brief periods in the Bastille, he spent a large portion of his life outside of France, in England, in Prussia as special guest of King Frederick the Great, and at his country estate which straddled the French-Swiss border. Voltaire skillfully used his brilliant talents and European reputation to fight against the evils of society. Opposing the popular argument, "Whatever is, is right," he made this the theme in 1759 of his most famous novel, *Candide,* portions of which appear in this reading. Visited at his country home in his later years by hundreds of the famous and near-famous, Voltaire at eighty-three returned in triumph to Paris and died there, exhausted by the tumultuous reception he received. From *The Works of Voltaire,* trans. T. Smollett (Paris, 1901).

I

Chapter I: How Candide Was Brought up in a Magnificent Castle and How He Was Driven Thence

In the country of Westphalia, in the castle of the most noble baron of Thunder-ten-tronckh, lived a youth whom nature had endowed with a most sweet disposition. His face was the true index of his mind. He had a solid judgment, joined to the most unaffected simplicity; and hence, I presume, he had his name Candide. The old servants of the house suspected him to have been the son of the baron's sister, by a very good sort of a gentleman of the neighborhood, whom that young lady refused to marry, because he could produce no more than threescore and eleven quarterings in his arms; the rest of the genealogical tree belonging to the family having been lost through the injuries of time.

The baron was one of the most powerful lords in Westphalia; for his castle had not only a gate, but even windows; and his great hall was hung with tapestry. He used to hunt with his mastiffs and spaniels instead of greyhounds; his groom served him for huntsman; and the parson of the parish officiated as his private chaplain. He was called My Lord by all his people, and when he told a story every one laughed at it.

My lady baroness weighed three hundred and fifty pounds, consequently was a person of no small importance; and she did the honors of the house with a dignity that commanded universal respect. Her daughter was about seventeen years of age, fresh colored, pretty, plump, and desirable. The baron's son seemed to be a youth in every respect worthy of the father he sprung from. Pangloss, his tutor, was the oracle of the family, and little Candide listened to his instructions with all the simplicity natural to his age and disposition.

Master Pangloss taught the metaphysico-theologo-cosmolonigology. He could prove admirably that there is no effect without a cause; and that, in this best of all possible worlds, the baron's castle was the most magnificent of all castles, and my lady the best of all possible baronesses.

"It is demonstrable," said he, "that things cannot be otherwise than as they are; for as all things have been created for some end, they must necessarily be created for the best end. Observe, for instance, the nose is formed for spectacles, therefore we wear spectacles. The legs are visibly designed for stockings, accordingly we wear stockings. Stones were made to be hewn, and to construct castles, therefore My Lord has a magnificent castle; for the greatest baron in the province ought to be the best lodged. Pigs were intended to be eaten, therefore we eat pork all the year round: and they, who assert that everything is *right,* do not express themselves correctly; they should say that everything is *best.*"

Candide listened attentively, and believed implicitly; for he thought Miss Cunegund extremely beautiful, though he never had the courage to tell her so. He concluded that next to the happiness of being baron of Thunder-ten-tronckh, the next was that of being Miss Cunegund, the next that of seeing her every day, and the last that of hearing the doctrine of Master Pangloss, the greatest philosopher of the whole province, and consequently of the whole world.

One day when Miss Cunegund went to take a walk in a little neighboring wood which was called a park, she saw, through the bushes, the sage Doctor Pangloss giving a lesson in experimental philosophy to her mother's chambermaid, a little brown wench, very pretty, and very teachable. As Miss Cunegund took great interest in the sciences, she observed with the utmost attention the experi-

ments, which were repeated before her eyes; she perfectly well understood the force of the doctor's reasoning upon causes and effects. She retired greatly flurried, quite pensive and filled with the desire of knowledge, imagining that she might be a *sufficing reason* for young Candide, and he for her.

On her way back she happened to meet the young man; she blushed, he blushed also; she wished him a good morning in a flattering tone, he returned the salute, without knowing what he said. The next day, as they were rising from dinner, Cunegund and Candide slipped behind the screen. The miss dropped her handkerchief, the young man picked it up. She innocently took hold of his hand, and he as innocently kissed hers with a warmth, a sensibility, a grace—all very particular; their lips met; their eyes sparkled; their knees trembled; their hands strayed. The baron chanced to come by; he beheld the cause and effect, and without hesitation, saluted Candide with some notable kicks on the backside, and drove him from the castle. The lovely Miss Cunegund fainted away, and, as soon as she came to herself, the baroness boxed her ears. Thus, general consternation was spread over this most magnificent and most agreeable of all possible castles.

II

Chapter II: What Befell Candide among the Bulgarians

Candide, thus driven out of this earthly paradise, rambled a long time without knowing where he went; sometimes he raised his eyes, all bedewed with tears, toward heaven, and sometimes he cast a melancholy look towards the magnificent castle, where dwelt the fairest of young baronesses. He laid himself down to sleep in a furrow, heartbroken, and without

supper. The snow fell in great flakes, and, in the morning when he awoke, he was almost frozen to death. He crawled to the next village, which was called Waldberghoff-trarbk-dikdorff, without a penny in his pocket, and half dead with hunger and fatigue. There he stopped dejectedly at the door of an inn. He had not been long there, before two men dressed in blue, fixed their eyes steadfastly upon him. "Faith comrade," said one of them to the other, "there is a well-built young fellow, and of the right size." Upon which they went to Candide, and with the greatest politeness invited him to dine with them.

"Gentlemen," replied Candide, with most engaging modesty, "you do me much honor, but upon my word I have no money." "Money, sir!" said one of the blues to him, "young persons of your appearance and merit never pay anything; aren't you five feet five inches high?" "Yes, gentlemen, that is my height," replied he, making a low bow. "Come, then, sir, sit down along with us; we will not only pay your bill, but will never suffer such a clever young fellow as you to go short of money. Men were born to assist one another." "You are perfectly right, gentlemen," said Candide, "that is what Master Pangloss always told me, and I am convinced that everything is for the best."

His generous companions next entreated him to accept a few crowns, which he readily complied with, at the same time offering them his note for the payment, which they refused, and sat down to table. "Have you not a great affection for—" "Oh, yes! I have a great affection for the lovely Miss Cunegund." "May be so," replied one of the blues, "but that is not the question! We ask you whether you have not a great affection for the king of the Bulgarians?" "For the king of the Bulgarians?" said Candide. "Oh, Lord, not at all, why I never saw him in my life." "Why he is a most charming king! Come, we must drink his health." "With all my heart, gentlemen," says Candide, and off he tossed his glass. "Bravo!" cried the blues, "you are now the support, the defender, the hero of the Bulgarians; your fortune is made; you are in the high road to glory." So he was made to wheel about to the right, to the left, to draw his rammer, to return his rammer, to present, to fire, to march, and they gave him thirty blows with a cane; the next day he performed his exercise a little better, and they gave him but twenty; the day following he came off with ten, and was looked upon as a young fellow of surprising genius by all his comrades.

Candide was struck with amazement and could not for the soul of him conceive how he came to be a hero. One fine spring morning, he took it into his head to take a walk, and he marched straight forward, imagining it to be a privilege of the human species, as well as of the animals, to make use of their legs how and when they pleased. He had not gone six miles before he was overtaken by four other heroes, six feet high, who bound him neck and heels, and carried him to a dungeon. A court-martial was held and he was asked which he liked better, to run the gauntlet six and thirty times through the whole regiment, or to have his brains blown out with a dozen musket-balls? In vain he argued that the human will is free, and that he chose neither; they obliged him to make a choice, and he determined, in virtue of that divine gift called free will, to run the gauntlet six and thirty times. He underwent this discipline twice and, the regiment being composed of two thousand men, he received exactly four thousand strokes, which laid bare all his muscles and nerves from the nape of his neck to his rump.

As they were preparing to make him set out the third time our young hero, unable to stand it any longer, begged as a favor that they be so obliging as to shoot him through the head. The favor being granted, a bandage was tied over his eyes, and he was made to kneel down. At that very instant, his Bulgarian majesty happening to pass by stopped and inquired into the delinquent's crime. Being a prince of great penetration, he found, from what he heard of Candide, that he was a young metaphysician, entirely ignorant of the world, and, therefore, out of his great clemency he granted him pardon, for which his name will be celebrated in every journal and in every age. A skillful surgeon then cured the beaten-up Candide in three weeks by means of ointments first prescribed by Dioscorides. His sores were now skinned over and he was able to march, when the king of the Bulgarians gave battle to the king of the Abares.

Chapter III: How Candide Escaped from the Bulgarians and What Befell Him Afterwards

Never was anything so fine, so neat, so brilliant, and so well ordered as the two armies. The trumpets, fifes, oboes, drums, and blasts of artillery made such harmony as never was heard in hell itself. The entertainment began by a discharge of cannon, which, in the twinkling of an eye, laid flat about six thousand men on each side. The musket bullets swept away, out of the best of all possible worlds, nine or ten thousand scoundrels that infested its surface. The bayonet was next the sufficient reason of the deaths of several thousands. The whole losses amounted to thirty thousand souls. Candide trembled like a philosopher, and hid himself as well as he could during this heroic butchery.

At length, while the two kings were causing *Te Deums*—Glory to God—to be sung in their camps, Candide decided to go and reason somewhere else upon causes and effects. After passing over heaps of dead or dying men, the first place he came to was a neighboring village, in the Abarian territories, which had been burned to the ground by the Bulgarians, in accordance with international law. Here lay a number of old men covered with wounds, who watched their wives dying with their throats cut, and hugging their children to their breasts, all stained with blood. There several young virgins, whose bellies had been ripped open, after they had satisfied the natural desires of the Bulgarian heroes, breathed their last; while others, half burned in the flames, begged to be dispatched out of the world. The ground . . . was covered with the brains, arms, and legs of dead men.

Candide made all the haste he could to another village, which belonged to the Bulgarians, and there he found the heroic Abares had behaved in the same way. Thence continuing to walk over quivering limbs, or through ruined buildings, at length he left the theatre of war behind him. He had a little food in his knapsack and Miss Cunegund's image in his heart. . . .

III

[Candide arrived in Holland, had further misadventures, and then met a beggar "all covered with scabs, his eyes sunk in his head, the end of his nose eaten off, his mouth drawn on one side, his teeth as black as a coal, snuffling and coughing most violently, and every time he attempted to spit out dropped a tooth."]

Chapter IV: How Candide Found His Old Master Pangloss Again and What Happened to Him

. . . This shocking figure. . . looked at Candide very earnestly, shed tears and threw his arms about his neck. Candide started back aghast. "Alas!" said the one wretch to the other, "don't you know your dear Pangloss?" "What do I hear? Is it you, my dear master! you I behold in this dreadful condition? What awful misfortune has befallen you? What has made you leave the most magnificent and delightful of all castles? What has become of Miss Cunegund, the pearl of young ladies and nature's masterpiece?" "Oh Lord!" cried Pangloss, "I am so weak I cannot stand," upon which Candide instantly . . . procured him something to eat. As soon as Pangloss was a little refreshed, Candide began to repeat his inquiries concerning Miss Cunegund. "She is dead," replied the other. "Dead!" cried Candide, and immediately fainted away. His friend restored him by the help of a little sour vinegar, which he found by chance in the stable. Candide opened his eyes, and again repeated: "Dead! is Miss Cunegund dead? Ah, where is the best of worlds now? But of what illness did she die? Was it of grief on seeing her father kick me out of his magnificent castle?" "No," replied Pangloss, "her belly was ripped open by the Bulgarian soldiers, after they had ravished her as much as it was possible for a woman to be ravished. They broke the baron, her father's head for attempting to defend her; my lady, her mother, was cut in pieces; my poor pupil was treated in the same manner as his sister. And for the castle, they have not left one stone upon another; they have destroyed all the ducks, and the sheep, the barns, and the trees; but we have had our revenge, for the Abares have done the very same thing in a neighboring barony, which belonged to a Bulgarian lord."

At hearing this, Candide fainted away a second time, but, having come to his senses again, he said all that it became him to say. He inquired into the cause and effect, as well as into the sufficing reason that had reduced Pangloss to so miserable a condition. "Alas," replied the tutor, "it was love; love, the comfort of the human species; love, the preserver of the universe; the soul of all sensible beings; love, tender love!" "Alas," cried Candide, "I have had some knowledge of love myself, this sovereign of hearts, this soul of souls; yet it never cost me more than a kiss and twenty kicks on the backside. But how could such a beautiful cause produce such a hideous effect upon you?"

Pangloss answered in these terms: "O my dear Candide, you must remember Pacquette, that pretty girl, who waited on our noble baroness. In her arms I tasted the pleasures of paradise, which produced these hell-torments with which you see me devoured. She was infected with the disease, and perhaps has since died of it. She received this present of a learned churchman, who had traced it back to its source. He was indebted for it to an old countess, who had it of a captain of horse, who had it of a marchioness, who had it of a page. The page had it of a Jesuit, who, during his novitiate, had it in a direct line from one of the fellow-adventurers of Christopher Columbus. For my part I shall give it to nobody, for I am a dying man."

"O wise Pangloss," cried Candide, "what a strange genealogy is this! Isn't the devil at the root of it?" "Not at all," replied the great man, "it was an unavoidable thing, a necessary ingredient in the best of worlds; for if Columbus had not caught in an island in America this disease, which contaminates the course of generation, and frequently impedes propagation itself, and is evidently opposed to the great end of Nature, we should have had neither chocolate nor cochineal [a superior red dye]. . . ."

[Candide took Pangloss to a doctor who cured him—he "lost only an eye and an ear." Teacher and student then set sail for Lisbon, Portugal. A bad storm occurred and the ship sunk in Lisbon harbor. The two philosophers, however, clinging to a plank, managed to reach shore. Scarcely did they reach solid land when a violent earthquake began and 30,000 people were crushed in the falling ruins. Pangloss, as usual, consoled the survivors.]

"For," said he, "all this must necessarily be for the best. Since this earthquake is at Lisbon, it could not be anywhere else. It is impossible that things should not be where they are, because all is good."

A little man clad in black, who belonged to the Inquisition and sat at his side, took him up very politely, and said: "It seems, sir, you do not believe in original sin; for if all is for the best, then there has been neither fall nor punishment."

"I most humbly ask Your Excellency's pardon," answered Pangloss, still more politely, "for the fall of man and the punishment of Adam and Eve necessarily are a part of the best of possible worlds." "Then, sir, you do not believe there is free will," said the inquisitor. "Your Excellency will excuse me," said Pangloss, "free will is consistent with absolute necessity; for it was necessary we should be free; because, in short, the determinate will—"

Pangloss was in the middle of his sentence, when the inquisitor made a signal with his head to the tall armed footman in a cloak, who waited upon him.

Chapter VI: How a Fine Inquisition Was Staged To Prevent Earthquakes, and How Candide Was Whipped

After the earthquake, which had destroyed three-fourths of Lisbon, the wisemen of the country could not find any better means to prevent a total destruction, than to give the people a splendid inquisition. It had been decided by the university of Coimbra, that the spectacle of some persons burnt to death by a slow fire, with great ceremony, was an infallible antidote for earthquakes.

In consequence of this resolution, they had seized a Basque, convicted of having married his god-mother, and two Portuguese Jews, who had refused to eat bacon with their chicken. After dinner, they came and secured Dr. Pangloss, and his disciple Candide, the one for having spoke too freely, and the other for having listened with an air of approval. They were both conducted to separate rooms, extremely damp, and never inconvenienced by the sun. Eight days after, they were both clothed with a gown and had their heads adorned with paper crowns. Candide's crown and gown were painted with inverted flames and with devils that had neither tails nor claws; but Pangloss' devils had claws and tails, and the flames were pointed upwards. Thus dressed, they marched in procession and heard a very moving speech followed by fine music on a squeaking organ. Candide was whipped on the back in time with the music; the Basque and the two men who would not eat bacon were burnt; and Pangloss, though it was contrary to custom, was hanged. The same day, the earth shook anew, with a most dreadful noise.

Candide, terrified, confused, trembling and all bloody, said to himself: "If this is the best of possible worlds, what then can the rest be like? I have, of course, already been whipped among the Bulgarians; but, Oh, my dear Pangloss; thou greatest of philosophers, that it should be my fate to see you hanged without knowing the reason why! . . . Oh! Miss Cunegund! the jewel of ladies, was it really necessary for you to have been outraged and slain!"

Lanson: Voltaire as a Social Reformer

Gustave Lanson (1857–1934), French literary historian, wrote what many consider the "best brief survey of Voltaire's life and work." In these excerpts Lanson comments on Voltaire's involvement in social action and his concern with freedom. From Gustave Lanson, *Voltaire*, trans. Robert Wagoner (New York: John Wiley and Sons, Inc., 1960), pp. 151–152, 159–164.

I

The salient feature of Voltaire's life was his determination to be more than just a man of letters. In this respect he differed from Montesquieu, Diderot, and Rousseau, who were content to enlighten or inflame men's minds through their writings alone. No sooner was Voltaire quietly settled down in his canton of Gex and safe from harassment, or virtually so, than he became involved with others, not with mankind in general, but with specific individual cases which he regarded as either a result or a symptom of social abuses.

First, in 1759, it was the little affair, not widely publicized, of the six Crassy brothers whose inheritance Voltaire retrieved from the Jesuits of Ornex. Then in 1762 there was the Calas affair. It was on the 10th of March that Jean Calas, a textile merchant on the Rue des Filatiers in Toulouse, was put to death by being broken on the wheel after a long trial conducted first by the municipal magistrates and later by the *Parlement* of Toulouse. Calas was accused of murdering his eldest son, Marc-Antoine, who was found hanged in his father's shop October 13, 1761. The crime was attributed to the Calvinist family's horror at the thought that Marc-Antoine wanted to become a Catholic. Jean Calas died protesting his innocence.

Informed of this event on the 22nd of March by a businessman named Audibert, Voltaire first considered it an instance of Huguenot fanaticism. But further inquiry soon convinced him that he was in the presence of a judicial error. Thereupon Voltaire took personal charge of the case. He ran headlong into the indifference, skepticism, or open hostility of ministers, courtiers, and parliamentarians. So he turned to the public. With all kinds of writings, discussing the charges and facts in the case and developing his ideas of tolerance, Voltaire aroused and set in motion the great force of public opinion. He supported and directed from Ferney all the moves made by Mme Calas. He assisted the lawyers, Elie de Beaumont and Loyseau de Mauléon. On March 7, 1764, came the Council's first decree ordering a judicial review of the trial. On June 4, 1764, the judgment of Toulouse was reversed. On the 9th of March 1765 the fourth appellate judges of the Town Hall of Toulouse unanimously exonerated Calas, thereby clearing his name and restoring his family's civil and property rights. . . .

After the Calas case came that of the Sirven family. Again it was the same story. A young Huguenot girl had thrown herself into a well and was drowned. The father was condemned

"The Unfortunate Calas Family," a 1765 engraving. Mme Calas is seated to the left of her two daughters listening to her son read a letter about reparation.

by the fiscal attorney of Mazamet in southern France (1764). Fortunately, he was able to escape by fleeing with his wife and two surviving daughters. With his sharp, practical judgment, Voltaire chose not to move on behalf of Sirven until the Calas affair was terminated. Then he took hold of the case with the zeal of a crusader. He finished it by having Sirven and his wife fully cleared in 1771. . . .

There was the La Barre case. A crucifix had been mutilated at Abbeville (August 9, 1765). Several youths were suspects. The Chevalier d'Etallonde had fled. The Chevalier de La Barre was arrested and convicted. He was convicted only of not baring his head during the procession of the Holy Sacrament, of having sung some impious and obscene songs, of having recited *La Pucelle* [Voltaire], and of having in his possession such books as *La Religieuse en chemise* [a rather licentious novel, published anonymously] and *Le Dictionnaire philosophique portatif* [Voltaire]. For these offenses, aggravated by private grudges, the Seneschal's court of Abbeville condemned him to have his tongue torn out and then be beheaded. The sentence was upheld by the *Parlement* of Paris. La Barre was spared only the mutilation of his tongue. His body and head were burned on a pyre on which they also threw the *Dictionnaire philosophique* for good measure. Voltaire was thunderstruck. He appealed to the public. He befriended Etallonde and secured him a post in the service of Prussia. He tried later to quash the arrest warrant which condemned Etallonde by default. He was unsuccessful. He could only curse the judges of Abbeville in all his writings. And this he did not fail to do. . . .

In 1772 he took charge of the case of Mlle Camp, a Protestant girl whom the vicomte de Bombelle had married quietly in a remote rural area [Protestants were forbidden to meet in churches]. The wedding rite was performed by a Protestant pastor. The vicomte later abandoned her and their child in order to marry a wealthy Roman Catholic. He maintained that the first union was null and void. Voltaire was successful only in obtaining financial aid for the victim. . . .

When he learned that there were still *mainmortables* [serfs without property rights] in France, and that only a short distance from Ferney some 12,000 men were held in serfdom by twenty priests of Saint-Claude, Voltaire was horrified. From 1770 on, he besieged the king's councillor, Turgot, with pleas and petitions. He supported the lawyer Christin de

Besançon, who had decided to act on behalf of the serfs in the Jura mountains. Although he stirred up public opinion, his clients were not to win their freedom until the French Revolution. . . .

II

The Voltairian Revolution of France

If virtue resides only in social action, then the moral life is inconceivable without an involvement in politics, and the good man will be he who does good for everyone by working to improve society. And that is what Voltaire did, with unremitting fervor, during his last years. . . . Anxious for results, distrusting philosophical and theological systems, he did not apply himself, as Montesquieu and Rousseau had done, to the formulation of a political theory or to drawing up a plan for an ideal society. He did not refine on abstract principles. He was a realist to the highest degree, accepting France as she was with her social classes and her conditions so ripe for reform. He tried to discover what could be done immediately, what was within the realm of possibility, and limited his efforts to that end. He reviewed all phases of government and administration, criticizing them in the light of two or three moral principles of his own. He drew up a list of abuses and reforms, avoiding when possible any head-on collision with reality, the better to change it more effectively.

He regarded society as an established fact, a fact of life, and governments as the powers deriving from this fact. Governmental powers had, in the course of time, succeeded in disguising their rule by force as rule by law. But there is no law, save in the free consent of men, for men are by nature free and equal.

There is no divine right. Democracy is the most rational kind of government. But because it can survive only in small countries, and also because monarchy is the most ancient form of government in France, a concern for peace and order requires the Frenchman to be a royalist. A constitutional, representative regime is good in itself, but, for France, feudal anarchy had made a regime of absolute monarchy both useful and necessary. The force of royal power saved the people from petty tyrants. Yet one must require a respect for laws on the part of absolute royalty itself, and these laws must have as their object the preservation of freedom, the only "fundamental law of all nations." But general freedom, in practice, consists of a number of individual freedoms which must be guaranteed to each citizen through laws.

Here is Voltaire's list of required freedoms: (1) *Freedom of person:* slavery is against nature. (2) *Freedom of speech and the press,* even in matters of politics and religion. This freedom is the safeguard and basis of all others. Character assassination, outrages against authority and laws, even seditious libel, must be punished (3) *Civil liberty: habeas corpus* should be introduced. (4) *Freedom of conscience.* (5) *Security of private property:* if required for reasons of public utility, private property may be expropriated with compensation for the loss sustained. All citizens must have the right to possess private property, but there shall be no law enforcing an equal distribution of goods. (6) *Right to work* and to sell one's work or product to the highest bidder. Work is the property of those who lack property. . . .

We would also be wrong about Voltaire's spirit or intentions if we believed that they did not go beyond the reforms he championed. He was not a revolutionary or a visionary. He was an opportunist and a realist. He indicated what could be accomplished immediately, under the pressure of public opinion. Having achieved a certain limited objective, he did not give up asking for something else. He did not claim to be a republican. He did not call for a constitution on the English model. He did not expressly ask for the direct participation of property owners and industrialists in the management of public affairs. He did not ask for the right for Protestants to hold public office or be given the freedom of public worship. He did not demand that all professors be nominated by the state. But these were matters he regarded as altogether reasonable. He contented himself with declaring the right of the state to supervise religious communities. He did not demand their immediate dissolution, though he desired and hoped for it.

Voltaire was, beyond any doubt, a conservative. But he was conservative in the manner of any true liberal. He did not want a violent upheaval. He did not try to abolish social classes or the unequal distribution of wealth. He put France into the hands of the enlightened bourgeoisie, whose limits he would expand to include greater numbers of common people through the process of education. But his program, precisely because it was a practical one, contained nothing absolute or definitive. He maintained the constant attitude of seeking certain limited and realizable reforms, towards which he bent every effort, and then anticipating additional improvements made possible by having accomplished his first objectives. And thus it would continue to be so long as we find evil in the world and, with the aid of human reason, can conceive of something better. Thus it would

always be so long as humanity and justice are, in one place or another, wounded and suffering, and so long as society remains imperfect and men unhappy.

Voltaire Attacks Fanaticism

Voltaire was a master of propaganda. Many of his propagandist writings were collected in the form of a dictionary. Voltaire held that the most useful books were those in which "the reader did part of the work himself," in which he develops the author's thoughts if given the germ of an idea. In this reading from the *Portable Philosophical Dictionary,* the famous *philosophe* provided his readers with the concept of "fanaticism." From *Voltaire's Philosophical Dictionary* (New York, 1901), V, pp. 8, 11–12, 15–19.

It is dreadful to observe how the opinion that the wrath of heaven might be appeased by human massacre spread, after being once started, through almost every religion. . . .

The same spirit of fanaticism cherished the rage for distant conquests; scarcely had Europe repaired its losses when the discovery of a new world hastened the ruin of our own. At that terrible injunction, "Go and conquer," America was desolated and its inhabitants exterminated; Africa and Europe were exhausted in vain to repeople it; the poison of money and of pleasure having enervated the species, the world became nearly a desert and appeared likely every day to advance nearer to desolation by the continual wars which

were kindled on our continent, from the ambition of extending its power to foreign lands.

Let us now compute the immense number of slaves which fanaticism has made, whether in Asia, where uncircumcision was a mark of infamy, or in Africa, where the Christian name was a crime, or in America, where the pretext of baptism absolutely extinguished the feelings of humanity. Let us compute the thousands who have been seen to perish either on scaffolds in the ages of persecution, or in civil wars by the hands of their fellow citizens, or by their own hands through excessive austerities, and maceration. Let us survey the surface of the earth, and glance at the various standards unfurled and blazing in the name of religion; in Spain against the Moors, in France against the Turks, in Hungary against the Tartars; at the numerous military orders, founded for converting infidels by the point of the sword, and slaughtering one another at the foot of the altar they had come to defend. Let us then look down from the appalling tribunal thus raised on the bodies of the innocent and miserable, in order to judge the living, as God, with a balance widely different, will judge the dead.

In a word, let us contemplate the horrors of fifteen centuries, all frequently renewed in the course of a single one; unarmed men slain at the feet of altars; kings destroyed by the dagger or by poison; a large state reduced to half its extent by the fury of its own citizens; the nation at once the most warlike and the most pacific on the face of the globe, divided in fierce hostility against itself; the sword unsheathed between the sons and the father; usurpers, tyrants, executioners, sacrilegious robbers, and bloodstained parricides violating, under the impulse of religion, every convention divine or human—such is the deadly picture of fanaticism. . . .

We understand by fanaticism at present a religious madness, gloomy and cruel. It is a malady of the mind, which is taken in the same way as smallpox. Books communicate it much less than meetings and discourses. We seldom get heated while reading in solitude, for our minds are then tranquil and sedate. But when an ardent man of strong imagination addresses himself to weak imaginations, his eyes dart fire, and that fire rapidly spreads; his tones, his gestures, absolutely convulse the nerves of his auditors. He exclaims, "The eye of God is at this moment upon you; sacrifice every mere human possession and feeling; fight the battles of the Lord"—and they rush to the fight.

Fanaticism is, in reference to superstition, what delirium is to fever, or rage to anger. He who is involved in ecstasies and visions, who takes dreams for realities, and his own imaginations for prophecies, is a fanatical novice of great hope and promise, and will probably soon advance to the highest form, and kill man for the love of God.

Bartholomew Diaz was a fanatical monk. He had a brother at Nuremberg called John Diaz, who was an enthusiast adherent to the doctrines of Luther, and completely convinced that the pope was Antichrist, and had the sign of the beast. Bartholomew, still more ardently convinced that the pope was god upon earth, quits Rome, determined either to convert or murder his brother; he accordingly murdered him! Here is a perfect case of fanaticism. . . .

There is no other remedy for this epidemical malady than that spirit of philosophy, which, extending itself from one to another, at length civilizes and softens the manners of men and prevents the access of the disease. For when the disorder has made any progress, we should, without loss of time, fly from the seat of it, and wait till the air has become purified from contagion. Law and religion are not completely efficient against the spiritual pestilence. Religion, indeed, so far from affording proper nutriment to the minds of patients laboring under this infectious and infernal distemper, is converted, by the diseased process of their minds, into poison. . . .

Laws are yet more powerless against these paroxysms of rage. To oppose laws to cases of such a description would be like reading a decree of council to a man in a frenzy. The persons in question are fully convinced that the Holy Spirit which animates and fills them is above all laws; that their own enthusiasm is, in fact, the only law which they are bound to obey.

What can be said in answer to a man who says he will rather obey God than men, and who consequently feels certain of meriting heaven by cutting your throat? . . .

There has been only one religion in the world which has not been polluted by fanaticism and that is the religion of the learned in China. The different sects of ancient philosophers were not merely exempt from this pest of human society, but they were antidotes to it: for the effect of philosophy is to render the soul tranquil, and fanaticism and tranquility are totally incompatible. That our own holy religion has been so frequently polluted by this infernal fury must be imputed to the folly and madness of mankind. Thus Icarus abused the wings which he received for his benefit. They were given him for his salvation and they insured his destruction.

Voltaire Defends the Innocent: The Cases of Calas and Sirven (1762-1765)

The Calas case is in Voltaire, *Toleration and Other Essays,* trans., Joseph McCabe (New York, 1912), pp. 1-5.

I. SHORT ACCOUNT OF THE DEATH OF JEAN CALAS

The murder of Calas, which was perpetrated with the sword of justice at Toulouse on March 9, 1762, is one of the most singular events that deserve the attention of our own and of later ages. We quickly forget the long list of the dead who have perished in our battles. It is the inevitable fate of war; those who die by the sword might themselves have inflicted death on their enemies, and did not die without the means of defending themselves. When the risk and the advantage are equal astonishment ceases, and even pity is enfeebled. But when an innocent father is given into the hands of error, of passion, or of fanaticism; when the accused has no defense but his virtue; when those who dispose of his life run no risk but that of making a mistake; when they can slay with impunity by a legal decree—then the voice of the general public is heard, and each fears for himself. They see that no man's life is safe before a court that has been set up to guard the welfare of citizens, and every voice is raised in a demand of vengeance.

In this strange incident we have to deal with religion, suicide, and parricide. The question was, whether a father and mother had strangled their son to please God, a brother had strangled his brother, and a friend had strangled his friend; or whether the judges had incurred the reproach of breaking on the wheel an innocent father, or of sparing a guilty mother, brother, and friend.

Jean Calas, a man of sixty-eight years, had been engaged in commerce at Toulouse for more than forty years, and was recognized by all who knew him as a good father. He was a Protestant, as were also his wife and family, except one son, who had abjured the heresy, and was in receipt of a small allowance from his father. He seemed to be so far removed from the absurd fanaticism that breaks the bonds of society that he had approved the conversion of his son [Louis Calas], and had had in his service for thirty years a zealous Catholic woman, who had reared all his children.

One of the sons of Jean Calas, named Marc Antoine, was a man of letters. He was regarded as of a restless, sombre, and violent character. This young man, failing to enter the commercial world, for which he was unfitted, or the legal world, because he could not obtain the necessary certificate that he was a Catholic, determined to end his life, and informed a friend of his intention. He strengthened his resolution by reading all that had ever been written on suicide.

Having one day lost his money in gambling, he determined to carry out his plan on that very day. A personal friend and friend of the family, named Lavaisse, a young man of nineteen, well known for his candid and kindly ways, the son of a distinguished lawyer at Toulouse, had come from Bordeaux on the previous day, October 12, 1761. He happened to sup with the Calas family. The father, mother, Marc Antoine, the elder son, and Pierre, the second son, were present. After supper they withdrew to a small room. Marc Antoine disappeared, and when young Lavaisse was ready to go, and he and Pierre Calas had gone downstairs, they found, near the shop below, Marc Antoine in his shirt, hanging from a door, his coat folded under the counter. His shirt was unruffled, his hair was neatly combed, and he had no wound or mark on his body.

We will omit the details which were given in court, and the grief and despair of his parents; their cries were heard by the neighbours. Lavaisse and Pierre, beside themselves, ran for surgeons and the police.

While they were doing this, and the father and mother sobbed and wept, the people of Toulouse gathered round the house. They are superstitious and impulsive people; they regard as monsters their brothers who do not share their religion. . . . Some fanatic in the crowd cried out that Jean Calas had hanged his son Marc Antoine. The cry was soon repeated on all sides; some adding that the deceased was to have abjured Protestantism on the following day, and that the family and young Lavaisse had strangled him out of hatred of the Catholic religion. In a moment all doubt had disappeared. The whole town was persuaded that it is a point of religion with the Protestants for a father and mother to kill their children when they wish to change their faith.

The agitation could not end here. It was imagined that the Protestants of Languedoc had held a meeting the night before; that they had, by a majority vote, chosen an executioner for the sect; that the choice had fallen on young Lavaisse; and that, in the space of twenty-four hours, the young man had received the news of his appointment, and had come from Bordeaux to help Jean Calas, his wife, and their son Pierre to strangle a friend, son, and brother.

The captain of Toulouse, David, excited by these rumours and wishing to give effect to them by a prompt execution, took a step which is against the laws and regulations. He put the Calas family, the Catholic servant, and Lavaisse in irons. . . .

What great victories reason is winning among us! But would you believe, my dear friend, that the family of the Calas, so efficiently succored and avenged, was not the only one that religion accused of parricide —was not the only one sacrificed to the furies of religious persecution? . . .

II. SHORT ACCOUNT OF THE PERSECUTION OF THE SIRVEN FAMILY

A native of Castres, named Sirven, had three daughters. As the religion of the family is the so-called reformed religion, the youngest of the daughters was torn from the arms of her mother. She was put into a convent, where they beat her to help her to learn her catechism: she went mad: and threw herself into a well at a place not far from her parents' house. The bigots thereupon made up their minds that her father, mother, and sisters had drowned the child. The Catholics of the province are absolutely convinced that one of the chief points of the Protestant religion is that the fathers and mothers are bound to hang, strangle, or drown any of their children whom they suspect of any leaning toward the

Catholic faith. Precisely at the moment when the Calas were in irons, this fresh scaffold was uplifted.

The story of the drowned girl reached Toulouse at once. Everyone declared it to be a fresh instance of murderous parents. The public fury grew daily: Calas was broken on the wheel: Sirven, his wife, and his daughter were accused. Sirven, terrified, had just time to flee with his delicate family. They went on foot, with no creature to help them, across precipitous mountains, deep in snow. One of the daughters gave birth to an infant among the glaciers: and, herself dying, bore her dying child in her arms: they finally took the road to Switzerland.

The same fate which brought the children of the Calas to me, decided that the Sirvens should also appeal to me. Picture yourself, my friend, four sheep accused by the butchers of having devoured a lamb: for that is what I saw. I despair of describing to you so much innocence and so much sorrow. What ought I to have done? and what would you have done in my place? Could I rest satisfied with cursing human nature? I took the liberty of writing to the first president of Languedoc, a wise and good man: but he was not at Toulouse. I got one of my friends to present a petition to the vice-chancellor. During this time, near Castres, the father, mother, and two daughters were executed in effigy: their property confiscated and dissipated—to the last sou.

Here was an entire family—honest, innocent, virtuous—left to disgrace and beggary among strangers: some, doubtless, pitied them: but it is hard to be an object of pity to one's grave! I was finally informed that remission of their sentence was a possibility.

At first, I believed that it was the judges from whom that pardon must be obtained. You will easily understand that the family would sooner have begged their bread from door to door, or have died of want, than ask a pardon which admitted a crime too horrible to be pardonable. But how could justice be obtained? how could they go back to prison in a country where half the inhabitants still said that Calas' murder was just? Would there be a second appeal to Council? Would anyone try to rouse again the public sympathy which, it might well be, the misfortunes of the Calas had exhausted, and which would weary of refuting such accusations, of reinstating the condemned, and of confounding their judges?

Are not these two tragic events, my friend, so rapidly following each other, proofs of the inevitable decrees of fate, to which our miserable species is subject? A terrible truth, so much insisted on in Homer and Sophocles: but a useful truth, since it teaches us to be resigned and to learn how to suffer.

Shall I add that, while the incredible calamities of the Calas and the Sirvens wrung my heart, a man, whose profession you will guess from what he said, reproached me for taking so much interest in two families who were strangers to me? "Why do you mix yourself up in such things?" he asked; "let the dead bury their dead." I answered him, "If I found an Israelite in the desert—an Israelite covered in blood; suffer me to pour a little wine and oil into his wounds: you are the Levite, leave me to play the Samaritan. . . ."

I have only done in the fearful cases of the Calas and the Sirvens what all men do: I have followed my bent. A philosopher's lot is not to pity the unhappy—it is to be of use to them.

Voltaire Reflects on the Need for Good Laws

From Voltaire's *Philosophical Dictionary*, trans. H. I. Woolf (London: George Allen & Unwin Ltd., 1924).

No country has a good code of laws. The reason for this is evident: the laws have been made according to the time, the place, the need, etc.

When the needs have changed, the laws which have remained have become ridiculous. Thus the law which forbade the eating of pig and the drinking of wine was very reasonable in Arabia, where pig and wine are injurious. But it is absurd at Constantinople. . . .

To the shame of mankind, it is well known that the laws which govern our games are the only ones which are completely just, clear, inviolable, and enforced. Why is the Indian who gave us the rules of the game of chess willingly obeyed all over the world, and why are the popes' decretals, for example, today an object of horror and scorn? The reason is that the inventor of chess arranged everything with precision for the satisfaction of the players, while the popes, in their decretals, had nothing in view but their own interest. The Indian wished to exercise men's minds equally, and give them pleasure; the popes wished to besot men's minds. Also, the essence of the game of chess has remained the same for five thousand years, it is common to all the inhabitants of the earth; and the decretals are known only at Spoletto, Orvieto, Loretto, where the shallowest lawyer secretly hates and despises them.

Full of all these reflections, I like to think that there is a natural law independent of all human conventions: the fruit of my work must belong to me; I must honor my father and my mother; I have no right over my fellow's life, and my fellow has none over mine, etc. But when I reflect that from the days of Chedorlaomer to those of Mantzel everyone has gone about loyally killing and pillaging his neighbors, with a license in his pocket, I am very sad.

I am told that there are laws among thieves, and also laws of war. I ask what are these laws of war. I learn that they mean hanging a brave officer who has stood fast in a bad post without cannon against a royal army; that they mean having a prisoner hanged, if the enemy has hanged one of yours; that they mean putting to fire and sword villages which have not made their required contributions on an appointed day, according to the orders of the gracious sovereign of the district. "Good," say I, "this is the *Spirit of the Laws.*"

It seems to me that almost everyone has received from nature enough common sense to make laws, but that no one is just enough to make good laws.

STUDY QUESTIONS

1. What kind of person was Candide? Why was he always getting into difficulties? What was wrong with the philosophy of Dr. Pangloss? What specific points was Voltaire making?

2. *Candide* is a satire, that is a literary work ridiculing human vices and follies through the use of humor. How, in the first paragraphs, does Voltaire satirize Candide's mother, the baron and baroness, and Dr. Pangloss? Find examples of satire in other sections.

3. Satire, because its bite is softened by its humor, has proved an effective way of getting a message across in societies in which heavy censorship exists. In what ways is *Candide* a valuable source of information about the eighteenth century?

4. Do you think that Voltaire in *Candide* was opposed to the use of reason? To the idea of progress? To Locke's theory of how man learned?

5. Why did Voltaire interfere in social abuses? On what did he blame the Calas and Sirven injustices?

6. What was Voltaire's view of society? What did he mean by freedom? Do you agree with Lanson's appraisal of him as conservative?

7. What did Voltaire find wrong with laws? Do his articles on law and toleration have anything in common with the tale of *Candide*? In what ways is Voltaire a representative specimen of modern man?

Chapter 3

The Development of the Modern State, 1600–1815

The sense of man's relationship to society and the state was as profoundly altered by the economic and political revolutions of the seventeenth and eighteenth centuries as his sense of place in the cosmos had been by the gropings of early modern science. Behind this challenge to both the feudal order and the sacred monarchy lay the spurt in the growth of the European population, the opening of new lands on the steppes of Eurasia and in the vastness of the New World, and the relentless commercial and industrial revolution which brought to the bourgeoisie the wings of ambition and a widening concern for justice.

Two restless forces were at work in the undermining of the landscape of legalized social orders and the incredibly varied forms of monarchical and princely authority. The first force had its origin in the efforts of monarchs to modernize their governments, increase control over their subjects, and extend and defend their territory. In so doing, paradoxically, their debt to the bourgeoisie was enlarged. The second but critically important force was the effort of the bourgeoisie to alter the older form of monarchy and find a place for themselves in a social order whose privileges belonged largely with birth, and whose preponderant power rested with the owners of land.

England's development of machine technology had profoundly altered her own social order and offered her neighbors a new conception of the many ways in which power could be enjoyed and exploited. But in those recesses of Europe where the pall of serfdom and lordly authority over tiny villages remained unshaken, England's example was irrelevant. The scale and pace of her economic development was at that time without parallel and only the prescient few understood it as the harbinger of a new industrial order.

In France, the eighteenth-century movement toward modernization and democracy had a remarkable victory; one that polarized European society and opinion for a century. There the feudal order was toppled in 1789, and a constitutional covenant, reflecting the spirit of the Enlightenment, was established. But revolution and warfare in this new age sharply heightened the power of the state, which drew the support of an ever wider body of the citizenry, even as it increased its control over them. No one contributed to this process as much as did Napoleon who, though a child of the Revolution, takes his place with the monarchical founders of the nation-state.

1568–1648	Dutch revolt from Spain
1572	St. Bartholomew's Eve massacre
1588	Defeat of Spanish Armada
1598	Edict of Nantes
1603–1625	James I of England
1606–1669	Rembrandt van Rijn
1607	Jamestown, Virginia settled
1608–1674	John Milton
1613	Michael Romanov founds ruling dynasty in Russia
1618–1648	Thirty Years' War
1632–1687	Jean Baptiste Lully
1640–1649	English Civil War
1643–1715	Louis XIV, France
1649	Charles I (England) sentenced to death
1651	Hobbes, *Leviathan*
1652	Dutch colonists land at Capetown
1660	Restoration in England
1661	Versailles palace begun
1667–1668	Louis XIV goes to war over Spanish Netherlands
1672–1678	Louis XIV fights Holland
1683	Turks besiege Vienna
1685	Revocation of the Edict of Nantes
1685–1750	J. S. Bach
1685–1759	G. F. Handel
1688–1697	Louis XIV: War of the League of Augsburg
1689	Glorious Revolution in England
1689	Locke, *Of Civil Government, Second Treatise*
1697	Peter the Great visits the West
1701–1713	War of the Spanish Succession
1707	Mogul Empire in India disintegrates
1712	Thomas Newcomen engine
1717–1720	Mississippi Bubble in France
1733	Flying shuttle, John Kay
1740–1786	Frederick II, the Great, of Prussia
1754–1763	Seven Years' War
1765	Stamp Act Congress
1769	James Watt steam engine
1770	Boston Tea Party
1774	First Continental Congress
1774	Samuel Crompton spinning mule
1775–1783	American Revolutionary War
July 1776	Declaration of Independence
1776	Thomas Paine, *Common Sense*

1788	First British settlement in Australia
May 1789	Estates-General meets in France
July 14, 1789	Fall of the Bastille
August 27, 1789	Declaration of the Rights of Man
April 1792	Beginning of the wars, France vs. Europe
September 1792	France declared a republic
1793–1794	Reign of Terror
1804–1815	Napoleon Bonaparte, Emperor

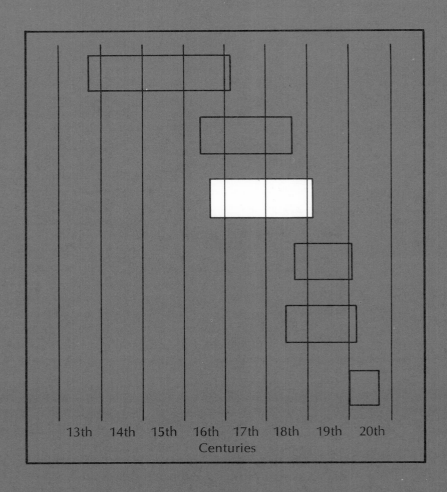

13th 14th 15th 16th 17th 18th 19th 20th
Centuries

TOPIC 16

SOVEREIGNTY AND THE NATION-STATE

There is a difference between that attachment to local authority and tradition which can be traced back to the beginnings of civilization and the special loyalty modern men give to the nation. The allegiance of traditional man was claimed by the tribal group to which he belonged, by the chieftain or king whom he served, or by the religion in which he believed rather than by his nationality. The rise of dynastic states in the fifteenth and sixteenth centuries, while still emphasizing the personal relation between ruler and ruled, was a necessary stage in the shift from traditional to modern society. These readings, therefore, seek to provide an understanding of the nature of the early modern state.

A. Organski: What Makes a Nation?

Study of political development in recent centuries presupposes an understanding of the basic modern governing unit, the nation-state. In the following reading A. F. K. Organski (1923–   ), American political scientist, discusses the factors that shape a particular group of people into a national unit. From *World Politics* by A. F. K. Organski. © copyright 1958, 1968 by A. F. K. Organski. Reprinted by permission of Alfred A. Knopf, Inc.

POLITICAL TIES

The nation is first and foremost a political unit. It is, more specifically, the largest political unit that recognizes no political superior. Members of the same nation can and usually do share much more than the same government and the same territory. They may have a common economy, a common language, a common culture, a common religion, a common political ideology, and a common history. . . . But it is important to notice that all these other traits, though usual, are not universal. One can think of exceptions in almost every case, nations whose members do *not* all speak the same language, have the same culture, and so on down the list. The one characteristic that all members of a nation share, and to this there can be no exception, is that they are all under the political jurisdiction of the same government.

Thus it is political behavior which defines the extent of each nation and the population it includes. In addition, political institutions play a large part in keeping the nation separate and distinct from other nations, in promoting unity within the nation, and in defending it against interference or attack from the outside.

To keep the nation separate from the rest of the world, political agencies watch over the national frontiers, arbitrary lines that separate the national territory and population from the outside world. They control the movement of people and goods across these lines, and they pass upon the applications of outsiders who wish to move into the national territory or to become members of the national group. To become an American or a Chinese or a German or a Brazilian, one must go through a political process and meet political standards. All national governments reserve to themselves the right to refuse admission or citizenship to any outsider they do not want.

National political agencies also act to prevent people and territory they control from breaking away from the nation. The only country that nominally grants its constituent units the legal right of secession is the U.S.S.R., but any student of Soviet politics knows that this right to secede is an illusion.

The right of the American states to secede was denied by war, and most national governments would treat in a similar manner any attempt by some of its citizens to take the territory they lived on and withdraw it and themselves from the control of the national government.

Even individuals who wish to depart without territory are limited in their right to do so. No matter how free the country, the granting of passports (without which it is impossible to travel abroad) is a right that national governments jealously guard, and while some governments allow some of their citizens to emigrate to other countries and become citizens there, other governments do not give passports to anyone whom they suspect of wanting to shift his political allegiance. To escape from such a nation, an individual must trick his government into giving him a passport or flee illegally across an armed border, and then, once he has moved himself beyond the reach of national officials, he must find another national government that will accept him despite the objections of his own nation. He must be under the control of one nation or another. He cannot simply secede from the nation-state system.

To promote unity within the nation, national governments engage in many different activities. They act to remove obstacles to the movement of men and goods within the national territory, to improve internal communications, and to spread and promote common characteristics of the people such as language, culture, and political ideology. They try to stamp out forms of localism that interfere with national unity, and they punish individual treason as the worst political crime a man can commit.

National governments provide and enforce many of the rules that allow the individuals in the nation to work together without getting in each other's way and doing one another harm. It seems obvious that, particularly in the great and complex industrial nations of modern times, life as we know it could not be carried on unless the government made and enforced rules governing the use of highways and railways and plane routes, of radio and television stations, of the mails, rules setting standards of safety and honesty in the production and distribution of goods and services, rules about money and banking and selling stocks, rules about labor relations, rules providing for the handicapped and underprivileged. All of these governmental activities are necessary to provide for the smooth functioning of a nationwide economy and a nationwide culture. Government rules help to minimize conflicts between individuals who are dependent on each other.

When conflict *does* occur, the government again stands by to set limits on the kind of struggle that can be permitted and to help settle or even to impose settlement of cases that cannot be left for private solution. In this area of governmental activity, it is usual to think first of institutions such as courts that are designed specifically for this task. However, in actuality, the process of settling important differences that might tear apart the fabric of national society goes on constantly in many political institutions. Not only jurists in the courts of law, but also political leaders at political conventions, lawmakers in legislatures, bureaucrats in executive offices, all are frequently engaged in settling differences, for the reconciliation of differences is an integral part of the political process.

If all goes well, differences within the nation are settled without the use of force, but in the last analysis the government controls a virtual monopoly of force in the form of military bodies and police. Even organized crime can defy governmental forces only on a hit and run basis, and for the ordinary citizen, such defiance is out of the question. Enlightened self-interest keeps the citizens of a nation working together a large percentage of the time, and a respect for law and order keeps them in line on most occasions when self-interest runs against the interests of others. But when self-interest and a respect for law are not enough, the overwhelming force at the disposal of the national government prevents a nation from dividing itself into warring camps.

There is still another way in which political institutions help to hold the nation together. They provide the symbols that evoke the idea of the nation in the minds of her citizens. The process through which people identify with the nation will be treated more fully later, but it should be noted at this point that the main national symbols, for example, the flag, the words of the national anthem, the king, the nation's founder, are all political symbols concerned with the national government, its personnel, and its actions. Without them, the expression of the emotional attachment which people feel for their nation would be difficult indeed.

In addition to separating the nation from the outside world and helping to unify its people, the national government performs the crucial function of protecting the nation from outside interference or attack. It is the government that has the exclusive right to deal with officials of other nations, and it is the government that mobilizes the population and resources of the nation in any armed combat with outsiders.

In short, the nation is primarily a political unit, for membership in it is defined in political terms, and political agencies have the main responsibility for defining the territorial boundaries, controlling movement across them, deciding who can belong to a nation's population and who cannot, preventing secession, promoting unity within the nation by encouraging internal trade and communication, making rules to keep the peace, settling disputes through control of a monopoly of force, providing the symbols that stand for the nation, and protecting it against outsiders. It is hard to overestimate the importance of political ties in binding a group of individuals into a nation. . . .

SHARED CHARACTERISTICS
—A SUMMARY

We have seen that individual members of a national group have many characteristics in common. Although these vary somewhat from one nation to another, it is possible to generalize. Most nations have a single national language, some have a predominant religion. All have a common culture, a common predominant political ideology, a common history and a certain amount of economic unity, and a tendency toward national differentiation along these lines is strengthened by governmental action. However, the major tie that holds the members of a nation together is political, for the nation is essentially and without exception a political unit.

Secondarily, it is a psychological unit, that is to say, it is a group of people who feel that they constitute a unit, who feel that they have many important characteristics in common, whether they actually do or not. It is a group

of people who choose to emphasize the ways . . . they are alike rather than the ways . . . they differ. This feeling of unity is every bit as important as the actual homogeneity upon which it is supposedly based. . . .

SOVEREIGNTY

"Sovereignty" is a word on many tongues. . . . We choose to define sovereignty as the possession of supreme power. . . . We have already defined power as the ability to influence the behavior of others in accordance with one's own ends. Sovereign power is supreme power, and within its territorial jurisdiction, the national government is sovereign, since it controls more power than any other group or individual. The nation is also sovereign in its dealings with other nations, since it recognizes no higher authority above itself. . . .

National sovereignty has two characteristics that will prove to be important. . . . First, power—and sovereign power is no exception—is always exercised in the interests of the powerful as they see that interest. Second, national power is rarely relinquished consciously and voluntarily. The first statement is not really open to argument. If power is defined as the ability to influence the behavior of others in accordance with one's own ends, then to exercise power simply means that one *does* influence the behavior of others in accordance with one's own ends. Of course, it is conceivable that a nation could be genuinely unselfish, that the goals of its foreign policy might be the welfare of humanity whether or not this benefited the nation concerned. However, no national government has ever *claimed* to be pursuing such a policy, and if it did, it could be sure that a sizeable delegation of its citizens would

descend upon the capital in rage, demanding that the government stop "selling out" the nation. What passes for national unselfishness is the kind of policy that benefits others without causing any damage at home, what Americans are fond of calling "enlightened self-interest" since it is supposed to result in long-range benefits for the nation in the form of good will, trade, and possibly alliances. In short, whether they are selfish or unselfish, farsighted, or shortsighted, the ends for which national power is exercised are the goals of those who wield the power. . . .

It follows that national power is rarely given up consciously and voluntarily, for if power is used to reach the goals of those who hold it, what reason can there be for giving it to others who may use it otherwise? Power changes hands, but it usually does so without the consent of those who lose it.

It must be understood that national sovereignty is not simply a matter of interest to diplomats and other government officials. The sovereign power of the national state affects deeply the everyday lives of the citizens who make up the nation. The state uses its power to organize the national society, to enforce the accepted ways of behavior, and to uphold a particular division of goods and services, offices and honors. On the international level, the national government uses its power to improve the well-being of its citizens, perhaps at the expense of others, and to protect their way of life as much as possible from outside interference. There is not a citizen whose life would not be influenced if his national government were to give up its sovereignty. For international and domestic power are but two sides of the same coin. One cannot give up power in international affairs and keep it at home.

Those who benefit from the existing distribution of power will oppose any shift that might injure them, but it is not primarily because of their "interests" that citizens support the nation state. The tie between the individual and the nation is far stronger than is realized by those who would explain it away by proving that the "true" interests of all individuals would best be served by a world state based upon a world community. The greatest obstacle to the abolition of national sovereignty lies, not in the rational self-interest of individuals, but in the sentiments of nationalism, for citizens would not submit so willingly to the power of the state at home nor cheer so heartily its acts abroad if they did not feel a tremendous psychological commitment to the nation. . . . This, then, is the reality of sovereignty. Supreme power within the nation is possessed by the national government, which exercises that power both internally and internationally in the interests of those it represents. . . .

The States of Europe in the Seventeenth and Eighteenth Centuries

The states of Europe formed the elements that shaped the kaleidoscope of international relations in the seventeenth and eighteenth centuries. Then as now internal and external policy were intimately linked, and it is impossible to consider the development of the modern state without considering both. The list of states briefly describes the condition of the European states at this time and is fol-

lowed by a commentary on the similarities and differences among them written by Laurence B. Packard (1887–1955), noted historian of this period. I. Compiled by the eds. II. From *The Age of Louis XIV* by Laurence Bradford Packard. Copyright 1929 by Holt, Rinehart and Winston, Inc. Copyright © 1957 by Laurence Bradford Packard. Reprinted by permission of Holt, Rinehart and Winston, Inc.

I. LIST OF STATES

France was the leading continental power following her victories over Spain in the first half of the seventeenth century. Under King Louis XIV (1643–1715) she dominated the European political scene and her power and influence continued to a lesser degree throughout the eighteenth century.

England in the seventeenth century remained on the fringes of European events. The struggle to consolidate royal power occupied much of the century and diverted English attention. Concern with the protection and expansion of commerce, however, involved the English increasingly in world affairs, and in the eighteenth century when England was governed by a coalition of commercial and landowning interests she superceded France as the most wealthy and powerful Western state.

Spain witnessed in both centuries continuing decline in power. In the sixteenth century under Charles V (1516–1558) and Phillip II (1558–1598) Spanish armed might, supported by the riches of the mines of the New World, had been feared by all of Europe. Deterioration caused chiefly by overextension, lack of leadership, and inability to accommodate to change was not halted by the replacement in 1701 of the moribund Hapsburg dynasty by the Bourbons. The European portions of the

Spanish Empire—the Netherlands, Burgundy, and large parts of Italy—had all either become independent (Holland, Sicily) or been transferred to rival states (Burgundy to France, Milan and the Southern Netherlands to the Austrian Hapsburgs) by the middle of the eighteenth century. Of Spanish glory the overseas possessions alone were left.

Austria was ruled by a more vigorous branch of the Hapsburg family. Her attempt in the seventeenth century to dominate Germany failed in thirty years of bloody conflict (Thirty Years' War, 1618–1648), but this did not obscure her position as the leading Central European power. In addition to possession of the more or less honorary title of Holy Roman Emperor, the Hapsburgs were rulers of millions of Germans, Hungarians, Italians, Slavs, and of what are today called Belgians. To the West they were invariably to be found arrayed against the French Bourbons in the struggle for European hegemony; to the East they fought for generations against the invading Turks (who even besieged the Hapsburg capital of Vienna in 1683) until the waning of Turkish power in the eighteenth century.

Germany did not exist as such. Instead there were hundreds of German states organized within the framework of the Holy Roman Empire. These states varied in size from the extensive territories of a Brandenburg-Prussia, Bavaria, Saxony, or Hanover to tiny baronies consisting literally of a hilltop castle with its appended village and varied in structure from principalities to church-states and self-governing free cities. Granted virtual independence at the conclusion of the Thirty Years' War, the German states actually presented a power vacuum, constantly fearful of the encroachment of Austria or the more powerful minor states. Most important of these was Brandenburg-Prussia, whose Hohenzollern rulers gradually fashioned a viable modern state out of separate possessions that spread across the German plain. Under Frederick II (1740–1786), an impressive military strategist who at one time campaigned successfully against France, Austria, and Russia, the state of Brandenburg-Prussia gained a European reputation.

Russia was an Asia-oriented state until forcibly brought into the Western orbit by her great Tsar Peter (1689–1725). Peter and his successors waged a series of wars in the eighteenth century to break Russia's landlocked condition and extend her boundaries through Swedish, Polish, and Turkish territory to the Baltic and Black Seas. Russia became increasingly involved in the affairs of Europe but her tremendous potential was as yet unfulfilled.

Italy, like Germany, consisted of a variety of states. The Renaissance city-states had remained geographically intact for the most part but were dominated by France, Spain, or Austria or even governed by members of the ruling families of these larger nations. The direct power of the Pope was confined to the area about Rome (Papal States) and his religious authority deteriorated after the Thirty Years' War even in Catholic countries such as France.

Other States: the Netherlands (Holland) gained independence from Spain in the sixteenth century to become the (unsuccessful) object of French aggression in the seventeenth. The small size of the Dutch homeland should not obscure the fact that Holland possessed an extensive empire, a large merchant marine, and was among the most prosperous of the European states. *Sweden* had played a major role in the Thirty Years' War but had overexerted herself and slowly relinquished her dream of a Baltic Empire under Prussian and Russian armed pressure. *Poland* was a large, weak state whose fiercely independent nobility prevented the elected kings from governing effectively. Poland's vulnerability encouraged constant intervention by her neighbors in her affairs. In the seventeenth century the *Ottoman Empire* (Turkey), in addition to large areas in Asia and Africa, controlled most of southeastern Europe from the Ukraine to Hungary. A constant threat to the Hapsburgs, Turkish power declined gradually during the eighteenth century.

II. POLICIES OF STATE

We may say that most of these European states fall into two groups according to the type of policy pursued by their governments. One group comprised the states which were struggling to defend their territories and independence; their policy might be described as passive, non-aggressive, and self-contained. The other group comprised the states aggressively endeavoring to expand their possessions and power. Generally speaking, Spain, most of the German states, Poland, Sweden, the Netherlands, and most of the Italian states were on the defensive, trying to maintain the status quo. France, Russia, the Turks, and among the German states, Brandenburg–Prussia, especially, were ambitiously on the offensive, aiming to expand territorially, and seeking more prestige and power. The Hapsburgs were, in a sense, in both groups; i.e., they were forced to be on the defensive by the nature of their dominions, the location, and the enterprise of their neighbors; at the same time, the Hapsburgs were ambitious, grasping, and aggressive. Their whole history is a maze of contradictions and inconsistencies, and it is not surprising to find them, paradoxically enough, in both groups of states. England hardly belongs in either category. She had no aggressive continental designs, and stood, on the continent, more or less on the defensive. She was concerned in the maintenance of the balance of power, and desired to see no state acquire a hegemony, nor did she intend to allow any strong state to lodge on the shore of the Low Countries. Economically, however, and in the colonial world, England was just beginning to take the initiative in acquisition. In these fields she was about to become decidedly aggressive.

What constitutes the explanation of such a difference between these seventeenth-century states? Why should the policy of one group be defensive, and of the other aggressive? Certainly, we may assume that as far as being eager for the glory and spoils of military victory is concerned, one state would be as prepared as any other to gain as much as possible. Limitations of size and resources, the weakness of their governments, and the proximity of strong neighbors, compelled many of them to remain on the defensive. What led the others to an aggressive policy? In other words, why were the larger and more powerful states constantly at war, or ready to fight? We must remember that most of the European states of the seventeenth century were controlled by dynasties, nearly absolute in power, and fortified by what they believed to be Divine Right. These dynasties could therefore conduct the policy of states as they saw fit. No consultation with their subjects was necessary, although it was true, of course, that important interests such as industry and commerce could at least present their desires to the sovereigns.

What was it that these dynastic kings pursued in their policies of state? For what purpose did they assume that God allowed them to reign over their respective states? Obviously, the answer given by any of them might have been: to protect their lands and peoples, to maintain law and order, to dispense justice, and to provide for the general welfare of their subjects. Such duties, we should say, as belonged to any government. Our search, however, is directed to the discovery of what these kings considered to be this *general welfare*. In this crucial question we find a most important bearing upon the whole history of royal dynasties, as well as of modern states. Seventeenth-century dynasties by Divine Right were commonly given to confusing the welfare of states and peoples with their own personal and family interests and ambitions, regarding them, in fact, as identical. What was good for the dynasty was good for the state.

The protection of lands and peoples, or security of the state as we now call it, was the chief professed concern of every government in the conduct of its relations with other states. Then, as now, ideas of security covered a multitude of possible interpretations. Instances are comparatively rare, since the sixteenth century, of wanton, unprovoked attack by one state upon another, and yet there have been innumerable wars, always declared by both sides to be wars of defence, of security. The explanation of this lies in the numerous possibilities in the interpretation of the meaning of what is necessary for security. The principle of security has generally been built on notions that the best defence is preparedness to fight. Such preparedness has frequently been carried to the extent of developing the theory that to attack first is necessary; an offensive will catch an enemy before he can attack, and thereby provide defence

against him. Finally, security consists in the conviction that certain territories lying perhaps just over the borders of a state are indispensable for adequate defence,—they are strategically valuable for military operations in defence, or they constitute a natural barrier. Such considerations, it may easily be seen, can be applied to justify almost any policy, from a glaringly aggressive undertaking to a bona fide striving for security.

This has been true from the first modern war to the latest international conflict. How slowly men come to face realities, and judge events with reason and not with prejudices and emotions! It is very easy to see how, when decisions rested almost entirely with the head of a royal dynasty, whose regard for the state was that of an owner for his property and rights, matters of security might be subject to the temper and impatience of a hasty, overzealous and unrestrained individual. Conceptions of right and defence of right, particularly where land and wealth were concerned, might be, and frequently were, used to cover ambition and aggressiveness. No restraints existed, except limitations of strength and fear of more powerful rivals, to curb dynasties in their interpretation of security.

Power was undoubtedly the principal ambition of dynasties,—power and what it implies in exalted position, enviable influence, and the consciousness of controlling men and resources. How could power be obtained? In attempting to answer this question, we are dealing with a problem which has confronted man from the day when he first began to fight, to the present moment. The acquisition of territories and peoples seemed the obvious way to acquire power. Since organized society began, probably, kings, or their equivalents, have fought with one another for the pos-

session of lands and peoples. It is only in very recent years that men have analysed this aim, and asked the question: Does the gaining of territories and peoples really mean the gaining of power; but in reckoning up the costs, and in attempting to estimate the effect of gains made by force upon the people involved, doubts have been cast upon the simple notion that vast territories, or numerous subjects, necessarily make for power,—or for the welfare of the state.

Mercantilist ideas . . . convinced seventeenth-century monarchs of the validity of these conceptions of power. They hold that more land and more people implied more resources, more labor, therefore more trade and consequently more precious metal; hence the state would be more powerful. A policy for power was clearly one of the characteristics of seventeenth-century absolute monarchy.

Heinz Lubasz: The Modern State

In his introduction to a collection of essays focusing on the development of the modern state, American historian Heinz Lubasz reminds his readers that there is no such thing as *the* modern state but instead there are a great number of modern states from which scholars construct a model that contains the essential characteristics of all these states. Reprinted with permission of The Macmillan Company from *The Development of the Modern State* by Heinz Lubasz. Copyright © by Heinz Lubasz 1964.

The modern state is a European, or more exactly, western European, creation. It gradually emerged in the course of the fifteenth and sixteenth centuries and found its first mature form in the seventeenth. It is worth noting that the modern state came into existence in the same area and during the same period as did modern capitalism, modern science and philosophy, and that specifically modern form of Christianity, Protestantism. The simultaneous emergence of distinctively new forms of political, economic, intellectual, and religious life is by no means a matter of mere coincidence. All forms of human activity are, as we know, to some degree interconnected, though the extent to which they display common features will, of course, vary a great deal. Suffice it to say that a remarkable change in the style and focus of human activity is discernible in western Europe in the era of the Renaissance, which leaves its mark on almost every aspect of civilization. Men's activities appear to become more systematic, intensive, and secular. Modern capitalism is more relentless in its pursuit of gain, and more proficient and advanced in its techniques, than medieval capitalism; modern science is less restrained in its quest for knowledge of *all* kinds, and more concerned with method, than medieval; and Protestantism, by drawing a sharper line between the sacred and the secular, between God and man, than medieval Christianity had done, allows men to pursue their worldly goals with almost undivided attention, even if it enjoins them to do so for the greater glory of God.

This increased attention to technical proficiency. . . coupled with a significant separation of this-worldly from other-worldly considerations, is also very much in evidence in political life. The state (which at first means the ruler, the prince) comes to employ ever more efficient means to pursue, with great

intensity and to the full extent of available resources, one principal objective: the accumulation of power. From its inception, the modern state seeks to acquire sole authority and effective power within a given territory, as well as autonomy vis-à-vis other states. Exclusive domination over a certain territory and its population (the ruler's domain, the dynasty's realm, the king's inheritance) and the power to be the arbiter of its own conduct in relations among states—that is the twin aspect of modern sovereignty, the Janus face of the modern state. The modern state is, first of all, the sovereign state.

Exclusive domination does not in itself mean unlimited or total domination. The modern state is, in fact, not only a sovereign state; it is also a state governed by a public and more or less stable system of law, which regulates an ever-growing number of activities and of relationships among individuals and groups in society, but also regulates the state itself and sets some sort of limit to the operations of government. The modern state claims exclusive and compulsory jurisdiction over its subjects or citizens, but it exercises this claim in accordance with set and known procedures, and, normally at least, it does not punish acts that have not previously been declared to be punishable. Furthermore, the modern state claims only to *regulate* or *control* economic, social, or even religious and cultural activities: it does not itself *undertake* these activities or attempt to absorb them into the state. There is a distinction between state and society, between the formal, public "organization of the community for the purposes of government," and society itself—the sum-total of citizens and their nongovernmental organizations and activities; a distinction, no matter how im-

perfectly, is absolutely fundamental to the modern state. It is the very foundation not only of the rights of the citizen or subject, but also of at least a measure of free economic, social, and cultural activity of whatever kind. The drawing of a distinction between state and society is, in short, itself a fundamental characteristic of the modern state.

In a similar way, the state's claim to be the sole arbiter of its own actions vis-à-vis other states does not necessarily mean that it claims to destroy all other states and to establish dominion over the whole globe. On the contrary, the modern state is, in fact, not only a sovereign state; it is also a state that recognizes, even if it does not always respect, the sovereignty of other states. Hence from the sixteenth century to the twentieth, Europe has more or less adhered to the principle of a balance of power and has developed an international law, not to prevent war, but to regulate the conduct of states in war as well as in peace. That the principle of balance of power frequently led to war is not an argument against it, since it was not intended, any more than international law was, to preserve the peace, but only to serve as a regulative principle that would allow many sovereign states to exist side by side. There is a difference between claiming sovereign autonomy and claiming world domination; between regarding another political entity as an adversary to be worsted or defeated, and regarding it as an enemy to be utterly vanquished or even destroyed. The recognition of this difference is absolutely fundamental to the modern state system, and hence to the existence of the modern state as a power-unit. It is the very foundation not only of limited war, but also of a regulated and orderly peace. The reciprocal recognition of sovereignty is, in short, likewise a fundamental characteristic of the modern state.

The first modern states arose in Italy, England, France, and Spain. The Italian principality, [city-state] partly because of its small size, did not as such serve as a model for later developments, though it was the first to evolve a number of institutions—notably the bureaucratic administration and the mercenary army—typical of the state throughout the modern era. Spain, which did exert considerable influence on the emerging patterns of the modern state in the sixteenth and seventeenth, and to some degree even in the eighteenth, centuries, both in Europe and overseas, subsequently went into decline, and its influence on the evolution of the modern state was thereafter very slight. England and France, however, which had been the strongest of medieval monarchies (a fact thoroughly relevant to their becoming the most powerful and influential of modern states) became, each in its way, models for other states. For the development of *European* states the example of France was paramount; as a continental state itself, its geopolitical situation and its economic and social conditions were in many ways similar to those of other continental states, and its political institutions were, as a result, widely imitated, both before the French Revolution (absolute monarchy) and after (constitutionalism). England, whose development during the Middle Ages and until the nineteenth century was in some important respects different from that of the continent, had a greater impact on the *non-European* world (largely via its colonies, especially the American colonies) than on Europe itself, though in the nineteenth century, if not indeed earlier, some of its institutions,

too, were adapted to continental practice. At the risk of considerable oversimplification we may say that England is the prototype of the parliamentary, constitutional state, in which local self-government provides for a substantial degree of decentralization; while France is the prototype of the authoritarian (which does not, of course, necessarily mean dictatorial) regime with a highly centralized, bureaucratic administration.

In France, and in most of the states of continental Europe, including the many small principalities, dukedoms, and kingdoms in Germany and Italy, a permanent bureaucracy and a standing army were the principal technical tools with which the modern state was built, and it was money that enabled the ruler to acquire them. The availability of fluid wealth made it possible for him to replace the feudal nobility, in the two functions that in the Middle Ages had made it indispensable to him, with hired professionals. With the rise of a professional bureaucracy and a professional army, the nobility also lost the important political role it had once held in the state. As it now had little actual power, either military or administrative, and as, by the terms of its own cherished privileges, it was largely exempt from substantial taxation (it simply collected the peasants' taxes) and therefore did not directly supply much of the state's income, the king could afford to ignore it politically. The great councils and the assemblies of estates, which had played so important a role in the medieval "monarchy of estates," were in the absolute monarchies of the seventeenth century gradually "put to sleep." For two centuries or more (i.e., until the era of the middle-class revolutions), the monarchs of continental Europe, including those of Prussia and Russia, even managed to

obtain the active or passive support of this nobility, by allowing it extensive social and economic privileges, and a very nearly free hand with the peasantry.

But the very element that had made it possible for the prince to build his state—to wit, money—also proved to be the source of his undoing. As the state expanded its activities, as it enlarged its army and its administration, and as funds were lavished on the pomp and luxury with which the absolute monarch liked to surround himself, the state's need for ready cash constantly grew. The principal producers of cash were the commercial and industrial middle class and the peasantry. Through both these classes felt the heavy hand of the tax collector and the oppressive weight of state-imposed restrictions and regulations of many kinds, and though both bitterly resented the privileges and the wealth of a largely unproductive, parasitical aristocracy, the bourgeoisie alone was able, in the late eighteenth and in the nineteenth century, to carry through revolutions which sharply curtailed or even abolished both the privileged status of the aristocracy and the authority of the monarch. Thus the bourgeoisie acquired a measure of control over the state which it had been so largely financing.

These revolutions radically transformed the conception of the state in respect of its physical and human foundations. The bourgeois revolutions were carried through in the name (though not to the benefit) of *all* the state's population, of the whole *nation,* in the name of natural rights and popular sovereignty. Thus the state, which had hitherto been thought of as the domain and personal inheritance of the king, as the king's land, was henceforward conceived to "belong" instead to the people who inhabited it, to the nation. It is with the era of the bourgeois revolutions that the state ceases to be, in fact as well as in conception, a *proprietary-territorial state* and becomes instead a *nation-state*. And just as it was France that had served as the principal model of the absolutistic, dynastic state, so it was chiefly France that inspired, by example and by reaction against it, the building elsewhere in Europe of the liberalistic nation-state.

Cardinal Richelieu Enunciates "Reason of State" (1642)

One of the great spokesmen for the principles that underlay the concept of the modern state was Armand du Plessis, Cardinal Richelieu, chief minister of France from 1624 until his death in 1642. The following selections are taken from his *Political Testament* which he wrote to serve as a guide after his death for his not very capable royal master, Louis XIII. The *Testament* is concerned with what Richelieu called *raison d'Etat,* or "reason of state," that is, the argument that the goal of governmental policy is the maintenance and increase of the power of the state. From *The Political Testament of Cardinal Richelieu,* trans. Henry B. Hill (Madison: The University of Wisconsin Press, 1961). Copyright © 1961 by the Regents of the University of Wisconsin.

I

Introduction

When Your Majesty resolved to admit me both to your council and to an important place in your confidence for the direction of your affairs, I may say that the Huguenots [Protestants] shared the state with you; that the nobles conducted themselves as if they were not your subjects, and the most powerful governors of the provinces as if they were sovereign in their offices.

I may say that the bad example of all of these was so prejudicial to the welfare of this realm that even the best courts were affected by it, and endeavored, in certain cases, to diminish your legitimate authority as far as it was possible in order to carry their own powers beyond the limits of reason.

I may say that everyone measured his own merit by his audacity; that in place of esteeming the benefits which they received from Your Majesty at their proper worth, they all valued them only as they satisfied the demands of their imaginations; that the most scheming were held to be the wisest, and often found themselves the most prosperous.

I may further say that foreign alliances were scorned, private interests being preferred to those of the public, and in a word, the dignity of the royal majesty was so disparaged, and so different from what it should be, because of the misdeeds of those who conducted your affairs, that it was almost impossible to recognize it. It was impossible, without losing all, to tolerate longer the conduct of those to whom Your Majesty had intrusted the helm of state; and yet everything could not be changed at once without violating the laws of prudence, which do not permit the passing from one extreme to another without preparation. . . .

Notwithstanding these difficulties which I explained to Your Majesty, knowing how much kings may do when they make good use of their power, I dared to promise you, with assurance, that you would soon find remedies for the disorders in your state, and that your prudence, your courage, and the benediction of God would give a new aspect to this realm. I promised Your Majesty to employ all my industry and all the authority which it should please you to give to me to ruin the Huguenot party, to abase the pride of the nobles, to bring all your subjects back to their duty, and to restore your reputation among foreign nations to the station it ought to occupy. . . .

II

Public Interest: The First Objective

The public interest ought to be the sole objective of the prince and his councillors, or, at the least, both are obliged to have it foremost in mind, and preferred to all private gain. It is impossible to overestimate the good which a prince and those serving him in government can do if they religiously follow this principle, and one can hardly imagine the evils which befall a state if private interest is preferred to the public good and actually gains the ascendency. True philosophy, as well as the precepts of both Christianity and sound politics, teach this truth so clearly that a prince's councillors can hardly too often remind him of so necessary a principle, nor the prince punish too severely those members of his council despicable enough not to practice it.

I cannot but remark in this regard that the prosperity which has invariably blessed Spain for several centuries is solely due to the fact that its council has given preference to the public interest above all other interests, while most of the misfortunes which have befallen

France have occurred because many of those employed in government administration have been more concerned with their own advancement than with that of the public welfare. The former has always pursued the public interest, which by its very nature has induced it to act in the fashion most advantageous to the state, while the latter, accommodating everything to their selfish profit or whims, have often twisted the execution of government programs in order to make them privately more agreeable or advantageous. . . .

If those in whose hands Your Majesty places the direction of your affairs have the ability and the probity of which I have spoken above, you have no more worries in this regard, which of itself offers no problems since the concern for the prince's own reputation and the public interest have a common end.

Princes ordinarily easily consent to the over-all plans proposed for their states because in so doing they have nothing in mind save reason and justice, which they easily accept when they meet no obstacle which turns them off the path. When the occasion arises, however, of putting into practical action the wise programs they have adopted, they do not always show the same firmness. Distracting interests, pity and compassion, favoritism and importunities of all sorts obstruct their best intentions to a degree they often cannot overcome sufficiently to ignore private consideration, which ought never influence public affairs. It is in such matters that they should summon up all their strength against inclinations toward weakness, keeping before their eyes the fact that those whom God has destined to protect others should have no characteristics but those advantageous to the public interest, and to which they should adhere inflexibly.

III

The Uses of Punishments and Rewards

It is a common but nevertheless true saying which has long been repeated by intelligent men that punishments and rewards are the two most important instruments of government in a realm. It is certain that, whatever else one may do in governing states, one must be inflexible in punishing those who fail to obey, and religiously scrupulous in rewarding those who perform notable services. In other words, one would not govern badly if guided by this precept since most people can be held to their duty through either fear or hope. I rate punishments, I must say, higher than rewards, because if it were necessary to dispense with one of these, it would be better to give up the latter than the former. The good ought to be adhered to for its own sake, and in all justice no one should be rewarded for this. But there is no crime which does not violate those precepts men are obligated to obey, so that the punishment to be expected for disobedience of this sort is therefore justified, and this obligation is so direct in many cases that to let the act go unpunished is to commit a further error. I speak here of things which injure the state and which have been premeditated, and not of those lesser offenses which result from chance or misfortune, toward which princes may and should often show indulgence. . . .

In this regard it is necessary to impress upon kings clearly the degree to which they are responsible to God when they bestow the principal offices of state solely on the basis of favoritism. This can lead to their being filled by mediocre men, to the prejudice of the well-being of their states. It is necessary to point out at this juncture that while one should not condemn out of hand all personal attachments which have no other foundation than the natural affection one feels more strongly for one person than for another, one cannot excuse princes who allow themselves to be carried away to the point of giving to those they thus like responsibilities in the discharge of which they can be as detrimental to the interests of the state as they can be useful to their own. . . .

The Power of the Prince

Power being one of the things most necessary to the grandeur of kings and the success of their governments, those who have the principal management of states are particularly obliged to omit nothing which could contribute to making their masters fully and universally respected. As goodness is the object of love, so power is the cause of fear. It is certain that of all the forces capable of producing results in public affairs, fear, if based on both esteem and reverence, is the most effective, since it can drive everyone to do this duty. If this principle is of great efficacy with regard to internal affairs, it is of no less value externally, since both foreigners and subjects take the same view of redoubtable power and both refrain from offending a prince whom they recognize as being able to hurt them if he so wishes. I have said already that this power of which I speak should be based on esteem and respect. I hasten to add that this is so necessary that if it is based on anything else there is the grave danger that instead of producing a reasonable fear the result will be a hatred of princes, for whom the worst possible fate is to incur public disapprobation.

There are several kinds of power which can make princes respected and feared—it is a tree with various branches, all nourished by the same root. The prince ought to be powerful because of his good reputation, because of a reasonable number of soldiers kept continuously under arms, because of a sufficient revenue to meet his ordinary expenses, plus a special sum of money in his treasury to cover frequent but unexpected contingencies, and, finally, because of the possession of the hearts of his subjects. . . .

Conclusion

In order to terminate this work happily it only remains for me to point out to Your Majesty that kings, being obliged to do many more things as sovereigns than they would have to do as private individuals, can never deviate even a little from their duty without committing more faults of omission than an ordinary person would be guilty of by commission. It is the same with those to whom sovereigns delegate a part of the powers of their governments, since this honor commits them to the same obligations as those possessed by their sovereigns. Both, when looked at as private individuals, are subject to the same faults as other men. But when one considers the public, for whose well-being they are responsible, their obligations are more numerous, for they cannot without sin fail to do any of the many things their offices charge them with. Thus it is that one who is both good and virtuous as a private individual can be a bad magistrate or sovereign because of the little regard he has for the fulfilling of the duties of his office.

In a word, if princes do not do everything within their power to keep in order the various classes in their states, if they are careless in the choice of members of their councils, if they ignore good advice, if they do not have a particular care to so conduct themselves as to appear the living embodiment of the law, if they are neglectful in establishing the reign of God, as well as of reason and justice, if they fail to protect the innocent, reward notable public services and punish the disobedience and crimes which endanger the disciplined order and security of states, if they do not apply themselves to their utmost in trying to foresee and prevent possible evils and divert by careful negotiations the storms which the wind often can carry farther than one would think, if favoritism prevents them from choosing carefully those whom they honor with the highest offices and principal dignities of the kingdom, if they do not firmly hold the reins of government with a view to giving the state the strength it ought to have, if on all occasions they do not give preference to the public interest over all private ones, though they otherwise be good, they find themselves much more culpable than those who transgress the laws and commandments of God either by commission or omission, it being certain, of course, that acts of commission and omission are really equally culpable. . . .

STUDY QUESTIONS

1. What is a state? What is a nation? What forces hold it together? What forces can tear it apart? Think of American examples.

2. Why doesn't a world state exist? Think of possible earlier attempts at forming one.

3. Define sovereignty. What is the connection between sovereignty and power? What does the nation-state chiefly use its power for?

4. Review the European state system of the seventeenth and eighteenth centuries. What, according to Packard, seems to determine state policy?

5. When did the modern state take shape? What countries served as models in its early development? What institutions were necessary to form the modern state? Why did they not exist earlier?

6. On the basis of your reading how was the seventeenth-century state ruled? How does Richelieu's *Testament* illustrate the problems of developing a modern state?

7. With the *Testament* as sole source, what problems appear to have faced the French king at the time that Richelieu became his chief minister? What did Richelieu advise should be done to maintain and increase the power of the state?

The Centralization of the French State

From H. C. Darby, "The Centralization of the State" in H. Butterfield, D. W. Brogan, H. C. Darby, and J. H. Jackson, *A Short History of France From Early Times to 1958* (New York: Cambridge University Press, 1959), pp. 51–58, 60–61.

An essential feature of French development from the tenth to the eighteenth centuries was the growth of centralized government. By the end of the fifteenth century the monarchy, with the aid of the bourgeois, was beginning to form a professional non-feudal administration. The assertion of Louis XI (1461–1483) was more than a mere claim: "to us alone belongs and is due the general government and administration of the realm." To keep in constant touch with his officials, and "to have careful information from every quarter," Louis created the *poste*; on all the main roads in the kingdom relays of four or five good horses, reserved for the king's riders, were arranged under the charge of *maîtres de la poste*.

But centralized government did not necessarily mean a centralized people. While the French monarchy became more and more absolute, France itself remained divided, and during the wars of religion in the sixteenth and seventeenth centuries some of these divisions came dangerously near the surface. The danger was averted and the administrative reforms of Richelieu, in the first half of the seventeenth century, prepared the way for the great measure of centralization under Louis XIV. Not that all differences were obliterated, for, until the Revolution, France retained many evidences of its former disunity.

RELIGIOUS WARS, 1562–1629

It was impossible for France to remain isolated from the general movement of religious reform in Europe during the sixteenth century. The writings of Luther and other reformers found earnest leaders, and, in spite of persecution, the reformed doctrines gained increasing support in France. On 29 January 1535 an edict ordered the extermination of the heretics, and with this began that emigration of Protestants which did not cease until the middle of the eighteenth century. The most famous of these exiles was John Calvin, who became pastor of the first French Protestant Church, founded in 1538 at Strasbourg by some 1500 refugees. The first Protestant church in France itself was that of Meaux (1546), organized on the lines of that at Strasbourg. . . .

Constant warfare with the Hapsburgs prevented any very complete execution of the edicts against heresy, but when peace was made with the Hapsburgs in 1559 a period of religious conflict began at home. Between 1562 and 1570 there was intermittent warfare which ended in the Treaty of St. Germain. The Huguenots [Protestants] now obtained, first, liberty of conscience and of worship, and then, as guarantee of the king's word, four fortified places—La Rochelle, a key to the sea; La Charité in the centre; Cognac and Montauban to the south. The religious strug-

---

ABSOLUTISM IN FRANCE

The efforts of Cardinal Richelieu to strengthen royal authority found fruition in the long reign (1643–1715) of Louis XIV, who identified perfectly his personal ambitions with "reason of state." In its striving for unity, Louis' France represents to a highly developed degree the early modern state. Centralization of authority in the place of feudalism, the coordination of state policy and mercantilism, religious conformity rather than tolerance, and, above all, the unashamed glorification of power were hallmarks of seventeenth-century man's readiness to accept state intervention as a way of ending disorder and insecurity. Religion added its blessing and the theory that absolute power was the rightful exercise of kings because it was the will of God. The readings trace the steps that led to royal absolutism in France and consider the achievements and shortcomings of this form of government in the person of its most illustrious representative.

gle seemed almost at an end, when in 1572, the unfortunate Charles IX was induced to sanction a general massacre of the Huguenots in Paris on the eve of St. Bartholomew (24 August). Other towns followed the example of the capital, and altogether nearly 20,000 victims fell.

The news of the massacre roused the survivors to a desperate resistance. Weakened by the loss of many leaders, they had but little chance of success. The government prepared forces to reduce those towns which refused obedience. La Rochelle held out for six and a half months against the Catholic army which was obliged to abandon the seige after losing more than 20,000 men. A policy of suppression was impossible to carry out, and an edict of July 1573 brought the war to an end by granting a general amnesty and by permitting Huguenot worship in [four towns]. . . . Hostilities, however, soon broke out again, and continued intermittently for the rest of the century.

During these years the issues of the Catholic-Protestant struggle were confused by political considerations. The Huguenot bourgeoisie, mostly drawn from the industrial districts of the south, joined hands with discontented nobles and anticlericals. The defence of a persecuted religion became more and more involved with a struggle for political power. The complications of the time were not diminished by the fact that each side obtained foreign assistance—the Spanish support of the Catholic party was particularly important. "Men", it was said, "were combatting not for faith, not for Christ, but for command."

At this time the heir to the throne was none other than Henry of Navarre who had become leader of the Huguenots, so that in 1589 when the house of Valois became extinct, the legitimate king was a Calvinist. At first it seemed an impossible situation, but the Catholics were so divided among themselves about an alternative that the result was complete confusion. Henry offered a solution—his own accession and religious toleration. In 1593 he decided the fate of France by formally adopting the Catholic faith, and in the following year, supported the extreme French Catholic party. All loyal Frenchmen rallied to his standard. In 1595 he was acknowledged by the Pope, and in 1598 the Treaty of Vervins ended the war with Spain. When peace was in sight, Henry turned to the question of the Huguenots. In 1598 the Edict of Nantes gave them liberty of conscience, full civil rights, and freedom of public worship in those places where it had been celebrated in 1577; it also gave them guarantees in the form of a large number of fortified places to be held for eight years, the cost of garrisoning them to be borne by the crown. Thus, after nearly forty years of dispute, a religious compromise was secured.

But an end to civil war had not yet been achieved, for the death of Henry IV in 1610 left his great work unfinished. During the minority of his successor, Louis XIII, power fell into the hands of counsellors who were only too ready to favour the Catholic party. The Huguenots once more took up arms in defence of their liberty. Their dissatisfaction was again as much political as religious. Aided by the weakness of the crown, the Huguenot towns had become virtually self-governing communes, independent of the central government. Huguenot organization had parcelled France out into districts ('circles') under regular officers. In the strong words attributed to Richelieu, the Huguenots shared the government of France with the king.

There were revolts in 1621–1622, in 1625–1626 and again in 1627–1629. The great Huguenot stronghold of La Rochelle was starved out after a gallant defence, and then it was a comparatively easy matter to crush the rebellion in Languedoc and in the district of the Cévennes. By the Treaty of Alain in June 1629, the Huguenots ceased to retain any political power. Their guaranteed towns were handed over to the government; their fortresses were dismantled; their organization was destroyed, and they ceased to exist as a political party; their liberty of worship alone remained unimpaired. The treaty marked the end of the period of religious wars, and constituted an important step forward in the centralization of the country.

ADMINISTRATIVE REFORM UNDER RICHELIEU, 1624–1642

Richelieu had come into power as the chief minister of Louis XIII in 1624, just in time to destroy the political power of the Huguenots. But there was yet much to be done before France was a unified state. As long as the administration of the provinces and the raising and control of the army were in the hands of the territorial nobility, a successful court intrigue was still liable to throw the country back into the state of anarchy. To obviate this danger Richelieu applied himself to the establishment of a bureaucracy—a civil service under the direct control of the crown. The abolition of duelling and the destruction of feudal castles in 1626; the substitution of royal administrative officers for those of the territorial nobles . . .; the direct administration by crown officials of the Huguenot towns after 1629; the development of a professional army;

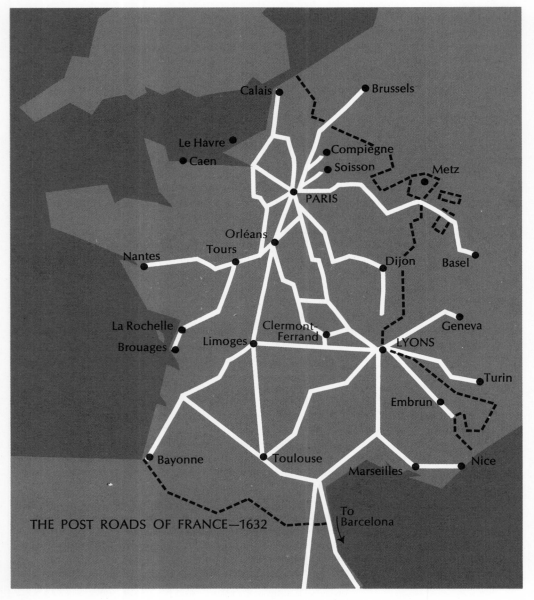

THE POST ROADS OF FRANCE—1632

the more complete establishment of a royal post throughout the kingdom in 1627—all these were steps in undermining the political power of the nobles and in centralizing royal authority more completely at Paris.

An indication of the way in which France was now being governed from the capital is provided by Tavernier's map of post roads in 1632. In Roman times, Lyons had been the chief route centre of Gaul; and during subsequent centuries Roman roads still provided the main routes from town to town. But the road network, considered as a system and not as individual stretches, had changed its character; by the seventeenth century the road centre had become Paris. French geographers themselves have emphasized the part that routes play in holding diverse regions together in one political unit. Thus it was that the main roads of France, and the organization of post services along them, were calculated to serve in this development are plain to see. In 1599 Henry IV's chief minister, Sully, took the new title of 'Chief Road Surveyor of France', and created the nucleus of the administrative machinery of the *Ponts et Chaussées*, the first national highway department of modern times. In 1627 Richelieu improved the post system; in 1672 the transport of letters became a state privilege. Although there was no great technical improvement in road making until the coming of the eighteenth century, the implications of Tavernier's map of 1632 are clear enough. The road system shows a considered combination of ways and means in accord with the centralizing policy of the state.

In order to consolidate his political despotism, Richelieu made use of the system of 'Intendants' established in the latter part of the sixteenth century. These intendants were commissioners sent out by the king to restore order in the provinces after the civil wars. Their functions were at first extraordinary and temporary, but some had been retained as permanent State officials. In 1637 Richelieu appointed intendants over the whole of France, and placed the complete financial, judicial and police administration in their hands. The centralized monarchy which grew up after the Hundred Years' War, under Louis XI and his successors, had divided France into *gouvernements,* each presided over by a governor whose functions were mainly military, but whose chief significance lay in the fact that he represented the crown against the disruptive tendencies of the old feudal nobility. The new intendants were even more strictly dependent on the crown, and were not drawn, like the governors, from the ranks of the provincial *noblesse.* Their duties became so extended that the power of the governors was reduced to a shadow. Their unit of administration was a new one, and, in effect, the new system created a permanent civil service that helped to centralize absolute power at the expense of local authority.

THE REIGN OF LOUIS XIV,
1643–1715

Richelieu died in 1642, and his death was followed by that of his royal master, Louis XIII, in the following year. The new king, Louis XIV, was but five years old, and France was once more weakened by a regency and by renewed intrigues on the part of the nobility. Under these circumstances there grew up the movement which is generally known as the 'Fronde'. It was, in effect, the last rally of the discontented elements of French society against the power of the monarchy under the *ancien régime.* It broke out in 1648; but under Riche-

Louis XIV holds court in the Hall of Mirrors at Versailles. Princes of the blood surround the Sun King as he receives homage from the Duke of Genoa.

lieu's successor, Cardinal Mazarin, it was brought to an end in 1653. Government by intendants was re-established, and the direct authority of the king was henceforward without rival in France. When Mazarin died in 1661, Louis XIV, now twenty-four years old, declared his intention to rule as well as to reign. For fifty-five years he not only controlled the destinies of France, but was the most prominent figure in Europe.

Many wars were fought during his reign, and the frontiers of France were greatly extended. But perhaps even more important than his wars and his diplomacy was the type of civilization that now developed in France. He was not a man of genius nor a really great statesman, but he was capable, energetic and dignified. So great did the prestige of the French monarchy become that its etiquette

and manners spread to all other courts in Europe. Moreover, the literary and intellectual movement which had begun in the days of Richelieu culminated in a blaze of glory, and critics in France became the arbiters of taste for all Europe. French drama reached its highest development in the hands of Corneille, Racine, and Molière; among the philosophers of the period were Descartes, Pascal, Bossuet, and Fénelon. The 'Age of Louis XIV' was not only the golden age of French literature but a landmark in the history of European culture; the domination of French thought over the European world of letters was complete.

In the midst of this efflorescence of culture, Louis lived surrounded by servility and adulation, and intoxicated by the idea of his own greatness and invincible power. Everything

225

was made to centre around the king and the court. Any form of opposition was unbearable; neither public nor private criticism was allowed; the police became the chief bulwark of the government. The States-General were never summoned. The centralized system of Richelieu and Mazarin was carried to its logical conclusion. Louis attempted to destroy the provincial differences of France, and to spread a uniform civilization as well as a uniform administration over the country. The destruction of municipal liberties was completed under the pretext of bad financial administration. The intendants were supported and strengthened against all local opposition. *L'Etat,'* said Louis, '*c'est moi*' [I am the state.]

The Huguenots became a particular object of the king's attention. Satisfied with the free exercise of their worship, many Huguenots of the middle class had devoted themselves with great success to industrial employments of various kinds. But now, impelled by his passion for uniformity and by an increasing devotion in the later years of his life, Louis began a repressive policy. In 1682 missions were established throughout France to convert the heretics, and edicts were issued closing Huguenot churches and schools. When numbers of the most industrious of the artisans of France began to leave the country, Louis forbade emigration. In desperation, the mountaineers of the Cévennes rose in tumult in 1683, and were suppressed with inhuman barbarities. Finally, in October 1685, came the Revocation of the Edict of Nantes; the reformed worship was suppressed, and its ministers expelled. Many Huguenots escaped and carried their thrift and skill to the enemies of France—thus Holland dates its industrial revival, and Brandenburg its industrial life, from 1685. It is said that over 400,000 inhabit-

The vastness of Versailles with its many ornate buildings and its park stretching behind is apparent in this 1722 view.

ants were thus lost to France. Those who were too poor or too ignorant to escape continued, in the fastness of the Cévennes, a desultory but fanatical struggle with their oppressor. From 1703 to 1711, under the name of the 'Camisards', they were able to hold their own, but ultimate triumph was with Louis. Not until 1801 did the Huguenots again attain a legal standing in France.

In Paris itself, Louis had refused to live any longer at the Louvre in the midst of the citizens, and built for himself the enormous palace of Versailles. This became the centre of national life and a model for foreign royalties. While the people groaned under taxes to support this royal magnificence, the nobles of France were content to hold the towel at the king's toilet. Although it had lost its independence under Richelieu, the nobility of France remained a rich body with great social influence. By destroying the political power of the nobles and yet leaving them their privileges, Richelieu and Louis XIV prepared the way for the Revolution.

Officials Are Sent To Inspect the State of the Nation (1663)

The broad prerogatives traditionally held by local authorities and the difficulties of communication between Paris and the outlying provinces created serious problems for effective royal control in seventeenth-century France. The king relied strongly on the services of special officials who were sent from the capital to inspect conditions in the provinces and to report back directly to him and his chief financial officer, Jean-Baptiste Colbert. This reading contains excerpts from Colbert's 1663 instructions to such traveling justices. From P. Clement, *Lettres, Instructions et Memoirs de Colbert* (Paris, 1867), Vol. IV. Trans. Thomas Mendenhall, Basil Henning, A. S. Foord, *Ideas and Institutions in European History 800–1715* (New York: Holt, Rinehart and Winston, 1948), pp. 309, 311–313.

The king wishing to be clearly informed concerning the state of the provinces of his realm, His Majesty has ordered that his memorandum be sent to the itinerant justices so that they may set themselves, each within the confines of his own district, to ascertain carefully and exactly the following information. . . .

Ecclesiastic: In regard to the Church, the names and numbers of dioceses; the cities, towns, villages, and parishes which are under their ecclesiastical jurisdiction, their temporal government and the towns and parishes of which this government is composed; particularly, if the bishop is temporal lord of the cathedral city; the name, age, estate, and disposition of the bishop; if he comes from that part of the country or not; if he makes his residence there; how he performs his episcopal visitations; what credit he has in his diocese, and what effect he might have in difficult times; what reputation he enjoys among his flock, if he confers the benefice of his chapter; if he is engaged in any lawsuit; the amount of his revenues; the names and the values of the benefices which he confers. . . .

Military Government: Concerning the military government, which concerns the nobility, which is the second order of his kingdom, although His Majesty knows all the talents of the governors and lieutenant-generals of his provinces he wishes nevertheless in order to make these reports complete that the itinerant justices begin their inquiry concerning the nobility and the name of the said governor general, his house and relationships in the province, whether they actually are in residence there; their good and bad conduct; if they are accused of taking money or of vexing the people in any other way; if these accusations are probable; if the people complain of them; what credit they have among the nobility and the lower classes. And since the principal and most important application that His Majesty wishes the governors of provinces to do is to insist upon justice and prevent the suppression of the weak and the violence of the strong, His Majesty wishes to be particularly informed of the past conduct of these governors in order to judge what he should do in the future. In case that some violent outbreak happened in some province, His Majesty wishes to be informed in detail along with the knowledge of how the governor conducted himself. . . .

Concerning Justice: And since it is assuredly the most important matter which there is to examine in the province, it will be good and even very necessary to know in detail the interests of the principal officers of these judicial bodies and particularly if those who led in the recent unpleasantness [the Fronde] are still living. . . . It is necessary first of all to be informed in detail of the kind of justice which that judicial body dispenses to the subjects of the King; if there is corruption or not; the cases and persons who are under suspicion. If the court has been guilty of any manifest injustice, which created any stir in the province or which resulted in the oppression of the weak in favor of any friend, relative, or any other vicious condition, His Majesty desires to be informed as well concerning the length of trials and any excessive judges' fees, not only in the superior courts but also in the lower courts, for it is necessary to know in detail concerning these two matters which can be such a burden to His Majesty's subjects. . . .

His Majesty, having often received complaints that the officers of the sovereign courts in diverse places sometimes make forced sales to themselves of the lands which are to provide their stipends. He will be very well pleased to be particularly informed of these cases or of anyone who practices this. It will be equally necessary to expose in the report all the resources in lands possessed by each one of the officers of the court. There remain the royal prosecutors concerning whom it is very necessary to know the intensions and the competency, above all if they have enough strength to make applications and the necessary pursuits to uphold justice with vigor and severity, being absolutely necessary to have people in these positions who will not let themselves be swayed by any consideration of personal gain and still less of influence. . . .

Revenues of the King: After having discovered the value of all the different kinds of revenue and by this means all that which the king collects annually in the provinces, it will be necessary to examine in detail all the difficulties encountered in collecting and fathering them. Whether they cause any lessening of the revenues or are prejudicial to the people. Concerning import and export duties which are regulated by tariff schedules, it is nevertheless very necessary to hear the complaints and to inform oneself exactly if they are well founded; for better understanding it will be good to communicate their complaints to the directors and principals of the tax farms who are always in the province.

It will be very necessary on this point to make a particular study and to examine in detail the basis of the merchant's complaints and the answers of the tax farmers because the former were accustomed to make great complaints and to search out all imaginable means to defraud the rights of the farms and the latter not only seek to defend themselves but even to plague unnecessarily the merchants on occasion; and since that farm concerns commerce to the establishment of which up and down his kingdom His Majesty gives his care in all matters, it is necessary that the justices examine carefully all that which has to do with the subject in the province for the satisfaction of His Majesty and for the good and advancement of his people. . . .

Bishop Bossuet Defines Divine Right Monarchy
(c. 1675)

Bishop Jacques Bossuet (1627–1704) was the tutor of Louis XIV's only son. As part of his job, he wrote an essay for his pupil entitled *Politics Drawn from the Very Words of Holy Scripture* which carefully defined the privileges and responsibilities of the individuals who had been chosen by God to rule over other men. Bossuet's essay is one of the clearest statements of the theory of divine right monarchy. From Bishop Jacques Bossuet, *Politics Drawn from the Very Words of Holy Scripture,* in J. H. Robinson, *Readings in European History* (New York, 1906), II, pp. 273–275.

We have already seen that all power is of God. The ruler, adds St. Paul, "is the minister of God to thee for good. But if thou do that which is evil, be afraid; for he beareth not the sword in vain: for he is the minister of God, a revenger to execute wrath upon him that doeth evil." Rulers then act as the ministers of God and as his lieutenants on earth. It is through them that God exercises his empire. Think ye "to withstand the kingdom of the Lord in the hand of the sons of David?" Consequently, as we have seen, the royal throne is not the throne of a man, but the throne of God himself. The Lord "hath chosen Solomon my son to sit upon the throne of the kingdom of the Lord over Israel." And again, "Solomon sat on the throne of the Lord. . . ."

It appears from all this that the person of the king is sacred, and that to attack him in any way is sacrilege. . . . The prince need render account of his acts to no one. "I counsel thee to keep the king's commandment, and that in regard of the oath of God. Be not hasty to go out of his sight: stand not on an evil thing for he doeth whatsoever pleaseth him. Where the word of a king is, there is power: and who may say unto him, What doest thou? Whoso keepeth the commandment shall feel no evil thing." Without this absolute authority the king could neither do good nor repress evil. It is necessary that his power be such that no one can hope to escape him, and, finally, the only protection of individuals against the public authority should be their innocence. . . .

God is infinite, God is all. The prince, as prince, is not regarded as a private person: he is a public personage, all the state is in him; the will of all the people is included in his. As all perfection and all strength are united in God, so all the power of individuals is united in the person of the prince. What grandeur that a single man should embody so much! . . .

John B. Wolf: Louis XIV and Royal Power

Consideration of seventeenth-century absolutism is impossible without focusing on the life of the man whose reign embodied the concept. Professor Wolf's outstanding biography of Louis XIV explains the period from the vantage point of the life of the grand monarch, whose upbringing imposed upon him the obligation to play out the role assigned to him by his heredity and his talents, his duty to God and to his state. Reprinted from *Louis XIV* by John B. Wolf by permis-

I. THE CULT OF THE KING

The great palace [of Versailles] was a keystone in the new cult of royalty. In the preceding eras the great constructions were usually to the glory of God; even Philip II, when he built his great palace, made it a monastery with the chapel as the center of interest. At Versailles the bedroom of the king is the center, identifying the king as the highest power on earth, while the chapel is to one side. The imposing grandeur of the château was evidence of the wealth of the kingdom; and its construction without walls and moats was proof of the power of the king's government. Versailles was a challenge, a defiance flung out at all Europe; as impressive a display of the wealth, power, and authority of the French king as were his armies and his warships. Europe did not miss this. In the century after the construction of Versailles, châteaus at Vienna, at Potsdam, at Dresden, at Munich, at St. Petersburg, and the very plans for the city of Washington, D. C., reflected the influence of the grandeur of Versailles. A sovereign who wished to flaunt his power could do no better than to imitate Louis XIV. Louis probably never dreamed of the fact that he had also built a monument that would become a lucrative tourist attraction for hundreds of years to come. He and his generation had the intention of housing the king, who was identifying himself with the kingdom in a way that would heighten his power and his authority in the world. . . .

The most important offices in the royal household were occupied by great noblemen and their wives. There were about 250 individuals—men, women, and children—who were classed as people of quality: the princes of the blood, the dukes and peers, the very wealthy noblemen of ancient lineage (usually with the title *marquis*), important clergymen, and soldiers with high rank in the king's army or navy. Some of these people had family histories as old as the royal family itself, for indeed the kings of France were of this stock, but the majority were of more recent creation. There were considerable gradations among them. The peers and dukes took their position from the date of the creation of the title, the simple persons of quality from positions in the household, the church, or the armed services. Louis assured these people the respect due to their status in society; in court functions, at the grand sessions of Parlement, or simply in the social setting of the court, the dukes and peers shared the grandeur of the king; they were his "cousins", they acted as if they were set apart from the rest of humanity. Under Louis XIV they acted out roles that helped to create the *mystique* necessary to justify the power that the king did, in fact, exercise. Their roles, however, were purely ceremonial, for they were excluded from the realities of power. As Saint-Simon contemplated this situation, he reached the conclusion that Louis XIV was deliberately attempting to destroy the dukes and the peers of the realm.

Most of these people of quality owed their positions to recent kings; only a very few of them could actually trace their lineage deep into the middle ages. The kings of France had long since been encroaching upon the traditional feudal orders. None of the lay peers still ruled their provinces as quasi-independent lords, for the crown had absorbed their powers. However, in the sixteenth and seventeenth centuries a new feudality struggled to establish itself out of the disorders of the "religious" war and the rebellions of the first half of the seventeenth century. As men with enormous wealth, with governorships and provinces made hereditary in their families, these "great ones" of the land had dangerously threatened the king's authority. Louis XIV was well aware of the problem through his own experiences during the *Fronde*. Like his father and grandfather he strove to curb these "great ones." One of the most effective means was to cheapen their ranks by the creation of new peers, and by the encroachment upon their real powers as governors or as holders of great fiefs through the action of royal intendants dependent upon the king and directed by his ministers. In this way the new feudality could be curbed; at the same time, by bringing these great ones to court and domesticating them as servants of the royal households, Louis gradually weakened their will to rebel.

All of the bowing and scraping, the pretentions to grandeur, could not conceal the fact that Louis had separated real power from social prestige. Elizabeth-Charlotte [Louis' sister-in-law] saw this most clearly: "I am not ignorant to the point of not knowing what difference there is between the Elector of Brandenburg and Monsieur [her husband], but in order to prevent Monsieur from seeing that he is only in a way a slave of his brother, one gives him a huge idea of his grandeur, to which nothing can approach and which nonetheless is without any foundation, and is purely imagination." In another place she wrote, "I hold grandeur as purely chimerical when great power is not joined to it." But what was left to the great ones? They were offered social prestige, ceremonial importance, grandeur—if they would act out roles that would supply the *mystique* for their king's exercise of power. If they refused to accept the offer, they also gave up the royal favor that was translated into patronage, pension, gratifications, and the *divertissements* of the court. . . .

The Wars of Louis XIV

It is probable that Louis XIV, had he been asked to name his greatest contribution to France, would have hesitated between the achievement of religious unity and the expansion of the frontiers. The monarchs of the sixteenth and seventeenth century regarded the nation as their personal property and were convinced that warfare and conquest redounded to the glory and power of king and state. France was at war for most of Louis' long life. The immediate rival was the Spanish and Austrian Hapsburgs, whose family union in the early sixteenth century posed the threat of European domination. Richelieu had intervened in the Thirty Years' War to prevent this, and in the Treaty of Westphalia (1648) France had gained a handful of fortress-towns on the outer edges of the Holy Roman Empire. War with Spain did not end until 1659 (Treaty of the Pyrenees) with the cession of considerable Spanish territory. France, thereafter, was unquestionably the leading European state. The Sun King's personal ambitions drove him to tip the continental balance of power further by attempting to gain what he considered the "natural boundaries" of France: the Alps, Pyrenees, and left bank of the Rhine River. In a series of wars in 1667–1688, 1672–1678, and 1688–1697, aimed primarily at reaching the Rhine, Louis gained the lands indicated on the map but united the nations of Europe against France. His final war (1701–1713) was a daring attempt to

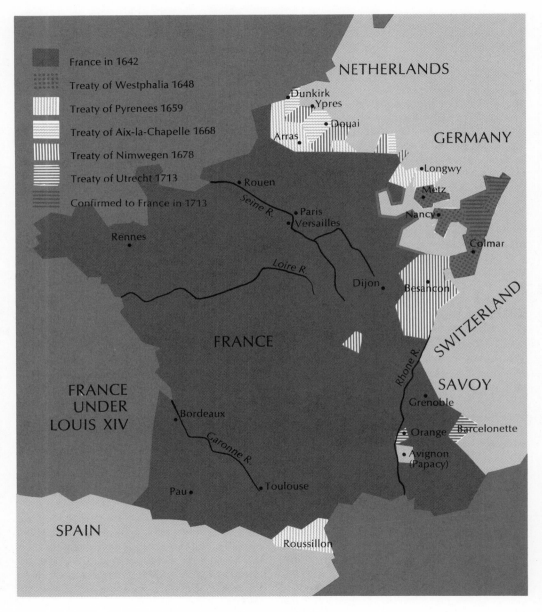

France in 1642

Treaty of Westphalia 1648

Treaty of Pyrenees 1659

Treaty of Aix-la-Chapelle 1668

Treaty of Nimwegen 1678

Treaty of Utrecht 1713

Confirmed to France in 1713

obtain the throne of Spain for his grandson after the death of the last of the Spanish Hapsburg line. In this Louis was successful after an enervating struggle. The remaining Spanish possessions in Europe were divided among his opponents at the Treaty of Utrecht and the Spanish colonies opened up to English trade. Two years later Louis died, leaving a larger but economically exhausted France.

While music, art, and drama gave pleasure to the court as well as helped to make an imposing facade for the monarchy, the men of letters and of science also received the bounty of the king and responded by praising his reign. Voltaire long ago pointed out that Louis' government stands like a shining light as the patron of art, literature, and science, in striking contrast to the government of his archfoe William of Orange, who became King of England. This is true. One has to wait until the establishment of the great American foundations like the Guggenheim, the Rockefeller, the Mellon, and others to see patronage of culture and science on the scale set by Louis XIV. Moreover the king's government was probably more important to the scientist and the artist than our contemporary foundations are. For today a man of letters can make a living from his royalties; a scientist, as a professor or an employee of a great corporation; and even an artist or a musician, as a teacher; whereas in the seventeenth century few such opportunities existed. Thus the king's bounty was very important. The list of the recipients of Louis' pensions and *gratifications* sounds like the roll call of the Guggenheim fellows: in one year there were three theologians, eight linguists, twenty-five French and three foreign "men of letters," five historians, one painter (most painters were employed by the *Batiments* on regular salaries), one lawyer, six students of physics, four surgeons and medical men, one botanist, one mathematician. . . .

Louis also sponsored academies of the dance, of painting, of science, of letters; but one often suspects that he knew little or nothing about these organizations. For example, he made only one visit to the observatory that he "built and supported"; the tapestry commemorating that event does not tell of its uniqueness. Obviously much of the king's sponsorship was the work of his ministers, but it does not really matter whether the inspiration came from the king, Colbert, one of the Le Telliers, or some other of Louis' creatures—it was done in his name and the intention was to bring prestige to the king and his regime. It was no accident that in the literary quarrel known as the "battle between the moderns and the ancients," men compared the age of Louis XIV with those of Pericles and of Augustus. Louis' efforts to support science and culture obviously paid off in terms of royal prestige, and as we shall see, his government needed his prestige as a *mystique* to cover the extensions of power that accompanied the creation of the military-police state. When the king's power grew to the point where another *Fronde* was simply out of the question, then also his prestige and grandeur, the *mystique* that justified power, had also to expand.

However, the doings at court and in the capitals of Europe were known to only a few. The *Gazette* printed stories of court functions, but it had a limited circulation. Thus there was the problem of carrying the message to the people of the kingdom. They were feeling the imposition of power that came with the development of the bureaucratic, military-police state; they had also to accept the *mystique* that justified the king's assumption of this power over the kingdom. The solution lay in the profoundly royalist sentiments of the French. The clergy, the professors, the literate had long explained that God gave the power to govern to kings while He retained the authority to himself, and that He would hold the king responsible for his acts. The king was the "father of his country", the object of admiration—perhaps veneration—a consecrated figure with functions that made him godlike. Even the more violent pamphleteers during the *Fronde* professed loyalty and love for the king; he was the object of their

Louis XIV liked to be portrayed as a military conqueror. Here, dressed in ornamental armor, the king stands before a battle scene.

desires. His role as a political agent, however, was not so clearly defined; there were many who believed that the centralizing tendencies of the royal governments were at least unfortunate and probably illegal. Since the last of the fourteenth century there had been a growing struggle in the kingdom between the decentralized sources of power (nobility, towns, guilds, etc.) and the centralizing tendencies of the monarchy. By Louis XIV's time this contest within the inherited pluralistic structure of politics had reached a crisis, a crisis that tipped the balance of force in favor of the central authority. This new balance had to be spelled out both in political institutions like the new army and the bureaucracy, and in the symbols and ceremony that gave to the people a visual apperception of political order. A most important factor in this vision was the image of the king in the popular mind.

The lives of most seventeenth-century men were lived out in a dull routine of traditional activity broken only by some colorful religious festival, an occasional arrival of a stranger, a troop of minstrels or players, a military cavalcade, or some such event. Thus the progressions of the court from one château to another that had long been the usual pattern of monarchy were "events" of importance in the lands through which the court moved. Anyone who has journeyed up the Nile on an excursion steamer, where he can see the seventeenth century juxtaposed to his own, will never forget the cries of the children and others who greet the weekly visit of the steamer as a contact with the outside world. How much more exciting must have been the cavalcade of soldiers and courtiers, the gay carriages, the wagons and mule trains, the fine gentlemen and bedecked ladies, with

the person of the king as the center of attraction. A newsletter from the court in 1683 tells the story of the royal voyage toward Fontainebleau:

> On the road from Chambor [d] . . . the King was loaded with presents of fruit and flowers that the people brought to him and for which they were liberally recompensed. One person . . . threw in front of the King's carriage the most beautiful lamb that you have ever seen . . . but it fled so quickly that no one could catch it . . .

It was a typical scene reflecting the popularity of the king—or perhaps the vacuum in the lives of the people. Kings were well advised to travel from place to place, to show themselves to the people, to allow the local clergy to tell their parishioners that this was the king that God had given them. It secured stability for their position and consent for their rule.

This was the age-old pattern. For centuries French kings had traveled through their lands, giving justice, receiving the blessings of the clergy, and the cheers of the people. During the reign of Louis XIV, in addition to this well-established relationship, new patterns developed—a new cult that associated the king more closely with the Godhead. This new cult foliated in the form of festivals, fireworks, statues, fountains, palaces, expositions, books, pamphlets, and religious services—all organized to glorify the king, to raise his throne to the steps of heaven, to remove his person from the ranks of ordinary human beings. . . .

This generation of princes and statesmen stood on the edge of a past that had been both difficult and disorderly; all over Europe the military and political pluralism inherited

from a yesterday had led to civil wars, rebellions, violence, contempt for the processes of law. Cloaked by religious flags, by demands for the recognition of "liberties," or simply by a brutal urge for pillage and plunder, these disorders had endangered the tranquility of the European world and the security of all men. The historian does not have to journey far in the years 1600–60 to understand why Hobbes decided that the Leviathan was the only hope for society; such disorder could be cured only by power. A Henry IV might try to govern the kingdom in the manner of a guerilla chieftain, but he had to realize that he shared his power with the men whose backs he slapped. Richelieu and Louis XIII could govern with erratic brutality, using picked panels of judges and the executioner to impose their will, but the headsman's sword cannot long replace the scepter if the king is not to appear a tyrant. This was the problem of the men around Louis XIV: they were willing to use force to give form to society, to break the will of rebellion, but they recognized that consent of the governed is most important for the ruler. Louis carefully explained to his son that it would be quite inconvenient to have to use force all the time to secure obedience. He had not read Machiavelli for nothing.

The vital forces of the kingdom seconded the royal will to restore order and break the political and military pluralism that had caused so much trouble in the past. The new army that Mazarin and his creatures were making was popular, for it could expel the "pillagers", as men called soldiers during the *Fronde*. The *Grand Jours* that invaded the provinces to bring malefactors to justice and peace to the land were welcome even though many of the criminals slipped through the nets. The intendants of police, justice, and taxation were well received when they began to inquire closely about the murders that passed as duels or accidents, the kidnappings that passed for elopements, and other acts of violence in the land. This was bringing order out of the *mêlée* and control over the pluralism that had created disorder. The new army and the bureaucracy were the agents of this action, but in addition there was needed a new image of royalty, a new *mystique,* and new sanctions for the power that it was exercising. This was the work of a propaganda that utilized all the vital forces of the kingdom. . . .

II. THE RELATION BETWEEN THE KING AND THE GOVERNING OF FRANCE

As is so often the case with Louis XIV, there is little direct evidence that will link the king as a person with the things that were done in his name or the processes that developed under the direction of his government. It is difficult to believe that Louis was personally responsible for the development of the *mystique* that raised the throne of the king to the foot of the throne of God and endowed his person with divine attributes; it is more likely that his creatures were responsible for this. By raising the throne far above the older centers of power, by placing the king in a unique and remote position instead of in the status of "first among equals" that had been true of the medieval feudal monarch, and finally, by identifying the person of the king with the vital forces in the kingdom, these men were preparing for the future state that would be able to exercise truly great power over the lives of its people. It would be interesting to know how much Louis was

the author of this drama; perhaps he was merely a clever actor who took his clues from the men who were giving characteristic form to the emerging bureaucratic military-police state of the West. Unfortunately we shall never really know which is the case.

Those who follow Louis XIV through the papers created by his government will quickly learn that the burden of work increased each decade at very near to a geometric ratio. Letters, minutes, orders, decrees, patents, grants, the registers of the household officials, and the correspondence of the secretaries of state all show the same pattern; the growing impact of the royal government upon the kingdom is reflected in an ever-increasing flow of paper. What could be cared for in 1661 by a secretary with an assistant and a few clerks, by 1685 required a small army of copyists, clerks, secretaries, and bureaucrats. The victory of the men of the pen over all competitors was complete. The secretaries and ministers who could be seen hurrying down the corridors of the royal châteaus to closet themselves with the king, exercised the power that formerly had belonged to princes of the blood, dukes and peers, marshals of France, municipal governments, and noblemen on their estates. Not all of the activity of these displaced persons had been usurped by the royal government, but enough had been to indicate the trends of the society that was in the process of becoming. The king himself was slowly but surely being subordinated to the procedures of his government; where his father had spoken of "my state", in the last twenty years of his life Louis XIV came increasingly to speak of "*the* state" of which he was the first servant.

In 1661 Louis ordered his collaborators not to sign or seal any order without his permis-

sion; by 1685 such an order, if literally obeyed, would have caused an impasse in the business of government. But by 1685 the king did not need to see every document; precedents had become established and bureaucratic procedures ironed out so that much business that formerly had required royal attention could now safely be cared for by a secretary. The king had enough to do in handling the important business of state, and the items of private affairs of his subjects that fascinated him; he could not look at everything. This fact becomes more and more apparent as we examine the flow of paper in the areas of foreign affairs, defense, commerce, police, religion, and the royal household. As the government's impact grew to include more and more of the life of the kingdom, the king, sometimes harassed by ill health, had to give much of the work to the team that helped him govern the state. Even a Louis XIV, who wanted to see everything himself, was brought to this situation by the growth of bureaucratic controls.

There was an enormous press of work for the government of the realm. These were the years when the great system of fortifications that rimmed the north and the east of the kingdom was built; guns, powder, magazines, soldiers, uniforms, and the whole paraphernalia of the emerging modern army came into the scope of the ministry of war. On the sea coast, in addition to the fortification of the great harbors, there were the naval arsenals where anchors, guns, rope, sails, and the host of other things needed for the new huge warships carrying 120 guns, were made or stored. The reports of the army of intendants, engineers, inspectors, clerks, and officers who were building these military institutions simply could not all come to the king's desk. Nor was that the end of the government's activity. This was the period when the chartered companies trading with Asia, Muscovy, America, the Levant, and elsewhere were burgeoning into important aspects of the political and economic society. Behind them was the whole economic structure that Colbert hoped to create to give France a primary place in the trade of the world. In another section of the château of Versailles the dispatches from French ambassadors, agents, and spies poured in telling of the activities and politics of France's neighbors, of the impact of French foreign policies, of the problems that were yet to come. Other servants of the king were concerned with religion, police and public order, the needs of the royal households, and the ceremonial activities of the court. Except for questions that particularly interested the king, many of these papers did not come to his desk unless the problems reached a stage of tension. Thus after 1680 it was surely possible that many things were done in his name without Louis' knowing much about them. Even today we cannot be sure whether his signature on many documents was written by him or someone who could sign his name even better than he could.

All this only underlines the fact that by the 1680's the business of the king's government had become the process of "mobilizing the potential power of the kingdom in the service of the state." Louis' government was the first to create "modern" military institutions, and thus was forced to develop the financial and administrative structures to support them. Even though this was important business of the realm, with the rise of bureaucratic institutions much of it could safely be left to the attention of administrators like Louvois, Colbert, and the *cadres* that they were de-

veloping in the wake of their drive for power. Louis discussed their projects with them both privately and in council, but he left the details to those who managed the bureaus.

As the royal authority extended over the kingdom, it brought new business for the king and his government. We find Louis, for example, writing to municipal officers asking for the names of men who would be suitable replacements for a position vacated by death. In former years these came under the supervision of the king. Louis was keenly aware of the importance of making good appointments, both to secure efficiency in government and to use political patronage properly. Even more common were the letters and minutes dealing with the extension of the police power. The countryside and the towns of France before the rise of Louis' police power were scenes of much disorder. Murders, assaults, robberies, kidnappings were all too common and too often unpunished, indeed, unnoticed by local authorities. Such things were still not uncommon by 1680, but there was a definite effort to curb and control crime. Many other problems came before the king as the highest judge of the land, but we often find him dismissing the request for royal intervention with the formula, "it is an affair for ordinary justice." However, we do see him acting in the role of "father of the country" to discipline errant sons at their father's request and to punish courtiers, noblemen, or others whose crimes did not come under the purview of the courts, as well as interesting himself in some spectacular crimes that came to his attention. The royal discipline was usually accomplished by a *lettre de cachet* by which the offender was summarily placed in a prison, a hospital, or a monastery for an indefinite period of time. . . .

Absolutism in Practice

Louis XIV penned his conception of the royal role in a memorandum to his young son about the year 1666. He wanted the boy to know early in life about the personal discipline that was necessary if one was to be an absolute monarch. He also wanted him to know something of the pleasures that came along with the job. In the second selection the Duc de Saint-Simon (1675–1755), member of a high-ranking French noble family, describes his own view of the king's role. Saint-Simon spent much of his life at Versailles where he kept extensive notes on the activities of the Court. A terrible gossip, his description of other nobles and of members of the royal family are witty and often extremely poisonous. I. From *A King's Lessons in Statecraft: Louis XIV; Letters to His Heirs,* trans. Herbert Wilson (London: Ernest Benn Limited, 1924), pp. 48–50. II. From Duc de Saint-Simon, *Memoirs of Louis XIV and the Regency,* trans. Bayle St. John (Washington, 1901), II, pp. 359–360.

I. LOUIS XIV DESCRIBES WHAT A KING DOES (c. 1666)

Two things without doubt were absolutely necessary: very hard work on my part, and a wise choice of persons capable of seconding it. . . .

I laid a rule on myself to work regularly twice every day, and for two or three hours each time with different persons, without counting the hours which I passed privately and alone, nor the time which I was able to give on particular occasions to any special affairs that might arise. There was no moment when I did not permit people to talk to me about them provided they were urgent. . . .

I cannot tell you what fruit I gathered immediately I had taken this resolution. I felt myself, as it were, uplifted in thought and courage; I found myself quite another man, and with joy reproached myself for having been too long unaware of it. This first timidity, which a little self-judgment always produces and which at the beginning gave me pain, especially on occasions when I had to speak in public, disappeared in less than no time. The only thing I felt then was that I was King, and born to be one. I experienced next a delicious feeling, hard to express, and which you will not know yourself except by tasting it as I have done.

For you must not imagine, my son, that the affairs of State are like some obscure and thorny path of learning which may possibly have already wearied you, wherein the mind strives to raise itself with effort above its purview, repugnant to us as much as its difficulty. The function of Kings consists principally in allowing good sense to act, which always acts naturally and without effort. What we apply ourselves to is sometimes less difficult than what we do only for our amusement. Its usefulness always follows. A King, however skillful and enlightened be his ministers, cannot put his own hand to the work without its effect being seen. Success, which is agreeable in everything, even in the smallest matters, gratifies us in these as well as in the greatest, and there is no satisfaction to equal that of noting every day some progress in glorious and lofty enterprises, and in the happiness of the people which has been planned and thought out by oneself. All that is most necessary to this work is at the same time agreeable; for, in a word, my son, it is to have one's eyes open to the whole earth; to learn each hour the news concerning every province and every nation, the secrets of every court, the mood and the weaknesses of each Prince and of every foreign minister; to be well-informed on an infinite number of matters about which we are supposed to know nothing; to elicit from our subjects what they hide from us with the greatest care; to discover interests of those who come to us with quite contrary professions. I do not know of any other pleasure we would not renounce for that. . . .

II. A NOBLE VIEWS THE KING (c. 1700)

Louis XIV was made for a brilliant Court. In the midst of other men, his figure, his courage, his grace, his beauty, his grand mien, even the tone of his voice and the majestic and natural charm of all his person, distinguished him till his death as the King Bee, and showed that if he had only been born a simple private gentleman, he would equally have excelled in *fêtes*, pleasures, and gallantry, and would have had the greatest success in love. The intrigues and adventures which early in life he had been engaged in had exercised an unfortunate influence upon him. He wished to reign by himself. His jealousy on this point unceasingly became weakness. He reigned, indeed, in little things; the great he could never reach: even in the former, too, he was often governed. . . . Naturally fond of trifles, he unceasingly occupied himself with the most petty details of his troops, his household, his mansions; would even instruct his cooks, who received, like novices, lessons they had known by heart for years. This vanity, this unmeasured and unreasonable love of admiration, was his ruin. His ministers, his generals, his mistresses, his courtiers, soon perceived his weakness. They praised him with emulation and spoiled him. Praises, or to say truth, flattery, pleased him to such an extent, that the coarsest was well received, the vilest even better relished. It was the sole means by which you could approach him. Those whom he liked owed his affection for them to their untiring flatteries. This is what gave his ministers . . . authority, and the opportunities they had for adulating him, of attributing everything to him, and of pretending to learn everything from him. Suppleness, meanness, an admiring, dependent, cringing manner—above all, an air of nothingness—were the sole means of pleasing him.

STUDY QUESTIONS

1. What factors made the process of centralization of the French state difficult?

2. What do Colbert's instructions to the itinerant justices tell about conditions in France in the mid-seventeenth century?

3. What was meant by "Divine Right of Kings"?

How would such a theory of kingship affect the relationship between government and people? Why was it widely accepted?

4. What role did Louis XIV play in the government of France? According to Wolf, the King, St. Simon?

5. Define absolutism. Ask yourself: What problems were the French rulers trying to solve? What forces opposed attempts to solve the problems? How did the rulers try to solve the problems? How successful were they? How absolute was Louis XIV?

6. Is there anything "modern" about seventeenth-century French absolutism?

Majesty of State

The real power of the state in the seventeenth and eighteenth centuries was expressed through the autocratic will of the monarch (in England and a few other regions by that of an aristocratic establishment). Through his agents the monarch set and collected taxes and established the law of the land, controlled the administration of justice and other aspects of governance, and levied and directed the forces of military and police. The cement that held together the apparatus of power was the *mystique* of kingship. The illustrations in this portfolio concentrate on the dramatic and aesthetic devices by which monarchy asserted its authority.

The most conspicuous evidence of majesty for most subjects were the vast and imposing palaces in which their kings, sultans and emperors lived and from whence the laws and edicts that shaped their lives flowed. The great palaces on this and the next page are typical.

Below, the baroque Queluz palace of the Braganza kings of Portugal; and, right the spreading Topkapi palace of the Ottoman sultans of Turkey.

The serenely beautiful Taj Mahal built by Shah Jehan of India in the seventeenth century as a memorial to his wife.

The royal palace in Bangkok in Thailand.

Left, the Dining Room of Ahmed III (1703–1730) in Topkapi. Its walls were paneled with colorful paintings of fruit and flowers, framed in mother-of-pearl. The ceiling featured an immense mirror.

The interiors of these palaces were showpieces for the wealth and power of their owners.

The Taj Mahal. Some of the handsomely carved ivory screens.

The Great Gallery of Schoenbrunn palace in Vienna. Its ceiling was covered by huge allegorical paintings similar to this decoration by Giovanni Battista Tiepolo (1696–1770) for the Palazzo Barbaro in Venice.

Baroque bedroom in the
Palazzo Sagredo, Venice.

A concert at Versailles in honor of the birthday of the dauphin, son of Louis XV.

Evening relaxation at the court of
Louis XIV in 1682.

An Indian prince riding on an elephant (late sixteenth century).

The status of the princely aristocracy reflected that of the potentates.

A Japanese daimyo (lord), accompanied by samurai (knights), other officers and attendants, on his way to the Imperial Court in Yedo (seventeenth century).

Above left, Queen Christina of Sweden (1632–1654), one of
Europe's first liberated women.

The monarchs themselves, whether from Europe, Asia, or
Africa, had in common the aura of command.

Above right, the ruler of the once-powerful African kingdom
of Benin (1680s). Right, Babar, founder of the Mogul Empire
in India, (1483–1530), conquering descendent of Tamerlane.
Far right, King Munza of the Niam tribe of Central Africa
(1870s).

Carved lacquer throne of Chinese Emperor Chien Lung (1736–1795).

Coronation throne of Anne of England (1701–1714).

The jewel-encrusted Peacock Throne of Iran.

Silver coronation throne of Christina, still used each year by the Swedish king when he formally opens Parliament.

Three Seventeenth-Century English Documents

TOPIC 18

CROWN VERSUS PARLIAMENT IN ENGLAND

The history of England in the seventeenth century contrasts sharply with that of France. Whereas in France, the challenge to the growing power of the king was successfully countered by Richelieu and Louis XIV; in England, the crown was unable to maintain itself against a similar attack by the aristocracy and other forces opposed to royal absolutism. There a storm brewed that neither force, patronage, nor bureaucracy could tame. The opposition to arbitrary government, gathered together in Parliament, was able to compel a constitutional settlement with the English monarchy. This settlement, known as the Glorious Revolution, exercised a powerful impact on the minds of men and eventually influenced significantly the political development of both the European continent and England's overseas colonies. The readings seek to discover the nature of the settlement and the circumstances under which it came about.

The first selection is from Prothero, *Statutes and Other Constitutional Documents* (London, 1894), pp. 293–294; the second and third selections are from Rushworth, *Historical Collections* (London, 1721), I, p. 53 and VII, pp. 1418–1419.

I. JAMES I CAUTIONS AGAINST CHALLENGING THE POWER OF KINGS (1610)

The state of monarchy is the supremest thing upon earth, for kings are not only God's lieutenants upon earth and sit upon God's throne, but even by God himself they are called gods. There be three principal similitudes that illustrate the state of monarchy: one taken out of the word of God, and the two others out of the grounds of policy and philosophy. In the Scriptures kings are called gods, and so their power after a certain relation compared to the Divine power. Kings are also compared to fathers of families: for a king is truly . . . the father of his people. And lastly, kings are compared to the head of this microcosm of the body of man. . . .

I conclude then this point touching the power of kings with this axiom of divinity, That as to dispute what God may do is blasphemy, . . . so is it sedition in subjects to dispute what a king may do in the height of his power. But just kings will ever be willing to declare what they will do, if they will not incur the curse of God. I will not be content that my power be disputed upon; but I shall ever be willing to make the reason appear of all my doings, and rule my actions according to my laws. . . .

But I would wish you to be careful to avoid three things in the matter of grievances. First, that you do not meddle with the main points of government; that is my craft; I must not be taught my office. Secondly, I would not have you meddle with such ancient rights of mine as I have received from my predecessors. . . . And lastly I pray you, beware to exhibit for grievance anything that is established by a settled law, and whereunto (as you have already had a proof) you know I will never give a plausible answer: for it is an undutiful part in subjects to press their king, wherein they know beforehand he will refuse them. . . .

II. PARLIAMENT MAKES A "GREAT PROTESTATION" (1621)

That the liberties, franchises, privileges, and jurisdictions of Parliament are the ancient and undoubted birthright and inheritance of the subjects of England; and that the arduous and urgent affairs concerning the King, state and defence of the realm, and of the Church of England, and the making and maintenance of laws, and redress of mischiefs and grievances, counsel and debate in Parliament: and that in the handling and proceeding of those businesses every member of the House hath, and of right ought to have . . . liberty and freedom to treat of those matters, in such order, as in their judgments shall seem fittest. . . .

III. CHARLES I (SON OF JAMES) IS SENTENCED TO DEATH (1649)

Whereas the Commons of England assembled in Parliament have by their late Act entitled an *Act of the Commons of England assembled in Parliament for erecting an High Court of Justice for the trying and judging of Charles Stuart, King of England,* authorized and constituted us an High Court of Justice . . . a charge of high treason and other high crimes was, in behalf of the people of England, exhibited against him and read openly unto him, wherein he was charged, that he, the said Charles Stuart, being admitted King of England, and therein trusted with a limited power to govern by and according to the law of the land and not otherwise; and by his trust, oath, and office being obliged to use the power committed to him for the good and benefit of the people, and for the preservation of their rights and liberties; yet, nevertheless, out of a wicked design to erect and uphold in himself an unlimited and tyrannical power to rule according to his will, and to overthrow the rights and liberties of the people . . . which by the fundamental constitutions of this kingdom were reserved on the people's behalf in the right and power of frequent and successive Parliaments, or national meetings in Council; he, the said Charles Stuart, for accomplishment of such his designs, and for the protecting of himself and his adherents in his and their wicked practices, to the same end hath traitorously and maliciously levied war against the present Parliament, and people therein represented. . . .

For all which treasons and crimes this Court doth adjudge that he, the said Charles Stuart, as a tyrant, traitor, murderer, and public enemy to the good people of this nation, shall be put to death by the severing of his head from his body.

From Despotism to the Glorious Revolution

From *A History of the Western World,* Volume I, *Ancient Times to 1715,* by S. B. Clough et al. Copyright ©, 1964, by D. C. Heath & Co., a division of Raytheon Education Co., Boston, Mass.

I

On the somber afternoon of January 30, 1649, a sense of dread had settled over Westminster and the city of London beside the icy Thames. Whitehall was thronged with silent people and grim-faced soldiers. One of the tall windows of the Banqueting Hall in the palace had been removed to form an entry to a scaffold draped in black. On the platform was a headman's block. A double line of hand-picked members of Cromwell's New Model Army held the open space between the palace of St. James and the spectral setting in Whitehall. Early that morning Charles I, King of England, had listened to the 27th Chapter of Matthew read to him by an Anglican bishop. The reading of Christ's trial and passion had been followed by Holy Communion. In midmorning, led by halberdiers, Charles had been moved to the Banqueting Hall, traditionally the site of so much gaiety, for the dreadful wait. In the midst of his progress, a citizen named Tench confronted him insolently and then scooped up the King's little spaniel, Rogue, which he later exhibited as a prize. Across the dreary Channel in Paris, Charles' wife, Queen Henriette, was lodged in an apartment in the Louvre, blockaded by the opening battles of the Fronde, a last-ditch aristocratic rebellion against the assertive absolutism in France.

For three hours the King waited, then he was brought out for his last confrontation with his people. On the scaffold two black-masked figures awaited him. They were his executioners. The composure of the King, his

This woodcut of the beheading of Charles I appeared in a contemporary account by Richard Brandon, the chief executioner of London. Brandon found it necessary to write a description of the execution after royalists spread the rumor that he had refused to participate out of loyalty to the king and that instead a puritan chaplain, or even Oliver Cromwell, had dealt the blow.

uncanny steadfastness in this extremity, need not have been unexpected by his enemies. Although his duplicity had convinced his opponents that no agreement could be reached with such an intriguer, he had dealt with all sides with but one intent: to maintain the power of the crown unfettered by Parliament or the common law or by those who used these institutions to challenge his will. He had been brought down by revolutionaries who, in the name of principle, had brought him to the scaffold.

Standing near his executioners, the King began a last and entirely futile defense. The Rump of the House of Commons which had tried him, he said, was an illegal body. The Army which now held power in England was an usurping government, a tyrannous element backed only by force. A Lieutenant-General was the unlawful chief of state. It was he, Charles, who had sought to uphold English tradition, now ruptured by this monstrous insurgency. His last words are said to have been: "If I would have given way to an arbitrary way, for to have all laws changed according to the power of the sword, I needed not to have come here. And therefore I tell you, and I pray to God it be not laid to your charge, that *I am the martyr of the people.*" Then the King's cloak was removed; he was placed on the block; the axe rose and fell. After a moment of shocked silence, one of the headsmen raised the bloody remnant to the sky. Thus on a wintry afternoon a few months after the signing of the Treaties of Westphalia and about ten years before the negotiation of the Peace of the Pyrenees and the definitive conclusion of the continental wars of fifty years, an English king was executed in England by one of the new armies of the seventeenth century.

On the continent, during the past forty years, kings had, here and there, been driven out of their realms; the ministers of one ruler had been thrown from a window; at least one king had been killed in battle; and Henry IV of France had been assassinated by a fanatic. But only in England had a king been brought to trial for high crimes against the state and condemned to death.

Charles I's unique position on January 30, 1649, illustrates the peculiar position of England *vis-à-vis* the rest of the European world. England was and is near Europe, but not of it. Although English history was moved by all of the economic, social, religious, political, and intellectual currents that swayed the continent, England managed to react in a special and insular way with rather different results.

In England, as on the continent, the seventeenth-century struggle between the modern principle of centralization and unification on the one hand and the idea of particularism and localism on the other went on amid considerable strife and bloodshed. Religious controversies raged as well. But England did not become directly seriously involved in the continental European wars of the early seventeenth century. In England, government was modernized and the religious question was to all intents and purposes settled before the century was over; but English modernization did not take the route toward royal, centralized absolutism followed by the most successful contemporary continental monarchies. What is more, the solutions to their political and religious problems that the English achieved in the seventeenth century proved to be remarkably durable; they persisted with only minor modifications until well into the nineteenth century. During the seventeenth century, the English seem to have worked a great deal of radicalism out of their systems; and came up with a moderate settlement. Perhaps it is because they had their fling at revolutionary radicalism early that later they seemed so conservative to foreign observers.

In the pages that follow, a brief description of the political developments in England from the death of Elizabeth I (1603) through the Glorious Revolution (1689) will be followed by an attempt to explain why the English underwent just this kind of revolutionary turmoil at this particular time. . . .

The Whole Story in Brief: England from 1603 to 1689

Charles' last futile defense of his rôle as protector of the people against the power of "the sword" was the logical outgrowth of the theory of absolutism shared by all the monarchs of his day. In France, the power of Louis XIV (1643–1715) was to be buttressed by the Sun King's official political theorist, Bishop Bossuet, who proved through massive reference to Scripture that God had intended his people to be ruled by anointed monarchs holding authority directly from God. The main trend of politico-constitutional development in early modern times was not, in fact, in the direction of greater and wider representation of the people in parliamentary bodies but towards the increasingly autocratic power of the king.

In England while a representative body sharing power with the king had made its appearance in the later Middle Ages, the kings had long been the effective rulers over their realms. The Tudor monarchs, Henry VII, Henry VIII, and Elizabeth, in their several ways ruled in an arbitrary manner—although through tact, cajolery, and craft they had avoided head-on clashes and had mesmerized the English people to feel that they were being led rather than pushed. James I, who came to the throne in 1603 on the death of Elizabeth, publicly announced his version of the Divine Right idea: "From God the King and from the King the Law." He was not content, as the Tudors had been, with the simple fact of absolute rule; he wanted it recognized that he was divinely appointed to rule absolutely.

James, who came to England from Scotland, was unfamiliar with his new subjects and their ways. His bitter struggle with Scottish Presbyterians made him overly wary of even moderate Puritans in England. The English parliamentary class was not willing to accept his notions about monarchy any more than many English religious dissidents were willing to accept his ideas concerning religious uniformity.

James called four Parliaments during his reign and his relations with them were often stormy. His son, Charles I, who entertained all the political and religious notions of his father but carried them to even greater extremes fared even worse. He called three Parliaments between 1625 and 1629. Each time he expected Parliament to supply funds; each time Parliament attempted to extract guarantees of its power in return.

In 1629, Charles dissolved his third Parliament and endeavored for eleven years to manage without that troublesome body, despite his pressing financial needs. He revived archaic medieval prerogatives as devices for raising funds, devices that were, the parliamentarians thought, clearly in violation of English constitutional precedent. Eventually the matter was brought to a test of arms in the 1640's. The royal forces were defeated: the King was executed and England entered upon

The deep antagonism between the royalists and the supporters of Parliament is reflected in this illustration from *A Dialogue or Parley between Prince Rupert's Dog Pudel and Tobie's Dog Pepper,* published in 1642. Rupert, royalist commander and the king's nephew, and his cavalier companions are distinguished by their curled hair and rich attire. The parliamentary forces and their dog have a more puritanical appearance.

an Interregnum, without a king (1649–1660), ruled by a military dictatorship under the name of Protectorate (1653–1660).

During the civil warfare of the 1640's, the English people chose sides. There was no clear division along class lines as we think of these today, though the overwhelming majority of business classes supported Parliament. The clearest divisions were religious: Roman Catholics and most Anglicans sided with the crown: Presbyterians, Congregationalists, and other Puritan groups* were parliamentarian. Geographically, the area to the

*Puritanism expressed the religious position of those in seventeenth-century English life who wanted a more democratic organization of their church and sought both simpler ritual and a closer adherence to Calvin's theology. From the time of James I, who tried to drive them out of the established Anglican church, they were to be found mainly among the Presbyterians, Independents (Congregationalists), Anabaptists, and a number of smaller sects—Eds.

north and west of England was royalist while the territory to the south and east was the stronghold of Parliament. Cromwell's Protectorate was a workable if dull government for England; but it did not provide effectively for its own perpetuation. When the dictator died, in 1658, therefore, the decision was made—partly by the Army—to bypass Cromwell's designated successor and to restore the Stuart line to the English throne. The first of the restored Stuarts, Charles II, managed to avoid serious conflict with people and Parliament but his brother and successor, James II, alienated the parliamentary group, partly because he seemed to entertain the same constitutional views as did his father and grandfather and partly because he was a Roman Catholic.

The politico-religious conflicts of the early part of the century were not yet fully resolved.

In 1688–1689 the dominant parliamentary group turned against James II and invited his Protestant daughter, Mary, and his son-in-law William of Orange, Stadtholder of the Netherlands, to ascend the throne of England as co-rulers. William and Mary accepted the invitation; James II was allowed to flee the country and England had its Glorious or Bloodless Revolution. The new monarchs signed a document, the famous Bill of Rights, in which they bound themselves and their heirs to a great number of prohibitions.

Almost entirely a negative document or list of things the monarchs should not do, the

Bill of Rights was derived from English memories of Stuart attempts at absolutism. On the positive side, it stated that Parliament should be called frequently: a few years later, it was enacted that Parliament should be called no less often than every three years. The levying of money without the consent of Parliament was, of course, declared illegal, as was the maintenance of a standing army without parliamentary assent. To ensure compliance with the latter stricture, Parliament established that the Mutiny Act, which gave the crown control over its military and naval forces, was to be passed for an interval of only one year at a time. The effect of this measure was to force the calling of annual Parliaments.

A contrast in English leadership in the seventeenth century: contemporary portraits of Oliver Cromwell and James II.

The Revolution of 1689 was "Glorious" mainly because it was accomplished neatly and by the "right" people. Members of Parliament, Lords and Commons, all people of substance, were the revolutionaries. James escaped intact, and no one of questionable background (save, perhaps, one of Cromwell's generals) or radical ideology was allowed to participate. From this time on throughout the eighteenth century and well into the nineteenth century England was effectively governed by an elite group in the Lords and Commons, often working in conjunction with the crown.

The above account of the main political events leading to the execution of Charles I in 1649 and the Glorious Revolution of 1689 is simple and well known. Latter-day historians are inclined to probe underneath these surface facts for explanation of *why* events occurred as they did. What, they wish to know, were the conditions underlying the affairs of state that made it come to pass that a constitutional monarchy was established in England, while, in the same period of history, an overwhelming absolutism triumphed across the Channel in France? Whereas the French experienced merely an abortive aristocratic revolt, the *Fronde*, the English went through something like a national revolution. Explanations of the English achievement must necessarily hinge on the answers to the question of why a truly revolutionary situation developed in England, as well as on how the political events unrolled.

II

The Background of the English Revolution

The English Revolution can be, and has been, thought of as part of the historical transition between agricultural and parochial Europe and the early modern forms of economy and social order, in which an expanded world of discovery, exploration, and commerce strengthened the position of urban and capitalist groups, while at the same time the remnants of the feudal nobility suffered further erosion of their power. It is probably true that during the late sixteenth century and into the seventeenth many English squires and merchants [the gentry] were improving their material position relative to that of the hereditary nobility, though how much is still a subject for debate. . . .

In the early seventeenth century the most active part of the gentry was the technically non-noble squirearchy which owned the overwhelming preponderance of English real estate. Under the Tudors, the squires had become the mainstay of the English government as ministers in the Royal Privy Council and as Justices of the Peace; and they dominated the Commons. Although the towns returned more members to the House than did the counties, the merchants in the enfranchised boroughs preferred to select their representatives from the country gentry who had the leisure for, and the habit of, parliamentary activity. Many of the gentry earnestly prepared themselves for this national service by attending the university and studying law. In the early seventeenth century this group acquired or developed some enlightened and dedicated leaders. . . .

What was there about these men of the seventeenth century that led them to forsake their calm acres and to run the risks involved in openly opposing the crown? Was it that they were infected with "the bourgeois spirit"? Probably not. The answer seems to be that they were imbued, rather, with the Puritan spirit. They were all anti-Roman Catholic; most were anti-episcopal; some were Presbyterian; and a few, like Oliver Cromwell, were Independent (Congregational). They were accustomed by heredity and training to political leadership in the counties and in Parliament. They thought of themselves not as revolutionaries but as the conservators of the English tradition. In the last years of Elizabeth's reign this conservative opposition began to express itself, in Parliament and out. . . . The Commons became increasingly stubborn over money matters and had to be held at bay by royal cajolery and intimidation. . . .

Shortly after James' accession, the prelude began to merge into Revolution. James demonstrated his ecclesiastical prejudices at the Hampton Court Conference of 1604 when he confronted the Puritans who presented a petition requesting toleration of their views with the curt observation, "No Bishop, no King." His son grew up in an atmosphere of assertive tactlessness. By the time Charles became King (1625), the temper of the English Puritans had moved from humble petition to outspoken criticism of the crown. . . .

When crisis came for Charles it was money which precipitated it. In what is known as the Ship-Money incident of 1634, he extended a traditional levy on the port-towns for the maintenance of the navy to the whole kingdom. Unquestionably, strengthening the defense of the kingdom was an upright intention; but there was no evidence that Charles actually intended to use the Ship Money for the fleet. His influential subjects were thoroughly alarmed at the possibilities if Charles were to carry off this, for him, potentially fruitful scheme. John Hampden spearheaded the opposition by publicly refusing to pay this new crown tax and forcing a test case. Charles was ready with a packed court. Hampden was found guilty; but the publicity gained by Hampden's stand and the injustice of the verdict made their impression on the country and solidified the opposition which determined to force the King, by fair means or foul, to call Parliament.

The hoped-for day came when Charles and Archbishop Laud tried to impose the Anglican prayer book on Scotland and promoted the Bishop's Wars (1639 and 1640). It is possible that some of the parliamentary squires played a part in stirring up these conflicts, for it was quite clear that in time of peace Charles could get along without Parliament. The Scottish revolt demanded counter-measures; counter-measures required an army; an army required money; and the result was the calling of two Parliaments in 1640. The first of these (the "Short Parliament") was dissolved after a few weeks. The second (the "Long Parliament") did not officially expire until 1660. . . .

In 1640–1641, the objectives of the active dissidents seem to have been to impose, first, a Presbyterian system on the Church and, second, some simple limitations on the monarchy. The opposition that moved under the leadership of John Pym was still moderate. Any liberal concession on the King's part might easily have precluded civil war. But such a concession would have been a voluntary limitation of royal prerogative; and this was too much to ask of a king raised on the theories of divine right absolutism.

Before Pym's death in 1643, his Militia Bill had been enacted and a parliamentary army had been created. His Grand Remonstrance had arraigned the monarchy as a tyranny. And in January, 1642, Pym had provoked the act that was to lose the King first London

and later his kingdom: Charles' imprudent attempt to seize five leading members of the Commons during a session. A king had desecrated the decorums, and his subjects proceeded to return the desecration in full.

In this moment of danger, Parliament took refuge in the City of London, appointed a Committee of Public Safety and began to raise its army. Taking with him 32 Peers and 65 members of the Commons, Charles fled to the North where he raised his own military force; and the war began. In this first stage of civil war, the inexperienced parliamentary army fared ill until its reorganization by the ambitious squire from Huntingdonshire, Oliver Cromwell. In time this "New Model" Army became an extraordinary military force characterised by order, discipline, purpose, and efficiency. Its leader, profoundly religious as were his men, saw the hand of Providence even in his most cruel and unnecessary acts. The New Model Army was made up of yeomen, and its chaplains assumed the role of prophets. The ideas of the soldiers of the New Model Army on religious matters were to the left of those of the Puritan squires and the Presbyterians; and some of them were downright religious radicals. These men became disenchanted with their parliamentary leadership when they learned that Parliament thought of replacing Anglicanism with Presbyterianism as the established church of England.

Modes of Radical Thought

The English Revolution produced political and social revisionism in religious vocabulary. The distinctive epithets of the day, "Leveller," "Digger," "Quaker," "Ranter," referred to various Christian religious types whose ideas may be broken down into three broad shades

of opinion. The conservatives were the "church types," who wished to establish one church (their own) as the national religion buttressed by the state and with authority in all spiritual matters. Lutherans, Anglicans, and Roman Catholics were "church-type." The more independent "sect-type" believed in complete separation of Church and State. He tended to idealize the primitive Christian church and was led by inspired preachers rather than ordained ones. Congregationalists and Anabaptists were "sect-type." The "spiritual-type," of which the "Diggers" and the primitive Quakers were the most notable examples, acted upon individual revelations from the Holy Spirit.

The program of the Presbyterian "church-types" was the most influential in the House of Commons. The Army, on the other hand, was dominated by the "sect-type" Independents or Congregationalists, of which Cromwell was one. Another "sect-type" group was the Levellers, whose most eloquent spokesman was John Lilburne. Lilburne translated Christian doctrine into political terms, advocating the reform of Parliament and the extension of the suffrage. The Levellers were organized as a "party," with a mass membership, weekly meetings, two weekly newspapers, and a color—sea green—to distinguish their adherents. A looser organization was the "spiritual-type" Society of Friends or "Quakers," formed by George Fox. Quakers sought God "experimentally"—as a personal experience. Fox referred contemptuously to Cambridge as the place where apprentices learned the "trade" of preaching. To him, education was neither necessary nor desirable for spiritual well-being or leadership. Any man, carpenter or shoemaker, could, if inspired, come to understand God's word. To the left of the Quakers were the spiritual communists, the "Diggers," whose leader was Gerrard Winstanley. Winstanley appeared in 1649 with a few followers on St. George's Hill in London and began to dig the commons to sow parsnips, carrots, and beans. Winstanley said that God had told him that only those who labor in the earth should enjoy its fruits—a frightening notion! Even wilder spirits among the radical religious personalities began to question conventional standards of morality.

Thus, as Lilburne and the Levellers attacked traditional English political institutions, Winstanley and the Diggers threatened the social order. Fox and the Quakers attacked Church authority and the educational system. Notwithstanding some of their exaggerated ideas which frightened the more conservative reformers in Parliament, "behind the mobs who hooted the King's half-pay captains in the Palace Yard and knocked down papists at the street corners, moved the humble men who were to inspire democracy for all time with its best peculiar hopes and ideals." Despite their contemporary failure the radical zealots made an enduring mark on English ideals of justice, right, and democracy. . . .

The Revolution Contained and the Interregnum

Cromwell presided ably over the unstable situation as Lord Protector until his death in 1658, warily experimenting with combinations of interests and individuals in an attempt to find a workable order for England. He seems to have considered his role as an interim one, "protector," not despot. He was sensitive to the vacuum created by regicide and understanding of the deep English undercurrent of loyalty to the symbol of monarchy. . . .

After his death . . . the title of Lord Protector passed, by previous arrangement, to his son, Richard, who was soon persuaded to resign his title. A confused situation developed in which one of the Major Generals (Monk) took the steps which led to a reassembling of all members of the Long Parliament still alive and the calling of a special Convention Parliament which decided to accept Charles II, son of the beheaded Charles, as King. The Interregnum was over. . . .

The Restoration and Glorious Revolution, 1660–1689

One of the great problems of the Restoration was the religion of the King. Charles was secretly a Roman Catholic who accepted bribes from the King of France. This was bad enough, but the fact that the next in line to the throne, James, Duke of York, the King's brother, was an avowed Roman Catholic was a more serious matter. The question of succession brought up the great parliamentary fight during Charles' reign when a bill was introduced (1679) that would have had the effect, if passed and accepted by the crown, of excluding James from the succession. The Whigs, led by the brilliant Earl of Shaftsbury, supported the bill; whereas the Tories opposed it. Charles was determined that it should not pass and roused himself sufficiently to employ his considerable political skill and influence to defeat it in Parliament. Those who could not reconcile themselves to the idea of a Roman Catholic King could comfort themselves in defeat by the observation that it was unlikely that the aging Duke of York would have any more children and that those he already had were Protestant. For the long haul, the Anglican religious settlement seemed safe.

Eventually (1685), Charles toyed his way to his death, in bed and still King of England. His brother and successor was not so fortunate. James II seems to have had all of the instincts of his father and grandfather. He seems to have wanted to reassert absolute monarchy by divine right. Yet he played into the hands of the opposition by appointing Roman Catholics to governmental posts and by asking for a larger army; and, then, he tried to confuse issues by pressing for toleration for Nonconformists as well as for Roman Catholics. He was as tactless as had been his forebears; and in just three years he squandered whatever good will had greeted his coronation. But his greatest crime was to beget, late in life, a healthy, male, Roman Catholic child. There was nothing for it except that James II had to go. Thus, under James, the crisis that Charles II had avoided precipitated itself, rather like a distorted and accelerated playback of the reign of the first James some eighty years before.

There were, however, certain basic differences. In the opening phases of the English Revolution, the revolutionary drive had come from men of the lesser aristocracy who were joined by some of the middle and lower orders of society. In the situation of 1688–1689 it was the great aristocratic grandees who directed the delicate operation of forcing James into flight rather than martyrdom. In the earlier stages of this nearly century-long revolutionary process, there had been basic disagreement on constitutional, economic, religious, and social questions. Now the real anxiety turned on whether James would make the boat at Dover! When a bumbling patriot caught and triumphantly returned James to London, the action verged on slapstick comedy. Thus, a nearly farcical conservative revolution finally established some of the important political ideas put forward in 1641 in the days of Pym: ministerial authority vested in Parliament with monarchy a revocable trust. Certainly the King was not turned into a figurehead by the Revolution of 1689, but a substantial step toward such a royal condition had been taken. The more radical ideas that had been expressed by the Levellers, Diggers, and others during the 1640's found no implementation in the Glorious Revolution and had to wait until the nineteenth century for further exploration. . . .

The Bill of Rights (1689)

In December of 1688, after the flight of James, William of Orange was authorized to hold elections for a new parliament. This Parliament in the next three years passed several pieces of legislation designed to resolve England's internal conflicts. The Bill of Rights, considered one of the great English Constitutional documents, was among the first. From E. P. Cheyney, *Readings in English History* (New York: Ginn and Company, 1922), pp. 545–547.

Whereas the said late King James II having abdicated the government, and the throne being thereby vacant, his Highness the prince of Orange (whom it hath pleased Almighty God to make the glorious instrument of delivering this kingdom from popery and arbitrary power) did (by the advice of the lords spiritual and temporal, and diverse principal persons of the Commons) caused letters to be written to the lords spiritual and temporal, being Protestants, and other letters to the several counties, cities, universities, boroughs, and Cinque Ports, for the choosing of such persons to represent them, as were of right to be sent to parliament, to meet and sit at Westminster upon the two and twentieth day of January, in this year 1689, in order to such an establishment as that their religion, laws, and liberties might not again be in danger of being subverted; upon which letters elections have been accordingly made.

And thereupon the said lords spiritual and temporal and Commons, pursuant to their respective letters and elections, being now assembled in a full and free representation of this nation, taking into their most serious consideration the best means for attaining the ends aforesaid, do in the first place (as their ancestors in like case have usually done), for the vindication and assertion of their ancient rights and liberties, declare:

1. That the pretended power of suspending laws, or the execution of laws, by regal authority, without consent of parliament is illegal.
2. That the pretended power of dispensing with the laws, or the execution of law by regal authority, as it hath been assumed and exercised of late, is illegal.
3. That the commission for erecting the late court of commissioners for ecclesiastical causes, and all other commissions and courts of like nature, are illegal and pernicious.
4. That levying money for or to the use of the crown by pretense of prerogative, without grant of parliament, for longer time or in other manner than the same is or shall be granted, is illegal.

5. That it is the right of the subjects to petition the king, and all commitments and prosecutions for such petitioning are illegal.
6. That the raising or keeping a standing army within the kingdom in time of peace, unless it be with consent of parliament, is against law.
7. That the subjects which are Protestants may have arms for their defense suitable to their conditions, and as allowed by law.
8. That election of members of parliament ought to be free.
9. That the freedom of speech, and debates or proceedings in parliament, ought not to be impeached or questioned in any court or place out of parliament.
10. That excessive bail ought not to be required, nor excessive fines imposed, nor cruel and unusual punishments inflicted.
11. That jurors ought to be duly impaneled and returned, and jurors which pass upon men in trials for high treason ought to be freeholders.
12. That all grants and promises of fines and forfeitures of particular persons before conviction are illegal and void.
13. And that for redress of all grievances, and for the amending, strengthening, and preserving of the laws, parliament ought to be held frequently.

And they do claim, demand, and insist upon all and singular the premises, as their undoubted rights and liberties; and that no declarations, judgments, doings, or proceedings, to the prejudice of the people in any of the said premises, ought in any wise to be drawn hereafter into consequence or example.

To which demand of their rights they are particularly encouraged by the declaration of his Highness the prince of Orange, as being the only means for obtaining a full redress and remedy therein.

Having therefore an entire confidence that his said Highness the prince of Orange will perfect the deliverance so far advanced by him, and will still preserve them from the violation of their rights, which they have here asserted, and from all other attempt upon their religion, rights, and liberties:

The said lords spiritual and temporal, and commons, assembled at Westminster, do resolve that William and Mary, prince and princess of Orange, be and be declared, king and queen of England, France, and Ireland, the dominions thereunto belonging, to hold the crown and royal dignity of the said kingdoms and dominions to them the said prince and princess during their lives, and the life of the survivor of them; and that the sole and full exercise of the regal power be only in, and executed by, the said prince of Orange, in the names of the said prince and princess, during their joint lives; and after their deceases, the said crown and royal dignity of the said kingdoms and dominions to be to the heirs of the body of the said princess; and for default of such issue to the princess Anne of Denmark, and the heirs of her body; and for default of such issue to the heirs of the body of the said prince of Orange. And the lords spiritual and temporal, and commons, do pray the said prince and princess to accept the same accordingly. . . .

Upon which their Majesties did accept the crown and royal dignity of the kingdoms of England, France, and Ireland, and the dominions thereunto belonging, according to the resolution and desire of the said lords and commons contained in the said declaration.

Cromwell's Army Debates Democracy (1647)

The Army which carried Charles to the scaffold and Cromwell to power was divided over the political and constitutional settlement it sought. Its differences reflected the social divisions within the Army itself, between those who were laborers, tradesmen, or artisans, and those who came from the more substantial propertied classes. The debates recorded in these minutes occurred in 1647 over a constitutional proposal, "Agreement of the People," drawn up by radical Independents known as Levellers. The position of the Levellers (here represented by Rainborough and Sexby) was rejected by Cromwell and his son-in-law Ireton; it remained a radical position in Western political practice well into the twentieth century. From A. S. P. Woodhouse, *Clarke Papers* in *Puritanism and Liberty* (Chicago: University of Chicago Press, 1951). Copyright © 1951 by the University of Chicago. This is published in Canada by J. M. Dent and Sons Ltd.

I. AN AGREEMENT OF THE PEOPLE

. . . In order whereunto we declare:

I   That the people of England, being at this day very unequally distributed by counties, cities, and boroughs, for the election of their deputies in Parliament, ought to be more indifferently proportioned, according to the number of inhabitants; the circumstances whereof, for number, place, and manner, are to be set down before the end of this present Parliament.

II That to prevent the many inconveniences apparently arising from the long continuance of the same persons in authority, this present Parliament be dissolved upon the last day of September, which shall be in the year of our Lord 1648.

III That the people do of course choose themselves a Parliament once in two years, *viz.,* upon the first Thursday in every second March, after the manner as shall be prescribed before the end of this Parliament, to begin to sit upon the first Thursday in April following, at Westminster (or such other place as shall be appointed from time to time by the preceding Representatives), and to continue till the last day of September then next ensuing, and no longer.

IV That the power of this, and all future Representatives of this nation is inferior only to theirs who choose them, and doth extend, without the consent or concurrence of any other person or persons, to the enacting, altering, and repealing of laws; to the erecting and abolishing of offices and courts; to the appointing, removing, and calling to account magistrates and officers of all degrees; to the making war and peace; to the treating with foreign states; and generally to whatsoever is not expressly or impliedly reserved by the represented to themselves.

Which are as followeth:

1. That matters of religion, and the ways of God's worship, are not at all entrusted

by us to any human power, because therein we cannot remit or exceed a title of what our consciences dictate to be the mind of God, without wilful sin; nevertheless the public way of instructing the nation (so it be not compulsive) is referred to their discretion.

2. That the matter of impressing and constraining any of us to serve in the wars is against our freedom, and therefore we do not allow it in our representatives; the rather because money (the sinews of war) being always at their disposal, they can never want numbers of men apt enough to engage in any just cause.

3. That after the dissolution of this present Parliament, no person be at any time questioned for anything said or done in reference to the late public differences, otherwise than in execution of the judgments of the present representatives, or House of Commons.

4. That in all laws made, or to be made, every person may be bound alike, and that no tenure, estate, charter, degree, birth, or place, do confer any exemption from the ordinary course of legal proceedings, whereunto others are subjected.

5. That as the laws ought to be equal, so they must be good, and not evidently destructive to the safety and well-being of the people.

These things we declare to be our native rights, and therefore are agreed and resolved to maintain them with our utmost possibilities against all opposition whatsoever, being compelled thereunto not only by the examples of our ancestors, whose blood was often spent in vain for the recovery of their freedoms, suffering themselves, through fraudu-

Parliament met in St. Stephen's Chapel in in Westminster Palace. This seventeenth-century scene shows the crowded hall with the Speaker of the House enthroned at its head, before him are parliamentary clerks. The sergeant at arms, who preserved order in the chamber, stands in the foreground.

lent accommodations, to be still deluded of the fruit of their victories, but also by our own woeful experience, who, having long expected, and dearly earned, the establishment of these certain rules of government, are yet made to depend for the settlement of our peace and freedom upon him that intended our bondage and brought a cruel war upon us.

II. THE DEBATES

Debate of October 29, 1647

[Major Rainborough] I desire we may come to that end we all strive after. I humbly desire you will fall upon that which is the engagement of all, which is the rights and freedoms of the people, and let us see how far we have made sure to them a right and freedom. . . .

(The paper called the Agreement read. Afterwards the first article read by itself.)

[Ireton] . . . It is said, they are to be distributed according to the number of inhabitants: "The people of England," etc. And this doth make me think that the meaning is, that every man that is an inhabitant is to be equally considered, and to have an equal voice in the election of those representatives, the persons that are for the general Representative; and if that be the meaning, then I have something to say against it. . . .

[Rainborough] . . . Really I think that the poorest he that is in England hath a life to live, as the greatest he; and therefore truly, sir, I think it's clear, that every man that is to live under a government ought first by his own consent to put himself under that government; and I do think that the poorest man in England is not at all bound in a strict sense to that government that he hath not had a voice to put himself under. . . .

[Ireton] . . . For my part, I think it is no right at all. I think that no person hath a right to an interest or share in the disposing of the affairs of the kingdom, and in determining or choosing those that shall determine what laws we shall be ruled by here—no person hath a right to this, that hath not a permanent fixed interest [property] in this kingdom, and those persons together are properly the represented of this kingdom, and consequently are also to make up the representers of this kingdom, who taken together do comprehend whatsoever is of real or permanent interest in the kingdom. And I am sure otherwise I cannot tell what any man can say why a foreigner coming in amongst us—or as many as will coming in amongst us, or by force or otherwise settling themselves here, or at least by our permission having a being here—why they should not as well lay claim to it as any other. We talk of birthright. Truly birthright there is thus much claim. Men may justly have by birthright, by their very being born in England, that we should not seclude them out of England, that we should not refuse to give them air and place and ground, and the freedom of the highways and other things, to live amongst us—not any man that is born here, though by his birth there come nothing at all (that is part of the permanent interest of this kingdom) to him. That I think is due to a man by birth. But that by a man's being born here he shall have a share in that power that shall dispose of the lands here, and of all things here, I do not think it a sufficient ground. I am sure if we look upon that which is the utmost (within any man's view) of what was originally the constitution of this kingdom, upon that which is most radical and fundamental, and which if you take away,

there is no man hath any land, any goods, or any civil interest, that is this: that those that choose the representers for the making of laws by which this state and kingdom are to be governed, are the persons who, taken together, do comprehend the local interest of this kingdom; that is, the persons in whom all land lies, and those in corporations in whom all trading lies. This is the most fundamental constitution of this kingdom. . . . Now I wish we may all consider of what right you will challenge that all the people should have right to elections. Is it by the right of nature? If you will hold forth that as your ground, then I think you must deny all property too, and this is my reason. For thus: by that same right of nature (whatever it be) that you pretend, by which you can say, one man hath an equal right with another to the choosing of him that shall govern him—by the same right of nature, he hath the same equal right in any goods he sees—meat, drink, clothes—to take and use them for his sustenance. He hath a freedom to the land, to take the ground, to . . . till it; he hath the same freedom to anything that any one doth account himself to have any propriety in. Why now I say then, if you, against the most fundamental part of the civil constitution (which I have now declared), will plead the Law of Nature, that a man should . . . have a power of choosing those men that shall determine what shall be law in this state, though he himself have no permanent interest in the state, but whatever interest he hath he may carry about with him—if this be allowed, because by the right of nature we are free, we are equal, one man must have as much voice as another, then show me what step or difference there is, why I may not by the same right take your property. . . .

[Rainborough] . . . Sir, to say because a man pleads that every man hath a voice by right of nature, that therefore it destroys by the same argument all property—this is to forget the Law of God. That there's a property, the Law of God says it; else why hath God made that law, *Thou shalt not steal?* I am a poor man, therefore I must be oppressed: if I have no interest in the kingdom, I must suffer by all their laws be they right or wrong. Nay thus: a gentleman lives in a country and hath three or four lordships, as some men have (God knows how they got them); and when a Parliament is called he must be a Parliament-man; and it may be he sees some poor men, they live near this man, he can crush them—I have known an invasion to make sure he hath turned the poor men out of doors; and I would fain know whether the potency of rich men do not this, and so keep them under the greatest tyranny that was ever thought of in the world. And therefore I think that to that it is fully answered: God hath set down that thing as to propriety with this law of his, *Thou shalt not steal.* And for my part I am against any such thought, and, as for yourselves, I wish you would not make the world believe that we are for anarchy.

[Cromwell] I know nothing but this, that they that are the most yielding have the greatest wisdom; but really, sir, this is not right as it should be. No man says that you have a mind to anarchy, but that the consequence of this rule tends to anarchy, must end in anarchy; for where is there any bound or limit set if you take away this limit, that men that have no interest but the interest of breathing shall have no voice in elections? Therefore I am confident on't, we should not be so hot one with another. . . .

[Sexby] I see that though liberty were our end, there is a degeneration from it. We have engaged in this kingdom and ventured our lives, and it was all for this: to recover our birthrights and privileges as Englishmen; and by the arguments urged there is none. There are many thousands of us soldiers that have ventured our lives; we have had little propriety in the kingdom as to our estates, yet we have had a birthright. But it seems now, except a man hath a fixed estate in this kingdom, he hath no right in this kingdom. I wonder we were so much deceived. If we had not a right to the kingdom, we were mere mercenary soldiers. There are many in my condition; . . . it may be little estate they have at present, and yet they have as much a birthright as those two [Cromwell and Ireton] who are their lawgivers, as any in this place. I shall tell you in a word my resolution. I am resolved to give my birthright to none. Whatsoever may come in the way, and whatsoever may be thought, I will give it to none. If this thing be denied the poor, that with so much pressing after they have sought, it will be the greatest scandal. There was one thing spoken to this effect: that if the poor and those in low condition were given their birthright it would be the destruction of this kingdom. I think this was but a distrust of Providence. I do think the poor and meaner of this kingdom—I speak as in relation to the condition of soldiers, in which we are—have been the means of the preservation of this kingdom. I say, in their stations, and really I think to their utmost possibility; and their lives have not been held dear for purchasing the good of the kingdom. And now they demand the birthright for which they fought. Those that act to this end are as free from anarchy or confusion as those that oppose it, and they have the Law of God and the law of their conscience with them.

J. H. Plumb: Sources of English Instability

J. H. Plumb, Professor of Modern English History at Christ's College, Cambridge, has made a significant contribution to our understanding of the sources of English political stability in the early eighteenth century. In the selection below he examines the conditions of English life before the Glorious Revolution. From J. H. Plumb, *The Growth of Political Stability in England, 1675–1725.* Copyright © 1967 by the Houghton Mifflin Company. This book is published in Canada by Macmillan & Company Ltd., London.

In every European country, even indeed where absolutism was most consistently developed, as in France, there were still many factors as well as many institutions making for incoherence and instability. In these England was richly endowed. The two most important institutions were Parliament and local government; far less important but not inconsiderable were two problems—Ireland and Scotland—and an enigma—the City of London. To these must be added the strong individualism created by chartered rights, liberties, and freeholds, all centuries old, and sanctified by law as well as time; nor must the turbulence natural to an agrarian society in which grinding poverty was the lot of most men be forgotten. Finally, there was a tradition of conspiracy, riot, plot, and revolt among the ruling class that stretched back to the Normans. By 1688, violence in politics was an Englishman's birthright.

The key to political instability was Parliament, a medieval institution launched by the Tudors into a world for which it was unfitted. The need to identify the authority of the ruling class with the acts of the Reformation arose out of the Tudors' own lack of a trained professional class of royal officials, capable of controlling and ordering provincial England. So long as the Crown, the gentry, and the merchants were involved in social revolution, religious crisis, and external danger, the relationship with Parliament, although often strained, worked. No permanent system of control of the Commons was devised; clientage and the creation of boroughs strengthened the Crown's influence but did not establish it, nor did it give any permanent security to the monarchy. Already in Elizabeth I's reign the Commons were managed with difficulty, and their capacity for intransigence, obstinacy, and violent criticism was frequently and amply demonstrated. After 1601, they were fundamentally out of hand—difficult to screw money from and a hotbed of criticism; no one could manage them for long, neither James I, Charles I, Cromwell, nor Charles II. Before the legislature, the executive was often impotent. Of course, attempts were made to control it: through managed elections—Charles I and Oliver Cromwell both tried that, but to no avail—or through exploitation of loyalty, well warmed with pension and place, and kept steady by a patriotic foreign policy; that too had been tried. . . .

Because of its inability to control Parliament, the monarchy was starved of its necessary supplies in the pursuit of profit and power throughout the seventeenth century. . . . The deep sense of independence, with its attendant suspicion of the Court, that ran through the Commons, was based on the position of the gentry and provincial merchants in local government. The extent of social, political, and judicial power in their hands was formidable; and behind this power lay the sanction of arms, for in the last resort they controlled the militia. As Sir Henry Capel told his fellow squires in the Commons in 1673, 'Our security is the militia: that will defend us and never conquer us. . . .'

The power of the seventeenth-century gentry was sanctioned by violence—riding out against their enemies, hamstringing their neighbour's dogs, beating their farmer's sons, or shooting down their riotous labourers. They played ducks and drakes with the law when it suited them, breaking with impunity what they were supposed to maintain. At Wigtown in 1708 the magistrates were involved with a large gang of smugglers who attacked and wounded the customs officers and seized a large cargo of brandy. Robert Walpole, a J. P. of Norfolk, had smugglers call regularly at his back door at Houghton and even used an Admiralty barge to run his wine up the Thames. He held government office at the time. Justices frequently closed alehouses for no other reason than that it drove customers to the one they owned themselves. Their quarrels, usually about rights of property, were frequent and bloody. A sea of turbulence washed about the gentry's lives, and they deeply resented any threat to the freedoms that they felt belonged to them as gentlemen. Since the days of the Tudors no government, royal or republican, had got to terms with them. Like Charles I or Charles II,

Cromwell had failed absolutely to take the gentry into his control, and so made Restoration inevitable. Charles II's failure nearly toppled his throne. James II's was more complete; they chased him out of his kingdom. To bring the independent country gentry into some ordered relationship with government, or to diminish their role in it, became an absolute necessity if political stability was ever to be achieved. The Bill of Rights, however, underscored their liberties and privileges no less heavily than Magna Carta had done for John's barons. . . . And in many ways the Bill of Rights makes more sense if seen in a medieval context of charters than as the cornerstone of the modern constitution. Parliament and the structure of local government were the key problems for centralizing monarchy, but there were others, less powerful but equally intractable, or so it seemed.

Firstly, there was Ireland and Scotland. Only Cromwell, backed by a well-trained professional army, had crushed them into subservience. And once he and his army had gone, the Irish erupted again, creating problems of law and order that necessitated a highly professional standing army that Parliament would not tolerate and Charles II could not afford. The Revolution of 1688 made things worse, not better, and opened a fresh era of civil war and rebellion. It seemed unlikely that Scotland or Ireland could be brought to heel without strong monarchy backed by force. And if they were not brought to heel, what government in England could ever feel secure? Cromwell's ruthless policy might solve a crisis, but it could never breed the security requisite for stability. . . .

And there was the enigma nearer at hand: the City of London had long been divided in itself; many of the great merchants who dominated the aldermanic bench were drawn to authoritative and patriarchal concepts of society, and a monarchy *à la française* would have held no terrors for them—indeed, many would have welcomed both Louis XIV and Colbert. The great trading companies—East India, Levant, African—depended upon royal charter for their monopolies, and these they wished to preserve against the growing threats of interlopers. . . . And there were Presbyterians as well as High Anglicans who had no wish to venture on radical courses. Throughout the Civil War and the Commonwealth the City magnates had shown a great suspicion of radicalism among the City's lower middle class. Some of their colleagues, however, were less happy about the *status quo* and they looked with longing at the power and security of their Dutch cousins in Amsterdam. Also, the lesser merchants, who played a conspicuous, if not a dominant, role in the Common Council, were as suspicious of the monarchy as they were of some of their own aldermen. They had helped to purge the City government time and time again in order to support first Parliament, then the Army, and finally Cromwell. Throughout the Commonwealth their power had grown and the Restoration did not deprive them of their political voice; indeed, the City was more democratic in 1660 than it had been in 1640 or was to be in 1730. . . . Political control, however, was not the only problem with regard to London that remained unsolved. The financial relations between the monarchy and the City, or rather between the central government and the City, for it was equally true of Cromwell, had never found a satisfactory basis. Without the financial resources of the City no government could hope to survive, but the relationship was ambivalent, subject to suspicion and extortion, and totally unsatisfactory.

As well as finance, there remained also the question of policy: men of business, great or small, were aware that government policy deeply influenced their prosperity; they wanted a sound monetary policy, although what it should be baffled them, and naturally they wished to pursue an aggressive economic policy in relation to the world's trade, although here again the situation was not simple, some merchants still fearing the Dutch more than the French. But in pursuing profit and power Cromwell had proved more reliable than the Stuarts, for Charles II's addiction to the French troubled many merchants as much in their pockets as in their consciences. In order to achieve political stability, London needed to be tamed, neutralized, or wooed. Although it played less part in the Revolution of 1688 than in any other upheaval of the seventeenth century, the implacable hostility towards the Stuarts of the majority of those Londoners who exercised political and social power in the City had been a major factor in their repeated defeats, and indeed rendered easy the accession of William and Mary. But even so, the City continued to present grave difficulties to any government, because like so many institutions in England's political life it was basically inimical to direct control, whether Whig or Tory or a mixture of both. Xenophobic, greedy, unsophisticated, and obstinate, the politically-minded citizens of London could be as suspicious of authority as the squires of Wales. . . .

In addition, some would add, as a final factor in the creation of political instability—tradition. The fact that Englishmen had for centuries rebelled against kings and ministers, conspired and plotted against them, risen often in riot and violence, had so conditioned them to a life of political instability that change might prove almost impossible. Traditions are quickly bred and quickly destroyed and they snap suddenly in a world of rapid social change. Historians too often think of rapid social change as creating conditions of turbulence; but societies can move as quickly into stability as into revolution, and between 1688 and 1725 Britain did just that. And traditions changed just as rapidly: by 1730 Englishmen were congratulating themselves on their tolerance, on their capacity for political compromise, on the preservation of their liberties. In 1688, however, it seemed as if the forces of political instability had won, for the Revolution had been undertaken by those forces in society that were thoroughly opposed to strong executive government. For the Revolution of 1688 was a monument raised by the gentry to its own intractable sense of independence.

GREAT SEAL OF ENGLAND, 1651.

Cut by Thom. Simon.

STUDY QUESTIONS

1. On the basis of the documents in Reading 102, which describe highlights in the course of English history in the first half of the seventeenth century, how does this history seem similar to or different from political development in France at the same time?

2. Would you consider the execution of Charles I a turning-point in Western political history? Why?

3. What seem to have been the major issues in seventeenth-century English history?

4. Do you think that James I and Charles I provoked a revolution? What evidence supports this view? Make a defense of the royal goals. Why did Parliament win in the end?

5. What was Parliament? What power did it have? Who belonged to it? What were its goals in the struggle with James I and Charles I? With James II?

6. How did religious issues affect the political struggle?

7. What conflicts did the Bill of Rights try to resolve? To what degree did it resemble Magna Carta?

8. Why was there so much argument over who would have the right to vote? Contrast the positions of Rainborough and Ireton. How might the dead Charles I have commented on this debate? What is the significance of the introduction of "natural law" into the argument?

9. Why was the balance of power radically different in England than in France; that is, why did the aristocracy dominate the monarchs in England while the kings dominated the nobles in France?

10. Do you think, after reading the Plumb article, that England could have avoided revolution?

THE HOUSE OF COMMONS, 1642.

Natural Law and Political Theory

From *A History of the Modern World*, by Robert R. Palmer and Joel Colton. Copyright 1950, © 1956, 1965 by Alfred A. Knopf, Inc. Reprinted by permission of the publisher.

TOPIC 19

THE FOUNDATIONS OF MODERN POLITICAL THEORY

Along with the development of modern states in the seventeenth and eighteenth centuries came new formulations in political theory to explain why government had taken the shape that it had and to suggest possible alternatives. Freedom versus authority was the great issue with which outstanding theorists like Bossuet, Hobbes, Locke, Montesquieu, and Rousseau wrestled in writings that captured the imagination of their time and have influenced political thought ever since. These writings reflect the political events and intellectual currents of the time in which they were written; revolutions in England, absolutism in France, the clash between science and religion, and the pervasive faith in the potential of natural law provide their base. The readings explore conflicting answers to such significant questions as what man was like in a state of nature, how government came about, what its purpose was, and what were the rights and duties of governors and governed.

Political theory can never be strictly scientific. Science deals with what does exist or has existed. It does not tell what ought to exist. To tell what society and government ought to be like, in view of man's nature and his capacity to be miserable or contented, is a main purpose of political theory. Political theory is in a sense more practical than science. It is the scientists and scholars who are most content to observe facts as they are. Practical men, and scientists and scholars so far as they have practical interests, must always ask themselves what ought to be done, what policies ought to be adopted, what measures taken, what state of affairs maintained or brought about. Conservatives and radicals, traditionalists and innovators, are alike in this respect. It is impossible in human affairs to escape the word "ought."

But political theory was affected by the scientific view. The Renaissance Italian, Niccolò Machiavelli (1469–1527), had opened the way in this direction. Machiavelli too had his "ought"; he preferred a republican form of government in which citizens felt a patriotic attachment to their state. But in his book, *The Prince,* he disregarded the question of the best form of government, a favorite question of Christian and scholastic philosophers of the Middle Ages. He separated the study of politics from theology and moral philosophy.

He undertook to describe how governments and rulers actually behaved. He observed that successful rulers behaved as if holding or increasing power were their only object, that they regarded all else as means to this end. Princes, said Machiavelli, kept their promises or broke them, they told the truth or distorted or colored it, they sought popularity or ignored it, they advanced public welfare or disrupted it, they conciliated their neighbors or destroyed them, depending merely on which course of action seemed the best means of advancing their political interests. All this was bad, said Machiavelli; but that was not the question, for the question was to find out what rulers really did. Machiavelli, in *The Prince,* chose to be non-moral in order to be scientific. To most readers he seemed to be simply immoral. Nor was it possible to draw the line between *The Prince* as a scientific description of fact and *The Prince* as a book of maxims of conduct. In telling how successful rulers obtained their successes, Machiavelli also suggested how rulers *ought* to proceed. And though governments did in fact continue to behave for the most part as Machiavelli said, most people refused to admit that they ought to.

Political theory in the seventeenth century did not embrace the cynicism attributed to Machiavelli. Nor did it fall into the skepticism of those who said that the customs of one's country should be passively accepted, or that one form of government was about as good as another. It directly faced the question, What is right? The seventeenth century was the classic age of the philosophy of natural right or of natural law.

The idea of natural law has underlain a good deal of modern democratic development, and its decline in the last century has been closely connected with many of the troubles of recent times. It is not easy to say in what the philosophy of natural law essentially consisted. It held that there is, somehow, in the structure of the world, a law that distinguishes right from wrong. It held that right is "natural," not a mere invention of men. This right is not determined, for any country, by its heritage, tradition, or customs, nor yet by its actual laws (called "positive" laws) of the kind that are enforced in the law courts. All these may be unfair or unjust. We detect unfairness or injustice in them by comparing them with natural law as we understand it; thus we have a basis for saying that cannibalism is bad, or that a law requiring forced labor from orphan children is unjust. Nor is natural law, or the real rightness of a thing, determined by the authority of any person or people. No king can make right that which is wrong. No people, by its will as a people, can make just that which is unjust. Right and law, in the ultimate sense, exist outside and above all peoples. They are universal, the same for all. No one can make them up to suit himself. A good king, or a just people, are a king or people whose actions correspond to the objective standard. But how, if we cannot trust our own positive laws or customs, or our leaders or even our collective selves, can we know what is naturally right? How do we discover natural law? The answer, in the natural law philosophy, is that we discover it by reason. Man is considered to be a rational animal. And all men are assumed to have, at least potentially and

when better enlightened, the same powers of reason and understanding—Germans or English, Siamese or Europeans. This view favored a cosmopolitan outlook, and made international agreement and general world progress seem realizable goals. As time went on, the premises of this philosophy came to be questioned. By the twentieth century it was widely thought that man was not an especially rational being, but was motivated by drives or urges or instincts, and that human differences were so fundamental that men of different nationalities or classes could never expect to see things in the same way. When this happened the older philosophy of natural law lost its hold on many minds. In the seventeenth and eighteenth centuries it was generally accepted. . . .

Hobbes Sees Government as a Leviathan (1651)

Thomas Hobbes (1588–1679) was acquainted with many famous men of his time, among them Galileo, Descartes, and Bacon. He supported the royalist cause during the English Civil War and had to flee the country. While in exile he wrote a book on political theory in which the sense of insecurity and the author's generally pessimistic view of mankind reflect the conflict that was taking place in the British Isles. Hobbes entitled his book *Leviathan,* thus recalling the powerful monster described in the Old Testament (Job 41) as a necessary evil. From *The Works of Thomas Hobbes,* ed. W. Molesworth (London, 1839), Vol. III.

I

Of the Natural Condition of Mankind as concerning Their Happiness and Misery

Nature hath made men so equal, in the faculties of the body, and mind; as that though there be found one man sometimes manifestly stronger in body, or of quicker mind than another; yet when all is reckoned together, the difference between man, and man, is not so considerable, as that one man can thereupon claim to himself any benefit, to which another may not pretend, as well as he. For as to the strength of body, the weakest has strength enough to kill the strongest, either by secret machination, or by confederacy with others, that are in the same danger with himself. . . .

In the nature of man, we find three principal causes of quarrel. First, competition; secondly, diffidence; thirdly, glory.

The first, maketh men invade for gain; the second, for safety; and the third, for reputation. The first use violence, to make themselves masters of other men's persons, wives, children, and cattle; the second, to defend them; the third, for trifles, as a word, a smile, a different opinion, and any other sign of undervalue, either direct in their persons, or by reflection in their kindred, their friends, their nation, their profession, or their name.

Hereby it is manifest, that during the time men live without a common power to keep them all in awe, they are in that condition which is called war; and such a war, as is of every man, against every man. . . .

Whatsoever therefore is consequent to a time of war, where every man is enemy to every man; the same is consequent to the time, wherein men live without other security, than what their own strength, and their own invention shall furnish them withal. In such condition, there is no place for industry; because the fruit thereof is uncertain: and consequently no culture of the earth; no navigation, nor use of the commodities that may be imported by sea; no . . . building; no instruments of moving, and removing, such things as require much force; no knowledge of the face of the earth; no account of time; no arts; no letters; no society; and . . . worst of all, continual fear, and danger of violent death; and the life of man, solitary, poor, nasty, brutish, and short. . . .

II

To this war of every man, against every man, this also is consequent; that nothing can be unjust. The notions of right and wrong, justice and injustice have there no place. Where there is no common power, there is no law: where no law, no injustice. Force, and fraud, are in war the two cardinal virtues. Justice, and injustice are none of the faculties neither of the body, or mind. If they were, they might be in a man that were alone in the world, as well as his senses, and passions. They are qualities, that relate to men in society, not in solitude. It is consequent also to the same condition, that there be no propriety, no dominion, no *mine* and *thine* distinct; but only that to be every man's, that he can get; and for so long, as he can keep it. And thus much for the ill condition, which man by mere nature is actually placed in; though with a possibility to come out of it, consisting partly in the passions, partly in his reason. . . .

Of the Causes, Generation, and Definition of a Commonwealth

The final cause, end, or design of men, who naturally love liberty, and a dominion over others, in the introduction of that restraint upon themselves, in which we see them live in commonwealths, is the foresight of their own preservation, and of a more contented life thereby; that is to say, of getting themselves out from that miserable condition of war, which is necessarily consequent, as hath been shown in Chapter XIII, to the natural passions of men, when there is no visible power to keep them in awe, and tie them by fear of punishment, to the performance of their covenants, and observation of those laws of nature. . . .

For the laws of nature, as *justice, equity, modesty, mercy,* and, in sum, *doing to others, as we would be done to,* of themselves, without the terror of some power, to cause them to be observed, are contrary to our natural passions, that carry us to partiality, pride, revenge, and the like. And covenants, without the sword, are but words, and of no strength to secure a man at all. Therefore notwithstanding the laws of nature, which every one hath then kept, when he has the will to keep them, when he can do it safely, if there be no power erected, or not great enough for our security; every man will, and may lawfully rely on his own strength and art, for caution against all other men. . . .

III

The only way to erect such a common power, as may be able to defend [men] from the invasion of foreigners, and the injuries of one another, and thereby to secure them in such sort, as that by their own industry, and by the fruits of the earth, they may nourish themselves and live contentedly; is, to confer all their power and strength upon one man, or upon one assembly of men, that may reduce all their wills, by plurality of voices, unto one will: which is as much as to say, to appoint one man, or assembly of men, to bear their person; and every one to own, and acknowledge himself to be author of whatsoever he that so beareth their person, shall act, or cause to be acted, in those things which concern the common peace and safety; and therein to submit their wills, every one to his will, and their judgments, to his judgment. This is more than consent, or concord; it is a real unity of them all, in one and the same person, made by covenant of every man with every man, in such manner, as if every man should say to every man, *I authorise and give up my right of governing myself, to this man, or to this assembly of men, on this condition, that thou give up thy right to him, and authorise all his actions in like manner.* This done, the multitude so united in one person, is called a COMMONWEALTH. . . . And he that carrieth this person, is called SOVEREIGN, and said to have *sovereign power;* and every one besides, his SUBJECT.

Liberty of Subjects

The obligation of subjects to the sovereign, is understood to last as long, and no longer, than the power lasts, by which he is able to protect them. For the right men have by nature to protect themselves, when none else can protect them, can by no covenant be relinquished. . . . And though sovereignty, in the intention of them that make it, be immortal; yet it is in its own nature, not only subject to violent death, by foreign war; but also through the ignorance and passions of men, it has in it, from the very institution, many seeds of a natural mortality, by [internal] discord.

Locke Champions Representative Government

Like Thomas Hobbes, John Locke (1632–1704), the author of the *Essay Concerning Human Understanding*, wrote his *Treatises on Civil Government* while in political exile from England. Unlike Hobbes, however, he supported the forces that opposed the Stuart kings. A member of the Whig faction, Locke was able to return triumphantly to England after the victories of Parliament and William of Orange in the Glorious Revolution. The struggle with the Stuarts greatly influenced his political thinking, a fact that should be kept in mind in reading *On Civil Government*. From *The Works of John Locke* (London, 1824), Vol. IV.

CHAPTER II: OF THE STATE OF NATURE

To understand political power right, and derive it from its original, we must consider what state all men are naturally in, and that is, a state of perfect freedom to order their actions and dispose of their possessions and persons, as they think fit, within the bounds of the law of nature; without asking leave, or depending upon the will of any other man.

A state also of equality, wherein all the power and jurisdiction is reciprocal, no one having more than another; there being nothing more evident, than that creatures of the same species and rank, promiscuously born to all the same advantages of nature, and the use of the same faculties, should also be equal one amongst another without subordination or subjection; unless the lord and master of them all should, by any manifest declaration of his will, set one above another, and confer on him, by an evident and clear appointment, an undoubted right to dominion and sovereignty. . . .

But though this be a state of liberty, yet it is not a state of license: though man in that state has an uncontrollable liberty to dispose of his person or possessions, yet he has not liberty to destroy himself, or so much as any creature in his possession, but where some nobler use than its bare preservation calls for it. The state of nature has a law of nature to govern it, which obliges every one: and reason, which is that law, teaches all mankind, who will but consult it, that being all equal and independent, no one ought to harm another in his life, health, liberty, or possessions: for men being all the workmanship of one omnipotent and infinitely wise Maker; all the servants of one sovereign master, sent into the world by his order, and about his business; they are his property, whose workmanship they are, made to last during his, not another's pleasure. . . .

CHAPTER IV: OF SLAVERY

The natural liberty of man is to be free from any superior power on earth, and not to be under the will or legislative authority of man, but to have only the law of nature for his rule. The liberty of man, in society, is to be under no other legislative power, but that established, by consent, in the commonwealth; nor under the dominion of any will, or restraint of any law, but what that legislative shall enact, according to the trust put in it. Freedom then is not what Sir Robert Filmer tells us, "a liberty for every one to do what he lists, to live as he pleases, and not to be tied by any laws:" but freedom of men under government is, to have a standing rule to live by, common to every one of that society, and made by the legislative power erected in it; a liberty to follow my own will in all things, where the rule prescribes not; and not to be subject to the inconstant, uncertain, unknown, arbitrary will of another man: as freedom of nature is, to be under no other restraint but the law of nature. . . .

CHAPTER VI: OF PROPERTY

God, who hath given the world to men in common, hath also given them reason to make use of it to the best advantage of life, and convenience. The earth, and all that is therein, is given to men for the support and comfort of their being. And though all the fruits it naturally produces, and beasts it feeds, belong to mankind in common, as they are produced by the spontaneous hand of nature; and nobody has originally a private dominion, exclusive of the rest of mankind, in any of them, as they are thus in their natural state; yet being given for the use of men, there must of necessity be a means to appropriate them some way or other, before they can be of any use, or at all beneficial to any particular man. . . .

Though the earth, and all inferior creatures, be common to all men, yet every man has a property in his own person: this nobody has any right to but himself. The labour of his body, and the work of his hands, we may say, are properly his. Whatsoever then he removes out of the state that nature hath provided, and left it in, he hath mixed his labour with, and joined to it something that is his own, and thereby makes it his property. . . .

He that is nourished by the acorns he picked up under an oak, or the apples he gathered from the trees in the wood, has certainly appropriated them to himself. Nobody can deny but the nourishment is his.

I ask then, when did they begin to be his? when he digested? or when he brought them home? or when he picked them up? and it is plain, if the first gathering made them not his, nothing else could. That labour put a distinction between them and the common: that added something to them more than nature, the common mother of all, had done; and so they became his private right. . . .

But the chief matter of property being now not the fruits of the earth, and the beasts that subsist on it, but the earth itself; as that which takes in, and carries with it all the rest; I think it is plain, that property in that too is acquired as the former. As much land as a man tills, plants, improves, cultivates, and can use the product of, so much is his property. He by his labour does, as it were, enclose it from the common. Nor will it invalidate his right, to say every body else has an equal title to it, and therefore he cannot appropriate, he cannot enclose, without the consent of all his fellow commoners, all mankind. God, when he gave the world in common to all mankind, commanded man also to labour, and the penury of his condition required it of him. God and his reason commanded him to subdue the earth, i.e., improve it for the benefit of life, and therein lay out something upon it that was his own, his labour. He that, in obedience to this command of God, subdued, tilled, and sowed any part of it, thereby annexed to it something that was his property, which another had no title to, nor could without injury take from him. . . .

CHAPTER IX: OF THE ENDS OF POLITICAL SOCIETY AND GOVERNMENT

If man in the state of nature be so free, as has been said; if he be absolute lord of his own person and possessions, equal to the greatest, and subject to nobody, why will he part with his freedom? Why will he give up his empire, and subject himself to the dominion and control of any other power? To which it is obvious to answer, that though in the state of nature he hath such a right, yet the enjoyment of it is very uncertain, and constantly exposed to the invasion of others; for all being kings as much as he, every man his equal, and the greater part no strict observers of equity and justice, the enjoyment of the property he has in this state is very unsafe, very insecure. This makes him willing to quit a condition, which, however free, is full of fears and continual dangers: and it is not without reason, that he seeks out, and is willing to join in society with others, who are already united, or have a mind to unite, for the mutual preservation of their lives, liberties, and estates, which I call by the general name, property.

The great and chief end, therefore, of men's uniting into commonwealths, and putting themselves under government, is the preservation of their property. . . .

CHAPTER XIX: OF THE DISSOLUTION OF GOVERNMENT

The reason why men enter into society, is the preservation of their property; and the end why they choose and authorize a legislative, is, that there may be laws made, and rules, set, as guards and fences to the properties of all the members of the society: to limit the power, and moderate the dominion, of every part and member of the society: for since it can never be supposed to be the will of the society, that the legislative should have a power to destroy that which every one designs to secure by entering into society, and for which the people submitted themselves to legislators of their own making; whenever the legislators endeavour to take away and destroy the property of the people, or reduce them to slavery under arbitrary power, they put themselves into a state of war with the people, who are thereupon absolved from any farther obedience, and are left to the common refuge, which God hath provided for all men, against force and violence. Whensoever therefore the legislative shall transgress this fundamental rule of society; and either by ambition, fear, folly or corruption, endeavour to grasp themselves, or put into the hands of any other, an absolute power over the lives, liberties, and estates of the people; by this breach of trust they forfeit the power the people had put into their hands for quite contrary ends, and it devolves to the people, who have a right to resume their original liberty, and, by the establishment of a new legislative, (such as they think fit) provide for their own safety and security, which is the end for which they are in society. What I have said here, concerning the legislative in general, holds true also concerning the supreme executor, who having a double trust put in him, both to have a part in the legislative, and the supreme execution of the law, acts against both, when he goes about to set up his own arbitrary will as the law of the society. . . .

Montesquieu Urges Separation of Power in Government (1748)

Charles Louis de Secondat, Baron de Montesquieu (1689–1755), gained his reputation with the *Persian Letters,* a satire on French society, supposedly penned by two inquisitive Persians who wrote home describing the odd customs they witnessed in France. A visit to England in 1730 turned Montesquieu into a fervent admirer of English institutions and society. Many of his impressions are reflected in the political theories spelled out in *The Spirit of the Laws,* his major work, that took him five years to complete. From Baron de Montesquieu, *The Spirit of the Laws,* trans. T. Nugent (New York, 1900).

I

In order to have a perfect knowledge of these laws, we must consider man before the establishment of society: the laws received in such a state would be those of Nature.

The law which, impressing on our minds the idea of a Creator, inclines us toward him, is the first in importance, though not in order, of natural laws. Man in a state of nature would have the faculty of knowing, before he had acquired any knowledge. Plain it is that his first ideas would not be of a speculative nature; he would think of the preservation of his being before he would investigate its origin. Such a man would feel nothing in himself at first but impotency and weakness; his fears and apprehensions would be excessive; as appears from instances (were there any necessity of proving it) of savages found in forests, trembling at the motion of a leaf, and flying from every shadow.

In this state every man, instead of being sensible of his equality, would fancy himself inferior. There would therefore be no danger of their attacking one another; peace would be the first law of nature. . . .

As soon as man enters into a state of society he loses the sense of his weakness; equality ceases. . . .

Fear, I have observed, would induce men to shun one another; but the marks of this fear being reciprocal, would soon engage them to associate. Besides, this association would quickly follow from the very pleasure one animal feels at the approach of another of the same species. . . . and the natural inclination they have for each other would form [another] law.

Beside the sense or instinct which man possesses in common with brutes, he has the advantage of acquired knowledge; and thence arises a second tie, which brutes have not. Mankind have therefore a new motive of uniting [which] results from the desire of living in society. . . .

There are three species of government: republican, monarchical, and despotic. In order to discover their nature, it is sufficient to recollect the common notion, which supposes three definitions, or rather three facts: that a republican government is that in which the body, or only a part of the people, is possessed of the supreme power; monarchy, that in which a single person governs by fixed and established laws; a despotic government, that in which a single person directs everything by his own will and caprice. . . .

When the body of the people is possessed of the supreme power, it is called a democracy. When the supreme power is lodged in the hands of a part of the people, it is then an aristocracy. . . .

In an aristocracy the supreme power is lodged in the hands of a certain number of persons. These are invested both with the legislative and executive authority; and the rest of the people are, in respect to them, the same as the subjects of a monarchy in regard to the sovereign. . . .

In every government there are three sorts of power: the legislative; the executive in respect to things dependent on the law of nations; and the executive in regard to matters that depend on the civil law.

By virtue of the first, the prince or magistrate enacts temporary or perpetual laws, and amends or abrogates those that have been already enacted. By the second, he makes peace or war, sends or receives embassies, establishes the public security, and provides against invasions. By the third he punishes criminals, or determines the disputes that arise between individuals. The latter we shall call the judiciary power, and the other simply the executive power of the state.

The political liberty of the subject is a tranquility of mind arising from the opinion each person has of his safety. In order to have this liberty, it is requisite that the government be so constituted that one man need not be afraid of another.

When the legislative and executive powers are united in the same person, or in the same body of magistrates, there can be no liberty, because apprehensions may arise lest the same monarch or senate should enact tyrannical laws, to execute them in a tyrannical manner.

Again, there is no liberty if the judiciary power be not separated from the legislative and executive. Were it joined with the legislative, the life and liberty of the subject would be exposed to arbitrary control; for the judge would be then the legislator. Were it joined to the executive power, the judge might behave with violence and oppression. There would be an end of everything, were the same man or the same body, whether of the nobles or of the people, to exercise these three powers: that of enacting laws, that of executing the public resolutions, and of trying the causes of individuals.

II

As in a country of liberty, every man who is supposed a free agent ought to be his own governor; the legislative power should reside in the whole body of the people. But since this is impossible in large states, and in small ones is subject to many inconveniences, it is fit that the people should transact by their representatives what they can not transact by themselves.

The inhabitants of a particular town are much better acquainted with its wants and interests than with those of other places; and are better judges of the capacity of their neighbours than of that of the rest of their countrymen. The members, therefore, of the legislature should not be chosen from the general body of the nation; but it is proper that in every considerable place a representative should be elected by the inhabitants.

The great advantage of representatives is their capacity of discussing public affairs. For this the people collectively are extremely unfit, which is one of the chief inconveniences of a democracy. . . .

In such a state there are always persons distinguished by their birth, riches, or honours; but were they to be confounded with the common people, and to have only the weight of a single vote like the rest, the common liberty would be their slavery, and they would have no interest in supporting it, as most of the popular resolutions would be against them. The share they have, therefore, in the legislature ought to be proportioned to their other advantages in the state, which happens only when they form a body that has a right to check the licentiousness of the people, as the people have a right to oppose any encroachment of theirs. . . .

The executive power ought to be in the hands of a monarch, because this branch of government, having need of despatch, is better administered by one than by many; on the other hand, whatever depends on the legislative power is oftentimes better regulated by many than by a single person.

But if there were no monarch, and the executive power should be committed to a certain number of persons selected from the legislative body, there would be an end then of liberty; by reason that the two powers would be united, as the same persons would sometimes possess, and would be always able to possess, a share in both. . . .

Rousseau Explains the Social Contract (1762)

Jean-Jacques Rousseau's most famous work, *The Social Contract,* built on and extended the contract theory which underlay seventeenth- and eighteenth-century thinking on how government developed. Rousseau (1712–1778) had made his reputation in 1749 with an essay in which, contrary to general opinion among the *philosophes,* he argued that man was good by nature but had been corrupted by civilization. The first selection is taken from the later (1755) essay on the subject, "A Discourse on the Origins of Inequality." *The Social Contract* was one of the most influential political treatises ever written, its conclusions have been interpreted in widely different ways. From *The Social Contract and Other Discourses* by Jean-Jacques Rousseau. Translated by G. D. H. Cole. Everyman's Library Edition. Reprinted by permission of E. P. Dutton & Co., Inc. This is published in Canada by J. M. Dent & Sons Ltd.

I. GOOD MAN AND EVIL SOCIETY (1755)

If the reader . . . traces the lost and forgotten road, by which man must have passed from the state of nature to the state of society, . . . he cannot fail to be struck by the vast distance which separates the two states. . . . We are taught nothing on this subject, by reflection, that is not entirely confirmed by observation. The savage and the civilized man differ so much in the bottom of their hearts and in their inclinations, that what constitutes the supreme happiness of one would reduce the other to despair. The former breathes only peace and liberty; he desires only to live and be free from labour. . . . Civilized man, on the other hand, is always moving, sweating, toiling and racking his brains to find still more laborious occupations: he goes on in drudgery to his last moment, and even seeks death to put himself in a position to live, or renounces life to acquire immortality. He pays his court to men in power, whom he hates, and to the wealthy, whom he despises; he stops at nothing to have the honour of serving them; he is not ashamed to value himself on his own meanness and their protection; and, proud of his slavery, he speaks with disdain of those, who have not the honour of sharing it. . . .

It is not to my present purpose to insist on the indifference to good and evil which arises from this disposition, in spite of our many fine works on morality, or to show how, everything being reduced to appearances, there is but art and mummery in even honour, friendship, virtue, and often vice itself, of which we at length learn the secret of boasting; to show, in short, how, always asking others what we are, and never daring to ask ourselves, in the midst of so much philosophy, humanity and civilization, and of such sublime codes of morality, we have nothing to show for ourselves but a frivolous and deceitful appearance, honour without virtue, reason without wisdom, and pleasure without happiness. It is sufficient that I have proved that this is not by any means the original state of man, but that it is merely the spirit of society, and the inequality which society produces, that thus transform and alter all our natural inclinations.

II. THE RIGHT OF THE
STRONGEST
(1762)

Man is born free; and everywhere he is in chains. One thinks himself the master of others, and still remains a greater slave than they. How did this change come about? I do not know. What can make it legitimate? That question I think I can answer.

If I took into account only force, and the effects derived from it, I should say: "As long as a people is compelled to obey, and obeys, it does well; as soon as it can shake off the yoke, and shakes it off, it does still better; for, regaining its liberty by the same right as took it away, either it is justified in resuming it, or there was no justification for those who took it away." But the social order is a sacred right which is the basis of all rights. Nevertheless, this right does not come from nature, and must therefore be founded on conventions. Before coming to that, I have to prove what I have just asserted. . . .

The strongest is never strong enough to be always the master, unless he transforms strength into right, and obedience into duty. Hence the right of the strongest, which, though to all seeming meant ironically, is really laid down as a fundamental principle.

But are we never to have an explanation of this phrase? Force is a physical power, and I fail to see what moral effect it can have. To yield to force is an act of necessity, not of will—at the most, an act of prudence. In what sense can it be a duty?

Suppose for a moment that this so-called "right" exists. I maintain that the sole result is a mass of inexplicable nonsense. For, if force creates right, the effect changes with the cause: every force that is greater than the first succeeds to its right. As soon as it is possible to disobey with impunity, disobedience is legitimate; and, the strongest being always in the right, the only thing that matters is to act so as to become the strongest. But what kind of right is that which perishes when force fails? If we must obey perforce, there is no need to obey because we ought; and if we are not forced to obey, we are under no obligation to do so. Clearly, the word "right" adds nothing to force: in this connection, it means absolutely nothing. . . .

III. THE MAKING OF A
SOCIAL COMPACT (1762)

I suppose men to have reached the point at which the obstacles in the way of their preservation in the state of nature [are greater] . . . than the resources at the disposal of each individual for his maintenance in that state. That primitive condition can then subsist no longer; and the human race would perish unless it change its manner of existence.

But, as men cannot engender new forces, but only unite and direct existing ones, they have no other means of preserving themselves than the formation, by aggregation, of a sum of forces great enough to overcome the resistance. These they have to bring into play by means of a single motive power, and cause to act in concert.

This sum of forces can arise only where several persons come together: but, as the force and liberty of each man are the chief instruments of his self-preservation, how can he pledge them without harming his own interests, and neglecting the care he owes to himself? This difficulty, in its bearing on my present subject, may be stated in the following terms:

The problem is to find a form of association which will defend and protect with the whole common force the person and goods of each associate, and in which each, while uniting himself with all, may still obey himself alone, and remain as free as before.

This is the fundamental problem of which the *Social Contract* provides the solution.

The clauses of this contract are so determined by the nature of the act that the slightest modification would make them vain and ineffective; so that, although they have perhaps never been formally set forth, they are everywhere the same and everywhere tacitly admitted and recognized, until, on the violation of the social contract, each regains his original rights and resumes his natural liberty, while losing the conventional liberty in favour of which he renounced it.

These clauses, properly understood, may be reduced to one—the total alienation of each associate, together with all his rights, to the whole community; for, in the first place, as each gives himself absolutely, the conditions are the same for all; and, this being so, no one has any interest in making them burdensome to others. . . .

Finally, each man, in giving himself to all, gives himself to nobody; and as there is no associate ever which he does not acquire the same right as he yields others over himself, he gains an equivalent for everything he loses, and an increase of force for the preservation of what he has.

If then we discard from the social contract what is not of its essence, we shall find that it reduces itself to the following terms:

> Each of us puts his person and all his power in common under the suprème direction of the general will, and, in our corporate capacity, we receive each member as an indivisible part of the whole. . . .

IV. WHETHER THE GENERAL WILL IS FALLIBLE (1762)

It follows from what has gone before that the general will is always right and tends to the public advantage; but it does not follow that the deliberations of the people are always equally correct. Our will is always for our own good, but we do not always see what that is; the people is never corrupted, but it is often deceived, and on such occasions only does it seem to will what is bad.

There is often a great deal of difference between the [majority] will and the general will; the latter considers only the common interest, while the former takes private interest into account, and is no more than a sum of particular wills. . . .

HOW TO CHECK THE USURPATIONS OF GOVERNMENT

What we have just said . . . makes it clear that the institution of government is not a contract, but a law; that the depositaries of the executive power are not the people's masters, but its officers; that it can set them up and pull them down when it likes; that for them there is no question of contract, but of obedience; and that in taking charge of the functions the State imposes on them they are doing no more than fulfilling their duty as citizens, without having the remotest right to argue about the conditions.

When therefore the people sets up an hereditary government, whether it be monarchical and confined to one family, or aristocratic and confined to a class, what it enters into is not an undertaking: the administration is given a provisional form, until the people chooses to order it otherwise. . . .

I am here assuming what I think I have shown; that there is in the State no fundamental law that cannot be revoked, not excluding the social contract itself; for if all the citizens assembled of one accord to break the contract, it is impossible to doubt that it would be very legitimately broken.

STUDY QUESTIONS

1. What is the purpose of political theory? Does theory influence men to act or simply justify actions they have already taken?

2. Why was seventeenth- and eighteenth-century political theory closely related to the concept of natural law?

3. According to each author, what was man like in a state of nature? Why did they differ in their views of man?

4. According to each, how did government come about? What was the social contract? Did each man agree with this concept?

5. What kind of government did each author propose? What did each think was the chief purpose of government? What are the rights of man? Under what conditions can the contract be broken?

6. What is the difference between the position of Hobbes and that of Divine Right?

7. What did Rousseau mean by the General Will?

Frederick the Great
States the Duties of a Sovereign (1781)

TOPIC 20

ENLIGHTENED ABSOLUTISM

The political theorists whose ideas were expressed in the preceding topic were Western Europeans trying to draw from their own experiences a notion of the forms of government most desirable and workable for men. The most common form for Europeans living in the eighteenth century, however, was what is variously known as benevolent despotism or enlightened absolutism. Based on utilizing the absolutist powers of monarchy in order to achieve some of the goals popularized by the Enlightenment, enlightened absolutism was accepted by many intellectuals as the best form attainable under existing circumstances. The average citizen was not prepared to think of making radical changes in his government either, and local grievances rarely threatened the power of territorial sovereigns. The readings describe the reigns of several enlightened monarchs and provide evidence from which to judge the strengths and weaknesses of this approach to government.

Frederick II of Prussia, called "The Great," was ruler of what had long been a poor and remote area of Germany. A succession of administratively able predecessors had exploited a favorable position at the close of the Thirty Years' War to maintain an efficient standing army, construct an effective bureaucracy, and knit disparate territories into a union that permitted Prussia to play a role in European politics beyond the normal potential of its sandy acres and small population (4,000,000 in 1740). Frederick (1740–1786) was equally successful in war and peace, almost doubling the territory of his country and advancing agriculture and industry. In this reading the Prussian ruler explains his views on the role of a king in the eighteenth century. From "Essay on the Forms of Government and on the Duties of Sovereigns," in *Posthumous Works of Frederick II, King of Prussia,* trans. Thomas Holcroft, (London, 1789), IX, p. 198.

We have observed that citizens have only granted preeminence to one of their fellows in consideration of the services they expect from him; these services consist in maintaining the laws, in seeing that justice is strictly observed, in opposing the corruption of morals to the utmost of his power, in defending the State against its enemies. . . . Princes, sovereigns and kings are not, therefore, invested with supreme authority in order to plunge with impunity into debauchery and luxury; they are not raised above their fellow citizens in order to satisfy their pride by ostentatious display, thus contemptuously

insulting those who live in simplicity of manner, poverty, or destitution; they are not at the head of the State in order to maintain around themselves a crowd of hangers-on, whose idleness and uselessness will beget all manner of vices. . . .

The sovereign is bound by indissoluble bonds to the body of the State; in consequence, he suffers the repercussion of all the ills that afflict his subjects, and society in its turn suffers from the misfortunes that affect its sovereign. There exists only one welfare, which is that of the State in general. If the prince loses provinces, he is no longer in a condition to assist his subjects as heretofore, and if misfortune has obliged him to incur debts, his poor citizens will have to discharge them; on the other hand if his people are few in number and sunk in destitution, the sovereign is debarred from all renown. These are truths so incontestable that it is needless to dwell further on them.

I repeat, then, the sovereign represents the State; he and his people form one single body, which can only be happy in so far as it is harmoniously united. The prince stands in relation to the society over which he rules as the head stands to the body; he must see, think, and act for the community, in order to procure for it all the advantages which it is capable of enjoying. If the monarchical form of government is to prevail over the republican, the sovereign's duty is clear; he must be active and upright, and gather together all his strength to follow the path that is prescribed for him. This is the view I take of his duties. . . . That he may never swerve from them, he must remember that he is a man, like the humblest of his servants; if he is the first judge, the first general, the first financier and the first minister of society, it is not in order that he should represent it, but that he may fulfill its duties. He is merely the first servant of the State, obliged to act with probity, wisdom and complete disinterestedness, as though at any moment, he might be called upon to give an account of his administration to his fellow citizens.

Enlightened Despotism in Theory and Practice

From *A History of the Western World,* Vol. II, *1715 to the Present,* by S. B. Clough et al. Copyright ©, 1964, by D. C. Heath & Co., a division of Raytheon Education Co., Boston, Mass.

The activities and policies of those late eighteenth-century monarchs who attempted to overhaul and to rationalize their governments and the societies they dominated constituted the historical phenomenon known as enlightened or benevolent despotism and represented an early stage in the pattern of revolutionary developments under consideration. . . . The work of these monarchs also represented a further step in the process of early modern centralized state-making.

Despite the fact that enlightened despotism was in no case a complete success and despite the fact that some enlightened despots were nearly absolute failures, this phenomenon has proven to be one of the most interesting and most studied aspects of late eighteenth-century European history. One wonders, quite naturally, why this striking pattern of government fell nearly simultaneously across so much of Europe. There were at least four reasons. First, the social and economic stresses . . . produced a turmoil of social change, and the monarchs felt called upon to make their regimes square with the new facts of life. Second, the economic and political wounds that resulted from the great wars of mid-century made the need for reforms of some kind particularly obvious. Third, a surprising number of the monarchs of the day were sensitive, alert, and active human beings who were willing and anxious to rule effectively. Fourth, there came out of the Enlightenment a pattern of thought that emphasized that reform was both possible and desirable.

THE IDEA BEHIND ENLIGHTENED DESPOTISM

Enlightened political thought had developed in such a way as to emphasize the idea that it was the monarch who should be the creator, that in him was deposited the collective "human reason" that would undertake the needed reform. Instead of maintaining that he was the state, the enlightened despot tended to believe, as Frederick II of Prussia put it, that he was simply the first servant of the state. He wielded his power for the welfare of the state which was something other than himself, and the welfare of the state depended upon the welfare of the people. The enlightened despots felt called upon, therefore, to improve the conditions under which their subjects worked and lived.

By way of illustration, one may refer to Frederick the Great's *Essay on Forms of Government* (1777) to see how the most interesting practitioner of the enlightened despotic art thought about himself. At the outset of this privately printed essay, Frederick said that the state and laws came into being when savage families united "that they might secure their possessions by mutual defense." Then he went on to remark that because "laws could neither be maintained nor executed unless someone should incessantly watch for their preservation, magistrates arose . . . whom the people elected. . . ." Frederick emphasized that the true origin of sovereign power was an election.

Different people, he said, have created different kinds of sovereignties—aristocracies, oligarchies, democracies, despotisms, and monarchies. There are various kinds of monarchy, among them the medieval feudal monarchy, which had happily disappeared except in Poland; the despotic monarchy like that in Turkey where the sovereign "may with impunity commit the most atrocious cruelties" and is often strangled in return; and what he called "true" monarchical government which is "the best or the worst of all others, accordingly as it is administered." Again, he repeated that "men granted pre-eminence to one of their equals in expectation that he should do them certain services." . . .

ENLIGHTENED DESPOTISM IN PRACTICE

Frederick's reign falls naturally into two parts. The first, from 1740 to 1763, was almost entirely taken up with war; the second, from 1763 until his death in 1786, was a time of peace during which he could indulge his paternalistic propensity for rational reforms from above. This sort of tender-loving-care was badly needed by Prussia as well as by the other combatant countries at the time. The series of wars terminated by the Treaties of Paris and Hubertusburg (1763) had really begun as early as 1733. These conflicts had become increasingly taxing and had involved more countries as they succeeded one another; and the upshot was a general fatigue and disorganization in the early 1760's as the several combatant countries returned to peace-time footing. . . .

FREDERICK II AND THE WAR FOR SILESIA

After an upbringing at the hand of a loutish, single-minded but capable father (Frederick William I) that would have driven most sensitive children to bedlam, young Frederick (ruled 1740–1786) almost miraculously made his accommodation to the world as his father ordered it; and after an intensive, enforced apprenticeship in administration and after a good deal of covert study of French enlightened books, of music and economics, he acceded to the throne in 1740. The territories that he inherited, though small and sparsely populated, were spread non-contiguously over no less than 18 degrees of longitude from the Rhine on the west to the Niemen on the east and possessed no logic other than the determination and the fortunes of Frederick's ancestors who had acquired them.

Shortly after he came to his throne, this 28-year-old prince, who had just written that a ruler should fight only just wars and should not covet his neighbor's territory, threw the magnificent army created by his father into 23-year-old Maria Theresa's fair province in the valley of the upper Oder—Silesia. Why? "It was," he said later, "a means of acquiring reputation and of increasing the power of the state."

The enterprise so blithely started in 1740 took 23 years and nearly cost Frederick his life and everything that his ancestors had so patiently accumulated. At one point, while Frederick was contending against the grand alliance of France, Austria, and Russia—after defeat in the Battle of Kunersdorf (1759) —Frederick wrote to one of his ministers: "All is lost . . . I shall not survive the ruin of the Fatherland. Adieu forever!" But he recovered; his armies gained some important victories; the Russians left the coalition against him; and in 1763 he was confirmed by the statesmen of an exhausted Europe in his possession of Silesia.

Later Frederick wrote about the cost of taking and keeping this province with its million and a half population: whole provinces devastated, deserted farms, ruined cities, scarcity of food and commerce, industry and finance at a standstill. Even more serious, Frederick thought, was a moral collapse resulting from the war. Discipline and the habit of work had fled the land. Moreover, although the Prussian state had gained territory from the war, East Prussia was still not connected with the heart of the Hohenzollern lands (the Mark Brandenburg); the frontiers still lacked natural boundaries and lay open to invasion on every side. Frederick could feel no more territorially secure in 1763 than he had in 1740.

RECONSTRUCTION OF THE ARMY

In view of this insecurity, then, his greatest and first care was to cultivate that which for Prussia took the place of mountain ranges, channels, and contiguously coherent territories: the army. Having lost 180,000 soldiers and 1,500 of its best officers killed (not to speak of other casualties) in 16 pitched battles

during the Seven Years' War alone, this army desperately needed rehabilitation. The enormity of these war losses can best be understood if one realizes that Frederick calculated that in order to discourage the cupidity of his richer and far larger neighbors (Russia, Austria, and France) he needed a peace-time army personnel exactly as numerous as his wartime losses. The dead make poor soldiers; the total Prussian population in 1763 was only about 5 million; and in order to ensure that crops were planted and harvested in his realms, Frederick was forced after the war to furlough soldiers for agricultural work.

The secret of Frederick's success in rebuilding his shattered army was the fact that although his kingdom was nearly ruined by the war, his royal treasury was still ample, his magazines of war-supplies were full, remounts and draft animals for the army in good supply. All he needed was men; and with money he could buy some of these abroad—especially in western and southern Germany. Others his officers kidnapped—fine, tall men, preferably—surprised by Prussian "recruiting" parties as they emerged from church in Mecklenburg or Saxony. By whatever method, the recruits came in at the rate of seven to eight thousand per year. To supplement his precious Junker nobles, generations of whom had been sacrificed to Silesia, Frederick found officers where he could, as long as they were noble. Only desperation would lead him to use non-noble officers who, Frederick believed, lacked the necessary bravado and habit of command. Prussian noble boys were trained in *Cadettenhausen* (military schools). Spring and autumn the regiments maneuvered under the King's watchful eye; and what had been in 1763 a wreck of 151,000 dispirited men became by

Frederick reviews his troops.

1771 a polished weapon 186,000 strong, and Frederick's war treasury was bulging with cash.

ECONOMIC RECONSTRUCTION

The tremendous tax-income needed to support this army could be raised only in an economically healthy land. Economic reconstruction, then, had been as essential as the recruitment of soldiers. To replace the 500,000 farmers and workers lost during the war,

Frederick followed his father's example and encouraged immigration of foreign colonists to such effect that ten years after the end of the war the devastated provinces had greater populations than in 1756. To enable these colonists as well as the previous residents to produce, the government made available horses, seed, and cattle and established banks to supply credit for rural improvements. The upshot of this carefully administered and supervised program was quick rebuilding of

the villages and an increase of agricultural production to the point where Prussia became a substantial exporter of grain.

Industry, too, profited from the energetic zeal of this soldier-accountant king who provided flexible mercantilist support for infant industries. High protective tariffs on imported goods and government subsidies for what the King considered desirable new industries, along with exemption from excise taxes for the products of these enterprises, were the main features of this support. To make credit available to industrial entrepreneurs, Frederick created more banks which served to reduce interest rates to reasonable levels. But government subsidy and tax-exemption was not something that Prussian entrepreneurs could hope to enjoy indefinitely. The King watched the new industries grow: when they seemed to be able to stand on their own feet their privileges were suppressed.

Within ten years after the conclusion of the war, Frederick's industrial and agricultural policy, along with a program of internal improvements, had produced an economically rebuilt country, enjoying a highly favorable balance of trade. In 1740 there had been a trade deficit of 600 thousand *thalers*; in 1775 this had changed to a credit of 4,400,000 *thalers*. The incoming payments helped to provide ample grist for the tax-collector's mill, swelled the treasury, and fed the army. Withal, the population—even including the nobility—remained relatively poor. Nor could it be otherwise when such a small population was supporting such a large army.

To relieve his subjects of their cash, Frederick imported the most skillful and experienced tax-collectors that he could find—Frenchmen. One of these—de Launay—was paid three times as much as any other Prussian civil servant. Experts in the creation and imposition of indirect taxes, these French collectors managed to increase the annual royal revenues by three million *thalers* between 1763 and 1775 to the grand total of 21,700,000 *thalers*. Of this sum the King immediately set aside two million for his war-chest, spent 3,700,000 on fortifications and put two million back into the economy by way of subsidies. The remaining 14 million went to pay for administration, public services, and the army. No other major European government could boast anything like a comparable financial position despite the fact that their territories were far larger and their populations were greater and richer.

All this was very efficient, but not particularly Enlightened; and many of Frederick's contemporaries thought of his kingdom as little more than a garrison. On a visit to Berlin, Goethe, a non-Prussian German, compared Prussia to a military anthill or an immense clockwork machine and took the first opportunity to flee home to Weimar. Frederick himself was not content with his reputation as a first-rate accountant and soldier; he also wished to be thought of as a philosopher-king, his kingdom a land of discipline and cultivation.

DISCIPLINE AND EDUCATION

Discipline first of all. Among the peasants a proper subserviency and stability was to be achieved primarily by maintaining the accustomed relationships between peasant and landlord. Although he wrote in 1772 that serfdom was a barbarous custom, he did nothing to abrogate it on those private estates where it existed and where it served to support the nobility upon which he depended

absolutely for his army officers and civil servants. Thus most east Elbian Prussian peasants not only paid about 40 per cent of their income to the state; they also continued to owe virtually unlimited service to the landlords.

For the population at large, including the nobility and bourgeoisie as well as peasants, discipline was to be sought through education. In 1763 the Prussian government promulgated the *Landschulreglement* (Rural School Law) which stipulated that elementary education was obligatory for all children. Frederick's Minister of Public Instruction, K. S. von Zedlitz, tried conscientiously to implement this law; but there seems to have been some difference of opinion between the King and Prussian *Aufklärern* (Enlighteners) who had drafted the measure. In Frederick's view, education for the masses should not lead so much to enlightenment as to social stability and loyalty to the state. Schoolmasters, Frederick wrote, should "teach the youngsters religion and morality. . . . It is enough for the people in the country to learn only a little reading and writing." They should be instructed in practical matters like the cultivation of mulberry trees (the King was anxious to see silk produced in Prussia); but above all, they should be imbued, said this deistic disciple of Voltaire, with a true fear of God. . . . This tendency to emphasize the practical in education was, of course, according to the formula prescribed by the French *philosophes* and squared, for instance, with the ideas of Diderot and the other *Encyclopedistes* with whose work Frederick was entirely familiar. On paper, the Prussian educational system from the compulsory rural schools to the universities was an admirable and forward-looking structure

which could have freed the people from ignorance and superstition. But the massive sums of money necessary for true universal education were simply not available. . . .

ENLIGHTENED DESPOTISM IN PRUSSIA

To achieve a high degree of civilization in his kingdom, Frederick resorted—as he did for expert tax-collectors—to imports from France. It was as though he felt that his subjects had so much to do in performing the economic, social, administrative, and military tasks he assigned to them that they had no time left over for the arts and letters. Actually, Frederick knew relatively little about German culture. He tended to speak, write, and think in French; he was thoroughly familiar with French writers, but he was hardly aware of his great German literary contemporaries: Lessing, Goethe, and Schiller for instance. He rejuvenated the Royal Academy at Berlin which had been neglected by his father and drew to it illustrious foreigners as academicians. French drama, French paintings were brought to Berlin and to Frederick's little French palace at Potsdam where the flute-playing king carried on his famous correspondence with French intellectuals.

As philosopher-king, Frederick held to the principle of freedom of conscience. Above all, he wrote, the sovereign must not interfere in the religious beliefs of his subjects:

Nay, Toleration is itself so advantageous to the people . . . that it constitutes the happiness of the state. As soon as there is that perfect freedom of opinion, the people are all at peace; whereas persecution has given birth to the most bloody civil wars, and such as have been the most inveterate and the most destructive.

So much for theory. In practice, Frederick lived up to his formula insofar as he encouraged people of all beliefs to enter his realms and did not interfere with their worship. Even Jews were tolerated (though the King disliked them and considered them useless to the state) as long as they paid particular and high taxes to compensate the state for their uselessness. But tolerance stopped at this point. A Prussian could believe anything—or not believe—as he saw fit as long as he didn't say or write anything that would disturb discipline or otherwise endanger the state. The censor saw to that. The censor was the King. Free expression was limited to the royal dinner table and there to the King alone.

Enlightened despotism, Prussian model, was, then clearly a despotism. It was efficient because its generating power, the King, was efficient. It depended upon the tireless personal attention of a single, severe, yet strangely sensitive man. Its guiding principle was the protection and expansion of the Hohenzollern lands and power. . . .

THE HAPSBURG MONARCHY

The Austrian experiment in enlightened despotism was, on two counts, quite a different affair. First, Joseph II, unlike Frederick, was not willing to compromise his principles and was determined to do a thorough job. Second, his work did not take place . . . in a small and, therefore, easily supervised state like Prussia. The Hapsburg monarchy was a widespread and complicated accumulation of kingdoms, archduchies, and sovereignties of various kinds in which at least eleven different lan-

Frederick the Great not only furthered the arts in Prussia, he actively participated in them, writing French verse and composing music. He was a lover of the flute and an accomplished player, frequently performing his own compositions before the court.

guages were spoken* in addition to countless dialects. Many of the provinces ruled by the Hapsburgs had, in addition to their own languages, their particular customs, traditional privileges and legislative bodies.

*German, Magyar, Polish, Italian, Czech, Slovakian, Slovenian, Serbo-Croatian, Romanian, Flemish, and French—Eds.

Maria Theresa

To balance this liability of diversity, Joseph II had one great asset: his charmingly capable mother. Enlightened despotism was not in Austria a one-shot operation, at least as far as despotism was concerned. Like Frederick II in Prussia, who was able to superimpose his Enlightenment on top of the police state established by his dour, drill-sergeant father,

Joseph profited from the work of the beautiful and persuasive Maria Theresa. This "empress" who reigned for forty years (1740–1780) had, with the help of her great ministers Counts Haugwitz and Kaunitz, accomplished in the years between 1749 and 1763 a considerable administrative reform. A congeries of principalities had very nearly been molded into a unit before Joseph came of age. The new Austrian administration, modelled after the Prussian original, was highly centralized in Vienna; and meetings of estates and diets in most parts of Maria Theresa's empire had been quietly suspended.

This good, high-minded, and pious woman was anxious to promote the well-being of her people. In this endeavor her government substantially reduced the labor services that landlords were permitted to exact from peasant-serfs, and it managed to subject nobles to taxation so that they would bear at least part of the burden of government. However, Maria Theresa was afraid of the ideas of the *philosophes* which, she believed, represented a threat to her imperial power. Accordingly, while her son and young men in the University of Vienna eagerly read and talked about "natural law," she tried through censorship to prevent these dangerous ideas from circulating in her realm.

When in 1765 the Emperor Francis, Maria Theresa's beloved husband, died, the sorrowful widow admitted her son, Joseph, to a co-regency with her in the rule of the Hapsburg heritage. The young man became Holy Roman Emperor as well. During the remaining fifteen years of her life she entrusted her old servant Kaunitz with the task of keeping Joseph and his dangerous ideas within the bounds of prudence. Partially effective as long as she lived, this control terminated with her death in 1780.

Joseph II

Joseph was also good, high-minded, and pious but, unlike his mother, he was a doctrinaire child of the Enlightenment. He believed passionately in the necessity for and the possibility of organizing life on earth rationally. He believed that he spoke for the state and was possessed both of the "right reason" to decide what should be accomplished and the power to get it done. His "reason" was humanitarian and egalitarian. He was deeply revolted by injustice; he abhorred the exploitation of the many weak by the few strong. Injustice and exploitation resulted, he thought, from the workings of unnatural and outmoded institutions carried over from the past. All these should be destroyed and replaced by the beneficent and watchful state. Negatively, he would eliminate serfdom, destroy the guilds, and terminate the privileged corporativeness of the church, of the aristocracy, and of all other constituted bodies—except the state. Positively, he would establish equality of taxation as well as religious, civil, economic, and intellectual liberty—complete freedom, that is, from everything except the police. This was a big program, probably far too ambitious for the time and place and certainly more than he could have achieved during the ten short years (1780–1790) that remained to him after his mother's death.

That decade was full of activity as Joseph attempted to realize his vision through his own arduous toil and that of his increasingly intimidated bureaucracy. No usage, no institution, and no rights (except what he decided were "natural rights") were sacred in his view. His methods were drastic and arbitrary. His intentions were socially revolutionary.

As the thousands of edicts that issued from his office in Vienna after 1780 changed time-honored usages and eliminated ancient privileges, Joseph's enemies multiplied. Many Roman Catholics were appalled when he decreed religious toleration for Protestant and Eastern Christians, as well as for Jews, and when he closed monasteries and put the clergy on the government payroll. When he moved not only to liberate the serfs but also to free the peasantry from all forced labor, landlords joined the resistance. Hungarians, Bohemians, Belgians, and Italians resented the loss of their autonomy and the upsetting of their local customs, and they protested the policy designed to make German the official language of the entire empire. Even the peasants, who were the primary objects of Joseph's benevolence, became confused by agrarian reforms that they did not fully understand and rose in revolt. As resistance increased so did Joseph's determination to have his way and the prisons of this liberally enlightened monarchy became stuffed with political prisoners.

The immediate upshot of Joseph's revolution from above was failure and revolt. While he wore himself out with work, rebellion broke out in the Austrian Netherlands and in Hungary. Rioting Bohemian peasants were slaughtered by Joseph's army. Landlords, ecclesiastics, and intellectuals all opposed him. His mother's old minister refused to see him, even on his deathbed. To add to his agony, the ambitious foreign policy which Joseph had directed toward aggrandizing Hapsburg prestige and power also ended in failure. Returning from an unsuccessful military campaign in the Balkans late in 1788, Joseph took to his bed, broken in health at age 48. He died a year later clearly aware that his vast rational-humanitarian storm had failed to destroy the old edifices. It remained for his much more conservative brother and successor, Leopold, to salvage some small parts of Joseph's program and to try to regroup the Hapsburg empire to withstand the new revolutionary winds that were already blowing from France.

There is a certain irony implicit in Joseph's tragedy. No other ruler, enlightened, benevolent, or otherwise, seems to have understood more clearly the desires of the late eighteenth-century bourgeoisie. He had a vision of a society where power and rank would be open to talent, a vision of economic activity freed from artificial restraints. He worked harder than any other monarch to make this vision a reality, and yet he was rejected by his own subjects.

Saul Padover: Joseph II of Austria

The professional interests of Saul Padover (1905–   ) have included extensive government service, writing, and teaching. Particularly interested in social movements and ideas, Professor Padover is the author of several biographies, the subjects of which range from Thomas Jefferson to the model enlightened monarch, Joseph II. Selections from the latter make up this reading. From Saul K. Padover, *The Revolutionary Emperor: Joseph II of Austria,* revised edition (Hamden, Connecticut: Archon Books, 1967), pp. 128–132, 133–134, 135.

Joseph's aim was to create a centralized and unified bureaucracy wholly devoted to the state and its ideas. The officials had to fill out a questionnaire every six months, giving their outside incomes, years of service, abilities, effort, conduct, knowledge—fifteen questions in all. To assure them economic security, the emperor decreed, in March, 1781, that they be eligible for pensions at the end of ten years of service. . . .

The officials were peremptorily informed that henceforth they were nothing but servants, servants of the state. Nor were they allowed, if they were German, to feel any superiority to their non-Teutonic colleagues. 'All jealousies and prejudices between province and province, nation and nation, must cease,' the emperor decreed in his Pastoral Letter; 'in body politic the whole suffers when even one member is sick. The distinctions between nations and religions must disappear, and all citizens must consider each other as brothers.' The officials were to give their bodies and souls to the state; they were to have no outside interests or occupations. 'In the business of the state,' Joseph rules, 'personal inclinations should not have the slightest influence. Everybody must give his best and carry out his duties regardless of rank or ceremony.' Everything and everybody for the service of the state, was his motto. 'The State,' he said in a phrase that was to become famous, meant 'the greatest good for the greatest number.' He realized that his conditions were hard; hence he warned those who could not sacrifice themselves 'to leave an office of which they were neither worthy nor capable'.

The emperor strove to establish an officialdom that was honest, educated, and efficient. Family, position, or high connections were no longer a recommendation. A man must have merit to be appointed and promoted. He warned Kolowrat, Chancellor of Bohemia, that appointments to the Aulic Council should go only to those 'who possess a knowledge of the country', and who had ability and experience.

No official was safe from the emperor's interference or wrath. One could never tell when he would drop in for inspection. On a cold November morning Joseph once unexpectedly walked into the office of the Austro-Bohemian chancery and grimly sat down with paper and pencil to take notes. 'You will excuse me,' he said to the flustered chancellor, 'if I listen-in to-day.' One winter morning, on his way to a meeting, the emperor met a councillor going up the stairs. 'Ah,' said the monarch to the embarrassed official, 'we are both late to-day.' At a prolonged administrative session, a councillor surreptitiously glanced at his watch; it was three o'clock. The emperor also looked at his watch. 'Indeed,' he remarked to the official, 'it is somewhat late, but , you know, time passes quickly when one is in good company.' On a sudden inspection at the Vienna Municipal Hospital Joseph found the man in charge in his shirt-sleeves reading a newspaper. Without being permitted to put on his coat, the mortified official had to take his emperor through all the corridors and rooms of the building. But the joke the emperor relished most, and gleefully repeated, was the one about the government official and the priest. The bureaucrat asked a priest why the clergy had become too proud to employ the humble mount of the Saviour. 'We are forced to have recourse to horses,' the clergyman answered coldly, 'because the emperor has taken so many jackasses into his employ that there are few left for us to use.'

Joseph could be blunt to the point of brutality, especially to the nobles. When he deprived Prince Furstenberg of the governorship of Bohemia, he told Princess Furstenberg harshly: 'I must tell you, Madame, that in future, things can no longer go on in Austria as formerly . . . Give your consort the assurance of my regard, and at the same time remind him, that, in future, in matters relating to the state, I expect his own immediate reports; I am not accustomed, in affairs of my empire, to correspond with—ladies.'

Joseph did not even spare Kaunitz's chancery. Once when a note of his to the foreign office took four months before it was attended to, he burst into fury. 'Nothing is done,' he stormed, 'but only bare facts and obstacles . . . When, after experience, I make certain propositions, I expect them to be accepted, and not considered merely as a lamentation of mine on which you should utilize your wits for the sole purpose of making a lawyerish plea for the preservation of precedents.' His letters to Leopold are full of complaints against the bureaucracy. 'I find difficulties and bitter work,' he wrote. 'There is an absolute lack of men who can conceive and will; almost no one is animated by zeal for the good of the fatherland; there is no one to carry out my ideas.' Leopold, who was wise, cool, and without much faith, told his brother calmly that his great design of simplifying, clarifying, and unifying the administration was admirable; 'but the work which you have undertaken is most formidable, difficult, and discouraging, for you will find infinite obstacles among the employees, accustomed to the old regime, who do not like any innovations.'

Complain as he might of his officials, and urge them, as he did, to go to the university 'to improve their ignorance' yet the despotic son of Maria Theresa brooked neither interference nor independent thinking on the part of his bureaucracy. The Chotek incident showed this. The experienced Count Chotek did not agree with the emperor's revolutionary tax patent of 1789. He protested that the economic ideas in the tax reform were un-sound and dangerous. Joseph ignored his subordinate's plea, and Chotek, after eighteen years of service, found himself compelled to resign. 'I realize,' he sadly wrote to his emperor, 'that with eight children and a moderate income my resignation will be hard on my family; but there are circumstances in life when a man of honour has to sacrifice everything to preserve his self-respect, which he could not do if he remained in a position where he would be forced to act against his principles.' This is strangely reminiscent of Joseph's own struggles with his mother. But did the emperor sympathize?

> Whatever your decision, [was the imperial answer], I will not change my actions, not even out of respect for you. . . . Accustomed as I am to ingrates, this does not surprise me. But that a man of spirit like you, out of sheer obstinacy and quixotism, should take such a step when, even if the tax patent were really harmful, the blame would not fall on you—that, I admit, has astonished me.

With or without aid and co-operation, the absolutist monarch instituted a regular 'paper regime.' Edict followed edict with lightning rapidity. At the end of the ten-year reign there were six thousand decrees, and over eleven thousand new laws, filling eleven hundred and forty-seven folio pages. Every conceivable and inconceivable matter was regulated, legislated for, re-arranged, and prescribed. The emperor was trying to create a rational, mechanized state, soul-less and will-less, but one that should function like some monstrous well-greased machine. The thoroughness with which he went to work on this monster, which he called the State, is appalling. Nothing was left to chance, imagination, or initiative. He meant well, of course. His people were to be made happy in spite of themselves. He was to be to them a father, a harsh and brooding, but just and solicitous father.

In 1784 Joseph issued minute instructions for the guidance of his district commissioners who were to travel through the land for periodic inspections. They were to observe:

Whether the censual and vital statistics registers were kept.

Whether the houses were numbered.

What was the condition of the buildings.

Whether the population was industrious or lazy; well-to-do or poor; and why.

Whether the conscription books were kept in order.

Whether the barracks were habitable.

How many men could be quartered among citizens and peasants.

Whether the army behaved properly towards the civil population.

Whether the population had sufficient protection.

Whether the toleration edicts were observed.

Whether there was any superstition.

Whether the clergy were respected, and what their discipline was.

Whether divine services were properly carried out and whether the churches were in good condition.

Whether the preachers delivered indiscreet sermons.

Whether anyone cared for the orphans, foundlings, and homeless children.

Whether anything was being done for the blind, deaf, and crippled children to make them ultimately self-supporting.

What was the condition of the schools.

Whether there were roving clowns and jugglers on the land.

Whether the restrictions against drunkenness were carried out.

Whether there was a need for more workhouses and prisons.

Whether the laws were carried out.

Whether the judges were obedient to the superior courts.

Whether the roads were cleared.

Whether there were sufficient precautions in the sale of poisons.

Whether the sale of contraceptive methods was prohibited.

Whether the church penances and the dishonouring punishments of unfortunate girls were abolished, and whether there were institutions for the saving of such girls, and foundlings.

The officials had to investigate, observe, and report upon hundreds of such questions, which the emperor drew up himself. He would leave nothing to the doubtful intelligence of his subalterns.

Nor was this all. With his mania for systematization, the eternally suspicious despot created a far-flung espionage system and re-organized the official police. Previously, the police had been under the administration of the provincial governments. In 1786 the emperor unified all the police in his lands, except Hungary. Provincial police chiefs were to report to Count Pergen, the minister of the interior, in Vienna, and Pergen was to com-municate directly to Joseph to whom he had access at all hours. Pergen received ten thousand gulden every three months for his secret service. To each provincial capital Joseph sent a specially trained police commissioner who was to work together with the governor, without, however, being responsible to the latter. The secret police, which became the basis for the notorious state-police under Metternich, a generation later, was not created to watch revolutionists, but to keep tab on the officials, the army, and the clergy. . . .

The secret police were to keep an eye 'on the doings of the officials and to discover how the public is satisfied with them, whether they receive bribes, whether they have relatives abroad with whom they correspond, whether they have contact with suspicious strangers to whom they give official secrets'. Such findings should be reported to Pergen. The agents were to find out 'what the public says of the monarch and his government, what its mood is from time to time, and whether there are any malcontents'. The army was to be watched to see whether 'there are any individuals who are in communication with foreign powers.' Furthermore, 'the clergy, whose tendencies, in general, are hierarchical, are to be strictly watched to see whether or not they promulgate principles which are contrary to their subjection to the ruler and to the interest of the state'. The agents should observe whether 'the laws of the land are neglected . . . whether money is being taken out of the country, and whether anything else is done to the prejudice of the state'. An eye should be 'kept on suspicious foreign persons, false recruiters, spies and forgers'. The frontier police were to go over all private correspondence 'for interesting news . . . and also to track down unfaithful officials'. This, however, was to be done carefully so 'that the police should not compromise itself'. Observations were to be made 'on those who underhandedly try to spread sectarianism and errors among the credulous mob'. 'Particularly suspicious persons' on their way to Vienna should be reported immediately.

The second half of the instructions dealt with 'ways and means'. The police should keep a list of all suspects. Everybody, particularly strangers, should be registered. Servants should be carefully employed to spy on their masters. This, the emperor pointed out, would serve a double purpose: 'it would keep this class in order', and it would be easy for the police to watch them. The post should be placed in the hands 'of persons on whose uprightness and dependability the police can rely'. The police should employ anybody who could be of any use, no matter what their position: 'Messengers, drivers, nay, under certain circumstances, even Jews who sometimes do good service. Nobody should be considered too low.' No consideration was to be shown to suspects, 'because the duties to the state permit no mercy and no regard. . . .'

Despite his police regime and his distrust, Joseph was democratic and always accessible to his subjects. He encouraged direct complaints and his antechambers were crowded with petitioners who never had long to wait. 'I was accustomed,' the emperor said, 'to pass too many hours in my father's antechamber not to know from experience how unpleasant such a detention must be to others.' The monarch was not only unaffected but cordial, sympathetic to the poor, and ready to grant prompt aid or redress wrong.

'Your Majesty,' a trembling peasant addressed the emperor [concerning a corrupt tax collector], 'the rascal, I beg your pardon, has

Joseph felt that a prince should be accessible to his subjects. Here, the emperor is surrounded by the grateful members of a large family to whom he had given financial assistance.

gone off with my last piece, money and beast; we are reduced, my wife and children, to beggary. I always said: Our emperor would not allow this: but he answered: Our emperor has nothing to do with it. We gave him all we could, and now he wants more money or forced labour. You must wait, I said to him, I am going to see the emperor, and I'll tell him'.

Emperor Joseph II replied: 'That is enough, my good man. Do you know reading and arithmetic?'

'Yes, Sire; I can show you.'

'I believe you; wait a moment. Give this rescript to that honest collector; you take his position.'

'Must I deprive him of his bread?'

'Do not let it bother you. That man gets only what he deserves.'

The emperor was not so generous, however, to aristocrats, officials and snobs.

'What do you wish, madame?' he brusquely asked the widow of an official. 'You have heard of the suppression of the pension.'

'How can I live on five hundred florins? I demand justice from Your Majesty.'

'It is precisely because of justice that you will not get that pension.'

'I thought that the services of my late husband, and the standards to which I am accustomed, would militate in my favour.'

'The services of your husband,' the emperor replied dryly, 'were recompensed by a salary. As to your standards, or those which you believe you are entitled to, I must consider also my other subjects. I am not merely the sovereign of Vienna, and you are not the only person I have to serve. Am I to assist you at the expense of the unfortunate poor? Justice demands that I should not accord to you what could support five or six thrifty families.'

'But what will become of my daughter? She is without resources.'

'She can go to work.'

'My daughter—work! But Your Majesty. . . !'

'Work,' snapped the emperor, 'yes, work! I, too, work!'

Some Eighteenth-Century Enlightened Monarchs: Spain, Portugal, and Baden

From *The Enlightened Despots* by Geoffrey Bruun. Copyright 1929 by Holt, Rinehart and Winston, Inc. Copyright © 1957 by Geoffrey Bruun. Reprinted by permission of Holt, Rinehart and Winston, Inc.

CHARLES III OF SPAIN

Charles III of Spain (1759–1788) was trained for his royal office by an apprenticeship in Italy. The untiring intrigues of his mother, Elizabeth Farnese, secured for him the throne of Naples and Sicily in 1734, and for twenty-five years he strove to promote in that backward and priest-ridden state the principles of enlightened government. Charles was himself a devout Catholic; but clerical opposition to his reforms made him an enemy of the Church. With the aid of his energetic Minister Tanucci, he labored perseveringly to reduce the power of the priesthood and to increase the prosperity of his subjects.

Called to the Spanish throne in 1759 by the death of his half-brother Ferdinand, Charles transferred his attention to the mightier task of arresting Spain's decline and turning that country from the path of decadence to which the blind policies of earlier monarchs had committed her. Stirred by stories of his benevolence the Spanish people prepared to welcome him with loyal enthusiasm, but his appearance must have disappointed them a little. Short and round-shouldered, with dark skin, small eyes, and a toothless mouth, he looked more like a broken-down clerk than a king. Court functions and military reviews interested him little. He dressed shabbily, and hated ceremonies. At heart he was an administrator, a king of the new type, honest, conscientious, and deeply absorbed in his responsibilities. In his desire to remodel outworn institutions and to promote the welfare of his people by wise legislation he was a true prince of the Enlightenment; in his jealous retention of authority and his impatience at opposition he was a true despot.

The turbulent conditions in his capital called forth some of Charles' first efforts at reform. Madrid had all the pageantry and picturesqueness, the color and the squalor, of a medieval city. Many of the streets were narrow, dirty, and unsanitary. Badly lighted at night, without police protection, they often proved dangerous to wayfarers, for murder and robbery were common occurrences. In this favorable atmosphere private feuds flourished, for an assailant, wrapped in the anonymous security of a Spanish cloak and sombrero, could achieve his revenge and escape unrecognized, leaving the footpads to shoulder the blame for another deed of violence. In an attempt to remedy this state of affairs Charles ordered the streets cleaned and lighted, organized a police force, and forbade the wearing of long cloaks and broad-brimmed hats. But this last order, crowning as it did a series of reforms which the Spaniards regarded as foreign innovations, stirred the people of Madrid to riot and bloodshed. Frightened by the hostile demonstrations Charles fled from the capital; the unpopular edict was withdrawn, and Squillaci, the minister responsible for its enforcement, was exiled in disgrace. . . .

POMBAL IN PORTUGAL

If the Portuguese kingdom enjoyed a period of enlightened despotism in the second half of the eighteenth century the credit belongs less to Joseph I (1750–1777) than to his able but tyrannical minister, Sebastian Joseph Cavalho, Marquis of Pombal. Under the direction of this vigorous statesman the whole internal administration of Portugal was revolutionized. From 1755, the year of the great Lisbon earthquake, when Pombal's presence of mind in the face of the disaster earned him the complete confidence of his king, until the latter's death in 1777, Pombal remained the virtual dictator of Portugal. Under his direction the finances were balanced, the legal machinery simplified, and the educational system improved. In his desire to see Portugal recover something of her waning greatness he reorganized the army and attempted to build up a stronger connection with the Portuguese colonies, a project which he sought to further by establishment of commercial companies with special privileges. The Jesuits, already engaged in the colonial trade, resented his interference, and fostered opposition to his plans both in Portugal and America, a policy which hastened the general disaster so soon to overtake their order.

The fame which Pombal won by his energetic reforms, and his patriotic endeavors to liberate Portugal from foreign influences, has been clouded over by the stories of his unbridled despotism. For those who ventured to oppose him he had no mercy; his political enemies spent years in secret dungeons; and he did not hesitate on occasion to strike terror into his foes by an act of summary punishment. In particular the affair of the Tavoras, still wrapped away from the historian by terrible clouds of mystery, has invested his name with an atmosphere of horror.

On the night of September 3, 1758, as Joseph I was driving back to his palace after a love tryst, his carriage was fired upon from the shadows and the king seriously wounded. Three months later followed the arrest of the Marquis Tavora with his wife and children, the Duke of Aveiro and others, all charged with a conspiracy to assassinate the king. After a secret trial the accused were sentenced to death, the women to be beheaded, the men broken on the wheel. The sentence was carried out in public on January 3, 1759, with all the infamous ritual the law prescribed for the punishment of regicides. The secrecy surrounding the proceedings, the fact that Pombal kept in his possession the record of the trial, and the later discovery that parts of it had been destroyed, led his opponents to declare the whole conspiracy an invention of his imagination. Real or imagined there is no doubt that it served him well in his war against the Jesuits. A half-crazed Jesuit monk named Malagrida, confessor to the Tavoras, was implicated in the conspiracy and burned; and in 1759, Joseph, who was already out of patience with the Jesuits for their intrigues in his American colonies, was persuaded to banish the Order from all the dominions of the Portuguese crown.

CHARLES FREDERICK OF BADEN

The brilliant personality of Frederick the Great of Prussia has overshadowed the fame of those lesser German princes of the eighteenth century who strove to prove themselves enlightened rulers; but from such oblivion the name of Charles Frederick of Baden, at least, deserves to be retrieved. Frederick himself declared that he respected Charles above all his princely contemporaries and Frederick's judgment of men was seldom at fault.

Among the many problems to which Charles Frederick gave his attention during his long reign—1748–1816—his agrarian reforms claimed the first place. In 1769 he wrote to the Marquis de Mirabeau, seeking advice on some vexatious questions of political economy. He was soon in regular communication not only with Mirabeau but with Dupont de Nemours as well, the latter becoming for a time a member of his council and tutor to his son. This connection with the Physiocrats encouraged Charles in his projects of reform and concentrated his attention on agriculture as the basis of national wealth.

Believing with Mirabeau that poor peasants make a poor kingdom and that serfdom was not only unjust but economically unsound, Charles Frederick determined to liberate all the serfs on his personal domains. He desired to establish as the foundation of the social and economic order in his state a contented class of small independent farmers. Technical improvements in agriculture, the introduction of new crops, and the encouragement of trade and manufacture, enabled him to promote the prosperity of Baden while maintaining peace with his neighbors. The population was increased by settlers who came from all parts of Germany, attracted by the religious toleration and the legal protection which Charles was able to assure his subjects. At the same time an intelligent fiscal system reduced the taxation, and the progress of education, and of the arts and sciences, made Baden, under Charles Frederick, one of the most prosperous and enlightened of the German states.

STUDY QUESTIONS

1. What problems did Frederick the Great face and how did he attempt to solve them?

2. What did Frederick think the role of the sovereign was? Did he live up to his own ideas of what a ruler should be? Was he an effective ruler?

3. How would you define "enlightened absolutism?" What were the enlightened monarchs trying to achieve?

4. Why was this form of government prevalent in the eighteenth century? Why was it found in Central and Eastern Europe rather than in France and England?

5. Compare the efforts of Joseph II with those of Frederick. Who was more "enlightened"? Who was more successful? Why?

6. What do the examples of Charles III of Spain, Marquis Pombal of Portugal, and Charles Frederick of Baden contribute toward understanding the strengths and limits of enlightened absolutism?

7. What were the strengths and limitations of enlightened absolutism?

Robert Heilbroner: The Economic Revolution

From Robert L. Heilbroner, *The Worldly Philosophers*. Copyright, 1953, by Robert L. Heilbroner. Reprinted by permission of Simon & Schuster, Inc. pp. 6–24, 38–42, 44–51.

I

Since he came down from the trees, man has faced the problem of survival, not as an individual but as a member of a social group. His continued existence is testimony to the fact that he has succeeded in solving the problem; but the continued existence of want and misery, even in the richest of nations, is evidence that his solution has been, at best, a partial one.

Yet man is not to be too severely censured for his failure to achieve a paradise on earth. It is hard to wring a livelihood from the surface of this planet. It staggers the imagination to think of the endless efforts which must have been expended in the first domestication of animals, in the discovery of planting seed, in the first working of surface ores. It is only because man is a socially cooperative creature that he has succeeded in perpetuating himself at all.

But the very fact that he has had to depend on his fellow man has made the problem of survival extraordinarily difficult. Man is not an ant, conveniently equipped with an inborn pattern of social instincts. On the contrary, he is pre-eminently endowed with a fiercely self-centered nature. If his relatively weak physique forces him to seek cooperation, his untamed unconscious drives constantly

---

TOPIC 21

THE RISE OF A MARKET ECONOMY

Interlaced with the new intellectual attitudes and views on government that characterized the early modern world was a basic shift in man's concept of the nature of the economic sector of his life. Economic change cannot be pinpointed in time like scientific discoveries, or inventions, or by the publication of a book that alters the thinking of men. Nonetheless, at the time in which the theories of Copernicus, Galileo, Descartes, and Newton were revolutionizing traditional thought, a similarly world-shaking development was taking place in economic life with the appearance of the market system. These readings constitute a commentary on this development, taken chiefly from the writings of Robert L. Heilbroner (1919–   ), an eloquent American economist who possesses the gift of making economics easily intelligible to the average reader. Avoiding the examination of economic theory within a vacuum remote from the realities of everyday life, Professor Heilbroner presents theory as it fits into the flow of history but at the same time selects his historical narrative to "illustrate and substantiate the abstractions of theory."

threaten to disrupt his social working partnerships.

In primitive society, the struggle between aggression and cooperation is taken care of by the environment; when the specter of starvation looks a community in the face every day—as with the Eskimos or the African hunting tribes—the pure need for self-preservation pushed society to the cooperative completion of its daily tasks. But in an advanced community, this tangible pressure of the environment is lacking. When men no longer work shoulder to shoulder in tasks directly related to survival—indeed when half or more of the population never touches the tilled earth, enters the mines, keeps cattle, or builds with its hands—the perpetuation of the human animal becomes a remarkable social feat.

So remarkable, in fact, that society's existence hangs by a hair. A modern community is at the mercy of a thousand dangers: if its farmers should fail to plant enough crops, if its railroad men should take it into their heads to become bookkeepers; . . . if too few should offer their services as miners, puddlers of steel, candidates for engineering degrees—in a word, if any of a thousand intertwined tasks of society should fail to get done—industrial life would soon become hopelessly disorganized. Every day the community faces the possibility of breakdown—not from the forces of nature, but from sheer human unpredictability.

Over the centuries man has found only three ways of guarding against this calamity.

He has ensured his continuity by organizing his society around tradition, by handing down the varied and necessary tasks from generation to generation according to custom and usage: son follows father and a pattern is preserved. In ancient Egypt, says Adam Smith, "every man was bound by a principle of religion to follow the occupation of his father, and was supposed to commit the most horrible sacrilege if he changed it for another." Similarly, in India, until recently, certain occupations were traditionally assigned by caste; in fact, in much of the unindustrialized world, one is still born to one's metier.

Or society can solve the problem differently. It can use the whip of central authoritarian rule to see that its tasks get done. The pyramids of ancient Egypt did not get built because some enterprising contractor took it into his head to build them, nor do the Five Year Plans of the Soviet Union get carried out because they happen to accord with hand-me-down custom or individual self-interest. Both Russia and Egypt are authoritarian societies: politics aside, they have ensured their *economic survival* by the edict of one authority and by the penalties that supreme authority sees fit to issue.

For countless centuries man dealt with the problem of survival according to one or the other of these solutions. And as long as the problem of survival was handled by tradition or command, the economic problem never gave rise to that special field of study called economics. . . . For the economists waited upon the invention of a third solution to the problem of survival. They waited upon the development of an astonishing game in which society assured its own continuance by allowing each individual to do exactly as he saw fit—provided he followed a central guiding rule. The game was called the "market system," and the rule was deceptively simple: each should do what was to his best monetary advantage. In the market system the lure of gain, not the pull of tradition or the whip of authority, steered each man to his task. And yet, although each was free to go wherever his acquisitive nose directed him, the interplay of one man against another resulted in the necessary tasks of society getting done.

It was this paradoxical, subtle, and difficult solution to the problem of survival which called forth the economist. For unlike the simplicity of custom and command, it was not at all obvious that with each man out only for his own gain, society could in fact endure. It was by no means clear that all the jobs of society—the dirty ones as well as the plush ones—would be done if custom and command no longer ran the world. When society no longer obeyed one man's dictates, who was to say where it would end?

It was the economists who undertook to explain this puzzle. But until the idea of the market system itself had gained acceptance, there was no puzzle to explain. And until a very few centuries ago, men were not at all sure that the market system was not to be viewed with suspicion, distaste, and distrust. The world had gotten along for centuries in the comfortable rut of tradition and command; to abandon this security for the dubious and perplexing security of the market system, nothing short of a revolution was required.

It was the most important revolution, from the point of view of shaping modern society, that ever took place—fundamentally more disturbing by far than the French, American, or even the Russian Revolutions. To appreciate its magnitude, to understand the wrenching which it gave society, we must immerse ourselves in that earlier and long-forgotten world from which our own society finally sprang. Only then will it be clear why the economists had so long to wait.

Dealers in shoes, gold vessels, and clothing display goods at the annual Lendit Fair in Paris in the late fourteenth century. Symbols of their wares protrude above the merchants' tents.

First stop: France. The year, 1305.

It is a fair we visit. The traveling merchants have arrived that morning with their armed guard, have set up their gaily striped tents, and are trading among themselves and with the local population. A variety of exotic goods is for sale: silks and taffetas, spices and perfumes, hides and furs. Some have been transported from the Levant, some from Scandinavia, some from only a few hundred miles away. Local lords and ladies frequent the stalls, eager to relieve the tedium of their boring, draughty, manorial lives; along with the strange goods from Araby they are eagerly acquiring new words from that incredibly distant land: divan, syrup, tariff, artichoke, spinach, jar.

But inside the tents we meet with a strange sight. Books of business, open on the table, are barely more than notebooks of transactions; a sample extract from one merchant reads: "Owed ten gulden by a man since Whitsuntide. I forgot his name." Calculations are made largely in Roman numerals and sums are often wrong; long division is reckoned as something of a mystery and the use of zero is not clearly understood. And for all the gaudiness of the display and the excitement of the people, the fair is a small thing. The total amount of goods which comes into France in a year over the Saint Gothard pass (on the first suspension bridge in history) would not fill a modern freight train; the total amount of merchandise carried in the great Venetian fleet would not fill one modern steel freighter.

Next stop: Germany. The year, 1550 odd.

Andreas Ryff, a merchant, bearded and fur-coated, is coming back to his home in

A German merchant pays toll. The merchant in this miniature from Nuremburg, although it dates from the sixteenth century, represents a somewhat earlier age than that of Andreas Ryff.

Baden; he writes in a letter to his wife that he has visited thirty markets and is troubled with saddle-burn. He is even more troubled by the nuisances of the times; as he travels he is stopped approximately once every six miles to pay a customs toll; between Basle and Cologne he pays thirty-one levies.

And that is not all. Each community he visits has its own money, its own rules and regulations, its own law and order. In the area around Baden alone there are 112 different measures of length, 92 different square measures, 65 different dry measures, 163 different measures for cereals and 123 for liquids, 63 special measures for liquor, and 80 different pound weights.

We move on: we are in Boston in the year 1644.

A trial is in progress; one Robert Keane, "an ancient professor of the gospel, a man of eminent parts, wealthy and having but one child, and having come over for conscience' sake and for the advancement of the gospel," is charged with a heinous crime: he has made over sixpence profit on the shilling, an outrageous gain. The court is debating whether to excommunicate him for his sin, but in view of his spotless past it finally relents and dismisses him with a fine of two hundred pounds. But poor Mr. Keane is so upset that before the elders of the Church he does "with tears acknowledge his covetous and corrupt heart." The minister of Boston cannot resist this golden opportunity to profit from the living example of Keane's avarice to thunder forth in his Sunday sermon on some *false* principles of trade. Among them are these:

I. That a man might sell as dear as he can, and buy as cheap as he can.

II. If a man lose by casualty of sea, etc., in some of his commodities, he may raise the price of the rest.

III. That he may sell as he bought, though he paid too dear. . . .

All false, false, false, cries the minister; to seek riches for riches' sake is to fall into the sin of avarice.

We turn back to England and France.

In England a great trading organization, The Merchant Adventurers Company, has drawn up its articles of incorporation; among them are these rules for the participating merchants: no indecent language, no quarrels among the brethren, no card playing, no keeping of hunting dogs. No one is to carry unsightly bundles in the streets. This is indeed an odd business firm; it sounds more nearly like a fraternal lodge.

In France there has been entirely too much initiative displayed of late by the weaving industry, and a *reglement* has been promulgated by Colbert in 1666 to get away from this dangerous and disruptive tendency. Henceforth the fabrics of Dijon and Selangey are to contain 1,408 threads including selvages, neither more nor less. At Auxerre, Avallon, and two other manufacturing towns, the threads are to number 1,376; at Chatillon, 1,216. Any cloth found to be objectionable is to be pilloried. If it is found three times to be objectionable, the merchant is to be pilloried instead.

There is something common to all these scattered fragments of bygone worlds. It is this: first, the idea of the propriety (not to say the necessity) of a system organized on the basis of *personal gain* has not yet taken root. Second, a separate, self-contained economic world has not yet lifted itself from its social context. The world of practical affairs is inextricably mixed up with the world of political, social, and religious life. Until the two worlds separate, there will be nothing that resembles the tempo and the feeling of modern life. And for the two to separate, a long and bitter struggle must take place.

It may strike us odd that the idea of gain is a relatively modern one; we are schooled to believe that man is essentially an acquisitive creature and that left to himself he will behave as any self-respecting businessman would. The profit motive, we are constantly being told, is as old as man himself.

But it is not. The profit motive as we know it is only as old as "modern man." Even today the notion of gain for gain's sake is foreign to a large portion of the world's population, and it has been conspicuous by its absence over most of recorded history. Sir William Petty, an astonishing seventeenth-century character (who was in his lifetime cabin boy, hawker, clothier, physician, professor of music, and founder of a school named Political Arithmetick), claimed that when wages were good, labor was "scarce to be had at all, so licentious are they who labor only to eat, or rather to drink." And Sir William was not merely venting the bourgeois prejudices of his day. He was observing a fact which can still be remarked among the unindustrialized peoples of the world: a raw working force, unused to wagework, uncomfortable in factory life, unschooled to the idea of an ever-rising standard of living, will not work harder if wages rise; it will simply take more time off. The idea of gain, the idea that each man not only may but should constantly strive to better his material lot, is an idea which was quite foreign to the great lower and middle strata of Egyptian, Greek, Roman, and medieval cultures, only scattered throughout Renaissance and Reformation times, and largely absent in the majority of Eastern civilizations. As a ubiquitous characteristic of society, it is as modern an invention as printing.

Not only is the idea of gain by no means as universal as we sometimes suppose, but the social sanction of gain is an even more modern and restricted development. In the Middle Ages the Church taught that "No Christian ought to be a merchant," and behind that dictum lay the thought that merchants were a disturbing yeast in the leaven of society. In Shakespeare's time the object of life for the ordinary citizen, for everybody, in fact, except the gentility, was not to advance his station in life, but to maintain it. Even to our Pilgrim forefathers, the idea that gain might be a tolerable—even a useful—goal in life would have appeared as nothing short of a doctrine of the devil.

Wealth, of course, there has always been, and covetousness is at least as old as the Biblical tales. But there is a vast deal of difference between the envy inspired by the wealth of a few mighty personages and a general struggle for wealth diffused throughout society. Merchant adventurers have existed as far back as the Phoenician sailors, and can be seen all through history, in the speculators of Rome, the trading Venetians, the Hanseatic League, and the great Portuguese and Spanish voyagers who sought a route to the Indies and to their personal fortunes. But the adventures of a few are a far different thing from an entire society moved by the venture spirit. . . .

Take, for example, the fabulous family of the Fuggers, the great bankers of the sixteenth century. At their height, the Fuggers owned gold and silver mines, trade concessions, and even the right to coin their own money; their credit was far greater than the wealth of the kings and emperors whose wars (and household expenses) they financed. But when old Anton Fugger died, his eldest nephew, Hans Jacob, refused to take over the banking empire on the ground that the business of the city and his own affairs gave him too much to do; Hans Jacob's brother, George, said he would rather live in peace; a third nephew, Christopher, was equally uninterested. None of the potential heirs apparent to a kingdom of wealth apparently thought it was worth the bother.

Apart from kings (those that were solvent) and a scattering of families like the Fuggers, the early capitalists were not the pillars of society, but the outcasts. . . . Here and there an enterprising lad like St. Godric of Finchale would start as a beachcomber, gather enough wares from the wrecks of ships to become a merchant, save his money and eventually buy his own ship to trade as far afield as from Scotland to Flanders. But such men were few. As long as the paramount idea was that life on earth was only a trying preamble to Life Eternal, the business spirit was neither encouraged nor did it find spontaneous nourishment. Kings wanted treasure and for that they fought wars; the nobility wanted land and since no self-respecting nobleman would willingly sell his ancestral estates, that entailed conquest, too. But most people—serfs, village craftsmen, even the masters of the manufacturing guilds—wanted to be left alone to live as their fathers had and as their sons would in turn.

The absence of the idea of gain as a normal guide for daily life—in fact the positive disrepute with which the idea was held by the Church—constituted one enormous difference between the strange world of the tenth to sixteenth centuries and the world that began, a century or two before Adam Smith, to resemble our own. But there was an even more fundamental difference. The idea of "making a living" had not yet come into being. Economic life and social life were one and the same thing. Work was not yet a means to an end—the end being money and the things it buys. Work was an end in itself, encompassing, of course, money and commodities, but engaged in as a part of a tradition, as a natural way of life. In a word, the great social invention of "the market" had not yet been made. . . .

There was a reason for this blindness. The Middle Ages, the Renaissance, the Reformation—indeed the whole world until the sixteenth or seventeenth centuries—could not envisage the market system for the thoroughly sound reason that Land, Labor, and Capital—the basic agents of production which the market system allocates—did not yet exist. Land, labor, and capital in the sense of soil, human beings, and tools are of course coexistent with society itself. But the idea of abstract land or abstract labor did not immediately suggest itself to the human mind, any more than did the idea of abstract energy or matter. Land, labor, and capital as "agents" of production, as impersonal, dehumanized economic entities, are as much modern conceptions as the calculus. Indeed, they are not much older.

Take, for example, land. As late as the fourteenth or fifteenth century there was no land, at least in the modern sense of freely salable, rent-producing property. There were lands, of course—estates, manors, and principalities—but these were emphatically not real estate to be bought and sold as the occasion warranted. Such lands formed the core of social life, provided the basis for prestige and status, and constituted the foundation for the military, judicial, and administrative organization of society. Although land was salable under certain conditions (with many strings attached), it was not generally *for sale*. A medieval nobleman in good standing would no more have thought of selling his land than a respectable honorary society or exclusive club today would think of selling memberships. Every society takes some objects of value and places them outside the orbit of transactions; for the Middle Ages, land was one of these.

And the same was true for labor. When we talk of the labor market today, we mean the endless bargaining process in which individuals sell their services to the highest bidder. There simply was no such process in the precapitalist world. There was a vast hodgepodge of serfs, apprentices, and journeymen who labored, but most of this labor never entered a market to be bought and sold. In the country, the peasant lived tied to his lord's estate; he baked at the lord's oven and ground at the lord's mill, tilled the lord's fields and served his lord in war, but he was rarely if ever paid for any of his services: these were his *duties* as a serf, not the "labor" of a freely contracting agent. In the towns the apprentice entered the service of a master; the length of his apprenticeship, the number of his colleagues, his rate of pay, his hours of work, the very methods he used were all regulated by a guild. There was little or no bargaining between servant and master except for sporadic strikes when conditions became intolerable. This was no more of a labor market than is provided by interns in a hospital.

Or take capital. Certainly capital existed in the precapitalist world, in the sense of private wealth. But although the funds existed, there was no impetus to put them to new and aggressive use. Instead of risk and change, the motto was safety first. Not the shortest and most efficient, but the longest and most labor-consuming process was the preferred technique of production. Advertising was forbidden and the idea that one master guildsman might produce a better product than his colleagues was regarded as treasonable. In sixteenth-century England, when mass production in the weaving trade first reared its ugly head, the guilds protested to the king. The wonder workshop—two hundred looms and a service staff including butchers and bakers to take care of the working force—was thereupon outlawed by His Majesty: such efficiency and concentration of wealth would set a bad precedent.

Hence the fact that the medieval world could not conceive the market system rested on the good and sufficient reason that it had not yet conceived the abstract elements of production itself. Lacking land, labor, and capital, the Middle Ages lacked the market; and lacking the market (despite its colorful local marts and traveling fairs), society ran by custom and tradition. The lords gave orders and production waxed and waned accordingly. Where no orders were given, life went on in its established groove. . . .

There would be nothing for any economist to do for several centuries—until this great self-reproducing, self-sufficient world erupted into the bustling, scurrying, free-for-all of the eighteenth century. "Erupted" is perhaps too dramatic a word, for the change would take place over centuries rather than in a single violent spasm. But the change, long drawn out though it was, was not a peaceful evolution; it was an agonized convulsion of society, a revolution.

Just to commercialize the land—to convert the hierarchy of social relationships into so many vacant lots and advantageous sites—required nothing less than the uprooting of an entrenched feudal way of life. To make "workers" out of the sheltered serfs and apprentices—no matter how exploitative the cloak of paternalism may have been—required the creation of a frightened disoriented class called the proletariat. To make capitalists out of guild masters meant that the laws of the jungle had to be taught to the timid denizens of the barnyard.

Hardly a peaceful prospect, any of this. Nobody *wanted* this commercialization of life. How bitterly it was resisted can only be appreciated if we take one last journey back to watch the economic revolution taking place.

We are back in France: the year, 1666.

The capitalists of the day face a disturbing challenge which the widening market mechanism has inevitably brought in its wake: change.

The question has come up whether a guild master of the weaving industry should be allowed to try an innovation in his product. The verdict: "If a cloth weaver intends to process a piece according to his own invention, he must not set it on the loom, but should obtain permission from the judges of the town to employ the number and length of threads that he desires, after the question has been considered by four of the oldest merchants and four of the oldest weavers of the guild." One can imagine how many suggestions for change were tolerated.

Shortly after the matter of cloth weaving has been disposed of, the button-makers guild raises a cry of outrage; the tailors are beginning to make buttons out of cloth, an unheard-of thing. The government, indignant that an innovation should threaten a settled industry, imposes a fine on the cloth-button makers and even on those who wear cloth buttons. But the wardens of the button guild are not yet satisfied. They demand the right to search people's homes and wardrobes and even to arrest them on the streets if they are seen wearing these subversive goods.

And this dread of change and innovation is not just the comic resistance of a few frightened merchants. Capital is fighting in earnest against change, and no holds are barred. In England a revolutionary patent for a stocking frame is not only denied in 1623, but the Privy Council orders the dangerous contraption abolished. In France the importation of printed calicoes is threatening to undermine the clothing industry. It is met with measures which cost the lives of sixteen thousand people! In Valence alone on one occasion 77 persons are sentenced to be hanged, 58 broken on the wheel, 631 sent to the galleys, and one lone and lucky individual set free for the crime of dealing in forbidden calico wares.

But capital is not the only agent of production which is frantically seeking to avoid the dangers of the market way of life. What is happening to labor is still more desperate.

Let us turn back to England.

It is the end of the sixteenth century, the great era of English expansion and adventure. Queen Elizabeth has made a triumphal tour of her kingdom. But she returns with a strange plaint. "Paupers are everywhere!" she cries.

Masters gather to discuss gild policy. In this case they are the directors of a seventeenth-century Dutch wine handlers gild painted by Ferdinand Bol.

This is a strange observation, for only a hundred years before, the English countryside consisted in large part of peasant proprietors tilling their own lands, the yeoman, the pride of England, the largest body of independent, free, and prosperous citizens in the world. Now, "Paupers are everywhere!" What has happened in the interim?

What has happened has been an enormous movement of expropriation—or, rather, the beginning of such a movement, for it was then only in its inception. Wool has become a new, profitable commodity, and wool demands grazing pastures for the wool producer. The pastures are made by enclosing the common land; the patchwork crazy quilt of small scattered holdings (unfenced and recognizable only by a tree here and a rock there dividing one man's land from another) and the common lands on which all might graze their cattle or gather peat, are suddenly declared to be all the property of the lord of the manor and no longer available to the whole parish. Where before was a kind of communality of ownership, now there is private property. Where there were yeomen, now there are sheep. One John Hales in 1549 wrote: "... where XL persons had their lyvings, now one man and his shepherd hath all. ... Yes, those shepe is the cause of all theise meschieves, for they have driven husbandrie out of the countries, by the which was encreased before all kynde of victuall, and now altogether shepe, shepe."

It is almost impossible to imagine the scope and impact of the process of enclosure. As early as the middle of the sixteenth century riots had broken out against it: in one such uprising, 3,500 people were killed. By the mid-eighteenth century, the process was still in full swing; not until the mid-nineteenth would it run its terrible historic course. Thus in 1820, nearly fifty years after the American Revolution, the Duchess of Sutherland dispossessed 15,000 tenants from 794,000 acres of land, replaced them with 131,000 sheep, and by way of compensation rented her evicted families an average of two acres of submarginal land each.

But it was not merely the wholesale land-grabbing which warrants attention. The tragedy is what happened to the yeoman. Driven off the land, he was at a total loss. He could not become a wage earner in the modern sense, for there were no factories ready to receive him, and nothing like large-scale industry available to absorb him. Deprived of his independent farm, the yeoman became a robber, beggar, vagabond, pauper, a miserable agricultural laborer, or a tenant. Terrified at the flood of pauperism throughout the country, the English Parliament tried to deal with the problem by localizing it. It

tied paupers to their parishes for a pittance of relief and dealt with wanderers by whipping, branding, and mutilation. A social reformer of the time of Adam Smith seriously proposed to deal with the migrant pauper by confining him to institutions for which he candidly suggested the name Houses of Terror. But what was worst of all was that the very measures which the country took to protect itself from the pauper—tying him to his local parish where he could be kept alive on poor relief—prevented the only possible solution to the problem. It was not that the English ruling classes were utterly heartless and cruel. Rather, they failed to understand the concept of a fluid, mobile labor force which would seek work wherever work was to be found according to the dictates of the market. At every step, the commercialization of labor, like the commercialization of capital, was feared, fought, and misconceived.

The market system with its essential components of land, labor, and capital was born in agony—an agony that began in the thirteenth century and did not run its course until well into the nineteenth. Never was a revolution less well understood, less welcomed, less planned. But the great market-making forces would not be denied. Insidiously they ripped apart the mold of custom, insolently they tore away the usages of tradition. For all the clamor of the button makers, cloth buttons won the day. For all the action of the Privy Council, the stocking frame became so valuable that in another seventy years the same Privy Council would forbid its exportation. For all the breakings on the wheel, the trade in calicoes increased apace. Over last-ditch opposition from the Old Guard, economic land was created out of ancestral estates, and over the wails of protest from employees and

masters alike, economic labor was ground out of unemployed apprentices and dispossessed farm laborers.

The great chariot of society, which for so long had run down the gentle slope of tradition, now found itself powered by an internal combustion machine. Transactions, transactions, transactions and gain, gain, gain provided a new and startlingly powerful motive force.

II

What forces could have been sufficiently powerful to smash a comfortable and established world and institute in its place this new unwanted society?

There was no single massive cause. The new way of life grew inside the old, like a butterfly inside a chrysalis, and when the stir of life was strong enough it burst the old structure asunder. It was not great events, single adventures, individual laws, or powerful personalities which brought about the economic revolution. It was a process of internal growth.

First, there was the gradual emergence of national political units in Europe. Under the blows of peasant wars and kingly conquest, the isolated existence of early feudalism gave way to centralized monarchies. And with monarchies came the growth of the national spirit; in turn this meant royal patronage for favored industries, such as the great French tapestry works, and the development of armadas and armies with all their necessary satellite industries. The infinity of rules and regulations which plagued Andreas Ryff and his fellow sixteenth-century traveling merchants gave way to common laws, common measurements, common currency.

An aspect of the political change which was revolutionizing Europe was the encouragement of foreign adventure and exploration. In the thirteenth century, the brothers Polo went as unprotected merchants on their daring journey into the land of the great Khan; in the fifteenth century Columbus sailed for what he hoped would be the same destination under the royal auspices of Isabella. The change from private to national exploration was part and parcel of the change from private to national life. And in turn the great national adventures of the English and Spanish and Portuguese sailor-capitalists brought a flood of treasure and treasure-consciousness back to Europe. "Gold," Christopher Columbus had said, "is a wonderful thing! Whoever possesses it is master of everything he desires. With gold one can even get souls into heaven." The sentiments of Christopher Columbus were the sentiments of an age and hastened the advent of a society oriented toward gain and chance and activated by the chase after money. Be it noted, in passing, that the treasures of the East were truly fabulous. With the share received as a stockholder in Sir Francis Drake's voyage of the *Golden Hynd,* Queen Elizabeth paid off all England's foreign debts, balanced its budget, and invested abroad a sum large enough, at compound interest, to account for Britain's entire overseas wealth in 1930!

A second great current of change was to be found in the slow decay of the religious spirit under the impact of the skeptical, inquiring, humanist views of the Italian Renaissance. The world of Today elbowed aside the world of Tomorrow, and as life on earth became more important, so did the notion of material standards and ordinary comforts. Behind the change in religious tolerance was the rise of Protestantism, which hastened a new attitude toward work and wealth. The

Church of Rome had always regarded the merchant with a dubious eye and had not hesitated to call usury a sin. But now that this merchant was every day climbing in society, now that he was no longer a mere useful appendage but an integral part of a new kind of world, some re-evaluation of his function became necessary. The Protestant leaders paved the way for an amalgamation of spiritual and temporal life. Far from eulogizing the life of poverty and spiritual contemplation, as separate from worldly life, it became the part of positive piety to make the most of one's God-given talents in daily business. Acquisitiveness became a recognized virtue—not immediately for one's private enjoyment, but for the greater glory of God. From here it was only a step to the identification of riches with spiritual excellence, and of rich men with saintly ones.

In the twelfth century a local folk take tells of a usurer about to be married who was crushed by a falling statue as he was entering the church. On examination, the statue was also of a usurer, thus revealing God's displeasure with dealers in money. Even in the mid-1600s, as we may remember, poor Robert Keane collided head on with the Puritan religious authorities because of his business practices. In such an atmosphere of hostility, it was not easy for the market system to expand. Hence the gradual acceptance by the spiritual leaders of the innocuousness, indeed the benefits, of the market way was essential for the full growth of the system.

Still another deep current lies in the slow social changes which eventually made the market system possible. We are accustomed to thinking of the Middle Ages as a time of stagnation and lack of progress. Yet in five hundred years, the medievalists fathered one

thousand towns (an immense achievement), connected them with rudimentary but usable roads, and maintained their populations with food brought from the countryside. All this developed the familiarity with money and markets and the buying and selling way of life.

Progress was not only a matter of this slow urbanization. There was technical progress, too, of a vastly important sort. The commercial revolution could not begin until some form of rational money-accounting had developed; although the Venetians of the twelfth century were already using sophisticated accounting devices, the merchants in Europe were little better than schoolboys in their accounting ignorance. It took time for the recognition of the need for bookkeeping to spread; not until the seventeenth century was double entry a standard practice. And not until money was rationally accounted for could large-scale business operations run successfully.

Perhaps most important of all in the pervasiveness of its effect was a rise in scientific curiosity. Although the world would wait until the age of Adam Smith for its cataclysmic burst of technology, the Industrial Revolution could not have taken place had not the ground been prepared by a succession of basic subindustrial discoveries. The precapitalist era saw the birth of the printing press, the paper mill, the windmill, the mechanical clock, the map, and a host of other inventions. The idea of invention itself took hold; experimentation and innovation were looked on for the first time with a friendly eye.

No single one of these currents, acting by itself, could have turned society upside down. Indeed, many of them may have been as much the effects as the causes of a great convulsion in human organization. History turns no sharp corners, and the whole vast upheaval sprawled out over time. Evidences of the market way of life sprang up side by side with older traditional ways, and remnants of the former day persisted long after the market had for all practical purposes taken over as the guiding principle of economic organization. Thus guilds and feudal privileges were not finally abolished in France until 1790, and the Statute of Artificers which regulated guild practices in England was not repealed until 1813.

But by the year 1700, twenty-three years before Adam Smith was born, the world which had tried Robert Keane, prohibited merchants from carrying unsightly bundles, worried over "just" prices, and fought for the privilege of carrying on in its fathers' footsteps was on the wane. In its place society has begun to heed a new set of "self-evident" dicta. Some of them are:

> Every man is naturally covetous of lucre.
>
> No laws are prevalent against gaine.
>
> Gaine is the Centre of the Circle of Commerce.

A new idea has come into being: "economic man"—a pale wraith of a creature who follows his adding-machine brain wherever it leads him. The textbooks will soon come to talk of Robinson Crusoes on desert isles who will organize their affairs as if they were so many penny-pinching accountants.

In the world of affairs a new fever of wealth and speculation has gripped Europe. In France in 1718 a Scottish adventurer named John Law organized a wild blue-sky venture known as the Mississippi Company, selling shares in an enterprise which would mine the mountains

of gold in America. Men and women fought in the streets for the privilege of winning shares, murders were committed, fortunes made overnight. One hotel waiter netted thirty million *livres*. When the company was about to topple with frightful losses for all investors, the government sought to stave off disaster by rounding up a thousand beggars, arming them with picks and shovels, and marching them through the streets of Paris as a band of miners off for the Land of Eldorado. Of course the structure collapsed. But what a change from the timid capitalists of a hundred years ago to the get-rich-quick mobs jostling in the Rue de Quincampoix; what a money-hungry public this must have been to swallow such a bare-faced fraud!

No mistake about it, the travail was over and the market system had been born. The problem of survival was henceforth to be solved neither by custom nor by command, but by the free action of profit-seeking men bound together only by the market itself. The system was to be called capitalism. And the idea of gain which underlay it was so firmly rooted that men would soon vigorously affirm that it was an eternal and omnipresent attitude.

Population and Food Supply

From pp. 83–85, *Western Civilization: The Struggle for Empire to Europe in the Modern World,* edited by William Langer. Copyright © 1968 by William Langer, Paul MacKendrick, Deno J. Geanakoplos, J. H. Hexter, and Richard Pipes. By permission of Harper & Row, publishers.

In the early modern era Europe found that it had to produce more food and clothing than it had in the late Middle Ages, simply because there were more people to feed and clothe. Although it is not possible to measure the population increase that occurred in early modern Europe with anywhere near the accuracy with which present-day demographers measure trends, it is known that the general pattern was one of gradual and relatively steady growth for about two hundred years after 1450. The rate of growth would have been more striking were it not that periods of turmoil—civil wars, foreign invasion, and famines caused by bad weather and ravaging armies—reduced the populations of several countries at various times. Germany during the Thirty Years' War, France during the Wars of Religion and the War of the Spanish Succession, and Russia during the Time of Troubles after the death of Ivan the Terrible, all suffered major declines in population. In the 1600s population growth appears to have become irregular all over Europe, and until well after 1700 it was spotty and subject to local reverses. England continued a slow growth, and Spain underwent a steady decline throughout the sixteenth century. Nowhere, however, did the population fall back to the low levels of the early fifteenth century.

Sometime after 1700 a general upswing in population began. By 1750 almost all Europe was more thickly settled than ever before in its history. From the Urals to the Atlantic, Europe was on the verge of a population explosion that was to continue with increasing force for more than a hundred years. At the beginning of the eighteenth century, it

EUROPEAN POPULATION FIGURES

	1700	1800	% OF INCREASE
France	19	27	42
Germany	15	25	67
Russia	12	30	150
		(expanded boundaries)	
Italy	11	18.1	65
England, Wales, Scotland	6.7	10.5	57
Spain	6	10.5	75

Accurate population in figures is difficult to obtain. These figures (in millions) are taken from R. R. Palmer, *Atlas of World History* (New York: Rand McNally and Company, 1957), p. 193.

is doubtful that there were 20 percent more Frenchmen than there had been four hundred years before, but during that century, up to the outbreak of the Revolution in 1789, the population of France increased almost 45 percent. More significant than the gross increase was the rate of growth. In France the population was growing ten times as rapidly in the eighteenth century as it had grown in the previous four centuries. Give or take a little, the same pattern of a steeply rising rate of population growth held true for the whole Western world. . . .

The increased population of Europe had, naturally, to be fed, but the increase in demand does not seem to have led to any general improvement in farming methods up to the beginning of the eighteenth century. Except in a few areas, the three-field system and three-crop rotation—spring crop and winter crop of grain for human consumption followed by a year when the fields lay fallow—persisted in Europe's richest farm lands, so that each year a third of the best soil produced nothing but scanty pasturage for cattle.

The overseas expansion of Europe added somewhat to the available food supply. Three of the most important overseas products that the European learned to enjoy—coffee, tea, and tobacco—did not, however, add to his stock of nourishment, though they undoubtedly increased his pleasures in life. America's most revolutionary contribution to European diet and agriculture, the potato, was long considered by many a decorative but inedible plant. As late as 1700, only two American products contributed much to the nourishment of Europe—cane from the Caribbean islands, and cod from the Grand Bank of Newfoundland and the New England coast. The products of the cane benefited the European in three ways. Sugar sweetened his tea and coffee, rum warmed his stomach and lightened his head, and molasses mixed with sulphur supposedly cured him of many ills. The North Atlantic cod, dried or salted, served a double purpose. The better part of the catch supplemented the North Sea salt herring and helped provide Europeans with fish when the supply of salt meat gave out in Lent. The worse part—the refuse—helped to keep the Negro slaves of the Caribbean alive and thus ensured the production of sugar. . . .

The growth of Europe's population was limited not only by the slow increase of the food supply, but by high infant mortality, high childbearing mortality for mothers, and low adult resistance to the ravages of diseases. Drastic population growth waited on radical improvement in farming methods to raise yields per acre and per farm worker and on the adoption of elementary sanitary measures in midwifery and infant care.

Profit-Seeking and the Mississippi Bubble

The "Mississippi Bubble" is the name given the period of wild stock speculation in France from 1717 to 1720. John Law (1671–1729), a persuasive Scotsman, gained the approval of the debt-ridden French government to seek financial recovery by increasing trade rather than by the usual tactic of repudiating the debt. Among other measures, he organized the Company of the West (Mississippi Company), which was granted a monopoly of trade with the Louisiana Territory. Government creditors were pressured to convert their notes into Company stock that, under the glowing promises of immense profits circulated by Law, rapidly rose in value. The scheme offered advantages for all involved: the government was able to retire much of its indebtedness while creditors could expect a profit greater than the interest on the notes they had surrendered. Law's propaganda, however, led to incredible speculation as Frenchmen of all classes hastened to get some of the easy money. Within two years shares of the Company stock rose 3000 percent over their original selling price, until the realization that they could not possibly earn enough to justify their cost brought a sudden collapse. The money hunger of the day and its social impact is apparent in this early nineteenth-century account. From J. P. Wood, *Memoirs of the Life of John Law of Lauriston* (Edinburgh, 1824), pp. 118–120, 121–122.

A footman had gained so much that he provided himself with a fine carriage; but the first day it came to the door, he, instead of stepping into the vehicle, mounted up to his old station behind. Another, in a similar predicament, brought himself well off by pretending he got up only to see if there was room on the back for two or three more lackeys, whom he was resolved to hire instantly. Mr. Law's coachman had made so great a fortune that he asked a dismission from his service, which was readily granted, on condition of procuring another as good as himself. The man thereupon brought two coachmen to his master, they were both excellent drivers, and desired him to make choice of one, at the same time saying that he would take the other for his own carriage. One night at the opera, a Mademoiselle de Begond, observing a lady enter magnificently dressed, and covered with diamonds, jogged her mother, and said, "I am much mistaken if this fine lady is not Mary, our cook." The report spread through the theatre, till it came to the ears of the lady, who, coming up to Madame de Begond, said, "I am indeed Mary your cook, I have gained large sums in the rue Quincampoix [stock market]. I love fine clothes and fine jewels, and am accordingly dressed in them. I have paid for everything, am in debt to nobody, and pray what has any person in this place to say to this?" At another time, some persons of quality beholding a gorgeous figure alight from a most splendid equipage, and inquiring what great lady that was, one of her lackeys answered, "A woman who has tumbled from a garret into a carriage." One of these upstarts, finding himself enriched beyond his utmost expectations, hastened to a coachmaker's and ordered a berlin to be made in the finest taste, lined with the richest crimson velvet and gold fringe, and went away after leaving 4,000 livres as earnest. The coachmaker running after him to inquire what arms were to be put on the carriage, was answered, "Oh, *the finest—the finest* by all means." . . .

It may, perhaps, require some explanation how so many low persons should acquire large fortunes from nothing, in so short a time; but, independent of the rise in the price of actions, various, indeed, were the ways of doing so during the Mississippi contagion. Some, either unable or unwilling to go to the rue Quincampoix to dispose of their shares, trusted them to others, who received orders to sell for a certain sum. On their arrival, they commonly found the price risen, and without scruple put the price in their own pockets. A gentleman, falling sick, sent his servant to dispose of 250 shares for 8,000 livres each; and he sold them at the rate of 10,000 livres, making a profit of 500,000 livres, which he appropriated to himself, and, by other lucky adventures, increased that sum to upwards of two millions. A person deputed to sell 200 shares for another, kept himself concealed for some days, during which time their price rose so high that he cleared near a million of livres of profit, giving back to his employer, who had been hunting him in vain, only the market rate of the day on which he was sent to dispose of the actions. One De Josier, trusted with the like number of shares to sell for 550 livres each, disappeared, but coming back when the system was at its height, profited immensely.

STUDY QUESTIONS

1. Why is the problem of economic survival so complex? How has man met the problem over the centuries?

2. What is meant by the market system? Why was it considered revolutionary in comparison with practices in the past? Why was personal gain (profit motive) generally suspect in the traditional world?

3. Why are modern concepts of land, labor, and capital essential for the development of a market system? How do these modern concepts differ from those in traditional society?

4. How does Heilbroner explain the appearance and growth of the market system?

Lewis Mumford: The Religion of the Machine

During the last thousand years the material basis and the cultural forms of Western Civilization have been profoundly modified by the development of the machine. How did this come about? Where did it take place? What were the chief motives that encouraged this radical transformation of the environment and the routine of life: what were the ends in view: what were the means and methods: what unexpected values have arisen in the process? These are some of the questions that the present study seeks to answer.

While people often call our period the "Machine Age," very few have any perspective on modern technics or any clear notion as to its origins. Popular historians usually date the great transformation in modern industry from Watt's supposed invention of the steam engine; and in the conventional economics textbook the application of automatic machinery to spinning and weaving is often treated as an equally critical turning point. But the fact is that in Western Europe the machine had been developing steadily for at least seven centuries before the dramatic changes that accompanied the "industrial revolution" took place. Men had become mechanical before they perfected complicated machines to express their new bent and interest; and the will-to-order had appeared once more in the monastery and the army and the counting-house before it finally manifested itself in the factory. Behind all the great material inventions of the last century and a half was not merely a long internal development of technics: there was also a change of mind. Before the new industrial processes could take hold on a great scale, a reorientation of wishes, habits, ideas, goals was necessary.

To understand the dominating role played by technics in modern civilization, one must explore in detail the preliminary period of ideological and social preparation. Not merely must one explain the existence of new mechanical instruments: one must explain the culture that was ready to use them and profit by them so extensively. For note this: mechanization and regimentation are not new phenomena in history: what is new is the fact that these functions have been projected and embodied in organized forms which dominate every aspect of our existence. Other civilizations reached a high degree of technical proficiency without, apparently, being profoundly influenced by the methods and aims of technics. All the critical instruments of modern technology—the clock, the printing press, the water-mill, the magnetic compass, the loom, the lathe, gunpowder, paper, to say nothing of mathematics and chemistry and mechanics—existed in other cultures. The Chinese, the Arabs, the Greeks, long before the Northern European, had taken most of the first steps toward the machine. And although the great engineering works of the Cretans, the Egyptians, and the Romans were carried

---

THE PROCESS OF ECONOMIC MODERNIZATION

The growing market for goods placed increasing strain on traditional methods of production. The machine and the rational organization of production within the modern factory system was the answer to the demand for greater productivity. It is the combination of these elements, and new sources of power, that created what is frequently called the "Industrial Revolution." As the readings below indicate, however, neither the machine nor the factory is a modern invention. Rather it was their intensive and efficient exploitation to meet new needs that marks a radical departure from the past. The readings that follow examine the process of eighteenth-century economic modernization and the new social group it brought to power.

out mainly on an empirical basis, these peoples plainly had an abundance of technical skill at their command. They had machines; but they did not develop "the machine." It remained for the peoples of Western Europe to carry the physical sciences and the exact arts to a point no other culture had reached, and to adapt the whole mode of life to the pace and the capacities of the machine. How did this happen? How in fact could the machine take possession of European society until that society had, by an inner accommodation, surrendered to the machine?

Plainly, what is usually called *the* industrial revolution, the series of industrial changes that began in the eighteenth century, was a transformation that took place in the course of a much longer march. . . .

THE DUTY TO INVENT

The principles that had proved effective in the development of the scientific method were, with appropriate changes, those that served as a foundation for invention. Technics is a translation into appropriate, practical forms of the theoretic truths, implicit or formulated, anticipated or discovered, of science. Science and technics form two independent yet related worlds: sometimes converging, sometimes drawing apart. . . .

The unwillingness to accept the natural environment as a fixed and final condition of man's existence had always contributed both to his art and his technics: but from the seventeenth century, the attitude became compulsive, and it was to technics that he turned for fulfillment. Steam engines displaced horse power, iron and concrete displaced wood, aniline dyes replaced vegetable dyes, and so on down the line, with here and there a gap. Sometimes the new product was superior practically or esthetically to the old, as in the infinite superiority of the electric lamp over the tallow candle: sometimes the new product remained inferior in quality, as rayon is still inferior to natural silk: but in either event the gain was in the creation of an equivalent product or synthesis which was less dependent upon uncertain organic variations and irregularities in either the product itself or the labor applied to it than was the original.

Often the knowledge upon which the displacement was made was insufficient and the result was sometimes disastrous. The history of the last thousand years abounds in examples of apparent mechanical and scientific triumphs which were fundamentally unsound. One need only mention bleeding in medicine, the use of common window glass which excluded the important ultra-violet rays, the establishment of the post-Liebig dietary on the basis of mere energy replacement, the use of the elevated toilet seat, the introduction of steam heat, which dries the air excessively—but the list is a long and somewhat appalling one. The point is that invention had become a duty, and the desire to use the new marvels of technics, like a child's delighted bewilderment over new toys, was not in the main guided by critical discernment: people agreed that inventions were good, whether or not they actually provided benefits, just as they agreed that childbearing was good, whether the offspring proved a blessing to society or a nuisance. . . .

The religion of the machine needed such support as little as the transcendental faiths it supplanted: for the mission of religion is to provide an ultimate significance and motive-force: the necessity of invention was a dogma, and the ritual of a mechanical routine was the binding element in the faith. In the eighteenth century, Mechanical Societies sprang into existence, to propagate the creed with greater zeal: they preached the gospel of work, justification by faith in mechanical science, and salvation by the machine. Without the missionary enthusiasm of the enterprisers and industrialists and engineers and even the untutored mechanics from the eighteenth century onward, it would be impossible to explain the rush of converts and the accelerated tempo of mechanical improvement. The impersonal procedure of science, the hard-headed contrivances of mechanics, the rational calculus of the utilitarians—these interests captured emotion, all the more because the golden paradise of financial success lay beyond. . . .

PRACTICAL ANTICIPATIONS

From the beginning, the practical value of science was uppermost in the minds of its exponents, even in those who single-mindedly pursued abstract truth, and who were as indifferent to its popularization as Gauss and Weber, the scientists who invented the telegraph for their private communication. "If my judgment be of any weight," said Francis Bacon in *The Advancement of Learning*, "the use of history mechanical is of all others the most radical and fundamental towards natural philosophy: such natural philosophy as shall not vanish in the fume of subtile, sublime, or delectable speculation, but such as shall be operative to the endowment and benefit of man's life." And Descartes, in his *Discourse on Method*, observes: "For by them [general restrictions respecting physics] I perceived it to be possible to arrive at knowledge highly useful in life . . . and thus render ourselves the lords and possessors of nature. And this is a result to be desired, not only in order to the invention of an infinity of arts, by which we might be able to enjoy without any trouble the fruits of the earth, and all its comforts, but also especially for the preservation of health, which is without doubt of all blessings of this life the first and fundamental one. . . ."

So confident in the results of the new approach was Hooke that he wrote: "There is nothing that lies within the power of human wit (or which is far more effectual) of human industry which we might not compass; we might not only hope for inventions to equalize those of Copernicus, Galileo, Gilbert, Harvey, and others, whose names are almost lost, that were the inventors of Gunpowder, the Seaman's Compass, Printing, Etching, Graving, Microscopes, Etc., but multitudes that may far exceed them: for even those discovered seem to have been the product of some such methods though but imperfect; what may not be therefore expected from it if thoroughly prosecuted? Talking and contention of Arguments would soon be turned into labors; all the fine dreams and opinions and universal metaphysical nature, which the luxury of subtle brains has devised, would quickly vanish and give place to solid histories, experiments, and works. . . ."

By the seventeenth century the note of confidence had increased, and the practical impulse had become more universal and urgent. The works of Porta, Cardan, Besson, Ramelli, and other ingenious inventors, engineers, and mathematicians are a witness both to increasing skill and to growing enthusiasm over technics itself. . . . "To them that come after us," said Glanvill, "it may be as ordinary to buy a pair of wings to fly to remotest regions, as now a pair of boots to ride a journey; and to confer at the distance of the Indies by sympathetic conveyances may be as usual in future times as by literary correspondence." Cyrano de Bergerac conceived the phonograph. Hooke observed that it is "not impossible to hear a whisper a furlong's distance, it having been already done; and perhaps the nature of things would not make it more impossible, although that furlong be ten times multiplied." Indeed, he even forecast the invention of artificial silk. And Glanvill said again: "I doubt not posterity will find many things that are now but rumors verified into practical realities. It may be that, some ages hence, a voyage to the Southern tracts, yea, possibly to the moon, will not be more strange than one to America. . . . The restoration of grey hairs to juvenility and the renewing the exhausted marrow may at length be effected without a miracle; and the turning of the now comparatively desert world into a paradise may not improbably be effected from late agriculture." (1661)

Technology and the Industrial Revolution

From William H. McNeill, *The Rise of the West, A History of the Human Community* (Chicago: University of Chicago Press, 1963). Copyright © 1963 by the University of Chicago Press.

The advance of technology, which gathered speed throughout the seventeenth and eighteenth centuries, played a direct and tangible role in remaking society. Technology affected men's lives bit by bit, without any over-all plan or deliberate purpose of reordering society. Yet some thinkers proclaimed a firm faith in the beneficent effect of just such piecemeal technical change. The English empirical tradition proved particularly hospitable to such an outlook; for such men as Francis Bacon (d. 1626) and the founders of the Royal Society (1660) looked forward with complete confidence to the benefits they expected to arise from technical improvements arrived at through careful observation and experiment. Yet, in fact, it was only slowly that scientific theory came to have much bearing upon the processes of economic production. Until chemistry achieved a precision which it lacked in the eighteenth century, abstract science had little to contribute to the industrial arts. But theory was not really needed. Rough-and-ready empiricism, finding expression in a general willingness to reconsider traditional practices, to tinker with new devices, and to try different procedures, materials, or tools, was quite enough to work cumulatively enormous changes in European technology; and the rate of such advance was vastly accelerated by the new custom of recording, measuring, comparing, and publishing results in professional journals.

Most basic of all economic activities was agriculture; and here such simple procedures as systematic selection of seed, careful breeding of animals for specific traits, and the introduction or spread of new crops like clover, turnips, potatoes, maize, cotton, and tobacco worked enormous increases in the productivity of farm land. Deliberate tests to discover the best shapes for plowshares and other implements promoted the efficiency of cultivation. Gentlemen farmers systematically and enthusiastically explored the benefits of repeated tillage, elimination of weeds, tile drainage, and application of manures and other fertilizers. England took the lead in this development; for English landowners were in a position to impose new methods upon farm laborers; whereas in most other parts of Europe, a routine-bound peasantry continued to adhere to old methods and only slowly adopted improved agricultural techniques.

Road and canal construction were much improved by the same trial-and-error procedure, although here government initiative was far more important than it was in agricultural development. France led the way in constructing tolerable all-weather roads and a canal system that linked the major rivers of the country into an interlocking pattern of navigable waterways. England followed suit only toward the close of the eighteenth century, while the rest of Europe (except Holland) lagged appreciably behind. Ship, wagon, and passenger coach construction improved steadily; and railroad cars, drawn either by men or by horses, came into general use for short hauls of heavy or bulky materials.

As in earlier times, mining constituted a major growth point for technology. By the eighteenth century, English coal mines took over the technical leadership formerly held by Germans. As shafts were sunk deeper into the ground and the scale of coal mining increased, the need for heavy machinery for hoists and for pumps to keep the pits from flooding taxed engineering ingenuity. The need for powerful prime movers spurred experiments with steam engines. As a result, Thomas Newcomen's engine (1712) led to the first practicable use of coal to energize pumping systems for the mines. During the following decades, the usefulness of these engines increased with improvements in details of their construction and a rapid increase in

their size and power. Then in the 1760's, James Watt revolutionized steam engine design by driving a piston with live steam. He patented his invention in 1769; but in the following decades diversifications of design, together with the adaptation of his engine for uses other than pumping, greatly increased its value.

The practical success of steam engines depended upon techniques for shaping metal accurately, so that piston and cylinder walls could be made to match closely enough to prevent serious loss of pressure. These and other technical problems were solved practically, rather than theoretically, by a small bank of ingenious artificers and mechanics with little or no formal scientific training. Nevertheless, the routine of the workshop itself constituted a type of training, and in fact the co-ordination of human activity necessary to the large-scale production of such complicated machinery as a steam engine was at least as significant as technological details of the new invention. Scores and soon hundreds of men had to be disciplined to make a large variety of metal parts that would ultimately fit together into an engine: this required precise measurement at every stage of manufacture and the skilful use of file and calipers until just the right dimensions had been achieved. Ancient individual artisan skills of hand and eye were, in effect, linked together to produce an end result that no single man could achieve without an extravagant expenditure of time. And this linkage was itself created by an unprecedentedly abstract and precise mesh of dimensional specifications for the separate parts—valves and valve seats, pistons and cylinders, rods and bearings—that, when assembled, made a steam engine that really worked.

Metallurgy also underwent fundamental development, again primarily in England,

where the shortage of wood for charcoal had long hindered steelmaking. During the second half of the eighteenth century, the use of coke as a substitute fuel solved this problem for the steel industry. Other technical improvements permitted a more uniform quality and increased scale of production; and as steel became cheaper, it found new uses in bridge building and structural work as well as for machinery. Thus England and Scotland were already plunging headlong toward the age of coal and iron when the French Revolution began.

The most spectacular technical development, however, was reserved to the textile trades, where a series of inventions, from John Kay's flying shuttle (1733) to Samuel Crompton's spinning mule (1774), made possible the mechanization of spinning and weaving and thereby enormously mutiplied rates of output while cheapening the finished cloth. The cotton industry, which was new in England and thus uninhibited by long artisan tradition, most readily adopted these new processes. As a result, by the last decades of the eighteenth century, English cotton cloth was beginning to undersell the products of Indian looms, even in India itself.

England and Scotland thus began to surge ahead of the rest of Europe in important branches of technology. The Industrial Revolution, which was to remake the face of Europe and of the world, had begun. . . :

The Duty To Invent

The brief selection from Daniel Defoe's *Robinson Crusoe*, published in 1719, provides a hint of how this best-selling novel (four editions within the first four months of publication) reflected the interests and attitudes of the English reading public. The passage describes Crusoe's outlook after his shipwreck on the deserted island. In the second selection Anglican minister Edmund Cartwright (1743–1823) explains how he came to invent the prototype of the modern loom. I. From Daniel Defoe, *The Life and Strange Surprising Adventures of Robinson Crusoe of York, Mariner* (London, 1719), pp. 79–81. II. From Richard Guest, *A Compendious History of the Cotton Manufacture* (London, 1823), pp. 44–45.

I. ROBINSON CRUSOE MASTERS LIFE ON A DESERT ISLAND (1719)

Having now brought my mind a little to relish my condition, and given over looking out to sea to see if I could spy a ship; I say, giving over these things, I began to apply myself to accommodate my way of living, and to make things as easy to me as I could. . . .

So I went to work; and here I must needs observe, that as reason is the substance and original of the mathematicks, so by stating and squaring every thing by reason, and by making the most rational judgment of things, every man may be in time master of every mechanick art. I had never handled a tool in my life, and yet in time, by labour, application, and contrivance, I found at last that I wanted nothing but I could have made it, especially if I had had tools; however, I made abundance of things, even without tools, and some with no more tools than an adze and a hatchet, which perhaps were never made that way before, and that with infinite labour. For example, if I wanted a board, I had no other way but to cut down a tree, set it on an edge before me, and hew it flat on either side with my axe, till I had brought it to be thin as a

plank, and then dubb it smooth with my adze. It is true, by this method I could make but one board out of a whole tree, but this I had no remedy for but patience, any more than I had for the prodigious deal of time and labour which it took me up to make a plank or board. But my time or labour was little worth, and so it was as well employ'd one way as another. . . .

II. THE REV. EDMUND CARTWRIGHT DESCRIBES HIS INVENTION OF THE POWER-LOOM (1785)

Happening to be at Matlock, in the summer of 1784, I fell in company with some gentlemen of Manchester, when the conversation turned on Arkwright's spinning machinery. One of the company observed, that as soon as Arkwright's patent expired, so many mills would be erected, and so much cotton spun, that hands never could be found to weave it. To this observation I replied that Arkwright must then set his wits to work to invent a weaving mill. This brought on a conversation on the subject, in which the Manchester gentlemen unanimously agreed that the thing was impracticable; in defence of their opinion, they adduced arguments which I certainly was incompetent to answer or even to comprehend, being totally ignorant of the subject, having never at that time seen a person weave. I controverted, however, the impracticability of the thing, by remarking that there

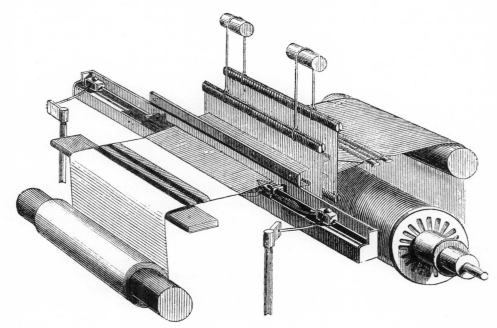

Cartwright's power-loom.

had lately been exhibited in London, an automaton figure, which played at chess. Now you will not assert, gentlemen, said I, that it is more difficult to construct a machine that shall weave, than one which shall make all the variety of moves which are required in that complicated game.

Some little time afterwards, a particular circumstance recalling this conversation to my mind, it struck me, that, as in plain weaving, according to the conception I then had of the business, there could only be three movements, which were to follow each other in succession, there would be little difficulty in producing and repeating them. Full of these ideas, I immediately employed a carpenter and smith to carry them into effect. As soon as the machine was finished, I got a weaver to put in the warp, which was of such materials as sail cloth is usually made of. To my great delight, a piece of cloth, such as it was, was the produce.

As I had never before turned my thoughts to anything mechanical, either in theory or practice, nor had ever seen a loom at work, or knew anything of its construction, you will readily suppose that my first loom must have been a most rude piece of machinery.

The warp was placed perpendicularly, the reed fell with a force of at least half an hundred weight, and the springs which threw the shuttle were strong enough to have thrown a Congreve rocket. In short, it required the strength of two powerful men to work the machine at a slow rate, and only for a short time. Conceiving in my great simplicity, that I had accomplished all that was required, I then secured what I thought a most valuable property, by a patent, 4 April, 1785. This being done, I then condescended to see how other people wove; and you will guess my astonishment, when I compared their easy modes of operation with mine. Availing myself, however, of what I then saw, I made a loom in its general principles, nearly as they are now made. But it was not till the year 1787, that I completed my invention, when I took out my last weaving patent, August 1st of that year.

Robert Bakewell Improves Cattle Breeding (1771)

Technical development occurred in agriculture as well as in industry. The rapid growth of population in the eighteenth century encouraged a search for means of increasing the production of food. Improved farm implements, more efficient methods of planting, and a better quality crop were some of the results of applied observation and experimentation. In this reading Arthur Young (1741–1820), a prominent publicist of the new methods, describes the astounding improvements in the breeding of cattle made by an English landowner. From Arthur Young, *The Farmer's Tour Through the East of England* (London, 1771), I, pp. 110–111.

Mr. Bakewell of Dishley, one of the most considerable farmers in this country, has in so many instances improved on the husbandry of his neighbors, that he merits particular notice in this journal.

His breed of cattle is famous throughout the kindgom; and he has lately sent many to *Ireland*. He has in this part of his business many ideas which I believe are perfectly new; or that have hitherto been totally neglected. This principle is to gain the beast, whether sheep or cow, that will weigh most in the most valuable joints:—there is a great difference between an ox of 50 stone [700 pounds], carrying 30 in roasting pieces, and 20 in coarse boiling ones—and another carrying 30 in the latter and 20 in the former. And at the same time that he gains the shape, that is, of the greatest value in the smallest compass; he asserts, from long experience, that he gains a breed much hardier, and easier fed than any others. These ideas he applies equally to sheep and oxen.

In the breed of the latter, the old notion was, that where you had much and large bones, there was plenty of room to lay flesh on; and accordingly the graziers were eager to buy the largest boned cattle. This whole system Mr. Bakewell has proved to be an utter mistake. He asserts, the smaller the bones, the truer will be the make of the beast—the quicker she will fat—and her weight, we may easily conceive, will have a larger proportion of valuable meat: *flesh*, not *bone*, is the butcher's object. Mr. Bakewell admits that a large boned beast, may be made a large fat beast, and that he may come to a great weight; but justly observes, that this is no part of the profitable enquiry; for stating such a simple proposition, without at the same time showing the expence of covering those bones with flesh, is offering no satisfactory argument. The only object of real importance, is the proportion of *grass* to *value*. I have 20 acres; which will pay me for those acres best, large or small boned cattle? The latter fat so much quicker, and more profitably in the joints of value; that the query is answered in their favour from long and attentive experience. . . .

Richard Arkwright Creates the Modern Factory (1768–1792)

Excerpted from *The Industrial Revolution in the Eighteenth Century* by Paul Mantoux, translated by Marjorie Vernon. Reprinted by permission of Harcourt, Brace & World, Inc. and the Executors of the Estate of Paul Mantoux. This is published in Canada by Jonathan Cape Limited.

Richard Arkwright was born at Preston on December 23rd, 1732, the youngest of a large and poor family. While still quite young, he was apprenticed to a barber and wig-maker, and just found time in which to learn to read and write. At fifty, he was taking lessons in grammar and spelling. In 1750, he set up at Bolton, a few miles from his native town, where for a long time he plied his trade of barber, first of all in a basement, and then in a very humble shop. He was twice married. His first wife came from Leigh, between Warrington and Bolton—a detail of some interest. The second brought him some money, which enabled him to leave his shop and to go in for a more paying occupation, that of a dealer in hair. He attended markets, and visited farms in order to buy the hair of country girls. He then treated it with a dye of his own making and resold it to the wig-makers who, in that century of wigs, were ready buyers.

This story of Arkwright's early life is not only interesting in itself, but gives us an insight into his character and thus helps us to judge of the part he actually played. We must first note that there is nothing about him which suggested an inventor's career. He had no technical experience, for he was not a weaver like John Kay and Hargreaves, or a carpenter and mechanic like Wyatt. He must have learnt everything he knew of the textile industry . . . through conversations in his barber's shop or during his rounds in Lancashire villages. On the other hand, he displayed very early those qualities which explain his success. He was anxious to better himself, he had fertile brains for devising means of rising

in the world, and he knew how to drive a good bargain. . . .

The origins of his main invention are wrapped in curious obscurity. . . . No end of ridiculous and conflicting stories, which he was careful never to deny, were circulated during his lifetime by his admirers. According to some people, the principle of the spinning machine had been suggested to him by a cylindrical wire-drawing machine. . . . According to others, he had studied at Derby the

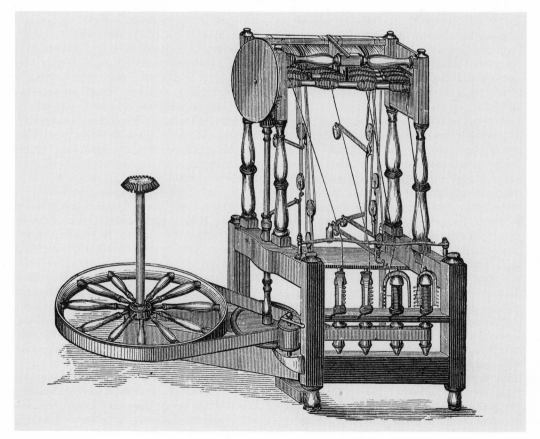

Arkwright's spinning-frame.

working of the silk-throwing machines, or, in his barber's shop, he had overheard a sailor describe a machine used by the Chinese. . . . While the history of the invention is so obscure, the story of Arkwright's ventures is clear and easy to follow. The machine was made, in 1768, in a room adjoining the Free Grammar School at Preston. Arkwright had enlisted the help of a Warrington clockmaker, a namesake of Kay the inventor of the fly shuttle. As we shall see, this collaboration accounts for many things. Apparently Arkwright had great difficulty in raising the necessary funds. He first turned to a scientific-instrument-maker, who refused to take him seriously, and then to one of his friends, a publican called John Smalley. The next year [1769] he took out his patent of invention, valid for fourteen years.

We can not only read the text of this patent, but also see the original model of the machine itself, preserved at the South Kensington Museum [London]. It is made entirely of wood, and is about thiry-two inches high. As far as we can judge, it is very like the machine invented in 1733 by John Wyatt, and improved by Lewis Paul. A wheel sets in motion four pairs of rollers of increasing rapidity of rotation. The top cylinder of each pair is covered with leather, whilst the lower one is ribbed or grooved lengthwise. After it has gone through the rollers, whose progressive acceleration stretches it more and more, the thread is twisted and wound on vertical spindles. Generally speaking, this machine only differs in its details from that of Wyatt. These trifling differences cannot explain Arkwright's triumphal success in a line where more ingenious men than he had been hopeless failures. His success was due to his business capacity, of which he gave proof almost at once.

It was, above all, necessary to raise capital. Smalley was not rich enough, and Arkwright already dreamed of big business. For this reason . . . he migrated to Nottingham. We know that this town was the center of the stocking-frame industry, in which a capitalistic organization had followed the development of mechanical equipment. Arkwright succeeded in interesting in his schemes the local bank of Wright Brothers. . . . But profits no doubt did not follow rapidly . . . for at the end of a year the Wrights withdrew their support. Arkwright knew how to extricate himself from his difficulties. In 1771 he entered into a contract with two rich hosiers, Need of Nottingham and Strutt of Derby. Need and Strutt belonged to the class of merchant manufacturers. They employed a large number of workers in their own homes, and also had workshops where stockings were knitted on frames. Thus it was on a system of production akin to "manufacture," if not on "manufacture" itself, that the factory system was grafted.

The first workshop set up by Arkwright at Nottingham was hardly larger than the one Wyatt and Paul had established in Birmingham thirty years before. It had but a few machines, which were worked by horses. It was in 1771, the year he joined forces with Need and Strutt, that Arkwright settled at Cromford, near Derby . . . on the Derwent [where water power was available]. . . . In a few years the Cromford spinning mill had grown up, and by 1779 it contained several thousand spindles and employed three hundred workmen.

That which made the success of the undertaking quite certain was not only the rapidity but the quality of the production. The new machine (the water frame as it was called, to distinguish it from the jenny, which was worked by hand) produced a much stronger thread than the most skilled spinner. . . . Instead, therefore, of weaving materials which were partly linen and only partly cotton, it became possible to weave pure cotton goods, which were as perfect, in every respect, as their Indian models. At first the Cromford factory was only an appendage to those of Need and Strutt. All the thread it spun was used solely for making stockings. But in 1773, Arkwright and his partners set up weaving workshops in Derby, where, for the first time, pure cotton calicoes were made. . . .

Here Arkwright ran into trouble. Jealous competitors appealed to the Act of 1735, which forbade the manufacture of pure cotton goods for excise reasons. Arkwright was forced to defend his industry before Parliament. Soon after this obstacle was overcome (1774), he ran into patent difficulties. One Thomas Highs charged that Arkwright had stolen his spinning machine from one he had made in 1767; John Kay, the clockmaker who had assisted Arkwright in his first model, testified on Highs' behalf. Highs, a born inventor without business acumen, came from Leigh, the home of Arkwright's first wife, and Arkwright had known him for years. The case continued until June, 1785, when the court condemned Arkwright and declared his patent to have lapsed. Thus it appears "that Arkwright's chief invention, to which he owed most of his wealth and fame, was not really his."

This trial, together with the judgment, would have utterly crushed any other man than Arkwright. But he was not so easily daunted. Deprived of his patent, he was still the richest cotton-spinner in England, and his factories were the most numerous, the most important and the best run. He went on developing his undertakings. In 1784, with David Dale [Robert Owen's father-in-law], he founded the New Lanark spinning mills, which derived their power from the falls of the Clyde. He set up others at Wirksworth and Akewell near Cromford, and he did not neglect the old ones . . . In Nottingham . . . he first made use of the steam engine. Honors too became his portion. In 1786 . . . he was knighted . . . [and became] Sheriff of the County of Derby. He died in 1792, leaving a capital of half a million. One of his factories, that at Bakewell, brought his heirs in £20,000 a year . . . big figures, in days when great millionaire manufacturers had not yet been heard of. . . .

His success, in fact, best illustrates what he really achieved, and what his place in economic history should be. He was no inventor. At the most he arranged, combined and used the inventions of others, which he never scrupled to appropriate for his own ends. . . . He was the first who knew how to make something out of other men's inventions, and who built them up into an industrial system. In order to raise the necessary capital for his undertakings, in order to form and dissolve those partnerships which he used successively as instruments with which to make his fortune, he must have displayed remarkable business ability, together with a curious mixture of cleverness, perseverance and daring. In order to set up large factories, to engage labor, to train it to a new kind of work, and to enforce strict discipline in the workshops, he needed an energy and an activity not often met with. These were qualities which most inventors never had, and without which their inventions could not have resulted in the building of a new industrial system. It was

Arkwright who . . . really created the modern factory. He personified the new type of great manufacturer, neither an engineer nor a merchant, but adding to the main characteristics of both, qualifications peculiar to himself: those of a founder of great concerns, an organizer of production, and a leader of men. Arkwright's career heralded a new social class and a new economic era.

Robert Heilbroner: The Rise of the New Men

Robert L. Heilbroner, *The Making of Economic Society*, © 1962. Reprinted by permission of Prentice-Hall, Inc., Englewood Cliffs, New Jersey.

Why did the Industrial Revolution originally take place in England and not on the continent? To answer the question we must look at the background factors which distinguished England from most other European nations in the eighteenth century.

The first of these factors was simply that England was relatively wealthy. In fact, a century of successful exploration, slave-trading, piracy, war, and commerce had made her the richest nation in the world. Even more important, her riches had accrued not merely to a few nobles, but to a large upper-middle stratum of commercial bourgeoisie. England was thus one of the first nations to develop albeit on a tiny scale, a prime requisite of an industrial economy: a "mass" consumer market. As a result, a rising pressure of demand inspired a search for new techniques. [Very typically, the Society for the Encouragement of Arts and Manufactures (itself a significant child of the age) offered a prize for

a machine that would spin six threads of cotton at one time, thus enabling the spinner to keep up with the technologically more advanced weaver. It was this which led, at least in part, to Arkwright's spinning jenny, of which we shall hear more shortly.]

Second, England was the scene of the most successful and thorough-going transformation of feudal society into commercial society. A succession of strong kings had effectively broken the power of the local nobility and had made England the strongest encouragement to the rising mercantile classes. Then too, as we have seen, the enclosure movement, which gained tempo in the seventeenth and eighteenth centuries, expelled an army of laborers to man her new industrial establishments.

Third, England was the locus of a unique enthusiasm for science and engineering. The famous Royal Academy, of which Newton was an early president, was founded in 1660 and was the immediate source of much intellectual excitement. Indeed, a popular interest in gadgets, machines, and devices of all sorts soon became a mild national obsession: *Gentlemen's Magazine*, a kind of *New Yorker* of the period, announced in 1729 that it would henceforth keep its readers "abreast of every invention"—a task which the mounting flow of inventions soon rendered quite impossible. No less important was an enthusiasm of the British landed aristocracy for scientific farming: English landlords displayed an interest in . . . crop rotation and fertilizer which their French counterparts would have found quite beneath their dignity.

Then there were a host of other background causes, some as fortuitous as the immense resources of coal and iron ore on which the British sat; others as purposeful as the development of a national patent system which deliberately sought to stimulate and protect the act of invention itself. And then, as the Revolution came into being, it fed upon itself. The new techniques (especially in textiles) simply destroyed their handicraft competition around the world and thus enormously increased their own markets. But what finally brought all these factors into operation was the energy of a group of New Men who made of the latent opportunities of history a vehicle for their own rise to fame and fortune.

One such, for instance, was John Wilkinson. The son of an old-fashioned small-scale iron producer, Wilkinson was a man possessed by the technological possibilities of his business. He invented a dozen things: a rolling mill and a steam lathe, a process for the manufacture of iron pipes, and a design for machining accurate cylinders. Typically, he decided that the old-fashioned leather bellows used in the making of iron itself were not efficient, and so he determined to make iron ones. "Everybody laughed at me," he later wrote. "I did it and applied the steam engine to blow them and they all cried: 'Who could have thought of it?'"

He followed his success in production with a passion for application: everything must be made of iron: pipes, bridges, even ships. After a ship made of iron plates had been successfully launched, he wrote a friend: "It answers all my expectations, and has convinced the unbelievers, who were nine hundred and ninety-nine in a thousand. It will be a nine-days wonder, and afterwards, a Columbus' egg."

But Wilkinson was only one of many. The most famous was, of course, James Watt, who, together with Matthew Boulton, formed the first company for the manufacture of steam engines. Watt was the son of an architect,

shipbuilder, and maker of nautical instruments. At thirteen he was already making models of machines, and by young manhood he was an accomplished artisan. He planned to settle in Glasgow, but the guild of hammermen objected to his making mathematical instruments—the last remnants of feudalism thus coming into an ironic personal conflict with the man who, more than any other, would create the invention that would destroy guild organization. At any rate, Watt found a haven at the university and there, in 1764, had his attention turned to an early and very unsatisfactory steam engine invented by Newcomen. In his careful and systematic way, Watt experimented with steam pressures, cylinder designs, and valves, until by 1796 he had developed a truly radical and (by the standards of those days) extraordinarily powerful and efficient engine. Interestingly, Watt could never have done so well with his engines had not Wilkinson perfected a manner of making good piston-cylinder fits. Previously, cylinders and pistons were made of wood and rapidly wore out. Typically, too, it was Wilkinson who bought the first steam engine to be used for purposes other than pumping: it blew the famous iron bellows.

There was needed, however, more than Watt's skill. The new engines had to be produced and sold, and the factory that made them had to be financed and organized. Watt at first formed a partnership with John Roebuck, another iron magnate, but it shortly failed. Thereafter luck came his way. Matthew Boulton, already a wealthy and highly successful manufacturer of buttons and buckles, took up Roebuck's contract with Watt, and the greatest combination of technical skill and business acumen of the day was born.

Even then the firm did not prosper immediately. Expenses of development were high,

and the new firm was not out of debt for twelve years. Yet from the beginning, interest was high. By 1781 Boulton was able to claim that the people of London, Birmingham, and Manchester were all "steam mill mad"; and by 1786, when two steam engines were harnessed to fifty pairs of millstones in the largest flour mill in the world, all of London came to see and marvel.

The steam engine was the greatest single invention, but by no means the sole mainstay, of the Industrial Revolution. Hardly less important were a group of textile inventions, of which the most famous was Arkwright's jenny.

Arkwright's career is, in itself, interesting. A barber, he plied his trade near the weaving districts of Manchester and so heard the crying need for a machine that would enable the cottage spinners to keep up with the technically more advanced weavers. Good fortune threw him into contact with a clockmaker named John Kay, whom he hired to perfect a machine that Kay had already begun with another employer-inventor. What happened thereafter is obscure: Kay left the business accused of theft and embezzlement, and Arkwright appeared as the "sole inventor" of a spinning jenny in 1769.

He now found two rich hosiers, Samuel Need and Jedediah Strutt, who agreed to set up business with him to produce jennies, and in 1771 the firm built its own spinning mill. It was an immense success; by 1779 it had several thousand spindles, more than 300 workmen, and ran night and day. Within not many years Arkwright had built an immense fortune for himself and founded an even more immense textile industry for England. "O reader," wrote Carlyle, looking back on his career, "what a historical phenomenon is that bag-cheeked, pot-bellied, much enduring, much inventing barber! . . . It was this man that had to give England the power of cotton."

THE INDUSTRIAL ENTREPRENEUR

It is interesting, as we watch the careers of the New Men, to draw a few generalizations concerning them. For these were an entirely new class of economically important persons. Peter Onions, who invented the puddling process, was an obscure foreman; Arkwright was a barber, Benjamin Huntsman, the steel pioneer, was originally a maker of clocks; Maudslay, who invented the automatic screw machine, was a bright young mechanic at the Woolwich Arsenal. None of the great industrial pioneers came of noble lineage; and with few exceptions, such as Matthew Boulton, none even possessed money capital. In agriculture, the new revolutionary methods of scientific farming enjoyed aristocratic patronage and leadership, especially from the famous Sir Jethro Tull and Lord Townshend; but in industry, the lead went to men of humble origin and descent.

Let us note, therefore, that this required a social system flexible enough to permit the rise of such obscure "adventurers." It is not until we see the catalytic effect of unleashing and harnessing the energies of talented men in the lower and middle ranks of the social order that we begin to appreciate the immense liberating effect of the preceeding economic and political revolutions. In the medieval hierarchy the meteoric careers of such new men would have been unthinkable. In addition, the new men were the product of the unique economic preparation of England itself. They were, of course, the beneficiaries of the rising demand and the technical inquisitiveness of the times. Beyond that, many of the small manufacturers were,

themselves, former small proprietors who had been bought out during the late period of the enclosure movement and who determined to use their tiny capital in the promising area of manufacture.

Many of these new men made great sums of money. A few, like Boulton and Watt, were modest in their wants. Despite an iron-clad patent, they charged for their engines only the basic cost of the machine and installation plus one-third the saving in fuel which the customer got. Some, like Josiah Wedgwood, founder of the great china works, actually refused, on principle, to take out patents. But most of them did not display such fine sensibilities. Arkwright retired a multi-millionaire living in ostentatious splendor; Huntsman, Wilkinson, Samuel Walker (who began life as a nailsmith and stole the secret of cast steel)— all went on to roll up huge fortunes. [In contrast to the manufacturers, the inventors did not usually fare successfully. Many of them, who did not have Watt's good fortune in finding a Boulton, died poor and neglected, fruitlessly suing for stolen inventions, unpaid royalties, ignored claims.] Indeed, Wilkinson's iron business became a minor industrial state with a credit stronger than many German and Italian principalities. It even coined its own money, and its copper and silver tokens (with a profile and legend of John Wilkinson, Ironmaster) were much in use between 1787 and 1808.

Beyond mere avarice, the manufacturers have been described by the economic historian, Paul Mantoux, as "tyrannical, hard, sometimes cruel: their passions and greeds were those of upstarts." They had the reputation of being heavy drinkers and of having little regard for the honour of their female employees. They were proud of their newly acquired wealth and lived in great style with

footmen, carriages and gorgeous town and country houses.

Pleasant or unpleasant, the personal characteristics fade beside one overriding quality. These were all men interested in expansion, in growth, in investment for investment's sake. All of them were identified with technological progress, and none of them disdained the productive process. An employee of Maudslay's once remarked, "It was a pleasure to see him handle a tool of any kind, but he was *quite splendid* with an 18-inch file." Watt was tireless in experimenting with his machines; Wedgwood stomped about his factory on his wooden leg scrawling, "This won't do for Jos. Wedgwood," wherever he saw evidence of careless work. Richard Arkwright was a bundle of ceaseless energy in promoting his interests, jouncing about England over execrable roads in a post chaise driven by four horses, pursuing his correspondence as he traveled.

"With us," wrote a French visitor to a calico works in 1788, "a man rich enough to set up and run a factory like this would not care to remain in a position which he would deem unworthy of his wealth." This was an attitude entirely foreign to the rising English industrial capitalist. His work was its own dignity and reward; the wealth it brought was quite aside. Boswell, on being shown Watt and Boulton's great engine works at Soho, declared that he never forgot Boulton's expression as the latter declared, "I sell here, sir, what all the world desires to have—Power."

The New Men were first and last *entrepreneurs*—enterprisers. They brought . . . a new energy, as restless as it proves to be inexhaustible. In an economic, if not a political, sense, they deserve the epithet "revolutionaries," for the change they ushered in was nothing short of total, sweeping, and irreversible.

STUDY QUESTIONS

1. What factors explain the growing reliance on technology in the eighteenth century? What is meant by "the religion of the machine?"

2. How did the advance of technology affect the lives of eighteenth-century men?

3. Why do you think *Robinson Crusoe* was a best seller? Analyze the process by which the Reverend Cartwright invented the power loom. What do these men have in common?

4. What do the attitudes of the inventors and experimenters tell you about values and goals in their day?

5. How did the career of Richard Arkwright symbolize the connection between technology and economic growth?

6. Why did economic changes occur most spectacularly in Great Britain?

7. What does Heilbroner mean by the "new men"? What were they like? Why could they get ahead more easily in the eighteenth century than previously? How did they justify their careers?

8. On the basis of these readings how did economic growth affect traditional values?

This scene of fireworks on the Pont-Neuf in Paris in 1745 catches the mix of urban pride and *ancien regime* grandeur that epitomizes the eighteenth century.

M. S. Anderson: The Structure of Eighteenth-Century Society

British scholar M. S. Anderson has taken on the challenge of comparative history. Here he examines the structure of eighteenth-century European society as a whole, still essentially rural and traditional, but increasingly under assault by the forces of intellectual, economic, and political change. From *Europe in the Eighteenth Century 1713–1783* by M. S. Anderson. Copyright © 1961 by M. S. Anderson. Reprinted by permission of Holt, Rinehart and Winston, Inc., New York.

TOPIC 23

CONTINUITY AND CHANGE IN SOCIETY

Despite the marked economic changes brought about in England, France, and the Netherlands by commerce and industry, the European social order still bore the stamp of its feudal past. Nobility, peasantry, and townsmen were cast in relationships hardened by the passage of time, and the further eastward one traveled in Europe the more rigid those relationships became. Nonetheless, as the readings indicate, these ties were challenged in the eighteenth century by new wealth and changing aspirations. By the time the century had come to a close, the traditional social order had been profoundly shaken.

I

Over most of Europe, society during this period was still in essentials what it had been for generations. Its traditional character is visible above all in the continuing vital importance of a great variety of small, closely-knit groups, and in the persistence of regional differences so numerous and varied as to defy classification or adequate description. . . . Moreover in many parts of the continent the traditional clear-cut division of society into orders, distinct from one another and essentially though not completely hereditary in character, had lost very little of its original force. In Central Europe, where the growth of powerful unified States was slow or even non-existent the vitality of tradition in this respect was especially marked. . . .

The Peasants

In almost every eighteenth-century State, society was still in the main rural, and the workers on the land (who may be conveniently if not altogether accurately referred to as 'peasants') were the largest social group.

The peasant's economic and social status, his standard of living and the degree of personal freedom he enjoyed, varied enormously in different areas. They depended on whether he was a free man or a serf, on the way in which he held his land, on whether that land was adequate to maintain him and his family, and on a host of other factors.

From the social (though not necessarily the economic) point of view the critical distinction was that between the peasant who was personally free and his fellow who was a serf. This was largely a distinction between the western and eastern halves of the continent. In the British Isles, the Iberian peninsula and Italy, legal serfdom no longer existed. (Though how far a labourer in Connaught or Calabria was a free man in any real sense of the term is quite another matter.) In France it was a serious factor only in a few eastern areas (in 1750 there were in all about 950,000 serfs in the country). . . .

Serfdom in eastern and northern Germany and in Russia differed essentially from that in France and western Germany. In the latter it was a medieval institution surviving with increasing difficulty in a changing social and economic climate, of little apparent value to the State and more and more the target for the criticisms of reformers. This period saw its legal abolition in Lorraine, Savoy and Baden. East of the Elbe, on the other hand, it was a relatively new institution which had developed rapidly in the seventeenth century. In Brandenburg and Saxony its spread was accelerated by the devastation of the Thirty

Years War, and above all by the critical shortage of labour which the war had produced. This, coupled with a growing demand for grain both for export and for distilling, led the landowners in these areas to extend and intensify their control over the peasant population. As well as being obliged to provide labour-services, the peasant thus lost in many parts of eastern Germany the right to choose his employment, to work outside the lord's estate without the latter's consent, or even to marry without the payment to him of a small tax. His subjection was facilitated by a growing tendency towards the union in the hands of the landowning class of landowner-ship and rights of jurisdiction. This meant that in the eighteenth century the landlord was usually a judicial and administrative official, and often an army officer as well. Against this concentration of authority, and still more against the power given the landowner by the dependence on him of the Prussian administration and army for their efficient functioning, the peasant was almost helpless. . . .

In Russia serfdom had originated in a somewhat different way. There it arose from the efforts of the government, from the second half of the sixteenth century onwards, to pin down a scanty and shifting population in a vast undeveloped country and extract from it the money and services required for State purposes. This process was completed in the reign of Peter I by the introduction of a system of military conscription from 1705 onwards, and above all by the imposition on the Russian peasantry in 1719 of the poll-tax (literally "soul tax"). Peter made the landowner responsible for the collection of this tax and for the supply of recruits from his estates. By so doing he greatly increased the lord's authority over his serfs. The nature of

serfdom in Russia was thus fundamentally changed. From being primarily an attachment to the soil, as it had been under the legislation of the sixteenth and seventeenth centuries, it became increasingly one to the person of the landlord, and hence approximated to slavery. This was emphasized in 1762, when Peter III gave the lords the power to transfer serfs from one estate to another, in this way depriving the serf of his traditional right to the land he cultivated. The abolition of slavery as a recognized legal status in 1723 thus indicated a decline in the position of the serf rather than a rise in that of the slave. Russia indeed was the one European State in which the legal position of the serf changed clearly and decisively for the worse in this period. . . .

Areas such as the Habsburg provinces, Poland and Russia, where serfdom was onerous and the authority of the central government hard to enforce, were the natural breeding-ground of peasant revolts. All of them suffered during this period from disturbances of this type. In Bohemia there was a serious rising in 1775, and another broke out in Transylvania in 1784. In the Polish Ukraine there was a very savage revolt, provoked by the antagonism between an Orthodox and Uniate peasantry and a mainly Catholic landowning class, in the 1730's. In Russia above all agrarian discontent and disorder were endemic throughout the century, especially in its second half. Seventy-three peasant risings, most of them of purely local importance, are known to have taken place in 1762–1769; and the widespread rural disorder which marked the early years of the reign of Catherine II culminated in the revolt led by the Cossack Pugachev which broke out in 1773 and was not completely suppressed till

1775. This revolt was the greatest outburst of the social protest anywhere in Europe during this period. In the Baltic provinces there was serious rural unrest in 1778 and 1783, and in another great wave of discontent in 1796–1797 in Central Russia 278 separate outbreaks were recorded.

None of these revolts, however, in Russia or elsewhere, had any real programme beyond that of removing some or all of the burdens which weighed so heavily on the peasant. Most of them were little more than inarticulate outbursts of hatred and resentment. Occurring as nearly all of them did in areas where towns were few and small they were deprived of the urban leadership which alone might have brought them some degree of success. In the same way the flight of peasants to foreign States or thinly-populated border areas, though it sometimes reached considerable proportions—200,000 cases of this kind were officially recorded in Russia in 1719–1727 and there must have been many more which escaped official notice—could not seriously menace the social system from which they fled. . . .

II

The Nobility

The structure, numbers and influence of the landowning class (the term 'nobility', though its use cannot always be avoided, is too narrow to be really accurate) varied enormously in different parts of Europe. Almost everywhere, except in Britain and the United Provinces, it enjoyed important legal privileges—rights of jurisdiction, immunity from certain forms of particularly severe or degrading punishment or from some types of taxation. In many States legal barriers were opposed to the acquisition by commoners of 'noble land'. In the eastern and central parts of the continent in particular the legal superiority of the landlords to other social groups was marked. Thus in Poland they retained until 1768 powers of life and death over their serfs, and in Hungary succeeded in 1731 in asserting their right to pay no taxes at all. In many countries the landowning class was tending, as the century progressed, to become more self-conscious, more jealous of its rights and more anxious to prevent commoners from achieving privileged status. This is perhaps seen most clearly in Sweden, where the constitution of 1720 severely limited the ruler's right to ennoble commoners.

In most parts of Europe it had originated as a knightly class with important military functions; and military traditions and ambitions still counted for much in the outlook of many of its members in the eighteenth century. Its real military effectiveness, however, had now shrunk to very small proportions. No European army in the eighteenth century could afford to base its organization entirely on a single class or to exclude commoners completely from its commissioned ranks. This created, in many States, an implicit conflict between military efficiency and what many members of the privileged class, especially many of its poorer members, thought of as their right to monopolize commissions. . . .

The landowning class had more than merely military importance in the eighteenth century. It not only provided the bulk of the officers for the armies (and to a lesser extent the navies) of nearly all European States, but played a large, sometimes an indispensable, part in the running of their administrative machines. In Prussia, where the junkers were being transformed in the later seventeenth and early eighteenth centuries into a class of

hereditary State servants, the whole administration increasingly reflected their virtues and vices. A very similar position was to be found in Russia. There Peter I had succeeded, in the face of much opposition, in asserting the principle that every landowner was bound, as a condition of holding his land, to serve the State for an unlimited period in the armed forces or the civil administration. In this way alone could the officers and administrators needed for the creation of powerful armed forces and a centralized bureaucracy be found, and Russia be enabled to play the role of a great power in Europe. . . .

In France the position was somewhat different. There, as the old military and landed nobility, the *noblesse de l'épée,* showed itself less and less able to administer a State dominated by complex social and financial problems, it was supplemented and to some extent replaced by a new administrative nobility, the *noblesse de la robe.* This class, of comparatively recent origin and led by the holders of a number of great legal offices, was now growing in wealth and influence. It provided many of the Secretaries of State who controlled during this period the workings of most of the different departments of the central administration. . . . Equally important, it dominated the *parlements*—great, conservative and largely hereditary legal corporations, twelve in number, which could possess great political importance. On the other hand, since it was composed mainly of bourgeois who had purchased government offices carrying with them the privileges of nobility, or their descendants, the *noblesse de la robe* tended to be looked down upon by the older noble families and has sometimes been considered by historians as merely the highest stratum of the French bourgeoisie. Nor had it much access to or influence at the court, or within

the charmed circle immediately surrounding the royal family. Its very abilities, indeed, to some extent told against it; for learning or genuine intellectual interests seemed to many Frenchmen the qualities of a commoner, qualities with which a true nobleman could dispense. Nevertheless it was one of the most important elements in French society during this period. Able, conservative and self-interested, it had become by the years before 1789 perhaps the greatest of all obstacles to the radical overhaul of the governmental system which was now clearly needed.

In Britain also the influence of the aristocracy and squirearchy on the government and administrative system was profound. Throughout the century the House of Lords retained a political influence and position in popular esteem little if at all inferior to those possessed by the House of Commons. The latter in any case consisted almost completely of landowners; its members were very often related to those of the Upper House and owed their seats to the money and influence of some peer. Moreover to the end of this period and long after the Cabinet remained a predominantly aristocratic body. The younger Pitt, when he took office as Prime Minister in 1783, was the only member of his own Cabinet who sat in Commons; and as late as 1830 that of Lord Grey contained thirteen peers or sons of peers, a baronet, and only one untitled commoner. In English local government also the dominance of the landowning class through the Justices of the Peace was the central fact of this period.

The use of the words 'nobility' or 'landowning class' must not, however, be taken as implying that a homogeneous social group is being discussed. There were vast differences between the 'nobilities' of different countries. The Polish and Hungarian squires exacting directly or through manorial officials labour-services from their peasants, had not much resemblance to the aristocrats of England or Sweden, whose lands were for the most part leased to tenant-farmers over whom they had relatively little control. The service-nobilities of Russia and Prussia had little in common with the increasingly functionless aristocrats of Spain and Italy. There were also important distinctions between the different sections and subdivisions of each national 'nobility'. In England, where the peerage was a small and relatively homogeneous body separated by a clear line of division from non-noble landowners however wealthy, the position was relatively straight forward. In most other countries, however, the number of people who could lay claim to the privileges of nobility was very large, and the disparities between them in wealth, education and political power might be very great.

Thus in France, where the noblesse towards the end of this period numbered in all perhaps some 250,000 people, there were probably as few as 4,000 noble families which had any share, however small, in the life of the court, or any direct access to the monarch. Between a great noble who could obtain for himself and his protégés the appointments, honours and pensions which only court influence could secure, and the poor provincial squire, the *hobereau*, who might live and work in conditions no better than those enjoyed by many peasants, the gulf was wide indeed. Only in a purely legal sense can they be regarded as belonging to the same social class. . . .

Similarly in Spain, where in the census of 1787 half a million people (about 5 per cent of the total population) claimed to be of noble status, the difference between the poor *hidalgos* who made up the vast majority of

this total and the tiny group of great land-owners at the apex of the social pyramid, such as the Dukes of Infantado and Medina-Sidonia, was immense. Within those major divisions of the Spanish privileged class, moreover, there were further subdivisions: the grandees, the highest stratum of the nobility numbering little more than a hundred in all, were classified, at least in theory, in three distinct groups. Contrasts of this type were equally sharp in Poland. There the privileged class, the *szlachta*, was before the partitions an enormous group of almost a million people, the vast majority of whom were poor and many of whom owned little or no land. Many of them, to the casual observer, were distinguishable from peasants only by their possession of the right to wear a particular type of dress and by the fact that special seats were reserved for them in church. Between 'barefoot *szlachta*' of this type and the two dozen or so really great magnates who ruled the country (in so far as it was ruled at all before the partitions) there could be no real equality. A Prince Radziwill, owning land greater in extent than many of the German States, or a member of one of the other great Polish families, the Czartoryskis, the Potockis, the Sapiehas, was a different being from the ignorant and impoverished squires who followed and depended on him. . . .

III

The Towns and the Middle Class

The social importance of the towns, and of the merchant class by which most of them were ruled throughout this period, also differed enormously in different parts of Europe. In the United Provinces the patriciate of Amsterdam had long been a dominant group, enjoying great political influence as

well as great wealth. In England a somewhat similar development was visible before the end of the seventeenth century; during the two generations or more which followed, great London bankers, financiers or merchants . . . had on occasion very real influence on the development of government policy. In the realm of public finance, in particular, ministers normally depended heavily on the support, and were compelled to pay attention to the advice, of a small number of great capitalists. Many of these were of Jewish, Dutch or Huguenot extraction. Moreover there was a strong tendency for this group, by intermarriage or by purchase of land, to become closely connected with and eventually assimilated to, the greater landowners. . . . The emergence of a similar class, even smaller in numbers but in some ways equally important, can be seen almost simultaneously in France.

The growth of an *haute bourgeoisie* was encouraged in France (and elsewhere in Europe) by the system of tax-farming, which undoubtedly brought vast profits to a small number of wealthy families and individuals. In the later years of this period the immense expansion of French colonial trade which followed the peace of 1763 added to its ranks an increasing number of great merchant families such as the Gradis and Bonnaffé of Bordeaux or the Roux of Marseilles. Both in Britain and France, however, this class depended almost entirely on trade, above all overseas trade, and on financial dealings of various kinds, for the wealth which made it important. No English industrialist, not even an Arkwright, a Boulton, or a Wilkinson, had the social status or political influence of a great banker or merchant. In France the entire period saw only two industrial dynasties of more than local importance; the De Wendels

POPULATION DENSITIES PER SQUARE MILE
IN LATE 18th CENTURY EUROPE

with their great interests in the iron industry, and the Van Robais textile magnates.

On a smaller scale the growth of a commercial and financial upper middle class similar to that of Britain and France can be seen in a few other areas of Europe—Tuscany, Genoa, some West German cities. Elsewhere it was almost entirely lacking. Overwhelmingly agrarian countries with few towns, small merchant marines and little capital, such as Prussia, the Habsburg territories, Poland and Russia, could produce little of this kind. . . . The influence of the urban population was further reduced by the fact that it was largely composed of aliens—Jews or Germans in Poland, Greeks or Rumanians in Hungary. All over Eastern and much of Central Europe, moreover, the position of the towns was weakened by the fact that landowners, using the raw materials produced by their estates and the forced labour of their serfs, often set up in the countryside industrial establishments which competed with urban factories and workshops.

It must not be thought that the importance of the towns in this period lay solely in their production of a wealthy upper middle class. This social group was not only confined in the main, as has been pointed out, to a few great West European cities, but was often unable to dominate even these. Thus in London the smaller merchants, tradesmen and craftsmen, who controlled the Common Council and elected the city's four Members of Parliament, tended as a rule to be hostile to the urban magnates whose close connexions with the government and the aristocracy they distrusted and envied. . . .

The position in the great cities of France was in essentials rather similar, and in its political repercussions much more important.

France was the one European country in which an urban middle class of this type, composed of merchants, professional men, and even in a few cases industrialists, was both large enough to be a really powerful element in society and at the same time completely excluded from political power. In the United Provinces the government had long ceased to be dominated by the nobility, though the greatest merchant families of Amsterdam and a few other cities formed a kind of aristocracy which aroused a good deal of envy and bad feeling in those a little farther down the social scale. In Britain a bourgeois, if he were wealthy enough, would eventually be accepted more or less as an equal by the landed gentry. The great cities and the interests which dominated them could always make their voices heard in the House of Commons. In France, by contrast, society and the political structure were still overwhelmingly aristocratic in tone, and the safety-valves for bourgeois envy and resentment which existed in Britain (and were by no means completely effective there) were almost non-existent. It was not unheard-of for a French merchant, banker, or even industrialist to be ennobled. In 1767, perhaps with a vague realization that middle-class discontent was beginning to gather strength, the government promised that henceforth rights almost equivalent to those of nobility should be granted each year to two important merchants, provided that their fathers and grandfathers had also been merchants. This, however, was a very half-hearted attempt to solve a very intractable problem. The obstacles in the way of the urban middle class, however well-to-do, attaining nobility are illustrated by the fact that in Brittany, a province which possessed such substantial ports as Brest and

L'Orient, only twenty-two businessmen were ennobled in the three generations before 1789.

Indeed the generation before the Revolution saw a deepening and widening of the gulf which separated noble and bourgeois, a growing self-consciousness and exclusiveness on the part of the nobility which intensified the frustrations already inherent in the structure of French society. It became increasingly difficult for any but the wealthiest merchants or professional men to buy really important government posts. All Louis XVI's intendants (great officials each of whom superintended an area known as a *généralité*) were noble: it would have been impossible for Louvois or Colbert to rise to high office under him as they did under Louis XIV. . . .

In many West European States during this period the towns, even if not independent as the German free cities and Italian city-states were, continued to enjoy a considerable degree of autonomy in their relations with the central government. This meant that their internal organization continued to be of real political and social importance. That organization varied enormously, but was usually complex and designed to avoid any concentration of real power in the hands of an individual or a small group of individuals. . . . Certain characteristics, however, were common to most European towns during this period. In the majority of them an important role in government was played by the guilds. In Strasbourg, for example, the twenty guilds each elected fifteen members of the Council of Three Hundred and, of more practical importance, one member of the Senate. In most French towns indeed the ruling body was composed mainly or entirely of representatives of the craft and merchant guilds. Though there were some important German cities (Frankfort for instance) in whose government guild influence was slight, here too the guilds were usually powerful and often dominant. In practice, however, every West European town during this period, whatever its constitution, tended to be ruled by an oligarchy of its wealthier citizens, an oligarchy which was usually largely hereditary. Thus in Berne, where the hereditary element was unusually strong, there were only about 250 families which were classified as capable of ruling: of these about seventy really controlled the city. In many other towns the same names can be seen recurring for generation after generation in the membership of the ruling bodies—the Dietrichs and Wenckers in Strasbourg for example.

Eighteenth-century cities were able to retain their inherited social and administrative structure because few of them, at least until late in the century, were predominantly industrial. Nowhere in Europe even at the end of this period, except in a few restricted areas such as the textile-producing parts of Lancashire or the metal-working region around Liège and Dinant, could there be found large towns whose populations included considerable numbers of industrial workers of a modern type. A proletariat in the Marxist sense was coming into existence in many of the cities of Europe, one which in some areas suffered considerable hardship and oppression. It was however a proletariat organized in terms of workshops far more than of factories. The fact that many of such large-scale industrial enterprises as did exist—the Ural ironworks in Russia are a leading example—were situated in areas far removed from any large town also helped urban life to retain its mercantile and handicraft character almost everywhere down to the end of this period.

The still largely traditional and static society described in this chapter was doomed to rapid decay. The network of communities, orders, privileges, peculiarities and exemptions, of which it was composed, could not hope to withstand indefinitely the forces of change which were growing stronger throughout this period. From the middle of the century at latest it was being steadily though very slowly eroded by the demands of governments for larger revenues and greater administrative efficiency. It was also being undermined, more rapidly and perhaps more fundamentally, by the development of Europe's economic life. For a society based on customs and traditions which were everywhere different was slowly being supplanted by one based on abstract ideas which were everywhere the same. . . .

Elements of Flux in the Mid-Eighteenth Century

From *A History of the Western World,* Vol. I, *Ancient Times to 1715,* by S. B. Clough et al. Copyright ©, 1964, by D. C. Heath & Co., a division of Raytheon Education Co., Boston, Mass.

In 1763, at the end of the Seven Years' War, European life and society doubtless seemed stable enough to the casual contemporary observer. The ponderous ceremonial of court life ground serenely on around great kings and petty princes who appeared secure on their thrones. Established religious institutions—whether Roman Catholic, Lutheran, Anglican, Orthodox, or even Calvinist—buttressed the civil power. Society seemed to be composed of the traditional strata: several ranks of nobles, a few layers of bourgeois, a relatively small number of urban and rural workers, and a very large social base of peasants.

At the top, nobles were dissolute, ignorant, arrogant, frivolous, rich, restrained, educated, humble, humanitarian, or poor—or almost any combination of these qualities—but they were noble, and cherished noble privileges of all kinds. In the middle, bourgeois businessmen contrived, kept their books, saved, and then, frequently, bought titles, country estates, or honorific positions to dignify their names. By and large it was still true that only a person who did not work at a gainful employment, except for supervision of farming or very large-scale overseas trading or financial enterprises, could be considered "a gentleman." At the bottom, peasants and workers labored at production or service and were thought of by their superiors as somewhat less than human. Now and again, the peasants rose up in smaller or larger rebellions but order was always restored. Most peasants farmed much as their forefathers had been doing since the later Middle Ages.

Nor did government in general seem to operate very differently from the way it had for many decades. Still not quite despotic and not really absolute, late eighteenth-century governments tended to carry on their work through the agency of a horde of appointed officials (although in England the unpaid local Justice of the Peace still carried the major burden of English administration.) The policies of these governments continued to be highly competitive. Each great power tended to organize itself internally so as to be able to expand at the expense of its neighbors. Mercantilistic regulation internally and war externally were still the main results of this aggressiveness.

What, then, was there in the apparently stable compound of western civilization of about 1763 which would react to produce the violent upheavals of the revolutionary era which followed?

ELEMENTS OF FLUX IN THE 1760's

In addition to the yeasty ideas of the Enlightenment and the beginnings of the Industrial Revolution which have already been discussed, the potentially revolution-making elements were (1) a remarkable population increase, (2) an equally significant upward movement of prices accompanied by (3) increased business activity of all kinds, all of which led to (4) social mutations affecting all classes, from the aristocracy down to the peasantry. . . .

Population Increase

European population has experienced three periods of substantial population increase. The first of these took place in the High Middle Ages after what had been a long era of stagnation or even of decline during the later Roman Empire and early Middle Ages. This medieval increase stopped around 1300 and European population remained stable or, perhaps, decreased for 150 years; but after 1450 social changes leading to earlier marriages, agricultural improvements, and capitalistic rationalization of certain business procedures touching on the distribution of goods and services led to another substantial increase (estimated at 30 per cent over the next 150 years). Then, about 1600, European population seems to have encountered a ceiling set by the limits of food supply, by high infant and maternal mortality as well as

by the static and relatively short life span expected by most people.

During the latter part of the seventeenth century and onward into the eighteenth, this ceiling seems to have been raised. In the first place, births increased as, for one reason or another, young people tended, once again, to marry earlier. In addition, scientific and medical advances permitted more infants to survive. What had been the homely art of obstetrics began to receive more learned attention in this period; before 1700 schools were established on the continent for the training of midwives; physicians published books on the subject and read papers before the 1670's; and new French regulations required that midwives should remove their rings and wash their hands before touching a patient. Many states endeavored to control the spread of infectious disease (particularly the plague) by elaborate quarantine regulations; and as the power of the central government increased it became more nearly possible to enforce public health measures. All these factors, combined with technological-economic changes . . . led to the beginning of our great modern European population swell. The population of Europe in 1650 was about 100 million; in 1750, 140 million; in 1800, 187 million.

Prices and Business Activity

As population was increasing on the eve of the revolutionary era, so were the prices of commodities. After a period of roughly 70 years (1660–1730) during which the price trend had been downward, prices in France started to go up and showed a steady if gradual increase to about 1763 when they increased sharply. Between 1730 and 1789 French grain prices increased 60 per cent. There is no reason to believe that prices in

other countries or in other commodities acted very differently on the eve of the revolutions.

Among those who suffer most from price increases are those who live on fixed incomes or those, as in the case of landed aristocrats, whose revenues are set contractually over long periods of time and cannot rapidly be adjusted to the changing price structure. Peasants who have commodities to sell are usually gainers—if the ruling classes permit the laws of the marketplace to operate—in a period of rising prices, as are businessmen generally. In a period of rising prices (all other things remaining equal) wages tend to rise less rapidly than prices and consequently the opportunities are attractive to the entrepreneurs who can make great profits under such circumstances. In fact, while prices in France increased 60 per cent between 1730 and 1789, wages increased only about 22 per cent. The bourgeoisie of the time seem to have responded as the economists tell us they should have done; and the outward and visible signs of this response were the new factories of the industrial revolution and the model farms of the agricultural revolution. These factories and rationalized farms brought with them more than simple technological change; they also led to significant social mutations as large numbers of workers in France and England left their cottages and migrated to the new industrial cities and as reforming landlords endeavored with varying degrees of success to "enclose" their estates.

Despite the fact of an enclosure movement in England, there is no conclusive evidence that the lot of the statistically "average" English peasant was worsening in the late eighteenth century. On the contrary French peasants were better off than they had been in their own recent past; the northern Italian peasant was prospering; the burdens laid upon the west Elbian German peasant were probably not more than he could carry comfortably. Moreover, serfdom, which had long since entirely vanished from England, was limited to not more than a few hundred thousand . . . in France, was disappearing in northern Italy, and had nearly vanished in west Elbian Germany. In Iberian Spain and Portugal, in southern peninsular Italy, in east Elbian Germany, in Danubian Europe (Bohemia, Austria and Hungary), and across the plains of Poland and Russia, however, most peasants were sunk in abysmal servitude and poverty, their lot tending to get worse rather than to improve.

Aristocratic Consolidation

The traditional ruling orders had been two in number: the clergy and the nobility, representing spiritual and civil authority. Over the course of late medieval and early modern times, the clergy and the nobility had come increasingly under the control of the central government, especially in those areas—England, Spain, Prussia, Austria, and France, for instance—where the process of centralized state-making was most advanced. . . . In the eighteenth century the upper clergy were generally selected by European monarchs from among the aristocracy. The great aristocratic ecclesiastics—archbishops, bishops, abbots—often lived splendidly on vast incomes and sometimes paid very little attention to spiritual matters. These were tended to by humble parish priests or pastors who had little in common with their superiors. Obviously, then, the clergy was not a unit.

The noble order, likewise, was not homogeneous. Some ancestor-proud nobles lacked power, lived as peasants and were unable even to get their sons into the army as officers.

MARRIAGE À LA MODE (1745) by William Hogarth, English painter, engraver, and satirist.

1. The Marriage Contract

The marriage of wealth and birth in eighteenth-century England is described in these scenes by Hogarth. In the first, an alderman of London negotiates a marriage for his daughter to the son of a great lord. The lord, who points to a family tree that goes back to William the Conqueror, is willing to marry his son to a commoner if the financial settlement is adequate. Neither of the young people involved seems concerned with the other. The young noble toys with his snuff-box and ring, catching a side-glance at himself in the mirror. The young lady, in conversation with her lawyer, toys cooly with her own ring. The lack of affection for one another of the prospective bripe and groom apparently is of no concern to their fathers.

2. Breakfast Scene

The second scene, after the marriage, is one of disorder in the noble's household. The wife has just gotten up, although candles are burning and the clock indicates that it is afternoon. The husband, sprawled in a chair, appears just to have come home. He betrays signs of a night of dissipation—a broken sword on the floor and a woman's cap in his pocket. A distraught servant carries a stack of bills, only one of which has been paid and filed.

3. The Countess' Dressing Room

The wife becomes countess after the death of her father-in-law and pursues her social life in the style of the nobility. Her friends, in various attitudes of rapture or sleep, listen to two Italian musicians that have been hired to entertain the countess. Only the footman, serving chocolate, shows his contempt for the scene. The lawyer has become the countess' paramour and his portrait hangs on the wall. Other paintings display the revels of love.

4. Death of the Nobleman

Her lover rents a room where they spend the night. The suspicious earl has followed her there and is himself stabbed when he tries to kill the lawyer and avenge his honor. Her lover escapes through the window. The countess is alarmed and perhaps contrite as the earl collapses before her.

5. Death of the Countess

With this Hogarth concludes his satire on the deficiencies of upper-class life. The countess returns to her father's house and takes her own life. A vial of poison brought by a servant lies on the floor next to the last written words of the lawyer, whom we assume has also to pay for his sins. An apothecary scolds the servant for having procured the poison for the countess but seems as much disturbed by having arrived too late to gain profit from the situation. Her child clings to the dying mother as the greedy alderman removes a diamond ring from his daughter's hand.

1. The Marriage Contract

2. Breakfast Scene

3. The Countess' Dressing Room

4. Death of the Nobleman

5. Death of the Countess

Others were rich and powerful. Feudal nobility, like the feudal military levy, had in reality vanished long since as a functional and viable social institution. In England the Peers of the Realm corresponded in theory to the medieval barons, but in point of fact there were almost no eighteenth-century Lords who could trace their noble ancestry farther back than the sixteenth century; and the English king could and did create new Peers at will. In France, by regulation of 1760, only those who could establish noble descent dating from 1400 were received by the king at court. There were probably fewer than 1000 families who could meet this test; but the French court nobility did not include all the powerful aristocrats, many of whom were judges (nobility of the robe) or others whose recent ancestors had purchased job and title. Furthermore, many of the French nobles were too poor to appear at court. In Hungary, to take another example, an early eighteenth-century constitution separated the nobility into three groups: first, some 200 magnates; second, about 15,000 landed gentry; and, third, a large number of landless "sevenplumtree" nobles. The constitution of the Spanish nobility, the work of a king, Charles I, dated from the early sixteenth century and, likewise, specified three categories: the *grandees* at the top, then the *titulos* (titled nobles) and, finally, a great swarm of idle and often impecunious *hidalgos* (nobles without title).

It is difficult to generalize about European aristocracy because old traditions and current developments varied from place to place. For instance, it has been said that eighteenth-century English peers enjoyed power without privilege, that the French nobility had privilege without power and that the Prussian and Austrian nobility partook of both. One could put this another way by saying that nobles as nobles seldom enjoyed power, but that some nobles who were part of the aristocratic establishment did.

Thus, "aristocracy" has a wider meaning than nobility. Nobility had to do with birth and, though highly modified by modern usage and law, harked back to medieval tradition. Aristocracy was modern and existed in places like Switzerland, New York, and Virginia that had never known feudal nobility. Aristocrats filled the important offices of church, state, army and navy and often profited greatly at public expense. Many rich and influential people, including merchants, financiers, and intellectuals, sought and often achieved noble titles as outward and visible signs of their success and as keys to open the doors to greater wealth and power. . . .

The paths of upward social mobility were open to fortunate, witty, and aggressive adventurers. The road up existed, but the gates were narrow; the newly-ennobled found that they had to put up with insults from those on whose patents of nobility the ink was only a bit drier. Moreover, the *parvenu* was the exception to the rule which was becoming increasingly hereditary. For example, in France, government administrative service had in the seventeenth century been a well-climbed social ladder, and under Richelieu (before the 1640's) most of the powerful Intendants had been recruited from the non-noble and non-aristocratic lawyer class; but under Louis XVI after 1774 all of the 30-odd Intendants were aristocrats of judicial families and 14 of them were sons of Intendants. In England, where passage upward to aristocratic and noble status had traditionally been easier than elsewhere, there was probably less circulation after 1750 than had been the case earlier. This pattern of rigidification seems to have developed in the late eighteenth century in a general way from Poland on the East to British North America on the West.

Now, at the very time that this aristocracy-patriciate was closing its ranks against infiltration, population was growing; prices were increasing; entrepreneurial activity was on the rise; manufacturers were making fortunes; and a growing number of capable, fortunate, and rich people were clamoring for titles of nobility and were finding them increasingly difficult to get.

Many of the deprived *élites* believed that this situation was unjust and unnatural. As men they knew themselves to be equal or superior to the hereditary aristocrats; it was only natural, therefore, that their talents and their contributions to the wealth and welfare of the body politic should be recognized. These bourgeois or middle-class people began to think in terms of opening the aristocracy so that they, too, could belong. Many of these people were literate and were familiar with the enlightened ideas which tended to reinforce their claims. The ends they sought included an end of unnatural privilege, equality of taxation, and the rationalization of society to permit the free circulation of the *élites*.

Several late eighteenth-century monarchs, some of whom read the enlightened books, responded in a well-intentioned if highly authoritarian way to the same stimuli. It would be far too neat to say that their aims coincided with those of the disaffected bourgeoisie; but the more perceptive princes could not fail to recognize the fact that a privileged and closed aristocracy limited the royal freedom of action and represented a conflicting power within the state. If these reforming monarchs of the last decades of the *ancien régime* did not seek to abolish the aristocracy, at least they sought further to tame it and to accommodate it to their ideas of what was the proper form for the state and what was the reasonable structure for society. . . .

The French Nobility Raises Barriers to Social Mobility

The Marquis de Bouillé (1739–1800), author of this account, was an enlightened nobleman. Loyal to Louis XVI during the French Revolution, he took a leading part in the

unsuccessful attempt of the royal family to escape in 1791. From Marquis de Bouillé, *Mémoires,* ed. F. Barrière (Paris, 1859), p. 123. The *French Revolution as Told by Contemporaries,* copyright, 1938, by E. L. Higgins. Reprinted by permission of the publisher, Houghton Mifflin Company.

The immense riches brought [by commerce] to the kingdom were distributed only to the

These eighteenth-century paintings present aspects of that privileged existence that the French nobility zealously tried to restrict to themselves. At the right, gourmets consume oysters and wine in a lavishly decorated dining hall. At the left, aristocrats take a break during a hunt. Paintings by Jean François de Troy and Carle Van Loo.

commoners, since the prejudices of the nobles excluded them from commerce and from all the mechanical and liberal arts. This very increase in wealth, in augmenting the currency, had contributed to the impoverishment of the nobles, and that of landed proprietors in general. Moreover, the cities were considerably enlarged: commercial centers were established, such as Lyons, Nantes, Bordeaux, and Marseilles, becoming as important and as rich as the capitals of some neighboring states. Paris had increased in a terrific manner; and while the nobles were quitting their estates to ruin themselves in Paris, the commoners were piling up wealth by means of their industry. All the little provincial towns had become more or less commercial; almost all had manufactures or some special commercial product. All were peopled with *petits bourgeois,* who were richer and more industrious than the nobles, and who had found the way, themselves or their fathers, to enrich themselves in the administration or in the leasing of the fiefs and lands of the great lords and nobles, or even in their service, when they could not take part in greater speculations. They received, in general, an education which was more necessary for them than for gentlemen, since the latter, by their birth and by their wealth, obtained the leading posts in the state without possessing either merit or talent, while the former were destined to languish in secondary positions in the army. Thus, in Paris and in the large cities, the bourgeoisie was superior in wealth, in talent, and in personal merit. In the provincial towns they possessed the same superiority over the country nobility. Although they were well aware of this superiority, they were humiliated continually. They found themselves excluded by military regulations from positions in the army. In the same way they were excluded from the upper clergy by the choice of bishops and Vicars-general from among the nobility. In general they were excluded from most cathedral chapters. [In the magistrature] the judges rejected them as equals and in fact most of the sovereign courts admitted only nobles to their membership.

Two Englishmen View France

The first reading contains an excerpt from a letter written in Paris by John Moore, an English physician who spent a year on the continent as traveling companion to the young Duke of Hamilton. The second selection is from the diary of Arthur Young, the agricultural reformer. Young traveled in France in 1787, 1788, and again in 1789 to study "the cultivation, resources, and national prosperity" of that country. I. From John Moore, *A View of Society and Manners in France, Switzerland and Germany* (London, 1803), Vol. I, pp. 27–28. II. From *Arthur Young's Travels in France* (London, 1892), pp. 197–198.

I. JOHN MOORE (1779)

A candid Englishman, of whatever rank in life he may be, must see with indignation, that every thing in this kingdom is arranged for the accommodation of the rich and the powerful; and that little or no regard is paid to the comfort of citizens of an inferior station. This appears in a thousand instances, and strikes the eye immediately on entering Paris.

I think I have seen it somewhere remarked, that the regular and effectual manner in which the city of London is lighted at night, and the raised pavements on the sides of every street for the security and conveniency of foot passengers, seem to indicate, that the body of the people, as well as the rich and great, are counted of some importance in the eye of the government. Whereas Paris is poorly and partially lighted; and except on the Pont Neuf and Pont Royal, and the quays between them, is not provided with footways for the accommodation and safety of those who cannot afford carriages. They must therefore grope their way as they best can, and skulk behind pillars, or run into shops, to avoid being crushed by the coaches, which are driven as near the wall as the coachman pleases; dispersing the people on foot at their approach, like chaff before the wind.

It must be acknowledged, that monarchy (for the French do not love to hear it called despotism, and it is needless to quarrel with them about a word) is raised in this country so very high, that it quite loses sight of the bulk of the nation, and pays attention only to a few, who, being in exalted stations, come within the Court's sphere of vision.

II. ARTHUR YOUNG (1789)

July 12th. Walking up a long hill, to ease my mare, I was joined by a poor woman, who complained of the times, and that it was a sad country; demanding her reasons, she said her husband had but a morsel of land, one cow, and a poor little horse, yet they had a *franchar* (42 lb.) of wheat, and three chickens, to pay as a quitrent to one Seigneur; and four *franchar* of oats, one chicken and 1 shilling to

This view of Fenchurch Street with Ironmongers Hall, c.1760, presents the well-groomed London John Moore described. A less inspiring aspect of eighteenth-century London is seen in Hogarth's "Gin Lane".

pay to another, besides very heavy tailles and other taxes. She had seven children, and the cow's milk helped to make the soup. . . . It was said, at present, that something was to be done by some great folks for such poor ones, but she did not know who nor how, but God send us better, *car les tailles et les droits nous ecrasent* [the taxes and special privileges are destroying us].—This woman, at no great distance, might have been taken for sixty or seventy, her figure was so bent, and her face so furrowed and hardened by labour—but she said she was only twenty-eight. An Englishman who has not travelled, cannot imagine the figure made by infinitely the greater part of the countrywomen in France; it speaks, at the first sight, hard and severe labour; I am inclined to think that they work harder than the men, and this, united with the more miserable labour of bringing a new race of slaves into the world, destroys absolutely all symmetry of person and every feminine appearance. To what are we to attribute this difference in the manners of the lower people in the two kingdoms? To GOVERNMENT.

Rousseau Dines with a French Peasant (1732)

Rousseau was twenty at the time of this incident. He was on his way through central France, going from Paris to Lyons, without work and, as usual, with little money. From J. J. Rousseau, *Confessions* (London, 1904), Book IV, Vol. I, pp. 148–149.

One day, amongst others, having purposely turned out of my way to get a nearer view of a spot which appeared worthy of admiration, I was so delighted with it, and went round it so often that, at last, I completely lost myself. After several hours of useless walking, tired, and dying of hunger and thirst, I entered a peasant's hut, not much to look at, but the only dwelling I saw in the neighborhood. I expected to find it the same as in Geneva, or Switzerland, where all the well-to-do inhabitants are in a position to show hospitality. I begged him to give me dinner, and offered to pay for it. He offered me some skimmed milk and coarse barley bread, saying that that was all he had. I drank the milk with delight, and ate the bread, husks and all; but it was not very invigorating fare for a man exhausted by fatigue. The peasant, who examined me closely, estimated the truth of my story by my appetite, and immediately afterwards declared that he could see that I was a good and honourable young man, who had not come there to betray him for money. He opened a little trapdoor near the kitchen, went down, and come up a minute afterwards with a nice brown wheaten loaf, a very tempting-looking ham, although considerably cut down, and a bottle of wine, the sight of which rejoiced my heart more than all the rest; to this he added a substantial omelette, and I made a dinner such as none but a pedestrian ever enjoyed. When it came to the question of payment, his uneasiness and alarm returned; he would take none of my money, and refused it with singular anxiety; and the amusing thing was that I could not imagine what he was afraid of. At last, with a shudder, he uttered the terrible words, "Revenue-officers and excisemen." He gave me to understand that he hid his wine on account of the excise, that he hid his bread on account of the tax, and that he was a lost man, if anyone had a suspicion that he was not starving. All that he said to me on this subject, of which I had not the least idea, made an impression upon me which will never be forgotten. It was the germ of the inextinguishable hatred which subsequently grew up in my heart against the oppression to which these unhappy people are subject, and against their oppressors. This man, although in good circumstances, did not dare to eat the bread which he had obtained by the sweat of his brow, and could only escape utter ruin by displaying the same poverty as prevailed around him. I left his house, equally indignant and touched, lamenting the lot of these beautiful countries, upon which Nature has only lavished her gifts to make them the prey of barbarous farmers of taxes. . . .

A German Duke Purchases a Farm (1777)

From W. H. Bruford, *Germany in the Eighteenth Century* (New York: Cambridge University Press, 1952), pp. 95–96.

A relative of the mistress of . . . the duke of Pfalz-Zweibrücken (Karl II August) owned a farm near Homburg that she wished to sell. The duke was accordingly persuaded to visit

A ducal country residence such as that described in the reading. This *Lustschloss,* or pleasure palace, near Dresden was built for the Elector of Saxony in the early eighteenth century.

it one day. It was made to look very attractive. The farmer and his family and all their servants were working in their picturesque Sunday clothes, the finest of cattle were brought there for the visit, delicious cream and butter were served and by good fortune the weather was glorious. The court doctor assured the prince that it would be impossible to be ill in such surroundings, and the ladies and gentlemen-in-waiting could not sufficiently praise the view. The duke easily fell a victim. Next day [his official architect] was summoned to him. The stables and byres had to be enlarged, a cottage for the farmer and his family had to be built, the rooms needed structural alterations, decoration, and furnishing. An English garden had to be made of the woods, valleys and meadows near the house. In a few weeks the farm had already grown into quite a village, for the crowds of workmen who were needed had to be accommodated, with their families, in specially built huts, where you saw their wives washing their linen out of doors and their children playing and dancing. . . . At first the duke just drove over every afternoon, but presently he wanted to dine there. This necessitated further alterations—a new kitchen wing, a large dining room. And so the farm grew and grew until the duke was living there permanently. Soon a regular [palace] had been built, with stables for a thousand horses, kennels for a thousand dogs, an enormous riding-school, with quarters for the equerries, grooms, keepers, cooks and servants; an 'orangerie' with rooms for the gentlemen-in-waiting, pages, officers, doctors, chaplains and gardeners; a picture gallery and library, a theatre, a zoological garden, and barracks for 1400 men. Finally a whole town had to be called into being, to accommodate all those whose services were required by the duke and his court. All this happened in about ten years. It is said to have cost the duke fourteen million Gulden— the income of the duchy was 800,000! . . .

STUDY QUESTIONS

1. What was the European social structure like in the eighteenth century? To what extent was each of the social classes essentially traditional?

2. According to Anderson, what were the principal forces that were influencing the structure of eighteenth-century society? Are they the same as those called "elements of flux" in Reading 126?

3. What was the general economic condition of Europe at this time? Why did population increase rapidly? What effect did economic expansion, rising prices, population growth, and movement from country to towns have on the various social classes?

4. What is meant by aristocratic consolidation? Why should this process speed up in the eighteenth century? What might be the consequences of the speedup?

5. To what extent do Readings 127–130 support the issues raised in the first reading? What tensions between classes emerge in each?

Europe Migrates Outward

From William H. McNeill, *The Rise of the West* (Chicago: University of Chicago Press, 1963), pp. 653, 656–657, 661–663, 664–665, 667–668. Copyright © 1963 by the University of Chicago Press.

TOPIC 24

THE AMERICAN REVOLUTION

While absolutism, enlightened or otherwise, was the common form of government on the European continent in the eighteenth century, Great Britain was ruled by an oligarchy of the well-born, who dominated Parliament. These were successful and prosperous years on the whole for Britain, years of accelerating economic growth and expanding Empire. In 1763, three-quarters of a century of armed rivalry with France ended with the virtual expulsion of the French from the Western Hemisphere. Within little more than a decade, however, the English inhabitants of the North American coast had risen in revolt against the mother country. The American Revolution, fed by English constitutional development and the political theorizing of the Enlightenment, provided a stirring example for the challenge to the established order by the new economic, social, and political forces of the eighteenth century. The readings are concerned with why this challenge occurred and with the shape that it assumed.

By 1700, the wealth and power at Europe's command clearly surpassed anything that other civilized communities of the earth could muster; and European society had attained a precarious equilibrium resting upon intensification as well as extension of enterprise at home and abroad. The New World offered the greatest single field for European expansion, although no part of the habitable globe entirely escaped attention. Between 1700 and 1850, such vast regions as northern Asia, Australia, South Africa, India, and the Levant all in varying degrees became satellites of the European political-economic system. Only in the Far East did massive civilized societies retain full autonomy; and even there, China and Japan began to experience creeping internal crisis that prepared the way for a definitive collapse of the traditional social order in the Far East shortly after 1850. . . .

The multifarious aspects of European expansion in the seventeenth and eighteenth centuries may, without unduly drastic schematization, be reduced to three types of exploitation of the lands and peoples with which Europeans came in contact. First and farthest-ranging, Europeans continued to penetrate regions where readily available local products had value for European or other civilized markets. Furs from the frozen northlands of Asia and America plus gold and diamonds from the Brazilian jungles were the most important such products in the period 1650–1789. Second, in certain tropical and sub-tropical lands, especially the West and East Indies, Europeans reorganized local economies to produce commodities in demand upon the world market. This involved drastic interference with pre-existing social relationships, for European enterprise was based upon slavery or other forms of forced labor and sometimes involved massive population transfers. Third, in temperate regions, primarily in North and South America and in the western parts of the Eurasian steppe, European settlements developed from crude beginnings into genuine transplants of a European style of society, even when separated from the heartland of Europe by thousands of miles. . . .

THE SPREAD OF EUROPEAN SETTLEMENT

In diverse parts of the earth, European settlers produced a series of mutations from the social patterns of their homelands. The rigorous slavery of a West Indian sugar plantation and the rude egalitarianism of a New England frontier community represent extremes of a spectrum along which many intermediate social forms may be discerned. The harsh slavery of Barbados shaded into the less rigorous conditions of servitude that prevailed on Spanish or Portuguese plantations in Central America and Brazil. The neo-

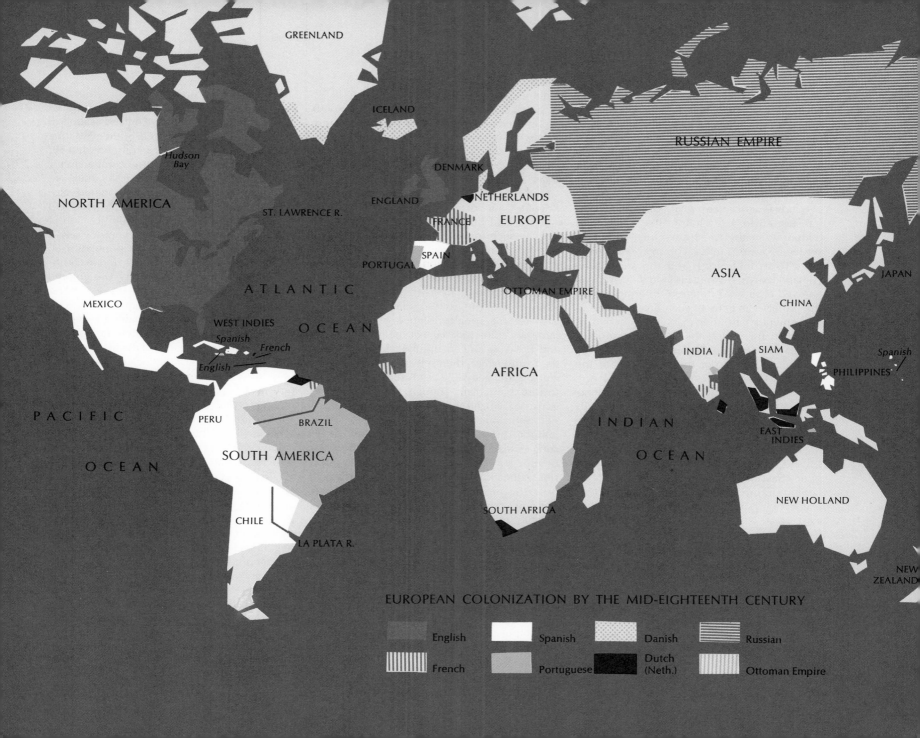

GREENLAND

RUSSIAN EMPIRE

ICELAND

Hudson Bay

DENMARK

ENGLAND

NETHERLANDS

NORTH AMERICA

ST. LAWRENCE R.

FRANCE

EUROPE

ASIA

JAPAN

SPAIN

PORTUGAL

CHINA

ATLANTIC

MEXICO

OTTOMAN EMPIRE

INDIA

SIAM

WEST INDIES

OCEAN

Spanish

French

Spanish

PHILIPPINES

English

AFRICA

PACIFIC

PERU

BRAZIL

INDIAN

EAST INDIES

SOUTH AMERICA

OCEAN

OCEAN

CHILE

NEW HOLLAND

SOUTH AFRICA

LA PLATA R.

NEW ZEALAND

EUROPEAN COLONIZATION BY THE MID-EIGHTEENTH CENTURY

English   Spanish   Danish   Russian

French   Portuguese   Dutch (Neth.)   Ottoman Empire

serfdom of eastern Europe and the forced labor exacted from the Indians of Spanish America represented a milder form of compulsory service, in law if not always in fact; and once again the Spanish case was milder, if only because the weight of government regulation stood on the side of Indian rights. Workmen indentured for a term of years—a common practice in early Virginia—and felons transported to Australia or Siberia occupied midpoints in the spectrum. Finally, the free settler of a proprietary colony, owing quit-rents to a noble lord, and the small New England farmer, owning his land in fee simple, enjoyed a personal freedom inferior only to the ultimate anarchy of such diverse types as the American frontiersman, the Siberian or Canadian fur trader, the Brazilian bandiera, the gaucho of the Argentine pampas, the Ukrainian Cossack, or the buccaneer of the Spanish Main.

On any advancing frontier, labor shortage is always a major problem. Diametrically opposite solutions offer: drastic compulsion to sustain social stratification; or equally drastic liberty with concomitant regression toward an egalitarian neo-barbarism. Each policy has advantages and drawbacks. Drastic compulsion may be required to sustain specialists who are needed if the society is to exist at all. Thus without hard-driving economic entrepreneurs, plantations could not arise; and without a professional military class, agricultural settlements on the western parts of the Eurasian steppelands could not have been defended. Moreover, an upper class sustained by compulsory labor may rapidly attain a comparatively high degree of culture and lend the society as a whole a veneer of elegance otherwise unattainable. Such achievements are easily underrated in

a democratic age, when men are more likely to sympathize with the slave or serf than with his master. Yet civilization first arose only through the direction of the labor of one group by another; and by a similar process, civilized societies repeatedly were able to transcend constricting geographical barriers—whether long ago in Hittite Asia Minor and Roman Gaul, or more recently in Spanish America and Russian Ukraine. Yet the drawback to such forcible propagation of civilization is always serious; for a culture which excludes the great majority of the inhabitants remains necessarily precarious.

We are far more likely to admire the other alternative of the frontier: drastic egalitarianism. Yet the rough violence of such communities, directed against helpless natives and breaking out in drunken brawls among the frontiersmen themselves, meant a degeneration of erstwhile civilized populations toward barbarism. Though armed with the guns of civilized workshops, European frontiersmen sloughed off nearly all the legal and cultural restraints of civilized society. To be sure, civilized life gradually arose in the wake of rude pioneers through social differentiation, education, and technical advance. Moreover, this process undoubtedly worked itself out more rapidly and regularly than the comparable process of cultural filtering down from a cultivated aristocracy. In this lay the real superiority of anarchic frontier liberty as against its alternative of wholesale compulsion. But during the seventeenth and eighteenth centuries the advantages of the plunge toward anarchism remained almost wholly potential, while the shorter-range successes of compulsion were evident and undeniable. Assuredly, the cultivated elegance of aristocratic Virginia, New Spain, Hungary, and Russia—based . . . upon compulsory labor—far over-balanced the modest beginnings of civilization along the New England seaboard.

Yet the New England and Middle Atlantic colonies of North America compensated for their cultural crudity by the comparatively large number of European (or rather ex-European) settlers they accommodated. Nowhere else in the world did such large and compact agricultural communities arise. Nonetheless, the eighteenth century saw a substantial growth of Spanish population in the La Plata region of Argentina; and in southern Brazil, Portuguese settlers pre-empted wide territories. But in both these regions, ranching was more prominent than agriculture, so that settlement remained comparatively thin. In Canada, French farmers remained close to the banks of the St. Lawrence; and backwoods farming began to develop only toward the end of the eighteenth century, in large part through the initiative of Tory refugees from the American Revolution. In South Africa, Dutch colonists landed at Capetown in 1652. When the British took over the colony in 1795, Dutch ranchers had penetrated far inland; while near the Cape itself a fairly substantial farming community had taken root. In 1789 the first English settlers landed in Australia. Thus except for New Zealand, first colonized in 1840, all the major overseas centers of European population had begun their development by the end of the eighteenth century.

The movement of European settlers across the world's oceans was spectacular and pregnant for the future; but the simultaneous settlement of the western Eurasian steppelands probably involved a more massive migration and was no less significant in changing the cultural balance of the world. In the

318

This eighteenth-century engraving presents a highly imaginative view of the planning of Savannah, Georgia with non-existent mountains towering in the background, but it does clearly show the settlers at work reclaiming the wilderness. The plan and details of construction, the process of land clearing, and the utilization of slave labor blend aspects reflecting the culture of two worlds.

In contrast to the men who carried Europe with them to the New World, Russians found the process of Westernization a more traumatic experience. In this illustration one of Tsar Peter's soldiers forcibly cuts off the beard of a nobleman to make him look more like a Western European. An avid Westerner, Peter imported hundreds of foreign craftsmen and technicians and was the first Russian ruler to travel widely in Western Europe.

seventeenth and eighteenth centuries, millions of pioneers broke the vast grasslands between central Hungary and western Siberia to the plow. At the extreme edges of this eastward movement, anarchic frontier conditions arose comparable to those of the New World. Russian settlers in Siberia, for example, escaped all but nominal control and lived rough lives as hunters, fishers, and agriculturalists much like those of American frontiersmen. . . .

The expansion of European civilization after 1648 proceeded, not only by occupation of new ground, but also by acculturation to European styles of life in outlying regions already within Europe's sphere of influence. By 1789, this process had brought large parts of Russia and the New World to full member-ship in what henceforth must be called Western, rather than merely European civilization. This addition of America and Russia to the European-centered body politic of the West increased the variety and diluted or perhaps even debased the quality of Western civilization. Yet despite persistent differences between the old centers of European civilization and the outliers, a basic community of culture more and more united the American, western European, and Russian peoples, and set them off from the civilized communities of the rest of the world.

The acculturation of Russia and the Americas to a European style of civilization proceeded by remarkably different paths. Russians had first to cast off much of their peculiar cultural heritage—a violent and painful process—before they could embrace the West. By contrast, the American descendants of European immigrants were merely reclaiming what their ancestors had in varying measure sloughed off by succumbing to rude conditions of frontier existence; and no deep psychological strains were involved in once again sharing more fully in European civilization. . . .

Even at the end of the eighteenth century, the English, ex-English and French colonies lagged far behind Spanish America. Mexico City, with 112,926 inhabitants in 1793, eclipsed anything to the north and indeed surpassed in size any city of contemporary France and England except Paris or London. Indeed, the population of Mexico exceeded by a substantial margin that of all thirteen English colonies together; and the splendor, elegance, and cultivation of the Spanish colonial upper class surpassed anything yet achieved along the Atlantic coast of North America.

Yet the culturally laggard New England and Middle Atlantic colonies of North America represented the most thoroughgoing translation of European-type society to new ground to be found anywhere in the world. These English colonies developed rapidly from the small and isolated coastal lodgments of the early seventeenth century into a more or less continuous band of settlements stretching from New Hampshire to Georgia and, by the time of the American Revolution, extending inland to the Appalachians. Population grew very fast, partly by immigration but mainly through natural increase. By 1790, when the first United States census was taken, it totaled four million, not far short of half the population of Great Britain.

Britain's American Colonies

Excerpted from *Europe and America* by Solomon F. Bloom, © 1961 by Harcourt, Brace & World, Inc. and reprinted with their permission.

In England two revolutions in the seventeenth century had resulted in a compromise under which the mercantile classes, the landed classes, and the monarchy shared power in a ratio which fluctuated with circumstances. The power of the monarchy was still ample—at the beginning of the eighteenth century Queen Anne was still vetoing acts of Parliament—but the ruler could not collect taxes or control the army without parliamentary consent. Nor could he suspend laws. Under the common law, the state had to defend the validity of its acts in courts. The nobility and gentry continued to control the countryside while the trading and shipping classes helped to shape economic and colonial policy. . . .

The representative institutions of Britain prevailed in her colonies on the American mainland. These colonies had been founded by royal charters and grants, some of which were constitutions in miniature. There was a very restricted suffrage, resting generally on the ownership of landed property, but since property was more widely distributed and inheritance laws were more egalitarian than at home, a greater proportion of the colonists was represented in their assemblies than of Englishmen in the House of Commons. . . .

THE IMPACT OF THE ENLIGHTENMENT

The Enlightenment promoted an easy interchange of ideas. It made the European world, and particularly the countries bordering on the North Atlantic, a single cultural community. The leading men of France, Holland, Great Britain, and the American colonies maintained contact with one another by correspondence and visits. Locke and Newton were the patron saints of the French and American as well as the English Enlighten-

ment. Montesquieu and Voltaire were widely read on both sides of the Channel, and on both sides of the ocean. In France, Anglomania and, later, enthusiasm for everything American were common. Businessmen crossed borders easily, and it was customary for investors and enterprisers to function with facility in several Atlantic countries. There were men who enjoyed citizenship and the privileges of natives in two or three countries simultaneously.

In each country the Enlightenment was naturally colored by local characteristics. In England the touch of empiricism was especially strong. France paid her traditional homage to logic, precision, and clarity. The American colonies were at once behind and ahead of England and France. They were both cultural and political dependencies, for they imported their reading matter and scientific knowledge, like their manufactured goods and luxuries, from Europe. Even their Bibles were European; it was not until 1777 that the first English version of the New Testament was published in the colonies. The Enlightenment crossed the ocean rather slowly, but the American had one advantage over the European: he was born more than half enlightened. In *Letters from an American Farmer* (1782), the fond eulogy of the French essayist and agronomist Hector St. John de Crèvecoeur (1735–1813), the American was a "new man." He had left behind

. . . all his ancient prejudices and manners, receives new ones from the new mode of life he has embraced, the new government he obeys, and the new rank he holds. . . . From involuntary idleness, servile dependence, penury, and useless labor, he has passed to toils of a different nature, rewarded by ample subsistence. This is an American.

The transatlantic society was

> not composed, as in Europe, of great lords who possess everything, and a herd of people who have nothing. Here are no aristocratical families, no courts, no kings, no bishops, no ecclesiastical dominion, no invisible power giving to a few a very visible one; no great manufactures employing thousands, no great refinements of luxury. The rich and the poor are not so far removed from each other as they are in Europe.

Nor were the various nationalities. "I could point out to you," wrote Crèvecoeur, "a man whose grandfather was an Englishman, whose wife was Dutch, whose son married a French woman, and whose present four sons have now four wives of different nations." In America, "individuals of all nations are melted into a new race of men," deriving from that "strange mixture of blood, which you will find in no other country." . . .

Apart from breeding an easier and more democratic atmosphere, America contributed to the Enlightenment a tart homeliness of expression. Benjamin Franklin (1706–90), the self-made printer and businessman of Philadelphia who was also a journalist, scientist, inventor, and politician, was the prototype of the enlightened American. His popular mouthpiece, Poor Richard of the *Almanac*, observed, "Kings and bears often worry their keepers," "Poverty, poetry, and new titles of honor make men ridiculous," and "Love and lordship hate companions." Franklin wrote,

> In old times it was no disrespect for men and women to be called by their

Benjamin Franklin, "prototype of the enlightened American," wears the fur cap of the American frontier in this contemporary portrait by John Trumbull.

own names. Adam was never called Master Adam; we never read of Noah Esquire, Lot Knight, and Baronet, nor the Right Honorable Abraham, Viscount Mesopotamia, Baron of Canaan. No, no, they were plain men, honest country graziers, that took care of their families and their flocks.

Franklin's young compatriot Thomas Jefferson remarked with a rough directness, "It does me no injury for my neighbor to say that there are twenty gods, or no god. It neither picks my pocket nor breaks my leg."

There were two other ways in which American experience made a significant contribution to the Enlightenment. Some of the colonies had charters or "contracts" with the Crown which laid down procedures of government and lawmaking; thus the concept of written constitutions took root in the New World. Secondly, while representation in European parliaments or estates was often based on rank, class, office, or prescription, the need to grant representation to frontier settlers accustomed the American colonists to the idea of representation exclusively by township or territory. This idea became central in modern parliamentarianism. . . .

ENGLISH CONSTITUTIONAL QUESTIONS

In the preceeding century two revolutions had advanced the power of Parliament, although they left the monarch with considerable strength. They had led to the entrenchment in ministerial office of a group of princely landlords, supported by mercantile interests and religious dissenters. This Whig oligarchy opposed the interference of the king in the conduct of affairs, which it came to regard as its monopoly. The first Hanover-

ENGLISH RULERS FROM CHARLES II
TO GEORGE III

Charles II	1660–1685
James II	1685–1688
William and	1689–1702
Mary	1689–1694
Anne	1702–1714
George I	1714–1727
George II	1727–1760
George III	1760–1820

ian kings, George I (1714–1727) and George II (1727–1760), were much more interested in governing their native German state than England. By a kind of disuse and indifference, influence slipped from the Crown to Whig ministers.

On the whole, Whig rule was liberal and successful, although its political means were questionable. The ministers controlled Parliament, either through the purchase of seats—many were available on the market at about £2000—or through the dispensing of offices, pensions, sinecures, and outright gifts to members. The laws against religious dissent lost much of their severity in a loose enforcement. An easygoing rule preserved the traditional liberties of the country. Commercial and maritime interests were vigorously prosecuted.

At the moment of their greatest triumphs, the Whigs met their match in the young King George III (1760–1820). Unlike his two predecessors, George III was a native Briton. He had been brought up to resent the ascendancy of the Whig families. His mind was limited and intermittently unbalanced, but he had great earnestness and persistence. He ascended the throne in 1760 determined to emancipate the Crown and to rule as well as reign. Although the Whig ministers had governed under his predecessors, the cabinet system was not yet fully developed. Ministers could disagree on policy and vote on opposite sides in Parliament. It was recognized that the king had a right to choose the ministers, although his choices had to be approved by a majority in the House of Commons.

The methods of George III and "the King's friends," a group of noblemen and politicians who flocked to his support, were not revolutionary. They did not propose to revive the claim of a royal prerogative to act without parliamentary sanction, which had cost the Stuart dynasty two thrones and a royal head in the preceding century. Rather, they proposed that the King act like many another aristocratic politician—that is, that he control blocks of seats in the Commons by purchase or by influencing the electors to vote for his nominees. In such a game, however, the monarch had a great and, it seemed to his opponents, an unfair advantage, for he had at his disposal large funds from the state treasury.

The combination of royal and parliamentary influence would make the power of the King and his "friends" irresistible. It would diminish the distinction between legislative and executive power which was one of the principal guarantees of liberty. Although his methods were conventional, therefore, the success of George III as a political leader, with a party of his own, held distinct dangers for the constitutional development of Great Britain. The situation was worsened by the fact that the King and his supporters pursued their aims with an obstinacy that jarred political sensibilities and spilled over into the area of policy. . . .

However, before the liberals could check "the King's friends" at home, colonial self-respect was roused to do them battle. The royal power was no less dangerous at home than in the colonies, where indeed it introduced fewer innovations; but these innovations confirmed exactions which had long been regarded as oppressive and therefore appeared in the unpleasant guise of imperialism.

THE AMERICAN ISSUE

The Whig oligarchy had treated the English colonies in North America with a salutary offhandedness. Until the middle of the eighteenth century the thirteen colonies had been neither rich enough nor populous enough to invite intensive exploitation; the West Indian islands, with their profitable sugar plantations and the ancillary slave trade, had attracted greater attention and interest. The king, as we have seen, usually appointed the governors of the American colonies, except for a few cases in which governors were elected or "proprietors" exercised executive powers on the basis of royal charters. The lower houses of the legislatures were everywhere elected by the colonists, while members of the upper houses were appointed by the governors. The colonists supplied the bulk of the administrators. The salaries of elected officials, and of most of the royal appointees, depended on the approval of the assemblies, a system which gave the colonists a measure of self-government and control over the executive. The corruption of politics in England was not matched in the overseas colonies. All in all, the colonies enjoyed a somewhat more liberal political system than the mother country.

However, the economic regulations imposed by the distant government in London were onerous. The American market was reserved for British manufactures, and local industries which competed with home enterprises were forbidden. The colonists were compelled to purchase most of their imports in England. When they were allowed to buy elsewhere, they had to transship through a British port, paying a substantial tribute to the British exchequer and a middleman's profit to British merchants, warehousemen, and factors. Many a colonial staple could be exported only to the mother country. Parliament sweetened the pill of these Navigation Acts by granting bounties on some important American staples which Britain needed, by giving the colonies a favored position in the British

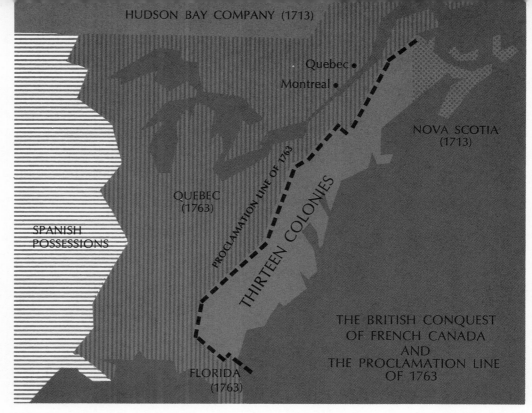

HUDSON BAY COMPANY (1713)

Quebec •
Montreal •

NOVA SCOTIA
(1713)

QUEBEC
(1763)

PROCLAMATION LINE OF 1763

THIRTEEN COLONIES

SPANISH
POSSESSIONS

FLORIDA
(1763)

THE BRITISH CONQUEST
OF FRENCH CANADA
AND
THE PROCLAMATION LINE
OF 1763

market as compared with foreign competitors, and by promoting and protecting colonial as well as British shipping. But the greatest "compensation" for these controls was their lax enforcement. Smuggling was common in that age everywhere, but it was practiced most widely in the New World, where it was hardest to check. The American colonists engaged tacitly in what amounted to an informal trade with non-British colonies and Continental countries, notably Holland. . . .

Of the immediate issues that aroused the colonists, one was an irritation and the other a provocation. As a result of her defeat in [1763, in the latest of a series of colonial wars between them,] France had ceded to Great Britain the large area which lay between the Allegheny Mountains and the Mississippi River. By the Proclamation of 1763, Britain closed this region to American settlement, ostensibly to obviate conflict with the Indian tribes. . . . The colonists feared that the government might assign huge estates in the territory to a few favorites and courtiers, a fear which, under the prevailing system of government, was only too likely to become a reality. Small folk became restless, although the government could not easily prevent them from settling on the frontier. Speculative companies were particularly disturbed, for they had hoped to buy large tracts and hold them for inflated sales to settlers. In a new and growing country, land represents the most important form of investment, and some of the leading capitalists and politicians held stock in such companies.

Of greater immediate consequence was the attempt to raise more money in the colonies. The British government was determined to compel Americans to contribute toward the support of imperial armed forces and to ensure their cooperation in time of crisis. It

therefore attempted to strengthen the central authority. New laws and administrative orders issued in 1763–1765 provided for the strict enforcement of trade regulations. New revenues to help defray the salaries of the royal governors and their appointees were raised— not, as formerly, by royal requisitions addressed to the colonial assemblies and approved by them, but by the action of the legislature at London. If both Parliament and the colonial assemblies could pass tax measures, the utmost circumspection was called for, in order to avoid a conflict. Yet the measures were approved by Parliament with hardly any discussion. The Americans protested immediately, and with a vehemence that astonished both the government and the opposition in England.

The colonists were even more deeply disturbed by Britain's evident intention to enforce and extend mercantilist controls and exploitation than by the fiscal program. But the right of the Parliament in London to regulate trade and impose external taxes— customs duties, for example—was securely established and recognized and could not be challenged. The colonists therefore selected the Stamp Act, among the many measures of 1763–1765, as the main target of their attack. This law provided that no legal document was valid in a court unless it carried a stamp of a value proportionate to the financial transaction involved. The tax was not large, but such "internal" imposts had customarily been imposed only by the colonial assemblies. It was also a conspicuous tax, affecting poor men as well as rich, professional men and journalists—especially vocal groups—as well as landowners and businessmen: everyone who had to make a will, a contract, or a loan. In October 1765 a congress of delegates from nine colonies drew up a protest against internal taxes imposed from the outside: ". . . it is inseparably essential to the freedom of a people, and the undoubted right of Englishmen, that no taxes be imposed on them but with their own consent, given personally or by their representatives." . . .

The substance of the American case, then, was rather different from its formalities. In essence, the colonists were insisting that they be treated on an equal basis with the Englishmen at home. They wished their assemblies to be able to bargain with and check royal power as the English Parliament could. They had come to think of America not as an inferior appendage of England, but as another England, or, better, a distinct commonwealth. Some of them believed that the British Empire must evolve toward a federal system.

The colonists arrived at this conception at least a century before any European government put it into practice. In the late eighteenth century, the government of England hardly shared their vision, although many enlightened men did. The controversy sharpened the constitutional issue in England. The King was at a great advantage, for, since many English groups profited from colonial control, he could defend his policy as patriotic. But his victory would be also a victory over the Whig theory of government as it had developed earlier in the century. Thus the issue of colonial freedom became one with that of enlightened reform and Parliamentary supremacy—and they were resolved together.

Even though the colonists were thus defending the cause of English as well as Ameri-

can liberty, the Parliamentary opposition to the King's policies could not help them much. The Whigs were in the minority. Besides, they were chary of diminishing the jurisdiction of Parliament, for whose independence they were striving. They therefore wished to retain the right, and continue the practice, though in attenuated form, of commercial controls. This was the position of the imperialist William Pitt, who applauded American resistance but added:

> Let the sovereign authority of this country over the colonies be asserted in as strong terms as can be made to extend to every point of legislation whatsoever. That we may bind their trade, confine their manufactures, and exercise every power whatsoever, except that of taking their money out of their pockets without their own consent. . . .

Since the Americans had not challenged the right of the mother country to regulate their commerce, there was room for compromise. But George III and his compliant Prime Minister, Lord North (1732–1792), who headed the government from 1770 to 1782, were resolved not to compromise. They treated the colonists with condescension. The Americans retaliated by ignoring the Stamp Act, intimidating the distributors of the stamps into inactivity, and agreeing to cease buying English goods. The Stamp Act was thereupon repealed, in 1766, but a Declaratory Act was simultaneously passed, asserting the right of Parliament to regulate the colonies in all matters. Since the Americans were contending for a real case, not a formal one, they enjoyed their practical victory. But in the following year Parliament passed the Townshend Acts, which provided

for the collection of a variety of customs duties, partly in order to pay the salaries of royal officials in the colonies. The old argument was reopened, but this time the colonial assemblies clashed with the governors, and commercial intercourse with England was diminished by voluntary agreement among the colonies.

From this point, it was goad on one side and defiance on the other. The Americans resented particularly the revival of an old law under which they might be taken to England to be tried for treason. When the Townshend duties were repealed in 1770, a small tax on tea was retained in order to demonstrate the claim that Parliament could tax the colonies. Three years later the East India Company had an oversupply of tea on hand. The government remitted the duty collected upon imports into England and allowed the Company to reship its cargo to the colonies, where a somewhat smaller duty would be charged. Although the Americans would thus obtain unusually cheap tea, the incident illustrated some of the worst features of imperialism: favoritism to well-connected interests and discriminatory treatment of colonists. When the ships arrived in Boston Harbor, a group of disguised colonists boarded them and threw overboard the whole cargo of 340 chests. England's answer to the "Boston Tea Party" was coercion. The port was closed and the authority of the royal governor strengthened. The colonies promptly drew together in the First Continental Congress (1774), which denounced the enforcement of these measures and organized a commercial boycott of England. Organizations of patriots multiplied: Committees of Correspondence, to keep the colonies in close touch with one another and to coordinate their policies and activities; Committees of Safety, to take over

American colonists resist British imperialism by dumping tea into Boston Harbor. In this nineteenth-century illustration, the "Indians" are encouraged from the wharves by their fellow patriots.

Five colonists were killed by British troops in the Boston Massacre, March 5, 1770. According to one eye-witness, the "mulatto" Crispus Attucks (center) probably was the first to fall. The attack by soldiers on a milling crowd brought sympathy to the anti-British movement. A contemporary broadside by Paul Revere.

the functions of government or to exert pressure upon the existing colonial parliaments or officials; and "Sons of Liberty," to press for direct resistance and to intimidate the "loyalist" partisans of the English government. The royal troops were bested by colonial volunteers in the first clash, which occurred at Lexington, near Boston, in April 1775. In August the King branded the colonists as rebels, and they beseiged his army in Boston. The die was cast—yet many conservative Americans still struggled between loyalty and risk.

Into this inflammable situation a brilliant English pamphleteer, newly arrived in America, cast a lighted match. In *Common Sense* Thomas Paine (1737–1809) argued boldly for a rupture with the mother country. Hereditary monarchy, Paine asserted, has no basis either in natural or in divine right. The Lord was a republican, he reminded a generation which was familiar with the Old Testament, for He had tried to argue the Hebrews out of their demand to be given a king: "Your wickedness is great, which ye have done in the sight of the Lord, in asking for a king. . . ." Royalty, wrote Paine, was born in conquest, usurpation, and robbery. Between such an institution and America there was no room for compromise. In independence only, and independence at once, lay the safety of the colonists and the best hope, not only of America, but of the whole Western world: "Freedom hath been hunted around the globe. Asia, and Africa, have long expelled her. Europe regards her like a stranger, and England hath given her warning to depart. O! receive the fugitive, and prepare in time an asylum for mankind." George Washington said that *Common Sense* "worked a powerful change in the minds of many men."

Waverers took sides. Most of the colonists split into supporters of independence and uncompromising loyalists. The former had the advantage of vigor and represented a broad cross section of the population. By the spring of 1776 royal authority had collapsed nearly everywhere, and the elected assemblies, seconded or rivaled by more spontaneous organizations, had informally taken over executive and even judicial functions. Separation was a fact, and in July 1776 the Second Continental Congress openly declared the independence of America and instructed the colonies to establish new governments and write constitutions.

Thomas Paine Argues That Independence Makes Common Sense
(January 1776)

Thomas Paine (1737–1809) had already protested against royal authority in England before coming to America in 1774. Here he quickly made the cause of the rebellious colonists his own and in January, 1776 published a famous pamphlet, *Common Sense*, which urged immediate independence from Great Britain. Between 1776 and 1783 he wrote another sixteen essays on *The American Crisis*. Paine's writings, idealistic, radical, and polemic, captured the imagination of the public and contributed to the American determination to gain independence. Paine, himself, later participated in the French Revolution. The selection from *Common Sense* that follows is taken from the third part of the pamphlet, in which the author presents his arguments for immediate independence. From *Life and Writings of Thomas Paine,* ed. D. E. Wheeler (New York, 1908), II, *Common Sense,* pp. 29–34, 41–44, 54–55, 57–58.

In the following pages I offer nothing more than simple facts, plain arguments, and common sense; and have no other preliminaries to settle with the reader, than that he will divest himself of prejudice and prepossession, and suffer his reason and his feelings to determine for themselves; that he will put on, or rather that he will not put off, the true character of a man, and generously enlarge his views beyond the present day. . . .

The Sun never shone on a cause of greater worth. 'Tis not the affair of a city, a county, a province, or a kingdom, but of a continent—of at least one eighth part of the habitable globe. 'Tis not the concern of a day, a year, or an age; posterity are virtually involved in the contest, and will be more or less affected even to the end of time, by the proceedings now. Now is the seed-time of continental union, faith and honour. The least fracture now will be like a name engraved with the point of a pin on the tender rind of a young oak; the wound will enlarge with the tree, and posterity read it in full grown characters. . . .

Sons of Liberty express their solidarity with the movement for independence by pulling down a statue of George III in New York City, July 1776. There appear to be loyalists in the crowd.

I have heard it asserted by some, that as America has flourished under her former connection with Great Britain, the same connection is necessary towards her future happiness, and will always have the same effect. Nothing can be more fallacious than this kind of argument. We may as well assert that because a child has thrived upon milk, that it is never to have meat, or that the first twenty years of our lives is to become a precedent for the next twenty. But even this is admitting more than is true, for I answer roundly, that America would have flourished as much, and probably much more, had no European power taken any notice of her. The commerce by which she hath enriched herself are the necessaries of life, and will always have a market while eating is the custom of Europe.

But she has protected us, say some. That she hath engrossed us is true, and defended the continent at our expense as well as her own, is admitted; and she would have defended Turkey from the same motives, *viz.* for the sake of trade and dominion. . . .

But Britain is the parent country, say some. Then the more shame upon her conduct. Even brutes do not devour their young, nor savages make war upon their families; wherefore the assertion, if true, turns to her reproach; but it happens not to be true, or only partly so, and the phrase *parent* or *mother country* hath been jesuitically adopted by the King and his parasites, with a low papistical design of gaining an unfair bias on the credulous weakness of our minds.

Europe, and not England, is the parent country of America. This New World hath been the asylum for the persecuted lovers of civil and religious liberty from *every part* of Europe. Hither have they fled, not from the tender embraces of the mother, but from the cruelty of the monster; and it is so far true of England, that the same tyranny which drove the first emigrants from home, pursues their descendants still. . . .

It is repugnant to reason, to the universal order of things, to all examples from former ages, to suppose that this continent can long remain subject to any external power. The most sanguine in Britain doth not think so. The utmost stretch of human wisdom cannot, at this time, compass a plan, short of separation, which can promise the continent even a year's security. Reconciliation is *now* a fallacious dream. Nature hath deserted the connection, and art cannot supply her place. For, as Milton wisely expresses, "never can true reconcilement grow where wounds of deadly hate have pierced so deep." . . .

Small islands not capable of protecting themselves are the proper objects for government to take under their care; but there is something very absurd in supposing a continent to be perpetually governed by an island. In no instance hath nature made the satellite larger than its primary planet; and as England and America . . . reverse the common order of nature, it is evident that they belong to different systems. England to Europe—America to itself.

I am not induced by motives of pride, party, or resentment to espouse the doctrine of separation and independence; I am clearly, positively, and conscientiously persuaded that it is the true interest of this continent to be so; that every thing short of *that* is mere patchwork, that it can afford no lasting felicity,—that it is leaving the sword to our children, and shrinking back at a time when a little more, a little further, would have rendered this continent the glory of the earth. . . .

But where, say some, is the King of America? I'll tell you, friend, He reigns above, and doth not make havoc of mankind like the royal brute of Great Britain. Yet that we may not appear to be defective even in earthly honours, let a day be solemnly set apart for proclaiming the charter; let it be brought forth placed on the Divine Law, the Word of God; let a crown be placed thereon, by which the world may know, that so far as we approve of monarchy, that in America *the law is king*.

For as in absolute governments the king is law, so in free countries the law ought to be king; and there ought to be no other. But lest any ill use should afterwards arise, let the Crown at the conclusion of the ceremony be demolished, and scattered among the people whose right it is.

A government of our own is our natural right: and when a man seriously reflects on the precariousness of human affairs, he will become convinced, that it is infinitely wiser and safer, to form a constitution of our own in a cool deliberate manner, while we have it in our power, than to trust such an interesting event to time and chance. . . .

Ye that tell us of harmony and reconciliation, can ye restore to us the time that is past? Can ye give to prostitution its former innocence? Neither can ye reconcile Britain and America. The last cord is now broken; the people of England are presenting addresses against us. There are injuries which nature cannot forgive; she would cease to be nature if she did. As well can the lover forgive the ravisher of his mistress, as the continent forgive the murders of Britain. The Almighty hath implanted in us these unextinguishable feelings for good and wise purposes. They are the guardians of His image in our hearts. They distinguish us from the herd of common animals. The social compact would dissolve, and justice be extirpated from the earth, or have only a casual existence, were we callous to the touches of affection. The robber and the murderer would often escape unpunished, did not the injuries which our tempers sustain, provoke us into justice.

O! ye that love mankind! Ye that dare oppose not only the tyranny but the tyrant, stand forth! Every spot of the old world is overrun with oppression. Freedom hath been hunted round the globe. Asia and Africa have long expelled her, Europe regards her like a stranger, and England hath given her warning to depart. O! receive the fugitive, and prepare in time an asylum for mankind.

The Declaration of Independence (July 4, 1776)

From *Messages and Papers of the Presidents*, ed. James B. Richardson (New York, 1897), I, pp. 1–2, 5.

THE UNANIMOUS DECLARATION OF THE THIRTEEN UNITED STATES OF AMERICA

When in the course of human events, it becomes necessary for one people to dissolve the political bands which have connected them with another, and to assume among the powers of the earth the separate and equal station to which the Laws of Nature and of Nature's God entitle them, a decent respect to the opinions of mankind requires that they should declare the causes which impel them to the separation.

We hold these truths to be self-evident, that all men are created equal, that they are endowed by their Creator with certain unalienable rights, that among these are life, liberty, and the pursuit of happiness. That to secure these rights, governments are instituted among men, deriving their just powers from the consent of the governed. That whenever any form of government becomes destructive of these ends, it is the right of the people to alter or to abolish it, and to institute new government, laying its foundation on such principles and organizing its powers in such form, as to them shall seem most likely to effect their safety and happiness. Prudence, indeed, will dictate that governments long established should not be changed for light and transient causes; and accordingly all experience hath shown, that mankind are more disposed to suffer, while evils are sufferable,

John Trumbull completed his oil painting of the signing of the Declaration of Independence during the lifetime of most of the signers.

than to right themselves by abolishing the forms to which they are accustomed. But when a long train of abuses and usurpations, pursuing invariably the same object evinces a design to reduce them under absolute despotism, it is their right, it is their duty, to throw off such government, and to provide new guards for their future security. Such has been the patient sufferance of these Colonies; and such is now the necessity which constrains them to alter their former systems of government. The history of the present King of Great Britain is a history of repeated injuries and usurpations, all having in direct object the establishment of an absolute tyranny over these States. To prove this, let facts be submitted to a candid world. . . .

[There follows a list of twenty-seven oppressions attributed to George III.]

We, therefore, the Representatives of the United States of America, in General Congress assembled, appealing to the Supreme Judge of the world for the rectitude of our intentions, do, in the name, and by authority of the good people of these Colonies, solemnly publish and declare, That these United Colonies are, and of right ought to be Free and Independent States; that they are absolved from all allegiance to the British Crown, and that all political connection between them and the State of Great Britain is and ought to be totally dissolved; and that as Free and Independent States they have full power to levy war, conclude peace, contract alliances, establish commerce, and to do all other acts and things which independent States may of right do. And for the support of this declaration, with a firm reliance on the protection of Divine Providence, we mutually pledge to each other our lives, our fortunes and our sacred honor.

R. R. Palmer: The Forces in Conflict in the American Revolution

Noted American historian Robert R. Palmer here describes the confrontation of forces in the Thirteen Colonies that led to revolution. The selection is taken from his two-volume work, *The Age of the Democratic Revolution,* which analyzes and compares parallel currents of change in the Western world during the last half of the eighteenth century. From *The Age of the Democratic Revolution: A Political History of Europe and America, 1760–1800,* by R. R. Palmer (Copyright © 1959 by Princeton University Press; Princeton Paperback, 1969), Vol. I, pp. 190–192, 194–197, 199–201, 202. Reprinted by permission of Princeton University Press.

I

The American Revolution may be seen as a conflict of forces some of which were old, others brought into being by the event itself.

The oldest of these forces was a tradition of liberty, which went back to the first settlement of the colonies. It is true that half of all immigrants into the colonies south of New England, and two-thirds of those settling in Pennsylvania, arrived as indentured servants; but indentured servitude was not a permanent status, still less a hereditary one; the indentures expired after a few years, and all white persons soon merged into a free population.

Politically, the oldest colonies had originated in a kind of *de facto* independence from the British government. Even after the British made their colonial system more systematic, toward the close of the seventeenth century, the colonies continued to enjoy much local self-determination. Only five per cent of the laws passed by colonial assemblies were disallowed in Great Britain, and, while these often concerned the most important subjects, the infrequency of the British veto was enough to make it the exception. The elected assemblies, as already noted, were the most democratically recruited of all such constituted bodies in the Western World. In general, it was necessary to own land in order to have the right to vote for a member of the assembly, but small owner-farmers were numerous, most of all in New England; and recent studies all tend to raise the estimates of the proportion of those enjoying the franchise before the Revolution. It seems to have been above eighty per cent of adult white males in Massachusetts, half or more in New Jersey, perhaps a little under half in Virginia. Many who had the right to vote did not often use it, and this was in part because the procedure of elections was not made convenient for the ordinary hard-working man; but nonvoting also suggests an absence of grievances, or perhaps only that the common man neither expected nor feared much from government. The elected assemblies enjoyed what in Europe would be thought a dangerously popular mandate. By 1760, decades of rivalry for power between the assemblies and the governors had been resolved, in most of the colonies, in favor of the assemblies. The idea of government by consent was for Americans a mere statement of fact, not a bold doctrine to be flung in the teeth of government, as in Europe. Contrariwise, the growing assertiveness of the assemblies made many in England, and some in America, on the eve of the Revolution, believe that the time had come to stop this drift toward democracy—or, as they would say, restore the balance of the constitution. In sum, an old sense of liberty in America was the obstacle on which the first British empire met its doom. Here the most sophisticated latest researches seem to return to the old-fashioned American patriotic historical school.

From the beginnings of British America there had also been a certain rough kind of equality. Except for slaves, the poor were less poor than in Europe, and the rich were not so wealthy. Almost a quarter of the population of England were classified as paupers in 1688; almost a tenth in 1801. There was no pauperism in America, accepted and institutionalized as such; anyone not hopelessly shiftless, or the victim of personal misfortune, could make a living. At the other extreme, on the eve of the Revolution, there were men who owned hundreds of thousands of acres, mostly vacant, the main values being speculative and in the future. It is hard to say how wealthy a wealthy colonial was. A fortune of £30,000 was thought very large in Massachusetts; Joseph Galloway of Pennsylvania was said to possess £70,000. In England in 1801 there were probably 10,000 families with an average income of £1,500 a year or more, of which the capital value would be about £30,000. There is ground for believing that in England at this time, as in the United States in 1929, five per cent of the population received over thirty-five per cent of the income. The distribution of wealth in colonial America was far more equal.

There were recognized inequalities of social rank. But rank somehow lacked the magic it enjoyed in Europe. In the migration from England and Europe, the well-situated and the high-born had been notably absent. There were Americans of aristocratic pretentions, but the most ambitious genealogy led only to some middling English gentleman's manor house; most Americans were conscious of no lineage at all, American genealogy being largely a nineteenth-century science. No American could truthfully trace his ancestry to the mists of time or the ages of chivalry—nor, indeed, could many British peers or French noblemen. It was the complaint of Lord Stirling, as the New Jersey revolutionary, William Alexander, was called, that he was *not* recognized as a lord in England. A Swedish clergyman arriving in New Jersey in 1770, to take over the old Swedish congregation on the Delaware, found that well-to-do farmers were like lesser gentry in Sweden, in their use of fine linen and fondness for good horses. The significant thing for America was that people of this style of life did not, as in Sweden, consider themselves nobles. Everyone worked, and to the Swedish newcomer it seemed that "all people are generally thought equally good."

The simplicities in which British America had originated gave way to more complex forms of society in the eighteenth century. A liberty almost like that of the "state of nature," a liberty defined by the remoteness of government, gradually changed, especially after the British revolution of 1688, into the more organized and channelized liberty of British subjects under the British constitution. There was a bias toward equality in the foundations. The superstructure, as it was raised, exhibited palpable inequalities. As America became more civilized it began to have, like all civilized countries, a differentiation of social classes. Even the once unmanageable

Quakers took on new social refinements. The Philadelphia Yearly Meeting of 1722 officially declared its "decent respect" for "ranks and dignities of men," and called for honor and obedience "from subjects to their princes, inferiors to superiors, from children to parents, and servants to masters." Increasingly there was a kind of native American aristocracy. No question was of more importance for the future than the way in which this new aristocracy would develop.

The colonial aristocracy, as it took form in the eighteenth century, owed a good deal to close association with government. From New Hampshire to the far South, . . . there were intermarried families which monopolized seats in the governor's councils, in some cases, now, to the third and fourth generation. There were Americans, close to the British authorities, who regarded themselves as the natural rulers of the country. Sometimes, like Englishmen of the class to which they would compare themselves, they expected to draw a living from public offices, to which they need devote only part of their time. This practice has been most closely studied for Maryland, where there were a number of offices in which a man could live like a gentleman, with a good deal of leisure, for £150 a year.

More generally, the wealth of the growing American upper class came from early land grants, or from inheritance of land in a country where land values were always rising, or from mercantile wealth in the half-dozen seaboard cities, all of which except Charleston lay from Philadelphia to the North, or from the ownership of plantations and Negro slaves in the South. New York and the Southern provinces, because of their systems of landholding, were the most favorable to the growth of aristocratic institutions, but an upper class existed everywhere in the settled regions. In places where landed and mercantile wealth came together, as at New York and Charleston, people mixed easily with mutual regard; there was no standoffishness between "trade" and "gentry."

Without the rise of such a colonial aristocracy there could have been no successful movement against England. There had to be small groups of people who knew each other, who could trust each other in hazardous undertakings, who had some power and influence of their own, who could win attention and rally followers, and who, from an enlarged point of view, felt a concern for the welfare of the provinces as a whole. "While there are no noble or great and ancient families . . . they cannot rebel," as an observer of New England remarked in 1732. A generation later such "great" families, if not noble or very ancient, could be found everywhere in the colonies.

On the other hand, the rise of such an aristocracy brought class friction and internal tension. "In many a colony in 1764," according to [one historian], "civil war seemed more likely than war with Britain." There was everlasting bickering over land titles, quitrents, debts, and paper money. There was complaint, in the western part of several provinces, at under-representation in the elected assemblies, or at the long distances it was necessary to go to cast a vote or to be present in a court of law. Rich and poor were not so far apart as in Europe, but they were far enough apart to cause trouble. Western Massachusetts, suspicious of Boston, was not hostile to Britain until 1774. There was a great rent riot in the Hudson valley in 1766, directed against the manorial system on which the Van

Rensselaers and the Livingstons grew wealthy. A thousand angry western Pennsylvania farmers marched on Philadelphia in 1764, enraged that the over-represented East, and its opulent and pacifistic Quaker aristocracy, begrudged them military protection at the time of Pontiac's Indian war. . . .

Loyalists are tarred and feathered as patriots impose revolutionary justice. From a line engraving, "The Procession," of the period.

Conflicting forces were therefore at work in America, when the Stamp Act added the conflict between America and Great Britain. Americans all but universally opposed the Stamp Act. Most of those who eventually became loyalists disapproved of British policy in the ten years before the Revolution. The doctrine of parliamentary supremacy was an innovation, accepted in England itself only since the revolution of 1689; the trend toward centralization of the empire under parliamentary authority, with attendant plans for reordering the colonial governments, was a modern development, a new force, much less old than the American liberties. On this Americans could agree. They began to disagree on the means used to uphold the American position. It was one thing to sit in meetings or submit petitions to Parliament; it was another to persist stubbornly in defiance, to insult or intimidate the King's officers, stop the proceedings of law courts, and condone the violence of mobs. Whether the British constitution really assured no taxation without representation was, after all, uncertain. It was far more certain that the British constitution secured a man against physical violence, against his having his house plundered and wrecked by political adversaries, or against being tarred and feathered for refusing to join a non-import agreement decided on by some unauthorized assembly which had no right to use force. As events unfolded, men took sides, and Americans found themselves disputing with each other on a new subject, the attitude to be taken to British law. . . .

II

It is not easy to say why some Americans warmly embraced the Revolution, or why others opposed it, or how many there were on each side. Independence made it . . . necessary to choose between loyalty and rebellion. . . . The bulk of American opinion, after July 1776, seems to have been actively or potentially for independence. Positive and committed loyalists were a minority, but not therefore unimportant. They had the strength of the British empire on their side, and much also in the American tradition to support them. They believed in liberties for the colonies, and in old and historic rights under the British constitution, which, however, they felt to be less threatened by Parliament than by unruly new forces in America itself.

It is not possible to explain the division between patriot and loyalist by other or supposedly more fundamental divisions. The line coincided only locally or occasionally with the lines of conflict that had appeared before the war. Families divided, brothers often went different ways. Doubtless many a man marked himself for a lifetime by the impulsive decision of a moment. Economic and class motivations are unclear. The most firmly established merchants and lawyers tended to loyalism, but there were respected merchants and lawyers who embraced the revolution. New York and Virginia were both full of great landowners, but New York was the most loyalist province, Virginia one of the most revolutionary. Ironmasters, who had reason to object to British controls on the American iron industry, wound up in both camps. . . . Religion of the Calvinist type was a force working against England, but the Presbyterians of the Carolina frontier, not eager to be governed by their own gentry, supplied many soldiers to the King. National origin had no general influence, for the Middle Colonies, the least English in origin, were stronger centers of loyalism than New England or the South. The young men, if we may judge by the infinitesimal proportion who were in the colleges, were ardently patriot. The colleges, from Harvard to William and Mary, were denounced by loyalists as hotbeds of sedition.

An obvious explanation, quite on the surface, is as good as any: that the patriots were those who saw an enlargement of opportunity in the break with Britain, and the loyalists were in large measure those who had benefited from the British connection, or who had organized their careers, and their sense of duty and usefulness, around service to the King and empire. These would include the American-born governors, Thomas Hutchinson in Massachusetts and William Franklin in New Jersey. There were also the families that customarily sat on the governors' councils or held honorific or lucrative offices under the crown. There were some in the rising American upper class who admired the way of life of the aristocracy in England, and who would imitate it as best they could. Such was surely their right as British subjects, but it might alienate them from Americans generally, even many of the upper class, who were willing to have social distinctions in America develop in a new way. . . .

The war itself polarized the issues. Each side needed strength, and the revolutionary leaders looked for it in the mass of the population, the loyalists among the ruling circles of Great Britain. In legal form, the struggle was between the sovereignty of the former colonies and the sovereignty of the British King-in-Parliament. Rebellious leaders, however, clothed themselves in the sovereignty of the "people," both in form and to a large degree in content. The social content of Parliament in the eighteenth century needs no further elaboration. The struggle, whatever men said, and whatever has been said since, was inseparable from a struggle between democratic and aristocratic forces. If the rebellion was successful, democracy in America would be favored. If it failed, if Parliament and the loyal Americans had their way, development in America would move in an aristocratic direction. In this respect the American Revolution resembled the revolutions in Europe. . . .

STUDY QUESTIONS

1. In what ways did European settlement in the New World resemble and in what ways did it diverge from the European model?

2. How did English constitutional and political problems affect the lives of Englishmen abroad?

What was the American case in the quarrel with Britain? How good was this case in your opinion?

3. What reasons did Paine advance in support of immediate American independence rather than reconciliation with Great Britain?

4. In what ways does the Declaration of Independence represent typical eighteenth-century beliefs?

5. What conflicting forces in the Thirteen Colonies influenced the outbreak of revolution according to Palmer?

6. What determined the position Americans took in the American Revolution? In what sense was it a war "of the people"?

Revolution Erupts in France

From *A History of the Modern World* by R. R. Palmer and Joel Colton. Copyright 1950, © 1956, 1965 by Alfred A. Knopf, Inc. Reprinted by permission of the publisher.

I

In 1789 France fell into revolution, inaugurating an age of social upheaval and war that lasted for over a quarter of a century and raising ideas and concepts of government that exercised a profound and continuing influence on the history of the European world. Unlike the Russian Revolution of 1917, the French Revolution occurred in the most advanced country in Europe. With a population of some 24,000,000, the French in 1789 were the most numerous of all European peoples under a single government. They may also have been the wealthiest, though not per capita. French exports to Europe were greater than those of Great Britain. It is said that half the goldpieces circulating in Europe were French. Paris was the center of the intellectual movement of the Enlightenment. The French language was universally spoken in intellectual and aristocratic circles. The established classes of Europe were in the habit of taking ideas from France, and therefore were the more horrified and astounded when revolution broke out in that country.

The Old Regime—The Three Estates

. . . The essential fact about the Old Regime [in France] was that it was still legally aristocratic and in many ways feudal. Everyone belonged legally to an "estate" or "order" of society. The First Estate was the clergy, the Second Estate the nobility, and the Third Estate included everyone else—from the wealthiest business and professional classes to the poorest peasantry and city workers. These categories were important in that the individual's legal rights and personal prestige depended on the category to which he belonged. Politically, they were obsolescent; not since 1614 had the estates assembled in an Estates-General of the whole kingdom, though in some provinces they had continued to meet as provincial bodies. Socially, they were obsolescent also, for the threefold division no longer corresponded to the real distribution of interest, influence, property, or productive activity among the French people.

Conditions in the church and the position of the clergy have been much exaggerated as a cause of the French Revolution. The church in France levied a tithe on all agricultural products, but so did the church in England; the French bishops often played a part in government affairs, but so did the bishops in England through the House of Lords. The French bishoprics of 1789 were in reality no wealthier than those of the Church of England were found to be when investigated forty years later. In actual numbers, in the secular atmosphere of the Age of Enlightenment, the clergy, especially the monastic orders, had greatly declined, so that by 1789 there were probably not more than 100,000 Catholic clergy of all types in the entire population. But if the importance of the clergy has often

---

TOPIC 25

THE OUTBREAK OF THE FRENCH REVOLUTION

The most severe social and political crisis of the eighteenth century occurred in France, the wealthiest nation in continental Europe and second only to Russia in population. The French social order had increasingly during the century been under assault, a condition to which her intellectual traditions and financial practices both contributed. The nation that had come to the aid of the American rebels was rocked by its own revolution a little more than a decade later, a revolution in which all social classes participated. Before it ended the French Revolution overwhelmed the defenders of Europe's old order and became a movement of world-wide significance. The readings present some of the reasons for the outbreak of revolution.

The ceremonial costume of the clergy, nobility, and commoners visibly distinguished members of the three estates.

higher church offices, army, parliaments, and most other public and semi-public honors were almost monopolized by the titled aristocracy in the time of Louis XVI, who, it will be recalled, had mounted the throne in 1774. Repeatedly, through parliaments, provincial estates, or the assembly of the clergy dominated by the noble bishops, the aristocracy had blocked royal plans for taxation and shown a desire to control the policies of state. At the same time the bourgeoisie, or upper crust of the Third Estate, had never been so influential. The fivefold increase of French foreign trade between 1713 and 1789 suggests the growth of the merchant class, and of the legal and governmental classes associated with it. As members of the bourgeoisie became stronger, more widely read and more self-confident, they resented the distinctions enjoyed by the nobles. Some of these were financial: nobles were exempt from the most important direct tax, the *taille*, on principle, whereas bourgeois obtained exemption with more effort, but so many bourgeois enjoyed tax privileges that purely monetary self-interest was not primary in their psychology. The bourgeois resented the nobleman for his superiority and his arrogance. What had formerly been customary respect was now felt as humiliation. And they felt that they were being shut out from office and honors, and that the nobles were seeking more power in government as a class. The Revolution was the collision of two moving objects, a rising aristocracy and a rising bourgeoisie.

The common people, below the commercial and professional families in the Third Estate, were probably as well off as in most countries. But they were not well off compared with the upper classes. Wage earners had by no means shared in the wave of busi-

been overemphasized, still it must be said that the church was deeply involved in the prevailing social system. For one thing, church bodies — bishoprics, abbeys, convents, schools, and other religious foundations— owned between five and ten per cent of the land of the country, which meant that collectively the church was the greatest of all landowners. Moreover, the income from church properties, like all income, was divided very unequally, and much of it found its way into the hands of the aristocratic occupants of the higher ecclesiastical offices. For while the mass of the parish clergy was

of lower-class origin . . . the better positions were reserved for the nobles. Every bishop of Louis XVI's time was a nobleman—a state of affairs unknown before the eighteenth century. It need only be added that in the Age of Enlightenment the church no longer expressed the ideas of many thinking—and unthinking—people.

The noble order, which in 1789 comprised about 400,000 persons, including women and children, had enjoyed a great resurgence since the death of Louis XIV in 1715. The intendants, usually commoners a century before, were now usually nobles. Government service,

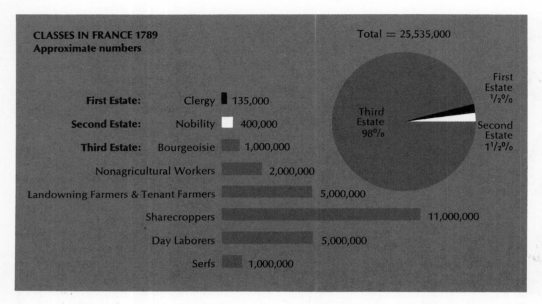

CLASSES IN FRANCE 1789
Approximate numbers

Total = 25,535,000

First Estate:	Clergy	135,000
Second Estate:	Nobility	400,000
Third Estate:	Bourgeoisie	1,000,000
	Nonagricultural Workers	2,000,000
	Landowning Farmers & Tenant Farmers	5,000,000
	Sharecroppers	11,000,000
	Day Laborers	5,000,000
	Serfs	1,000,000

First Estate ½%

Third Estate 98%

Second Estate 1½%

ness prosperity. Between the 1730's and the 1780's the prices of consumer's goods rose about 65%, whereas wages rose only 22%. Persons dependent on wages were therefore badly pinched, but they were less numerous than today, for in the country there were many small farmers, and in the towns many small craftsmen, both of which groups made a living not by wages, but by selling the products of their own labor at market prices. Yet in both town and country there was a significant wage-earning or proletarian element, which was to play a decisive part in the Revolution.

II

The Agrarian System of the Old Regime

Over four-fifths of the people were rural. The agrarian system had developed so that there was no serfdom in France, to be sure, as it was known in eastern Europe. The relation of lord and peasant in France was not the relation of master and man. The peasant owed no labor to the lord—except a few token services in some cases. The peasant worked for himself, either on his own land or on rented land; or he worked as a sharecropper; or he hired himself out to the lord or to another peasant.

The manor, however, still retained certain surviving features of the feudal age. The noble owner of a manor enjoyed "hunting rights," or the privilege of keeping game preserves, and of hunting on his own and the peasant's land. He usually had a monopoly over the village mill, bakeshop, or wine press, for the use of which he collected fees, called *banalités.* He possessed certain vestigal powers of jurisdiction in the manorial court, and certain local police powers, from which fees and fines were collected. These seigneurial privileges were of course the survivals of a day when the local manor had been a unit of government and the noble had performed the functions of government, an age that had long passed with the development of the centralized modern state.

There was another special feature to the property system of the Old Regime. Every owner of a manor (there were some bourgeois and even wealthy peasants who had purchased manors) possessed what was called a right of "eminent property" with respect to all land located in the manorial village. This meant that lesser landowners within the manor "owned" their land in that they could freely buy, sell, lease out, bequeath or inherit it; but they owed to the owner of the manor, in recognition of his "eminent property" rights, certain rents, payable annually, as well as transfer fees that were payable whenever the land changed owners by sale or death. Subject to these "eminent" property rights, land ownership was fairly widespread. Peasants directly owned about two-fifths of the soil of the country; bourgeois a little under a fifth. The nobility owned perhaps a little over a fifth, and the church somewhat under a tenth, the remainder being crown lands, wastelands, or commons. Finally, it must be noted that all property rights were subject also to certain "collective" rights, by which villagers might cut firewood or run their pigs in the commons, or pasture cattle on land belonging to other owners after the crops were in, there being usually no fences or enclosures.

All this may seem rather complex, but it is important to realize that property is a changing institution. Even today, in industrialized countries, a high proportion of all property is in land, including natural resources in and below the soil. In the eighteenth century property meant land even more than it does today. Even the bourgeois class, whose wealth was so largely in ships, merchandise, or commercial paper, invested heavily in land, and in France in 1789 enjoyed ownership of almost as much land as the nobility, and of more than the church. The Revolution was to revolutionize the law of property by freeing the private ownership of land from all the indirect encumbrances described—manorial fees, eminent property rights, communal village agricultural practices, and church tithes. It also was to abolish other older forms of property, such as property in public office or in masterships in the gilds, which had become useful mainly to closed and privileged groups. In final effect the Revolution established the institutions of private property in the modern sense, and benefited, therefore, most especially the landowning peasants and the bourgeoisie.

The peasants not only owned two-fifths of the soil, but occupied almost all of it, working it on their own initiative and risk. That is to say, land owned by the nobility, the church, the bourgeoisie, and the crown was divided up and leased to peasants in small parcels. France was already a country of small farmers. There was no "big agriculture" as in England, eastern Europe, or the plantations of America. The manorial lord performed no economic function. He lived, not by managing an estate and selling his own crops or cattle, but by receiving innumerable dues, quitrents, and fees. During the eighteenth century, in connection with the general aristocratic resurgence, there took place a phenomenon often called the "feudal reaction." Manorial lords, faced with rising living costs, and acquiring higher living standards because of the general material progress, collected their dues more rigorously or revived old ones that had fallen into disuse. Leases and sharecropping arrangements also became less favorable to the peasants. The farmers, like the wage earners, were under a steadily increasing pressure. At the same time the peasants resented the "feudal dues" more than ever, because they regarded themselves as in many cases the real owners of the land, and the lord as a gentleman of the neighborhood who for no reason enjoyed a status different from their own. The trouble was that much of the property system no longer bore any relation to real economic usefulness or activity.

The political unity of France, achieved over the centuries by the monarchy, was likewise a fundamental prerequisite, and even a cause, of the Revolution. Whatever social conditions might have existed, they could give rise to nation-wide public opinion, nation-wide agitation, nation-wide policies, and nation-wide legislation only in a country already politically unified as a nation. These conditions were lacking in central Europe. In France a French state existed. Reformers did not have to create it, but only capture and remodel it. Frenchmen in the eighteenth century already had the sense of membership in a political entity called France. The Revolution saw a tremen-

The damage to peasants' crops caused by the hunting "rights" of the nobility is shown in this emotional seventeenth-century German scene of nobles trampling down the ripening grain.

dous stirring of this sense of membership and of fraternity, turning it into a passion for citizenship, civic rights, voting powers, use and application of the state and its sovereignty for the public advantage. At the very outbreak of the Revolution people saluted each other as *citoyen* and shouted *vive la nation!*

III

The Financial Crisis

The Revolution was precipitated by a financial collapse of the government. What overloaded the government was by no means the costly magnificence of the court of Versailles. Only five per cent of public expenditures in 1788 was devoted to the upkeep of the entire royal establishment. What overloaded all governments was war costs, both current upkeep of armies and navies and the burden of public debt, which in all countries was due almost totally to the war costs of the past. In 1788 the French government devoted about a quarter of its annual expenditure to current maintenance of the armed forces, and about a half to the payment of its debts. British expenditures showed almost the same distribution. The French debt stood at almost four billion *livres*. It had been greatly swollen by the War of American Independence. Yet it was only half as great as the national debt of Great Britain, and less than a fifth as heavy per capita. It was less than the debt of the Dutch Republic. It was apparently no greater than the debt left by Louis XIV three quarters of a century before. At that time the debt had been lightened by repudiation. No responsible French official in the 1780's even considered repudiation, a sure sign of the progress in the interim of the bourgeois class, who were the main government creditors.

Yet the debt could not be carried, for the simple reason that the French budget did not balance. Taxes and other revenues fell short of necessary expenditures. This in turn was not due to national poverty, but to the tax exemptions and tax evasions of privileged elements, especially the nobles. We have already described how the most important tax, the *taille,* was generally paid only by the peasants—the nobles being exempt by virtue of their class privilege, and office holders and bourgeois obtaining exemption in various ways. The church too insisted that its property was not taxable by the state; and its periodic "free gift" to the king, though substantial, was less than might have been obtained from direct taxation of the church's land. Thus, although the country itself was prosperous, the government treasury was empty. The social classes which enjoyed most of the wealth of the country did not pay taxes corresponding to their income, and, even worse, they resisted taxation as degrading.

A long series of responsible persons—Louis XIV himself, John Law, Maupeou, Turgot—had seen the need of taxing the privileged classes. Jacques Necker, a Swiss banker made director of the finances in 1777 by Louis XVI, made moves in the same direction, and, like his predecessors, was dismissed. His successor, Calonne, as the crisis mounted, came to even more revolutionary conclusions. In 1786 he produced a program in which enlightened despotism was tempered by a modest resort to representative institutions. He proposed, in place of the *taille,* a general tax to fall on all landowners without exception, a lightening of indirect taxes and abolition of internal tariffs to stimulate economic production, a confiscation of some properties of the church, and the establishment, as a means of interest-

ing the propertied elements in the government, of provincial assemblies in which all landowners, noble, clerical, bourgeois, and peasant, should be represented without regard to estate or order.

This program, if carried out, might have solved the fiscal problem and averted the Revolution. But it struck not only at privileges in taxation—noble, provincial, and others—but at the threefold hierarchic organization of society. Knowing from experience that the Parliament of Paris would never accept it, Calonne in 1787 convened an "assembly of notables," hoping to win its endorsement of his ideas. The notables insisted on concessions in return, for they wished to share in control of the government. A deadlock followed; the king dismissed Calonne and appointed as his successor Loménie de Brienne, the exceedingly worldly-wise archbishop of Toulouse. Brienne tried to push the same program through the Parliament. The Parliament rejected it, declaring that only the three estates of the realm, assembled in an Estates-General, had authority to consent to new taxes. Brienne and Louis XVI at first refused, believing that the Estates-General, if convened, would be dominated by the nobility. Like Maupeou and Louis XV, Brienne and Louis XVI tried to break the parliaments, replacing them with a modernized judicial system in which the law courts should have no influence over policy. This led to a veritable revolt of the nobles. All the parliaments and provincial estates resisted, army officers refused to serve, the intendants hesitated to act, noblemen began to organize political clubs and committees of correspondence. With his government brought to a standstill, and unable to borrow money or collect taxes, Louis XVI on July 5, 1788, promised to call the

Estates-General for the following May. The various classes were invited to elect representatives and also to draw up lists of their grievances.

From Estates-General to National Assembly

Since no Estates-General had met in over a century and a half, the king asked all persons to study the subject and make proposals on how such an assembly should be organized under modern conditions. This led to an outburst of public discussion. Hundreds of political pamphlets appeared, many of them demanding that the old system by which the three estates sat in separate chambers, each chamber voting as a unit, be done away with, since under it the chamber of the Third Estate was always outnumbered. But in September 1788 the Parliament of Paris, restored to its functions, ruled that the Estates-General should meet and vote as in 1614, in three separate orders.

The nobility, through the Parliament, thus revealed its aim. It had forced the summoning of the Estates-General, and in this way the French nobility initiated the Revolution. The Revolution began as another victory in the aristocratic resurgence against the absolutism of the king. The nobles actually had a liberal program: they demanded freedom of speech and press, freedom from arbitrary arrest and confinement. Many now were even prepared to give up special privileges in taxation; this might have worked itself out in time. But in return they hoped to become the preponderant political element in the state. It was their idea, not merely to have the Estates-General meet in 1789, but for France to be governed in all the future through the Estates-General,

a supreme body in three chambers, one for nobles, one for a clergy in which the higher officers were also nobles, and one for the Third Estate.

This was precisely what the Third Estate wished to avoid. Lawyers, bankers, business men, government creditors, shopkeepers, artisans, workingmen, and peasants had no desire to be governed by lords temporal and spiritual. Their hopes of a new era, formed by the philosophy of the Enlightenment, stirred by the revolution in America, rose to the utmost excitement when "good king Louis" called the Estates-General. The ruling of the Parliament of Paris in September 1788 came to them as a slap in the face—an unprovoked class insult. The whole Third Estate, turned on the nobility with detestation and distrust. The Abbé Sieyès in January 1789 launched his famous pamphlet, *What is the Third Estate?*, declaring that the nobility was a useless caste which could be abolished without loss, that the Third Estate was the one necessary element of society, that it was identical with the nation, and that the nation was absolutely and unqualifiedly sovereign. Through Sieyès the ideas of Rousseau's *Social Contract* entered the thought of the Revolution. At the same time, even before the Estates-General actually met, and not from the books of *philosophes* so much as from actual events and conditions, nobles and commoners viewed each other with fear and suspicion. The Third Estate, which had at first supported the nobles against the "despotism" of the king's ministers, now ascribed to them the worst possible motives. Class antagonism poisoned the Revolution at the outset, made peaceful reform impossible, and threw many bourgeois without delay into a radical and destructive mood. And the mutual suspicion between classes,

produced by the Old Regime and inflamed by the Revolution, has troubled France ever since.

The Estates-General met as planned in May 1789 at Versailles. The Third Estate, most of whose representatives were lawyers, boycotted the organization in three separate chambers. It insisted that deputies of all three orders should sit as a single house and vote as individuals; this procedure would be of advantage to the Third Estate, since the king had granted it as many deputies as the other two orders combined. For six weeks a deadlock was maintained. On June 13 a few priests, leaving the chamber of the First Estate, came over and sat with the Third. They were greeted with jubilation. On June 17 the Third Estate declared itself the "National Assembly." Louis XVI, under pressure from the nobles, closed the hall in which it met. The members found a neighboring indoor tennis court, and there, milling about in a babel of confusion and apprehension, swore and signed the Oath of the Tennis Court on June 20, 1789, affirming that wherever they foregathered the National Assembly was in existence, and that they would not disband until they had drafted a constitution. This was a revolutionary step, for it assumed virtually sovereign power for a body of men who had no legal authority. The king ordered members of the three estates to sit in their separate houses. He now somewhat tardily presented a reforming program of his own, too late to win the confidence of the disaffected, and in any case continuing the organization of French society in legal classes. The self-entitled National Assembly refused to back down. The king faltered, failed to enforce his commands promptly, and allowed the Assembly to remain in being. In the following days,

A triumph of fraternity in an act of civil disobedience, Jacques Louis David's painting of the Oath of the Tennis Court places defecting members of the clergy in the foreground. In the painter's romantic perspective, members of the Third Estate exult in their revolutionary action.

at the end of June, he summoned about 18,000 soldiers to Versailles.

What had happened was that the king of France, in the dispute raging between nobles and commoners, chose the nobles. It was traditional in France for the king to oppose feudalism. For centuries the French monarchy had drawn strength from the bourgeoisie. All through the eighteenth century the royal ministers had carried on the struggle against the privileged interests. Only a year before, Louis XVI had been almost at war with his rebellious aristocracy. In 1789 he failed to assert himself. He lost control over the Estates-General, exerted no leadership, offered no program until too late, and provided no symbol behind which parties could rally. He failed to make use of the profound loyalty to himself felt by the bourgeoisie and common people, who yearned for nothing so much as a king who would stand up for them, as in days of yore, against an aristocracy of birth and status. He tried instead, at first, to compromise and postpone a crisis; then he

found himself in the position of having issued orders which the Third Estate boldly defied; and in this embarrassing predicament he yielded to his wife, Marie Antoinette, to his brothers, and to the court nobles with whom he lived, and who told him that his dignity and authority were outraged and undermined. At the end of June Louis XVI undoubtedly intended to dissolve the Estates-General by military force. But what the Third Estate feared was not a return to the old theoretically absolute monarchy. It was a future in which the aristocracy should control the government of the country. There was now no going back; the revolt of the Third Estate had allied Louis XVI with the nobles, and the Third Estate now feared the nobles more than ever, believing with good reason that they now had the king in their hands.

The Lower Classes in Action

The country meanwhile was falling into dissolution. The lower classes, below the bourgeoisie, were out of hand. For them too the convocation of the Estates-General had seemed to herald a new era. The grievances of ages, and those which existed equally in other countries than France, rose to the surface. Short run conditions were bad. The harvest of 1788 had been poor; the price of bread, by July 1789, was higher than at any time since the death of Louis XIV. The year 1789 was also one of depression; the rapid growth of trade since the American war had suddenly halted, so that wages fell and unemployment spread while scarcity drove food prices up. The government, paralyzed at the center, could not take such measures of relief as were customary under the Old Regime. The masses were everywhere restless. Labor trouble broke out; in April a great riot of workingmen devastated a wallpaper factory in Paris. In the rural districts there was much disorder. Peasants declared that they would pay no more manorial dues, and were likewise refusing taxes. In the best of times the countryside was troubled by vagrants, beggars, rough characters, and smugglers who flourished along the many tariff frontiers. Now the business depression reduced the income of honest peasants who engaged in weaving or other domestic industries in their homes; unemployment and indigence spread in the country; people were uprooted; and the result was to raise the number of vagrants to terrifying proportions. It was believed, since nothing was too bad to believe of the aristocrats (though it was not true), that they were secretly recruiting these "brigands" for their own purposes to intimidate the Third Estate. The economic and social crisis thus became acutely political.

The towns were afraid of being swamped by beggars and desperadoes. This was true even of Paris, the largest city in Europe except London. The Parisians were also alarmed by the concentration of troops about Versailles.

Head of the Marquis de Launey, Governor of the Bastille, drawn at the scene of execution.

An excited group of Parisians take arms on the night of July 12, 1789 to defend the city as rumors spread of troop concentration at Versailles.

They began to arm in self-defense. All classes of the Third Estate took part. . . . Crowds began to look for weapons in arsenals and public buildings. On July 14 they came to the Bastille, a stronghold built in the Middle Ages to overawe the city, like the tower of London in England. It was used as a place of detention for persons with enough influence to escape the common jails, but was otherwise in normal times considered harmless; in fact there had been talk, some years before, of tearing it down to make room for a public park. Now, in the general turbulence, the governor had placed cannon in the embrasures. The crowd requested him to remove his cannon, and to furnish them with arms. He refused. Through a series of misunderstandings, reinforced by the vehemence of a few firebrands, the crowd turned into a mob, which assaulted the fortress, and which, when helped by a handful of trained soldiers and five artillery pieces, persuaded the governor to surrender. The mob, enraged by the death of ninety-eight of its members, streamed in and murdered six soldiers of the garrison in cold blood. The governor was murdered while under escort to the Town Hall. The mayor of Paris met the same fate. Their heads were cut off with knives, stuck on the ends of spikes, and paraded about the city. While all this happened the regular army units on the outskirts of Paris did not stir, their reliability being open to question, and the authorities being in any case unaccustomed to firing on the people.

The capture of the Bastille, though not so intended, had the effect of saving the assembly at Versailles. The king, not knowing what to do, accepted the new situation in Paris. He recognized a citizens' committee, which had formed there, as the new munici-pal government. He sent away the troops that he had summoned, and commanded the recalcitrants among nobles and clergy to join in the National Assembly. In Paris and other cities a bourgeois or national guard was established to keep order. The Marquis de Lafayette, "the hero of two worlds," received command over the guard in Paris. For insignia he combined the colors of the city of Paris, red and blue, with the white of the house of Bourbon. The French tricolor, emblem of the Revolution, thus originated in a fusion of old and new.

In the rural districts matters went from bad to worse. Vague insecurity rose to the proportions of panic in the Great Fear of 1789, which spread over the country late in July in the wake of travelers, postal couriers, and others. The cry was relayed from point to point that "the brigands were coming," and peasants, armed to protect their homes and crops, and gathered together and working upon each other's feelings, often turned their attention to the manor houses, burning them in some cases, and in others simply destroying the manorial archives in which fees and dues were recorded. The Great Fear became part of a general agrarian insurrection, in which the peasants, far from being motivated by wild alarms, knew perfectly well what they were doing. They intended to destroy the manorial regime by force.

The Initial Reforms of the National Assembly

The Assembly at Versailles could restore order only by meeting the demands of the peasants. To wipe out all manorial payments would deprive the landed aristocracy of most of its income. Many bourgeois also owned manors. There was therefore much perplexity. A small group of deputies prepared a surprise move in the Assembly, choosing an evening session from which many would be absent. Hence came the "night of August 4." A few liberal noblemen, by pre-arrangement, arose and surrendered their hunting rights, their banalités, their rights in manorial courts, and feudal and seigneurial privileges generally. What was left of serfdom and all personal servitudes were declared ended. Tithes were abolished. Other deputies repudiated the special privileges of their provinces. All personal tax privileges were given up. On the main matter, the dues arising from "eminent property" in the manors, a compromise was adopted. These dues were all abolished, but compensation was to be paid by the peasants to the former owners. The compensation was in most cases never paid. Eventually, in 1793, in the radical phase of the Revolution, the provision for compensation was repealed. In the end French peasant landowners rid themselves of their manorial obligations without cost to themselves. From the cocoon of the manor the French peasant democracy emerged intact, in contrast to what later happened in most other countries, where peasants, when in turn liberated from manorial obligations, either lost part of their land or were crushed under installment payments lasting many years.

The decree summarizing the resolutions of August 4 announced flatly that "feudalism was abolished." In its place the Assembly proceeded to map out the new order. The first step was to issue, on August 26, 1789, the Declaration of Rights of Man and Citizen. This document affirmed the principles of the new state, which were essentially the rule of law, equal individual citizenship, and collective sovereignty of the people. . . .

Violence Demolishes the Feudal System (1789)

The first account was written by the Marquis de Ferrières, a conservative nobleman and deputy in the Estates-General. The second is taken from the memoirs of J. S. Bailly (1736–1793), leading member from the Third Estate to the Estates-General. Bailly was president of that body when it became the National Assembly and Mayor of Paris after the taking of the Bastille. He was executed during the Reign of Terror. *The French Revolution as Told by Contemporaries,* copyright, 1938, by E. L. Higgins. Reprinted by permission of the publisher, Houghton Mifflin Company.

I. THE GREAT FEAR BRINGS A PEASANT UPRISING
(Summer, 1789)

One hundred and fifty châteaux in Franche-Comté, Mâconnais, and Beaujolais were already burned! The conflagration threatened to consume all the estates. . . . Shall I speak of murders, of atrocities committed against the nobles? . . . M. de Baras, cut into pieces before his wife . . . M. de Montesson, shot after having seen his father-in-law's throat cut! A nobleman, paralyzed, abandoned on a funeral-pile! Another whose feet they burned to make him give up his title deeds! The unfortunate M. de Belsunce massacred at Caen! Mme. de Berthilac, forced, the ax over her head, to give up her land! Mme. la Princesse de Listenois, constrained to the same sacrifice, with a scythe at her neck, and her two daughters fainting at her feet! The Marquis de Tremand, an infirm old man, chased at night from his chateau, hunted from

Nobility and clergy rejoice in the renunciation of their feudal rights, August 4, 1789. This medal was struck four months later to commemorate this event.

city to city, arriving at Basel [Switzerland], almost dying, with his broken-hearted daughters! The Comte de Montessu and his wife, with pistols at their heads for three hours, and asking for death as a favor, taken from their carriage to be thrown into a pond! The Baron de Mont-Iustin, suspended in a well, and hearing the question deliberated as to whether he should be allowed to fall or made to perish in another manner! . . . Alsace, Champagne, and Dauphiné a prey to the fury of a troop of brigands sent from Paris; and to authorize

these sanguinary atrocities, deputies of the commons wrote to their bailiwicks that the nobles wished to blow up the hall of the Assembly at a time when there was no one present but the commons! They told the peasants that the nobles were against the king; they sent supposed orders to burn the châteaux, to massacre the nobles. . . . These odious means prepared the session of the 4th of August [abolition of feudalism]. It was while surrounded by the bodies of nobles massacred in the light of the flames that devoured their châteaux that the Assembly pronounced the decrees violating the sacred rights of legitimate property!

II. THE NATIONAL ASSEMBLY ACTS TO ABOLISH FEUDALISM (night of August 4)

During the evening M. Target read a draft of the proclamation intended to stop the pillaging and burning of the châteaux, and require the payment of taxes, rents, and feudal dues, which were no longer being paid voluntarily.

This proclamation was the occasion of a majestic deliberation and a scene that was veritably grand, absorbingly interesting, and forever memorable. It was declared that both the refusal to pay feudal dues and the burning of title deeds resulted from hatred of the feudal régime with its burden upon the peasants.

The Vicomte de Noailles Proposes to Abolish Feudal Rights

How can one hope, gentlemen, to calm the agitation in the provinces, assure public liberty, and confirm proprietors in their true rights without knowing the cause of the insurrection manifesting itself in the interior of the kingdom? And how can it be remedied without applying the remedy to the malady which causes it? . . . The kingdom vacillates between two alternatives, the destruction of society and a governmental system which will be the admiration of all Europe.

How can this government be established? By calming the people. How can this be realized? By showing the people that no one opposes them except where conservatism is necessary. To bring about this extremely necessary quiet, I propose an announcement declaring that the representatives of the nation have decided the impost shall be paid by every individual in the kingdom in proportion to his income; that all public burdens will in the future be equally supported by all; that all feudal rights be redeemable . . . in money or exchangeable at a fairly estimated price; and that the seignioral *corvées*, mortmains, and other personal servitudes be abolished without compensation. . . .

The Assembly Abolishes the Feudal System

Article I. The National Assembly completely abolishes the feudal system. It decrees that, in the rights and dues that are feudal as well as rental, those which maintain real or personal mortmain and personal servitude, and those which pertain to them, shall be abolished without compensation. All others are declared redeemable, and the amount and manner of redemption shall be fixed by the National Assembly. Of the said rights, those which are not suppressed by this decree shall continue to be collected until indemnified.

Declaration of the Rights of Man and of the Citizen (August 27, 1789)

From *Translations and Reprints from the Original Sources of European History*, ed. by the Department of History of the University of Pennsylvania (Philadelphia, 1897), I, no. 5, pp. 6-8.

I

The representatives of the French people, organized as a National Assembly, believing that the ignorance, neglect or contempt of the rights of man are the sole cause of public calamities and of the corruption of governments, have determined to set forth in a solemn declaration the natural, inalienable and sacred rights of man, in order that this declaration, being constantly before all the members of the social body, shall remind them continually of their rights and duties; in order that the acts of the legislative power, as well as those of the executive power, may be compared at any moment with the ends of all political institutions and may thus be more respected; and, lastly, in order that the grievances of the citizens, based hereafter upon simple and incontestable principles, shall tend to the maintenance of the constitution and redound to the happiness of all. Therefore the National Assembly recognizes and proclaims, in the presence and under the auspices of the Supreme Being, the following rights of man and of the citizen:—

1. Men are born and remain free and equal in rights. Social distinctions may only be founded upon the general good.
2. The aim of all political association is the preservation of the natural and imprescriptible rights of man. These rights are liberty, property, security and resistance to oppression.
3. The principle of all sovereignty resides essentially in the nation. No body nor individual may exercise any authority which does not proceed directly from the nation.

4. Liberty consists in the freedom to do everything which injures no one else; hence the exercise of the natural rights of each man has no limits except those which assure to the other members of the society the enjoyment of the same rights. These limits can only be determined by law.

5. Law can only prohibit such actions as are hurtful to society. Nothing may be prevented which is not forbidden by law, and no one may be forced to do anything not provided for by law.

6. Law is the expression of the general will. Every citizen has a right to participate personally or through his representative in its formation. It must be the same for all, whether it protects or punishes. All citizens, being equal in the eyes of the law, are equally eligible to all dignities and to all public positions and occupations, according to their abilities, and without distinction except that of their virtues and talents.

II

7. No person shall be accused, arrested or imprisoned except in the cases and according to the forms prescribed by law. Any one soliciting, transmitting, executing or causing to be executed any arbitrary order shall be punished. But any citizen summoned or arrested in virtue of the law shall submit without delay, as resistance constitutes an offence.

8. The law shall provide for such punishments only as are strictly and obviously necessary, and no one shall suffer punishment except it be legally inflicted in virtue of a law passed and promulgated before the commission of the offence.

9. As all persons are held innocent until they shall have been declared guilty, if arrest shall be deemed indispensable, all harshness not essential to the securing of the prisoner's person shall be severely repressed by law.

10. No one shall be disquieted on account of his opinions, including his religious views, provided their manifestation does not disturb the public order established by law.

11. The free communication of ideas and opinions is one of the most precious of the rights of man. Every citizen may, accordingly, speak, write, and print with freedom, but shall be responsible for such abuses of this freedom as shall be defined by law.

12. The security of the rights of man and of the citizen requires public military force. These forces are, therefore, established for the good of all and not for the personal advantage of those to whom they shall be entrusted.

13. A common contribution is essential for the maintenance of the public forces and for the cost of administration. This should be equitably distributed among all the citizens in proportion to their means.

14. All the citizens have a right to decide, either personally or by their representatives, as to the necessity of the public contribution; to grant this freely; to know to what uses it is put; and to fix the proportion, the mode of assessment, and of collection, and the duration of the taxes.

15. Society has the right to require of every public agent an account of his administration.

16. A society in which the observance of the law is not assured, nor the separation of powers defined, has no constitution at all.

17. Since property is an inviolable and sacred right, no one shall be deprived thereof except where public necessity, legally determined, shall clearly demand it, and then only on condition that the owner shall have been previously and equitably indemnified.

Alexis de Tocqueville: How the French Enlightenment Influenced the Revolution

Alexis de Tocqueville (1805–1859), thoughtful commentator on the course of Western civilization, gained fame with his *Democracy in America* published in 1835 after a pioneering trip to the New World. Although Tocqueville stemmed from an old French noble family and was a defender of the monarchical system he was even more a spokesman for justice and good government. One of his major works was the study of the French Revolution and its consequences from which this reading is taken. From *The Old Regime and the French Revolution* by Alexis de Tocqueville, translated by Stuart Gilbert. Copyright © 1955 by Doubleday & Company, Inc. Reprinted by permission of the publisher.

For a long while the French had been the most literary-minded of all the nations of Europe, but so far our writers had not displayed that intellectual brilliance which won them world-wide fame toward the middle of the eighteenth century. True, they did not play an active part in public affairs, as English writers did; on the contrary, never had they kept so steadily aloof from the political arena. In a nation teeming with officials none of the men of letters held posts of any kind, none was invested with authority.

Nevertheless, they did not (like most of their German contemporaries) resolutely turn their backs on politics and retire to a world apart, of *belles lettres* and pure philosophy. On the contrary, they were keenly interested in all that concerned the government of nations; this, one might almost say, was an obsession with them. Questions such as the origin of human society, its earliest forms, the original rights of citizens and of authority, the "natural" and the "artificial" relations between men, of the legitimacy of custom, and even the whole conception of law—all these bulked large in the literature of the day. As a result of this incessant probing into the bases of the society in which they lived, they were led both to examine its structure in detail and to criticize its general plan. Not all our writers, it is true, made these vast problems their exclusive study; indeed, the great majority dealt with them casually, even, one might say, toyed with them. But all took notice of them in one way or another. This kind of abstract, literary politics found its way, in varying proportions, into all the writings of the day, and there was none, from the most ponderous treatise to the lightest lyric, that had not at least a grain of it.

The political programs advocated by our eighteenth-century writers varied so much that any attempt to synthesize them or deduce a single coherent theory of government from them would be labor lost. Nonetheless, if, disregarding details, we look to the directive ideas, we find that all these various systems stemmed from a single concept of a highly general order, their common source, and that our authors took this as their premise before venturing on their personal, often somewhat eccentric solutions of the problem of good government. Thus, though their ways diverged in the course of their researches, their starting point was the same in all cases; and this was the belief that what was wanted was to replace the complex of traditional customs governing the social order of the day by simple, elementary rules deriving from the exercise of the human reason and natural law.

When we look closely into it we find that the political philosophy of these writers consists to all intents and purposes in ringing the changes on this one idea. It was no new one; it had haunted men's imaginations off and on for three millennia, but never until now had it succeeded in making itself accepted as a basic principle. How was it that at this particular point of time it could root itself so firmly in the minds of the writers of the day? Why, instead of remaining as in the past the purely intellectual concept of a few advanced thinkers, did it find a welcome among the masses and acquire the driving force of a political passion to such effect that general and abstract theories of the nature of human society not only became daily topics of conversation among the leisure class but fired the imagination even of women and peasants?

And why was it that men of letters, men without wealth, social eminence, responsibilities, or official status, became in practice the leading politicians of the age, since despite the fact that others held the reins of government, they alone spoke with accents of authority? These questions I shall now try to answer, and at the same time I shall draw attention to the remarkable, not to say formidable, influence these men's writings (which at first sight might seem to concern the history of our literature alone) had on the Revolution, and, indeed, still have today.

It was not by mere chance that our eighteenth-century thinkers as a body enounced theories so strongly opposed to those that were still regarded as basic to the social order; they could hardly be expected to do otherwise when they contemplated the world around them. The sight of so many absurd and unjust privileges, whose evil effects were increasingly felt on every hand though their true causes were less and less understood, urged or, rather, forced them towards a concept of the natural equality of all men irrespective of social rank. When they saw so many ridiculous, ramshackle institutions, survivals of an earlier age, which no one had attempted to co-ordinate or to adjust to modern conditions and which seemed destined to live on despite the fact that they had ceased to have any present value, it was natural enough that thinkers of the day should come to loathe everything that savored of the past and should desire to remold society on entirely new lines, traced by each thinker in the sole light of reason.

Their very way of living led these writers to indulge in abstract theories and generalizations regarding the nature of government, and to place a blind confidence in these. For living as they did, quite out of touch with practical politics, they lacked the experience which might have tempered their ·enthusiasms. Thus they completely failed to perceive the very real obstacles in the way of even the most praiseworthy reforms, and to gauge the perils involved in even the most salutary revolutions. That they should not have had the least presentiment of these dangers was only to be expected, since as a result of the total absence of any political freedom, they had little acquaintance with the realities of public life, which, indeed, was *terra incognita* to them. Taking no personal part in it and unable to see what was being done by others in that field, they lacked even the superficial acquaintance with such matters which comes to those who live under a free régime, can see what is happening, and hear the voice of public opinion even though they themselves take no part whatever in the government of the country. As a result, our literary men became much bolder in their speculations, more addicted to general ideas and systems, more contemptuous of the wisdom of the ages, and even more inclined to trust their individual reason than most of those who have written books on politics from a philosophic angle.

When it came to making themselves heard by the masses and appealing to their emotions, this very ignorance served them in good stead. If the French people had still played an active part in politics (through the Estates-General) or even if they had merely continued to concern themselves with the day-to-day administration of affairs through the provincial assemblies, we may be sure that they would not have let themselves be carried away . . . by the ideas of the writers of the day; any experience, however slight, of public affairs would have made them chary of accepting the opinions of mere theoreticians.

Similarly if, like the English, they had succeeded in gradually modifying the spirit of their ancient institutions without destroying them, perhaps they would not have been so prompt to clamor for a new order. As it was, however, every Frenchman felt he was being victimized; his personal freedom, his money, his self-respect, and the amenities of his daily life were constantly being tampered with on the strength of some ancient law, some medieval usage, or the remnants of some antiquated servitude. Nor did he see any constitutional remedy for this state of affairs; it seemed as if the choice lay between meekly accepting everything or destroying the whole system. . . .

STUDY QUESTIONS

1. What were the causes of the French Revolution? Differentiate between general and specific causes.

2. What did each social class want at the time of calling the Estates General? Do you find ideas common to the Enlightenment among their objectives?

3. How was it possible that the government of a wealthy country such as France could go bankrupt? Why was financial reform so difficult?

4. Why didn't Louis XVI take strong action to settle French problems? Why did he eventually support the nobility instead of the middle class? Could he have stopped the Revolution?

5. What was the significance of agricultural conditions in bringing on revolution? What part was played by chance? Why did the nobility agree to abolish feudalism?

6. What enlightened ideas are found in the Declaration of the Rights of Man?

7. Was there any special significance in ending the Declaration with the subject contained in Article 17? Is this in harmony with the abolition of feudalism by the National Assembly?

8. What position does Tocqueville take on the influence of the writers and thinkers of the Enlightenment on the outbreak of the Revolution? Do you agree with this position?

A Brief Account of the Revolution

TOPIC 26

THE COURSE OF THE FRENCH REVOLUTION

The stages of revolutions have received as much attention as their causes. In one view, after a period of mounting attack by social critics has destroyed public confidence in the government and left it especially vulnerable to economic or political crisis, sudden acts of violence intimidate the ruling group to grant sweeping concessions. Power is transferred to moderate revolutionists but the pace of reform rapidly accelerates and more radical leaders emerge. Civil war may likely result, during which the extremists seize control of the government and try to impose radical changes. Reaction ultimately sets in and the revolution is halted. The course of the French Revolution has suggested this kind of model, and the readings examine the context in which the revolution passed through these stages.

From Geoffrey Parsons, *The Stream of History* (New York: Charles Scribner's Sons, 1934), pp. 521–524.

The French Revolution began in 1789 and lasted ten years, till Napoleon seized the reins and ended the rule of the people in a dictatorship. It began in orderly fashion, with no thought of overturning the monarchy. The Estates-General, composed of the clergy, nobility, and the third estate, were called by the king to meet at Versailles in May to consider the desperate problems of taxation which confronted the nation. The first dispute ended in a complete victory for the third estate, which by sheer boldness organized itself into the first National Assembly of France. The weak, hesitating Louis XVI first opposed and then surrendered to the third estate's insistence that it sit until a constitution be prepared.

In July the first disorder broke out at Paris, where the Bastille was captured and razed on the 14th. The spirit of revolt spread to the provinces, and a number of chateaux were burned by the peasants to destroy the records of feudal dues. As a result the Assembly at Versailles speeded up its labors, and the remaking of France was accomplished in the month of August. Here was no mere shift of political sovereignty, as in the American Revolution. Serfdom was abolished, taxation was reformed so as to bear upon all alike, the Church tithes were abolished, and the old provinces were replaced by departments, ending the old feudal diversity for all time.

The Declaration of the Rights of Man wrote into the law of the land the ideals of equality and liberty which Rousseau had preached. The sovereignty of the people was asserted, and freedom of speech and religious liberty were established.

Once again Louis XVI hesitated. As a result, a Paris mob, composed chiefly of women, marched to Versailles to ask for bread, and brought him and his family back to Paris with them. Thereafter he was virtually a prisoner in the Tuileries. But still there was no thought of deposing him. The National Assembly also moved to Paris, and in the more radical atmosphere of the city blundered into its first excesses. It passed laws altering the organization of the Church and seizing its property. At the end of the first year the nobility were abolished. Thereafter the *émigrés* over the border conspired to start a counter-revolution which would restore the old order. Even so, the second year ended with the populace still loyal to the king. The turning-point came in June, 1791, when the king and queen committed the unpardonable blunder of attempting to escape from France. By chance they were halted near the border and brought back ingloriously to Paris. This final act of the dull Louis XVI sealed his doom. Republican sentiment now began for the first time to develop after two years of revolution. During this early period the moderates had been in control of the Assembly under the leadership of Mirabeau, an aristocrat, a moderate, and one of the ablest Parliamentary leaders of France.

The third year saw a swift turn toward the extremists. Most potent in stirring radical sentiment was the war commenced by the monarchical powers of Europe to rescue Louis XVI and his queen, Marie Antoinette, sister of the emperor of Austria. As a consequence all Paris was stirred by fear and wrath. The Jacobin clubs gained control of the Assembly, mobs invaded the Tuileries, and in September, 1792, the Paris Commune, the radical city government, which had usurped the powers of the Assembly, committed one of the most dastardly crimes in history. It massacred in prisons several thousands of alleged sympathizers of the Austrians and the *émigrés*. In the same month the monarchy was abolished by a Constitutional Convention and a republic proclaimed. In the spirit of fantastic radicalism which now seized Paris, a new republican calendar was created. The king was convicted of treason—he had unquestionably treated with other rulers who wished to invade France—and executed in January, 1793. There succeeded the terrible year of the Terror, from April, 1793, to July, 1794, the fifth year of the Revolution. If the early years of the Revolution were based on the doctrines of the Rationalists, of Voltaire, of Diderot, and Montesquieu, it was the emotionalism preached by Rousseau which now engulfed Paris. A Committee of Public Safety was formed whose primary duty was to save France from the invading armies. It accomplished this end in an extraordinarily successful military campaign, thanks largely to Carnot. Meantime the Terror was turned against alleged enemies at home. Revolt against the radical rule at Paris flared in the provinces, and as a result the Committee of Public Safety was forced to fight a civil war at home while defending the frontiers against foreigners.

Thousands were executed by the guillotine in Paris and many more in the provinces. Marie Antoinette was put to death in October, 1793. The climax of the Reign of Terror came in June and July, 1794. In the reaction, the fanatical Robespierre, leader of the Terror, was himself guillotined, and the slaughter was over.

The Revolution passed through five more years of relative quiet, disturbed by occasional uprisings and violence. The lesson of representative rule was hard to learn. Finally in November, 1799, Napoleon Bonaparte (1769–1821), a young general of Italian ancestry, a Corsican by birth and a Frenchman by the chance of Corsica's annexation a year before his birth, returned from campaigns in Egypt and Syria, executed a military coup d'état, threw out the legislators at the point of the bayonet, and established himself as the virtual sovereign of France. . . .

1789
May 5   Opening of the Estates-General
June 20   Tennis Court Oath (formation of National Assembly)
July 14   Fall of the Bastille
August 4   Nobles surrender feudal rights
August 27   Declaration of the Rights of Man
October 5–6   Women's bread march to Versailles
1790
July 14   Louis XVI "accepts" the Constitutional Monarchy
1791
June 20   Attempted flight of royal family
THE LEGISLATIVE ASSEMBLY (Constitutional monarchy until suspended in September 1792. Assembly elected with property qualifications and proviso that

no person could serve who had been in National Assembly. Rising influence of the Parisian population.)
October   Opening of Legislative Assembly
1792
April 20   War with Austria (until 1797) and Prussia (until 1795)
July 11   Manifesto of Duke of Brunswick (threatening Paris if royal family harmed)
August 10   Mob storms Tuileries Palace
Sept. 2–7   September massacres (hunting down of suspected royalists)
1792–1795
THE NATIONAL CONVENTION (Height of Revolution. Republic. Reign of Terror and Reaction. Successfully waged war.)
1792
Sept. 21   France declared a Republic
1793
Jan. 21   Execution of Louis XVI
Feb. 1   Declaration of War on England, Spain, and Holland
April 6   Organization of Committee of Public Safety
June 2   Arrest of Girondins (moderates)
1794
Spring   Height of Terror
July 27   Execution of Robespierre
December   Return of moderates to Convention
1795
August 22   Constitution of Year III
Oct. 5   Napoleon's "whiff of grapeshot"
Oct. 26   Convention dissolves
1795–1799
THE DIRECTORY (Republic headed by five directors. Middle classes recover influence. Internal dissension. Increasing power of army. Rise of Napoleon.)

The Moderates Achieve Their Goals

The abolishment of feudalism and the enactment of the Declaration of the Rights of Man by the National Assembly ushered in a period of several years during which the moderate revolutionaries were in control of the French government. The lawyers and merchants who were the backbone of the articulate Third Estate sought to establish a constitutional monarchy in which ability rather than birth would be the determinant of power. That ability was largely defined in terms of wealth is apparent in the selections below. In the first selection, the most outstanding of the moderate leaders, Count Mirabeau (1749–1791) explains his conception of the nature of property. The second selection recounts the reaction of the municipal administration of Paris to the attempt of working people to form labor unions to meet problems of unemployment and inflation. A law abolishing such unions (Loi de Chapelier) was passed by the National Assembly in June 1791. The third selection contains passages from the Constitution of 1791 pertaining to voting requirements. In this constitution the so-called active citizens chose electors who selected the actual representatives in the Assembly. I. From Paris, Moniteur, II, 123 in Thomas C. Mendenhall, Basil Henning, and Archibald Foord, The Quest for a Principle of Authority in Europe: 1715–Present, Select Problems in Historical Interpretation (New York: Holt, Rinehart and Winston, Inc., 1948), p. 61. II. From P. J. B. Buchez and P. C. Roux-Lavergne, Histoire parliamentaire de la revolution française (Paris, 1834–1838), IX, pp. 44–45 in Mendenhall, Henning, and Foord, p. 62. III. From The French Revolution as Told by Contemporaries, copyright, 1938, by E. L. Higgins. Reprinted by permission of the publisher, Houghton Mifflin Company.

I. COUNT MIRABEAU EXPLAINS THE NATURE OF PRIVATE PROPERTY (November, 1789)

If I consider property, in its relation to individuals, in its nature, in its effects, and its relation to . . . law, I discover: . . .

That the right on which private properties is founded is, so to speak, coexistent with the establishment of the society, since it has its source in this faculty which every individual has of participating in the advantages which all the other members with whom he is forming a political association will have. . . .

That special laws are not necessary to assure the domain of private property, for, by want of ordering in principle a community of possessions, the establishment and the guarantee of individual possessions are a necessary consequence of the very foundation of society. . . .

Finally, I discover that each individual enjoys his property not by title of contract, since he can dispose of it; nor as depositary, since he can dissipate it; nor as usufructer, since he can destroy it; but as absolute master, just as he can dispose of his will, his arms, his thought. . . .

II. THE MUNICIPAL GOVERNMENT OF PARIS WARNS THE WORKING PEOPLE (April, 1791)

The municipal authorities have learned that the workers in some trades are meeting daily in great numbers and are combining instead of spending their time at work; that they are debating and making decrees by which they are arbitrarily setting a day's wages; that many of them are circulating around in the various shops and spreading their supposed decrees to those who had not cooperated and are using threats and violence against these others in order to make them join the movement and stop work.

The suppression [of tolls on foodstuffs entering towns] is of benefit to all citizens. To lower the pay of workers because of this suppression, on the grounds that their food is now cheaper and that their masters will have to pay the taxes which of necessity will have to replace the tolls, this would be to put things back where they were and to betray the will of the nation by making the law work only to the advantage of the rich. The employers and masters certainly do not suggest this injustice.

But if it is just and reasonable that the workers should gain by the ending of tolls, is it right that they should take this opportunity to burden the owners or employers, by forcing them to raise wages? All citizens have equal rights but they are not (nor will they ever be) equal in ability or in talents; nature has not wished it. It is thus impossible that they should hope to make the same gains. A law which would remove the hope of making more than the next fellow would thus be an unjust law. A coalition of workmen to fix a uniform daily pay and to force their fellow workmen to submit to this scale would obviously be against their real interests. In addition such a coalition would be a violation of the law, the annihilation of public order, a threat to the public interest, and the means of reducing those who advocated it to poverty by means of the halt or cessation of work which would result. In every respect the result would be a tragedy. . . .

III. THE CONSTITUTION OF 1791 SETS VOTING REQUIREMENTS

Section II: Primary Assemblies— Nomination of Electors

I. In order to form a National Legislative Assembly, the active citizens shall meet every two years, in primary assemblies, in the towns and cantons. . . .

II. To be an active citizen it is necessary,

To be born, or to have become, a Frenchman;

To be twenty-five years of age complete;

To have resided in the city or canton during the time determined by the law;

To pay, in any part of the kingdom, a direct contribution [tax] at least equal to the value of three days' labor, and to produce the acquittance;

Not to be in a menial capacity; namely, that of a servant receiving wages;

To be inscribed, in the municipality of the place of residence, in the list of the national guards;

To have taken the civic oath.

III. Every six years the legislative body shall fix the *minimum* and the *maximum* of the value of a day's labor, and the administrators of the departments shall determine the rate for every district. . . .

VII. No man can be named elector, if, to the conditions necessary in order to be an active citizen, he does not join the following: In towns of more than 6000 inhabitants, that of being proprietor or life-renter of a property valued on the rolls of the contribution at a revenue equal to the local value of 150 days' labor. . . .

And in the country, that of being proprietor or life-renter of a property valued on the rolls of contribution at a revenue equal to the local value of 150 days' labor, or of being a farmer of lands valued, on the same rolls, at the value of 400 days' labor. . . .

The Revolution Turns to Terror

The attempted flight from Paris of the royal family undermined faith in constitutional monarchy, and the outbreak of war with Austria and Prussia in 1792 accelerated the transfer of decision-making from the moderates to the more radical revolutionaries. Foremost among these was Maximilien Robespierre (1758–1794), a lawyer from the provinces, who became the dominant figure in the Committee of Public Safety established to guard against subversion at home while France was waging war.

In the first selection below Robespierre explains why the Revolution had to adopt the tactics of terror. The law on suspects, sections of which are included in the second selection, provided guidelines for the detection of subversives and enlarged the powers of the courts in dealing with them. Approximately 17,000 death sentences were meted out by the revolutionary tribunals for political offenses during the fifteen months of terror. The last two selections provide data on these executions, the first written by a conservative member of the Legislative Assembly (Comte de Vaublanc, 1756–1845) and the second a statistical analysis of roughly 85 percent of the executions. I. From *Pageant of Europe,* revised edition, by Raymond P. Stearns, copyright,

1947, © 1961, by Harcourt, Brace and World, Inc. and reprinted with their permission. II. From F. M. Anderson, *The Constitutions and Other Select Documents Illustrative of the History of France, 1789–1907* (Minneapolis, 1908), 2d ed., pp. 186–187. III. Reprinted by permission of the publishers from Donald Greer, *The Incidence of the Terror during the French Revolution,* Cambridge, Mass.: Harvard University Press, Copyright 1935 by the President and Fellows of Harvard College; 1963 by Donald Malcolm Greer, p. 166. IV. *The French Revolution as Told by Contemporaries,* copyright, 1938, by E. L. Higgins. Reprinted by permission of the publisher, Houghton Mifflin Company.

I. ROBESPIERRE EXPLAINS THAT SUCCESSFUL REVOLUTION REQUIRES BOTH VIRTUE AND TERROR (Speech of February 5, 1794)

It is time to mark clearly the aim of the Revolution and the end toward which we wish to move; it is time to take stock of ourselves, of the obstacles which we still face, and of the means which we ought to adopt to attain our objectives. . . .

What is the goal for which we strive? A peaceful enjoyment of liberty and equality, the rule of that eternal justice whose laws are engraved, not upon marble or stone, but in the hearts of all men.

We wish an order of things where all low and cruel passions are enchained by the laws, all beneficent and generous feelings aroused; where ambition is the desire to merit glory and to serve one's fatherland; where distinctions are born only of equality itself; where the citizen is subject to the magistrate, the magistrate to the people, the people to justice; where the nation safeguards the welfare

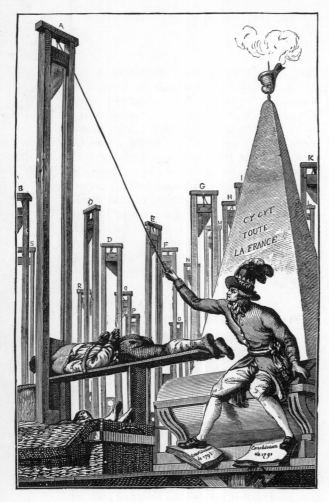

Robespierre guillotining the executioner and stepping on the Constitutions of 1791 and 1793. The caption reads, "Robespierre, after having had all the French guillotined, beheads the executioner with his own hand." This caricature cost the engraver his life.

In our country we wish to substitute morality for egotism, probity for honor, principles for conventions, duties for etiquette, the empire of reason for tyranny of customs, contempt for vice for contempt for misfortune, pride for insolence, the love of honor for the love of money . . . that is to say, all virtues and miracles of the Republic for all the vices and snobbishness of the monarchy.

We wish in a word to fulfill the requirements of nature, to accomplish the destiny of mankind, to make good the promises of philosophy . . . that France, hitherto illustrious among slave states, may eclipse the glory of all free peoples that have existed, become the model of all nations. . . . That is our ambition; that is our aim.

What kind of government can realize these marvels? Only a democratic government. . . . But to found and to consolidate among us this democracy, to realize the peaceable rule of constitutional laws, it is necessary to conclude the war of liberty against tyranny and to pass successfully through the storms of revolution. Such is the aim of the revolutionary system which you have set up. . . .

Now what is the fundamental principle of democratic, or popular government—that is to say, the essential mainspring upon which it depends and which makes it function? It is virtue: I mean public virtue . . . that virtue which is nothing else but love of fatherland and its laws. . . .

The splendor of the goal of the French Revolution is simultaneously the source of our strength and of our weakness: our strength, because it gives us an ascendancy of truth over falsehood, and of public rights over private interests; our weakness, because it rallies against us all vicious men, all those who in their hearts seek to despoil the people. . . . It is necessary to stifle the domestic and foreign enemies of the Republic or perish with them. Now in these circumstances, the first maxim of our politics ought to be to lead the people by means of reason and the enemies of the people by terror.

If the basis of popular government in time of peace is virtue, the basis of popular government in time of revolution is both virtue and terror; virtue without which terror is murderous, terror without which virtue is powerless. Terror is nothing else than swift, severe, indomitable justice; it flows, then, from virtue.

II. THE LAW ON SUSPECTS
(September 17, 1793)

1. Immediately after the publication of the present decree all the suspect persons who are in the territory of the Republic and who are still at liberty shall be placed under arrest.

2. Those are accounted suspect persons; 1st, those who by their conduct, their connections, their remarks, or their writings show themselves the partisans of tyranny or federalism and the enemies of liberty; 2nd, those who cannot, in the manner prescribed by the decree of March 21st last, justify their means of existence and the performance of their civic duties; 3rd, those who have been refused certificates of civism; 4th, public functionaries suspended or removed from their functions by the National Convention or its commis-

of each individual, and each individual proudly enjoys the prosperity and glory of his fatherland; where all spirits are enlarged by the constant exchange of republican sentiments and by the need of earning the respect of a great people; where the arts are the adornment of liberty, which ennobles them; and where commerce is the source of public wealth, not simply of monstrous opulence for a few families.

sioners and not reinstated, especially those who have been or shall be removed in virtue of the decree of August 14th last; 5th, those of the former nobles, all of the husbands, wives, fathers, mothers, sons or daughters, brothers or sisters, and agents of the *émigrés*, who have not constantly manifested their attachment to the Revolution; 6th, those who have emigrated from France in the interval from July 1, 1789, to the publication of the decree of March 30–April 8, 1792, although they may have returned to France within the period fixed by that decree or earlier.

3. The committees of surveillance established according to the decree of March 21st last, or those which have been substituted for them, either by the orders of the representa-tives of the people sent with the armies and into the departments, or in virtue of special decrees of the National Convention, are charged to prepare, each in its district, the list of suspect persons, to issue warrants of arrest against them, and to cause seals to be put upon their papers. The commanders of the public force to whom these warrants shall be delivered shall be required to put them into execution immediately, under penalty of removal. . . .

10. The civil and criminal tribunals can, if there is need, cause to be arrested and sent into the above-mentioned jails persons ac-cused of offenses in respect of whom it may have been acquitted of the accusations brought against them.

III. A CALENDAR OF THE TERROR

DATE	NOBLES		UPPER MIDDLE CLASS		LOWER MIDDLE CLASS		CLERGY	
March–September, '93	39	8%	60	12%	64	12%	30	6%
October, '93–May, '94	607	6%	1243	11%	1035	10%	534	5%
June–July, '94	501	20%	626	24%	333	13%	327	13%
August, '94	10	12%	28	29%	1	1%	17	20%
No Date Given	1	1%	27	24%	5	5%	12	11%
Totals	1158	8¼%	1964	14%	1488	10½%	920	6½%

DATE	WORKING CLASS		PEASANTS		NO GIVEN STATUS		TOTAL
March–September, '93	170	33%	137	26%	18	3%	518
October, '93–May, '94	3638	34%	3570	33%	135	1%	10812
June–July, '94	535	21%	195	8%	37	1%	2554
August, '94	19	22%	27	31%	4	5%	86
No Date Given	27	25%	32	29%	6	5%	110
Totals	4389	31¼%	3961	28%	200	1½%	14080

A CALENDAR OF TERROR

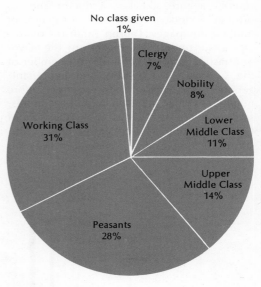

THE CLASS OF THOSE
WHO DIED IN THE TERROR

IV. A CONTEMPORARY RECALLS FIVE WEEKS IN THE REIGN OF TERROR (Winter 1793–1794)

[There were executed] from December 2, 1793, to January 11, 1794, two shoemakers, a clerk from the ministry of the interior, a doctor, a woman, Kersaint and Rabaut (depu-ties of the Convention), a brigadier, Mme. Dubarry, a Paris banker and two sons, a deputy of the Convention, a Swiss, two tailors, two persons undescribed, a former page, four women, the Duc de Châtelet, a servant, three men of the household of the Duc de Mont-morency, a grocer, a cooper, a wigmaker, a tailor, two nobles, a chief of army *dépôts,* a justice of the peace of the Constituent Assembly, a *curé*, a baker, a doctor and his brother, a clerk, a clockmaker, a director of military equipages, Lebrun (minister of foreign affairs under the Convention), the mayor of Strasbourg, the Duc de Biron (member of the Constituent Assembly and lieutenant-general), an excise collector, two more nobles, a woman, a transfer agent, a commissary, two priests, two women, the son of General Custine, a lieutenant-colonel, a substitute of the procurator-general of the *cour des aides*, Marshal Lückner (convicted according to the sentence, of having delivered several strongholds over to the enemy), a soap manufacturer, a noble, a priest, a sergeant, a substitute in the Convention, a man of letters, a woman, a printer, the former commander of Sainte-Lucie, the president of the revolutionary committee of Montpellier (an accomplice of the Brissotins, according to the sentence), and Lamourette (constitutional bishop). Total 89, of which thirteen were women.

The head of Louis XVI is raised above an enthusiastic crowd after the king's execution in the Place de la Revolution, January 1793. The square would later be called the Place de la Concorde. A contemporary engraving.

Foreign Invasion Shapes the Revolution

The wars that began in 1792 were decisive for the direction taken by the French Revolution. In the following year the government initiated a system of mass conscription, soon to be imitated by other nations, that would result in the largest army seen in Europe since Roman times. This decree of 1793 is presented in the first reading. The second reading consists of excerpts from the letters to his mother of a young patriotic conscript. Sentiments such as those expressed by Joliclerc were undoubtedly reinforced on hearing the stirring words and music of *The Marseillaise*, written to inspire the French republicans in the war against the conservative forces of Austria and Prussia. *The Marseillaise* is now the French national anthem. The translation used here was by the English romantic poet Shelley. I. From F. M. Anderson, *The Constitutions and Other Select Documents Illustrative of the History of France, 1789–1907* (Minneapolis, 1908), 2d ed., pp. 184–185. II. From H. F. Stewart and P. Desjardins, eds., *French Patriotism in the Nineteenth Century*, Daniel Resnick, trans. (New York: Cambridge University Press, 1923), pp. 21–23. III. From *The Complete Poetical Works of Percy Bysshe Shelley* (Boston, 1901), p. 561.

I. THE LEVEE EN MASSE
(August 23, 1793)

1. From this moment until that in which the enemy shall have been driven from

the soil of the Republic, all Frenchmen are in permanent requisition for the service of the armies.

The young men shall go to battle; the married men shall forge arms and transport provisions; the women shall make tents and clothing and shall serve in the hospitals; the children shall turn old linen into lint; the aged shall betake themselves to the public places in order to arouse the courage of the warriors and preach the hatred of kings and the unity of the Republic.

2. The national buildings shall be converted into barracks, the public places into workshops for arms, the soil of the cellars shall be washed in order to extract therefrom the saltpeter.

3. The arms of the regulation caliber shall be reserved exclusively for those who shall march against the enemy; the service of the interior shall be performed with hunting pieces and side arms.

4. The saddle horses are put into requisition to complete the cavalry corps; the draft horses, other than those employed in agriculture, shall convey the artillery and the provisions.

5. The Committee of Public Safety is charged to take all the necessary measures to set up without delay an extraordinary manufacture of arms of every sort which corresponds with the ardor and energy of the French people. It is, accordingly, authorized to form all the establishments, factories, workshops, and mills which shall be deemed necessary for the carrying on of these works, as well as to put in requisition, within the entire extent of the Repub-

Royalists in western France were not "pacified" until 1799 and government conscripts were sent out to fight against them. Here a royalist band blocks a bridge by overturning a manure cart. The action took place in 1793 and was an early episode in the wars of the Vendée.

lic, the artists and workingmen who can contribute to their success. . . .

6. The representatives of the people sent out for the execution of the present law shall have the same authority in their respective districts, acting in concert with the Committee of Public Safety; they are invested with the unlimited powers assigned to the representatives of the people to the armies.

7. Nobody can get himself replaced in the service for which he shall have been requisitioned. The public functionaries shall remain at their posts.

II. CONSCRIPT FRANCOIS-XAVIER JOLICLERC WRITES TO HIS MOTHER

13 December, 1793

My dear mother,

You continue to point out to me, in all your letters, that we must get out of the army, cost what it may. Here are the difficulties and the obstacles that I can see.

First of all, it is difficult to find replacements despite the enormous sums that are expended for this purpose. Secondly, we have just had a call-up of men eighteen to twenty-five; and the call-up of those from twenty-five to thirty-five is being prepared. As soon as we got home, we would have to get ready to go back, regretting the money we had spent. Thirdly, when *la patrie* calls us to her defense, we ought to fly there as if running to a good meal. Our life, our wealth, and our talents do not belong to us. It is to the nation, *la patrie*, that all that belongs.

I know well that you and all the others in our village do not share these sentiments. They are not aroused by the cries of an outraged fatherland, and all that they do results from being compelled to. But I have been brought up in conscience and thought, and have always been republican in spirit, although obliged to live in a monarchy. These principles of love for *la patrie, la liberté, la république,* are not only engraved in my heart, but are deeply etched and will remain there as long as it will please the Supreme Being to sustain in me the breath of life.

Even if it cost me three quarters of my possessions to have you share these sentiments with me, I would gladly part with them and consider it a very small sacrifice. Oh, if only one day you could know the price of liberty and lose your senseless attachment to material things.

30 May, 1794

What about my lot? I am at my post, where I ought to be, and every good man who knows what's what ought to fly to the aid of his country in danger. If I should perish there, you ought to rejoice. Can one make a finer sacrifice than to die for one's country? Can one die for a more just, glorious, and fairer cause? No! Would you rather see me die on a mattress of straw in my bed at Froidefontaine [his home village] working with wood or stone?

No, dear mother. Think that I am at my post and you will be consoled. If your conscience reproaches you in some way, sell even the last of your petticoats for *la patrie*. She is our only rudder, and it is she who guides us and gives us happiness. . . .

Your son, Joliclerc

III. THE MARSEILLAISE URGES THE CITIZENS TO ARMS (1792)

Ye sons of France, awake to glory!
Hark! Hark! the people bid you rise!
Your children, wives, and grandsires hoary,
Behold their tears and hear their cries!
Shall hateful tyrants, mischief breeding,
With hireling hosts, a ruffian band,
Affright and desolate the land
While liberty and peace lie bleeding?

To arms! To arms! ye brave!
The avenging sword unsheathe!
March on! March on! all hearts resolved
On victory or death!

Now, now, the dangerous storm is rolling,
Which treacherous kings confederate raise!
The dogs of war, let loose, are howling,
And, lo! our fields and cities blaze.
And shall we basely view the ruin,
While lawless force, with guilty stride,
Spreads desolation far and wide,
With crimes and blood his hands imbruing?

To arms! To arms! ye brave! etc.

O Liberty, can man resign thee,
Once having felt thy generous flame?
Can dungeons, bolts, or bars confine thee,
Or whips thy noble spirit tame?
Too long the world has wept, bewailing,
That Falsehood's dagger tyrants wield;
But Freedom is our sword and shield,
And all their arts are unavailing.

To arms! To arms! ye brave! etc.

A revolutionary music-sheet of the "March of the Marseillais."

John H. Stewart: Consequences of the French Revolution

John Hall Stewart's (1904–   ) special area of historical interest is eighteenth- and nineteenth-century France. In this reading he contrasts the apparent and actual achievements of the French Revolution. Reprinted with permission of The Macmillan Company from *A Documentary Survey of the French Revolution* by John H. Stewart. Copyright 1951 by The Macmillan Company.

One of the striking features of historical writing on the French Revolution is a tendency to *omit* "conclusions." Historians have dwelt at length on the causes of the Revolution, and have traced in detail the course of its history. But few have ventured to provide a summary estimate of its outcome. . . .

This does not mean that those who have written about the French Revolution have no opinions on the subject; in fact, quite the contrary is the case. On the one hand, there are those who believe that the Revolution was a mistake, that it was a "bad thing" for France and for Europe, that it was reactionary, antidemocratic, and nonprogressive. On the other hand, there are those who contend that it was the greatest event in modern history, that it was essentially a "good thing" for all concerned, that it laid the liberal, democratic, and progressive foundations of the life of modern Europe. And each group of advocates produces apparently substantial and irrefutable evidence to verify its claims. . . .

The immediate consequences of the French Revolution may be determined . . . by examining the extent to which the Revolution was successful in achieving its original objectives. And this may be done most effectively by contrasting the institutional life of France in 1799 with what it had been in 1789—political, economic, social, religious, and intellectual.

Politically, in 1789 France was a monarchical state, with a long tradition of divine-right absolutism. It lacked anything approximating the "free" parliamentary institutions of England—even the existence of recognized constitutional foundations was a matter of controversy. Liberties, such as they were, were conceived principally in terms of the old Latin "libertas," i.e., "privilege." "Liberties of the subject" were unknown, and there was no official statement of either "rights" or "duties" of citizens. The remark attributed to Louis XIV might still explain the relation of the king to his subjects: "I am the State" was as applicable, in many respects, as it had been a century earlier. Little that might be identified as political democracy or political liberty existed. The people were governed by the king and his bureaucracy mainly for the benefit of the privileged classes.

In the field of local government, most of the work was done by appointed royal officials, responsible only to the central government; and what remained of local autonomy was restricted to a few areas. In both local and national government, election of public officials was virtually unknown, and participation in affairs of state was limited to a chosen few. There was no uniform code of laws for France as a whole. An appointed and venal judiciary applied a variety of legal procedures with slight heed for the "rights" or physical well-being of the individual. Laws were frequently cruel, and their administra-

tion arbitrary. Moreover, laws were the product, not of a representative or responsible legislature, but of a king, the only check on whose powers were the aristocrats who controlled the higher courts. In much of what it did the State was aided and abetted by the Church, with which a working agreement had existed for many years. And, as yet, provincialism, rather than nationalism, characterized the attitude of the average Frenchman.

To many students the foregoing remarks may appear ridiculous. Well may they inquire, "Why seek in the France of *1789* the political features of the *modern* liberal-democratic state?" But that is one of the very reasons why the French Revolution is so important! It pointed the way, for France and for Europe, the way which much of the modern world now takes for granted, but which in 1789 was little more than hope and faith in the minds of a few men. The first serious evidences of the realization of that hope and faith were already visible in *1799.* By that year divine-right, absolute monarchy had yielded to a republic, with at least a quasi-democratic form of government, and with popular sovereignty widely accepted in principle. By that time France not only possessed a constitution, and a written one at that, but she had had *three* such documents, had tried two of them, and was about to experiment with a fourth! For the most part these constitutions represented the work of regularly selected constitutional conventions, three of them carried declarations of rights of the individual, and one included a statement of *duties.*

New standards of political life had become known—freedom of action, security of property, protection of persons. Codes of law (ultimately further integrated by Napoleon) had supplanted the chaos and confusion of an earlier day. An elected judiciary, the principle of habeas corpus, trial by jury, humanized penalties all had come into being. Law had come to symbolize the general will, and equality *before* the law had taken the place of privilege. In local affairs a decentralized system, likewise with elected officials, and with a high degree of local autonomy, had taken the place of the intendants. And everywhere much experience had been gained in voting for candidates, running for office, discussing public issues, and participating in the affairs of government. A consciousness of a common national destiny had been fostered by the exigencies of war, a war to defend the Revolution against its enemies; and widespread attempts to substitute the French language for local dialects contributed further to the maturing of national feeling. Moreover, the war had brought into being a citizen army, in which everybody served in one capacity or another, either local or national. This took the place of the part-volunteer, part-professional army of the Old Regime; and the new dispensation replaced office holding based on social position and inheritance by tenure based on competence.

Economically, in 1789 France was still essentially an agrarian state. The economy rested upon an outmoded manorialism, one of the holdovers of the feudal regime, characterized by burdensome and inflexible features. Land was still very much a monopoly of privileged classes and corporations; and there was a vast gap—political, economic, and social—between those who owned it and those who worked it. The system, moreover, tended to perpetuate archaic agricultural techniques which, combined with natural conditions, frequently left France desperately short of food.

In commerce and industry France was the leading continental state. But those activities were hampered by numerous internal duties and customs, which added greatly to the cost of land transport of commodities; and so far as foreign trade was concerned, there was little in the form of a regular tariff system. In industry, progress was impeded by the outworn methods and traditions of the guilds, a survival of the middle ages. And in all phases of the economy everyone suffered from the lack of a uniform system of weights and measures.

In fiscal and financial matters there was no budget worthy of the name before the 1780's. The national treasury and the king's purse were substantially the same thing, and the steadying effect of a civil list was lacking. Taxes were inefficiently assessed and collected, they existed in variety and inequity, and both taxes and state finances were adversely affected, to a considerable extent, by the existence of the parasitical privileged classes. There was no apparent relationship between the economy and social problems.

By 1799, however, manorialism and all that it represented (the so-called "feudal regime") had been abolished, never to return, and "free" agriculture had taken its place. Land had ceased to be a monopoly of the few, and, although it was not redistributed as some would have wished, at least it was made available to all who could afford to buy it. Internal duties and customs had been disestablished, and France had become domestically what Colbert had tried to make it in the seventeenth century—a free-trade entity. On the frontiers a national tariff now provided protection to local industry and revenue for national government. The guilds had fallen along with other corporations, and

industrial activity had received a mighty impetus from its connection with the war effort. In place of diversity and confusion in weights and measures, by 1799 the now universally used metric system had come into being; and its significance far transcended the limits of things economic. Socialism, however abortive, had raised its head to indicate the inevitable and inseparable relationship between the economic and social activities of the community. Budgets and civil lists (the latter, of course, only so long as the monarchy continued) had become commonplace. Taxes had been reduced in form and number, and serious efforts had been made to assess them equitably and collect them efficiently. Control of finances, in so far as there was any, had passed from the upper classes to the middle class. And the franc had replaced older standards of money for the nation as a whole.

Socially, in 1789 France was a class society; moreover, it was a class-*conscious* society. The privileged minority enjoyed most of the benefits and prerogatives, while the unprivileged majority shared but little in those features of life. The upper classes rode high; the middle class waited, impatiently, for their chance to rise to power; the peasants kept on working. Slavery existed in the colonies, but perhaps that was to be expected at the time. The common man counted for little, and whatever social reform there was usually took place under the aegis of the Church.

By 1799 classes had given way to equality, an equality more pronounced than that in politics—though, as in *Animal Farm* some were "more equal than others." The bourgeoisie were coming into their own, while the lower levels of society, both urban and rural, were slowly rising, although they still had a long way to go. In any case, labor was presumably a free commodity, and laborers relatively free people. One of the most significant developments of the decade was the revolutionary idea of "careers open to talents." This meant that one's natural gifts could enable one to cross all lines of caste, wealth, inheritance, and family. Humanitarianism had taken form in many ways, notably in the improvement of conditions in prisons and in the abolition of slavery in the colonies. The common man had been recognized as a human being, as an individual. And social reforms of very considerable consequence had been undertaken by the State. In the social sphere may be seen, perhaps more clearly than in any other, one of the major features of the Revolution, the revolt against privilege.

Religiously, in 1789 France was burdened by a condition of intolerance which had apparently been growing since the middle of the seventeenth century. Non-Catholics labored under all sorts of disabilities, civil as well as religious. The Church was, in many respects, a strong arm of the State. It enjoyed vast power, numerous privileges, and much property. Controlling education, censorship, and the recording of vital statistics as it had done for many years, it was a force to be reckoned with. And, as might be expected of the time, the idea of civil marriage or of the dissolution of marital bonds by civil authorities, was not only frowned upon—it was not permitted.

By 1799 all this had changed. Since 1791 there had been more than tolerance, there had been *liberty* in religion. For Jew and Protestant alike, religious and civil limitations disappeared. Freedom replaced restriction. Moreover, the power of the Church in the State had been reduced, its privileges virtually eliminated, and its material wealth confiscated. To all intents and purposes it had become a branch of the civil service. The State had taken over many of the functions hitherto performed by clerics—education, censorship, and the recording of vital statistics. And, although France remained nominally a Catholic country, the forces of secularism were fast making themselves felt—two outstanding examples of which tendency were the establishment of civil marriage and the legalization of divorce.

Intellectually, in 1789 France suffered from widespread restrictions, and the fact that she *had* a most vigorous cultural life was a triumph for the intelligentsia. Education, as already indicated, was under the hand (sometimes a dead one) of the Church. A periodical press scarcely existed. Few opportunities were available for obtaining educational or other cultural advantages. And what encouragement existed for arts and letters was usually of a limited variety dispensed by the king and the aristocracy.

By 1799, however, Frenchmen had had the experience of enjoying, at least in theory, freedom of speech and freedom of the press. Education had been reorganized along the lines which it still follows in most modern states—free, compulsory, universal, and secular. The Revolution had given rise to an extensive, if not always great, periodical press. Lack of opportunities had yielded to the "careers open to talents" already mentioned, and such talents were encouraged and brought to fruition through public prizes, state patronage, and similar devices. Moreover, while there had been few museums and libraries prior to 1789, the revolutionaries established many more, planned still additional ones, and endeavored to integrate them with the educational system.

It might safely be said that never in human history, or at least never prior to 1799, had so much been achieved by one people in such a short span of time! Yet, lest the uninformed naively assume that between 1789 and 1799 some divine force had transformed France from a purgatory into a paradise, the foregoing impressive list of apparent achievements must be balanced against the *actual* accomplishments. In other words, how much of what was done progressed beyond the "paper" stage, how much failed in the effort? And, it must be admitted, here the opponents of the Revolution find much of their material for criticism. A few significant examples will suffice as evidence.

Politically, constitutionalism had been accepted, but the constitution of 1799 was a farce; declarations of rights had been made three times, but each time they had been more form than substance, and in 1799 they were omitted entirely; democracy had never been really tried—1799 inaugurated a dictatorship; the liberties of the subject had been flagrantly violated during the Terror; in 1799 it appeared that equality and security were preferable to liberty; and protection of property had been of little help to the clergy or the *émigrés*.

Economically, "free" land was a reality only for those who possessed the wherewithal to purchase it; agricultural reforms were still in the future; workers lacked the right to organize and to strike; and the fiscal and financial situation left by the Directory was worse than that facing the Estates-General—stability was still lacking.

Socially, the bourgeoisie had supplanted the clergy and nobles, but the common man still awaited his due; class consciousness persisted, and privilege was still sought; many of the social reforms proposed never passed outside the legislative halls; and socialism was a dead issue.

Religiously, France was still Catholic, and neither the Revolution nor its attempt at a synthetic faith had altered the situation; anti-Protestantism and anti-Semitism were by no means obliterated; and the revolutionary legislation affecting the Church had produced a schism which remained for Napoleon to heal.

Finally, despite a brief taste of the several freedoms, France was entering upon a period in which censorship was to keep news of Trafalgar from the columns of the *Moniteur,* and education was to become little more than Bonapartist propaganda; in fact, the educational projects of the Revolution remained, for the most part, decently interred in statute books.

Yet this situation was by no means abnormal. It should neither encourage the counter-revolutionary nor discourage the revolutionary. As fundamental change, the Revolution inevitably worked through a three-fold process: *disestablishment* (of outmoded old institutions); *innovation* (through badly needed new institutions); and *compromise* (by adaption of existing institutions to the necessities of the moment). The original objectives—which, for convenience, may perhaps best be summed up as *liberty, equality,* and *order*—could be achieved in no other way. What appears to be failure is nothing more than proof that in such movements the forces of reaction are strong, and the ambitions of men usually far exceed the ability of those same men to put their plans to practical use.

One thing, however, is certain—in 1789 liberty, equality, and order had been mere words; in 1799 they had become sufficiently accepted in principle and tried in practice that, come what might, they were to persist as permanent, if not universally accepted, elements of French life!

Obviously, as a crusade for universal "good" and against universal "bad," the French Revolution could not be confined within the territorial limits of any one state. If not universal, at least it was west European in its appeal. Both the Old Regime and the Enlightenment—the institutional and intellectual sources of the Revolution—were as much European as they were French! True, the differences between the Europe of 1789 and that of 1799 were neither as apparent nor as real as the corresponding differences in France. On the surface at least, they seemed to be more in diplomacy and territory than in ideas or institutions. Yet these latter aspects of west European life were undergoing change. The Revolution was setting an example and disseminating propaganda. And when, in the decade *following* 1799, Bonaparte overran Europe, he furthered the process by imposing upon his satellites those features of the Revolution in which he believed. Never again was west Europe able to continue along the path of the Old Regime—always was she to be diverted from that course by the spirit of the French Revolution. This diversion, and eventual arrival at the *real* goal may be seen in the ultimate consequence.

STUDY QUESTIONS

1. Through what stages did the Revolution go? Evaluate critically the position taken by the author of the brief account.

2. What were the goals of the moderate revolutionaries? Who would such goals satisfy?

3. Why, according to Robespierre, did terror tactics have to be used? What did he consider the goals of the Revolution? How realistic do these goals seem?

4. Who seems to have suffered in the Reign of Terror? How can you explain the wide distribution of executions?

5. How did the invasion of France by foreign armies affect the shape taken by the Revolution? Why, for instance, is young Joliclerc more patriotic than his fellow villagers?

6. How would a song like the "Marseillaise" strengthen the revolutionary ardor of the French? Might such songs contribute to French military victories?

7. How is the success of the French Revolution to be judged? In what sense is it part of a continuing revolution?

France and Europe under Napoleon

TOPIC 27

THE NAPOLEONIC ERA

With the overthrow of Robespierre in 1794 the French Revolution entered a period of consolidation. Executive power was distributed among five "Directors." Domestic unrest continued, however, and the continuing wars with foreign states threw growing political weight toward the military men who were leading the French campaigns in Germany and Italy. Most versatile of the generals was Napoleon Bonaparte (1769–1821) who made himself dictator of France in 1799. Born of an Italian family on the Mediterranean island of Corsica the year after its ownership passed to France, Napoleon was educated in French military schools and rose rapidly after suppressing a popular uprising against the Directory in 1795 with a "whiff of grapeshot." Napoleon always claimed to be a child of the Revolution, and certainly it was the Revolution that made his phenomenal rise possible. The readings describe highlights of his career and raise questions concerning his motives, goals, and actual accomplishments.

From William H. McNeill, *History Handbook of Western Civilization* (Chicago: University of Chicago Press, 1953). Copyright © 1953 by the University of Chicago Press.

1795–1799
DIRECTORY

1797
Peace with the Austrians after Italian campaign. Only Great Britain remained at war with France

1798
Second coalition formed: Britain, Austria and Russia

1799
Babeuf plot at home

1799
Coup d'Etat of Napoleon. Overthrow of the Republic. Establishment of the Consulate

1799–1804
CONSULATE

1801
Austria makes peace with France

1801
Peace with Austria and Papal Concordat

1802
Great Britain makes peace with France. Peace on all fronts for first time since 1792

1803
Great Britain declares war on France

1804–1814
EMPIRE

1803–1805
Third coalition raised against Napoleon (Austria, Russia, Sweden, and later Prussia)

1805
British naval victory at Trafalgar. Napoleon begins economic blockade of England (Continental System)

1806
Napoleon achieves supremacy on land in Europe

1807
Franco-Russian agreement on spheres of influence in Europe (Tilsit)

1808–1812
Guerrilla war in Spain against the French occupier (Peninsular War)

1807–1813
Liberalizing reforms in Prussia

1812
Napoleon invades Russia

1812–1813
Victorious fourth coalition forms against Napoleon: Russia, Prussia, Great Britain, Austria, and many smaller states

1814–1815
Bourbons returned to power in France (First Restoration). Napoleon confined to island of Elba

1815
Napoleon returns to power for Hundred Days. Defeat at Waterloo terminates Napoleon's political career

1821
Death of Napoleon at St. Helena

The men who overthrew Robespierre in 1794 had no idea of abandoning the revolution, and most Frenchmen agreed with them. But they did feel, generally, that the revolution had gone far enough within France, and were prepared to abandon the plans and proposals for yet further innovation which Robespierre and other Jacobins had been nourishing. . . .

But abroad, the policy of the government after Thermidor was as revolutionary as it was conservative at home. The French armies, organized in the white heat of the revolution, continued to win victory after victory. In 1795 Spain and Prussia withdrew from the war and Holland became a republic under French protection. In 1797, after a brilliant campaign in Italy, Napoleon Bonaparte compelled the Austrians to make peace, and only Great Britain remained at war with the victorious French. The next year Napoleon persuaded the Directory to equip an army and send it to Egypt under his command. The expedition was successful at first, despite precarious communications with the homeland. Napoleon's victories in Egypt soon came to stand out in high relief against a series of failures which beset the Directory at home.

In 1798 a new coalition (the Second) was formed by Britain, Austria and Russia. In the following year the armies of the coalition were able to defeat the French in Italy and Switzerland and once more threatened the borders of France itself. At home the government of the Directory was discredited by unblushing corruption and by the fact that public order had not been very successfully maintained. Royalist and reactionary plots were rife; and on the extreme left a conspiracy was formed under the leadership of François Babeuf (1760–97). Babeuf advocated public ownership of all land in order to establish economic as well as political equality. The conspiracy came to nothing and Babeuf was arrested and executed; but his ideas became one of the sources for the later development of socialism.

Failure in war and the threat of disturbances at home seemed to indicate that the Republic was in need of a stronger and more resolute rule. Napoleon saw this as his opportunity. When news of French reverses in Italy reached him, he hastily left Egypt and within a month of his arrival in France was able to organize a *coup d'état* (1799). With the help of the veteran Abbé Sieyès, who had become one of the Directors, Napoleon established himself as supreme military commander and First Consul of the Republic, drew up a new Constitution (the Consulate) and submitted it to ratification by plebiscite. The theory of popular sovereignty was retained in the phrases of the new constitution, but the reality of power rested in Napoleon's hands. He not only commanded the armies, conducted administration at home and diplomacy abroad, but also proposed all laws, which were then accepted or rejected by an intricately designed set of legislative chambers.

Napoleon speedily justified the faith which the French people had shown in him when they overwhelmingly ratified the new system of government. Once again he invaded Italy and defeated the Austrian armies (Marengo). Russia had already withdrawn from the war; Austria made peace in 1801 and Great Britain followed suit in the next year (Treaty of Amiens). For the first time since 1792 France was everywhere at peace and everywhere victorious.

Napoleon's brilliant successes were due in part to his personal qualities. He was a great general, who knew how to choose efficient officers and how to win the devotion of his soldiers. He built on the military tradition of the French revolutionary armies, and developed further the tactics which had been evolved by others before him. The chief technical innovation Napoleon made in warfare was his greater use of field artillery. Lighter field guns which could keep pace with marching infantry had been designed by French ordnance experts, and as a result artillery, instead of bogging down several miles behind the lines of battle, could be brought into play even before the infantry engaged. Until his opponents imitated French guns, and began to employ them in similar numbers, Napoleon's armies had a decisive advantage, quite apart from the additional edge in numbers and enthusiasm which general conscription and revolutionary feeling secured for the French.

As a young artillery officer, Napoleon had sympathized with the Jacobins, and when he became the ruler of France he claimed to be a true son of the revolution. Formal deference was paid to popular sovereignty even when Napoleon assumed the title of Emperor, and all his changes of the constitution were submitted to plebiscite for ratification. But Napoleon was more interested in order than in liberty, and his rule was almost from the start despotic.

begun to draw up, was brought to completion—the Code Napoleon. In its provisions the enduring changes wrought by the revolution were spelled out in detail, and a logical, relatively simple system of law was brought into operation in all parts of France, and in all regions which French armies conquered as well. A national public school system was established, and all educational institutions were brought under the supervision of a central administrative body called the University of France. Numerous public works were constructed, and a vigorous administration checked graft and speculation among public officials and maintained the solvency of the government. Control of currency and financial policy was vested in the Bank of France, organized in 1800.

Local government was strictly centralized. The departments were placed under prefects whom Napoleon appointed; and all towns of over 5000 inhabitants were headed by mayors appointed in the same way. A central police force was created to keep order in all the large towns and to seek out and check plots against

In one respect Napoleon broke with the revolutionary tradition. The religious policy of the successive revolutionary bodies had resulted in the division of France between Catholics and revolutionists. Napoleon therefore began negotiations with the pope, and in 1801 reached an agreement with him (Concordat) which governed the relation between the French government and the papacy until 1905. By the Concordat of 1801 the pope recognized the loss of Church property in France and admitted Napoleon's right to nominate bishops, whom the pope then installed in office. Salaries were to be paid by the state, and Catholicism was recognized as the religion of "the majority of Frenchmen" but was not accorded any legal monopoly. Actually Napoleon also subsidized other religious groups from state funds.

In most other respects, Napoleon retained and systematized the work of the revolution. A code of law, which the Convention had the power of the new ruler of France. A rigorous censorship of newspapers prevented opposition from achieving any public expression.

A few royalists and a fringe of Jacobins remained dissatisfied, but Napoleon succeeded in winning the support of the great majority of the French population. The First Consul had brought peace, order, and glory; and if revolutionary liberty had been curtailed, the equality of all classes before the law and the fraternity of patriotism had been retained and consolidated. In 1802 a grateful nation conferred the Consulship on Napoleon for life; two years later, after still more splendid victories, he was crowned Emperor of the French.

In 1803, scarcely more than a year after peace had been signed, Great Britain declared war again. The immediate issue was the British refusal to surrender Malta (as they were bound to do by the treaty of Amiens). The underlying and more important causes for the renewal of hostilities, however, were the British suspicion of Napoleon's effort to restore a French empire in Louisiana and Haiti, and the activities of the French government in Holland, Italy and Switzerland, where Napoleon was setting up puppet states. For several months after the renewal of war, Napoleon busied himself with preparations for an invasion of England; but when British subsidies and diplomacy raised a Third Coalition against the French (Austria, Russia, Sweden and, later, Prussia) he diverted his armies to meet his continental foes. In a series of brilliant victories (Ulm, Austerlitz, Jena, Friedland) Napoleon defeated all his land enemies. By 1806 he was supreme on the continent. He used his power to reduce Austria and Prussia to the level of second-rate powers by taking from them large slices of territory. With the Russians he came to an agreement (Tilsit) by which Europe was divided between Czar Alexander I (1801–1825) and the Emperor of the French.

On the sea, however, the British had won a decisive victory at Trafalgar (1805), and Napoleon thenceforth abandoned his hope of challenging British naval supremacy or of invading England. Instead he resorted to an

The French lost twenty-two ships and all hope of waging a war beyond the shores of Europe in the Battle of Trafalgar (1805) near the Straits of Gibraltar. Although the outnumbered British force did not lose a single vessel, their commander, Admiral Nelson, lost his life (right foreground.) An oil painting by D. Dighton.

economic blockade (the Continental System), hoping to bring the 'nation of shopkeepers' to terms by ruining British trade.

Between 1806 and 1812 Napoleon used his power to reorganize the state system of Europe. The borders of France were enlarged and at their greatest extent included Holland and the North Sea coast of Germany at one extreme and the Illyrian Provinces (along the east coast of the Adriatic Sea) at the other. Moreover France was ringed round by a series of satellite states. Italy was completely under French control. Some territories (including Rome itself) were annexed to France; the rest of the peninsula was divided between a kingdom of Italy of which Napoleon was himself

king, and a kingdom of Naples, entrusted to one of Napoleon's relatives. After assuming the title of Emperor, Napoleon crowned his infant son King of Rome, in imitation of the medieval practices of the Holy Roman Emperors. Napoleon tried to reduce Spain to similar dependency after 1808, but was not successful for long.

Napoleon's most lasting territorial changes were made in Germany. With the co-operation of some of the larger states of Germany, Napoleon suppressed several hundred of the small principalities, free cities and ecclesiastical states into which Germany had been divided for centuries. He united the German states adjacent to France into a Confederation

of the Rhine, and in north central Germany created a new kingdom of Westphalia, ruled by one of his brothers. Finally, territory taken from Prussia and Austria was formed into a Grand Duchy of Warsaw—a rump of the former kingdom of Poland which had been wiped from the map during the last quarter of the 18th century.

French influence in all of these dependent areas was very strong. Reforms of government and society were carried through on the French model, roads and other public works were built, and a familiarity with the leading ideas of the French revolution was acquired by many segments of the population. In Germany and Italy the new order was not unpopular at first, and it was only after Napoleon had suffered military defeat that he lost the support of the new states which he had established in those regions.

But French reform and example were two-edged weapons. Further east in Europe states-

THE CORONATION OF JOSEPHINE
Having placed the crown upon his own head, Napoleon turned to his wife Josephine at the ceremonies in the Cathedral of Notre Dame on December 2, 1804. The artist David made this step in the creation of a ruling dynasty the visual center of his huge canvas. In contradiction of David's portrayal, Pope Pius VII did not raise his hand to bless the Emperor, but instead, walked out later in the ceremony. Two of Napoleon's sisters were obliged reluctantly to carry the train of Josephine's imperial mantle. The Emperor's mother has been placed as a spectator in the center of the gallery, while his uncle, Cardinal Fesch, raises his cross. A more legitimate link to royalty was acquired in 1810 when Napoleon, having divorced Josephine, married the Austrian Archduchess, Marie-Louise.

men were impelled to imitate many things which the French had done in order to make their own nations strong to resist further French aggression. Prussia and Austria, smarting under defeat, began an extensive reorganization of their governments and military establishments, supplementing long service professional troops with conscript armies like the French. Great Britain, too, despite economic difficulties caused by Napoleon's blockade, remained supreme on the sea, and fanned every spark of discontent. In Russia, the admiration which Czar Alexander had conceived for Napoleon when first they met in 1806 gradually cooled, for Alexander found that Napoleon was not willing to give him a free hand to conquer the decaying Ottoman Empire; and he also discovered that the blockade of British goods, which he had agreed should be imposed, was seriously hurting the Russian economy.

All these factors worked to undermine the supremacy which Napoleon had won. But perhaps the most significant element in his eventual downfall was the stimulus to nationalism which the French example provided for all the peoples of Europe. Germans and Italians began to feel that if France could be strong, united and powerful their countries could and should be so too; and the frequent presence of French troops, which regularly lived off the country, helped to stimulate a detestation of the foreign conquerors not only among the ruling classes (who had hated and feared the French from the first) but among the common people as well. Thus the resistance to Napoleon gradually transformed itself from an effort of governments to an effort of whole peoples united behind their governments. In such wars the French revolutionary élan was encountered, and even

Forced southward by Russian pressure, the retreating French army came to the Berezina River in Central Russia in November 1812. Attacked by the Russians as they were crossing the river, the French lost more than 20,000 men, but Napoleon and remnants of the Grand Army managed to escape. This early nineteenth-century illustration shows the panic of the crossing.

surpassed by the patriotic enthusiasm of the opponents.

It was above all else in Spain and in Prussia that the new sense of nationalism weakened Napoleon's position. In 1808 Napoleon persuaded the Spanish king to abdicate and turn over his throne to one of Napoleon's brothers. This transaction stirred the Spanish people to revolt, and a long and bitter guerilla war ensued (the Peninsular War, 1808–14). A British expeditionary force under Sir Arthur Wellesley (later Duke of Wellington) came to the aid of the rebels, and the British and Spaniards between them were able to keep up a running battle against the French occupation troops until Napoleon's final downfall.

Something close to revolution, conducted from the top, came to Prussia between 1807 and 1813. Serfdom was abolished and many

of the liberal principles of the French revolution were written into law. Most important of all, a new army was carefully and painstakingly trained; and a spirit not only of Prussian but of German nationalism was cultivated. . . .

It was not until 1812 that military defeat caught up with Napoleon. In that year he invaded Russia in order to punish the Czar for having lifted the blockade against British goods. The march to Moscow and Napoleon's dismal retreat in the dead of winter are too well known to require description. Napoleon's defeat in Russia stirred Prussia to attack; a fever of national patriotism swept Germany and other German states soon followed the example set by the Prussians. A new coalition arose, this time including Russia, Prussia, Great Britain and Austria. After many battles, of which the 'Battle of the Nations' near

Leipzig was the greatest, Napoleon was driven back inside France and compelled to abdicate (April, 1814).

The victorious coalition restored the brother of Louis XVI as king of France . . . . A diplomatic congress was assembled at Vienna to settle the future of Europe. Negotiation at the Congress did not proceed smoothly. The great powers seemed near to splitting up over the question of the disposition of Poland and Saxony. This situation, and widespread dissatisfaction in France with the restoration of the Bourbons, persuaded Napoleon to leave the island of Elba (where the powers had given him a miniature state to govern) and land once more in France. The return of Napoleon did indeed rally the French nation behind him; but he had miscalculated the reaction of the European powers. They promptly buried their differences and took the field together against the renewed Napoleonic danger. In June 1815, Napoleon marched to meet an allied army under the Duke of Wellington. The two armies met near the village of Waterloo in Belgium, and after a hard day's battle Napoleon's army was routed. Four days later Napoleon abdicated for the second time. He surrendered himself to the commander of a British warship, and, without touching foot on dry land, was transported to the desolate island of St. Helena in the South Atlantic. There he died in 1821. . . .

Napoleon Administers France

Napoleon was an innovative administrator. His quick mind sparked ideas, and he sought to buttress his authority by achieving domestic prosperity and stability for France. Three examples of his approach to internal problems are included in this reading. The first was written to his brother Lucien, who was Minister of the Interior in the period following the coup d'état of 1799. The second was addressed to the judiciary of the Department of the Seine, while the third was dictated while he was in exile on St. Helena. From R. M. Johnston, ed., *The Corsican: A Diary of Napoleon's Life in His Own Words* (Boston, 1910), pp. 118–121, 128–129, 486–487.

I. HOW TO REVIVE THE PROSPERITY OF FRANCE
(December, 1799)

If war were not a necessity, my first care would be to found the prosperity of France on the communes [village units]. It is a much simpler matter, when reconstructing a nation, to deal with one thousand of its inhabitants at a time instead of striving romantically for the individual happiness of every one. In France a commune stands for 1000 inhabitants. To work at the prosperity of 36,000 communes is to work at the prosperity of the 36,000,000 inhabitants, while simplifying the question, and reducing the difficulty by the proportion that exists between 36,000 and 36,000,000.

The Minister of the Interior will carefully consider the following ideas:

Before the Revolution the commune belonged to the lord and to the priests; the vassal and the parishioner had no right to the roads; no ditches, nor fields for pasturing their cows or their sheep. Since 1790, when, suddenly and righteously, these common rights of communication and pasturage were snatched from the hands of the feudal lord, each municipality has, under the protection of the laws, become a real person, having the right to hold, to acquire, and to sell property, and to perform every deed known to our law for the benefit of the municipal community. France was therefore suddenly divided into 36,000 individualities, each one of which was subject to all the instincts of the proprietor, which are to increase his possessions, to improve his products, to swell his revenue. The root of the prosperity of France, therefore, lay at that point.

The reason why nothing has grown from this root is this: that an individual proprietor is always alive to his interests, while a community is, on the contrary, sleepy and sterile; the interests of an individual are a matter of simple instinct; those of a commune demand virtue, and virtue is rare. Since 1790 the 36,000 communes are but 36,000 orphans, heiresses of the old feudal privileges, neglected or plundered these ten years by the municipal tutors of the Convention, and of the Directory. They have stolen from the roads, from the pathways, from the trees, from the churches. What would become of the communes if this went on another ten years? The first duty of a Minister of the Interior is to stop an evil which will otherwise infect these 36,000 members of the social body.

The first condition, when dealing with a great evil, is to diagnose carefully its gravity and its incidents. The Minister of the Interior will therefore begin by drawing up a general schedule of the situation of the 36,000 communes of France. We have never had such a schedule. . . .

When this schedule is drawn up, the prefect will be notified that the whole effort of the administration must be brought to bear on the communes that are in debt, and that the mayors who do not come into line with these ideas of communal improvement must be removed. The prefect is to visit these communes at least twice a year, and the sub-prefect four times a year, under penalty of removal from office. A monthly report shall be sent to the minister of what is being done and of what remains to be done in these communes.

Every year the fifty mayors who have done most to free their communes, or to increase their resources, shall be brought to Paris at the expense of the State and presented ceremonially to the three Consuls. A column erected at the expense of the Government at the principal entrance of the city or village will hand the name of the mayor down to posterity. On it shall be inscribed: "A grateful country to the guardian of his commune!"

II. NAPOLEON STATES HIS CONCEPT OF JUSTICE AND LAW (May, 1800)

While France was torn by factions, justice was badly administered, as was indeed inevitable. For ten years have these conditions lasted; it is for you to bring them to an end. You are never to ask to what party the man who demands justice belongs; but you are to weigh the rights of all men with severe impartiality. It is for the army to secure peace between our citizens. You are appointed for life; no one has the right to remove you; you are responsible for your judgments only to your conscience; you will be as impassive as the law. With laws that actually interfere with the action of justice, I myself am compelled to prosecute disorders that affect the security of the state and to repress them arbitrarily.

Penal laws should read as though engraved on tables of marble, and should be as concise as the Decalogue.

A law should always lay down a general principle; it would be futile to attempt to foresee all possible cases.

III. THE TREASURES OF NAPOLEON ARE FOUND IN HIS PUBLIC WORKS (September, 1816)

You want to know the treasures of Napoleon? They are enormous, it is true, but in full view. Here they are: the splendid harbour of Antwerp, that of Flushing, capable of holding the largest fleets; the docks and dykes of Dunkirk, of Havre, of Nice; the gigantic harbour of Cherbourg; the harbour works at Venice; the great roads from Antwerp to Amsterdam, from Mainz to Metz, from Bordeaux to Bayonne; the passes of the Simplon, of Mont Cenis, of Mont Genèvre, of the Corniche, that give four openings through the Alps; in that alone you might reckon 800 millions. The roads from the Pyrenees to the Alps, from Parma to Spezzia, from Savona to Piedmont; the bridges of Jena, of Austerlitz, of the Arts, of Sèvres, of Tours, of Lyons, of Turin, of the Isère, of the Durance, of Bordeaux, of Rouen; the canal from the Rhine to the Rhone, joining the waters of Holland to the Mediterranean; the canal that joins the Scheldt and the Somme, connecting Amsterdam and Paris; that which joins the Rance and the Vilaine; the canal of Arles, of Pavia, of the Rhine; the draining of the marshes of Bourgoing, of the Cotentin, of Rochefort; the rebuilding of most of the churches pulled down during the Revolution, the building of new ones; the construction of the Louvre, of the public granaries, of the Bank, of the canal of the Ourcq; the water system of the city of Paris, the numerous sewers, the quays, the embellishments and monuments of that great city; the public improvements of Rome; the

reestablishment of the manufactories of Lyons. . . .

These are monuments to confound calumny! History will relate that all this was accomplished in the midst of continuous wars, without raising a loan, and with the public debt actually decreasing day by day.

Napoleon Plans a United Europe

In exile on St. Helena, Napoleon had ample time to reflect on his accomplishments. In this reading he muses on what he described as a great unfulfilled dream—the creation of a federation of European nations. From *Memoirs of Napoleon*, ed. F. M. Kircheisen, trans. F. Collins (New York: Dodd, Mead and Company, 1929), pp. 230–232.

One of my favourite ideas was the fusion, the federation of the nations, which had been separated by revolutions and politics. There are in Europe more than 30 million French, 15 million Spaniards, as many Italians, and 30 million Germans. I wanted to unite them all into one strong, national body. The accomplisher of this work would be awarded by posterity with its most beautiful wreath, and I felt myself strong enough and called on to undertake this work. When this was done people could devote themselves to the realization of the ideal, at present only a dream, of a higher civilization. Then there would be no more vicissitudes to fear, for there would be only one set of laws, one kind of opinion, one view, one interest, the interest of mankind. Then perhaps one could realise for Europe the thought of an amphictyony, a North American Congress. And what views

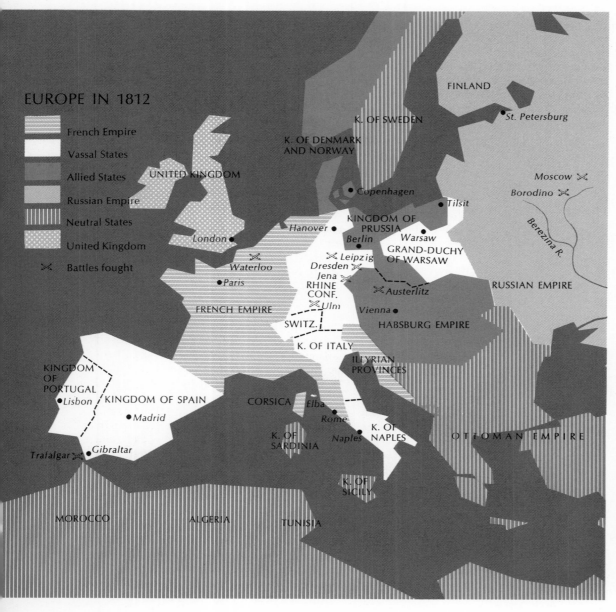

EUROPE IN 1812

- French Empire
- Vassal States
- Allied States
- Russian Empire
- Neutral States
- United Kingdom
- ⚔ Battles fought

FINLAND

K. OF SWEDEN

St. Petersburg

K. OF DENMARK
AND NORWAY

Moscow ⚔

Borodino ⚔

UNITED KINGDOM

Copenhagen

Tilsit

Berezina R.

Hanover

KINGDOM OF
PRUSSIA

Berlin

Warsaw

GRAND-DUCHY
OF WARSAW

London

Leipzig ⚔

Dresden

Jena ⚔

Waterloo ⚔

RHINE
CONF.

RUSSIAN EMPIRE

Paris

Austerlitz ⚔

FRENCH EMPIRE

⚔ Ulm

Vienna

SWITZ.

HABSBURG EMPIRE

K. OF ITALY

KINGDOM
OF
PORTUGAL

ILLYRIAN
PROVINCES

CORSICA

Elba

Lisbon

KINGDOM OF SPAIN

Rome

Madrid

K. OF
SARDINIA

K. OF
NAPLES

Naples

OTTOMAN EMPIRE

Trafalgar ⚔

Gibraltar

K. OF
SICILY

MOROCCO

ALGERIA

TUNISIA

would then be opened out, what a spectacle the world would present!

The fusion of the 30 million Frenchmen under one law had already taken place, that of the Spaniards being on the point of completion; for one must not judge a thing, as is generally done, by its result. . . . Spain was not lost to me through her resistance, nor by means of England's help, but in consequence of my own mistakes, and the misfortunes which I met with, but especially because I was so careless as to remove myself and my whole power a thousand leagues from Spain [to Russia in 1812]. Had it not been for this mistake Spain would have been pacified in three or four years. Peace would have returned to the Peninsula, a new and happy period of intellectual and social freedom for the country would have begun, and, instead of hating me, the new-born nation would have blessed me, that nation for which the most frightful struggles are now in store.

In Italy the fusion was almost completed. Here one only needed to watch quietly, the thing was thriving there alone. Every day was bringing the fruits of unity, legislation, and the new flight in thought and feeling to maturity. The union of Piedmont, Parma, Tuscany, and the Papal States with France was only transitory, and had no other purpose than to facilitate the completion of the national education of the Italians, and to keep the whole under one's eye.

And so the South of Europe was already approaching very close to the great goal, and then, when the thing was complete, what would the South have to fear from the North? Must not every human effort break against such walls?

The unification of Germany required more time. Here also I would have had to begin

370

with the simplification of its huge composition, not just because the people are not yet ripe for national ideas, but lest they should give themselves up too violently to the thing that was long germinating in their hearts. It is incomprehensible to me that no German Prince up to the present had had the idea of unifying the whole. If destiny had made me a German Prince, I would have rescued this nation from the storms of our days under one sceptre. With thirty million Germans surrounding my throne, as I know them, if I had been chosen and appointed by them as their ruler, I would never have been forsaken. As their Emperor I would never have been brought to St. Helena.

This plan of bringing about a union of the nations—and it is the noblest, most courageous and highest-minded plan—was wrecked through my misfortune and fall, like so many others in the execution of which I was hindered, but it is not lost for all that. The start has been given, the force of circumstances will carry it out, and nothing can prevent it. In the first great general war that breaks out, the ruler who understands how to unite his interests with those of the common people, will see himself in a moment head of all Europe, and will then be able to do what he likes in this respect.

Eugene Tarlé: The Russian People Face the French Invasion

Napoleon's imperial designs shattered on the nationalistic fervor aroused everywhere in Europe by the French conquests. French patriotic spirit and love of country were quickly transferred to Germans, Spaniards, and Russians, when they saw their homelands occupied by the foreigner. In this reading, Eugene Tarlé (1874–1955), noted Russian historian, describes the reaction of the Russian peasantry to the invasion of 1812. From Eugene Tarlé, *Napoleon's Invasion of Russia* (New York: Oxford University Press, 1942), pp. 256–258, 260, 267–269.

At first glance, we are confronted by a paradox; the peasants who loathed their servitude, who protested by murders of landowners recorded in annual statistics, and by revolts, which had, only 37 years before, imperiled the entire feudal order by the Pugachev insurrection—the same peasants met Napoleon as a fierce enemy, fighting with all their strength, as no other peasants had fought him except those of Spain. They refused to trade with the enemy, burned their grain and hay, even their huts, particularly if there were any French foragers inside; and actively assisted the guerrillas.

And yet there is definite evidence that as early as 1805–07, and at the beginning of the invasion of 1812, rumours associating Napoleon with dreams of emancipation circulated among the Russian peasantry (above all, among servants and near the cities). There was talk of a letter Napoleon had allegedly sent to the Tsar, warning him that until he liberated the peasants, there would be war and no peace. How then shall we account for so decisive a change in the peasant outlook?

It must be remembered that Napoleon burst upon Russia as a conqueror, a beast of prey, a ruthless destroyer, and that he never had the slightest intention of liberating the serfs. For the Russian peasants, the defence of Russia from the invading enemy was a defence of their lives, their families, their property.

At the beginning of the war, when the French army occupied Lithuania and White Russia, the White Russian peasants revolted, hoping to liberate themselves from the *Pani,* their tyrannical White Russian masters. In July and August 1812, White Russia was swept by stormy peasant agitation, which in places passed into open rebellion. In panic, landowners fled to the cities—to the Duke of Bassano in Vilna, to Marshal Davout in Moghilev, to General Dombrowski in Minsk, to the Emperor himself in Vitebsk. They asked for armed help against the peasants, pleaded for punitive expeditions, since the newly established Polish and Lithuanian gendarmery was not strong enough to maintain order. The French command promptly crushed the peasants and restored all the feudal rights. Napoleon's actions in Lithuania and White Russia had thus shown that he had no intention of helping the peasants in their efforts to throw off their chains, and would use his might to uphold the serf-owning nobles. This was in accord with his policy: he considered the Polish and Lithuanian nobles the basic political force in these places and had no desire to frighten them away by inspiring their peasants with the idea of liberation. . . .

The wholesale pillaging by the conquering army, by countless marauders, and sometimes by criminal bands of French deserters, caused the peasants' hatred of the enemy to grow from day to day.

The successive recruiting levies evoked no complaints; on the contrary, they were greeted with unprecedented enthusiasm. On 12 December 1812, the order went out to choose 8 recruits from every 500 men throughout the country. This, counting the militia levies, was the third general levy—at least, for some of the governments. In ordinary times, recruiting was viewed with loathing and horror. But now, after the loss of Moscow, it aroused quite other feelings. . . .

After the burning of Moscow, the bitterness of the peasants was intense. Despite appeals and enticements, the peasants round Moscow refused to trade with the French, and they savagely killed the alien foragers and marauders who fell into their hands. They even attacked French prisoners convoyed by Cossacks. When the foraging parties were escorted by large convoys, the peasants burned their provisions, sometimes entire villages, and fled to the woods. Those caught resisted desperately and perished. The French took no prisoners among the peasants, and sometimes on approaching a village would open fire to crush the possibility of resistance.

The guerrilla movement, which began immediately after Borodino, achieved its tremendous success only through the active, voluntary, and zealous assistance of the Russian peasantry. But this unquenchable hatred of the despoilers, destroyers, murderers, and ravishers manifested itself, above all, in the enthusiasm with which peasants joined the army and fought. The national character of this war was at once revealed in organized forms—in the army. In Spain, the national war assumed quite other forms, because in that country much time passed before military units could be organized. But in their indomitable hatred of the foreign ravishers and pillagers, in their thirst to give their lives for the destruction of a cruel and predatory foe, in their firm consciousness of their inner right, the Russian people was not a whit behind the Spanish people.

The French invaders of Spain also faced popular resistance. Bloody guerrilla warfare went on for years. The Spanish artist Goya captured the brutalizing effect of such fighting on human beings in a series of drawings done between 1808 and 1814 that he called *The Disasters of War*. This picture is entitled "Y Son Fieras" ("And They Are Wild Beasts").

In describing the retreat of the Grand Army, I shall speak in detail about the guerrilla war. But it must be noted here that the peasants had begun partisan warfare during the first half of the war, before the chief pioneer of the movement, Denis Davydov, had come forward with his plan. Stepan Eremenko, a private of the Moscow infantry regiment, wounded and abandoned at Smolensk, escaped from prison and organized a peasant guerrilla detachment of 300 men. Samus collected about 2,000 peasants and made bold attacks on the French. The peasant Ermolai Vasilyev gathered a force of about 600 men, arming them with rifles and sabres seized from the French.

These national heroes did not chase after glory, and their deeds have not been systematically recorded. A peasant woman of a Sokolovo village, in the Government of

Smolensk, alone defended herself against six Frenchmen, slew three of them, including a colonel, with a pitchfork, and put the remaining three to flight. She is known to us only by her first name, Praskovya.

This Praskovya, at the head of a small group of peasants of both sexes, energetically attacked detachments sent out by the French to requisition grain and hay in the Dukhovshchin district of Smolensk Government.

On entering Smolensk in November, Napoleon was apprised of the lack of provisions. In his rage, he ordered Siaufat, the commissary officer, to be shot, and another commissary officer, Villeblanche, to be put on trial. Siaufat was shot; the other was saved, when Jomini informed the Emperor that he was not so much to blame, as the peasants of the region had attacked the French foragers with particular ferocity and destroyed them; in his report he mentioned Praskovya and her astonishing feats. As a result, Napoleon stopped the proceedings against Villeblanche.

'The National War' is not a mere chapter in the history of the year 1812. The entire war against the invader was from start to finish a national war. Napoleon's strategy had counted his own troops and Alexander's troops, but he had to fight the Russian people, whom he had not counted. It was the hand of the Russian people that inflicted the irreparable, mortal blow. . . .

In the Austrian Alps the Tirolean peasants revolted under the leadership of Andreas Hofer, son of an innkeeper. Betrayed to the French, Hofer was taken to Italy and executed in 1809.

Napoleon Acknowledges the Source of His Power

Napoleon made the following admission in a conversation in 1811. From *The Mind of Napoleon*, ed., J. Christopher Herold (New York: Columbia University Press, 1955), pp. 241–242.

Five or six families are sharing the thrones of Europe, and they are pained to see a Corsican taking a seat on one of them. I cannot keep my place except by using force. I cannot accustom them to look upon me as an equal except by keeping them under my yoke. As soon as I cease to be feared, my Empire is destroyed. Thus I must repress whatever they undertake. I cannot let them threaten me and not strike back. What would be an indifferent matter to a king of an old dynasty is very serious to me. I shall persist in this attitude so long as I live, and if my son does not become a great warrior, if he does not resemble me, he will have to come down from the throne to which I shall have raised him—for it takes more than one man to consolidate a monarchy. Louis XIV, despite all his earlier victories, would have lost his crown at the end of his life if he had not been the heir of a long line of kings. Among the anciently established sovereigns, war aims never go beyond possession of a province or a fortress. With me, the stake is always my existence and that of the whole Empire.

In domestic matters, my position is entirely different from that of the long-established sovereigns. They can live indolently in their palaces; they can abandon themselves shamelessly to all the debauches of riotous living. Nobody challenges their legitimate rights; nobody dreams of replacing them; nobody accuses them of ingratitude, since nobody has helped them to attain the throne. As for me, everything is different: there is no general but believes he has the same rights to the throne as I. There is no influential man who doesn't give himself the credit for having guided my conduct on the Eighteenth Brumaire. Consequently, I must be very stern toward those people. If I were familiar with them, they would soon share my power and the public treasury. They don't like me—but they fear me, and that's good enough for me. I admit them into the army, I give them commands—but I also keep an eye on them. They wanted to escape my yoke; they wanted to federalize France. One word from me was enough to stifle their plot. So long as I live, they will never be dangerous. If I suffered a defeat, they would be the first to desert me.

At home as abroad, I reign only through the fear I inspire. If I renounced this system, I would be dethroned before long. This is my position, and these the motives that guide me.

Napoleon Carves His Niche in History

Napoleon's sensitivity to how his career would be judged by posterity was revealed in constant allusions to his achievements and unrealized objectives and in his conscious effort on St. Helena to create a Napoleonic "legend." A brief statement by Napoleon is followed in this reading by a summation of his historical role by J. Christopher Herold (1919–1964), editor and author, who was fascinated by the life and times of the French emperor. I. From R. M. Johnston, ed., *The Corsican: A Diary of Napoleon's Life in His Own Words* (Boston, 1910), p. 493. II. From *The Horizon Book of the Age of Napoleon,* © copyright 1963 by American Heritage Publishing Co., Inc. Reprinted by permission.

I. NAPOLEON ASSESSES HIS REPUTATION (March, 1817)

In spite of all the libels, I have no fear whatever about my fame. Posterity will do me justice. The truth will be known; and the good I have done will be compared with the faults I have committed. I am not uneasy as to the result. Had I succeeded, I would have died with the reputation of the greatest man that ever existed. As it is, although I have failed, I shall be considered as an extraordinary man: my elevation was unparalleled, because unaccompanied by crime. I have fought fifty pitched battles, almost all of which I have won. I have framed and carried into effect a code of laws that will bear my name to the most distant posterity. I raised myself from nothing to be the most powerful monarch in the world. Europe was at my feet. I have always been of the opinion that the sovereignty lay in the people. In fact, the imperial government was a kind of republic. Called to the head of it by the voice of the nation, my maxim was, *la carrière est ouverte aux talens* [advancement in life is open for all those who are capable] without distinction of birth or fortune, and this system of equality is the reason that your oligarchy hates me so much.

II. J. C. HEROLD: LEGACY AND LEGEND

Napoleon's impact on the modern imagination has been incalculably great. Who would have dreamed of being a Napoleon before Napoleon? After him, the dream lacked originality. Undoubtedly Hitler, one of the most mediocre figures in world history, dreamed of being Napoleon. One might think that such a disciple would bring his master into disrepute. On the contrary, a comparison between Napoleon and Hitler can only increase one's admiration for Napoleon's sanity, moderation, and economy of cruelty. Napoleon loved only himself, but, unlike Hitler, he hated nobody. In good as in evil, he was without emotion, and he did only so much of either as he believed necessary for his purposes. Moreover, he was the only great dictator of modern times who was not the slave of a particular political doctrine.

As a self-made man and demigod, Napoleon is unique in history and therefore, as it were, timeless. But what of his impact on the modern world—not as a symbol or a mythological figure but as a historical force? How did he find the world, and how did he leave it? Was he . . . an anachronistic intrusion upon the modern world, or was he a modern, a pathbreaker for a new age? Did his adventure merely interrupt the historic process for two decades, or did it further that process? These are complex questions, and only tentative answers to them are possible.

When he began his career, he found the world in chaos and convulsion. The old order was collapsing; the new order had failed to materialize. Like the hero of some myth or fairy tale, he picked up the pieces of the old order, took advantage of others' quarrels to make himself their master, won kingdoms and vast fortunes, gave wealth and honor to his brothers, sisters, and in-laws, reached for ever more since it was so easy and finally overreached himself. When his career ended, he left the world still subject to the same explosive tensions that had eased his way to power but so exhausted from his exploits that it postponed its search for a new order by half a century. Perhaps, had he not appeared on the stage, the old order would have been restored fifteen years earlier than it was; on the other hand it is doubtful that the forces that were then shaping today's world—industrial and technological progress, the resulting prosperity of the middle class and the grievances of the laboring class, the general trend toward political equality and national unification—would have been appreciably slower to make themselves felt.

In many ways (though my no means in all), Napoleon was insensitive to the forces that were shaping the future. Except in some scattered remarks he made at St. Helena, when he had time to reflect on the age, he was blind to the potentialities of steam power and of other inventions that were changing the world. A conservative by temperament, he distrusted innovations of any sort. He sought to establish a dynasty when monarchy was beginning to go out of fashion—and the dynasty he wished to establish was based on the Carolingian model, at that; he created a nobility after a revolution had been fought to abolish it; and in restoring the Church he gave it a position which, as subsequent history has shown, was out of keeping with modern trends.

He disparaged all theories of progress. He paid no attention to the masses—the *canaille* [rabble], as he called them—and he willfully ignored the national pride and aspirations of Italians, Germans, Spaniards, Poles, and Russians. He was equally conservative in warfare; his innovations in that art, including his use of unprecedented masses of troops and artillery and his masterly logistics, which made the employment of such masses possible, were important innovations, to be sure, but they grew out of circumstances rather than a wish to revolutionize warfare. In general, he never looked farther ahead than the next day and regarded all experiment as dangerous nonsense. In all these respects—except, perhaps, the military—he cannot be said to have been a modern or to have made a significant contribution to the modern age.

Yet to see in him an anachronistic reincarnation of a hero of antiquity is equally incorrect. His vision of a universal empire may recall Augustus and Diocletian rather than modern times, but who would say that Augustus and Diocletian were not more modern than Talleyrand or Metternich? His passion for uniformity and standardization was decidedly modern. But his main achievement, if it may be called that, was the revolution he brought about in the techniques of power and of manipulating men. His use of the press and

of propaganda, his mastery of applied psychology to make people do what he wanted them to do, his rhetoric, his bulletins, his genius at self-dramatization, his flair for pageantry, his superb exploitation of human vanity, ambition, and gullibility, his genius at fanning fear and greed by turns, and, finally, his artful creation of his own legend—all this places him squarely in our own times. Nor has any successful dictator since Napoleon neglected the techniques that he was the first to apply in a systematic way.

In the science of manipulating men, Napoleon was undoubtedly ahead of his times—a dubious merit. But what was his influence on the historic process of his own times and the decades following? It is generally contended that while he set back the Revolution in France, he promoted the spread of its principles elsewhere, notably in Germany, Italy, and Spain. This he assuredly did, though not always wittingly or deliberately. The importance of the Civil Code in extending the concept of legal equality has been somewhat exaggerated by Napoleon's apologists. If he helped to sweep away the remnants of feudalism and to arouse the political consciousness of the peoples of Europe, he accomplished this in a negative way. His victories and conquests demonstrated the decrepitude of old institutions and the need for reform; his oppression, his insensitiveness to the national pride of nations other than the French, eventually roused them to action and gave them a sense of dignity and importance that no Holy Alliance could suppress. The Spanish uprising of 1808, the Russian resistance of 1812, the German War of Liberation of 1813 can hardly be said to have been intended by Napoleon; yet they were direct

results of his actions, and they changed the world.

Napoleon was not eager to liberate Latin America; yet his aggression in Spain did just that. He was not anxious to make a world power of the United States; yet his sale of the Louisiana Territory did just that. He had no desire to create German unity; yet by reducing the number of sovereignties from more than three hundred to thirty-six (in order to create useful puppet states rather than to benefit Germany) and by fanning German nationalism, which was directed against him, he did more for German unity than any man except Bismarck. There is no evidence that he wished to unite Italy, but he gave the Italians just enough taste of national independence to set the Risorgimento in motion. . . . The last thing he desired to do was to undermine the institution of monarchy . . . ; yet . . . by demonstrating the utter moral decay of European monarchy, and by his own anachronistic imperial mummery Napoleon dealt monarchy as destructive a blow as did the executioner who beheaded Louis XVI.

One feels at a loss, trying to fit the brief era of Napoleon's domination into the scheme of history. Somehow he does not seem to belong there. His positive achievements merely continued the centralizing trends set by Richelieu and Louis XIV. In nearly all other respects, his historical role was that of an unconscious tool of destruction, clearing the way for a modern age that little resembled the age he thought he was creating. The first of the modern dictators, he was less the creature of his times than were his successors and imitators, and he remains unique. . . .

STUDY QUESTIONS

1. What kind of man was Napoleon? What special abilities did he have? What shortcomings? How did his abilities and shortcomings affect his career?

2. What were Napoleon's objectives? What is the relationship between these and his actual accomplishments?

3. Napoleon called himself "a child of the revolution." To what extent did he carry out the revolutionary ideals?

4. In what ways did he carry on the policies of the old French monarchy? Compare his reign with that of Louis XIV. Could Napoleon be called an "enlightened despot"? On what did his power rest?

5. Why didn't Napoleon exploit the revolutionary potential that would be connected with liberating the Russian serfs?

6. How modern was Napoleon? What was the significance of the following: Code Napoleon; administrative reforms; propaganda; the policy of "career open to talent"; Continental System; the goal to create a united Europe; "Liberty, Equality, Fraternity *and* Order?"

7. What were Napoleon's greatest (most lasting) achievements?

8. How can military occupation serve as a transmitter of culture, custom, and ideas? What has been the American experience in Europe and Japan? Where, in the area of French expansion beyond 1789, would you expect French influence to have been most lasting?

An English cartoon of 1814 pictures Czar Alexander I of Russia turning the grindstone as John Bull holds Napoleon's nose to the wheel. The rulers of Europe watch in satisfaction as the man who has ground them down for years receives his due.

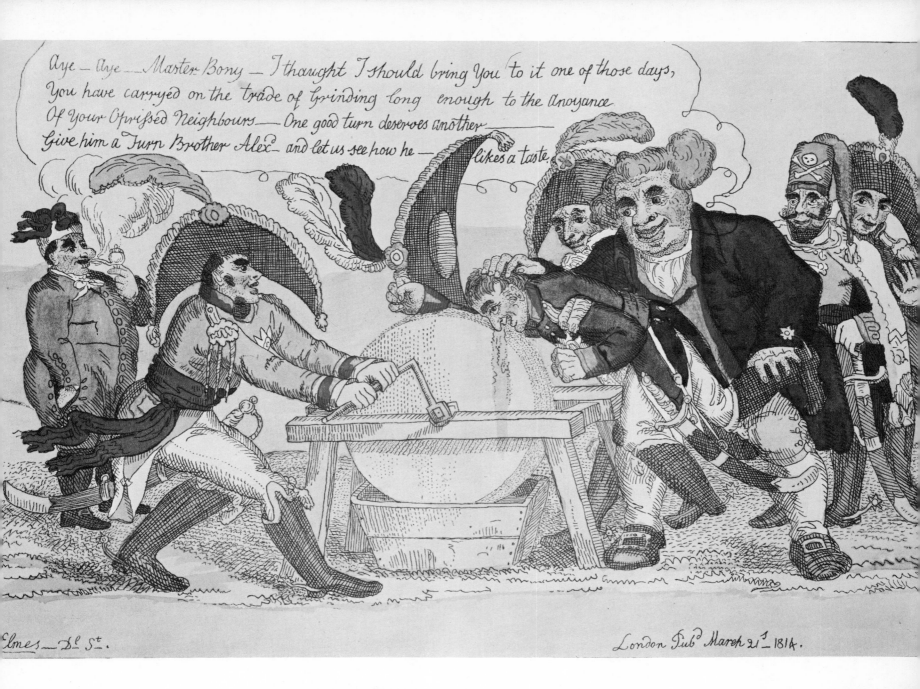

Chapter 4

Industrial Growth and Society,
1776–1914

The roots of our modern society extend back to the great scientific discoveries of the seventeenth century, to the technological improvements of the eighteenth century, and to the special political and intellectual development that accompanied them.

The nineteenth century saw a rapid acceleration of all these factors, a rushing current that produced a society essentially different from that which had previously existed. Economic growth, in particular, fostered the steady expansion of the middle classes and spawned a new class of industrial proletariat. Bound in a common origin by the machines that had created them, these two groups followed widely differing paths in their development. The middle classes, increasingly dominating the economic life of the century, struggled to enlarge their share of political power that in 1800 was still largely in the hands of the landowning aristocracy. The new industrial proletariat, on the contrary, was faced with the more immediate problems of maintaining simple existence. Only gradually did the incoherent mass of laboring poor forge a common identity that enabled it to exert pressure on the governing classes and participate in the social, economic, and political benefits of Western society.

The readings in this chapter are concerned with the economic, social, and political repercussions that followed the phenomenal expansion of the market system in the late eighteenth and the nineteenth centuries.

1770–1870	First stage of Industrial Revolution
1772–1837	Charles Fourier, phalanstery community
1776	Adam Smith publishes *Wealth of Nations*
1789–1832	Jeremy Bentham
1798	Malthus, Essay on the *Principle of Population*
1800–1828	Robert Owen in New Lanark
1810	Founding of Krupp works, Essen
1811–1816	Luddite rioting
1819	Peterloo Massacre
1818–1883	Karl Marx
1821	Saint-Simon, *Du Système Industriel*
1830	July Revolution, France
1831	Sadler Investigation Committee
1832	First British Parliamentary Reform Bill
1833	Britain abolishes slavery
1841–1847	Brook Farm
1846	Repeal of Corn Laws
1847–1848	Karl Marx and Friedrich Engels, *Communist Manifesto*
1848	France abolishes slavery
1848	Seneca Falls Convention on women's rights
1848	French Second Republic
1848	June Days, France
1859	Darwin, *Origin of Species*
1859	John Stuart Mill, *On Liberty*
1859	Karl Marx, *Das Kapital*
1859	Samuel Smiles, *Self-Help*
1861	Emancipation of Russian serfs
1863	United States abolishes slavery
1869	John Stuart Mill, *On the Subjection of Women*
1870–1914	Second stage of Industrial Revolution
1881	Germany introduces social welfare legislation
1886	American Federation of Labor
1891	Bernstein and Evolutionary Socialism
1896	Fabian Socialist Program
1902	Lenin, "What is to be Done?"
1905	Violence first used by British suffragettes
1909	Lloyd George's budget

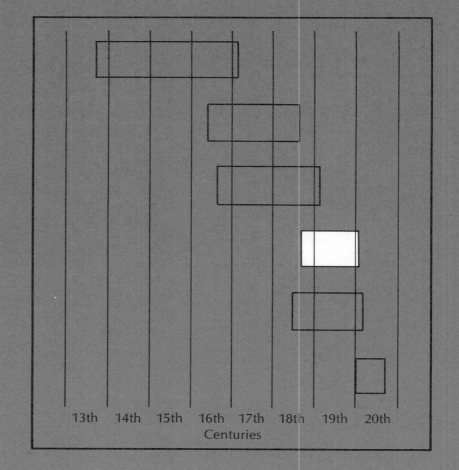

13th 14th 15th 16th 17th 18th 19th 20th
Centuries

TOPIC 28

THE THEORY OF THE MARKET

The amazing growth of the market system in the early modern world has been described in Topics 47 and 48. Those who benefitted from the flourishing market economy did not at first ask for elaborate elucidations of its functioning. By the seventeenth and eighteenth centuries, however, several explanations had been advanced. For many years the most successful of these was that called mercantilism, a concept based on government intervention in the economy to assure a favorable balance of trade and the accumulation of bullion. A counter-theory based on the idea of natural law was introduced in the late eighteenth century by the Scottish economist Adam Smith (1723–1790) whose work has provided the foundation for modern "classical" economics. The readings present these theories but lay stress on the contributions of Smith in providing a rational justification for the competitive market.

Thomas Mun Advocates Mercantilism (1630)

An early attempt to provide an explanation of how to retain and increase the wealth engendered by the market has become known as the mercantile theory of economics, or mercantilism. Proceeding from the medieval assumption that the total wealth of the world was fixed in amount, the mercantilists urged that as large as possible a share of that wealth be gained through government supervision of the economy. This accumulation of wealth was to be achieved primarily by creation of a favorable balance of trade, as is explained in this reading taken from the writings of Thomas Mun (1571–1641), a leading English mercantilist. From Thomas Mun, *England's Treasure by Forraign Trade* (London, 1664), pp. 543–545.

The means to enrich this Kingdom, and to encrease our Treasure.

Although a Kingdom may be enriched by gifts received, or by purchase taken from some other Nations, yet these are things uncertain and of small consideration when they happen. The ordinary means therefore to encrease our wealth and treasure is by *FORRAIGN TRADE*, wherein wee must ever observe this rule; to sell more to strangers yearly than wee consume of theirs in value.

The particular ways and means to encrease the exportation of our commodities, and to decrease our Consumption of forraign wares.

The revenue or stock of a Kingdom by which it is provided of forraign wares is either *Natural* or *Artificial*. The Natural wealth is so much only as can be spared from our own use and necessities to be exported unto strangers. The Artificial consists in our manufactures and industrious trading with forraign commodities, concerning which I will set down particulars as may serve for the cause we have in hand.

1. First, although this Realm be already exceeding rich by nature, yet might it be encreased by laying the waste grounds (which are infinite) into such employments as should no way hinder the present revenues of other manufactured lands, but hereby to supply ourselves and prevent the importations of Hemp, Flax, Cordage, Tobacco, and divers other things which now we fetch from strangers to our great impoverishing.

2. We may likewise diminish our importations, if we would soberly refrain from excessive consumption of forraign wares in our diet and rayment, with such often change of fashions as is used, so much the more to encrease the waste and charge; which vices at this present are more notorious amongst

us than in former ages. Yet might they easily be amended by enforcing the observation of such good laws as are strictly practised in other Countries against the said excesses; where likewise by commanding their own manufactures to be used, they prevent the coming in of others, without prohibition, or offence to strangers in their mutual commerce. . . .

4. The value of our exportations likewise may be much advanced when we perform it our selves in our own Ships, for then we get only not the price of our wares as they are worth here, but also Merchants gains, the charges of ensurance, and fraight to carry them beyond the seas. . . .

5. The frugal expending likewise of our own natural wealth might advance much yearly to be exported unto strangers; and if in our rayment we will be prodigal, yet let this be done with our own materials and manufactures, as Cloth, Lace, Embroideries, Cutworks and the like, where the excess of the rich may be the employment of the poor, whose labours notwithstanding of this kind, would be more profitable for the Commonwealth, if they were done to the use of strangers.

6. The Fishing in his Majesties seas of *England, Scotland* and *Ireland* is our natural wealth, and would cost nothing but labour, which the *Dutch* bestow willingly, and thereby draw yearly a very great profit to themselves by serving many places of Christendom with our Fish, for which they return and supply their wants both of forraign Wares and Mony, besides the multitude of Mariners and Shipping, which hereby are maintain'd. . . .

8. Also wee ought to esteem and cherish those trades which we have in remote or far Countreys, for besides the encrease of Shipping and Mariners thereby, the wares also sent thither and receiv'd from thence are far more profitable unto the kingdom than by our trades neer at hand; . . . Neither is there less honour and judgment by growing rich (in this manner) upon the stock of other Nations, than by an industrious encrease of our own means, especially when this later is advanced by the benefit of the former, as we have found in the *East Indies* by sale of much of our Tin, Cloth, Lead and other Commodities, the vent whereof doth daily encrease in those Countreys which formerly had no use of our wares. . . .

12. Lastly, in all things we must endeavor to make the most we can of our own, whether it be *Natural* or *Artificial;* And forasmuch as the people which live by the Arts are far more in number than they who are masters of the fruits, we ought the more carefully to maintain those endeavors of the multitude, in whom doth consist the greatest strength and riches both of King and Kingdom: for where the people are many, and the arts good, there the traffique must be great, and the Countrey rich. . . .

Adam Smith Finds the Key to the Wealth of Nations (1776)

Adam Smith (1723–1790) was a Scottish economist whose famous work, *An Inquiry into the Nature and Causes of the Wealth of Nations,* had tremendous influence on later economic and political theory. He taught for years at the University of Glasgow in Scotland, resigning his post in 1764 to serve as private instructor of the young Duke of Buccleuch. Smith and Buccleuch spent two years in Europe, mostly in France where they met many of the *philosophes* including Turgot and Voltaire. Perhaps most important as an influence on Smith was his acquaintance with François Quesnay, the spokesman for the Physiocrats. These were a group of *philosophes* who believed that true wealth was more than the mere accumulation of large amounts of gold or silver, but rather came from the proper use of land for agricultural production. Adam Smith, looking at this from his knowledge of what was going on in Britain, felt that an even greater source of wealth came from industrial production. He spent ten years after his return from Europe polishing his argument, and the *Wealth of Nations* was published in 1776, the same year as the American Declaration of Independence. Smith was a life-long bachelor and was so absent-minded that he once wandered out of his house in his bathrobe and trudged on fifteen miles before he realized the state of his dress. But he had a sharp eye for what he was interested in and was a typical man of the Enlightenment, who tried to apply reason to the solving of pressing human problems which in Smith's view were those created by the spreading Industrial Revolution. From Adam Smith, *An Inquiry into the Nature and Causes of the Wealth of Nations* (London, 1802), I, pp. 1–4, 9, 82–87. II, 181–182. III, 42–43.

I. THE ADVANTAGES OF SPECIALIZATION

The greatest improvement in the productive powers of labour, and the greater part of any skill, dexterity, and judgment with which it is any where directed, or applied, seem to have been the effects of the division of labour.

The effects of the division of labour, in the general business of society, will be more easily understood, by considering in what manner it operates in some particular manufactures. . . .

To take an example, therefore, from a very trifling manufacture; but one in which the division of labour has been very often taken notice of, the trade of the pin-maker; a workman not educated to this business (which the division of labour has rendered a distinct trade), nor acquainted with the use of the machinery employed in it (to the invention of which the same division of labour has probably given occasion), could scarce, perhaps, with his utmost industry, make one pin in a day, and certainly could not make twenty. But in the way in which this business is now carried on, not only the whole work is a peculiar trade, but it is divided into a number of branches, of which the greater part are likewise peculiar trades. One man draws out the wire, another straights it, a third cuts it, a fourth points it, a fifth grinds it at the top for receiving the head; to make the head requires two or three distinct operations; to put it on, is a peculiar business, to whiten the pins is another; it is even a trade by itself to put them into the paper; and the important business of making a pin is, in this manner, divided into about eighteen distinct operations, which, in some manufactories, are all performed by distinct hands, though in others the same man will sometimes perform two or three of them. I have seen a small manufactory of this kind where ten men only were employed, and where some of them consequently performed two or three distinct operations. But though they were very poor, and therefore but indifferently accommodated with the necessary machinery, they could, when they exerted themselves, make among them about twelve pounds of pins in a day. There are in a pound upwards of four thousand pins of a middling size. Those ten persons, therefore, could make among them upwards of forty-eight thousand pins in a day. Each person, therefore, might be considered as making four thousand eight hundred pins in a day. But if they had all wrought separately and independently, and without any of them having been educated to this peculiar business, they certainly could not each of them have made twenty, perhaps not one pin in a day; that is, certainly, not the two hundred and fortieth, perhaps not the four thousand eight hundredth part of what they are at present capable of performing, in consequence of a proper division and combination of their different operations. . . .

This increase in the quantity of work, which, in consequence of the division of labour, the same number of people are capable of performing, is owing to three different circumstances; first, to the increase of dexterity in every particular workman; secondly, to the saving of the time which is commonly lost in passing from one species of work to another; and lastly, to the invention of a great number of machines which facilitate and abridge labour, and enable one man to do the work of many.

II. THE LAWS OF THE MARKET

There is in every society or neighbourhood an ordinary or average rate both of wages and profit in every different employment of labour and stock. This rate is naturally regulated, as I shall show hereafter, partly by the general circumstances of the society, their riches or poverty, their advancing, stationary or declining condition; and partly by the particular nature of each employment. . . .

When the price of any commodity is neither more nor less than what is sufficient to pay the rent of the land, the wages of the labour, and the profits of the stock employed in raising, preparing, and bringing it to market, according to their natural rates, the commodity is then sold for what may be called its natural price.

The commodity is then sold precisely for what it is worth, or for what it really costs the person who brings it to market; for though in common language what is called the prime cost of any commodity does not comprehend the profit of the person who is to sell it again, yet if he sells it at a price which does not allow him the ordinary rate of profit in his neighbourhood, he is evidently a loser by the trade; since by employing his stock in some other way he might have made that profit. His profit, besides, is his revenue, the proper fund of his subsistence. As, while he is preparing and bringing the goods to market, he advances to his workmen their wages, or their subsistence; so he advances to himself, in the same manner, his own subsistence, which is generally suitable to the profit which he may reasonably expect from the sale of his goods. . . .

The actual price at which any commodity is commonly sold is called its market price. It may either be above, or below, or exactly the same with its natural price.

The market price of every particular commodity is regulated by the proportion between the quantity which is actually brought to market, and the demand of those who are willing to pay the natural price of the commodity, of the whole value of the rent, labour, and profit, which must be paid in order to bring it thither. Such people may be called the effectual demanders, and their demand the effectual demand; since it may be sufficient to effectuate the bringing of the commodity to market. . . .

When the quantity of any commodity which is brought to market falls short of the effectual demand, all those who are willing to pay the whole value of the rent, wages, and profit, which must be paid in order to bring it thither, cannot be supplied with the quantity which they want. Rather than want it altogether, some of them will be willing to give more. A competition will immediately begin among them, and the market price will rise more or less above the natural price, according as either the greatness of the deficiency, or the wealth and wanton luxury of the competitors, happen to animate more or less the eagerness of the competition. Among competitors of equal wealth and luxury the same deficiency will generally occasion a more or less eager competition, according as the acquisition of the commodity happens to be of more or less importance to them. Hence the exorbitant price of the necessaries of life during the blockade of a town or in a famine.

When the quantity brought to market exceeds the effectual demand, it cannot be all sold to those who are willing to pay the whole value of the rent, wages and profit, which must be paid in order to bring it thither. Some part must be sold to those who [will not buy unless they] pay less, and the low price which they give for it must reduce the price of the whole. The market price will sink more or less below the natural price, according as the greatness of the excess increases more or less the competition of the sellers, or according as it happens to be more

or less important to them to get immediately rid of the commodity. The same excess in the importation of perishables, will occasion a much greater competition than in that of durable commodities, in the importation of oranges, for example, than in that of old iron.

When the quantity brought to market is just sufficient to supply the effectual demand and no more, the market price naturally comes to be either exactly, or as nearly as can be judged of, the same with the natural price. The whole quantity upon hand can be disposed of for this price, and cannot be disposed of for more. The competition of the different dealers obliges them all to accept of this price, but does not oblige them to accept of less.

The quantity of every commodity brought to market naturally suits itself to the effectual demand. It is the interest of all those who employ their land, labour, or stock, in bringing any commodity to market, that the quantity never should exceed the effectual demand; and it is the interest of all other people that it never should fall short of that demand.

If at any time it exceeds the effectual demand, some of the component parts of its price must be paid below their natural rate. If it is rent, the interest of the landlords will immediately prompt them to withdraw a part of their land: and if it is wages or profit, the interest of the labourers in the one case, and of their employers in the other, will prompt them to withdraw a part of their labour or stock from this employment. The quantity brought to market will soon be no more than sufficient to supply the effectual demand. All the different parts of its price will rise to their natural rate, and the whole price to its natural price.

If, on the contrary, the quantity brought to market should at any time fall short of the

effectual demand, some of the component parts of its price must rise above their natural rate. If it is rent, the interest of all other landlords will naturally prompt them to prepare more land for the raising of this commodity; if it is wages or profit, the interest of all other labourers and dealers will soon prompt them to employ more labour and stock in preparing and bringing it to market. The quantity brought thither will soon be sufficient to supply the effectual demand. All the different parts of its price will soon sink to their natural rate, and the whole price to its natural price.

The natural price, is therefore, as it were, the central price, to which the prices of all commodities are continually gravitating. Different accidents may sometimes keep them suspended a good deal above it, and sometimes force them down even somewhat below it. But whatever may be the obstacles which hinder them from settling in this center of repose and continuance, they are constantly tending towards it. . . .

III. THE INVISIBLE HAND

As every individual, therefore, endeavours as much as he can both to employ his capital in the support of domestic industry, and so to direct that industry that its produce may be of the greatest value; every individual necessarily labours to render the annual revenue of the society as great as he can. He generally, indeed, neither intends to promote the public interest, nor knows how much he is promoting it. By preferring the support of domestic to that of foreign industry, he intends only his own security; and by directing that industry in such a manner that its produce may be of the greatest value, he intends only his own security; and by directing that industry in such a manner that its produce may be of the greatest value, he intends only his own gain, and he is in this, as in many other cases, led by an invisible hand to promote an end which was not part of his intention. Nor is it always the worse for the society that it was no part of it. By pursuing his own interest he frequently promotes that of the society more effectually than when he really intends to promote it. I have never known much good done by those who affected to trade for the public good. It is an affectation, indeed, not very common among merchants, and very few words need be employed in dissuading them from it.

Every individual, it is evident, can, in his local situation, judge much better than any statesman or law-giver the kind of domestic industry which his capital can employ and of which the produce is likely to be of the greatest value. The statesman, who should attempt to direct private people in what manner they ought to employ their capitals, would not only load himself with a most unnecessary attention, but assume an authority which could safely be trusted, not only to no single person, but to no council or senate whatever, and which would nowhere be so dangerous as in the hands of a man who had folly and presumption enough to fancy himself fit to exercise it. . . .

IV. THE GOVERNMENT'S ROLE

All systems either of preference or of restraint, therefore, being thus completely taken away, the obvious and simple system of natural liberty establishes itself of its own accord. Every man, as long as he does not violate the laws of justice, is left perfectly free to pursue his own interest his own way, and to bring both his industry and capital into competition with those of any other man, or order of men. The sovereign is completely

discharged from a duty, in the attempting to perform which he must always be exposed to innumberable delusions, and for the proper performance of which no human wisdom or knowledge could ever be sufficient; the duty of superintending the industry of private people, and of directing it towards the employments most suitable to the interest of the society. According to the system of natural liberty, the sovereign has only three duties to attend to; three duties of great importance, indeed, but plain and intelligible to common understandings: first, the duty of protecting the society from the violence and invasion of other independent societies; secondly, the duty of protecting, as far as possible, every member of the society from the injustice or oppression of every other member of it, or the duty of establishing an exact administration of justice; and, thirdly, the duty of erecting and maintaining certain public works and certain public institutions, which it can never be for the interest of any individual, or small number of individuals, to erect and maintain; because the profit could never repay the expence to any individual or small number of individuals, though it may frequently do much more than repay it to a great society. . . .

Robert Heilbroner: The Wonderful World of Adam Smith

From Robert Heilbroner, *The Worldly Philosophers* (New York: Simon and Schuster, Inc., 1961), pp. 38–42, 44–51. Copyright, 1953 by Robert L. Heilbroner. Reprinted by permission of Simon and Schuster, Inc.

Two great problems absorb Adam Smith's attention. First, he is interested in laying bare the mechanism by which society hangs together. How is it possible for a community in which everyone is busily following his self-interest not to fly apart from sheer centrifugal force? What is it which guides each individual's private business so that it conforms to the needs of the group? With no central planning authority and no steadying influence of age-old tradition, how does society manage to get those tasks done which are necessary for survival?

These questions lead Smith to a formulation of the laws of the market. What he sought was "the invisible hand," as he called it, whereby "the private interests and passions of men" are led in the direction "which is most agreeable to the interest of the whole society."

But the laws of the market will be only a part of Smith's inquiry. There is another question which interests him: whither society? The laws of the market are like the laws which explain how a spinning top stays upright; but there is also the question of whether the top, by virtue of its spinning, will be moved along the table.

To Smith and the great economists who followed him, society is not conceived as a static achievement of mankind which will go on reproducing itself, unchanged and unchanging, from one generation to the next. On the contrary, society is seen as an organism which has its own life history. To discover the shape of things to come, to isolate the forces which impel society along its path—this is the grand objective of economic science. . . .

Adam Smith's laws of the market are basically simple. They tell us that the outcome of a certain kind of behavior in a certain social framework will bring about perfectly definite and foreseeable results. Specifically they show us how the drive of individual self-interest in an environment of similarly motivated individuals will result in competition; and they further demonstrate how competition will result in the provision of those goods that society wants, in the quantities that society desires, and at the prices society is prepared to pay. Let us see how this comes about.

It comes about in the first place because self-interest acts as a driving power to guide men to whatever work society is willing to pay for. "It is not from the benevolence of the butcher, the brewer, or the baker that we expect our dinner," says Smith, "but from their regard to their self-interest. We address ourselves, not to their humanity, but to their self-love, and never talk to them of our necessities, but of their advantages."

But self-interest is only half the picture. It drives men to action. Something else must prevent the pushing of profit-hungry individuals from holding society up to exorbitant ransom: a community activated only by self-interest would be a community of ruthless profiteers. This regulator is competition, the socially beneficial consequence of the conflicting self-interests of all the members of society. For each man, out to do his best for himself with no thought of social cost, is faced with a flock of similarly motivated individuals who are in exactly the same boat. Each is only too eager to take advantage of his neighbor's greed if it urges him to exceed a common denominator of acceptable behavior. A man who permits his self-interest to run away with him will find that competitors have slipped in to take his trade away; if he charges too much for his wares or if he refuses to pay as much as everybody else for

his workers, he will find himself without buyers in the one case and without employees in the other. Thus very much as in the *Theory of Moral Sentiments,* the selfish motives of men are transmuted by interaction to yield the most unexpected of results: social harmony.

Consider, for example, the problem of high prices. Suppose we have one hundred manufacturers of gloves. The self-interest of each one will cause him to wish to raise his price above his cost of production and thereby to realize an extra profit. But he cannot. If he raises his price, his competitors will step in and take his market away from him by underselling him. Only if all glove manufacturers combine and agree to maintain a solid front will an unduly high price be charged. And in this case, the collusive coalition could be broken by an enterprising manufacturer from another field—say, shoe-making—who decided to move his capital into glove manufacture where he could steal away the market by shading his prices.

But the laws of the market not only impose a competitive price on products. They also see to it that the producers of society heed society's demands of the *quantities* of goods it wants. Let us suppose that consumers decide they want more gloves than are being turned out, and fewer shoes. Accordingly the public will scramble for the stock of gloves on the market, and the shoe business will be dull. As a result glove prices will tend to rise as consumers try to buy more of them than there are ready at hand, and shoe prices will tend to fall as the public passes the shoe stores by. But as glove prices rise, profits in the glove industry will rise, too; and as shoe prices fall, profits in shoe manufacturing will slump. Again self-interest will step in to right

the balance. Workers will be released from the shoe business as shoe factories contract their output; they will move to the glove business where business is booming. The result is quite obvious: glove production will rise and shoe production will fall.

And this is exactly what society wanted in the first place. As more gloves come on the market to meet demand, glove prices will fall back into line. As fewer shoes are produced, the surplus of shoes will soon disappear and shoe prices will again rise up to normal. Through the mechanism of the market, society will have changed the allocation of its elements of production to fit its new desires. Yet no one has issued a dictum, and no planning authority has established schedules of output. Self-interest and competition, acting one against the other, have accomplished the transition.

And one final accomplishment. Just as the market regulates both prices and quantities of *goods* according to the final arbiter of public demand, so it also regulates the *incomes* of those who cooperate to produce those goods. If profits in one line of business are unduly large, there will be a rush of other businessmen into that field until competition has lowered surpluses. If wages are out of line in one kind of work, there will be a rush of men into the favored occupation until it pays no more than comparable jobs of that degree of skill and training. Conversely, if profits or wages are too low in one trade area, there will be an exodus of capital and labor until the supply is better adjusted to the demand.

All this may seem somewhat elementary. But consider what Adam Smith has done, with his impetus of self-interest and his regulator of competition. First, he has explained how prices are kept from ranging arbitrarily away from the actual cost of producing a good. Second, he has explained how society can induce its producers of commodities to provide it with what it wants. Third, he has pointed out why high prices are a self-curing disease, for they cause production in those lines to increase. And finally, he has accounted for a basic similarity of incomes at each level of the great producing strata of the nation. In a word, he has found in the mechanism of the market a self-regarding system for society's orderly provisioning. . . .

But the laws of the market are only a description of the behavior which gives society its cohesiveness. Something else must make it go. Ninety years after the *Wealth of Nations,* Karl Marx was to make the portentous announcement that he had unearthed "laws of motion" which described how capitalism proceeded slowly, unwillingly, but ineluctably to its doom. But the *Wealth of Nations* already had its own laws of motion. However, quite unlike the Marxist prognosis, Adam Smith's world went slowly, quite willingly, and more or less inevitably to Valhalla [heaven].

Valhalla would have been the last destination that most observers would have predicted. Sir John Byng, touring the North Country in 1792, looked from his coach window and wrote: "Why, here now, is a great flaring mill . . . all the Vale is disturb'd. . . . Sir Richard Arkwright may have introduced Much Wealth into his Family and into his Country, but, as a Tourist, I execrate his Schemes, which having crept into every Pastoral Vale, have destroyed the course, and the Beauty of Nature." "Oh! What a dog's hole is Manchester," said Sir John on arriving there.

In truth, much of England was a dog's hole. The three centuries of turmoil which had prodded land, labor, and capital into existence seemed to have been only a preparation for still further upheaval, for the recently freed agents of production began to be combined in a new and ugly form: the factory. And with the factory came new problems. Twenty years before Sir John's tour, Richard Arkwright, who had gotten together a little capital peddling women's hair to make wigs, invented (or stole) the spinning throstle. But having constructed his machine, he found it was not so easy to staff it. Local labor could not keep up with the "regular celerity" of the process—wagework was still generally despised and some capitalists found their new-built factories burned to the ground out of sheer blind malice. Arkwright was forced to turn to children—"their small fingers being active." Furthermore, since they were unused to the independent life of farming or crafts, children adapted themselves more readily to the discipline of factory life. The move was hailed as a philanthropic gesture—would not the employment of children help to alleviate the condition of the "unprofitable poor"?

For if any problem absorbed the public mind, besides its mixed admiration for and horror at the factory, it was this omnipresent problem of the unprofitable poor. In 1720 England was crowded with a million and a half of them—a staggering figure when we realize that her total population was only twelve or thirteen million. Hence the air was full of schemes for their disposition. Despairing schemes, mostly. For the common complaint was the ineradicable sloth of the pauper, and this was mixed with consternation at the way in which the lower orders aped their betters. Working people were actually drinking tea! The common folk seemed to prefer wheaten bread to their traditional loaf of rye or barley! Where would all this lead to, asked the thinkers of the day; were not the wants of the poor ("which it would be prudence to relieve, but folly to cure," as a contemporary pamphlet expressed it) essential for the welfare of the state? What would happen to Society if the indispensable gradations of society were allowed to disappear?

But if consternation described the prevalent attitude of the day toward the great amorphous mass of working England, it certainly did not describe Adam Smith's philosophy. "No society can surely be flourishing and happy, of which by far the greater part of the numbers are poor and miserable," he said. And not only did he have the temerity to make so radical a statement, but he proceeded to demonstrate that society was in fact constantly improving; that it was being propelled, willy-nilly, toward a positive goal. It was not moving because anyone willed it to, or because Parliament might pass laws, or England win a battle. It moved because there was a concealed dynamic beneath the surface of things which powered the social whole like an enormous engine.

For one salient fact struck Adam Smith as he looked at the English scene. This was the tremendous gain in productivity which sprang from the minute division and specialization of labor. Going into a pin factory, this is what Smith saw:

> One man draws out the wire, another straights it, a third cuts it, a fourth points it, a fifth grinds it at the top for receiving the head; to make the head requires two or three distinct operations; to put it on is a peculiar business; to whiten it is another; it is even a trade by itself to put them into paper. . . . I have seen a small manufactory of this

THE PIN FACTORY I

A pin factory was the classic example adduced by Adam Smith to illustrate the advantages of a division of labor. How long, he asked rhetorically, would it take to make a pin if one workman performed every step himself?

"Pins were made from wire, and since steel wire was prohibitively expensive, and iron wire insufficiently ductile, the best grade of pins was made of brass. Drawing out brass wire (Fig. 2), although it looks the simplest of tasks, required experience and a very sure touch. Everything depended on the precise alignment and spacing of the arrangement of nails (Fig. 2, *d*) through which the wire is pulled. The farther apart they were and the more obtuse the angle, the thicker was the wire and the heavier the pin. Each drawer made his own "engine" every time the order came down to change the characteristics of the pin and to make a different weight.

A good drawer could pull 60 feet of wire a minute off the reel, after which it passes in lengths to the cutters (Figs. 3 & 4) who snip it into pin lengths. The men were supposed to cut 70 pins a minute, 4,200 an hour. Pointing the pins is a simple matter of grinding one end of the shank (Figs. 5 & 6). The wheel at the right (Fig. 9) is used for heading, as will appear in the plate that follows."

kind where ten men only were employed and where some of them consequently performed two or three distinct operations. But though they were very poor, and therefore but indifferently accommodated with the necessary machinery, they could, when they exerted themselves, make among them about twelve pounds of pins in a day. There are in a pound upwards of four thousand pins of a middling size. Those ten persons, therefore, could make among them upwards of forty-eight thousand pins in a day. . . . But if they had all wrought separately and independently . . . they certainly could not each of them make twenty, perhaps not one pin in a day. . . .

There is hardly any need to point out how infinitely more complex present-day production methods are from those of the eighteenth century. Smith, for all his disclaimers, was sufficiently impressed with a small factory of ten people to comment on it; what would he have thought of one employing ten thousand! But the great gift of the division of labor is not its complexity—indeed it simplifies most toil. Its advantage lies in its capacity to increase what Smith calls "that universal opulence which extends itself to the lowest ranks of the people." That universal opulence of the eighteenth century looks like a grim existence from our modern vantage point. But if we view the matter in its historical perspective, if we compare the lot of the work-

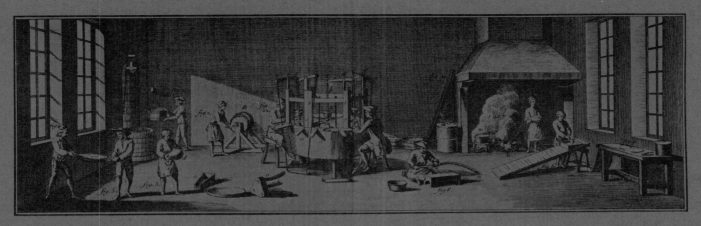

THE PIN FACTORY II

The central operation here is heading. Heading-wire from Fig. 9 is cut into spiral coils. The but of the pin-shank catches in the spiral, two turns of which are left around the shank, and then the head is flattened into a button by annealing (Fig. 7, *n*) and pounding it against the miniature anvils of the machine shown as Fig. 12 below. This was a complicated and precise piece of machinery, a sort of tiny drop-forge.

To blanch the pins, they must finally be tin-coated. For this they are packed in layers in tinfoil (Fig. 9) and boiled in a dilute solution of salts of tartrate (Fig. 7, *m*) from which they emerge to be washed (Fig. 1), dried (Fig. 2), polished by mutual friction (Fig. 5), and sorted and packed in quart jugs for shipping (Fig. 3)."

(From C. C. Gillispie, ed., *A Diderot Pictorial Encyclopedia of Trades and Industry*, 2 volumes (New York: Dover Publishers, Inc., 1929), Volume I, Plates 185 and 186 with text.)

ingman in eighteenth-century England to his predecessor a century or two before, it is clear that mean as his existence was, it constituted a considerable advance. Smith makes the point vividly. . . .

Were we to examine . . . all the different parts of his dress and household furniture, the coarse linen shirt which he wears next to his skin, the shoes which cover his feet, the bed which he lies on . . . the kitchen-grate at which he prepares his victuals, the coals which he makes use of for that purpose, dug from the bowels of the earth, and brought to him perhaps by a long sea and a long land carriage, all the other utensils of his kitchen, all the furniture of his table, the knives and forks, the earthen or pewter plates upon which he serves up and divides his victuals, the different hands employed in preparing his bread and his beer, the glass window which lets in the heat and the light, and keeps out the wind and the rain, with all the knowledge and art requisite for preparing that beautiful and happy invention; . . . if we examine, I say, all those things . . . we shall be sensible that without the assistance and cooperation of many thousands, the very meanest person in a civilized country could not be provided, even according to what we very falsely imagine, the easy and simple manner in which he is commonly accommodated. Compared indeed with the more extravagant luxury of the great, his accommodation must no doubt appear extremely simple and easy; and yet it may be true, perhaps, that the accommodation of a European prince does not always so much exceed that of an industrious and frugal peasant, as the accommodation of the latter exceeds that of many an African king, the absolute master of the lives and liberties of ten thousand naked savages.

What is it that drives society to this wonderful multiplication of wealth and riches? Partly it is the market mechanism itself, for the market harnesses man's creative powers in a milieu which encourages him, even forces him, to invent, innovate, expand, take risks. But there are more fundamental pressures behind the restless activity of the market. In fact, Smith sees deep-seated laws of evolution which propel the market system in an ascending spiral of productivity.

The first of these is the Law of Accumulation.

Let us remember that Adam Smith lived at a time when the rising industrial capitalist could and did realize a fortune from his investments. Richard Arkwright, apprenticed to a barber as a young man, died in 1792 leaving an estate of 500,000 pounds. Samuel Walker, who started a forge going in an old nailshop in Rotherham, left a steel foundry on that site worth 200,000 pounds. Josiah Wedgwood, who stumped about his pottery factory on a wooden leg scrawling "This won't do for Jos. Wedgwood" wherever he saw evidence of careless work, left an estate of 240,000 pounds and much landed property. The Industrial Revolution in its early stages provided a veritable grab bag of riches for whoever was quick enough, shrewd enough, industrious enough to ride with its current.

And the object of the great majority of the rising capitalists was first, last, and always, to accumulate their savings. At the beginning of the nineteenth century, 2,500 pounds was collected in Manchester for the foundation of Sunday schools. The sum total contributed to this worthy cause by the single largest employers in the district, the cotton spinners, was 90 pounds. The young industrial aristocracy had better things to do with its money than contribute to unproductive charities—it had to accumulate, and Adam Smith approved wholeheartedly. Woe to him who did not accumulate. . . .

But Adam Smith did not approve of accumulation for accumulation's sake. He was, after all, a philosopher, with a philosopher's disdain for the vanity of riches. Rather, in the accumulation of capital Smith saw a vast benefit to society. For capital—if put to use in machinery—provided just that wonderful division of labor which multiplies man's productive energy. Hence accumulation becomes another of Smith's two-edged swords: the avarice of private greed again redounding to the welfare of the community. . . . Accumulate and the world will benefit, says Smith. And certainly in the lusty atmosphere of his time there was no evidence of any unwillingness to accumulate on the part of those who were in a position to do so.

But—and here is a difficulty—accumulation would soon lead to a situation where further accumulation would be impossible. For accumulation meant more machinery and more machinery meant more demand for workmen. And this in turn would sooner or later lead to higher and higher wages, until profits—the source of accumulation—were eaten away. How is this hurdle surmounted?

It is surmounted by the second great law of the system: the Law of Population.

To Adam Smith, laborers, like any other commodity, could be produced according to the demand. If wages were high, the number of work-people would multiply; if wages fell, the number of the working class would decrease.

Nor is this quite so naive a conception as it appears at first blush. In Smith's day infant mortality among the lower classes was shockingly high. "It is not uncommon," says Smith, ". . . in the Highlands of Scotland for a mother who has borne twenty children not to have two alive." In many places in England, half the children died before they were four, and almost everywhere half the children only lived to the age of nine or ten. Malnutrition, evil living conditions, cold, and disease took a horrendous toll among the poorer element. Hence although higher wages may have affected the birth rate only slightly, it could be expected to have a considerable influence on the number of children who would grow to working age.

Hence if the first effect of accumulation would be to raise the wages of the working class, this in turn would bring about an increase in the number of workers. And now the market mechanism takes over. Just as higher prices on the market will bring about a larger production of gloves and the larger number of gloves in turn press down the higher prices of gloves, so higher wages will bring about a larger number of workers, and the increase in their numbers will set up a reverse pressure on the level of their wages. Population, like glove production, is a self-curing disease—as far as wages are concerned.

And this meant that accumulation might go safely on. The rise in wages which it caused and which threatened to make further accumulation unprofitable is tempered by the rise in population. Accumulation leads to its own undoing, and then is rescued in the nick of time. The obstacle of higher wages is undone by the growth in population which those very higher wages made feasible. There is something fascinating in this automatic process of aggravation and cure, stimulus and response, in which the very factor which seems to be leading the system to its doom is also slyly bringing about the conditions necessary for its further health.

And now observe that Smith has constructed for society a giant endless chain. As regularly and as inevitably as a series of interlocked mathematical propositions, society is started on an upward march. From any starting point the probing mechanism of the market first equalizes the returns to labor and capital in all its different uses, sees to it that those commodities demanded are produced in the right quantities, and further ensures that prices for commodities are constantly competed down to their costs of production. But further than this, society is dynamic. From its starting point accumulation of wealth will take place, and this accumulation will result in increased facilities for production and in a greater division of labor. So far, all to the good. But accumulation will also raise wages as capitalists bid for workers to man the new factories. As wages rise further accumulation begins to look unprofitable. The system threatens to level off. But meanwhile workmen will have used their higher wages to rear their children with fewer mortalities. Hence the supply of workmen will increase. As population swells, the competition between workmen will press down on wages again. And so accumulation will continue, and another spiral in the ascent of society will begin.

This is no business cycle which Smith describes. It is a long term process, a secular evolution. And it is wonderfully certain. Provided only that the market mechanism is not tampered with, everything is inexorably determined by the preceding link. A vast reciprocating machinery is set up with all of society inside it: only the tastes of the public—to guide producers—and the actual physical geography of the nation are outside the chain of cause and effect.

And observe, furthermore, that what is foreseen is a constantly improving state of affairs. True, the rise in the working population will always force wages back toward a subsistence level. But *toward* is not *to*; as long as the accumulation process continues—and Smith sees no reason why it should cease—there is a virtually endless opportunity for society to improve its lot. Smith did not imply that this was the best of all possible worlds: he had read Voltaire's *Candide* and was no Dr. Pangloss himself. But there was no reason why the world should not *move* in the direction of improvement and progress. Indeed, if one left the market mechanism alone and allowed it and the great social laws to work themselves out, it was inevitable that progress would result. . . .

STUDY QUESTIONS

1. How did Mun propose to assure a favorable balance of trade? Do you think the kind of measures he advised would greatly increase the wealth of England,

2. Why did Adam Smith argue for the division and specialization of labor? Are there disadvantages to this practice? Why, in Smith's analysis, must efficiency be the goal of industrial organization?

3. What did Smith mean by "natural price" and "market price"? What "laws" affect "market price"? What would Smith think of government subsidies or minimum wage laws?

4. How, according to Smith, does a man achieve good for society by seeking benefits for himself? What is the "invisible hand"? Are the goals of self-interest and public welfare in harmony in *The Wealth of Nations*?

5. To what areas did Smith limit government activity? Do you think such a limitation in the role of government is practical today? Was it acceptable in the eighteenth century?

6. Why did Smith seek laws to explain the workings of the economy?

7. What problems were created by the industrial revolution? How, in general, did Smith propose to deal with them? Did he underestimate or overlook any of the problems?

8. In what way could Smith be called "a typical man of the Enlightenment"? Why do you think *The Wealth of Nations* appealed to its readers?

Prince Albert Proclaims the Achievements of Science and Industry (1851)

THE SPREAD OF THE INDUSTRIAL REVOLUTION

The burgeoning economic growth that moved Adam Smith to find a rationale that would fit it into a world plan continued apace in the nineteenth and twentieth centuries. The quality of this growth was uneven, however, and affected certain sections of the population and certain geographic areas more than others. It made the West unchallenged leader of the world, which was increasingly divided into economically developed and economically "backward" regions. The readings examine the contours of this relentless industrial change.

Prince Albert (1819–1861) was the husband of Queen Victoria of England (reigned 1837–1901). He was seriously interested in the changes that resulted from increasing scientific discovery and expanding economic growth, and he enthusiastically supported the plans for a large-scale industrial exhibition which would display the industrial achievements of all nations. The Great Exhibition of 1851 with its motto of "Progress, Work, Religion, Peace" could be considered the first world's fair. The following is from a speech made by the Prince. From *Principal Speeches and Addresses of H. R. H. the Prince Consort* (London, 1862), pp. 110–112.

Nobody . . . who has paid any attention to the peculiar features of our present era, will doubt for a moment that we are living at a period of most wonderful transition, which tends rapidly to accomplish that great end, to which, indeed, all history points—*the realization of the unity of mankind*. Not a unity which breaks down the limits and levels of the peculiar characteristics of the different nations of the earth, but rather a unity, the *result and product* of those very national varieties and antagonistic qualities.

The distances which separated the different nations and parts of the globe are rapidly vanishing before the achievements of modern invention, and we can traverse them with incredible ease; the languages of all nations are known, and their acquirement placed within the reach of everybody; thought is communicated with the rapidity, and even by the power, of lightening. On the other hand, the *great principle of division of labour*, which may be called the moving power of civilization, is being extended to all branches of science, industry, and art.

Whilst formerly the greatest mental energies strove at universal knowledge, and that knowledge was confined to the few, now they are directed on specialities, and in these, again, even to the minutest points; but the knowledge acquired becomes at once the property of the community at large; for, whilst formerly discovery was wrapped in secrecy, the publicity of the present day causes that no sooner is a discovery or invention made than it is already improved upon and surpassed by competing efforts. The products of all quarters of the globe are placed at our disposal, and we have only to choose which is the best and the cheapest for our purposes, and the powers of production are intrusted to the stimulus of *competition and capital*.

So man is approaching a more complete fulfillment of that great and sacred mission which he has to perform in this world. His reason being created after the image of God, he has to use it to discover the laws by which the Almighty governs His creation, and, by making these laws his standard of action, to conquer nature to his use; himself a divine instrument.

Science discovers these laws of power, motion, and transformation; industry applies them to the raw matter, which the earth yields us in abundance, but which becomes valuable only by knowledge. Art teaches us the im-

This photograph of the Crystal Palace was taken in 1862. The appearance of illumination in the fountains is caused by the long-time exposure necessary for photography at the time.

An interior view of the Crystal Palace, taken from the originals of the Great Exhibition painted for Prince Albert in 1851, shows the variety of models and machinery displayed.

mutable laws of beauty and symmetry, and gives to our productions forms in accordance to them.

Gentlemen—the Exhibition of 1851 is to give us a true test and a living picture of the point of development at which the whole of mankind has arrived in this great task, and a new starting-point from which all nations will be able to direct their further exertions.

The Industrial Revolution "Takes Off"

Part I. From L. S. Stavrianos, *The World since 1500: A Global History,* © 1966. Reprinted by permission of Prentice-Hall, Inc., Englewood Cliffs, New Jersey. II. Tables.

I

The material culture of mankind has changed more in the past two hundred years than it did in the preceding five thousand. In the eighteenth century man was living in essentially the same manner as the ancient Egyptians and Mesopotamians. He was still using the same materials to erect his buildings, the same animals to transport himself and his belongings, the same sails and oars to propel his ships, the same textiles to fashion his clothes, and the same candles and torches to provide light. But today metals and plastics supplement stone and wood; the

railroad, the automobile, and the airplane and atom power drive ships in place of wind and manpower; a host of synthetic fabrics compete with the traditional cottons, woolens, and linens; and electricity has eclipsed the candle and has become a source of power available for a multitude of duties at the flick of a switch.

The origins of this epochal transformation are to be found partly in the scientific revolution . . . and partly in the so-called Industrial Revolution. The reason for the qualifying "so-called" is that there has been much uneasiness over the use of the term *Industrial Revolution*. It has been pointed out that, in certain respects, the Industrial Revolution had gotten under way before the eighteenth century, and that, for all practical purposes, it has continued to the present day. Obviously, then, this was not a revolution in the sense of a spectacular change that began and ended suddenly.

Yet the fact remains that during the 1780's a breakthrough did occur in productivity, or, as economists now put it, there was "a take-off into self-sustained growth." More specifically, there was created a mechanized factory system that produced goods in such vast quantities and at such rapidly diminishing cost as to be no longer dependent on existing demand but to create its own demand. An example of this now common, but hitherto unprecedented, phenomenon, is the automobile industry. It was not the demand for automobiles existing at the turn of the century that created the giant automobile industry of today, but rather the capacity to build the cheap model T Ford which stimulated the modern mass demand for them.

This Industrial Revolution is of prime importance for world history because it provided the economic and military basis for Europe's world hegemony in the nineteenth century, as well as the main goal for the underdeveloped world in the twentieth century. The aim of every new country today, having successfully "taken off" in the sense of independent political existence, is likewise to "take off" into a corresponding independent economic existence. . . .

Industrial Revolution: First Stage, 1770–1870

The Industrial Revolution cannot be attributed merely to the genius of a small group of inventors. Genius doubtless played a part, but more significant was the combination of favorable forces operating in late eighteenth century England. Inventors seldom invent except under the stimulus of strong demand. Many of the principles on which the new inventions were based were known centuries before the Industrial Revolution, but they were not applied to industry because the incentive was lacking. This was the case, for example, with steam power. It was known, and even applied, in Hellenistic Egypt, but merely to open and close temple doors. In England, however, a new source of power was urgently needed to pump water out of mines and to turn the wheels of the new machinery. The result was a series of inventions and improvements until finally a commercially feasible steam engine was developed. . . .

The historical significance of the steam engine can scarcely be exaggerated. It provided a means for harnessing and utilizing heat energy to furnish driving power for machines. Thus, it ended man's age-old dependence on animal, wind, and water power.

A vast new source of energy now was available, and before long man was also to tap the other fossil fuels locked up in the earth—namely, oil and gas. In this manner began the trend that has led to the present situation in which Western Europe has 11.5, and North America has 29, times as much energy available per capita as Asia. The meaning of these figures is apparent in a world in which economic and military strength is dependent directly upon the energy resources available. Indeed, it may be said that Europe's domination of the globe in the nineteenth century is based more upon the steam engine than upon any other single device or force.

The new cotton machines and steam engines required an increased supply of iron, steel, and coal—the need was met by a series of improvements in mining and metallurgy. Originally, iron ore had been processed in small furnaces filled with charcoal. The depletion of the forests compelled the manufacturers to turn to coal, and it was at this point—in 1709—that Abraham Darby discovered that coal could be reduced to coke just as wood had been to charcoal. Coke proved to be as effective as charcoal and was much cheaper. Darby's son developed a huge bellows driven by a waterwheel, thus producing the first mechanically operated blast furnace and greatly reducing the cost of iron. . . . Meanwhile, coal-mining methods also had been improved in order to keep up with the rising demands of the iron industry. Most important was the use of the steam engine to pump water out of mines, and the invention in 1815 of Sir Humphry Davy's safety lamp, which greatly reduced mining hazards.

As a result of these various developments Britain was producing by 1800 more coal and iron than the rest of the world together. More specifically, Britain's coal output rose from 6 million tons in 1770 to 12 million tons in 1800 to 57 million tons in 1861. Likewise, her iron output increased from 50,000 tons in 1770 to 130,000 tons in 1800 to 3,800,000 tons in 1861. Iron had become sufficiently plentiful and cheap to be used for general construction purposes, and man had entered the Age of Iron as well as the Age of Steam.

The expansion of the textile, mining, and metallurgical industries created a need for improved transportation facilities to move the bulky shipments of coal and ore. The first significant step in this direction was taken in 1761, when the Duke of Bridgewater built a seven-mile canal between Manchester and the coal mines at Worsley. The price of coal in Manchester fell by half, and the Duke extended his canal to the Mersey River, offering rates one-sixth those charged by land carriers. These spectacular results generated a canal-building fever that endowed England with 2,500 miles of canals by 1830.

The canal era was paralleled by a great period of road building. Roads were so primitive that people traveled on foot or on horseback, and wagons loaded with merchandise could scarcely be drawn over them during the rainy seasons. After 1750 a group of road engineers—John Metcalf, Thomas Telford, and John McAdam—evolved methods of building hard-surfaced roads that would bear traffic all through the year. Travel by coach increased from four miles an hour to six, eight, or even ten. Travel by night also became possible, so that the journey from Edinburgh to London, which had once taken fourteen days, now required only forty-four hours.

After 1830 both roads and waterways were challenged by the railroad. The new mode of transportation came in two installments. First

was the plate or rail track, in common use by the mid-eighteenth century for moving coal from the pit head to some waterway or to the place where it was to be burned. It was claimed that on a track, a woman or a child could pull a cart laden with three quarters of a ton, and that one horse could do as much work as twenty-two horses did on an ordinary road. The second stage was the installation of the steam engine to the cart. The chief figure here was a mining engineer, George Stephenson, who first used an engine to pull coal trucks from a mine to the River Tyne. In 1830 his *Rocket* pulled a train thirty-one miles from Liverpool to Manchester at an average speed of fourteen miles per hour. Within a few years the railroad dominated long-distance traffic, being able to move passengers and freight faster and cheaper than was possible on roads or canals. By 1838 Britain had 500 miles of railroad; by 1850, 6,600; and by 1870, 15,500.

The steam engine was applied also to water transportation. From 1770 onward, inventors in Scotland, France, and the United States experimented with engines afloat. The first commercially successful steamship was built by an American, Robert Fulton, who went to England to study painting but turned to engineering after meeting James Watt. In 1807 he launched his *Clermont* on the Hudson River. Equipped with a Watt engine that operated paddle wheels, it steamed 150 miles up the river to Albany. Other inventors followed Fulton's example, notably Henry Bell of Glasgow, who laid the foundations of Scottish shipbuilding industry on the banks of the River Clyde. The early steamships were used only for river and coastal runs, but in 1833 the *Royal William* steamed from Nova Scotia to England. Five years later the *Sirius* and the

Great Western crossed the Atlantic in the opposite direction, taking $16\frac{1}{2}$ and $13\frac{1}{2}$ days respectively, or about half the time required by the fastest sailships. In 1840 Samuel Cunard established a regular transatlantic service, announcing beforehand dates of arrival and departure. Cunard advertised his enterprise as an "ocean railway" which had replaced the "maddening irregularity inseparable from the days of sail." By 1850 the steamship had bested the sailship in carrying passengers and mails, and was beginning to compete successfully for freight traffic.

The Industrial Revolution produced a revolution in communication as well as transportation. Hitherto a message could be sent to a distant place only by wagon, postrider, or boat. But in the middle of the nineteenth century the electric telegraph was invented, the work chiefly of an Englishman, Charles Wheatstone, and two Americans, Samuel F. B. Morse and Alfred Vail. In 1866 a transatlantic cable was laid, establishing instant communication between the Old and New Worlds.

Man thus conquered both time and space. Since time immemorial he had defined distances between places as involving so many hours travel by wagon, by horse, or by sailboat. But now he strode over the earth in seven-league boots. He could cross oceans and continents by steamship and railroad, and he could communicate with fellow-beings all over the world by telegraph. These achievements, and the others that enabled man to harness the energy in coal, to produce iron cheaply, and to spin one hundred threads of yarn at one time—all suggest the impact and significance of this first stage of the Industrial Revolution. It united the globe to an infinitely greater degree than it had been united

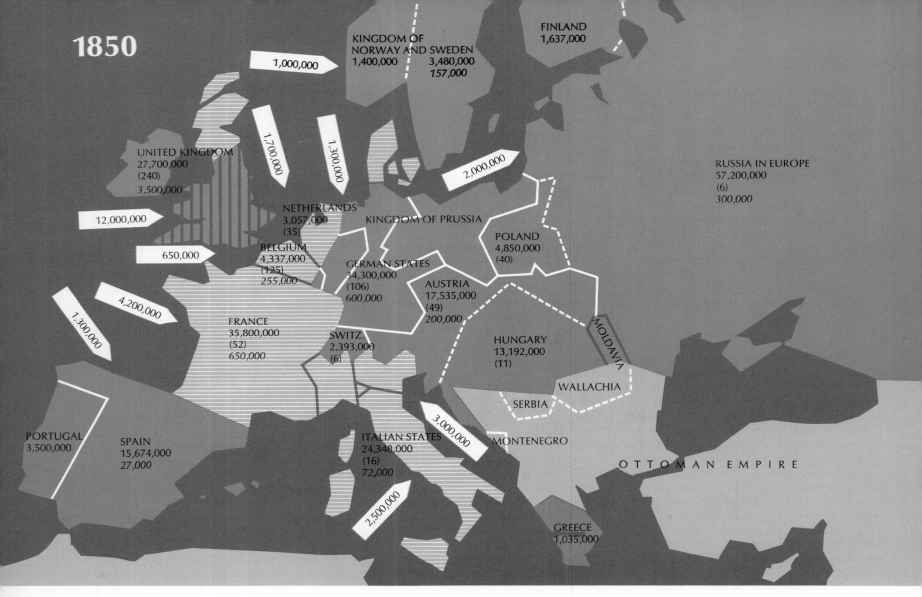

1850

FINLAND
1,637,000

KINGDOM OF
NORWAY AND SWEDEN
1,400,000   3,480,000
            157,000

1,000,000

RUSSIA IN EUROPE
57,200,000
(6)
300,000

UNITED KINGDOM
27,700,000
(240)
3,500,000

1,700,000

1,300,000

2,000,000

12,000,000

NETHERLANDS
3,057,000
(35)

KINGDOM OF PRUSSIA

POLAND
4,850,000
(40)

650,000

BELGIUM
4,337,000
(125)
255,000

GERMAN STATES
34,300,000
(106)
600,000

AUSTRIA
17,535,000
(49)
200,000

4,200,000

FRANCE
35,800,000
(52)
650,000

SWITZ.
2,393,000
(6)

HUNGARY
13,192,000
(11)

MOLDAVIA

1,300,000

WALLACHIA

SERBIA

PORTUGAL
3,500,000

SPAIN
15,674,000
27,000

ITALIAN STATES
24,348,000
(16)
72,000

3,000,000

MONTENEGRO

OTTOMAN EMPIRE

2,500,000

GREECE
1,035,000

INDUSTRIALIZATION OF EUROPE, 1850

20% of population in cities of 100,000 or more	5% or less of population in cities of 100,000 or more
6-10% of population in cities of 100,000 or more	

Explanation of Figures

 1,300,000 ship tons in port

51,958,000—population in 1910

(240)—Railroad mileage per million of population

200,000—Pig iron production in metric tons

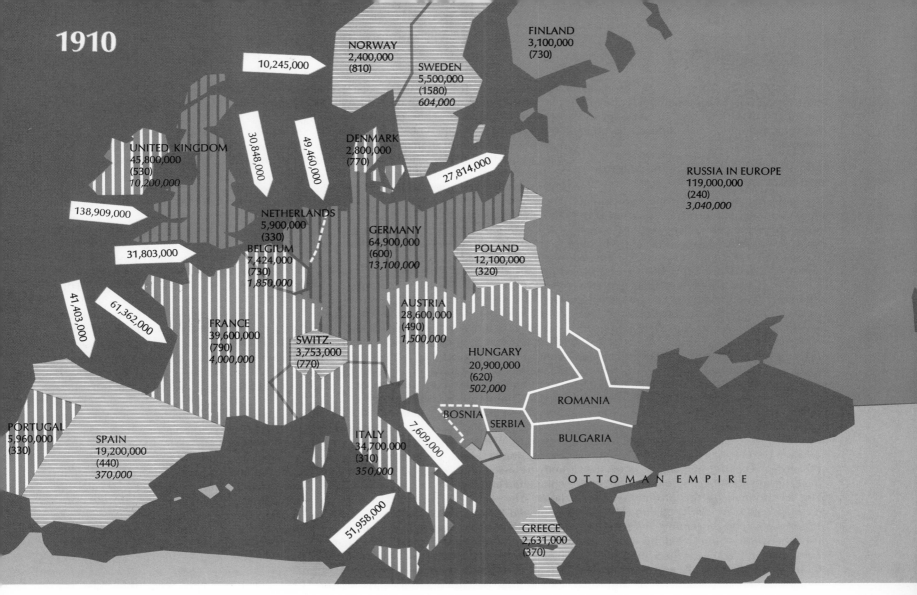

1910

NORWAY
2,400,000
(810)

10,245,000

SWEDEN
5,500,000
(1580)
604,000

FINLAND
3,100,000
(730)

30,848,000

49,460,000

DENMARK
2,800,000
(770)

27,814,000

RUSSIA IN EUROPE
119,000,000
(240)
3,040,000

UNITED KINGDOM
45,800,000
(530)
10,200,000

138,909,000

NETHERLANDS
5,900,000
(330)

GERMANY
64,900,000
(600)
13,100,000

POLAND
12,100,000
(320)

31,803,000

BELGIUM
7,424,000
(730)
1,850,000

41,403,000

61,362,000

FRANCE
39,600,000
(790)
4,000,000

SWITZ.
3,753,000
(770)

AUSTRIA
28,600,000
(490)
1,500,000

HUNGARY
20,900,000
(620)
502,000

ROMANIA

PORTUGAL
5,960,000
(330)

SPAIN
19,200,000
(440)
370,000

ITALY
34,700,000
(310)
350,000

7,609,000

BOSNIA

SERBIA

BULGARIA

OTTOMAN EMPIRE

51,958,000

GREECE
2,631,000
(370)

INDUSTRIALIZATION OF EUROPE 1910

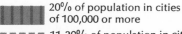 20% of population in cities
of 100,000 or more

6-10% of population in cities of
100,000 or more

11-20% of population in cities
of 100,000 or more

5% or less of population in cities
of 100,000 or more

**Explanation
of
Figures**

 7,609,000 ship tons in port

12,100,000—Population in 1910

(330) Railroad mileage
per million of population

4,000,000—Pig iron production
in metric tons

397

in the times of the Romans or the Mongols, and it made possible the European domination of the globe that was to last until the Industrial Revolution had diffused to other regions.

Industrial Revolution: Second Stage, 1870–1914

The Industrial Revolution which got under way in the late eighteenth century has continued steadily and relentlessly to the present day. Hence it is essentially artificial to divide its evolution into various periods. Yet a case can be made for considering 1870 as a transition date. It was about that time that two important developments occurred—science began to affect industry significantly, and mass-production techniques were perfected and applied. . . .

The impact of science was felt by all industries after 1870. In metallurgy, for example, a number of processes were developed (Bessemer, Siemens-Martin and Gilchrist-Thomas) that made possible the mass production of high-grade steel from low-grade iron ore. The power industry was revolutionized by the harnessing of electricity and by the invention of the internal combustion engine which uses chiefly oil and gasoline. Communications also were transformed by the invention of the wireless, or radio. In 1896, Guglielmo Marconi devised a machine for sending and receiving messages without wires, but his work was based on the researches of the Scottish physicist James Clerk Maxwell, and the German physicist Heinrich Hertz. The oil industry developed rapidly as a result of the work of geologists who located oilfields with remarkable accuracy, and of chemists who devised ways to refine crude oil into naphtha, gas, kerosene, and both light and heavy lubricating oils. One of the most spectacular examples of the effect of science on industry may be seen in the case of the coal derivatives. In addition to yielding coke and a valuable gas that was used for illumination, coal also gave a liquid, or coal tar. Chemists discovered in this substance a veritable treasure trove, the derivatives including hundreds of dyes and a host of other by-products such as aspirin, wintergreen, saccharin, disinfectants, laxatives, perfumes, photographic chemicals, high explosives, and essence of orange blossom.

The second stage of the Industrial Revolution was also characterized by the development of mass-production techniques. The United States led in this field as Germany did in the scientific. Certain obvious advantages explain U. S. primacy in mass production: the great storehouse of raw materials; the abundant supply of capital, both native and European; the constant influx of cheap immigrant labor; and the vast home market of continental proportions and with a rapidly growing population and a rising standard of living.

Two principal methods of mass production were developed in the United States. One was the making of standard interchangeable parts, and the assembling of these parts into the completed unit with a minimum of handicraft labor. The American inventor Eli Whitney employed this system at the very beginning of the nineteenth century in manufacturing muskets for the government. His factory, based on this novel principle, attracted wide attention and was visited by many travelers. One of these described well the basic feature of Whitney's revolutionary technique: "For every part of the musket he has a mould; and there is said to be so much exactitude in the finishing, that every part of any musket may be adapted to all the parts of any other."

During the decades following Whitney, machines were made more and more accurate, so that it became possible to produce parts that were not nearly alike but exactly alike. The next step, early in the twentieth century, was the working out of the assembly line. Henry Ford gained fame and fortune by devising the endless conveyor belt that carried car parts to the place where they were needed by the assembly workmen. . . .

Science and mass-production methods affected agriculture as well as industry. Again it was Germany that led in the application of science, and the United States in mass production. German chemists discovered that to maintain the fertility of the soil it was necessary to replace the nitrogen, potassium, and phosphorus that was taken out by plants. At first guano was used for this purpose, but toward the end of the nineteenth century it gave way to purer forms of the necessary minerals. As a result, world production of the minerals increased between 1850 and 1913 from insignificant amounts to 899,800 net tons of nitrate (three-fourths of which was used for fertilizer), 1,348,000 metric tons of potash, and 16,251,213 tons of superphosphates.

In the United States the large size of the farms and the lack of sufficient rural labor stimulated the invention of agricultural machinery. The tractor which replaced the horse could pull a rotary plow that plowed as much as fifty acres a day. The combine could automatically cut, gather, thresh, and clean the grain, and even bundle it in sacks ready for the market. As important as these new machines were the grain elevators, the canning factories, the refrigerated cars and ships, and the rapid transportation facilities, which resulted in a world market for agricultural as well as for industrial products. The wheat of

Canada, the mutton of Australia, the beef of Argentina, and the fruits of California were to be found in markets throughout the world. Thus, the farmer was as much affected by the agricultural revolution as the artisan had been by the Industrial. Agriculture, which traditionally had offered a means of independent livelihood, was becoming a large-scale business enterprise geared to production for national and international markets.

Diffusion of the Industrial Revolution

During the nineteenth century the Industrial Revolution spread gradually from England to the Continent of Europe, and even to the non-European portions of the globe. At first there were various obstacles in the way of diffusion. A British law forbade the exportation of machinery, and conditions on the Continent were not conducive to industrialization, particularly because of the strength of the guilds and the disturbances connected with the Revolutionary and Napoleonic Wars. But the wars ended in 1815, and the British law was repealed in 1825. Soon the railway-building fever, which got under way in England in the 1830's was affecting the Continent. Furthermore, British industrialists by this time were accumulating surplus capital and were on the look-out for investment opportunities on the Continent. By 1830, fifteen to twenty thousand British workers were employed in France alone to man the new machines.

Once the Industrial Revolution began to spread, certain factors determined the pattern of diffusion. Most important were an adequate supply of natural resources, particularly iron and steel, and a free and mobile working population, unencumbered by either guild restrictions or feudal obligations. Belgium met both these requirements and hence was the first country on the Continent to be industrialized. The process began before 1830, and proceeded so rapidly that by 1870 the majority of Belgians lived in cities and were directly dependent upon industry or trade. As early as 1830 Belgium was producing 5 million tons of coal per year, and by 1913 the figure had risen to 23 million tons. Other branches of industry grew so fast, however, that from 1840 onward Belgium had to import coal from England.

France followed after Belgium, though—for several reasons—at a much more leisurely pace. . . . Nevertheless, industrialization did gradually affect France, especially in the north of the country—in Alsace-Lorraine and in the regions about Lille, Rouen, and Paris. The number of steam engines increased from 15 in 1815 to 625 in 1830, 26,146 in 1871, and 82,238 in 1910. The most rapid tempo of industrialization came after 1870, when the value of manufactured products rose from 5 billion francs in that year to 15 billion in 1897. Yet the fact remains that by 1914 France was not so thoroughly industrialized as Belgium, England, or Germany.

The pattern of industrialization in Germany was very different from that in France. Because of the political disunity, the poor transportation facilities, the strong guilds, and other considerations, Germany started very slowly. But after 1871 German industry advanced in such giant strides that all the other economies of Europe, including that of Britain, were left behind. The formation of the German Empire in 1871 contributed to this remarkable progress. The acquisition of Alsace-Lorraine at the same time added valuable iron reserves to Germany's plentiful natural resources. Germany also had the advantage of starting off with new and up-to-date machinery which was more efficient than Britain's older equipment. And the German government aided substantially by building a network of canals and railroads, providing tariff protection and subsidies when they were needed, and establishing an efficient educational system which turned out a stream of well-trained scientists and technicians. These factors enabled Germany by 1914 to surpass all other European states in the iron, steel, chemical, and electrical industries, and to follow after Britain in coal and textiles. In 1914 the number of workers in German industry had risen to two-fifths of the total labor force, and that in agriculture had fallen to one-third.

Several other European countries had developed substantial industries by 1914, the most important being Russia, Austria-Hungary, and Italy. Among the overseas countries, the United States had advanced at a phenomenal rate, while Japan, Canada, and Australia had made appreciable progress. The United States, especially, with its unique advantages previously noted, by the beginning of the twentieth century had become the first industrial power in the world. In steel production, for example, the United States in 1910 was producing 26,512,000 metric tons as against 13,698,000 by Germany, her closest competitor, and in coal her output was 617 million metric tons as against 292 million tons by Great Britain, who was in second place.

We may conclude that by 1914 the Industrial Revolution had spread significantly from its original center in the British Isles. In fact, the diffusion reached such proportions that Britain now not only faced formidable competition, but had been surpassed by two other countries, Germany and the United States. . . .

Effect of the Industrial Revolution on Europe

Increase of Population

Another effect of the Industrial Revolution on Europe was to make possible an unprecedented increase in population. In spite of the emigration overseas of millions of Europeans during the nineteenth century, the population of the Continent in 1914 was well over three times that of 1750. The reasons for this population explosion are economic and medical. The great increase of productivity in both agriculture and industry meant increased means of subsistence in terms of food, cloth-

ing, shelter, and other necessities of life. Famine in most parts of Europe west of Russia became a memory of the past. Even if crops failed, the new transportation facilities ensured adequate supply from outside. The population increase was due also to the advances of medical science and to the adoption of numerous public health measures. There was little or no increase in the birth rate, but the death rate was sharply reduced by preventing or curing diseases. Vaccination, segregation of infected persons, safeguarding of water supplies, knowledge of antiseptics— all these reduced the death rate in northwestern Europe from at least 30 per 1,000

persons in 1800 to about 15 in 1914. Thus Europe's population climbed steeply from 140 million in 1750 to 188 million in 1800, 266 million in 1850, 401 million in 1900, and 463 million in 1914. This rate of increase in Europe was so much higher than in the other regions of the world that it altered the global population balance (see Table 1).

Urbanization

The Industrial Revolution led also to an unprecedented urbanization of world society. Cities date back to the Neolithic period when the invention of agriculture produced a food surplus that could support urban centers. During the following millennia the size of cities depended on the amount of food that the surrounding land could produce. Thus the most populous cities were to be found in the valleys and flood plains, like the Nile, the Fertile Crescent, the Indus, and the Hwang Ho. With the development of large-scale river and sea transport, cities were able to specialize in trade and industry and thus to expand their populations beyond the limits of their agricultural hinterlands.

Far more significant, however, is the modern worldwide urbanization produced by the Industrial Revolution. The replacement of the putting-out system by the factory system led to a mass influx into the new centers of industry. The large new urban populations could be fed because food supplies now were available from all parts of the world. Technological and medical advances made it possible to eliminate the plagues that previously had decimated cities, and even to make city living relatively endurable and pleasant. The more important of these advances include ample provision of pure water, perfection of centralized sewerage and waste disposal systems,

Table 1 ESTIMATED POPULATION OF THE WORLD*

MILLIONS	1650	1750	1850	1900	1950
Europe	100	140	266	401	593
U.S. & Canada	1	1	26	81	168
Latin America	12	11	33	63	163
Oceania	2	2	2	6	13
Africa	100	95	95	120	199
Asia	330	479	749	937	1,379
TOTAL	545	728	1,171	1,608	2,515
PERCENTAGES					
Europe	18.3	19.2	22.7	24.9	24.0
U.S. & Canada	.2	.1	2.3	5.1	6.7
Latin America	2.2	1.5	2.8	3.9	6.5
Oceania	.4	.3	.2	.4	.5
Africa	18.3	13.1	8.1	7.4	7.9
Asia	60.6	65.8	63.9	58.3	55.4
TOTAL	100.0	100.0	100.0	100.0	100.0

*These figures show that Europe's percentage of the total world population rose from 18.3 in 1650 to 24.0 in 1950. But by the latter date, most of the population of the United States, Canada, and Oceania was of European origin, and at least half of the population of Latin America was also. Accordingly, it is more meaningful to say that by 1950 the percentage of Europeans and people of European origin had risen to about one-third of the world total. From *United Nations Demographic Yearbook*. Copyright, United Nations (1957). Reproduced by permission. Adapted from A. M. Carr-Saunders, *World Population* (Oxford: Clarendon Press, 1936) by permission of Barnes and Noble. This is published in Canada by Frank & Co. Ltd.

insurance of an adequate food supply, and prevention and control of contagious diseases. Thus cities all over the world grew at such a rate that by 1930 they included 415 million people or one-fifth of the human race. This represents one of the great social transformations in human history, for city-dwelling meant an entirely new way of life. Many Western countries, such as Britain, Belgium, Germany, and the United States, had by 1914 a substantial majority of their people living in cities. The pace and scope of urbanization during the nineteenth century is reflected in the figures presented in Table 2.

Increase of Wealth

The Industrial Revolution, with its efficient exploitation of human and natural resources on a worldwide scale, made possible an increase in productivity that is without precedent in all history. Great Britain, who first was affected in this respect, increased her capital from 500 million pounds sterling in 1750 to 1,500 million pounds in 1800, to 2,500 million pounds in 1833, and to 6,000 million in 1865. In the latter part of the nineteenth century the entire world felt the impact of the increasing productivity. The wool of New Zealand, the wheat of Canada, the rice of Burma, the rubber of Malaya, the jute of Bengal, and the humming factories of Western Europe and eastern United States—all these resources were enmeshed in a dynamic and constantly expanding global economy. . . .

Table 2 POPULATION OF SELECTED CITIES*

(In Thousands)

	17th c.	1800	1850	1880	1900	1950 (CITY)	1950 (METRO)
New York	5	64	696	1,912	3,437	7,900	13,300
London	150	959	2,681	4,767	6,581	8,325	10,200
Paris	200	600	1,422	2,799	3,670	4,950	6,350
Moscow	unknown	250	365	612	1,000	4,700	6,500
Berlin	20	172	500	1,321	2,712	3,345	3,900
Manchester	under 15	77	303	341	544	700	1,965
Vienna	100	247	444	1,104	1,675	1,615	1,900
Rome	130	153	175	300	463	1,625	1,625

*R. R. Palmer, ed., *Atlas of World History* (Chicago: Rand McNally & Company, 1962), pp. 194–95. Reprinted by permission.

II. TABLES OF SELECTED NINETEENTH-CENTURY STATISTICS

Table 3 INFANT MORTALITY*

(Deaths per Thousand Infants under One Year Old)

	U.S.A.	ENGLAND & WALES	GERMANY	FRANCE	JAPAN
1870		154		178	
1880		149		172	
1890		142		166	
1900		153		164	170
1910		128	186	132	156
1920	76	76	123	95	161
1930	68	68	94	89	137
1940	47	57	64	91	90
1950	29	30	55	47	60

* *Annuaire Statistique de la France,* 1945, Partie Internationale, p. 23.

Table 4 LIFE EXPECTANCY AT BIRTH (FEMALES)*

(Number of Years)

	U.S.A.	ENGLAND & WALES	GERMANY	FRANCE	JAPAN
18th c.				27	
1825				41	
1845		42		41	
1875		45	39		
1885		47	40	44	
1895		48	44		
1905	51	52	48	49	45
1920	57	60		56	43
1930	61	63	60	59	46
1950	71	72	69	69	60

* *Annuaire Statistique de la France,* 1954, Partie Internationale, p. 18.

Table 5 CONQUERED DISEASES*

(*Deaths per Million of Population from Typhoid Fever*)

	U.S.A.	ENGLAND & WALES	DENMARK	FRANCE	JAPAN
1870			672		
1880		325	478		
1890		179	192		
1900	313	175	111		138
1910	225	70	38	114	130
1920	76	13	13	59	223
1930	45	9	9	48	145
1940	11	3	2	26	104
1950	1	5	1	8	9

*Annuaire Statistique de la France, 1954, Partie Internationale, pp. 25–35.

Table 6 COAL PRODUCTION*

(*Thousands of Metric Tons*)

	U.S.A.	GREAT BRITAIN	U.S.S.R.	GERMANY	FRANCE
1860	13,358	81,322		12,348	
1870	29,978	112,197		26,398	13,180
1880	64,850	149,021	3,240	46,974	19,362
1890	143,100	184,529	6,015	70,238	26,083
1900	244,600	228,784	16,156	109,290	33,405
1910	455,000	268,677	24,930	152,828	38,350
1920	597,178	233,205	7,642	131,356	34,672
1930	487,078	247,775	48,817	142,699	68,293
1940	462,045	227,898	166,000	173,043	40,984
1950	505,313	219,796	260,000	111,137	67,620

*Annuaire Statistique de la France, 1954.

Table 7 RAILWAY MILEAGE*

(*Thousands of Miles*)

	U.S.A.	GREAT BRITAIN	GERMANY	RUSSIA	INDIA
1850	9.0	6.6	3.7	.4	.0
1860	30.6	10.4	7.2	1.0	.9
1870	52.9	15.5	12.2	7.0	4.8
1880	93.3	18.0	21.0	15.0	9.3
1890	163.4	20.0	26.7	20.2	16.8
1900	193.3	21.9	31.9	31.7	23.7
1910	240.3	23.4	38.0	41.2	32.1
1920	252.8	20.3	35.9	36.6	37.0
1930	249.1	21.4	36.4	52.0	41.5
1940	233.7	19.9	36.7	62.5	41.0

*W. S. Woytinsky and E. S. Woytinsky, *World Commerce and Governments*, The Twentieth Century Fund, New York, 1955, p. 342.

TABLE 8 SPEED OF TRANSPORTATION*

(*Miles per Hour*)

	HORSE COACH	CANAL TUG	RIVER BOAT	OCEAN SHIP	RAIL-ROAD	AUTO	AIRPLANE
1840	5	2	5	10	31		
1860	5	2	6	15	40		
1880	5	3	8	20	50		
1900	5	4	10	25	60	30	
1910	5	4	10	30	60	45	50
1920	5	4	11	30	65	55	110
1930	5	4	11	30	70	60	185
1940	5	4	11	35	100	75	300

*W. S. Woytinsky and E. S. Woytinsky, *World Commerce and Governments*, The Twentieth Century Fund, New York, 1955, p. 308.

E. J. Hobsbawm: Toward an Industrial World

British historian E. J. Hobsbawm (1909–   ) here analyzes the fundamental changes that were taking place in the economy of the Western world in the first half of the nineteenth century. Reprinted by permission of The World Publishing Company from *The Age of Revolution* by E. J. Hobsbawm. Copyright © 1962 by E. J. Hobsbawm. This is published in Canada by George Weidenfeld & Nicholson Ltd.

I

After about 1830 . . . the rate of economic and social change accelerated visibly and rapidly. Outside Britain the period of the French Revolution and its wars brought relatively little immediate advance, except in the USA, which leaped ahead after its own war of independence, doubling its cultivated area by 1810, multiplying its shipping sevenfold, and in general demonstrating its future capacities. (Not only the cotton-gin, but the steamship, the early development of assembly-line production—Oliver Evans' flour-mill on a conveyor-belt—are American advances of this period.) The foundations of a good deal of later industry, especially heavy industry, were laid in Napoleonic Europe, but not much survived the end of the wars, which brought crisis everywhere. On the whole, the period from 1815 to 1830 was one of setbacks, or at the best of slow recovery. States put their finances in order—normally by rigorous deflation (the Russians were the last to do so in 1841). Industries tottered under the blows of crisis and foreign competition; the American cotton industry was very badly hit. Urbanization was slow: until 1828 the French rural population grew as fast as that of the cities. Agriculture languished, especially in Germany. Nobody observing the economic growth of this period, . . . would judge that any country other than Britain and perhaps the USA was on the immediate threshold of industrial revolution. To take an obvious index of the new industry: outside Britain, the USA, and France the number of steamengines and the amount of steam power in the rest of the world in the 1820s was scarcely worth the attention of the statistician.

After 1830 (or thereabouts) the situation changed swiftly and drastically; so much so that by 1840 the characteristic social problems of industrialism—the new proletariat, the horrors of uncontrolled break-neck urbanization—were the commonplace of serious discussion in Western Europe and the nightmare of the politician and administrator. The number of steam-engines in Belgium doubled, their horsepower almost trebled, between 1830 and 1838: from 354 (with 11,000 hp) to 712 (with 30,000). By 1850 the small, but by now very heavily industrialized, country had almost 2,300 engines of 66,000 horsepower, and almost 6 million tons of coal production (nearly three times as much as in 1830). In 1830 there had been no joint-stock companies in Belgian mining; by 1841 almost half the coal output came from such companies.

It would be monotonous to quote analogous data for France, for German states, Austria, or any other countries and areas in which the foundations of modern industry were laid in these twenty years: Krupps of Germany, for instance, installed their first steam-engine in 1835, the first shafts of the great Ruhr coalfield were sunk in 1837, and the first coke-fired furnace was set up in the great Czech iron centre of Vîtkovice in 1836, Falck's first rolling-mill in Lombardy in 1839–1840. . . . 1830–1848 marks the birth of industrial areas, of famous industrial centres and firms whose names have become familiar from that day to this, but hardly even their adolescence, let alone their maturity. Looking back on the 1830s we know what that atmosphere of excited technical experiment, of discontented and innovating enterprise, meant. It meant the opening of the American Middle West; but Cyrus McCormick's first mechanical reaper (1834) and the first 78 bushels of wheat sent eastwards from Chicago in 1838 only take their place in history because of what they led to after 1850. In 1846 the factory which risked manufacturing a hundred reapers was still to be congratulated on its daring: 'it was difficult indeed to find parties with sufficient boldness or pluck and energy, to undertake the hazardous enterprise of building reapers, and quite as difficult to prevail upon farmers to take their chances of cutting their grain with them, or to look favourably upon such innovation.' It meant the systematic building of the railways and heavy industries of Europe, and, incidentally, a revolution in the techniques of investment; but if the brothers Pereire had not become the great adventurers of industrial finance after 1851, we should pay little attention to the project of '*a lending and borrowing office*' where industry will borrow from all capitalists on the most favourable terms through the intermediary of the richest bankers acting as guarantors, which they vainly submitted to the French government in 1830.

As in Britain, consumer goods—generally textiles, but also sometimes foodstuffs—led these bursts of industrialization; but capital goods—iron, steel, coal, etc.—were already more important than in the first British industrial revolution: in 1846, 17 per cent of Belgian industrial employment was in capital-goods industries as against between 8 and 9 per cent in Britain. By 1850 three-quarters of all Belgian industrial steam-power was in mining and metallurgy. As in Britain, the average new industrial establishment—factory, forge, or mine—was rather small, surrounded by a great undergrowth of cheap, technically unrevolutionized, domestic, putting-out or sub-contracted labour, which grew with the demands of the factories and the market and would eventually be destroyed by the further advances of both. . . .

The industrial landscape was thus rather like a series of lakes studded with islands. If we take the country in general as the lake, the islands represent industrial cities, rural complexes (such as the networks of manufacturing villages so common in the central German and Bohemian mountains), or industrial areas: textile towns like Mulhouse, Lille, or Rouen in France, Elberfeld-Barmen (the home of Frederick Engels' pious cottonmaster family) or Krefeld in Prussia, southern Belgium or Saxony. If we take the broad mass of independent artisans, peasants turning out goods for sale in the winter season, and domestic or putting-out workers as the lake, the islands represent the mills, factories, mines, and foundries of various sizes. The bulk of the landscape was still very much water; or—to adapt the metaphor a little more closely to reality—the reed-beds of small scale or dependent production which formed round the industrial and commercial centres.

Domestic and other industries founded earlier as appendages of feudalism also existed. Most of these—e.g., the Silesian linen industry—were in rapid and tragic decline. The great cities were hardly industrialized at all, though they maintained a vast population of labourers and craftsmen to serve the needs of consumption, transport, and general services. Of the world's towns with over 100,000 inhabitants, apart from Lyon, only the British and American ones included obviously industrial centres: Milan, for instance, in 1841 had a mere two small steam-engines. In fact the typical industrial centre—in Britain as well as on the Continent—was a small or medium-sized provincial town or a complex of villages.

II

At the opposite extreme . . . stood the USA. The country suffered from a shortage of capital, but it was ready to import it in any quantities, and Britain stood ready to export it. It suffered from an acute shortage of manpower, but the British Isles and Germany exported their surplus population, after the great hunger of the middle forties, in millions. It lacked sufficient men of technical skill; but even these—Lancashire cotton workers, Welsh miners and iron-men—could be imported from the already industrialized sector of the world, and the characteristic American knack of inventing labour-saving and above all labour-simplifying machinery was already fully deployed. The USA lacked merely settlement and transport to open up its apparently endless territories and resources. The mere process of internal expansion was enough to keep its economy in almost unlimited growth, though American settlers, governments, missionaries, and traders already expanded overland to the Pacific or pushed their trade—

backed by the most dynamic and second largest merchant fleet of the world—across the oceans, from Zanzibar to Hawaii. Already the Pacific and the Caribbean were the chosen fields of American empire.

Every institution of the new republic encouraged accumulation, ingenuity, and private enterprise. A vast new population, settled in the seaboard cities and the newly occupied inland states, demanded the same standardized personal, household and farm goods and equipment, and provided an ideally homogeneous market. The rewards of invention and enterprise were ample: and the inventors of the steamship (1807–1813), the humble tack (1807), the screw-cutting machine (1809), the artificial denture (1822), insulated wire (1827–1831), the revolver (1835), the idea of the typewriter and sewing machine (1843–1846), the rotary printing press (1846), and a host of pieces of farm machinery, pursued them. No economy expanded more rapidly in this period than the American, even though its really headlong rush was only to occur after 1860.

Only one major obstacle stood in the way of the conversion of the USA into the world economic power which it was soon to become: the conflict between an industrial and farming North and a semi-colonial South. For while the North benefited from the capital, labour, and skills of Europe—and notably Britain—as an independent economy, the South (which imported few of these resources) was a typical dependent economy of Britain. Its very success in supplying the booming factories of Lancashire with almost all their cotton perpetuated its dependence, comparable to that which Australia was about to develop on wool, the Argentine on meat. The South was for free trade, which enabled it to sell to Britain and in return to buy cheap British goods; the North, almost from the beginning (1816), protected the home industrialist heavily against any foreigner—i.e., the British competed for the territories of the West—the one for slave plantations and backward self-sufficient hill squatters, the other for mechanical reapers and mass slaughterhouses; and until the age of the transcontinental railroad the South, which controlled the Mississippi delta through which the Middle West found its chief outlet, held some strong economic cards. Not until the Civil War of 1861–65—which was in effect the unification of America by and under Northern capitalism—was the future of the American economy settled.

The other future giant of the world economy, Russia, was as yet economically negligible, though forward-looking observers already predicted that its vast size, population, and resources must sooner or later come into their own. The mines and manufactures created by eighteenth-century tsars, with landlords or feudal merchants as employers, serfs as labourers, were slowly declining. The new industries—domestic and small-scale textile works—only began a really noticeable expansion in the 1860s. Even the export of corn to the West from the fertile black-earth belt of the Ukraine made only moderate progress. Russian Poland was rather more advanced,

but, like the rest of Eastern Europe, from Scandinavia in the north to the Balkan peninsula in the south, the age of major economic transformation was not yet at hand. Nor was it in Southern Italy and Spain, except for small patches of Catalonia and the Basque country. . . .

One part of the world thus swept forward towards industrial power, another lagged. But the two phenomena are not unconnected with each other. Economic stagnation, sluggishness, or even regression was the product of economic advance. For how could the relatively backward economies resist the force—or in certain instances the attraction—of the new centres of wealth, industry, and commerce? The English and certain other European areas could plainly undersell all competitors. To be the workshop of the world suited them. Nothing seemed more 'natural' than that the less advanced should produce food and perhaps minerals, exchanging these non-competitive goods for British (or other West-European) manufactures. 'The sun,' Richard Cobden told the Italians, 'is your coal.' Where local power was in the hands of large landowners or even progressive farmers or ranchers, the exchange suited both sides. Cuban plantation-owners were quite happy to make their money by sugar, and to import the foreign goods which allowed the foreigners to buy sugar. Where local manufacturers

could make their voice heard, or local governments appreciated the advantages of balanced economic development or merely the disadvantages of dependence, the disposition was less sunny. . . .

Of all the economic consequences of the age of dual revolution this division between the 'advanced' and the 'under-developed' countries proved to be the most profound and the most lasting. Roughly speaking by 1848 it was clear which countries were to belong to the first group, i.e., Western Europe (minus the Iberian peninsula), Germany, Northern Italy, and parts of Central Europe, Scandinavia, the USA, and perhaps the colonies settled by English-speaking migrants. But it was equally clear that the rest of the world was, apart from small patches, lagging, or turning—under the informal pressure of Western exports and imports or the military pressure of Western gunboats and military expeditions—into economic dependences of the West. Until the Russians in the 1930s developed means of leaping this chasm between the 'backward' and the 'advanced,' it would remain immovable, untraversed, and indeed growing wider, between the minority and the majority of the world's inhabitants. No fact has determined the history of the twentieth century more firmly than this.

STUDY QUESTIONS

1. Why was Prince Albert so optimistic in 1851?

2. What does the author of Reading 155 consider the prime importance of the industrial revolution? Why does he divide it into two stages?

3. What factors determined the speed of industrialization? What advantages did the countries

that industrialized later have over Great Britain?

4. Evaluate the changes that occurred in Europe as a result of accelerated economic growth. What advantages resulted? What problems were created?

5. What do Tables 5 and 6 (in Reading 155) imply about future economic development?

6. What brakes to Albert's optimism are applied by Hobsbawm? What did he mean in describing the industrial landscape in 1850 as "a series of lakes studded with islands"?

7. To what degree does Hobsbawm agree with the account in Reading 155? In what way does he differ and why is this significant?

IN THE WAKE OF THE INDUSTRIAL REVOLUTION

The pattern of industrialization which emerged in Great Britain in the latter part of the eighteenth century rapidly spread in little more than 200 years from a small island to the entire globe. Standardization, specialization, the concentration of labor in factories, and a great investment in capital equipment have all been part of this process. The goal of industrialization has been to reduce the cost per unit of producing goods and services and to increase as a result the output per man-hour of labor. The American worker today produces in a half hour what the British factory hand required a whole working day to achieve a century ago. At the same time the industrial capital behind him has increased more than tenfold.

Within the most technologically advanced societies the mechanization, specialization, and uniformity required by the industrial mode have often resulted in boredom, frustration, and anger at the tyranny of machines, sometimes drowning out the voices of those who see technology as morally neutral, materially enriching, and a liberator of leisure. For most of the world's population, however, industrialization has continued to provide the most effective way to meet the pressing problems of poverty and the limits of traditional society.

Above, the spinning wheel. Even in the twentieth century Mahatma Gandhi, the Indian leader, shown here with a *Charka,* encouraged impoverished villagers to take up traditional hand spinning as a means of self-help. Textiles, one of the first areas to benefit from industrialization, are today one of India's principal exports.

Right, a modern spinning mill in Japan.

Industrialization transformed mining

Miners in the eighteenth century sometimes
took the risk of easing their work by blasting.
It was safer, however, to build a bonfire to
loosen the rocks as this example from
Diderot's *Encyclopédie* shows. At the right a
man carries away the ore in a wheelbarrow.

Below, today massive machines drill into the
rock and, left, mechanized cars transport the
ore in the Swedish mining region of Kiruna.

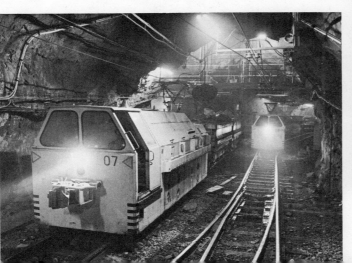

The machine replaced manual labor

Diamonds were laboriously sorted from the soil by hand at the famous Kimberley digs in South Africa in the 1870s.

Diamonds are separated from earth on a greasebelt in this modern recovery plant of the Consolidated Diamond Mines of South-West Africa.

Machines became complex

In this eighteenth-century machine shop for
threading screws, the man in figure 1 is hammering out a thread pattern on a steel rod.
Figures 3 and 4 depict machines for threading
larger screws. That in figure 4 is turned by a
foot-driven wheel (5) which is regulated to
reverse rotation while moving back and forth
the width of the thread with each turn.

A modern machine tool, the largest facing
lathe in Europe, used in the French Creusot
Steel Corporation.

The Middle Classes Inherit the Earth

TOPIC 30

THE MIDDLE CLASS VALUE SYSTEM

The rapid expansion of the market economy produced a new class of men in Western society, the merchants, manufacturers, and allied professional people whose status was not based on hereditary rights but on the wealth that they accrued by their own labors and through the profits of invested capital. These men were known collectively as the middle classes or bourgeoisie, a term that derived from the medieval stronghold, or burg, which offered protection to the traders and craftsmen who sprang up with the revival of commerce but did not have a legitimate place in the feudal system. The readings in Topic 58 examine the rise of the bourgeoisie in the eighteenth and early nineteenth centuries and seek to define the values they held.

Historically . . . the middle classes originally consisted of freemen and townsmen, as distinguished from the privileged aristocracy, and from the peasants riveted to the land. In the early modern period (1500–1789), however, social readjustments necessitated a more elastic definition, a definition concisely expressed by Gretton as "that portion of the community to which money is the primary condition and the primary instrument of life." Under this category came the commercial, industrial, and professional groups as distinguished from the nobility, the peasants, and the wage-earners. Today, all class boundaries have become even more difficult to define, because traditional privileged persons for the most part have disappeared, groups have moved from one stratum into another, individuals have risen and fallen in status, modern society has become so complex that persons may belong to more than one class at a time. Consequently, a certain section within the old bourgeoisie is now called the middle class. It refers . . . to the "not-so-rich and not-so-poor individuals between the proletariat-labor group and the wealthy capitalist and social aristocracy." Such a "sandwich" definition indicates how difficult it is to characterize the middle classes. . . .

HERALDS OF PROGRESS

"Antiquity deserveth that reverence that men should make a stand thereupon and discover what is the best way; but when the discovery is well taken, then to make progression." In thus begging men to cease worshipping the past and to look forward to a new day, the far-seeing Francis Bacon (1561–1626) was but one of the heralds of progress who caused an intellectual revolt against cultural tradition and so paved the way for the French Revolution and the triumph of bourgeois individualism. This attack upon "authority" was aided by such seventeenth-century scientists as Newton and Descartes. In thought Descartes left no place for the "authority of tradition." Not believing in the "wisdom of prejudice," he substituted for it faith in the power of our thoughts today. If we use the proper method, he wrote, we shall be able to outstrip our ancestors. The golden age is not behind us. Not only is progress possible, but there are no limits that can be assigned to it in advance. Such a philosophy could not help but appeal to a large part of the middle classes of his day. . . .

The scientists initiated a constructive instead of a destructive movement. It is true that their successors, as we shall see later in this chapter, demanded the overturn of those institutions, consecrated by the past, which in their opinion were unjust. But at this time there existed the "idea of progress as a guiding principle in seeking solutions for the difficult problems which were harassing the minds of men." This progressive idea was gladly accepted by the pragmatic middle classes, who realized that before they could attain a position in society satisfactory to their ego, the idea of Providence, the basis of the aristocratically organized society of the Middle Ages, must be obliterated. In its place must be substituted the belief in growth, "which included the gradual enlightenment of man's nature, the evolution of his intelligence, the expansion of his moral sense, and the improvement of his well-being." Possessed by this view, the publicists (the so-called philosophers of the eighteenth century) strove for intellectual and religious freedom, for political rights, and for economic independence. Desirous of well-being, they fostered above everything else the conception of the dignity of the individual as achieved through self-determination and self-expression. This assumption was primarily utilitarian, an outgrowth of the Puritan view that an individual should mold his own destiny. The inevitable result was the acceptance of the idea of success measured in commercial enterprise and in the attainment of economic liberty.

The middle classes soon found that it was the economic foundation of their social order that had to be reoriented; in essence, economic factors lay at the basis of the multifarious political, social, religious, and intellectual institutions. In some new way they had to enhance the life of labor, to raise it far above the supercilious life of the dilettante aristocrats. For practical reasons, too, they deemed it necessary for the expansion of their businesses that the regulations which maintained the old order be swept away or greatly altered. Opposition to the barrier of classes became more pronounced. The erection of an ideal civil society became an absorbing purpose. Having reached the conclusion that economic aspects dominated all phases of earthly existence, they welcomed most enthusiastically the birth of a new social science, economics, which explained and justified their position, a theory which they hoped would enable them more than ever to supplant the old regime by developing national governments under their own control. . . .

No writer of the eighteenth century equaled Voltaire in the expression of bourgeois ideas. Although he attacked kingly tyranny, he never advocated the substitution of a French republic. What he tried to do was to clear the way for the rise of the business classes by restricting the sphere of the church to non-secular matters and by limiting the function of the state to maintaining the status quo in property relations. . . .

In the political field, Voltaire's visions were limited to an abiding faith in benevolent despotism; at no time did he attack despotism as an "unnatural" form of government. Here he contrasted with other intellectuals, notably John Locke of England, who in the seventeenth century maintained that the ultimate source of the government was the people or their representatives, rather than a king ruling by grace of God. Voltaire's countryman, Montesquieu (1689–1755), supported Locke's views and, in his *Spirit of the Laws*, praised the English type of limited monarchy. His books made such institutions as parliament, the right of the legislature to control finances, and the *habeas corpus* proceedings familiar to the middle-class men throughout the continent. Despite the limitations of his political ideas, Voltaire, on the whole, believed confidently in enlightenment and progress through reason rather than through tradition. To the middle classes his ideas were very welcome.

To Jean Jacques Rousseau (1712–1778), more than to Voltaire, went the honor of being the peerless prophet of bourgeois democracy. True enough, Rousseau, in urging a return to nature, that is, in turning his back upon the forward movement of arts and sciences and demanding the overthrow of the existing civilization which, he believed, had demoralized mankind, was more radical than the average member of the middle classes. If, however, he meant the overthrow of the obsolescent, decadent, feudal-classical compromise—the absolute state—as the "degenerate Athens" of the eighteenth century and desired the establishment of a Sparta, where men would lead sober, industrious, and thrifty lives, then he was bourgeois. Rousseau's emphasis upon "the simple life" appealed to the middle classes, for the bourgeoisie necessarily led basically simple lives. Theirs was the applause of rationalizers. Above all, his belief in the sovereignty of the people earned for him popular commendation. By "the people" Rousseau, according to the business classes, meant those unprivileged but ambitious individuals who had money but lacked blue blood. They, not the king, were to make the laws. . . .

But Adam Smith (1723–1790) was by far the outstanding bourgeois philosopher of the eighteenth century. Maintaining in his *Wealth of Nations* (1776) that the true strength of a nation lay in the prosperity of its citizens, Smith contended that unrestricted enterprises

407

promoted the accumulation of riches by the individual. In direct opposition to mercantilism, he asserted that restrictions were useless and even harmful; each man knew best how to acquire wealth; and if he were permitted to adopt a policy of self-interest, the nation would become rich. The individual, therefore, should be allowed freedom in business unhampered by governmental regulation. To its advocates this doctrine of *laissez faire* constituted the expression of economic liberty.

Smith was the agent for a concept which arose out of many intellectual streams of thought. From the theologians came the doctrine that there was no need for the state to intrude in every-day life. From the political teachings of Locke and Rousseau came the theory that the state had no right to intervene in economic matters. From the French Physiocrats came the assertion that it was inexpedient for the government to interfere with or regulate business. To some economic writers governmental interference was not only unwise but immoral. Man had natural rights, which it was criminal to deny. Every individual, for example, had the right to make money, unhampered by political and social restrictions. No rules or regulations should stand in the way of a man engaged in the production of wealth. At the same time private property was sacred and inviolate. Once wealth was in his possession, no one should have the right to deprive him of it against his will. This, in essence, was the shrewd economic philosophy of the right to have and to hold.

Bourgeois capitalism was endangered by such wholehearted acceptance of individualism. The workers soon announced that these so-called rights included that of possessing employment and of receiving a larger share of the fruits of their labor. Thereupon the employers invoked the concept of "natural law" to defend their position. According to this philosophy, inasmuch as natural physical laws had been formulated for the movements of the stars, planets, and in fact all forms of nature, did it not follow that certain natural laws should determine social conditions? Such deduction, of course, had all the falsity of reasoning by analogy. Natural laws explained why some nations and individuals were wealthy and others were poor. Poverty would always exist, for if poor men were given larger wages, they would have larger families and more mouths to feed; *ergo*, poverty would persist. Man-made regulations, maintained the orthodox advocates of this philosophy, could not overcome the law of supply and demand. It was a natural law. How could wage-earners be saved from poverty if some were predestined to be rich and others to be poor? The exponents of *laissez faire* left the solution to the individual. Bourgeois individualism made economic salvation possible through the practice of thrift, self-denial, and hard work. Other things being equal, a self-made man who followed these precepts could enter the paradise of the middle classes. If by cleverness, shrewdness, or good luck, he obtained a large share of the wealth of a nation, then as a rich man he was entitled to a place in a special section of paradise reserved for monied aristocrats. . . .

REACTION AFTER NAPOLEON

After the fall of Napoleon, most people, especially those of the governing classes, did not immediately realize that they were living in a new era. Still firmly entrenched in power, they looked with horror upon the French Revolution, with its violence, bloodshed, and chaotic confusion. In their opinion the old régime stood for law and order, while the new spirit was for anarchy and devilment. To them the attacks upon the church signified the establishment of a "Godless Age." They maintained that the French Revolution had resulted only in bloodshed and misery. Alarmed over its violent consequences, they bitterly opposed its spread and tried to return in so far as possible to the "good old pre-revolutionary days." Few of them were able to divine that the Revolution had not yet spent itself, that the disorders would continue, that normalcy and sound prosperity would not and could not return until a definitely new and different order was instituted.

Disregarding, for the most part, the very idea of the recent changes, representatives of the powers responsible for the overthrow of Napoleon, under the leadership of the Austrian and British clever diplomats, Metternich and Castlereagh, sought at the Congress of Vienna (1815) to restore the past. They realized that the great majority of the people wanted peace above all else and were not especially interested in the creation of an earthly paradise for the future. Famines, pestilences, crime, and disease—the effects of the great wars—caused churchmen, business men, wage-earners, and peasants to place emphasis upon the present and to demand law, order, and peace. Peace could be attained, claimed the conservatives, provided the pre-revolutionary conditions, under which people supposedly had been happy and contented and had lived in harmony with one another, could be restored. Therefore, most of them opposed such revolutionary and bourgeois principles as constitutionalism, legal equality, equitable taxation, religious toleration, and intellectual liberty and proceeded to recreate as far as they were able to Europe of 1789. . . .

Despite these reactionary sentiments, a general revival of liberalism was under way by 1820. In England and France, the bourgeoisie were again attacking the old régime; while throughout Europe and the Americas, liberals, representing numerous classes, were advocating various kinds of liberty, such as national unity, constitutional government, democracy, and freedom for slaves and serfs. In England, bourgeois liberalism made its greatest advance when, between 1815 and 1830, another group among the middle classes challenged the right of the autocrats and the commercial plutocrats to dominate affairs in England and in France. These new protagonists were the manufacturers, the so-called "Captains of Industry," who, dependent for success on intelligence rather than on social position, joined the commercial classes in supporting Adam Smith's doctrine of the *laissez faire*. The Textile Revolution, offering a new way whereby a man could accumulate a fortune, made possible their success. Originally wage-earners or yeomen, these men were able to save or borrow a small amount of money; with it they purchased new machines and became the owners of small factories, each factory employing a few workmen. From these humble beginnings rose some of the powerful and wealthy manufacturing families of the nineteenth century.

During the late eighteenth century these men had the good as well as the bad characteristics of pioneers. In England a "mill owner" was a "hard-bitten north-country workingman" of no education and great force of character, taking little stock of his social or political relations with the outer world. He refused to enjoy leisure or recreation for himself, nor would he allow his workers any free time. . . . At no time did he concern himself about the physical welfare of the children he employed, except in so far as it made or marred his own fortune.

When Napoleon was overthrown, the mill owners of the second generation were originating an "industrial bourgeoisie of a new and enterprising type." Better educated and possessing a wider outlook than "his grim old father," the young captain of industry determined to enjoy more fully the political and social benefits which, he believed, wealth should bestow on him. To achieve these ends he welcomed an alliance with the gentry and the clergy around him. Moreover, he expressed ideas which often ran counter to the view of the aristocrats. He believed, for example, in the abolition of slavery; he opposed church rites, income taxes, and the Corn Laws. Ardently he subscribed to the bourgeois ideas expressed in the *Edinburgh Review*.

A middle-class family of the 1860s listens as the Bible is read on Sunday night.

The manufacturer, however, did not accept the philosophy of wealth of the commercial bourgeoisie. Adopting the puritanical suspicion of the life of leisure and personal pleasure, the mill owner stressed the godliness of hard work, self-denial, and the accumulation of wealth "for its own sake." Like the commercial patricians he balked at the attempts of labor to assert its rights. Unions received his stern disfavor, and although a few mill owners, like Robert Owen, recognized the necessity of social reform, the great majority clung stubbornly to the doctrine of individualism so far as the relations between capital and labor were concerned.

In the early nineteenth century, there were also the lesser middle classes in the various cities and towns of Europe. They consisted of the small business men, such as local shopkeepers, artisans, salesmen, and professional classes (doctors and lawyers). These elements, dependent on the profit system, soon took a personal interest in public affairs. Denied the ballot for the most part, they read newspapers, which were becoming popular at that time, and discussed the various topics of the day. The petty bourgeoisie also imitated their wealthy brothers by supporting churches and by enjoying such bourgeois comforts as vacations and social and intellectual avocations. Most of them accepted the bourgeois philosophy of individualism and worshipped at the shrine of the captain of industry—the self-made man.

Perhaps the greatest of the early nineteenth-century bourgeois liberals was Jeremy Bentham (1748–1832). A sincere exponent of Adam Smith's doctrine of benevolent selfishness as the road to social progress, he advocated in his *Principles of Morals and Legislation* and *Universal and Perpetual Peace* the abolition of all laws and institutions which stood in the way of individual economic advancement. He asserted that existing institutions should be judged not for their antiquity but for their utility in promoting "the greatest happiness of the greatest number." Since each individual is actuated by selfish motives, and since the welfare of the majority is the only sensible objective of society, the dominance of the majority is an inevitable premise to progress. He believed, therefore, that political democracy was justifiable and desirable.

Bentham did more than any other writer to put liberalism on a practical business basis. Merchants and industrialists often became inspired exponents of his utilitarianism. The sanctions of tradition and of reason were ignored and keen-minded business men decided that everything must rise, stand, or fall on the basis of its utility. Few institutions of the old régime could pass this test. Feudal laws, aristocracy, autocracy, and theocracy were now attacked by the utilitarian exponents of plutocracy who were determined to establish a bourgeois state.

But what was the bourgeois state? Primarily it was a country ruled by those who supported and were affected by the government—the taxpayers. The revolutionary slogan of "no taxation without representation" was revived by these nineteenth-century leaders of the Third Estate who were convinced that regardless of the form of government—constitutional monarchy or republic—they must possess political control. Under the tutelage of Smith, Bentham, and other writers, the bourgeoisie also had developed rather definite ideas as to the duties of the state. In their opinion the state should maintain "law and order," defend its citizens against alien attacks, and conduct certain public enterprises which private individuals could not maintain. All other governmental activities, they believed, should be abolished, especially mercantilistic restrictions on commerce, industry, and agriculture. Each person should work out his own salvation. The law of supply and demand should be observed so that capital could "find its most lucrative course, commodities their fair price, industry and intelligence their natural reward, idleness and folly their natural punishment." The function of government was merely to protect life and property "at a minimum of cost. . . ."

The bourgeois stress upon freedom was a vital factor in the spread of nationalism as well as of secular education in the early nineteenth century. . . . Between 1815 and 1848 it became impossible to disregard nationalism. The patriotic movements that had formerly stirred up the French, the Poles, the Portuguese, the Spaniards, the Italians, and the Germans in their opposition to Napoleon now influenced them to claim freedom and unity for all of their nationality. These demands could no longer be ignored, for the new political, economic, and social systems introduced into Europe during the Revolutionary and Napoleonic periods enabled the middle classes to gain political control of their governments. Their supremacy hastened the formation of new national states. After these governments were established, the liberal exponents of Western civilization were in a position to lead their nations in the conquest and Europeanization of the entire world.

This tremendous expansion of the middle-class system, however, would not have been possible without the aid of science. The early nineteenth century witnessed the real beginning of modern technocracy. According to the eminent German economist, Sombart, this modern technocracy was "founded upon the application of the natural sciences to technology and the consequent transformation of empirical experience into rational knowledge." In other words, scientific research and formulation resulted in inventions and engineering (the application of theoretical science). These developments had as their goal the "complete replacement of *Quality by Quantity.*" Therefore, mechanical inventions applied to industry would enable the middle classes to emphasize quantity ahead of quality production, and by so doing extend the scope of their operations and the amount of their wealth. Furthermore, the transformation from human power to steam and electric power would completely emancipate these classes. Hitherto they had been largely dependent upon the local labor supply for their help and upon local markets for raw materials and the sale of the goods. The steam engine and the steamship opened the world to their enterprise. Markets, production, and profits seemed unlimited. They had the world to gain!

Samuel Smiles Prescribes Self-Help (1859)

Samuel Smiles (1812–1904) turned into a book a series of lectures that he had presented before middle-class audiences, dealing with men who rose by their own efforts from simple beginnings to fortune and power. *Self-Help* was one of the most popular books in the nineteenth century and over 250,000 copies were sold. From Samuel Smiles, *Self-Help* (London, 1859), pp. 1–2, 232–234.

"Heaven helps those who help themselves" is a well-tried maxim, embodying in a small compass the results of vast human experience. The spirit of self-help is the root of all genuine growth in the individual; and, exhibited in the lives of many, it constitutes the true source of national vigour and strength. Help from without is often enfeebling in its effects, but help from within invariably invigorates. Whatever is done *for* men or classes, to a certain extent takes away the stimulus and necessity of doing for themselves; and where men are subjected to over-guidance and over-government, the inevitable tendency is to render them comparatively helpless.

Even the best institutions can give a man no active aid. Perhaps the utmost they can do is, to leave him *free* to develop himself and improve his individual condition. But in all times men have been prone to believe that their happiness and well-being were to be secured by means of institutions rather than by their own conduct. Hence the value of legislation as an agent in human advancement has always been greatly over-estimated. To constitute the millionth part of a Legislature, by voting for one or two men once in three or five years, however conscientiously this duty may be performed, can exercise but little active influence upon any man's life and character. Moreover, it is every day becoming more clearly understood, that the function of Government is negative and restrictive, rather than positive and active; being resolvable principally into protection—protection of life, liberty, and property. Hence the chief "reforms" of the last fifty years have consisted mainly in abolitions and disenactments. But there is no power of law that can make the idle man industrious, the thriftless provident, or the drunken sober; though every individual can be each and all of these if he will, by the exercise of his own free powers of action and self-denial. Indeed all experience serves to prove that the worth and strength of a State depend far less upon the form of its institutions than upon the character of its men. For the nation is only the aggregate of individual conditions, and civilization itself is but a question of personal improvement.

National progress is the sum of individual industry, energy, and uprightness, as national decay is of individual idleness, selfishness, and vice. What we are accustomed to decry as great social evils, will, for the most part, be found to be only the outgrowth of our own perverted life; and though we may endeavour to cut them down and extirpate them by means of Law, they will only spring up again with fresh luxuriance in some other form, unless the conditions of human life and character are radically improved. If this view be correct, then it follows that the highest patriotism and philanthropy consist, not so much in altering laws and modifying institutions, as in helping and stimulating men to elevate and improve themselves by their own free and independent action. . . .

Sound was the advice given by Mr. Bright to an assembly of working men in 1847, when . . . he used the following words: "There is only one way that is safe for any man, or any number of men, by which they can maintain their present position if it be a good one, or raise themselves above it if it be a bad one,—that is, by the practice of the virtues of industry, frugality, temperance, and honesty." . . . What is it that has made, that has in fact created, the middle class in this country, but the virtues to which I have alluded? There was a time when there was hardly any class in England, except the highest, that was equal in condition to the poorest class at this moment. How is it that the hundreds of thousands of men now existing in this our country of the middle class, are educated, comfortable, and enjoying an amount of happiness and independence, to which our forefathers were wholly unaccustomed? Why, by the practice of those very virtues; for I maintain that there has never been in any former age as much of these virtues as is now to be found amongst the great middle class of our community. When I speak of the middle class, I mean that class which is between the privileged class, the richest, and the very poorest in the community; and I would recommend every man to pay no attention whatever to public writers or speakers, whoever they may be, who tell them that this class or that class, that this law or that law, that this Government or that Government, can do all these things for them. I assure you, after long reflection and much observation, that there is no way for the working classes of this country to improve their condition but that which so many of them have already availed themselves of,— that is, by the practice of those virtues, and by reliance upon themselves.

There is no reason why the condition of the average workman in this country should not be a useful, honourable, respectable, and happy one. The whole body of the working classes might (with few exceptions) be as frugal, virtuous, well-informed, and well-conditioned as many individuals of the same class have already made themselves. What some men are, all without difficulty might be. Employ the same means, and the same results will follow. That there should be a class of men who live by their daily labour in every state is the ordinance of God, and doubtless

is a wise and righteous one; but that this class should be otherwise than frugal, contented, intelligent, and happy, is not the design of Providence, but springs solely from the weakness, self-indulgence, and perverseness of man himself. The healthy spirit of self-help created amongst working people would more than any other measure serve to raise them as a class, and this, not by pulling down others, but by levelling them up to a higher and still advancing standard of religion, intelligence, and virtue.

Sir Titus Salt Provides the Model for a Successful Nineteenth-Century Businessman

Titus Salt (1803–1876) was a prosperous textile manufacturer who served as mayor of Bradford, near Manchester. He was knighted in 1869. His reputation as a model employer and a good citizen is commemorated by a marble statue which still stands before the Bradford town hall. From R. Balgarnie, *Sir Titus Salt, Baronet: His Life and Its Lessons* (London, 1877), pp. 80–85.

He was a very *early riser*, and his unvarying rule was to be at the works before the engine was started. Is it not written, "the hand of the diligent maketh rich"? and here is a signal illustration of it. It used to be said in Bradford, "Titus Salt makes a thousand pounds before other people are out of bed." Whether the sum thus specified was actually realised by him we cannot say, but it is the habit of early

rising we wish to point out, and inculcate on those whose business career is about to begin. In these times of artificiality and self-indulgence, when the laws of nature are often wantonly violated, the chances of success are dead against those who follow such a course. Let young men especially avoid it; yea, let them take Mr. Titus Salt as an example of early rising. . . .

It is almost superfluous to mention that this early presence at "the works" exercised a high moral influence over his workpeople. Well they knew they had not merely to do with delegated authority, but with that which was supreme. If any of them were late, it was the master's rebuke they feared. If any were conspicuous above the rest for regularity and skill in their duties, it was the master's approval they expected, and this approval was shewn by the promotion of those who served him best. Some who entered his employment in the humblest capacity have been raised to the highest positions in it. There was thus a personal acquaintance formed, and a mutual sympathy established, that greatly helped to bridge the gulf which too often has separated master and workpeople, and sometimes placed them in an attitude of antagonism to each other. Throughout his manufacturing career he had great moral power in attaching the workpeople to himself; they all looked up to him as a friend rather than a master, and they obeyed and served him with all the devotion of a Highland clan to their noble chieftain. . . .

Another striking feature of his character, and one which enabled him to accomplish so much work, was his *punctuality*. Never was military despot more rigid than he in the observance of this rule: when he made an engagement he was punctual to the minute,

Bust of Sir Titus Salt in Bradford.

and he expected the same in others who had dealings with him. . . . Such was his punctuality that he was hardly ever known to miss a train, or to be in a hurry for one. It was the same at home as in business: the hour of meals was observed with precision, and all other domestic arrangements were conducted on the same principle of order. With watch in hand he would await the time for evening prayers, and then the bell was instantly rung for the household to assemble. When the usual hour arrived for his family and household to retire to rest, the signal was at once given and observed. . . . When guests were staying at his house, he was the timekeeper of their movements, and in regulating themselves accordingly they were seldom mistaken. When a journey was to be taken with his wife and family, say to the metropolis or the seaside, nothing was left to chance; but the day and hour of starting, together with other minor arrangements, were written down some time beforehand.

Another marked characteristic in the prosecution of his immense business was his *methodical exactness:* but for this habit, which was natural to him, he never could have personally controlled the various departments in connection with "the works." He was scrupulously exact in the arrangement of his papers, and knew where to lay his hand on any document when required. His letters were always promptly answered. He was exact in his accounts, exact in the words he spoke—which never had the colour of exaggeration about them—exact in his purchases and sales. When he had fixed his price he stood by it, so that no one ever thought of arguing with him to take a farthing less. . . .

But if we were to sum up all the qualities that conduced to his success at this period, all those mental characteristics that enabled him to prosecute his immense business single-handed, it would be expressed in the word *whole-heartedness.* . . . How many men drag out a miserable existence, owing to the very consciousness that they have been mistaken in their occupation? As a consequence of this, they have never followed it with their whole heart, they have always hankered after some-thing else, and that to which they have originally put their hands, has, of course, turned out a failure. Better for a young man carefully to watch the bias of his mind, and the particular taste evinced; then in that direction his future course ought to be steered. This is just nature giving a broad hint, and what she thus indicates is likely to prosper; then let him determine to succeed, and succeed he must. It was thus with Mr. Salt; his early proclivities found their true sphere in the occupation he now pursued.

Jeremy Bentham Champions Utilitarianism (1789–1832)

Jeremy Bentham (1748–1832) was an English reformer whose life spanned the Enlightenment, the French Revolution, and the post-Napoleonic era. *An Introduction to the Principles of Morals and Legislation* appeared in the year in which the Revolution erupted and exercised great influence on nineteenth-century reformers. The doctrine of utilitarianism, which Bentham described in this work (the first selection below), was applied to specific subjects in his numerous later books. The second selection is taken from one of these, the *Manual of Political Economy,* written late in his life. From *The Works of Jeremy Bentham,* ed. J. Bowring (Edinburgh, 1843), I, p. 103. II, p. 33.

I. THE PRINCIPLE OF UTILITY (1789)

I. Nature has placed mankind under the governance of two sovereign masters, *pain* and *pleasure*. It is for them alone to point out what we ought to do, as well as to determine what we shall do. On the one hand the standard of right and wrong, on the other the chain of causes and effects, are fastened to their throne. They govern us in all we do, in all we say, in all we think; every effort we can make to throw off our subjection, will serve but to demonstrate and confirm it. . . . The *principle of utility* recognizes this subjection, and assumes it for the foundation of that system, the object of which is to rear the fabric of felicity by the hands of reason and of law. . . .

II. By the principle of utility is meant that principle which approves or disapproves of every action whatsoever, according to the tendency which it appears to have to augment or diminish the happiness of the party whose interest is in question. . . .

III. By utility is meant that property in any object whereby it tends to produce benefit, advantage, pleasure, good, or happiness . . . as to prevent the happening of mischief, pain, evil, or unhappiness to the party whose interest is considered: if that party be the community in general, then the happiness of the community; if a particular individual, then the happiness of that individual. . . .

V. It is in vain to talk of the interest of the community without understanding what is the interest of the individual. A thing is said to promote the interest, or to be for the interest of an individual, when it tends to add to the sum total of his pleasures; or, what comes to the same thing, to diminish the sum total of his pains.

VI. An action then may be said to be conformable to the principle of utility, or, for shortness sake, to utility (meaning with respect to the community at large), when the tendency it has to augment the happiness of the community is greater than any it has to diminish it.

VII. A measure of government (which is but a particular kind of action, performed by a particular person or persons) may be said to be conformable to or dictated by the principle of utility, when in like manner the tendency which it has to augment the happiness of the community is greater than any which it has to diminish it.

VIII. When an action, or in particular a measure of government, is supposed by a man to be conformable to the principle of utility, it may be convenient, for the purposes of discourse, to imagine a kind of law or dictate, called a law or dictate of utility; and to speak of the action in question as being conformable to such law or dictate. . . .

II. UTILITY APPLIED TO ECONOMICS (1832)

According to the principle of utility in every branch of the art of legislation, the object or end in view should be the production of the maximum of happiness in a given time in the community in question.

In the instance of this branch of the art [legislation concerning economic matters], the object or end in view should be the production of that maximum of happiness, in so far as this more general end is promoted by the production of the maximum of wealth and the maximum of population.

The practical questions, therefore, are— how far the measures respectively suggested by these two branches of the common end agree?—how far they differ, and which requires the preference?—how far the end in view is best promoted by individuals acting for themselves?—and in what cases these ends may be best promoted by the hands of government? . . .

With the view of causing an increase to take place in the mass of national wealth, or with a view to increase of the means either of subsistence or enjoyment, without some special reason, the general rule is, that nothing ought to be done or attempted by government. The motto, or watchword of government, on these occasions, ought to be—*Be quiet.*

For this quietism there are two main reasons:

1. Generally speaking, any interference for this purpose on the part of the government is needless. The wealth of the whole community is composed of the wealth of the several individuals belonging to it taken together. But to increase his particular portion is, generally speaking, among the constant objects of each individual's exertions and care. Generally speaking, there is no one who knows what is for your interest so well as yourself—no one who is disposed with so much ardor and constancy to pursue it.

2. Generally speaking, it is moreover likely to be pernicious, viz., by being unconducive, or even obstructive, with reference to the attainment of the end in view. Each individual, bestowing more time and attention upon the means of preserving and increasing his portion of wealth than is or can be bestowed by government, is likely to take a more effectual course than what, in his instance and on his behalf, would be taken by government.

It is, moreover, universally and constantly pernicious in another way, by the restraint or constraint imposed on the free agency of the individual. Pain is the general concomitant of the sense of such restraint, wherever it is experienced. . . .

With few exceptions, and these not very considerable ones, the attainment of the maximum of enjoyment will be most effectually secured by leaving each individual to pursue his own maximum of enjoyment, in proportion as he is in possession of the means. Inclination in this respect will not be wanting on the part of anyone. Power, the species of power applicable to this case— viz., wealth, pecuniary power—could not be given by the hand of government to one without being taken from another; so that by such interference there would not be any gain of power upon the whole. . . .

David Thomson: Nineteenth-Century Liberalism and Democracy Defined

Basic to the value system of the nineteenth-century bourgeoisie were the philosophical principles known as liberalism. Here David Thomson, British historian and political scientist, defines the term and describes its genesis and its restless relationship in the early nineteenth century with its fellow traveler, democracy. From *Europe Since Napoleon,* by David Thomson. © Copyright 1957, 1962 by David Thomson. Reprinted by permission of Alfred A. Knopf, Inc.

Liberalism, in its continental European sense more clearly than its English or American sense, was like nationalism in that it rested on the belief that there should be a more organic and complete relationship between government and the community, between state and society, than existed under the dynastic regimes of the eighteenth century. Instead of government and administration existing above and in many respects apart from society—the exclusive affair of kings and their ministers and officials—they should rest on the organized consent of at least the most important sections of the community, and they ought to concern themselves with the interests of the whole community. The ideas that Americans had asserted in 1776 had still not been accepted by European governments: ideas that "governments are instituted among men" to secure individual rights, and derive "their just powers from the consent of the governed." European liberals stood, fundamentally, for these American ideals. The biggest obstacles to a broader basis of government were the powers and privileges of the aristocracy and the Church, and the lack of privileges of the merchant, business, and manufacturing classes. Thus the spearhead of the liberal attack against feudal rights and clericalist power was, in each European country, the underprivileged middle and professional classes. It was these classes, backed in the course of events by the peasants and by the Paris mob, that had been the central driving force of the French Revolution, and the chief gainers from it.

In doctrine, therefore, continental liberalism derived from the rationalist movement of the eighteenth century which had made so corrosive an attack upon inequality and arbitrary power. Its most characteristic method was parliamentary government; it sought in constitutional arrangements and in the rule of law a means of expressing middle-class interests and opinion, a vehicle of social reform, and a safeguard against absolutist government. It was distinct from democracy, or radicalism, in that it favored ideas of the sovereignty of parliamentary assemblies rather than of the sovereignty of the people; it wanted an extension of the franchise to include all men of property but to exclude men without property; it valued liberty more highly than equality; and it appealed to broadly the same classes as the growing sense of nationalism. . . .

Democracy resembled liberalism in that it derived its ideals from eighteenth-century rationalism and was equally opposed to the inequalities of the old order. It differed from it in holding to the view that sovereignty lay not in constitutional systems or in representative parliamentary assemblies, but in the "general will" of the whole people, as Rousseau had taught. It favored universal male suffrage, the subordination of parliamentary bodies to the will of the electorate as a whole, and even devices of direct democracy such as the plebiscite or the referendum. It was devoted to the ideal of equality of political and civil rights. In its more extreme forms it even demanded greater social and economic equality. Like liberals, democrats demanded equality of all before the law and equality of opportunity for all; but unlike liberals, they wanted to secure these rights even at the cost of greater economic leveling. For this reason, in the first half of the century democracy was treated as a more revolutionary and frightening doctrine than liberalism. The fear of Jacobinism, which haunted the conservative governments of Europe between 1815 and

1848, was partly the fear of the resurgence of French power; it was even more the fear of radical democracy. To resist this menace, liberals were often ready to join with conservatives to crush popular movements and uprisings that favored democratic ideals. The nearest twentieth-century counterpart to this fear was the universal fear of bolshevism after 1917: a fear irrational enough to produce strange alliances of otherwise incompatible and hostile forces, yet well enough founded to create a series of violent revolutions and savage repressions. Democracy, even more than liberalism, was a central cause of change and revolution in the century after Waterloo. . . .

John Stuart Mill Defines Liberty (1859)

John Stuart Mill (1806–1878) was a disciple of Bentham and was probably the most influential of English liberals. His classic and thoughtful defense draws the line between tyranny, liberty, and majority rule. From J. S. Mill, *On Liberty* (London, 1859), Chapter 1.

The subject of this Essay is not the so-called Liberty of the Will, so unfortunately opposed to the misnamed doctrine of Philosophical Necessity; but Civil, or Social Liberty: the nature and limits of the power which can be legitimately exercised by society over the individual. . . .

The struggle between Liberty and Authority is the most conspicuous feature in the portions of history with which we are earliest familiar, particularly in that of Greece, Rome, and England. But in old times this contest was between subjects, or some classes of subjects, and the Government. By liberty, was meant protection against the tyranny of the political rulers. . . . The aim, therefore, of patriots was to set limits to the power which the ruler should be suffered to exercise over the community; and this limitation was what they meant by liberty. . . .

In time, however, a democratic republic came to occupy a large portion of the earth's surface, and made itself felt as one of the most powerful members of the community of nations; and elective and responsible government became subject to the observations and criticisms which wait upon a great existing fact. It was now perceived that such phrases as "self-government," and "the power of the people over themselves," do not express the true state of the case. The "people" who exercise the power are not always the same people with those over whom it is exercised; and the "self-government" spoken of is not the government of each by himself, but of each by all the rest. The will of the people, moreover, practically means the will of the most numerous or the most active *part* of the people; the majority, or those who succeed in making themselves accepted as the majority; the people, consequently, *may* desire to oppress a part of their number; and precautions are as much needed against this as against any other abuse of power. The limitation, therefore, of the power of government over individuals loses none of its importance when the holders of power are regularly accountable to the community, that is, to the strongest party therein. This view of things, recommending itself equally to the intelligence of thinkers and to the inclination of those important classes in European society to whose real or supposed interests democracy is adverse, has had no difficulty in establishing itself; and in political speculations "the tyranny of the majority" is now generally included among the evils against which society requires to be on its guard.

Like other tyrants, the tyranny of the majority was at first, and is still, vulgarly, held in dread, chiefly as operating through the acts of the public authorities. But reflecting persons perceive that when society is itself the tyrant—society collectively, over the separate individuals who compose it—its means of tyrannizing are not restricted to the acts which it may do by the hands of its political functionaries. Society can and does execute its own mandates: and if it issues wrong mandates instead of right, or any mandates at all in things with which it ought not to meddle, it practises a social tyranny more formidable than many kinds of political oppression, since, though not usually upheld by such extreme penalties, it leaves fewer means of escape, penetrating much more deeply into the details of life, and enslaving the soul itself. Protection, therefore, against the tyranny of the magistrate is not enough: there needs protection also against the tyranny of the prevailing opinion and feeling; against the tendency of society to impose, by other means than civil penalties, its own ideas and practises as rules of conduct on those who dissent from them; to fetter the development, and, if possible, prevent the formation, of any individuality not in harmony with its ways, and compel all characters to fashion themselves upon the model of its own. There is a limit to the legitimate interference of collective opinion with individual independence: and to find that limit, and maintain it against encroachment, is as indispensable to a good condition of human affairs, as protection against political despotism. . . .

The object of this Essay is to assert one very simple principle, as entitled to govern absolutely the dealings of society with the individual in the way of compulsion and control, whether the means used be physical force in the form of legal penalties, or the moral coercion of public opinion. That principle is, that the sole end for which mankind are warranted, individually or collectively, in interfering with the liberty of action of any of their number, is self-protection. That the only purpose for which power can be rightfully exercised over any member of a civilised community, against his will, is to prevent harm to others. His own good, either physical or moral, is not a sufficient warrant. He cannot rightfully be compelled to do or forbear because it will be better for him to do so, because it will make him happier, because, in the opinions of others, to do so would be wise, or even right. These are good reasons for remonstrating with him or reasoning with him, or persuading him, or entreating him, but not for compelling him, or visiting him with any evil in case he do otherwise. To justify that, the conduct from which it is desired to deter him, must be calculated to produce evil to someone else. The only part of the conduct of anyone, for which he is amenable to society, is that which concerns others. In the part which merely concerns himself, his independence is, of right, absolute. Over himself, over his own body and mind, the individual is sovereign.

STUDY QUESTIONS

1. What was the bourgeoisie? How is its growth connected with the scientific revolution? How were the middle classes affected by such Enlightenment ideas as progress, the social contract, popular sovereignty, and Adam Smith's economic theories?

2. What were the values of the middle classes?

3. Why were the writings of Samuel Smiles so popular in the nineteenth century? What view of society did Smiles have? How would he have evaluated the life of Titus Salt? Does Salt seem like a modern businessman?

4. What did Bentham mean by the principle of utility? By the "happiness of the community"? Could you make an argument that Bentham is a transitional figure between the eighteenth and nineteenth centuries? Why did his theories appeal to the bourgeoisie?

5. Define the meaning of liberalism in the early nineteenth century on the basis of today's readings. How did liberalism differ from democracy? What did the middle classes want and to what were they opposed?

6. How did Mill define liberty? What did he mean by "tyranny of the majority"?

TOPIC 31

POLITICS AND THE MIDDLE CLASSES

The new economic and social eminence gained by the middle classes in the industrializing countries of Western Europe did not, however, easily open to them the doors of political power. In the early nineteenth century the right of participation in government remained limited to hereditary landowners and the very rich. Thus defense of constitutional liberties and extension of the right to vote were natural goals to which the middle classes directed their attention. These goals men preferred to attain by peaceable reform of existing institutions, but when the forces of the status quo refused to bend, the middle classes turned to revolutionary action. The readings examine both paths to political change by focusing on England and France in the 1820s and 1830s.

The Middle Class Seeks Political Power

From *Europe Since Napoleon,* by David Thomson. © Copyright 1957, 1962 by David Thomson. Reprinted by permission of Alfred A. Knopf, Inc.

I. LAND AS A BASIS FOR POLITICAL POWER

The upheavals of the years between 1789 and 1815 in France brought an unprecedented transference of landed property from great landowners and great corporations (particularly the Church) to a number of smaller property owners. . . . When Napoleon came to power he found large stocks of land still not sold or granted away, and from this he endowed a new Napoleonic aristocracy. It was drawn mainly from middle-class people who as soldiers, lawyers, or bureaucrats served his dictatorship. Usually these new landowners simply stepped into the shoes of the old, and leased the land for rent to farmers who cultivated it. The general effect seems to have been considerable acquisitions of land by the middle classes, and some acquisition by the peasants. . . . At the restoration there were still unsold national lands, and these were mostly returned to their former aristocratic owners. It was impossible for the king to meet the nobles' demands that their property rights be completely restored, for even to attempt this would have alienated too large a proportion of the population. But by repurchase and regrant, it is thought that by 1820 the old nobility had made good about half its losses—a proportion big enough to give the returned *émigrés* great political power.

The limited diffusion of landed property involved a correspondingly limited extension of political rights. The equation between land and political power remained intact. It was, on the whole, the old aristocracy, the wealthy capitalist bourgeoisie, and the most substantial peasant proprietors who gained from the redistribution of land. The bulk of the land of France was still, therefore, owned by a relatively small class, though it was a differently constituted and somewhat larger class than in 1789. Political power was confined to this class by the simple device of fixing the qualification for voting for the new French parliament in terms of the amount of money paid annually in direct taxation. The vote for the Chamber of Deputies went only to citizens who were 30 years of age or more and paid at least 300 francs a year in direct taxation. The electorate was thus only some 90,000 in a population of 30 million. To be a deputy a man had to be over 40 and pay at least 1000 francs a year in direct taxation, and he was indirectly elected. In addition, parliamentary power was shared with an upper chamber, the House of Peers, in which sat the higher aristocracy and clergy. The rights of landed wealth were in these ways deeply entrenched in the new monarchy, and this was a guarantee that its whole policy would be intensely conservative. . . . Between 1814 and 1830 the restored monarchy rested on a balance between the powers of the old aristocracy, now much depleted and impoverished, and the power of the new business oligarchy, rapidly growing in power. . . . The aristocracy became more an office-holding than a landowning class. It shared power, in effect with the wealthy *bourgeois* who owned a landed estate on which he paid heavy taxes, and the wealthier manufacturer who paid taxes on his membership in a corporation.

The regime represented a balance and a compromise between aristocracy and oligarchy, and the working of the corrupt parliament held little interest for the mass of the nation. The Chamber of Deputies had a permanent majority on the right, and a permanent minority on the left. No party system was possible, and opposition had to content itself with spasmodic attacks and a running fire of verbal criticism of the government, without prospect of assuming ministerial responsibilities. As under the *ancien régime,* government remained exclusively the job of the king and his ministers, and the principle of ministerial responsibility to parliament was neither fully understood nor practically possible.

In Britain, where demands for parliamentary reform had been smothered by the exigencies of the long wars against France and by the reaction against the ideas of Jacobinism, similar arrangements existed. There, too, the landed aristocracy of the eighteenth century, reinforced by the ennobled generals, admirals, and administrators of the war years and by the faster-growing class of financiers, merchants, and manufacturers, virtually monopolized state power. The House of Lords, from which most ministers of the Crown were still drawn, preserved its control over legislation. Through individual influence and patronage the aristocracy controlled a large share of the borough representation in the House of Commons. The electorate was determined by an antiquated and complicated system of property qualifications which gave the vote to only some 400,000 men, and effective power to the landed gentry in the countryside and the large landowners and men of wealth in the towns. The regular system of patronage, corruption, and intimidation secured the return of a high proportion of placemen and younger sons of the nobility. The Landed Property Qualification Acts stipulated that members of Parliament for the counties must own a landed estate of at least £600 a year; and for the boroughs, a landed estate of £300 a year.

The larger part played by trade and industry in the life of Britain than in the life of France was reflected in the fact that in Britain the *bourgeoisie* had staked for themselves a larger share in power, alongside the aristocracy. But the principles on which the regime rested were very similar. Parliament existed to represent not persons but property: despite the clamor of radical reformers, the changes made before 1815 had merely admitted certain forms of wealth other than landed property to a very limited share in power. The predominance of the landed and agricultural interests in 1815 is shown well enough by the Corn Law passed in that year; it gave farmers protection by prohibiting the import of corn from abroad until the price at home had reached the high level of 80 shillings a quarter. It is shown, too, by the maintenance of the harsh Game Laws, which made it illegal for anyone to buy and sell game. In 1816 these old restrictions were added to; a new law provided that the cottager caught with his snares at night, in quest of a hare or a rabbit, could be transported for seven years. . . .

II. THE RESTORED MONARCHY IN FRANCE

The restoration [in France] rested on a Charter, granted by Louis XVIII in 1814, and in this respect it was fundamentally different from the monarchy of Louis XVI. The existing Legislature drew up a draft constitution that, on May 2, 1814, Louis XVIII accepted in principle. He announced that he was returning to his ancestral throne, but that he would invite members of the Senate and the Legislative Body to help him to draw up a constitution. This was duly done by June 4. Its first articles guaranteed certain fundamental liberties: equality before the law and equal eligibility for civil and military office; freedom from arbitrary arrest and trial, freedom of conscience, worship, and expression; inviolability of private property, including purchases of the national lands. Political opinions and actions prior to the restoration would not be inquired into. France was given a system of parliamentary government with two chambers and responsibility of ministers. The restored monarchy was in form a constitutional, parliamentary regime, designed to safeguard individual rights.

On the other hand, the forms and ideas of an absolute and hereditary monarchy were also preserved alongside these provisions. Louis claimed that he had really been king since his brother's execution, and referred to 1814 as "the nineteenth year of our reign." He insisted in the preamble to the constitution that it was granted "voluntarily, and by the free exercise of our royal authority." Whereas royalists could point out that what the king had given he could also take away, constitutionalists could point to the king's oath that he would keep the conditions laid

The specter of a return to a church-dominated state and a feudal social order was raised by Charles X's coronation at Rheims. After receiving his crown from the Archbishop, Charles received homage from his eldest son. The Duke of Orleans, later to reign as Louis-Philippe, awaits his turn to the left of the king.

down in it. These ambiguities and inconsistencies of the new regime betray its effort to find a compromise between monarchy and liberalism.

Divine right and constitutional limitations were uneasy bedfellows. Yet they might have reached eventual harmony had Louis been succeeded by a monarch of equal tact and similar determination not to go on his travels again. The Bourbon restoration in France repeated the story of the Stuart restoration in England after 1660. Just as Charles II was succeeded by his more intransigent brother, James II, who forfeited the throne after three years, so Louis XVIII was succeeded in 1824 by his unstatesmanlike brother, Charles X, who forfeited the throne after six years. . . .

A further factor of importance was France's relative inexperience with working parliamentary institutions. In this respect France was very different from Great Britain. British constitutional government was able to de-velop, even during the period of die-hard conservatism and repression, because behind it lay centuries of practical experience in how representative institutions could impose controls on kings and parliamentary procedures on their ministers. French parliamentary traditions were only a quarter of a century old in 1815, and the record of representative assemblies in France was broken, turbulent, and inconclusive. In Britain a series of subtle conventions, not laid down in any charter, determined the conditions on which governments could secure a reliable parliamentary majority, the circumstances in which they must resign or in which they could expect the monarch to dissolve parliament and appeal to the electorate, the procedures of parliamentary debate, and above all the responsibilities of ministers, individually and collectively, to the House of Commons. Some of these conventions and almost tacit understandings were of fairly recent date; but by 1815 they were accepted without challenge. . . .

When Charles X succeeded to the throne [of France] in September, [1814] the ultra-conservatives felt that they had a free hand. . . . They proceeded to carry out much of their original program. Control of education was given to the Church by making a bishop minister of education. An indemnity, amounting in practice to some 650,000 francs, was paid to the *émigrés* who had lost their estates. The first of these measures flouted the anticlericalist sentiments of the *bourgeoisie*, the second attacked their pockets. The money was found by converting 5 per cent annuities into annuities of 3 per cent.

Charles insisted on being crowned at Reims with the elaborate ritual of the *ancien régime*, and this was taken as symbolic of his intention to revive the whole of the prerevolutionary order. When the Jesuits reappeared and sacrilege was made a crime punishable by death, widespread fears of an extreme clericalist reaction were aroused. The government's attacks on its liberal critics, the prosecutions of publishers and the imprisonment of journalists, solidified liberal opposition. Though opposition was not strong inside parliament, it gained in strength in the country. The extremist policy, moreover, split the

ranks of the royalists themselves, for many churchmen feared and opposed the power of the Jesuits. At the elections of 1827 the opposition gained a majority of 60. . . .

The open clash came in March, 1830, when the Chamber reminded the king that "the permanent harmony of the political views of your Government with the wishes of your people is the indispensable condition for the conduct of public affairs." That was the permanent constitutional issue of the restoration: should ministers be responsible to the king alone, or to parliament? When Charles dissolved the Chamber, he was asserting that they must be responsible to him alone; and when the elections of July returned an opposition that was 53 stronger than before, the king was obliged to fall back on royal prerogatives and attempt a virtual *coup d'état.* In itself an admission that constitutional monarchy had failed in France under a Bourbon king, this was a signal for open battle between king and country. The result, the Revolution of July, is described below. . . .

THE QUESTION OF POLITICAL REFORM IN BRITAIN

The comparison with contemporary happenings in Britain is illuminating. There, with parliamentary traditions, conventions, and habits well established and generally accepted, constitutional government worked more smoothly. Tory [Conservative] governments held power under Lord Liverpool until 1827, and then under George Canning, Lord Goderich, and the Duke of Wellington until 1830. Prudent financial policies and the businesslike handling of public affairs encouraged a revival of economic prosperity after the agricultural depression of 1815–1816 and the commercial crisis of 1819. In Britain, as in

France, more liberal and radical reforms were stubbornly resisted. But conservatism in Britain was more ready than was royalism in France to make timely concessions and to place public welfare above party interests. . . .

Toryism had, too, a certain philosophy. It regarded social distress and economic depression as evils entirely divorced from politics—as afflictions that any society must from time to time suffer because of bad harvest or disturbance of trade. Political agitation that played upon conditions of social distress and held out hopes of betterment through political reform seemed, therefore, both irresponsible (since it might endanger public order) and hypocritical (since it raised false hopes). The purpose of. . .repression in general was to prevent political agitation from penetrating lower socially than the relatively well-educated middle classes. For popular orators to preach radicalism to mass meetings of hungry and ill-educated men in the winter of their distress was little short of revolutionary activity. This attitude was shared by Tories and Whigs alike: the growing mass of the laboring classes were unfit to take any responsible or intelligent part in politics; in time, with prudent government, their lot might improve; but radicalism and democracy bred only dangerous delusions.

In the 1820's radicalism in England became more quiescent. The harshness of repression had scared off many agitators. Improvements in material prosperity softened the economic distress that had nourished popular excitement. A generous though wasteful system of poor relief, administered locally and financed by poor rates, saved the most destitute from starvation. Interest in parliamentary reform declined until 1830, when the revolution in France and the fall of the Bourbon monarchy

Ten of the demonstrators were killed and hundreds injured as armed troops attacked a crowd of people gathered to hear speeches on parliamentary reforms at St. Peter's Field in Manchester in August 1819. The event, known as the Peterloo Massacre, was followed by more repressive legislation.

revived hopes of democratic advance. George IV died on June 26, 1830, and the general elections that followed took place amid the exciting news from Paris.

The London Radical Reform Association and the Birmingham Political Union directed the excitement toward hopes of parliamentary reform in England. Once again conservatives came to feel that some kind of overhaul of the electoral system could not much longer be postponed. When that autumn the Duke of Wellington went out of his way to defend the existing constitution, his government was defeated within a fortnight. The Whig minis-

try headed by Lord Grey, which succeeded him, was from the outset pledged to a reform bill. Grey held that timely concession to a sustained and widespread popular demand was the right policy, not in the sense that it should be a first step toward broader democracy but rather that it should be a final settlement and reconciliation between the governing aristocracy and the nation. His ministry was solidly aristocratic in its composition, and when rural disturbances and urban strikes broke out the government repressed them with all the old severity. The Whigs were at one with the Tories in resisting democracy

and in crushing popular movements; they differed from the Tories only in a more realistic readiness to forestall more violent pressures by the timely granting of moderate reforms, which would 'afford sure ground of resistance to further innovation.''. . .

THE REVOLUTIONARY TIDE

The second half of the year 1830 saw revolutions in France, Belgium, parts of Germany, Italy, and Switzerland, and in Poland. In Portugal and Spain civil war began, which lasted in Spain until 1840. These revolutions were unlike the risings of 1820, which were liberal revolts led by broader elements of the wealthy middle classes. They were primarily protests against the rigidities and shortcomings of the conservative policies adopted since 1815; and the limited extent of their purposes and their success derived from the economic conditions already described. What they had in common was a desire to bring governments into closer relationship with society, as society had developed up to that date. When the course of events carried the revolutionary movements beyond that point, they lost impetus and were checked.

The July Revolution in France

In France the liberal opposition to the ultra-conservative government of Charles X was able to take its stand on the Charter of 1814. As a result of the elections of July, 1830, the liberal opposition in the Chamber grew from 221 to 274. Polignac's ministry decided on a *coup d'état*. It took the legitimist royalist form of issuing a set of five Ordinances of July 25. These dissolved the newly elected Chamber before it could meet, reduced the electorate from 100,000 to 25,000, called for new elections on this basis, and forbade any publication not authorized by the government. In spirit, if not entirely in the letter, they destroyed the Charter and the existing constitution. The liberal politicians and journalists, led by men like Adolphe Thiers, Francois Guizot, and the banker Jacques Laffitte, met to draw up protests, defy the prohibition of free publication, and bring the force of public opinion to bear upon the king. On the day after the fateful Ordinances appeared, crowds formed in the streets of Paris; and on the day after that the republican groups . . . organized bands of students and workers to throw up the barricades. On July 28 these groups captured the Hôtel de Ville (seizure of the city hall being the traditional prelude to Paris revolutions). They raised the tricolor flag, the red, white and blue of the revolution, and paraded in the boulevards. The royal troops were without guidance or direction because of the inaction of the king and his ministers, and lost control of the city. By July 30 the rebels had complete mastery of the capital, and Charles X abdicated in favor of his grandson, the Duke of Bordeaux, henceforth known to his supporters as "Henry V." The downfall of the Bourbons was almost bloodless.

The insurgents were divided as to what to do next. The more democratic republicans, with headquarters at the Hôtel de Ville, wanted to set up a republic under the presidency of the eminent Lafayette, now 74, the "hero of two worlds" and idol of the National Guard. The liberal politicians and journalists, as the parliamentary majority under the existing constitution, wanted to make the Duke of Orleans king. . . . Descended from a younger brother of Louis XIV, the Orleans family had been the traditional rivals to the Bourbon kings. The Duke's father, "Equality

Philip" (*Philippe Egalité*) had conspired against Louis XVI, and during the Revolution he had adopted republican and revolutionary ideas—though these had not saved him from the guillotine in 1793. The Duke himself had known poverty and exile, but was now a wealthy, thrifty man of 57. He resolved to play the role of citizen king, model of bourgeois virtues and respectful of constitutional liberties. . . . He captured republican support by visiting Lafayette at the Hôtel de Ville on July 31, relying on the fact that that conservatively minded hero preferred monarchy to Jacobinism. When he appeared on the balcony with Lafayette and the two men embraced one another wrapped in an enormous tricolor, the Paris crowds went mad with delight. This kiss won him republican support as well as the support of the National Guard, of which Lafayette was now commander. Charles X fled to England, prudently taking his grandson with him, and a week later parliament declared the throne to be vacant. Within two days it proclaimed Orleans king as Louis Philippe, "King of the French by the Grace of God and the will of the nation." Consolidation of the constitutional monarchy seemed complete, and the revolution, skillfully manufactured in Paris, was accepted with little resistance by the whole of France.

With the form of the regime so quickly settled by the "Three Glorious Days" (July 27–29) the parliament now proceeded to revise the Charter and impose it upon the new king. The revisions indicate clearly the liberal ideals of the majority. The Chamber of Peers was weakened in its hereditary character by being turned into an upper house of life members only, nominated by the king, and a batch of new peers were created to guarantee the change. The electorate was

widened by lowering the age qualification for voters to 25 instead of 30, and the property qualification from 300 francs to 200. Citizens were eligible to become deputies at the age of 30 instead of 40. Censorship was abolished, cases involving the press were referred to trial by jury, and extraordinary tribunals or judicial commissions were prohibited. Roman Catholicism was recognized as the religion of "the majority of Frenchmen," but the connection between altar and throne was ended, some religious orders were expelled, and provision was made for state-aided primary schools to be set up in each commune.

The men who imposed these conditions on the king had clear ideas of what they wanted. They did not want universal suffrage or democracy; they did not want a republic, too closely associated in France with Jacobinism and extreme democracy; they did not want to found the new regime on revolution, or even on a plebiscite—hence the maneuvers, engineered by Laffitte and his friends, to place on the throne a man who combined the necessary credentials of royal descent with a personal readiness to accept the restraints of the Charter and of ministerial responsibility to parliament. The merit of the new regime, in their eyes, was that it got rid of the absolutist and clericalist proclivities of the Bourbons while guaranteeing property and public order against the encroachments of democracy and republicanism. It held a balance between liberty and order, parliamentarism and authority. It would from the outset have bitter enemies—the clerical and the legitimist royalists, who regarded Louis Philippe and his supporters as traitors; the republicans, who felt cheated; the surviving enthusiasts for Bonapartism. Like every other regime France has had since 1815, it was confronted with a large and disloyal opposition, which regarded it as a fraud and a betrayal. But it would, its supporters hoped, give France a period of peace, prosperity, and settled order in which trade and industry could flourish and men could grow rich in security. This, the king knew, was the commission he had been given. His personal tastes and inclinations coincided happily with these expectations. His chief interests were to stay on the throne and to stay rich. . . . He was, in short, everything that a liberal king in 1830 could be expected to be: middle class, respectable, and unspectacular. . . .

Parliamentary Reform in Great Britain

The British counterpart to the liberal revolutions of these years was the great parliamentary Reform Bill passed in 1832. As already described, the ministry of Lord Grey came to power in the autumn of 1830 pledged to promote a bill for reform of the electoral system. The first bill he introduced passed the House of Commons by a majority of only one vote, and Grey demanded fresh elections, which were fought amid great excitement on the main issue of parliamentary reform. This reference of a major constitutional issue to the electorate was itself an implicit concession to liberal ideas. These elections gave the Whigs, led by Grey, a majority in the House of Commons, but the bill was twice defeated in the House of Lords, which had a Tory majority. It was only after Grey had forced the Lords into passing the bill, by the threat that the king would create enough new peers to give the Whigs a majority in the Lords, that they gave way; William IV had agreed to so drastic a threat only because there was no other practicable alternative; Grey had already resigned and Wellington, the Tory leader, not

having the confidence of the country, had refused to take office. The bill was in this way prefaced by events that vividly coerced both king and Lords into bowing to the wishes of the Commons and of public opinion. . . .

The "Act to amend the representation of the people in England and Wales," which eventually passed through parliament in 1832, was very much less democratic in effect than either its title or the stormy events that preceded its enactment might suggest. The most substantial change it made was to redistribute the strength of the constituencies. The House of Commons consisted, as before, of 658 members elected for boroughs and counties. But whereas 262 boroughs had returned 465 members, only 257 now returned 399; and whereas county members had been 188 they now numbered 253. The universities of Oxford, Cambridge, and Dublin each returned two representatives. These changes, which strengthened the power of the country gentry and the big towns at the expense of the landed proprietors and boroughmongers who had controlled scores of small borough constituencies, gave more weight in politics to the wealthy business and commercial classes of the large northern towns, hitherto greatly underrepresented in parliament. Of the small towns, 86 lost the right to return either one or two members to the Commons. These included some, such as the notorious Old Sarum, which had long ceased to be towns at all and whose representatives had been virtually nominated by the "borough owner." At the same time 22 new boroughs were allowed to return two members each, and 21 others one member each; and these were the big new towns, mostly in the north, which had grown up around the ports, industries, and mines. These changes were not great enough to destroy the preponderance of the

landed interest. There remained nearly 50 boroughs and well over 60 members still directly dependent on the peers and landowners of England and Wales. But the men whose wealth depended on trade and manufacturing were given a share of parliamentary power alongside the old landed interest—a share large enough to enable them to assert their interests, as subsequent legislation was to show.

At the same time the Act protected both landed and industrial interests against the dangers of democracy by a host of other provisions, the chief of which were the changes in the qualification for voting. These remained complex, but all depended on property qualifications. In the boroughs a voter had to be owner or tenant of a property worth at least £10 annual value. This effectively kept out of the electorate all the working classes, confined it to men of some wealth and social standing. The old electorate of less than half a million was increased by about 50 per cent in England and Wales. No provision was made for secret ballot, which meant that the old methods of bribery, influence, and intimidation at elections remained as effective as ever. . . . Yet the electoral system succeeded in returning to the Commons, now enhanced in its prestige and powers in relation to king or Lords, men who broadly represented the main interests and opinions of the country. The radical democrats, whose agitation had done so much to bring about the reform, remained as bitterly disappointed as were the contemporary republicans of France after the July Revolution. It was the Whigs who had won the day; though by effecting this first deliberate overhaul of the parliamentary system they had made it more difficult, in future, to resist further such changes when the mass of opinion in the country demanded them. . . .

Frenchmen Call for Resistance against Charles X (July 1830)

The July Ordinances of the reactionary ministers of Charles X suspended the freedom of the press, dissolved the French legislature, and reduced the size of the electorate. On July 27, 1830, more than sixty deputies issued the protest found in the first selection. The political leadership of the revolution came from the disaffected bourgeoisie, whose cause, championed by the press and the parliamentary opposition, ultimately led to a show of force in the streets of Paris. The heaviest street fighting took place, however, in the most congested sections of the city where the young and the poor provided most of the rebels at the barricades. The poor had joined the political agitation for reasons of their own. A serious depression beginning in 1828 brought growing unemployment, rising bread prices, and general misery. Typical of hundreds of handbills distributed among the Parisian populace is the call to resistance in the second selection. I. From Jean Duvergier (ed.), *Collection complète des lois de 1788 à 1830* (Paris, 1834–1906), v. 30, p. 81 in John Hall Stewart, *The Restoration Era in France, 1814–1830* (Princeton, N.J., 1968; Van Nostrand), p. 168. II. In the collection of the Bibliotheque Nationale, reproduced in Charles Ledré, *La presse à l'assaut de la monarchie, 1815–1848* (Paris: Armand Colin, 1960) p. 111. Trans. D. P. Resnick.

I. PROTEST OF PARIS DEPUTIES, JULY 27, 1830

The undersigned . . . consider themselves absolutely obliged by their duty and their honor to protest against the measures that the councillors of the crown have recently brought into effect for the overthrow of the legal system of elections and the ruin of the freedom of the press.

The said measures, contained in the ordinances of July 25, are, in the eyes of the undersigned, directly contrary to the constitutional rights of the Chamber of Peers, to

the public law of the French, to the prerogatives and decrees of the courts, and are calculated to throw the entire State into a confusion that would compromise both present peace and future security.

Accordingly, the undersigned, inviolably faithful to their oath, protest with one accord, not only against the said measures, but also against all acts which may be the consequence thereof.

And seeing, on the one hand, that the Chamber of Deputies, not having been constituted, cannot be legally dissolved; and on the other, that the attempt to form another Chamber of Deputies by a new and arbitrary method is in formal contradiction to the Constitutional Charter and the acquired rights of the electors, the undersigned declare that they still consider themselves as legally elected . . . and that they cannot be replaced except by virtue of elections conducted according to the principles and forms determined by law.

If the undersigned do not effectively exercise the rights and do not perform all the duties that derive from their legal action, it is because they have been prevented from so doing by physical violence.

II. PARIS HANDBILL,
JULY, 1830

Frenchmen!
All means of defense are legitimate. Remove the paving stones from the streets. Scatter them here and there about a foot apart to slow down the charge of the cavalry and infantry. Carry as many paving stones as possible to the second, third, and all floors above, piling up at least twenty to thirty at each window. Wait quietly until the troops are pinned down in the middle of the streets before letting go.

All Frenchmen should leave their doors, hallways and alleyways open as a place of refuge for our own fighters and come to their aid. Be calm and without fear. The troops will never dare to enter, certain as they must be of the death that awaits them.

It would be well that one person remain at each door to assist the safe passage of our fighters.

Frenchmen! Our salvation is in our own hands. Would we want to abandon it? Who among us would not prefer death to slavery?

III. AN ARTIST CAPTURES THE SPIRIT OF THE JULY REVOLUTION

The Romantic movement in art was at its height in 1830. Eugene Delacroix (1798–1863) caught the romantic fervor of the 1830 revolution in his famous painting *Liberty Leading the People*. Note Delacroix' inclusion of the unlikely allies that found themselves united on the barricades. At Liberty's right is a top-hatted member of the bourgeoisie followed by sturdy representatives of the working class; at her left a pistol-packing Paris street urchin. Participation of the lower classes in revolt against authority, welcomed momentarily by the bourgeoisie, offered a less desirable portent for the bourgeois future.

Francois Guizot Assesses the Revolutionary Movement (1831 and 1834)

Francois Guizot was Professor of Modern History at the Sorbonne under the Restoration and a leader of its political opposition. After the Revolution of 1830 in which he participated, he began a varied career in public office, serving as prime minister for the last eight years of the Constitutional Monarchy (1840–1848). He was an ardent defender of the French bourgeoisie and in his historical writings praised its contribution to the development of France. The selections below are taken from two speeches made before the French parliament. From M. Guizot, *Histoire parlementaire de France* (Paris, 1863), pp. 220–225 in T. Mendenhall, B. Henning, and A. Foord, *The Quest for a Principle of Authority in Europe, 1715–Present* (New York: Holt, Rinehart and Winston, Inc., 1948), pp. 144–145, 147.

I. THE MIDDLE CLASS AND POLITICAL REVOLUTION, 1831

Each epoch has its special task. The Revolution of 1789 was under obligation to destroy the *ancien régime;* it accomplished this with principles and powers which were adequate for the job, but when it tried to apply these principles and these powers to something else, when it tried to establish its own government with these principles and powers which had just destroyed the *ancien régime,* it was able to give us nothing but tyranny mixed with anarchy. We had this combination in two forms, powerful under the Convention, weak under the Directory.

The Revolution destroyed the *ancien régime* but was unable to do more. The Empire arose to re-establish order, order of an exterior, material sort which was the basis of the civil society as the Revolution had founded it. The Empire spread this idea throughout all of Europe; this was its mission and it succeeded at it. It was incapable, however, of establishing a lasting political government; the necessary conditions were lacking. The Empire fell in its turn, to be succeeded by the Restoration.

What did the Restoration [of the Bourbons in 1814] promise? It promised to resolve the problem, to reconcile order with liberty. It was under this banner that the charter was granted. The Restoration bore a principle within itself. It had accepted principles of liberty in the charter; it had promised to establish them, but it made this promise under the cloak of the *ancien régime,* on which there had been written for so many centuries: *Divine Right.* It was unable to solve the problem. It died in the process, overwhelmed by the burden.

It is on us, on the Revolution of July, that this job has been imposed; it is our duty and responsibility to establish definitively, not order alone, not liberty alone, but order and liberty at the same time. There is no way of escaping this double duty. Yes, gentlemen, our duty is twofold. We are commissioned to establish at the same moment the principle and the institutions of order, the principle and the institutions of liberty: there is the promise of the Revolution of July. . . .

It has many ways to accomplish this task, this twofold mission; but in its own nature, in the nature of the events which created it, it runs into great obstacles. It is unquestionably the most necessary, the most legitimate, of the revolutions which have been accomplished in the world; but essentially, it is a revolution, that is to say, a tremendous overthrow of the government and of society through the intervention of material force. Now these are the basic facts of our revolution which produced on the one hand its glory and on the other its peril. The greatest difficulty, perhaps, which it had to overcome, the source of nearly all its present problems, is that it was the work of material force; not the work of an established power, of a legal force, it was the result of popular action, a glorious title, but at *the* same time one contrary to the regular state of society. Every revolution accomplished in this manner is by its very nature an antisocial fact from which it is difficult to escape. . . .

II. THE MIDDLE CLASS AND SOCIAL REVOLUTION, 1834

The French Revolution, as has been often said, was less of a political revolution than a social revolution. It changed, displaced, upset property, influence, and power. It established the middle class upon debris of the old aristocracy. If the middle class, once arrived at this position, had barricaded itself, had shut itself up behind a triple hedge of privilege, monopolies, and exclusive rights, as was the case three or four hundred years ago, I would then understand the revolt, the upheaval which would have been attempted against this class by some other section of our society. But there is nothing in it, absolutely nothing. The middle class has remained without privileges, without monopolies, and does not even possess (if you will allow me to say so) a sufficiently energetic awareness of its own

The smugness, scorn, and indifference of the ruling elite are reflected in the features of Louis-Philippe, as caricatured by Daumier (1834). The king closes his eyes benignly to the past, blindly scorns the present, and gazes with trepidation at the future. His somewhat pear-shaped head was a favorite butt of cartoonists.

rights and its own power. What the middle class lacks among us is enough self-confidence in itself and its power. It is still timid and uncertain; it does not know how to exercise, with sufficient resolution, all the political power which belongs to it and which

can only belong to it. It is therefore a little strange to accuse this class of privilege and tyranny, to say that it is the middle class that is halting the forward movement of society. Gentlemen, I do not understand how such words can be seriously said in an assembly of enlightened men. With us liberty is found at every level; the forward movement is nowhere arrested. With work, common sense, and good conduct one rises, one rises as high as is possible in our social scale. The middle class, therefore, has not succeeded to the situation and to the privileges of the old aristocracy.

Nevertheless, gentlemen, war has been declared against this class; beneath your very eyes a new social revolution is being attempted, a new effort made to relocate property, influence, and power. Several times the property and the family have been directly attacked. When this direct attack has resulted in general disapproval, indirect methods are then used; it is said that wealth is poorly distributed, that the relations between the proletariat and the men of property are poorly arranged. Some sort of theory concerning workers and wastrels is invented in order to carry the war to the middle class. . . .

Whoever does not work with his hands, or does not write, is a wastrel. You, gentlemen, who come here to give your time and money, your leisure in the public service, you are wastrels. (*Laughter from the center*) You are wastrels who devour the substance of the working classes. . . .

This, gentlemen, is the new theory in political economy, which has been developed to attack the middle class; these are the absurd, even primitive arguments which are used to trouble our society, to menace us with a new social revolution.

The English Reform Bill of 1832

In R. R. Palmer, ed., *Atlas of World History* (Chicago: Rand McNally and Company, 1957).

The map shows the counties or shires of England, which have not changed appreciably since the tenth century. It also reduces to simple terms the great Reform Bill of 1832. From the origins of Parliament in the thirteenth century down to 1832 there had never been any general rearrangement of representation in the House of Commons. Each English county sent two members to the House. Towns having the right to be represented were called boroughs; most boroughs sent two members each. Many old boroughs had declined or failed to grow since the Middle Ages. Many rapidly growing towns, like Manchester, were not boroughs, and hence were represented only through their county members. Population had also grown substantially in the north, where before the eighteenth century it had always been very thin.

The map shows the net effect of the Reform Bill. The figure within each county shows the number of seats in the House of Commons (both county and borough seats) gained or lost by that county. Note that almost all losses were in the south, and that almost all gains were in the Midlands and in the north where population was accumulating in the course of the Industrial Revolution. The abolition of decayed boroughs made seats available for redistribution without increasing the size of the House.

The Reform Bill of 1832 marked a great social transformation, not because it enlarged

ENGLISH REFORM BILL 1832

Counties gaining six or more county and borough members of the House of Commons in 1832

Counties gaining five or less

Counties sustaining a net loss through reduction of boroughs and those sustaining no net change

SCOTLAND

Northumberland
+3

Durham
+6

Cumberland
+3

Westmorland
−1

North Riding
0

YORK

Lancashire
+11

West Riding
+6

East Riding
−1

Cheshire
+7

Derby
+2

Lincoln
+1

Nottingham
+2

Shropshire
0

Stafford
+8

Leicester
+2

Rutland
0

Norfolk
0

WALES

Worcester
+2

Warwick
+4

North-ampton
−1

Huntingdon
0

Cambridge
+1

Hereford
−1

Bedford
0

Suffolk
−5

Monmouth
0

Oxford
0

Buckingham
−3

Hertford
+1

Essex
+4

Gloucester
+5

Middlesex
+4

Berkshire
0

Wiltshire
−15

Surrey
−3

Kent
0

Somerset
−4

Hampshire
−7

Sussex
−10

Devon
−4

Dorset
−6

Cornwall
−28

the electorate, which it did only slightly, but because by its redistribution of seats it shared political power between the landed aristocracy and the new business interests of Lancashire and the Midlands. Democratization began with the Reform Bill of 1867, by which about a third of adult males in the United Kingdom received the vote.

Thomas Macaulay Supports Parliamentary Reform (1831)

Thomas Babington Macaulay (1800–1859) is remembered as one of England's foremost historians. He was also a reforming liberal and was a member of Parliament at the time of the agitation for the Great Reform Bill. The following speech was made on March 2, 1831, early in the struggle to get the Bill passed. From *Speeches of Lord Macaulay* (London, 1875).

I

One noble Lord has to-night told us that the town of Aldborough, which he represents, was not larger in the time of Edward the First than it is at present. The line of its walls, he assures us, may still be traced. It is now built up to that line. He argues, therefore, that as the founders of our representative institutions gave members to Aldborough when it was as small as it now is, those who would disfranchise it on account of its smallness have no right to say that they are recurring to the original principle of our representative institutions. But does the noble Lord remember

429

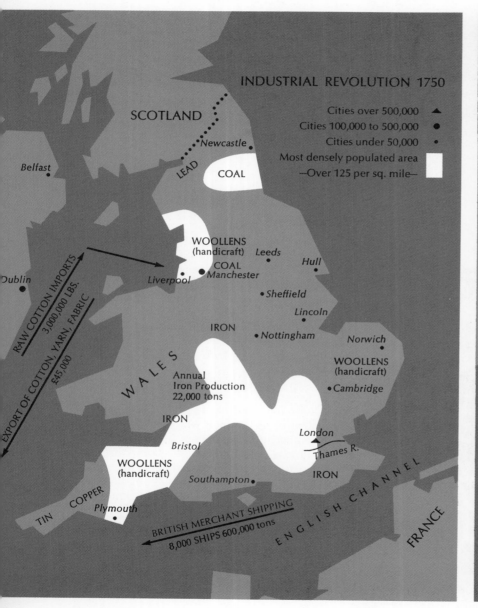

INDUSTRIAL REVOLUTION 1750

SCOTLAND

Belfast

Newcastle

LEAD

COAL

Cities over 500,000 ▲
Cities 100,000 to 500,000 ●
Cities under 50,000 ·
Most densely populated area
—Over 125 per sq. mile—

Dublin

WOOLLENS
(handicraft)

Leeds

Hull

COAL

Liverpool *Manchester*

RAW COTTON IMPORTS
3,000,000 LBS.

EXPORT OF COTTON, YARN, FABRIC
£45,000

Sheffield

Lincoln

IRON

Nottingham

Norwich

W A L E S

Annual
Iron Production
22,000 tons

WOOLLENS
(handicraft)

Cambridge

IRON

WOOLLENS
(handicraft)

Bristol

London
Thames R.

IRON

Southampton

COPPER

TIN

Plymouth

BRITISH MERCHANT SHIPPING
8,000 SHIPS 600,000 tons

E N G L I S H   C H A N N E L

FRANCE

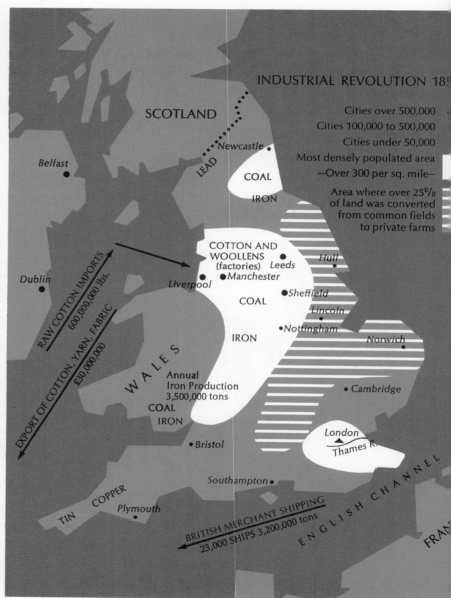

INDUSTRIAL REVOLUTION 185[0]

SCOTLAND

Belfast

Newcastle

LEAD

COAL

IRON

Cities over 500,000
Cities 100,000 to 500,000
Cities under 50,000
Most densely populated area
—Over 300 per sq. mile—

Area where over 25%
of land was converted
from common fields
to private farms

Dublin

COTTON AND
WOOLLENS
(factories)

Leeds

Hull

Liverpool *Manchester*

COAL

Sheffield

Lincoln

IRON

Nottingham

Norwich

RAW COTTON IMPORTS
600,000,000 lbs.

EXPORT OF COTTON, YARN, FABRIC
£30,000,000

W A L E S

Annual
Iron Production
3,500,000 tons

COAL

IRON

Cambridge

London
Thames R.

Bristol

Southampton

COPPER

TIN

Plymouth

BRITISH MERCHANT SHIPPING
23,000 SHIPS 3,200,000 tons

E N G L I S H   C H A N N E L

FRANC[E]

the change which has taken place in the country during the last five centuries? Does he remember how much England has grown in population, while Aldborough has been standing still? Does he consider, that in the time of Edward the First [13th century], the kingdom did not contain two millions of inhabitants? It now contains nearly fourteen millions. A hamlet of the present day would have been a town of some importance in the time of our early Parliaments. Aldborough may be absolutely as considerable a place as ever. But compared with the kingdom, it is much less considerable, by the noble Lord's own showing, than when it first elected burgesses. . . .

We talk of the wisdom of our ancestors; and in one respect at least they were wiser than we. They legislated for their own times. They looked at the England which was before them. They did not think it necessary to give twice as many members to York as they gave to London, because York had been the capital of Britain in the time of Constantius Chlorus; and they would have been amazed indeed if they had foreseen that a city of more than a hundred thousand inhabitants would be left without representatives in the nineteenth century, merely because it stood on ground which in the thirteenth century had been occupied by a few huts. They framed a representative system, which, though not without defects and irregularities, was well adapted to the state of England in their time. But a great revolution took place. The character of the old corporations changed. New forms of property came into existence. New portions of society rose into importance. There were in our rural districts rich cultivators, who were not freeholders. There were in our capital rich traders, who were not livery-men. Towns

shrank into villages. Villages swelled into cities larger than the London of the Plantagenets. Unhappily while the natural growth of society went on, the artificial polity continued unchanged. The ancient form of the representation remained; and precisely because the form remained, the spirit departed. Then came that pressure almost to bursting, the new wine in the old bottles, the new society under the old institutions. It is now time for us to pay a decent, a rational, a manly reverence to our ancestors, not by superstitiously adhering to what they, in other circumstances, would have done. All history is full of revolutions, produced by causes similar to those which are now operating in England. A portion of the community which had been of no account expands and becomes strong. It demands a place in the system, suited, not to its former weakness, but to its present power. If this be granted, all is well. If this is refused, then comes the struggle between the young energy of one class and the ancient privileges of another. Such was the struggle between the Plebeians and the Patricians of Rome. Such was the struggle of the Italian allies for admission to the full rights of Roman citizens. Such was the struggle of our North American colonies against the mother country. Such was the struggle which the Third Estate of France maintained against the aristocracy of birth. Such was the struggle which the Roman Catholics of Ireland maintained against the aristocracy of creed. Such is the struggle which the free people of colour in Jamaica are now maintaining against the aristocracy of skin. Such, finally, is the struggle which the middle classes in England are maintaining against an aristocracy of mere locality, against an aristocracy the principles of which is to invest a hundred drunken

potwallopers in one place, or the owner of a ruined hovel in another, with powers which are withheld from cities renowned to the farthest ends of the earth for the marvels of their wealth and of their industry. . . .

My hon. friend, the member for the University of Oxford, tells us that if we pass this law England will soon be a republic. The reformed House of Commons will, according to him, before it has sat ten years, depose the King and expel the Lords from their House. Sir, if my hon. friend could prove this, he would have succeeded in bringing an argument for democracy infinitely stronger than any that is to be found in the works of Paine. My hon. friend's proposition is in fact this: that our monarchical and aristocratical institutions have no hold on the public mind of England; that these institutions are regarded with aversion by a majority of the middle class. This, Sir, I say, is plainly deducible from his proposition; for he tells us that the representatives of the middle class will inevitably abolish royalty and nobility within ten years: and there is surely no reason to think that the representatives of the middle class will be more inclined to a democratic revolution that their constituents. Now, Sir, if I were convinced that the great body of the middle class in England look with aversion on monarchy and aristocracy, I should be forced, much against my will, to come to this conclusion, that monarchical and aristocratical institutions are unsuited to my country. Monarchy and aristocracy, valuable and useful as I think them, are still valuable and useful as means, and not as ends. The end of government is the happiness of the people; and I do not conceive that, in a country like this, the happiness of the people can be promoted by a form of government in which the middle classes place no confidence, and which exists only because the middle classes have no organ by which to make their sentiments known. But, Sir, I am fully convinced that the middle classes sincerely wish to uphold the Royal prerogatives and the constitutional rights of the Peers.

II

What facts does my hon. friend produce in support of his opinion? One fact only; and that a fact which has absolutely nothing to do with the question. The effect of this Reform, he tells us, would be to make the House of Commons all-powerful. It was all-powerful once before, in the beginning of 1649. Then it cut off the head of the King, and abolished the House of Peers. Therefore, if it again has the supreme power, it will act in the same manner. Now, Sir, it was not the House of Commons that cut off the head of Charles the First; nor was the House of Commons then all-powerful. It had been greatly reduced in numbers by successive expulsions. It was under the absolute dominion of the army. A majority of the House was willing to take the terms offered by the King. The soldiers turned out the majority; and the minority, not a sixth part of the whole House, passed those votes of which my hon. friend speaks, votes of which the middle classes disapproved then, and of which they disapprove still. . . .

Turn where we may, within, around, the voice of great events is proclaiming to us, Reform, that you may preserve. Now, therefore, while everything at home and abroad forebodes ruin to those who persist in a hopeless struggle against the spirit of the age; now, while the crash of the proudest throne of the Continent [France] is still resounding in our ears; now, while the roof of a British palace affords an ignominious shelter to the exiled heir of forty kings; now, while we see on every side ancient institutions subverted and great societies dissolved; now, while the heart of England is still sound; now, while old feelings and old associations retain a power and a charm which may too soon pass away; now, in this your accepted time; now, in this your day of salvation, take counsel, not of prejudice, not of party spirit, not of the ignominious pride of a fatal consistency, but of history, of reason, of the ages which are past, of the signs of this most portentous time. Pronounce in a manner worthy of the expectation with which this great debate has been anticipated, and of the long remembrance which it will leave behind. Renew the youth of the State. Save property, divided against itself. Save the multitude, endangered by its own ungovernable passions. Save the aristocracy, endangerd by its own unpopular power. Save the greatest, and fairest, and most highly civilised community that ever existed from calamities which may in a few days sweep away all the rich heritage of so many ages of wisdom and glory. The danger is terrible. The time is short. If this bill should be rejected, I pray to God that none of those who concur in rejecting it may ever remember their votes with unavailing remorse amidst the wreck of laws, the confusion of ranks, the spoliation of property, and the dissolution of social order.

STUDY QUESTIONS

1. What is the relationship between political development and a nation's social and economic needs? Compare (1) the structure of society, (2) the political institutions, and (3) the attitudes of the groups in power in France and Great Britain in the period between 1800 and 1830.

2. Why was there a revolution in France in 1830? What happened? What was the result? What role was played by the middle classes?

3. At whom was the Paris handbill aimed? What portents of the future for the middle classes do it and the Delacroix painting contain?

4. Of what was Guizot afraid in assessing the revolutionary movement? How did he defend the middle classes?

5. What accounts for the fact that France experienced violent revolution in 1830 while England underwent relatively peaceful change in 1832?

6. On what grounds did Macaulay argue that there should be a change in the British electoral system? How do the maps in Reading 166 help to understand the issue involved?

7. What did Macaulay mean by "Reform so that you may preserve"? Was the goal of change in either Britain or France liberalism or democracy? What is the relation between the two?

The Material and Social Effects of Industrialization

From E. R. Tannenbaum, *European Civilization Since the Middle Ages* (New York: John Wiley and Sons, Inc., 1965), pp. 374–379.

Although the new mode of production did not yet affect the majority of people in the most advanced countries by 1850, it was already changing the lives of a growing minority. We shall have to distinguish the material and social effects of industrialization on the new proletariat from those of concurrent and in part independent developments like urbanization and population growth. What would the effects of the "population explosion" and overcrowded cities have been *without* an increase in machine manufactures that could be exchanged for food? We shall also see that the growth of the industrial proletariat was soon to be matched by a proliferation of service and professional people, white-collar workers, civil servants, and engineers. The middle class became larger and much more heterogeneous, and the nobility and the peasants did not disappear. Industrialization made European society more complex and added new class antagonisms to existing ones.

Morally the Industrial Revolution was neutral. Degraded working and living conditions went far back into history, and neither the possession of capital nor the extensive use of machines were needed to make men callous and brutal. Some men had been that way from time out of mind. On the other hand, the human agents who promoted industrialization had no more far-sighted visions for the betterment of humanity than the human agents who caused the increase in the population. Only the public authorities, learning by experience with the new conditions of industrialization and rapid urbanization, could take action to alleviate the squalor and insecurity that these conditions imposed on masses of helpless workers. Such action came slowly.

WORKING CONDITIONS

The factory system created a new type of industrial proletariat. There had been some landless workers with nothing to sell but their labor since the late Middle Ages, but these journeymen had worked on the fringes of the traditional craft guilds. There had also been a few large workshops, such as those that turned out armaments or refined sugar, in which traditional unmechanized labor operated under supervision. The Industrial Revolution not only greatly increased the size of the proletariat, it also concentrated it in larger work units. In the new mills and factories power-driven machines produced goods formerly fashioned by hand. And the term "hand" came to mean an interchangeable operative who simply tended the machines.

At first the handicraft workers hated the machines. Would they not do away with work, create unemployment, and reduce wages? The weavers and finishers of wool cloth reacted especially violently. In both England and France they sent petitions to the government, marched in protest demonstrations, and sometimes went so far as to smash the machines. The most notorious machine-

---

TOPIC 32

WORKING CLASS CONDITIONS AND THE ORGANIZATION OF PROTEST

To the problems created by rapid population growth and urban crowding, industrialization added its own special overlay. The industrial system expanded without plan or pattern, offering new opportunities for employment and increasing the output of goods, but simultaneously generating uncontemplated social distress. The condition of the working man and the first attempts to alleviate his distress and to protest the structure of society that had permitted such conditions to develop are examined in these readings.

a

b

c

a) Medieval high-warp loom.
b) Seventeenth-century weaving.
c) The revolutionary change caused by industrialization is well illustrated by these three scenes. The mechanized spinning mill of 1835 produced quantities of cloth while reducing the craftsmen of previous centuries to the status of service personnel for the machines.

wreckers were the "Luddites" (named after their legendary leader Ned Ludd), who spread terror in the English Midlands in 1811-1812. It took an army as large as the one Wellington was leading in Spain to put them down. As time went on, the workers saw that machines did not eliminate the need for labor, and the wrecking rampages finally ceased. But each technological innovation thereafter met with the same initial hostility.

It is difficult today to imagine the adjustment the factory required of its new workers.

434

In pre-industrial shops and home workrooms craftsmen had worked just as hard, but at their own pace. Now the relentless click-clack of the machine set the pace. Boulton managed to discipline his workers to operate with such a degree of regularity that the slightest dissonance in the noise of the hammers and bellows indicated a stoppage or an accident. Furthermore, everybody now had to begin work on time. Today we expect everyone and everything to be on time, but in the early years of the Industrial Revolution the inexorable demands of the clock seemed inhuman. When the Duke of Bridgewater reproached his factory workers for being late in returning

A Luddite leader, disguised as a woman, urges his followers to destroy machines and factories.

from the midday break, they excused themselves by saying that they had failed to hear the stroke of one; the Duke immediately had the clock altered so that henceforth it struck thirteen. The workers were taught not to be late or absent by having their wages docked severely for each offense. They also had to learn not to leave their posts without permission and not to gossip on the job. This new type of worker was supervised and disciplined by the foreman, a new offshoot of an older breed, the drill sergeant.

The worst evils of the early factory system were not the pace of the machines and the harsh discipline of the foremen. Most workers eventually got used to these demands. Nor were low wages, long hours, or the exploitation of women and children anything new. The worst evils were unsafe and unsanitary working conditions and a complete lack of any kind of security against unemployment, injury, illness, or old age. . . .

Only gradually, and in the face of vigorous resistance, did the British government try to alleviate the appalling working conditions of the early factory system. Its regulatory laws of 1802 and 1816 had no effect because they were not enforced. The first effectively applied law was the Factory Act of 1833. It forbade the employment of children under nine years, restricted the labor of those between nine and thirteen to 48 hours a week or 9 in a single day, and those from thirteen to eighteen years to 69 hours a week or 12 in a day. Children under thirteen years were to have 2 hours of schooling a day. A system of paid inspectors was set up to enforce these and other provisions. In 1844 another law tried to reduce the numerous accidents that women and children suffered in the factories. It required the shielding of dangerous moving

parts of the machines and said that women and children should not be allowed to clean them until the machines were stopped. Similar laws were soon adopted in France and Germany. Like many laws, these early factory acts tell us more about the conditions they were supposed to remedy than they do about their own effectiveness. . . .

LIVING CONDITIONS

The wage earners lost most in housing. Urban slums were nothing new. But the simultaneous growth of cities and industry multiplied them at an astronomical rate, despite all the belated efforts of civic-minded municipalities to alleviate the squalor and overcrowding. In the newer mill and mining towns, houses were built back-to-back along narrow alleys, or around courtyards closed in on all four sides and entered by a tunnel. Most of these tenements had no running water and had to rely upon water carriers, selling by the pail. There were no fountains in picturesque town squares. In fact, there were no squares or other open spaces at all. Inside the houses, lack of ventilation intensified the stench of garbage and excrement. Here is a description of a working class tenement in Stockton:

Shepherd's Buildings comprise two rows of houses with a street seven yards wide between them. Each row consists of two lines of houses back-to-back. . . . There is one outside toilet for each row. . . . Each house contains two rooms, a common room, and a bedroom above it; each room is three yards square. In a typical house there are nine people belonging to the same family, and the mother about to give birth to a tenth. There are 44 houses in the two rows and 22 cellars all the same size.

Those people who could not afford, or find, a room lived in the cellars and courtyards. In 1850, 15,000 people lived in cellars in Manchester; in Liverpool 39,000 people lived in 7,800 cellars and 86,000 in 2,400 courtyards. A few years later 3,000 of the 3,600 cellars in the working-class district of Lille, France "housed" over 15,000 people within their damp, leaky walls. . . .

Living conditions in the urban slums were not necessarily worse than in the rural slums from which most of their inhabitants came, but they had more harmful social effects. Again, we must distinguish between the effects of industrialization and the effects of urbanization and population growth. Life in a cellar in Manchester was undoubtedly preferable to death on the roadside in overpopulated Ireland. Still, the fact that father, mother, and children spent most of their waking hours in a factory broke down family life, and the lack of community and church life in the jerry-built urban slums made matters worse. Children received practically no moral or religious instruction, and those who did not work played in the streets with no supervision. They also lacked the warm contacts with older relatives that country children had. There was no grandmother to tell them folk tales, and they usually did not see their father even on Sunday, for he was often drinking up the remainder of the wages he had received the night before. The mother, or sometimes an older sister, bore the whole burden of keeping the family together. Rural folklore created the old woman who lived in a shoe and had so many children she didn't know

what to do. In Stockton or Glasgow her plight was a great deal more visible to well-meaning reformers.

Many urban people ate better food and lived longer than their country cousins, but they were often less healthy. Lack of sleep and exercise stunted their growth; foul air and indoor work gave them a sickly pallor and bad lungs. Worst of all, overcrowding and

hopelessly inadequate sanitation facilities exposed them constantly to contagious diseases.

The cholera epidemic of 1831–1832 struck rural as well as urban areas, but it took a heavy toll in mining towns like Newcastle, where housing conditions and sanitation were particularly bad. It also struck the older cities with better municipal facilities, causing 1,400

Working-class tenement yards, back to back. An illustration by Gustave Doré for Blanchard Jerrold's *London: A Pilgrimage* (1872).

Urban slum in Orange Court, Drury Lane. An illustration by Gustave Doré for Blanchard Jerrold's *London: A Pilgrimage* (1872).

deaths in Berlin, 6,700 in London, and 18,600 in Paris. The poor people of Paris accused the authorities of poisoning them in order to reduce their swelling numbers. . . .

Industrialization, urbanization, and population growth seemed to divide the most advanced countries into two hostile "nations." On the one side were the "haves," from the rich noblemen and bankers to the small independent farmers and shopkeepers. On the other side were the "have nots," the "other nation" of landless workers completely dependent on their uncertain wages for survival. The concentration of this growing proletariat in cities and mill towns made it more visible to the "haves" and reinforced the workers' own sense of deprivation and injustice.

Parliament Investigates Conditions in English Industry

The appalling working conditions in British industry and the exploitation of the British masses led to a series of parliamentary investigations in England in the 1830s and 1840s. The report of the Sadler Committee in 1831 led to the drafting of the Factory Act of 1833 that placed some restrictions on child labor. The first part of this reading presents the testimony of Michael Crabtree, a workingman, before the Sadler Committee. The second excerpt is from testimony given to the Ashley Committee of 1842. From *Parliamentary Papers* (London, 1832), XV, pp. 95–97 and (London, 1842), XV–XVII, Appendix 2, p. 107.

I. EVIDENCE GIVEN BEFORE THE SADLER COMMITTEE (1831)

[Matthew Crabtree is questioned. The committee's questions are followed by his answers.]

What age are you? — Twenty-two.

What is your occupation? — A blanket manufacturer.

Have you ever been employed in a factory? — Yes.

At what age did you first go to work in one? — Eight.

How long did you continue in that occupation? — Four years.

Will you state the hours of labor at the period when you first went to the factory, in ordinary times? — From 6 in the morning to 8 at night.

Fourteen hours? — Yes.

With what intervals for refreshment and rest? — An hour at noon.

When trade was brisk what were your hours? — From 5 in the morning to 9 in the evening.

Sixteen hours? — Yes.

With what intervals at dinner? — An hour.

How far did you live from the mill? — About two miles.

Was there any time allowed for you to get your breakfast in the mill? — No.

Did you take it before you left your home? — Generally.

During those long hours of labor could you be punctual; how did you awake? — I seldom did awake spontaneously; I was most generally awoke or lifted out of bed, sometimes asleep, by my parents.

Were you always in time? — No.

What was the consequence if you had been too late? — I was most commonly beaten.

Severely? — Very severly, I thought.

In those mills is chastisement towards the latter part of the day going on perpetually? —Perpetually.

So that you can hardly be in a mill without hearing constant crying? — Never an hour, I believe.

Do you think that if the overlooker were naturally a human person it would still be found necessary for him to beat the children, in order to keep up their attention and vigilance at the termination of those extraordinary days of labor? — Yes; the machine turns off a regular quantity of cardings [combed cotton fibre], and of course they must keep as regularly to their work the whole of the day; they must keep with the machine, and therefore however human the slubber [chief carding operator] may be, as he must keep up with the machine or be found fault with, he spurs the children to keep up also by various means; but that which he commonly resorts to is to strap them when they become drowsy.

At the time when you were beaten for not keeping up with your work, were you anxious to have done it if you possibly could? — Yes; the dread of being beaten if we could not keep up with our work was a sufficient impulse to keep us to it if we could.

When you got home at night after this labor, did you feel much fatigued? — Very much so.

Had you any time to be with your parents, and to receive instructions from them? — No.

What did you do? — All that we did when we got home was to get the little bit of supper that was provided for us and to go to bed immediately. If the supper had not been ready directly, we should have gone to sleep while it was preparing.

Did you not, as a child, feel it a very grievous hardship to be roused so soon in the morning? — I did.

Were the rest of the children similarly circumstanced? — Yes, all of them; but they were not all of them so far from their work as I was.

And if you had been too late you were under the apprehension of being cruelly beaten? — I generally was beaten when I happened to be too late, and when I got up in the morning the apprehension of that was so great, that I used to run, and cry all the way as I went to the mill.

II. EVIDENCE GIVEN BEFORE LORD ASHLEY'S MINES COMMISSION (1842)

[Patience Kershaw, age 17, is questioned. The Committee noted: "This girl is an ignorant, filthy, ragged, and deplorable-looking object, such a one as the uncivilized natives of the prairies would be shocked to look upon."]

A contemporary cartoon broadcasts the findings of the Sadler Committee. Previous regulatory laws initiated by Sir Robert Peel did not effectively curb the abuse of child labor as the cartoon suggests.

A girl hurries coal in the English mines. An illustration from the book, *The White Slaves of England* (1853).

My father has been dead about a year. My mother is living and has ten children, five lads and five lasses; the oldest is about thirty, the youngest is four. Three lasses go to the mill. All the lads are colliers, two getters [diggers] and three hurriers [carriers]. One lives at home and does nothing. Mother does nothing but look after home.

All my sisters have been hurriers, but three went to the mill. Alice went because her legs swelled from hurrying in cold water [ground water in mines] when she was hot. I never went to day-school; I go to Sunday-school, but I cannot read or write. I go to the pit at five o'clock in the morning and come out at five in the evening. I get my breakfast of porridge and milk first. I take my dinner with me,

a cake, and eat it as I go. I do not stop or rest any time for the purpose. I get nothing else until I get home, and then have potatoes and meat, not meat every day.

I hurry in the clothes I have now got on, trousers and ragged jacket. The bald place upon my head is made by thrusting the corves [the coal was pulled in baskets (corves) fastened to the head and shoulders by a chain]. My legs have never swelled, but my sisters' did when they went to the mill. I hurry the corves a mile and more under ground and back; they weigh 300 cwt. I hurry 11 a day. I wear a belt and chain at the workings to get the corves out. The getters that I work for are naked except their caps; they pull off all their clothes. I see them at work when I

go up. Sometimes they beat me, if I am not quick enough, with their hands; they strike me upon my back. The boys take liberties with me; sometimes they pull me about. I am the only girl in the pit; there are about 20 boys and 15 men. All the men are naked. I would rather work in a mill than in a coalpit.

Eyewitnesses Report on the Consequences of Industrialization

Industrial conditions were increasingly debated as attacks mounted on the consequences of industrialism. Observers of the system differed sharply in their appraisals as can be seen in the two eyewitness accounts that compose this reading. The first selection is from Dr. Gaskell's, *The Manufacturing Population of England,* which told in detail about the deteriorating physical condition of the working class. Andrew Ure, author of the second selection, was a Scottish philosopher whose *The Philosophy of Manufactures* extolled the benefits of the factory system. I. From P. Gaskell, *The Manufacturing Population of England* (London, 1833). II. From Andrew Ure, *The Philosophy of Manufactures* (Edinburgh, 1835), p. 301.

I. DR. GASKELL IS SHOCKED (1833)

Any man who has stood at twelve o'clock at the single narrow doorway, which serves as the place of exit for the hands employed in the great cottonmills, must acknowledge that an uglier set of men and women, of boys and girls, taking them in mass, it would be

Public attention was directed to the physical condition of working people by well-known writers such as Mrs. Frances Trollope, who published her *Life and Adventures of Michael Armstrong* in 1840. In this mill scene a tattered child worker thanks middle-class Michael for a kindness.

impossible to congregate in a smaller compass. Their complexion is sallow and pallid—with a peculiar flatness of feature, caused by the want of a proper quantity of adipose substance to cushion out the cheeks. Their stature low—the average height of four hundred men, measured at different times and different places, being five feet six inches. Their limbs, slender, and playing badly and ungracefully. A very general bowing of the legs. Great numbers of girls and women walking lamely or awkwardly, with raised chests and spinal flexures. Nearly all have flat feet, accompanied with a down-tread, differing very widely from the elasticity of action in the foot and ankle, attendant upon perfect formation. Hair thin and straight—many of the men having but little beard, and that in patches of a few hairs, much resembling its growth among the red men of America. A spiritless and dejected air, a sprawling and wide action of the legs, and an appearance, taken as a whole, giving the world but "little assurance of a man," or if so, "most sadly cheated of his fair proportions. . . ."

II. ANDREW URE APPROVES
(1835)

I have visited many factories, both in Manchester and in the surrounding districts, during a period of several months, entering the spinning rooms, unexpectedly, and often alone, at different times of the day, and I never saw a single instance of corporal chastisement inflicted on a child, nor indeed did I ever see children in ill-humour. They seemed to be always cheerful and alert, taking pleasure in the light play of their muscles,—enjoying the mobility natural to their age. The scene of industry, so far from exciting sad emotions in my mind, was always exhilarating.

It was delightful to observe the nimbleness with which they pieced the broken ends, as the mule-carriage began to recede from the fixed roller-beam, and to see them at leisure, after a few seconds' exercise of their tiny fingers, to amuse themselves in any attitude they chose, till the stretch and winding-on were once more completed. The work of these lively elves seemed to resemble a sport, in which habit gave them a pleasing dexterity. Conscious of their skill, they were delighted to show it off to any stranger. As to exhaustion by the day's work, they evinced no trace of it on emerging from the mill in the evening; for they immediately began to skip about any neighbouring play-ground, and to commence their little amusements with the same alacrity as boys issuing from a school. It is moreover my firm conviction, that if children are not ill-used by bad parents or guardians, but receive in food and raiment the full benefit of what they earn, they would thrive better when employed in our modern factories, than if left at home in apartments too often ill-aired, damp, and cold. . . .

John Stuart Mill Asserts the Limits of Representative Government (1861)

John Stuart Mill's early acceptance of Jeremy Bentham's theories on how to promote the good of the community became more critical as he viewed the growing problems of the nineteenth century. In the selection below,

Factory girls spinning yarn in 1820.

Mill's democratic beliefs are balanced by his fears of a society dominated by the masses. From J. S. Mill, *Representative Government* (London, 1861), pp. 160–176.

It is by political discussion that the manual labourer, whose employment is a routine, and whose way of life brings him in contact with no variety of impressions, circumstances, or ideas, is taught that remote causes, and events which take place far off, have a most sensible effect even on his personal interests; and it is from political discussion, and collective political action, that one whose daily occupations concentrate his interests in a small circle round himself, learns to feel for and with his fellow-citizens, and becomes consciously a member of a great community. But political discussions fly over the heads of those who have no votes, and are not endeavouring to acquire them. Their position, in comparison with the electors, is that of the audience in a court of justice, compared with the twelve men in the jury-box. It is not *their* suffrages that are asked, it is not their opinion that is sought to be influenced; the appeals are made, the arguments addressed, to others than them; nothing depends on the decision they may arrive at, and there is no necessity and very little inducement to them to come to any. Whoever, in an otherwise popular government, has no vote, and no prospect of obtaining it, will either be a permanent malcontent, or will feel as one whom the general affairs of society do not concern; for whom they are to be managed by others; who 'has no business with the laws except to obey them,' nor with public interests and concerns except as a looker-on. What he will know or care about them from this position, may partly be measured by what an average woman of the middle class knows and cares about politics, compared with her husband or brothers. . . .

No arrangement of the suffrage, therefore, can be permanently satisfactory, in which any person or class is peremptorily excluded; in which the electoral privilege is not open to all persons of full age who desire to obtain it.

There are, however, certain exclusions, required by positive reasons, which do not conflict with this principle, and which, though an evil in themselves, are only to be got rid of by the cessation of the state of things which requires them. I regard it as wholly inadmissible that any person should participate in the suffrage, without being able to read, write, and, I will add, perform the common operations of arithmetic. Justice demands, even when the suffrage does not depend on it, that the means of attaining these elementary requirements should be within the reach of every person, either gratuitously, or at an expense not exceeding what the poorest, who earn their own living, can afford. . . .

It is also important, that the assembly which votes the taxes, whether general or local, should be elected exclusively by those who pay something towards the taxes imposed. Those who pay no taxes, disposing by their votes of other people's money, have every motive to be lavish, and none to economize. As far as money matters are concerned, any power of voting possessed by them is a violation of the fundamental principle of free government; a severance of the power of control, from the interest in its beneficial exercise. It amounts to allowing them to put their hands into other people's pockets, for any purpose which they think fit to call a public one. . . .

In the long run, therefore (supposing no restrictions to exist but those of which we have now treated), we might expect that [almost] all . . . would be in possession of votes, so that the suffrage would be, with that slight abatement, universal. That it should be thus widely expanded, is, as we have seen, absolutely necessary to an enlarged and elevated conception of good government. Yet in this state of things, the great majority of voters, in most countries, and emphatically in this, would be manual labourers; and the twofold danger, that of too low a standard of political intelligence, and that of class legislation, would still exist, in a very perilous degree. It remains to be seen whether any means exist by which these evils can be obviated.

They are capable of being obviated, if men sincerely wish it; not by any artificial contrivance, but by carrying out the natural order of human life, which recommends itself to every one in things in which he has no interest or traditional opinion running counter to it. In all human affairs, every person directly interested, and not under positive tutelage, has an admitted claim to a voice, and when his exercise of it is not inconsistent with the safety of the whole, cannot justly be excluded from it. But though every one ought to have a voice—that every one should have an equal voice is a totally different proposition. . . . An employer of labour is on the average more intelligent than a labourer; for he must labour with his head, and not solely with his hands. A foreman is generally more intelligent than an ordinary labourer, and a labourer in the skilled trades than in the unskilled. A banker, merchant, or manufacturer, is likely to be more intelligent than a tradesman, because he has larger and more complicated interests to manage. In all these cases it is not the having merely undertaken the superior function, but the successful performance of it, that tests the qualifications; for which reason, as well as to prevent persons from engaging nominally in an occupation for the sake of the vote, it would be proper to require that the occupation should have been perservered in for some length of time (say three years). Subject to some such condition, two or more votes might be allowed to every person who exercises any of these superior functions. The liberal professions, when really and not nominally practised, imply . . . a still higher degree of instruction; and wherever a sufficient examination, or any serious conditions of education, are required before entering on a profession, its members could be admitted at once to a plurality of votes. The same rule might be applied to graduates of universities. . . .

Socialism and Social Reform

Reprinted with permission of The Macmillan Company from *A History of Civilization* by Gerrit P. Judd. Copyright © by Gerrit P. Judd 1966.

The socialist movement arose early in the nineteenth century as a response to the problems of industrialism and as a protest against liberalism. The word "socialist" first appeared in the English language in 1833, and "socialism" in 1839. In general, socialism was a reassertion of the preliberal tradition that society should operate for the benefit of all its members, a tradition with roots in the gild and manorial systems of the Middle Ages. Socialists viewed the social evils of the Industrial Revolution with mounting concern. In the great debate on the rights of man precipitated by the Enlightenment and accentuated by the French Revolution, the socialists insisted on the overriding importance of social questions. They opposed the liberal emphasis on individualism and competition and the liberal concepts of *laissez–faire* and natural economic laws, which they believed had permitted the social misery of industrial workers. Instead they believed in social collaboration and a planned economy, developed, especially in England, from existing political institutions. Many of the early social theories and proposals were fumbling attempts to solve the new economic problems. But at least they represented a stirring of conscience and a sincere effort to cope with the unprecedented economic changes. . . .

In France a bold aristocrat, the Count of Saint-Simon (1760–1825), who had fought for the American patriots and had supported the French Revolution, was the first to realize that industrialism created new problems which required new social thought. He was a pioneer in emphasizing the importance of economic organization in the historical process. He also emphasized the continuing struggle between privileged and unprivileged groups. A believer in the brotherhood of man, he wished to apply scientific analysis to society so that the state might organize the means of production for the benefit of the people as a whole. The eccentricity of his followers, who created a moralistic cult, brought notoriety to his work but discredited the significance and originality of his thinking. . . .

Pierre Joseph Proudhon (1809–1865), a self-educated anarchist of French peasant stock, was an influential, if often inconsistent, advocate of social reform. He was especially hostile to private property and to the state, which he regarded as an instrument of oppression. In his voluminous and eloquent writings he advocated active rebellion against centralized political authority. Instead of the state he favored small, loosely connected communities in which the family had a prominent role. It was his hope that in time mankind's ethical progress would remove the necessity for any government at all.

England's most famous early socialist was Robert Owen (1771–1858), a successful Manchester textile manufacturer. Precisely because he was a successful businessman, members of Europe's governing classes read his works with attention and respect. Owen believed that an improved environment, in particular better education, would lead to human progress. Unlike the majority of other socialists, Owen had the money to put his ideas to a practical test. In 1800 he established a model textile mill at New Lanark, about 20 miles southeast of Glasgow in Scotland. Here, in the dark early days of the Industrial Revolution, he insisted on working conditions which were excellent by contemporary standards, along with good housing, sanitation, and schools. His experiment succeeded, for at New Lanark he made substantial profits. In 1825 he sponsored a communistic American colony in Indiana called New Harmony. This costly experiment failed within a few years after its foundation. Nonetheless, Owen's career as a whole provided a brilliant demonstration that intelligently applied socialism could be a practicable way of life. . . .

In the early stages of the Industrial Revolution English workmen remained for the most part apathetic and politically indifferent. But

New Lanark, Owen's model factory town, was viewed by over 20,000 curious visitors including many continental dignitaries in the years between 1815 and 1825.

Robert Owen offered elementary education at New Lanark for adults as well as children. In so doing he set a pattern that some factory owners would later follow. The illustration shows a factory school for mill operatives in Manchester in 1862.

as time passed the writings of radicals like Cobbett and Paine, taken in conjunction with depressed working conditions, awakened them to a mood of rising discontent. After the repeal of the Combination Acts in 1824 a number of trade (labor) unions arose. Their agitation and strikes caused much alarm among employers. Accordingly in 1825 a new law restricted union activity by making it hard to take collective action without incurring severe legal penalties. Despite this setback the labor movement continued. In 1834 Robert Owen founded the Grand National Consolidated Trades Union, which tried to unite the members of all English unions. That same year six laborers in Tolpuddle, Dorset, received sentences of seven years penal servitude in Australia for administering secret oaths during the formation of an agricultural branch of the Grand National Union. The case of the so-called Tolpuddle Martyrs caused much protest. But it led to the dissolution of the Grand National Union and for the time

The Chartists march in protest in April 1848.

Isaiah Berlin: Utopian Socialism

Sir Isaiah Berlin (1909–   ) is a noted British scholar in the field of social and political theory. President of Wolfson College, Oxford, he has been visiting professor at a number of American universities. He has written widely on the philosophy of history and has been concerned with the liberating power of ideas in Western thought. From Isaiah Berlin, *Karl Marx, His Life and Environment,* Third Edition (New York, 1963: Oxford University Press) pp. 90–97.

Saint-Simon was a thinker of bold and original views: he was the first writer to assert that the development of economic relationships is the determining factor in history—and to have done this in his day in itself constitutes a sufficient claim to immortality—and further to analyse the historical process as a continuous conflict between economic *classes,* between those who, at any given period, are the possessors of the main economic resources of the community, and those who lack this advantage and come to depend upon the former for their subsistence. According to Saint-Simon, the ruling class is seldom sufficiently able or disinterested to make rational use of its resources, or to institute an order in which those most capable of doing so apply and increase the resources of the community, and seldom flexible enough to adapt itself, and the institutions which it controls, to the new social conditions which its own activity brings about. It therefore tends to pursue a short-sighted and egoistic policy, to form a close caste, accumulate the available wealth in a few hands, and by means of the

being checked the union movement as a whole.

After 1834 labor leaders turned to political action. They were deeply disappointed that workingmen had not received the vote in the Reform Act of 1832. They believed further that social reform could come only when popularly elected representatives replaced the upper-class and bourgeois members of House of Commons. In 1838 an association of workmen in London drew up the People's Charter, a sixfold program of political reform. The Charter called for manhood suffrage, the secret ballot, abolition of property qualifications for members of Parliament, salaries for members of Parliament, equal electoral districts, and annual Parliaments annually elected. In later years all but the last point became law. But, as might have been anticipated, in 1839 Parliament rejected the Charter, accompanied as it was by a huge petition containing many fictitious names. In 1848 Parliament rejected a second Chartist petition. The Chartist movement failed because of the strength of its opponents and the disunity and inexperience of its leaders.

The failure of Chartism symbolized the temporary defeat of labor by the landed and liberal groups. But the labor movement persisted. Throughout the West, discontented workmen continued their struggle for social reform by peaceful or violent means.

prestige and power thus obtained, to reduce the dispossessed majority to social and economic slavery. The unwilling subjects naturally grow restive and devote their lives to the overthrow of the tyrannical minority; this, when the conjunction of circumstances favours them, they eventually succeed in doing. But they grow corrupted by the long years of servitude, and become incapable of conceiving ideals higher than those of their masters, so that when they acquire power, they use it no less irrationally and unjustly than their own former oppressors; in their turn they create a new proletariat, and so at a new level the struggle continues. Human history is the history of such conflicts: due ultimately—as Adam Smith and the eighteenth-century French philosophers would have said—to the blindness of both masters and subjects to the coincidence of the best interests of both under a rational distribution of economic resources. Instead of this the ruling classes attempt to arrest all social change, lead idle and wasteful lives, obstructing economic progress in the form of technical invention, which, if only it were properly developed, would, by creating unlimited plenty and distributing it scientifically, swiftly ensure the eternal happiness and prosperity of mankind. Saint-Simon, who was a far better historian than his encyclopaedist predecessors, took a genuinely evolutionary view of human society, and estimated past epochs, not in terms of their remoteness from the civilization of the present, but in terms of the adequacy of their institutions to the social and economic needs of their own day; with the result that his account of, for example, the Middle Ages is far more penetrating and sympathetic than that of the majority of his liberal contemporaries. He saw human progress as the inventive, creative activity of men

in society, whereby they transform and enlarge their own nature and its needs and the means of satisfying them, both spiritual and material; human nature is not, as the eighteenth century had assumed, a fixed entity, but a process of growth, the direction of which is determined by its own failures and successes. Hence he noted that a social order which responded to genuine needs in its own day might tend to hamper the movements of a later time, becoming a straitjacket, the nature of which is concealed by the classes protected by its existence. The army and the Church, organic and progressive elements in the mediaeval hierarchy, are now obsolete survivals, whose functions are performed in modern society by the banker, the industrialist, and the scientist; with the consequence that priests, soldiers, *rentiers,* can survive only as idlers and social parasites, wasting the substance and holding up the advance of the new classes; they must therefore be eliminated. In their place industrious and skilful experts, chosen for their executive ability, must be placed at the head of society: the financiers, engineers, organizers of large, rigorously centralized, industrial and agricultural enterprises, must constitute the government. The Saint-Simonians taught that the laws of inheritance which lead to undeserved inequalities of wealth must be abolished: but on no account must this be extended to private property in general: every man has a right to the fruit of his own personal labour. Like the makers of the Revolution, and Fourier and Proudhon after them, Saint-Simon and his disciples firmly believed that the ownership of property furnished at the same time the sole incentive to energetic labour and the foundation of private and public morality. Bankers, company promoters, industrialists, inventors, scientists, engineers, thinkers, art-

ists, poets, must be adequately rewarded by the State in proportion to their efficiency: once the economic life of the society is rationalized by the experts, the natural virtue of progressive human nature, the natural harmony of the interests of all, will guarantee universal justice, security, contentment and equality of opportunity for all men alike.

Saint-Simon lived at a time when the last relics of feudalism in Western Europe were finally disappearing before the advance of the bourgeois *entrepreneur* and his new mechanical devices. He had endless faith in the immense possibilities of technical invention and in its naturally beneficent effect on human society: he saw in the rising middle class able and energetic men animated by a sense of justice and disinterested altruism, hampered by the blind hostility of the landowning aristocracy and of the Church, which trembled for their own privileges and possessions, and so became enemies to all justice and to all scientific and moral progress.

This belief was not so naïve then as it may now seem to be. As Marx was himself later to repeat, in the actual moment of struggle for social emergence, the vanguard of the rising class in a nation naturally identifies its own cause with the whole mass of the oppressed, and feels, and to a certain degree is, the disinterested champion of a new ideal, fighting at the furthest outposts of the progressive front. Saint-Simon was the most eloquent prophet of the rising bourgeoisie in its most generous and idealistic mood. He naturally set the highest value on industry, initiative, inventiveness, and the capacity for large-scale planning: but he also sharply formulated the theory of the class struggle, little knowing to what application this portion of his doctrine would one day be put. He was himself a landed nobleman of the eighteenth century, ruined by the Revolution, who had chosen to identify himself with the advancing power, and so to explain and justify the supersession of his own class.

His most celebrated ideological rival, Charles Fourier, was a commercial traveller who lived in Paris during those first decades of the new century, when the financiers and industrialists, upon whom Saint-Simon had placed all his hopes, so far from effecting social reconciliation, proceeded to sharpen class antagonism by creation of strongly centralized monopolist concerns. By obtaining control of credit, and employing labour on an unprecedented scale, they created the possibility of mass production and mass distribution of goods, and so competed on unequal terms with the smaller traders and artisans, whom they systematically drove out of the open market, and whose children they absorbed into their factories and mines. The social effect of the Industrial Revolution in France was to create a rift and a state of permanent bitterness between the *grande* and the *petite bourgeoisie,* which dominates the history of that country from that date. Fourier, a typical representative of the ruined class, inveighs bitterly against the illusion that capitalists are the predestined saviours of society. His older contemporary, the Swiss economist Sismondi, had defended, with an immense mass of historical evidence, at a period when it required something akin to genius to have perceived it, the view that, whereas all previous class struggles occurred as a result of the scarcity of goods in the world, the discovery of new mechanical means of production would flood the world with excessive plenty, and would themselves, unless checked, lead to a class war before which previous conflicts would pale into insignificance. The necessity of marketing the ever-growing produce would lead to a continual competition between the rival capitalists, who would be forced systematically to lower wages and increase the working hours of the employees in order to secure even temporary advantage over a slower rival, which in turn would lead to a series of acute economic crises, ending in social and political chaos, due to the internecine wars between groups of capitalists. Such artificial poverty growing in direct proportion with the increase of goods, above all the monstrous trampling on those very fundamental human rights, to guarantee which the great revolution was made, could only be prevented by State intervention, which must curtail the right of accumulating capital and of the means of production. But whereas Sismondi was an early 'New Dealer', who believed in the possibility of a centrally organized, rationally and humanely conducted society, and confined himself to general recommendations, Fourier distrusted all central authority, and declared that bureaucratic tyranny is bound to develop, if the government units are too large; he proposed that the earth should be divided into small groups which he called phalansteries, each self-governing and federated into larger and larger units; all machinery, land, buildings, natural resources should be owned in common. His vision, an odd blend of eccentricity and genius, at its most apocalyptic moments remains elaborate and precise: a great central electric plant will by its power do all the mechanical labour of the phalanstery: profits should be divided between labour, capital and talent in the strict proportion $5:3:2$, and its members, with no more than a few hours of daily work, will thus be free to occupy themselves with developing their intellectual, moral and artistic faculties to an extent hitherto unprecedented in history. The exposition is at times interrupted by bursts of pure fantasy, such as the prophecy of the emergence in the immediate future of a new race of beasts, not dissimilar in appearance to existing species, but more powerful and more numerous—'anti-lions', 'anti-bears', 'anti-tigers', as friendly and attached to man as their present ancestors are hostile and destructive, and doing much of his work with the skill, intelligence and foresight wanting to mere machines. The thesis is at its best at its most destructive. In the remorseless exactness of its analysis of the self-destructive effects of free competition; in the intense quality of its indignation and its sense of genuine horror at the wholesale disregard for the life and liberty of the individual by the monstrous régime of financiers and their hirelings, the judges, the soldiers, the administrators, Fourier's indictment is the prototype of all later attacks on the doctrine of the unchecked *laissez-faire,* of the great denunciations of Marx and Carlyle, of Daumier's cartoons and Büchner's plays, no less than of the communist, fascist, and Christian protests against the substitution of new forms of privilege for old, and against the enslavement of the individual by the very machinery designed to set him free.

The Revolution of 1830, which expelled Charles X and brought Louis Philippe to the throne of France, revived public interest in social questions once more. During the decade which followed, an endless succession of books and pamphlets poured from the presses, attacking the evils of the existing system, and suggesting every kind of remedy, from the mildly liberal proposals of Lamartine or Crémieux to the more radical semi-socialist demands of Marrast or Ledru Rollin, and the developed State socialism of Louis Blanc, and ending with the drastic programmes of Barbès and Blanqui, who in their journal *L'Homme*

Libre, advocated a violent revolution and the abolition of private property. Fourier's disciple Considérant proclaimed the imminent collapse of the existing system of property relations; and well-known socialist writers of the time, Pecqueur, Louis Blanc, Dézami, and the most independent and original figure among them, Proudhon, published their best known attacks on the capitalist order between 1839 and 1842, and were in their turn followed by a host of minor figures who diluted and popularized their doctrines. In 1834, the Catholic priest Lamennais published his Christian socialist *Words of a Believer,* and in 1840 appeared the *Bible of Freedom* by the Abbé Constant, fresh evidence that even in the Church there were men unable to resist the great popular appeal of the new revolutionary theories. . . .

The subsequent fate of these movements is of small importance. The Saint-Simonists, after some years of desultory existence, dis- appeared as a movement: some of them became highly prosperous railway magnates and *rentiers,* fulfilling at least one aspect of their master's prophecy. The more idealistic Fourierists founded communist settlements in the United States, some of which, like the Oneida community, lasted for some decades and attracted leading American thinkers and writers; in the sixties they had considerable influence through their newspaper, the *New York Tribune.* . . .

STUDY QUESTIONS

1. What is meant in Reading 168 by the "moral neutrality" of the Industrial Revolution? In what sense are urbanization, population growth and industrialization distinct in character? What do they have in common?

2. What were working and living conditions like in industrialized society? Which features were the worst? Why? Compare these conditions with those of rural society in the same age. With preindustrialized society in general. With conditions in newly emerging nations today.

3. What seem to have been the most pressing problems experienced by Michael Crabtree and Patience Kershaw and described by Dr. Gaskell? Was Ure's account of factory conditions, in comparison, untruthful?

4. Why did Mill wish to extend the right to vote? What reservations did he have? What was his attitude toward democracy? Do you think his was a satisfactory solution for the problems of the working class?

5. What other solutions were put forth? Why did the early socialists oppose the objectives of liberalism?

6. What did Saint Simon and Fourier see as the major problems of industrial society? In what sense were their social theories radical? What elements of the capitalist system did they support?

E. J. Hobsbawm: The Laboring Poor

TOPIC 33

MARXIAN SOCIALISM: A RESPONSE TO INDUSTRIALISM

As E. J. Hobsbawm points out in the first of the readings below, when the possibilities of improving their lot within the existing structure of early industrial society were closed to the vast majority of workingmen, they had either to accept their fate or rebel against it. For an active minority, outright rebellion was the chosen response to oppression. The man who more than any other was responsible for providing a rationale for working class revolution was Karl Marx on whose philosophy and program the readings in this topic focus.

Reprinted by permission of the World Publishing Company from *The Age of Revolution* by E. J. Hobsbawm. Copyright © 1962 by E. J. Hobsbawm. This is published in Canada by George Weidenfeld and Nicholson Ltd.

Three possibilities were . . . open to such of the poor as found themselves in the path of bourgeois society, and no longer effectively sheltered in still inaccessible regions of traditional society. They could strive to become bourgeois; they could allow themselves to be ground down; or they could rebel.

The first course, as we have seen, was not merely technically difficult for those who lacked the minimum entrance fee of property or education, but profoundly distasteful. The introduction of a purely utilitarian individualist system of social behaviour, the theoretically justified jungle anarchy of bourgeois society with its motto 'every man for himself and the devil take the hindmost,' appeared to men brought up in traditional societies as little better than wanton evil. 'In our times,' said one of the desperate Silesian handloom linen-weavers who rioted vainly against their fate in 1844, 'men have invented excellent arts to weaken and undermine one another's livelihood. But alas, nobody thinks any longer of the Seventh Commandment, which commands and forbids as follows: Thou shalt not steal. Nor do they bear in mind Luther's commentary upon it, in which he says: We shall love and fear the Lord, so that we may not take away our neighbour's property nor money, nor acquire it by false goods and

trading, but on the contrary we should help him guard and increase his livelihood and property.' Such a man spoke for all who found themselves dragged into an abyss. . . .

There were of course labouring men who did their best to join the middle classes, or at least to follow the precepts of thrift, self-help, and self-betterment. The moral and didactic literature of middle-class radicalism, temperance movements, and Protestant endeavour is full of the sort of men whose Homer was Samuel Smiles. And indeed such bodies attracted and perhaps encouraged the ambitious young man. The Royton Temperance Seminary, started in 1843 (confined to boys—mostly cotton operatives—who had taken the pledge of abstinence, refused to gamble, and were of good moral character), had within twenty years produced five master cotton spinners, one clergyman, two managers of cotton mills in Russia 'and many others had obtained respectable positions as managers, overlookers, head mechanics, certified schoolmasters, or had become respectable shopkeepers.' Clearly such phenomena were less common outside the Anglo-Saxon world, where the road out of the working class (except by migration) was very much narrower—it was not exceptionally broad even in Britain—and the moral and intellectual influence of the Radical middle class on the skilled worker was less.

On the other hand there were clearly far more who, faced with a social catastrophe they did not understand, impoverished, exploited, herded into slums that combined

Apathetic workingmen stop for a rest at noon. Drawn by German artist Kaethe Koll-witz in 1909.

bleakness and squalor, or into the expanding complexes of small-scale industrial villages, sank into demoralization. Deprived of the traditional institutions and guides to behaviour, how could many fail to sink into an abyss of hand-to-mouth expedients, where families pawned their blankets each week until payday and where alcohol was 'the quickest way out of Manchester' (or Lille or the Borinage). Mass alcoholism, an almost invariable companion of headlong and uncontrolled industrialization and urbanization, spread 'a pestilence of hard liquor' across Europe. Perhaps the numerous contemporaries who deplored the growth of drunkenness, as of prostitution and other forms of sexual promiscuity, were exaggerating. Nevertheless, the sudden upsurge of systematic temperance agitations, both of a middle- and working-class character, in England, Ireland, and Germany around 1840 shows that the worry about demoralization was neither academic nor confined to any single class. Its immediate success was shortlived, but for the rest of the century the hostility to hard liquor remained something which both enlightened employers and labour movements had in common. . . .

The alternative to escape or defeat was rebellion. And such was the situation of the labouring poor, and especially the industrial proletariat which became their nucleus, that rebellion was not merely possible, but virtually compulsory. Nothing was more inevitable in the first half of the nineteenth century than the appearance of labour and socialist movements, and indeed of mass social revolutionary unrest. The revolution of 1848 was its direct consequence.

That the condition of the labouring poor was appalling between 1815 and 1848 was not

450

denied by any reasonable observer, and by 1840 there were a good many of these. That it was actually deteriorating was widely assumed. In Britain the Malthusian population theory, which held that the growth of population must inevitably outrun that of the means of subsistence, was based on such an assumption, and reinforced by the arguments of Ricardian economists. Those who took a rosier view of working-class prospects were less numerous and less talented than those who took the gloomy view. In Germany in the 1830s the increasing pauperization of the people was the specific subject of at least fourteen different publications, and the question whether 'the complaints about increasing pauperization and food shortage' were justified was set for academic prize essays. (Ten of sixteen competitors thought they were and only two that they were not.) The very prevalence of such opinions is itself evidence of the universal and apparently hopeless misery of the poor.

No doubt actual poverty was worst in the countryside, and especially among landless wage-labourers, rural domestic workers, and, of course, land-poor peasants, or those who lived on infertile land. A bad harvest, such as in 1789, 1795, 1817, 1832, 1847, still brought actual famine, even without the intervention of additional catastrophes such as the competition of British cotton goods, which destroyed the foundation of the Silesian cottage linen industry. After the ruined crop of 1813 in Lombardy many kept alive only by eating manure and hay, bread made from the leaves of bean plants and wild berries. . . .

But in fact the misery—the increasing misery as so many thought—which attracted most attention short of total catastrophe such

as the Irish, was that of the cities and industrial areas where the poor starved less passively and less unseen. Whether their real incomes fell is still a matter of historical debate, though, as we have seen, there can be no doubt that the general situation of the poor in cities deteriorated. Variations between one region and another, between different types of workers and between different economic periods, as well as the deficiency of statistics, make such questions

difficult to answer decisively, though any significant absolute general improvement can be excluded before 1848 (or in Britain perhaps 1844), and the gap between the rich and the poor certainly grew wider and more visible. The time when Baroness Rothschild wore one and a half million francs worth of jewellery at the Duke of Orléans' masked ball (1842) was the time when John Bright described the women of Rochdale: '2,000 women and girls passed through the streets singing hymns—it

Irish potato famine of 1847. Crop failure meant rents could not be paid. Evicted peasant families took refuge in burrows dug two to three feet beneath the earth and covered over with sticks and turf. The burrows or "scalps" shown in this illustration served as homes for the Clare and Connemara peasantry during the famine.

Capital and labor as portrayed in *Punch* in 1847.

was a very singular and striking spectacle . . . they are dreadfully hungry—a loaf is devoured with greediness indescribable and if the bread is nearly covered with mud it is eagerly devoured.' . . .

Materially the new factory proletariat was likely to be somewhat better off. On the other hand it was unfree, under the strict control and the even stricter discipline imposed by the master or his supervisors, against whom they had virtually no legal recourse and only the very beginnings of public protection. They had to work his hours or shifts, to accept his punishments and the fines with which he imposed his rules or increased his profits. In isolated areas or industries they had to buy in his shop, as often as not receiving their wages in *truck* (thus allowing the unscrupulous employer to swell his profits yet further), or live in the houses the master provided. No

doubt the village boy might find such a life no more dependent and less impoverished than his parents'; and in Continental industries with a strong paternalist tradition, the despotism of the master was at least partly balanced by the security, education, and welfare services which he sometimes provided. But for the free man entry into the factory as a mere 'hand' was entry into something little better than slavery, and all but the most famished tended to avoid it, and even when in it to resist the draconic discipline much more persistently than the women and children, whom factory owners therefore tended to prefer. And, of course, in the 1830s and part of the 1840s even the material situation of the factory proletariat tended to deteriorate.

Whatever the actual situation of the labouring poor, there can be absolutely no doubt

that every one of them who thought at all—*i.e.,* who did not accept the tribulations of the poor as part of fate and the eternal design of things—considered the labourer to be exploited and impoverished by the rich, who were getting richer while the poor became poorer. And the poor suffered *because* the rich benefited. The social mechanism of bourgeois society was in the profoundest manner cruel, unjust, and inhuman. 'There can be no wealth without labour' wrote the *Lancashire Co-operator.* 'The workman is the source of all wealth. Who has raised all the food? The half-fed and impoverished labourer. Who built all the houses and warehouses, and palaces, which are possessed by the rich, who never labour or produce anything? The workman. Who spins all the yarn and makes all the cloth? The spinner and weaver.' Yet 'the labourer remains poor and destitute, while those who do not work are rich, and possess abundance to surfeiting.' And the despairing rural labourer (echoed literally even today by the Negro gospel-singer) put it less clearly, but perhaps even more profoundly:

> If life was a thing that money could buy
> The rich would live and the poor might die.

The Song of the Lower Classes (c. 1854)

One of the leaders of the Chartist movement, which unsuccessfully tried to stir the English working class to revolt in the 1830s and 1840s, was Ernest Jones. His poem catches the defiant disillusion of the exploited working masses.

We plough and sow—we're so very, very low
   That we delve in the dirty clay,
Till we bless the plain—with the golden grain,
   And the vale with the fragrant hay.
Our place we know—we're so very low,
   'Tis down at the landlord's feet:
We're not too low—the bread to grow,
   But too low the bread to eat.

Down, down we go—we're so very, very low,
   To the hell of the deep sunk mines,
But we gather the proudest gems that glow
   Where the crown of a despot shines.
And whenever he lacks—upon our backs
   Fresh loads he deigns to lay:
We're far too low to vote the tax,
   But not too low to pay.

We're low—we're low—mere rabble, we know,
   But at our plastic power
The mould at the lordlings' feet will grow
   Into palace and church and tower—
Then prostrate fall—in the rich man's hall,
   And cringe at the rich man's door:
We're not too low to build the wall,
   But too low to tread the floor.

We're low—we're low—we're very, very low,
   Yet from our fingers glide
The silken flow—and the robes that glow
   Round the limbs of the sons of pride.
And what we get—and what we give—
   We know, and we know our share:
We're not too low the cloth to weave,
   But too low the cloth to wear!

We're low—we're low—we're very, very low,
   And yet when the trumpets ring,
The thrust of a poor man's arm will go
   Through the heart of the proudest king.
We're low—we're low—our place we know
   We're only the rank and file,
We're not too low to kill the foe,
   But too low to touch the spoil.

Empress Eugénie of France and her ladies-in-waiting by Franz Winterhalter, court painter and fashionable artist for British, French, and German royalty.

Honoré Daumier's "The Third Class Carriage," an oil painting of lower-class life by the famous lithographer and caricaturist.

Karl Marx Justifies Revolutionary Change

(1848)

Karl Marx (1818–1883) was the son of a lawyer of moderate means in the Rhineland territories of pre-industrial and reactionary Prussia. His first interests were law and philosophy, and he maintained these interests through his university years. It was then that the winds of rapid economic change and of political revolution sweeping in from the west engulfed the young man. After a brief and unsuccessful effort at journalism in Cologne, he moved to Paris. Until he was forced to leave two years later, he lived there among the competing currents of socialist thought he would later attack as Utopian. *The Communist Manifesto* was the first full statement of his view of the past, present, and future. It contained the essential ideas of Marx as a scholar and revolutionary—his view of history, his criticism of contemporary social thought, and his program for the new working class created by the factory system. Written in collaboration with Friedrich Engels, it was first published in February 1848, after the cycle of revolutions of that year had already begun. Marx' enormous stature as a nineteenth-century thinker remains unchallenged despite the continuing controversy that surrounds his philosophy of history. In the portions of the *Manifesto* reproduced here, the great impact on the young Marx of the transformation of Europe through industrial technology and political revolution is clearly visible. From Karl Marx and Friedrich Engels, *Manifesto of the Communist Party,* trans. Samuel Moore (London, 1888).

A family portrait in the 1860s. Karl Marx and Friedrich Engels stand behind Marx's daughters Jenny, Eleanor, and Laura.

BOURGEOIS AND PROLETARIANS

The history of all hitherto existing society is the history of class struggles. . . .

In the earlier epochs of history, we find almost everywhere a complicated arrangement of society into various orders, a manifold gradation of social rank. In ancient Rome we have patricians, knights, plebeians, slaves; in the Middle Ages, feudal lords, vassals, guild-masters, journeymen, apprentices, serfs; in almost all of these classes, again, subordinate gradations. . . .

Our epoch, the epoch of the bourgeoisie, possesses, however, this distinctive feature: It has simplified the class antagonisms. Society as a whole is more and more splitting up into two great hostile camps, into two great classes directly facing each other—bourgeoisie and proletariat. . . .

The discovery of America, the rounding of the Cape, opened up fresh ground for the rising bourgeoisie. The East-Indian and Chinese markets, the colonization of America, trade with the colonies, the increase in the means of exchange and in commodities generally, gave to commerce, to navigation, to industry, an impulse never before known, and thereby, to the revolutionary element in the tottering feudal society, a rapid development. . . .

Meantime the markets kept ever growing, the demand ever rising. Even manufacture no longer sufficed. Thereupon, steam and machinery revolutionized industrial production. The place of manufacture was taken by the giant, modern industry, the place of the industrial middle class, by industrial millionaires, the leaders of whole industrial armies, the modern bourgeoisie. . . .

Each step in the development of the bourgeoisie was accompanied by a corresponding political advance of that class. An oppressed class under the sway of the feudal nobility, it became an armed and self-governing association in the medieval commune; here independent urban republic (as in Italy and Germany), there taxable "third estate" of the monarchy (as in France); afterwards, in the period of manufacture proper, serving either the semi-feudal or the absolute monarchy as a counterpoise against the nobility, and, in fact, cornerstone of the great monarchies in general—the bourgeoisie has at last, since the establishment of modern industry and of the world market, conquered for itself, in the modern representative state, exclusive political sway. The executive of the modern state is but a committee for managing the common affairs of the whole bourgeoisie.

The bourgeoisie has played a most revolutionary role in history.

The bourgeoisie, wherever it has got the upper hand, has put an end to all feudal, patriarchal, idyllic relations. It has pitilessly torn asunder the motley feudal ties that bound man to his "natural superiors," and has left no other bond between man and man than naked self-interest, than callous "cash payment." It has drowned the most heavenly ecstasies of religious fervor, of chivalrous enthusiasm, of philistine sentimentalism, in the icy water of egotistical calculation. It has resolved personal worth into exchange value, and in place of the numberless indefeasible chartered freedoms, has set up that single, unconscionable freedom—Free Trade. In one word, for exploitation, veiled by religious and political illusions, it has substituted naked, shameless, direct, brutal exploitation. . . .

The bourgeoisie has through its exploitation of the world market given a cosmopolitan character to production and consumption in every country. To the great chagrin of reactionaries, it has drawn from under the feet of industry the national ground on which it stood. All old-established national industries have been destroyed or are daily being destroyed. They are dislodged by new industries, whose introduction becomes a life and death question for all civilized nations, by industries that no longer work up indigenous raw mate-

Doré, in this mid-century cartoon, shared Marx's view of the callousness of bourgeois society. Bound together and helpless, the laborers are treated like piles of chips on the playing table.

rial, but raw material drawn from the remotest zones; industries whose products are consumed, not only at home, but in every quarter of the globe. In place of old wants, satisfied by the production of the country, we find new wants, requiring for their satisfaction the products of distant lands and climes. In place of the old local and national seclusion and self-sufficiency, we have intercourse in every direction, universal interdependence of nations. And as in material, so also in intellectual production. The intellectual creations of individual nations become common property. National one-sidedness and narrow-mindedness become more and more impossible, and from the numerous national and local literatures there arises a world literature.

The bourgeoisie, by the rapid improvement of all instruments of production, by the immensely facilitated means of communication, draws all nations, even the most barbarian, into civilization. The cheap prices of its commodities are the heavy artillery with which it batters down all Chinese walls, with which it forces the barbarians' intensely obstinate hatred of foreigners to capitulate. It compels all nations, on pain of extinction, to adopt the bourgeois mode of production; it compels them to introduce what it calls civilization into their midst, *i.e.,* to become bourgeois themselves. In a word, it creates a world after its own image.

The bourgeoisie has subjected the country to the rule of the towns. It has created enormous cities, has greatly increased the urban population as compared with the rural, and has thus rescued a considerable part of the population from the idiocy of rural life. Just as it has made the country dependent on the towns, so it has made barbarian and semi-barbarian countries dependent on the civil-ized ones, nations of peasants on nations of bourgeois, the East on the West. . . .

The bourgeoisie, during its rule of scarce one hundred years, has created more massive and more colossal productive forces than have all preceding generations together. Subjection of nature's forces to man, machinery, application of chemistry to industry and agriculture, steam-navigation, railways, electric telegraphs, clearing of whole continents for cultivation, canalization of rivers, whole populations conjured out of the ground—what earlier century had even a presentiment that such productive forces slumbered in the lap of social labor?

We see then that the means of production and of exchange, which served as the foundation for the growth of the bourgeoisie, were generated in feudal society. At a certain stage in the development of these means of production and of exchange, the conditions under which feudal society produced and exchanged, the feudal organization of agriculture and manufacturing industry, in a word, the feudal relations of property became no longer compatible with the already developed productive forces; they became so many fetters. They had to be burst asunder; they were burst asunder.

Into their place stepped free competition, accompanied by a social and political constitution adapted to it, and by the economic and political sway of the bourgeois class.

A similar movement is going on before our own eyes. Modern bourgeois society with its relations of production, of exchange and of property, a society that has conjured up such gigantic means of production and of exchange, is like the sorcerer who is no longer able to control the powers of the nether world whom he has called up by his spells. For many a decade past the history of industry and commerce is but the history of the revolt of modern productive forces against modern conditions of production, against the property relations that are the conditions for the existence of the bourgeoisie and of its rule. It is enough to mention the commercial crises that by their periodical return put the existence of the entire bourgeois society on trial, each time more threateningly. In these crises a great part not only of the existing products, but also of the previously created productive forces, are periodically destroyed. In these crises there breaks out an epidemic that, in all earlier epochs, would have seemed an absurdity—the epidemic of overpopulation. Society suddenly finds itself put back into a state of momentary barbarism; it appears as if a famine, a universal war of devastation had cut off the supply of every means of subsistence; industry and commerce seem to be destroyed. And why? Because there is too much civilization, too much means of subsistence, too much industry, too much commerce. The productive forces at the disposal of society no longer tend to further the development of the conditions of bourgeois property; on the contrary, they have become too powerful for these conditions, by which they are fettered, and no sooner do they overcome these fetters than they bring disorder into the whole of bourgeois society, endanger the existence of bourgeois property. The conditions of bourgeois society are too narrow to comprise the wealth created by them. And how does the bourgeoisie get over these crises? On the one hand by enforced destruction of a mass of productive forces; on the other, by the conquest of new markets, and by the more thorough exploitation of the old ones. That is to say, by paving the way for more extensive and more destructive crises, and by diminishing the means whereby crises are prevented.

The weapons with which the bourgeoisie felled feudalism to the ground are now turned against the bourgeoisie itself.

But not only has the bourgeoisie forged the weapons that bring death to itself; it has also called into existence the men who are to wield those weapons—the modern working class—the proletarians.

In proportion as the bourgeoisie, *i.e.,* capital, is developed, in the same proportion is the proletariat, the modern working class, developed—a class of laborers, who live only so long as they find work, and who find work only so long as their labor increases capital. These laborers, who must sell themselves piecemeal, are a commodity, like every other article of commerce, and are consequently exposed to all the vicissitudes of competition, to all the fluctuations of the market.

Owing to the extensive use of machinery and to division of labor, the work of the proletarians has lost all individual character, and, consequently, all charm for the workman. He becomes an appendage of the machine, and it is only the most simple, most monotonous, and most easily acquired knack, that is required of him. Hence, the cost of production of a workman is restricted, almost entirely, to the means of subsistence that he requires for his maintenance, and for the propagation of his race. But the price of a commodity, and therefore also of labor, is equal to its cost of production. In proportion, therefore, as the repulsiveness of the work increases, the wage decreases. Nay, more, in proportion as the use of machinery and division of labor increases, in the same proportion the burden of toil also increases, whether by prolongation of the working hours, by increase of the work exacted in a given time, or by increased speed of the machinery, etc.

Modern industry has converted the little workshop of the patriarchal master into the great factory of the industrial capitalist. Masses of laborers, crowded into the factory, are organized like soldiers. As privates of the industrial army they are placed under the command of a perfect hierarchy of officers and sergeants. Not only are they slaves of the bourgeois class, and of the bourgeois state; they are daily and hourly enslaved by the machine, by the overlooker, and, above all, by the individual bourgeois manufacturer himself. The more openly this despotism proclaims gain to be its end and aim, the more petty, the more hateful and the more embittering it is. . . .

The lower strata of the middle class—the small tradespeople, shopkeepers, and retired tradesmen generally, the handicraftsmen and peasants—all these sink gradually into the proletariat, partly because their diminutive capital does not suffice for the scale on which modern industry is carried on, and is swamped in the competition with the large capitalists, partly because their specialized skill is rendered worthless by new methods of production. Thus the proletariat is recruited from all classes of the population.

The proletariat goes through various stages of development. With its birth begins its struggle with the bourgeoisie. At first the contest is carried on by individual laborers, then by the work people of a factory, then by the operatives of one trade, in one locality, against the individual bourgeois who directly exploits them. They direct their attacks not against the bourgeois conditions of production, but against the instruments of production themselves; they destroy imported wares that compete with their labor, they smash machinery to pieces, they set factories ablaze, they seek to restore by force the vanished status of the workman of the Middle Ages. . . .

But with the development of industry the proletariat not only increases in number; it becomes concentrated in greater masses, its strength grows, and it feels that strength more. The various interests and conditions of life within the ranks of the proletariat are more and more equalized, in proportion as machinery obliterates all distinctions of labor and nearly everywhere reduces wages to the same low level. The growing competition among the bourgeois, and the resulting commercial crises, make the wages of the workers ever more fluctuating. The unceasing improvement of machinery, ever more rapidly developing, makes their livelihood more and more precarious: the collisions between individual workmen and individual bourgeois take more and more the character of collisions between two classes. Thereupon the workers begin to form combinations (trade unions) against the bourgeoisie; they club together in order to keep up the rate of wages; they found permanent associations in order to make provision beforehand for these occasional revolts. Here and there the contest breaks out into riots.

Now and then the workers are victorious, but only for a time. The real fruit of their battles lies, not in the immediate results, but in the ever expanding union of the workers. This union is furthered by the improved means of communication which are created by modern industry, and which place the workers of different localities in contact with one another. It was just this contact that was needed to centralize the numerous local struggles, all of the same character, into one national struggle between classes. But every class struggle is a political struggle. And that union, to attain which the burghers of the Middle Ages, with their miserable highways, required centuries, the modern proletarians, thanks to railways, achieve in a few years.

This organization of the proletarians into a class, and consequently into a political party, is continually being upset again by the competition between the workers themselves. But it ever rises up again, stronger, firmer, mightier. It compels legislative recognition of particular interests of the workers, by taking advantage of the divisions among the bourgeoisie itself. Thus the ten-hour bill in England was carried.

Altogether, collisions between the classes of the old society further the course of development of the proletariat in many ways. The bourgeoisie finds itself involved in a constant battle. At first with the aristocracy; later on, with those portions of the bourgeoisie itself whose interests have become antagonistic to the progress of industry; at all times with the bourgeoisie of foreign countries. In all these battles it sees itself compelled to appeal to the proletariat, to ask for its help, and thus, to drag it into the political arena. The bourgeoisie itself, therefore, supplies the proletariat with its own elements of political and general education, in other words, it furnishes the proletariat with weapons for fighting the bourgeoisie. . . .

The social conditions of the old society no longer exist for the proletariat. The proletarian is without property; his relation to his wife and children has no longer anything in common with bourgeois family relations; modern industrial labor, modern subjection to capital, the same in England as in France, in America as in Germany, has stripped him of every trace of national character. Law, morality, religion, are to him so many bourgeois prejudices, behind which lurk in ambush just as many bourgeois interests.

All the preceding classes that got the upper hand sought to fortify their already acquired status by subjecting society at large to their conditions of appropriation. The proletarians cannot become masters of the productive forces of society, except by abolishing their own previous mode of appropriation. They have nothing of their own to secure and to fortify; their mission is to destroy all previous securities for, and insurances of, individual property.

All previous historical movements were movements of minorities, or in the interest of minorities. The proletarian movement is the self-conscious, independent movement of the immense majority, in the interest of the immense majority. The proletariat, the lowest stratum of our present society, cannot stir, cannot raise itself up, without the whole superincumbent strata of official society being sprung into the air. . . .

The essential condition for the existence and sway of the bourgeois class, is the formation and augmentation of capital; the condition for capital is wage-labor. Wage-labor rests exclusively on competition between the laborers. The advance of industry, whose involuntary promoter is the bourgeoisie, replaces the isolation of the laborers, due to competition, by their revolutionary combination, due to association. The development of modern industry, therefore, cuts from under its feet the very foundation on which the bourgeoisie produces and appropriates products. What the bourgeoisie therefore produces, above all, are its own gravediggers. Its

fall and the victory of the proletariat are equally inevitable. . . .

PROGRAM

We have seen above, that the first step in the revolution by the working class, is to raise the proletariat to the position of ruling class, to establish democracy.

The proletariat will use its political supremacy to wrest, by degrees, all capital from the bourgeoisie, to centralize all instruments of production in the hands of the state, *i.e.*, of the proletariat organized as the ruling class; and to increase the total of productive forces as rapidly as possible.

Of course, in the beginning, this cannot be effected except by means of despotic inroads on the rights of property, and on the conditions of bourgeois production; by means of measures, therefore, which appear economically insufficient and untenable, but which, in the course of the movement, outstrip themselves, necessitate further inroads upon the old social order, and are unavoidable as a means of entirely revolutionizing the mode of production.

These measures will of course be different in different countries.

Nevertheless in the most advanced countries, the following will be pretty generally applicable.

1. Abolition of property in land and application of all rents of land to public purposes.
2. A heavy progressive or graduated income tax.
3. Abolition of all right of inheritance.
4. Confiscation of the property of all emigrants and rebels.
5. Centralization of credit in the hands of the state, by means of a national bank

with state capital and an exclusive monopoly.

6. Centralization of the means of communication and transport in the hands of the state.

7. Extension of factories and instruments of production owned by the state; the bringing into cultivation of waste lands, and the improvement of the soil . . . in accordance with a common plan.

8. Equal obligation of all to work. Establishment of industrial armies, especially for agriculture.

9. Combination of agriculture with manufacturing industries; gradual abolition of the distinction between town and country, by a more equable distribution of the population over the country.

10. Free education for all children in public schools. Abolition of child factory labor in its present form. Combination of education with industrial production, etc.

When, in the course of development, class distinctions have disappeared, and all production has been concentrated in the hands of a vast association of the whole nation, the public power will lose its political character. Political power, properly so called, is merely the organized power of one class for oppressing another. If the proletariat during its contest with the bourgeoisie is compelled, by the force of circumstances, to organize itself as a class; if, by means of a revolution, it makes itself the ruling class, and, as such sweeps away by force the old conditions of production, then it will, along with these conditions, have swept away the conditions for the existence of class antagonisms, and of classes generally, and will thereby have abolished its own supremacy as a class.

In place of the old bourgeois society, with its classes and class antagonisms, we shall have an association, in which free development of each is the condition for the free development of all. . . .

CONCLUSION

In short, the Communists everywhere support every revolutionary movement against the existing social and political order of things.

In all these movements they bring to the front, as the leading question in each case, the property question, no matter what its degree of development at the time.

Finally, they labor everywhere for the union and agreement of the democratic parties of all countries.

The Communists disdain to conceal their views and aims. They openly declare that their ends can be attained only by the forcible overthrow of all existing social conditions. Let the ruling classes tremble at a Communist revolution. The proletarians have nothing to lose but their chains. They have a world to win.

Workingmen of all countries, unite!

Adam Ulam: The Unfinished Revolution

Adam B. Ulam has long been interested in the context in which socialist ideologies have developed. He brings to his study of Marxism a specific concern for the psychological and material needs of industrializing nations. From *The Unfinished Revolution,* by Adam B. Ulam. © Copyright 1960 by Adam B. Ulam. Reprinted by permission of Random House, Inc.

I

It is only since World War II that we have realized that we are in the midst of a yet unfinished revolution. Its character is more complex than commonplace Communist propaganda would have it; and it also defies the usual Western editorializing, which always sees in revolutionary stirrings the result of an inadequate standard of living, or corruption and oppression by a particular government. The conditions underlying the current revolution are in many ways similar to those that disturbed and transformed Western European society during the first half of the nineteenth century. Under different conditions and in a different world situation, we see parts of Asia, Africa, and Latin America entering the initial or intermediate stages of the Industrial Revolution. The birth pains of modern industrial society, which Marx often mistook for the death throes of capitalism are being enacted before our eyes. We can see more clearly what Marxism was *about* than could the generations for whom it was a movement of protest against capitalism, an obsolete economic theory, or a philosophical justification for an international Communist conspiracy. Also, in another dimension, within the context of a highly industrialized society, both the insights and the limitations of Marxism are more clearly perceptible now that a society based on Marxist ideology is challenging the greatest nonsocialist state for industrial and political supremacy.

In other words, we can begin to see Marxism not only as a set of theories and prophecies postulated by its author and his disciples, but as something that "exists in nature" as well . . . a thinker may be supremely important and his thought of world significance not only because he formulates historical laws, but also because his thought reflects the essence of the mood of great historical periods. This has been the great significance of Marx, Philosopher, economist, a would-be politician and revolutionary, his ideas are still alive and important because they are attuned to the two greatest tendencies of the industrial age: the worship of science and mechanization and limitless faith in their power to transform mankind; and the very opposite—protest against the soullessness and destructiveness of the machine age. Every society reaching for industrialization and modernization has its "Marxist" period, when some of the ideas of Marx are relevant to its problems and are reflected in everyday sentiments of the masses of people, even though the name of Marx and his movement may be unknown to them. Hence the attraction for Marxism, and the quasi-Marxist character of social protest in many areas of the world. . . .

Marxism, then, is not only the complex of theories bequeathed by Marx and Engels and developed, interpreted, and acted out in countless ways by countless theorists, parties, and movements. To use an analogy from physics: science has learned to produce in the laboratory elements found in nature. Imperfect as such comparisons must be, Marxism to a remarkable degree reproduces the social psychology of the period of transition from a preindustrial to an industrial society. If this is correct, then it is not surprising that Marxian socialism found little response in late nineteenth-century England and a great deal in Russia at the turn of the century. The industrialized United States has experienced Marxism in the last generation only as an intellectual reaction to the Depression; but large parts of Latin America, drawn increasingly into modern economy and its con-

comitants, are experiencing social and political turbulence which, while not directed by Marxists and not necessarily inspired by socialism or communism, is Marxist in its mood if not in its postulates. . . .

II

The class struggle is the salt of Marxism, its most operative revolutionary part. As a historical and psychological concept, it expresses a gross oversimplification, but it is the oversimplification of a genius. The formula of the class struggle seizes the essence of the mood of a great historical moment—a revolution in basic economy—and generalizes it into a historical law. It extracts the grievances of groups of politically conscious workers in Western Europe, then a very small part of the whole proletariat, and sees in it the portent and meaning of the awakening of the whole working class everywhere. The *first* reaction of the worker to industrialization, his feelings of grievance and impotence before the machine, his employer, and the state which stands behind the employer, are assumed by Marx to be typical of the general reactions of the worker to industrialization. What does change in the process of the development of industry is that the worker's feeling of impotence gives way to class consciousness, which in turn leads him to class struggle and socialism. Marx's worker is the historical worker, but he is the historical worker of a specific period of industrial and political development.

Even in interpreting the psychology of the worker of the transitional period, Marx exhibited a rationalistic bias. The worker's opposition to the capitalist order is a total opposition to its laws, its factories, and its government. But this revolutionary conscious-

ness of the worker is to take him next to Marxist socialism, where he will accept the factory system and the state, the *only* difference being the abolition of capitalism. Why shouldn't the revolutionary protest of the worker flow into other channels: into rejection of industrialism as well as capitalism, into rejection of the socialist as well as the capitalist state? It is there that Marx is most definitely the child of his age, the child of rationalistic optimism: the workers will undoubtedly translate their anarchistic protests and grievances into a sophisticated philosophy of history. They will undoubtedly realize that the forces of industrialism and modern life, which strip them of property, status, and economic security, are in themselves benevolent in their ultimate effects and that it is only capitalism and the capitalists which make them into instruments of oppression. The chains felt by the proletariat are the chains of the industrial system. The chains Marx urges them to throw off are those of capitalism. Will the workers understand the difference? And if they do, will they still feel that in destroying capitalism they have a "world to win"?

How different will the better world of socialism be from the old one of capitalism? Marx and Engels have notoriously little to say about the wonderful new world their criticism and theories imply. The wealth of observations and historical data illustrating the nature of capitalism is paralleled by a skimpiness of reference concerning socialism: a few epigrammatic statements about the general nature of socialist society, a few items of the political program for the socialist parties, incidental references to the contemporary socialist movements and such revolutions as the Paris Commune, and that is all. The task of expounding the Marxist canon in the very un-Marxist world of Western Europe of the 1880's fell mainly to Engels. He wrote chattily and attractively, a fact that makes him, rather than his great companion, the favorite of the popularizers of Marxism. His thought on the main issues had, of course, for a long time merged with that of Marx. There is in Engels, at the same time, a certain dilettantism and a tendency to write around rather than to address himself directly to the most important theoretical issues. At his death in 1895, the canon of Marxism was frozen, and the vital questions of the socialist role in parliamentarianism, of the nature of transition from capitalism, and of socialism itself, remained to be fought over by the Revisionists and the orthodox Marxists. The fight, although accompanied by continuous invocation of the scriptures, points up the really enigmatic and ambiguous nature of the Marxist argument as it touches the actual problem of socialism.

The apparent enigma disappears if one refuses to be distracted by the revolutionary phraseology of Marxism into believing that *from the economic point of view* the stage of socialism represents a drastic break with capitalism. Quite the contrary: socialism, once it assumes power, has as its mission the fullest development of the productive resources of society. Though private ownership of the means of production and the profit motive are abolished, the state takes on the mission, formerly performed by individual capitalists, of creating "those material conditions which alone can form the real basis of a higher form of society." The logic of the doctrine implies that in so doing the state will in no wise proceed differently from the capitalist: i.e., it will take the worker's surplus labor in the form of surplus value and will sink it in further investment. From the earliest, most revolutionary writings of Marx and Engels until the very end of their activity, there is no indication that society, until full material abundance is achieved (whatever that may be), can dispense with the organization of labor and production typical of capitalism. What, then, is socialism? *It is simply capitalism without the capitalists*. There is no need for elaborate descriptions of socialism. Except for the abolition of private property in the means of production (its rationalization), socialism continues and intensifies all the main characteristics of capitalism. The Bolsheviks and especially Stalin have been accused of perverting Marxism into state capitalism. Yet we need not burden Marx and Engels with the responsibility for Stalinism to perceive that the notion of socialism as state capitalism is found in the canon of Marxism under all the revolutionary and anarchistic phraseology.

When they wrote the *Communist Manifesto,* Marx and Engels were very young men. They could not deny themselves a certain youthful bravado ("Communism is already acknowledged by all European powers to be itself a power."—a ridiculous statement in the Europe of 1848) and a most literal attempt to *épater les bourgeois* ("The Communists have no need to introduce community of women; it has existed almost from time immemorial."). Yet even in the midst of all this pathos, so typical of revolutionary manifestoes mushrooming all over Europe in 1848, there is a chilling reminder:

> The proletariat will use its political supremacy to wrest, by degrees, all capital from the bourgeoisie, to centralize all instruments of production in the hands of the state, i.e., of the proletariat organized as a ruling class; and to increase the total of productive forces as rapidly as possible.

Even at the most revolutionary moment in their career, Marx and Engels do not envisage the worker getting away from the treadmill of the factory system, do not allow the industrial system other functions than the ceaseless race for more and more production, more and more accumulation. Nothing in *the logic* of Marxism should enable the worker to expect his standard of life to rise *immediately* following the revolution. Nothing in the doctrine extends to the worker the prospect of greater control over conditions of his work once socialism is established. The state runs the factories; and the socialist state, as much if not more than the capitalist, is interested in increasing production and productivity. The devices of workers' control, industrial democracy, and profit sharing by the workers receive in Marxism all the sympathy they would receive from an early nineteenth-century capitalist. To be sure, the worker will have the pleasure of seeing "the expropriators expropriated," and crises and unemployment will disappear once the profit motive is eliminated. Yet the worker remains subject to factory discipline. Socialism demands that everybody work, but it repudiates the idea that everybody should be paid equally. The emphasis on technology and productivity promises, as a matter of fact, that there will be a very considerable inequality in wages and salaries under Marxist socialism. How many proletarians would be likely to stir into revolutionary action if the logic of Marxism were thus expounded to them?

STUDY QUESTIONS

1. What possibilities were open to the poor in the nineteenth century? What made social and economic advancement so difficult? Why was work as a factory hand "little better than slavery"?

2. What attitudes toward the workingman's social condition are expressed in Ernest Jones' poem?

3. In what sense, according to Marx, have the bourgeoisie played a revolutionary role in history? How have they helped to further the growth and revolutionary potential of the proletariat?

4. What were the specific measures Marx proposed in his program for a victorious proletariat? Which would the established classes be likely to resist most strenuously? How revolutionary is each today?

5. What was wrong with laissez-faire economics according to Marx?

6. Who, of the authors we have read, seem to have influenced Marx' thinking?

7. What does Ulam mean by his statement that Marx mistakenly took "the birth pains of modern industrial society" as "the death throes of capitalism"?

8. How does Ulam explain the continuing appeal of Marxism in the developing countries? In what sense, according to him, is Marxian socialism like capitalism?

Steel mill conditions about 1880
in a Krupp plant in Germany

MASS DEMOCRACY AND THE WANING OF LAISSEZ-FAIRE

"Workers of the world unite!" Karl Marx had urged in the *Communist Manifesto*. The year 1848 gave promise of bearing out his predictions. A cycle of revolutions, touched off in over fifty European cities by a spark from Paris, revealed the combustible tinder in Europe's new industrial society. To be sure, the goals of the revolutionary movement varied from country to country. In the portions of Western Europe undergoing industrialization, the movement had a dual focus: to extend the vote and to improve the lot of the working people. Further eastward, in the less developed portions of Europe, revolutions were fought for freedom from foreign control, for national unity and the right to a constitution.

Such movements were either crushed by force, or reduced to failure for lack of mass support and effective leadership. The one apparent exception, France, achieved a Republic and universal suffrage, but when concerned republican leaders pushed a markedly social program they opened the floodgates of reaction. The blood had hardly dried on the barricades before, as elsewhere in Europe, an authoritarian government became the main beneficiary of the turmoil of revolution.

The lessons of 1848 were drawn all over Europe. It seemed obvious that liberal, national and socialist programs could not be realized by disorganized masses of citizens, or even by educated élites. The ideal of a broader social and national community was no match for the narrower interests of class and region which had been so well defended by police and army. For many more decades, fear of revolution drove the bourgeoisie to defend what it called order and to reject out of hand programs fathered by the socialists.

Nevertheless, the constitutional, social and national programs of 1848 were not buried with their defenders. The state that emerged at mid-century found it necessary to realize many of the programs it had earlier fought. An explanation for this seeming paradox is to be found in both the pattern of Europe's social, economic and political development, and in the shortcomings and contradictions of the *laissez-faire* philosophy. The readings examine the response of government to organized political pressure, and the corollary effect of prosperity, trade unionism, and a responsive government on the character and goals of the socialist movement.

E. H. Carr: The Growth of State Intervention

The English historian E. H. Carr (1892–) was a member of the Foreign Office for many years. He has written widely on subjects that range from studies of Dostoevski and Bakunin to surveys of world politics between the wars and a monumental history of Soviet Russia. In this reading Professor Carr inspects the path that led from the *laissez-faire* doctrine of unfettered competition in the nineteenth century to the planned economy of contemporary society. From E. H. Carr, *The New Society* (New York: St. Martin's Press, 1951), pp. 21–25, 26. This book is published in Canada by Macmillan & Co. Ltd.

There is no more fascinating theme in contemporary history than to follow the stages through which the *laissez-faire* "night-watchman state" of the nineteenth century has been transformed into the "welfare state" of today—at one and the same time its logical opposite and its logical corollary. The process was, of course, gradual and had begun long before the twentieth century or the first world war. While the industrial revolution was still in its infancy, Robert Owen had issued a warning against the danger of giving it its head and pleaded for state action to curb some of its consequences:

> The general diffusion of manufactures throughout a country [he wrote in 1817] generates a new character in its inhabitants; and, as this character is formed on a principle quite unfavourable to individual or general happiness, it will produce the most lamentable and permanent evils unless its tendency be counteracted by legislative interference and direction.

The humanitarian movement which led to extensive factory legislation to protect, at first the child worker and the woman worker, and later workers in general, against extreme forms of physical exploitation, were well under way in Britain in the 1840's. In the 1880's Herbert Spencer was already fighting a losing rearguard action in defence of the night-watchman state when he listed a number of recent enactments of the British parliament which contravened sound liberal and *laissez-faire* principles: these included measures prohibiting the employment of boy chimney-sweeps, imposing compulsory vaccination, and permitting local authorities to establish free public libraries paid for out of the local rates. About the same time Bismarck was sponsoring the introduction in Germany of the first system of compulsory social insurance for the workers, and thus helping to prevent, forty years later, a German Bolshevik revolution. The first social insurance measure in Britain came in the 1890's in the form of compulsory insurance of workers against industrial accidents.

Social pressures brought about these enactments in the most advanced and densely populated industrial countries before any widespread conscious departure from the *laissez-faire* philosophy could be discerned. But they were symptoms of a profound underlying refusal to accept the continued validity of that philosophy and of the presuppositions on which it rested. The conception of a society where success was, in Macaulay's terminology, the "natural reward" of "industry and intelligence", and failure the "natural punishment" of "idleness and folly", was not particularly humane. But it was clear-cut, logical and coherent on one hypothesis—namely that the free and equal individuals who competed for these rewards and punishments did, in fact, start free and equal. What ultimately discredited the philosophy which Macaulay had so confidently enunciated was the realization that the competitors did not start free and equal and that, the longer the competition continued, the less scope was left for freedom and equality, so that the moral foundation on which *laissez-faire* rested was more and more hopelessly undermined. How had this happened? How could the logic of *laissez-faire* lead straight to a system which seemed its opposite and its negation?

In Great Britain and in the chief European countries, the industrial revolution broke in on a long-standing traditional order based on social hierarchy. The economic and social inequalities left behind by the *ancien régime* made impossible anything like the clean start between the competitors which was assumed by the exponents of *laissez-faire*. But this flaw, much less in evidence in the new world of America than in old Europe, was not very important. What was far more serious was that the revolution, which purported to wipe out the old inequalities and did in large measure wipe them out, soon bred and tolerated new inequalities of its own. . . . In every society, however egalitarian in principle, inherited advantages quickly set in motion the process of building up a ruling class, even if the new ruling class has not the additional asset of being able in part to build on the foundations of the old. And so it happened in the industrial society of the nineteenth

Horatio Alger's young heroes who began as bootblacks or newsboys always had their diligence and industry rewarded by success. The young lad on the cover of the *Luck and Pluck Series* (1869) waves good-bye to family and farm to seek his fortune in the city.

This real-life boy worker in Pittsburgh, Pennsylvania, at the outset of the twentieth century had less expectation of material success.

century; and the story of the industrious errand-boy who became the managing director and of the lazy son of the managing director who became an errand-boy was soon an agreeable myth which took little or no account of the facts of life. But, when this myth was exploded, it carried away with it whatever moral justification had existed for the non-intervention of the state in a society where industry and intelligence were automatically rewarded and idleness and folly automatically punished.

Nor did the trouble stop there. What was much worse than any inequality of initial opportunity was the fact that individuals engaged in the economic process obstinately refused to remain individuals. Instead of competing against one another on equal terms for the good of all, they began to combine with one another in groups for their own exclusive profit. . . .

The nightmare of competition has been replaced by the dream of monopoly. During this long period the individual business man has been ousted by the company, the company by the cartel and the trust, the trust by the super-trust. In this process the sky is the limit; nothing short of monopoly, first national, then, in favoured cases, international, is the ultimate goal. . . . The continuous and progressive replacement of the smaller by the larger unit has been the typical trend of economic organization in our time. . . .

This summary outline is enough to show that contemporary forms of economic organization, while they are in one sense a direct negation of the *laissez-faire* system, in another sense proceed directly from it. The result of free competition has been to destroy competition; competing individuals have replaced themselves by monopolistic groups as the economic units. The further, however, this process advances, the more untenable becomes the conception of non-interference by the state. The philosophy of *laissez-faire* presupposed the free competition of individual employer and individual worker on the labour market. The capitalist system in its maturity offers the picture of a class struggle between two vast power-groups; the state must intervene to bring about that modicum of harmony which *laissez-faire* so conspicuously failed to produce, and to mitigate the harshness of a struggle which, carried to its extreme conclusion, would wreck the foundations of the existing order. Hence the development of factory legislation, social insurance, wage-fixing and legislation against strikes. . . .

Germany Adopts Social Welfare Legislation (1881)

Against the opposition of the liberals, the German government passed a series of social welfare laws in the 1880s. The first of these was a bill to provide accident insurance. Otto von Bismarck (1815–1898), the conservative prime minister, justified the action of the government in a speech to the Reichstag (parliament) in March 1881. From W. H. Dawson, *Bismarck and State Socialism* (London, 1891).

Herr Richter [a liberal member of the Reichstag] has called attention to the responsibility of the State for what it does. But it is my opinion that the State can also be responsible for what it does not do. I do not think that doctrines like those of "*Laissez-faire, laissez-aller,*" "Pure Manchesterdom in politics," "Every man for himself and the devil take the hindmost," "As you make your bed, so must you lie," "To him that hath shall be given, and from him that hath not shall be taken away even that which he hath"—that doctrines like these should be applied in the State, and especially in a monarchically paternalistic State. On the contrary, I believe that those who profess horror at the intervention of the State for the protection of the weak lay themselves open to the suspicion that they are desirous of using their strength—be it that of capital, that of rhetoric, or whatever it be—for the benefit of a section for the oppression of the rest, for the introduction of party domination, and that they will be annoyed as soon as this design is disturbed by any action of the government.

I ask you what right had I to close the way to the throne against these people? The kings of Prussia have never been by preference kings of the rich. Frederick the Great said when Crown Prince: "When I become king, I will be a true king of the poor." He undertook to be the protector of the poor, and this principle has been followed by our later kings. At their throne suffering has always found a refuge and a hearing. . . .

I am not antagonistic to the rightful claims of capital; I am far from wanting to flourish a hostile flag; but I am of opinion that the masses, too, have rights which should be considered. . . .

Give the working-man the right to work as long as he is healthy; assure him care when he is sick; assure him maintenance when he is old. If you do that, and do not fear the sacrifice, or cry out at State Socialism directly the words "Provision for old age" are uttered,—if the State will show a little more Christian solicitude for the workingman, then I believe that the [socialists] will sound their birdcall in vain, and that the thronging to them will cease as soon as workingmen see that the Government and legislative bodies are earnestly concerned for their welfare. . . .

I will further every endeavour which positively aims at improving the condition of the working classes. . . . As soon as a positive proposal comes from the Socialists for fashioning the future in a sensible way, in order that the lot of the workingman might be improved, I would not at any rate refuse to examine it favourably, and I would not even shrink from the idea of State help for the people who would help themselves. . . .

British Liberals Tax the Land (1909)

David Lloyd George (1863–1945), a spirited member of the middle-class Liberal Party in England, was prime minister during the First World War. In 1909 he was Chancellor of the Exchequer (Secretary of the Treasury) in a reform-minded Liberal government. In order to get money needed in part to provide old age pensions for the British working classes, he proposed to establish new taxes on land. The landowners were furious at this direct attack on their income and power. In a famous speech to a packed crowd of four thousand, Lloyd George defended his budget by mounting a devastating assault on the possessing classes. From David Lloyd George, "The Budget and the People," *London Daily Chronicle*, July 30, 1909.

The Budget, as your chairman has already so well reminded you, is introduced not merely for the purpose of raising barren taxes, but taxes that are fertile, taxes that will bring forth fruit—the security of the country which is paramount in the minds of all. The provision for the aged and deserving poor—was it not time something was done? It is rather a shame that a rich country like ours—probably the richest in the world, if not the richest the world has ever seen—should allow those who have toiled all their days to end in penury and possibly starvation. It is rather hard that an old workman should have to find his way to the gates of the tomb, bleeding and footsore, through the brambles and thorns of poverty. We cut a new path for him—an easier one, a pleasanter one, through fields of waving corn. We are raising money to pay for the new road—aye, and to widen it so that 200,000 paupers shall be able to join in the march. There are many in the country blessed by Providence with great wealth, and if there are amongst them men who grudge out of their riches a fair contribution towards the less fortunate of their fellow-countrymen they are very shabby rich men. . . .

Some of our critics say, "The taxes themselves are unjust, unfair, unequal, oppressive—notably so the land taxes." They are engaged, not merely in the House of Commons, but outside the House of Commons, in assailing these taxes with a concentrated and a sustained ferocity which will not allow even a comma to escape with its life. Now, are these taxes really so wicked? Let us examine them; because it is perfectly clear that the one part of the Budget that attracts all this hostility and animosity is that part which deals with the taxation of land. Well, now let us examine it. . . .

Not far from here, not so many years ago, between the Lea and the Thames, you had hundreds of acres of land which was not very useful even for agricultural purposes. In the main it was a sodden marsh. The commerce and the trade of London increased under Free Trade, the tonnage of your shipping went up by hundreds of thousands of tons and by millions; labour was attracted from all parts of the country to cope with all this trade and business which was done here. What happened? There was no housing accommodation. This Port of London became overcrowded, and the population overflowed. That was the opportunity of the owners of the marsh. All that land became valuable building land, and land which used to be rented at £2 or £3 an acre has been selling within the last few years at £2,000 an acre, £3,000 an acre, £6,000 an acre, £8,000 an acre. Who created that increment? Who made that golden swamp? Was it the landlord? Was it his energy? Was it his brains—a very bad lookout for the place if it were—his forethought? It was purely the combined efforts of all the people engaged in the trade and commerce of the Port of London—trader, merchant, shipowner, dock labourer, workman—everybody except the landlord. Now, you follow that transaction. Land worth £2 or £3 an acre running up to thousands. During the time it was ripening the landlord was paying his rates and his taxes not on £2 or £3 an acre. It was agricultural land, and because it was agricultural land a munificent Tory Government voted a sum of two millions to pay half the rates of those poor distressed landlords, and you and I had to pay taxes in order to enable those landlords to pay half their rates on agricultural land, while it was going up every year by hundreds of pounds through your efforts and the efforts of your neighbours.

This is now coming to an end. . . . These things I tell you of have only been possible up to the present through the "fraud" of the few and the "folly" of the many. What is going to happen in the future? In future those landlords will have to contribute to the taxation of the country on the basis of the real value—only one halfpenny in the pound! Only a halfpenny! And that is what all the howling is about. . . .

Now, unless I am wearying you I have just one other land tax to speak to you about. The landlords are receiving eight millions a year by way of royalties. What for? They never deposited the coal in the earth. It was not they who planted those great granite rocks in Wales. Who laid the foundations of the mountains? Was it the landlord? And yet he, by some divine right, demands as his toll—for merely the right for men to risk their lives in hewing those rocks—eight millions a year!

I went down to a coalfield the other day, and they pointed out to me many collieries there. They said: "You see that colliery. The first man who went there spent a quarter of a million in sinking shafts, in driving mains and levels. He never got coal, and he lost his quarter of a million. The second man who came spent £100,000—and he failed. The third man came along and he got the coal." What was the landlord doing in the meantime? The first man failed; but the landlord got his royalty, the landlord got his deadrent—and a very good name for it. The second man failed, but the landlord got his royalty.

These capitalists put their money in, and I asked, "When the cash failed, what did the landlord put in?" He simply put in the bailiffs. The capitalist risks, at any rate, the whole of his money; the engineer puts his brains in; the miner risks his life. Have you been down a coal mine? I went down one the other day. We sank down into a pit a half mile deep. We then walked underneath the mountain, and we had about three-quarters of a mile of rock and shale above us. The earth seemed to be straining—around us and above us—to crush us in. You could see the pit-props bent and twisted and sundered, their fibres split in resisting the pressure. Sometimes they give way, and then there is a mutilation and death. Often a spark ignites, the whole pit is deluged in fire, and the breath of life is scorched out of hundreds of breasts by the consuming flame. In the very next colliery to the one I descended, just a few years ago, 300 people lost their lives in that way; and yet when the

Prime Minister and I knock at the doors of these great landlords, and say to them: "Here, you know these poor fellows who have been digging up royalties at the risk of their lives, some of them are old, they have survived the perils of their trade, they are broken, they can earn no more. Won't you give something towards keeping them out of the work-house?" They scowl at us. We say, "Only a ha'penny, just a copper." They retort, "You thieves!" And they turn their dogs on to us, and you can hear their bark every morning. If this is an indication of the view taken by these great landlords of their responsibility to the people who, at the risk of life, create their wealth, then I say their day of reckoning is at hand. . . .

The ownership of land is not merely an enjoyment, it is a stewardship. It has been reckoned as such in the past, and if the owners cease to discharge their functions in seeing to the security and defence of the country, in looking after the broken in their villages and in their neighborhoods, the time will come to reconsider the conditions under which land is held in this country. No country, however rich, can permanently afford to have quartered upon its revenue a class which declines to do the duty which it was called upon to perform since the beginning. . . .

Parliamentary Democracy Responds to Demands for Reform

From *Europe Since Napoleon,* by David Thomson. © Copyright 1957, 1962 by David Thomson. Reprinted by permission of Alfred A. Knopf, Inc.

THE NEW ELECTORATES

In almost the whole of western and central Europe, parliamentary institutions developed between 1871 and 1914. They varied widely in form and in effectiveness, in their electoral basis and in the extent of their control over governments. . . . But they were at least a provisional solution to the old problem, which had agitated European civilization since 1815, of how to establish a closer mutual relationship between state and society, between government and governed.

France was ahead of all other countries in having effective universal male suffrage from 1871 onward. The electoral laws of 1848, which were revived in 1871 and again in 1875, gave the vote to some ten million Frenchmen. The electorate of the United Kingdom after the reform acts of 1867–68 numbered only between two and a half and three million. But in 1884 Gladstone passed a further act which extended the electorate to about five million, or roughly one sixth of the population. This made the rural electorate as democratic as the urban, and was the first clear recognition of the radical principle that the individual, regardless of property qualification, was entitled to a vote. . . . Together with the secret ballot, which had been instituted in 1872, these reforms launched Britain on the broad road toward political democracy. In neither Britain nor France were women given the parliamentary vote before 1914, and in Britain nearly a quarter of even the adult male population remained voteless until 1918. But because the general principles of universal personal suffrage had now won the day, it was to be only a matter of time before they permeated the electoral systems of both countries.

Other western states, having instituted parliamentary systems in the years before 1870, developed along comparable lines. Switzerland had universal male suffrage after 1874. In Belgium until 1893 property qualifications restricted the electorate to less than 5 percent of the population, but a reform of that year established universal male suffrage with the addition of plural voting for men with special property or educational qualifications. In the Netherlands, reforms of 1887 and 1896 extended the electorate from 2 percent to 14 percent of the population but universal suffrage came only in 1917. Spain introduced universal male suffrage in 1890, Norway in 1898. . . . Of the German states, Baden adopted universal suffrage in 1904, Bavaria and Württemberg two years later. In Italy, on the other hand, the constitutional monarchy retained its mid-nineteenth-century restrictiveness, and even the electoral reform of 1882 widened the electorate to only about two million, or 7 percent of the population. Most Italian men gained the vote, at last, in 1912. Whereas the age for voting rights was 21 in the United Kingdom and France, in most other countries it was more. In the German *Reich* it was as high as 25; and in Italy, even in 1914, it was 30. . . .

Behind the whole checkered story, in spite of all the many divergences and restrictions, there can be discerned a great tide of movement. Democracy was advancing everywhere in Europe, and by 1914 it was lapping the frontiers of Asia. The symbol was the right of the individual citizen to vote—a right increasingly buttressed from the 1800's onward by secrecy of the ballot. The vote was often endowed, by enthusiastic radicals and frightened conservatives alike, with a magic power. Too many radicals expected universal suffrage to bring the millenium—to sweep away before it the last relics of feudalism, of aristocratic and plutocratic privilege, of popular squalor and ignorance. Too many conservatives and moderate liberals took the radicals at their word, and feared that democracy would demolish monarchy, church, religion, public order, and all that they cherished. Therefore the struggles for extensions of the franchise and secrecy of the ballot were often long and bitter, raising exaggerated hopes on one side, excessive fears on the other. . . .

Growth of Population

The new electorates of Europe were large, not only because of extensions of the franchise, but also because of the growth of populations. The immense increase of population in earlier decades was now producing the most momentous of all modern European phenomena—"the age of the masses". This, even more than the spread of democratic ideas, compelled every state to overhaul its machinery of government and administration. The accumulated consequences of this fact were to make the twentieth century unique in its problems and its opportunities. Between 1870 and 1914 Europe as a whole maintained the dizzy speed of its growth, and grew at an average rate of more than 1 percent each year. The 293 million in 1870 became 490 million by 1914. The last three decades of the nineteenth century, which saw the increase of Europe's inhabitants by nearly one third, saw also the emigration of 25 million more to North America, South America, and Australia. The earlier rate of increase tended to slow down in the western nations but to accelerate in the central and eastern nations. Between 1871 and 1914 the population of the

United Kingdom increased by nearly half, that of Germany by more than half, that of Russia by nearly three quarters. Italy grew more slowly than Germany, from 27 to 35 million; but France grew more slowly still, from 37 to only 40 million. Many Italians emigrated, whereas in France immigration constantly exceeded emigration. The significance of these differences . . . for internal politics was that every European government now had to administer and serve the interests of larger and denser agglomerations of people than ever before in the history of mankind. When the First World War began, the United Kingdom was still, as she had been since 1815, the most highly urbanized country in Europe, whereas France clung stubbornly to her rural character. But after her political unification Germany swung over sharply from a population almost as rural as the French to a position in which three out of five Germans lived in towns. This "flight to the towns" had begun before 1871, but it now took place in Germany at a speed unrivaled by any other nation.

These changes in greater or lesser degree affected all European countries. In terms of politics and administration they meant that all governments were confronted with problems that British governments had been obliged to tackle earlier in the century. These were problems of how to govern densely populated industrial towns; how to ensure adequate provision for public health and sanitation, public order, and police; how to protect industrial workers against bad conditions of working and living. Perplexing social problems were forced upon every government by the course of events; and the parallel growth of democratic ideas and of wider electorates ensured for these problems a high priority of attention. . . .

Social Reforms

Accordingly, the politics and policies of all European states came, in these years, to be greatly concerned with social problems. This pressure of demand for a more active state came into conflict, especially in western countries, with the recently dominant tendencies toward free trade, *laissez-faire,* and a divorce of politics from economic and social affairs. The more doctrinaire liberals, wedded to notions of free trade and free enterprise, found themselves being pushed from the left—partly by more radical-minded liberals and partly by the growing parliamentary socialist movements and labor organizations. In the novel circumstances of large popular electorates for whose votes rival political parties had to compete, there was a strong temptation for politicians to outbid one another. For this reason many of the social welfare measures passed in these years were the work of conservative parties, or of liberal parties obliged to yield to the pressure of their more radical supporters. Larger towns and larger electorates conspired to change the whole purport of state activity, as well as to make it more democratic.

A host of important consequences followed. Parliaments became busier passing legislation that imposed upon governments new kinds of work and organization; local authorities and officials blossomed into fresh life; and new sources of taxation had to be tapped to finance such activities. . . .

By 1914 every European country outside Russia and the Balkans had relatively well-developed codes of factory and labor legislation, comparable with the British and French. Austria set up a system of national factory inspection in 1883, and in 1907 issued an

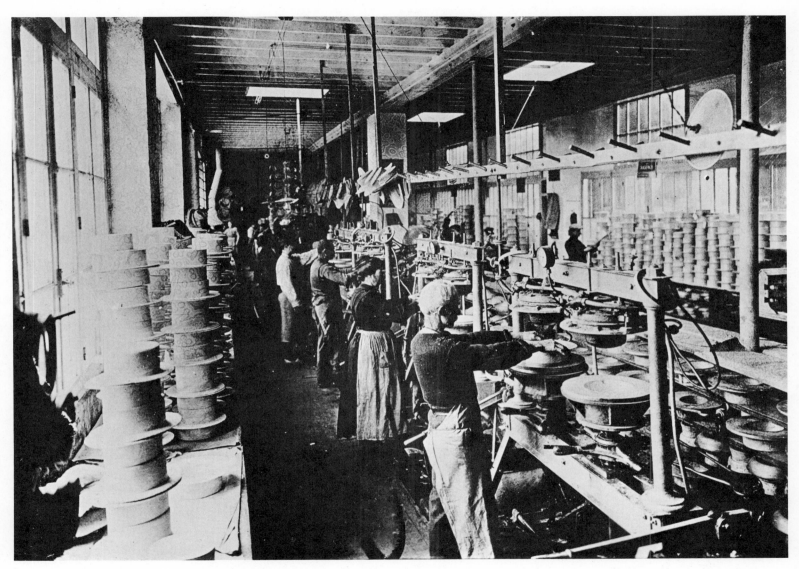

A hat factory near London, c.1900. Hazardous moving parts have been shielded, and the plant—considered modern in its day—is reasonably clean and well-lighted.

elaborate industrial code consolidating regulations that prohibited employment of children under twelve, prescribed an eleven-hour day in industry, and provided for good sanitation and protection against injury. Separate Swiss cantons, led by Zürich, followed the same course, and by 1877 a comprehensive federal statute was passed, applying to all cantons. In the same decade the Netherlands and Belgium introduced comparable laws. Italy and Spain lagged far behind other countries, but between 1886 and 1904 they too made some progress in labor legislation, the Italian being closely modeled on the German.

Just as Germany provided the most spectacular example, in these years, of massive and speedy industrial expansion, so she also set the pace in systematic social legislation. The emphasis in the German system . . . aimed at a comprehensive national provision for security against the three commonest vicissitudes of urban life—sickness, accident, and incapacity in old age. Acts tackling successively these three problems were passed in 1883, 1884, 1889. In 1911 the whole law of social insurance was codified and extended to various classes of nonindustrial workers, such as agricultural laborers and domestic servants. Before these laws were passed, a multitude of local provisions had been made voluntarily by benefit societies, guilds, burial clubs, and parishes. The *Reich* system utilized these older forms but gradually absorbed and replaced them by new local and factory associations which administered the insurance schemes. By 1913 some 14½ million persons were insured in this way. To the sickness and pension funds, both workers and employers contributed and both were represented on their management. In the course of time such benefits as free medical attendance and hospital care were extended, and by 1914 codes of factory legislation and of child labor were at last added. Although the prewar *Reich* did not set up unemployment insurance, it set up labor exchanges, and some municipalities had local schemes of insurance and relief for unemployed workers. Germans were pioneers in the thoroughness and extent of their welfare system. When war began, German workers were better protected against the hazards of an industrial society than those of any other country. This was a not unimportant element in her national solidarity and strength.

Germany's neighbors, impressed by these further developments, were quick to imitate them in whole or in part. Belgium and Denmark, as well as the United Kingdom, imitated all three forms of insurance. Austria adopted accident and sickness insurance in 1887–88, Italy and Switzerland in the 1890's. In these same years Britain, France, Norway, Spain, and the Netherlands introduced legislation that obliged employers to compensate their workers for accidents that occurred during work. Everywhere the state shouldered new kinds of responsibility for the safety and well-being of its citizens, and the principle of contributory insurance helped to reconcile *laissez-faire* individualism with the spectacular growth of state activity.

George Bernard Shaw Reports on Fabian Policy (1896)

George Bernard Shaw (1856–1950), the famous playwright, was an active member of the Fabian Society, a group of socialist intellectuals who were influential in founding the British Labour Party. The following report was written by Shaw for a meeting of the International Socialist Workers' Congress in London. From George Bernard Shaw, *Report on Fabian Policy, Fabian Tract No. 70* (London, 1896).

THE MISSION OF THE FABIANS

The object of the Fabian Society is to persuade the English people to make their political constitution thoroughly democratic and so to socialize their industries as to make the livelihood of the people entirely independent of private Capitalism. . . .

FABIAN CONSTITUTIONALISM

The Fabian Society is perfectly constitutional in its attitude; and its methods are those usual in political life in England.

The Fabian Society accepts the conditions imposed on it by human nature and by the national character and political circumstances of the English people. It sympathises with the ordinary citizen's desire for gradual, peaceful changes, as against revolutionary, conflict with the army and police, and martyrdom. . . .

FABIAN COMPROMISE

The Fabian Society, having learnt from experience that Socialists cannot have their own way in everything any more than other people, recognises that in a Democratic community Compromise is a necessary condition of political progress.

FABIAN SOCIALISM

Socialism, as understood by the Fabian Society, means the organization and conduct of the necessary industries of the country and the appropriation of all forms of economic rent of land and capital by the nation as a whole, through the most suitable public authorities, parochial, municipal, provincial, or central. . . .

FABIANS AND THE MIDDLE CLASS

In view of the fact that the Socialist movement has been hitherto inspired, instructed, and led by members of the middle class or "bourgeoisie," the Fabian Society, though not at all surprised to find these middle class leaders attacking with much bitterness the narrow social ideals current in their own class, protests against the absurdity of Socialists denouncing the very class from which Socialism has sprung as specially hostile to it. The Fabian Society has no romantic illusions as to the freedom of the proletariat from these same narrow ideals. Like every other Socialist society, it can only educate the people in Socialism by making them conversant with the conclusions of the most enlightened members of all classes. The Fabian Society, therefore, cannot reasonably use the words "bourgeois" or "middle class" as terms of reproach, more especially as it would thereby condemn a large proportion of its own members.

FABIAN NATURAL PHILOSOPHY

The Fabian Society endeavours to rouse Social compunction by making the public conscious of the evil condition of society under the present system. This it does by the collection and publications of authentic and impartial statistical tracts, compiled, not from the works of Socialists, but from official sources. The first volume of Karl Marx's *Das Capital,* which contains an immense mass of carefully verified facts concerning modern capitalistic civilization, and practically nothing about Socialism, is probably the most successful propagandist work ever published.

The Fabian Society, in its endeavours to continue the work of Marx in this direction, has found that the guesses made by Socialists at the condition of the people almost invariably flatter the existing system instead of, as might be suspected, exaggerating its evils. The Fabian Society therefore concludes that in the natural philosophy of Socialism, light is a more important factor than heat.

A Fabian Satirizes Self-Help (1889)

Sidney Webb (1859–1947), author of this satire, was a prominent member of the Fabian Society. Philosophically he was a believer in Bentham's concept of "utility" although his interpretation of what constituted the "happiness of the community" was far broader than that of Bentham. From Sidney Webb, *Socialism in England* (Baltimore, 1889), pp. 116–117.

Our unconscious acceptance of this progressive Socialism is a striking testimony to the change which has come over [England]. . . . The "practical man", oblivious or contemptuous of any theory of the Social Organism or general principles of social organisation, has been forced by the necessities of the time, into an ever-deepening collectivist channel. Socialism, of course, he still rejects and despises. The Individualist Town Councillor will walk along the municipal pavement, lit by municipal gas and cleansed by municipal brooms with municipal water, and seeing by the municipal clock in the municipal market that he is too early to meet his children coming from the municipal school hard by the county lunatic asylum and municipal hospital, will use the national telegraph system to tell them not to walk through the municipal park but to come by the municipal tramway, to meet him in the municipal reading-room by the municipal art gallery, museum and library, where he intends to consult some of the national publications in order to prepare his next speech in the municipal town hall, in favour of the nationalization of the canals and the increase of the government control over the railway system. "Socialism, sir," he will say, "don't waste the time of a practical man by your fantastic absurdities. Self-help, sir, individual self-help, that's what's made our city what it is." . . .

A Marxist Espouses Evolutionary Socialism (1899)

By the end of the century a number of Marx' followers had grown skeptical of the impending collapse of capitalism. As trade union organizations grew in strength and workers began to share in the prosperity of the economy, socialist demands became less militant. Eduard Bernstein (1850–1932), a prominent German socialist, became a spokesman for those who challenged the need for revolution as a program for the working class. Excerpts from his argument for evolutionary socialism appear in this reading. From Eduard Bernstein, *Evolutionary Socialism: A Criticism and Affirmation,* trans. E. Harvey (London, 1909), pp. ix–xiv.

I set myself against the notion that we have to expect shortly a collapse of the bourgeois economy, and that social democracy should be induced by the prospect of such an imminent, great, social catastrophe to adapt its tactics to that assumption. That I maintain most emphatically.

The adherents of this theory of a catastrophe, base it especially on the conclusions of the *Communist Manifesto*. This is a mistake in every respect.

The theory which the *Communist Manifesto* sets forth of the evolution of modern society was correct as far as it characterised the general tendencies of that evolution. But it was mistaken in several special deductions, above all in the estimate of the time the evolution would take. . . . But it is evident that if social evolution takes a much greater period of time than was assumed, it must also take upon itself forms and lead to forms that were not foreseen and could not be foreseen then.

Social conditions have not developed to such an acute opposition of things and classes as is depicted in the *Manifesto*. It is not only useless, it is the greatest folly to attempt to conceal this from ourselves. The number of members of the possessing classes is to-day not smaller but larger. The enormous increase of social wealth is not accompanied by a decreasing number of large capitalists but by an increasing number of capitalists of all degrees. The middle classes change their character but they do not disappear from the social scale. . . .

In all advanced countries we see the privileges of the capitalist bourgeoisie yielding step by step to democratic organisations.

Under the influence of this, and driven by the movement of the working classes which is daily becoming stronger, a social reaction has set in against the exploiting tendencies of capital, a counter-action which, although it still proceeds timidly and feebly, yet does exist, and is always drawing more departments of economic life under its influence. Factory legislation, the democratising of local government, and the extension of its area of work, the freeing of trade unions and systems of cooperative trading from legal restrictions, the consideration of standard conditions of labour in the work undertaken by public authorities—all these characterise this phase of the evolution.

But the more the political organisations of modern nations are democratised the more the needs and opportunities of great political catastrophes are diminished. He who holds firmly to the catastrophic theory of evolution must, with all his power, withstand and hinder the evolution described above, which, indeed, the logical defenders of that theory formerly did. But is the conquest of political power by the proletariat simply to be by a political catastrophe? Is it to be the appropriation and utilisation of the power of the State by the proletariat exclusively against the whole non-proletarian world? . . .

If not, and if one subscribes to his conclusions, one cannot reasonably take any offence if it is declared that for a long time yet the task of social democracy is, instead of speculating on a great economic crash, "to organize the working classes politically and develop them as a democracy and to fight for all reforms in the State which are adapted to raise the working classes and transform the state in the direction of democracy." . . .

Lenin Defends Militant Party Leadership (1902)

The conditions which prompted socialist leaders to accept existing governments did not exist in the same form in more backward and reactionary Russia. The ideology of revisionism was a threat to the influence of Lenin and fellow radicals within both the Russian Social Democratic Party and the international socialist movement. In the pamphlet "What Is To Be Done?" (1902), from which this selection is drawn, V. I. Lenin (1870–1924) met the threat head-on, and established his claim to the leadership of the Communist movement in the developing world. From V. I. Lenin, *Selected Works* (Moscow: Foreign Languages Publishing House, 1947), I, 166, 167–168, 172–173, 175.

We have said that our movement, much wider and deeper than the movement of the 'seventies, must be inspired with the same devoted determination and energy that inspired the movement at that time. Indeed, no one, we think, has up to now doubted that the strength of the modern movement lies in the awakening of the masses (principally, the industrial proletariat), and that its weakness lies in the lack of consciousness and initiative among the revolutionary leaders. . . .

We said that *there could not yet be* Social-Democratic consciousness among the workers. This consciousness could only be brought to them from without. The history of all countries shows that the working class, exclusively by its own effort, is able to develop only trade union consciousness, *i.e.*, it may itself realize the necessity for combining in unions, for fighting against the employers and for striving to compel the government to pass necessary labour legislation, etc.

The theory of Socialism, however, grew out of the philosophic, historical and economic theories that were elaborated by the educated representatives of the propertied classes, the intellectuals. According to their social status, the founders of modern scientific Socialism, Marx and Engels, themselves belonged to the bourgeois intelligentsia. Similarly, in Russia, the theoretical doctrine of Social-Democracy arose quite independently of the spontaneous growth of the labour movement; it arose as a natural and inevitable outcome of the development of ideas among the revolutionary Socialist intelligentsia. . . . Hence, simultaneously, we had both the spontaneous awakening of the masses of the workers, the awakening to conscious life and struggle, and the striving of the revolutionary youth, armed with the Social-Democratic theories, to reach the workers. . . .

Instead of calling upon the workers to go forward towards the consolidation of the revolutionary organization and to the expansion of political activity, they began to call for a *retreat* to the purely trade union struggle. They announced that "the economic basis of the movement is eclipsed by the effort never to forget the political ideal," and that the watchword for the movement was "Fight for an economic position" or what is still better, "The workers for the workers." It was declared that strike funds "are more valuable for the movement than a hundred other organizations," and so forth. Catchwords like: "We must concentrate, not on the 'cream' of the workers, but on the 'average,' mass worker"; "Politics always obediently follows economics," etc., etc., became the fashion, and exercised an irresistible influence upon the masses of the youth who were attracted to the movement, but who, in the majority of cases, were acquainted only with legally expounded fragments of Marxism.

Consciousness was completely overwhelmed by spontaneity—the spontaneity of the "Social-Democrats". . . , the spontaneity of those workers who were carried away by the arguments that a kopek added to a ruble was worth more than Socialism and politics, and that they must "fight, knowing that they are fighting not for some future generation, but for themselves and their children.". . .

This shows that *all* worship of the spontaneity of the labour movement, all belittling of the role of "the conscious element," of the role of the party of Social-Democracy, *means*, *quite irrespective of whether the belittler likes it or not, strengthening the influence of the bourgeois ideology among the workers.* All those who talk about "exaggerating the importance of ideology," about exaggerating the role of the conscious elements, etc., imagine that the pure and simple labour movement can work out an independent ideology for itself, if only the workers "take their fate out of the hands of the leaders." But this is a profound mistake. . . .

Since there can be no talk of an independent ideology being developed by the masses of the workers in the process of their movement *the only choice is:* either the bourgeois or the Socialist ideology. . . . Hence to belittle the Socialist ideology *in any way,* to *turn away from it in the slightest degree* means to strengthen bourgeois ideology. There is a lot of talk about spontaneity, but the *spontaneous* development of the labour movement leads to its becoming subordinated to the bourgeois ideology. . . . Hence, our task, the task of Social-Democracy, is to *combat spontaneity,* to *divert* the labour movement from its spontaneous, trade unionist striving to go under the wing of the bourgeoisie, and to bring it under the wing of revolutionary Social-Democracy. . . .

STUDY QUESTIONS

1. What factors discredited the laissez-faire economic philosophy? Where did free competition lead?

2. Why should officials of the established order like Bismarck and Lloyd George champion sweeping changes? How were they able to get the bills passed by legislatures in which the middle classes held a majority?

3. Why did the number of people who could vote steadily increase? What effect did this have on the process of change?

4. What is meant by the term "welfare state"? How does it differ from Enlightenment concepts of government? Nineteenth-century middle-class concepts of government? Which elements of the modern welfare state can be seen in European political practices before 1914?

5. What influence did welfare legislation exercise on the socialist movement?

6. How does Fabian Socialism relate to Marxist philosophy? To what extent are Bernstein's views different from those of Shaw and Webb?

7. How did Lenin diagnose the danger to the Marxist movement? How would he prevent undermining the workers' movement?

Chapter 5

The Evolution of Nationalism, 1789–1918

The sovereign European nation-state was a dynamic element in the forging of European society in the nineteenth century. Attacking the restraints of traditional society, the new spirit of nationalism was first allied with the liberal impulses of the century. Nationalism not only created a larger community of feeling within the boundaries of individual states but it also generated increasing distrust of minorities inside the national unit and hostility to other nation-states outside. Under the pressures created by the raging competition for wealth, the growth of military and industrial power, and the new Darwinian social science, nationalism became in the latter part of the century increasingly a threat to the peace of the world. By 1914, few would recognize in a world at war the vision of the century's first liberal nationalists.

The rapid industrialization and rampant nationalism of the West had momentous consequences for the rest of the world. Africa was rapidly divided among the European states. Asia was increasingly faced with a similar prospect. Only in the island empire of Japan were Western concepts and methods cleverly adapted to ward off the threat of Western dominance. All over, however, the process of Westernization was transforming the face of the world. These readings examine the changing landscape of nationalistic feeling and power in the nineteenth century against the background of economic and democratic progress developed in earlier chapters.

1749–1832	J. W. von Goethe
1770–1827	L. v. Beethoven
1783–1830	Simón Bolívar
1792	*Marseillaise*, Rouget de Lisle
1793	Chi'en Lung Emperor letter to George III
1796	Napoleon's first Italian campaign
1798	Napoleon in Egypt
1804	Saint Dominique establishes its independence from France, first black nation in Caribbean
1807–1808	Fichte's "Addresses to the German Nation"
1808–1825	Spanish-American colonies win independence
1812	Napoleon invades Russia
1813–1883	Richard Wagner
1814–1815	Congress of Vienna
1815	Waterloo
1820	Liberal nationalist outbreaks in Italy and Spain
1822	Liberia established
1823	Monroe Doctrine
1830–1833	Charles Lyell, *Principles of Geology*
1831	Mazzini founds *Young Italy*
1839–1842	Opium War
1846–1848	U.S. War with Mexico
1848–1849	Nationalist revolutions in Europe
1848	Louis Napoleon president of France
1852–1870	Napoleon III
1853–1854	Perry expedition to Japan
1854–1856	Crimean War
1859	Franco-Austrian War
1860	Development of Impressionism in painting
1861–1865	American Civil War
1862	Bismarck argues "blood and iron"
1870–1871	Franco-Prussian War
1870–1924	Nicolai Lenin
1871	Darwin, *Descent of Man*
1875–1878	Russo-Turkish War
1879	Alliance between Germany and Austria
1884–1885	Berlin Conference, division of Africa
1888–1918	William II, German emperor
1890	Bismarck dismissed as Chancellor
1890s	Impressionism in Music—Debussy
1894	Franco-Russian Entente
1894–1895	Japan defeats China
1898	Spanish-American War

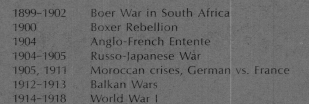

1899–1902	Boer War in South Africa
1900	Boxer Rebellion
1904	Anglo-French Entente
1904–1905	Russo-Japanese War
1905, 1911	Moroccan crises, German vs. France
1912–1913	Balkan Wars
1914–1918	World War I

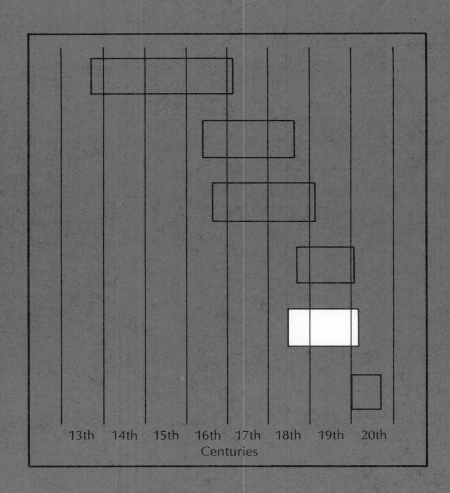

13th 14th 15th 16th 17th 18th 19th 20th
Centuries

TOPIC 35

Boyd Shafer: Toward an Understanding of Nationalism

EARLY STAGES OF NATIONALISM

The origins of national feeling are hotly contested by scholars who rarely agree even on the meaning of the concept of nationalism. Some have traced the genesis of British nationalism to both the period of Elizabethan expansion and the struggles of the English Civil War. None deny that nationalism was given new force by the French Revolution and had its temperature raised by the ensuing wars, conquests of foreign peoples, and occupations of foreign lands. The smoldering fires of national aspirations were further stirred by the reactionary peace settlement that followed the destruction of the Napoleonic Empire and they blazed openly in the European conflagration of 1848. The movement toward nationalism took on many forms, some of them contradictory, and these are explored in the readings.

Boyd C. Shafer (1907–) opens his *Nationalism: Myth and Reality* with the sentence: "A century of study of the group loyalty that has most powerfully motivated men in our time, nationalism, has produced no precise and acceptable definition." In this reading the historian of Modern Europe and former editor of the American Historical Review seeks tentatively to define a difficult concept. Excerpted from *Nationalism: Myth and Reality,* copyright © 1955, by Boyd C. Shafer. Reprinted by permission of Harcourt, Brace and World, Inc.

Nationalism is what the nationalists have made it; it is not a neat, fixed concept but a varying combination of beliefs and conditions. It may be in part founded on myth but myths like other errors have a way of perpetuating themselves and of becoming not true but real. The fact is that myth and actuality and truth and error are inextricably intermixed in modern nationalism. The only reasonable way to get at the nature of nationalism is to determine what beliefs—however true or false—and what conditions —however misinterpreted—are commonly— present. The following ten are here hypothetically advanced. No claim is laid for their infallibility or finality.

1. A certain defined (often vaguely) unit of territory (whether possessed or coveted).
2. Some common cultural characteristics such as language (or widely understood languages), customs, manners, and literature (folk tales and lore are a beginning). If an individual believes he shares these, and wishes to continue sharing them, he is usually said to be a member of the nationality.
3. Some common dominant social (as Christian) and economic (as capitalistic or communistic) institutions.
4. A common independent or sovereign government (type does not matter) or the desire for one. The "principle" that each nationality should be separate and independent is involved here.
5. A belief in a common history (it can be invented) and in a common origin (often mistakenly conceived to be racial in nature).
6. A love or esteem for fellow nationals (not necessarily as individuals).
7. A devotion to the entity (however little comprehended) called the nation, which embodies the common territory, culture, social and economic institutions, government, and the fellow na-

tionals, and which is at the same time (whether organism or not) more than their sum.

8. A common pride in the achievements (often the military more than the cultural) of this nation and a common sorrow in its tragedies (particularly its defeats).

9. A disregard for or hostility to other (not . . . all) like groups, especially if these prevent or seem to threaten the separate national existence.

10. A hope that the nation will have a great and glorious future (usually in territorial expansion) and become supreme in some way (in world power if the nation is already large). . . .

The nation-state, or the political organization of the nation, came into being and became dominant in part because that form of institution fitted the economic organization and the state of transportation and communication of modern times. Nation-states did not develop earlier because feudal, agricultural Europe did not need or foster them. The middle and working classes were not strong enough to demand them or did not desire them. The local nature and low level of industry, the trickle of trade and the bad roads did not demand or permit them. And the slow communication of ideas and the illiteracy of the bulk of the people prevented the rise of that national consciousness essential to their rise and growth. Conversely the nation-state and nationalism are possibly beginning to decline today because modern technology, the volume of industrial production and commerce, the speed of communication, and perhaps the enlightenment of many people are making national boundaries obsolete.

This is to say nothing more than that as a result of a multitude of historical, political, economic, and social forces a sentiment of unity grew within groups of people which expressed itself in devotion to what was called the nation. Nationalism, then, becomes a concept so complex and changing that it defies short, logical definition. At present by the word may be denoted that sentiment unifying a group of people who have a real or imagined common historical experience and a common aspiration to live together as a separate group in the future. This unifying sentiment expresses itself in loyalty to the nation-state whatever the government, in love of native land however little known, in pride in common culture and economic and social institutions though these may not be understood, in preference for fellow nationals in contrast to disregard for members of other groups, and in zeal not only for group security but for glory and expansion. In its most modern form it requires, as Rousseau advocated as early as the eighteenth century, almost absolute devotion to and conformity with the will of the nation-state as this is expressed by the ruler or rulers (autocratic or democratic), and it demands the supremacy (in watchmaking or military might) of the nation to which the nationalist belongs. . . .

Carlton Hayes: A Short History of Nationalism
1789–1870

With time out to serve as American ambassador to Spain, Carlton J. H. Hayes (1882–1964) taught history for almost fifty years at Columbia University. His interest in nationalism, on which subject he was the author of four books, was aroused by the outbreak of the First World War, the underlying nationalistic passions of which made a deep impression on him. In *Nationalism: A Religion,* Professor Hayes argues that modern nationalism has provided a new faith with which men can fill the religious void in their lives. The present reading surveys the growth of nationalism in Europe between the French Revolution and the year 1870. Reprinted with permission of The Macmillan Company from *Nationalism: A Religion* by Carlton J. H. Hayes. © by Carlton J. H. Hayes 1960.

I

French Revolution: Religious Emblems and Crusading Zeal

The great French Revolution in the last decade of the eighteenth century is a bulking landmark in the history of modern nationalism. . . .

Quasi-religious emblems attended the revolutionary progress of nationalism in France. A national flag—the tricolor—was compounded in 1789 of the red-and-blue of Paris and the white of the Bourbon king. A national holiday was celebrated every year on July 14, anniversary both of the destruction of the Bastille and of the Paris Federation Fete. A national anthem—the rousing *Marseillaise*—was composed by Rouget de Lisle in 1792 and first sung by a band of soldiers from Marseilles marching in Paris for the overthrow of the monarchy. Other emblems cropped up: liberty caps, Phrygian caps, Roman fasces, trees of liberty, long-pants uniforms (*sans-culottes*) for patriots, altars to the fatherland.

The Declaration of the Rights of Man and of the Citizen was treated as a national catechism, and profession of faith in it was prescribed by the Constitution of 1791. Anyone refusing to swear to it was cut off from the community by civil excommunication; and foreigners who swore loyalty to it were admitted to the ranks of the faithful and enrolled as in a communion of saints. At the first session of the Legislative Assembly, in the autumn of 1791, "twelve old men went in procession to seek the Book of the Constitution. They came back, having at their head the archivist Camus, who, holding up the book with his two hands and resting it on his breast, carried with slow and measured tread the new Blessed Sacrament of the French. All the deputies stood up and bared their heads. Camus, with meditative mien, kept his eyes lowered." The same Assembly decreed in June, 1792, that "in all the communes an altar to the fatherland shall be raised and on it shall be written the Declaration of Rights, with the inscription: "The citizen is born, lives, and dies for *la patrie*." Two years earlier, at Strasbourg, a rite of "civic baptism" was introduced jointly by a priest, a minister and a rabbi. "Civic marriages" and "civic funerals" came later, and likewise the many, many graves of soldier citizens with the epitaph, *Mort pour la patrie*—"Dead for the fatherland"! . . .

How can one understand the crusading zeal with which foreign war was waged by French revolutionaries without perceiving a main motivation in religious nationalism. Doubtless the first declaration of war, in April, 1792, was occasioned by the threatening attitude of the Austrian Emperor and his henchman, the King of Prussia. But it was accompanied by a long novel pronunciamento, at once idealistic and

French troops under Dumouriez and Kellerman turn back the troops of the king of Prussia on September 20, 1792, at Valmy, a village in the Argonne. Scenes from the battle were a favorite in the patriotic art of the period. The painting is by J. B. Mauzaisse.

propagandist: "that the French nation, faithful to the principles consecrated by its constitution 'not to undertake any war with a view to conquest nor ever to employ its forces against the liberty of any people,' only takes up arms for the maintenance of its liberty and independence; that the war which it is forced to prosecute is not a war of nation against nation . . .; that the French nation never confuses its brethren with its real enemies; that it will neglect nothing which may reduce the curse of war, spare and preserve property, and cause all the unhappiness inseparable from war to fall alone upon those who have conspired against its liberty; that it adopts in advance all foreigners, who, abjuring the

cause of its enemies, shall range themselves under its banners and consecrate their efforts to the defense of liberty; and that it will promote by all means in its power their settling in France. . . ."

Alas, no appreciable number of foreigners (except a minority in the Belgian Netherlands) abjured the cause of Austrian emperor and Prussian king. Armies of these sovereigns invaded France and were only halted in September, 1792, at Valmy. This was occasion for the September massacres at Paris, for the convocation of the Republican National Convention, and, two months later, for the issuance of a new and quite different pronunciamento concerning the war. "The French nation declares," we are now told, "that it will treat as enemies every people who, refusing liberty and equality or renouncing them, may wish to maintain, recall, or treat with the prince and the privileged classes; on the other hand, it engages not to subscribe to any treaty and not to lay down its arms until the sovereignty and independence of the peoples whose territory the troops of the Republic shall have entered shall be established, and until the people shall have adopted the principles of equality and founded a free and democratic government."

French armies were presently ensuring the incorporation of Savoy and Nice and of the Belgian Netherlands in revolutionary France, while against them Austria and Prussia were being joined by Sardinia, Great Britain, the Dutch Netherlands, and Spain. Simultaneously, revolts of conservatives and Catholics broke out within France, particularly at Lyons and in La Vendée and Brittany. The Revolutionaries replied with the Reign of Terror, with conscription, with totalitarian war. A decree of August, 1793, called for military service of all Frenchmen between the ages of eighteen and twenty-five, with the added instruction: "The young men shall go to battle; the married men shall forge arms and transport provisions; the women shall make tents and clothing and shall serve in the hospitals; the old people shall betake themselves to the public places in order to arouse the courage of the warriors and to preach hatred of kings and unity of the Republic."

Four months later a young warrior, a certain Francois Xavier Joliclerc, was writing his mother: "When the country calls us for its defense, we ought to hasten to it as I would hasten to a good meal. Our life, our goods, our talents do not belong to us. All such

belong to the nation, to *la patrie*. . . . Principles of love of country, love of liberty, love of the Republic are not only engraved on my heart; they are enshrined there, and there they will remain as long as it will please the Supreme Being to keep a breath of life in me." . . .

Under the First Napoleon

Napoleon Bonaparte was at least a stepson of the French Revolution. Beginning as a Corsican patriot, he grew up to combine French revolutionary nationalism with vaulting personal ambition. During his amazing career, from the first Italian campaign in 1796 to the last engagement at Waterloo in 1815, in turn career general, Consul of the Republic, and Emperor of the French, he personified revolutionary and nationalist principles. He maintained for the French the principle, if not the practice, of national democratic sovereignty, of equality and fraternity if not of liberty. He kept the national tricolor flag, and the "Marseillaise" as the national anthem. He stirred his armies with patriotic speeches, impressed the public with patriotic ritual, founded the patriotic Legion of Honor. He gave permanency to leveling social reforms of the Revolution by incorporating them in the monumental *Code Napoléon.*

He actually inaugurated what such revolutionaries as Talleyrand and Condorcet had proposed—the putting of the nation in state schools. He continued and developed to the full the putting of the nation (and all possible allies) in arms. . . .

In 1792, when the revolutionary wars began, there had been relatively slight nationalist spirit among the masses on the European Continent outside of France. But as the wars went on, and especially under Napoleon, it

was aroused and spread by several means. First, extensive areas were incorporated into France—the Belgian Netherlands, the German Rhineland, the Italian districts of Savoy and Nice—and for twenty years they shared intimately in its revolutionary heritage. Secondly, a string of dependent and allied territories came under French tutelage—the Italian peninsula, the Dutch Netherlands, nearly half of Germany (the "Confederation of the Rhine"), Denmark, Poland (the "Grand Duchy of Warsaw"), the "Illyrian provinces" (a strip of what is now Yugoslavia along the Adriatic), and (briefly) Spain and Portugal. Even in Sweden a Napoleonic Marshall, Bernadotte, was elected heir to the throne. Thirdly, peoples near France, and as far away from it as Austria and Russia, saw repeatedly the marching and camping of French armies and must have noted the patriotic ceremonies attending them. In time a goodly number of foreign troops—German, Italian, Polish, for instance—were intermixed, as allies, with Napoleon's nationalist French forces.

Most important for the spread of nationalism was the patriotic reaction on the part of foreign writers, statesmen, and eventually peoples, against the militancy of France, the Revolution, and Napoleon. . . .

Exponents of *German* nationalism grew numerous and noisy. Johann Gottlieb Fichte, while professor of philosophy at Jena in the 1790's had been a "fellow traveler" with the French revolutionaries, acclaiming their achievements and indoctrinating his university students with the principles of "liberty, equality, and fraternity." The Prussian defeat at Jena in 1806 changed Fichte. Henceforth, he was a bitter foe of Napoleon and the French and a strenuous advocate of German unity. His ultrapatriotic *Addresses to the Ger-*

man Nation were followed by his pamphlet entitled "The German Republic." He romantically described the worship he foresaw in the "national church" of the future: "On Sunday morning . . . when all parishioners have arrived, the church doors are thrown open and amid soft music the congregation enters. . . . When all are seated the great curtains at the altar are drawn aside, revealing the cannon, muskets, and other weapons which constitute the parish armory. For every German youth from his twentieth birthday to his death is a soldier. Then there appears before the congregation the justice of the peace, who unfurls the flag. . . ." It was a fitting end to Fichte that he died of cholera in 1814 while nursing soldiers in the War of Liberation, a martyr to the cause of German nationalism. . . .

Mention might similarly be made of such *Polish* patriots of the era as Thaddeus Kosciusko and Prince Adam Czartoryski, and of the *Greek* patriots Koraes and Rhigas and the Ypsilantis. A particularly striking example of nationalist reaction against Napoleon and the French was furnished by the popular *Spanish* uprising of "eighth of May" (1808). Here Britain furnished direct military aid, and the ensuing Peninsular War proved a major factor in Napoleon's overthrow. And notable among the fighting Spanish patriots was a young colonial from Venezuela, Simón Bolívar, who subsequently won fame as revolutionary "Liberator" of Spanish-American nations.

Then, too, from the burning of Moscow, which climaxed Napoleon's ill-fated invasion of Russia in 1812, the impressionable Tsar Alexander received, he said later, the patriotic "illumination" which moved him to assume leadership of what he regarded as a crusade against the French emperor. The decisive five-day battle at Leipzig in October of the next year has been appropriately dubbed the Battle of the Nations.

II

From Vienna Peace Settlement to the 1830's

The Congress of Vienna (1814–1815) registered the international peace settlement that terminated the Revolutionary and Napoleonic Wars which had ravaged Europe for twenty-three years. Its chief architect was Prince Metternich, who was no nationalist. Indeed he regarded nationalism as subversive of social security and the traditional state system of Europe, as inimical specifically to the polyglot nature of the Habsburg Empire he served, and as dangerous in general to European peace. For what would the triumph of nationalism entail? . . . He foresaw ruinous international wars, revolutionary rearrangement of boundaries, and partition of the Empire.

The settlement of 1815 corresponded, in the main, with Metternich's wishes. In the interest of a restored "balance of power," France was allowed to retain its frontiers of 1792 (including Alsace, but not Savoy or Nice), while, to hold France in check, the Rhineland and Westphalia were added to Prussia, and Belgium to the Dutch Netherlands. The nonnational Austrian Empire was bolstered and extended: it annexed outright two major Italian states (Venetia and Lombardy) and dominated the others into which the peninsula was redivided; and it secured hegemony over the several German states. Metternich thought in European, not in nationalist, terms. He was one of a dwindling number of cosmopolitan statesmen in Europe. . . .

Nevertheless, even while the Congress of Vienna was being held, and increasingly during the next few years, nationalism was inspiring widespread agitation and revolts. In 1814 an attempt was made by Norwegians to set up an independent national state, with a king of their own choosing. It failed, but the Swedish king, on annexing the country, promised to respect Norway's constitution and internal autonomy. In the same year a semisecret society, the Hetairia Philike, was founded for Greek national liberation. . . .

In the 1820's there were liberal nationalist outbreaks in Italy and Spain. They were repressed, but not so the revolt of the Spanish colonies on the American continents. In this instance nationalist Britain refused to cooperate with Metternich's "Concert of Europe" and backed the United States in proclaiming the famous "Monroe Doctrine."

In 1830–1831 a symbolic change occurred in France. The direct line of Bourbons that had been restored to the throne following Napoleon's downfall, while accepting certain principles of the French Revolution, had banned its flag and its anthem. Now, with forceful supplanting of the direct line of Bourbons with the Orleanist branch in the person of Louis Philippe, back came the revolutionary tricolor and "Marseillaise," and before long the new regime was encouraging a Napoleonic revival by pompous dedication of the Arc de Triomphe in honor of the emperor's victories and by solemn transport of his bones from faraway St. Helena to the crypt of the imposing Invalides on the banks of the Seine.

The revolutionary change in France was speedily followed by revolt of the Belgian Netherlands against their Dutch king and of Poles against their Russian "king," the Tsar.

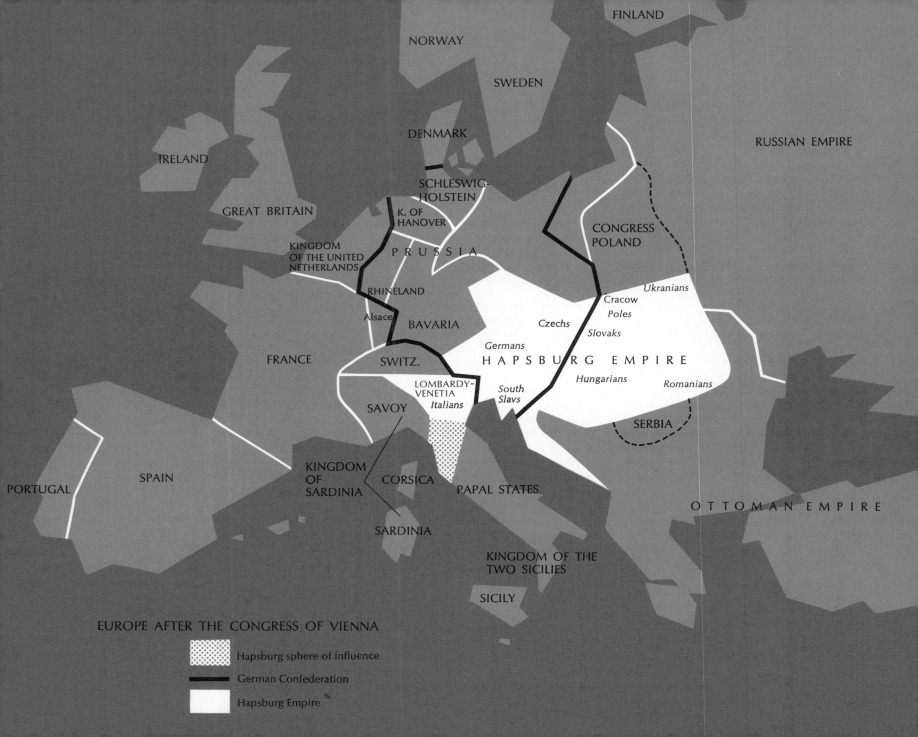

FINLAND

NORWAY

SWEDEN

RUSSIAN EMPIRE

DENMARK

IRELAND

SCHLESWIG-
HOLSTEIN

GREAT BRITAIN

K. OF
HANOVER

CONGRESS
POLAND

P R U S S I A

KINGDOM
OF THE UNITED
NETHERLANDS

Ukranians

RHINELAND

Cracow

Poles

Alsace

BAVARIA

Czechs

Slovaks

FRANCE

Germans

H A P S B U R G   E M P I R E

SWITZ.

Hungarians

Romanians

LOMBARDY-
VENETIA

*South
Slavs*

SAVOY

Italians

SERBIA

SPAIN

KINGDOM
OF
SARDINIA

CORSICA

PORTUGAL

PAPAL STATES

O T T O M A N   E M P I R E

SARDINIA

KINGDOM OF THE
TWO SICILIES

SICILY

EUROPE AFTER THE CONGRESS OF VIENNA

Hapsburg sphere of influence

German Confederation

Hapsburg Empire

The funeral procession of Napoleon (1840) nears the Invalides (left rear) where the remains of the Emperor are finally to rest in the French capital. An admirer kisses the velvet hangings of his carriage. Emblems over which the imperial eagle roosts (right foreground) commemorate his conquests.

Yet the storm passed with little apparent effect. The most significant thing about it was the conflict it raised between liberalism and nationalism. For example, while all the revolutionary rulers in the Habsburg Austrian Empire were professed liberals, they quarreled and fought over national questions. Austrian German liberals, striving to preserve traditional German domination of the polyglot Habsburg Empire, forcefully and successfully resisted the efforts of Italian liberals to unify their country. Magyar liberals, intent upon preserving intact the historic realm of Hungary, followed the leadership of the ultra-patriotic Louis Kossuth not only in demanding national independence for themselves but in denying the autonomous claims of their non-Magyar liberal subjects—Rumanian liberals in Transylvania and Slavic liberals in Croatia, Slovakia, and the Banat. Then the liberal Slavic Czechs and Slovenes of the Austrian crown-lands, hitherto at odds with the German liberal regime at Vienna, joined it in fighting Kossuth's liberal Hungary, whose end was hastened by armed intervention of Slavic Russia.

The upshot by 1849 was the restoration of the unitary Habsburg Empire as it had been under Metternich, with apparent suppression of both liberalism and nationalism. The Pan-Slavic Congress at Prague, under the presidency of the Czech patriot and historian Palacký, proved a comic-tragic affair. The self-appointed delegates, finding that they couldn't understand one another in their different Slavic tongues, fell back on their common knowledge of German as the vehicle for drafting a rhetorical declaration of the assumed freedom-loving national character of Slavs. Whereupon the Congress came to a speedy and inglorious end with the shooting,

The former succeeded because it was supported by Great Britain and France. The latter failed because Russia, Austria, and Prussia made common cause against it. Lines appeared sharply drawn between western Europe where nationalism was political and militant, as well as cultural, and central and eastern Europe where the older institutions and practices of empire were exemplified by Austria, Russia, and Turkey. . . .

Nationalism in Revolutions of 1848–1849

In 1848 a fierce thunderstorm of liberal nationalism broke over Europe. Rioting was epidemic in Paris, Milan, Vienna, Berlin, Rome; it was embryonic in Dublin and threatened in London. Metternich, chased out of Vienna, took refuge in England.

Liberal constitutional governments were quickly set up in the Habsburg Empire for Germans, Czechs, and Hungarians, in the several Italian states, in Prussia and most of the other German states, in Denmark and the Netherlands. Simultaneously, a National Assembly met at Frankfurt to arrange for the unification of Germany; a Pan-Slavic Congress assembled at Prague; and plans were put forth for Italian union or federation.

Civil war in Paris, Avenue Port Royal, February 1848. Members of the bourgeois National Guard joined by some workingmen attack a fortified building. Its defenders are out-numbered.

A scene from the Berlin insurrection of March 1848. Bourgeoisie and workingmen join in defense at the barricades. Paving stones from the rooftops rain on the Prussian troops.

Rome, attack on the Quirinal Palace, November 16, 1848. The Pope was forced to appoint a ministry more sympathetic to the reformers.

Prague, June 12, 1848. The first clash of Czech and imperial forces. Citizens on foot were no match for the cavalry and artillery under the command of Prince Windischgrätz.

by street rioters, of the wife and son of the German military governor of Bohemia, who, with perhaps pardonable ire, retaliated against the rioters and sent the Pan-Slavic delegates scurrying home.

Nor did success attend the effort of liberal Germans to create a unified national German state. In the Frankfurt Assembly they did adopt a nationalistic "Declaration of the Rights of the German Citizen" and a liberal constitution for a projected German Empire. But liberal Germany warred with liberal Denmark over the border provinces of Schleswig-Holstein, only to be stopped by the threat of Anglo-Russian intervention; and the resulting discomfiture of the Frankfurt Assembly was intensified by rivalry between Prussia and Austria, and finally completed by the restoration of conservative regimes in both those major states. Remnants of armed liberal opposition were crushed by Prussian troops in 1849, and the loose confederation of German states, under Austrian presidency, was reestablished. . . .

III

The Third Napoleon as Nationalist, 1848–1870

The French Revolution of 1848 had features reminiscent of the Jacobinism of the Great Revolution of 1789–1799. It dethroned Louis Philippe, the "bourgeois" king and last of French Bourbon monarchs, and it established a Second Republic with universal manhood suffrage. The democracy, thus proclaimed, was attended by a popular resurgence of nationalism. The expelled king and his prime minister had not been militantly patriotic. The new chief of state was the choice of an overwhelming majority of the democratic electorate, partly because he promised a re-

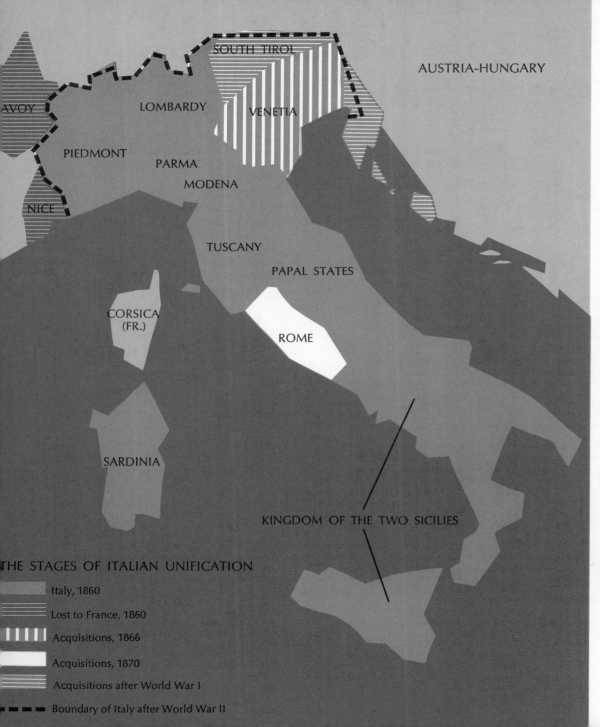

AUSTRIA-HUNGARY

SOUTH TIROL

SAVOY

LOMBARDY

VENETIA

PIEDMONT

PARMA

MODENA

NICE

TUSCANY

PAPAL STATES

CORSICA
(FR.)

ROME

SARDINIA

KINGDOM OF THE TWO SICILIES

THE STAGES OF ITALIAN UNIFICATION

Italy, 1860

Lost to France, 1860

Acquisitions, 1866

Acquisitions, 1870

Acquisitions after World War I

Boundary of Italy after World War II

gime of law and order, but chiefly because his name carried to the French masses a connotation of national glory. He was Prince Louis Napoleon Bonaparte, nephew of the general and emperor, and heir to the "Napoleonic Legend" which had been spun at St. Helena concerning the emperor's heroic efforts in behalf of peace and oppressed peoples. . . .

Napoleon III was a nationalist not only in regard to France. He was one on principle, dreaming of a Europe refashioned, under French tutelage, on the basis of self-determination for each nationality. Hence he was looked to for support by liberal patriots throughout the Continent, just as reactionary sovereigns had previously looked to Metternich. And like a knight-errant of nationalism, he repeatedly responded. To be sure, he combined with idealistic knight-errantry a politic ambition to obtain "compensations" of territory and prestige that would heighten French pride and strengthen his Empire.

The story of Napoleon III has been told many times and in great detail. We here merely note his major efforts and achievements in the realm of nationalism. First, in alliance with Great Britain, he waged the Crimean War, thereby halting Russian aggression in the Near East, and then reasserting French primacy by having the peace congress held at Paris. From the Crimean War came, too, the Emperor's interest in the Rumanian people and his diplomatic moves that eventuated in the establishment of an independent Rumania.

Second, pressed by Cavour and other Italian patriots, he went to war with the Habsburg Empire and pushed its armies out of Lombardy. Thus was inaugurated the steady swift course by which, within two years, a free and united Italy came into being. As "compensation" for the services he rendered, Napoleon III obtained Savoy and Nice for France.

Third, the Emperor expressed sympathy for Polish national aspirations. He might have supported the Polish revolt of 1863 against Russia if the latter had not been backed by both Prussia and Austria and if his own forces had not been heavily engaged at the moment in Mexico.

Fourth, he reconstructed for France an overseas colonial empire. In the face of opposition from the United States, he failed, we know, to retain Mexico. But he succeeded in establishing French control of Algeria, Indo-China, and certain islands in the Pacific. This national imperialism of Napoleon III's foreshadowed what was to become, in the era after 1870, a conspicuous mark of nationalism among the great powers of Europe, and incidentally a prime means of exporting nationalism to other continents.

Finally, Napoleon III fatefully contributed to the creation of the nationalist Hohenzollern Empire of William I and Bismarck. His youthful schooling in a German gymnasium, his inherent romanticism, and his general interest in the principle of nationality, specifically exemplified in his concern with Italians, Rumanians, and Poles, all predisposed him to sympathize with the cause of German unification. He stood aside while Prussia fought it out with Austria in 1866 for German hegemony, imagining that victorious Prussia, under Bismarck, would "compensate" France by agreeing to its incorporation of Belgium or the Rhineland or at least Luxembourg. He was now aging, and the younger Bismarck

outwitted and balked him at every turn. At last he acquiesced in popular French clamor for a showdown with Prussia (which was immediately provoked by Bismarck), and the ensuing Franco-Prussian War of 1870–1871 brought disaster to Napoleon III, and humiliation to France. The Emperor lost his throne, and France lost Alsace-Lorraine, while in the Hall of Mirrors of Louis XIV's splendid palace at Versailles a glittering assemblage of German princes and generals hailed the Hohenzollern king of Prussia as emperor of a united —and very nationalist—Germany.

Napoleon III, though usually classed as a dictator, was a comparatively mild one. He had imbibed in his youth liberal and democratic ideas to which he at least paid lip service during his whole public career. He particularly adhered to the principle of national and democratic self-determination, holding popular plebiscites on fundamental matters of government within France and likewise on transfers of territory from one state to another. In unifying Italy, and in annexing Savoy and Nice to France, he saw to it that local inhabitants should be consulted and should approve by majority vote. He also got Prussia to promise in 1866 that a similar plebiscite would be held in the duchy of Schleswig to determine whether it should be retained by Prussia or returned to Denmark, from which it had been seized.

The fall of Napoleon III and of France changed matters. Victorious Germany ignored the promised plebiscite in Schleswig, and annexed Alsace-Lorraine without consulting its inhabitants and against their clamorous protests. A new era was opening, marked throughout Europe by nationalism more blatant, more intolerant, and more forceful.

Giuseppe Mazzini Agitates for Italian Unification

Giuseppe Mazzini (1805–1872) was an ardent Italian patriot and democrat. His life was a long struggle to create a united and democratic republic out of an Italy divided into many small states and ruled by authoritarian and usually foreign princes. In exile most of his life, Mazzini in 1831 founded a secret society he called Young Italy to fight for independence and unity. His use of conspiratorial tactics was a failure, even his seizure of Rome during the 1848 Revolution came to an ill-starred end. But Mazzini's strength lay in his moral message and his great propagandistic talents that quickened the national consciousness of the divided inhabitants of the Italian peninsula. These moral and humanitarian qualities are apparent in the first selection written in exile in London in 1858. The second selection is taken from the General Instructions for the Members of Young Italy: Liberty-Equality-Humanity-Independence-Unity (1831). I. From Giuseppe Mazzini, *The Duties of Man* (London, 1858). II. From *Life and Writings of Joseph Mazzini* (London, 1890), I, pp. 101–103.

I. DUTIES TOWARD YOUR COUNTRY (1858)

You tell me, you cannot attempt united action, distinct and divided as you are in language, customs, tendencies, and capacity. The individual is too insignificant, and Humanity too vast. The mariner of Brittany prays to God as he puts to sea: *Help me, my God! my boat is so small and Thy ocean so wide!* And this prayer is the true expression of the condition of each one of you, until you find the means of infinitely multiplying your forces and powers of action.

This means was provided for you by God when he gave you a country; when, even as a wise overseer of labour distributes the various branches of employment according to the different capacities of the workmen, he divided Humanity into distinct groups or nuclei upon the face of the earth, thus creating the germs of Nationalities. Evil governments have disfigured the Divine design. Nevertheless you may still trace it, distinctly marked out—at least as far as Europe is concerned—by the course of the great rivers, the direction of the higher mountains, and other geographical conditions. They have disfigured it by their conquests, their greed, and their jealousy even of the righteous power of others; disfigured it so far that, if we except England and France—there is not perhaps a single country whose present boundaries correspond to that Design.

These governments did not, and do not, recognise any country save their own families or dynasty, the egotism of caste. But the Divine design will infallibly be realised. Natural divisions, and the spontaneous innate tendencies of the peoples, will take the place of the arbitrary divisions sanctioned by evil governments. The map of Europe will be re-drawn. The countries of the Peoples, defined by the vote of free men, will arise upon the ruins of the countries of kings and privileged castes, and between these countries harmony and fraternity will exist. And the common work of Humanity, of great amelioration, and the gradual discovery and application of its law of life, being distributed according to local and general capacities, will be wrought out in peaceful and progressive development and advance.

Then may each one of you, fortified by the power and the affection of many millions, all speaking the same language, gifted with the same tendencies, and educated by the same historical tradition, hope even by your own single effort to be able to benefit all Humanity.

O my brothers, love your Country! Our country is our Home, the House that God has given us, placing therein a numerous family that loves us, and whom we love; a family with whom we sympathize more readily, and whom we understand more quickly, than we do others; and which, from its being centered round a given spot, and from the homogeneous nature of its elements, is adapted to a special branch of activity. . . .

Be your country your Temple. God at the summit; a people of equals at the base.

Accept no other formula, no other moral law, if you would not dishonour alike your country and yourselves. Let all secondary laws be but the gradual regulation of your existence by the progressive application of this supreme law.

And in order that they may be such, it is necessary that *all* of you should aid in framing them. Laws framed only by a single fraction of the citizens, can never, in the very nature of things, be other than the mere expression of the thoughts, aspirations, and desires of that fraction; the representation, not of the Country, but of a third or fourth part, of a class or zone of the Country.

The laws should be the expression of the *universal* aspiration, and promote the universal good. They should be a pulsation of the heart of the Nation. The entire Nation should, either directly or indirectly, legislate.

By yielding up this mission into the hands of a few, you substitute the egotism of one class for the Country, which is the Union of all classes.

Country is not a mere zone of territory. The true Country is the Idea to which it gives birth; it is the Thought of love, the sense of communion which unites in one all the sons of that territory.

So long as a single one amongst your brothers has no vote to represent him in the development of the National life, so long as there is one left to vegetate in ignorance where others are educated, so long as a single man, able and willing to work, languishes in poverty through want of work to do, you have no Country in the sense in which Country ought to exist—the Country of all for all. . . .

II. METHODS BY WHICH YOUNG ITALY WILL ATTAIN ITS GOALS (1831)

The means by which Young Italy proposes to reach its aim are education and instruction, to be adopted simultaneously, and made to harmonize with each other.

Education must ever be directed to teach by example, word, and pen, the necessity of insurrection. Insurrection, whenever it can be realized, must be so conducted as to render it a means of national education. . . .

The instructions and intelligence indispensable as preparatory to action will be secret, both in Italy and abroad.

The character of the insurrection must be national; the program of the insurrection must contain the germ of the program of future Italian nationality. Wheresoever the

This idealistic young French student carrying a banner recalling the February 1848 uprising in Paris differs only in nationality from the members of Young Italy who swore their oath of fealty "in the name of God and of Italy." A daguerreotype of 1848.

initiative of insurrection shall take place, the flag raised, and the aim proposed, will be Italian.

That aim being the formation of a nation, the insurrection will act in the name of the nation, and rely upon the people, hitherto neglected, for its support. That aim being the conquest of the whole of Italy, in whatever province the insurrection may arise, its operations with regard to other provinces will be conducted on a principle of invasion and expansion the most energetic, and the broadest possible.

Desirous of regaining for Italy her rightful influence among the peoples, and her true place in their sympathy and affection, the insurrection will so direct its action as to prove the identity of her cause with theirs.

Convinced that Italy is strong enough to free herself with external help; that, in order to found a nationality, it is necessary that the feeling and consciousness of nationality should exist; and that it can never be created by any revolution, however triumphant, if achieved by foreign arms; convinced, moreover, that every insurrection that looks abroad for assistance, must remain dependent upon the state of things abroad, and can therefore never be certain of victory—Young Italy is determined that, while it will ever be ready to profit by the favorable course of events abroad, it will neither allow the character of the insurrection nor the choice of the moment to be governed by them.

Young Italy is aware that revolutionary Europe awaits a signal, and that this signal may be given by Italy as well as by any other nation. It knows that the ground it proposes to tread is virgin soil; and the experiment untried. Foregone insurrections have relied upon the forces supplied by one class alone, and not upon the strength of the whole nation.

The one thing wanting to twenty millions of Italians, desirous of emancipating themselves, is not power, but *faith*.

Young Italy will endeavor to inspire this faith—first by its teachings, and afterwards by an energetic initiative.

Young Italy draws a distinction between the period of insurrection, and that of revolution. The revolution begins as soon as the insurrection is triumphant.

Therefore, the period which may elapse between the first initiative and the complete liberation of the Italian soil, will be governed by a provisional dictatorial power, concentrated in the hands of a small number of men.

The soil once free, every authority will bow down before the national council, the sole source of authority in the state.

Insurrection—by means of guerrilla bands—is the true method of warfare for all nations desirous of emancipating themselves from a foreign yoke. This method of warfare supplies the want—inevitable at the commencement of the insurrection—of a regular army; it calls the greatest number of elements into the field and yet may be sustained by the smallest number. It forms the military education of the people, and consecrates . . . the native soil by the memory of some warlike deed.

Guerrilla warfare opens a field of activity for every local capacity; forces the enemy into an unaccustomed method of battle; avoids the evil consequences of a great defeat; secures the national war from the risk of treason, and has the advantage of not confining it within any defined and determinate basis of operations. It is invincible, indestructible. . . .

Count Cavour Links Railroads and National Unity (1846)

Count Camillo Cavour (1810–1861) was a liberal aristocrat from the northern Italian kingdom of Piedmont (Savoy). He had a burning sense of Italian patriotism and, as prime minister of his little state after 1852, was largely responsible for the unification of Italy under Piedmontese leadership. A combination of adroit power politics and the use of armed force proved necessary to end Austrian power in Italy, but Cavour realized that a real sense of Italian "oneness" had also to be created among all Italians in their various petty states that stretched from the Alps to Sicily. He, therefore, welcomed the opportunity to write a magazine review of a new book, *Railroads in Italy*, published in 1846. Portions from this review follow. From Count C. Cavour, "Review of Railroads in Italy," from *Europe in the Nineteenth Century*, 1815–1914 edited by Eugene N. Anderson, Stanley J. Pincetl, Jr. and Donald J. Ziegler, copyright © 1961 by The Bobbs-Merrill Co., Inc., reprinted by permission of the publishers.

I

No one with common sense contests the utility or even the necessity of railroads today. A few years have been sufficient to bring about a complete revolution of public opinion in their favor. The doubts that they inspired among statesmen and the uncertainties even the boldest of speculators felt about their financial success have been replaced by unlimited confidence. The public

has gone directly from suspicion to such enthusiasm that there is hardly a place in Europe so poor or a group of interests so insignificant that it does not expect in time to participate directly in the benefits of this marvelous conquest of the nineteenth century. . . .

The steam engine is a discovery which may be compared for the importance of its consequences only with printing, or, better yet, with the discovery of the American continent. These great discoveries are already almost four centuries old, yet their potential is still far from realized. The same will be true of the conquest made in transforming steam into a power supply unlimited in its action and applications. It will be many generations before we can determine all of its significance. No one has yet tried to calculate completely the changes this new power should effect in the economy of civilized peoples.

The influence of railroads will extend all over the world. In the nations which have reached a high level of civilization they will furnish immense impetus to industry; their economic results will be impressive from the beginning, and they will accelerate progress. But the social results which should take place, greater to us than the material results, will be especially remarkable in those nations which have remained backward. For them the railroads will be more than a means of self enrichment; they will be a powerful ally, with whose help they will triumph over the forces holding them in a dismal state of industrial and political immaturity. We are convinced that the locomotive is destined to diminish, if not abolish altogether, the humiliating inferiority to which many branches of the great Christian family are reduced. Thus considered, it fills a providential role; perhaps this is why we see it triumph so easily and so quickly over obstacles which have long prevented it from penetrating into certain regions.

If this is true, no nation has more right than Italy to place great hope in the potential of the railroads. The extensive political and social consequences which should result from them will testify better in this beautiful country than elsewhere to the great role they will play in the world's future. We therefore believe it will be of interest to our readers to see treated in some detail the questions connected with the establishment of railroads in Italy. . . .

The railroad from Turin to Chambery, across the highest mountains of Europe, will be the masterpiece of modern industry; it will be the most impressive triumph of the steam engine, the culmination of its glory. After subduing

An early railroad winds across the Alps in this 1868 illustration. At the right is the Italian side of the entrance to the Mont Blanc automobile tunnel which was opened in 1965, piercing seven miles through the mountainous border between France and Italy. This tunnel, located close to the railway route championed by Cavour, is a modern counterpart of the Italian statesman's dream of using railroads to remove a major obstacle to trade and the easy exchange of peoples.

the swiftest of rivers and the stormy seas, it has only to master the eternal snows and glaciers which create insurmountable barriers between peoples. This road will be one of the wonders of the world; it will immortalize the name of King Charles-Albert, who will have had the courage to undertake it and the energy to carry it out. The incalculable benefits which should result from it will cause the memory of his already glorious reign to be cherished forever, not only by his own subjects but by all Italians.

We may be criticized for exaggerating the importance of this route, but when one reflects that it will abolish the distances separating Venice, Milan, Genoa, Turin, and all of the other principal Italian cities from the leading cities of Europe, one will have to agree that we have underestimated rather than overestimated the influence of the "Railroad of the Alps" upon the industrial and political future of Italy.

This line will make Turin, situated at the base of the Alps where the Italian plains terminate, a European city. It will be the junction point of north and south, where the peoples of the German and Latin races will exchange products and ideas—an exchange especially profitable to the Piedmontese state, which already shares the qualities of both races. This magnificent destiny Turin will owe to the enlightened policy of the kings whose faithful capital it has been for centuries. . . .

II

Yet no matter how great the material benefits that the railroads will bring Italy, the psychological effects which they should produce will be still greater.

A few brief considerations will suffice to justify this assertion for those who know Italy.

Italy's misfortunes are of long standing. We will not try to set forth their historical background. Such a task would be out of place here as well as beyond our capabilities. But it is certainly true that they must be attributed primarily to the political influence exercised among us for centuries by foreigners. The principal obstacles to our freeing ourselves from this distressing influence are the internal divisions, the rivalries, even hostility among the members of the great Italian family. Next comes the distrust between the national princes and the most energetic segment of the population. This segment has a desire for progress, which is often too great, a lively national spirit, and a strong patriotism—all of which makes it, if not the principal instrument, the indispensable auxiliary of all efforts for emancipation.

If the railroads should reduce these obstacles—perhaps even make them disappear—they will be among the factors most favorable to the spirit of Italian nationalism. A communication system permitting the constant movement of persons in all directions must necessarily connect populations once strangers to each other and should contribute much to the destruction of petty municipal rivalries born of ignorance and prejudice— already disappearing through the efforts of enlightened Italians. This deduction is too obvious to be denied.

The primary psychological effect of the establishment of railroads on the Italian peninsula is so great that it would be enough to justify the enthusiasm railroads arouse among all true friends of Italy.

The second psychological effect expected has still more importance, although it will be harder to appreciate its significance at first.

The division of Italy at the time of the Congress of Vienna was as arbitrary as it was

imperfect. This august assemblage, acting solely on the basis of "might makes right," raised a political edifice without moral foundation. Their act was based not on any guiding principle, or on legality, which was violated in the case of Genoa and Venice, or on national interest or popular will; they recognized neither geographical situations nor the general and particular interests created by twenty years of revolution.

Only bitter fruit could come from such an act. Despite the benevolent conduct of several national princes, the discontent provoked by the new development grew rapidly during the years following the Restoration, and a storm threatened to break out in the near future. The fiery agitators and innovators, exploiting the bellicose passions developed by the Empire and finding support among liberal sentiments affronted by the decrees of the Congress of Vienna, fomented the unfortunate movements of 1820 and 1821.

These revolutionary efforts were easily repressed because the upper classes were divided and the masses took but little part in them, but their consequences were nonetheless deplorable for Italy. Although the attempts did not make the governments of the region tyrannical, they aroused in them a strong distrust of all nationalist ideas and stopped the development of the natural progressive tendencies already manifest. Weakened, discouraged, deeply divided, for a long time after that Italy could not hope to ameliorate her lot. . . .

The revolutionary doctrines of young Italy have little appeal to classes so strongly interested in the maintenance of the social order. Except for a few youthful spirits whose schoolboy ardor is not yet dampened by experience, there are in Italy only a small number of persons seriously disposed to practice the exalted principles of a sect embittered by misfortune. We believe that a good number of very determined opponents and extreme republicans would appear in the front ranks of the conservative party if the social order were truly menaced and the great principles on which it rests were in real danger. . . .

This future for which we yearn is the achievement of national independence. Italy can gain this supreme goal only through the united efforts of all her children. Without this she cannot hope for any real and lasting amelioration of her political condition, nor can she walk firmly on the road to progress. . . .

All history proves that no people can attain a high degree of intelligence and morality unless its spirit of nationalism is strongly developed. This remarkable fact is a necessary consequence of the laws governing human nature. The intellectual life of the masses moves within a highly restricted circle of ideas. Of those which they can acquire, the most noble and elevating other than religious ones are the concepts of patriotism and nationality. If the political circumstances of a country prevent these concepts from being manifest or give them false direction, the masses are plunged into a state of deplorable inferiority. But that is not all; if a people cannot be proud of nationality, a feeling of personal dignity exists only incidentally among a few privileged individuals. The majority, occupying the humblest social positions, need a feeling of national greatness to acquire a consciousness of their own dignity. At the risk of shocking hidebound political writers, we might even say that this consciousness is an essential element of morality for the people as well as for individuals.

For the sake of the great issue of emancipation for Italy, all issues dividing us must vanish and all special interests fall silent; this must be accomplished so that our country can achieve not only power and glory but a level of intellectual and moral development equal to that of the most civilized nations. . . .

In this regard we need only cite what is happening in Piedmont. The growth of primary education, the establishment of several chairs in social and political science, the encouragement given the corporate spirit in the arts as well as industry, and several other measures in addition to the railroads suffice to show that this distinguished and brilliant monarch has decided to maintain the glorious statecraft which has made his family the leading Italian dynasty in the past and should carry it to yet higher destinies in the future.

But more than any other administrative reform, and as much as large political concessions, the construction of railroads will contribute to consolidating that mutual confidence between governments and peoples which is the foundation of our hopes for the future. In giving these powerful instruments of progress to the nations whose destinies they rule, the governments only demonstrate their benevolence and feeling of security. Grateful for so great a benefaction, the people on their part will come to have complete faith in their sovereigns; tractable—though full of enthusiasm—they will permit their leaders to guide them to national independence.

If these arguments have some foundation, we must be justified in placing the moral achievements of the railroads in Italy above their material achievements and hailing their introduction among us as the harbinger of a better future. This is why . . . we like to include them among the principal "aspirations" of our homeland.

STUDY QUESTIONS

1. What is nationalism? Why is it difficult to define? How nationalist is the United States by Shafer's criteria?

2. How did the French Revolution further nationalism? In what sense was revolutionary nationalism a religious faith?

3. How did Napoleon affect the nationalism movement? Why did the powers who defeated Napoleon oppose nationalism after 1815? To whom did nationalism appeal? Who opposed it?

4. What was the relationship between nationalism and liberalism? Why was nationalism ignored at the Congress of Vienna? How would you evaluate the success of the national uprisings between 1815 and 1849?

5. What were the most important duties of man, according to Mazzini? How was love of one's own nation related to love of God? Did love of one's own nation make one an enemy of other countries?

6. By what tactics did Mazzini hope to pursue national unification? Were they contradictory?

7. Why did Cavour place so much stress on the development of railroads? What did he understand by nationalism?

8. How did Mazzini and Cavour differ in their approach to nationalism? To what extent were their goals similar?

9. Was Napoleon III more like Mazzini or Cavour? What importance did his policies have for the future of European nationalism?

Carlton Hayes: Forceful Nationalism and Industrialized Society

Reprinted with permission of The Macmillan Company from *Nationalism: A Religion* by Carlton J. H. Hayes. © by Carlton J. H. Hayes 1960.

TOPIC 36

LATER STAGES OF NATIONALISM

The once liberal and romantic notions that fostered national self-determination took on sharper and less utopian contours in the second half of the nineteenth century. This was particularly visible in the attitudes and behavior of the more powerful industrialized states. There the combination of industrial and military power threatened to substitute its own methods and goals for those of the earlier nationalism. Mazzini's view of nation-states living in peaceful harmony with one another was replaced by a chauvinism and xenophobia that undermined liberal values and the peace of nations. The emergence of nationalism from its liberal cocoon is traced in these readings. German nationalistic development has been chosen to illustrate the movement toward an armed camp of nations.

I

New and Competitive Militarism

The nationalism which swept like a tidal wave in the first two-thirds of the nineteenth century from western Europe over central and into eastern Europe, was associated and tinctured with the romantic liberalism of the era. Its political advocates held out to mankind an invigorating liberal promise—one which for a while seemed realizable—that every nationality should and would exercise a right of self-determination, ridding itself of alien control and imperialism, setting up a free national state of its own people. It would guarantee personal liberties to each citizen, establish parliamentary government, promote education, public works, and public health, and forward material well-being and prosperity. And as part of the prospect was the pleasant picture of peace between and among free national states and peoples. There would be free trade, free travel and migration, friendly rivalry in good works, limitation of armaments, judicial settlement of international disputes. A favorite subject for contemporary lithographs and amateur paintings was the lamb lying peacefully down with the lion. In 1842 Tennyson brought out *Locksley Hall,* containing its famous apostrophe to commerce and to the time when

The war drum throbbed no longer and battle flags were furl'd
In the Parliament of man, the Federation of the world. . . ."

. . . The events of 1848–49 indicated that to save the lamb from the lion, to say nothing of federating the world, force would be required. Not by simple and pacific self-determination would the map of central and eastern Europe be redrawn along the lines of nationality, but only through war, and then imperfectly. The Crimean War of 1854–1856 inaugurated an independent and united national state for Rumanians; the Franco-Austrian War of 1859, a like state for Italians. And the chief agent of both was Napoleon III, who, as we have seen, was a democrat and liberal of sorts, and an exponent of the right of national self-determination.

Not so the foremost European statesman of the generation following Napoleon's. Otto von Bismarck was a nationalist of a different kind; and the means he employed to erect and ensure a powerful German Empire gave tone and character to the intensifying nationalism in Europe during the half century from 1864 to 1914. Bismarck detested the Frankfurt Assembly of 1848 which had tried and failed to create a liberal, unified Germany. He stood for a national German state which would be dominated by his own conservative Prussia and from which Austria would be excluded. He would rely on the Prussian army, not on plebiscites, to achieve his ends.

Hence, against the opposition of German liberals, Bismarck fostered Prussian militarism.

He arbitrarily established compulsory and effective army service for all able-bodied Prussians and triumphantly utilized it in three aggressive wars. First was the War of 1864, by which Denmark was ousted from the duchies of Schleswig-Holstein. Second was the Seven Weeks' War of 1866 by which the German Confederation that had been headed by Austria, and supported by most of the other German states, was destroyed and supplanted by a tighter federation dominated by an enlarged Prussia. Third was the Franco-Prussian War of 1870–1871, which not only ended the French Empire of Napoleon III but inaugurated the nationalistic German Empire of the Prussian Hohenzollerns by absorbing the South German states and appropriating from France the territory of Alsace-Lorraine.

"Nothing succeeds like success," Bismarck, from being in 1864 a most unpopular Prussian minister, became in the 1870's a hero of the German nation. There continued to be some dislike and criticism of his methods and policies on the part of minority groups in the German Empire, for example Socialists, Catholics, Radical Democrats, Poles, and Alsatians, but acclaim was loudly voiced by the majority parties of "National Liberals" and "Free Conservatives." His militarism, once resented, was now generally accepted both at home and abroad, for peacetime as well as for wartime. To uphold the prestige of the newly created German Empire among the European great powers, and to safeguard it against any "war of revenge" by France, Bismarck insisted that it must retain, and from time to time increase, the size and efficiency of its armed forces—and it did so. . . .

Though the European great powers managed to preserve an "armed peace" between each other during the years from 1871 to 1914,

Edward Hicks (1780–1849), an American Quaker, painted about eighty versions of "The Peaceable Kingdom," a detail of which is reproduced here.

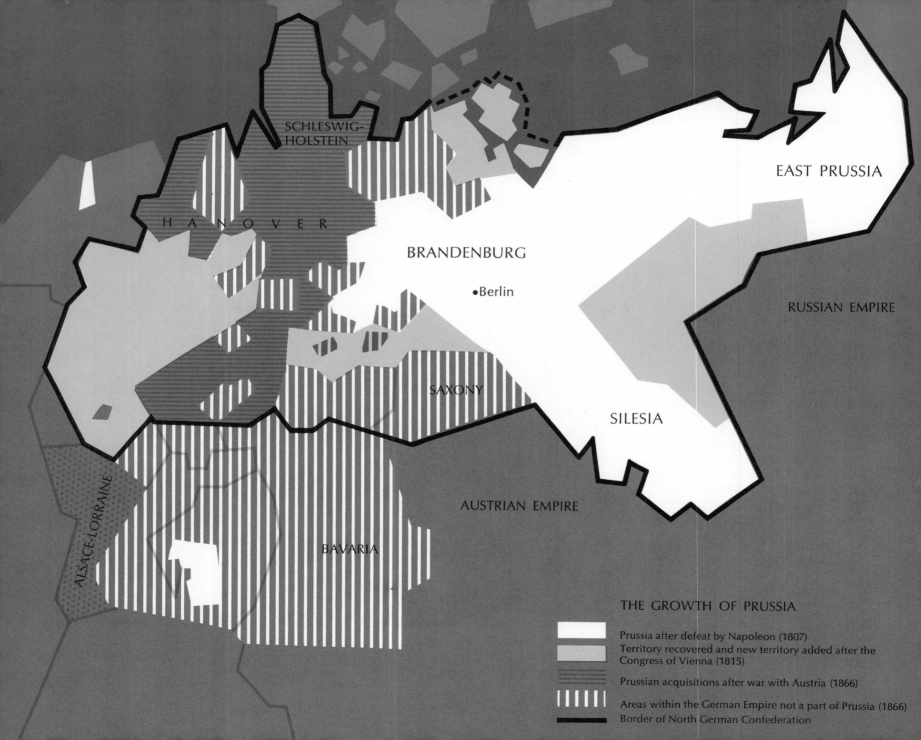

SCHLESWIG-
HOLSTEIN

EAST PRUSSIA

H A N O V E R

BRANDENBURG

•Berlin

RUSSIAN EMPIRE

SAXONY

SILESIA

ALSACE-LORRAINE

AUSTRIAN EMPIRE

BAVARIA

THE GROWTH OF PRUSSIA

Prussia after defeat by Napoleon (1807)

Territory recovered and new territory added after the
Congress of Vienna (1815)

Prussian acquisitions after war with Austria (1866)

Areas within the German Empire not a part of Prussia (1866)

Border of North German Confederation

the period was repeatedly punctuated by nationalist wars which affected the balance of power and exacerbated national rivalry. In 1875 both Bulgarians and Bosnian Serbs rose in arms against the Ottoman Empire. Followed the Russo-Turkish War of 1877–1878, concluding with expansion of Russia in Bessarabia and the Caucasus, recognition of full independence of Serbia and Rumania and autonomy for Bulgaria, and, in the nature of consolation prizes for Austria-Hungary and Great Britain, the "military occupation" of Bosnia-Herzegovina by the former and of Cyprus by the latter.

In 1885 Serbia warred with Bulgaria. In 1897 Greece fought to obtain Crete from the Turks. In 1898 was waged the Spanish-American War, and from 1889 to 1902 the war between British and Dutch in South Africa. Failure marked the international Peace Conferences at The Hague in 1899 and 1907. Instead there came in quickening succession the Russo-Japanese War of 1904–1905, the Italian-Turkish War of 1911–1912, the two Balkan Wars of 1912–1913—and the terrible World War I of 1914–1918.

Militarism did not keep the peace as its proponents sometimes argued it would. But it did stimulate and gravely heighten nationalist fervor in Europe and throughout traditional Christendom.

Effects of Industrial Revolution

Modern nationalism had arisen in a preponderantly agricultural and commercial society. Its original champions had belonged to the landed gentry or to the professional middle class of traders, lawyers, civil servants, scholars, and journalists. As for the masses, those in rural areas seem to have been less responsive than those in urban centers where intercommunication was relatively easy and

means of propaganda more available. Such had notably been the case in the England of the sixteenth and seventeenth centuries, and also in revolutionary France of the late eighteenth century. Much the same social pattern underlay the spread of cultural and then political nationalism in central and eastern Europe during the first two-thirds of the nineteenth century.

In the last third of the century, however, the development of technology and large-scale machine industry—what we call the "Industrial Revolution"—was transforming the traditional pattern of European society and laying foundation for a more rampant nationalism. To be sure, the revolution had gotten under way in England in the eighteenth century, and by 1848 it was already beginning to furnish the European Continent—and the United States—with steam-powered factories and locomotives, with railway lines and telegraph wires. But outside of England the social and national consequences of the revolution were not widely or deeply impressive until the 1860's and 1870's. Then the shift of population from farm to factory, from countryside to city, from peasantry to "proletariat," grew apace. So did the means of transportation and communication; so, too, the rivalry of peoples for economic advantage.

All this had bearing on the nationalist struggles of the time. It was England's industrial primacy which was mainly responsible for her triumph over Revolutionary and Napoleonic France, and also for the mighty prestige she enjoyed for at least a century afterward. Moreover, the American Civil War of 1861–1865, the longest and most destructive struggle in the hundred years from Napoleon to the First World War, was won by the more

industrialized and hence wealthier North; and it resulted not only in "preserving" the Union but in establishing its coercive supremacy over the several states. It was likewise the more industrialized Germany which defeated France in 1870–1871 and wrested from her the provinces of Alsace-Lorraine. And without increasing and spreading industrialization, it would have been impossible to maintain the mounting competitive armaments which major nations possessed from the 1860's and 1870's. An industrial nation could now be, indeed, a "great power." On the other hand, industrial backwardness might be calamitous, as indicated by successive defeats and losses of the Ottoman Empire in 1877–1878 and 1911–1913, of Spain in 1898, and of the South African Boers in 1899–1902. . . .

Possibly if the whole world could have been industrialized simultaneously and uniformly, with the same standard of living prevailing everywhere, national differences might not have been emphasized, and full economic liberalism, with its promise of "peace and universal brotherhood," might have been realized. What a Utopian dream! Actually, no two countries have been at any given time in exactly the same stage of industrialization, and especially after 1880 each partially industrialized country utilized the sentiment of nationalism and the power of national government to protect by tariffs and bounties its own industry against foreign competition, and by labor legislation and restriction of foreign immigration to raise the standard of living of its own people.

This is the *economic nationalism* which was significantly pursued by Bismarckian Germany and by post-Civil-War United States. It has since been adopted and applied by nation after nation. It is basic to the "welfare state," as exemplified by Germany in the 1880's, by Great Britain in the early 1900's, by the United States in the 1930's, and, in most drastic form by Communist Russia.

In fine, the Industrial Revolution served in many ways to spread and intensify nationalism. It increased the wealth and power of national states in Europe and America where it began and chiefly developed. It accentuated economic rivalry among them, and it contributed to a competitive imperialism which led eventually to nationalist reaction in Asia and Africa. . . .

II

Intolerance toward Minorities

Contemporary with the new national [ism] was a manifold display of nationalist intolerance. Back of this was the drive of heated patriots for national strength and power, and their conviction that tolerance of dissent and division within a nation would gravely weaken it. Hence the entire population of a country should be trained and obliged to conform with the characteristics and beliefs of the major or dominant nationality. Minorities who didn't conform were suspect; they obviously lacked the requisite hundred per cent of national patriotism and therefore merited treatment as inferior, second-class citizens if not as downright traitors. . . .

Nationalist intolerance in the era after 1870 was not only religious but racial. Earlier nationalists had frequently used the word "race," but in a loose way without pretense to scientific exactitude. Ever since Friedrich Schlegel, early in the nineteenth century, had delivered the dictum that there are as many races as there are languages, it had become commonplace to speak of a German race, a French race, a Slavic race, a Celtic race, an Anglo-Saxon race, and so on. This was, with most people, a merely conventional use of "race" as a synonym for nationality. . . .

The problem of finding out what the different human races were . . . seemed soluble through a combination of two methods. One was to classify races, superior and inferior, according to mental and spiritual traits and then discover to which a man belonged by observing his behavior and measuring his intelligence. The other method was to classify races according to physical features. Combination of the methods appeared to confirm "scientifically," that Germans, who had recently triumphed over France, belonged to a peculiarly valorous and superior race. Hence anyone who displayed "German" qualities of energy and bravery must belong to that race; and, conversely, anyone, who, like the prevalent physical type of North German, was tall, blond, blue-eyed, and long-headed, must possess superior qualities of courage and intellect. This was quite consistent with, and reassuring to, German nationalism. . . .

The Aryan myth—as such German racialism is properly described—was accepted and preached outside the German Empire. In France, for instance, it was expounded at length by the Comte de Gobineau, an aristocrat proud of the Germanic origins of his class and fearful of the leveling and corrupting influence of "inferior" races in his country. . . .

English and American publicists of presumably Anglo-Saxon lineage attributed the greatness of their countries to that stock—that superior Aryan and Teutonic race. Sir John Seeley in his *Expansion of England* (1883) proclaimed the British Empire to be the very embodiment of Anglo-Saxon superiority. To him and to numerous fellow imperialists, the motive force in all of England's greatness—political, commercial, industrial, and moral, no less than naval and colonial—was the "Anglo-Saxon race." And what easier explanation could be put forth of the growing strength and expansionist activity of the United States? "If I read not amiss," declared a Congregational clergyman of New England in 1885, "this powerful race will move down upon Mexico, down upon Central and South America, out upon the islands on the sea, over upon Africa and beyond. And can anyone doubt that the result of this competition of races will be the 'survival of the fittest'?"

Racialism gave new vigor and direction to anti-Jewish prejudice. Dislike of Jews and discrimination against them had long existed. They were everywhere a minority who preserved a good deal of clannishness and a good many traditions and customs different from the majority's. Christians were apt to dislike their religious recalcitrance; farmers, their urbanmindedness; conservatives, their flocking with liberals or Marxians. Yet at least in western and central Europe there had been a remarkable dwindling of anti-Jewish discrimination and prejudice in the first two-thirds of the nineteenth century and until the rise of racialism. Then anti-Jewish sentiment was rationalized and intensified as anti-Semitism. The Jews, it was now claimed, belonged to a Semitic *race* because the Hebrew spoken by their ancestors was a Semitic language, and their Semitic race couldn't help but transmit physical, mental, and moral traits different from the Aryan and irreconcilable with it. Hence there was no hope of changing Jewish habits and every reason for safeguarding Aryan nations against the degrading influence of Semitic minorities. . . .

While nationalist intolerance was displayed toward a supranational religion such as Catholic Christianity and toward a supposedly racial grouping such as Jews, its principal manifestation had to do with ethnic minorities. We should bear in mind that, despite the progress made since the French Revolution in redrawing the map of Europe along lines of nationality and in creating unified national states, no European state as yet embraced, or was confined to, a single nationality. Many German people were still outside the German Empire (chiefly in Austria, Switzerland, and Russia's Baltic provinces), while within it were Poles, Danes, and French-speaking Lorrainers. Italy lacked important "irredentas," and so did every one of the Balkan states. Belgium was bilingual, and Switzerland trilingual. Spain included Catalans and Basques as well as Castilians, and France a variety of "submerged" and "forgotten" peoples. Irish, Scots, and Welsh were joined with Englishmen in the "United Kingdom." Austria-Hungary and the Russian and Ottoman Empires, though dominated respectively by Germans and Magyars, by Russians, and by Turks, were not national states at all: they were polyglot and imperial.

This halting in the political sphere between a partially and an entirely nationalized Europe occurred when "the state" was assuming unprecedented functions and authority. It occurred likewise when doctrines and examples of forcefulness, racialism, and overseas imperialism were convincing dominant and "successful" nationalities that they were superior, and in duty bound to curb any agitation of "inferior" peoples for separate statehood and to keep them under the higher civilizing tutelage of the existing state. In other words, *raison d'état* compromised the working out of the principle of nationality. "National self-determination" gave way to "determination by superior peoples." Nationalism became imperialistic not only overseas but within Europe (and America).

J. G. Fichte Idealizes the German Love of Freedom (1808)

Johann Gottlieb Fichte (1792–1814) was a Prussian patriot who tried to whip up a spirit of German nationalism during the Napoleonic years. The "Addresses to the German Nation" were given in Berlin in 1807–1808, at a time when the city was occupied by the victorious troops of Napoleon. In order to avoid French censorship Fichte's lectures were focused on the Romans but his audience understood that he meant the French. From J. G. Fichte, *Addresses to the German Nation*, trans. R. F. Jones and G. H. Turnbull (La Salle, Illinois: The Open Court Publishing Co., 1922), pp. 136, 143–145.

The noble-minded man will be active and effective, and will sacrifice himself for his people. Life merely as such, the mere continuance of changing existence, has in any case never had any value for him; he has wished for it only as the source of what is permanent. But this permanence is promised to him only by the continuous and independent existence of his nation. In order to save his nation he must be ready even to die that it may live, and that he may live in it the only life for which he has ever wished. . . .

In this belief our earliest common forefathers . . . the Germans, as the Romans called them, bravely resisted the oncoming world dominion of the Romans. Did they not have before their eyes the greater brilliance of the Roman provinces next to them and the more refined enjoyments. . . . Were not the Romans willing enough to let them share in all these blessings? . . . To those who submitted the Romans gave marks of distinction in the form of kingly titles, high commands in their armies, and Roman orders. . . . Had they no appreciation of the advantages of Roman civilization. . . . They cannot be charged with ignorance or lack of consideration of any one of these things. Their descendants, as soon as they could do so without losing their freedom, even assimilated Roman culture, so far as this was possible without losing their individuality. Why, then, did they fight for several generations in bloody wars, that broke out again and again with ever renewed force? A Roman writer puts the following expression into the mouths of their leaders: "What was left for them to do, except to maintain their freedom or else to die before they became slaves?" Freedom to them meant just this: remaining Germans and continuing to settle their own affairs, independently and in accordance with the original spirit of their race, going on with their development in accordance with the same spirit, and propagating this independence in their posterity. All those blessings which the Romans offered them meant slavery to them because then they would have to become something that was not German, they would have to become half Roman. They assumed as a matter of course that every man would rather die than become half a Roman, and that a true German could only want to live in order to be, and to remain, just a German and to bring up his children as Germans.

They did not all die; they did not see slavery; they bequeathed freedom to their children. It is their unyielding resistance which the whole modern world has to thank for being what it now is. Had the Romans succeeded in bringing them also under the yoke and in destroying them as a nation, which the Romans did in every case, the whole development of the human race would have taken a different course, a course that one cannot think would have been more satisfactory. It is they whom we must thank—we, the immediate heirs of their soil, their language, and their way of thinking—for being Germans still, for being still borne along on the stream of original and independent life. It is they whom we must thank for everything that we have been as a nation since those days, and to them we shall be indebted for everything that we shall be in the future, unless things have come to an end with us now and the last drop of blood inherited from them has dried up in our veins. . . .

The present problem, the first task . . . is simply to preserve the existence and continuance of what is German. All other differences vanish. . . .

Seeking a folk hero from the days of their earliest ancestors, German nationalists made much of Hermann, or Arminius, who annihilated three Roman Legions in the depths of the Teutoberg Forest in A.D. 9 and ended Roman plans to add Germany beyond the Rhine to the Empire. This nineteenth-century painting shows Hermann in triumph after the victory.

Carl Schurz Anticipates a Democratic Germany (1848)

Carl Schurz (1829–1905) was studying at the University of Bonn when the Revolution of 1848 erupted. His exuberant description of the immediate reaction of students and professors in the little Rhineland town to the events in Paris reflects the mixture of liberalism and nationalism that characterized the continental crusade for self-determination. Schurz, along with many other disappointed democrats, was later forced by the collapse of the Revolution to flee to the United States where he had a long and impressive political career. From Carl Schurz, *Reminiscences* (New York, 1907), I, pp. 112–114.

One morning toward the end of February 1848, I sat quietly in my attic chamber, working hard at my tragedy of *Ulrich von Hutten*, when suddenly a friend rushed breathlessly into the room, exclaiming: "What, you sitting here! Do you not know what has happened?"

"No; what?"

"The French have driven away Louis Philippe and proclaimed the republic."

I threw down my pen—and that was the end of *Ulrich von Hutten*. I never touched the manuscript again. We tore down the stairs, into the street, to the market square, the accustomed meeting place for all the student societies after their midday dinner. Although it was still forenoon, the market was already crowded with young men talking excitedly. There was no shouting, no noise, only agitated conversation. What did we want there? This probably no one knew. But since the French had driven away Louis Philippe and proclaimed the republic, something of course must happen here, too. Some of the students had brought their rapiers along, as if it were necessary to make an attack or to defend themselves. We were dominated by a vague feeling as if a great outbreak of elemental forces had begun, as if an earthquake were impending of which we had felt the first shock, and we instinctively crowded together. Thus we wandered about in numerous bands—to the *Kneipe,* where our restlessness, however, would not suffer us long to stay; then to other pleasure resorts, where we fell into conversation with all manner of strangers, to find in them the same confused, astonished, and expectant state of mind; then back to the market square, to see what might be going on there; until finally late in the night fatigue compelled us to find the way home.

The next morning there were the usual lectures to be attended. But how profitless! The voice of the professor sounded like a monotonous drone coming from far away. What he had to say did not seem to concern us. The pen that should have taken notes remained idle. At last we closed our notebooks with a sigh and went away, impelled by a feeling that now we had something more important to do—to devote ourselves to the affairs of the fatherland. And this we did by seeking again as quickly as possible the company of our friends, in order to discuss what had happened and what was to come. In these conversations, excited as they were, certain ideas and catchwords worked themselves to the surface, which expressed more or less the feelings of the people. Now had arrived in Germany the day for the establishment of "German Unity," and the founding of a great, powerful national German empire.

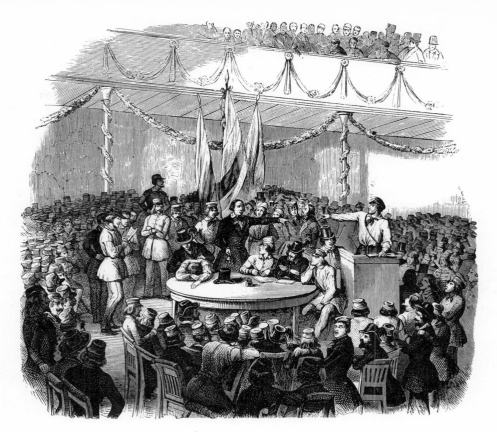

German students like those Carl Schurz described argue the objectives of the revolution in 1848.

First in line the convocation of a national parliament. Then the demands for civil rights and liberties, free speech, free press, the right of free assembly, equality before the law, a freely elected representation of the people with legislative power, responsibility of ministers, self-government of the communes, the right of the people to carry arms, the formation of a civic guard with elective officers and so on—in short, that which was called a "Constitutional form of government on a broad democratic basis." Republican ideas were at first only sparingly expressed. But the word democracy was soon on all tongues, and many, too, thought it a matter of course that if the princes should try to withhold from the people rights and liberties demanded, force would take the place of mere petition. Of course the regeneration of the country must, if possible, be accomplished by peaceable means. A few days after the outbreak of this commotion I reached my nineteenth birthday. I remember to have been so entirely absorbed by what was happening that I could hardly turn my thoughts to anything else. Like many of my friends, I was dominated by the feeling that at last the great opportunity had arrived for giving to the German people the liberty which was their birthright and to the German fatherland its unity and greatness, and that it was now the first duty of every German to do and to sacrifice everything for this sacred object. We were profoundly, solemnly, in earnest. . . .

Otto von Bismarck Offers Prussian Blood and Iron (1862)

Otto von Bismarck (1815–1898) was the chief figure in the unification of Germany under Prussian military leadership. He was not primarily interested in uniting Germany but in preserving conservative control within Prussia, one of the largest German states. The revolutions in 1848–1849 had failed in part because the liberal nationalists lacked the power to force the various German states to give up their sovereignty and submerge themselves into a united Germany. The smaller states were backed up by powerful Austria, who had no interest in the creation of a German national state since the majority of Austrian subjects were non-German and would be excluded from such a state. German liberals consequently turned in the 1850s to Prussia, the only other state that could challenge Austrian power. A good chance existed that the liberals could gain control of the Prussian government and then use this control to unite a Germany under what they

called "a policy of moral conquest." The decades of the 1850s and 1860s were a period of rapid economic development in Germany with the resultant growth of a prosperous middle class whose liberal representatives by 1862 had a majority in the Prussian parliament. The presence of this majority created an impasse with the conservative ruler of Prussia, William I. Prevented in his attempts to run the army in the way he wanted, William threatened to abdicate. This would have given the liberals a signal victory, a possibility made even more appalling to conservatives by the fact that the heir to the throne had liberal tendencies. At this moment the court called in Bismarck, a noted conservative, at the time Prussian ambassador to France. Bismarck's objective was to defeat the liberals; his tactic was to use the weapon of nationalism (and Prussian leadership in the movement to unify Germany) to divert their popular support. I. In *Bismarck, The Man and the Statesman. Reflections and Reminiscences of Otto Prince von Bismarck* (London, 1898), pp. 290–293, 309–310; II. From *Bismarck's Table Talk*, ed. Charles Lowe (London, 1895), pp. 60–61.

I. FROM BISMARCK'S REMINISCENCES

I arrived in Berlin in the morning of September 20. . . . I was received at [the palace] on September 22, and the situation only became clear to me when his Majesty defined it in some such words as these: "I will not reign if I cannot do it in such a fashion as I can be answerable for to God, my conscience, and my subjects. But I cannot do that if I am to rule according to the will of the present majority in parliament, and I can no longer find any ministers prepared to conduct

my government without subjecting themselves and me to the parliamentary majority. I have therefore resolved to lay down my crown, and have already sketched out the proclamation of my abdication. . . ." The King showed me the document in his own handwriting lying on the table, whether already signed or not I do not know. His Majesty concluded by repeating that he could not govern without suitable ministers.

I replied that his Majesty had been acquainted ever since May with my readiness to enter the ministry. . . . After a good deal of consideration and discussion, the King asked me whether I was prepared as minister to advocate the reorganization of the army, and when I assented he asked me further whether I would do so in opposition to the majority of parliament and its resolutions. When I asserted my willingness, he finally declared, "Then it is my duty, with your help, to attempt to continue the battle, and I shall not abdicate. . . ."

I succeeded in convincing him that, so far as he was concerned, it was not a question of Liberal or Conservative of this or that shade, but rather of monarchical rule or parliamentary government, and that the latter must be avoided at all costs, if even by a period of dictatorship. I said: "In this situation, I shall, even if your Majesty commands me to do things which I do not consider right, tell you my opinion quite openly; but if you finally persist in yours, I will rather perish with the King than forsake your Majesty in the contest with parliamentary government." This view was at that time strong and absolute in me, because I regarded the negations and phrases of the Opposition of that day as politically disastrous in face of the national task of Prussia. . . .

In the beginning of October I went . . . to meet the King, who had been at Baden-Baden for September 30, his wife's birthday. . . . My object in taking this opportunity for an interview was to set his Majesty at rest about a speech made by me in the Budget Commission [of the Prussian Parliament] on September 30, which had aroused some excitement and which, though not taken down in shorthand, had still been reproduced with tolerable accuracy in the newspapers. . . .

I had indicated plainly enough the direction in which I was going. Prussia—such was the point of my speech—as a glance at the map will show, could no longer wear unaided on its long narrow figure the panoply which Germany required for its security; that must be equally distributed over all German people. We should get no nearer the goal by speeches, associations, decisions of majorities; we should be unable to avoid a serious contest, a contest which could only be settled by blood and iron. In order to secure our success in this, the deputies must place the greatest possible weight of blood and iron in the hands of the King of Prussia, in order that according to his judgment he might throw it into one scale or the other. I had already given expression to the same idea in the House of Deputies in 1849. . . .

II. BISMARCK'S SPEECH BEFORE THE PRUSSIAN PARLIAMENTARY BUDGET COMMITTEE

Within a fortnight of his [arrival in Berlin], Bismarck had made his first speech at a sitting of the Budget Committee.

Military reform, he argued, was above all things requisite for a "national policy."

To this the objection was urged that it would be much better of the Government to aim at making moral conquests in Germany by a Liberal policy.

Thereupon Bismarck produced his pocketbook, and took from it a little twig with a few dried leaves upon it.

"I brought this olive-leaf with me from Avignon," he said, "in order to offer it to the Progressives [Liberals] as a symbol of peace, but I see that I am much too soon with it."

And on this assurance being only received with a smile, Bismarck roused himself to sterner speech.

"Germany," he said, "does not look to the liberalism, but to the power of Prussia, and Prussia must pull herself together so as not again to miss the favourable moment. Not by speechifying and resolutions, as in 1848 and 1849, can the great questions of the time be decided, but by *blood and iron.*"

And with that he crushed the withered olive leaves in the palm of his hand, sprinkling their dust upon the floor—such the history of the famous olive-twig which characterised the policy that was to [unify] Germany. . . .

Heinrich von Treitschke Demands the Return of Germany's Lost Brethren (1870)

Von Treitschke (1834–1896) was a German nationalist historian. Alsace-Lorraine, the borderlands between France and Germany, had belonged to France since its conquest by Louis XIV in the seventeenth century. Most of the inhabitants, particularly in Alsace, still spoke German as well as French at the time of the Franco-Prussian War (1870–1871). The "return" of Alsace-Lorraine was for many Germans one of the conditions of peace. The reading is taken from an article written by von Treitschke in 1870, entitled, "What We Demand from France." From H. von Treitschke, *Zehn Jahre deutscher Kämpfe: Schriften zur Tagespolitik* (Berlin, 1874), pp. 289–291.

In view of our obligation to secure the peace of the world, who dares object that the people of Alsace and Lorraine do not wish to belong to us? In face of the sacred necessity of these great days, the doctrine of the right of self-determination for all branches of the German race—that alluring solution proposed by demagogues without a country—becomes a pitiable and shameful thing. These provinces are ours by the right of the sword, and we shall dispose of them by a higher right— the right of the German nation, which cannot allow its lost children to remain forever alien to the German Empire. We Germans, knowing Germany and France, know better than these unfortunates themselves what is to the advantage of the people of Alsace, who, because of the misleading influence of their French life, have no knowledge of the new Germany. Against their will we shall restore them to their true selves.

With joyful wonder, we have watched the immortal progress of the moral forces of history in the awful changes of these days, and we have done so too often to be capable of belief in the unconditional value of mere popular disinclination. The spirit of a nation embraces not only contemporary generations, but those also who are before and behind it! We appeal from the misguided wills of those who now live in Alsace to the desires of those who lived there before them. We call upon all those stout Germans who once set the seal of our spirit upon the speech and the customs, the art and the communal life of the upper Rhine—and, before the nineteenth century comes to an end, the world will recognize that the spirit . . . still lives and that, though we set at naught the will of the present generation of Alsatians, we did so merely in obedience to the dictates of national honor. . . .

Paul Rohrbach Justifies the Spread of the German Idea in the World (1912)

Paul Rohrbach was an influential German journalist in the period preceding World War I who urged the spread of what he considered superior German culture through a policy of political expansion. From Paul Rohrbach, *The German Idea in the World* (Berlin, 1912), p. 6.

There is no need to state concerning the German idea, as of the Roman idea, that it can only be mistress of the world or not be at all. But we can press the comparison further and say: she will only conquer and dominate as the auxiliary of universal civilization, or not at all. It is easy to state the reasons for this. The Anglo-American element has today grown to such an extraordinary extent that, based on those countries belonging to it, on its means of action and on its internal power,

it seems on the way to establish its dominion over the world's civilization. Russia, the greatest and most numerous of political communities after the Anglo-Americans, appears to us stripped of its old hopes of a world policy because of its internal barbarism and its fragile structure. France has of its own accord renounced competition in the future with the other world powers. By the side of the Anglo-Americans, only the German nation has developed in such a fashion that she now appears sufficiently numerous and strong internally for her national thought to claim her formal right of a share in the shaping of the future. How can we understand this? We must know that we can only preserve our energy and our strength by an endless increase of the German idea. For us there can be no halt, no immobility. We cannot give up, even for a moment, the widening of our living space. We have only the choice between the alternative of relapsing into the ranks of the territorial peoples (bound by narrow boundaries) and that of conquering by force a place beside the Anglo-Americans (on the world scale). . . .

Hajo Holborn: Europe in the Age of Nationalism

In *The Political Collapse of Europe,* that appeared after the Second World War, Hajo Holborn (1902–1969) of Yale University, who left his native Germany at the time of the Nazi takeover, analyzed the combination of ele-

ments that transformed European civilization in the nineteenth and twentieth centuries. He examines the interrelationship of industrialism, militarism, and nationalism. From *The Political Collapse of Europe,* by Hajo Holborn. Copyright 1951 by Hajo Holborn. Reprinted by permission of Alfred A. Knopf, Inc.

Although capitalism became a world-wide movement, it utterly failed to destroy nationalism. On the contrary, the capitalistic epoch became the age of nationalism above all others. Everywhere capitalism preserved and solidified the existing national states and endowed them with an infinitely greater internal and external power than they had ever owned before. To this extent modern capitalism reaffirmed the historical pattern of Europe. Furthermore, it threw the national diversity of the Continent into bold relief. Various European nations found various solutions for granting political representation to the new wealth-producing classes. In Britain the *bourgeoisie* acquired political power, and the same happened in France, but in Austria-Hungary and Germany the *bourgeoisie* did not directly share political responsibility, acting instead as a mighty pressure group on the half-absolutistic governments. There were other distinctions. Britain sacrificed her agriculture to such an extent that she became almost an exclusively industrial state, whereas Germany, in spite of her greater industrial production, managed to retain an agriculture of considerable importance. France also remained a country in which agricultural and industrial production were more evenly matched. . . .

Modern industrial capitalism changed the social structure of the individual European states, but it did not basically transform the national motivations of international affairs. It altered, however, both the forms and the range of international relations.

We have already reviewed the changing forms of diplomacy in the age of imperialism; we must discuss one more development of importance, the militarization of the modern European states. The period between 1871 and 1914 has often been called the period of "armed peace." In a way any age of European history could be given this name, but the military element was at that time more conspicuous than in earlier ages. Modern industrial capitalism in an era of growing population and prosperity enabled the states to organize bigger navies and armies than ever before. In the eighteenth century, France was the first European power whose army was as big as the Roman army under Emperor Augustus. After 1815 every great continental state could boast of such an army. After 1850 and again after 1871 peacetime armies grew even larger. Modern industries could equip these armies with ever deadlier weapons. The frightful casualties of the Austro-Prussian and Franco-German wars showed how machines were multiplying man's destructive capacity. And the new mass forces and the increased fire power were made even more effective by modern communications. . . .

Napoleon aimed at the annihilation of the armed forces of his enemies and achieved it at what he called "lightning" speed and at great risk. He had at his disposal greater manpower and financial resources than the absolute monarchs had commanded. Napoleon did not hesitate to use all the resources of France and of any country that he conquered in order to gain absolute decisions on the battlefield and dictate peremptory political terms to the defeated. Military action, Napo-leon demonstrated, could not only conquer provinces and colonies but also destroy old and great nations in a single morning of combat.

The fearful lesson was not forgotten, though it was somewhat repressed after Napoleon's final defeat. Economic exhaustion and political reaction combined to keep modern militarism within bounds. Large armies had been built during the French Revolution. Carnot's *leveé en masse* had introduced the revolutionary idea that the right of modern national citizenship found its complement in the obligation of all the citizens to lend their strength to the defense of the nation. Napoleon had toned down the Jacobin principle of universal national service very considerably by granting special exemptions to the *bourgeoisie,* but the draft had allowed him to build up the big armies that he led to many victories. . . .

Prussia adopted universal military service in the years of liberation from Napoleon. The small and poor state could hope to create a large army only through conscription. The Prussian reformers expected that a citizens' army would display a higher morale than the mercenaries of Prussian absolutism. Since they also hoped that the new military system would help create a civic spirit in Prussian citizens, they wanted the conscript to serve in the army and army reserve only for relatively few years. Thereafter he was to join a national guard that was to have its own officers and was to be linked to the organs of local self-government introduced after 1807.

The idea of liberalizing the Prussian state through the reorganization of the army failed, as did many other liberal reform plans of the years 1807–19. Once the political reaction established its hold over the government the national guard idea was not further developed. Finally, William I's war minister Roon presented in the early 1860's an army bill that made universal military service nothing but a convenient system of recruitment for the standing army and its war reserve. And Bismarck's policy assured to the *Junker* officer corps complete control over Prussia's armed forces, which were directly subject to the king.

It was this reorganized army, resting on national conscription but converted into an instrument of a homogeneous professional officer class, that won the wars of 1866 and 1870–71 under Moltke. Under the influence of the German victories all the continental European states introduced universal military service as the most effective system for the organization of mass armies, and it formed the common basis of the subsequent expansion of the European armies.

Moltke's strategy had created in the heart of the Continent a new and powerful empire, and this fact by itself provided other nations with an incentive to arm. But it had also laid bare the terrifying effects that military might could produce in the age of modern capitalism. As late as 1840 it would have taken many weeks to assemble the whole Prussian army at a given place, since it was spread from Aachen to Tilsit. In 1866 the Prussian army was fully deployed along the Bohemian frontier in two weeks, and Moltke had even withdrawn the Prussian troops from the Rhine, since he trusted that in case of need he could move the army from Bohemia to southern Germany fast enough to meet a French military intervention. The railroads and the many new highways made mobility as well as concentration of forces possible.

But even more disquieting was the new relationship of war and peace that came thereby into being. Since the speed of mobilization was of vital significance, plans of mobilization had to be drawn up long beforehand. Every member of a nation liable for military duty had to know his place in the war machinery before war broke out. Whereas Napoleon made his military decisions on the battlefield, the modern European generals planned their campaigns and battles in peacetime and called upon their governments to implement their plans not only by granting them the necessary numbers of troops but by building the necessary railroad lines for their timely deployment. Thus an ever growing part of the peacetime activities of governments was absorbed by war preparations.

It is not enough to conceive of the process of militarization as the enlarging of armies in relative proportion to the growing population and the resources of the European nations. The changes caused by the militarization of Europe were structural as well. Previously merchants or travellers could cross all political frontiers without special permits and passports except in Russia; but militarization laid the groundwork for treating the national societies as independent, isolated entities. In the contracting geographical conditions of the age of modern capitalism the national states, for reasons of defense, grew more like medieval cities. The walls, gates, and moats were not visible as yet, but their blueprints were under way. In retrospect we can easily discern the beginnings of social organization for total war. The military leaders of the age, being themselves children of the social order that industrial capitalism had produced, thought they possessed the answer to the dangers that war posed to modern civilization. They believed that the existing social conditions would be strained to the breaking point by a long general war among the great powers. But they were confident that the modern war organization and strategy would make future wars short armed conflicts, like Moltke's wars of 1866 and 1871.

But the keen apprehension felt about any change of the balance of military forces resulted in the race of armaments and diplomatic alliances. The growth of army expenditure in the British empire between 1870 and 1890 was about 350 per cent, in France 250 per cent, in Russia 400 per cent, in Austria-Hungary almost 450 per cent, in Italy almost 350 per cent, in Germany 1,000 per cent. The strength of the highly industrialized states was reflected in the per capita cost of the military expenditure. The individual Britisher contributed $3.74 in 1870, $4.03 in 1890, $8.53 in 1914, the German $1.33, $2.95, $8.52, the Frenchman $3.03, $4.87, $7.33; the comparative figures for Russia were $1.34, $1.32, $2.58, and for Italy, $1.44, $2.63, $3.81.

The size of the military establishment and the assumed conditions of future warfare profoundly affected the conduct of diplomatic relations. The eighteenth century had called war the *ultima ratio regum.* One may reject this specious label, yet admit that the wars of the eighteenth century, though often enough grossly materialistic, still were to a much higher degree instruments of a rational policy than are modern wars. The gigantic power amassed in the military juggernauts and the dramatic speed required for their effective application hung like the sword of Damocles over the heads of the statesmen of the pre-World-War-I era. Their freedom of action was gravely handicapped. . . .

STUDY QUESTIONS

1. What was the promise of nationalism? Why was it difficult to fulfill? Could national aspirations have been achieved in the nineteenth century without the use of force? How were they affected by industrialization?

2. What was the relationship between nationalism and racism? Where did the ideals of liberalism and nationalism come in conflict?

3. Compare the views on German nationalism of the authors of Readings 191–195. What seems to be happening to the concept of nationalism?

4. What feelings and desires did Fichte try to evoke by his lectures on the relationship of Germans and Romans? How might leaders of emerging nations today react to his argument?

5. What did Schurz see as the relationship between liberalism and nationalism in 1848?

6. How did Bismarck propose to unite Germany? What alternatives did he reject by a call for "blood and iron"? How might the successful use of such tactics influence the future course of nationalism?

7. How did Treitschke justify the seizure of Alsace-Lorraine? Why was he opposed to allowing the residents of the provinces a free choice?

8. How did Rohrbach view the German role in the world? Were there any limits to his goals? Was his a peculiarly German view?

9. What was the relationship between industrialism, militarism, and nationalism? What effect did this relationship have on the priority given to military expenditures? On the life of the citizenry? On international relations?

China

A Chinese caricature of an English foraging party in the first half of the nineteenth century.

The Chinese frequently referred to Europeans as the "hairy ones." Here a Chinese has sketched a smoke-belching English sailor in 1839, shortly before the outbreak of the Opium War.

This newspaper cartoon of ca. 1891 reflects the hostile response of many Chinese to the proselytizing activity of Christian missionaries. In the lower left corner the Bible is being burned, while above a missionary is receiving rough and ready justice.

Nationalism in the Eyes of the Cartoonist

Cartoons with their use of exaggeration to make a point often capture far better than words the sense of ethnic superiority and condescension that marked the advanced stages of nationalism. The cartoons on this and the following pages supply a few typical Chinese, British, European, and American reactions toward their non-countrymen.

[Literal Translation of Characters.]
"The bloody hogs calling themselves foreign missionaries fool both the heavens and the earth. They try to destroy the dignity of our ancestry and our ancient religion. If they were riddled with bullets and cut up with swords, the punishment would not be too great. The dirty dogs! the wild beasts! the foul books! the hypocrites destroying the religion of the angels for their savage doctrines! Every kind of people in every land and on every sea want to see them punished!"

Great Britain

In 1845 the United States possessed the naiveté, in British eyes, to dispute the possession of the Northwest (Oregon) Territory.

This Japanese drawing was reproduced in a British book in 1874 by A. Humbert, *Japan and the Japanese* with the sarcastic caption ridiculing the credulous orientals, "Japanese Idea of a Railway Train." In point of fact the earliest English trains had closely resembled the illustration.

LIFE IN AN AMERICAN HOTEL?

A British view of the primitive state of American society (Punch, 1856).

Europe

Many Europeans sympathized with the underdog South African Boers during the British efforts to dominate them that ended in the Boer War of 1899–1902. Here the German cartoonist, Thomas Heine, pictures a muscular Queen Victoria at the time of the abortive Jameson Raid in 1895 being flattened by the imperturbable Paul Kruger, the Boer leader, while the South African imperialist Cecil Rhodes watches in growing dismay (left).

A German view of Russian imperialism in China. China conceded Russia the right to build a branch of the Trans-Siberian Railroad across Manchuria in 1896. The caption reads: "Russia has finally succeeded in belling the cat. (bottom)"

This Spanish cartoon from *Hojas Selectas* in 1901 portrays Theodore Roosevelt as the rising sun of Yankee imperialism. Note the implication that Roosevelt's simultaneous wielding of sword and olive branch has gained him both territory and votes (below center).

A common European view of the United States as prospering by the misfortunes of others is repeated in the Austrian satirical monthly *Kikeriki* in 1925 (below right).

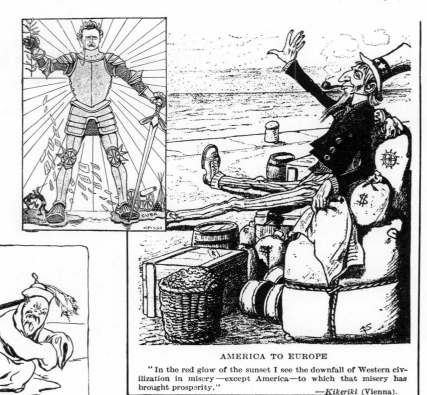

AMERICA TO EUROPE

"In the red glow of the sunset I see the downfall of Western civilization in misery —except America—to which that misery has brought prosperity."

—*Kikeriki* (Vienna).

"WHAT SHALL WE DO WITH OUR BOYS?"

The octopus-armed Chinese laborer monopolizing industrial production and sending his earnings back to China at the expense of unemployed Americans and the accompanying rise in juvenile delinquency was frequently cited as a reason for anti-Asian sentiment in the United States.

Uncle Sam extends a warm welcome to a somewhat disreputable group—(from right) a Jew, Italian, Spaniard, Dutchman, Balkan Slav, and Russian—while excluding a neatly dressed Japanese.

"WE DRAW THE LINE AT JAPANESE"

Nationalistic conceit pervades these cartoons of 1905 and 1914. Above is pictured a Rip van Winkle-like China awakened from his long sleep by the ringing alarm clock of Western progress. Right is presented a widely held American viewpoint that the nations of the world used the United States as a dumping ground for their undesirables.

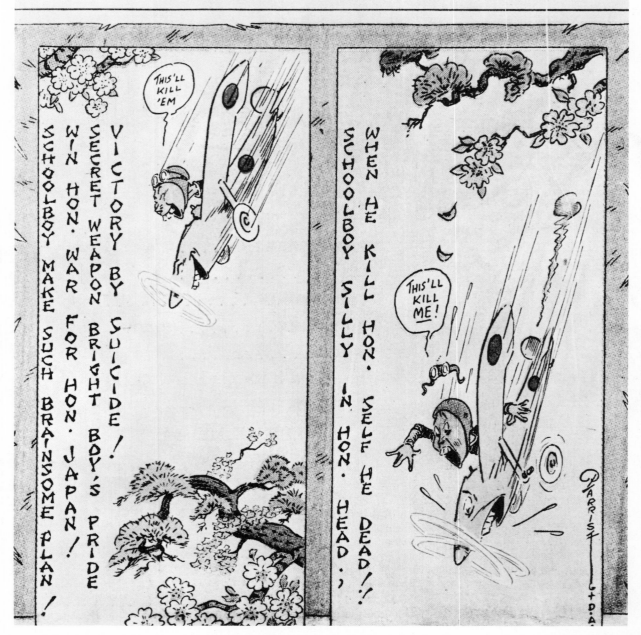

A 1945 cartoon lampoons the Japanese military code which highly honored personal sacrifice in the national interest.

A Revolution Takes Place in Biology

L. S. Stavrianos, *The World Since 1500: A Global History*, © 1966. Reprinted by permission of Prentice-Hall, Inc., Englewood Cliffs, New Jersey.

TOPIC 37

EVOLUTION AND ITS RESIDUE

No scientific writer had greater impact on the national and social struggles of late-nineteenth-century Europe than Charles Darwin. For some of his borrowers and popularizers the laws of evolution and natural selection became the key to understanding the hostility of nation-state relations and the ruthless competition of individuals. The vulgarizers of Social Darwinism provided evidence of the power of science and excuses for the persistence of *laissez-faire* attitudes and the belligerent and imperialist tendencies of nationalism. The readings that follow examine the place of Darwinist thought in the world view of the late nineteenth century, and its challenge to the ethical norms of both the Enlightenment and the Judaeo-Christian tradition.

I

As Isaac Newton dominated seventeenth century science with his discovery of the laws governing the bodies of the universe, so Charles Darwin (1809–1882) dominated nineteenth, for he discovered the laws governing the evolution of man himself.

The concept of evolution, however, was by no means new with Darwin: it had been propounded and applied in various fields of science. Jean de Lamarck (1744–1829) had earlier challenged the traditional notion of the immutable fixity of species created at one time and existing ever since. Instead he envisioned a comprehensive evolution from worm to man, and sought to explain the process of evolution with the theory of acquired characteristics. Horses acquired their speedy legs from the need to run fast, giraffes their long necks from the need to feed on tall branches. And any such body changes are handed on by hereditary processes to be the starting point for the next generation.

Then came Charles Lyell with his classic three-volume *Principles of Geology* (1830–1833), which popularized the "uniformitarian" or evolutionary theory of the formation of the earth's surface. Hitherto it had been believed that the surface had been formed by past catastrophes such as volcanoes, earthquakes, and floods. The existence of seashells in high mountainous regions was conveniently attributed to Noah's flood. Lyell, by contrast, held that the present surface of the earth is the product of the operation during countless millennia of geologic forces such as glaciation, wind and water erosion, and freezing and thawing.

The concept of evolution was prominent at this time in the social sciences as well as the physical. From the 1840's, Karl Marx was writing that all social institutions were in constant process of change. Since the beginning of human history one type of society had given way to another—primitive tribalism to ancient slavery to feudal serfdom, to modern capitalism and as he confidently predicted, to the socialism of the future. Much more influential was the all-embracing doctrine of evolution propounded by Herbert Spencer (1820–1903). He applied his doctrine to all things, material, biological, cultural, and social. In his *Progress, its Law and Cause*, published in 1857, Spencer wrote, "Whether it be in the development of Society, of Government, of Manufactures, of Commerce, of Language, Literature, Science, Art, this same evolution of the simple into the complex, through successive differentiations, holds throughout."

This was the atmosphere in which Darwin worked out his epoch-making theories. Darwin came from a family in which scientific ability had already appeared in two generations (and has since appeared in two more). He attended Cambridge University where he spent less time on his studies than on collecting and studying animals and insects. A professor who recognized his potentialities recommended him for an unsalaried post as naturalist on the government ship *Beagle,* which was starting on a scientific expedition around the world. During this voyage, which lasted from 1831 to 1836, Darwin was impressed by the numerous variations that he observed in individual species. On the isolated Galapagos Islands, for example, he found species that obviously had come from ancestors on the mainland but had somehow grown different. This eliminated the old theory of the fixity of species, but left unanswered the question of how and why variation occurred.

Two years after his return from the expedition, he derived a clue from the book by Thomas Malthus* propounding the theory that the human race tends to outrun its means of subsistence unless the redundant individuals are eliminated.

In October 1838 I happened to read for amusement Malthus on Population, and

*Thomas Malthus (1766–1834) was a pioneer in modern population study. He maintained that population tends to grow more rapidly than the food supply available, which is held down by the limited amount of fertile land on the earth. The only way to even the ratio of people to food was through wars and natural calamities. Malthus' theory was popular among the middle classes because it justified the existence of so many poor people in the world —Eds.

being well prepared to appreciate the struggle for existence which everywhere goes on from long continued observation of the habits of animals and plants, it at once struck me that under these circumstances favourable variations would tend to be preserved, and unfavourable ones to be destroyed. The result of this would be the formation of new species. Here then I had a theory by which to work.

Darwin developed this theory with his customary caution and painstaking care. In 1839 he began a draft; three years later it was still only a 35-page abstract in pencil. By 1844 he had expanded it to a 230-page study. . . .

But still Darwin could not bring himself to publish his findings. He continued to gather further evidence until 1858, when he received a staggering letter from another naturalist, Alfred Russel Wallace (1823–1913). Wallace had spent many years in Brazil and in the Dutch East Indies, where he had absorbed a vast store of zoological knowledge. In Febru-

MALTHUSIAN THEORY

ary, 1858, as he lay suffering from malaria at Ternate in the Moluccas, his mind turned to Malthus whom he also had read, and suddenly there flashed upon him the idea of the survival of the fittest as the mechanism by which evolution was effected. Being of an entirely different temperament from Darwin, he immediately put his thoughts to paper. The same evening, while still racked with fever, he drafted his new theory. On two succeeding evenings he elaborated upon it, and then he sent it to Darwin, with whom he had frequently corresponded.

Darwin received the manuscript in June 1858, and was stupefied to read a summary of what he already had written. "I never saw a more striking coincidence," he wrote to Charles Lyell; "if Wallace had my manuscript sketch written out in 1842, he could not have made a better short abstract! Even his terms now stand as heads of my chapters." Darwin no longer hesitated to make public his researches. He read his own essay and that of Wallace before a learned society in London on July 1, 1858, and the so-called Darwinian hypothesis of evolution was launched. Darwin set forth his ideas at greater length in his chief book, *On the Origin of Species by Means of Natural Selection, or the Preservation of Favoured Races in the Struggle for Life,* published in 1859.

II

Darwin's central thesis—his doctrine of evolution—was that animal and vegetable species in their present diverse forms are not immutably fixed as results of separate special acts of creation but are different and changing natural outcomes of a common original source. Darwin believed that the chief manner in which variation took place was by

The mottled wings of an oak beauty moth on a lichen-covered tree trunk aid in the insect's survival.

Charles Darwin Explains the Origin of Species (1859)

From Charles Darwin, *The Origin of Species* (New York, 1909) II, pp. 79–80, 81–84, 90–94, 97, 507–509.

GEOMETRICAL RATIO OF INCREASE

A struggle for existence inevitably follows from the high rate at which all organic beings tend to increase. . . . As more individuals are produced than can possibly survive, there must in every case be a struggle for existence, either one individual with another of the same species, or with the individuals of distinct species, or with the physical conditions of life. . . . Although some species may be now increasing . . . in numbers, all cannot do so for the world would not hold them.

There is no exception to the rule that every organic being naturally increases at so high a rate, that, if not destroyed, the earth would soon be covered by the progeny of a single pair. Even slow-breeding man has doubled in twenty-five years and at this rate in less than a thousand years there would literally not be standing-room for his progeny. Linnaeus has calculated that if an annual plant produced only two seeds—and there is no plant so unproductive as this—and their seedlings next year produced two, and so on, then in twenty years there would be a million plants. The elephant is reckoned the slowest breeder of all known animals, and I have taken some pains to estimate its probably minimum rate of natural increase; it will be safest to assume that it begins breeding when thirty years old,

"natural selection." He defined this process as follows:

> As many more individuals of each species are born that can possibly survive, and as, consequently, there is a frequently recurring struggle for existence, it follows that any being, if it vary however slightly in any manner profitable to itself, under the complex and sometimes varying conditions of life, will have a better chance of surviving, and thus be *naturally selected*. From the strong principle of inheritance, any selected variety will tend to propagate its new and modified form.

It may be hard to conceive of all the variety in nature as being the product of what appears to be such an inordinately slow process of change as that afforded by "natural selection." Yet statistical calculations show that even if a mutation resulted in only a one per cent better chance of survival, it would establish itself in half the individuals of a species in a hundred generations. In other words, if a hundred and one individuals with this mutation survived for every hundred without it, it would spread through the species in what is biologically speaking, a short time. A specific example of how "natural selection" operates is provided by a small moth which appears in light and dark colorations. It has been noticed that the light variety is about six times more common in light birch forests than the *dark* variety, and, conversely, that the dark variety is sixteen times commoner in dark pine forests than the light variety. Evidence of the functioning of "natural selection" has been found in the coloration of the moth wings left by the birds in the two types of forests. . . .

bringing forth six young in the interval, and surviving till one hundred years old; if this be so, after a period of from 740 to 750 years there would be nearly nineteen million elephants alive, descended from the first pair.

. . . Every single organic being may be said to be striving to the utmost to increase in numbers; that each lives by a struggle at some period of its life; that heavy destruction inevitably falls either on the young or old, during each generation or at recurrent intervals. Lighten any check, mitigate the destruction ever so little, and the number of the species will almost instantaneously increase to any amount.

NATURE OF THE CHECKS TO INCREASE

The amount of food for each species of course gives the extreme limit to which each can increase; but very frequently it is not the obtaining food, but the serving as prey to other animals, which determines the average numbers of a species. . . .

Climate plays an important part in determining the average numbers of a species and periodical seasons of extreme cold or drought seem to be the most effective of all checks. I estimated (chiefly from the greatly reduced numbers of nests in the spring) that the winter of 1854–5 destroyed four-fifths of the birds in my own grounds; and this is a tremendous destruction, when we remember that ten per cent is an extraordinarily severe mortality from epidemics with man. The action of climate seems at first sight to be quite independent of the struggle for existence; but in so far as climate chiefly acts in reducing food, it brings on the most severe struggle between the individuals, whether of the same or of distinct species, which subsist on the same kind of food. Even when climate, for instance extreme cold, acts directly, it will be the least vigorous individuals, or those which have got least food through the advancing winter, which will suffer most. . . .

When a species, owing to highly favoured circumstances, increases inordinately in numbers in a small tract, epidemics—at least, this seems generally to occur with our game animals—often ensue, and here we have a limiting check. . . .

STRUGGLE FOR LIFE MOST SEVERE BETWEEN INDIVIDUALS AND VARIETIES OF THE SAME SPECIES

As the species of the same genus usually have . . . much similarity in habits and constitution, and always in structure, the struggle will generally be more severe between them if they come into competition with each other, than between the species of distinct genera. We see this in the recent extension over parts of the United States of one species of swallow having caused the decrease of another species. The recent increase of the missel-thrush in parts of Scotland has caused the decrease of the song-thrush. How frequently we hear of one species of rat taking the place of another species under the most different climates. . . . All that we can do, is to keep steadily in mind that each organic being is striving to increase in a geometrical ratio; that each at some period of its life, during some season of the year, during each generation or at intervals, has to struggle for life and to suffer great destruction. When we reflect on this struggle, we may console ourselves with the full belief, that the war of nature is not incessant, that no fear is felt, that death is generally prompt, and that the vigorous, the healthy, and the happy survive and multiply. . . .

NATURAL SELECTION; OR THE SURVIVAL OF THE FITTEST

Let it . . . be borne in mind how infinitely complex and close-fitting are the mutual relations of all organic beings to each other and to their physical conditions of life; and consequently what infinitely varied diversities of structure might be of use to each being under changing conditions of life. Can it, then, be thought improbable, seeing that variations useful to man have undoubtedly occurred, that other variations useful in some way to each being in the great and complex battle of life, should occur in the course of many successive generations? If such do occur, can we doubt (remembering that many more individuals are born than can possibly survive) that individuals having any advantage, however slight, over others, would have the best chance of surviving and of procreating their kind? On the other hand, we may feel sure that any variation in the least degree injurious would be rigidly destroyed. This preservation of favourable individual differences and variations, and the destruction of those which are injurious, I have called Natural Selection, or the Survival of the Fittest. . . .

It may . . . be said that natural selection is daily and hourly scrutinising, throughout the world, the slightest variations; rejecting those that are bad, preserving and adding up all that are good; silently and insensibly working, *whenever and wherever opportunity offers,* at the improvement of each organic being in relation to its organic and inorganic conditions of life. We see nothing of these slow changes in progress, until the hand of time has marked the lapse of ages, and then so imperfect is our view into long-past geological ages, that we see only that the forms of life are now different from what they formerly were. . . .

CONCLUSION

In the survival of favoured individuals . . . during the constantly-recurrent Struggle for Existence, we see a powerful and ever-acting form of Selection. The struggle for existence inevitably follows from the high geometrical ratio of increase which is common to all organic beings. . . . More individuals are born than can possibly survive. A grain in the balance may determine which individuals shall live and which shall die,—which variety or species shall increase in number, and which shall decrease, or finally become extinct. As the individuals of the same species come in all respects into the closest competition with each other, the struggle will generally be most severe between them; it will be almost equally severe between the varieties of the same species, and next in severity between the species of the same genus. . . . The slightest advantage in certain individuals, at any age or during any season, over those with which they come into competition, or better adaptation in however slight a degree to the surrounding physical conditions, will, in the long run, turn the balance. . . .

As geology plainly proclaims that each land has undergone great physical changes, we might have expected to find that organic beings have varied under nature, in the same way as they have varied under domestication. And if there has been any variability under nature, it would be an unaccountable fact if natural selection had not come into play. It has often been asserted, but the assertion is incapable of proof, that the amount of varia-

tion under nature is a strictly limited quantity. Man, though acting on external characters alone and often capriciously, can produce within a short period a great result by adding up mere individual differences in his domestic productions; and every one admits that species present individual differences. But, besides such differences, all naturalists admit that natural varieties exist, which are considered sufficiently distinct to be worthy of record in systematic works. . . .

If then, animals and plants do vary, let it be ever so slightly or slowly, why should not variations or individual differences, which are in any way beneficial, be preserved and accumulated through natural selection, or the survival of the fittest? If man can by patience select variations useful to him, why, under changing and complex conditions of life, should not variations useful to nature's living products often arise, and be preserved or selected? What limit can be put to this power, acting during long ages and rigidly scrutinising the whole constitution, structure, and habits of each creature,—favouring the good and rejecting the bad? I can see no limit to this power, in slowly and beautifully adapting each form to the most complex relations of life. The theory of natural selection, even if we look no farther than this, seems to be in the highest degree probable. . . .

Darwin Comes to Conclusions about the Descent of Man (1871)

From Charles Darwin, *The Descent of Man* (London, 1871), pp. 32, 54–57, 69–74, 183–186.

I

The Bodily Structure of Man

It is notorious that man is constructed on the same general type or model as other mammals. All the bones in his skeleton can be compared with corresponding bones in a monkey, bat, or seal. So it is with his muscles, nerves, bloodvessels and internal viscera. The brain, the most important of all the organs, follows the same law, as shown by Huxley and other anatomists. . . .

With respect to the causes of variability, we are in all cases very ignorant; but we can see that in man as in the lower animals, they stand in some relation to the conditions to which each species has been exposed, during several generations. . . .

The Direct and Definite Action of Changed Conditions

This is a most perplexing subject. It cannot be denied that changed conditions produce some, and occasionally a considerable effect, on organisms of all kinds; and it seems at first probable that if sufficient time were allowed this would be the invariable result. . . .

In the United States, above 1,000,000 soldiers, who served in the late war, were measured, and the States in which they were born and reared were recorded. From this astonishing number of observations it is proved that local influences of some kind act directly on stature; and we further learn that "the State where the physical growth has in great measure taken place, and the State of birth, which indicates the ancestry, seem to exert a marked influence on the stature." For instance, it is established, "that residence in the Western States, during the years of growth, tends to produce increase of stature." On the other hand, it is certain that with sailors, their life delays growth, as shewn "by the great difference between the statures of soldiers and sailors at the ages of seventeen and eighteen years." . . . When we compare the differences in stature between the Polynesian chiefs and the lower orders within the same islands, or between the inhabitants of the fertile volcanic and low barren coral islands of the same ocean, or again between the Fuegians on the eastern and western shores of their country, where the means of subsistence are very different, it is scarcely possible to avoid the conclusion that better food and greater comfort do influence stature. . . .

Natural Selection

We have now seen that man is variable in body and mind; and that the variations are induced, either directly or indirectly, by the same general causes, and obey the same general laws, as with the lower animals. Man has spread widely over the face of the earth, and must have been exposed, during his incessant migration, to the most diversified conditions. . . . The early progenitors of man must also have tended, like all other animals, to have increased beyond their means of subsistence; they must, therefore, occasionally have been exposed to a struggle for existence, and consequently to the rigid law of natural selection. . . . We know, for instance, that the muscles of our hands and feet, which determine our powers of movement, are liable, like those of the lower animals, to incessant variability. If then the progenitors of man inhabiting any district, especially one undergoing some change in its conditions, were divided into two equal bodies, the one half which included all the individuals best adapted by their powers of movement for gaining subsistence, or for defending themselves, would on an average survive in greater numbers, and procreate more offspring than the other and less well endowed half.

Man in the rudest state in which he now exists is the most dominant animal that has ever appeared on this earth. He has spread more widely than any other highly organised form: and all others have yielded before him. He manifestly owes this immense superiority to his intellectual faculties, to his social habits, which lead him to aid and defend his fellows, and to his corporeal structure. The supreme importance of these characters has been proved by the final arbitrament of the battle for life. Through his powers of intellect, articulate language has been evolved; and on this his wonderful advancement has mainly depended. . . .

There can be no doubt that the difference between the mind of the lowest man and that of the highest animal is immense. An anthropomorphous ape, if he could take a dispassionate view of his own case, would admit that though he could form an artful plan to plunder a garden—though he could use stones for fighting or for breaking open nuts, yet that the thought of fashioning a stone into a tool was quite beyond his scope. Still less, as he would admit, could he follow out a train of metaphysical reasoning, or solve a mathematical problem, or reflect on God, or admire a grand natural scene. Some apes, however, would probably declare that they could and did admire the beauty of the coloured skin and fur of their partners in marriage. They would admit, that though they could make other apes understand by cries some of their perceptions and simpler wants, the notion of expressing definite ideas by definite sounds had never crossed their minds. They might insist that they were ready to aid their fellow-apes of the same troop in many ways, to risk their lives for them, and to take charge of their orphans; but they would be forced to acknowledge that disinterested love for all living creatures, the most noble attribute of man, was quite beyond their comprehension.

Nevertheless the difference in mind between man and the higher animals, great as it is, certainly is one of degree and not of kind. We have seen that the senses and intuitions, the various emotions and faculties, such as love, memory, attention, curiosity, imitation, reason, etc., of which man boasts, may be found in an incipient, or even sometimes in a well-developed condition, in the lower animals. They are also capable of some inherited improvement, as we see in the domestic dog compared with the wolf or jackal. If it could be proved that certain high mental powers, such as the formation of general concepts, self-consciousness, etc., were absolutely peculiar to man, which seems extremely doubtful, it is not improbable that these qualities are merely the incidental results of other highly-advanced intellectual faculties; and these again mainly the result of the continued use of a perfect language. . . .

General Conclusion

The main conclusion here arrived at, and now held by many naturalists who are well competent to form a sound judgment is that man is descended from some less highly organised form.

II

The grounds upon which this conclusion rests will never be shaken, for the close similarity between man and the lower animals in

THE LION OF THE SEASON.

ALARMED FLUNKEY. "MR. G-G-G-O-O-O-RILLA!"

embryonic development, as well as in innumerable points of structure and constitution, both of high and of the most trifling importance,—the rudiments which he retains, and the abnormal reversions to which he is occasionally liable,—are facts which cannot be disputed. They have long been known, but until recently they told us nothing with respect to the origin of man. Now when viewed by the light of our knowledge of the whole organic world, their meaning is unmistakable. The great principle of evolution stands up clear and firm, when these groups or facts are considered in connection with others, such as the mutual affinities of the members of the same group, their geographical distribution in past and present times, and their geological succession. It is incredible that all these facts should speak falsely. He who is not content to look, like a savage, at the phenomena of nature as disconnected, cannot any longer believe that man is the work of a separate act of creation. He will be forced to admit that the close resemblance of the embryo of man to that, for instance, of a dog—the construction of his skull, limbs and whole frame on the same plan with that of other mammals, independently of the uses to which the parts may be put—the occasional re-appearance of various structures, for instance of several muscles, which man does not normally possess, but which are common to the Quadrumana—and a crowd of analogous facts—all point in the plainest manner to the conclusion that man is the co-descendant with other mammals of a common progenitor. . . .

The main conclusion arrived at in this work, namely, that man is descended from some

A contemporary cartoon from *Punch*.

lowly organised form, will, I regret to think, be highly distasteful to many. But there can hardly be a doubt that we are descended from barbarians. The astonishment which I felt on first seeing a party of Fuegians on a wild and broken shore will never be forgotten by me, for the reflection at once rushed into my mind—such were our ancestors. These men were absolutely naked and bedaubed with paint, their long hair was tangled, their mouths frothed with excitement, and their expression was wild, startled, and distrustful. They possessed hardly any arts, and like wild animals lived on what they could catch; they had no government, and were merciless to every one not of their own small tribe. He who has seen a savage in his native land will not feel much shame, if forced to acknowledge that the blood of some more humble creature flows in his veins. For my own part I would as soon be descended from that heroic little monkey, who braved his dreaded enemy in order to save the life of his keeper, or from that old baboon, who descending from the mountains, carried away in triumph his young comrade from a crowd of astonished dogs—as from a savage who delights to torture his enemies, offers up bloody sacrifices, practises infanticide without remorse, treats his wives like slaves, knows no decency, and is haunted by the grossest superstitions.

Man may be excused for feeling some pride at having risen, though not through his own exertions, to the very summit of the organic scale; and the fact of his having thus risen, instead of having been aboriginally placed there, may give him hope for a still higher destiny in the distant future. But we are not here concerned with hopes or fears, only with the truth as far as our reason permits us to discover it; and I have given the evidence to the best of my ability. We must, however, acknowledge, as it seems to me, that man with all his noble qualities, with sympathy which feels for the most debased, with benevolence which extends not only to other men but to the humblest living creature, with his god-like intellect which has penetrated into the movements and constitution of the solar system—with all these exalted powers—man still bears in his bodily frame the indelible stamp of his lowly origin.

Social Darwinism

L. S. Stavrianos, *The World Since 1500: A Global History,* © 1966. Reprinted by permission of Prentice-Hall, Inc., Englewood Cliffs, New Jersey.

Darwin's theory was far from generally accepted during his lifetime. . . . There was bitter opposition in certain quarters, particularly amongst the churchmen. This was understandable, because just as the Copernican system of astronomy had deposed the earth from its central place in the universe, so Darwinism seemed to dethrone man from his central place in the history of the earth. Such was the natural conclusion of the churchmen when Darwin published another book, *The Descent of Man,* in 1871. In this work he marshaled the evidence that man is related to all animal life, and concluded that "he who is not content to look, like a savage, at the phenomena of nature as disconnected, cannot any longer believe that man is the work of a separate act of creation." Darwin, in other words, was denying the act of divine creation. He was denounced, with less than fairness, for undermining human dignity, morality, and religion, and for saying that men came from monkeys. Benjamin Disraeli solemnly declared that if it were a choice between apes and angels, he was on the side of the angels.

Despite this hostile reception in religious and other circles, Darwinism had profound repercussions upon Western society. The basic reason is that its emphasis on survival of the fittest and struggle for survival fitted in admirably with the temper of the times. In politics, for example, this was the period when Bismarck was unifying Germany by blood and iron. His nationalistic admirers in all countries believed that Darwinism offered them support and justification. They held that in politics, as in nature, the strongest are victorious, and that war-like qualities decide who will win in the international "struggle for survival". In economic life this was the period of free enterprise and rugged individualism. The upper and middle classes, comfortable and contented, stoutly opposed any state intervention for the promotion of greater social equality. They argued that they deserved their blessings and prosperity because they had proven themselves "fitter" than the shiftless poor, and, furthermore, the absorption of smaller concerns by big business was a part of the "struggle for survival". The late nineteenth century was also the golden age of colonial expansion, and Darwinism was used to justify imperialism. It was argued that colonies were necessary for the prosperity and survival of a Great Power, and also that native peoples, judged in terms of worldly success, were weak, inferior, and in need of the protection and guidance of the superior and stronger Europeans.

This application of Darwin's theories to the social scene is known as Social Darwinism. Darwin himself had never dreamt, let alone intended, that his findings would be exploited in this fashion. But the fact remains that they were, and the reason is that they seemed to offer scientific buttressing to the materialism or *Realpolitik,* that came over Europe at this time from other causes. Darwinism, in short, fitted in conveniently with Kipling's dictum

That they should take who have the power
And they should keep who can.

Philip Gosse Faces the Dilemma of Evolution versus Creation (1859)

Philip Gosse (1810–1888) was a respected English natural scientist. The dilemma presented to pious Christians by Darwinian theory is apparent in the following description of Gosse written by his son. Gosse tried to resolve the dilemma by developing a hypothesis that God, when creating the earth, gave it the appearance of a planet that had existed for millions of years. Gosse's theory (which he called "Omphalos") thus provided an explanation for the presence of fossils on the earth. It did not explain, however, why God would go to such great trouble to deceive man, and the theory was ridiculed by fundamentalist Christians and evolutionists alike. Reprinted with the permission of Charles Scribner's Sons from *Father and Son,* pages 128–129, by Edmund Gosse. Copyright 1907 Charles Scribner's Sons; renewal copyright 1935 Philip Gosse. This is published in Canada by William Heinemann Ltd.

Up to this point in [my father's] career, he had . . . nourished the delusion that science and revelation could be mutually justified, that some sort of compromise was possible. With great and ever greater distinctness, his investigations had shown him that in all departments of organic nature there are visible the evidences of slow modification of forms, of the type developed by the pressure and practice of eons. This conviction had been borne in upon him until it was positively irresistible. Where was his place, then, as a sincere and accurate observer? Manifestly, it was with the pioneers of the new truth, it was with Darwin, Wallace and Hooker. But did not the second chapter of "Genesis" say that in six days the heavens and earth were finished, and the host of them, and that on the seventh day God ended his work which he had made?

Here was a dilemma! Geology certainly *seemed* to be true, but the Bible, which was God's word, *was* true. If the Bible said that all things in Heaven and Earth were created in six days, created in six days they were,—in six literal days of twenty-four hours each. The evidences of spontaneous variation of form, acting, over an immense space of time, upon ever-modifying organic structures, *seemed* overwhelming, but they must either be brought into line with the six-day labour of creation, or they must be rejected. I have already shown how my Father worked out the ingenious "Omphalos" theory in order to justify himself as a strictly scientific observer who was also a humble slave of revelation. But the old convention and the new rebellion would alike have none of his compromise. . . .

Andrew Carnegie Praises Variety over Uniformity (1908)

Andrew Carnegie (1835–1919) was one of America's greatest nineteenth-century capitalists. Son of a Scottish weaver, he emigrated to the United States at the age of thirteen where he got a job as a bobbin boy in a Pittsburgh cotton factory. Carnegie's rise was rapid and based on Smiles' formula of self-help. A millionaire at forty, he ultimately became the single largest steel manufacturer in the world. Carnegie came to believe that men of wealth had a responsibility to the community: before his death he had given away over $350,000,000. Carnegie was, nonetheless, a convinced Social Darwinist, as shown by excerpts taken from his writings. This reading is part of an article, "Variety versus Uniformity," written in 1908. From Andrew Carnegie, *Problems of Today: Wealth, Labor, Socialism* (New York, 1908), pp. 124–126, 132.

By selection and cultivation of the exceptional animal or plant—that showing the greatest "variation" from the ordinary type—breeders and cultivators develop the higher orders of life. Thus has come man from the brute. The race has been allowed to develop in freedom, hence, while still savage, the stronger physically was the foremost, and later, under civilization, the strongest mentally have become the leaders, from whom have arisen the select few whose names stand out in history as the exceptional members of our race, whose labors and example, in all the higher domains of human effort, have slowly lifted the race to its present position, infinitely higher than it was only a few hundreds of years ago.

Not uniformity, but infinite diversity, ensured this progress, and as far as we can see, it is through diversity alone that the race can continue its upward march. The exceptional man in every department must be permitted and encouraged to develop his unusual powers, tastes and ambitions in accordance with the laws which prevail in everything that lives or grows. The "survival of the fittest" means that the exceptional plants, animals, or men which have the needed "variations" from the common standard, are the fructifying forces which leaven the whole. Among these are the great teachers and lawgivers, the poets and statesmen, physicians and historians, the inventors and discoverers, who lead the mass of more uniform pattern onward and upward. The contrast between Shakespeare and the ordinary specimen of humanity is as great as that between the average civilized man and the barbarian.

A few pages of this book would hold the names of the truly exceptional men who have distinctly moved the human race forward since history began. Many indeed have contributed thereto, and in the widest sense no individual can live a good, useful life without contributing his mite to the general weal, but those who have achieved a decided advance in any one of the innumerable paths of human effort have been few in number, although they built upon the work of many predecessors. Burbank grows hundreds of thousands of plants, sometimes millions, before the exceptional variation appears from which a new variety can be developed, capable of producing superior fruit. So with man, who must be left in perfect freedom, as long as he infringes not upon the freedom of others, nor injures the State, free to choose his career and live his own life in his own way, the rule being perfect freedom, limitation of that always exceptional and only exercised when overpowering reasons arise rendering interference necessary to protect the freedom of others, and thus prevent greater evils to the body politic. . . .

One point is clear. Nothing should be done that would tend to reduce diversity of talents in our race, and everything should be done to increase it if possible; for it is through "variation" the progress of the race has been achieved and is to come, and the progress is the chief end of existence. This is what we are here for, as is proven by the fact that progress from the lower to the higher has prevailed from the time this earth cooled and life began to appear. This is our God-like mission, that every individual in his day and generation push on this march upward, so that each succeeding generation may be better than the preceding. . . .

F. von Bernhardi Justifies the Right To Make War (1911)

Friedrich von Bernhardi (1849–1930) was a German general and military writer whose *Germany and the Next War,* written just before World War I, has been widely quoted as an example of German innate aggressiveness. More accurately, it represents a widely held interpretation of the meaning of Darwin's survival of the fittest. Similar expressions can be found in the writings of other European contemporaries. From *Germany and the Next War,* by Friedrich von Bernhardi, Copyright 1914, Longman's Green Co., pp. 18–21. Used by permission of David McKay Company, Inc.

The struggle for existence is, in the life of Nature, the basis of all healthy development. All existing things show themselves to be the result of contesting forces. So in the life of man the struggle is not merely the destructive, but the life-giving principle. "To supplant or to be supplanted is the essence of life," says Goethe, and the strong life gains the upper hand. The law of the stronger holds good everywhere. Those forms survive which are able to procure themselves the most favourable conditions of life, and to assert themselves in the universal economy of Nature. The weaker succumb. This struggle is regulated and restrained by the unconscious sway of biological laws and by the interplay of opposite forces. In the plant world and the animal world this process is worked out in unconscious tragedy. In the human race it is consciously carried out, and regulated by social ordinances. The man of strong will and strong intellect tries by every means to assert himself, the ambitious strive to rise, and in this effort the individual is far from being guided merely by the consciousness of right. The life-work and the life-struggle of many men are determined, doubtless, by unselfish and ideal motives, but to a far greater extent the less noble passions—craving for possessions, enjoyment and honour, envy and the thirst for revenge—determine men's actions. Still more often, perhaps, it is the need to live which brings down even natures of a higher mould into the universal struggle for existence and enjoyment.

There can be no doubt on this point. The nation is made up of individuals, the State of communities. The motive which influences each member is prominent in the whole body. It is a persistent struggle for possessions, power, and sovereignty, which primarily governs the relations of one nation to another, and right is respected so far only as it is compatible with advantage. So long as there are men who have human feelings and aspirations, so long as there are nations who strive for an enlarged sphere of activity, so long will conflicting interests come into being and occasions for making war arise.

The natural law, to which all laws of Nature can be reduced, is the law of struggle. All intrasocial property, all thoughts, inventions, and institutions, as, indeed, the social system itself, are a result of the intrasocial struggle, in which one survives and another is cast out. The extra-social, the super-social struggle which guides the external development of societies, nations, and races, is war. The internal development, the intrasocial struggle, is man's daily work—the struggle of thoughts, feelings, wishes, sciences, activities. The outward development, the super-social struggle, is the sanguinary struggle of nations—war. In what does the creative power of this struggle consist? In growth and decay, in the victory of the one factor and in the defeat of the other! This struggle is a creator, since it eliminates.

That social system in which the most efficient personalities possess the greatest influence will show the greatest vitality in the intrasocial struggle. In the extrasocial struggle, in war, that nation will conquer which can throw into the scale the greatest physical, mental, moral, material, and political power, and is therefore the best able to defend itself. War will furnish such a nation with favourable vital conditions, enlarged possibilities of expansion and widened influence, and thus promote the progress of mankind; for it is clear that those intellectual and moral factors which insure superiority in war are also those which render possible a general progressive development. They confer victory because the elements of progress are latent in them. Without war, inferior or decaying races would easily choke the growth of healthy budding elements, and a universal decadence would follow. "War," says A. W. von Schlegel, "is as necessary as the struggle of the elements in Nature". . . .

Struggle is, therefore, a universal law of Nature, and the instinct of self-preservation which leads to struggle is acknowledged to be a natural condition of existence. "Man is a fighter." Self-sacrifice is a renunciation of life, whether in the existence of the individual or in the life of States, which are agglomerations of individuals. The first and paramount law is the assertion of one's own independent existence. By self-assertion alone can the State maintain the conditions of life for its citizens, and insure them the legal protection which each man is entitled to claim from it. This duty of self-assertion is by no means satisfied by the mere repulse of hostile attacks; it includes the obligation to assure the possibility of life and development to the whole body of the nation embraced by the State.

Strong, healthy, and flourishing nations increase in numbers. From a given moment they require a continual expansion of their frontiers, they require new territory for the accommodation of their surplus population. Since almost every part of the globe is inhabited, new territory must, as a rule, be obtained at the cost of its possessors—that is to say, by conquest, which thus becomes a law of necessity. . . .

Thomas Huxley Challenges the Ethics of Social Darwinism (1893)

Thomas Huxley (1825–1895) was a prominent English biologist who became the principal spokesman for Darwinism in England. To Huxley human evolution extended beyond physical changes, a thesis he argued in *Evolution and Ethics,* one of many volumes devoted to Darwinian ideas. From Thomas Huxley, *Evolution and Ethics* (London, 1893), pp. 79–83, 85.

I think I do not err in assuming that, however diverse their views on philosophical and religious matters, most men are agreed that the proportion of good and evil in life may be very sensibly affected by human action. I never heard anybody doubt that the evil may be thus increased, or diminished; and it would seem to follow that good must be similarly susceptible of addition or subtraction. Finally, to my knowledge, nobody professes to doubt that, so far forth as we possess a power of bettering things, it is our paramount duty to use it and to train all our intellect and energy to this supreme service of our kind.

Hence the pressing interest of the question, to what extent modern progress, . . . and, more especially, the general outcome of that progress in the doctrine of evolution, is competent to help us in the great work of helping one another? . . .

There is [a] fallacy which appears to me to pervade the so-called "ethics of evolution." It is the notion that because, on the whole, animals and plants have advanced in perfection of organization by means of the struggle

The question of what could be considered the fittest predated Huxley and even Darwin. This humorous cartoon of 1830, entitled "Awful Changes—Man Found Only in a Fossil State," was provided with the following caption: —A Lecture— "You will at once perceive," continued Professor Ichthyosaurus, "that the skull before us belonged to some of the lower order of animals. The teeth are very insignificant, the power of the jaws trifling, and altogether it seems wonderful how the creature could have procured food."

multiplication goes on without cessation, and involves severe competition for the means of support. The struggle for existence tends to eliminate those less fitted to adapt themselves to the circumstances of their existence. The strongest, the most self-assertive, tend to tread down the weaker. But the influence of the cosmic processes on the evolution of society is the greater the more rudimentary its civilization. Social progress means a checking of the cosmic process at every step and the substitution for it of another, which may be called the ethical process; the end of which is not the survival of those who may happen to be the fittest, in respect of the whole of the conditions which obtain, but of those who are ethically the best.

As I have already urged, the practice of that which is ethically best—what we call goodness or virtue—involves a course of conduct which, in all respects, is opposed to that which leads to success in the cosmic struggle for existence. In place of ruthless self-assertion it demands self-restraint; in place of thrusting aside, or treading down, all competitors, it requires that the individual shall not merely respect, but shall help his fellows; its influence is directed, not so much to the

for existence and the consequent "survival of the fittest"; therefore men in society, men as ethical beings, must look to the same process to help them towards perfection. I suspect that this fallacy has arisen out of the unfortunate ambiguity of the phrase "survival of the fittest." "Fittest" has a connotation of "best"; and about "best" there hangs a moral flavour. In cosmic nature, however, what is "fittest" depends upon the conditions. Long since, I ventured to point out that if our hemisphere were to cool again, the survival of the fittest might bring about, in the vegetable kingdom,

a population of more and more stunted and humbler and humbler organisms, until the "fittest" that survived might be nothing but lichens, diatoms, and such microscopic organisms as those which give red snow its colour; while, if it became hotter, the pleasant valleys of the Thames and Isis might be uninhabitable by any animated beings save those that flourish in a tropical jungle. They, as the fittest, the best adapted to the changed conditions, would survive.

Men in society are undoubtedly subject to the cosmic process. As among other animals, survival of the fittest, as to the fitting of as many as possible to survive. It repudiates the gladiatorial theory of existence. It demands that each man who enters into the enjoyment of the advantages of a polity shall be mindful of his debt to those who have laboriously constructed it; and shall take heed that no act of his weakens the fabric in which he has been permitted to live. Laws and moral precepts are directed to the end of curbing the cosmic process and reminding the individual of his duty to the community, to the protection and influence of which he owes, if not existence itself, at least the life of something better than a brutal savage. . . .

Ethical nature may count upon having to reckon with a tenacious and powerful enemy as long as the world lasts. But, on the other hand, I see no limit to the extent to which intelligence and will, guided by sound principles of investigation, and organized in common effort, may modify the conditions of existence, for a period longer than that now covered by history. And much may be done to change the nature of man himself. The intelligence which has converted the brother of the wolf into the faithful guardian of the flock ought to be able to do something towards curbing the instincts of savagery in civilized men. . . .

George E. Simpson: Darwin and Social Darwinism

George E. Simpson (1904–   ), American sociologist and anthropologist, has varied interests in race and culture. In the article below he surveys the uses of Darwinian ideas in national and racist theory. From George E. Simpson, "Darwin and 'Social Darwinism,'" *Antioch Review,* XIX (Spring 1959), pp. 33–45. Reprinted by permission of The Antioch Press.

EARLY SOCIAL DARWINISM

The application of Darwin's principle of natural selection to human society, with special emphasis on competition and struggle, became known as "Social Darwinism." This doctrine, congenial to the intellectual climate of the end of the nineteenth century, was endorsed by the advocates of unrestricted competition in private enterprise, the colonial expansionists, and the opponents of voluntary social change. Among others, Ernest Haeckel provided scientific sanction for this point of view.

> The theory of selection teaches that in human life, as in animal and plant life, everywhere and at all times, only a small and chosen minority can exist and flourish, while the enormous majority starve and perish miserably and more or less prematurely. . . . The cruel and merciless struggle for existence which rages through living nature, and in the course of nature *must* rage, this unceasing and inexorable competition of all living creatures is an incontestable fact; only the picked minority of the qualified fittest is in a position to resist it successfully, while the great majority of the competitors must necessarily perish miserably. We may profoundly lament this tragical state of things, but we can neither controvert nor alter it. "Many are called, but few are chosen." This principle of selection is as far as possible from democratic, on the contrary it is aristocratic in the strictest sense of the word.

Herbert Spencer and William Graham Sumner were prominent in advancing the doctrine of the social Darwinists. Despite differences in their philosophies, both saw the poor as the "unfit." Because they are the result of the operations of the laws of evolution, they cannot be assisted and efforts to help them through legislation, public charity, and social reconstruction are evil. According to Spencer, "The whole effort of nature is to get rid of them, and make room for better. . . . If they are sufficiently complete to live, they do live, and it is well they should live. If they are not sufficiently complete to live, they die, and it is best they should die."

Although Darwin pointed out that militarism and war occasion reverse selection by exposing the biologically soundest young men to early death or preventing them from marrying during the prime of life and, at the same time, by providing those with poorer constitutions with greater opportunity to marry and propagate their kind, many of the social Darwinists praised war as a means of furthering social progress. . . . An English scientist, Karl Pearson, wrote: "History shows me one way and one way only, in which a high state of civilization has been produced, namely the struggle of race with race, and the survival of the physically and mentally fitter race. If men want to know whether the lower races of man can evolve a higher type, I fear the only course is to leave them to fight it out among themselves."

Nineteenth century imperialists, calling upon Darwinism in defense of the subjugation of "backward" races, "could point to *The Origin of Species* which had referred in its sub-title to *The Preservation of Favored Races in the Struggle for Life.* Darwin had been talking about pigeons but they saw no reason why his theories should not apply to men, and the whole spirit of the naturalistic world-view seemed to call for a vigorous and un-relenting thoroughness in the application of biological concepts." Darwinian theory was utilized to justify the conflicts of rival empires, the ententes and the alliances of the "balance of power." Bismarck in Germany, Chamberlain in England, and Theodore Roosevelt in the United States found in social Darwinism a sanction for their theories of force and expansion.

Another aspect of social Darwinism at the turn of the century was the eugenics movement. Like other early social Darwinists, the eugenicists equated the "fit" with the upper classes and the "unfit" with the poor. Believing that disease, poverty, and crime are due largely to heredity, they warned against the high reproductive rates of the lower classes. . . .

SOCIAL DARWINISM IN RECENT YEARS

Adolf Hitler's racism and Nazism have been called perversions of Darwinism. Hitler's virulent doctrines were the culmination of a half-century of social Darwinistic thinking in Germany. One of his most influential immediate predecessors was General Friedrich von Bernhardi, who said of the Germans that "no nation on the face of the globe is so able to grasp and appropriate all the elements of culture, to add to them from the stores of its own spiritual endowment, and to give back to mankind richer gifts than it received." . . . Bernhardi glorified war as a biological necessity, as the greatest factor in the furtherance

of culture and power, and claimed that the Germans could fulfill their great and urgent duty toward civilization only by the sword.

Hitler's doctrines are so well-known that extended reference to them here is unnecessary. According to *Mein Kampf,* the "Aryan" alone "furnishes the great building-stones and plans for all human progress." The Aryan had subjugated "lower races" and made them do his will, the Jew's "intellect is never constructive," "the mingling of blood . . . is the sole reason for the dying-out of old cultures," and hyperindividualism had cheated Germany of world domination and a peace "founded on the victorious sword of a lordly people. . . ." Hitlerism represents the most extreme variety of social Darwinism and the one which has had the most powerful effects on the destinies of modern peoples. . . .

CRITICISMS OF SOCIAL DARWINISM

The Russian sociologist, Jacques Novicow (1849–1912), was one of the first writers to devote himself to the refutation of the doctrine that unmitigated struggle for existence is the chief factor in human progress. In Novicow's view, the struggle for existence becomes in human society primarily an intellectual rather than a physical type of conflict. He predicted that intellectual conflict within societies would increase, be accompanied by an increase of justice and sympathy and a decrease of hatred, and bring about the survival of the best individuals.

In 1902, Petr Kropotkin wrote of the two aspects of animal life in Eastern Siberia and Northern Manchuria which had impressed him most—the severity of the struggle for existence against a formidable Nature, and

the absence of the bitter struggle for existence among animals of the same species in spots where animal life was abundant. Under the former conditions, the distinctive feature was under-population rather than over-population. Wherever he observed scores of species and millions of individuals (colonies of rodents, flights of birds, a migration of fallow-deer), he saw mutual aid and mutual support which led him to conclude that this feature was highly important for the maintenance of life and the preservation and further evolution of each species. He saw further that when animals have to struggle mightily against scarcity of food (e.g., semi-wild cattle and horses, wild ruminants, squirrels), the portion of the species affected by the calamity "comes out of the ordeal so much impoverished in vigor and health that no progressive evolution of the species can be based on such periods of keen competition." Consequently, Kropotkin was unable to accept the view that the struggle for the means of subsistence, of every animal against all other animals of its own species, and of every man against all other men, was a natural law. Instead he was convinced that the practice of mutual aid has created the conditions of social life, "in which man was enabled to develop his arts, knowledge, and intelligence". . . .

THE PRESENT STATUS OF THE CONCEPT OF NATURAL SELECTION

The view that "life is a struggle for existence in which only the fit survive, the fittest being those who have whatever it takes to survive" has been called "the Darwinian fallacy." The concept of natural selection has not been discarded, but it has undergone revision. . . .

To J. B. S. Haldane the application of Darwinism to contemporary capitalist society would be that the poor are fitter than the rich because they leave more offspring behind them in each generation. Replying to Mr. Haldane, Bernhard Stern called attention to the importance of social tradition (e.g., knowledge of birth control, influence of religious tradition, changing attitudes concerning family life) in determining family size.

Darwin's opposition to birth control, on the ground that "overmultiplication was useful, since it caused a struggle for existence in which only the strongest and the ablest survived," seems outmoded. Geoffrey West remarks that now "intelligent birth control is as much a factor for survival as co-operation."

In shaping the genetic equipment of homo sapiens in the past, natural selection contributed to the development of culture. Culture has been such a successful nonbiological adaptive instrument that man has become specialized to live in man-made environments. Despite the claims of the social Darwinists, social improvement seems to be due mainly to advances in technology and social organization rather than to breeding or selective elimination. Self-preservation is no longer a sufficient motive for living. Modern man determines what "the conditions and standards of a tolerable existence" are.

In no human society has it been possible to breed genetic types selectively which would be adapted to different statuses. Societies change at different rates, but even during relatively stable periods social life is a complex matter. Those who show the greatest adaptability have an enormous advantage in meeting the demands of life in any type of society. . . .

CONCLUSION

One hundred years after the publication of *The Origin of Species,* and eighty-eight years after the appearance of *The Descent of Man,* natural selection remains an important concept in biology, anthropology, sociology, even in international relations. Modern man is subject to selection, natural and artificial. If this were not so, all human genotypes would produce surviving children in the same ratio as the occurrence of these genotypes in existing populations. Today the adaptive value of co-operation is more widely acknowledged and the role of ruthless aggression as a factor in the evolution of man, society, and culture is given smaller significance. Social Darwinistic thinking has not disappeared, but increasingly the "nature, red in tooth and claw" version of natural selection is regarded as an outdated brand of Darwinism.

STUDY QUESTIONS

1. In what sense had the climate for Darwin's discoveries been prepared by other researchers? What were the specific contributions of Lyell and Malthus?

2. What developments in nature does the theory of natural selection seek to explain? Would the concept of evolution have been accepted in a traditional society?

3. Why didn't Darwin want to interfere with the process of natural selection? How do you think modern medicine and warfare affect the process of selection among human beings?

4. On what grounds did Darwin believe that the theory of evolution could be applied to man? What, according to Darwin, distinguished man from the higher animals?

5. What problems for the Biblical view of creation were posed by Darwin's findings?

6. What did Carnegie draw from Darwinian theories? Was his Darwinism consistent with his individualism? How would these attitudes have influenced his behavior towards labor unions?

7. What inferences does Bernhardi draw from Darwinian theories that affect the relationship of nations? Can war be scientifically justified?

8. In what sense, for Huxley, does civilization require a redefinition of who is "fittest"? What helps to promote "the ethical process" in civilized society?

9. How has Darwinism affected social and economic thought? In what sense have technology and culture limited the application of natural selection to the evolution of human society?

Europe Takes over Africa

L. S. Stavrianos, *The World Since 1500: A Global History*, © 1966. Reprinted by permission of Prentice-Hall, Inc., Englewood Cliffs, New Jersey.

TOPIC 38

IMPERIALISM

While European contact with the non-Western world has an ancient history, the occupation by Europeans of large areas beyond the shores of their continent did not take place before the modern world had transformed Western society. The irruption of the developed nations upon traditional peoples living in Africa and Asia reached its first peak in Europe's age of imperialism in the second half of the nineteenth century. Respect for traditional social patterns and values gave way before the Western impact. By presenting samples of the varying perspectives of Africans, Asians, and Westerners on the relationship of ruler and ruled, the readings provide an opportunity to appraise the place of imperialism in the modernization and Westernization of the non-European world.

I

For centuries the most valuable of African resources for Europeans were the slaves. . . . The typical voyage of the slave traders was triangular. The first leg was from the home port to Africa, with a cargo including salt, cloth, firearms, hardware, beads, and rum. These goods were bartered for slaves brought by fellow-Africans from the interior to the coast. The unfortunate victims were packed under atrocious conditions in the vessels and shipped across the Atlantic on the so-called "middle passage." At their New World destinations the slaves were either sold at once or held in stockades to be retailed on demand. The final lap was the voyage home with plantation produce such as sugar, molasses, tobacco, or rice.

Thanks to the prevailing trade winds the "middle passage" was normally swift and brief. Nevertheless, the average death rate during the trip was over 10 per cent. The casualties were brought about by the inhuman crowding, the stifling heat, and the poor food. Maize and water once every twenty-four hours was the standard diet. If the slaves refused to eat they were lashed, and, if that failed, hot irons were used to force them to eat. When epidemics broke out, as they often did under the foul conditions, the sick slaves were drowned in order to prevent infection from spreading. Not infrequently the slaves jumped overboard rather than endure the misery. Indeed, this became so common that nets were fixed all around the decks to prevent suicides. It is revealing that slave ships carried insurance against the death of slaves and also against insurrections aboard ship.

Even greater casualties were suffered earlier, during the overland march to the coast. Raiding parties plundered villages and broke up families in their search for strong young men and women. The captives were then driven from dawn to dusk in the blazing heat and pouring rain, through thick jungles or over dry plains, and tormented by stinging insects that gave them no peace. If they faltered through sheer exhaustion they were mercilessly beaten, and if they failed to stumble on, they were finished off by a sword or a club. The survivors who reached the coast were driven naked into the market like cattle. Then they were branded with the name of the company or buyer, and herded into the forts to await shipment across the ocean. It is not surprising that for every 1,000 Africans kidnapped from their villages, an estimated 300 survived to work in the Americas. Five hundred normally perished during the march to the coast, 125 in the packed holds of the slave ships, and another 75 died soon after landing in the New World.

Despite these horrors, Europeans continued to buy and sell Africans for over four centuries. The profits were so great that powerful vested interests resolutely opposed any proposals for control or abolition. There were first of all the African chiefs who received as much as £20 or 30 for a single able-bodied slave. One of the chiefs, when told to stop his trade said, "What! Can a cat stop catching mice? Will not a cat die with a mouse in its mouth? I will die with a slave in my mouth." The African middlemen who had reaped handsome profits from the trade were violently opposed to all abolition proposals. Indeed, riots against Europeans were organized on African soil in defiance of the abolition movement.

The plantation owners in the Americas likewise supported the slave trade, especially the Barbados planters who held an important bloc of seats in the British Parliament in the eighteenth century. There were European vested interests also that championed the slave trade, both amongst the traders and the various merchants at home who provided the rum and the manufactured goods. According to one estimate, Britain shipped to Africa manufactures valued at one million pounds a year, and the other European countries sent an equal amount for the same purpose. The return on this outlay was so extraordinarily high that in the eighteenth century the prosperity of cities such as Liverpool and Bristol depended heavily on this traffic. A considerable number of distilleries were built to provide the slave ships with rum. English woolens, and later, cottons, also were shipped in large quantities to Africa. The metallurgical industry provided chains, locks, bars, and guns of all kinds. The shipyards, too, were kept busy by the slave trade, since over 200 English ships alone were engaged at the end of the eighteenth century. . . .

Despite these formidable obstacles, a small group of reformers campaigned vigorously for abolition. In 1787 they established in England the Society for the Abolition of the Slave Trade. In 1823 they founded the Anti-Slavery Society to end the institution of slavery as well as the slave trade. These abolitionists were aided by the progress of the Industrial Revolution, which was rendering slavery obsolete. Advancing technology called for overseas markets rather than for a cheap supply of human power. In fact, the abolitionists argued that the slave trade was inefficient, and insisted that a more profitable "legitimate" trade could be developed in Africa.

The first success of the abolitionists was a law in 1807 providing that no British ships could participate in the slave trade, and prohibiting the landing of slaves in British colonies. Finally, in 1833 Parliament passed a decree completely abolishing slavery on

Overland March to the Coast.

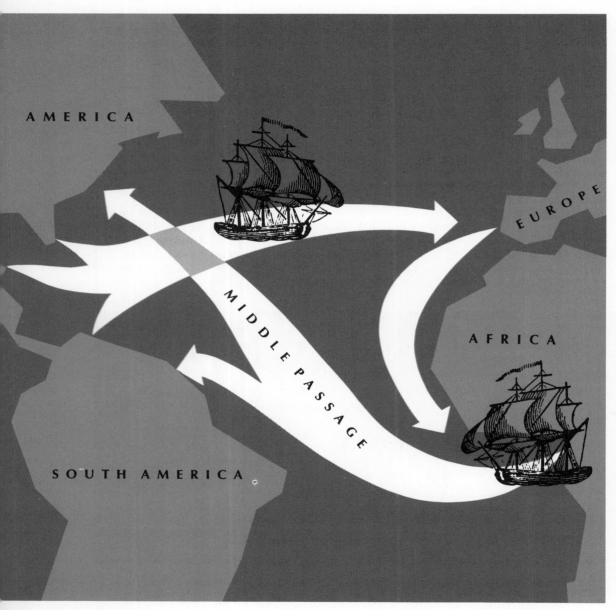

AMERICA

EUROPE

MIDDLE PASSAGE

AFRICA

SOUTH AMERICA

British territory, and providing 20 million pounds as compensation for the slaveholders. The British government went further and persuaded other European countries to follow its example in allowing British warships to seize slave ships flying other flags. . . . Needless to say, many traders continued to slip through the blockade, lured on by the fortunes awaiting them in the Americas. Complete success was not possible until the various countries in the New World gradually abolished slavery as an institution—as did Haiti in 1803, the United States in 1863, Brazil in 1888, Cuba at about the same time, and so forth. . . .

Exploration and Partition of Africa

The agitation for the abolition of slavery contributed directly to the exploration and opening up of the "Dark Continent." The abolitionists hoped to curtail the slave trade by pushing into the interior where the slaves were captured and they sought to develop "legitimate" or regular commerce that would replace the traffic in slaves. At the same time, a growing scientific fad for geography made Europeans intensely curious about unexplored lands. These factors all combined to bring to Africa in the nineteenth century a number of remarkable and colorful explorers. . . .

Prior to 1870 the European powers had insignificant holdings in Africa. They consisted mostly of seaports and fortified trading stations, together with bits of adjacent territory acquired as adjuncts to trade rather than as bases for territorial expansion. With the termination of the European slave trade, most of these coastal footholds were virtually abandoned since the legitimate trade was insufficient to support them. The only significant exceptions to this general picture were at the opposite ends of the continent, in French Algeria and British South Africa, where actual colonization was taking place. But even there the activities were haphazard, with no definite plans for expansion and annexation. . . .

After 1870 a combination of factors produced a reversal of this anticolonial attitude. Colonies now were regarded as assets for the mother country, and the continent of Africa, being unoccupied and defenseless, became the vortex of imperialist aspirations. A typical expression of the new colonialism was that of the French economist Paul Leroy-Beaulieu, who wrote in 1874, "Colonization is for France a question of life and death: either France will become a great African power, or in a century or two she will be no more than a secondary European power; she will count for about as much in the world as Greece and Roumania in Europe."

The leader of the imperialist drive in Africa was King Leopold of Belgium. A shrewd monarch, he sensed the opportunities offered by the great interior plateaus that were being opened up by the explorers. In 1876 he convened a conference in Brussels, ostensibly to help introduce civilization into Africa. In his opening address he declared, "The object which unites us here today is one of those which deserve in the highest degree to occupy the friends of humanity. To open to civilization the only part of our globe where it has not penetrated, to pierce the darkness which envelops entire populations, is, I venture to say, a crusade worthy of this century of progress." The Brussels Conference resulted in the founding of the International Association for the Exploration and Civilization of Central Africa. Although ostensibly an association of several national groups, the executive committee was controlled by Leopold. . . .

The immediate effect of Leopold's machinations was to jolt the other European leaders to action. The French already had sent their famous explorer, Count de Brazza, to the lower Congo, and he was able to acquire for his country the lands to the north of the river. The Germans also entered the race, obtaining in 1884 South-West Africa, Togoland, and the Cameroons. Now the Portuguese joined in, especially since they had been claiming for some time the west coast as far north as 5° 12'S., that is, both sides of the Congo mouth and inland indefinitely. Britain never had been willing to recognize these Portuguese claims but she now changed her mind in hopes of checking the aggressive Belgians and French. So an Anglo-Portuguese Convention was signed on February 26, 1884 recognizing Portuguese sovereignty over the mouth of the Congo and providing for Anglo-Portuguese control of navigation on the river.

The treaty was furiously denounced by the other powers, so an international conference was held in Berlin in 1884–1885 to prepare rules for the further acquisition of African territories. It was agreed that no power should annex land or establish a protectorate without first giving notice of intent; that recognition of territorial claims must depend on effective occupation; and that disputes were to be settled by arbitration. The conference also recognized the Congo Basin, to be known as the Congo Free State. Finally, high-sounding declarations were made about uplifting the natives, spreading the Gospel, and stamping out slavery. All these were to be conspicuous by their absence in the so-called Free State.

Now that an international code for territorial aggrandizement was agreed upon, the entire continent was partitioned in less than two decades. In the Congo, Leopold bought out in 1887 all non-Belgian interests in order to eliminate possible criticism of his enterprise. Then he reimbursed himself by reserving a crown district of the richest rubber lands, ten times the size of Belgium. Here, as elsewhere in the Congo, special monopolies for the exploitation of natural products, including rights of native labor, were awarded to commercial concerns in most of which Leopold was a heavy stockholder. His profits, therefore, were derived both from the stipends paid to the state by the concessionaires and from the dividends earned in the course of their immensely successful operations. In the final analysis, the fortunes that were made in the Congo were extracted by ruthless exploitation of the native peoples. So unbelievably brutal were the various methods of forced labor that the population of the Congo declined by one-half (from 20 to 10 million) between 1885 and 1908 when it was ruled by Leopold. . . .

In the rest of West Africa the French were the most active. Starting from their old trading posts on the Ivory Coast, in Dahomey, and on the north bank of the Congo, they conceived a grand plan for pushing inward and founding a French West African Empire that would stretch from Algeria to the Congo and from the Senegal to the Nile or even the Red Sea. Since the Germans and the British also had footholds along the west coast, the French had to outflank their rivals in a race for the hinterland. By and large they were successful. Only the British in Nigeria and the Germans in the Cameroons were able to expand significantly into the interior. All the rest of West Africa, together with the vast Sahara, became a great French domain ruled from Paris. . . .

In East Africa the Portuguese had held Mozambique since the sixteenth century and France had claims to Madagascar. The chief rivals for the remaining territory were the Germans and the British. At the end of 1884, while the Berlin Conference was in session, a young German colonial enthusiast, Dr. Carl Peters, landed secretly in East Africa. Within ten days he had persuaded the local chiefs to sign away more than 60,000 square miles, an area almost one-third the size of his own homeland. The following year the German government proclaimed a protectorate over the region obtained by Carl Peters.

The German activities aroused the British who proceeded to sign treaties giving them the territory in the Kenya area. This land grabbing drew repeated protests from the Sultan of Zanzibar who for long had held sovereignty over the East African coast opposite his island. Both the British and the Germans ignored his protests and signed two agreements in 1886 and 1890 settling their respective territorial disputes. . . .

Meanwhile, the Italians had belatedly joined the scramble for African territory. They managed to obtain two barren colonies on the Red Sea coast, Eritrea and Somaliland, and later, in 1896, they gambled for higher stakes by sending an army to conquer the kingdom of Ethiopia. The Christian Ethiopians were not a primitive tribal people like those in most other parts of Africa. Their Emperor Menelik had an army of 80,000 men trained by French officers and armed with French weapons. He was able to defeat the small Italian army of 10,000, and his kingdom remained free from European rule. Except for the small republic of Liberia on the west coast, by 1914 Ethiopia

was the only independent state on the whole continent. And even Liberia, set up in 1822 as a settlement for freed American Negroes (named from the Latin *liber*, meaning "free!"), became a virtual United States protectorate in 1911 because of bankruptcy and internal disorders.

The net result of this unprecedented territorial aggrandizement was the partitioning of the entire continent of Africa among the European powers. The only exceptions, as noted above, were the precarious states of Liberia and Ethiopia. Table 1 gives a specific analysis of the African continent in 1914.

II

Europe's Impact

Economic

Since economic motives were prominent in the partitioning of Africa, it is not surprising that drastic economic changes followed the partitioning. Europe no longer was content with boatloads of slaves at the coastal ports. The industrialized West no longer needed human slaves; technology had provided an abundance of the mechanical variety. Instead the West had need for the raw materials found in the interior of Africa, and it now had

TABLE 1 POLITICAL DIVISIONS IN AFRICA IN 1914

		SQUARE MILES
French	Tunisia, Algeria, Morocco, French West Africa, French Congo, French Somaliland, Madagascar	4,086,950
British	Union of South Africa, Basutoland, Bechuanaland, Nyasaland, Rhodesia, British East Africa, Uganda, Zanzibar, Somaliland, Nigeria, Gold Coast, Sierra Leone, Gambia, Egypt, Anglo-Egyptian Sudan	3,701,411
German	East Africa, South-West Africa, Cameroon, Togoland	910,150
Belgian	Congo State	900,000
Portuguese	Guinea, West Africa, East Africa	787,500
Italian	Eritrea, Italian Somaliland, Libya	600,000
Spanish	Rio de Oro, Muni River Settlements	79,800
Independent States	Liberia, Ethiopia	393,000
TOTAL		11,458,811

the technological means to extract these materials.

The first important step in the exploitation of Africa's resources came with the discovery of diamonds in Kimberley (1867) and gold in the Witwatersrand (1884). Equally great mineral wealth was discovered in the Rhodesias (gold and copper) and in the Congo (gold, copper, and diamonds). Many portions of the west coast yielded rich supplies of such tropical forest products as palm oil, rubber, and ivory. European and American companies bought vast plantations in such regions as the Congo, the Cameroons, and French Equatorial Africa, one example being the Firestone Corporation, which in 1926 was given a 90-year lease on 100,000 acres of land in Liberia.

Not only did foreign companies lease large tracts of land, but foreign settlers took over much of the good agricultural land. Explorers had reported that some of the interior plateaus had fertile soil as well as a pleasant climate. Consequently, European settlers flocked in, particularly to Southern Rhodesia and East Africa. Before long they had gained possession of the most desirable agricultural properties in these regions.

In order to transport the minerals and the agricultural commodities now being produced, the Europeans proceeded to build a network of railways in Africa as they already had done in Asia. These railways were designed to facilitate the export of produce rather than to stimulate general economic development. Thus the railway system in West Africa ran only north to south, with no direct connection between east and west. . . .

All of these economic developments naturally had profound effects upon the native peoples. The inhabitants of the temperate plateau areas were affected most by the loss of the lands taken by white settlers. In some

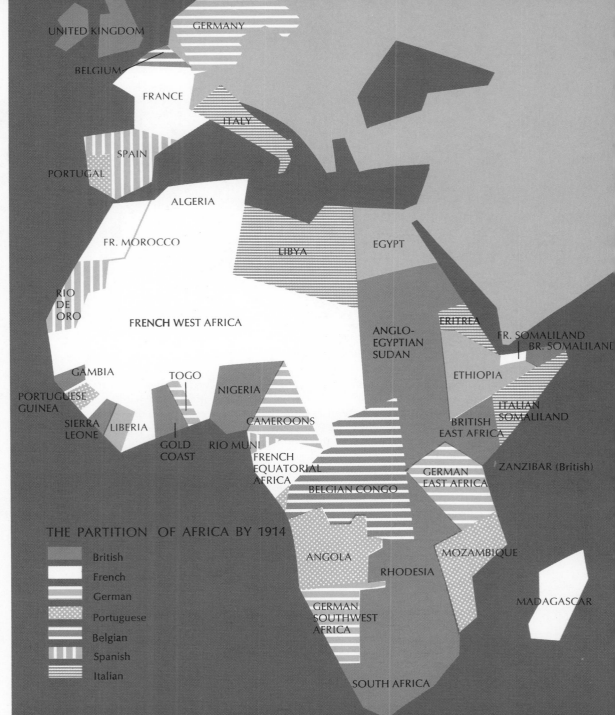

THE PARTITION OF AFRICA BY 1914

British
French
German
Portuguese
Belgian
Spanish
Italian

Europeans direct the native laborers in this 1888 photograph of gold mining in South Africa.

cases whole districts were reserved for exclusive white use, and the land could not be tilled by the Africans, even though it sometimes lay fallow. Consequently, the Africans were forced to work for wages on the white man's plantations, while some even "squatted" on the land of the white farmers for whom they worked to gain the privilege of tilling a small plot for themselves. In other regions the Africans found it necessary to leave their families and go to work in the mines. If the Africans refused to provide the labor needed for the plantations and mines, various types of forced labor were used. The most common was the levying of a head tax compelling the African to work in order to earn the money to pay the tax. These various developments reduced the traditional economic self-sufficiency of the African. No longer did he work simply to feed himself and his family, increas-

ingly he was involved in a money economy and was affected by world economic conditions. For example, a depression in the industrialized countries immediately affected the operation of copper mines, while a slump in the world price for palm oil immediately lowered the income of a large number of individual producers in West Africa. We can see, then, that the effect of Europe's economic impact was twofold: to entangle the Africans in a world-wide money economy, and to subordinate them, directly or indirectly, to the white man who was everywhere the "boss."

Cultural

Together with the trader, the investor, and the settler from Europe came the European missionary. He had a profound effect upon African culture because he was the first European

who consciously sought to change it. The others affected it indirectly and incidentally, as when they forced Africans to leave their ancestral villages to work in cities or mines. But the missionary came with the avowed purpose of changing the African way of life, and he used three instruments to carry this out: education, medicine, and religion.

Schools offering a Western education and Western ideals were an integral part of every mission station. These schools were particularly influential since most colonial governments left education to the missionaries. In many respects the mission schools were constructive in their influence: often they taught the pupils how to build better houses, improve their agricultural methods, and observe the rudiments of hygiene and sanitation. They also taught reading and writing in African as well as European languages. The missionaries

A contemporary missionary, member of the Lorogurno Catholic mission in Kenya, supplies medical education to women of the nomadic Turkana tribe.

reduced the African languages to writing and so laid the foundations for *indigenous* African literature. The great majority of those Africans who chose literary careers were educated in missionary schools.

On the other hand, these schools inevitably had a subversive influence on the African people; they often taught that the traditional way of life was primitive and wrong. In time the students listened less to their parents and elders and more to their European teachers whom they learned to respect. In addition, the mission schools used European books that taught more about Europe than about Africa. Early history text books used in the French colonies began with lessons dealing with "our ancestors the Gauls." Missionary education encouraged individualism, which was contrary to the communal African way of life. It is not surprising that Africans subjected to several years of this type of education were usually loathe to return to their villages. Instead they looked for jobs with the colonial governments, missions, or private businesses, thus moving further away from their traditional culture.

Political

Europe's imprint was as marked in the political field as it was in the economic and cultural fields. To start, the boundaries of the various colonies had to be fixed (here the outcome depended purely upon the European balance of power). No attention was paid to the indigenous people concerned, so that they often found themselves under the rule of two or even three European powers. Some of the Somali, for example, were ruled by the French, others by the British, still others by the Italians, and a number even found themselves within the boundaries of Ethiopia.

A Masai Tribal Council in Kenya.

Once the boundaries had been settled, the problem of organizing some administrative system arose. The European governments did not have enough manpower to rule directly all the peoples of the vast African continent, so they resorted to . . . indirect rule; administration was conducted through tribal chiefs who were allowed to retain some of their authority. Usually the British allowed the chiefs more leeway than did the French, but even the French could not control everything because their African possessions were so vast and their supply of officials was so limited.

On the surface, then, the Africans retained their traditional political institutions. They still had their councils of elders, their laws, their courts, and their chiefs. But in practice this political structure was undermined. The chiefs could be appointed or removed by the local European administrators, and their decisions no longer had the force of law since tribesmen could go over their heads to the European officials whose word was final. . . .

The most serious and direct challenge to the traditional tribal authorities came from the class of Western educated Africans that gradually developed in almost all the colonies. They tended to challenge not only the native chiefs but also the European officials. They usually were the first to demand that educated Africans should be allowed to participate in the administration of their countries. These people were the first nationalists; they laid the foundations for the powerful nationalist movement of today. They did so because they had imbibed in Western schools certain political ideas such as individual liberty and political freedom, and they saw no reason why the principles of liberalism and nationalism should be applicable in Europe and not in Africa. . . .

Jomo Kenyatta: A Response to Imperialism

Jomo Kenyatta, a leader of the East African Kikuyu tribe, became the first president of the independent Republic of Kenya in 1964. Previously he had been found guilty by the British of leading the bloody Mau Mau rebellion (1953–1961) and had been sentenced to life imprisonment. This fable describes the response of Africans to the European take-over of their continent. Reprinted from *Facing Mt. Kenya,* by Jomo Kenyatta, by permission of Random House, Inc. All rights reserved under International and Pan-American copyright conventions. This is published in Canada by Martin Secker & Warburg Limited.

Once upon a time an elephant made a friendship with a man. One day a heavy thunderstorm broke out, the elephant went to his friend, who had a little hut at the edge of the forest, and said to him: "My dear good man, will you please let me put my trunk inside your hut to keep it out of this torrential rain?" The man, seeing what situation his friend was in, replied: "My dear good elephant, my hut is very small, but there is room for your trunk and myself. Please put your trunk in gently." The elephant thanked his friend, saying: "You have done me a good deed and one day I shall return your kindness." But what followed? As soon as the elephant put his trunk inside the hut, slowly he pushed his head inside, and finally flung the man out in the rain, and then lay down comfortably inside his friend's hut, saying: "My dear good friend, your skin is harder than mine, and as there is not enough room for both of us, you can afford to remain in the rain while I am protecting my delicate skin from the hailstorm."

The man, seeing what his friend had done to him, started to grumble, the animals in the nearby forest heard the noise and came to see what was the matter. All stood around listening to the heated argument between the man and his friend the elephant. In this turmoil the lion came along roaring, and said in a loud voice: "Don't you know that I am the King of the Jungle! How dare anyone disturb the peace of my kingdom?" On hearing this the elephant, who was one of the high ministers in the jungle kingdom, replied in a soothing voice, and said: "My Lord, there is no disturbance of the peace in your kingdom. I have only been having a little discussion with my friend here as to the possession of this little hut which your lordship sees me occupying." The lion, who wanted to have "peace and tranquillity" in his kingdom, replied in a noble voice, saying: "I command my ministers to appoint a Commission of Enquiry to go thoroughly into this matter and report accordingly." He then turned to the man and said: "You have done well by establishing friendship with my people, especially with the elephant who is one of my honourable ministers of state. Do not grumble any more, your hut is not lost to you. Wait until the sitting of my Imperial Commission, and there you will be given plenty of opportunity to state your case. I am sure that you will be pleased with the findings of the Commission." The man was very pleased by these sweet words from the King of the Jungle, and innocently waited for his opportunity, in the belief, that naturally the hut would be returned to him.

The elephant, obeying the command of his master, got busy with other ministers to appoint the Commission of Enquiry. The following elders of the jungle were appointed to sit in the Commission: (1) Mr. Rhinoceros; (2) Mr. Buffalo; (3) Mr. Alligator; (4) The Rt. Hon. Mr. Fox to act as chairman; and (5) Mr. Leopard to act as Secretary to the Commission. On seeing the personnel, the man protested and asked if it was not necessary to include in this Commission a member from his side. But he was told that it was impossible, since no one from his side was well enough educated to understand the intricacy of jungle law. Further, that there was nothing to fear, for the members of the Commission were all men of repute for their impartiality in justice, and as they were gentlemen chosen by God to look after the interest of races less adequately endowed with teeth and claws, he might rest assured that they would investigate the matter with the greatest care and report impartially.

The Commission sat to take the evidence. The Rt. Hon. Mr. Elephant was first called. He came along with a superior air, brushing his tusks with a sapling which Mrs. Elephant had provided, and in an authoritative voice said: "Gentlemen of the Jungle, there is no need for me to waste your valuable time in relating a story which I am sure you all know. I have always regarded it as my duty to protect the interests of my friends, and this appears to have caused the misunderstanding between myself and my friend here. He invited me to save his hut from being blown away by a hurricane. As the hurricane had gained access owing to the unoccupied space in the hut, I considered it necessary, in my friend's own interests, to turn the undeveloped space to a more economic use by sitting in it myself; a duty which any of you would undoubtedly have performed with equal readiness in similar circumstances."

After hearing the Rt. Hon. Mr. Elephant's conclusive evidence, the Commission called Mr. Hyena and other elders of the jungle, who all supported what Mr. Elephant had said. They then called the man, who began to give his own account of the dispute. But the Commission cut him short, saying: "My good man, please confine yourself to relevant issues. We have already heard the circumstances from various unbiased sources; all we wish you to tell us is whether the undeveloped space in your hut was occupied by anyone else before Mr. Elephant assumed his position?" The man began to say: "No, but—" But at this point the Commission declared that they had heard sufficient evidence from both sides and retired to consider their decision. After enjoying a delicious meal at the expense of the Rt. Hon. Mr. Elephant, they reached their verdict, called the man, and declared as follows: "In our opinion this dispute has arisen through a regrettable misunderstanding due to the backwardness of your ideas. We consider that Mr. Elephant has fulfilled his sacred duty of protecting your interests. As it is clearly for your good that the space should be put to its most economic use, and as you yourself have not yet reached the stage of expansion which would enable you to fill it, we consider it necessary to arrange a compromise to suit both parties. Mr. Elephant shall continue his occupation of your hut, but we give you permission to look for a site where you can build another hut more suited to your needs, and we will see that you are well protected."

The man, having no alternative, and fearing that his refusal might expose him to the teeth and claws of members of the Commission, did as they suggested. But no sooner had he built another hut than Mr. Rhinoceros charged in with his horn lowered and ordered the man to quit. A Royal Commission was again ap-

pointed to look into the matter, and the same finding was given. This procedure was repeated until Mr. Buffalo, Mr. Leopard, Mr. Hyena and the rest were all accommodated with new huts. Then the man decided that he must adopt an effective method of protection, since Commissions of Enquiry did not seem to be of any use to him. He sat down and said: "Ng'enda thi ndeagaga motegi," which literally means, "there is nothing that treads on the earth that cannot be trapped," or in other words, you can fool people for a time, but not forever.

Early one morning, when the huts already occupied by the jungle lords were all beginning to decay and fall to pieces, he went out and built a bigger and better hut a little distance away. No sooner had Mr. Rhinoceros seen it than he came rushing in, only to find that Mr. Elephant was already inside, sound asleep. Mr. Leopard next came in at the window, Mr. Lion, Mr. Fox, and Mr. Buffalo entered the doors, while Mr. Hyena howled for a place in the shade and Mr. Alligator basked on the roof. Presently they all began disputing about their rights of penetration, and from disputing they came to fighting, and while they were embroiled together the man set the hut on fire and burnt it to the ground, jungle lords and all. Then he went home, saying "Peace is costly, but it's worth the expense," and lived happily ever after.

Rudyard Kipling Reminds Men of the White Man's Burden (1899)

Rudyard Kipling (1856–1936), British author and poet, invoked the commitment of the

Europeans in what has become a classic explanation of the imperialistic spirit. From *Collected Verse of Rudyard Kipling* (New York, 1907), pp. 215–217.

Take up the White Man's burden—
Send forth the best ye breed—
Go bind your sons to exile
To serve your captives' need;
To wait in heavy harness,
On fluttered folk and wild—
Your new-caught, sullen peoples,
Half-devil and half-child. . . .

Take up the White Man's burden—
The savage wars of peace—
Fill full the mouth of Famine
And bid the sickness cease,
And when your goal is nearest
The end for others sought,
Watch sloth and heathen Folly
Bring all your hopes to nought. . . .

Take up the White Man's burden—
And reap his old reward;
The blame of those ye better,
The hate of those ye guard—
The cry of hosts ye humour
(Ah, slowly!) toward the light:—
"Why brought he us from bondage,
Our loved Egyptian night?"

Take up the White Man's burden—
Ye dare not stoop to less—
Nor call too loud on Freedom
To cloke your weariness;
By all ye cry or whisper,
By all ye leave or do,
The silent, sullen peoples
Shall weigh your Gods and you.

Take up the White Man's burden—
Have done with childish days—
The lightly proffered laurel,
The easy, ungrudged praise.
Comes now, to search your manhood
Through all the thankless years,
Cold, edged with dear-bought wisdom,
The judgment of your peers!

Two Indians Debate the English Occupation of India

The first two selections are by Dadabhai Naoroji (1825–1917), who was known as "the Grand Old Man of India." Naoroji spent much of his life in England, where in 1892 he became the first Indian elected to the British parliament (as a Liberal from London.) He devoted his life to educating the British public on Indian Conditions. He returned frequently to India and was three times elected president of the India National Congress, a group dedicated to gaining Indian self-government. The third selection is by a more extreme Indian nationalist, Bal Gangadhar Tilak. In Wm. Theodore de Bary, Stephen Hay, Royal Weiler and Andrew Yarrow, eds., *Oriental Civilization, Sources of Indian Tradition* (New York: Columbia University Press, 1958), pp. 671–673, 720–723.

I. MEMORANDUM WRITTEN BY D. NAOROJI (1880)

Europeans occupy almost all the higher places in every department of government. . . . While in India they acquire India's money, experience, and wisdom, and when they go they carry both away with them, leaving India so much poorer in material and moral wealth. Thus India is left without, and cannot have, those elders in wisdom and experience who in every country are the natural guides of the rising generations in their national and social conduct and of the destinies of their country— and a sad, sad loss this is!

Every European is isolated from the people around him. He is not their mental, moral, or social leader, or companion. For any mental or moral influence or guidance or sympathy with the people, he might just as well be living in the moon. The people know not him, and he knows not nor cares for the people. Some honorable exceptions do now and then make an effort to do some good, . . . but in the very nature of things, these efforts are always feeble . . . and of little permanent effect. . . .

The Europeans are not the natural leaders of the people. They do not belong to the people. They cannot enter into their thoughts and feelings; they cannot join or sympathize with their joys or griefs. On the contrary, every day the estrangement is increasing. Europeans deliberately and openly widen it more and more. There may be very few social institutions started by Europeans in which natives, however fit and desirous to join, are not deliberately and insultingly excluded. The Europeans are and make themselves strangers in every way. . . .

The power that is now being raised by the spread of education, though yet slow and small, is one that in time must, for weal or woe, exercise great influence. In fact, it has already begun to do so. . . .

The educated find themselves simply so many dummies, ornamented with the tinsel of school education. . . . What must be the inevitable consequence? A wild, spirited horse without curb or reins will run away wild and kill and trample upon everyone that comes in his way. A misdirected force will hit anywhere and destroy anything. The power that the rulers are raising will . . . recoil against themselves, if with this blessing of education they do not do their whole duty to the country which trusts to their righteousness and thus turn this good power to their own side. . . . The voice of the power of the rising education is, no doubt, feeble at present. Like the infant, the present dissatisfaction is only crying at the pains it is suffering. Its notions have not taken any form or shape or course yet, but it is growing. Heaven only knows what it will grow to! If the present material and moral destruction of India continues, a great convulsion must inevitably arise by which either India will be more and more crushed under the iron heel of despotism and destruction, or may succeed in shattering the destroying hand and power. . . .

II. SPEECH BY D. NAOROJI TO INDIA NATIONAL CONGRESS (1886)

We have assembled to consider questions upon which depend our future. . . . It is our good fortune that we are under a rule which makes it possible for us to meet in this manner. (Cheers.) It is under the civilizing rule of the Queen and people of England that we meet here together, hindered by none, and are freely allowed to speak our minds without the least fear and without the least hesitation. Such a thing is possible under British rule and British rule only. (Loud cheers.) Then I put the question plainly: Is this Congress a nursery for sedition and rebellion against the British Government (cries of "no, no"); or is it another stone in the foundation of the stability of that Government (cries of "yes, yes")? There could be but one answer, and that you have already given. We are thoroughly sensible [aware] of the numberless blessings conferred upon us, of which the very existence of this Congress is a proof in a nutshell. (Cheers.) Were it not for these blessings of British rule I could not have come here, as I have done, without the least hesitation and without the least fear that my children might be robbed and killed in my absence; nor

could you have come from every corner of the land, having performed, within a few days, journeys which in former days would have occupied as many months. (Cheers.) These simple facts bring home to all of us at once some of those great and numberless blessings which British rule has conferred upon us. But there remain even greater blessings for which we have to be grateful. It is to British rule that we owe the education we possess. The people of England were sincere in the declarations made more than half a century ago that they were bound to administer for the good of India, to the glory of their own name, and the satisfaction of God. (Prolonged cheering.)

III. SPEECH BY B. G. TILAK (1906)

One fact is that this alien government has ruined the country. In the beginning, all of us were taken by surprise. We were almost dazed. We thought that everything that the rulers did was for our good and that this English government has descended from the clouds to save us from the invasions of Tamerlane and Chingis Khan, and, as they say, not only from foreign invasions but from internecine [civil] warfare. We felt happy for a time, but it soon came to light that the peace which was established in this country did this . . .—that we were prevented from going at each other's throats, so that a foreigner might go at the throat of us all. *Pax Britannica* [British peace or rule] has been established in this country in order that a foreign government may exploit the country. That this is the effect of this *Pax Britannica* is being gradually realised in these days. It was an unhappy circumstance that it was not realised sooner. . . . English education, growing poverty, and better familiarity with our rulers, opened our eyes and our leaders. . . .

Your industries are ruined utterly, ruined by foreign rule; your wealth is going out of the country and you are reduced to the lowest level which no human being can occupy. In this state of things, is there any other remedy by which you can help yourself? The remedy is not petitioning but boycott! We say prepare your forces, organize your power, and then go to work so that they cannot refuse you what you demand. . . . Every Englishman knows that they are a mere handful in this country and it is the business of everyone of them to befool you in believing that you are weak and they are strong. This is politics. We have been deceived by such policy so long. What the new party wants you to do is to realize the fact that your future rests entirely in your own hands. If you mean to be free, you can be free. . . . We shall not give them assistance to collect revenue and keep peace. We shall not assist them in fighting beyond the frontiers or outside India with Indian blood and money. We shall not assist them in carrying on the administration of justice. We shall have our own courts, and when time comes we shall not pay taxes. Can you do that by your united efforts? If you can, you are free from tomorrow. . . . Some gentlemen who spoke this evening referred to half a bread as against the whole bread. I say I want the whole bread, and that immediately. . . .

Barbara Ward: The Rich Nations and the Poor Nations

Barbara Ward (1914–   ) is a widely published and distinguished writer and lecturer. She has contributed greatly to public reflec-

The chief point that distinguishes tribal and traditional society is that all the internal impulses to modernization have been largely lacking. And yet today these societies are everywhere in a ferment of change. How has this come about? Where did the external stimulus come from? There is only one answer. It came, largely uninvited, from the restless, changing, rampaging West. In the last 300 years, the world's ancient societies, the great traditional civilizations of Latin America and the tribal societies of Africa, have all, in one way or another, been stirred up from outside by the new, bounding, uncontrollable energies of the Western powers which, during those same years, were undergoing concurrently all the revolutions—of equality, of nationalism, of rising population, and of scientific change—which make up the mutation of modernization.

The great world-wide transmitter of the modernizing tendency has been without doubt—for good and evil—Western colonialism. It is typical, I think, of the way in which the changes have come about that, again and again, Western merchants were the forerunners of upheaval. They went out to bring back the spices and silks and sophistications of the Orient to cold and uncomfortable Europe. At first, they had no intentions of conquering anything. They simply tried to establish monopoly positions for themselves—hardly surprising when you could earn a 5,000-percent profit on a shipload of nutmeg making landfall in Europe—and to drive the traders of other nations away. They fought each other ferociously at sea but on land controlled only 'factories'—clusters of warehouses, port installations, and dwelling houses held on sufferance from the local ruler. And so the position might have remained. But Dutch pressure was too great for the frail political structure of Java in the seventeenth century and little by little, by backing compliant sultans and deposing sullen ones, the Dutch became political masters of all the rich 'spice islands.'

In the following century, the Mogul superstructure collapsed in India and in their maneuvering to destroy French influence the British found themselves assuming power by a similar route, first backing local contenders, then, saddled with them as puppets or incompetents, gradually assuming the power which slipped from their enfeebled grip. The Europeans had come out to trade. Imperial control was a by-product—and an increasingly ruinous one in commercial terms—yet as late as 1850 the nominal ruler in India was still a merchant corporation—'John Company,' the East India Company.

Colonial control, developing from its origins in trade, began to set the whole revolution of modernization into motion. It launched the radical changes brought about by a rapidly increasing growth in population. Western control introduced the beginnings of medical science. It ended internal disorder. A crowding into the big cities began. There were some attempts at more modern sanitation.

Towards the close of the nineteenth century a spurt of population began throughout India and the Far East. But this spurt had a different consequence from the comparable increase in the West. Western lands were relatively underpopulated—North America absolutely so—when the processes of modernization began. The growth in numbers was a positive spur to economic growth; it brought laborers into the market and widened the market. At the same time the new machines, the new developing economy based on rising productivity, expanded the possibilities of creating wealth in a way that more than outstripped the growth in population. But in the Far East, in India, where population was already dense, the effect of the colonial impact was to increase the rate of the population's growth without launching a total transformation of the economy. More births, longer lives, sent population far beyond the capabilities of a stumbling economy. Today the grim dilemma has appeared that population is so far ahead of the means of satisfying it that each new wave of births threatens in each generation to wipe out the margin of savings necessary to sustain added numbers. The West, where growth in population acted as a spur to further expansion, has not faced this dilemma, and in the East it is not yet clear how so grave a dilemma *can* be faced.

Colonial rule brought in the sense of a this-worldly concern for the advantages of material advance by the simplest and most direct route—the 'demonstration effect.' The new merchants, the new administrators, lived better, lived longer, had demonstrably more materially satisfying lives. The local people saw that this was so and they began to wonder why and whether others might not live so too. Above all, the local leaders saw vividly that the new scientific, industrial, and technological society enjoyed almost irresistible power. This, too, they naturally coveted.

At the same time, the colonial system did set in motion some definite beginnings in the processes of technical change and economic growth. There was some education of local people in the new techniques of Western life. Some merchants in the old societies, the Compradors in China, for instance, or the Gujaratis in India, began to exercise their talents as entrepreneurs in a new, settled, commercial society. Some of the preliminaries of industrialization—railways, ports, roads, some power—the preliminaries we call 'infrastructure'—were introduced to the benefit of the new colonial economy. Some export industries expanded to provide raw materials for the West. Virtually nothing was done about basic agriculture; but plantation systems did develop agricultural products—tea, pepper, ground-nuts, jute—for the growing markets of Europe.

Above all, the new political ideas streamed in. Western education gave an *élite* a first look at Magna Charta. In their school-books in India the sons of Indians could read Edmund Burke denouncing the depradations of Englishmen in India. The new sense of equality, inculcated by Western education, was reinforced by the daily contrast between the local inhabitants and the colonial representatives who claimed to rule them. Personal equality fused with the idea of national equality, with the revolt educated men increasingly felt at being run by another nation. The whole national movement of anti-colonialism was stirred up by Western ideas of national rights and national independence, and by the perpetual evidence that the rights were being denied.

Everywhere there was ferment; everywhere there was the beginning of change; everywhere a profound sense that the old ways were becoming inadequate, were in some way no longer valid or viable for modern man. And this feeling stirred up an equally violent reaction. Men rose up to say that the old ways were better and that the new-fangled fashions would destroy all that was valuable and profound in indigenous civilization. Between the modernizers and the traditionalists, between the young men who wanted to accept everything and the old men who wanted to reject everything, the local community threatened to be distracted by contradictory leadership. A crisis of loyalty and comprehension superimposed itself on all the other crises. It was rare for a country to achieve the national coherence that was achieved in India under the leadership of Gandhi in whom ancient vision and the modern idea of equality could coexist, and around whom old and new were thus able to unite.

The important point to remember, however, if one wishes to grasp the present contrast between the rich nations and the poor, is that all these changes, introduced pell-mell by colonialism, did not really produce a new and coherent form of society, as they had done in the West. There was no 'take-off,' to use Professor Rostow's phrase, into a new kind of society. The colonial impact introduced problems that seemed too large to be solved, or, at least, problems that offered immense difficulty to any solution. . . .

STUDY QUESTIONS

1. How did the slave trade begin? What vested interests supported it? What was the relationship between the slave trade and the Western conquest of Africa?

2. What made Western conquest of Africa possible? What impact did the European presence have on African development?

3. "Translate" Kenyatta's fable into an African's account of how Europeans took over his lands. Why was the native unable to retain respect for Western law? What is Kenyatta's suggested solution to the problem of Western aggression?

4. What did Kipling consider as the "White Man's Burden"? What response to his presence could the White Man expect from native peoples? Why, according to Kipling, must the White Man persevere?

5. What attitude did Naroji express toward British rule in his two statements? Were they in conflict and if so, why? What was Tilak's critique of British rule, and by what tactics did he believe independence should be pursued?

6. Define imperialism. How was it connected to the industrial revolution, nationalism, social Darwinism?

7. How did colonial rule produce a revolution of modernization?

8. Did the benefits of modernization justify colonization? Make an argument for or against the proposition that this was so.

TOPIC 39

IMPERIAL CHINA AND THE WEST

Although the great plateaus, deserts, and mountains that ring the vast area of eastern Asia called China encouraged the welding together into a single empire of the peoples who inhabited the interior, they also contributed to traditional China's relative isolation from the rest of the world. Intermittently making contact with other great civilizations of antiquity—India, Persia, and Mediterranean Europe—China's own highly developed and venerable civilization was then largely self-contained. During the Middle Ages, Western merchants, like the Polos, along with Christian missionaries, were present in limited numbers. The European voyages of discovery in the sixteenth century brought the Portuguese

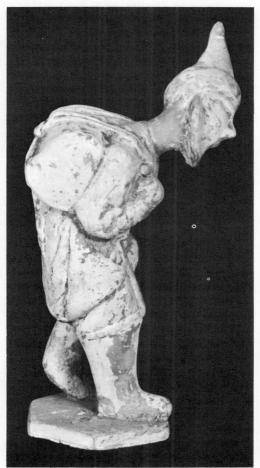

China's trade contacts with Mediterranean peoples are evoked by this clay figurine of a Semitic merchant, T'ang period (618–906). A large foreign community was resident in China during Carolingian times. According to a contemporary Arab merchant, more than 100,000 Mohammedans, Christians, Parsees, and Jews were massacred at Hang Chou during the latter part of the ninth century.

and Spaniards who established trading posts and bolstered the activities of missionaries, chiefly Jesuit, who had by 1700 converted a third of a million Chinese to Catholicism. For its part, China under the Yüan and Ming dynasties (1279–1644) periodically invaded neighboring areas, and her naval expeditions sailed as far as the Persian Gulf and the East African coast. The Chinese, however, always controlled the number of foreigners permitted within the country, and severely restricted the freedom of European merchants. By the end of the eighteenth century, the foreign traders were confined to a small area in the port of Canton, obliged to deal with special officials and forbidden to learn the Chinese language. The Westerners coveted the profitable Chinese trade—tea, silk, and cotton; the Chinese spurned any intrusion on their time-tested way of life. These relationships were first brought to a state of crisis in the opium wars of the last century. Our readings explore the difficult choices open to Imperial China in her confrontation with the more technologically advanced nations of the West.

The Value System of Imperial China

Traditional China had its own unique value system, here described by contemporary American Sinologists. The first selection is from John K. Fairbank, *East Asia, The Modern Transformation* (Boston, Houghton Mifflin, 1965), pp. 82, 84. Copyright © 1965 by the Houghton Mifflin Company. Reprinted by permission of the publisher. The second selection is from the introduction to *The China Reader,* Vol. 1; *Imperial China: The Decline of the Last Dynasty and the Origins of Modern China,* eds. Franz Schurmann and Orville Schell (New York, Random House, 1966), pp. xv-xvii. Copyright © 1966 by Random House, Inc. Reprinted by permission of the publisher.

Big, happy family was blessing in old China

The Chinese invented paper during the Han dynasty (207 B.C.-220 A.D.). Windows in Chinese homes were covered by thin paper made half transparent with a coating of tung oil. Colored paper cuttings such as this were pasted on the windows to brighten up the rooms. Usually the subject matter was symbolic of good fortune. This cutting makes the point that a big, happy family was a blessing in old China.

I

Our perspective will be aided if we first note the traditional view that the Chinese held of themselves and of the cosmos—the self-image that was so violently shattered in the course of the nineteenth century. This was the psychological starting point for the long series of unexpected defeats and bitter humiliations brought by Western contact.

In her own tradition, China was and had always been in the center of the civilized world, surrounded by peoples of lesser culture who invariably acknowledged the cultural superiority of *Chung-kuo* (literally, "the Central Country," the Chinese name for China).

China's superiority was ascribed to her success in approximating, more closely than "barbarian" lands, the natural order of the cosmos. This was manifest in the order and

harmony enjoined by the Confucian Classics—for example, the Five Relationships or Bonds that connected and subordinated subject to ruler, wife to husband, son to father, and younger to elder brother, and related friend to friend; or the distinction between the superior men who labor with their minds and the small men who labor with their muscles; or the hierarchy of classes which ranked them in the order of scholar-official, farmer, artisan and merchant.

Proper conduct in daily life, according to the classical teachings, would maintain this social order of status and hierarchy. Conduct was molded by the family system. The individual was at all times subordinate to his family, which encompassed all members within five generations, including even third

cousins. This extended family system provided economic support, social contact and recreation, education, and religious focus in the reverence solemnly paid to the ancestors. . . .

This social order, though based on the premise that individuals are not equally endowed, offered opportunity for the able and ambitious man. His advancement could come through self-cultivation, especially through learning based on study of the Classics, which would enable him to act like and to be a superior man and, through the government examination system, to become a degree-holder and even an official. In the early nineteenth century, local district examinations, held in two years out of every three, provided each time a total of about 25,000 degree-holders at the lowest regular level, who might thereafter compete in a ramified series of higher examinations to qualify for official posts.

The principles of the Confucian order, handed down through the Classics and inculcated by the family and the examinations, were also maintained from day to day by the benevolent rule of the emperor. As Son of Heaven he stood at the apex of the human scene and by his virtuous conduct set the example for mankind. The emperor's power was believed to be exerted primarily through this example. His virtuous conduct of itself moved others, including even outer "barbarians," to act correctly, and thus the social order was kept intact and in tune with the whole natural order of which it was a part. Rewards and punishments were necessary to control small men but were secondary to the power of right conduct which influenced superior men. The emperor therefore admonished his people as to the norms of proper conduct. . . .

II

China is a country and a civilization distant from our own Western traditions. Over three thousand years ago she began to develop her own civilization, at times borrowing from neighboring cultures, notably Buddhism from India. But unlike the lands of Europe which for centuries looked to each other, China just sent her pilgrims to India to bring back what was desirable. When Buddhism took root in China and became a great Chinese religion, the Chinese forgot about India, and from the Sung Dynasty to recent times India was as remote from China as was Europe. The Chinese traditionally regarded themselves as at the center of the universe, and the outer galaxies, except when they bothered China were of no concern to her.

The Chinese believed they had devised man's most perfect system of government and society. If they were not always perfect in practice, that was just because man could not live up to his ideals. They regarded the universe as made up of harmonious balances; thus if man understood the laws of the universe, and the learned man were given authority, then there was no reason for everything not to be in harmony: individual, family empire. In no civilization did education hold so central a place nor did learned men enjoy such political authority as in China.

Enlightenment, however, was not accessible to all. Human society was forever divided into "gentlemen" and "small men." Some of the latter, through hard work and study, might attain the rank of the gentlemen, but the great mass of small men would forever remain where they were. It was the gentleman's duty to exercise benevolent rule over the small men: emperor over his subjects, magistrate over the people, husband over wife and children. If all men accepted the wisdom of the *Tao* (the Way), then peace would prevail. The old Chinese conception of peace was expressed through the word "flat": no disturbances in the realm, the village, or the home, no passion in the life of man, serenity in old age where death calmly supplanted life. . . .

Reason and passion came to old China from two directions: the West and the small men of China.

The prosperity of imperial China is reflected in this Cantonese scene.

Toward the end of the nineteenth century the Chinese finally convinced that there was a universe beyond China's confines. For decades the Chinese had had contacts with Westerners, but regarded them as little more than modern versions of the ancient nomadic invaders. But then, as had been the case with Indian Buddhism fifteen hundred years earlier, they began to realize that peoples outside of China had discovered secrets about man, society, and cosmos of which the Chinese were entirely unaware. Both the Chinese discovery of India and of the West came during times of breakdown in China, but there was an important difference. Buddhism's Indian missionaries went quietly to China, set up monasteries, and translated scriptures. Westerners who went to China in the nineteenth century subjected the Chinese to humiliation of the deepest sort, branding them an inferior race, beating them militarily, reviling them as heathen whose souls had to be transformed before they could become fully human. What made the humiliation even harder to bear was the realization that the Westerners' spiritual horizons were broader than any the Chinese had ever known, and that they experienced a world of emotions which the Chinese denied themselves in the interests of Confucian harmony. . . .

Humiliation from the West was accompanied by the degeneration of Chinese society itself. The rebellious currents of the late eighteenth century led from the Taiping Rebellion, to the Boxers, to the Kuomintang, and finally to the Communists. The small men of China—peasants, merchants, workers, women, and the young—burst forth in murderous hatred of their rulers. One has only to compare the Taipings' proclamations with the official documents of the Imperial suppressors of revolution to see the gulf separating new and old. The Taipings, with their millenarian beliefs, projected a world of love, joy, and hatred: the enemies of the people would be smashed, all men would be made equal, the wealth would be shared, and a good society would come into being. The Imperial documents are detailed battle reports about "bandit suppression," proposals about improving conditions, and schemes for restoring harmony. . . .

The Chinese Assert Their Traditional Values

These values stemmed in part from the teachings of great Chinese philosophers such as Confucius (K'ung Fu-tzu, 551–479 B.C.) and Mencius (Meng-tzu, 371–289? B.C.) who taught that man was innately good and naturally loved his fellow-men. Man's full potential could only be realized through education, hence the traditional Chinese reliance on the scholar-official who served as guide and conscience of the ruler. It was the duty of the state to ensure the prosperity of its subjects, for only when material wants were assuaged and social stability assured could man find peace of mind. Rulers were judged on the degree of success they exhibited in following the Way of Confucius and providing the good life for their people. The first selection is taken from "The Book of Mencius" in William de Bary, Wing-tsit Chan, and Burton Watson, eds., *Sources of Chinese Tradition* (New York, Columbia University, 1960), pp. 92–93.

The philosophers provided the Chinese not only with a rationale that explained the nature of man and society but with the workings of the whole universe. Thus it is not surprising that the Chinese on the eve of their violent collision with modern civilization showed a condescending disdain for foreign ways. The second selection contains excerpts from a letter of the Ch'ien Lung Emperor (1736–1795) to George III of Great Britain in response to the request of the British envoy for representation at Peking and the opening of China to British commerce. From H. F. MacNair, ed., *Modern Chinese History, Selected Readings* (Shanghai: Commercial Press Ltd., 1923), pp. 2–4.

I. MENCIUS DESCRIBES HUMANE GOVERNMENT (4th Century B.C.)

Mencius went to see King Hui of Liang. The king said: "You have not considered a thousand *li* too far to come, and must therefore have something of profit to offer my kingdom?" Mencius replied: "Why must you speak of profit? What I have to offer is humanity and righteousness, nothing more. If a king says, 'What will profit my kingdom?' the high officials will say, 'What will profit our families?' and the lower officials and commoners will say 'What will profit ourselves?' Superiors and inferiors will try to seize profit one from another, and the state will be endangered. . . . Let your Majesty speak only of humanity and righteousness. Why must you speak of profit?"

Mencius said: "It was by virtue of humanity that the Three Dynasties won the empire, and by virtue of the want of humanity that they lost it. States rise and fall for the same reason. Devoid of humanity, the emperor would be unable to safeguard the four seas, a feudal lord would be unable to safeguard the altars of land and grain [that is, his state], a minister would be unable to safeguard the ancestral temple [that is, his clan-family], and the individual would be unable to safeguard his four limbs. Now people hate destruction and yet indulge in want of humanity—this is as if one hates to get drunk and yet forces oneself to drink wine."

Mencius said: "An overlord is he who employs force under a cloak of humanity. To be an overlord one has to be in possession of a large state. A king, on the other hand, is he who gives expression to his humanity through virtuous conduct. To be a true king, one does not have to have a large state. T'ang [founder of the Shang dynasty] had only a territory of seventy *li* and King Wen [founder of the Chou] only a hundred. When men are subdued by force, it is not that they submit from their hearts but only that their strength is unavailing. When men are won by virtue, then their hearts are gladdened and their submission is sincere, as the seventy disciples were won by the Master, Confucius. This is what is meant in the *Book of Odes* when it says:

From east and west,
From north and south,
Came none who thought of disobedience.

Mencius said: "States have been won by men without humanity, but the world, never."

II. THE CH'IEN LUNG EMPEROR COMMUNICATES WITH KING GEORGE III (1793)

You, O King, live beyond the confines of many seas, nevertheless, impelled by your humble desire to partake of the benefits of our civilization, you have dispatched a mission respectfully bearing your memorial. Your Envoy has crossed the seas and paid his respects at my Court on the anniversary of my birthday. To show your devotion, you have also sent offerings of your country's produce.

I have perused your memorial: the earnest terms in which it is couched reveal a respectful humility on your part, which is highly praiseworthy. In consideration of the fact that your Ambassador and his deputy have come a long way with your memorial and tribute, I have shown them high favor and have allowed them to be introduced into my presence. To manifest my indulgence, I have entertained them at a banquet and made them numerous gifts. . . .

As to your entreaty to send one of your nationals to be accredited to my Celestial Court and to be in control of your country's trade with China, this request is contrary to all usage of my dynasty and cannot possibly be entertained. It is true that Europeans, in the service of the dynasty, have been permitted to live at Peking, but they are compelled to adopt Chinese dress, they are strictly confined to their own precincts and are never permitted to return home. You are presumably familiar with our dynastic regulations. Your proposed Envoy to my Court could not be placed in a position similar to that of Europeans in Peking who are forbidden to leave China, nor could he, on the other hand, be allowed liberty of movement and the privilege of corresponding with his own country; so that you would gain nothing by his residence in our midst.

Emperor Ch'ien Lung in his chair of state.

Moreover, Our Celestial dynasty possesses vast territories, and tribute missions from the dependencies are provided for by the Department for Tributary States, which ministers to their wants and exercises strict control over their movements. It would be quite impossible to leave them to their own devices. Supposing that your Envoy should come to our Court, his language and national dress differ from that of our people, and there would be no place in which to bestow him. It may be suggested that he might imitate the Europeans permanently resident in Peking and adopt the dress and customs of China, but, it has never been our dynasty's wish to force people to do things unseemly and inconvenient. Besides, supposing I sent an Ambassador to reside in your country, how could you possibly make for him the requisite arrangements? Europe consists of many other nations besides your own: if each and all demanded to be represented at our Court, how could we possibly consent? The thing is utterly impracticable. How can our dynasty alter its whole procedure and system of etiquette, established for more than a century, in order to meet your individual views? . . .

Swaying the wide world, I have but one aim in view, namely, to maintain a perfect governance and to fulfill the duties of the state: strange and costly objects do not interest me. If I have commanded that the tribute offerings sent by you, O King, are to be accepted, this was solely in consideration for the spirit which prompted you to dispatch them from afar. Our dynasty's majestic virtue has penetrated unto every country under heaven, and kings of all nations have offered their costly tribute by land and sea. As your Ambassador can see for himself, we possess all things. I set no value on objects strange or ingenious, and have no use for your country's manufac-

tures. This then is my answer to your request to appoint a representative at my Court, a request contrary to our dynastic usage, which would only result in inconvenience to yourself. I have expounded my wishes in detail and have commanded your tribute Envoys to leave in peace on their homeward journey. It behoves you, O King, to respect my sentiments and to display even greater devotion and loyalty in future, so that, by perpetual submission to our Throne, you may secure peace and prosperity for your country hereafter.

John K. Fairbank: Tribute and Trade

The nations of the West long desired a free hand to develop trade with China, but it was only in the nineteenth century that rapidly advancing industrialization made it possible for them to force their desires upon the Chinese. In this selection John K. Fairbank (1907–   ), a highly respected Sinologist, describes the conditions under which outsiders were permitted to do business with the Chinese and sets the stage for the emerging conflict. A major point of friction stemmed from the fact that, whereas Western nations proceeded from acceptance of the concept of legal equality among sovereign states, China regarded all other peoples in principle as tributary to the Empire. Reprinted with permission of the publisher from John K. Fairbank, *The United States and China,* 3d ed. (Harvard University Press, Cambridge, 1971), pp. 125–126, 137–142. Copyright 1971 by the President and Fellows of Harvard College.

The West approached China through the medium of China's foreign trade. The Western impact can be understood only against this commercial background. The sixteenth cen-

The Great Wall. Begun in the third century B.C. to defend China from barbarian invasions, it stretches for more than 2000 miles between Mongolia and China. Twenty to fifty feet high and between fifteen and twenty-five feet wide, it remains one of the most impressive monuments to China's ancient glory.

tury Portuguese and the seventeenth century Dutch and British adventurers and merchants who opened the China trade discovered unknown regions, just as their colleagues of the same generations were opening up the New World. The all-important difference was that Eastern Asia, far from being a virgin continent, was already the center of an enormous and ramified commercial life of its own. The early Western ventures of exploration and trade were but small increments in channels of commerce already centuries old. It is a striking fact that British trade was opened at Canton in 1637, within a very few years of the founding of New England. Yet British trade with China was not able to expand outside of Canton until the nineteenth century, when New England had long since become part of a new and independent nation ready itself to aid in expanding the Canton trade.

The contrast between European expansion in America and its retardation in China must be understood from the Asian as well as the European side. It was not solely that European expansionist hopes and rivalries became more easily focused upon the wide open opportunities of the New World. The very size and richness of the Far Eastern empires, China and Japan, made them at first too strong to coerce, too sophisticated and too self-sufficient to best in trade.

[With the onset of the Industrial Revolution in the West, however, the Chinese position rapidly deteriorated.]

During a full century, from 1842 to 1943, China labored under the handicap of the unequal treaties by which she was opened to Western commercial and religious enterprise. . . .

To understand the one-sidedness and inequality of the unequal treaties which the Western powers imposed upon the Chinese empire, one must look at the ancient tribute system which China first imposed upon Western visitors. This old Chinese system was just as unequal as the treaty system that supplanted it.

The tribute system was an application to foreign affairs of the Confucian doctrines by which Chinese rulers gained an ethical sanction for their exercise of political authority. Just as the virtuous ruler by his moral example had prestige and influence among the people of the Middle Kingdom, so he irresistibly attracted the barbarians who were outside the pale of Chinese culture. To a Confucian scholar it was inconceivable that the rude tribes of the frontier should not appreciate China's cultural superiority and therefore seek the benefits of Chinese civilization. Since the Emperor exercised the Mandate of Heaven to rule all mankind, it was his function to be compassionate and generous to all "men from afar." The imperial benevolence should be reciprocated, it was felt, by the humble submission of the foreigner.

Once the foreigner had recognized the unique position of the Son of Heaven it was unavoidable that these reciprocal relations of compassionate benevolence and humble submission should be demonstrated in ritual form, by the ceremonial bestowal of gifts and of tribute respectively. Tribute thus became one of the rites of the Chinese court. It betokened the admission of a barbarian to the civilization of the Middle Kingdom. It was a boon and privilege, and not ignominious. As the original Chinese culture-island spread through the centuries, from the ancient nuclear area over the rest of China, to absorb barbarian tribes, the formalities of tribute relations were developed into a mechanism by which barbarous regions outside the empire might be given their place in the all-embracing Sinocentric cosmos.

When Europeans first came to China by sea these formalities were naturally expected of them. According to the collected statutes of the Manchu dynasty, a tributary ruler of a foreign state should receive an imperial patent of appointment which acknowledged his tributary status. There should also be conferred upon him a noble rank and an imperial seal for use in signing his memorials, which should be dated by the Chinese calendar. When his tribute missions came, they should be limited in size to one hundred men, of whom only twenty might proceed to the capital, by the imperial post. At the capital the mission was lodged, carefully protected, and entertained. Eventually it was received in audience by the Emperor. This was the time of all others when the tribute envoys performed the kowtow.

Early European envoys, like the unhappy Hollanders who presented tribute at the Manchu court in 1795, were inclined to feel that this calisthenic ceremony more than offset the imperial benevolence which filtered down to them through the sticky hands of the officials who had them in charge. The full kowtow was no mere prostration of the body but a prolonged series of three separate kneelings, each one leading to three successive prostrations, nose upon the floor. The "three kneelings and nine prostrations" left no doubt in anyone's mind, least of all in the performer's, as to who was inferior and who superior. Egalitarian Westerners usually failed to appreciate that this abasement of the individual who kowtowed was a normal aspect of the ceremonial life in a society of status. The Emperor kowtowed to Heaven and his parents, the highest grandees kowtowed to the Emperor. In a less formal way friends

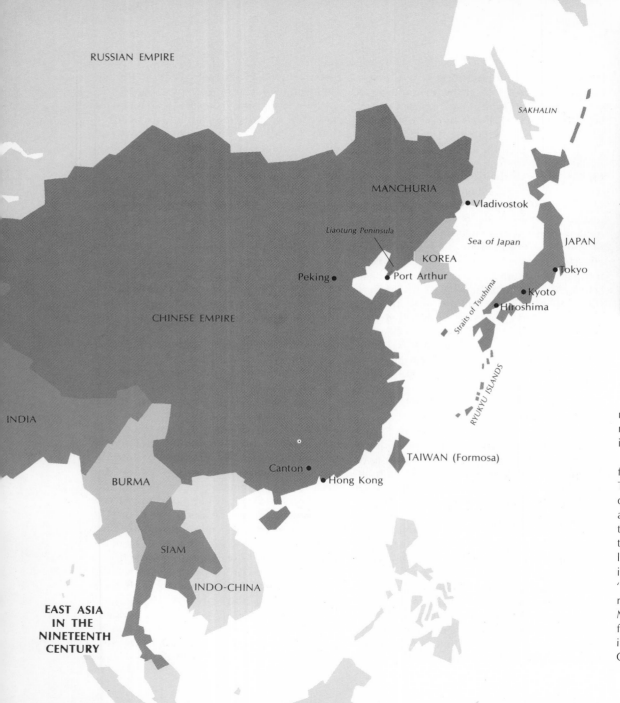

EAST ASIA IN THE NINETEENTH CENTURY

RUSSIAN EMPIRE

SAKHALIN

MANCHURIA

● Vladivostok

Liaotung Peninsula

Sea of Japan

KOREA

JAPAN

Peking ●   ● Port Arthur

● Tokyo

CHINESE EMPIRE

Straits of Tsushima

● Kyoto
● Hiroshima

RYUKYU ISLANDS

INDIA

TAIWAN (Formosa)

Canton ●

BURMA   ● Hong Kong

SIAM

INDO-CHINA

This scene from the motion picture "Anna and the King of Siam," while not Chinese, catches the sense of inferiority and debasement which the kowtow induced.

might kowtow to each other, as polite Japanese almost do today. From a tribute bearer it was therefore no more than good manners.

The secret of the tribute system was the fact that it had become a vehicle for trade. The Ming chroniclers, by including the long defunct Roman East, fictitious principalities, and border tribes, had listed more than 120 tributaries. The Manchus put the border tribes under a special office and reduced their list of genuine tributaries to less than a dozen including the still shadowy countries of the "Western Ocean" whose merchants had already appeared at Canton. Because the Manchu empire chiefly sought stability in its foreign relations, it dealt only with neighboring countries or with those who came to China. If foreign merchants came and their ruler wanted to promote their trade, he could present tribute. It was as simple as that.

The trading states of East Asia presented tribute to the Chinese court in order to maintain their trade and friendly relations and were duly enrolled as tributaries. Certain ports and markets were designated for them. Thus tribute and trade from Korea came by land through Shanhaikuan, from the Liu-ch'iu (Ryukyu) Islands through Foochow, from Siam through Canton. When the first Europeans reached Canton, they were similarly enrolled and almost without realizing it became part of China's tributary firmament. Until the nineteenth century the diplomatic missions sent from Western powers to China, although they totaled more than a score, did little or nothing to shatter the Chinese institution of tribute and the conviction of superiority which it signified. It was still possible for the Ch'ien-lung Emperor, in his famous mandate of 1793 to King George III, to compliment the barbarian ruler on his "respectful humility" while at the same time refusing to permit any exchange of diplomatic representatives or expansion of British trade outside Canton.

The Canton System and its Collapse

The old Canton trade in its heyday (c. 1760-1840) was carried on under a working compromise between the Chinese system of tributary trade and European mercantilism. During the Napoleonic wars one of the great survivors of the mercantilist era, the British East India Company, based on India, beat out its Continental competitors and brought the growing tea exports of Canton into a profitable triangular trade between England, India, and China. Fleets of East Indiamen voyaged annually from London to Canton, where the company by its charter monopolized all British trade and dealt with a comparable monopoly on the Chinese side—a licensed guild of about a dozen firms, or "hongs." These Chinese hong merchants were responsible to the imperial officials for the foreign trade and traders. The foreigners in turn were restricted by various regulations which, for example, confined them largely to their factories and kept them outside the walls of Canton. Thus by mutual agreement during most of the eighteenth century, in spite of continual disputes, the old Canton trade proved mutually profitable within the limits imposed by two, Chinese and foreign, systems of trade regulation.

Western expansion, and free trade in particular, disrupted the Canton system after the East India Company lost its monopoly of Britain's China trade in 1833. Unfortunately for the repute of private enterprise in the Orient, it reached the China coast at this time chiefly in the form of the opium trade conducted by private traders. This historical circumstance has poisoned Sino-Western relations ever since.

The opium was grown and taxed chiefly in areas under East India Company jurisdiction in India. Opium was carried to China by private British and Indian traders, as well as by Americans who competed as best they could by buying opium in Turkey. They usually found Chinese merchants and mandarins eager to flout the Emperor's prohibitions of smoking and importation. The result was an illegal trade—openly connived at by British, American, Chinese, and other merchants and officials—too valuable to the British Indian exchequer to be refrained from, too necessary to the balancing of the tea export trade to be given up by the merchants, and too profitable to them and to venal Chinese officials to be easily suppressed. . . .

In the Chinese view, the Western barbarians have always been outlandish in their physical characteristics, generally uncouth and smelling of mutton fat. In slang they have been called "foreign devils" (fan-kuei or yang-kuei-tzu), "big noses" (ta-pi-tzu), or "hairy ones" (mao-tzu). The official history of the Ming had described in some detail the Portuguese method of boiling and eating little Chinese children. Nineteenth century mission orphanages were thought to make medicine out of children's eyes and hearts. Foreign diplomats seemed to the mandarins wily and inscrutable, unpredictable "as dogs and sheep." Peasant mothers used to shield their babies from a foreigner's unlucky glance and especially the black magic of his camera. All in all, the white peril in nineteenth century China was a good deal more sinister than the yellow peril of the 1900's in America.

Warren Cohen: The Opium Trade

Professor Cohen points out that the opium trade provided the occasion rather than the cause of open hostilities between China and the Western powers. In this selection, taken from his monograph on the emerging role of the United States in China, he describes the significance of the trade in opium for both Western merchants and Imperial China. In Warren I. Cohen, *America's Response to China* (John Wiley & Sons, New York, 1971), pp. 3–7. Copyright © 1971 by John Wiley & Sons, Inc. Reprinted by permission.

By the time the Americans arrived on the scene, the tribute system had long been a vehicle for trade and the Manchus had

The only legal outlet for trade with China until after the Opium War was this stretch of waterfront in Canton, where foreign nations were permitted to erect warehouses for their goods. Merchants were restricted to the area.

worked out a variation for dealing with the barbarians who came by sea. Satisfied with the Western merchants' acceptance of the inferior role necessitated by tributary status, the Chinese government did not require the tribute mission to the capital. Whereas the court had traditionally sought the prestige derived from the ritual, by the eighteenth century both Peking and the local officials found sufficient advantage in the revenue derived from the trade. Nonetheless, the barbarians could certainly not be allowed free rein within the empire. They were contemptible not only as foreigners but also as businessmen—a class of low standing in the Confucian hierarchy.

If the barbarian traders persisted in coming to peddle their wares, to purchase some of the products of the superior Chinese civilization, they had to be restricted to one small area in Canton. Here the possibility of contamination was limited, the disease quarantined, the Chinese people protected. Here Chinese officials would not be bothered by the barbarians but could leave the management of the foreign merchant in the hands of the Chinese merchant.

Hemmed in by restrictions, left without recourse to settle disputes, unprotected by his government, the American businessman, like his European colleagues, remained in China. Obviously, the profits were worth the bother. And at times the bother was considerable, as in the notorious Terranova case of 1821, in which a seaman on an American ship was seized and executed by Chinese authorities in retaliation for a death for which he may have had no responsibility whatever. When Chinese officials demanded that Terranova be turned over to them in connection with the death of a woman allegedly struck by debris discarded from the American vessel, the merchants at first refused. Advised that refusal would mean exclusion of Americans from trade with China, the American business community decided to allow Terranova to be seized after a show of protest. Terranova was tried secretly, with no American present, and sentenced to death by strangulation. After the sentence was carried out, the American government did not protest and the Americans in Canton were commended by the local Viceroy for their properly submissive behavior. Such was the state of Sino-American relations under the tribute system, during the years when the Chinese dictated the terms of contact. . . .

[In addition to the humiliating status he was forced to accept, the] American businessman faced the problem of finding some article to sell. Furs, sandalwood, and even ginseng (which aging Chinese gentlemen sought in their never-ending search for a means to restore fading potency) had but limited markets, and all together failed to match the value of the items that the West in general sought to purchase. Like the Englishman, the American merchant was increasingly forced to fall back on the sale of opium—though some Americans, to be sure, would neither touch nor condone the drug traffic.

As the decade of the 1830's neared its end, the opium trade became a critical problem for the Chinese government. Obviously, some Chinese officials were deeply concerned about the moral and physical effects of drug addiction. In addition, the very reason for the opium traffic—the fact that the drug provided the West with a marketable commodity, whose sales exceeded the value of Western imports from China—created a financial problem for the Chinese government. In short, commerce with the West, which had traditionally left China with a favorable balance of payments, was now draining China of its hard currency.

The Chinese had no alternative but to put an end to the importation of opium. The English merchants who were largely responsible for the opium trade seemed convinced that there was no alternative to the continuation of this profitable enterprise, and the lines of conflict were drawn. Lacking diplomatic relations with the Chinese government and unable to persuade Chinese officials to receive a diplomatic mission, the traders had no channel through which to arrange a peaceful settlement of the dispute. With the Chinese determined to use force if necessary to put an end to a trade proscribed since 1800, the English merchants petitioned successfully for military support from their government. Thus the two countries, China and Great Britain, were drawn into conflict, into the "Opium War."

Given the perspective time grants to the historian, it is readily apparent that conflict between China and the West was inevitable. It is equally apparent that opium provided the occasion rather than the cause of that conflict. So long as the Chinese remained too arrogant to study these barbarians carefully, too arrogant to realize that England in particular had become powerful enough to make good the demand for diplomatic equality—for that long the point of Sino-Western contact could be but a powder keg awaiting a spark. Industrialization and the growth of nationalism had made the West more powerful and more assertive at a time when the Chinese had passed the peak of their power. The phenomenon of dynastic decline, so much a part of China's historical record, had not bypassed the Manchus.

The locus of power had shifted, but China's

mandarins had not perceived this. The "foreign devils," the "big noses"—those whom the Chinese thought of as savages and treated hardly better—were no longer willing to respond to the arbitrary exercise of authority obediently or submissively. Had the Chinese been able to conceive of diplomatic equality among nations, they might have been spared the "Opium War" and the century of humiliation that followed.

By the time the war broke out in 1839, the Chinese "barbarian experts," specialists on the West, had at least solved the problem of telling Westerners apart. Though they all looked alike, the Chinese had learned that Americans were not Englishmen and that in fact there existed a heritage of ill will between the United States and Great Britain. Having learned a little about the American Revolution and the War of 1812, Chinese officials concluded that their traditional policy of playing barbarians off against each other (*i-i-chih-i*) might well work here—and called upon loyal and obedient Americans to bring in English heads. Unhappily for the Chinese, the American community in Canton remained out of the action, preferring to take over the local trade, including opium, while the British were otherwise occupied.

The Treaty of Nanking, which restored peace after the British victory, signalled a new phase in the history of China: the end of the tribute system and the beginning of the treaty system. Unfortunately, the new system, though based in theory on the Western concept of diplomatic equality, proved as unequal as the old. For the next hundred years, the barbarian dictated the terms of Sino-Western contact. China's pretensions to universal hegemony vanished in an age in which the Chinese were widely scorned—a once-proud empire reduced to semicolonial status.

The Opium War "Opens" China (1839-1842)

Although profit-seeking Chinese merchants and corrupt officials had cooperated with Western merchants in the growing opium trade, the Imperial government had long opposed it on moral grounds and by the 1830's was also becoming increasingly alarmed at the rising drain on Chinese silver needed to buy it. In 1839 the Emperor sent a special commissioner, Lin Tse-hsü, to Canton with orders to stamp out the trade. Lin forced the Western merchants to surrender their stocks of the drug on hand, which were promptly destroyed. The traditional Chinese policy of combining tactics of coercion and persuasion is evident in the letter from the commisioner to Queen Victoria that forms the first selection. To the British, who were most affected, the issue was as much one of freedom of trade, diplomatic equality and the legal rights of their nationals as of the disputed drug, and they promptly retaliated by bombarding the Chinese coast at various points and seizing important fortifications. Chinese ignorance of Western power is amply illustrated in the second selection in which a high official smugly dismisses the British military threat. The third selection supplies examples of the ease with which superior British gun power worsted the defenders. The first reading is reprinted by permission of the publishers from Ssu-yu Teng and John K. Fairbank, *China's Response to the West, A Documentary Survey 1837–1923* (Cambridge, Mass.: Harvard University Press, 1954), pp. 24–27. Copyright 1954 by the President and Fellows of Harvard College. The second is from P. E. Kuo, *A Critical Study of* the *First Anglo-Chinese War with Documents* (Commercial Press, Ltd., Shanghai, 1935), pp. 260–261; and the third, Captain Sir Edward Belcher, *Narrative of a Voyage Round the World* (London, 1843), II pp. 141–143, 150–154.

I. COMMISSIONER LIN WRITES TO QUEEN VICTORIA (1839)

A communication: magnificently our great Emperor soothes and pacifies China and the foreign countries, regarding all with the same kindness. If there is profit, then he shares it with the peoples of the world; if there is harm, then he removes it on behalf of the world. This is because he takes the mind of heaven and earth as his mind.

The kings of your honorable country by a tradition handed down from generation to generation have always been noted for their politeness and submissiveness. We have read your successive tributary memorials saying "In general our countrymen who go to trade in China have always received His Majesty the Emperor's gracious treatment and equal justice," and so on. Privately we are delighted with the way in which the honorable rulers of your country deeply understand the grand principles and are grateful for the Celestial grace. For this reason the Celestial Court in soothing those from afar has redoubled its polite and kind treatment. The profit from trade has been enjoyed by them continuously for two hundred years. This is the source from which your country has become known for its wealth.

But after a long period of commercial intercourse, there appear among the crowd of barbarians both good persons and bad, unevenly. Consequently there are those who smuggle opium to seduce the Chinese people and so cause the spread of the poison to all provinces. Such persons who only care to profit themselves, and disregard their harm to others, are not tolerated by the laws of heaven and are unanimously hated by human beings. His Majesty the Emperor, upon hearing of this, is in a towering rage. He has especially sent me, his commissioner, to come to Kwangtung, and together with the governor-general and governor jointly to investigate and settle this matter. . . .

We find that your country is sixty or seventy thousand *li* [three *li* make one mile, ordinarily] from China. Yet there are barbar-

This nineteenth-century print shows Commissioner Lin overseeing the destruction of opium on the wharves at Canton, an act which led to the First Opium War.

ian ships that strive to come here for trade for the purpose of making a great profit. The wealth of China is used to profit the barbarians. That is to say, the great profit made by barbarians is all taken from the rightful share of China. By what right do they then in return use the poisonous drug to injure the Chinese people? Even though the barbarians may not necessarily intend to do us harm, yet in coveting profit to an extreme, they have no regard for injuring others. Let us ask, where is your conscience? I have heard that the smoking of opium is very strictly forbidden by your country; that is because the harm caused by opium is clearly understood. Since it is not permitted to do harm to your own country, then even less should you let it be passed on to the harm of other countries— how much less to China! Of all that China exports to foreign countries, there is not a single thing which is not beneficial to people: they are of benefit when eaten, or of benefit when used, or of benefit when resold: all are beneficial. Is there a single article from China which has done any harm to foreign countries? Take tea and rhubarb, for example; the foreign countries cannot get along for a single day without them. . . .

Now we have set up regulations governing the Chinese people. He who sells opium shall receive the death penalty and he who smokes it also the death penalty. Now consider this: if the barbarians do not bring opium, then how can the Chinese people resell it, and how can they smoke it? The fact is that the wicked barbarians beguile the Chinese people into a death trap. How then can we grant life only to these barbarians? He who takes the life of even one person still has to atone for it with his own life; yet is the harm done by opium limited to the taking of one life only? Therefore in the new regulations, in regard to those barbarians who bring opium to China, the penalty is fixed at decapitation or strangulation. This is what is called getting rid of a harmful thing on behalf of mankind. . . .

Our Celestial Dynasty rules over and supervises the myriad states, and surely possesses unfathomable spiritual dignity. . . . The barbarian merchants of your country, if they wish to do business for a prolonged period, are required to obey our statutes respectfully and to cut off permanently the source of opium. They must by no means try to test the effectiveness of the law with their lives. May you, O King, check your wicked and sift your vicious people before they come to China, in order to guarantee the peace of your nation, to show further the sincerity of your politeness and submissiveness, and to let the two countries enjoy together the blessings of peace. How fortunate, how fortunate indeed! After receiving this dispatch will you immediately give us a prompt reply regarding the details and circumstances of your cutting off the opium traffic. Be sure not to put this off.

II. A HIGH OFFICIAL PREDICTS EIGHT WEAKNESSES OF THE BRITISH (1840)

Indulging their petty skill, the rebellious barbarians come to invade our frontiers and capture our cities. What they rely upon is nothing but sturdy ships and large guns. But it is forgotten that the said barbarians run counter to principles of military success in eight points. Provisions being transported over thousands of miles, the soldiers do not have good rest or enough food. Moreover, separated by a long sea route, upon the exhaustion of their original store, it is hard for them to fetch further supplies. This is one weakness.

To cross the seas takes a long time—often over a year on the way back and forth. And amidst the huge waves they can hardly station their troops. In case of the defeat of the first fleet, rescue can scarcely be expected from a near-by force. This is the second weakness.

In the said barbarian country the government is rich while the people are poor. In times of peace, the soldiers are not well cared for. Should these be dispatched to fight tens

The primitive state of the weaponry with which the Chinese faced the British is illustrated by this gingal, a type of early musket that needed to be supported in order to fire. Note the spears, shields, bow and arrows.

of thousands of miles away from their home, how can they, who have no brotherly love at first, possess the spirit to fight enemies? This is their third weakness.

Although the cannons of the said barbarians are fierce, yet the guns are not adapted to shooting skyward. Take, for instance, our fort of Woosung. From the bottom upward, there are the stone base, then the clay base, and finally the fort itself. It is an elevation far above the level of the barbarian ships. If they should shoot upward, the bullets would go down and consequently lose the force of shooting. Moreover, the ships toss up and down with the waves, which fact makes it hard to hit right. This is their fourth weakness.

Although the said barbarians, who take the ships as their home, are at their best in sailing amidst the waves and winds, yet their ships are unwieldy, taking water to a great depth. The line of sand bars is unfamiliar to them. If they are not guided by native pilots, their ships are apt to stand erect once they sail into the shallow waters and the sand bars. That makes them unable to move. This is their fifth weakness.

It is true that their ships are strong. But what fares well with water does not fare well with fire. If our soldiers attack them with fire, their ships can be burned outright. This is their sixth weakness.

The said barbarians are versed in naval warfare. But in waging battles they rely exclusively upon guns. They do not know how to use fists or swords. Moreover, their waist is stiff and their legs straight. The latter, further bound with cloth, can scarcely stretch at will. Once fallen down, they cannot again stand up. It is fatal to fighting on the land. This is their seventh weakness.

The said barbarians were born and bred in foreign countries, and consequently are not used to the climate of China. I have been informed that after the occupation of Tinghai, sickness was widespread and miasma prevailed. Every day there died some barbarians. This is their eighth weakness. The said barbarians having these eight weaknesses, we can surely count upon their defeat.

III. AN ENGLISH COMMANDER DESCRIBES NAVAL OPERATIONS IN CHINA (1840–1841)

[Dec. 1840] Chuenpee, or Shakok, is supposed to be the outer defence to Canton river, but ships can easily pass it, and even through in the direction of Tycocktow (or Taikok) without much danger from shot from either battery. The first battery on the crest of Chuenpee, in the hands of practised gunners with good ordnance, would be a serious obstruction.

The island of Chuenpee is entirely composed of small hills, rising from a general level, which affords good valley passes for troops. By a reconnaissance, almost overlooking the enemy's works, it was evident that troops could advance, if covered by shipping on the west to create a diversion, and that the hill of Chuenpee once in our hands, the batteries beneath were untenable. . . .

The divisions landed about half-past eight. The Samarang led her division in gallant style, direct for the centre of the battery, anchoring within half a cable's length of the walls, followed by the Modeste, Druid, and Columbine; and quickly and gallantly was their work achieved. Queen and Nemesis were duly placed, and dropped their shells prettily, the Queen firing the first shot, or "opening the ball," as Jack had it, when Calliope, Hyacinth, and Larne, anchored and opened on the Lower Chuenpee.

On observing the marines about to enter the upper battery, I transferred myself to Nemesis, and pushed on with our division of boats for the junks, giving Lower Chuenpee a dose of grape and canister, within pistol range. The Nemesis, drawing not more than five and a half or six feet, enabled us to get close up with the junks before opening fire, when several well-directed guns put them completely into confusion. The first rocket pitched into the magazine of the ship next the admiral, and she blew up in great style.

This settled the affair. The boats then moved on, and set fire to the junks in the lower part of the river, but in ascending the main branch, those retreating under canvass kept up a very spirited fire on the chasing boats, very gallantly kept in check by Lieut. Watson, of the Calliope. The increase of force soon decided their fate; two ran on shore, and the remainder made their escape. . . .

[Jan. 1841] Having passed the light squadron during the night, and obtained some observations on Sampanchow, the Calliope, Samarang, Herald, and Alligator, passed up, and about four we rejoined them off Wangtong. A reconnaissance of the enemy's works was immediately made from the southern Wangtong, which they had neither fortified nor occupied; and preparations were accordingly made for constructing a howitzer battery on the saddle neck of that island. . . .

As the breeze was light, and scarcely gave steerage way, the squadron did not move as early as was expected. At daylight Captain Knowles, R. A., opened with his howitzers from South Wangtong, and kept the enemy pretty well amused throughout their lines. About nine o'clock I visited his battery, and took a fair view of the enemy's works, and as soon as the breeze freshened, repaired on board the Calliope. Passing close to the western battery, she was anchored within musket-shot, on its N.W. flank, opposing her broadside to the new works which had been thrown up on that face of the island. Samarang took up her station very prettily under her stern, and the cross fire of the two vessels was beautiful; it acted like masons chipping off the alternate angles of the nearest embrasure.

In a few minutes the enemy were flying; when, by Captain Herbert's direction, I passed to the commodore, and found Wellesley and Druid punishing the western heavy fort. Having communicated "that there was no further opposition," I was ordered to see the troops landed immediately. It required but the sight of our despatch boat to set all the landing boats in motion, forcing my gig high and dry.

On landing, I immediately took possession of the pass above the western battery, and prevented any advance until a commanding officer was found to lead the troops; many of the landing boats' crews having quitted their boats, were sent back. I then directed Commander Fletcher to take the battery at the beach, and moved on with the troops.

Opposition there was none. The unfortunate Chinese literally crammed the trenches, begging for mercy. I wish I could add that it was granted. The Sepoys [Indian troops] fired into them. Wishing to rescue some of them, I went into the trench and drew three out, motioning them to come amongst our troops, and they would be safe. Two were shot down whilst holding by my skirts; and one of my gig's crew, perceiving my danger, dragged me away, exclaiming, "They will shoot you next, sir." Thus much for employing troops who cannot understand English, and will only be commanded by their own officers! . . .

Before sunset the enemy were driven from every post, even from their hill encampment; and the British were the only colours in sight. . . .

An Official Urges That China Learn from the West (1861)

The Opium War ended with the cession of the island of Hong Kong to Great Britain and the liberalization of relations between China and the West, based thereafter on treaties assuring most-favored-nation status to one after another of the Western powers. Chinese reluctance to treat the "barbarians" as equals and the ambition of the West to increase its privileges led to a second war in 1858–1860, in the course of which the British and French captured both Canton and the Imperial capital of Peking. Once again the Chinese were compelled to cede territory and grant even more extensive commercial and legal concessions to the foreigners. These years also saw the great popular rising, the T'ai Ping rebel-

British bombardment of the war junks at Chuenpee Creek.

lion (1850–1864), during which some twenty million people lost their lives. That the government would maintain a rigid attitude toward the Western powers during such a crisis underlines the depth of contempt in which the Court held the West and the disregard of the lessons of 1839. More thoughtful officials, however, saw in China's humiliation an opportunity for a national regeneration that would redirect Chinese energies and return the country to Confucian paths of social discipline and moral awareness. Many of these officials joined in the "self-strengthening" movement that sought to preserve the traditional Chinese way of life through selective adaptation of Western values. A leading spokesman for the movement, Feng Kuei-fen (1809–1874), excerpts from whose writings make up this selection, argued that China must learn to exploit the scientific knowledge and technological development on which Western superiority was based. From William de Bary, Wing-tsit Chan, and Burton Watson, eds., *The Sources of Chinese Tradition* (New York: Columbia University Press, 1960), II, pp. 46–48.

I. WHY WE MUST LEARN FROM THE WEST

According to a general geography compiled by an Englishman, the territory of China is eight times that of Russia, ten times that of the United States, one hundred times that of France, and two hundred times that of Great Britain. . . . Yet we are shamefully humiliated by the four nations, not because our climate, soil, or resources are inferior to theirs, but because our people are inferior. . . . Now, our inferiority is not something allotted us by Heaven, but is rather due to ourselves. If it were allotted us by Heaven, it would be a shame but not something we could do anything about. Since the inferiority is due to ourselves, it is a still greater shame, but something we can do something about. And if we feel ashamed, there is nothing better than self-strengthening. . . .

Why are the Western nations small and yet strong? Why are we large and yet weak? We must search for the means to become their equal, and that depends solely upon human effort. With regard to the present situation, several observations may be made: in not wasting human talents, we are inferior to the barbarians; in not wasting natural resources, we are inferior to the barbarians; in allowing no barrier to come between the ruler and the people, we are inferior to the barbarians; and in the matching of words with deeds, we are also inferior to the barbarians. The remedy for these four points is to seek the causes in ourselves. They can be changed at once if only the emperor would set us in the right direction. There is no need to learn from the barbarians in these matters.

We have only one thing to learn from the barbarians, and that is [how to construct] strong ships and effective guns. . . . Funds should be allotted to establish a shipyard and arsenal in each trading port. A few barbarians should be employed, and Chinese who are good in using their minds should be selected to receive instruction so that in turn they may teach many craftsmen. When a piece of work is finished and is as good as that made by the barbarians, the makers should be rewarded with an official *chü-jen* degree, and be permitted to participate in the metropolitan examinations on the same basis as other scholars. Those whose products are of superior quality should be rewarded with the *chin-shih* degree [ordinarily conferred in the metropolitan examinations], and be permitted to participate in the palace examinations like others. The workers should be paid double so that they will not quit their jobs.

Our nation's emphasis on civil service examinations has sunk deep into people's minds for a long time. Intelligent and brilliant scholars have exhausted their time and energy in such useless things as the stereotyped examination essays, examination papers, and formal calligraphy. . . . We should now order one-half of them to apply themselves to the manufacturing of instruments and weapons and to the promotion of physical studies. . . . The intelligence and ingenuity of the Chinese are certainly superior to those of the various barbarians; it is only that hitherto we have not made use of them. When the government above takes delight in something, the people below will pursue it further: their response will be like an echo carried by the wind. There ought to be some people of extraordinary intelligence who can have new ideas and improve on Western methods. At first they may take the foreigners as their equals; finally they may move ahead and surpass them. Herein lies the way to self-strengthening. . . .

Some have asked why we should not just purchase the ships and man them with [foreign] hirelings, but the answer is that this will not do. If we can manufacture, repair, and use them, then they are our weapons. If we cannot manufacture, repair, or use them, then they are still the weapons of others. . . . In the end the way to avoid trouble is to manufacture, repair, and use weapons by ourselves. Only thus can we pacify the empire; only thus can we become the leading power in the world; only thus can we restore our original strength, redeem ourselves from former humiliations, and maintain the integrity of our vast territory so as to remain the greatest country on earth.

II. HOW WE MUST LEARN FROM THE WEST

Western books on mathematics, mechanics, optics, light, and chemistry contain the best principles of the natural sciences. In the books on geography, the mountains, rivers, strategic points, customs, and native products of the hundred countries are fully listed. Most of this information is beyond the reach of the Chinese people. . . .

If we wish to use Western knowledge, we should establish official translation bureaus in Canton and Shanghai. Brilliant students not over fifteen years of age should be selected from those areas to live and study in these schools on double allowances. Westerners should be appointed to teach them the spoken and written languages of the various nations, and famous Chinese teachers should be engaged to teach them classics, history, and other subjects. At the same time they should learn mathematics. (Note: All Western knowledge is derived from mathematics. . . . If we wish to adopt Western knowledge, it is but natural that we should learn mathematics). . . . China has many brilliant people. There must be some who can learn from the barbarians and surpass them.

It is from learning that the principles of government are derived. In discussing good government, the great historian Ssu-ma Ch'ien said: "Take the latter-day kings as your models." This was because they were nearer in time; their customs had changed from the past and were more similar to the present; and their ideas were not so lofty as to be impracticable. It is my opinion that today we should also take the foreign nations as our examples. They live at the same time and in the same world with us; they have attained prosperity and power by their own efforts. Is

it not fully clear that they are similar to us and that their methods can easily be put into practice? If we let Chinese ethics and Confucian teachings serve as the foundation, and let them be supplemented by the methods used by the various nations for the attainment of prosperity and power, would it not be the best of all solutions? . . .

Imperial China Seeks a Solution (1890)

In the years of comparative calm that succeeded the second Anglo-Chinese War, life in China continued at its traditional pace, seemingly unperturbed by the Western incursions. Beneath the surface, however, the Imperial system was under growing pressure. The helplessness of China became obvious in her quick military defeat in 1894–1895 by Japan, her Asiatic neighbor. Japan had rapidly adopted Western ways after being forced into contact with the West in the 1850s. China, in defeat, ceded to Japan the large island of Formosa (Taiwan) and acknowledged the independence of her long-time vassal state, Korea. Japan's victory set off a race among the European nations to obtain territory and special privileges; by the end of the decade China's continuing existence as a nation seemed doubtful. The government's desperate response, expressed in the fanatical Boxer Uprising of 1900, was to try to drive all foreigners out of the country. The consequence, however, was even more stringent foreign dictation and ultimately, in 1911, revolution and the establishment of a republic.

Under the shadow of Chinese impotence in the 1890s a vigorous internal debate took place concerning the proper policy to follow. Conservatives like Yeh Te-hui (1864–1927) defended the existing order as a manifestation of the Confucian Way. The outstanding reformer K'ang Yu-wei (1858–1927) championed the need for thoroughgoing institutional reform and preached the merits of constitutional monarchy. For a short period (the Hundred Days of 1898) K'ang was placed in a position as chief minister to put his ideas into effect until reactionary forces compelled him to flee the country. Chang Chih-tung (1837–1909), a leading scholar-official, took the more moderate position that though reform was necessary it must be accomplished gradually within the traditional structure of Confucian teaching. The selections are from William de Bary, Wing-tsit Chan, and Burton Watson, eds., *Sources of Chinese Tradition* (Columbia University Press, New York, 1960), II, pp. 71–73, 79–86.

I. YEH TE-HUI PRAISES THE SUPERIORITY OF CHINA

Of all countries in the five continents China is the most populous. It is situated in the north temperate zone, with a mild climate and abundant natural resources. Moreover, it became civilized earlier than all other nations, and its culture leads the world. The boundary between China and foreign countries, between Chinese and barbarians, admits of no argument and cannot be discussed in terms of their strength or our weakness.

Of the four classes of people the scholars are the finest. From the beginning of the present dynasty until today there have been numerous great ministers and scholars who rose to eminence on the basis of their examination essays and poems. Although special

The outstanding figure in China from 1861 to 1908 was the Dowager Empress Tz'u Hsi who dominated the weak emperors and stubbornly refused to countenance change. Symbolic of the decline of the Manchu dynasty is this marble boat that she had constructed at her summer palace in Peking, using funds that had been designated for the building of a modern navy.

examinations have been given and other channels of recruitment have been opened, it is mostly from the regular civil service examinations that men of abilities have risen up. The Western system of election has many defects. Under that system it is difficult to prevent favoritism and to uphold integrity. At any rate, each nation has its own governmental system, and one should not compel uniformity among them.

An examination of the causes of success and failure in government reveals that in general the upholding of Confucianism leads to good government while the adoption of foreignism leads to disorder. If one keeps to kingly rule [relying on virtue], there will be order; if one follows the way of the overlord [relying on power], there will be disorder. . . .

[Mencius said:] "The people are the most important element in a nation," not because the people consider themselves important, but because the sovereign regards them as important. And it is not people's rights that are important. Since the founding of the Ch'ing dynasty our revered rulers have loved the people as their own children. Whenever the nation has suffered from a calamity such as famine, flood, and war, the emperor has immediately given generous relief upon its being reported by the provincial officials. For instance, even though the treasury was short of funds recently, the government did not raise any money from the people except for the *likin* [internal customs duty] tax. Sometimes new financial devices are proposed by ministers who like to discuss pecuniary matters, but even if they are approved and carried out by order of the department concerned, they are suspended as soon as it is learned that they are troubling the people. How vastly different is this from the practice of Western countries where taxes are levied in all places, on all persons, for all things, and at all times?

Confucianism represents the supreme expression of justice in the principles of Heaven and the hearts of men. In the future it will undoubtedly be adopted by civilized countries of both East and West. The essence of Confucianism will shine brightly as it renews itself from day to day.

II. K'ANG YU-WEI URGES THE EMPEROR TO INITIATE REFORM

A survey of all states in the world will show that those states which undertook reforms became strong while those states which clung to the past perished. The consequences of clinging to the past and the effects of opening up new ways are thus obvious. If Your Majesty, with your discerning brilliance, observes the trends in other countries, you will see that if we can change, we can preserve ourselves; but if we cannot change, we shall perish. Indeed, if we can make a complete change, we shall become strong, but if we only make limited changes, we shall still perish. If Your Majesty and his ministers investigate the source of the disease, you will know that this is the right prescription.

Our present trouble lies in our clinging to old institutions without knowing how to change. In an age of competition between states, to put into effect methods appropriate to an area of universal unification and laissez-faire is like wearing heavy furs in summer or riding a high carriage across a river. This can only result in having a fever or getting oneself drowned. . . .

It is a principle of things that the new is strong but the old weak; that new things are fresh but old things rotten; that new things are active but old things static. If the institutions are old, defects will develop. Therefore there are no institutions that should remain unchanged for a hundred years. . . .

Nowadays the court has been undertaking some reforms, but the action of the emperor is obstructed by the ministers, and the recommendations of the able scholars are attacked by old-fashioned bureaucrats. If the charge is not "using barbarians' ways to change China," then it is "upsetting the ancestral institutions." Rumors and scandals are rampant, and people fight each other like fire and water. A reform in this way is as ineffective as attempting a forward march by walking backward. It will inevitably result in failure. Your Majesty knows that under the present circumstances reforms are imperative and old institutions must be abolished. I beg Your Majesty to make up your mind and to decide on the national policy. After the fundamental policy is determined, the methods of implementation must vary according to what is primary and what is secondary, what is important and what is insignificant, what is strong and what is weak, what is urgent and what can wait. . . . If anything goes wrong, no success can be achieved.

After studying ancient and modern institutions, Chinese and foreign, I have found that the institutions of the sage-kings and Three Dynasties [of Hsia, Shang, and Chou] were excellent, but that ancient times were different from today. I hope Your Majesty will daily read Mencius and follow his example of loving the people. The development of the Han, T'ang, Sung, and Ming dynasties may be learned, but it should be remembered that the age of universal unification is different from that of sovereign nations. As to the republican governments of the United States and France and the constitutional governments of Britain and Germany, these countries are far away and their customs are different from ours. Their changes occurred a long time ago and can no longer all be traced. Consequently I beg Your Majesty to adopt the purpose of Peter the Great of Russia as our purpose and to take the Meiji Reform of Japan as the model for our reform. The time and place of Japan's reform are not remote and her religion and customs are somewhat similar to ours. Her success is manifest; her example can be easily followed.

III. CHANG CHIH-TUNG ADVISES MODERATION

The crisis of China today has no parallel either in the Spring and Autumn period [that is, the time of Confucius] or in all the dynasties from the Ch'in and Han down through the Yüan and Ming. . . . Our imperial court has shown the utmost concern over the problem, living in anxiety and worry. It is ready to make changes and to provide special opportunities for able ministers and generals. New schools are to be established and special examinations are to be held. All over the land men of serious purpose and sincere dedication have responded with enthusiasm and vigor. Those who seek to remedy the present situation talk of new learning; those who fear lest its acceptance should destroy the true Way hold fast to the teachings of the ancients. Both groups are unable to strike the mean. The conservatives resemble those who give up all eating because they have difficulty in swallowing, while the progressives are like a flock of sheep who have arrived at a road of many forks and do not know where to turn.

The former do not know how to accommodate to special circumstances; the latter are ignorant of what is fundamental. Not knowing how to accommodate to special circumstances, the conservatives have no way to confront the enemy and deal with the crisis; not knowing the fundamental, the innovators look with contempt upon the teachings of the sages. . . .

Following the Proper Order

If we wish to make China strong and preserve Chinese learning, we must promote Western learning. But unless we first use Chinese learning to consolidate the foundation and to give our purpose a right direction, the strong will become rebellious leaders and the weak, slaves. The consequence will be worse than not being versed in Western learning.

Scholars today should master the Classics in order to understand the purpose of our early sages and teachers in establishing our doctrine. They must study history in order to know the succession of peace and disorder in our history and the customs of the land, read the philosophers and literary collections in order to become familiar with Chinese scholarship and fine writing. After this they can select and utilize that Western learning which can make up for our shortcomings and adopt those Western governmental methods which can cure our illness. In this way, China will derive benefit from Western learning without incurring danger.

STUDY QUESTIONS

1. What values determined the way of life in Imperial China? In what ways did these values encourage China's isolation from the rest of the world?

2. Why, specifically, did the Ch'ien Lung Emperor refuse to establish diplomatic relations with Great Britain? How does his letter illustrate the functioning of the tribute system?

3. What arguments can be made on each side in the dispute about the opium trade between the Chinese government and the Western traders? Might a working agreement have been reached? If so, how?

4. Why does Feng believe that China must learn from the West? What does he see as the most important thing to be learned?

5. How do Yeh, K'ang, and Chang differ in their solutions to China's problems? Could a solution be found in Imperial China without abandoning the foundations upon which the Empire was based?

The Transformation of Japan into a Modern State

Reprinted from Edward McNall Burns and Philip Lee Ralph, *World Civilizations From Ancient to Contemporary*, 3d. ed. (New York: 1964, Norton), II, pp. 366–369, 370–371, 373, 376–381. By permission of W. W. Norton & Co. Inc. Copyright 1964 by W. W. Norton & Co., Inc.

TOPIC 40

THE JAPANESE RESPONSE TO THE WEST

Like China the island empire of Japan had long followed a policy of isolation from the rest of the world. Japan's modern history began in 1853–1854 when the gunboats of American Commodore Matthew Perry forced its military over-lord, the Shogun, whose Tokugawa clan had dominated emperor and empire since the early seventeenth century, to open the country to Western commerce. Unlike China, however, the noble families of Japan quickly recognized Western technological superiority and readily adopted those Western ways that seemed necessary for national self-preservation. The Japanese—industrious, adaptable, proud and sensitive—sought acceptance as equals among the Great Powers. They faced serious obstacles, however, in reaching their goal. Racial prejudice and foreign imperialism threatened Japan's future. The legacy of the struggle posed by this challenge shaped the course of Japanese history in the first half of the twentieth century.

The first important effect of the opening of Japan was that it led to the abolition of the Shogunate, making possible a reorganization of the government along modern lines. The heads of the great "western clans" (Choshu, Satsuma, Hizen, and Tosa) had long been awaiting an opportunity to displace the Tokugawa family from its dominant position. The action of the Shogun in yielding to the

The American expedition commanded by Commodore Perry lands in Tokyo Bay in July, 1853. Perry's instructions were to gain protection from the Tokugawa Shogunate for ship-wrecked American sailors and permission for American ships to refuel and trade in Japan. The Japanese constructed a special enclosure (with conical roofs) to receive the foreigners but stationed a large number of troops (background) on the beach. Perry kept the guns of his two frigates trained on the shore. He commissioned W. Heine, an artist who accompanied the expedition, to sketch this drawing of the encounter.

The Japanese were fascinated by the appearance of the foreign "long noses" as seen in these drawings of the 1860s. Left, children dancing for a foreign audience, by Yoshikazu. Below, an American naval officer and his wife, by Yoshitora.

Western powers provided just such an opportunity. Before signing the treaties the Shogun had taken the unprecedented step of going to Kyoto to consult the emperor. The clan leaders subsequently demanded that the emperor should be restored to his rightful position as ruler, denounced the Shogun for his weakness in submitting to the foreigners, and raised the cry that the "barbarians" must be expelled. The antiforeignism of the western clan leaders was broken by direct action on the part of the "barbarians." In 1863, after an Englishman had been slain by people of the Satsuma *Daimyo* [clan], British vessels bombarded the Satsuma capital. Duly impressed, the Satsuma leaders immediately voiced the desire to acquire a navy like that of Britain. The feudal lords of Choshu were similarly chastened and reoriented in their thinking in 1864 when British, French, Dutch, and United States men-of-war unleashed a joint action upon Shimonoseki. In a remarkably short time the key men of the great feudal estates dropped their attitude of uncompromising hostility to the foreigners, meanwhile becoming more determined than ever to end the outmoded dual system of government.

In 1867 the Shogun was prevailed upon to surrender his prerogatives to the emperor. . . . Upon the abolition of the Shogunate, which had existed for almost 700 years, the imperial residence was moved from Kyoto to Edo, renamed Tokyo ("Eastern Capital"), and the old castle of the Shogun was converted into an imperial palace. This series of events constituted what is known as the Meiji Restoration.

It so happened that the Emperor Mutsuhito, a lad of fifteen at the time of the Restoration, proved to be an extremely capable person who helped materially in the task of reorganizing Japanese institutions. The years of his reign, known as the Meiji or "Enlightened" era (1867–1912), witnessed the emergence of Japan as a modern and powerful state. Nevertheless, it would be a mistake to attribute Japan's transformation to the initiative of the emperor. As in previous periods of the country's history, effective leadership was supplied by less exalted figures, who used the throne as a symbol to promote a sentiment of national solidarity and to give the sanction of authority to their program. Quite understandably, the leaders in the political field were recruited chiefly from the

ranks of feudal society, although they included some members of the old court nobility. In spite of their aristocratic backgrounds, however, the leaders were quick to perceive the necessity of breaking with the past if genuine progress along Western lines was to be achieved. Some of the western clans voluntarily liquidated feudal institutions within their own jurisdiction, urging others to follow their example, and in 1871 the emperor formally abolished the whole feudal system. . . .

The sweeping political, social, economic, and intellectual changes which took place in Japan during the Meiji era were sufficient to constitute a revolution. However, they were not the result of a mass movement or of any tumultuous upheaval from the bottom of society. The revolution was one directed and carefully controlled from above. The fact that the Tokugawa regime had already unified the country and through its discipline had instilled habits of docility in the population facilitated the work of the Restoration leaders. The majority of the population played only a passive role in the transformation, even though they were profoundly affected by it.

In carrying out their carefully channeled

This seventeenth century helmet and mask symbolize the feudal system that held sway in Japan until the Meiji era.

revolution, Japan's leaders made a painstaking study of the institutions of all the major Western nations and copied, with adaptations, what seemed to be the best features of each. In the political sphere, they reached the conclusion that the principles of constitutional monarchy should be introduced. A bold but somewhat ambiguous statement of policy known as the Emperor's Charter Oath (1868), had hinted at the establishment of a deliberative assembly; but when plans for the drafting of a constitution were announced, it was made clear that any concessions would be in the nature of a gift from the throne rather than in recognition of inherent popular rights. A handpicked commission drafted a constitution which, promulgated by the emperor in 1889, was patterned somewhat after the model of the German Imperial Constitution of 1871. . . . In spite of some liberal features, the conservative character of the new government was unmistakable. So high was the property qualification for voting that only about 1 per cent of the population was enfranchised. The position of the emperor was declared to be inviolable; he retained supreme command of the army and navy, directed foreign affairs, and could veto bills passed by the Diet. Notably lacking was the principle of parliamentary control over the executive; ministers were responsible not to the Diet but to the emperor. . . .

The economic changes of the Meiji era were perhaps even more significant than the political. In Tokugawa feudal days Japan was far from being a purely agrarian nation, and before the Restoration of 1867 an urban economy, chiefly mercantile and capitalistic, had come into being. When the new regime undertook to strengthen the state and secure the benefits of Westernization, an ambitious program was launched for the development

of industry and a modern system of communications. Because private capital was not available in sufficient quantities to do the job quickly and because Japanese patriotism frowned upon extensive borrowing from foreign investors, the government assumed the initiative in constructing railroads, telegraph

In a move to familiarize the population with highlights of Western culture, illustrated commentaries were produced, such as this Yokahama print which drolly depicts the moment when John James Audubon returns from a trip and finds his manuscript, entailing years of labor, eaten up by mice.

and telephone lines, docks, shipyards, and even manufacturing plants, while it also aided private industry by loans and subsidies. There was no tradition of *laissez faire* in Japan to stand in the way of government participation in the economic sphere, and public officials were anxious to move ahead as rapidly as possible. However, many enterprises which had been fostered by the state were eventually transferred to private hands, although the state retained control of railways and communications for strategic and security reasons. Hence, in Japan, economic progress led to the growth of a capitalist class, but one which did not correspond exactly with similar classes in the Western industrial nations. The members of the new capitalist class, like the prominent political figures, were drawn largely from the old aristocracy. . . .

Industrial developments in Japan in the late nineteenth and early twentieth centuries differed in several respects from the typical pattern of economic change in the West. In the first place, they were so rapid that in one generation the country was producing a surplus of manufactured goods, and foreign markets had become essential to the national economy. Second, the Industrial Revolution was transported to Japan after it had already reached an advanced stage in the Western nations, and consequently characteristics of the First and Second Industrial Revolutions were intermingled. The employment of women in industry at low wages, the lack of organization among the laborers or of legal safeguards to protect them, and the working conditions in factories and mines were parallel to the early stages of the Industrial Revolution in the West. On the other hand, the projection of the government into the business sphere and the appearance of finance

capitalism were phenomena that were only beginning to manifest themselves in Western Europe and the United States. To a considerable extent in Japan, finance capitalism preceded industrial capitalism, because there had not been time for financial reserves to accumulate from the savings effected by a gradual mechanization of industry. The wealth of the aristocracy and of merchant and banking houses—essentially unproductive classes—was drawn upon to expedite industrial progress, and the fortunate members of these groups were in a position to dominate the productive enterprises of mining, manufacturing, and distribution as these grew to maturity. . . .

In passing successfully through the difficult years of the Restoration period, the Japanese gave abundant evidence of vitality, courage, and versatility. In many fields they had come abreast of the Western nations, while they had also retained their own distinctive cultural heritage. At the same time, the accomplishments were not an unmixed good, and social problems had arisen which could not be easily solved. . . . Scientific knowledge, improved sanitation and medical facilities, and especially the impact of the Industrial Revolution induced a terrific increase in a population that had remained almost stationary for over a century. Between 1867 and 1913, the population grew from about 30 million to more than 50 million, and from this time on the rate of growth was still more rapid. There was not enough arable land in Japan to produce food for such large numbers, even under the most efficient methods of cultivation. While a brisk foreign trade could correct the deficiency, not only was a sufficient volume of trade difficult to maintain but the profits from manufacturing and commerce were concentrated in the hands of

The blessings of Western Civilization are introduced to Japan. This woodcut by Yoshifuji shows a locomotive and foreign sailing ships in the harbor of Yokahama.

a small group. The standard of living of the farmers—the great majority of the population—remained almost at a standstill while the total national income was rising. . . .

Japan's external relations during the Meiji era were directly related to, and appreciably affected by, her internal development. It is not strange that Japan, in the process of becoming a modern state, adopted a policy of imperialism, in view of her agility in assimilating the techniques of Western nations and also in view of the stresses created by the industrialization of the country. . . .

Japanese expansion in Eastern Asia would almost inevitably be at the expense of the decadent Chinese Empire. In 1876, the Japanese government took direct steps to end the isolation of Korea, a "hermit nation" which had been as tightly sealed against outside influences as Japan under the Tokugawa Shogunate. Copying a page from the Western book, the Japanese negotiated a treaty with the Seoul government which accorded them extraterritoriality and other rights, as well as opening Korea to commercial intercourse. The treaty also recognized Korea as an independent state, in total disregard of the fact that the Peking government considered the peninsula a tributary dependency of the Manchu Empire. Actually the Manchu officials

had neglected to enforce their claims, and their belated attempt to recover their position by counterintrigue against the Japanese was almost certain to provoke a clash with Japan. Korea, at this time, was an ideal breeding ground for war. In spite of brilliant episodes in its past, the kingdom had degenerated into one of the most backward regions of Asia. The administration was corrupt and predatory, the peasants ignorant and wretched, and conditions in general thoroughly belied the country's poetic name—Chosen ("Land of the Morning Calm"). Japan's interest in Korea was both economic and strategic, the latter because Russia had acquired the Maritime Province on the Pacific coast directly north of the Korean border and had already attempted to intervene in Korea's troubled affairs. After a local rebellion had furnished the excuse for both China and Japan to rush troops into Korea, the Sino-Japanese war was precipitated.

It could be—and has been—argued that, beginning with her swift victory over China in 1895, Japan's policy in Asia was one of territorial aggression. In the treaty of Shimonoseki, Japan required from China not only recognition of Korean independence and the payment of an indemnity but also the cession of Formosa, the Pescadores Islands, and the southern projection of Manchuria—the Liaotung Peninsula. Japan joined in the scramble for concessions in China, acquiring a sphere of interest in Fukien province opposite Formosa. When harassed by the advance of Russian imperialism in Korea, Japan attacked Russia in 1904 and, after defeating her on land and sea, annexed the southern half of Sakhalin Island and obtained economic concessions in Manchuria. These facts, however, are only part of the story, which in its entirety indicates that the Japanese were adept in mastering the object lessons of European diplomacy and power politics. Following the

In spite of the vast changes during the Meiji Era, the rural masses continued their traditional way of life.

JAPAN TO THE GREAT BEAR: "Twinkle, twinkle, little star; how I wonder what you are up to!"

Japanese concern about Russian intentions in Manchuria is illustrated in this cartoon of 1904 in the Chicago *Tribune*.

Sino-Japanese war, under pressure from Russia, France, and Germany, Japan had been forced to relinquish her claim to the Liaotung Peninsula, on the ground that occupation of this region by a foreign power would threaten the safety of the Peking government. Almost immediately afterward, Russia, by a treaty of alliance with China, secured control of the very region she had denied to Japan and converted practically all Manchuria into a Russian sphere of interest. Several attempts on the part of the Japanese government to reach an accommodation with Russia in regard to Korea and Manchuria were frustrated by the recklessness and duplicity of the Tsar's agents. Nevertheless, some influential Japanese considered war with Russia too dangerous an undertaking, and the government would probably not have dared to attack

Russia except for the fact that the Anglo-Japanese Alliance of 1902 assured Japan of the friendly backing of the world's greatest naval power. The British welcomed Japan's accession to a position of strength as a means of checking Russian expansion in the Far East. During the Russo-Japanese war, sentiment in both Great Britain and the United States was prevailingly in favor of Japan, largely because of the devious and bullying tactics that the Russians had been pursuing. President Theodore Roosevelt's sympathy for Japan helped in terminating the hostilities, and the peace treaty was negotiated at Portsmouth, New Hampshire.

Japan's victory over Russia seemed for a time to restore a balance of power in the Far East. Russia, shaken by her Revolution of 1905, and Japan, her financial reserves drained by the war, quickly agreed on apportioning their respective spheres in Manchuria—publicly affirming, of course, that they had no intention of violating China's territorial integrity. But the balance of power proved to be unstable. The outbreak of the European war in 1914, necessitating a "retreat of the West" from Asia, provided Japan with a golden opportunity to consolidate and extend her position.

Japanese Arms Defeat a Western Power (1905)

The rapid successes of the Japanese army and navy in the war with Russia (1904–1905) amazed the nations of the West. One of the most spectacular feats was the total destruction of the Russian fleet in the Straits of Tsushima between Japan and Korea, after it had moved halfway around the world from its base in the Baltic Sea. The Russian command, confident that the Japanese would have to disperse their navy to protect the various approaches to the home islands, carelessly opted to proceed by the shortest route to Vladivostok. They were taken by surprise by the entire Japanese fleet in a relatively narrow area where the advantages of maneuverability lay with the defenders. Superior speed, handling, and fire power clinched the Japanese victory. In the first selection captured Russian officers, interviewed by an American journalist, estimate the reasons for their defeat. From George Kennan, "The Destruction of the Baltic Fleet," *Outlook* (July, 1905), pp. 818–819. A Japanese assessment is provided in the second selection. From *The New York Times*, August 1, 1905, p. 1.

I. THE RUSSIANS ACKNOWLEDGE JAPANESE SUPERIORITY

The reasons assigned by the Russian officers for their disastrous defeat are briefly, as follows:

1. Insufficient information with regard to the whereabouts and disposition of Admiral Togo's ships.

2. The superior speed of the Japanese vessels, which enabled them to take the positions that were most advantageous and to fight, throughout the engagement, at ranges of their own choosing. The Russian ships had been cleaned as well as was possible to clean them without docking facilities, but their bottoms were all foul, and not one of them could make anything like its record speed.

3. The surprising and extraordinary accuracy of the Japanese gun-fire at long ranges.

This, the officers of the Orel think, was the decisive factor in the contest. They agree in stating that their ships were overwhelmed and defeated by gun-fire long before a torpedo-boat was brought into action. . . .

"At a distance of four miles," said Lieutenant X_____, "the Japanese gunners seemed to hit us with almost every shot that they fired, and if you've been through the Orel, you know what they did to us. Our men had not had practice enough to shoot accurately at such ranges. We hoped that we might be able to crowd Togo's ships up toward the land on the Japan side of the strait, and so get nearer to them; but they were too fast for us. They circled around ahead of us, and knocked us to pieces at such long ranges that we were barely able to see them through the mist. . . ."

4. The extraordinary efficiency and destructiveness of shells loaded with Shimose powder. I have already described the effects produced by these shells, and need only add here that the officers of the Orel fully confirmed my judgment with regard to them. They attribute the disabling of their ships largely to the explosive peculiarities of these projectiles.

5. The amount of interior woodwork in many of the Russian ships—particularly the battle-ships—and the presence of coal in bags on their decks. Everything combustible was set on fire by the Shimose shells, and the conflagrations that ensued demoralized the crews, distracted their attention from their proper work, and sometimes enshrouded the vessels in such dense clouds of smoke that the officers and gunners could see nothing whatever of the fight. "We suffered less from this cause than some of the other ships did," said Lieutenant X_____, "because we had less woodwork, but even on the Orel everything seemed to burn, down to the very

paint. In the first stage of the battle the Kniaz Suvaroff appeared to be burning, with a clear flame, from one end to the other."

6. The neutral gray paint of the Japanese ships, which, in the gray mist that hung over the sea on the 27th, made them almost invisible at distances of three and four miles. The Russian battle-ships were painted black.

Finally, the Russian officers attribute their defeat in general to good judgment and great skill on the Japanese side. "Looking at it from their point of view," said Lieutenant X_____, "it would be hard to imagine a better-planned or better-fought battle."

II. THE JAPANESE ATTRIBUTE THEIR VICTORY TO THE EMPEROR

Three hundred of the leading Japanese in New York gathered at the Nippon Club, 44 West Eighty-fifth Street, last night to listen to addresses by some of the heroes of the fleet that smashed the Russian navy about Port Arthur and in the Sea of Japan. The peace envoys kept away from the reception, where the topic was to be war and the retelling of Japan's amazing victory.

The Japanese naval officers, Commander Kamimura, Commander Oguro, and Lieut.

A Japanese woodcut of the sinking of the Russian battleship Petropavlovsk during the Russo-Japanese War.

Commander Sato, told the stories of their exploits in the simplest and most unassuming manner. The guests sat silent, as they listened to the stories of their country's triumphs, with lips apart like children listening to the story of Jack the Giant Killer. There were no shouts of "Banzai."

When the story of the victory was being told the Japanese would laugh for the pure joy of it and then clap their hands because Jack had bested the Giant. Throughout the addresses, which were short, the men of the navy of Japan interjected frequently Togo's phrase that it had happened because of "the virtue of the Emperor of Japan." These observations were reverently received and accepted as the true explanation of the great victory.

At the conclusion of the addresses a reception was held in the parlors of the club, where there was not one battleflag to be seen. There was no singing of the Japanese national anthem. Vice President Arie of the club acted as Chairman and introduced the speakers. Commander Kamimura of the armored cruiser Tokiwa, who received the surrender of the Russian battleships, said in part:

"Through the virtue of the Emperor our ships were in splendid shape, and our crews worked at the guns, in the bowels of the ships, and wherever men had duties to perform, just as if it had been a drill. There was no one afraid, and every man of the fleet was fit and ready for his work.

"Through the virtue of the Emperor we had the advantage of position with the sunlight shining in the faces of a foe we had trapped. There was no escape for him, even if he was brave.

"Through the virtue of the Emperor, we had had target practice in all sorts of weather, and could shoot straight in a rough sea as well as a smooth one. It was in this way that we won.

"Through the virtue of the Emperor, it was my honor to take charge of the surrendered Russian battleships. Admiral Togo could not spare many of us, and so when we took charge it was a big task. Some of our officers could speak a little Russian, French, and English. The Russians could speak almost any language in a way. They acted in good faith, but it was a difficult job at skillful navigation, with wounded ships under commanders who could not always make their orders understood.

"Through the virtue of the Emperor you may rely on the army and the navy of your native land. It remains for you to be industrious in studying the ways of American success in commerce for the glory of Japan and the peace of the world."

The other speakers likewise ascribed every success to the virtue of the Emperor.

The Japanese Experience Racial Prejudice

Tied by treaty to Great Britain since 1902 and encouraged by the friendly support of the Roosevelt administration in the United States in bringing the war to an end, the Japanese felt that their stunning victory over Russia had earned them recognition as an equal member of the Western community of powers. To their confusion they learned that their successes led to growing suspicion of Japanese foreign policy and to a conspicuous increase in white racism. Three examples of these racial attitudes are included in this reading. The first selection describes an attempt of the San Francisco Board of Education to segregate Japanese students within the school system. There was marked anti-Japanese feeling in California, stemming partly from racial antipathy as the numbers of Japanese immigrants grew (by 1900, 12,000 Japanese were arriving annually) but also from the fears of organized labor for Japanese competition. Rapid deterioration of Japanese-American relations was prevented only by the exertions of President Theodore Roosevelt who managed to get the San Francisco resolution reversed in 1907. The second selection relates an episode from the world cruise of the American battleship fleet in 1907–1909. President Roosevelt was desirous of dramatizing the fighting strength of the new American navy both to the American public and to foreign nations; the enthusiastic welcome received by the fleet in New Zealand and Australia betrayed deep anti-Oriental sentiments. Reprinted from Thomas A. Bailey, *Theodore Roosevelt and the Japanese-American Crises* (Stanford University Press, 1934), pp. 14–15, 28–29, 281–284, with the permission of the publisher. Copyright © 1971 by the Board of Trustees of Leland Stanford Junior University.

The third selection is drawn from a somewhat later period. At the conference meeting at Paris in 1919 to draft terms of peace following the World War, the Japanese representatives vainly attempted to add a statement on racial equality to the Covenant of the League of Nations. They were no more successful when they reduced their request to recognition of "the principle of equality

Racial prejudice on the Pacific coast is reflected in this magazine illustration of San Francisco idlers molesting a Chinese laborer.

for nations and just treatment of their nationals." The selection describes the treatment of this "hot potato" by the men who were championing the creation of a new world at Versailles. From Roy W. Curry, *Woodrow Wilson and Far Eastern Policy, 1913–1921* (New York, Bookman Associates, 1957) pp. 253–257. Copyright 1957 by Bookman Associates. Reprinted by permission of the publisher.

I. THE SAN FRANCISCO SCHOOL BOARD ORDERS SEGREGATION (1906)

The first significant move in the direction of segregation was made on April 1, 1905. On that day, a year and a half before the final order, the San Francisco Board of Education presented to the Board of Supervisors a budget which provided for the construction of added facilities at the Chinese school, which, it was proposed, all the Japanese chil-

dren throughout the city should attend. But since the Board of Supervisors could not overstep the one-dollar tax-rate limit imposed by the charter, the money for this purpose was not made available. . . .

A cartoon in the English humor magazine *Punch* in 1906 raises a serious political issue: Did the United States have the power to compel the individual states to conform to the terms of the treaties it made with other sovereign nations? The Japanese Government has complained that its treaty with the United States has been infringed by the refusal of the Californian high schools to admit Japanese children. The federal government, however, has apparently no power to enforce obedience, on the part of individual American states, to the terms of its own treaty.

JAPAN: May I ask, are you the "United" States?
UNCLE SAM: Waal, I can't say right away, I'm just consultin' California on that vurry point.

Nothing daunted by this obstacle in the way of its first step toward segregation, the Board of Education passed a resolution on May 6, 1905, which read:

RESOLVED, That the board of education is determined in its efforts to effect the establishment of separate schools for Chinese and Japanese pupils, not only for the purpose of relieving the congestion at present prevailing in our schools, but also for the higher end that our children should not be placed in any position where their youthful impressions may be affected by association with pupils of the Mongolian race.

In the meantime, the leadership of the anti-Japanese movement in San Francisco had fallen into the hands of union labor, which then held the city in its grip. Meetings were called, and the boycotting of Japanese or those who employed them was urged. On May 7, 1905—a day of great significance in the history of Pacific Coast anti-Japanese agitation—a mass meeting was held at which the Japanese and Korean Exclusion League was launched. The major objective of this organization was to secure, through propaganda and various other kinds of pressure, and extension of the Chinese exclusion laws to the Japanese. Late in 1906 the League claimed a membership of 78,500 in California alone, three-fourths of whom were said to live in San Francisco. This organization also worked for a boycott of the Japanese, and on October 22, 1905, instructed its executive committee to appear before the Board of Education and petition that body to carry out the League's avowed policy of segregating the Mongolian children of the city.

On August 23, 1906, the Exclusion League again made representations to the Board of

Education, on this occasion protesting against the alleged crowding of white children in the schools by the Japanese. The Board replied that every effort was being made to seat the whites first but that a lack of funds prevented the erection of a separate building for the Japanese. Then it was that the Chinese school, which had been rebuilt after the fire,* provided the Board with an opportunity to take the action that it had long been contemplating. When this school was reopened, fewer Chinese children enrolled than had previously done so. There was room, apparently, for the ninety-three Japanese pupils elsewhere in attendance in the public schools of the city. Accordingly, at its meeting of October 11, 1906, the Board passed the following resolution, which was soon to produce international repercussions:

> RESOLVED, That in accordance with Article X, section 1662, of the school law of California, principals are hereby directed to send all Chinese, Japanese, or Korean children to the Oriental Public School, situated on the south side of Clay street, between Powell and Mason streets, on and after Monday, October 15, 1906.

II. AUSTRALIANS CHEER THE AMERICAN "WHITE" FLEET (1908)

After a week in Hawaii, during which the picturesque hospitality of the islands was lavished upon the officers and men, the fleet began its long voyage to Auckland, New Zealand, which was reached on August 9, 1908. The overwhelming exuberance of the reception there led an eyewitness to write: "Cali-

*San Francisco had been devastated by a massive earthquake followed by widespread fires in April, 1906 [eds.].

fornia went mad; New Zealand not only went fleet mad but it developed a new disease—fleetitis." Admiral Sperry told the London *Times* correspondent that the Auckland reception was more enthusiastic than any encountered on the western coast of America. The welcome of Sydney [Australia], where the fleet arrived on August 20, 1908, was even more unrestrained. By the time the ships had left Melbourne and Albany, Admiral Seaton Schroeder could write that "no possible vehicle of greeting was left unharnessed"; and Roosevelt later described as "wonderful" the "considerate, generous, and open-handed hospitality" of these people.

The white Australian ideal . . . was widely interpreted in the United States as the fundamental reason for the hysterical greeting. . . . Facing the teeming Orient, the Australians had for some time lived in dread of a yellow inundation, and this fear accounted for their "white Australia" policy and the recently developed emphasis on national defense. The renewal of the Anglo-Japanese alliance in

1905 had led to some misgivings in Australia that England was weakening in her support of the white ideal, and the greeting given the Americans may well have been an attempt to remind the mother country of her imperial obligations. In July, 1908, the Prime Minister of New Zealand, Sir Joseph Ward, made a speech in which he expressed the belief that in the future fight to determine white or Oriental supremacy the United States would stand shoulder to shoulder with the Australians. Shortly after the Australian invitation had been extended, the Melbourne *Age*, perhaps the most influential newspaper in Australia, observed:

> Ever since the renewal of the Anglo-Japanese alliance the naval supremacy of the Pacific has been in the hands of Japan . . . the effect . . . has been to place our rich, sparsely settled, and as yet undefended country more or less at the mercy of a colored race whom our "white Australian" ideal has bitterly offended.

The U.S. fleet passes Samoa.

The amazing advance of Japan into the rank of a first class Power and her newly conceived colonising ambitions, fortunately for us, have aroused our American cousins, and persuaded them to make a bid to recapture for the Anglo-Saxon blood the naval predominancy in the Pacific which Britain lately relinquished. Japan is at present our Imperial ally. . . . Nevertheless we are unfeignedly glad that America has invaded the Pacific. It is a move that cannot help but lessen our danger of Asiatic aggression and strengthen the grounds of our national security.

III. THE PRINCIPLE OF RACIAL EQUALITY IS DEFEATED AT VERSAILLES (1919)

The day following the opening session of the League of Nations Commission under the chairmanship of Wilson, Makino and Chinda [Japanese delegates] came to solicit the good offices of Colonel House [President Wilson's confidant] for support of their project to include guarantees of racial equality in the Covenant. The Colonel advised them to prepare two resolutions: one containing their full desires and another comprising the minimum they would accept. The following day, they brought the resolutions to House who showed them to Wilson. After discussing the two resolutions, the President made some changes in the acceptable proposal and said he wished to discuss the matter with his colleagues. Chinda then brought a new draft on the race question, since the Japanese legal adviser said the former proposals were innocuous. Birdsall suggests that they had learned that Prime Minister William H. Hughes of Australia had resolved to resist unalterably any provision suggesting racial

equality in the treaty, and thereupon realized the inability of the United States to stand for the desired clause. They then decided to advance an unacceptable demand on the point so as to gain respect at home. Hunter Miller thought the Japanese refused the House-Wilson draft because it was but a stated principle and had no legal effect. He observed that any draft on racial equality having a real legal obligation had no chance of approval. Lord Robert Cecil, the House of the British delegation told the Colonel that the "British would not agree to it at all, probably not in any form."

The Japanese on February 13, attempted to amend Article 19 of the original draft of the League Covenant containing the statement: "The High Contracting Parties agree that they will make no law prohibiting or interfering with the free exercise of religion, and that they will in no way discriminate either in law or in fact (against any religion). . . ." To this the Japanese desired to insert also racial equality. This was a reasonable request, but they were persuaded to drop it. The following day the League Covenant was presented at the plenary session, and immediately thereafter Wilson left for Washington to sign bills and take care of administrative affairs at the end of session.

On the day Wilson left Washington to return to Paris, March 4, 1919, Japanese Ambassador Ishii handed Breckenridge Long a memorandum for the President concerning racial equality. Long managed to get it to the White House within the hour of Wilson's leaving. In the memorandum the Japanese Government expressed its appreciation for the President's "sympathy and support" in abolishing racial discrimination. Japan regarded it as a basic principle and should it "fail of general recognition the Japanese Government do not see how a perpetual

friction and discontent among nations and races could possibly be eliminated." Therefore, their representatives at Paris would continue to agitate for its adoption and Tokyo hoped the President would support them in the matter. . . .

The Japanese appeal for the President's support of racial equality was followed on March 14 by an address of Ambassador Ishii at a dinner of the Japan Society in New York. Ishii attempted to allay the public fear that such a provision in the League would interfere with American immigration policy. Telegrams from the Japanese residents of Hawaii and from thirty-seven Japanese Associations in Tokyo petitioning for racial equality were presented to the Council session. In late March, Marquis Okuma, "the grand old man of Japanese politics," prepared a discourse on racial equality which was read at a mass meeting in Tokyo. While he indorsed Wilson's idea of the League, he stated the solution of the racial question was essential "in order to avoid future strife among nations arising out of the present unequal distribution of natural riches. . . ."

The Tokyo Embassy informed Washington that Marquis Okuma, in a press interview, stated the issue of racial equality was vital to Japan and, though she might wait for a considerable time, "if not finally conceded by the Powers Japan should resolve to withdraw from the League of Nations." At this time, Benjamin Fleisher, a correspondent in Tokyo, found the race equality question the leading topic of discussion there. The Japanese Government through *Kokusai*, the leading news service, and other channels was "disseminating (the) race equality discussion broadly through many countries in Asia." The *Nippon Dempo* agency was circulating to the local and country press ridiculous statements of

American arms shipments to China. Meanwhile, fearing that racial equality would be written into the League, the San Francisco Board of Supervisors sent resolutions to Washington and to Paris opposing any such action.

The racial equality issue came to a decision on April 11, when Baron Makino proposed an insertion in the preamble endorsing "the principle of equality of nations and just treatment of their nationals." This was a mild statement, and Wilson was willing to agree with it; but House passed the President a note, "The trouble is that if this Commission should pass it, it would surely raise the race issue throughout the world." Cecil, the British representative, under instructions from his government, shamefacedly objected to it. Hughes had threatened to make an issue of any such concession to the Japanese. Wilson realized the Hughes threat was no idle one; he had learned much of the strength of the opposition in Washington during his return trip in February; he possibly recalled the racial issue in California; it was not a problem foreign to American politics; the British were unalterably opposed. House was right. The President, who was chairman of the body, then spoke opposing the proposal as unnecessary, maintaining that controversies outside the Commission would be entailed in the amendment, and that equality need not be mentioned since it was a fundamental principle of the League—the very spirit of its Covenant. Makino insisted on a vote, and eleven of the seventeen members favored the Japanese proposal. Since the order of the Commission on the League called for unanimous consent, the amendment was rejected. No contrary vote was taken. British and American abstinence from voting had defeated one of the strongly-held objectives of the Japanese mission—racial equality.

Akira Iriye: Japan Assesses its Position in the World

The Japanese were thus faced with a dilemma that challenged the very meaning of the Meiji Restoration. Should Japan, her policy-makers deliberated, continue to follow a policy that assumed that the Westernized Asiatic state would be regarded as an equal in a Western-dominated world? Or did the covert racism at Versailles and America's own stake in the Pacific islands (Hawaii, the Philippines, Guam) indicate instead that Japan's future lay in championing a policy of Asia for Asians, pursued through a growth in Japan's influence over China? How American behavior and the political uncertainties it engendered affected the thinking of Japan's leaders is the subject of this reading taken from Professor Akira Iriye's (1934–) study of the genesis of American-Japanese antagonism. From Akira Iriye, *Across the Pacific: An Inner History of American-East Asian Relations*, (New York: Harcourt Brace Jovanovich, 1967), pp. 111–112, 114–117. Copyright © by Harcourt Brace Jovanovich. Reprinted by permission of the publisher.

In 1908 Hara Kei, a prominent Japanese politician, visited the United States for the first time. He was deeply impressed with America's economic might and its latent but unmistakable influence in world politics. He felt that even Europe, which he had seen in 1886 and now revisited, had come under America's political, economic, and even cultural influence. He vowed that an understanding with the United States would be a basic prerequi-site for Japanese policy. This was because America represented the inevitable trend in human affairs; to him it seemed obvious that the vitality of the American people, nurtured by democratic institutions, indicated the wave of the future. Japan's task was to identify itself with the trend; friendship with America was thus a logical necessity. Ten years later, in 1918, Hara became Japan's prime minister. His image of the United States had stayed with him, but to his dismay he found how difficult it was to effect understanding with America. Relations between the two countries had deteriorated during the preceding decade, and self-conscious antagonism between Japanese and Americans had become as much a fact of international relations as American-Japanese co-operation and compatibility before 1905. . . .

The Japanese had assumed that they could continue to count on friendly relations with the United States. As in the past, they believed that Japan's rights on the [Asian] continent, now vastly augmented, would require political understanding with and economic assistance of Western nations. "Japan must try at least to satisfy and obtain the sympathies of Britain and the United States," said Itō Hirobumi [1841–1909, leading Japanese statesman of the Meiji period] in 1906. It was imperative to eschew adventurism in Asia, which would cause the nation to lose the confidence of the Western powers, and to deepen economic ties with them so as to finance the newly acquired empire. The acceptance of the military and political status quo after the war, and of economic interdependence with Western powers, was the basic framework of Japanese foreign policy. To their dismay, however, Japan's leaders soon came to feel that the policy was not producing results as in the past. For instance, at the end of 1907, the year when Japan had successfully entered into political agreements with France and Russia to uphold their mutual rights in East Asia, Itō had to admit, "Japan's position in the world is most grievous. The situation is such that there is an unmistakable trend toward Japanese isolation." Despite the alliance with Britain and the agreements with France and Russia, he felt there was abroad an underlying suspicion of Japan and that the nation was not accepted as an equal. Contrary to the general belief in Japan's role between East and West, its position seemed more precarious than ever before. Itō was particularly dismayed by the racial prejudice displayed by certain groups in the United States.

The response of Japan's governmental leaders to the anti-Japanese moves in America is most illuminating. The anti-Japanese movement was naturally a blow to the Japanese, who felt they had done all they could to allay the Western fear of a yellow peril and to continue to act within the framework of understanding with the West. The only way they could explain the apparently incomprehensible phenomenon of race prejudice was by regarding it as a product of irrational minorities in America. As Foreign Minister Hayashi Tadasu wrote, the anti-Japanese agitation was attributable to irresponsible journalists and labor leaders in certain parts of the United States; it could not conceivably lie deeper. It must be a temporary and transient phenomenon, which would pass in due course. Hayashi dismissed war scares on both side of the Pacific as nonsense. The whole immigration episode would soon be forgotten as an unhappy but by no means inevitable page in the otherwise friendly history of Japanese-American relations. Much more important were the two countries' economic interdependence and general agreement on the status quo in East Asia.

Such a line of reasoning was behind Tokyo's eagerness to show evidence of its continued interest in understanding with the United States. The Root-Takahira agreement of 1908, mutually recognizing the status quo in the Pacific and proclaiming Japan's adherence to the Open Door principle, was one such attempt. Another was the rousing welcome the Japanese gave to the United States fleet in 1909, when it visited East Asia as part of its world cruise. . . . As the Japanese naval attaché in Washington wrote, the world cruise of the American fleet was obviously intended to demonstrate American naval power in the Pacific. Under the circumstances, he wrote, the best tactic for Japan was to impress American visitors with Japan's genuine interest in peace between the two peoples, so that the American people would give up their anti-Japanese prejudice. The naval and civilian leaders in Tokyo fully agreed and did all they could to show their sincere and friendly sentiments to the visitors. . . .

Nevertheless, many Japanese were coming to the realization that their relations with America were no longer what they had been. No matter how hard they tried to minimize the racial question, no matter how desperately they clung to an image of East and West harmonized through Japan, Western prejudice did not seem to abate. The gentlemen's agreements, in which Japan pledged to prohibit the emigration of laborers to the United States, did not satisfy the west coast agitators, who pushed for restrictive measures against Japanese already in America. Tokutomi Sohō, who had earlier preached Japan's mission between East and West, now came to admit that the country had no true friend in the world. Writing in 1911, he said that despite alliances and ententes Japan was merely an isolated entity. More than that, there seemed to be no real value in international sympathy and understanding. Japan must henceforth be resolute and carry out what it believed to be in its interests, regardless of other nations' attitudes. As though suddenly shaken out of his illusion, he now concluded that universal brotherhood, East-West harmony, and similar notions had merely expressed Japan's wishful thinking, derived from a sense of insecurity.

If the immigration dispute with the United States brought to the Japanese the awareness of irrational factors in international relations, developments in China likewise forced them to re-examine the policy of co-operative action with the West in East Asia. These were years of momentous political change in China, leading to the overthrow of the Manchu dynasty in 1912. This was also the time when the Chinese began their serious attempt at halting the tide of foreign encroachment. These two currents—the political crisis and the "rights recovery movement"—confronted the powers with serious new problems. Japan in particular was deeply involved, since the country had been a haven for Chinese revolutionaries, and since the Chinese nationalists began resorting to the boycotting of Japanese goods to protest against Japan's expansionistic policy in Manchuria and elsewhere. It was in this connection that some in Japan came to advocate a pan-Asianist approach. Instead of trying to co-ordinate action with the Western powers, they said, Japan should act unilaterally in order to safeguard and extend its position in China. Tanaka Giichi, who, as a staff member of the General Staff's operations section, was instrumental in drafting postwar military policy, believed that Japan should behave as a "continental nation." It was the nation's destiny to establish a predominant position in China. Considerations of understanding with the powers should not be allowed to stand in the way, if a favorable opportunity presented itself for obtaining such an end. Tanaka specifically noted that in its continental expansionism Japan might collide with the United States, since the latter, too, seemed intent on extending its interests in China. Japan must be prepared to implant its influence in south China so as to prevent the United States from doing so.

Two Statesmen Promote the Merits of Pan-Asianism

Asian leadership meant for some Japanese the military conquest of China. For others, like Prince Yamagata Aritomo (1838–1922), honored elder statesman, the slogan "Asia for the Asians" implied limited cooperation with China while maintaining continued friendly relations with the West to preclude a possible anti-Oriental coalition. Yamagata had been the chief organizer of the modern Japanese army and had the reputation of a militarist and reactionary. His views on foreign policy in 1914–1915, contained in the first selection show, nonetheless, a cautious and reflective mind. From Ryusaka Tsunoda, William T. de Bary, and Donald Keene, eds., *Sources of Japanese Tradition* (New York: Columbia University Press, 1958), pp. 714–715, 717. That the pan-Asian concept of Chinese-Japanese

collaboration could be attractive as well to the Chinese is shown in the second selection that describes a speaking tour of Japan made in 1924 by Sun Yat-sen, the revolutionary leader of the new China. Reprinted from Marius B. Jansen, *The Japanese and Sun Yat-sen* (Stanford University Press, 1954), pp. 210–211, with the permission of the publisher. Copyright © 1954 by the Board of Trustees of Leland Stanford Junior University.

I. A JAPANESE STATESMAN RECOMMENDS REACHING AN UNDERSTANDING WITH CHINA (1914–1915)

[August, 1914] There are people in our country who rely excessively on the military prowess of our empire and who believe that against China the application of force alone will suffice to gain our objectives. But the problems of life are not so simple as to permit of their solution by the use of force alone. The principal aim of our plan today should be to improve Sino-Japanese relations and to instill in China a sense of abiding trust in us. . . .

The recent international situation points to an increasing intensity in racial rivalry from year to year. It is a striking fact that the Turkish and Balkan wars of former years and the Austro-Serbian and the Russo-German wars of today [World War I] all had their inception in racial rivalry and hatred. The anti-Japanese movement in the state of California in the United States, and the discrimination against Hindus in British Africa are also manifestations of the same racial problem. Thus, the possibility of the rivalry between the white and colored races henceforth growing in intensity and leading eventually to a clash between them cannot be ruled out entirely.

When the present great conflict in Europe is over and when the political and economic order are restored, the various countries will again focus their attention on the Far East and the benefits and rights they might derive from this region. When that day comes, the rivalry between the white and the non-white races will become violent, and who can say that the white races will not unite with one another to oppose the colored peoples?

Now among the colored peoples of the Orient, Japan and China are the only two countries that have the semblance of an independent state. True, India compares favorably with China in its expansive territory and teeming population, but she has long since lost her independence, and there seems to be no reason today to believe that she will recover it. Thus, if the colored races of the Orient hope to compete with the so-called culturally advanced white races and maintain friendly relations with them while retaining their own cultural identity and independence, China and Japan, which are culturally and racially alike, must become friendly and promote each other's interests. . . .

In the formulation and execution of our Chinese policy, an indispensable consideration is our American policy. America is rich, and of late she is giving great attention to the commerce, industry, and trade of China. Moreover, the great European war has not deterred her in the least. On the contrary, America enjoys, because of the war, the full advantages of the proverbial fisherman (who makes off with the catch while the birds quarrel over it). And the government of China, suspicious of the true motives of our empire, and as a means of restraining our activities in China, has been turning to America. If we fail to dissipate China's suspicion of us, she will rapidly turn against us and instead turn more and more to America. America herself will take advantage of such a situation and will increasingly extend her influence over China.

The immigration problem in California has made for an unhappy situation in the relations between the empire and America. It is regrettable that this problem still awaits settlement. But the empire has never regarded America as a foe. Therefore, it is advisable, for the realization of our China policy, not to aggravate America's feelings toward us nor needlessly to arouse her suspicions over our actions. For the maintenance of peace in the Orient in the future, and the promotion of China's independence, I deem it a matter of utmost importance to negotiate in a frank and open manner with America. . . .

[May, 1915] In their essence Sino-Japanese relations are extremely simple and clear. What I should like to explain to Yuan [Yuan Shih K'ai, Chinese President 1912–1916] is that the cause of war in various parts of the world today is, in general, racial in character. . . . The racial problem is likewise the key to the solution of the Asia problem. Now, are not Japan and China the only true states in Asia? Is it not true that other than these two countries there is no other which can control all of Asia? In short, we must attempt the solution of our myriad problems on the premise of "Asia for the Asians." However, Japan is an island country. She is a small, narrow island country which cannot hope to support within its island confines any further increase in population. Thus, she has no alternative but to expand into Manchuria or elsewhere. That is, as Asians the Japanese must of necessity live in Asia. China may object to the Japanese setting foot in Manchuria, but had not Japan fought and repelled Russia from

Manchuria, even Peking might not be Chinese territory today. Thus, while the expansion of Japan into Manchuria may be a move for her own betterment and that of her people, it would also be a necessary move for the self-protection of Asians and for the co-existence and co-prosperity of China and Japan.

II. A CHINESE LEADER URGES THAT JAPAN CHOOSE THE "ORIENTAL RULE OF RIGHT" (1924)

Sun's last major address in Japan was delivered to a large audience in the Kobe Prefectural Girls School on November 28, 1924. He took as his subject Pan-Asianism. As on previous Japanese trips, Tai T'ien-ch'ou was his interpreter. The English *Mainichi* editor was obviously stirred by the talk.

> Dr. Sun delivered in Chinese a thundering address on "Great Asia." He completely carried his whole audience off the floor. Warmed by his own enthusiasm and that of his audience, Dr. Sun, in the course of his address, was obliged to take off one of his coats. When the meeting came to an end, the whole house rose and spontaneously gave three deafening *Banzai's* for the Chinese leader.

Sun's speech was, in the main, a restatement of his beliefs about the basic superiority of Asian culture and virtues. He pointed out that Asia was the source of the world's civilization, and that the Greek and Roman civilizations had been transmitted from Asia. Despite Asia's historic role, however, it had grown weaker at the very time that Europe had gained in strength. As a result a steady decline had set in for all Asian nations. Out

of this decline they had been newly awakened by the rise to independence of Japan; "the day when the unequal treaties were abolished by Japan was a day of regeneration for all Asiatic peoples." Japan's victory over Russia had indebted Asia further to her. "We regarded that Russian defeat by Japan as the defeat of the West by the East."

Sun then turned his attention to westerners who considered the rising of the East as a revolt against civilization. He refuted them by pointing out that Western civilization was based upon scientific materialism which resulted in a rule of force. This cult of Might was far inferior to the Oriental culture which was based on virtues of benevolence, justice, and morality—the Kingly Way. The problem of Pan-Asianism was a cultural problem of the conflict of the Occidental rule of Might with the Oriental rule of Right. There was, for Sun, no question of their intrinsic strength. Nepal, for instance, had sent tributary missions for centuries to China of her own volition. But if England should fall, all her contact with Nepal would cease overnight.

Benevolence alone, however, would not conquer the West; Asia was indebted to its two sentinels, Japan and Turkey, who had armed themselves. Similar measures should also be taken by China. Together with those progressive forces in Western countries that had begun to see the primacy of benevolence, Asian arms would then ensure Asian liberation. Already, progressive forces were to be found in most Western nations; one entire country had already reoriented her policy to insist on the rule of right and advocate the principles of benevolence and justice. For this reason, Russia was now being shunned by Europe. She [Europe] had subscribed to the Oriental values.

Sun's final words were addressed to his hosts of the evening:

> We advocate the avenging of the wrong done to those in revolt against the civilization of the rule of Might, with the aim of seeking a civilization of peace and equality and the emancipation of all races. Japan today has become acquainted with Western civilization of the rule of Might, but retains the characteristics of the Oriental civilization of the rule of Right. Now the question remains whether Japan will be the hawk of the Western civilization of the rule of Might or the tower of strength of the Orient. This is the choice which lies before the people of Japan.

The Government Contrasts "Japanism" with Western Values (1937)

The dismay of Japanese leaders that Western racial and imperialist attitudes seemed directed at preventing the continued expansion of the island empire was compounded by the growing conviction among the postwar generation that basic Japanese values were being eroded by wholesale acceptance of Western ideas and institutions. Sun Yat-sen had urged that Japan champion the Oriental Way and reject the role of "hawk"; the Japanese nationalists were convinced that the superiority of Japanese values gave their nation both the right and duty to establish hegemony in East Asia. Those who believed this exercised ever greater control of the government in the 1920s and 1930s. In 1937 the Ministry of Education published a brochure on the "Fundamentals of Our National Polity," which sought to make clear to the populace the essential meaning of "Japanism" and why certain Western values had to be rejected. Over two million copies of the document, excerpts from which follow, were sold, and it became a basic unit of ideological instruction for young and old. From Ryusaku Tsunoda, William T. de Bary, and Donald Keene, eds., *Sources of Japanese Tradition* (New York: Columbia University Press, 1958), pp. 786–787, 789–790, 792–793, 795.

INTRODUCTION

The various ideological and social evils of present-day Japan are the result of ignoring the fundamental and running after the trivial, of lack of judgment, and a failure to digest things thoroughly; and this is due to the fact that since the days of Meiji so many aspects of European and American culture, systems, and learning, have been imported, and that, too rapidly. As a matter of fact, the foreign ideologies imported into our country are in the main ideologies of the Enlightenment that have come down from the eighteenth century, or extensions of them. The views of the world and of life that form the basis of these ideologies are a rationalism and a positivism, lacking in historical views, which on the one hand lay the highest value on, and assert the liberty and equality of, individuals, and on the other hand lay value on a world by nature abstract, transcending nations and races. Consequently, importance is laid upon human beings and their groupings, who have become isolated from historical entireties, abstract and independent of each other. It is political, social, moral, and pedagogical theories based on such views of the world and of life, that have on the one hand made contributions to the various reforms seen in our country, and on the other have had deep and wide influence on our nation's primary ideology and culture. . . .

LOYALTY AND PATRIOTISM

Our country is established with the emperor, who is a descendant of Amaterasu Ōmikami, as her center, and our ancestors as well as we ourselves constantly have beheld in the emperor the fountainhead of her life and activities. For this reason, to serve the emperor and to receive the emperor's great august Will as one's own is the rationale of making our historical "life" live in the present; and on this is based the morality of the people.

Loyalty means to reverence the emperor as (our) pivot and to follow him implicitly. By implicit obedience is meant casting ourselves aside and serving the emperor intently. To walk this Way of loyalty is the sole Way in which we subjects may "live," and the fountainhead of all energy. Hence, offering our lives for the sake of the emperor does not mean so-called self-sacrifice, but the casting aside of our little selves to live under his august grace and the enhancing of the genuine life of the people of a State. . . . An individual is an existence belonging to a State and her history which forms the basis of his origin, and is fundamentally one body with it. . . .

HARMONY

When we trace the marks of the facts of the founding of our country and the progress

The Japanese ruler was regarded as divine by his people. Here Emperor Hirohito at his coronation in 1928 is wearing the traditional ceremonial robes of his ancestors, yellow in color with huge butterfly-like sleeves.

of our history, what we always find there is the spirit of harmony. Harmony is a product of the great achievements of the founding of the nation, and is the power behind our historical growth; it is also a humanitarian Way inseparable from our daily lives. The spirit of harmony is built on the concord of all things. When people determinedly count themselves as masters and assert their egos, there is nothing but contradictions and the setting of one against the other; and harmony is not begotten. . . . Harmony as in our nation is a great harmony of individuals who, by giving play to their individual differences, and through difficulties, toil and labor, converge as one. . . .

THE MARTIAL SPIRIT

And then, this harmony is clearly seen also in our nation's martial spirit. Our nation is one that holds *Bushidō* [military code of conduct that emphasizes loyalty, courage, and suicide (hari kari) before dishonor] in high regard, and there are shrines deifying warlike spirits. . . . But this martial spirit is not (a thing that exists) for the sake of itself but for the sake of peace, and is what may be called a sacred martial spirit. Our martial spirit does not have for its objective the killing of men, but the giving of life to men. This martial spirit is that which tries to give life to all things, and is not that which destroys. That is to say, it is a strife which has peace at its basis with a promise to raise and to

The bushido code of courage and self-sacrifice is here illustrated by a kamikaze suicide attack on an American warship during World War II.

develop; and it gives life to things through its strife. Here lies the martial spirit of our nation. War, in this sense, is not by any means intended for the destruction, overpowering, or subjugation of others; and it should be a thing for the bringing about of great harmony, that is, peace, doing the work or creation by following the Way. . . .

CONCLUSION

Every type of foreign ideology that has been imported into our country may have been quite natural in China, India, Europe, or America, in that it has sprung from their racial or historical characteristics; but in our country, which has a unique national polity, it is necessary as a preliminary step to put these types to rigid judgment and scrutiny so as to see if they are suitable to our national traits. . . .

To put it in a nutshell, while the strong points of Occidental learning and concepts lie in their analytical and intellectual qualities, the characteristics of Oriental learning and concepts lie in their intuitive and aesthetic qualities. These are natural tendencies that arise through racial and historical differences; and when we compare them with our national spirit, concepts, or mode of living, we cannot help recognizing further great and fundamental differences. . . .

The greater part of Occidental theories of State and political concepts so evolved do not view the State as being a nuclear existence that gives birth to individual beings, which it transcends, but as an expedient for the benefit, protection, and enhancement of the welfare of individual persons. . . . As a result, there have arisen types of mistaken liberalism and democracy that have solely sought untrammeled freedom and forgotten moral freedom, which is service. Hence,

wherever this individualism and its accompanying abstract concepts developed, concrete and historical national life became lost in the shadow of abstract theories; all states and peoples were looked upon alike as nations in general and as individuals in general; such things as an international community comprising the entire world and universal theories common to the entire world were given importance rather than concrete nations and their characteristic qualities; so that in the end there even arose the mistaken idea that international law constituted a higher norm than national law, that it stood higher in value, and that national laws were, if anything, subordinate to it. . . .

OUR MISSION

Our present mission as a people is to build up a new Japanese culture by adopting and sublimating Western cultures with our national polity as the basis, and to contribute spontaneously to the advancement of world culture. Our nation early saw the introduction of Chinese and Indian cultures, and even succeeded in evolving original creations and development. This was made possible, indeed, by the profound and boundless nature of our national polity; so that the mission of the people to whom it is bequeathed is truly great in its historical significance.

The Japanese Decide on War with the West

In the 1930s the course that the Japanese "mission" was to take moved from debate to action. The civilian government proved in-

effectual before the ambitions of soldiers who construed pan-Asianism to mean "East Asia for Japan." A number of prominent politicians were assassinated by ultranationalists and even army headquarters was not always in full control of the junior officers. In the face of feckless protests from the League of Nations, the northern Chinese province of Manchuria was invaded and occupied in 1931–1932 and a satellite state erected. Japanese forces continued to test the Chinese frontiers until the "China incident" of July 1937 launched open warfare that led ultimately to Pearl Harbor and the short-lived Greater East Asia Co-Prosperity Sphere. In the first selection, Hashimoto Kingorō, spokesman for the extremist army elements, argues the need for further expansion in 1939. In the second, Tokutomi Iichirō, a prominent nationalist writer, comments on the Imperial declaration of war against the United States in December 1941. From Ryusaku Tsunoda, William T. de Bary, and Donald Keene, eds., *Sources of Japanese Tradition* (New York: Columbia University Press, 1958), pp. 796–798, 800–801.

I. HASHIMOTO: JAPAN HAS THE RIGHT TO EXPAND (1939)

We have already said that there are only three ways left to Japan to escape from the pressure of surplus population. We are like a great crowd of people packed into a small and narrow room, and there are only three doors through which we might escape, namely emigration, advance into world markets, and expansion of territory. The first door, emigration, has been barred to us by the anti-Japanese immigration policies of other countries. The second door, advance into world markets, is being pushed shut by tariff barriers and the abrogation of commercial treaties. What should Japan do when two of the three doors have been closed against her?

It is quite natural that Japan should rush upon the last remaining door.

It may sound dangerous when we speak of territorial expansion, but the territorial expansion of which we speak does not in any sense of the word involve the occupation of the possessions of other countries, the planting of the Japanese flag thereon, and the declaration of their annexation to Japan. It is just that since the Powers have suppressed the circulation of Japanese materials and merchandise abroad, we are looking for some place overseas where Japanese capital, Japanese skills and Japanese labor can have free play, free from the oppression of the white race.

We would be satisfied with just this much. What moral right do the world powers who have themselves closed to us the two doors of emigration and advance into world markets have to criticize Japan's attempt to rush out of the third and last door?

If they do not approve of this, they should open the doors which they have closed against us and permit the free movement overseas of Japanese emigrants and merchandise. . . .

At the time of the Manchurian incident, the entire world joined in criticism of Japan. They said that Japan was an untrustworthy nation. They said that she had recklessly brought cannon and machine guns into Manchuria, which was the territory of another country, flown airplanes over it, and finally occupied it. But the military action taken by Japan was not in the least a selfish one. Moreover, we do not recall ever having taken so much as an inch of territory belonging to another nation. The result of this incident was the

establishment of the splendid new nation of Manchuria. The Powers are still discussing whether or not to recognize this new nation, but regardless of whether or not other nations recognize her, the Manchurian empire has already been established, and now, seven years after its creation, the empire is further

consolidating its foundations with the aid of its friend, Japan.

And if it is still protested that our actions in Manchuria were excessively violent, we may wish to ask the white race just which country it was that sent warships and troops to India, South Africa, and Australia and

Young recruits for the "military action" in Manchuria wave flags in farewell as they leave the Tokyo railroad station. The other side of the coin is reflected by the probable fate of this Chinese prisoner.

slaughtered innocent natives, bound their hands and feet with iron chains, lashed their backs with iron whips, proclaimed these territories as their own, and still continues to hold them to this very day?

They will invariably reply, these were all lands inhabited by untamed savages. These people did not know how to develop the abundant resources of their land for the benefit of mankind. Therefore it was the wish of God, who created heaven and earth for mankind, for us to develop these undeveloped lands and to promote the happiness of mankind in their stead. God wills it.

This is quite a convenient argument for them. Let us take it at face value. Then there is another question that we must ask them.

Suppose that there is still on this earth land endowed with abundant natural resources that have not been developed at all by the white race. Would it not then be God's will and the will of Providence that Japan go there and develop those resources for the benefit of mankind?

And there still remain many such lands on this earth.

II. TOKUTOMI:
JAPAN WILL BE THE LEADER
OF EAST ASIA (1941)

In Nippon resides a destiny to become the Light of Greater East Asia and to become ultimately the Light of the World. However, in order to become the Light of Greater East Asia, we must have three qualifications. The first is, as mentioned previously, strength. In other words, we must expel Anglo-Saxon influence from East Asia with our strength.

To speak the truth, the various races of East Asia look upon the British and Americans as superior to the Nippon race. They look upon Britain and the United States as more powerful nations than Nippon. Therefore, we must show our real strength before all our fellow-races of East Asia. We must show them an object lesson. It is not a lesson in words. It should be a lesson in facts.

In other words, before we can expel the Anglo-Saxons and make them remove all their traces from East Asia, we must annihilate them. In this way only will the various fellow races of Greater East Asia look upon us as their leader. I believe that the lesson which we must first show to our fellow-races in Greater East Asia is this lesson of cold reality.

The second qualification is benevolence. Nippon must develop the various resources of East Asia and distribute them fairly to all the races within the East Asia Co-Prosperity Sphere to make them share in the benefits. In other words, Nippon should not monopolize the benefits, but should distribute them for the mutual prosperity of Greater East Asia.

We must show to the races of East Asia that the order, tranquillity, peace, happiness, and contentment of East Asia can be gained only by eradicating the evil precedent of the encroachment and extortion of the Anglo-Saxons in East Asia, by effecting the real aim of the co-prosperity of East Asia, and by making Nippon the leader of East Asia.

The third qualification is virtue. East Asia embraces various races. Its religions are different. Moreover, there has practically been no occasion when these have mutually united to work for a combined aim. It was the favorite policy of the Anglo-Saxons to make the various races of East Asia compete and fight each other and make them mutually small and powerless. We must, therefore, console them, bring friendship among them, and make them all live in peace with a boundlessly embracing virtue. . . .

STUDY QUESTIONS

1. What were the characteristics of the Meiji "revolution"? Why do you think that the Japanese reaction to Western pressure was so different from that of the Chinese?

2. What were the goals of Japanese foreign policy?

3. To what can Japanese success in the war against Russia be attributed?

4. How did Western racism influence the shaping of Japanese policy?

5. What benefits, according to Yamagata, could Japan hope for in pursuing a conciliatory policy with China? Why did he warn against antagonizing the United States?

6. To what extent did Sun Yat-sen's position complement that of the Japanese?

7. What did the Japanese in the 1930s consider the most significant values?

8. In the light of the readings in this topic, what answer could one make to Hashimoto and Tokutomi?

Henry Commager: The End of the Victorian Age

TOPIC 41

THE END OF THE NINETEENTH CENTURY

Europe's sense of confidence in her continuing security and expansion was based on marked industrial leadership, rising wealth, and an energetic population. These qualities, nonetheless, masked grave failings in the handling of disputes among nations and barely managed to contain the national and social tensions that threatened existing governments. In the decades before World War I, the volatile arms race and the rigid system of alliances made the European world a powder keg. Its explosion in 1914 brought down the admired pillars of nineteenth-century progress and created a holocaust from which the European world never fully recovered. The coming of the War and its impact on participants are examined in the readings.

American historian Henry Steele Commager (1902–   ) has written widely both on American thought and values and on the relationship of past to present. In the essay that follows, Professor Commager casts his gaze on a larger Western community. From Henry Steele Commager, "1900–1950: From Victorian to Atomic Age," *The New York Times Magazine* (December 25, 1949), pp. 3–7. Copyright © 1949 by the New York Times Company. Reprinted by permission.

The twentieth century opened with Queen Victoria (Ruler 1837–1901) still on her throne. Already she had given her name to an era, and already men were beginning to pronounce that era the best, the most prosperous, and the most enlightened in history, forgetting or ignoring the poverty and misery, the cruelty, oppression and wars, that had stained its history. "Whatever may be thought of the nineteenth century," wrote the editor of the new *World's Work,* "when it can be seen in the perspective of universal history, it seems the best time to live that has so far come."

And as men looked back over the years since the defeat of Napoleon at Waterloo they had some reason for pride in the past, and for confidence in the future. The nineteenth century had seen the abolition of slavery throughout the English-speaking world, and the end of serfdom in Russia. It had seen the emergence of the backward peoples of the world, the development of a more benevolent imperialism, the growth of justice and the acknowledgement of international law. Science had at last come into its own, and science promised the conquest of disease and of want and the creation of a world incomparably richer than any that men had known in the past.

The standard of living had been raised everywhere, and there were no material wants that science and technology could not supply. Popular education had spread throughout the Western world, and universal education was about to be realized. The ravages of the industrial revolution, it was felt, were being overcome, and industry tamed; everywhere reformers were busy christianizing the social order, and among the "dark Satanic mills" men were building a new Jerusalem.

Not only had the Victorian Era created what appeared to be a general prosperity, it had created a new international order and brought about an era of peace. It was a bit awkward to insist upon the dawn of peace, to be sure, what with the Chinese-Japanese war, the Spanish-American war, the Boer War, and half a dozen minor wars in Africa, all in the decade of the Nineties, but men could argue, at least, that there had been no general war since Napoleon, and that wars seemed, now, to be banished to the fringes of western civilization. And throughout the western world there was free movement of men, money and goods—an achievement the full significance of which only a later generation would appreciate.

The nineteenth century had been a century of mounting nationalism, and of imperialism, but both, now, it seemed, were tempered and tamed. A balance of power had been achieved, and nations no longer needed to struggle for their places in the sun, while great new powers like the United States and Japan could advance without necessarily infringing on other nations.

The naked imperialism of the bad old days was giving way to an enlightened imperialism. The imperialism of the white man's burden . . . seemed to be justifying itself by its good works in the backward areas of the earth. The British Empire stood as a vindication of imperialism. It was the empire on which the sun never set; of it men could repeat the proud boast of Horace Walpole after the great triumphs of 1763: "Burn your Greek and Roman books, histories of little people." And Britain had learned her lesson; the empire was gradually being transformed into a commonwealth of nations, bound together by common ideals and loyalties, stronger by far than when it was held together by force.

The nineteenth century had seen, too, enormous strides toward democracy. It was not merely that suffrage was extended more widely—even to women in some more enlightened countries—but that the principle of popular government was acknowledged everywhere in the western world, and the machinery for making democracy effective was rapidly being perfected. The United States had led the way, and the triumph of the North in the Civil War had gone far to vindicate democracy in the Old World. In the last quarter of the century democracy had come on with a rush in many European countries—notably Scandinavia and Britain and France, and in the British dominions. As the nineteenth century melted into the twentieth,

liberals could congratulate themselves that the long struggle for democracy was all but won and could look forward confidently to the spread of democratic rule everywhere on the globe.

And along with democracy went humanitarianism and reform. There was little doubt in the minds of contemporaries that the forces of righteousness were triumphing over the forces of evil. The enlightened social conscience was at work in every field and in every country, improving the lot of the laborer, championing the welfare of women and children, eliminating poverty and slums, eradicating disease, spreading education, lifting up the backward peoples, caring for the dangerous and the perishing classes, realizing the teachings of Christianity.

Not only had the nineteenth century achieved such progress as men could scarcely imagine, it had vindicated the philosophy of progress. That philosophy had been formulated in the eighteenth century, but its formulation was on the basis of philosophy now discarded. The nineteenth century had furnished a new and sounder scientific foundation for the doctrine of progress and, what was more, it had found a scientist-philosopher who proved that progress was a scientific fact. This was Herbert Spencer, who—so it was asserted by his rapt contemporaries—boasted the most capacious intellect of all time, and whose genius surpassed that of Aristotle and Newton, as the telegraph surpassed the carrier pigeon. Spencer succeeded in bringing all human phenomena within the framework of scientific laws and of proving that evolution implacably imposed progress on man. "Progress," he wrote, "is not an accident but a necessity. . . . Always toward

perfection is the mighty movement—toward a complete development and a more unmixed good."

Then, gradually, a haze drew over the bright Victorian skies. One by one the buoyant hopes of the Victorians were doomed to disappointment. Within less than half a century prosperity gave way to ruin, universal peace to universal war, certainty to fear, security to insecurity, the ideal of progress to the doubt of survival. Never before in history had such bright hopes been so ruthlessly shattered; never had the philosophical temper undergone so profound a change. . . .

As the telescope and mathematics disclosed a universe so vast that it defied computation except in thousands of millions of light years and reduced the earth to a grain of pollen floating in illimitable space; as the microscope discovered a universe surging about each atom; as biology found the source of life in a series of apparently fortuitous chemical reactions; as the psychologists reduced the most profound thoughts of man, his highest flights of genius, to merely chemical impulses and uncontrollable reactions—the cosmic system familiar to the Victorians in which man possessed a soul, found meaning in life, and was sure of progress and of destiny, slipped quietly away. . . .

It is the misfortune of every philosophy and every science to be vulgarized, and it was not, perhaps, the fault of the new physicists or the new psychologists, that their versions of the nature of man and the relation of man to the universe struck almost mortal blows at authority of all kinds—the authority of law, of morality and of reason. Yet the convulsions that overtook the world in the generation after 1914 and especially in the years after

1930—the rejection of law, the abandonment of morals, the ruthless destruction of life—were not unconnected with these new philosophical and scientific ideas. . . .

Soon it was a truism that science had outrun social science. . . . That science saved millions of lives, enabled millions of others to live who could not otherwise have been supported, released energies, provided leisure, enhanced man's enjoyment of life, could not for a moment be doubted. That it would be put to evil as well as to beneficent uses was no new idea. What was new was the fear that Adams expressed, that "science is to wreck us, and that we are like monkeys monkeying around with a loaded shell." The generation that lived in the shadow of atomic and bacteriological warfare was not one that could take the beneficence of science for granted. . . .

Peter Viereck: Roots of the European Catastrophe

From Peter Viereck, "The Revolution in Values: Roots of the European Catastrophe, 1870–1952." Reprinted with permission from the *Political Science Quarterly*, September, 1952, Vol. LXII, No. 3, pp. 341–345. Also reprinted in a later work of the author, *Shame and Glory of the Intellectuals*, G. Putnam's Sons, Capricorn Paperback, New York 1965.

Both socialism and nationalism had long been present in Europe. A bit of socialism and a lot of nationalism had modified—to left or right—the liberalism of the various uprisings of 1848. But to a great extent the original pre-Marx socialism and the original pre-Bismarck nationalism had been peaceful, conciliatory, tolerant, evolutionary, in the great liberal tradition. The pre-Marxist socialists—Robert Owen (1771–1858), Saint-Simon (1760–1825), Fourier (1772–1837), . . . and the rest—have been dismissed by Marxist . . . writers as mere "utopians." The label "utopian socialist" continues to cling mockingly to non-Marxist socialists, who hope to bring about socialism peacefully without class war. The label is not one to be ashamed of. Its advocates claim that only through peaceful evolution—as in the current socialist reforms in Scandinavia—can socialism be achieved without sacrifice of civil liberties. In contrast, Marxist socialism and Bismarckian nationalism have in common a resort to force, a contempt for tolerant parliamentary solutions. After the 1870's, these are the dominant kinds of socialism and nationalism.

The pre-Bismarck nationalists—like Herder (1744–1803) in Germany and Mazzini (1805–1872) in Italy—are known as "liberal" nationalists. Like their historical brethren, the utopian socialists, they had tried and failed in the revolutions of 1848. Their nationalism was one not of hate for other races but of tolerant cooperation of all nationalities in a peaceful nondespotic Europe.

In deriding the attempt to achieve socialism through parliamentary means, Marx (1818–1883) and Soviet writers are exactly as scathing as Bismarck was in deriding his "liberal nationalist" predecessors. Marx and Lenin might have said on behalf of class war and of the proletariat what Bismarck said on behalf of national war and of Prussia in his often quoted speech of 1862, attacking peaceful parliamentary methods: "The eyes of Germany are fixed not upon Prussia's liberalism, but upon her armed might. . . . The great questions of the day will not be decided by speeches or by majority decisions—that was the mistake of 1848 and 1849—but by blood and iron!"

The "blood and iron" nationalism that followed 1870 culminated eventually in Nazi Germany and Fascist Italy. The "blood and iron" Marxist socialism of the 1870's culminated eventually in Soviet Russia and in an Iron Curtain advancing over Europe and Asia. Preferring state omnipotence to individualism and preferring quick violent change to gradual parliamentary change, these are the two new value-systems that arose from the ethical revolution. They arose to challenge the traditional ethics and values of Europe and America. . . .

In the words of Cavour (1810–1861), who achieved the Italian territorial revolution: "If we did for ourselves what we do for our country, what rascals we would be!" That sentence might be taken as the motto for the whole ethical revolution and for the two world wars that followed.

Contrast the Bernhardi credo about "no power above the state" with its direct opposite: Thomas More's dying words on the scaffold, "I die the king's good servant, but God's first." Substitute "the nation-state" for "king" and substitute "universal ethics" for "God", and you have the perfect contrast between our value-heritage and the revolt against values.

Nationalized ethics has crushed internationalism on the one hand and individualism on the other. This made it the appropriate creed for that new power-group, the middle-class nationalists created by the industrial and territorial revolutions.

So-called Machiavellianism—ruthlessness in world affairs—is, of course, nothing new; it has always been with us. But not until after 1870 was it systematized so thoroughly, or thought out so deliberately. Never before the age of Hitler and Stalin was it practiced with such efficient total coordination. Never before was it accepted so popularly and widely as replacing Christianity as a religion and system of ethics.

At the same time, a scientific revolution—the "new Science" associated with Darwinism—not merely changed the science of Europe but had important indirect repercussions on its political and social ethics. Political and social misuses of Darwin's theory of "evolution through natural selection" gave a seemingly scientific justification to the ruthlessness accompanying the ethical revolution. National war and class war, the political militarism that followed Bismarck and the social militarism that followed Marx, could now claim to serve man's evolution by weeding out the allegedly "unfit" nations, races, or classes. . . .

The history of Europe after 1870 relates the decline—not necessarily fall—of Europe. . . . At first the value-system known as "Europe" did seem to tame the two revolutionary forces of nationalism and socialism, extracting from them what was valuable, changing national frontiers and social frontiers without sacrificing personal liberties. It was a good example of "challenge and response." A seemingly successful absorption of the challenge, a case of practical evolutionary conservatism,

marked the history of Europe from 1870 up to World War I. Reactionary tsars and kaisers and revolutionary socialists and nationalists were all making ever handsomer concessions (no matter how grudgingly) to reasonableness and to parliamentary processes.

By 1914, socialism and nationalism seemed "house-broken". Marxist socialist parties had relaxed into "Social Democrats"; most nationalistic hotheads were calming down into national democrats; for a while, there was more talk of the Hague Peace Conferences than of the approaching war. To a great extent, the leading parties of socialism and likewise of nationalism had been assimilated into the European parliamentary system, working in lawful, gradual, parliamentary fashion for the changes they demanded.

That is why World War I was a tragedy so irrevocable. It cut suddenly short the slow, patient taming-process. . . .

Europe Builds the Road to War (1871–1914)

From William H. McNeill, *History Handbook of Western Civilization* (Chicago: University of Chicago Press, 1953). Copyright 1953 by the University of Chicago Press.

Industrialism grew at an accelerated tempo after 1871, especially in Germany, which within a few years of the formation of the German empire became the leading industrial as well as the leading military state of Europe.

The military and economic rise of Germany worked a fundamental change in the Euro-

pean political balance. As long as Bismarck remained Chancellor of the new German state, his skillful diplomacy, playing upon long-standing rivalry between France and Britain, and between Russia and Britain, kept potential enemies of Germany separated. At the same time he was able to form alliances with Austria (1879) and Italy (1882), and he maintained friendly relations with Russia.

Bismarck's dominance on the continent was made easier by the fact that the other great powers of Europe were engaged in imperialistic rivalries. France and Great Britain were frequently at loggerheads over Africa, the most notable crises coming in 1882, when the British asserted control over Egypt, and in 1898, when rival French and British expeditions met one another in the Sudan at Fashoda. A similar tension existed between Great Britain and Russia. In central Asia, the two powers intrigued against one another in Afghanistan and Persia; and in the Near East, Russia, Austria, and Great Britain indulged in a three-cornered contest for influence and control over the Ottoman empire.

The situation in the Balkan peninsula was further complicated by the development of fiery nationalism among the Balkan peoples themselves. Greeks, Serbs, Rumanians, Bulgars, Albanians, and Turks, each in turn began to awake to European ideas of national self determination during the course of the 19th century; and each people developed the ambition to create a new or enlarged state which would embrace all fellow nationals. Such ambitions were, of course, mutually conflicting; yet the various Balkan nationalities were able to find champions for their cause among the interested great powers. . . .

Not only in the Near East, but in Africa, China and Oceania as well, German traders and German diplomats began to rival the older imperial powers. Germany's entrance upon an imperialistic career had the effect of bringing a fundamental change in the European balance of power, for the appearance of a newcomer had the effect of bringing together the other imperial nations. Their rivalries and mutual suspicions were gradually compromised and overcome, so that during the first decade of the 20th century a new and powerful grouping of France, Russia and Great Britain came to be arrayed against the Germans and their allies.

This new turn of events became particularly evident after William II (1888–1918) came to the German throne. In 1890 Bismarck was dismissed from his post as Chancellor, and the young Emperor undertook personally to direct the German government. William was determined to make his mark on history, and was deeply impressed by the arguments of Admiral Mahan in favor of sea power. Consequently, he determined to build up a powerful German navy that could rival the British on the high seas; and at the same time he began to extend vigorous support to German imperialistic plans, especially in Turkey.

The effect of his policies was to bring together a powerful coalition opposed to Germany. Against the Triple Alliance of Germany, Austria and Italy, which Bismarck had formed, there arose the Triple Entente—France, Russia and Great Britain. The formation of the Triple Entente was a difficult matter, for it required compromises to regulate the powers' respective 'spheres of influence.' Such compromises were not always easy to achieve. In 1894 France and Russia formed an alliance without difficulty; the French-British compromise came only after prolonged negotiation, and even then the British were not

A super battleship of the period before the First World War, the British vessel *H.M.S. Hibernia.*

willing to sign a definite treaty binding them automatically to warlike action. Consequently all that was achieved was an understanding —an *entente cordiale* in the language of diplomacy (1904). Three years later a settlement of disputed claims in central Asia and in the Near East brought Great Britain and Russia together in a similar entente.

Thus from 1907 onward Europe was divided: Germany, Austria and Italy faced France, Russia and Great Britain. The balance of power between the two groups was very nearly equal, and any slight alteration produced tremors throughout the entire state system of Europe. The consequence was that periodic crises arose which more than once

threatened war. In 1905 and again in 1911 the German government intervened in Morocco, where the French government was busy extending and consolidating a protectorate. Both these acts engendered much bad feeling, but were settled peacefully.

Each time one or the other of the great powers backed down in a crisis, its leaders resolved not to do so again—resolved also to prepare militarily so that a further diplomatic set-back need not be endured. Consequently a growing arms race developed between the major powers. When the Germans began to build a navy, the British decided to outbuild them; when a new and more efficient type of warship—the dreadnaught—was introduced, both Germans and British decided to build more of them than the other did. On land a similar rivalry developed. The size of standing armies was increased by prolonging the period of training to which conscripts were subjected; and the decisions of one government came to be tied to the decisions made by a rival.

Thus the stage was set for the outbreak of World War I. The actual occasion was almost trivial: in June, 1914 the heir to the Austrian throne was assassinated at Sarajevo in the recently annexed province of Bosnia. The Austrian government accused the Serbs of complicity in the crime, demanded satisfaction, and when their demands were not wholly met, the Austrian armies mobilized and marched against Serbia. But this time the Russians were resolved not to give in, as they had done in 1908, and came to Serbia's aid against the Austrians. Thereupon the whole chain of alliances was brought into operation. Germany came to Austria's help; France and Great Britain joined with Russia; and, to the surprise and bewilderment of many, in the early days of August, 1914, almost all Europe found itself engaged in a bitter war which had originated with a political assassination in an obscure Balkan town six weeks earlier.

Herman Kahn: How World War I Started

Herman Kahn (1922–   ) is a policy analyst and planner whose defense studies have made him a controversial public figure. He is best known for his application of the methods and assumptions of rational analysis to international relations and warfare. A good sample of his contribution may be found in the selection that follows. From *On Thermonuclear War*, by Herman Kahn (Copyright © 1960 by Princeton University Press). Reprinted by permission of Princeton University Press.

The most interesting thing about World War I in addition to its technology and tactics is the prewar situation, the manner in which the war got started. The last really big European war had ended in 1815 with the defeat of Napoleon. The last moderately large war in Europe, the Franco-Prussian, had terminated in 1871. The next forty-three years, until 1914, were for the European continent years of almost complete peace, marred only by small wars between relatively unimportant Balkan nations and a relatively innocuous war between the Russians and the Turks in 1877. That is, Europe had had about a century of relative peace and almost half a century of almost complete peace. The thought of war had grown unreal to the governments involved. They got used to making threats to go to war, either directly or by implication, and they even got used to getting their way when they made these threats strong enough. There were a number of crises which made newspaper headlines and scared both governments and people, but after a while even these became unreal and the armies were thought of more as pieces in a game played by diplomats (called "let's find a formula") than as tools to be used. Even though the two sides snarled ferociously at each other, one side was always expected to give way graciously, or ungraciously, before it came to a trial of arms. Both consciously and unconsciously, all the top decision makers were afraid of being involved in a large war. In spite of the optimistic calculations of some of the military, there was a feeling in all the governments that the war would be big and that it was too risky an activity to engage in unless the odds were overwhelmingly in one's favor, and none of the nations felt the odds were sufficiently high in 1914. Therefore, *just because neither side really wanted war, one side or the other would presumably withdraw before things got out of hand.*

As far as I know, just about all modern historians agree on this thesis—that none of the top statesmen or the rulers and very few, if any, of the soldiers wanted a world war in 1914 (though some wanted a war somewhat later, after certain preparations had been made), and only the Serbs and the Austrians wanted even a small war. And yet war came. How did it happen?

The British historian A. J. P. Taylor described the prewar situation in an article in *The Observer*. . . .

> The Statesmen of Europe with one accord, accepted the theory of "the deterrent": the more strongly and firmly they threatened, the more likely they were both to preserve the peace of Europe and get their way. . . .
>
> The German rulers were firmly wedded to the theory of the deterrent. A resolve to go to war, loudly proclaimed; and the other side would give way. In Jagow's words: "The more boldness Austria displays, the more strongly we support her, the more likely Russia is to keep quiet." Those who condemn the German policy should reflect that Sir Edward Grey did the opposite from the Germans: he failed to make his position

clear in advance. And for this he has often been saddled with responsibility for the war. . . .

The amateur strategist, devising actions without inquiring whether they were technically possible, was a recurring theme in July 1914. . . . It was no doubt the penalty for forty years of peace, years in which armies and campaigns had been weapons of diplomacy, not of war.

The most striking feature of the July crisis was the total lack of contact in every country between the political and military leaders. Military plans were at their most rigid in the railway age; yet no statesman had the slightest idea what the timetables involved. Their sensations, when diplomacy collapsed, were those of a train passenger who sees the express thundering through the station at which he intended to alight.

As Taylor says, World War I was a railroad war. It was a war for which the general staffs of the four great continental powers had spent decades planning meticulous timetables. The war plans were literally cast in concrete in the sense that governments built railroads according to the requirements of the war plans. One could look at a nation's railroads and get a very accurate idea of what its war plans were. All nations except Britain had very large numbers of trained reserves available that were quite different from the kind of manpower we refer to as reserves today; the 1914 conscripts were prepared to be mobilized into fighting armies. As soon as they were called to the colors, most of them could march into battle on an equal footing with the best professional troops available.

This ability to increase one's force by a large factor and in a very short period of time gave a disasterous instability to the situation, because it promised to give the nation that mobilized first a crucial advantage.

As General Boisdeffre, the assistant chief of the French General Staff explained to Tsar Nicholas:

> The mobilization is the declaration of war. To mobilize is to oblige one's neighbor to do the same. . . . Otherwise, to leave a million men on one's frontier, without doing the same simultaneously, is to deprive oneself of all possibility of moving later; it is placing oneself in a situation of an individual who, with a pistol in his pocket, should let his neighbor put a weapon to his forehead without drawing his own.

While the Tsar answered that that was his understanding also, his general staff in 1912 decided that the belief that "the proclamation of mobilization is equivalent to the declaration of war," had serious disadvantages for the Russians, since it took them so long to mobilize. Therefore, they formally annulled the rule and instructed the Foreign Office, "It will be advantageous to complete concentration without beginning hostilities, in order not to deprive the enemy irrevocably of the hope that war can still be avoided. Our measures for this must be masked by clever diplomatic negotiations, in order to lull to sleep as much as possible the enemy's fears."

While the above is a perfectly reasonable "military requirement," since it is very valuable to be able to steal a march on the enemy, it is not a reasonable diplomatic requirement. The Foreign Office felt that the enemy was just not going to be fooled by soothing words

while the Russians prepared to draw (rather noisily) their pistols. As a matter of fact the Russian Foreign Office was wrong. They did succeed, in the crisis of July 1914, in holding off a German mobilization for about a week while the Russians went through preparatory moves. They did this not by being superlatively clever, but by not knowing themselves what they really intended to do and managing to transmit the confusion to the Germans. . . . As long as the situation was ambiguous, [the German government] was not willing to make an irrevocable step, and no temporizing measures had been prepared, so the German government did nothing while its enemies stole a march on it. . . .

Thus it turned out that the German plan for protecting themselves by quick countermeasures failed. There were many reasons for this failure. We have mentioned the first and most important, the Germans' failure to react quickly. This is, of course, the standard problem in dealing with any situation in which there might be false alarms and in which the reaction to a false alarm is costly. One may be unwilling to react. Countries are usually reluctant to go to war except at a time and manner of their own choosing, and as long as there is any chance of peace they usually feel obligated to discount the signals they are getting; because they do not want to be premature, they accept the risk of giving the enemy precious time until the threat becomes unambiguous.

A second reason that the timing of the German plan was thrown off was that the Russians turned out to be somewhat better at mobilizing than expected. In addition to mobilizing faster than the experts thought they could, the Russians attacked before being fully prepared. Either out of enlightened self-interest or possibly from loyalty to their alliance they were determined to create a diversion that would help the French, even if it meant attacking prematurely and risking a disaster (which it did). This, too, is a standard problem. Whenever a plan depends on a very precise estimate of either the enemy's capability or his willingness to run risks, it is automatically unreliable.

Like the Germans, the Russians had a rather rigid war plan. All their thinking had been devoted to the problem of how to attack Germany and Austria together, and they had not considered any other kind of large war. In particular, they had made no plans for attacking just Austria-Hungary. The Russian government found, to its surprise and consternation, that it could not even carry out a partial mobilization for the purpose of threatening Austria without threatening the Germans by troop movements on their frontier and at the same time leaving themselves helpless before a German mobilization or attack, because they could not reverse their movements. The rigidities and pressures toward pre-emptive action contained in the Russian and German war plans proved disastrous in the events that followed. In much the same way, careless and rigid plans today by either the Russians or the Americans to use certain kinds of quick reaction as a defense might be disastrous.

Many people realized then that the basic situation was unstable and that a chain of events could erupt into a conflagration, but I think relatively few people took the possibility seriously; that is, few of the decision makers "cared" until events had gone too far. The possibility of war by miscalculation was too hypothetical; the civilians tended to leave such matters to the military and the military tended to take a narrow professional view of the risks. The fact that the hypothetical situation could be predicted made it seem even more impossible that it would happen. People do not deliberately walk off cliffs; they believe that only hidden cliffs are dangerous. Only it did not prove to be really like that. . . .

The more historians examine World War I, the more it seems to be clear that this was a war none of the responsible governments wanted, a war set in motion by relatively trivial circumstances, a motion which, given the state of the world, could not be stopped. It is quite possible that if there had been a really great statesman in a responsible position the war could have been averted. But there was no such statesman, and so the automatic machinery that had been set in motion ground on to its inevitable conclusion.

Because the whole concept of a war by accident, or a miscalculation is so important, and because there seem to be many valid analogies between July 1914 and almost any crisis month in the 1960–1975 period, I should like, at the risk of belaboring the obvious, to list some of the analogies:

1. The need to meet or even beat the enemy's mobilization timetable has a number of similarities to many current quick reaction schemes. We have today, even more than in 1914, the possibility of setting into motion a series of self-confirming signals generated by reactions and counteractions taken on almost sheerly technical grounds without much reference to further developments in policy. There is also the opposite problem (which paradoxically can occur simultaneously). The dangerous counteractions may not be adequate as peacetime training maneuvers, as moderate measures undertaken to reduce vulnerability, or as bargaining threats to bluff the opponent into acquiescence.

2. The need to have a quick victory or stalemate to prevent a situation in which both sides lost. It is interesting to note that Schlieffen recognized this and suggested that if the initial campaign against the French failed, the Germans should try for a negotiated peace. Unfortunately for the moderates, the consequences of not terminating hostilities were not recognized by the decision makers; the desire for victory and "the honor of the battlefield" was too strong.

3. The rigidity of the war plans. In 1914 this occurred because they were so complicated that the general staffs felt that they could not draw up more than one. This single war plan was then made even more rigid because it depended on such detailed railroad schedules. In 196X there is a fair chance that the war plan will be handled by a high-speed computer—if we have not made a real effort, nothing could be more rigid. While there will doubtless be opportunities for human intervention, events may move so quickly that these opportunities may be formal rather than of real effect. It is also likely that there will be only one plan because some planners find it hard to take seriously the thought of a number of different situations. They want to examine and plan for only the most obvious one, and ignore the others.

4. As in 1914, in 196X the various governments, having seen the world go

through so many false alarms and crises, will have become blasé. Most people today, in and out of government, find it difficult to believe that any sane decision maker would deliberately initiate a thermonuclear war, no matter how tense the crisis. Therefore, temptation for both sides to take firm (and incompatible) positions is likely to become irresistible.

5. Even more than in 1914, governments in our day are likely to be ignorant of the technical details of war and the tactical measures that can or cannot (or, more important, must or must not) be taken in various specialized situations. In peacetime the study and preparation of these measures will be relegated to military staffs as being narrow and technical. As a result they may be considered in a narrow and technical way. In 196X the ignorance of major decision makers is likely to be more profound than in 1914, because at that time the ignorance was related mainly to disuse; there was no philosophical and doctrinaire position that war was "unthinkable." The study of the strategy and tactics of the actual fighting as opposed to deterrence was considered an eminently practical and respectable subject. Today, on the contrary, it is almost impossible to get people interested in the tactics and strategy of thermonuclear war. It is now believed that only the prewar moves are of interest, and even these are not too important because deterrence is supposed to be so close to "automatic." Also, war is technically more complex today than in 1914, and the technological situation changes rapidly.

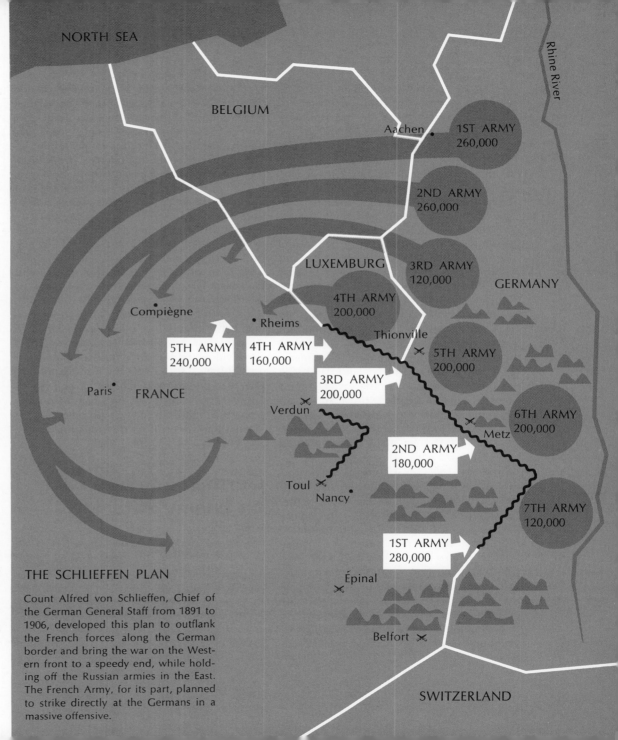

THE SCHLIEFFEN PLAN

Count Alfred von Schlieffen, Chief of the German General Staff from 1891 to 1906, developed this plan to outflank the French forces along the German border and bring the war on the Western front to a speedy end, while holding off the Russian armies in the East. The French Army, for its part, planned to strike directly at the Germans in a massive offensive.

6. The year 196X should have at least as many chances for decision makers to make mistakes due to having been under physical and emotional strain and pressures for quick reaction. The issues are bigger, crises develop faster, and the time for reaction may be less.

7. Probably the most important similarity between 1914 and 196X is the ease with which small powers and allies may be able to manipulate the major powers for their own ends. Instead of Serbia and Austria, we can think of China and almost any Asiatic power; West Germany and East Germany; France and the Middle East; and so on. On the other hand, the military situation is such that allies are both more firmly tied and less important to the United States and the Soviet Union than they once were to Germany, Russia, France, and England. With the possible exception of the Soviet Union's relations to China (Khrushchev's announced policy to support the Chinese in the Formosa dispute), neither country really has to sign "blank checks" to hold its allies.

There are, of course, major differences between 1914 and today. On the stabilizing side, the most important difference is that the thermonuclear balance of terror is much more effective than the 1914 fear of defeat or revolution. However, for that reason, the balance of terror is also more likely to be strained since blackmail, firm positions, reckless actions, and sheer ignorance of the details all look safer. *It is reasonably likely that the passage of time will see a gradual growth in the willingness of all parties to be both provoking and careless about their actual capabilities.*

The other differences seem to be mostly on the destabilizing side and made the balance more precarious. Today, because both sides are in effect permanently mobilized, it may be possible to strike without giving any internal or external advance signals. In addition, there are now so many ways to destroy a nation or its armed forces that the danger of unconventional attacks or the exploitation of unconventional effects is ever-present. . . . Sometimes these unconventional attacks, while seeming to be bizarre or reckless, are still more calculable than was a 1914 offensive. Even with the most careful mutual and unilateral arrangements, the possibility of accidents or errors by relatively minor officials, setting off a disastrous chain of events, will exist. In addition, measures designed to limit this last possibility will themselves create new vulnerabilities of either a physical or psychological sort. Lastly and most important, the fear of future instability caused by an insufficiently controlled arms race is so great and growing that it may create pressures for preventive war or other destabilizing moves.

German Soldiers Face an Enemy Attack

Trench warfare was a shattering experience, as this letter from a collection of German students' letters from the front indicates. August Hopp, a theology student before the war, was twenty-three when he wrote the letter, seventeen days before he was killed in the battle of Combres. From the book *German Students' War Letters* translated and arranged from the original edition of Dr. Philipp Witkop by A. F. Wedd. Published by E. P. Dutton & Co., Inc. and reprinted with their permission. This is published in Canada by Methuen & Co. Ltd.

It was a pitch-dark night. We marched slowly up the steep incline in bottomless mud. Every second one stumbled into a shell-hole. Thank God the enemy's shells were dropping farther back, the French evidently thinking that they were already in possession of the hill. . . .

At last came the order: 'The Company will at once relieve a Company of the 154th in the recaptured trench.' Under the guidance of a Lieutenant of the 154th, who knew the forward terrain thoroughly, we started, through a boyau* to a trench half-way down the northern slope of the wooded hill. And there the real tragedy began. Already, while in the reserve position, we had occasionally, in the darkness of the night, stumbled over some of the dead bodies which were scattered all over the side of the hill, but in these trenches one saw death in a hundredfold most frightful forms. Right at the entrance lay one of the 130th, leaning against the breastwork, as if he had dropped asleep as he fell, a little bloody hole in his forehead, cold and stark. And then we forced ourselves along, for we had to get through to the far side of the left flank, one behind the other, through the trench, on the bottom of which were stagnating pools of blood in which lay, in wildest confusion, corpses of Germans and French, almost blocking the way every few steps, so that one had to clamber over the heaped-up bodies, constantly finding one's hands and

---

*A short connecting trench running at right angles and frequent intervals between the lines of trenches—Eds.

face in contact with ghastly, bleeding wounds. A mixture of blood and mud was smeared over our boots and clothes and hands. One couldn't walk upright, one *must* not, for down in the gully, 30 yards away, lay the French trenches. As soon as even the spike of a helmet showed above the parapet— bang, bang!—a bullet whistled over our heads. At the same time we saw the terrible effect of the artillery-fire, for not a tree was left standing in the upper part of the wood behind or in front of the trenches. The ground looked as if there had been an earthquake; the trench was here and there a chaos of earth, stones, tree-trunks and corpses, and the nearer we got to the left wing the more ghastly it became, the thicker and thicker lay the bodies, and the more the bullets whistled.

The Lieutenant of the left flank, whose platoon I was to relieve, came to meet me and give me the most necessary instructions as quickly as possible: 'Cover your left as much as you can, it is badly threatened, and hold the trench! . . .'

I quickly divided up my men, four to the barrier, all the rest to the breastwork: 'The trench will be held to the last man!' I ordered six of my snipers and my smartest N.C.O. to protect my left flank. They had to lie absolutely flat, outside the trench, behind little hastily thrown-up mounds of earth, facing the enemy's flanking-trenches. I took them out myself and showed each sniper his position, crawling from one to the other. And just then we got our first greeting! I had carelessly raised myself up to get a better view across— and how it crackled and hissed and hummed and whistled! The mud splashed up into my eyes. Bullets were pitching all round me and then a murderous rattle started over there— that meant a machine-gun. They were shoot-ing with their pipes in their mouths. My snipers and I did not allow ourselves to get flustered. Nobody was hit. Over there the képis kept bobbing up incautiously, to look across, and each of my men aimed at a képi, fired, and many a képi gave a bounce into the air and disappeared for good. But the machine-gun kept on rattling, especially by the barrier. If only we had more cover! How will the day end?

It was 9 a.m., and the so-called trench was full of corpses and all sorts of equipment. We stood and sat on bodies as if they were stones or logs of wood. Nobody worried if one had its head stuck through or torn off, or a third had gory bones sticking out through its torn coat. And outside the trench one could see them lying in every kind of position. There was one quite young little chap, a Frenchman, sitting in a shell-hole, with his rifle on his arm and his head bent forward, but he was holding his hands, as if to protect himself, in front of his chest in which there was a deep bayonet wound. And so they lay, in all their different positions, mostly Frenchmen, with their heads battered in by blows from mallets and even spades, and all around rifles, equipment of all kinds and any number of képis. The 154th had fought like furies in their attack, to revenge themselves for the shell-fire.

A heap of five corpses lay just this side of the barrier; we were constantly having to tread on them to try and squash them down into the mud, because, in consequence of the gun-fire, we couldn't get them out of the trench. Suddenly I noticed with horror that one of the supposed corpses, lying underneath three others, was beginning to move —he was a big bearded Frenchman—opened his eyes and began to groan hideously. He must have lain insensible all night beneath the corpses. We dragged him out, screaming with pain. I gave him a drink, but we couldn't do anything else for him, and he soon sank back into a deep swoon. Our feelings gradually became quite blunted.

I had received orders from the Company Commander, on behalf of the Battalion, to storm the opposite trench with three parties of volunteers: 'The trench must be taken by 11 o'clock!' The necessary dispositions were at once made, the smartest men being chosen. One's heart quaked a little. I was going to begin the attack from the boyau, and at the same moment the 10th Company was to start from the opposite side. The most important thing was to make sure whether the boyau was clear of the enemy, in order to begin the attack from there. I myself climbed over the barrier into the boyau; enemy shots flickered by, but didn't hit me. The boyau was full of bodies. Holding my revolver in front of me, I advanced—5, 10, 20 yards. At that point the way was barred by a barbed-wire obstruction, so there was no choice but to scramble over the traverse. I succeeded in doing this unnoticed. I could see that beyond the traverse there were none of the enemy, so that I could bring my attacking party as far as here and get the enemy's trench almost on the flank. If the French had been already in the boyau, it would certainly have been all up with me. So I went back to the barrier and told the men to climb over it, one by one, into the boyau.

That went off splendidly, unnoticed by the enemy; I had my thirty-two little men safely in the boyau and all ready. 'Fix bayonets! There will be no shooting, but with one spring we shall be in the enemy's trench and everybody in it will be killed or taken prisoner. Only we must not be seen beforehand, so be careful!'

Those were my orders. I couldn't see any sign of the 10th Company advancing, which seemed ominous!

We proceeded soundlessly, in single file, along the trench until we reached that damned barbed-wire obstruction, where we had got to climb over the traverse. It wasn't so easy for thirty-two men to do that unobserved as it had been for one, with the French not 30 yards away. I was in front and got safely over; my rifle was handed to me by the man behind and the next 1, 2, 3, 4, 5, 6, 7, 8 also got over all right. Then, just as the 9th man, who had perhaps humped his back up too high, was in the act of clambering over, all of a sudden a crackling machine-gun and rifle-fire was directed at this very spot. The bullets came rattling against the thin layer of earth. The 9th man got safely over simply by letting himself fall into the trench, and at the same moment the whole front of the trench

French troops, like their German counterparts in the reading, advance across barbed wire as shells explode.

was struck by a murderous volley. We ducked down as well as we could—there was no question of going farther, and then—what the devil is that? All at once there was a whistling of bullets over us from behind. The shots were being fired from our rear position against the French trench where the boyau which we already occupied ran into the French communication trenches—our men evidently not knowing that we were trying to attack by the boyau. It was a horrible situation, caught between the fire from our own side and the enemy's. . . .

The attack was brought to a standstill, and I breathed again! Suddenly there was a shout from below: 'urrah!' Furious firing again! But what's that? Field-Greys below there! My Lance-Corporal shouted to me: 'Herr Fähnrich,* it's the 10th Company!' Heavens, we were firing on our own men who had attacked! 'Cease fire, cease fire!' I bellowed as loud as ever I could. German discipline caused an instantaneous lull!

Yes, they really are Field-Greys down there; one could see their helmets. With one spring I was out of the trench and down towards the 10th Company. But hardly was I out of the trench than it began to whistle and clatter all round me, so that I could neither see nor hear, and even as I dropped to the ground I perceived quite close to me six fellows in helmets, hidden behind tree-trunks. The devil! what a dirty trick! One bullet hit the iron on the heel of my boot. With one single movement I was up, stumbled and fell back into the trench. Lance-Corporal Rössle, with two shots, killed two of the rascals dead as

---

*Fähnrich = Ensign. A youth of good family, qualifying for a commission.

mutton. It is to be hoped that the other four didn't get away either: they had German helmets and overcoats on to deceive us. My men shot simply as fast as the bullets could quit the rifle, and down in the gully we heard cries and great confusion.

All at once there was silence. Not a Frenchman stirred. And we too could stop and puff a bit. We were black with gunpowder-smoke and dripping with sweat. The men too were quite out of breath in consequence of having accompanied all their shots with a continual stream of abuse and curses in real Bavarian dialect! . . . The French had evidently had enough. Out in front one could hear wounded whimpering pitifully. . . .

But the worst was still to come! The bombardment! It was just like the one we had seen yesterday, only this time we were in the middle of it. It started at 3 o'clock, and at the same time they poured in a terrific flanking fire on our left. One after another of my brave men met his fate, either from artillery or infantry fire. It was ghastly; I had to keep urging the men to stick it out, not to lose courage, knowing all the time that I might be hit myself at any moment.

I crawled out again to the flank position, where there was no cover at all, and encouraged the men who were lying there—Corporal Seckinger and Privates Platzr and Plemmer—to keep a good look out, so that the enemy should not suddenly fall upon our flank in case the awful artillery fire should be too much for us. I had to shout into their ears, such a thunder was going on all round. Then, just as I had crawled down again into the trench, I was thrown over by a fearful concussion. Up above, where the three were lying, a soft, gurgling sound was heard; the legs of the one nearest me jerked convulsively

once; then all was deathly still! Platzr, who had been lying between Seckinger and Plemmer, came creeping down into the trench, his face deathly pale and streaming with blood. 'Seckinger and Plemmer don't move!' was all he said. Three men hit by one shell!

And so came the turn of one after another. In front, by the barrier, one man got a bullet through the chest. I gave him a drink and he died directly after. Yet another got a shell-splinter in the heart; he remained, sitting on the breastwork, as if he were asleep; once or twice in the night I was just going to wake him up. I told another to fire, because Frenchmen were showing themselves down below. Tearfully he answered, 'Sir, I can't,' and held out the shattered stump of his right hand. The cry burst from my lips: 'O God, help us!' But we didn't budge from the trench, while it thundered and rattled unceasingly.

There was a panic on the right: the men imagining that the whole left wing was smashed up. 'The French are coming!' one of the wounded had shouted in his bewildered excitement. For one moment the ranks were shaken, they all made a rush to the right, with the one idea of escaping from this horrible, agonizing hell in the trench. I sprang to the right. My platoon was alone, isolated. Then I snatched my revolver out of my pocket, leapt as far as possible to the right and drove them all back again to the left. They went of their own accord when they saw that I was still alive. If the French had attacked at that moment it might have gone badly with us. Nerves had given way for a moment, but we quickly pulled ourselves together again. This will give you some idea of the intensity of the fire.

About 9 o'clock I heard that the Company on our right had been withdrawn. Firing continued till half-past five. After that we all lay with our nerves strung up, waiting for the attack for which we supposed the artillery fire had been preparing. But it didn't come. In spite of it all they would have found us at our posts, although they were still firing on our flank and killing and wounding many. But one gets by degrees so callous about death that one hardly looks round when anybody falls. The thing one minds most is the lamentations of the badly wounded when one can't do anything for them. The afternoon cost us thirty men, eleven being dead and the rest mostly severely wounded, the greater number being of my platoon. I was reinforced, at my request, from another platoon.

I have never in my life so longed for nightfall as on this 21st of February; but it brought us no rest, not to mention sleep. The rifle-fire went on rattling too, but the gracious darkness protected us from the frightful gun-fire. My platoon was relieved by the 2nd for the night. My men were allowed to shift along to the right flank of the Company where it was less dangerous. I remained to hand over. The stretcher-bearers also came at last to fetch the wounded. Some of them died on the difficult, painful journey through the narrow trench. Seckinger and Plemmer were not dead but frightfully wounded. Seckinger had a shell-splinter right through his eyes. It had torn out both eyes and injured the brain. And the poor chap was still alive and even conscious as I pressed his hand in a last farewell, saying: 'You were faithful unto death. I commend you into God's hands.' 'Goodbye,' he answered. . . .

The night passed. We sat on corpses without worrying—as long as one didn't have to sit in the mud! . . .

A French Soldier Loses His Faith in Human Progress

A highly sensitive rendering of the terror and demoralization of the war appeared in a novel by Jules Romains (1885–   ) that reached the French public in book form in 1938. Part of the series *Men of Good Will,* it contributed to the examination of French society and values in the war and interwar period. From *Verdun,* by Jules Romains, trans. by Gerard Hopkins. Copyright 1939 and renewed 1967 by Alfred A. Knopf, Inc. Reprinted by permission of the publisher.

Courage is by no means incompatible with terror, with the general nervousness of the trenches. The irreverent laughter induced in us by the spectacle of life prevents us from taking our own individual lives too seriously. Men in the mass are seen to be like a shoal of fish or cloud of locusts swarming to destruction. The individual man is less than nothing—certainly not worth worrying about. The act of clinging to life is merely so much extra and useless trouble. We just let ourselves be swept along; the tide of danger picks us up and carries us with it. It will leave us high and dry precisely where it chooses and how it chooses: dead, mutilated, made prisoner, or even still living—not that that really settles anything.

This, it seems to me, is the one irreparable loss. It has taken civilization centuries of patient fumbling to teach men that life, their own and that of others, is something sacred. Well, it's been so much work thrown away.

We shan't, you'll see, get back to that attitude in a hurry.

For people like us, this particular disaster is but one aspect of a far more extensive disaster, from the effects of which I, for one, shall never recover. How can I explain what I mean without making the sceptics smile? . . . Let me put it this way: Without subscribing to the cruder forms of the belief in progress, we did think—I hope you don't mind my saying "we"—that the last few centuries of Western civilization had given to human nature an orientation, a culture, that, no matter how one viewed it from the point of view of metaphysics, had had certain very important practical results. If we anticipated a continuance of the process, we could not, I think, be accused of undue stupidity. But that's a thing of the past. The anticipation, like everything else, has been swept away. My most haunting horror is not that I see men now willing to suffer and to act as they do, but that having so seen them, I shall never again be able to believe in their good intentions. Look at the thing how you will, it is now proved beyond power of contradiction that millions of men can tolerate, for an indefinite period and without spontaneously rising in revolt, an existence more terrible and more degrading than any that the numberless revolutions of history were held to have terminated for ever. They obey and they suffer as unquestioningly as the slaves and victims of the most bestial periods known to us. Don't let us blind ourselves to the truth by saying that at least they know why they are doing it, and that the fact of their free will saves their human dignity. We have no reason to affirm that the slaves and victims of past societies did not, between their rations of stripes, receive doses of moral drugs, injections of powerful suggestion, which created in them an attitude of consent. The slaves of the Pyramids may have been filled with admiration for the architectural ambitions of Pharoah. The Hindu widows who were burned on the funeral pyres of their husbands were no doubt persuaded that those who hoisted them on to the piles of aromatic wood were only helping them to accomplish a painful duty. All our talk of man's dignity is but mockery unless and until a day comes when certain things will under no circumstances be required of him or accepted by him as inevitable. I can no longer believe that any such day will ever come. You have often laughed at my optimism, at my Rousseauism; well, I am now in a state of mind that forces me to a deep distrust of man, of everything he may enforce as master or consent either to do or to endure as slave. . . .

STUDY QUESTIONS

1. How well had the goals of Prince Albert (Reading 154) been realized by the end of the century?

2. What kinds of developments, in Commager's and Viereck's analysis, were challenging the values and achievements of the past?

3. How did the arms race and the alliance system pave the road to world war? What other forces contributed?

4. How is it possible for a general war to break out that neither side desires? Why did a strategy of deterrence fail? Could it happen again?

5. What was trench warfare like? What impact did exposure to ground fighting in World War I have on the value system of the soldiers? Do you think that the onslaught on liberal values can be traced to earlier developments in the nineteenth century?

Chapter 6

Acceleration in History:
The Twentieth Century

The pace of industrial progress in the twentieth century has exceeded the dreams of its nineteenth-century apostles, extending Western techniques and values to the furthest reaches of a shrinking globe. This astounding diffusion could not conceal, however, a growing uneasiness among Westerners about their ability to preserve and enhance the civilization created so arduously and over so many centuries. Primary among these creators of doubt was the dismal record of two world wars waged on an unprecedented scale.

From a Western perspective, the First World War deserves to be called the worst single catastrophe in human history. The precarious peace that followed could not overcome the war's legacy, and twenty-five years later the peace was again broken. The Second World War brought not only enormous losses of population and devastation of great urban centers, but a surrender of power by the established European nations. On their periphery, Russia and America emerged as superpowers, and in the developing continents, former colonies entered the world of sovereign nation-states.

The postwar decades, although they saw the decline of European political and economic dominance, were also years of triumph for the West. Her science and technology remained sources of hope to the great bulk of mankind, still looking to Western techniques for aid in industrial growth. Equally important, the concern for human rights, so significant in the Western tradition, was taken up in the constitutions and aspirations of countless new nations. Despite the fear created by the macabre wedding of science and military technology in the advanced industrial nations, faith persisted in the ability to improve our civilization by knowledge and reason. Like their predecessors three hundred years earlier, the explorers of space hoped they were making "a giant step for mankind."

1903	Wright brothers' first flight
1911	Frank L. Wright, Taliesin
1911	Collapse of Manchu Empire
1913	Stravinsky's *Rite of Spring*
1916	Einstein publishes his general theory of relativity
1917	Russian Revolution
1918	British women granted limited suffrage
1919	League of Nations
1919	Treaty of Versailles
1920	United States 20th Amendment grants female suffrage
1924	Lenin dies
1924	Schönberg first uses 12-tone technique
1925	Kafka, *The Trial*
1926–1953	Stalin dominates Russia
1929	Stock Market Crash; Great Depression begins
1931–1932	Japanese occupy Manchuria
1933	Hitler comes to power
1936–1939	Spanish Civil War
1937	Japanese declare war on China
1937	*Guernica* by Pablo Picasso
1938	Munich Agreement
1939	German invasion of Poland
1939–1945	World War II
1945	Atomic bomb dropped on Japan
1945	United Nations Charter
1947	Marshall Plan
1948–1949	Berlin Airlift
1949	North Atlantic Treaty Organization
1949	Russia tests atomic bomb
1950–1953	Korean War
1955	Warsaw Pact
1955	Bandung Conference of Asian and African nations
1956	Soviet reoccupation of Hungary
1957	Common Market
1957	Sputnik
1960s	Most African colonies win independence
1961	Berlin Crisis
1962	Cuban Missile Crisis
1965	United States' escalation in Vietnam
1967	Six-Day War in the Near East
1969	United States astronauts land on moon
1969	Soviet invasion of Czechoslovakia
1971	India-Pakistan War
1972	Nixon trip to China

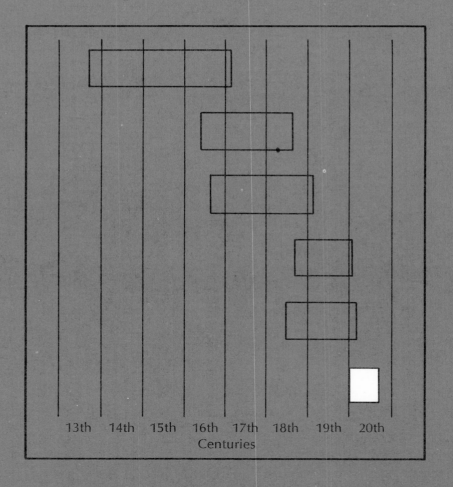

13th 14th 15th 16th 17th 18th 19th 20th

Centuries

TOPIC 42

VOICES OF THE TWENTIETH CENTURY

Many thoughtful Europeans traced the decline of European civilization in this century to the First World War. Winston Churchill wrote of that war: "Injuries were wrought to the structure of human society which a century will not efface." In a similar vein, the French writer Jules Romains harked back to the war for the origins of decline: "It was on August 2, 1914, that the real front was broken, the front held by civilization against barbarism." In their pessimism, however, some of the finest European minds sought an explanation that would get at the very sources of human behavior. Sigmund Freud, a Viennese physician, was in this company. Other voices in the interwar period, echoing the sentiments of the American statesman Woodrow Wilson, maintained their faith in the inherent desire of man to do what is right and relied on international agreements and the principle of collective security embodied in the structure of Wilson's League of Nations to keep the peace. Following a brief survey of the years between the two world wars this Topic presents these voices of hope and their counterparts of violence and destruction.

The Period between Wars

This article, contributed by the editors of this book, provides an introduction to the interwar years.

Europe, which had blundered into the First World War, felt the cost of that blunder for generations to come. Ten million men never returned from the battlefield and twenty million more were wounded, but casualties were far greater even than these and were found as well among the living—the demoralized recipients of official telegrams announcing the deaths of sons and husbands, the disoriented survivors of years in uniforms, and the confused laborers in a European economy weakened by the catastrophe.

Of crucial importance among the results of the war was the transformation that had been effected in the European state, which controlled the lives of its citizens to a greater extent than ever before. In order to assure more effective participation in the war new, wide-ranging instruments of state control had been introduced by the European governments. Propaganda had sold an increasingly unpopular war to the citizen, rationing had affected his access to consumer goods, conscription had shaped his way of life, and security measures had limited his freedom to dissent. Not least among the losses was the freedom to travel. During the war passports had been introduced to limit movement across the borders of Europe's nation-states. Like many of the measures introduced at this time its use was continued in peacetime.

While the European state was being transformed internally, the place of Europe in the world was also being altered. No longer could Western Europeans claim political and military precedence over all other nations. It was the entrance of the United States into the war in 1917 that had turned the tide of battle in favor of the democratic forces. And yet after 1919 the United States refused to assume the responsibilities of leadership to which her power obligated her. Giant Russia, too, was isolated from the Western community of nations after a revolution in 1917 that overthrew the tsar and established a communist dictatorship. The European states could pretend to ignore these facts in the 1920s and 30s, but no major effort to control aggression in the world could be successful without the support of these two powers on the periphery.

The seeds of a new war had been planted in the Treaty of Versailles, the agreement that brought World War I to a close. The seeds developed, however, only because of the fertile soil into which they were thrown. The Treaty of Versailles recognized the existence of several new nations in central and eastern Europe, created at the expense of the defeated German and Austro-Hungarian Empires and a Russia torn by civil war and revolution. The security of these new states—Czechoslovakia, Poland and Yugoslavia, and the Baltic republics of Latvia, Lithuania and Estonia—lying between Germany and Russia seemed to depend either on Russia's and Germany's continuing willingness to respect the terms of the settlement or the ability of a collective security agreement, like that proposed for the League of Nations, to deter aggression. However, an isolationist American Senate vetoed United States participation in the League, Britain refused to guarantee the frontiers of the new nations, and Bolshevik Russia was excluded from discussions of European security.

Nonetheless, the decade of the 1920s was generally a peaceful and prosperous one. A new German republican government subscribed to the terms of the Versailles settlement and began to repay the victors the losses to property caused by the war. There were border conflicts on the edge of Europe, some involving aggression by a great power, but no conflict between major powers developed. Rather it was the great depression of 1929 that brought to the surface the unresolved issues in Europe, terminated her peace and prosperity, and brought the world to a second catastrophe.

The fateful crash came in October of 1929, and revealed the interdependence of the global economy of the twentieth century and the pivotal role of American banks within it. During the First World War, for the first time in her history, the United States had become a creditor nation. The effects of that development were revealed when five thousand American banks closed down in four years. The sound of those closing doors had echos around the world far greater than the gunshot which was heard at Lexington. The German economy, which had been helped along by short-term American loans, was hardest hit. When these were called in the German economy collapsed, and by 1931 six million unemployed restlessly walked the streets. Other nations followed the lead of the United States in cheapening currency by going off the gold standard. Nations turned inward, raising tariffs to protect industry and jobs at home and using the depreciation of currency to make home-produced goods more competitive abroad.

Widespread unemployment, on a scale never known before in the industrialized states, had profound consequences. It diminished the respect enjoyed by the father of the family now no longer a breadwinner, heightened discontent with national leadership, and made the average citizen willing and even eager to have the state assume a more protective role in his life. In those European countries in which the experience with democracy was recent and incomplete, in nations like Germany and Italy, this discontent was exploited by fascist dictators.

Adolf Hitler and Benito Mussolini used the discontent created by the war settlement and the depression to create powerful one-party states. The power of the state over the individual was carried furthest in Germany. Dissenters were isolated and punished, children were turned into informers against their parents, the government monopolized communications, education, and economic opportunity. A Jewish minority within the German state was made the scapegoat for Germany's war losses, economic difficulties, and international position. The new system of political control by bureaucracy and terror touched the average citizen far more than had authoritarian rule in earlier periods. Similar instruments of control were developed in Soviet Russia, though for other reasons. Because of these similarities, Germany and Russia, with quite different ideologies, can be described together as totalitarian states.

In the 1930s Germany turned against the terms of the Versailles Treaty. Hitler, who

The Fascist dictators meet, Benito Mussolini and Adolf Hitler.

came to power in 1933, had been quick to sense the dissatisfaction in Germany with a treaty that bound her to a second-class status among nations. He was quick to sense as well the possibilities of exploiting in Germany's interest the portions of the Treaty that guaranteed national self-determination. For the treaty-makers had frequently sacrificed that ideal to the complementary one of economic self-sufficiency for the new states.

Locked within the boundaries of the new state of Czechoslovakia, for example, were a minority of three and a half million Germans. After announcing the creation of a standing army, sending troops back into the Rhineland, and annexing Austria, all in contravention of the Versailles agreement, Hitler turned his attention to Germany's unguaranteed frontiers in central Europe. The first victim was Czechoslovakia. The Munich agreement of 1938, by which France and Britain ceded Czech territory to Germany without the participation of Czechoslovakia and in the absence of Russia, symbolized the weakness of Europe's security system between the wars.

The second victim was Poland, and it was Germany's invasion of Poland on September 1, 1939 that triggered the Second World War. The United States was brought into the conflict two years later, after another expanding state, Japan, attacked Pearl Harbor, an important American naval installation in the Pacific. The war raged for six years, in jungles, on mountains, in the sea, and high above the earth. Civilian and military losses in the war were even greater than in 1914–1918. The full commitment of the United States and Russia— the same commitment they had withheld from peace efforts between the wars—was required in military efforts before the Second World War could be brought to a close. Germany and her allies were defeated, but the barbarism of a war marked by the attempted extermination of a whole people, the devastation of cities, and the use of atomic weapons against a civilian population left the taste of victory a bitter one. For Europe, there was despair amid the ruins.

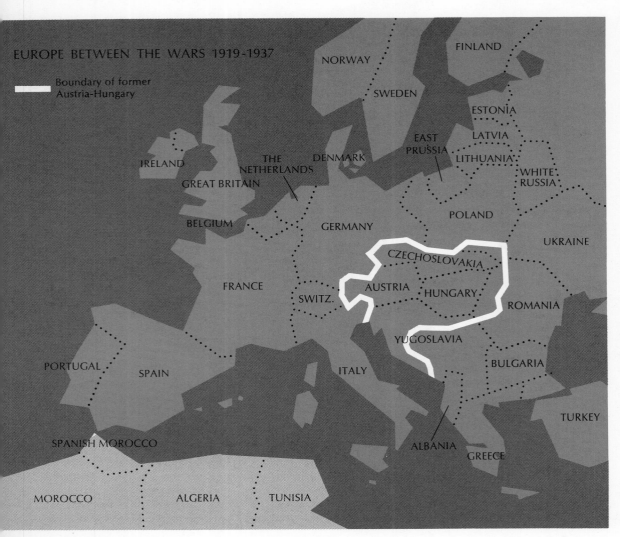

EUROPE BETWEEN THE WARS 1919–1937

Boundary of former
Austria-Hungary

NORWAY

FINLAND

SWEDEN

ESTONIA

LATVIA

EAST
PRUSSIA

LITHUANIA

IRELAND

THE
NETHERLANDS

DENMARK

WHITE
RUSSIA

GREAT BRITAIN

BELGIUM

GERMANY

POLAND

UKRAINE

CZECHOSLOVAKIA

FRANCE

AUSTRIA

HUNGARY

SWITZ.

ROMANIA

YUGOSLAVIA

PORTUGAL

SPAIN

ITALY

BULGARIA

TURKEY

SPANISH MOROCCO

ALBANIA

GREECE

MOROCCO

ALGERIA

TUNISIA

Sigmund Freud Argues the Limits of Reason

Sigmund Freud (1865–1939) was one of the great thinkers of modern times. His work in psychoanalysis has had wide impact on education, art, and literature. While Freud is best known for his essays on the influence of childhood on later behavior, particularly on sexual behavior, his theories are generally concerned with the limits of human reason and with the antagonism between the demands of instinct and the restrictions imposed upon man by civilization. The first selection, written during World War I, focuses upon the dislocation caused by war. The second is taken from one of his most influential works, *Civilization and Its Discontents*, in which Freud examines the relation between civilization and human behavior patterns. I. pp. 292–295 of "Thoughts for the Times on War and Death," Chapter XVII of Volume IV of *The Collected Papers of Sigmund Freud*, edited by Ernest Jones, M.D., Basic Books, Inc., Publishers, New York, 1959. II. Reprinted from *Civilization and Its Discontents* by Sigmund Freud. Translated from the German and edited by James Strachey. By permission of W. W. Norton & Company, Inc. Copyright © 1961 by James Strachey. Both I and II are published in Canada by The Hogarth Press Ltd.

I. THE DISILLUSIONMENT OF THE WAR (1915)

The war in which we had refused to believe broke out, and brought—disillusionment. Not only is it more sanguinary and more destructive than any war of other days, because of the enormously increased perfection of weapons of attack and defence; but it is at least as cruel, as embittered, as implacable as any that has preceded it. It sets at naught all those restrictions known as International Law, which in peace-time the states had bound themselves to observe; it ignores the prerogatives of the wounded and the medical service, the distinction between civil and military sections of the population, the claims of private property. It tramples in blind fury on all that comes in its way, as though there were to be no future and no goodwill among men after it has passed. It rends all bonds of fellowship between the contending peoples, and threatens to leave such a legacy of embitterment as will make any renewal of such bonds impossible for a long time to come.

Moreover, it has brought to light the almost unbelievable phenomenon of a mutual comprehension between the civilized nations so slight that the one can turn with hate and loathing upon the other. Nay, more—that one of the great civilized nations [Germany] is so universally unpopular that the attempt can actually be made to exclude it from the civilized community as 'barbaric,' although it long has proved its fitness by the most magnificent co-operation in the work of civilization. . . .

Nations are in a measure represented by the states which they have formed; these states, by the governments which administer them. The individual in any given nation has in this war a terrible opportunity to convince himself of what would occasionally strike him in peace-time—that the state has forbidden to the individual the practice of wrong-doing, not because it desired to abolish it, but because it desires to monopolize it, like salt and tobacco. The warring state permits itself every such misdeed, every such act of violence, as would disgrace the individual man. It practises not only the accepted strategems, but also deliberate lying and deception against the enemy; and this, too, in a measure which appears to surpass the usage of former wars. The state exacts the utmost degree of obedience and sacrifice from its citizens, but at the same time treats them as children by maintaining an excess of secrecy, and a censorship of news and expressions of opinion that renders the spirits of those thus intellectually oppressed defenceless against every unfavourable turn of events and every sinister rumour. It absolves itself from the guarantees and contracts it had formed with other states, and makes unabashed confession of its rapacity and lust for power, which the private individual is then called upon to sanction in the name of patriotism.

Nor may it be objected that the state cannot refrain from wrong-doing, since that would place it at a disadvantage. It is no less disadvantageous, as a general rule, for the individual man to conform to the customs of morality and refrain from brutal and arbitrary conduct; and the state but seldom proves able to indemnify him for the sacrifices it exacts. It cannot be a matter for astonishment, therefore, that this relaxation of all the moral ties between the greater units of mankind should have had a seducing influence on the morality of individuals; for our conscience is not the inflexible judge that ethical teachers are wont to declare it, but in its origin is 'dread of the community' and nothing else. When the community has no rebuke to make, there is an end of all suppression of the baser passions, and men perpetrate deeds of cruelty, fraud, treachery and barbarity so incompatible with their civilization that one would have held them to be impossible.

Well may that civilized cosmopolitan, therefore, of whom I spoke, stand helpless in a world grown strange to him—his all-embracing patrimony disintegrated, the common estates in it laid waste, the fellow-citizens embroiled and debased!

In criticism of his disillusionment, nevertheless, certain things must be said. Strictly speaking, it is not justified, for it consists in the destruction of—an illusion! We welcome illusions because they spare us emotional distress, and enable us instead to indulge in gratification. We must not then complain if now and again they come into conflict with some portion of reality, and are shattered against it.

Two things in this war have evoked our sense of disillusionment: the destitution shown in moral relations externally by the states which in their interior relations pose as the guardians of accepted moral usage, and the brutality in behaviour shown by individuals, whom, as partakers in the highest form of human civilization, one would not have credited with such a thing. . . .

II. CIVILIZATION AND ITS DISCONTENTS (1930)

. . . Men are not gentle creatures who want to be loved, and who at the most can defend themselves if they are attacked; they are, on the contrary, creatures among whose instinctual endowments is to be reckoned a powerful share of aggressiveness. As a result, their neighbour is for them not only a potential helper or sexual object, but also someone who tempts them to satisfy their aggressiveness on him, to exploit his capacity for work without compensation, to use him sexually without his consent, to seize his possessions, to humiliate him, to cause him pain, to torture and to kill him. . . . As a rule this cruel aggressiveness waits for some provocation or puts itself at the service of some other purpose, whose goal might also have been reached by milder measures. In circumstances that are favourable to it, when the mental counter-forces which ordinarily inhibit it are out of action, it also manifests itself spontaneously and reveals man as a savage beast to whom consideration towards his own kind is something alien. Anyone who calls to mind the atrocities committed during the racial migrations or the invasions of the Huns, or by the people known as Mongols under Jenghiz Kahn and Tamerlane, or at the capture of Jerusalem by the pious Crusaders, or even, indeed, the horrors of the recent World War —anyone who calls these things to mind will have to bow humbly before the truth of this view.

The existence of this inclination to aggression, which we can detect in ourselves and justly assume to be present in others, is the factor which disturbs our relations with our neighbour and which forces civilization into such a high expenditure [of energy]. In consequence of this primary mutual hostility of human beings, civilized society is perpetually threatened with disintegration. The interest of work in common would not hold it together; instinctual passions are stronger than reasonable interests. Civilization has to use its utmost efforts in order to set limits to man's aggressive instincts and to hold the manifestations of them in check by physical reaction-formations. Hence, therefore, the use of methods intended to incite people into identifications and aim-inhibited relationships of love, hence the restriction upon sexual life, and hence too the ideal's commandment to love one's neighbour as one-self—a commandment which is really justified by the fact that nothing else runs so strongly counter to the original nature of man. In spite of every effort, these endeavours of civilization have not so far achieved very much. It hopes to prevent the crudest excesses of brutal violence by itself assuming the right to use violence against criminals, but the law is not able to lay hold of the more cautious and refined manifestations of human aggressiveness. The time comes when each one of us has to give up as illusions the expectations which, in his youth, he pinned upon his fellow-men, and when he may learn how much difficulty and pain has been added to his life by their ill-will. At the same time, it would be unfair to reproach civilization with trying to eliminate strife and competition from human activity. These things are undoubtedly indispensable. . . .

In all that follows I adopt the standpoint, therefore, that the inclination to aggression is an original, self-subsisting instinctual disposition in man, and I return to my view that it constitutes the greatest impediment to civilization. At one point in the course of this enquiry . . . I was led to the idea that civilization was a special process which mankind undergoes, and I am still under the influence of that idea. I may now add that civilization is a process in the service of Eros [the instinct for life in Man], whose purpose is to combine single human individuals, and after that families, then races, peoples and nations, into one great unity, the unity of mankind. Why this has to happen, we do not know; the work of Eros is precisely this. These collections of men are to be libidinally bound to one another. Necessity alone, the advantages of work in common, will not hold them together. But man's natural aggressive instinct, the hostility of each against all and of all against each, opposes this programme of civilization. This aggressive instinct, is the derivative and the main representative of the death instinct which we have found alongside of Eros and which shares world-dominion with it. And now, I think, the meaning of the evolution of civilization is no longer obscure to us. It must present the struggle between Eros and Death, between the instinct of life and the instinct of destruction, as it works itself out in the human species. This struggle is what all life essentially consists of, and the evolution of civilization may therefore be simply described as the struggle for life of the human species. . . .

Collective Security Provides a Means To Preserve Peace

One of the most hopeful developments of the postwar era was the reliance placed on the concept of collective security as an instrument to preserve future peace. The idea of collective security was not new. It was popularized and given contemporary form, however, by the idealistic American president, Woodrow Wilson (1856–1924), who was determined to utilize the victory of the democracies to establish a just and lasting peace which would contain a built-in mechanism to make it unnecessary for the world ever to go to war again. Collective security correctly assumes that aggression can only be stopped by superior force. It provides that force by achieving mutual agreement among nations that it is their duty to act automatically against all aggression no matter by whom or for whatever reason. A center to coordinate the actions of the states of the world was created by the establishment of the League of Nations, the covenant of which formed the first section of the Versailles peace settlement. Passages from a Wilson speech in Columbus, Ohio, to rally support for the treaty in America are followed by excerpts from the Covenant of the League. I. From *Selected Literary and Political Papers and Addresses of Woodrow Wilson,* vol. II [New York: Grosset and Dunlap, 1927 (by arrangement with Harper and Row, Publishers)], pp. 353-354. II. From *Papers Relating to the Foreign Relations of the United States: The Paris Peace Conference, 1919,* vol. XIII, (Washington D.C., 1947), pp. 72, 83-84, 88-90.

I. PRESIDENT WILSON DEFENDS VERSAILLES AS AN ATTEMPT TO PUT AN END TO WAR (SEPTEMBER, 1919)

For, my fellow citizens, this treaty is not meant merely to end this single war. It is meant as a notice to every government which in the future will attempt this thing that mankind will unite to inflict the same punishment. There is no national triumph sought to be recorded in this treaty. There is no glory sought for any particular nation. The thought of the statesmen collected around that table was of their people, of the sufferings that they had gone through, of the losses they had incurred—that great throbbing heart which was so depressed, so forlorn, so sad in every memory that it had had of the five tragical years that have gone. Let us never forget those years, my fellow countrymen. Let us never

forget the purpose—the high purpose, the disinterested purpose—with which America lent its strength not for its own glory but for the defense of mankind.

As I said, this treaty was not intended merely to end this war. It was intended to prevent any similar war. I wonder if some of the opponents of the league of nations have forgotten the promises we made our people before we went to that peace table. We had taken by processes of law the flower of our youth from every household, and we told those mothers and fathers and sisters and wives and sweethearts that we were taking those men to fight a war which would end business of that sort; and if we do not end it, if we do not do the best that human concert of action can do to end it, we are of all men the most unfaithful, the most unfaithful to the loving hearts who suffered in this war, the most unfaithful to those households bowed in grief and yet lifted with the feeling that the lad laid down his life for a great thing and, among other things, in order that other lads might never have to do the same thing. That is what the league of nations is for, to end this war justly, and then not merely to serve notice on governments which would contemplate the same things that Germany contemplated that they will do it at their peril, but also concerning the combination of power which will prove to them that they will do it at their peril. It is idle to say the world will combine against you, because it may not, but it is persuasive to say the world is combined against you, and will remain combined against the things that Germany attempted. The league of nations is the only thing that can prevent the recurrence of this dreadful catastrophe and redeem our promises. . . .

II. THE TREATY OF VERSAILLES SPELLS OUT HOW COLLECTIVE SECURITY WILL WORK (1919)

Part I: The Covenant of the League of Nations

The High Contracting Parties, In order to promote international cooperation and to achieve international peace and security

by the acceptance of obligations not to resort to war,

by the prescription of open, just and honourable relations between nations,

by the firm establishment of the undertakings of international law as the actual rule of conduct among Governments,

and by the maintenance of justice and a scrupulous respect for all treaty obligations in the dealings of organized peoples with one another,

Agree to this Covenant of the League of Nations.

Article 10

The Members of the League undertake to respect and preserve as against external aggression the territorial integrity and existing political independence of all Members of the League. In case of any such aggression or in case of any threat or danger of such aggression the Council shall advise upon the means by which this obligation shall be fulfilled.

Article 11

1. Any war or threat of war, whether immediately affecting any of the Members of the League or not, is hereby declared a matter of concern to the whole League, and the League shall take any action that may be deemed wise and effectual to safeguard the peace of nations. In case any such emergency should

arise the Secretary-General shall on the request of any Member of the League forthwith summon a meeting of the Council.

2. It is also declared to be the friendly right of each Member of the League to bring to the attention of the Assembly or of the Council any circumstance whatever affecting international relations which threatens to disturb international peace or the good understanding between nations upon which peace depends.

Article 12

1. The Members of the League agree that if there should arise between them any dispute likely to lead to a rupture they will submit the matter either to arbitration *or judicial settlement* or to enquiry by the Council, and they agree in no case to resort to war until three months after the award by the arbitrators *or the judicial decision* or the report by the Council.

Article 16

1. Should any Member of the League resort to war in disregard of its covenants under Articles 12, 13, or 15, it shall *ipso facto* be deemed to have committed an act of war against all other Members of the League, which hereby undertake immediately to subject it to the severance of all trade or financial relations, the prohibition of all intercourse between their nationals and the nationals of the covenant-breaking State and the nationals of any other State, whether a Member of the League or not.

2. It shall be the duty of the Council in such case to recommend to the several Governments concerned what effective military, naval, or air force the Members of the League shall severally contribute to the armed forces to be used to protect the covenants of the League.

3. The Members of the League agree, further, that they will mutually support one another in the financial and economic measures which are taken under this Article, in order to minimize the loss and inconvenience resulting from the above measures, and that they will mutually support one another in resisting any special measures aimed at one of their number by the covenant-breaking State, and that they will take the necessary steps to afford passage through their territory to the forces of any of the Members of the League which are cooperating to protect the covenants of the League.

4. Any Member of the League which has violated any covenant of the League may be declared to be no longer a Member of the League by a vote of the Council concurred in by the Representatives of all the other Members of the League represented thereon.

The Views of Adolf Hitler

Adolf Hitler (1889–1945), demagogue and fascist dictator of Germany from 1933 to 1945, gained power in part through his insight into the weaknesses of the twentieth-century world. Extracts from four of his speeches present a sampling of his thinking. In *Hitler's Words,* ed. Gordan Prange (Washington, 1944), pp. 4, 10–11, 80. Reprinted by permission of the American Council on Public Affairs.

I. ONLY FORCE RULES (1926)

The fundamental motif through all the centuries has been the principle that force and power are the determining factors. All development is struggle. Only force rules. Force is the first law. A struggle has already taken place between original man and this primeval world. Only through struggle have states and the world become great. If one should ask whether this struggle is gruesome, then the only answer could be: For the weak, yes, for humanity as a whole, no.

World history proves that in the struggle between nations, that race has always won out whose drive for self-preservation was the more pronounced, the stronger. . . . Unfortunately, the contemporary world stresses internationalism instead of the innate values of race, democracy and the majority instead of the worth of the great leader. Instead of everlasting struggle the world preaches cowardly pacifism, and everlasting peace. These three things, considered in the light of their ultimate consequences, are the causes of the downfall of all humanity. The practical result of conciliation among nations is the renunciation of a people's own strength and their voluntary enslavement.

II. MAN MUST KILL (1929)

If men wish to live, then they are forced to kill others. The entire struggle for survival is a conquest of the means of existence which in turn results in the elimination of others from these same sources of subsistence. As long as there are peoples on this earth, there will be nations against nations and they will be forced to protect their vital rights in the same way as the individual is forced to protect his rights.

There is in reality no distinction between peace and war. Life, no matter in what form, is a process which always leads to the same result. Self-preservation will always be the goal of every individual. Struggle is ever-present and will remain. This signifies a constant willingness on the part of man to sacrifice to the utmost. Weapons, methods, instruments, formations, these may change, but in the end the struggle for survival remains. . . .

One is either the hammer or the anvil. We confess that it is our purpose to prepare the German people again for the role of the hammer. For ten years we have preached, and our deepest concern is: How can we again achieve power? We admit freely and openly that, if our Movement is victorious, we will be concerned day and night with the question of how to produce the armed forces which are forbidden us by the peace treaty. We solemnly confess that we consider everyone a scoundrel who does not try day and night to figure out a way to violate this treaty, for we have never recognized this treaty.

A major menace to German racial purity in Nazi eyes was the Jew, but as this early photograph demonstrates, there were other internal enemies as well. The banner reads: "We will permit no sabotage of the Fuehrer's (Hitler's) work of reconstruction." Beneath are caricatures of (left to right) opponents of sterilization, conservative landowners who yearn for the imperial past, Nordic women who fraternize with Jews, playboys, and Catholic religious orders (nun carrying entrance fee to Heaven).

We admit, therefore, that as far as we are concerned the German army in its present form is not permanent. For us it will serve only as a great cadre army, that is, as a source of sergeants and officers. And in the meantime we will be continuously at work filling in the ranks. We will take every step which strengthens our arms, which augments the number of our forces, and which increases the strength of our people.

We confess further that we will dash anyone to pieces who should dare to hinder us in this undertaking. . . . Our rights will never be represented by others. Our rights will be protected only when the German Reich is again supported by the point of the German dagger.

III. WORLD DISCORD IS GERMANY'S OPPORTUNITY (1930)

We Germans have no reason to wish, even in the slightest degree, that through events, no matter of what nature they might be, a so-called "World Peace" should be preserved which makes possible, indeed confirms . . . the most terrible plundering and extortion as the only possible fate for our

people. If a victor of superior strength expresses a desire for rest after a hard war, that is understandable. The tiger needs time to devour his victim. But that the victim should also wish that the tiger should not be disturbed in the act of devouring him is an unnatural desire. . . .

Germany can have only one ardent wish, namely, that the spirit of misfortune should hover over every conference, that discord should arise therefrom, and that finally a world peace which would otherwise ruin our nation should dissolve in blood and fire. And one can hope that out of this struggle the possibility might arise for Germany to enter upon the stage of world historical events as a performer. . . .

IV. RACIAL PURITY (1937)

The main plank in the National Socialist program is to abolish the liberalistic concept of the individual and the Marxist concept of humanity and to substitute therefor the folk community, rooted in the soil and bound together by the bond of its common blood. This is a very simple statement, but it involves a principle that has tremendous consequences. This is probably the first time and this is the first country in which the people are being taught to realize that, of all tasks which we have to face, the noblest and most sacred for mankind is that each racial species must preserve the purity of the blood which God has given it. . . . The greatest revolution which National Socialism has brought about is that it has rent asunder the veil which hid from us the knowledge that all human failures and mistakes are due to the conditions of the time and therefore can be remedied, but that there is one error which cannot be remedied once men have made it, namely, the failure

to recognize the importance of conserving the blood and the race free from intermixture and thereby the racial aspect and character which are God's gift and God's handiwork. It is not for men to discuss the question of why Providence created different races, but rather to recognize the fact that it punishes those who disregard its work of creation. . . .

Rudolf Hoess Describes Mass Murder at Auschwitz (1938-1943)

Rudolf Hoess, who had been in charge of Auschwitz Concentration Camp, was tried as a war criminal by the Allied powers after the defeat of Germany. Hoess' statement below was presented as evidence at his trial. He was later executed. From *Nazi Conspiracy and Aggression,* vol. VI, compiled by the Office of United States Chief of Counsel for Prosecution of Axis Criminality, International Military Trials—Nuremberg (Washington, D.C.: U.S. Government Printing Office, 1946), pp. 787–789.

I, Rudolf Franz Ferdinand Hoess, being first duly sworn, depose and say as follows:

I am forty-six years old, and have been a member of the NSDAP [Nazi Party] since 1922; a member of the SS since 1934; a member of the Waffen-SS since 1939. I was a member from December 1, 1934, of the SS Guard Unit, the so-called Deathshead Formation (*Totenkopf Verband*).

I have been constantly associated with the administration of concentration camps since 1934, serving at Dachau until 1938; then as

Adjutant in Sachsenhausen from 1938 to May 1, 1940, when I was appointed Commandant of Auschwitz. I commanded Auschwitz until December 1, 1943, and estimate that at least 2,500,000 victims were executed and exterminated there by gassing and burning, and at least another half million succumbed to starvation and disease making a total of dead of about 3,000,000.

This figure represents about 70% or 80% of all persons sent to Auschwitz as prisoners, the remainder having been selected and used for slave labor in the concentration camp industries. Included among the executed and burnt were approximately 20,000 Russian prisoners of war (previously screened out of Prisoner of War cages by the Gestapo) who were delivered at Auschwitz in Wehrmacht (army) transports operated by regular Wehrmacht officers and men. The remainder of the total number of victims included about 100,000 German Jews, and great numbers of citizens, mostly Jewish, from Holland, France, Belgium, Poland, Hungary, Czechoslovakia, Greece, and other countries. We executed about 400,000 Hungarian Jews alone at Auschwitz in the summer of 1944. . . .

The "final solution" of the Jewish question meant the complete extermination of all Jews in Europe. I was ordered to establish extermination facilities at Auschwitz in June 1941. At that time, there were already in the General Government [of Poland] three other extermination camps: Belzek, Treblinka and Wolzek. I visited Treblinka to find out how they carried out their extermination. The Camp Commandant at Treblinka told me that he had liquidated 80,000 in the course of one-half year. He was principally concerned with liquidating all the Jews from the Warsaw ghetto. He used monoxide gas and I did not think that his methods were very efficient. So when I set up the extermination building at Auschwitz, I used Cyclon B, which was a crystallized prussic acid which we dropped into the death chamber from a small opening. It took from 3 to 15 minutes to kill the people in the death chamber, depending upon climatic conditions. We knew when the people were dead because their screaming stopped. We usually waited about one-half hour before we opened the doors and removed the bodies. After the bodies were removed our special commandos took off the rings and extracted the gold from the teeth of the corpses.

Another improvement we made over Treblinka was that we built our gas chambers to accommodate 2,000 people at one time, whereas at Treblinka their 10 gas chambers only accommodated 200 people each. The way we selected our victims was as follows: we had two SS doctors on duty at Auschwitz to examine the incoming transports of prisoners. The prisoners would be marched by one of the doctors who would make spot decisions as they walked by. Those who were fit to work were sent into the camp. Others were sent immediately to the extermination plants. Children of tender years were invariably exterminated, since by reason of their youth they were unable to work. Still another improvement we made over Treblinka was that at Treblinka the victims almost always

Ovens in the concentration camp at Lublin, Poland, in which the bodies of victims of the gas chambers were cremated. After some experimentation, the furnaces were able to produce a temperature of 1500°C and the bodies were reduced to ashes in an efficient twenty-five minutes.

knew that they were to be exterminated and at Auschwitz we endeavored to fool the victims into thinking that they were to go through a delousing process.

Of course, frequently they realized our true intentions and we sometimes had riots and difficulties due to that fact. Very frequently women would hide their children under their clothes but of course when we found them we would send the children in to be exterminated. We were required to carry out these exterminations in secrecy but of course the foul and nauseating stench from the continous burning of bodies permeated the entire area and all of the people living in the surrounding communities knew that exterminations were going on in Auschwitz. . . .

The Atom Bomb Falls on Hiroshima (1945)

The director of Hiroshima Communications Hospital, Dr. Michihiko Hachiya, was wounded in the devastating American atomic attack that destroyed his city on August 6, 1945. While recuperating he wrote an account of the explosion's aftermath, the opening pages of which are reproduced in this reading. From Michihiko Hachiya, *Hiroshima Diary*, trans. and ed. Warner Wells (Chapel Hill: University of North Carolina Press, 1955), pp. 1–3, 14–16.

6 AUGUST 1945

The hour was early; the morning still, warm, and beautiful. Shimmering leaves, reflecting sunlight from a cloudless sky, made a pleasant contrast with shadows in my garden as I gazed absently through wide-flung doors opening to the south.

Clad in drawers and undershirt, I was sprawled on the living room floor exhausted because I had just spent a sleepless night on duty as an air warden in my hospital.

Suddenly, a strong flash of light startled me—and then another. So well does one recall little things that I remember vividly how a stone lantern in the garden became brilliantly lit and I debated whether this light was caused by a magnesium flare or sparks from a passing trolley.

Garden shadows disappeared. The view where a moment before all had been so bright and sunny was now dark and hazy. Through swirling dust I could barely discern a wooden column that had supported one corner of my house. It was leaning crazily and the roof sagged dangerously.

Moving instinctively, I tried to escape, but rubble and fallen timbers barred the way. By picking my way cautiously I managed to reach the *rōka* and stepped down into my garden. A profound weakness overcame me, so I stopped to regain my strength. To my surprise I discovered that I was completely naked. How odd! Where were my drawers and undershirt?

What had happened?

All over the right side of my body I was cut and bleeding. A large splinter was protruding from a mangled wound in my thigh, and something warm trickled into my mouth. My cheek was torn, I discovered as I felt it gingerly, with the lower lip laid wide open. Embedded in my neck was a sizable fragment of glass which I matter-of-factly dislodged, and with the detachment of one stunned and shocked I studied it and my blood-stained hand.

Where was my wife?

Suddenly thoroughly alarmed, I began to yell for her: "Yaeko-san! Yaeko-san! Where are you?"

Blood began to spurt. Had my carotid artery been cut? Would I bleed to death? Frightened and irrational, I called out again: "It's a five-hundred-ton bomb! Yaeko-san, where are you? A five-hundred-ton bomb has fallen!"

Yaeko-san, pale and frightened, her clothes torn and bloodstained, emerged from the ruins of our house holding her elbow. Seeing her, I was reassured. My own panic assuaged, I tried to reassure her.

"We'll be all right," I exclaimed. "Only let's get out of here as fast as we can."

She nodded, and I motioned for her to follow me.

The shortest path to the street lay through the house next door so through the house we went—running, stumbling, falling, and then running again until in headlong flight we tripped over something and fell sprawling into the street. Getting to my feet, I discovered that I had tripped over a man's head.

"Excuse me! Excuse me, please!" I cried hysterically.

There was no answer. The man was dead. The head had belonged to a young officer whose body was crushed beneath a massive gate.

We stood in the street, uncertain and afraid, until a house across from us began to sway and then with a rending motion fell almost at our feet. Our own house began to sway, and in a minute it, too, collapsed in a cloud of dust. Other buildings caved in or toppled. Fires sprang up and whipped by a vicious wind began to spread.

It finally dawned on us that we could not stay there in the street, so we turned our steps

Hiroshima, two months after the atomic attack. The center of the blast was approximately one mile from this area.

The second picture, taken from a Japanese movie (1953), captures the agony of nuclear victims seeking escape in the river.

towards the hospital. Our home was gone; we were wounded and needed treatment, and after all, it was my duty to be with my staff. This latter was an irrational thought—what good could I be to anyone, hurt as I was.

We started out, but after twenty or thirty steps I had to stop. My breath became short, my heart pounded, and my legs gave way under me. An overpowering thirst seized me and I begged Yaeko-san to find me some water. But there was no water to be found. After a little my strength somewhat returned and we were able to go on. . . .

7 AUGUST 1945

[Mr. Hachiya managed to get to a hospital which was still standing.]

. . . "Please tell us more of what occurred yesterday," [I said.]

"It was a horrible sight," said Dr. Tabuchi. "Hundreds of injured people who were trying to escape to the hills passed our house. The sight of them was almost unbearable. Their faces and hands were burnt and swollen; and great sheets of skin had peeled away from their tissues to hang down like rags on a scarecrow. They moved like a line of ants. All through the night, they went past our house, but this morning they had stopped. I found them lying on both sides of the road so thick that it was impossible to pass without stepping on them."

I lay with my eyes shut while Dr. Tabuchi was talking, picturing in my mind the horror he was describing. I neither saw nor heard Mr. Katsutani when he came in. It was not until I heard someone sobbing that my attention was attracted, and I recognized my old friend. I had known Mr. Katsutani for many years and knew him to be an emotional person, but even so, to see him break down made tears come to my eyes. He had come all the way from Jigozen to look for me, and now that he had found me, emotion overcame him.

He turned to Dr. Sasada and said brokenly: "Yesterday, it was impossible to enter Hiroshima, else I would have come. Even today fires are still burning in some places. You should see how the city has changed. When I reached the Misasa Bridge this morning, everything before me was gone, even the castle. These buildings here are the only ones left anywhere around. The Communications Bureau seemed to loom right in front of me long before I got anywhere near here."

Mr. Katsutani paused for a moment to catch his breath and went on: "I really walked along the railroad tracks to get here, but even they were littered with electric wires and broken railway cars, and the dead and wounded lay everywhere. When I reached the bridge, I saw a dreadful thing. It was unbelievable. There was a man, stone dead, sitting on his bicycle as it leaned against the bridge railing. It is hard to believe that such a thing could happen!"

He repeated himself two or three times as if to convince himself that what he said was true and then continued: "It seems that most of the dead people were either on the bridge or beneath it. You could tell that many had gone down to the river to get a drink of water and had died where they lay. I saw a few live people still in the water, knocking against the dead as they floated down the river. There must have been hundreds and thousands who fled to the river to escape the fire and then drowned.

"The sight of the soldiers, though, was more dreadful than the dead people floating down the river. I came onto I don't know how many, burned from the hips up, and where the skin had peeled, their flesh was wet and mushy. They must have been wearing their military caps because the black hair on top of their heads was not burned. It made them look like they were wearing black, lacquer bowls.

"And they had no faces! Their eyes, noses and mouths had been burned away, and it looked like their ears had melted off. It was hard to tell front from back. One soldier, whose features had been destroyed and was left with his white teeth sticking out, asked me for some water, but I didn't have any. He didn't say anything more. His plea for water must have been his last words. The way they were burned, I wonder if they didn't have their coats off when the bomb exploded."

It seemed to give Mr. Katsutani some relief to pour out his terrifying experiences on us, and there was no one who would have stopped him, so fascinating was his tale of horror. While he was talking, several people came in and stayed to listen. Somebody asked him what he was doing when the explosion occurred.

"I had just finished breakfast," he replied, "and was getting ready to light a cigarette, when all of a sudden I saw a white flash. In a moment there was a tremendous blast. Not stopping to think, I let out a yell and jumped into an air-raid dugout. In a moment there was such a blast as I have never heard before. It was terrific! I jumped out of the dugout and pushed my wife into it. Realizing something terrible must have happened in Hiroshima I climbed up onto the roof of my storehouse to have a look."

Mr. Katsutani became more intense and, gesticulating wildly, went on: "Towards Hiroshima, I saw a big black cloud go billowing up, like a puffy summer cloud. Knowing for sure then that something terrible had happened in the city, I jumped down from my storehouse and ran as fast as I could. . . ."

Escapism Through Film

A potent voice of the 20th century was the ubiquitious motion picture, which became an enormously influential vehicle for entertainment and propaganda in the period between the wars. Historical epics, romantic comedies, soap-opera dramas and detective thrillers all contributed to provide the average citizen with a means of escape from the problems of daily life.

The scenes from European and American films of the era include: below, the extravagant glitter of *The Gold Diggers of 1933;* on the following page, the unsophisticated Disney magic of *Snow White and the Seven Dwarfs* (1937); the horror of *Nosferatu* (1922) with its blood-sucking vampire Dracula; the poignant appeal of the triumphant "little man," Charlie Chaplin in *City Lights* (1931).

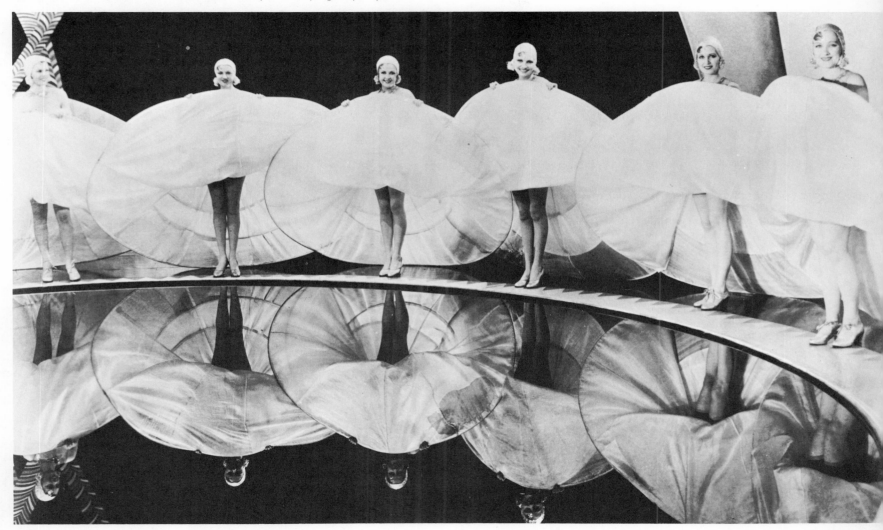

STUDY QUESTIONS

1. How did the world that followed World War I differ from that preceding? To what extent can blame be placed on the war for what happened in the thirty years that followed?

2. Why did Freud feel the war brought disillusionment? Why did he think this disillusion not justified?

3. What was Freud's view of the nature of man? How did it differ from that of Locke (third paragraph in Reading 80)?

4. Why did Freud conclude that there was a conflict between man and civilization? Was he opposed to civilization? Why did he think it had not been very successful?

5. How would Locke and the other Enlightenment figures have explained World War I? What would they have suggested as a solution for the future?

6. What is collective security? On what principles is it based? How does it work according to Articles 10–16 of the League Covenant? What are its shortcomings?

7. How would Freud explain the views of Adolf Hitler? Are Hitler's views "unwestern"? Why would people support him?

8. In what ways are Auschwitz and Hiroshima similar? In what ways dissimilar? How do the Enlightenment, Freud, Auschwitz, and Hiroshima illustrate the dilemma of modern man?

TOPIC 43

THE TOTALITARIAN STATE

Child of the twentieth century, the totalitarian state is the product of developments in political organization, technology, and terror that have made possible for the first time government that is, in fact, absolute. Totalitarian states have rejected the Western ideals of individual dignity and personal freedom, imposing instead the submission of man to the state and his powerlessness before it. The nightmare life of such regimes in Germany and Russia had certain common features despite their distinct and hostile ideologies. The readings consider the phenomenon of totalitarianism in both its fascist and communist forms, but concentrate on its development during the long dictatorship of Joseph Stalin.

Harry Shaffer: Communism and Fascism: Two Peas in a Pod?

American sovietologist Harry G. Shaffer prefaced his collection of interpretive articles on the Soviet system by attacking the assumption that one type of dictatorship is like every other. In this reading he points out the basic differences between fascism and communism. From *Queen's Quarterly*, Vol. LXIX, No. 1 (Spring 1962), cited in Shaffer: *The Soviet System in Theory and Practice*, New York: Copyright, 1965, Appleton-Century-Crofts, Division of Meredith Publishing Company, pp. 28–29, 30–33.

Born and raised in nations which, under a democratic, free enterprise system, have reached unparalleled economic affluence, the majority of Americans and Canadians have come to regard their political and economic system not only as the very best but as the only acceptable way of life for free men anywhere. Even moderate deviations towards the right or the left have been viewed traditionally with suspicion and apprehension, and changes are incorporated but slowly into the "American Way of Life." The extreme political left and the extreme political right, more often than not, are adjudged but poorly disguised tyrannies, alike in all respects except the names of the tyrants. Men like Hitler, Mussolini, Stalin, Khrushchev, Mao Tse-tung, and Castro tend to be treated as if they were identical in their philosophies and actions— all agents of the devil bent on enslaving suffering mankind for essentially similar purposes and by essentially similar means. Such men as Franco, Chiang Kai-shek, and Syngman Rhee, however, have (for reasons of political expediency) at one time or another received the luke-warm if not enthusiastic support of the American government, and the American public has been conditioned to accept them as defenders of Western Democracy with no questions asked.

As of now, well over one-third of the world's population is already within the Communist fold, and many other, smaller nations—both East and West—are ruled over by Fascist-type dictators. Under these circumstances, can we afford the erroneous assumption that Fascism and Communism— the two major radical challenges to twentieth-century Capitalist democracies of the liberal and of the more conservative type alike—are but two strands of poison ivy bearing different designations but demanding equal treatment and eradication? . . .

Fascism, its viewpoint somewhat reminiscent of that of the Tories during the American revolutionary period, denies the ability of people to govern themselves as free men in a democratic society. Mario Palmieri, Italian social scientist, refers to Democracy as "a bastard form of political and social organization. The mass of men," Palmieri proclaims, "is created to be governed and not to govern; is created to be led and not to lead; and is created finally to be slaves and not masters, slaves of their animal instincts, their physiological needs, their emotions and their passions." Mussolini explains that "Fascism asserts the irremediable, fruitful and beneficial inequality of men which can never be leveled permanently by a mere mechanical process such as universal suffrage." And Hitler sums

A sense of mass man in the service of the state pervades this photograph of a Nazi party rally in Nuremburg.

it up and draws a logical conclusion: "There must be no majority decision, but merely a body of responsible persons, and the word 'council' will revert to its ancient meaning. Every man shall have councillors at his side, but the *decision* shall be made by but one man."

The state, the all-powerful state which stands above the law, is the keystone of Fascist doctrine. "The state is not only the present," Mussolini shouted from his balcony, "it is also the past and above all it is the future. Transcending the brief spell of the life of individuals, the state stands for the immanent conscience of the nation." By superimposing the leadership principle upon the

theory of the omnipotence of the state, a system is created which, in Hitler's words, is based upon the maxim: "Authority of every leader towards below and responsibility towards above." The role of the *individual* in such a society was perhaps most clearly stated by one of Fascism's best known theoreticians, Alfredo Rocco: "For Fascism, society is the end, individuals the means, and its whole existence consists in using individuals as instruments for its ends. . . ."

In disagreement with the teachings of Fascism, Socialists and Communists of all shades and leanings believe in the perfectibility of all mankind. Man is basically good and capable of being master of his own destiny. Only

the economic, social, and political environment (with the stress on "economic") has prevented man from realizing the utmost limits of his capabilities both as a productive and as a social being.

Utopian thinkers and writers usually assumed that a change in environment in and of itself would be adequate to reform immediately what we generally refer to as "human nature." Karl Marx, father of "scientific socialism," was much more realistic. Fully aware that no revolutionary transformation of the economic, political, and social order could possibly usher in the stage of perfect freedom (which he prophesied would be the final destiny of mankind), Marx predicted the advent of an intermediate stage in society's development from Capitalist Democracy to pure Communism. This Intermediate Stage has been referred to by many designations, such as "Socialism" (as contrasted with "Communism"), "the Period of Transition." and, perhaps most frequently, "the Dictatorship of the Proletariat." It is this stage—not "Communism"—which the Soviet Union professes to be in at this moment. . . .

In marked distinction to Fascist ideology, no Communist ever proclaimed that a dictatorship would be the *final* goal of mankind. From Marx and Engels to present day Communist writers, this dictatorship is to be but preparatory for the time when, in Lenin's words, "mankind will inscribe on its banners: From each according to his ability, to each according to his needs." A pure Communist society, then, is mankind's promised land; a society without any government, police force, army, or jails; a society in which perfect freedom reigns; a society in which production will have been developed "to the n'th degree"; a society in which man will have been transformed into a "social being" who voluntarily and without special personal reward contributes to the best of his ability and takes from the common stores whatever he needs. It is this hope of an ideal order in which, quoting Lenin, "the *necessity* of observing the simple, fundamental rules of everyday social life in common will have become a *habit*"—it is this promise of a perfect world which Communism holds out to the hundreds of millions of its followers. To them, life under a "temporary" dictatorship does not seem too high a price to pay since most of them have known but little freedom in their native lands and most of their forefathers had lived and laboured under one or another type of tyranny since time immemorial. . . .

A Brief History of Communist Russia
(1917–1941)

From Crane Brinton, John B. Christopher, Robert L. Wolff, *Civilization in the West,* © 1964. Reprinted by permission of Prentice-Hall, Inc., Englewood Cliffs, New Jersey.

Why did the first successful Marxist revolution take place in Russia, where conditions according to Marx should have been least favorable, a backward agricultural country almost without an urban proletariat? Marx underestimated the revolutionary force latent in the Russian peasantry and lacked the imagination to conceive such a brilliant, ruthless, and lucky tactician as Lenin. Moreover, the Russian revolution was not wholly Marxist, but temporarily retreated into a kind of capitalism, and then spawned in Stalin a brutal dictator in whose policies nationalism and greed for personal power played as important a role as Marxism. At untold expense in human lives Stalin's programs created an industrial state fed by a collectivized agriculture. With much outside assistance, Russia withstood the savage attack that came from Adolf Hitler's Germany in June, 1941. The history of Russia between the First World War and the Second was, indeed, momentous.

THE MARCH REVOLUTION AND THE PROVISIONAL GOVERNMENT

World War I took a terrible toll in Russia, almost four million casualties in the first year alone. Munitions manufacture and supply were inefficient. With the Tsar at the front after 1915, and the Duma [parliament] prorogued, the Empress and her favorite, Rasputin, controlled the government, and adventurers and profiteers speculated in commissions, draft deferments, and commodities. Conservative patriots denounced the scandals, and in December, 1916, murdered Rasputin. Strikes and defeatism spread, while the armies bled to death at the front. The Tsar remained apathetic and refused all appeals to create a responsible ministry to clean up the mess.

The four days between March 8 and 12, 1914, saw a "leaderless, spontaneous, and anonymous revolution" in Petrograd (the new Russian name given to the capital city of St. Petersburg during the war). The troops of the Petrograd garrison refused to fire on workers striking in protest against food shortages and instead joined the strikers. A Soviet (council) of workers and soldiers with a 15-man executive committee took over the revolution, installed itself across the hall from the Duma, which remained in session, and asked that the Duma temporarily run the country. In consultation, Duma and Soviet created a "Provisional Government," . . . headed by a liberal, Prince Lvov, and including a radical labor lawyer and member of both Soviet and Duma, Alexander Kerensky. The Tsar abdicated and was arrested.

Between March and November 1917 the provisional government struggled against enormous difficulties: its members had no experience in government; they felt they had simultaneously to continue the war and democratize the huge unwieldy Russian Empire. The Soviet had the instruments of power, but would accept no responsibility. The provisional government did not have the tools to suppress its opponents, who multiplied especially in the provinces where local peasant-elected soviets sprang up. The peasants wanted land immediately, but the provisional

Lenin arrives at the Finland Station in Petrograd on April 16, 1917. In this later painting by M. Sokolov, omnipresent Joseph Stalin, who was not in the city at the time, stands in the train door behind Lenin.

government believed in legality and refused to sanction peasant seizures of land. Virtually all Russians wanted peace, but the provisional government felt in honor bound to continue the war. While waiting for a constituent assembly which was to be elected to give Russia a new constitution, the provisional government granted complete political liberty.

LENIN AND THE NOVEMBER REVOLUTION

Bolsheviks and other exiles began to return to Russia and to political life. The German general staff thought that the return of Lenin from Switzerland* would help disrupt the Russian war effort; so they permitted him to travel across Germany to the Baltic in a sealed railway car (April 16, 1917). Unlike most of his fellow [Marxists], who believed that a bourgeois parliamentary republic had to precede any eventual socialist revolution, Lenin had long advocated an alliance between workers and peasants to bring about an immediate uprising, from which the Bolsheviks would eventually emerge supreme. Lenin regarded himself as chief of the elite inner group of the Bolshevik party, which in turn would command the working class. The brilliant intellectual Leon Trotsky, who recognized Lenin's implicitly dictatorial tendencies, had long believed that the working class could move to power directly after the bourgeois revolution without waiting for the establishment of a bourgeois republic. In line with these ideas, Lenin returned to Russia,

*V. I. Lenin (1870–1924), the leader of the more extreme faction (Bolsheviks) of the Russian Marxists, had been exiled from Russia by the Tsarist authorities in 1907.

calling for the immediate seizure of power by the Soviets, much to the surprise of all but a very few of his followers. Calling for the immediate confiscation of estates and an immediate end to the war, he suited the popular mood; the army, the police, all government officials must go, and a republic of soviets must rise. Lenin galvanized the Bolsheviks into a revolutionary group waiting only the moment to seize power.

When an offensive on the front collapsed in July, and some troops rioted in the capital, the Soviet was too timid to take power. Kerensky became premier, and General Kornilov, commander-in-chief of the army, rallied conservative support, and planned a *coup* that would dispossess the Soviet. But railroad and telegraph workers sabotaged his movements, and his troops would not obey him. By September 14, Kornilov had been arrested; the only result of his efforts was increased pro-Bolshevik sentiment. The army mutiny got out of hand and peasant disorders mounted. Late in October, the Bolsheviks seized control of a military revolutionary committee originally chosen to defend the capital against the Germans, and now transformed by Trotsky into a general staff for the revolution. On November 7, with little bloodshed, the Bolsheviks took over Petrograd. . . . Lenin abolished landlords' property rights, proposed an immediate peace, and set up a Council of People's Commissars with himself as President, Trotsky was Foreign Commissar; a young Georgian named Joseph Djugashvili, who called himself Stalin, became Commissar of Nationalities. With varying speed, as most provincial garrisons helped them, the Bolsheviks seized power in Moscow, and in most of the provinces; Georgia, however, went Menshevik. Kornilov and some Duma poli-

ticians took refuge in Rostov-on-Don in southern Russia.

The Russian people were by no means pro-Bolshevik. When Lenin permitted elections for a constituent assembly, the first and last free elections in Russian history, the Bolsheviks polled only about 25 per cent of the vote. . . . Lenin permitted the assembly to meet only once (January 18, 1918); he dissolved it the next day by decree, and sent guards with rifles to disperse it. Thus he nullified the popular will. Russia did not have the high literacy rate, the tradition of debate, the respect for individual rights, or the large middle class usually associated with successful constitutional government. But it was Lenin's arbitrary use of force that ended the chance for true parliamentarism in Russia.

CIVIL WAR, 1917–1921

For the next three years, to the end of 1920, civil war raged in Russia, and foreign powers intervened to assist the enemies of the Bolsheviks, who changed their name to Communists and in 1918 shifted the capital to Moscow. The Bolsheviks at first believed that world revolution would soon begin in Germany, and then engulf other nations; so they treated foreign affairs casually. They completed the nationalization of all banks and all industrial enterprises employing more than ten workers by 1920. They requisitioned food from the peasants, mobilized the poorer ones against the richer peasants (*kulak*, meaning "fist," and implying hard-fisted usuriousness), and set up a secret police (the "*Cheka*," from the initials of the words meaning "extraordinary commission"). Early in 1918, they signed the Treaty of Brest-Litovsk with Germany . . . giving away one-third of Russia's population, 80 per cent of its iron, and 90 per cent of its coal (March 3, 1918). . . .

THE NEP, 1921–1928

By the end of the civil war, all vital services had broken down in Russia, and famine was raging; agricultural and industrial output had fallen disastrously. Anarchist revolts broke out, most notably at the naval base of Kronstadt (March, 1921), and were suppressed with much bloodshed; but they frightened Lenin into a change of policy. The "New Economic Policy" (always called NEP) adopted in 1921 and lasting until 1928, marked a temporary retreat from doctrinaire communist programs. Its chief aim was reconstruction, sought by appeasing the peasants and —since there had been no world revolution —by obtaining the resources of capitalist states.

The government now stopped requisitioning the whole of the peasant's crop above the minimum necessary to keep him alive. He paid a very heavy tax in kind, but could sell the rest of his crop to a private purchaser if he wished. Peasant agriculture became capitalist again, and the *kulaks* grew still richer, while the poor peasants often lost their land and hired out their labor. The state controlled heavy industry, banking, transportation, and foreign trade—what Lenin called the "commanding heights"—but allowed private enterprise in domestic trade and light industry. The partial return to capitalism brought economic recovery by 1926–1927.

Many leading communists hated NEP, and functionaries often subjected enterprising businessmen or farmers to petty persecution. Those who wanted to abolish NEP, liquidate those who profited by it, and push world revolution were called "Left deviationists:" They included Trotsky. Those who wanted to push the NEP program still further were the "Right deviationists:" Their chief spokesman was Nikolai Bukharin. The question agitated the communist leaders, especially as a result of the final illness of Lenin (1922–1924).

STALIN'S RISE TO POWER

The two leading contenders to succeed Lenin were Trotsky and Stalin. Toward the end of his life Lenin was urging that Stalin should be deprived of power, and only Lenin's death saved Stalin's career. To defeat Trotsky, Stalin first allied himself with Bukharin and argued for a kind of gradualism: peasant cooperatives but not collectives, no forced industrialization program, limited co-operation with capitalistic states and parties abroad. Having deprived Trotsky of influence, Stalin adopted many of Trotsky's ideas. Finding that agricultural production was not keeping pace with industry, he came out in 1927 for collectivization. He favored rapid industrialization and realized that this would involve huge investments of capital. Trotsky agrued that socialism in a single country could not succeed until world revolution brought communism to the industrial nations making their skills available to the cause; Stalin, on the other hand, maintained that Russia, while helping communist movements everywhere, could succeed as a "socialist" state by itself. His argument reflected his own Russian nationalism as well as his bid for popularity with the rank and file in Russia.

Stalin's victory, however, had less to do with the merits of the rival theories competing for acceptance in Russia during the 1920's than with his personal power. As Commissar of Nationalities he managed the destiny of almost half the population of the new Russian Soviet Republic and all the Asians in "republics" that he took charge of creating and that preserved and fostered native languages and cultures. In 1922 he sponsored the formation of the USSR (Union of Socialist Soviet Republics), with Moscow firmly controlling war, foreign policy, trade, and transport, coordinating finance, economy, food, and labor; but leaving justice, education, and agriculture in theory to the separate republics. A Council of Nationalities—with equal numbers of delegates from each ethnic group—became a second chamber, the Supreme Soviet being the first. Together they would appoint the administration, the Council of People's Commissars.

As chief of the Workers and Peasants' Inspectorate, Stalin could send his men anywhere in the government to eliminate inefficiency or corruption. He was also a member of the Politburo, the tight little group of Communist Party bosses, where his job was to manage the party: he prepared the agenda for meetings, passed on orders, controlled party patronage, maintained files on individuals' loyalty and achievement. This unobstrusive bureaucrat had in fact got hold of the real reins of power.

Trotsky was much more glamorous: Minister of War, creator of the Red Army, cultivated intellectual. But Stalin and two Bolshevik collaborators sent Trotsky's supporters to posts abroad, prevented the publication of Lenin's attacks on Stalin, and gradually deprived Trotsky of his positions. In 1927 Stalin had Trotsky expelled from the party and deported to Siberia, the first stage in a long exile that eventually brought him to Mexico, where an emissary from Stalin murdered him with an ice pick in 1940.

STALIN IN POWER: COLLECTIVIZATION

The same congress that expelled Trotsky in December, 1927, brought NEP to an end, and announced a "new socialist offensive" for 1928. Stalin became supreme, and the years between 1928 and 1941 would see the collectivization of agriculture, forced industrialization, the great political purges, and the building of an authoritarian state apparatus.

In 1929 Stalin declared war on the *kulaks* and virtually ended individual farming in Russia, proclaiming immediate full-scale collectivization. In exchange for locating and turning over to the state hidden crops belonging to the *kulaks,* the poorer peasants were promised places in collective farms to be made up of the *kulaks'* land and equipped with their implements. There were about two million *kulak* households in Russia, perhaps ten million people in all, who would now not only lose their property but be refused any place in the new collective. Peasants were gunned into submission, *kulaks* deported to Siberia or allowed to starve. Rather than join collectives peasants often burned their crops, broke their plows, and killed their cattle. Between one-half and two-thirds of the livestock in Russia were slaughtered. Famine took millions of human lives. In March, 1930, Stalin blamed local officials who had been "dizzy with success" for the tragedy. In one year 50 per cent of Russian farms had been thrown into collectives. Thereafter the process was more gradual and there were fewer excesses. By 1941 virtually all Russian farms had been

The SOVFOTO caption that accompanies this photo reads: "The collective farm system brought tremendous changes in the life of the peasant. His labor was made incomparably easier and more productive. Farm families now have high and steady incomes. Soviet farmers of today—for them wooden plows and the life-long hardships of their fathers are relics of the past."

The Russians, since their revolution, have placed major emphasis on the development of their heavy industry. They consider that development of a heavy industry base is a necessary first step to the full industrialization of their country. Here two Russian workers take part in manufacturing of a truck. The scene is from the Zis factory where trucks, cars, bicycles and refrigerators are made.

collectivised: there were 250,000 collectives, 900,000,000 acres in extent, supporting 19,000,000 families. . . .

THE FIVE-YEAR PLANS

In industry, 1928 saw the first of the Five-Year Plans, setting ambitious goals for production over the coming five years. Stalin appropriated ever bigger sums for capital investment, and often demanded impossibly high rates of growth. Partly the motive was to mechanize the new large-scale farms by the rapid production of tractors and by building power stations. Partly, Stalin wanted to create the mass industrial working class that Marxism taught was necessary for socialism. Additionally, he was determined to make socialism in Russia secure against outside attack, which he was sure menaced from all directions. Though the goals of the first Five-Year Plan were not attained by 1932, fulfillment was announced, and the second Plan for 1933–1937 went into effect. The third followed in due course, and was interrupted only by German invasion in 1941.

The Five-Year Plans emphasized heavy industry: steel, electric power, cement, coal, oil. Between 1928 and 1940 steel output went up four-and-one-half times, power eight, cement more than two, coal four, and oil almost three, with similar rises in chemical and machine production. Russia did in about twelve years what the rest of Europe had taken three-quarters of a century to do. Enthusiasm was whipped up by publicizing awards to especially productive workers. Yet the hardships were great. Inexperience and inefficiency cost heavily, and housing the workers, moving whole industries, and opening up new resources cost hundreds of thousands of lives. . . .

Russia by 1940 had one-third (instead of 18 per cent) of its people living in cities. Moscow and Leningrad (formerly St. Petersburg and Petrograd) almost doubled in size, and smaller towns grew even faster. The whole social picture had been changed. The prerevolutionary privileged classes had disappeared; the middle class, temporarily reprieved by NEP, vanished after 1928; most of the old intelligentsia, unable to stomach the dictatorship, emigrated. Those who stayed were forced into line with the new Soviet intellectual movements and were expected to concentrate their efforts on technological advances. Stalin's new system of incentives rewarded the small minority of skilled laborers, bureaucrats, and bosses [of collective farms], together with writers, artists, and entertainers, who formed the new elite. Although Soviet propaganda predicted the withering away of the state and reasserted that true communism was still the goal, the USSR fostered not Marxist equality but a new caste system.

STALIN'S DICTATORSHIP

Opposition to Stalin's ruthlessness existed, of course, but he imagined it to be everywhere. In 1934 the famous and mysterious purges began. Unlike the Jacobin terror in France, these did not begin until 17 years after the onset of the revolution; unlike Robespierre, Stalin survived. The murder of the party boss of Leningrad, Sergei Kirov (December 1, 1934) touched off the first purge. Kirov apparently had urged Stalin to relax his pressures, and Stalin probably arranged his murder. A series of trials, some of them secret, at intervals until 1938, and many executions without trial led to the death of every member of Lenin's Politburo except Stalin himself.

Most of the Soviet diplomatic corps, 50 of the 71 members of the Communist Party's Central Committee, judges, two successive heads of the secret police, and the prime ministers and chief officials of the non-Russian republics of the USSR—all were murdered or disappeared without a trace. It is doubtful whether any of the victims had actually conspired with Hitler, as some were accused of doing, though many of them certainly hated Stalin. Some who confessed publicly probably felt so deep a loyalty to the communist system that they sacrificed themselves for Stalin's Soviet state. Some doubtless hoped to save their families or even themselves; many may have hoped that the confessions were so ridiculous that nobody would believe them. Despite the upheaval no breakdown in the system took place for new bureaucrats quickly replaced the old. . . .

The period 1928–1941 saw a wholesale retreat from many of the ideas of the revolution. In the army traditional ranks were restored. Russia's national past was officially rediscovered and praised. The family, attacked by the old Bolsheviks who had made divorce and abortion easy, was rehabilitated; Stalin stressed the sanctity of marriage, made divorce more difficult to get, and encouraged children to obey their parents. In education, the authority of the teacher over the schoolroom was reaffirmed after a long period of classroom anarchy. But education became indoctrination as newspapers, books, theaters, movies, music, and art all plugged the party line. Censorship under Stalin outdid censorship under Nicholas I, since it prescribed that all artists constantly praise the system. Even the traditional militant atheism of the Bolsheviks was modified in 1937, as church-going no longer constituted reason for persecution or arrest. All these measures were designed partly to retain popular loyalty during the disruptive purges of the party and also to prepare for a German attack. Whatever the shift in views, Stalin dictated and managed it.

Nikita Khrushchev Attacks the Cult of the Individual (1956)

The last years of Stalin's life brought a recurrence of the tactics of terror of the 1930s. After his death in March 1953, the Soviet Union was ruled collectively by his leading lieutenants, who found it necessary to relax to some degree the tension of Russian society. But as Bertram Wolfe, respected authority on the Russian revolutionary movement, has noted: "Stalin's spirit was mighty, even in death. They, the priests of his cult, had made his figure so vast that they and all their deeds were dwarfed by it. Now they would have to cut him down to size." The unavoidable denunciation of Stalin was initiated at a secret session of the Twentieth Party Congress in Moscow on February 24, 1956 in an emotional speech by Nikita Khrushchev (1894–), Party First Secretary. Parts of this speech follow. Copyright © 1956 by The New York Times Company. Reprinted by permission. *Pravda's* hymn of praise to Stalin which prefaces Khrushchev's address is reprinted from *Problems of Communism*, March–April 1963, (United States Information Agency), p. 87.

Gigantic portraits of Stalin, such as this poster covering the side of a Moscow apartment house in 1936, were familiar sights in the Soviet Union.

I. A RUSSIAN NEWSPAPER HAILS THE AUTHOR OF CREATION (*Pravda*, August 28, 1936)

O Great Stalin, O leader of the Peoples,
Thou who didst give birth to man,
Thou who didst make fertile the earth,
Thou who dost rejuvenate the centuries,
Thou who givest blossom to the spring. . . .

II. KHRUSHCHEV DENOUNCES STALIN (February, 1956)

In December 1922 in a letter to the Party Congress Vladimir Ilyich [Lenin] wrote: "After taking over the position of Secretary General, Comrade Stalin accumulated in his hands immeasurable power and I am not certain whether he will be always able to use this power with the required care". . . .

When we analyze the practice of Stalin in regard to the direction of the Party and of the country, when we pause to consider everything which Stalin perpetrated, we must be convinced that Lenin's fears were justified. The negative characteristics of Stalin, which, in Lenin's time, were only incipient, transformed themselves during the last years into a grave abuse of power by Stalin, which caused untold harm to our Party.

We have to consider seriously and analyze correctly this matter in order that we may preclude any possibility of a repetition in any form whatever of what took place during the life of Stalin, who absolutely did not tolerate collegiality in leadership and in work, and who practiced brutal violence, not only toward everything which opposed him, but also toward that which seemed to his capricious and despotic character, contrary to his concepts.

Stalin acted not through persuasion, explanation, and patient cooperation with people, but by imposing his concepts and demanding absolute submission to his opinion. Whoever opposed this concept or tried to prove his viewpoint, and the correctness of his position—was doomed to removal from the leading collective and to subsequent moral and physical annihilation. This was especially true during the period following the XVIIth Party Congress, when many prominent Party leaders and rank-and-file Party workers, honest and dedicated to the cause of Communism, fell victim to Stalin's despotism. . . .

Stalin originated the concept "enemy of the people." This term automatically rendered it unnecessary that the ideological errors of a man or men engaged in a controversy be proven; this term made possible the usage of the most cruel repression, violating all norms of revolutionary legality, against anyone who in any way disagreed with Stalin, against those who were only suspected of hostile intent, against those who had bad reputations. . . .

Stalin . . . used extreme methods and mass repressions at a time when the revolution was already victorious, when the Soviet state was strengthened, when the exploiting classes were already liquidated and Socialist relations were rooted solidly in all phases of [the] national economy, when our Party was politically consolidated and had strengthened itself both numerically and ideologically. It is clear that here Stalin showed in a whole series of cases his intolerance, his brutality and his abuse of power. Instead of proving his political correctness and mobilizing the masses, he often chose the path of repression and physical annihilation, not only against actual enemies, but also against the Party and the Soviet government. Here we see no wisdom but only a demonstration of the brutal force which had once so alarmed V. I. Lenin. . . .

Facts prove that many abuses were made on Stalin's orders without reckoning with any norms of Party and Soviet legality. Stalin was a very distrustful man, sickly suspicious; we knew this from our work with him. He could look at a man and say: "Why are your eyes so shifty today," or "Why are you turning so much today and avoiding to look me directly in the eyes?" The sickly suspicion created in him a general distrust even toward eminent Party workers whom he had known for years. Everywhere and in everything he saw "enemies," "two-facers" and "spies."

Possessing unlimited power he indulged in great willfullness and choked a person morally and physically. A situation was created where one could not express one's own will.

When Stalin said that one or another should be arrested, it was necessary to accept on faith that he was an "enemy of the people." Meanwhile, Beria's gang, which ran the organs of the state security, outdid itself in proving the guilt of the arrested and the truth of materials which it falsified. And what proofs were offered? The confessions of the arrested, and the investigative judges accepted these "confessions." And how is it possible that a person confesses to crimes which he has not committed? Only in one way—because of application of physical methods of pressuring him, tortures, bringing him to a state of unconsciousness, deprivation of his judgement, taking away of his human dignity, In this manner were "confessions" acquired. . . .

The power accumulated in the hands of one person, Stalin, led to serious consequences during the Great Patriotic War. . . .

If we sharply criticize today the cult of the individual which was so widespread during Stalin's life and if we speak about the many negative phenomena generated by this cult which is so alien to the spirit of Marxism-Leninism, various persons may ask: How could it be? Stalin headed the Party and the country for 30 years and many victories were gained during his lifetime. Can we deny this? In my opinion, the question can be asked in this manner only by those who are blinded and hopelessly hypnotized by the cult of the individual, only by those who do not understand the essence of the revolution and of the Soviet State, only by those who do not understand, in a Leninist manner, the role of the Party and of the nation in the development of the Soviet society.

The Socialist revolution was attained by the working class and by the poor peasantry with the partial support of middle class peasants. It was attained by the people under the leadership of the Bolshevik Party. Lenin's great service consisted of the fact that he created a militant Party of the working class, . . . became its experienced leader, and led the working masses to power, to the creation of the first Socialist State.

You remember well the wise words of Lenin that the Soviet State is strong because of the awareness of the masses that history is created by the millions and tens of millions of people.

Our historical victories were attained thanks to the organizational work of the Party, to the many provincial organizations, and to the self-sacrificing work of our great nation. These victories are the result of the great drive and activity of the nation and of the Party as a whole; they are not at all the fruit of the leadership of Stalin, as the situation was pictured during the period of the cult of the individual.

If we are to consider this matter as Marxists and as Leninists, then we have to state unequivocally that the leadership practice which came into being during the last years of Stalin's life became a serious obstacle in the path of Soviet social development. . . .

Some comrades may ask us: Where were the members of the Political Bureau of the Central Committee? Why did they not assert themselves against the cult of the individual in time? And why is this being done only now?

First of all we have to consider the fact that the members of the Political Bureau viewed these matters in a different way at different times. Initially, many of them backed Stalin actively because Stalin was one of the strongest Marxists and his logic, his strength, and his will greatly influenced the cadres and Party work. . . .

In the situation which then prevailed I have talked often with Nikolai Aleksandrovich Bulganin; once when we two were traveling in a car, he said, "It has happened sometimes that a man goes to Stalin on his invitation as a friend. And when he sits with Stalin, he does not know where he will be sent next, home or to jail. . . ."

Hannah Arendt: Totalitarianism Seeks To Remake Man

German-born Hannah Arendt (1906–   ) is a provocative political theorist whose account of the origins of totalitarianism is widely recognized as a trenchant study of one of the modern world's most disturbing developments. In this selection Dr. Arendt analyses the striving toward total domination which she considers the salient feature of totalitarianism. Excerpted from *The Origins of Totalitarianism*, copyright © 1951, 1958, 1966 by Hanna Arendt. Reprinted by permission of Harcourt, Brace & World, Inc.

The concentration and extermination camps of totalitarian regimes serve as the laboratories in which the fundamental belief of totalitarianism that everything is possible is being verified. . . .

Total domination, which strives to organize the infinite plurality and differentiation of human beings as if all of humanity were just one individual, is possible only if each and every person can be reduced to a never-changing identity of reactions, so that each of these bundles of reactions can be exchanged at random for any other. The problem is to fabricate something that does not exist, namely, a kind of human species resembling other animal species whose only "freedom" would consist in "preserving the species." Totalitarian domination attempts to achieve this goal both through ideological indoctrination of the elite formations and through absolute terror in the camps; and the atrocities for which the elite formations are ruthlessly used become, as it were, the practical application of the ideological indoctrination—the testing ground in which the latter must prove itself—while the appalling spectacle of the camps themselves is supposed to furnish the "theoretical" verification of the ideology.

The camps are meant not only to exterminate people and degrade human beings, but also serve the ghastly experiment of eliminating, under scientifically controlled conditions, spontaneity itself as an expression of human behavior and of transforming the human personality into a mere thing, into something that even animals are not; for Pavlov's dog, which, as we know, was trained to eat not when it was hungry but when a bell rang, was a perverted animal.

Under normal circumstances this can never be accomplished, because spontaneity can never be entirely eliminated insofar as it is connected not only with human freedom but with life itself, in the sense of simply keeping alive. It is only in the concentration camps that such an experiment is at all possible, and therefore they are not only *"la société la plus totalitaire encore réalisée"* (David Rousset) but the guiding social ideal of total domination in general. Just as the stability of the totalitarian regime depends on the isolation of the fictitious world of the movement from the outside world, so the experiment of total domination in the concentration camps depends on sealing off the latter against the world of all others, the world of the living in general, even against the outside world of a country under totalitarian rule. This isolation explains the peculiar unreality and lack of credibility that characterize all reports from the concentration camps and constitute one of the main difficulties for the true understanding of totalitarian domination, which stands or falls with the existence of these concentration and extermination camps; for, unlikely as it may sound, these camps are the true central institution of totalitarian organizational power.

There are numerous reports by survivors. The more authentic they are, the less they attempt to communicate things that evade human understanding and human experience —sufferings, that is, that transform men into "uncomplaining animals." None of these reports inspires those passions of outrage and sympathy through which men have always been mobilized for justice. On the contrary, anyone speaking or writing about concentration camps is still regarded as suspect; and if the speaker has resolutely returned to the

Hospital section at Nordhausen, a slave labor camp where thousands died, on the day of liberation April 20, 1945.

The nightmare-like atmosphere of the concentration camp is poignantly revealed in this photograph of camp officials making their morning rounds at Yanovsky Camp in Poland while an orchestra, made up of prisoners who were later to be put to death, plays a rousing tune.

world of the living, he himself is often assailed by doubts with regard to his own truthfulness, as though he had mistaken a nightmare for reality.

This doubt of people concerning themselves and the reality of their own experience only reveals what the Nazis have always known: that men determined to commit crimes will find it expedient to organize them on the vastest, most improbable scale. Not only because this renders all punishments provided by the legal system inadequate and absurd; but because the very immensity of the crimes guarantees that the murderers who proclaim their innocence with all manner of lies will be more readily believed than the victims who tell the truth. The Nazis did not even consider it necessary to keep this discovery to themselves. Hitler circulated millions of copies of his book in which he stated that to be successful, a lie must be enormous—which did not prevent people from believing him as, similarly, the Nazis' proclamations, repeated *ad nauseam,* that the Jews would be exterminated like bedbugs (*i.e.,* with poison gas), prevented anybody from *not* believing them. . . .

It is the appearance of some radical evil, previously unknown to us, that puts an end to the notion of developments and transformations of qualities. Here, there are neither political nor historical nor simply moral standards but, at the most, the realization that something seems to be involved in modern politics that actually should never be involved in politics as we used to understand it, namely all or nothing—all, and that is an undetermined infinity of forms of human living-together, or nothing, for a victory of the concentration-camp system would mean the same inexorable doom for human beings as the use of the hydrogen bomb would mean the doom of the human race. . . .

II

It is in the very nature of totalitarian regimes to demand unlimited power. Such power can only be secured if literally all men, without a single exception, are reliably dominated in every aspect of their life. In the realm of foreign affairs new neutral territories must constantly be subjugated, while at home ever-new human groups must be mastered in expanding concentration camps, or, when circumstances require, liquidated to make room for others. The question of opposition is unimportant both in foreign and domestic affairs. Any neutrality, indeed any spontaneously given friendship, is from the standpoint of totalitarian domination just as dangerous as open hostility, precisely because spontaneity as such, with its incalculability, is the greatest of all obstacles to total domination over man. The Communists of non-Communist countries, who fled or were called to Moscow, learned by bitter experience that they constituted a menace to the Soviet Union. Convinced Communists are in this sense, which alone has any reality today, just as ridiculous and just as menacing to the regime in Russia, as, for example, the convinced Nazis of the Röhm faction were to the Nazis.

What makes conviction and opinion of any sort so ridiculous and dangerous under totalitarian conditions is that totalitarian regimes take the greatest pride in having no need of them, or of any human help of any kind. Men insofar as they are more than animal reaction and fulfillment of functions are entirely superfluous to totalitarian regimes. Totalitarianism strives not toward despotic rule over men, but toward a system in which men are superfluous. Total power can be achieved and safeguarded only in a world of conditioned reflexes, of marionettes without the slightest trace of spontaneity. Precisely because man's resources are so great, he can be fully dominated only when he becomes a specimen of the animal-species man.

Therefore character is a threat and even the most unjust legal rules are an obstacle; but individuality, anything indeed that distinguishes one man from another, is intolerable. As long as all men have not been made equally superfluous—and this has been accomplished only in concentration camps—the ideal of totalitarian domination has not been achieved. Totalitarian states strive constantly, though never with complete success, to establish the superfluity of man—by the arbitrary selection of various groups for concentration camps, by constant purges of the ruling apparatus, by mass liquidations. Common sense protests desperately that the masses are submissive and that all this gigantic apparatus of terror is therefore superfluous; if they were capable of telling the truth, the totalitarian rulers would reply: The apparatus seems superfluous to you only because it serves to make men superfluous.

The totalitarian attempt to make men superfluous reflects the experience of modern masses of their superfluity on an overcrowded earth. The world of the dying, in which men are taught they are superfluous through a way of life in which punishment is meted out without connection with crime, in which exploitation is practiced without profit, and where work is performed without product, is a place where senselessness is daily produced anew. Yet, within the framework of the totalitarian ideology, nothing could be more sensible and logical; if the inmates are vermin, it is logical that they should be killed by poison gas; if they are degenerate, they should not be allowed to contaminate the population; if they have "slave-like souls" (Himmler), no one should waste his time trying to re-educate them. Seen through the eyes of the ideology, the trouble with the camps is almost that they make too much sense, that the execution of the doctrine is too consistent.

While the totalitarian regimes are thus resolutely and cynically emptying the world of the only thing that makes sense to the utilitarian expectations of common sense, they impose upon it at the same time a kind of supersense which the ideologies actually always meant when they pretended to have found the key to history or the solution to the riddles of the universe. Over and above the senselessness of totalitarian society is enthroned the ridiculous supersense of its ideological superstition. Ideologies are harmless, uncritical, and arbitrary opinions only as long as they are not believed in seriously. Once their claim to total validity is taken literally they become the nuclei of logical systems in which, as in the systems of paranoiacs, everything follows comprehensibly and even compulsorily once the first premise is accepted. The insanity of such systems lies not only in their first premise but in the very logicality with which they are constructed.

The curious logicality of all isms, their simple-minded trust in the salvation value of stubborn devotion without regard for specific, varying factors, already harbors the first germs of totalitarian contempt for reality and factuality.

Common sense trained in utilitarian thinking is helpless against this ideological supersense, since totalitarian regimes establish a functioning world of no-sense. The ideological contempt for factuality still contained the proud assumption of human mastery over the world; it is, after all, contempt for reality which makes possible changing the world, the erection of the human artifice. What destroys the element of pride in the totalitarian contempt for reality (and thereby distinguishes it radically from revolutionary theories and attitudes) is the supersense which gives the contempt for reality its cogency, logicality, and consistency. What makes a truly totalitarian device out of the Bolshevik claim that the present Russian system is superior to all others is the fact that the totalitarian ruler draws from this claim the logically impeccable conclusion that without this system people never could have built such a wonderful thing as, let us say, a subway; from this, he again draws the logical conclusion that anyone who knows of the existence of the Paris subway is a suspect because he may cause people to doubt that one can do things only in the Bolshevik way. This leads to the final conclusion that in order to remain a loyal Bolshevik, you have to destroy the Paris subway. Nothing matters but consistency.

With these new structures, built on the strength of supersense and driven by the motor of logicality, we are indeed at the end of the bourgeois era of profits and power, as well as at the end of imperialism and ex-pansion. The aggressiveness of totalitarianism springs not from lust for power, and if it feverishly seeks to expand, it does so neither for expansion's sake nor for profit, but only for ideological reasons: to make the world consistent, to prove that its respective supersense has been right.

It is chiefly for the sake of this supersense, for the sake of complete consistency, that it is necessary for totalitarianism to destroy every trace of what we commonly call human dignity. For respect for human dignity implies the recognition of my fellow-men or our fellow-nations as subjects, as builders of worlds or cobuilders of a common world. No ideology which aims at the explanation of all historical events of the past and at mapping out the course of all events of the future can bear the unpredictability which springs from the fact that men are creative, that they can bring forward something so new that nobody ever foresaw it.

What totalitarian ideologies therefore aim at is not the transformation of the outside world or the revolutionizing transmutation of society, but the transformation of human nature itself. The concentration camps are the laboratories where changes in human nature are tested, and their shamefulness therefore is not just the business of their inmates and those who run them according to strictly "scientific" standards; it is the concern of all men. Suffering, of which there has been always too much on earth, is not the issue, nor is the number of victims. Human nature as such is at stake, and even though it seems that these experiments succeed not in changing man but only in destroying him, by creating a society in which the nihilistic banality of *homo homini lupus* is consistently realized, one should bear in mind the necessary limita-

Men become superfluous in a totalitarian world. Indifference to the act of killing is reflected in the faces of these ordinary German soldiers watching the execution of Czech patriots (Terezin, 1942).

627

tions to an experiment which requires global control in order to show conclusive results. . . .

The danger of the corpse factories and holes of oblivion is that today, with populations and homelessness everywhere on the increase, masses of people are continuously rendered superfluous if we continue to think of our world in utilitarian terms. Political, social, and economic events everywhere are in a silent conspiracy with totalitarian instruments devised for making men superfluous. The implied temptation is well understood by the utilitarian common sense of the masses, who in most countries are too desperate to retain much fear of death. The Nazis and the Bolsheviks can be sure that their factories of annihilation which demonstrate the swiftest solution to the problem of over-population, of economically superfluous and socially rootless human masses, are as much of an attraction as a warning. Totalitarian solutions may well survive the fall of totalitarian regimes in the form of strong temptations which will come up whenever it seems impossible to alleviate political, social, or economic misery in a manner worthy of man.

STUDY QUESTIONS

1. Compare the philosophy and goals of fascism and communism. How are they similar? How different? What are the attitudes of each toward the individual, the State, the nature of man, the economic sector, the social order, nationalism, the use of force?

2. Under what circumstances did the Russian Revolution take place? What was the difference between the March and November revolutions? Why wasn't the middle class able to establish a liberal democracy?

3. How did Lenin proceed to establish Marxian socialism in Russia? To what extent had he succeeded by his death? How did the views of Trotsky and Stalin differ? Why did Stalin win the power struggle?

4. What major programs did Stalin initiate? Why did he choose these and not others?

5. To what extent did Russia fit Marx's concept of socialism by 1941? How might Freud have explained the course of Russian history in these decades?

6. What aspects of Stalin's rule did Khrushchev attack in his speech? What did he mean by the "cult of the individual"? How did he get Stalin's successors "off the hook"?

7. To what end, according to Arendt, does totalitarianism seek to remake man? What means make this possible?

8. What is the appeal of totalitarian ideology to many men of the twentieth century?

The Course of the War

TOPIC 44

THE SECOND WORLD WAR

Twenty-five years after the outbreak of the First World War, Europe faced a second holocaust. Begun as an attack by Germany on Poland, the war soon engulfed scores of nations on six continents. At its close only the United States and the Soviet Union could still be regarded as world powers. A wartime alliance had developed new bonds between the two, and disputes were kept submerged during the joint struggle against fascism. The coming of the peace, however, left unresolved major differences about the structure of the postwar world and presented new questions about how the destructive weaponry developed during the war could be brought under man's control. The readings trace the history of the war, its impact on the nation-state, and its portent for the future.

In the early morning hours of September 1, 1939, the German forces launched the attack on Poland that initiated almost five years of ruthless and devastating warfare. Poland fell quick victim to the *Blitzkrieg* (lightning war) tactics of the German army and within nine months the Western European democracies of Norway, Denmark, the Netherlands, Belgium, and France had been overrun. Britain who now stood alone against the Nazi onslaught managed to ward off a massive aerial assault, but in the following spring the Germans turned their attention to southeastern Europe, conquered Yugoslavia and Greece and with the capture of Crete menaced the eastern Mediterranean. In this same spring of 1941, Hitler broke his nonaggression pact with Stalin and ordered a surprise attack on Russia that penetrated deep into the Ukraine and to the very gates of Moscow and Leningrad. This was the situation in Europe when the Japanese attacked America's Pacific outpost, Pearl Harbor, in December. The reading picks up the narrative when the United States entered the war. H. Stuart Hughes, *Contemporary Europe: A History*, © 1961. Reprinted by permission of Prentice-Hall, Inc., Englewood Cliffs, New Jersey.

THE GREAT COALITION

With the American intervention, the Second World War attained its final form. It became a coalition struggle of the two greatest democracies of the West in declared or tacit alliance with the homeland of Communism. These ill-assorted bedfellows had been thrown together by a series of historical accidents. Britain and the United States shared with the Soviet Union a common enemy in fascist terror and aggression, but there was little else to hold together two such radically different types of society, whose history during the previous quarter-century had been marked far more often by hostility than by friendship. On both sides, a massive legacy of distrust barred the way to harmonious cooperation. At the end of 1941, it was an open question whether the colossus of the East and the Anglo-Saxon powers would succeed in sinking their differences and in forming a solid fighting front. The next three years were to be punctuated by unremitting and constantly disappointed efforts on the part of Churchill and Roosevelt to establish with Stalin a true comradeship in arms.

At the outset the British served as the connecting link between the Russians and the Americans. The average Englishman was far more convinced than was his American counterpart of the advantages of an alliance with the Soviet Union—for one thing, he owed more to the Russians: with the German invasion in June, the *Luftwaffe's* attacks on British cities had come to an abrupt end. Hence Churchill voiced the sentiments of the overwhelming majority of his fellow citizens when, on the morrow of the Nazi attack, he pledged Stalin all the aid he could spare. In so doing, he did not repudiate his anti-Bolshevist past; he merely admitted frankly that to him the necessities of warfare overrode everything else. In the months that followed, he was generous in sending supplies—most of them going by the long, exposed sea route around the North Cape, where German aircraft based in Norway took a fearful toll of British convoys. With the signature of a mutual aid pact in mid-July, Britain and the Soviet Union became formally allied.

Roosevelt was unwilling to go that far. He well knew that an influential segment of the American people would never countenance an alliance with a communist state. But even before Pearl Harbor, he had agreed to ship supplies to the Soviet Union, using as precedent the lend-lease arrangements which had been made with Britain the previous spring. These marked a major turning point in the successive steps that had brought Roosevelt's policy into ever closer alignment with Churchill's war effort: in the summer of 1940 there had been the deal by which Britain conceded the use of overseas bases to the United States in return for fifty overage destroyers; a year later the American President had met the British Prime Minister at sea off Argentia in Newfoundland to sign the Atlantic Charter; and in September, 1941, the American navy had all but gone to war, when it was ordered to "shoot on sight" at submarines or other naval vessels threatening its convoy operations.

Still the American people continued to be profoundly divided: on the eve of Pearl Harbor, a clear majority opposed armed involvement on Britain's side. The Japanese attack [December 7] rescued Roosevelt from a cruel dilemma by forcing his hand: now the country had no alternative. The President was also spared the dangers of a congressional debate over whether to declare war on Germany and Italy as well as Japan; the two fascist states

themselves took the initiative by inaugurating hostilities with the United States in conformity with their Tripartite Pact with Tokyo.

Roosevelt and his military advisers made their crucial decision within a month after Pearl Harbor when they determined to give the defeat of Germany priority over dealing with Japan. Although this meant that some sort of coordination with the Russians was essential, the American government was resolved to limit such coordination to the military sphere. It would make no political or territorial commitments. Thus the British were left to deal with Stalin on the diplomatic front. From the beginning, he showed himself a tough negotiator. In late December, Anthony Eden, once again British foreign secretary, flew to Moscow to find out what the Russians wanted: he was astounded to learn that Stalin—who had barely saved his capital a fortnight before—insisted on retaining nearly all his gains from his pact with Hitler; the Soviet Union's rightful boundaries, he claimed, were those which existed at the time of the Nazi attack.

Temporarily, the British were able to put Stalin off by explaining—quite honestly—that the Americans would never consent to such a deal. To agree to the expanded Soviet boundaries of June, 1941, would be a direct violation of the Atlantic Charter, which promised self-determination to enslaved peoples. It meant consenting to the forced annexation of territories containing millions of Finns and Estonians, Lithuanians and Letts, Rumanians and Poles. Stalin's claims against Poland created a particularly embarrassing situation for Churchill and Roosevelt. Britain had gone to war in order to help the Poles, and now the Soviet leader was insisting on keeping the lands he had annexed at their country's fall.

True, he had signed an agreement with the Polish government-in-exile shortly after Hitler attacked him. This provided for the liberation of Polish prisioners whom the Red Army had captured in 1939 and their enrollment in a new army of liberation; but the agreement was vague on the question of postwar boundaries, and the Poles in London were displeased with the way in which the Russians were carrying it out.

Thus as early as the first month of American involvement in the war, the problem had arisen that was to poison relations within the grand alliance at its very end.

When the Red Army finally halted the German invasion in December, 1941, the situation of the Soviet Union seemed all but hopeless. It had lost its richest lands and more than half its industrial resources: the territory occupied by the Germans contained two-fifths of its population, its grain, and its railroad lines, plus two-thirds of its coal and iron. Over-all industrial production had fallen by more than half, and famine in the cities was beginning to take a dreadful toll.

Yet Stalin went on with his winter offensive. From December to May, the Red Army pushed forward, disengaging an ample protective zone before Moscow and dislodging the Germans from their advanced positions in the Ukraine. This campaign showed how much the Red Army had learned from the Winter War against Finland two years earlier: the Russians were now warmly clothed; they traveled light; and they knew how to operate in dispersed formation in the snow, infiltrating past the German outposts and cutting them off from their supplies and their escape routes to the rear.

This resiliency of the Russians—this ability to fight back after the terrible defeats of the summer and autumn—amazed and delighted their well-wishers in occupied Europe and in the West. It seemed to betoken some peculiar strength in the Soviet peoples, or in the system of government under which they lived. Thus the winter of 1941–1942 marked the beginning of a new wave of pro-Soviet and pro-Communist feeling in Europe. Stalin's pact with Hitler in 1939 had completely deflated his country's prestige. Now the rupture of that pact and Soviet resistance to the Nazi invasion brought a sharp and steady rise in Russia's standing: the years between 1941 and 1944 saw Soviet prestige higher than ever before.

From the perspective of the ordinary citizen who was no expert in military affairs, it looked as if Russia were doing all the fighting, while Britain and the United States were standing idly by. For nearly three years, the war in the East dwarfed the struggle in the West. The Nazi-Soviet conflict was without precedent in history. In the extent of territory it covered, in the forces engaged, in the ruthlessness displayed on both sides, certainly no modern war was comparable to it. Against the 150-odd divisions that the Germans and their satellites had sent to Russia, the Red Army had mobilized more than twice as many. These Soviet divisions were smaller and lighter than the German units, but as the war continued, and as Russia's population advantage began to tell, the weight of numbers fell ever more heavily on Stalin's side, despite the frightful losses that the Soviet peoples suffered. These again were without precedent: at the end of the war, total Soviet deaths—civilian and military—were estimated at twenty million. Millions had died in combat; millions more had starved or frozen to death. The Germans had slaughtered countless others among the

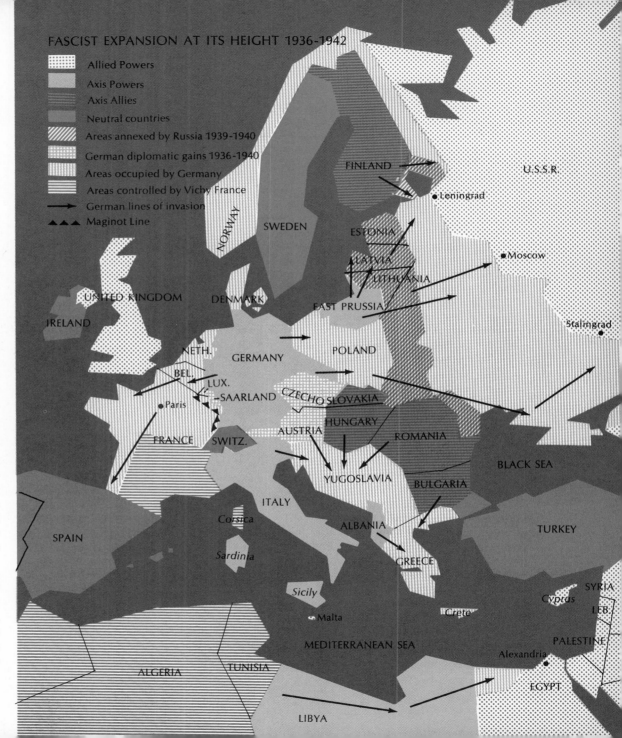

FASCIST EXPANSION AT ITS HEIGHT 1936-1942

Allied Powers
Axis Powers
Axis Allies
Neutral countries
Areas annexed by Russia 1939-1940
German diplomatic gains 1936-1940
Areas occupied by Germany
Areas controlled by Vichy France
→ German lines of invasion
▲▲▲ Maginot Line

civilian population behind the lines or worked them to death as prisoners of war. The Soviet Union was not a signatory of the Geneva Convention, and the Nazis saw no purpose in conforming to its provisions in dealing with enemies whom they regarded as subhuman. On neither side, then, had a prisoner much chance of humane treatment: in most cases, imprisonment meant brutality, hardship, and a lingering death.

With the Soviet Union carrying the brunt of the fighting, there was mounting pressure on the British and Americans to come to the aid of the Russians by opening a second front on the European continent. Stalin pleaded for it in terms that alternated between polite suggestion and peremptory demand. Public opinion in Britain and the United States clamored for it—here once again the average citizen could not see why his country was taking so long to do the obvious. Neither the Russians nor the Anglo-American public understood that the Western Allies were *already* contributing mightily to the common war effort, but this contribution was more dispersed and harder to grasp than the Russian, reflecting the complex and wide-ranging commitments of a truly global struggle.

The Red Army faced a comparatively simple situation in strategy and supply. It was fighting close to home, in the great "heartland" of the Eurasian continent. Its supply lines were short, and its soldiers required little beyond food, clothes, and war material. It had a clear and comprehensible task: to expel the invaders from its country. Thus when it had turned the tide and begun to advance, its strategy followed a simple pattern: it pushed on for about 300 miles until its supply lines were stretched to the limit, then it paused to consolidate and regroup for another ad-

vance. Only when the Russians reached their own frontiers in the summer of 1944 were they faced with the perplexing choices that had plagued the British and Americans from the start.

The Western democracies were fighting not one war, but several. In Asia and the Pacific, they were fighting a war against Japan, which in the early part of the year 1942 was a series of unbroken defeats. In this struggle, they had no help from the Soviet Union: Stalin, fully occupied in defending himself in Europe, was not anxious to engage another enemy, and he maintained a strict neutrality in the war with Japan. The British were also fighting in the Mediterranean, and they were mounting a constantly increasing air offensive against the Reich itself. This had begun even before the diversion of the *Luftwaffe's* major strength to the attack on Russia gave the British air superiority in the West: in November, 1940, Molotov's conversations in Berlin with the Nazi leaders had been rudely interrupted by an RAF raid. In late 1941 and 1942, the British bombing attacks extended steadily in scope: the great north German cities of Berlin, Cologne, Hamburg, and the Rühr were assailed repeatedly. By the beginning of 1943, the Americans were ready to give full-scale assistance. With the addition of American strength, the air offensive against Germany went into a new phase. Hitherto the British planes had restricted themselves to night attacks; the American bombers—the B-17's or Flying Fortresses—which were more heavily armored, could strike in daylight as well.

The Americans on all fronts, and the British on most of theirs, were operating at the end of supply lines that were thousands of miles in length. Hence they could not put the bulk of their military manpower into combat units,

as the Russians could do so readily. Throughout the war a discouragingly high percentage of the Anglo-Americans in uniform remained absorbed in manning supply lines. It was over such far-flung communications lanes that the Red Army received the tanks and trucks and jeeps that alone enabled it to fight on. Some came around the North Cape, some by the longer but safer route via the Persian Gulf that was opened in the autumn of 1942.

In either case, the trip by sea took weeks and tied up a whole flotilla of cruisers, destroyers, and corvettes in convoy duty. For the British and Americans had still another war to fight—the war at sea. Although Germany was primarily a land power with an army that had proved itself the finest in the world, it was also a formidable naval power. In over-all naval strength Germany now ranked fourth —after the United States and Britain and its own ally, Japan—but in certain strategic classes of vessels Germany had no peer. Its two great battleships, the *Bismarck* and the *Tirpitz*, were the strongest afloat. The *Bismarck* kept half the British Home Fleet immobilized simply in watching it, until one day in May, 1941, it eluded its guard, spreading terror through the North Atlantic and sinking Britain's largest warship, the *Hood,* before it was itself destroyed by combined air and naval attack. The *Tirpitz* remained in a Norwegian fjord, a constant source of anxiety to the Royal Navy, which failed time after time in its attempts to sink it from the air. The German submarine fleet was a still greater menace: at the end of 1942, Hitler had 400 submarines, which destroyed more than six million tons of merchant shipping in the course of the year. For many months, the German submarines sank ships faster than the Americans and British could build them. It was only in the autumn of 1942 that the Anglo-American production rate outstripped monthly losses.

Finally, the critics of British and American strategy forgot that all the prospective operations in the West involved an amphibious assault against a heavily defended coastline. Here history offered no precedents. The great democracies had almost to invent the technique of amphibious warfare; the Germans had not dared to launch "Sea Lion" against England; the Russians had no need for, or experience in, major landing operations. These were to become the Anglo-American specialty—their great contribution to the art of modern warfare. But the Western Allies could make their supreme attempt—a major cross-Channel invasion of France—only after gaining experience in the Mediterranean and in the Pacific. They also needed time to construct a great fleet of landing craft: again and again during 1943 and 1944 a shortage of landing craft was to be the crucial limitation on offensive operations. . . .

THE TURNING OF THE TIDE

In the autumn of 1942, the tide turned. For more than three years, events had moved in Hitler's favor. The war had been a long succession of German victories—the greatest the world had ever seen. The best his enemies had been able to do was to stop his advance in the air battle of Britain and before Moscow and to defeat his Italian ally in the Mediterranean. At the end of 1942, the trend was reversed: the Russians held firm at Stalingrad, the British broke out of Egypt, the Americans landed in French North Africa; in two widely separated theaters of combat, the Allies were preparing vast encircling operations that would bring the Nazis their first major de-

feats. From this point on, the victory of Britain and America and the Soviet Union was never in doubt: the only question was how long it would take—and the answer to that question depended on the great strategic decisions which the Allied leaders were to make in their efforts to fight a coalition war of unprecedented scope and intensity.

Hitler changed his military command after the failure before Moscow. His old field marshals, disappointed by the Führer's interference with their strategy, retired and were replaced by younger men, who were more pliable and closer to the Nazi party. And Hitler himself assumed the post of commander-in-chief.

Although the military amateur was now in charge, the plan for the campaign of 1942 showed a more coherent strategy than that pursued in 1941: the attack was to be on one front alone; the whole weight of German arms was to be concentrated in the south, where Hitler hoped to achieve the decisive results that had eluded him the previous year. In the north and center, his forces were to remain where they were: as the spring thaws set in, and military operations bogged down, Hitler could note with gratification that the Russian winter offensive had ended without dislodging his troops from any essential position. The Germans had been obliged to withdraw before Moscow, but they still had Leningrad in an iron grip. It was in the south, once the mud had dried, that Hitler was to make his supreme effort: he planned to drive from the Ukraine to Stalingrad on the Volga, and to the Caspian Sea, thereby literally cutting the Soviet Union in two. By seizing the Caucasus, he hoped both to deny the Red Army its major source of oil and to solve his own most urgent supply problem.

At first, the German tanks rolled forward as relentlessly as they had the previous summer. In early July, they took Sevastopol in the Crimea; at the end of the month, they were in Rostov and preparing to cross the Don. Once across the great river, they raced ahead almost without interruption: by late summer, they were just short of the oil center of Grozny in the north Caucasus, and their advanced patrols had reached the Caspian Sea.

Meanwhile, on August 22, the Battle of Stalingrad had begun. Stalingrad was a key city in every sense. It was dear to Stalin's heart: under its original name of Tsaritsin it was the place where he had first made a military reputation during the civil war. It was also a major industrial center—one of the new manufacturing complexes which had been built up safely remote from the Soviet frontiers during the Five Year Plans. Finally, it was a strategic position of first importance: situated on the Volga just where the Don bends closest to its sister river, it stood farthest east of the great cities of southern Russia. Beyond Stalingrad lay little but open steppe: should it fall into enemy hands, communication between the south and the center of the country would be effectively severed.

Stalin gave the order to hold at all costs. With their backs to Asia, the city's defenders stood their ground. But the Germans—suffering enormous losses—still inched steadily forward. By mid-September they were in the city itself: attackers and besiegers fought desperately at close quarters in streets and factories. For a few days the position of the defenders seemed hopeless.

Once again Stalin kept his nerve. Already he had given the order for a great pincers movement that would catch the Germans in a trap. On September 21, the first Soviet attack

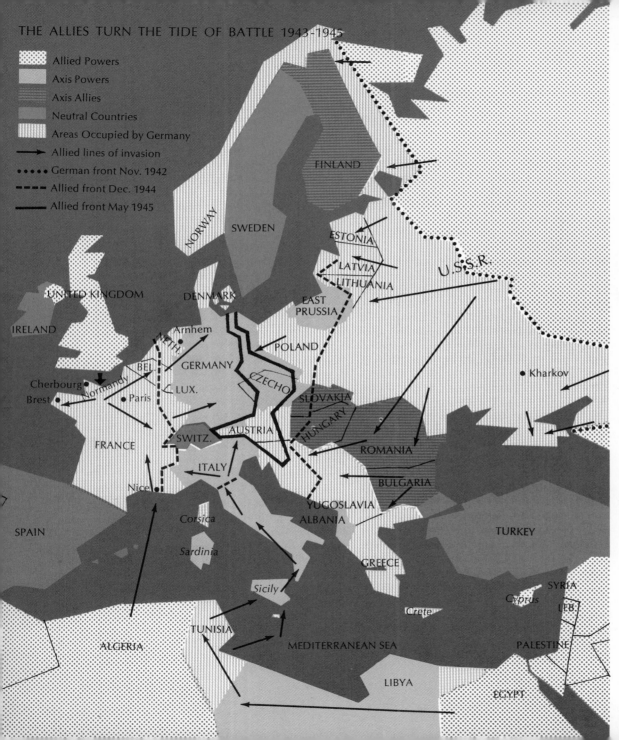

THE ALLIES TURN THE TIDE OF BATTLE 1943-1945

Allied Powers
Axis Powers
Axis Allies
Neutral Countries
Areas Occupied by Germany
Allied lines of invasion
German front Nov. 1942
Allied front Dec. 1944
Allied front May 1945

FINLAND
NORWAY
SWEDEN
ESTONIA
LATVIA
LITHUANIA
U.S.S.R.
UNITED KINGDOM
DENMARK
EAST PRUSSIA
IRELAND
Arnhem
NETH.
POLAND
BEL
GERMANY
CZECHO.
Kharkov
Cherbourg
Normandy
LUX.
Brest
Paris
SLOVAKIA
SWITZ.
AUSTRIA
HUNGARY
FRANCE
ITALY
ROMANIA
Nice
BULGARIA
Corsica
YUGOSLAVIA
SPAIN
Sardinia
ALBANIA
TURKEY
GREECE
Sicily
SYRIA
Cyprus
LEB.
Crete
TUNISIA
PALESTINE
ALGERIA
MEDITERRANEAN SEA
LIBYA
EGYPT

began: crossing the Volga north of Stalingrad, it advanced into the open plain between the two rivers. Ten days later, the second attack moved from the south. The Germans were caught off guard. Isolated at the end of a dangerously stretched communication line, the besiegers of Stalingrad now had to turn to face a new threat to the rear. In October and November, the Russian pincers began to close. If the Germans were to escape it had to be before winter set it. But Hitler refused to give the order for evacuation: he had resolved that his quarter-million soldiers at Stalingrad should die at their posts. It was full winter when the two Soviet advances met; the trap snapped shut—the rest was one long German martyrdom. Hunger, frost, and typhus took a mounting toll. By the new year, the Germans were reduced to a ragged rabble of sick and half-crazed men. On February 2, 1943, when the final surrender came, only 80,000 remained alive to be led off to captivity. . . .

TEHERAN AND THE GREAT STRATEGIC DECISIONS

Another decisive battle took place in North Africa at this time. Fascist and British forces had fought for possession of the desert between Libya and Egypt after Italy's entrance into the war in 1940. German activity in Africa was part of a grand strategy. German pressure at Stalingrad represented one tip of a gigantic pincers movement designed to win the entire Near East. The second pincer was finally blunted by the British at El Alamein, seventy miles from the mouths of the Nile, in the fall of 1942. At the same time the Americans, under General Dwight Eisenhower, landed in North Africa and by the succeeding fall the Allied Armies had pushed through Sicily into southern Italy. Rome itself was not reached until June, 1944. [Eds.]

After its victory at Stalingrad, the Red Army swept on to further winter triumphs. It drove back the German besiegers before Leningrad, cleared an additional zone west of Moscow, retook Rostov and began the liberation of the Ukraine. In the spring of 1943, however, as had happened the year before, the Germans struck back. In March, they captured the recently liberated city of Kharkov, and in early July they attacked 100 miles farther north in the region of Kursk and Orel. But this was their last effort; never again were the Germans to regain the initiative on the Eastern Front. In mid-July the Soviet summer offensive began to roll: it was the beginning of a colossal advance that continued almost two years and reached its end in the smoking ruins of Berlin. After freeing Kharkov once more, the Russians crossed the Dnieper and wrested Kiev from German control. By the end of the year, they had liberated more than half the Ukraine.

Victories such as these drew the two fronts closer together. With the British and Americans at last ashore on the European continent and with the Russians advancing relentlessly toward their own borders, a new coordination had become urgent. So long as the campaigns in the East remained widely separated from those in the West, it had been possible to treat them as two separate wars. Now it was essential to knit them together, and this was the purpose of the first of the two meetings that brought Churchill and Roosevelt into personal contact with Stalin—the meeting held in November and December, 1943, at the Persian capital of Teheran.

At Teheran, grand strategy was not the sole topic of discussion. Political questions were also touched on, and the outlines of an eventual settlement for Poland were sketched. Yet Roosevelt was still reluctant to make territorial commitments for the future: he preferred to wait until the end of the war, when the victorious Allies could deal with all major issues at once. This postponement suited Stalin far better than the Soviet leader was willing to admit: to delay a settlement meant to wait until the Russians had physical possession of the lands they demanded. Hence at Teheran Stalin advanced his territorial claims in rather perfunctory fashion: eventually he agreed with Roosevelt's desire for postponement. Churchill, rather, kept pushing for an early discussion of controversial issues; with his longer experience of international dealings, he realized better than Roosevelt that the time for bargaining was now, *before* the Red Army had the spoils of war in its hands.

In the same almost accidental fashion, Russian and American views on strategy coincided, whereas the British were more hesitant. For nearly two years Stalin had been pleading for a major second front—preferably in France—that would relieve German pressure on his own forces. This was also the desire of the American military leaders, whose only purpose was to find the shortest and speediest way to drive for the enemy's heart. Churchill, on the contrary, was always doubtful about a cross-Channel invasion: he dreaded a repetition of the fearful losses that the British had suffered in France in the First World War. Hence he favored operations in the Mediterranean and the Balkans that would strike at what he called the "soft under-belly of Europe." And—ever mindful of political considerations—he hoped that in this way he could keep at least part of East Central Europe free from Soviet control.

Roosevelt refused to listen to such arguments. The American President was less of a military expert than Churchill or Stalin; he did not try to run his war in the personal fashion they did, and he was far more dependent on the advice of his military chiefs. Hence he reflected their military impatience with political considerations and their desire to win the war in the shortest possible time by striking directly at Germany itself. This purely strategic reasoning—rather than any alleged "softness" toward Soviet Communism—brought Roosevelt into agreement with Stalin about a cross-Channel invasion of the Continent.

Hence the great achievement of the Teheran Conference was to overcome Churchill's last lingering objections and to confirm the tentative decision the British and Americans had reached six months earlier—a major landing would be made in France in May of 1944. The commander of the operation was to be General Eisenhower. Stalin—much gratified—promised to open a simultaneous offensive on the Eastern Front. The strategy had been established that would bring total victory in the last year and a half of the war. . . .

D-DAY

The landings began in the early morning of June 6 on a 60-mile arc along the broad indentation of the Norman coast between Cherbourg and Le Havre—close enough to the English coast to permit air fighter cover all the time. It was not the *Luftwaffe* that the invaders now had to fear; it was the Germans' artillery, their barbed wire, their underwater obstacles and mines—all the heavy defenses that they had been preparing for three years against just such an attack. Casualties were heavy on D-Day, and for hours the outcome

Allied Landing, D-Day, June 6, 1944.

hung in the balance. Yet the invaders were able to profit by German indecision: the enemy commander—Rommel, the legendary "desert fox" of North African fame—was calamitously deceived about their intentions. Believing that the Normandy landings were only a feint, and that the main invasion would come in the Calais area, where the Channel was narrowest, he kept his armored forces in reserve until it was too late. When they finally began to move, the harassing attacks of the French Resistance held them to a slow crawl.

Throughout June and most of July, Eisenhower's forces consolidated their beachhead and steadily increased their strength. Within a week of D-Day, more than 300,000 British and Americans were ashore, and through artificial harbors built off the beaches a steady stream of supplies began to flow in. The British under Montgomery were assigned the hard and unspectacular task of holding the main enemy attacks and hammering away at the city of Caen. The Americans, under General Omar Bradley, received the more attractive assignment of fighting their way out of the bridgehead and taking the Germans in the rear. On July 25, the American forces began the breakthrough at Saint-Lo. From there they went on to the cathedral town of Coutances, cutting off the enemy's retreat from the Cherbourg peninsula. By early August, the dashing tank commander, General George Patton, was out in open country, heading off on a great race across northern France.

With Patton's breakthrough, the campaign in France suddenly became fluid. In the next month and a half, nearly the whole country was liberated. On August 15 occurred the long-delayed descent on the Riviera beaches. Three American and seven French divisions —most of them withdrawn from the Italian campaign—poured ashore against light opposition. Within two weeks, they had taken Marseille and Nice and were beginning a triumphal advance up the Rhône Valley. Meanwhile central and southwestern France was liberating itself with its own resources; the Resistance fighters descended from the hills, harassing the frantic Germans who now had no thought but to escape from the enormous trap that was closing on them. Simultaneously, to the north Montgomery had beaten off the last German attacks and surrounded eight enemy divisions in a pocket near Falaise; the Americans were advancing through Brittany to free the vital seaport of Brest; and Patton's tanks, wheeling south of Paris, were already threatening to cut off the German forces in the capital.

At this point De Gaulle went into action. His prize armored division, under General Leclerc de Hauteclocque—which had been held in reserve for just such an eventuality—was given the order to advance on Paris. Here the Resistance had already risen: for ten days it fought bitter street battles with the occupying forces. Finally, Leclerc's tanks settled the issue. By August 26, the city was free. The day before, General de Gaulle—now universally recognized as the liberator and leader of the French—had arrived to take over authority: on a glorious summer afternoon he walked in triumph from the Etoile down the Champs Elysées to the Place de la Concorde, and then drove by car to Notre Dame, where the Te Deum of thanksgiving was interrupted by the desperate rifle shots of unyielding collaborationists.

In September, it seemed as if Germany might be defeated that very autumn. On the eleventh of the month the forces from the Normandy beachhead joined those coming up from the south to form a continuous front. During the next few days, they advanced together to reach the German border at several points. To the west, Montgomery's British and Canadians, after crossing the Seine and surrounding the frightfully devastated seaport of Le Havre, swept on to the Belgian frontier almost without opposition. In the first two weeks of September they liberated most of Belgium, and by the middle of the month they were advancing into the Netherlands. Now was the time to break the German defenses with one bold stroke. Yielding to Montgomery's eloquent pleas, Eisenhower decided to risk a great gamble on his left flank. An airborne operation—the largest yet attempted by either side—was to strike across the Rhine at Arnhem in the Netherlands, in an effort to leap the river obstacle and then carry the war into the heart of Germany.

The parachute attack at Arnhem began on September 17. The initial landings succeeded, but the operation was soon hampered by bad weather and the slowing of relief forces coming up from the south. The airborne troops held out for more than a week. Then the Germans closed in and the evacuation of the bridgehead became imperative; only a quarter of the original force reached the south bank of the Rhine alive. To the east meanwhile, Patton's tanks were running out of fuel, and the French and Americans who had come up from the south were meeting stern resistance in Alsace. By early October, it was clear that victory could not come until the following year. . . .

THE "BATTLE OF THE BULGE"

Then in mid-December the unexpected happened: the Germans struck back, powerfully and with stunning effect. For this—his last offensive effort—Hitler called on his most experienced commander, old Field Marshal von Rundstedt. Rundstedt's plan was bold and well conceived: he tried to cut through the Allied armies at their weakest point and, by capturing the great supply base of Antwerp, to demoralize them and disorganize their rear. The place he chose to strike was the same rugged and woody Ardennes where the Germans had breached the French defenses four and a half years before.

Rundstedt's plan came uncomfortably close to success. Favored by a spell of cloudy weather which prevented Allied planes from reconnoitering his troop concentrations, he caught the Americans thoroughly off guard. Soon a whole sector of the Allied line in Belgium and Luxemburg was staggering back: a great "bulge" opened which had to be closed at all costs. Eisenhower hastily summoned reserves from the south: this necessitated further strategic withdrawals. . . . It was a gloomy Christmas in Paris and Brussels: the victory which had seemed so close had once more been thrown into doubt. In London also there was fear as well as sorrow: the new V-missiles which the Germans launched from bases in the Netherlands were descending on the city with deadly accuracy.

By the third week of January, Eisenhower's forces had stopped the German offensive and pushed the attackers back out of the bulge. But the Battle of the Bulge, as it came to be called, had shaken the Allies and disorganized the timetable of their advance into the Reich. Once again it had made the Western war effort seem far less impressive than the Russian, for while the Americans and British were recovering from the shock they had received in the Ardennes, the Red Army was setting out on another spectacular winter offensive.

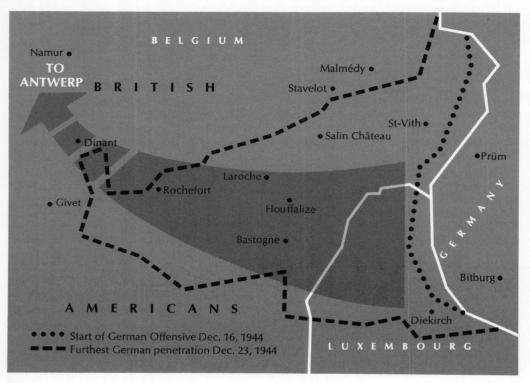

●●●● Start of German Offensive Dec. 16, 1944
▬ ▬ ▬ Furthest German penetration Dec. 23, 1944

Resuming the attack in Poland where they had broken it off five months earlier, the Russians captured Warsaw in mid-January, 1945, and then swept on 300 miles to penetrate deep into Germany itself. East Prussia and Upper Silesia were in their grasp: before them literally millions of Germans were fleeing in the bitter cold. The Red Army did not pause until it reached the Oder River, only 40 miles from Berlin. . . .

THE LAST CAMPAIGNS

Before Berlin, however, the greatest of the new Soviet commanders, Marshal Grigori Zhukov, had paused for two months, preparing his forces for the final assault. In front

of him lay Hitler's last hope—the most desperate and fanatical of his soldiers, whom he had ordered to stand their ground and die in defense of the Nazi capital. Berlin was now a mass of ruins. Indeed in the last winter of the war the Allied air forces had roamed at will over the Reich; virtually every city had been blasted again and again. With legitimate strategic targets exhausted, the British and American aviators struck almost at random, ruthlessly obliterating the architectural monuments of Germany's past and rendering millions homeless. The fire bombing of Dresden in February, 1945, in which tens of thousands lost their lives, ranks among the most terrible events of the entire war.

Still Hitler refused to recognize the inevitable. He decreed that the German people should go down with their leader in a macabre *Götterdämmerung,* and he immured himself in the air-raid bunker below the Reich Chancellery as the battle for Berlin began to rage above him.

During Zhukov's two-months pause, however, the military situation inside Germany had changed completely. The Americans had broken across the Rhine and now were almost as close to Berlin as he was. They were already on the Elbe, and the Red Army was still on the Oder. Between the two rivers lay the German capital. Toward the west Berlin was almost defenseless; its guardians were concentrated to the east against the threatened Soviet attack. The prize seemed to lie within Eisenhower's grasp. Why did he not reach out for it?

The answer is a mixture of strategic and diplomatic arguments, which seemed convincing at the time, but which in retrospect have been questioned again and again. From the strategic standpoint, the Supreme Allied Commander was worried about his supply lines, which had been stretched to the limit by his race across the Reich. He also felt the need of a clear line of demarcation between his own troops and the Russians, which the Elbe alone could provide. Finally he was constantly receiving reports that the Nazis were preparing to make their last stand in an Alpine redoubt in southern Germany and Austria, and he wanted to cut them off before they had time to consolidate this new position. Hence he ordered Bradley to stop at the Elbe and to wheel toward the south.

In fact the reports about the "redoubt" proved to be without substance. By mid-April, the German forces were far too disorganized to execute any such maneuver. There were also political aspects to the capture of Berlin which Eisenhower failed to appreciate: as a military man he had been taught that the fall of any particular city was always secondary to the main job of destroying the enemy forces. Churchill, on the contrary, fully understood the symbolic importance of capturing Berlin. He harried Eisenhower with ever stronger pleas to push on, but the Supreme Commander remained deaf to his entreaties. In Washington there was no longer the strong voice that might have supported Churchill. On April 12—the day after the Americans reached the Elbe—Roosevelt died, his last weeks overshadowed by mounting disputes with Stalin over Eastern Europe. With a power vacuum in Washington, Eisenhower was left to make his own decisions.

Vienna had already fallen to the Red Army on April 13. Here there was little that the Western Allies could have done, once they had rejected Churchill's reiterated proposals for an advance up from the Balkans or the Adriatic. Now before Berlin they chose to stand aside. On April 16, Zhukov opened his offensive. Nine days later he had the city surrounded. As the Russian tanks smashed into the capital, Hitler knew that the end had come. On the last day of April he shot himself, and his body was burned in the Chancellery courtyard.

The rest was a week-long mopping-up operation against scattered masses of German soldiery. As the American troops swung south, they had one more opportunity—the Czech capital of Prague, where the Resistance rose on May 5 and invited General Patton to enter. Eisenhower asked the Soviet command what he should do; the latter responded with a strong negative. Once again the American insistence of good relations with the Russians won the day. The Red Army did not reach Prague until May 9—two days after the German High Command, in a surrender ceremony at Eisenhower's headquarters at Reims, had finally brought the Second World War to a close. The six-year struggle with Nazism had ended—but the new contest over the future of Europe had already begun.

Alexandrinenstrasse in Berlin after peace came.

Winston Churchill Views the Atomic Bomb as "A Miracle of Deliverance"

Winston Churchill (1874–1965), the intrepid wartime prime minister of Great Britain, eloquently told the story of the war in a six-volume personal narrative. The final volume opened with the Anglo-American landings in Normandy and concluded with the complete defeat and occupation of the Axis nations and the establishment of a Russian foothold in Central Europe. Churchill entitled his book *Triumph and Tragedy* since "the overwhelming victory of the Grand Alliance has failed so far to bring general peace to our anxious world." The reading describes the strategic considerations behind the decision to use the atomic bomb in Japan. The successful detonation of the first bomb took place in the United States while the Allied leaders were in Potsdam, outside Berlin, conferring on problems left in the wake of Nazi defeat. From Winston S. Churchill, *The Second World War (Triumph and Tragedy)*. Copyright, 1955, by Houghton Mifflin Company. Reprinted by permission of the publisher.

On July 17 [1945] world-shaking news had arrived. In the afternoon Stimson [American Secretary of War] called at my abode and laid before me a sheet of paper on which was written, "Babies satisfactorily born." By his manner I saw something extraordinary had happened. "It means," he said, "that the experiment in the New Mexican desert has come off. The atomic bomb is a reality."

Although we had followed this dire quest with every scrap of information imparted to us, we had not been told beforehand, or at any rate I did not know, the date of the decisive trial. No responsible scientist would predict what would happen when the first full-scale atomic explosion was tried. Were these bombs useless or were they annihilating? Now we knew. The "babies" had been "satisfactorily born." No one could yet measure the immediate military consequences of the discovery, and no one has yet measured anything else about it.

Next morning a plane arrived with a full description of this tremendous event in the human story. Stimson brought me the report. I tell the tale as I recall it. The bomb, or its equivalent, had been detonated at the top of a phylon 100 feet high. Everyone had been cleared away for ten miles round, and the scientists and their staffs crouched behind massive concrete shields and shelters at about that distance. The blast had been terrific. An enormous column of flame and smoke shot up to the fringe of the atmosphere of our poor earth. Devastation inside a one-mile circle was absolute. Here then was a speedy end to the Second World War, and perhaps to much else besides.

The President invited me to confer with him forthwith. He had with him General Marshall and Admiral Leahy. Up to this moment we had shaped our ideas towards an assault upon the homeland of Japan by terrific air bombing and by the invasion of very large armies. We had contemplated the desperate resistance of the Japanese fighting to the death with Samurai devotion, not only in pitched battles, but in every cave and dugout. I had in my mind the spectacle of Okinawa island, where many thousands of Japanese, rather than surrender, had drawn up in line and destroyed themselves by hand-grenades after their leaders had solemnly performed the rite of *harakiri*. To quell the Japanese resistance man by man and conquer the country yard by yard might well require the loss of a million American lives and half that number of British—or more if we could get them there: for we were resolved to share the agony. Now all this nightmare picture had vanished. In its place was the vision—fair and bright indeed it seemed—of the end of the whole war in one or two violent shocks. I thought immediately myself of how the Japanese people, whose courage I had always admired, might find in the apparition of this almost supernatural weapon an excuse which would save their honour and release them from their obligation of being killed to the last fighting man.

Moreover, we should not need the Russians. The end of the Japanese war no longer depended upon the pouring in of their armies for the final and perhaps protracted slaughter. We had no need to ask favours of them. A few days later I minuted to Mr. Eden [British Foreign Secretary]: "It is quite clear that the United States do not at the present time desire Russian participation in the war against Japan." The array of European problems could therefore be faced on their merits and according to the broad principles of the United Nations. We seemed suddenly to have become possessed of a merciful abridgment of the slaughter in the East and of a far happier prospect in Europe. I have no doubt that these thoughts were present in the minds of my American friends. At any rate, there never was a moment's discussion as to whether the atomic bomb should be used or not. To avert a vast, indefinite butchery, to bring the war

Walter Millis: The Modern Nation-State at War

Stalin, Truman, and Churchill at Potsdam before the conference opened, July 17, 1945.

The Second World War was not only wider in geographic scope than any earlier armed conflict; it was also much more extensive in the means of warfare employed and the demands placed upon the populations of the nations involved. Walter Millis (1899–), noted American military historian, in his study of the role that war has played in shaping contemporary America, asks why the modern state was able successfully to make such demands upon its citizens. Reprinted by permission of G. P. Putnam's Sons from *Arms and Men: A Study in American Military History* by Walter Millis. Copyright © 1956 by Walter Millis.

I

The Second World War was unexpectedly enough, both a fluid war of machines and experts and also a total war of the regimented mass. Those military writers of the interwar years (the then Captain Charles de Gaulle was among them) who foresaw another conflict as one which would be fought to quick decision by small, highly trained "career" armies of air and tank specialists, were perhaps justified by the conquests of Poland and France; but their expectations were disappointed by the vast miseries which thereafter unrolled. In the Second War much greater total numbers were placed in uniform; total casualties (civilian and military) were doubtless vastly greater, even as the total volume of industrial war production mounted to colossally greater heights than in World War I. The destruction

to an end, to give peace to the world, to lay healing hands upon its tortured peoples by a manifestation of over-whelming power at the cost of a few explosions, seemed, after all our toils and perils, a miracle of deliverance.

British consent in principle to the use of the weapon had been given on July 4, before the test had taken place. The final decision now lay in the main with President Truman, who had the weapon; but I never doubted what it would be, nor have I ever doubted since that he was right. The historic fact remains, and must be judged in the after-time, that the decision whether or not to use the

atomic bomb to compel the surrender of Japan was never even an issue. There was unanimous, automatic, unquestioned agreement around our table; nor did I ever hear the slightest suggestion that we should do otherwise.

It appeared that the American Air Force had prepared an immense assault by ordinary air-bombing on Japanese cities and harbours. These could . . . have been destroyed in a few weeks or a few months, and no one could say with what very heavy loss of life to the civilian population. But now, by using this new agency, we might not merely destroy cities, but save the lives alike of friend and foe.

of physical capital values—homes, factory plant and equipment, communications and transport facilities—was on a correspondingly more enormous scale. These agonies and losses were, however, distributed more evenly than in the First War—as between the several nations involved, between the uniformed and civilian populations, between the age and sex groups. . . .

Out of this first war of both the mass and the machine, this first truly global conflict, one salient and shocking fact was to emerge: the almost unbelievable power of the modern centralized, managerial and nationalistic state to drain the whole physical, intellectual, economic, emotional and moral resources of its citizens to the single end of military victory. By the mid-'30's the Western world was acutely aware of the grim internal strength of the totalitarian regimes, ruling by dictatorial mass organization, by propaganda and by the secret police. What was less often appreciated was the extent to which, for the purposes of war, at least, these techniques were advancing in the British and American democracies. Triumphs of "monolithic" organization and direction which were quite out of the question in meeting the problems of the Great Depression were achieved overnight in meeting those of the Second War. Sacrifices, not only of life but of property, which Western governments in earlier wars would hardly have dreamed of asking, were imposed and accepted without question. Politics, which might be defined as the expression in society of individual difference, idiosyncrasy, variety and recalcitrance, were suspended everywhere for the "duration." The competitive economic system was temporarily abolished under rigid wage, price and raw material controls; even in the democ-

racies, severe limitations were placed upon the freedoms of thought, information and dissenting speech. It was not only in Russia and Germany but in Britain and the United States that war proved again the great forcing-bed of the unitary state. . . .

The modern nation-state had learned not only how to mobilize the entire emotional and material resources of its inhabitants for success in war, but also how to insure itself and its institutions against what might seem to be the probable results of the sacrifices thus demanded. The sacrifices of 1939–1945 were enormous, but so far from themselves producing revolutionary change, the most that can be said is that they were exploited by the revolutionary systems and states created in 1918 to secure advantage in struggles that long antedated 1939. Toward the end of the Napoleonic period, the Prussian Army reforms of Scharnhorst and Gneisenau were opposed by Prussian conservatives on the ground that to arm and train a whole people was to put a dangerous power in its hands. During the nineteenth century it was generally the liberals who were to be found on the side of the big, conscript mass army which, it was supposed, would keep military power in the control of the "people." In the preparedness agitation in the United States after 1914, the argument for universal conscription as the only "democratic" military system, and for military service itself as a democratic duty, was prominent. Liberals could be scornful of the "strutitudinous" excesses of Prussian militarism even while they were prepared to introduce its basic concepts into our own system. In the grimly ironic end, both liberals and conservatives alike were to be disappointed. The arming of the modern populace was to give it even less control than before

over its destinies. Its regimentation, on the other hand, was to give the propertied classes no more power to limit the advance of the welfare and egalitarian state than they had previously enjoyed.

The popular mass armies have not been without their effect upon social and economic policy. By their demands for adequate pay, pensions and recognition of their services they have made a considerable contribution—much greater, probably, than the leaders of the American Legion realize—to the modern welfare state. The "homes for heroes" which Lloyd George promised the British veterans in 1918, the benefits and bonus acts exacted by the American Legion in the interwar period, the GI Bill of Rights accorded the veterans of 1945 and 1953, were all highly "socialistic" if not communist measures, in that they recognized a communal responsibility for ardors and agonies suffered in the communal service of the state. That they encouraged the recognition of similar responsibilities to other large groups—the farmers, the unemployed wage workers, the "ill-housed," the Negro minority—who had also contributed to the national greatness, is obvious. Yet the mass army, as a political force, has been on the whole rather surprisingly neutralized in the modern community. Those who expected the Russian soldiers, returning from their contacts with the outer world, to cause trouble for the Kremlin were just as disappointed as was the Kremlin in its hopes of exporting Communist revolution with its soldiers. The Second World War was terrible in its spread of death and devastation, but it was singularly apolitical in its effects.

It was a revelation of the remarkable strength of the modern nationalistic state.

While the Napoleonic wars were the first great manifestations of popular nationalism, they were still fought by armies in which the mercenary was common, in which men of all nations found themselves suffering by choice or accident under strange flags, and in which internal dissension and even mutiny were not uncommon. In the American Civil War, the Northern copperheads and Southern appeasers and recalcitrants were constant problems for both governments. A draft act could still produce bloody riots and resistance in the North; a Southern effort to combine the railways into a national military transport system could still go to pieces on the rocks of individual initiative among the railway companies. . . .

II

In the crisis of 1914 the world was somewhat surprised when the socialist parties in all the belligerent nations enthusiastically backed that capitalist, imperialist (but also nationalist) war against which they were supposed to be aligned. The tremendous centripetal power of nationalism was so little understood as late as 1917 that many seriously doubted in that year whether the United States could conscript its citizens for battle. The doubt was unfounded; but popular dissent still had a powerful leverage upon history, especially when expressed by men with guns in their hands. The peace movement at the end of 1916 evoked a popular response which seriously alarmed the leaders in all the belligerent powers. It was the mutiny of the Russian soldiers and people in 1917 which overthrew the Czardom and took Russia out of the war. The French Army mutinies in the same year for a time virtually paralyzed the state. In 1918 it was the war weariness of the German people, brought to

a head by a mutiny in the German Navy, which shattered Ludendorff's nerve and so made plain the defeat to which the generals in fact had come. There were no similar episodes in 1945; the modern state, whether democratic or totalitarian, had learned to insure against their recurrence.

Since the great mobilization of the First War, a quasi-religious nationalism had been sedulously cultivated in the United States. It had acquired its creed (the oath of allegiance), its icons (the Flag), its ritual observances (the elaborate ceremonial drill with which patriotic societies like the American Legion, to say nothing of the armed forces, surrounded the nationalist symbols). At the end of the nineteenth century the scarcely radical New York *Journal of Commerce* had deplored the "artificial patriotism" being worked up at the time and the "remarkable fashion of hanging the flag over every schoolhouse and of giving the boys military drill." A half century later a national commander of the American Legion could nostalgically recall the days when people saluted the flag not just because they "had to"; and unaware that they frequently never saluted it at all, advocate a compulsory, ritual patriotism to restore the "old" faith.

The First War and its aftermath had converted most Americans to this ritualistic attitude toward the state. Its symbols were of great power, beauty and emotional force. Only a rather cheap cynicism could remain unmoved as the flag is brought down at sunset in some distant foreign post; or could fail to "salute the quarter deck" of a naval vessel whose people (in the old naval phrase) had, perhaps, done bloody and agonizing things in defense of their community. To hold that such rituals are meaningless would be

to deny much in our social heritage. But that they brought a powerful reinforcement to the monolithic and warlike state is hardly controvertible. By 1941 it was universally assumed that war would require the general conscription of manpower, heavy taxation distributed as equitably as possible among all, price controls, rationing and governmental allocation of raw materials, a massive governmental intervention directly into private industry with government-built armament plants and transportation facilities. The press bowed immediately to a voluntary censorship which was to be dutifully observed. No one doubted the necessity for a considerable secret police —the FBI—to protect against spies and saboteurs. Few even questioned so brutal an invasion of individual rights as the concentration and removal from the West Coast of some 80,000 American citizens of Japanese ancestry. A degree of regimentation and centralization which was never possible during the Civil War, which was still at least strange and disquieting after 1917, had by 1941 become no more than a normal and patently necessary order of affairs.

The centralized modern state had developed into an incomparable instrument for waging war. Whether in its totalitarian or democratic form, it could now mobilize its entire people, command all their loyalties and energies, provide them with weapons of incredible intricacy and give them command and staff organizations capable of utilizing their resources and their sacrifices with efficiency. The state could guarantee something like a just wage to its combatants, with paternal care thereafter. It could not avoid condemning a certain number of its citizens to being blasted or burned or shot to death, to enduring tortures by fire or evisceration possibly worse than those of earlier wars. But it was at least as economical as possible of such sacrifices, while the enormous strides of modern medicine enabled it to mitigate the agonies to a significant extent. It could provide its troops with clothing, housing, food and comforts of previously impossible excellence. By these and many other methods it demonstrated its capacity to hold the loyalty of its citizens through strains unparalleled in earlier wars; it was armored within as well as without; it had sufficiently reconciled its own internal struggles of class and interest to enter with confidence any war which might threaten it.

Unfortunately, in making itself into a superb instrument of scientific war, it had not been able to prevent other great states from doing the same thing. It had failed to reduce the institution of war itself to a usable and practicable instrument of policy—a means, that is to say, of adjusting the relations of peoples and securing the necessary decisions between their clashing interests at a bearable

cost in other human values. In the newly shattered world of late 1945, with the first atomic clouds drifting away like great question marks upon the sky, this fact stood starkly on the world's intellectual horizons.

For the Second World War, unlike any earlier struggle in its origins, its character and its development, was even more dramatically different in its end. The argument as to whether the Hiroshima and Nagasaki atomic bombs "caused" the Japanese surrender seems somewhat academic. There is much reason to believe that without them events would have proceeded much as they actually did; but whatever their influence upon the war just closing, their enormous significance was for the future. Here in the very last days of the great conflict the power of airborne demolition bombardment had been suddenly stepped up by a factor of 20,000. Nothing like this had ever happened before. The weapons and techniques developed in the course of earlier wars had usually carried important hints of coming change, but no one such

revolutionary change as this had actually been demonstrated. This eleventh-hour triumph of the embattled scientists altered at a stroke almost every calculation and every formula on which statesmen, strategists and military technicians had been accustomed to rely. The general staffs of 1914—highly trained, thoroughly expert and devoted men of war —had compounded a disaster for which there seemed no answer. So the mobilized scientists of 1945—also highly trained, expert and devoted to the furtherance of the country's interest—had compounded a terrible problem for which no rational solution was apparent to themselves or to anyone else. Science— building upon the work of the patriot democrats of 1776, upon the creators of the Napoleonic mass army, the steam engineers and technologists of the mid-nineteenth century, the managerial skills of the general staffs and big industry and much more beside—had produced in the nuclear weapon something which at least looked like the negation of all war. . . .

STUDY QUESTIONS

1. How did the alliance between the United States, Great Britain, and Russia develop? What did each participant gain from the alliance?

2. Why was there so much difficulty setting up a "second front"? Why did misunderstandings arise among the Allies?

3. In what sense was Stalingrad a turning-point in

the war? What other actions taken before the end of 1942 seemed to indicate that the tide was turning?

4. How successful was the second front opened by the Allies in June 1944? Why were the Germans able to prevent victory by Christmas?

5. How might the disposition of Russian troops at

the end of the war affect Russia's bargaining power in the postwar settlement? Why didn't the Western forces capture Berlin and Prague?

6. Why did the atomic bomb appear so desirable to the Allies in 1945?

7. In what ways did the two wars affect the control exercised by the nation-state over its citizens?

The Marshall Plan Launches European Economic Recovery

From *A Decade of Cooperation: Achievements and Perspectives. 9th Report of the O.E.E.C.* (Paris: The Organization for European Economic Co-operation, 1958), pp. 19–21, 24–28.

TOPIC 45

ECONOMIC REVIVAL

The massive destruction caused by the Second World War dealt what seemed at first a lethal blow to European economic and political vitality. Twenty years after the war, however, Europeans could point with pride to their economic resurgence and the reestablishment of their political importance. Behind Europe's economic revival lay sound planning and well-timed American aid. The first step in the American commitment to European economic recovery was the Marshall Plan, which went into effect in 1948. In its first two years, eight billion dollars were invested in the European economy. By 1950, overall production by the recipients of this aid had risen twenty-five percent above the prewar level. Out of the planning required of Europeans before American funds were to be allocated, came the design for a European Coal and Steel Community. This in turn stimulated other economic associations and in 1958 the European Common Market emerged. By the 1950s Western Europe was again the "workshop of the world." Utilizing to the full, past skills in finance, shipping, industry, and administration, its sixteen nations accounted for one quarter of the world's industrial output and forty percent of its trade. But the war had nonetheless irretrievably altered the world picture. The United States of America had emerged from the conflict as a global power with global interests and responsibilities, and Europe, in spite of tradition and potential, faced the challenge of the dynamic American system. The readings present highlights of the postwar economic picture.

Europe's requirements for the next three or four years of foreign food and other essential products—principally from America—are so much greater than her present ability to pay that she must have substantial additional help or face economic, social, and political deterioration of a very grave character.

It would be neither fitting nor efficacious for this Government to undertake to draw up unilaterally a programme designed to place Europe on its feet economically. This is the business of the Europeans. The initiative, I think, must come from Europe. The role of this country should consist of friendly aid in the drafting of a European programme and of later support of such a programme so far as it may be practical for us to do so. The programme should be a joint one, agreed to by a number of, if not all, European nations.

It was with the above words, spoken at Harvard on June 5, 1947, that General George C. Marshall, the United States Secretary of State, invited the nations of Europe to seek, with the moral and financial support of the United States, a co-operative solution to their immense problems of post-war reconstruction. This act of statesmanship was important not only for the aid which it offered; the United States and Canada had already given considerable assistance to Europe since the war's end. It was significant also because it brought a vision of a new spirit of co-operation with which Europe's problems could be tackled. And, as the last ten years have shown, this marked a turning-point in the relations among the nations that responded to the call.

In mid-1947 the recovery of the European economy was in great jeopardy. A feeling of frustration over post-war problems was widespread in many countries because the elimination of shortages, the removal of controls, the stopping of inflation and the rebuilding of destroyed and damaged property seemed so remote.

While much progress had been made in restoring production in most European countries, no headway had been made in a few, and further advance was everywhere hindered by serious shortages of coal, steel, and food. Agricultural output provided only three-quarters of the pre-war food supply per head of population. Large imports of scarce raw materials were required and the external payments deficit threatened to exhaust European foreign exchange reserves within a few months. During 1947 the European countries had suffered a series of crises. At the beginning of the year, the cold winter produced a severe fuel crisis and the drought in the summer brought many harvest failures. In the summer, too, came the failure of the British attempt at convertibility and the exhaustion of the American and Canadian loans to the United Kingdom. It had been hoped that

sterling convertibility would help Europe generally to emerge from bilateral and restrictive trade practices, but when the attempt failed, the prospects for freer trade seemed black indeed.

In spite of Europe's great need for industrial materials and food, governments were forced to keep total imports below pre-war levels. Production of export goods was inadequate,

Chart 1

"INDUSTRIAL PRODUCTION—1947"

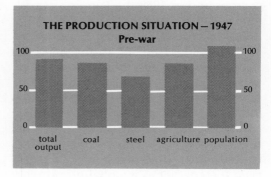

THE PRODUCTION SITUATION — 1947
Pre-war

total output | coal | steel | agriculture | population

In 1947 overall production of goods and services in Western Europe was still 7 per cent below pre-war. It had to be shared by a population some 8 per cent larger.

More importantly, recovery in certain key sectors such as coal and steel was lagging. The resulting bottlenecks presented serious obstacles to further recovery—particularly in export and investment goods industries. Agricultural production remained below pre-war. The shortages could only be made good by supplies from outside Europe.

but exports were needed in much greater volume than in pre-war years to compensate for the fall in European earnings from services such as shipping, insurance, and tourism and from foreign investment. Government spending abroad had also risen, and the high price of raw material imports had reduced considerably the purchasing power of European exports.

The economic and political dangers of the situation were very much in the minds of European statesmen, and their reaction to General Marshall's offer was immediate. . . . Only the Western European countries accepted this invitation and the conference was therefore unable to deal with the European problem as a whole. The countries participating hoped that other governments of Europe would eventually be able to associate themselves with the work undertaken.

The conference opened in Paris [July, 1947] under the chairmanship of Mr. Bevin. It set up a Committee of European Economic Co-operation (C.E.E.C.), supplemented by technical committees. The C.E.E.C. was established as a temporary body for the sole purpose of preparing a report on the European Recovery Programme. When the report was complete, a small group went to Washington in October 1947, at the request of the United States Government, to present it to the American Administration and to supply the latter with further information. The report outlined Europe's needs for the four years 1948–1952 as follows: i) to increase production, particularly in agriculture, energy, and heavy industry, ii) to eliminate inflation, iii) to promote economic co-operation, iv) to solve the dollar payments problem. . . .

The United States Government acted quickly, and detailed study began imme-

Chart 2

diately. A committee, headed by Secretary of Commerce Harriman, and consisting of economists, technicians, labour and business leaders, made a comprehensive report on all aspects of the problem and, after close scrutiny of the European proposals, suggested a 4-year programme of United States aid of between $12 and $17 billion. . . .

The Organisation for European Economic Co-operation (O.E.E.C.) was set up . . . as a means of ensuring the fulfilment of these general undertakings. Its functions were therefore of three kinds: to obtain increased co-operation between participating countries; to aid Member countries to fulfil their international undertakings and their national programmes; and to assist the United States Government in putting into effect its programme of aid to Europe.

Thus began an entirely new kind of international co-operation in Europe. Seventeen countries were determined to tackle their problems as a group and were willing to submit the whole range of their economic policy to the close scrutiny and criticism of their neighbours. They were determined to remove protective barriers created by almost two decades of depression, of war, and the aftermath of war, because they recognised that their mutual progress and prosperity were interdependent. The potential range of economic co-operation was almost unlimited, and the immediate tasks were all unanimously agreed and of great urgency. The Organisation set up by the Convention was an international body, and all decisions were to be taken unanimously. The O.E.E.C. did not set out with any set of binding general principles. The method of work was to be that of a group of good neighbours so well informed about each other's affairs that they could advise

THE REMAINS OF WAR DAMAGE—1947

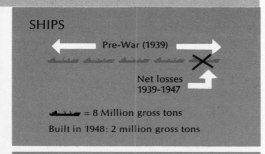

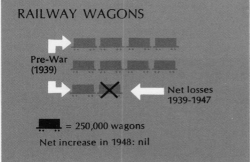

each other frankly to their mutual advantage. . . .

Between 1947 and 1957 industrial production in Europe had risen by 120 per cent,

An accurate statistical measure of total war damage is not possible. In particular the loss of industrial capacity cannot be evaluated. Although much had already been achieved, reconstruction needs in 1947 were still pressing.

The number of dwellings in 1947 in the Western European countries involved in the war was 7 per cent below pre-war. To make good this loss and to house the increased population would have required 7 million new dwelling units.

Europe's merchant fleet was 21 per cent, or four years of current construction, below pre-war. Moreover, in many cases, the ships that were in service were of wartime construction and they were ill-suited to peace-time conditions.

The number of railway wagons—often in poor condition—was 10 per cent below pre-war. Here current construction was little more than sufficient to make good obsolescence.

agricultural output by half, the volume of exports to the rest of the world by 180 per cent and gross national product per head by 55 per cent. The record in some O.E.E.C.

647

countries is better than in others, but in every one striking increases have been made in economic welfare. None of these achievements is the sole and direct result of action by the O.E.E.C., but none could have been attained so rapidly without the system of co-operation that has been developed by the O.E.E.C. over the past ten years. . . .

Chart 3

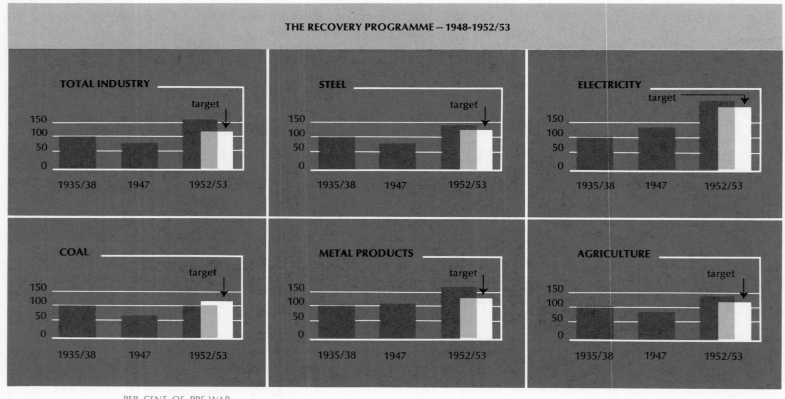

THE RECOVERY PROGRAMME — 1948-1952/53

PER CENT OF PRE-WAR		
	1952/53 TARGET	OUTPUT IN 1947
Total industry	130	94
Steel	129	69
Electricity	212	141
Coal	111	80
Metal Products	145	102
Agriculture	115	83

The "Interim Report on the European Recovery Programme" of 1948 set up targets for 1952–1953 for Western Europe as outlined in the table to the left.

Achievements substantially exceeded the targets in almost all fields, total industrial production rising 65 per cent above the 1947 level against the 40 per cent hoped for. With steel production well above expectations, production of machinery expanded roughly twice as much as had been foreseen, opening the way for new increases of output.

The success achieved in expanding electricity capacity enabled the enhanced requirements to be met. Coal production, however, did not grow as much as had been expected.

Agriculture exceeded the target of a 38 per cent increase on the 1947 level, permitting an increase in consumption at the same time as reduced imports.

All in all, the total output of goods and services reached about 128 per cent of the pre-war level against the 120 per cent indicated by the main sector targets.

Europe Savors the Affluent Society

From Ernest Hauser," Affluent Europe," in *The Saturday Evening Post,* February 10, 1962, pp. 17–18, 20, 22.

Europe is in the chips. An affluence undreamed of a few years ago is filling European pockets with hard cash, European kitchens with new gadgets, and European highways with new cars. Luxurious jet planes ferry busy men and women across the Alps, across the Rhine. People who used to ride the streetcar now drive to work. The stores are crammed with great quantities of the good things in life. Three hundred million human beings—the inhabitants of Europe on the sunny side of the Iron Curtain—are enjoying a prosperity that is unprecedented in the Old World's history.

Postwar reports of Europe's demise have since proved premature. That it was a narrow squeeze nobody here denies. "If we are still around at all," a ranking French official said, "it is most likely due to the forty-odd billion aid dollars the United States has lent or given Europe since the end of World War II. But we are now on our own. We've broken through. We have entered a new phase, and we are moving forward on our own momentum". . . .

The rise from rags to riches, to be sure, must be seen in its proper perspective. In several European countries expansion has been so spectacular largely because they had suffered heavy damage during World War II. Starting at the bottom, they came up fast, while our own economy was merely clambering from an already high plateau to a still higher one. Even today the average European is still "poor" by our standards, his annual income being roughly half the income of the average American in terms of real purchasing power.

Moreover there remain some ugly holes in the bright picture of Europe's new prosperity. Greece, Portugal, Southern Italy and parts of Spain are still beset by their old incubus, mass poverty. Slums, even cave dwellings, exist in many cities. There are regions where such necessities of life as electricity and running water are still considered luxuries. Even in Britain, Western Germany and France the electricity output per person is less than half our own. Housing, almost everywhere in Europe, is still distressingly inadequate, with many families living in one small room or sharing the homes of relatives. Last but not least, the distribution of wealth still leaves a lot to be desired, and abject misery frequently hides hard beneath the glittering surface.

Still, the great bulk of Western Europe's population is now immeasurably better off than in the recent past. Wages have gone up steeply in the last five years, and full employment has become a fact in almost every European country. In some industrial regions, such as the thriving Netherlands, there now are many more jobs than men to fill them. Switzerland, with a population of 5,000,000, employs as many as 500,000 foreign workers, most of them imported from Southern Italy and Spain. Western Germany has 750,000 registered job openings; and although wages there already are 13 percent higher than they were last year, a skilled man is worth almost any wage he asks for in what is known as the "gray labor market." Labor piracy has become a common practice in places like the Ruhr and Lombardy, where specialists are being lured from one job to another by pleading, desperate employers.

A static continent has turned dynamic. Cities have outgrown their old forms and spilled into the countryside. (Look down on any European capital from the air, and you will see its venerable body dwarfed by a brood of modern suburbs.) The birth rate has been climbing merrily since World War II—even old France, stagnant and over-age for decades, has spawned some record crops of babies, increasing her population from a pre-war 42,000,000 to 45,800,000. The accent is on youth. Everywhere one goes in Western Europe, one is impressed with the great number of young people, taller than their elders, and by the flocks of boisterously healthy children, dressed no longer like tiny adults but in dungarees and T shirts.

People are on the move. Farmers flock to the cities. Townsfolk become suburbanites. Touched by a magic wand, the great outdoors has come to life—long-silent forests swarm with campers, the lakes are white with sailboats, gingerbread mountain towns are packed with skiers. Anything that spells "hobby" and "outdoors"—from barbecue grills to records, stamps and movie cameras—is selling briskly. The money has come out of socks and mustard pots, and it circulates. . . .

The second-biggest annual show in Paris, after the autumn Automobile *Salon,* is the *Salon des Arts Menagers*—a sample fair of household gadgets and appliances which, every spring, fills the French capital with eager

Panorama of Krupp steel mills at Rheinhausen in the Ruhr.

visitors who come to ogle and to buy. Europe has gone appliance-happy. Refrigerators, washing machines, dishwashers, mixers, vacuum cleaners, record players and TV sets largely account for the fantastic rise in the turnover of consumer durables. While our own expenditure for this kind of hardware has increased by 20 per cent over the last decade, Europe's has doubled. . . .

Under the impact of the roaring '60's the map of Europe is changing almost as dramatically as it did in the Middle Ages, when townsmen built great castles and cathedrals and soon achieved ascendancy over less-enterprising neighbors.

Among the hitching posts of the new boom are Rotterdam, with its vast "Europort"; Zurich, which now plays banker to a large segment of the continent; Milan, the commercial capital of Italy; Turin, whose baroque palaces and churches are now eclipsed by the huge Fiat works; and Düsseldorf—"desk of the Ruhr."

It is in Düsseldorf that one receives perhaps the most impressive notion of what this age of affluence is all about. Fed by the mines and factories of the nearby Ruhr, whose corporations use it as a headquarters, the city—once a third-rate ducal residence—has turned into Exhibit A of what is known as the West German "miracle." Those of us who came through here at the end of World War II, when 65 percent of the city's built-up area was flattened, have trouble recognizing it. Wide, pleasant avenues, lined with glass-and-steel facades of modern buildings, have risen from the ruins of cramped quarters. Eleven junior skyscrapers have been completed or are being built; seventeen more are planned. Düsseldorf has made itself the principal emporium for ladies' coats and dresses on the continent; it boasts a "supermarket" for used cars; its stock exchange is now the continent's largest after Paris; its streetcars serve refreshments.

Almost everyone you see wears new, expensive clothes. The number of privately owned automobiles has more than doubled in the last five years. Along the chestnut-lined Königsallee, where swans float lazily in the canal that runs its length, shop windows overflow with all the attributes of the abundant life. From jewelry to hand-tooled leather goods, from furs and stylish shoes to chinaware and fancy chocolates, the German wage earner finds all his heart desires. Bank windows show on electronically operated boards the fluctuations of his favorite blue-chip stocks. In flower-trimmed side-walk cafes, housewives are apt to discuss, over ice cream and cake, the servant shortage or their Mediterranean cruise.

On the terrace of a fashionable restaurant, a German businessman was talking to me earnestly across the luncheon table. Below us the swift-flowing Rhine was filled with ships and barges laden with goods of every description. On the horizon the exhalations of a hundred furnaces were blending into a pink haze. "People should not call it a miracle," he said. "Nothing miraculous about it! We Germans are hard-working people, and we've had to work extra hard this time to prove to Russia and the prisoners behind the Iron Curtain that life is better where there is freedom." He drained his beaker while I waited for the rest which never came: We had to prove it also to ourselves. . . .

Will Europe stay her course? There is no reason, at this juncture, for concern. In spite of the unprecedented spending spree, savings are high; the factories are turning out the goods; there is no runaway inflation anywhere in Europe. Moreover, the Common Market—a solemn compact among European nations to scrap the trade barriers still separating them—is well out of the blueprint stage. As economic unity becomes a fact, as goods and people start to move across the map as freely as they do in the United States, the future holds the promise of an even more broadly based prosperity. . . .

Richard Mayne: Theory of the Larger Market

Richard Mayne (1926–   ), the first Englishman to become an official of the European Community, here presents the theory of economic integration as it developed in the Common Market. From Richard Mayne, *The Community of Europe* (London: Victor Gollancz Ltd, 1963), pp. 62–67.

America's industrial growth, indeed, was the most important quantitative factor in changing the pattern of world production between the wars. While Europe's share of total industrial output dwindled, that of North America as a whole not only caught up but even began to overtake it, rising from 36.5 per cent in 1913 to 42.1 per cent in 1929. By 1938, while industrial production in Great Britain, France, and Belgium stood respectively 54 per cent, 77 per cent and 79 per cent higher than in 1900, the comparable figure for the United States was 163 per cent. In Europe, only Germany, Italy and Sweden could match or outstrip the United States' growth rate, and no country could equal Canada's: in terms of absolute production figures, even Germany came well behind the United States. Moreover, despite the comparatively small proportion of North

The rebuilt Königsallee in Düsseldorf, the West German industrial capital, is famed for its elegance and luxury.

Prosperous citizens of Düsseldorf enjoy afternoon coffee along the busy Königsallee.

American products sold for export, these relative changes were also reflected in the trade figures. . . .

Among the explanations suggested to account for this disparity between American and European development, the size of the United States market was one that caught the attention of Europeans. As two astute commentators have put it, "The moment when the 'American era' began is significant: it coincides with the beginning of the process of disintegration in the world economy." While the American economy could develop on the basis of a single market of continental proportions, in Europe the advent of economic nationalism disturbed the multilateral equilibrium of international trade. Obviously, other factors played a part of the story, and it would be naive to presuppose a simple correlation between the size of the market and the rate of economic growth. But at a time when a return to free trade was clearly out of the question, Europeans certainly began to wonder whether they might not rival American prosperity if they could establish in their own continent a market of American size.

The basic idea, of course, was as old as the philosophy of free trade itself. Adam Smith had long ago stated that "the division of labour is limited by the extent of the market"; and the arguments for large markets were substantially those of the classical economists. Catering for a large market, they pointed out, would make possible economics of scale in mass production and distribution, resulting in lower costs; large-scale producers would have easier access to sources of capital, bigger research and training budgets, better planning facilities and therefore greater stability. Competition in a wider area would stimulate technical improvement and modernization, and would lead to the survival of the fittest; while this in turn would encourage greater specialization among firms and regions, so that industries would be more economically located and each would concentrate upon what it could do best.

Stated thus badly, the classical doctrine is crudely liberal and even rather brutal: but it makes some sense. Indeed, although early instances of larger markets added new elements to the old free-trading philosophy, they nevertheless lent colour to its general thesis. The suppression of internal economic barriers in France, the United Kingdom, and the Swiss Confederation undoubtedly made for greater prosperity, as it did in the U.S.A. The spread of the railways in Europe, creating larger markets by reducing travel costs, was an even more striking instance of the same process; and the Zollverein in nineteenth-century Germany, which gradually united into a single market a number of small principalities which hitherto had been divided by innumerable customs tariffs, laid the foundations for over a century of rapid economic growth.

At the same time, however, experience also suggested that the pure gospel of free trade stood in need of revision. This was due partly to practical changes in economic society, and partly to a growing sophistication of economic theory. Chief among the practical changes were the greater responsibilities of the state in economic affairs and the greater size and complexity of modern industry. On the one hand, the state's activities not only embraced such matters as labour laws, welfare projects, and indirect restraint or stimulus by means of taxes and tax reliefs, subsidies, marketing organizations, and monetary controls, but also direct participation in the economy itself. By 1955, indeed, the state's average current expenditure in Western Europe represented 28 per cent of the gross national product; and government ownership or participation affected central banks, railways, airlines, electricity, coalmining, oil, steel, transport equipment, and chemicals—to name only the most important industrial sectors. On the other hand, the nature of modern technology and modern finance had led to the formation, in all European countries, of industrial units and groupings far larger than any imagined by Adam Smith. Many of them—Siemens, I.C.I., Fiat, Unilever, Arbed, Sidelor, Brufina—are national household words; and many too have international ramifications.

Partly because of this altered context, moreover, classical economic theory had undergone drastic modifications, symbolized and in some degree accomplished by the so-called "Keynesian revolution". One of the essential elements of this revolution was its abandonment of the notion that a modern economy can rely on some quasi-automatic and self-regulating mechanism of prices and interests—what Adam Smith called "an invisible hand". While different Governments are pledged in theory to different degrees of "liberalism" or "planning", all in practice exercise a variety of controls, replacing the hidden hand by measures intended at most to ensure steady social and regional development and at least to iron out the cyclical booms and recessions which although still intractable are no longer accepted as inevitable. If economics was once little more than natural history, it is now coming more and more to resemble applied biology.

John Maynard Keynes (1883–1946), English economist, held that, contrary to Adam Smith, government intervention in the economy was necessary and beneficial. He argued that large-scale economic planning could prevent the boom-to-bust cycles characteristic of *laissez-faire* capitalism. Keynes counselled tax cuts, interest rate reductions, and heavy governmental spending to ward off recessions while advocating the reverse to hold down inflation. As he saw it, the key to prosperity lay in the continual full employment of all economic resources—men, machines, and materials—which could only be assured by a stable economy. [Eds.]

It is in taking account of these developments that theories of the larger market differ from classical theories of free trade. Free trade, like patriotism, is "not enough". The full implications of this change only emerged from practice in the moves towards economic integration in Europe which followed World War II; but some of them were already being expressed between the wars. As early as 1915, indeed, when the German theorist Friedrich Naumann proposed a customs union with Austria in his influential book *Mitteleuropa,* he argued: "No European nation, not even the German, by itself is large enough for an economic state of world standing. This is the result of the capitalist economic system. This economic state has its customs frontiers just as the military state has its trenches. Within these frontiers it tries to create a universally active exchange area. This involves an economic legislation, while advising the national governments on the remainder. The direct functions of the economic government include customs, cartel regulations, export arrangements, patent laws, protection of trade marks, control of raw materials, etc. Its indirect sphere of activity includes commercial legislation, social welfare and many other things. . . .

Walter Hallstein: The Goals of the Common Market (1959)

European affluence rested in good part on the efforts of the nations of Western Europe to cooperate in areas of mutual interest. High among these acts of international cooperation was the establishment of the European Economic Community or Common Market, which came into existence in 1957 with the signing of the Treaty of Paris by representatives of France, West Germany, Italy, Belgium, the Netherlands, and Luxembourg. The Community aimed at affecting a gradual economic union among its members that would lead ultimately to political union. Its headquarters were set up in Brussels, Belgium, and in the following years progressive steps were taken to eliminate internal tariff barriers and create a common external policy. Other objectives of the Common Market included the free movement of capital and labor, control of monopolies, and the extension of its provisions to achieve agricultural as well as industrial parity. The reading contains excerpts from a speech by the Community's first president, Walter Hallstein of Germany, delivered in New York on June 15, 1959, at a luncheon sponsored by the American Committee on United Europe. From Walter Hallstein, "The European Community: How Will It Fit Into the Atlantic Community?", in *Vital Speeches of the Day,* XXV, No. 19 (New York: City News Publishing Co., 1959), pp. 581–583.

Ladies and Gentlemen, an English statesman once declared that "many people prefer the existence of a problem which they cannot solve to an explanation of it which they cannot understand."

I have been asked today to say something about how the European Community, which is now a working reality on the eastern shore of the Atlantic, fits into that broader association which is the Atlantic Community. I hope that my explanation will not be more confusing than the problem I shall discuss.

At the end of the war, we in Europe arose among the ruins of our cities and rubbed our eyes, like men awakened from a nightmare. But it had been no nightmare. It had been the tragic culmination of a story of greed and folly and lust for power that had written finis to the old fragmented Europe.

The most complete expression of this line of thought, however, is to be found in a League of Nations study on customs unions, republished in 1947 by the United Nations. It declared: "For a customs union to exist, it is necessary to allow free movement of goods within the union. For a customs union to be a reality it is necessary to allow free movement of persons. For a customs union to be stable it is necessary to maintain free exchangeability of currency and stable exchange rates within the union. This implies, *inter alia,* free movement of capital within the union. When there is free movement of goods, persons, and capital in any area, diverse economic policies concerned with maintaining economic activity cannot be pursued. To assure uniformity of policy, some political mechanism is required. The greater the interference of the state in economic life, the greater must be the political integration within a customs union."

The cat was out of the bag at last. The theory of larger markets and customs unions led directly to the problem of political union.

Workers move freely in the Common Market. A sign in Italian is fixed to a streetcar window in West Germany to aid immigrant workers.

It was significant, indeed, that all the historical examples of larger markets—in France, in the United Kingdom, in Switzerland, in the German *Zollverein,* in Italy, and in the United States—had been preceded, accompanied, or followed, by pressure for political as well as economic integration. In the words of a young French economist deeply involved in the operations of the Common Market, "Political

union by itself soon proves impracticable without a corresponding economic union; economic union is only feasible if the states—or one of them—include it in their political programme. If the Keynesian revolution had thus in some sort remarried economics and politics, the history of Europe after World War II was to prove that the union was fertile.

We were confronted not only with the change but the necessity to build anew and to build better. With the generous help of your great country, we achieved a recovery that astounded even ourselves. New cities arose on the ruins of the old. New prosperity appeared where the grim specter of poverty and famine had once held sway.

In this year of grace of 1959, we can say with assurance that the process of recovery is ended, and that a new phase in Europe's history has begun. Today, we are no longer rehabilitating Europe; we are transforming Europe. Six nations—France, Germany, Italy, and the three Benelux countries—are in the process of welding their economies into a single unit, and laying the foundation of a future federation of states.

We have embarked upon this great adventure for two interrelated reasons—one economic and one political. I shall discuss each in turn.

The economic reason is obvious to anyone who has reflected upon the secret of American prosperity. As we Europeans look at your country, we naturally ask ourselves why our standard of living is still only half as high as yours. Are we less intelligent, do we work less hard, do we save less, have we less imagination than you? That—we tell ourselves—is not the answer. Your economy has reached its present heights in great part because you have created a huge home market which has per-

mitted you to make the fullest use of the techniques of specialization, automation, and mass production. We, on the other hand, with roughly the same number of people in our Community as there are in the United States, have lived for centuries in an area crisscrossed by national barriers that strangled trade and stifled output.

The Common Market is tearing down those barriers. It will make available to our industries a domestic market of 165 million people. As national barriers fall, new competition is already spurring modernization, increasing productivity, and lowering production costs.

The free movement of labor and capital is for the first time offering industry the chance to develop in those regions with natural advantages for productivity.

To enable everyone in every part of the Community to share in this new prosperity, the Common Market's Investment Bank is beginning to provide capital. Our Social Fund will give aid to those who need it, and our Overseas Development Fund will extend a helping hand to the Community's partners in Africa and elsewhere. We are creating a new economic frontier which, we believe, should generate the same dynamism, the same mobility and opportunity, the same sense of hope and adventure as did your Western frontier throughout your history. And we are creating that frontier, paradoxically enough, by the destruction of old national frontiers.

So much for the economic aims behind the Common Market. Its political aims are perhaps of even greater importance. In a rapidly shrinking world, challenged not only by the threat of Communism, but also by the growing needs of underdeveloped regions, the single nations of Europe can no longer afford to remain divided.

I am one of the many European admirers of that wise and witty man, Bob Hope. I remember that in one of his broadcasts he was challenged, as a so-called "strong man" in a circus, to tear a deck of cards in half. He accepted the challenge, and the listeners heard him straining and gasping. Suddenly there was a loud tearing sound. "Fine," said Mr. Hope, delightedly, "and now for the second card in the deck!"

Without wishing to accuse Mr. Hope of plagiarism, I believe that a similar story is told, in the ancient world, by Plutarch. But the lesson is as obvious now as it was then. Together we are strong: taken one by one, we are weak.

In combining for strength through the European Community, we are pooling not only our economic resources but our governmental policies. Our policies in the fields of transportation, energy, agriculture and cartels—in other words, all of the important aspects of economic policy—are being determined not with reference merely to the needs and importunities of individual small national states but in relation to the requirements of the Community as a whole. This is a political change of the first order of magnitude. It must inevitably be followed by a progressively greater unification of our policies in a widening area of activities.

In building a united Europe we do not seek to create a third force. For us, there is no such choice as between Communism and freedom. But we do wish to build an economic and political whole which will eliminate forever the wars and conflicts that twice in a single generation have come close to destroying the old world.

It seems clear to us that in this endeavor we are not acting selfishly. A family is not weakened; it is only benefitted, if one of the members grows well and strong. . . .

So, ladies and gentlemen, I can say to you categorically: The Common Market is here to stay. It is something more than a simple customs union. It is a political force. It is a reaction against the past, and one which could start a chain reaction.

Our aim is more than just to free trade: it is more than just to bring about a redistribution of resources. For the world economy, I am convinced, is not a cake to be cut and divided, but a vehicle to be set in motion. The industrialized regions of the world are its motor, and the Common Market will play its full part in helping to drive the vehicle and to steer it along the road of freedom, progress, and peace.

J.-J. Servan-Schreiber: The American Challenge

According to perceptive French critic J.-J. Servan-Schreiber (1924–   ) Europe, in the midst of unparalleled affluence, is losing the crucial race for technological progress and political autonomy. His book, *The American Challenge,* which appeared in France in 1967, lucidly described the European dilemma and suggested a possible, and characteristically Western, solution. From *The American Challenge* by J.-J. Servan-Schreiber, published by Atheneum and reprinted by permission of the publishers. Copyright © 1967 by Editions Denoel as *le Défi Américain:* English translation © 1968, 1969 by Atheneum House, Inc.

Fifteen years from now it is quite possible that the world's third greatest industrial power, just after the United States and Russia, will not be Europe, but *American industry in Europe.* Already, in the ninth year of the Common Market, this European market is basically American in organization.

The importance of U.S. penetration rests, first of all, on the sheer amount of capital invested—currently about $14 billion ($14,000,000,000). [In *fixed assets*—that is, plant and equipment, not including working capital (about as much again). Source: U.S. Department of Commerce.] Add to this the massive size of the firms carrying out this conquest. Recent efforts by European firms to centralize and merge are inspired largely by the need to compete with the American giants like International Business Machines (IBM) and General Motors. This is the surface penetration. But there is another aspect of the problem which is considerably more subtle.

Every day an American banker working in Paris gets requests from French firms looking for Frenchmen "with experience in an American corporation." The manager of a German steel mill hires only staff personnel "having been trained with an American firm." The British Marketing Council sends 50 British executives to spend a year at the Harvard Business School—and the British government foots the bill. For European firms, so conservative and jealous of their independence, there is now one common denominator: American methods.

During the past ten years Americans in Europe have made more mistakes than their competitors—but they have tried to correct them. And an American firm can change its methods in almost no time, compared to a European firm. The Americans have been reorganizing their European operations. Everywhere they are setting up European-scale headquarters responsible for the firm's Continental business, with sweeping powers of decision and instructions not to pay any attention to national boundaries.

These U.S. subsidiaries have shown a flexibility and adaptability that have enabled them to adjust to local conditions and be prepared for political decisions taken, or even contemplated, by the Common Market.

Since 1958 American corporations have invested $10 billion in Western Europe—*more than a third* of their total investment abroad. Of the 6,000 new businesses started overseas by Americans during that period, *half* were in Europe.

One by one, American firms are setting up headquarters to coordinate their activities throughout Western Europe. This is true federalism—the only kind that exists in Europe on an industrial level. And it goes a good deal farther than anything Common Market experts ever imagined.

Union Carbide set up its European headquarters in Lausanne in 1965. The Corn Products Company, which now has ten European branches, moved its coordinating office from Zurich to Brussels and transformed it into a central headquarters. IBM now directs all its European activities from Paris. The Celanese Corporation of America has recently set up headquarters in Brussels; and American Express has established its European central offices in London.

Standard Oil of New Jersey has put its European oil (Esso Europe) headquarters in London, and its European chemical (Esso Chemical SA) command in Brussels. Both have been told to "ignore the present division between the Common Market and the free trade zone [Britain, Scandinavia]." For Esso, Europe now represents a market *larger than the United States,* and one growing *three times faster. . . .*

The greater wealth of American corporations allows them to conduct business in Europe faster and more flexibly than their European competitors. This *flexibility* of the Americans, even more than their wealth, is their major weapon. . .

If American investment is only part of the phenomenon of power, the problem for Europe is to become a great power. What today seems like an enormous "rummage sale" of our industry to the Americans could, paradoxically, lead to our salvation.

American power is no longer what it was

The old and new are neighbors in Turkey. The Istanbul headquarters of International Business Machines looks down upon a mosque.

after the end of the war. Its scale and even its nature have changed. We are learning about it because we are feeling its impact right here on our shores. This is all to the good. While it is a shock, shock is better than surprise because it forces us to pay attention.

During the *past ten years,* from the end of the cold war and the launching of the first Sputnik, American power has made an unprecedented leap forward. It has undergone a violent and productive internal revolution. Technological innovation has now become the basic objective of economic policy. In America today the government official, the industrial manager, the economics professor, the engineer, and the scientist have joined forces to develop coordinated techniques for integrating factors of production. These techniques have stimulated what amounts to a permanent industrial revolution.

The originality of this revolution consists precisely in the effect this fusion of talents has on decisions made by government agencies, corporations, and universities. This takes us a long way from the old image of the United States—a country where business was not only separate from government but constantly struggling with it, and where there was a chasm between professors and businessmen. Today, to the contrary, this combination of forces has produced the remarkable integrated entity that John Kenneth Galbraith calls a "technostructure."

If we continue to allow the major decisions about industrial innovation and technological creativity—decisions which directly affect our lives—to be made in Washington, New York, Cambridge, Detroit, Seattle, and Houston, there is a real danger that Europe may forever be confined to second place. We may not be able to build one of those great industrial-intellectual complexes on which a creative society depends. What kind of future do we want?

It is time for us to take stock and face the hard truth. Some of those who watched the decline of Rome or Byzantium also caught a glimpse of the future that was coming. But that was not enough to change the course of history. If we are to be master of our fate, we will need a rude awakening. If this doesn't come, then Europe, like so many other glorious civilizations, will gradually sink into decadence without ever understanding why or how it happened. In 1923 Spengler mused over "The Decline of the West." Today we have barely time enough to comprehend what is happening to us.

What threatens to crush us today is not a torrent of riches, but a more intelligent use of skills. While French, German, or Italian firms are still groping around in the new open spaces provided by the Treaty of Rome, afraid to emerge from the dilapidated shelter of their old habits, American industry has gauged the terrain and is now rolling from Naples to Amsterdam with the ease and the speed of Israeli tanks in the Sinai desert.

Confronted with this conquering force, European politicians and businessmen do not know how to react. Public opinion, confused by their contradictory statements and mysterious shifts of policy, has no way of judging whether American investment is good or bad.

It is both. The stimulus of competition and the introduction of new techniques are clearly good for Europe. But the cumulative underdevelopment that could transform this assistance into a takeover is bad, very bad.

This unprecedented challenge has found us alone and unprepared, but not without resources. When power was measured by the number of men in arms and the number of legions, Europe was a leader. When power became industrial and was applied to the transformation of raw materials, Europe was still in the front rank. In 1940 nothing would have been able to defeat a coalition of Germany, Britain, and France, if they were really united. Even when plunged into the most terrible civil war of her history by Hitler's folly, this Europe, her body bled and her spirit drained, revived to make an extraordinary recovery after 1950, and can still aspire to a role of leadership. What our leaders have lacked in this postwar period is a rational ambition—an ambition that can be achieved.

During the years when American industry began its conquest of advanced technology, our political leaders were blind to new realities and the potential of the future. So blind that Britain and France were no better off than defeated Germany and Italy when confronted with the real winner who knew how to exploit his success and is now preparing his greatest triumph.

This new conquest almost perfectly defines the word "intangible." This no doubt explains why it has been misunderstood by leaders used to thinking is terms of tons of steel, machinery, and capital. The signs and instruments of power are no longer armed legions or raw materials or capital. Even factories are only an external symbol. Modern power is based on the capacity for innovation, which is research, and the capacity to transform inventions into finished products, which is technology. The wealth we seek does not lie in the earth or in numbers of men or in machines, but in the human spirit. And particularly in the ability of men to think and to create.

The scientist accepts this, but the politician, the civil servant, and the businessman understand it only with difficulty. It is fashionable today to praise profit indiscriminately. But as the economist François Perroux has shown, it is a catch-all for everything: returns on a business, monopoly gains, killings on a speculation. Healthy profit, real profit, for a business as for society as a whole, lies in the *fruits of innovation*.

The training, development, and exploitation of human intelligence—these are the real resources, and there are no others. The American challenge is not ruthless, like so many Europe has known in her history, but it may be more dramatic, for it embraces everything.

STUDY QUESTIONS

1. What was the Western world like after World War II? Why did economics play such a vital role in determining the future?

2. How did Europe again become "the workshop of the world" after the war? Why was the Marshall Plan needed and how did it work?

3. Why did the theory of the larger market have real impact on Europe only after the war? How did Keynesian thinking differ from classical economics?

4. What were the goals of the Common Market? What was the relation between it and the Marshall Plan? How does the Common Market function?

5. What did Hallstein see as the relationship between Europe's economic progress and her political future?

6. What did Servan-Schreiber mean by "the American challenge" to Europe? How was this challenge developed out of the last war specifically and the course of modern civilization generally?

THE DIVISION OF POWER

The European world was broken apart by the Second World War. Western Europe, liberated by the armies of the democracies, either quickly returned to the institutions and forms of the past or, in the case of Germany and Austria, was occupied by Allied troops. Eastern Europe received its postwar political identity as a result of the movement westward of Russian troops. By the spring of 1945 they stood behind a line running from the Elbe River to the Adriatic Sea and embracing almost all of the Balkan Peninsula. The Allied leaders, gathered at Yalta, accepted this military line as a temporary boundary between Western and Soviet influence in Europe. Russia's later tightening of political and economic control over her satellites was the major reason for the breakdown of the wartime alliance between Russia and America. The Cold War followed, separating further the western and eastern portions of Germany and hardening the line between Eastern and Western Europe.

By the winter of 1947–1948, the chill was everywhere. A fourth Communist International, the Cominform, was created. A Communist minority took over the government of Czechoslovakia in 1948, and Italian elections in the same year served as a battleground between East and West. The North Atlantic Treaty Organization (NATO) was founded the following year (1949) to defend the territorial integrity of its non-Communist member nations where necessary, and to otherwise deter the Soviet Union from extending itself further in Europe. As a countermove, Russia gathered her satellite forces into the Warsaw Pact. In the same year she too perfected the atomic bomb, thus ending the American nuclear monopoly. The next four years were grim. Tension continued over Berlin, a Western outpost behind the Iron Curtain; in Korea which had been divided in the Asian settlement, the Communist North invaded the South and the United States was soon again at war.

The first relaxation of the Cold War came in 1953 with the death of Stalin and the end of the Korean War. In that year, too, Russia exploded her first hydrogen bomb. A form of "peaceful coexistence" imposed itself by dint of the balance of terror created by the new weapons. Eastern Europe benefited from a relaxation of political control by Russia, even though an attempt at revolution in Hungary in 1956 was ruthlessly suppressed. By the 1960s the Cold War theater had shifted from Europe to the developing world. In Africa, Latin America, the Middle East, and Southeast Asia, the United States and the Soviet Union confronted one another and maneuvered for power and influence. The readings explore the origins and development of the Cold War and its effect on political decisions, considering in particular the problems created by America's role as "guardian of the peace."

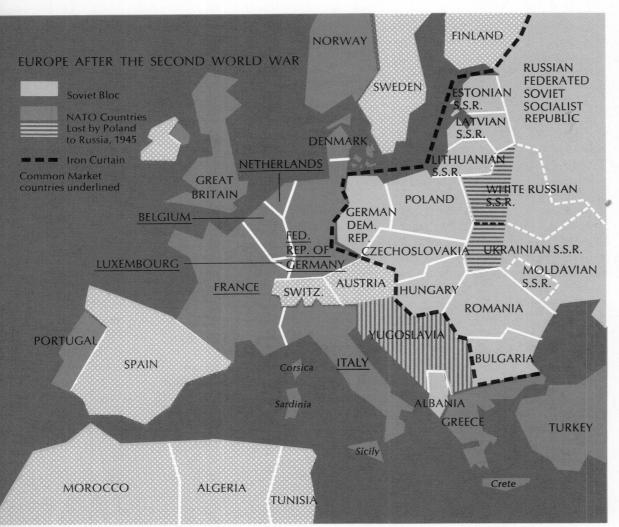

EUROPE AFTER THE SECOND WORLD WAR

Soviet Bloc

NATO Countries
Lost by Poland
to Russia, 1945

Iron Curtain

Common Market
countries underlined

NORWAY

FINLAND

SWEDEN

ESTONIAN
S.S.R.

RUSSIAN
FEDERATED
SOVIET
SOCIALIST
REPUBLIC

LATVIAN
S.S.R.

DENMARK

NETHERLANDS

LITHUANIAN
S.S.R.

GREAT
BRITAIN

POLAND

WHITE RUSSIAN
S.S.R.

BELGIUM

GERMAN
DEM.
REP.

FED.
REP. OF
GERMANY

CZECHOSLOVAKIA

UKRAINIAN S.S.R.

LUXEMBOURG

FRANCE

SWITZ.

AUSTRIA

HUNGARY

MOLDAVIAN
S.S.R.

ROMANIA

PORTUGAL

YUGOSLAVIA

BULGARIA

SPAIN

Corsica

ITALY

Sardinia

ALBANIA

GREECE

TURKEY

Sicily

MOROCCO

ALGERIA

TUNISIA

Crete

The United Nations Is Formed To Preserve Peace (1945)

Keystone of the effort after the Second World War to make future war impossible was the United Nations Organization. Launched in San Francisco in 1945, the United Nations was hamstrung from the start by the Russo-American conflict as well as by the limited power exercised by a body whose members had not given up their own sovereignty. As an instrument of peace-keeping, it was confined by the great powers to a role in areas where their own interests were not in direct conflict. The reading contains the preamble and part of the first article of the United Nations Charter. From the *Charter of the United Nations Together with the Statute of the International Court of Justice,* United States Department of State, Publication 2353, Conference Series 74.

PREAMBLE

We the peoples of the United Nations determined to save succeeding generations from the scourge of war, which twice in our lifetime has brought untold sorrow to mankind, and

to reaffirm faith in fundamental human rights, in the dignity and worth of the human person, in the equal rights of men and women and of nations large and small, and

to establish conditions under which justice and respect for the obligations arising from treaties and other sources of international law can be maintained, and

to promote social progress and better standards of life in larger freedom, and for these ends to practice tolerance and live together in peace with one another as good neighbors, and

to unite our strength to maintain international peace and security, and

to ensure, by the acceptance of principles and the institution of methods, that armed force shall not be used, save in the common interest, and

to employ international machinery for the promotion of the economic and social advancement of all peoples,

have resolved to combine our efforts to accomplish these aims. Accordingly, our respective Governments, through representatives assembled in the city of San Francisco, who have exhibited their full powers found to be in good and due form, have agreed to the present Charter of the United Nations and do hereby establish an international organization to be known as the United Nations.

PURPOSES AND PRINCIPLES

Article 1

The purposes of the United Nations are:

1. To maintain international peace and security, and to that end: to take effective collective measures for the prevention and removal of threats to the peace, and for the suppression of acts of aggression or other breaches of the peace, and to bring about by peaceful means, and in conformity with the principles of justice and international law, adjustment or settlement of international disputes or situations which might lead to a breach of the peace; . . .

2. To develop friendly relations among nations based on respect for the principle of equal rights and self-determina-

A view of United Nations headquarters with the skyscrapers of New York in the background. The complex is located on a six-block tract on the island of Manhattan.

The Security Council in session.

tion of peoples, and to take other appropriate measures to strengthen universal peace;

3. To achieve international coöperation in solving international problems of an economic, social, cultural, or humanitarian character, and in promoting and encouraging respect for human rights and for fundamental freedoms for all without distinction as to race, sex, language, or religion; and

4. To be a center for harmonizing the actions of nations in the attainment of those common ends.

Winston Churchill Warns That an Iron Curtain Has Descended in Europe (1946)

Out of office in the 1930s, Britain's Winston Churchill (1874–1965) had repeatedly warned the democratic peoples against resurgent Nazi Germany and urged united action to halt fascist aggression. After the war, his Conservative Party defeated at the polls, he reenacted his former role, this time directing his warning against the new threat of Soviet Russia. Churchill was a great phrase-maker. The speech below, which made the term "iron-curtain" a household word, was delivered in Missouri in March 1946, when, in the presence of President Truman, Churchill received an honorary degree at Westminster College. From Winston Churchill, Speech at Westminster College, Fulton, Missouri, March 5, 1946, in *Vital Speeches of the Day*, XII, No. 2 (New York: City News Publishing Co., 1946) 329–332.

A world organization has already been erected for the prime purpose of preventing war. United Nations Organization, the successor of the League of Nations, with the decisive addition of the United States and all that that means, is already at work. We must make sure that its work is fruitful, that it is a reality and not a sham, that it is a force for action and not merely a frothing of words, that it is a true temple of peace in which the shields of many nations can some day be hung and not merely a cockpit in a tower of Babel. Before we cast away the solid assurances of national armaments for self-preservation, we must be certain that our temple is built not upon shifting sands or quagmires, but upon the rock. Any one with his eyes open can see that our path will be difficult and also long, but if we persevere together as we did in the two world wars—though not, alas, in the interval between them—I cannot doubt that we shall achieve our common purpose in the end. . . .

EUROPE DIVIDED

A shadow has fallen upon the scenes so lately lighted by the Allied victory. Nobody knows what Soviet Russia and its Communist international organization intends to do in the immediate future, or what are the limits, if any, to their expansive and proselytizing tendencies. I have a strong admiration and regard for the valiant Russian people and for my war-time comrade, Marshal Stalin. There is sympathy and good will in Britain—and I doubt not here also—toward the peoples of all the Russias and a resolve to persevere through many differences and rebuffs in establishing lasting friendships. We understand the Russians need to be secure on her western frontiers from all renewal of German aggression. We welcome her to her rightful place among the leading nations of the world.

Above all we welcome constant, frequent and growing contacts between the Russian people and our own people on both sides of the Atlantic. It is my duty, however, to place before you certain facts about the present position in Europe—I am sure I do not wish to, but it is my duty, I feel, to present them to you.

From Stettin in the Baltic to Trieste in the Adriatic, an iron curtain has descended across the Continent. Behind that line lie all the capitals of the ancient states of central and eastern Europe. Warsaw, Berlin, Prague,

American and Russian soldiers greet each other enthusiastically as the Allied armies meet at Torgau in central Germany in 1945.

Vienna, Budapest, Belgrade, Bucharest and Sofia, all these famous cities and the populations around them lie in the Soviet sphere and all are subject in one form or another, not only to Soviet influence but to a very high and increasing measure of control from Moscow. Athens alone, with its immortal glories, is free to decide its future at an election under British, American and French observation.

The Russian-dominated Polish government has been encouraged to make enormous and wrongful inroads upon Germany, and mass expulsions of millions of Germans on a scale grievous and undreamed of are now taking place. The Communist parties, which were very small in all these eastern states of Europe, have been raised to pre-eminence and power far beyond their numbers and are seeking everywhere to obtain totalitarian control. Police governments are prevailing in nearly every case, and so far, except in Czechoslovakia, there is no true democracy. Turkey and Persia are both profoundly alarmed and disturbed at the claims which are made upon them and at the pressure being exerted by the Moscow government.

An attempt is being made by the Russians in Berlin to build up a quasi-Communist party in their zone of occupied Germany by showing special favors to groups of Left-Wing German leaders. At the end of the fighting last June, the American and British armies withdrew westward, in accordance with an earlier agreement, to a depth at some points 150 miles on a front of nearly 400 miles to allow the Russians to occupy this vast expanse of territory which the western democracies had conquered. If now the Soviet government tries, by separate action, to build up a pro-Communist Germany in their areas this will cause new serious difficulties in the

British and American zones, and will give the defeated Germans the power of putting themselves up to auction between the Soviets and western democracies. Whatever conclusions may be drawn from these facts—and facts they are—this is certainly not the liberated Europe we fought to build up. Nor is it one which contains the essentials of permanent peace.

The safety of the world, ladies and gentlemen, requires a new unity in Europe from which no nation should be permanently outcast. . . .

I have felt bound to portray the shadow which, alike in the West and in the East, falls upon the world. I was a minister at the time of the Versailles treaty and a close friend of Mr. Lloyd George. I did not myself agree with many things that were done, but I have a very vague impression in my mind of that situation, and I find it painful to contrast it with that which prevails now. In those days there were high hopes and unbounded confidence that the wars were over, and that the League of Nations would become all-powerful. I do not see or feel the same confidence or even the same hopes in the haggard world at this time.

On the other hand I repulse the idea that a new war is inevitable; still more that it is imminent. It is because I am so sure that our fortunes are in our own hands and that we hold the power to save the future, that I feel the duty to speak out now that I have an occasion to do so. I do not believe that Soviet Russia desires war. What they desire is the fruits of war and the indefinite expansion of their power and doctrines. But what we have to consider here today while time remains, is the permanent prevention of war and the establishment of conditions of freedom and democracy as rapidly as possible in all coun-

tries. Our difficulties and dangers will not be removed by mere waiting to see what happens; nor will they be relieved by a policy of appeasement. What is needed is a settlement and the longer this is delayed the more difficult it will be and the greater our dangers will become.

From what I have seen of our Russian friends and allies during the war, I am convinced that there is nothing they admire so much as strength, and there is nothing for which they have less respect than for military weakness. . . . If the western democracies stand together in strict adherence to the principles of the United Nations Charter, their influence for furthering these principles will be immense and no one is likely to molest them. If, however, they become divided or falter in their duty, and if these all-important years are allowed to slip away, then indeed catastrophe may overwhelm us all. . . .

President Truman Advocates American Intervention Against Communism (1947)

A year after Winston Churchill's Iron Curtain speech, American President Harry S Truman (1884–1972) enunciated the policy (Truman Doctrine) that would lead to a protracted attempt at global containment of Communism. The decision of the United States to intervene in the Balkans was made at a time when Greece faced a full-fledged civil war and Turkey was under Soviet pressure to permit establishment of a Russian base in the straits leading to the Mediterranean. Communist guerrillas in the northern mountains of Greece, aided by supporters in bordering Albania, Yugoslavia, and Bulgaria, were rebelling against the monarchy of Greece. The royal government had been aided in the past by Great Britain, but a British financial crisis had made further assistance impossible. In a speech to the Congress on March 12, 1947, President Truman requested support for an American economic and military commitment to Greece and went beyond this to describe conditions that would guide American intervention elsewhere. From "Recommendations on Greece and Turkey (Truman Doctrine)" in *A Decade of American Foreign Policy: Basic Documents, 1941–1949,* United States Senate Committee on Foreign Relations, Senate Document No. 123 (Washington, D.C., 1950), 1253–1257, pp. 619, 620, 621–623.

MR. PRESIDENT, MR. SPEAKER, MEMBERS OF THE CONGRESS OF THE UNITED STATES

The gravity of the situation which confronts the world today necessitates my appearance before a joint session of the Congress.

The foreign policy and the national security of this country are involved.

One aspect of the present situation, which I wish to present to you at this time for your consideration and decision, concerns Greece and Turkey.

The United States has received from the Greek Government an urgent appeal for financial and economic assistance. Preliminary reports from the American Economic Mission now in Greece and reports from the American Ambassador in Greece corroborate the statement of the Greek Government that assistance is imperative if Greece is to survive as a free nation. . . .

We have considered how the United Nations might assist in this crisis. But the situation is an urgent one requiring immediate action, and the United Nations and its related organizations are not in a position to extend help of the kind that is required. . . .

One of the primary objectives of the foreign policy of the United States is the creation of conditions in which we and other nations will be able to work out a way of life free from coercion. This was a fundamental issue in the war with Germany and Japan. Our victory was won over countries which sought to impose their will, and their way of life, upon other nations.

To insure the peaceful development of nations, free from coercion, the United States has taken a leading part in establishing the United Nations. The United Nations is designed to make possible lasting freedom and independence for all its members. We shall not realize our objectives, however, unless we are willing to help free peoples to maintain their free institutions and their national integrity against aggressive movements that seek to impose upon them totalitarian regimes. This is no more than a frank recognition that totalitarian regimes imposed upon free peoples, by direct or indirect aggression, undermine the foundations of international peace and hence the security of the United States.

The peoples of a number of countries of the world have recently had totalitarian regimes forced upon them against their will. The Government of the United States has made frequent protests against coercion and intimidation, in violation of the Yalta agreement, in Poland, Rumania, and Bulgaria. I must also state that in a number of other countries there have been similar developments.

At the present moment in world history nearly every nation must choose between alternative ways of life. The choice is too often not a free one.

One way of life is based upon the will of the majority, and is distinguished by free institutions, representative government, free elections, guaranties of individual liberty, freedom of speech and religion, and freedom from political oppression.

The second way of life is based upon the will of a minority forcibly imposed upon the majority. It relies upon terror and oppression, a controlled press and radio, fixed elections, and the suppression of personal freedoms.

I believe that it must be the policy of the United States to support free peoples who are resisting attempted subjugation by armed minorities or by outside pressures.

I believe that we must assist free peoples to work out their own destinies in their own way.

I believe that our help should be primarily through economic and financial aid which is essential to economic stability and orderly political processes.

The world is not static, and the *status quo* is not sacred. But we cannot allow changes in the *status quo* in violation of the Charter of the United Nations by such methods as coercion, or by such subterfuges as political infiltration. In helping free and independent nations to maintain their freedom, the United States will be giving effect to the principles of the Charter of the United Nations.

It is necessary only to glance at a map to realize that the survival and integrity of the

Greek nation are of grave importance in a much wider situation. If Greece should fall under the control of an armed minority, the effect upon its neighbor, Turkey, would be immediate and serious. Confusion and disorder might well spread throughout the entire Middle East.

Moreover, the disappearance of Greece as an independent state would have a profound effect upon those countries in Europe whose peoples are struggling against great difficulties to maintain their freedoms and their independence while they repair the damages of war.

It would be an unspeakable tragedy if these countries, which have struggled so long against overwhelming odds, should lose that victory for which they sacrificed so much. Collapse of free institutions and loss of independence would be disastrous not only for them but for the world. Discouragement and possibly failure would quickly be the lot of neighboring peoples striving to maintain their freedom and independence.

Should we fail to aid Greece and Turkey in this fateful hour, the effect will be far-reaching to the West as well as to the East.

We must take immediate and resolute action.

I therefore ask the Congress to provide authority for assistance to Greece and Turkey in the amount of $400,000,000 for the period ending June 30, 1948. In requesting these funds, I have taken into consideration the maximum amount of relief assistance which would be furnished to Greece out of the $350,000,000 which I recently requested that the Congress authorize for the prevention of starvation and suffering in countries devastated by the war.

In addition to funds, I ask the Congress to authorize the detail of American civilian and military personnel to Greece and Turkey, at the request of those countries, to assist in the tasks of reconstruction, and for the purpose of supervising the use of such financial and material assistance as may be furnished. I recommend that authority also be provided for the instruction and training of selected Greek and Turkish personnel. . . .

This is a serious course upon which we embark.

I would not recommend it except that the alternative is much more serious.

The United States contributed $341,-000,000,000 toward winning World War II. This is an investment in world freedom and world peace.

The assistance that I am recommending for Greece and Turkey amounts to little more than one-tenth of one per cent of this investment. It is only common sense that we should safeguard this investment and make sure that it was not in vain.

The seeds of totalitarian regimes are nurtured by misery and want. They spread and grow in the evil soil of poverty and strife. They reach their full growth when the hope of a people for a better life has died.

We must keep that hope alive.

The free peoples of the world look to us for support in maintaining their freedoms.

If we falter in our leadership, we may endanger the peace of the world—and we shall surely endanger the welfare of our own Nation.

Great responsibilities have been placed upon us by the swift movement of events.

I am confident that the Congress will face these responsibilities squarely.

West and East Organize Their Defenses: NATO and the Warsaw Pact

With the ratification of the NATO and Warsaw Pacts the Cold War was frozen into shape. The North Atlantic Treaty, a twenty-year collective security agreement, envisaging Russia as the potential aggressor, was signed by ten West European states, Canada, and the United States on April 4, 1949. In the next few years Turkey, Greece, and West Germany also joined. On May 14, 1955, the Soviet Union and seven nations within her sphere of influence signed a similar agreement. Portions of the texts appear below. I. From Royal Institute of International Affairs, *Atlantic Alliance* (London and New York, 1952), pp. 154–156; II. From "The Warsaw Security Pact" in *American Foreign Policy, 1950–1955*, United States Department of State, General Foreign Policy Series, vol. I, No. 117 (Washington, D.C., 1957), 1239–1241.

I. THE NORTH ATLANTIC TREATY
(1949)
Preamble

The Parties to this Treaty reaffirm their faith in the purposes and principles of the Charter of the United Nations and their desire to live in peace with all peoples and all Governments.

They are determined to safeguard the freedom, common heritage and civilization of their peoples, founded on the principles of democracy, individual liberty and the rule of law.

They seek to promote stability and well-being in the North Atlantic area.

They are resolved to unite their efforts for collective defence for the preservation of peace and security.

They therefore agree to this North Atlantic Treaty. . . .

Article 3

In order more effectively to achieve the objectives of this Treaty, the Parties, separately and jointly, by means of continuous and effective self-help and mutual aid, will maintain and develop their individual and collective capacity to resist armed attack. . . .

Article 5

The Parties agree that an armed attack against one or more of them in Europe or North America shall be considered an attack against them all and consequently they agree that, if such an armed attack occurs, each of them, in exercise of the right of individual or collective self-defence recognized by Article 51 of the Charter of the United Nations, will assist the Party or Parties so attacked by taking forthwith, individually and in concert with the other Parties, such action as it deems necessary, including the use of armed force, to restore and maintain the security of the North Atlantic area.

Any such armed attack and all measures taken as a result thereof shall immediately be reported to the Security Council. Such measures shall be terminated when the Security Council has taken the measures necessary to restore and maintain international peace and security.

II. THE WARSAW SECURITY PACT (1955)

The Contracting Parties,

reaffirming their desire for the establishment of a system of European collective se-

curity based on the participation of all European states irrespective of their social and political systems, which would make it possible to unite their efforts in safeguarding the peace of Europe;

mindful, at the same time, of the situation created in Europe by the ratification of the Paris agreements, which envisage the formation of a new military alignment in the shape of "Western European Union," with the participation of a remilitarized Western Germany and the integration of the latter in the North-Atlantic bloc, which increases the danger of another war and constitutes a threat to the national security of the peaceable states;

being persuaded that in these circumstances the peaceable European states must take the necessary measures to safeguard their security and in the interests of preserving peace in Europe;

guided by the objects and principles of the Charter of the United Nations Organization;

being desirous of further promoting and developing friendship, co-operation and mutual assistance in accordance with the principles of respect for the independence and sovereignty of states and of non-interference in their internal affairs,

have decided to conclude the present Treaty of Friendship, Cooperation and Mutual Assistance. . . .

Article 3

The Contracting Parties shall consult with one another on all important international issues affecting their common interests, guided by the desire to strengthen international peace and security.

They shall immediately consult with one another whenever, in the opinion of any one of them, a threat of armed attack on one or more of the Parties to the Treaty has arisen,

in order to ensure joint defence and the maintenance of peace and security.

Article 4

In the event of armed attack in Europe on one or more of the Parties to the Treaty by any state or group of states, each of the Parties to the Treaty, in the exercise of its right to individual or collective self-defence in accordance with Article 51 of the Charter of the United Nations Organization, shall immediately, either individually or in agreement with other Parties to the Treaty, come to the assistance of the state or states attacked with all such means as it deems necessary, including armed force. The Parties to the Treaty shall immediately consult concerning the necessary measures to be taken by them jointly in order to restore and maintain international peace and security.

Measures taken on the basis of this Article shall be reported to the Security Council in conformity with the provisions of the Charter of the United Nations Organization. . . .

Charles de Gaulle Extols French Nationalism (1965)

Charles de Gaulle (1890–1970), French patriot who headed the Free French forces while his homeland was occupied by the Germans in World War II, was called to power in 1958 at a time when civil war seemed to be threatening France. President de Gaulle's address reveals the challenge to American policy created by the persistence of European nationalism. From an *Address Delivered by General de Gaulle, President of the French Republic, over French Radio and Television on April 27, 1965,* Ambassade de France, Service de Presse et d'Information, French Affairs No. 175.

In today's world, where all problems arise, where the dangers could reach the infinite, where the needs and ambitions of States clash fiercely, what is the action of France?

Let us recognize that having once been a Colossus of a people by virtue of population, wealth and power, we are returning from afar to play our international role once more. For, one hundred years ago, our demographic and economic growth, and consequently our strength, began to decline. Then came, one after the other, the two world wars which ruined and decimated us, while two great countries, the United States and Russia, in their turn rose to the summit. In a situation of diminished strength at that time, the temptation to give up—which is to a weakened people what apathy is to a humiliated man—could have drawn us toward a decadence from which there would be no return. All the more as, having once been accustomed to being always in the forefront, sometimes not without presumptuousness, our relative decline might have caused us then to doubt ourselves too much. We might have become discouraged after comparing our statistics to those of the total population of each of the two giant countries, or the global production of their factories and their mines, or the number of satellites they are launching around the earth, or the mass of megatons which their missiles are capable of carrying for destruction.

Indeed, after the burst of French confidence and pride which lifted us from a fatal abyss during the last war and despite active forces which reappeared in our country with renewed vigor, a tendency toward self-effacement momentarily emerged to the point of being established in doctrine and in policy. That is why some partisans would have liked to bind us body and soul to the totalitarian empire. That is also why others professed that we must not only, as is sensible, remain the allies of our allies so long as a threat of domination stood in the East, but that we must also become absorbed into an Atlantic system, within which our defense, our economy and our commitments would necessarily depend on the American's weapons, material hold and policy. The same people, with the same intention, wanted our country—instead of participating, as is normal, in organized cooperation among the free nations of the Old Continent—to be literally dissolved in a Europe described as integrated which, lacking the incentives of sovereignty of the peoples and responsibility of the States, would automatically be subordinate to the protector across the ocean. Thus, there would doubtless still be French workers, farmers, engineers, professors, officials, Deputies and Ministers. But there would no longer be France. Indeed. The vital fact of these last seven years is that we have resisted the sirens of surrender and have chosen independence. . . .

From the viewpoint of security, our independence requires, in the atomic age we live in, that we have the necessary means to deter a possible aggressor ourselves, without detriment to our alliances, but without our allies' holding our fate in their hands. Now, we are giving ourselves these means [missiles]. Doubtless, they force us to an effort of renewal which is praiseworthy. But these means cost us no more than those which we would have to furnish for Atlantic integration, without thereby being sure of protection, if we were to continue to belong to it as subordinate auxiliaries. Thus we are reaching the point at which no State in the world could bring death to us without receiving it on its own land, which is without doubt the best possible guarantee.

In the economic, scientific and technical domain, to safeguard our independence, being required to face the enormous wealth of some—without, however, refusing to practice all types of exchanges with them—we must see that our activities, for the essential part, remain under French management and French control. We must also meet, at whatever cost, the competition in advanced sectors which determine the quality, the autonomy, the life of industry as a whole; which involve the maximum of studies, experiments and perfected tools; which require great numbers of the most highly qualified scientists, technicians and workers. Finally, when it is opportune, in order to combine our inventions, our capabilities and our resources in a given branch with those of another country, we must often choose one of those which is closest to us and whose weight we do not think will overwhelm us.

That is why we are imposing a financial, economic and monetary stability upon ourselves which frees us from resorting to outside aid; we are converting into gold the dollar surpluses imported into our country as a result of the American balance of payments; we have over the past six years multiplied by six the funds devoted to research; we are setting up a common industrial and agricultural market with Germany, Italy, Belgium, Holland and Luxembourg; we are tunneling through Mont Blanc in cooperation with the Italians; we are developing the Moselle River along with the people of Germany and Luxembourg; we are joining with England to build the world's first supersonic passenger aircraft; we are ready to extend this French-British collaboration to other types of civil and military aircraft; we have just concluded an agreement with Soviet Russia concerning the perfection and use of our color television process. In sum, however large may be the glass offered to us, we prefer to drink from our own, while touching glasses round about. . . .

Finally, the reappearance of a nation whose hands are free, which we have again become, obviously modifies the world interplay which, since Yalta, seemed to be limited to two partners. But since this division of the world between two great powers, and therefore into two camps, clearly does not benefit the liberty, equality and fraternity of peoples, a different order, a different equilibrium are necessary for peace. Who can maintain this better than we—provided we remain ourselves?

Men and women of France, as you can see, for us, for everyone, as ever, France must be France! . . .

President de Gaulle before his own people. In July 1969 he ended an eleven-year term as President of the Fifth Republic.

Nikita Khrushchev Encourages Peaceful Coexistence (1959)

Nikita Khrushchev (1894–1971), successor to Stalin in the Soviet Union, led the reaction to the excesses of Stalinism. Major events in his premiership (1958–1964) include the accelerated development of space exploration and the Cuban missile crisis with the United States. The speech below, written for the American journal, *Foreign Affairs,* introduced a new phase in Communist policy. From Nikita Khrushchev, "On Peaceful Coexistence," *Foreign Affairs,* XXXVIII (October 1959), pp. 3–4, 17–18. The copyright is held by the Council on Foreign Relations, Inc., New York.

From its very inception the Soviet state proclaimed peaceful coexistence as the basic principle of its foreign policy. It was no accident that the very first state act of the Soviet power was the decree of peace, the decree on the cessation of the bloody war.

What, then, is the policy of peaceful coexistence?

In its simplest expression it signifies the repudiation of war as a means of solving controversial issues. However, this does not cover the entire concept of peaceful coexistence. Apart from the commitment to non-aggression, it also presupposes an obligation on the part of all states to desist from violating each other's territorial integrity and sovereignty in any form and under any pretext whatsoever. The principle of peaceful coexistence also presupposes that political and economic relations between countries are to be based upon complete equality of the parties concerned, and on mutual benefit.

It is often said in the West that peaceful coexistence is nothing else than a tactical method of the socialist states. There is not a grain of truth in such allegations. Our desire for peace and peaceful coexistence is not conditioned by any time-serving or tactical considerations. It springs from the very nature of socialist society in which there are no classes or social groups interested in profiting by war or seizing and enslaving other people's territories. The Soviet Union and the other socialist countries, thanks to their socialist system, have an unlimited home market and for this reason they have no need to pursue an expansionist policy of conquest and an effort to subordinate other countries to their influence.

It is the people who determine the destinies of the socialist states. The socialist states are ruled by the working people themselves, the workers and peasants, the people who themselves create all the material and spiritual values of society. And people of labor cannot

The spirit of accomodation underlying coexistence between the democratic and communist worlds was furthered by visits of Soviet and American leaders to each others' homelands in 1959. Such meetings were not always models of good will, however, as this photograph of then Vice-President Richard Nixon arguing with Premier Krushchev before an astonished crowd at a Moscow fair demonstrates.

want war. For to them war spells grief and tears, death, devastation and misery. Ordinary people have no need for war.

Contrary to what certain propagandists hostile to us say, the coexistence of states with different social systems does not mean that they will only fence themselves off from one another by a high wall and undertake the mutual obligation not to throw stones over the wall or pour dirt upon each other. No! Peaceful coexistence does not mean merely living side by side in the absence of war but with the constantly remaining threat of its breaking out in the future. *Peaceful coexistence can and should develop into peaceful competition for the purpose of satisfying man's needs in the best possible way.*

We say to the leaders of the capitalist states: Let us try out in practice whose system is better, let us compete without war. This is much better than competing in who will produce more arms and who will smash whom. We stand and always will stand for such competition as will help to raise the well-being of the people to a higher level. . . .

What . . . is preventing us from making the principles of peaceful coexistence an unshakable international standard and daily practice in the relations between the West and East?

Of course, different answers may be given to this question. But in order to be frank to the end, we should also say the following: *It is necessary that everybody should understand the irrevocable fact that the historic process is irreversible.* It is impossible to bring back yesterday. It is high time to understand that the world of the twentieth century is not the world of the nineteenth century, that two diametrically opposed social and economic systems exist in the world today side by side, and that the socialist system, in spite of all the attacks upon it, has grown so strong, has developed into such a force, as to make any return to the past impossible.

Real facts of life in the last ten years have shown convincingly that the policy of "rolling back" Communism can only poison the international atmosphere, heighten the tension between states and work in favor of the cold war. Neither its inspirers nor those who conduct it can turn back the course of history and restore capitalism in the socialist countries. . . .

Peaceful coexistence is the only way which is in keeping with the interests of all nations. To reject it would mean under existing conditions to doom the whole world to a terrible and destructive war at a time when it is fully possible to avoid it.

Is it possible that when mankind has advanced to a plane where it has proved capable of the greatest discoveries and of making its first steps into outer space, it should not be able to use the colossal achievements of its genius for the establishment of a stable peace, for the good of man, rather than for the preparation of another war and for the destruction of all that has been created by its labor over many millenniums? Reason refuses to believe this. It protests. . . .

The existence of the Soviet Union and of the other socialist countries is a real fact. It is also a real fact that the United States of America and the other capitalist countries live in different social conditions, in the conditions of capitalism. Then let us recognize this real situation and proceed from it in order not to go against reality, against life itself. Let us not try to change this situation by interferences from without, by means of war on the part of some states against other states.

I repeat, there is only one way to peace, one way out of the existing tension: peaceful coexistence.

Ronald Steel: Pax Americana

The debate over the origins and course of the Cold War has been tied to a related concern with the cost and consequences of America's assumption of an imperial role. Ronald Steel (1931–   ), former Foreign Service officer and author of two important studies of America's role in world affairs, here examines the relationship between American rhetoric and principles and her actions in the postwar world. From *Pax Americana* by Ronald Steel. Copyright © 1967 by The Viking Press, Inc. All rights reserved. Reprinted by permission of The Viking Press, Inc.

I

"Sometimes people call me an idealist," Woodrow Wilson once said as he stumped the country trying to drum up support for the League of Nations. "Well, that's the way I know I am an American. America, my fellow citizens, . . . is the only idealistic nation in the world." Wilson, whose career is a tragic example of what happens when idealism is divorced from political realism, never spoke a truer word. America is an idealistic nation, a nation based upon the belief that the "self-evident truths" of the Declaration of Independence should be extended to unfortunate peoples wherever they may be.

For the first 170 years of our national existence, however, we were content to make this a principle rather than a program of action. America was, in John Quincy Adams' phrase, "the well-wisher to the freedom and independence of all," but "the champion and vindicator only of her own." With the exception of Mexico, the Philippines and a few brief adventures in the Caribbean, our national idealism did not go abroad in search of new fields to conquer. The great European war of 1914–1918 entangled us more against our will than by design. We entered it under the banner of idealism when neutrality became difficult, and we left Europe in disillusionment when power politics reared its ugly head at Versailles. Never again, we said. And never again we did, until the Japanese dragged us into a global war by the attack on Pearl Harbor.

From that time on, American idealism was transformed into a plan. The Word was given Flesh by the mating of American military power to a native idealism. For the first time in its history the nation had the ability to seek its idealistic goals by active intervention rather than merely by pious proclamation. The result was twin crusades, one in Europe, one in Asia: one to restore freedom to the West, one to bring it to the East. But the passing of one tyranny in Europe saw the rise of another; the defeat of Japan gave way to the resurgence of China. The triumph of the Second World War marked not the end of our labors, but only the beginning. It transformed a philosophical commitment to the principles of freedom and democracy into a political commitment to bring them about. American idealism was the foundation; American power was the instrument to achieve the ideals. From 1945 on, we were no longer simply the "well-wisher" to the world; we were its "champion and vindicator" as well. The moral purity of American isolationism gave way to the moral self-justification of American interventionism.

The change from the old isolationism to the new interventionism flowed almost inevitably from the Second World War. The unavoidable war against fascism revealed the bankruptcy of isolationism and destroyed the illusion that America could barricade herself from the immoralities of a corrupt world. It also provided the means for the dramatic growth of American military power which made the new policy of global interventionism possible. As a result of her participation in the war, America became not only a great world power but *the* world power. Her fleets roamed all the seas, her military bases extended around the earth's periphery, her soldiers stood guard from Berlin to Okinawa, and her alliances spanned the earth.

The Second World War threw the United States into the world arena, and the fear of communism prevented her from retreating. The old isolationism was buried and discredited. The crusade that was the war against fascism gave way to the new crusade that was the cold war against communism. Roused to a new sense of mission by the threat of Soviet communism, eager to bring her cherished values to the masses of mankind, a bit infatuated with the enormous power she possessed through the unleashing of the atom, America quickly accepted—and even came to cherish—her new sense of involvement in the fate of the world. The world of the early postwar era may not have been the One World of Wendell Willkie's dream, but America felt a unique sense of responsibility about its welfare.

A reaction to the old isolationism, the new globalism forced Americans to realize that they could no longer escape involvement in an imperfect world. But because the cold war, like the Second World War, was conceived as a moral crusade, it inflated an involvement that was essentially pragmatic into a moral mission. Since we were accustomed to victory in battle and were stronger than any nation had ever been in history, we believed that the world's problems could be resolved if only we willed hard enough and applied enough power. Convinced of the righteousness of our cause, we became intoxicated with our newly discovered responsibilities and saw them as a mandate to bring about the better world we so ardently desired. American military power, consecrated by the victory of the Second World War and reconfirmed by the development of the atomic bomb, joined forces with the power of American idealism to inaugurate a policy of global interventionism. . . .

The commitment to interventionism as a guiding principle has made it exceedingly difficult to distinguish between necessary and spurious motives for intervention—to determine which actions have a direct relation to the nation's security, and which merely represent wish-fulfillment on an international scale. In this respect it reflects a traditional weakness in American policy—a penchant for grandiose principles at the expense of a cool assessment of national interests, which has led the nation into painful involvements as a result of bold gestures carelessly made. The warning of John Quincy Adams has lately been forgotten in the intoxication of heady moral obligations, obligations which no one asked us to assume, and whose purpose we do not often understand. This is not the fault of the public but of its leaders, who are often tempted to use slogans to justify their actions, and then become prisoners of them. "American statesmen," as the historian Dexter Perkins has written,

> have believed that the best way to rally American opinion behind their purposes is to assert a moral principle. In doing so, they have often gone far beyond the boundaries of expediency. And perhaps it is fair to say that in underemphasizing security, they have helped to form a national habit which unduly subordinates the necessities of national defense to the assertion of lofty moral principles. . . .

II

The alignment of national goals with national interests—of our desires with our needs—is the most pressing task facing American diplomacy. It is a task that has become increasingly urgent with each expansion of our commitments. These commitments are to be found in a tangle of regional alliances, military pacts, verbal agreements, and even unilateral decisions. They can all, to one degree or another, be traced back to the Truman Doctrine of March 1947, when the United States made the ambiguous offer to defend threatened nations from aggression, whether direct or indirect. This led, through the back door of the European Recovery Program, to NATO, under which the United States is pledged to the defense of most of Europe and even parts of the Near East—from Spitzbergen to the Berlin Wall and beyond to the Asian borders of Turkey. From there the commitments become more vague, the situations more ambiguous, the countries themselves less crucial to American security.

From the seeds of the Truman Doctrine and the precedent of NATO came the Middle East Resolution, under which Congress gave President Eisenhower permission to protect the Arabs against communism; the CENTO and SEATO treaties that John Foster Dulles constructed to fill in the alliance gap from Iran to the Philippines; the ANZUS treaty with Australia and New Zealand; special defense arrangements with Japan and Korea; an unwritten obligation to protect India; the pledge for the defense of the entire western hemisphere under the Rio Pact; various peace-keeping functions under the United Nations; and, most recently, the Tonkin Gulf Resolution, a blank check given by Congress, allowing President Johnson to intervene as he sees fit in Southeast Asia. Early in 1967 the United States had 700,000 soldiers stationed in 30 countries, was a member of 4 regional defense alliances and an active participant in a fifth, had mutual defense treaties with 42 nations, was a member of 53 international organizations, and was furnishing military or economic aid to nearly 100 nations across the face of the globe. Put all this together and it leaves us, in James Reston's words, with "commitments the like of which no sovereign nation ever took on in the history of the world."

These entanglements happened more by accident than by design. The United States became involved in the defense of Western Europe because the defeat of Nazi Germany brought Stalin's armies into Central Europe. In Asia the disintegration of the Japanese Empire brought Russia into Manchuria and the United States into Japan, Okinawa, South Korea, and Taiwan. Later we advanced into Indochina when the French, despite our financial and military support, were unable to retain their Asian territories. We had no intention of virtually annexing Okinawa, of occupying South Korea, of preventing the return

American soldiers at the Berlin Wall.

672

American soldiers huddle on a rainy helicopter field in Vietnam. From a small military aid mission, they grew to a commitment of more than half a million.

of Taiwan to China, of fighting in Indochina, or of remaining in Western Europe. If someone had said in 1946 that twenty years later there would be 225,000 American soldiers in Germany, 50,000 in Korea, and a third of a million Americans fighting in Vietnam, he would have been considered mad. Yet so accustomed are we to our global commitments that we take this remarkable situation for granted.

Although the postwar vacuums are receding—with the resurgence of China, the recovery of Japan, and the revival of Europe—our commitment remains unchanged. We are still playing the same role of guardian that we played twenty years ago, when America and Russia were the only important powers in the world. Our diplomacy has not kept pace with the changes in the world power structure, and we are engaged far beyond our ability to control events. The result has been a dangerous gap in our foreign policy between our involvements and our means—

American soldiers in Vietnam. Despite rapid treatment of the wounded, the American death toll alone reached 40,000 at the beginning of the 70s.

between what we would like to accomplish and what we can reasonably hope to accomplish.

In a way it could be said that our foreign policy has been a victim of its own success. In the decision to rebuild and defend Western Europe, the United States acted with wisdom, humanity, and an enlightened conception of her own interests. The military alliance with Western Europe worked successfully because there was a clear community of interests between America and her allies. When we built our bases in Europe and sent our own soldiers to man the front lines, it was in the knowledge that we agreed with our allies on the dangers they faced and on the means by which they should be met. We came not as an army of occupation or as foreign mercenaries, but as friends joined in a common cause. We turned our back on the isolationism of the 1930s, put the American frontier right up to the Brandenburg Gate in Berlin, pledged our atomic weapons to the defense of our allies, added our own soldiers as guarantors of this pledge, and accepted the risk of nuclear devastation. We took this terrible risk because we had to: because neither strategically nor culturally could we accept the loss of Western Europe to our adversaries. The goal we sought in Western Europe in the early postwar period had three qualities essential for military intervention: it was vital to our interests, it was within our means to achieve, and it had the support of those we were trying to protect.

The difficulty, however, arose when the principles underlying NATO and the Marshall Plan were applied indiscriminately throughout the world—when it was assumed that the success of the Atlantic alliance could be duplicated in countries which shared neither our traditions, nor our interests, nor even our assessment of the dangers facing them. Too often American diplomacy has been engaged in the effort to create miniature NATO's and

Americans confront an uprooted population after the recapture of battered Hue, ancient capital of the Vietnamese, following the Tet offensive of January-February 1968.

Marshall Plans with countries that have only recently shaken off the yoke of Western rule, that are at a greatly inferior stage of economic and political development, that are as suspicious of us as they are of our adversaries, that are endemically poor and unstable, and that usually greet us as unwanted manipulators rather than as welcome friends.

If our policies were judged by a cold calculation of national interest, a good many of them might have been scrapped long ago. If the struggle with Russia were merely over geographical spheres of influence, if the cold war were nothing more than old-fashioned power politics on a global scale, our commitments could have been cut and our involvements drastically limited. But the cold war has not been simply a struggle of giants for supremacy; it has also been an ideological contest for the allegiance of mankind. Or so it has seemed to its leading participants. It is because we feel ourselves embroiled in a much greater struggle that we are involved in the sustenance and security of some hundred countries, that we have replaced the old isolationism with a sweeping policy of interventionism and are today fighting yet another land war in Asia.

We are there because we feel ourselves to be pledged to a world-wide struggle against communism, because we see ourselves as the defenders of freedom and democracy in the contest against tyranny, because we are, in President Kennedy's words, "by destiny rather than choice, the watchmen on the walls of world freedom." But this role of watchman is not, for all President Kennedy's noble rhetoric, imposed by destiny. It is imposed by ourselves and subject to whatever limitations we choose to put upon it. It can provide the excuse for our playing the role of global gendarme, or serve as a guideline for a measured calculation of the national interest. No task of global omniscience is imposed upon us that we do not choose for ourselves. . . .

STUDY QUESTIONS

1. On what concept of human nature was the United Nations based? How did it propose to preserve international peace?

2. What threat did the "iron curtain" pose for Western civilization? How did Churchill propose to meet the threat? How did he evaluate the role of the United Nations?

3. Under what conditions did the United States pledge herself to intervene in the affairs of other nations?

4. Compare the North Atlantic Treaty and the Warsaw Pact. Why were they drafted? On what principle were they based? What was their relationship to the United Nations? Do you think they would be an aid or an impediment to lasting peace?

5. Does de Gaulle sound more like a defender of the past or a spokesman for the future? What did nationalism mean to him? How would he define internationalism? Why was he not satisfied to trust France's future to the path charted by the UN and NATO?

6. What was Khrushchev's solution for the Cold War? What did he mean by peaceful coexistence? How did he visualize the shape of the future?

7. How did the practice of American interventionism develop? What are the dangers of confusing ideological doctrine with national interests?

POPULATION

□ REPRESENTS 1 MILLION
(Population Figures in Millions)

These maps of the world in the mid-1960s compare population with gross national product. What does such a comparison reveal about the advantages and problems of the Western nations in the world today? From Edwin O. Reischauer, *Beyond Vietnam: The United States and Asia* (New York, Knopf, 1967), pp. 48–51. Copyright © 1967 by Edwin O. Reischauer. Reprinted by permission of Alfred A. Knopf, Inc.

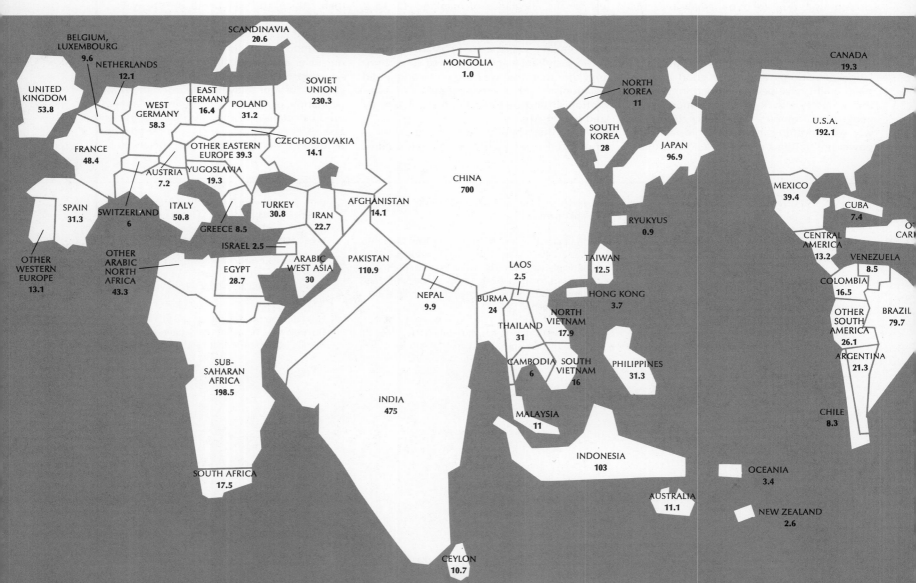

SCANDINAVIA 20.6

BELGIUM, LUXEMBOURG 9.6

NETHERLANDS 12.1

UNITED KINGDOM 53.8

EAST GERMANY 16.4

WEST GERMANY 58.3

POLAND 31.2

SOVIET UNION 230.3

MONGOLIA 1.0

NORTH KOREA 11

CANADA 19.3

FRANCE 48.4

OTHER EASTERN EUROPE 39.3

CZECHOSLOVAKIA 14.1

SOUTH KOREA 28

JAPAN 96.9

U.S.A. 192.1

AUSTRIA 7.2

YUGOSLAVIA 19.3

SPAIN 31.3

SWITZERLAND 6

ITALY 50.8

GREECE 8.5

TURKEY 30.8

IRAN 22.7

AFGHANISTAN 14.1

CHINA 700

MEXICO 39.4

CUBA 7.4

ISRAEL 2.5

RYUKYUS 0.9

CENTRAL AMERICA 13.2

OTHER WESTERN EUROPE 13.1

OTHER ARABIC NORTH AFRICA 43.3

EGYPT 28.7

ARABIC WEST ASIA 30

PAKISTAN 110.9

LAOS 2.5

TAIWAN 12.5

VENEZUELA 8.5

NEPAL 9.9

BURMA 24

HONG KONG 3.7

COLOMBIA 16.5

THAILAND 31

NORTH VIETNAM 17.9

OTHER SOUTH AMERICA 26.1

BRAZIL 79.7

SUB-SAHARAN AFRICA 198.5

INDIA 475

CAMBODIA 6

SOUTH VIETNAM 16

PHILIPPINES 31.3

ARGENTINA 21.3

MALAYSIA 11

CHILE 8.3

INDONESIA 103

OCEANIA 3.4

SOUTH AFRICA 17.5

AUSTRALIA 11.1

NEW ZEALAND 2.6

CEYLON 10.7

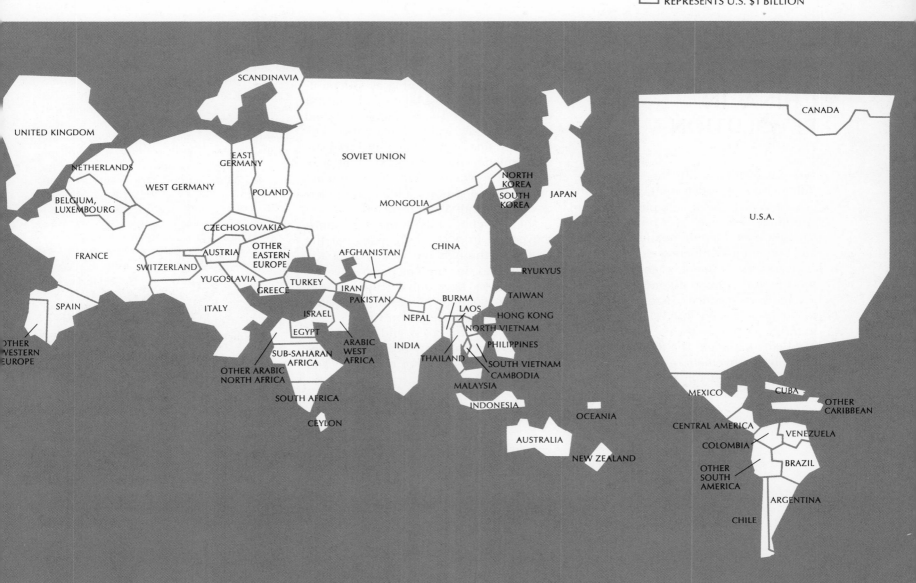

GROSS NATIONAL PRODUCT

☐ REPRESENTS U.S. $1 BILLION

SCANDINAVIA

UNITED KINGDOM

NETHERLANDS

EAST GERMANY

SOVIET UNION

CANADA

NORTH KOREA
SOUTH KOREA

JAPAN

BELGIUM, LUXEMBOURG

WEST GERMANY

POLAND

MONGOLIA

U.S.A.

FRANCE

CZECHOSLOVAKIA

CHINA

AUSTRIA

OTHER EASTERN EUROPE

AFGHANISTAN

SWITZERLAND

YUGOSLAVIA

TURKEY

IRAN

RYUKYUS

GREECE

PAKISTAN

TAIWAN

SPAIN

ITALY

ISRAEL

BURMA

LAOS

HONG KONG

OTHER WESTERN EUROPE

EGYPT

NEPAL

NORTH VIETNAM

ARABIC WEST AFRICA

INDIA

PHILIPPINES

OTHER ARABIC NORTH AFRICA

SUB-SAHARAN AFRICA

THAILAND

SOUTH VIETNAM

CAMBODIA

MEXICO

CUBA

OTHER CARIBBEAN

MALAYSIA

SOUTH AFRICA

INDONESIA

OCEANIA

CENTRAL AMERICA

VENEZUELA

CEYLON

COLOMBIA

AUSTRALIA

NEW ZEALAND

OTHER SOUTH AMERICA

BRAZIL

ARGENTINA

CHILE

A Story of Two Chinas

TOPIC 47

CHINA IN REVOLUTION

Western relations with the Chinese Republic seemed hopelessly tangled at the end of World War II, complicated by an enduring civil war in China and the struggle over the boundaries of Soviet and communist influence in Europe. The American government, eager to contain the Chinese communist movement and assure the emergence of a regime friendly to America's Pacific interests, allied itself in the civil war with the nationalist forces of Chiang Kai-Shek. The triumph of Mao Tse-Tung's movement, explored in these readings, severed for a period of more than twenty years close western ties with the Chinese mainland.

Within the developing nations of Asia and Africa, the Chinese Revolution took on more positive meaning as a demonstration of the possibilities of socialist development in a very underdeveloped and still largely rural and agrarian society. For the first time, Marxism-Leninism, augmented by the interpretations of Mao, could be applied in both theory and action to the conditions of life in an underdeveloped non-Western society.

These readings follow the communist movement from the birth pangs of the civil war, through the victory over the Japanese, to our present perspective on the Chinese Revolution. The readings have two goals in mind—to assess the effect of these changes on China's relationship with the West and to examine the relevance for other peasant societies of the Chinese model of revolution and modernization.

This reading is taken from *Thunder Out of China*, one of the best-sellers of the year 1946, by Theodore H. White (1915–   ). The author, a well-known American journalist, indicted the government of Generalissimo Chiang K'ai-shek, then favored by most Americans, as corrupt, self-perpetuating, and oblivious to the problems of the Chinese masses. "A revolution is stirring and shaking every province, every country, every village in the land." The author urged that the United States support this revolution and painted a favorable picture of the Communist followers of Mao Tse-tung as catalysts of change. The reading consists of selections from White's chapter on the rise to power of the Kuomintang party after the overthrow of the Manchu Empire and carries the subsequent struggle between Nationalists and Communists to 1937, eve of full-scale war with Japan. From Theodore H. White and Annalee Jacoby, *Thunder out of China* (New York: William Sloane Associates, 1946), pp. 34–42, 44–47. Reprinted by permission of William Morrow and Co., Inc. Copyright 1946, © 1961 by William Sloane Associates, Inc.

The collapse of the Manchu Empire in 1911 stripped China of her outward appearance of changelessness and stability. Within less than five years the first political lesson of government had been learned anew—that the state rests on force. That was the age of the war lords, and China broke up into a patchwork of blood and unhappiness. Each war lord had his own army, each army its district. The great war lords governed entire provinces; their generals governed parts of provinces; their captains governed counties, cities, towns. Three hundred men could keep a county in subjection, levy taxes on it, rape its women, carry off its sons, batten on its crops. All those who were accustomed to govern were gone, and the soldiers who took over found with astonishment that they were government. Their will was law; paper they printed was money. Among themselves they fought as the whim took them; coalitions formed and re-formed; ambition, treachery, and foul play became the code of Chinese politics. And each evil deed was sanctified by its perpetrator, who proclaimed it done for the unity of China. The only enduring legacy left by the war lords was their belief in force; the only conviction that Chiang K'ai-shek and the Communists have shared for twenty years is the conviction that armed strength is the only guarantee of security.

The war lords were purely destructive; in earlier ages such a period of anarchy might have lasted for generations before reintegration set in, but this was the twentieth century. All up and down the China coast and far up the rivers concessions had been wrung by foreign powers from the decadent Manchu government. On China's main rivers were steamers of foreign ownership, which were protected by gunboats flying foreign flags. Railways owned and managed by foreigners sucked profit out of China to foreign investors. China's tariffs were set and collected by foreigners; so was the most profitable of internal revenues, the salt tax. The foreigners who lived in China had enormous contempt for both the Manchus and the later war lords, but they could not exist in island communities in the vastness of China; for

their own purposes they had to create or convert to their use a body of Chinese who could act as a bridge between themselves and the nation they wished to plunder. Western businessmen created Chinese businessmen in their likeness. New Chinese banks were developed; old ones learned to substitute double-entry bookkeeping for beaded counting-boards. The factories, steamships, mines, and railways that foreigners controlled needed a host of skilled Chinese to operate them; their success caused Chinese businessmen to start similar projects, which needed the same kind of management and engineers. A new kind of Chinese began to appear, a naturalized citizen of the modern world; a middle class was developing in a feudal country.

No less forceful than the impact of Western armies and Western business was the impact of Western ideas. The new universities that were set up in China to teach the new sciences and skills created scholars and students of a new sort, who thought less of the Book of Odes and the millennial classics than they did of Adam Smith, Karl Marx, and Henry George. The adepts of the new learning smarted even more than the businessmen under the contempt, the brutality, and the indignity the imperial powers heaped on China; they gave brilliant intellectual leadership to the discontent within the land. The ferment seemed like a great undisciplined anarchy, more froth and foam than substance. But it arose from one basic problem—the statelessness of China. The problem had one basic solution—internal unity and strength in China.

The political instrument of the new merchant and educated class was the party known as the Kuomintang. The architect of

A view of the Shanghai Bund, once the foreign-dominated industrial and commercial heart of the city.

the early Kuomintang, its very soul, was a sad-eyed dreamer called Sun Yat-sen. It is customary now in intellectual circles to sneer at the naïvete with which he attacked world problems, but Sun Yat-sen was the first man to formulate a program of action for all the complex problems of the Chinese people. It was as if some Western thinker had attempted to devise one neat solution for the problems of feudalism, the Renaissance and Reformation, the industrial revolution, and the social unrest of today. Sun Yat-sen was a Cantonese who had been educated in Hawaii; he participated in almost every unsuccessful revolt against the Manchu dynasty in the last decade of its existence, and he had lived the life of a hunted exile in Japan, America, and Europe. Almost every war lord who verbally espoused unity adorned his ambition with quotations from Sun Yat-sen; almost all ended by betraying him. The wretchedness of China, the burning eloquence of Sun Yat-sen's cause within him, the examples of Western civilization in the countries of his exile, were all finally synthesized in his book *San Min Chu I,* or *Three Principles of the People.* . . .

The first was the Principle of Nationalism. China must win back her sovereignty and unity. The foreigners must be forced out of their concessions; they must be made to disgorge the spoils they had seized from the Manchus. China must have all the powers and dignities that any foreign nation had; she must be disciplined and the war lords purged. The second was the Principle of People's Democracy. China must be a nation in which the government serves the people and is responsible to them. The people must be taught how to read and write and eventually to vote. A system must be erected whereby their authority runs upward from the village to command the highest authority in the nation. The third was the Principle of People's Livelihood. The basic industries of China must be socialized; the government alone should assume responsibility for vast industrialization and reconstruction. Concurrently with the erection of the superstructure of a

modern economic system, the foundation had to be strengthened. The peasant's lot was to be alleviated; those who tilled the soil should own it. . . .

The years of exile and failure had been years of education for Sun Yat-sen. He began as a dreamer and an intellectual; but he learned, as all China did during the decade following the Manchu collapse, that dreams and theories alone were insufficient for the reorganization of the land. Thousands, perhaps millions, were willing to admit that his theories were right, even to join his party. But the party needed force—an armed tool to work its will. By the early 1920's history had conspired to give Sun the strength he needed. First, the Russians had succeeded in establishing their own revolution against feudalism and were interested in revolution everywhere; they were willing to send to China not only political mentors to aid Sun Yat-sen, but battle-seasoned soldiers who could fashion an army for him. Secondly, the decade-long violence within China had by now produced young soldiers and officers who were interested in more than loot and plunder; they were interested in their country as an end in itself, and they sought political leadership for their military skills.

In 1923, Sun Yat-sen was permitted by the local war lord to set up a nominal government in Canton. He had made such agreements before with other war lords when they had sought inspiring facades for practical despotism; each time he had been betrayed and cast out when he tried to exercise more than nominal authority. This time it was to be different. Within a year this new government of Sun Yat-sen was the seat of an incandescent revolutionary movement. Sun set up in Canton a center that was both military and political. Two Russian agents were his

most conspicuous advisers—Michael Borodin as political mentor and a general known as Galen for the new army. Communists were brought into the movement and made members of the Kuomintang. The political center was the training school for a host of flaming advocates of revolution, agents who were to circulate through all China in the next few years to preach the new doctrines. The real strength, however, was in a school on the banks of the muddy Whampoa River, where an academy for the training of revolutionary officers was set up. This was to produce men who, knowing how to wield force, would wield it not for the sake of force alone but in the name of a new China. To head this academy Sun Yat-sen chose a slim and cold-eyed Chekiang youth named Chiang K'ai-shek. . . .

In Canton Chiang was already the young hero of the revolution. The Russian advisers of Sun Yat-sen had been so taken with him that they had sent him to Moscow in 1923, for a six months' course in indoctrination. When he returned to head the Whampoa academy, he rose rapidly from comparative obscurity to dominance. The death of Sun Yat-sen in 1925 gave him almost unchallenged authority.

By the spring of 1926 the revolutionary armies of the Kuomintang were ready to set forth on the famous Northern March from Canton to the Yangtze Valley to reclaim China from the war lords. Chiang K'ai-shek was the commander-in-chief. It was a motley host armed with discarded weapons of every conceivable foreign manufacture. It was staffed with Russian advisers; some of its key armies were commanded by repentant war lords who had seen the light. Before it went the political agents, Communist and Kuomintang, organizing peasants and factory workers and

Above, flanked by Joseph Stalin and V. I. Lenin, this portrait of Sun Yat-sen indicates the respect given him by the Chinese Communists.

Right, Chiang Kai-shek in Nanking in 1929.

preparing the people of the country side for the dawn of a new day. The army swept north on the very crest of a wave of revolutionary enthusiasm and seized Hankow, whose workers had already been organized and begun to strike in late summer. From Hankow the armies turned east down the Yangtze Valley, swept through Nanking and on to Shanghai.

The advance of the revolutionary armies sounded like the hammers of doom to the foreign concession of Shanghai. From the interior came stories of riots, bloodshed, and butchery, of strikes that closed down all foreign shipping and factories, of Chinese soldiers killing white men and raping white women. The tide reached Shanghai in the spring of 1927. From within the city Communist agents organized the workers for a revolt, and on March 21, in a tremendous general strike, the entire city outside of the International Settlement closed down. The armed unions went on to make their strike one of the greatest of modern insurrections. They seized police stations, government buildings, and factories so rapidly that by the time Chiang's Kuomintang armies arrived at the suburbs, the workers were in complete control of the native city and turned it over to the revolutionary government.

Three weeks after the climactic victory the alliance of Communists and Kuomintang came to an end. What happened during those three weeks is a matter of mystery. Overnight the racketeering gangs of the water front and the underworld materialized in Chiang's support. Trembling foreign businessmen were quickly apprised that Chiang was indeed a "sensible" leader, and foreign arms and as-

681

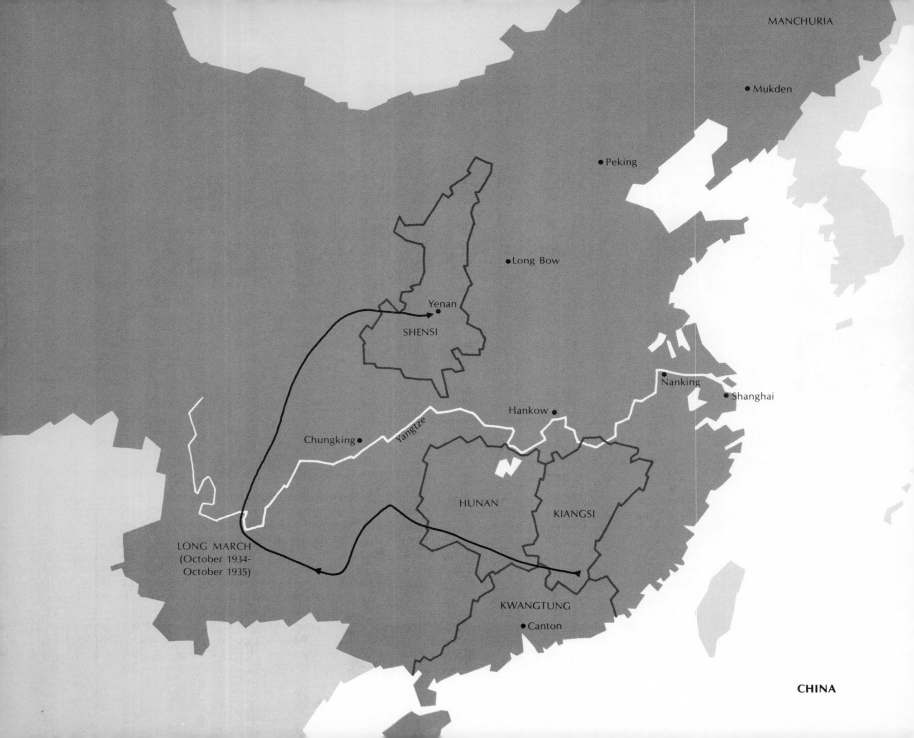

MANCHURIA

• Mukden

• Peking

• Long Bow

Yenan
SHENSI

Nanking
• Shanghai

Hankow •

Chungking •

Yangtze

HUNAN

KIANGSI

LONG MARCH
(October 1934–
October 1935)

KWANGTUNG

• Canton

CHINA

sistance were supplied him. The revolutionary forces were weak and vacillating; units of Chiang's own armies made overtures to the Communists, for they sensed an impending crisis. And then suddenly, without a word of warning, Chiang's deputies, assisted by cohorts from the underworld and blessed by foreign opinion, turned on the workers, disarmed them, executed their leaders, and forced the Communists underground by a purge that was to continue for years. . . .

What had happened? To understand the tragedy of the great uprising it is necessary to return to Canton and establish the personality of the historic antagonist of Chiang K'ai-shek—the Communist Party of China. Like the Kuomintang, the Chinese Communist Party was born of intellectual ferment. It appeared much later on the scene of Chinese history and took its analysis and solution of China's problems from the example of the Russian revolution. The Communists agreed completely with Sun Yat-sen and the Kuomintang that the foreigners must be thrown out, the war lords annihilated; but they went a step further. They asked: For whose benefit should China be reorganized? They answered: For the Chinese peasant himself.

To accomplish this it was necessary not only to achieve all the aims of the Kuomintang, but to go further, to smash in every village the shackles of feudalism that chained the peasant to the Middle Ages. In the cities the new industrial workers of the factories and mills were to be the constituents of the new era. The savage exploitation of labor by the coastal entrepreneurs would have to be ended before industry could be a blessing rather than a new curse to China. The Communists brought to their early alliance with the Kuomintang all the discipline and zealotry that are characteristic of their move-

ment everywhere. In its early days the Chinese Communist Party was organically linked with Moscow. The Russian delegation attached to Sun Yat-sen controlled the party completely and, under the strictest injunction from Moscow, committed it to unreserved subordination to the Kuomintang. Communist agents spearheaded the great organizing drives that led the triumphal Northern March of the revolutionary armies. They converted the areas of combat into quicksands for their war-lord enemies; peasant and labor unions developed almost overnight as the masses rose to the first leadership they had ever known as their own.

Chiang saw in the Communists a leadership as coldblooded and ruthless as his own. To his passionate nationalism their connection with Russia was wicked. His brief visit to Russia had given him an insight into the working of a dictatorial state along with a lasting dislike for the Russians. He saw the Communists as Russian agents, possessed of some magic formula that would tear the countryside apart in social upheaval—and he hated them. For the first three years of his alliance with the Communists he bided his time. He needed both Russian arms and peasant support; he could not afford a break. His march to the Yangtze Valley, however, brought him into contact for the first time with the highest rungs of the new Chinese industrial and commercial aristocracy. These men, no less than the foreigners, were terrified of strikes and labor unions; slogans of agrarian reform threatened to upset the entire system of rural commerce and landholding. Chiang suddenly found in the Shanghai business world a new base of support, a base powerful enough to maintain his party and his armies; with these men and their money behind him, he was no longer dependent on

Soldiers of the Red Army cross rugged snow-covered mountains on their "Long March".

Russian aid or agrarian revolution. When he makes up his mind, Chiang acts swiftly. Before the Communist leaders had any inkling of what was happening, their movement had been beheaded, and within a year of the Shanghai coup Communism was illegal from end to end of China.

Chiang K'ai-shek was the chief architect of the new China that emerged. Occasionally, in fits of sulkiness, he would withdraw from the government for a few months to prove that only he could hold its diverse elements together; he always returned with greater prestige and strength than before. The new Kuomintang government was a dictatorship.

It glossed itself with the phrases of Sun Yat-sen and claimed that it was the "trustee" of the people, who were in a state of "political tutelage." Its secret police were ubiquitous, while its censorship closed down like a vacuum pack over the Chinese press and Chinese universities. It held elections nowhere, for its conception of strengthening China was to strengthen itself, and it governed by fiat. This government rested on a four-legged stool—an army, a bureaucracy, the urban businessmen, the rural gentry. . . .

When Chiang forced the Communists underground, he cut them off from the workers of the city, but he could not break their contact with the agitated peasantry. South of the Yangtze the Communists found the memory of the revolution still green in the hearts of the villagers, and their troops proceeded to establish a miniature soviet republic. Chiang waged unceasing war against this soviet republic in southern China. With his government buttressed by loans from America, his troops, German-armed and trained, tightened their blockade about Communist areas each succeeding year. The very war against the Communists drew war lords into alliance with Chiang for mutual protection. The struggle against the Communists was savage and relentless. Within the areas that Chiang controlled, his police butchered Communist leaders; families of known Communist leaders were wiped out; students were watched and spied on, and possession of Communist literature was made a crime punishable by death. In Communist areas it was the village landlord who fared worst, and the hatred of the poor for the rich was given full rein.

By 1934 the pressure on the Communists had grown too great, and bursting out of Chiang's blockade line, they performed that spectacular feat known as the Long March. Men and women, with bag, baggage, and archives, the Communists marched from southern China to re-establish themselves in the northwest. The winding route of the main column of 30,000 was over 6000 miles long. The Long March was a savage ordeal that stands out in Chinese Communist history as an emotional mountain peak. The sufferings endured and the iron determination with which they were mastered are beyond description. The countryside through which the march passed is still dotted with stone blockhouses built by the government to hem in the Communists. The ferocity of the fighting ravaged the peasants in hundreds on hundreds of villages; in many districts in southern and central China the name of Communist is still hated for the destruction this march wreaked on the countryside. In certain other districts the Communists succeeded in creating a political loyalty among the poorer peasants that lingered for years. The Communists finally established themselves at the end of 1935 in the northwest, in the areas just north of Yenan in Shensi, which later became their chief base.

The Communists' arrival in Yenan coincided with a turning point both in their own history and in the party line. By now they had become an independent organization; their ties with Moscow were nominal. The Soviet Union had re-established friendly relations with Chiang K'ai-shek and left the Communist Party to fend for itself. From their new base the Communists raised a new call: Chinese unity against the Japanese! The response throughout China was instant, for the most profound emotion was touched. Japan had seized Manchuria in 1931, had pressed down past the Great Wall, was pouring opium into northern China, was flagrantly abusing every international standard of decency. China was being humiliated by the Japanese army in a way never experienced before; nothing, it seemed, would satisfy Japan except control over the whole vast country. . . .

Gradually the call for unity began to penetrate the army. In the north, where the civil war against the Communists was still being pushed, the campaign began to flag and finally came to a dead stop. Chiang, flying to Sian to revive it [December 1936] flew directly into a conspiracy and was kidnapped—not by Communists but by war lords who refused to fight against Communists any more when they might be fighting against the Japanese. During his two weeks' internment Chiang met the Communists personally for the first time since 1927. No one has ever recorded in full what actually happened during Chiang's kidnapping and at his meeting with the Communists, but the results were electric; the civil war came to an abrupt end. Chiang recognized the right of the Communists to govern their own areas in the north within the loose framework of the Central Government. Their armies were to be incorporated into the national armies. The Communists were to give up their program of revolution in the countryside. The government was to institute immediate democratic reforms, and Sun Yat-sen's program as set forth in *Three Principles of the People* was to be the code of the land.

This news came to the Japanese like an alarm in the night. Ever since China's Nationalist Revolution, Japan had been haunted by two prospects; one was the unity of China; the other, Communism in China. Japan knew that a united, resurgent China would ultimately be the leader of all Asia. Japan feared Communism, too. Her own empire was based on thin, rocky islands poor in every material resource except manpower. Her armed might rested on the unthinking obedience of civilians and soldiers, any system that challenged

Mao Tse-Tung Offers a Strategy for Revolution

工農商學兵聯合起來
打日本強盜!!!

The Communists tried to unite Chinese opinion against the Japanese even before the outbreak of hostilities in 1937. This anti-Japanese poster depicts (l. to r.) a farmer (sickle), student (writing brush), merchant (abacus), Nationalist and Red Army soldiers, and worker (hammer). The slogan reads: "Workers, peasants, merchants, students and soldiers, join together and strike the Japanese bandits!!!"

Mao Tse-tung (1893–   ), son of a well-to-do farmer, was born in the south-central Chinese province of Hunan. An avid student, deeply disturbed by the inequalities he witnessed in Chinese life, he became a Communist in 1920. Even in the years of cooperation between the Communists and the Kuomintang when for a short time he held various posts in the government, Mao, restless and radical, returned frequently to his Hunan homeland. There in the mid-twenties he became convinced, in contrast to the party line, that only a peasant-based revolution could be successful in China. In 1927, in the mountains of Hunan and neighboring Kiangsi, he organized the first rural revolutionary base area, expanded in 1931 into a "soviet republic" with himself as presiding chairman. Continuing attacks by the Kuomintang forces led ultimately to the famous Long March of 1934–1935 and the establishment of a new base in poor and isolated Shensi province in the northwest. During these years Mao wrote prolifically and effectively in defense of his thesis of agrarian revolution. The selection that follows is from *The Chinese Revolution and the Chinese Communist Party* (1939). From Mao Tse-tung, *Selected Works* (Peking: Foreign Languages Press, 1961), II, chap. 2.

We know that present-day Chinese society is a colonial, semi-colonial and semi-feudal society. Only when we grasp the nature of Chinese society will we be able clearly to understand the targets, tasks, motive forces and character of the Chinese revolution and its perspectives and future transition. A clear

them to thought was a menace to Japan. Thus, no matter which side won in China, Chiang K'ai-shek or Communism, Japan would lose. And to keep China permanently weak, disunited, and subordinate, Japan's continental armies had been constantly pressing down from the north, dabbling in war-lord politics, poisoning China with thousands of agents. The new accord between Chiang and the Communists meant that now

there was the possibility not only of a united China but of a united China in which Communism was tolerated and condoned. There was no time to be lost.

On the night of July 7, 1937, at the Marco Polo Bridge outside of Peking, Japanese garrison troops were engaged in field maneuvers. Someone fired a shot; the Japanese claimed they had been assaulted—the war had begun.

Sun Yat-sen and Chiang Kai-shek married into the illustrious Soong family. Above the three Soong sisters inspect the ruins of homes destroyed by Japanese air raids on Chungking. Mme. Sun is in the center, Mme. Chiang at the right. Their paths later diverged. Mme. Sun became a revolutionary heroine. She is shown in 1948 (below) with a group of children in the reading room of a child welfare center.

understanding of the nature of Chinese society, that is, of Chinese conditions, is therefore the key to a clear understanding of all the problems of the revolution.

Since the nature of present-day Chinese society is colonial, semi-colonial and semi-feudal, what are the chief targets or enemies at this stage of the Chinese revolution?

They are imperialism and feudalism, the bourgeoisie of the imperialist countries and the landlord class of our country. For it is these two that are the chief oppressors, the chief obstacles to the progress of Chinese society at the present stage. The two collude with each other in oppressing the Chinese people, and imperialism is the foremost and most ferocious enemy of the Chinese people, because national oppression by imperialism is the more onerous.

It is evident, then, that the enemies of the Chinese revolution are very powerful. They include not only powerful imperialists and powerful feudal forces, but also, at times, the bourgeois reactionaries who collaborate with the imperialist and feudal forces to oppose the people. Therefore, it is wrong to underestimate the strength of the enemies of the revolutionary Chinese people.

In the face of such enemies, the Chinese revolution cannot be other than protracted and ruthless. With such powerful enemies, the revolutionary forces cannot be built up and tempered into a power capable of crushing them except over a long period of time. With enemies who so ruthlessly suppress the Chinese revolution, the revolutionary forces cannot hold their own positions, let alone capture those of the enemy, unless they steel themselves and display their tenacity to the full. It is therefore wrong to think that the forces of the Chinese revolution can be built up in the twinkling of an eye, or that China's revolutionary struggle can triumph overnight.

The strength of the Chinese Communists lay in the support of the rural masses. Following the teaching of Mao, the Communists relied heavily on peasant guerrilla warfare. Here, far left, farmers are taught how to use a submachine gun; left, a smiling guerrilla holds a pair of home-made mines; and below, farmers, lacking rifles, arm themselves with the traditional "long knives" of the Chinese warrior.

In the face of such enemies, the principal means or form of the Chinese revolution must be armed struggle, not peaceful struggle. For our enemies have made peaceful activity impossible for the Chinese people and have deprived them of all political freedom and democratic rights. . . .

In the face of such enemies, there arises the question of revolutionary base areas. Since China's key cities have long been occupied by the powerful imperialists and their reactionary Chinese allies, it is imperative for the revolutionary ranks to turn the backward villages into advanced, consolidated base areas, into great military, political, economic and cultural bastions of the revolution from which to fight their vicious enemies who are using the cities for attacks on the rural districts, and in this way gradually to achieve the complete victory of the revolution through protracted fighting; it is imperative for them to do so if they do not wish to compromise with imperialism and its lackeys but are determined to fight on, and if they intend to build up and temper their forces, and avoid decisive battles with a powerful enemy while their own strength is inadequate. Such being the case, victory in the Chinese revolution can be won first in the rural areas, and this is possible because China's economic development is uneven (her economy not being a unified capitalist economy), because her

territory is extensive (which gives the revolutionary forces room to manoeuvre), because the counter-revolutionary camp is disunited and full of contradictions, and because the struggle of the peasants who are the main force in the revolution is led by the Communist Party, the party of the proletariat; but on the other hand, these very circumstances make the revolution uneven and render the task of winning complete victory protracted and arduous. Clearly then the protracted revolutionary struggle in the revolutionary base areas consists mainly in peasant guerrilla warfare led by the Chinese Communist Party. Therefore, it is wrong to ignore the necessity of using rural districts as revolutionary base areas, to neglect painstaking work among the peasants, and to neglect guerrilla warfare.

However, stressing armed struggle does not mean abandoning other forms of struggle; on the contrary, armed struggle cannot succeed unless co-ordinated with other forms of struggle. And stressing the work in the rural base areas does not mean abandoning our work in the cities and in the other vast rural areas which are still under the enemy's rule; on the contrary, without the work in the cities and in these other rural areas, our own rural base areas would be isolated and the revolution would suffer defeat. Moreover, the final objective of the revolution is the capture of the cities, the enemy's main bases, and this objective cannot be achieved without adequate work in the cities.

The Tasks of the Chinese Revolution

Imperialism and the feudal landlord class being the chief enemies of the Chinese revolution at this stage, what are the present tasks of the revolution?

Unquestionably, the main tasks are to strike at these two enemies, to carry out a national revolution to overthrow foreign imperialist oppression, the primary and foremost task being the national revolution to overthrow imperialism.

Lucien Bianco: The Communist Victory

The struggle against Japan (1937–1945) forced the Nationalists and Communists into temporary truce, but her defeat set off a race between them to seize as much Japanese-held territory and enemy equipment as possible. In this race the Nationalists with their superior forces and American financial and political support gained the larger portion. The United States insisted, however, that the two camps reach some degree of understanding, and a special mission led by General George Marshall was sent to China (December 1945–January 1947). The American efforts failed for they attempted to achieve the incompatible goals of reinforcing the autocratic Chiang government while urging fundamental social reforms that would cut the ground out from under the Communists. Armed conflict between the protagonists broke out in the summer of 1946 in Manchuria, where the commander of the Russian occupying forces had allowed the Communists to take possession of Japanese war supplies and territory, although denying them control of the industrial cities, which were turned over to the Nationalists. The Nationalist armies made striking progress at first, but soon became overextended; after mid–1947 the Communists were generally on the offensive. In a series of massive battles between September 1948 and January 1949 the Nationalists lost almost a million men, some of whom were killed in combat but many more captured or deserted. As Peking, Shanghai, Canton and the other great Chinese cities fell one after another to the Communists, Chiang K'ai-shek resigned as president and fled with the remnants of his armies to the island of Taiwan. On October 1, 1949 the People's Republic of China was proclaimed in Peking.

This reading is concerned with the reasons for the Communist victory. The author, Lucien Bianco, French social historian, carefully relates the revolutionary movement to the long-standing social crisis in China that spawned it. Reprinted from Lucien Bianco, *Origins of the Chinese Revolution 1915–1949*, tr. Marilyn Bell (Stanford University Press, 1971), pp. 179–180, 183–190, with the permission of the publisher. Copyright © 1971 by the Board of Trustees of Leland Stanford Junior University.

What made the Communists' victory possible? Although purely military considerations were far from negligible, they were decidedly less important than social and political factors. "The worse-equipped army will defeat the better-equipped army; the countryside will conquer the city; the party that does not receive foreign assistance will triumph over the party that does." Anyone who heard Red Army officers chanting these slogans with apparent conviction in early 1948 would have dismissed them as bluster intended to boost morale. Today they seem almost banal, and certainly less eloquent than the events they anticipated. For the Chinese Revolution ended in the conquest of a country the size of a continent by an army of beggars, and at a pace that dumbfounded military experts.

Less than a year passed between the capture of Mukden on October 30, 1948 and the capture of Canton on October 15, 1949—from Manchuria to the tropics in eleven and a half months!

Extraordinary as the victors' performance was, it is less striking than the disintegration of their foe. . . . Not only did the Nationalists underestimate their opponent, but they were incapable of adapting to the kind of war he was fighting. The Kuomintang strategists, like their French counterparts, can only be described as one war behind. To confront the Japanese and his domestic enemies, Chiang Kai-shek had slaved to build a modern army. In part he had succeeded; on the eve of the Second World War, his troops were not only the best in China, but a whole generation more modern than any other Chinese army. Most provincial armies still practiced a traditional and hence prestigious, if ineffective, form of warfare: marches and countermarches, elaborate feints and stratagems, few meaningful battles but many proclamations, and ultimately little bloodshed (except among the civilian population). To those acquainted with these vast, unwieldy premodern armies, the Generalissimo's German-equipped and German-organized elite corps appeared to represent the dynamism of the modern world. And yet the instrument to which Chiang gave such painstaking attention was outmoded as soon as it was ready. In part, of course, this was because his Wehrmacht advisers had based the Nationalist army's strategy on their own First World War experience with fixed-position and trench warfare. But Chiang's army was less outdated in relation to tanks, bombers, and Blitzkrieg tactics than in relation to the kind of revolutionary warfare practiced by the People's Liberation Army. . . .

The Communists' strategy was at once simple and clever, as bold as it was natural, and aimed, as we have noted, at destroying enemy forces rather than defending cities or expanses of territory. The Red Army was distinguished by its great mobility, or rather its total movability (everything could be rapidly dismantled and moved, leaving the enemy with a denuded area and a meaningless victory), as contrasted with the relative immobility of the Nationalist garrisons. Because of the Communists' overall numerical inferiority they eschewed full-scale or protracted battles, in which losses and gains would balance out, in favor of attacks in overwhelming force on small, isolated enemy units. At the same time, while applying the thousand and one tactics and tricks of the guerrilla trade, the

Chinese Communist soldiers perform the Yang-ko, a victory dance, on May 25, 1949, the day Shanghai fell. Note the American steel helmets taken from captured, American-armed Nationalist troops.

Red Army prepared for conventional warfare—including great battles and sieges of cities—when the time was right. . . .

Finally, the morale of the Red Army was as different from that of the forces of order as day from night. Conscription, a tragedy in the government-controlled areas, was an honor in the Liberated Areas. The Communists' morale was reinforced by their tactical successes in the thousand skirmishes and small-scale battles of the nameless war that so disconcerted the Nationalists, but no one would attribute the Communists' superior morale solely to military factors. Indeed, I may have exaggerated the victors' military virtues and underrated the extent to which the gradual crumbling of the enemy army facilitated the Communists' rapid and impressive victory. As we shall see, the collapse of the Nationalist army was hastened by the revolutionaries' social policy.

THE PEOPLE'S VICTORY

Guerrilla warfare is not a special form of the art of war, but the continuation of revolutionary struggle by military means. Mao said as much when he asserted that no matter how assiduously the Nationalists and their American military advisers studied the Communists' combat techniques, they could never hope to apply them successfully, because they depended on popular support, which the Communists' enemies were inherently incapable of winning. Popular support in China went to the Red Army. . . .

Did the fact that a war of national resistance had given way to civil war mean that would-be mobilizers of China's population must now stress social rather than national issues? In practice, both kinds of issues were exploited simultaneously. The Japanese invader was more or less supplanted in the

popular mind by the American imperialist, whose evil nature Communist soldiers could verify by inspecting the words "Made in U.S.A." on captured Nationalist weapons. If this familiar phrase was missing, as it was on captured bullets of Chinese manufacture, one could still resort to writing the character *mei* (America) on these bullets before distributing them to the soldiers. Many a guerrilla or militiaman, persuaded by such evidence, must have muttered the vengeful couplet

> Chiang Kai-shek has a stubborn heart,
> America is his father and mother. . .

Nationalism was thus far from a spent force. It made little difference if the terms of the appeal to nationalism were on the whole misleading; an argument is not necessarily the less persuasive for being specious.

After the hiatus of the united front period, social issues returned to the fore. But now it was no longer a question of exploiting popular issues for propaganda purposes; the order of the day was social war. Social revolution—terrifying, vast, and primitive— exploded throughout rural China. It did not break out everywhere at the same time. Sometimes the first move was made by the large landowners: on returning to a village they had fled seven or eight years before, they had their henchmen murder the peasants who has seized the land in their absence. At other times the peasants took the lead in settling accounts by lynching a village headman who had collaborated with the Japanese or a peasant who had spied on fellow villagers during the war, and perhaps also, for good measure, whoever happened to be collecting the land tax at the time. Sometimes the leaders of the revolution were outdistanced by the masses; sometimes they left the masses far behind. In 1945, the peasants'

insistence on immediate distribution of land dismayed the Communists, who were not eager, for example, to alienate an anti-Japanese landlord they had made local headman, or to lose the support of liberals who had not yet chosen sides. At other times, tenant farmers paralyzed by timidity and respect for the landed upper class had to be led by the hand to claim what Communist leaders pronounced to be their due.

Little by little, however, the peasants became bolder, the direction of the revolution became clearer, and the social conflict became more intense. As late as the spring of 1946, there were many areas in which the peasants' only concern was to avoid involvement in the warfare; when the Eighth Route Army left, the villagers stayed behind and welcomed the Nationalists. Soon, however, it became clear that the return of the Kuomintang meant the undoing of social and political advances the peasants had thought they could take for granted, the repeal of reforms relating to interest rates, land tax, and land rent that they had presumed to be part of any postwar government program, and worst of all, a return to the traditional social and political order. In addition, there was the threat of a resurgent White Terror, whose new victims would be former militiamen, local peasant leaders, members of the village Woman's Association, and the like.

The term Liberated Areas, by contrast, especially from 1947 on, when the CCP instituted an agrarian policy almost as radical as that of the Kiangsi period, became synonymous with the redistribution of land, the indictment of landlords, and the dictatorship of the Poor Peasants Association. During the winter of 1947–48, while many rich peasants were rallying to the side of the large landowners or trailing in the wake of government troops, some of the most wretched of the rural poor—tenant farmers, small proprietors, farm workers—flocked to the Communists. As the true direction of the revolution became clear, the struggle grew pitiless. When the villagers realized that their hour had come, that they had gone too far to turn back, years of accumulated hatred were unleashed. Landlords guilty of exploiting their tenants were paraded from village to village and slowly chopped to bits along the way by mobs armed with pitchforks, shears, pickaxes, and clubs, which then fought over the flesh of men alleged to have gorged themselves on the flesh of the people, and mutilated their remains. Some landowners hastened the destruction of their class by resorting to the kind of counter-terrorism used by the Algerian *pieds-noirs* in the spring of 1962. Furious and terrified, feeling their world crumbling beneath them, they took to murdering their more recalcitrant tenant farmers, whose numbers increased daily. Some had whole families of tenants buried alive (*huo-mai*), instructing their men to club back down any head that rose above ground level.

"A poor man has no right to speak," says an old Shansi maxim. When the dikes of silence and submission were swept away by revolution, the village square was inundated by a torrent of speeches and complaints. An avid audience attended, or rather participated in, "Speak Bitterness Meetings," meetings called by the Red Army at which individual peasants took turns recounting their woes and relating them to the general plight of the peasantry. The assembled village was at once the priest hearing confession, the chorus repeating and amplifying the complaint, and the avenger whose resolve was stiffened by this strange and simple ritual.

This public airing of grievances, which aroused or heightened the villagers' class-consciousness, is a good example of the originality of the Red Army, an army different from any that had gone before. Equally original was its use of information, not only about the movement of enemy forces but also, and more often, about conditions in a newly occupied village. The Red Army had a way of knowing the amount of taxes people owed, the names of farmers who had been evicted from their land or victimized by arbitrary treatment, even the names of women who were being ill-treated by their mothers-in-law. Such information was extremely useful in building a militia, a Women's Association, or a Poor Peasants Association, and in arriving at appropriate political and social policies.

The Red Army and the many local guerrilla units were not so much an army as a people in arms—a people, that is, from the numberless villages of the Northeast and the North China Plain. The enlistment rate closely reflected the progress of agrarian revolution; Manchuria, where the redistribution of land was carried out earliest and most thoroughly, furnished the People's Liberation Army with 1.6 million recruits between June 1946 and June 1948. Since the Red Army was an army of peasants, political education in the camps was handled much as it was in the villages. Even undermanned front-line regiments had in their ranks instructors and students, actors and actresses, and specialists in agrarian reform and rice-growing. A unit of the Eighth Route Army, wrote Jack Belden, an American war correspondent, was also "a school, theater, labor cooperative, and political club."

In a word, to millions of peasants, soldiers and civilians alike, the Red Army brought the immediate promise of a new existence, of liberation from all the evils of the old society. . . .

The People "Overturn" a Village (1946)

As Mao had correctly predicted, the essential element in the Communist victory was the support provided by the rural masses of China. To win the wholehearted allegiance of the peasantry had, therefore, been strategically indispensible for the Communist leadership. This was a formidable task since the masses, impoverished and exploited for the most part, had to be led by the party cadres from fatalistic acceptance of their lot to the realization that it was in their power to improve it. In their favor the Communist organizers had, of course, the burning resentment of the average peasant for the landholding elite. This reading describes a typical, local example of Communist efforts to prod the peasants into "settling accounts." The process of seizing the property of the landlords and driving them from the area was called *fanshen*, or "overturn." The incident described took place in January 1946. The Communists had organized an "Anti-Traitor Movement" to ferret out those Chinese who had collaborated with the Japanese. Now they cleverly turned the anger of the young patriots in the Movement against the landlord class. From William Hinton, *Fanshen* (New York, Vintage Books, 1966), pp. 128, 131–136.

Out of the confusion and near anarchy of the tempestuous Anti-Traitor Movement that followed the Japanese surrender came an assault on the land system itself. From chaotic revenge against collaborators, the young men of the resistance were led by the district Communist Party to a conscious planned attack on the landlords as a class. With this shift in emphasis, China's 20-year-old land revolution, temporarily suspended by the war, began again in earnest and rapidly gathered a momentum too great to be checked by any political party or leader.

The campaign in the Fifth District of Lucheng County started with a famous meeting in Li Village Gulch, the first settlement south of Long Bow on the road to Changchih. This meeting was held on January 16, 1946, in an effort to educate the young revolutionary cadres in the fundamentals of class relations and class consciousness so that they could, as they themselves said, "get at the root of calamity." All the young men who had just led the Anti-Traitor Movement to completion were brought together by the district leaders. The meeting lasted three days and three major issues were discussed: (1) Who depends upon whom for a living? (2) Why are the poor poor and the rich rich? (3) Should rent be paid to landlords? . . .

When the meeting broke up on the third day the three main questions had been settled in the minds of most: (1) The landlords depended on the labor of the peasants for their very life. (2) The rich were rich because they "peeled and pared" the poor. (3) Rent should not be paid to the landlords. . . .

In Long Bow the young men returned from the district meeting full of enthusiasm. Chang San-ch'ing, the secretary of the village government, who was one of the participants, later said: "I was very happy when I returned from Li Village Gulch. Up until that time I had been just a little afraid. I carried a burden on my back. I figured that if all those who had worked for the Japanese were to be struggled against, then I too would become a victim, for I had worked for a Japanese drug company for more than one year. But at that meeting we were told that the Anti-Traitor Movement was over. We decided that we would now struggle against the landlords who had oppressed us for so long. Everyone who had been oppressed or exploited, who had borrowed money or rented land could now make accusations and get revenge. I was very happy. I was no longer the least bit afraid for I thought—I too have been oppressed. From childhood my family suffered under loans at high interest and I worked out as a hired laborer for so many years, and later, when I went out to work, I just served the master of the shop. So all my life I have been oppressed and exploited. Now my time has come."

The first task faced by this group when they returned to the village was to organize a local Peasants' Association. This was a voluntary organization of all working peasants recognized by the Liberated Areas Government of Shansi-Honan-Hopei-Shantung as the only legal organ for carrying out agrarian policy, conducting the struggle against the landlords, receiving confiscated property, and distributing it to the landless and land poor.

Farm laborers, poor peasants, middle peasants, rural handicraftsmen, and impoverished intellectuals such as schoolteachers, letter writers, and clerks sympathetic to the new land policies were all entitled to join when approved by the elected committee of the Association. All members had the right to speak, vote, elect, and be elected, and also the right to criticize and replace elected officers. They were obligated to abide by the rules of the Association, carry out its decisions, and pay dues. These dues amounted to one catty [about 1 ½ lbs.] of millet a year.

Two cadres from the old Liberated Area in the Second District, where village Peasants' Associations had existed for a long time, came to help organize the local group in Long Bow. Thirty of the poorest peasants in the village were first called together. They included women whose sons had been killed in the fort, peasant families whose able-bodied members had been forced into rear service far from home, and long-term hired helpers who owned nothing but the clothes on their backs.

Some of these families had already received food and clothes as a result of the Anti-Traitor Movement. Fu-yuan and T'ien-ming explained to them that the preceding distributions were only the beginning, that such a small amount of goods could not solve any real problems, that they should tackle the land question itself. Fu-yuan posed to them the question of "who lives off whom?" He urged each member to tell his or her life story and to figure out for himself the root of the problem.

Once again Kuei-ts'ai led off. In order to move the others he told his own history. "In the past when I lived in Linhsien I stayed with my uncle," he said. "In order to get married my uncle borrowed 20 silver dollars. Within a year the interest plus the principal amounted to more than 300 dollars. We could not possibly repay this. The landlord seized all our lands and houses and I became a migrant wandering through the province looking for work."

This reminded poor peasant Shen T'ien-hsi of the loss of his home. "Once when we needed some money we decided to sell our house. We made a bargain with a man who offered a reasonable price, but Sheng Ching-ho, who lived next door, forced us to sell our house to him for almost nothing."

Then poor peasant Ta-hung's wife spoke up. "You had to sell your house, but my parents had to sell me. We lived in a prosperous valley but we owned no land. In the famine year we were starving and my parents sold me for a few bushels of grain. If we had had some land I could have found a husband and been properly married. Instead, I was sold like a donkey or a cow."

Story followed story. Many wept as they remembered the sale of children, the death of family members, the loss of property. The village cadres kept asking "What is the reason for this? Why did we all suffer so? Was it the 'eight ideographs' that determined our fate or was it the land system and the rents we had to pay? Why shouldn't we now take on

Left, the landlords' old title deeds are burned. Below, scene of a public trial in Shanpa Village, Kwangtung Province. The accused are village merchants and magistrates. Their alleged crimes are detailed on white aprons.

the landlords and right the wrongs of the past?"

T'ien-ming finally challenged them to action. "Now, the only question is, do we dare begin? The Eighth Route Army and the Liberated Areas Government stand behind us. Already in many places the landlords have been beaten down. We have only to follow the example of others. We have only to act with our own hands. Then we can all *fan-shen*."

"There are not enough of us," said one.

"Then we have to find more members. Each one here should go out and find others. All the poor are brothers together. If we unite no one can stand in our way."

Each of the 30 went home, visited with neighbor and friend, and each found two or three more peasants who could be approved by the whole group. Soon over 100 families had joined the peasants' Association. Most of them were poor, but among them were scattered a few middle peasants. . . .

Several days of intense activity followed the establishment of the new Association. Many active members neglected all their regular work in order to mobilize the majority of the people for the struggle to come. And so, toward the end of January, the campaign to "settle accounts" with the landlords finally began.

The committee of the Peasants' Association decided to tackle Kuo Ch'ung-wang first. He was not the richest man in the village but he was one of the meanest. His close association with the puppet Chief-of-Staff Chou Mei-sheng tarred him with the collaborationist brush. More important was the fact that while his tenants died of starvation during the famine year, he seized grain and hoarded it for speculation. The cadres, having learned from the failure of their first big meeting, held small group meetings ahead of time in order to gather opinions against Ch'ung-wang. Those with serious grievances were encouraged to make them known among their closest neighbors and were then mobilized to speak out at the village-wide meeting to come.

While the small meetings were in progress, the militia arrested Kuo Ch'ung-wang, searched his house and unearthed tons of grain. Much of it was rotten. On the day of the big meeting, the grain, which could have saved the lives of dozens of people, lay in the courtyard in a stinking mildewed heap. The people who crowded in to accuse walked over the grain and, as the courtyard filled up, some of them sat down on it. The smell and the sight of it reminded them of those who had died for want of a few catties and filled them with anger. Next to the grain stood two jars of salt water—salt that had been hoarded so long it had undergone hydrolysis. While the landless and the land poor went weeks without salt, Ch'ung-wang had let salt go to waste.

At this critical meeting, Fu-yuan, the village head, was the first to speak. Because he was a cousin of Ch'ung-wang, his words carried extra weight with the rest of the village. When a man was moved to accuse his own cousin, the provocation had to be serious.

"In the famine year," Fu-yuan began, talking directly to Ch'ung-wang, "my brother worked for your family. We were all hungry. We had nothing to eat. But you had no thought for us. Several times we tried to borrow grain from you. But it was all in vain. You watched us starve without pity."

Then Ho-pang, a militiaman, spoke up. His voice shook as he told how he had rented land from Ch'ung-wang. "One year I could not pay the rent. You took the whole harvest.

You took my clothes. You took everything." He broke down sobbing as a dozen others jumped up shouting.

"What was in your mind?"

"You took everything. Miao-le and his brother died."

"Yes, what were your thoughts? You had no pity. Didn't you hound P'ei Mang-wen's mother to her death?"

"Speak."

"Yes, speak. Make him talk. Let's hear his answers!"

But Ch'ung-wang had no answers. He could not utter a word. When the peasants saw that he could not answer them they realized that they had already won a victory. Many who had been afraid to open their mouths found themselves shouting in anger without thought of the consequences.

The meeting lasted all day. In the evening, when the committee reckoned up all the charges against Ch'ung-wang, they found that he owed one hundred bags of grain. That night, under a full moon, the militia went to the fields with measuring rods and measured Ch'ung-wang's land. They found that he had three acres more than were listed in his deeds and that for 20 years he had evaded taxes on that land while others had paid and paid. When they added this to the other damages claimed against him they realized that all his lands, all his houses, his grain, his clothes, his stock, and everything else that he owned would not be enough to settle the debt. Yet when they looked in his storeroom they found not hundreds, but only a paltry six bags of grain that could be seized.

The next morning when the people met again to carry on the campaign against Ch'ung-wang excitement ran high. Women even went so far as to bring food with them so that they and their families could stay right

through the day and not miss a single minute. Liang, the district leader, opened the attack. He said, "This is our only chance to settle the blood-and-sweat debt of the landlord. Even if you take all his property it will never be enough. Ask him where he has hidden his gold and silver. Make him give up his precious things."

"Yes, speak out. Where are the coins? Where have you buried the money?" came the shouts from the crowd. But Kuo refused to say anything beyond the fact that he had no silver and never had had any. Since nobody believed him, the militia were ordered into his house to make a search. They were joined by more than 60 peasant volunteers. They dug up the floors, ripped the mud bricks off the tops of the k'angs, tapped the walls. It was all in vain. They found nothing.

When the search proved fruitless, a few of the cadres took Ch'ung-wang aside. They told him that it was no use trying to hide his wealth. Since all his ordinary property was not enough to settle his account with the people, they would surely find his hidden wealth sooner or later. It would therefore be much safer and wiser for him to hand this over voluntarily than to face their wrath once they found it on their own. After several people had talked to him in the same vein Ch'ung-wang finally gave in. He told them where to dig. They found 50 silver dollars in an earthen crock.

When this money was brought before the people at the meeting, they became very angry. Here was proof that Ch'ung-wang had lied to them. Scores of people jumped up, ran forward, and began to beat him with whatever came to hand.

"Tell us where the rest is. You know that is not all," they shouted.

Someone struck him a blow in the face.

Ch'ung-wang held his bleeding mouth and tried to speak.

"Don't hit me. I'll tell you. I'll tell you right away. There is another 80 dollars in the back room."

The meeting adjourned immediately while the militia and their enthusiastic helpers again went to search. They very soon found another cache of coins, but this only whetted their appetites and angered them still further. Ch'ung-wang was playing with them as a cat plays with a mouse in spite of the fact that he was their prisoner. First grain, then salt, now silver dollars—the bastard was richer than they thought! When they got back to the courtyard, they beat him again.

That day he gave up more than 200 silver dollars.

The Revolution in Perspective: Twenty Years of Communism

The People's Republic was established in 1949. What has been accomplished in China in the intervening decades? Professor Ross Terrill (1939–   ), a native Australian teaching at Harvard, travelled to the mainland in 1971 and tells in this reading what life was like in China. From Ross Terrill, "The 800,000,000: Report from China" in *The Atlantic*, November, 1971. Pp. 118–120.

Leaving China by train through the technicolor lushness of Kwangtung's rounded hills,

I felt an emotion hard to understand, dangerous to trust. Fazed by South China's beauty on a summer morning, I did not yet see two diverse currents in this opaque emotion. First there was a feeling that rubs off from the buoyancy of corporate aspiration in China. The people seemed like Rousseau's "Spartan mother," putting country before self, living as lambs of Shepherd Mao—and that is ennobling. But—here was the second current— also a feeling of painful separation from the high pitch of collective spirit. I could not live like that—how can others do so? . . .

The individual in China, insofar as he reaches beyond the practicalities of life—I don't know how many do—is enveloped by an Idea, the Thought of Mao Tse-tung. The myth of Mao Thought has reached into homes and even spirits (which Leninism or Stalinism hardly did in Russia).

This near-total control is not by police terror. The techniques of Stalinist terror—armed cops everywhere, mass killings, murder of political opponents, knocks on the door at 3 A.M. and a shot soon after—are absent in China. Though force remains the ultimate basis of any state, control of the people in China is more nearly psychological than by physical coercion. Its extent would be hard to overstate. As these pages suggest, politics reaches into every corner. Yet the method of control is amazingly light-handed by Communist standards. The informal way PLA men mingle and work with the population is remarkable to see. Peking trusts its citizens in their millions with rifles at home (members of the militia). What it does not trust them with—for the Dictatorship is by Idea—is their own minds.

There is paradox in the impression, got especially in rural parts, that people proceed with their daily lives in a relatively unpres-

sured way. On one hand, Mao Thought pervades. On the other, the family (for instance) is extremely important to Chinese I met on this trip. The bridge is the age-old social discipline of the Chinese. The CCP has *used* the traditional bonds. An instance is reverence for ancestors. The Party does not stop the girls at the Nanking factory from visiting ancestors' graves, but it tries through propaganda to turn ancestor-reverence as much as possible toward *revolutionary martyrs*. . . .

Is it not worse in China than in Poland or Hungary, in that people cooperate in their own unfreedom? No, because the Idea fits the experience of most Chinese. At the Peking Chinese Medicine Hospital, I met a railway worker who'd been hit by a train, and the resulting spine disorder paralyzed him from the waist down. His legs had shrunk, his hope had dwindled, and he had lain in bed like a vegetable for eighteen years. In the Cultural Revolution, when doctors were urged to tackle "even the impossible," a team at the hospital began acupuncture treatment on 151 such half-paralyzed people. One hundred and twenty-four can now walk with a stick (fifteen of these without a stick; eight of the fifteen are at work again). Most had lain in bed for years, and the marks of the bedsores were on them like burns.

The railway worker hobbled across the room on crutches to greet me, and said: "I am out of bed because of Chairman Mao's Thought. Soon I will go back to work for the sake of the revolution." At that moment the remark seemed embarrassing, yet the Myth of Mao is functional to medicine and to much endeavor in China. . . . "Myth" is not falsehood but dramatization with a kernel of truth. The myth of Mao sums up bitter Chinese experience and lends hope. It seemed to give the railway worker a mental picture of a world he could rejoin, and his doctors that vital extra ounce of resourcefulness.

For the nation, it gives a recognizable (if distorted) summation of past struggles against landlords and foreigners, and an impulse to keep going further in the collective drama of China "standing up."

When Professor Fu at Sun Yat Sen University said his new research was aimed to serve "workers, peasants, and soldiers," he invoked a myth. This "Blessed Trinity" suffuses China today. Everything is weighed against its service to these three groups. . . .

Workers stands for industrialization. They come first, since according to Marx, workers make the revolution. Workers didn't in China, but modernizing China is a good part of the revolution's aims. Mao had not made an idol of industrialization as some Marxists have in Russia. But ever since the impact of the materially superior West shattered the Ch'ing Dynasty, China's opinion leaders have defined the national power they seek partly in terms of large-scale production. Here Marxist theory and national aspiration and the instinct of the "modern" Chinese mind all coincide.

Peasants stands for the reality of a China still 80 percent rural. The revolution came from the villages. It had to; there was no other adequate source. Mao became its leader by grasping this, and he still resists notions of development which would leave rural China lagging behind the industrial sector. Producing enough food for 800 million people is *the* great daily task of the Chinese nation; three quarters of Chinese spend their time growing their own food; the industrial and tertiary sectors are tiny beside the food-producing sector. To keep the country ticking over and hold it together, peasants are the key. To pursue equality, as Mao is doing, the peasants are also, of course, the key.

Soldiers stands for the international defense of the revolution, and also for a crucial fact about the politics of the revolution. Peking's leaders won power by the gun. . . . Soldiers are in this way central to China's revolutionary drama. But the People's Liberation Army is also the linchpin of China's politics today. For it is the *bridge between the peasant reality of China and the modernizing tasks*. It is a peasant army. As such it is the national institution which best represents the political reality of China. . . .

Workers, peasants, soldiers. Like so many slogans in China, it has a practical kernel. It ties together aims, methods, and resources. It is a myth with roots in reality.

I cannot say in blanket fashion whether this Mao Myth is "good or bad." For the ordinary Chinese it seems to give meaning to things. He can see such spectacular benefits from this present government that the collective drama—which the Mao Myth expresses—seems an acceptable way to try and get the further improvements in his life that he would like. It also stirs his national pride. The "privatistic" alternative, anyway, in a country with *per capita* income perhaps one twentieth of America's, is not a glittering one.

It is the intellectual who pays the big price. A scholar in a Chinese city, at the end of an evening's conversation, said three big things have happened since Liberation. China has "stood up." Class exploitation has gone. The nation is being "proletarianized." The first two he elaborated effectively, but he didn't convey much of the third. Either the idea seemed forced, elusive to him, or he had regrets about the way it has worked out.

Was he thinking of how the Mao Myth had "proletarianized" his field of study, twisting bits of the past to prettify the collective drama? I thought of his daughter, a bright graduate of a major university now working as a farm laborer. He had said of her in a rather flat way: "We hope that later she may be given a job that will make use of her abilities." For this man, the Mao Myth leaves high and dry his own concerns (and those of three of his children, and many of his colleagues). Whether the spoiling of these "careers" is worthwhile for the sake of the Chinese millions whose interests are put first—it is a question of values. . . .

People ask, "Is China free?", but there is no objective measure of the freedom of a whole society. Observation in China, as study of China, suggests that the revolution has been good for workers and peasants but problematic for intellectuals. It is hard to go on from there and make overall value judgments that are honest. . . .

It is easy for the rich man to scorn the loose morals of the poor man who steals his dinner. Easy for the pluralist America, which has 6 per cent of world population and about 35 per cent of its wealth, to attack the regimentation of China, which has about 25 per cent of world population and 4 per cent of its wealth. Easy, too, for tired America to shake its head at the psychological simplicities of China's nation-building mood, and forget that America was itself once in a proud, naïve stage of nation-building, bristling with a sense of innocence and mission. Yet at one point we and China face the same value judgment. Which gets priority: the individual's freedom or the relationships of the whole society? Which *unit* is to be taken for policy and moral judgment alike: the nation, trade union, our class, my cronies, me? This is the hinge on which the whole issue turns. . . .

I am not a good guide here. I felt the double emotion on the train from Canton because I am both moved by the collective priorities of China's new order *and* sad at the lack of individuality and choice. As a democratic socialist (not an American, but an Australian), I am (not to use caricatures) against both the "jungle" of capitalism and the "prison" of Communism. . . .

After leaving China, I met in Hong Kong a young man caught between "jungle" and "prison." Vincent swam from Kwangtung Province to Hong Kong, ten hours by night in the water, mainly to get better educational opportunities. (In 1971 some 20,000 will leave China for Hong Kong, many of them young people who wanted to go to college and got

sent to a village instead.) But his father, a teacher of Japanese in Hong Kong, would not or could not pay the big sum of money needed to educate him, so Vincent went to work in a factory. Now he is disillusioned with Hong Kong. "I work hard—and for nothing. To work hard for my country, that's all right. But here, it's not for China; it's not for anything. All you can do in Hong Kong is spend." Vincent is capable, and left China because he wasn't using abilities there. Now the lack of social purpose and the jumbled priorities of Hong Kong weigh on him. As we parted he asked my advice—should he go back?

I am not going to end with moral judgments, because history is just now scrambling up our moral categories rather drastically, not least those used between Americans and Chinese. A symbol catches the change. In Taiwan today you watch Chinese boys play cricket—Britain's game. This year Peking launched its new America policy with table tennis—China's game. The point is that China, so long the object of our policies and our judgments, is no longer a passive but an active factor in the world. Moral judgments are inescapable, but the formulation of the issues is often at history's mercy.

STUDY QUESTIONS

1. What did the Kuomintang offer to the Chinese people and why was its promise unfulfilled?

2. On what grounds did Mao champion a peasant revolution based in the countryside?

3. According to Bianco what made the Communist victory possible?

4. How did the Communists gain the support of the villagers of Long Bow? Why had they not "settled accounts" earlier?

5. What is the "Mao Myth"? What do the Chinese seem to have gained from the Revolution? What reservations does Terrill raise about life in China today?

A thaw in Peking. Chinese workers sweep away the snow during the first visit by an American President to Communist China, March 1, 1972.

The parade movements of this honor guard form part of the welcoming ceremony for visiting foreign dignitaries.

Peking, one of the world's oldest cities, contains an enormous paved public square of ninety-eight acres, which can hold more than a million people. The Tien An Men (Gate of Heavenly Peace) Square has been the scene of many anti-American rallies since the Korean War. Signs on the wall to the rear right read "Long live the Peoples Republic of China," "Long live the peoples of the world united together." Marchers carry signs wishing a long life to Chairman Mao. A colossal statue of Communist Party Chairman Mao Tse-Tung dominates this scene of a National Day Parade in 1967.

Shopping stall in the commercial district of Shanghai, still a major port. The so-called "Mao jacket," made popular by Sun Yat-Sen, who wore it with a stiff collar, is available in drab hues of grey and blue, as well as in black. It has four big pockets and is produced, with or without a lining, in cotton and wool.

In this Shanghai hardware store, busts of Mao take their place on the shelves with the other merchandise. This photo was taken by a member of a visiting trade mission.

A Chinese family relaxes at home. Li Po-yu (right), a member of a production brigade in a People's Commune in Sanwui, his wife, brother, and sister-in-law, all work on the land while his mother (left) tends the house.

(Below, left) Eleven Chinese children, in clothing whose varied patterns contrast sharply with those of their elders, are taken for a stroll on a Shanghai street.

(Below) Nursery schools are commonly attached to industries, like the one we see here, part of a large sewing machine factory in Canton. Children with toy guns as props perform a dance and song: "We are determined to liberate Taiwan." Note the picture of Chairman Mao in the rear right. September, 1971.

Men, women and children crowd the parks, walks, and other open areas for daily exercise. This photo was taken recently in Peking.

Acupuncture, an ancient method of inserting needles into a patient's nerve centers to relieve pain, is widely used in China. Here medical workers are helping students grasp the techniques of the skill by practicing on themselves.

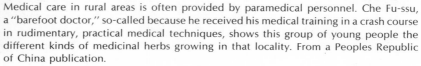

Medical care in rural areas is often provided by paramedical personnel. Che Fu-ssu, a "barefoot doctor," so-called because he received his medical training in a crash course in rudimentary, practical medical techniques, shows this group of young people the different kinds of medicinal herbs growing in that locality. From a Peoples Republic of China publication.

Welding operations on a modest scale are carried out by this Chinese woman in the China-Cuba Friendship People's Commune of Peking. Women are widely employed as machinists and factory hands.

Hand-painting of vases, an ancient Chinese art once dominated by men, continues to flourish in modern Communist China. The lions and dragons on the vase are traditional motifs suggesting prosperity and good fortune. Photo taken in Peking.

At Shanghai's "Circus," a theatre in the round, performances by acrobats are an essential part of a variety program which includes a mixture of theatre and political propaganda. Acrobats have long provided a popular form of entertainment in China. Performances are well attended and seats cheap. This show lasted two hours, played to a "standing room only" crowd, and the "best" seats cost the equivalent of twenty cents.

Taste in popular music among young people remains preelectronic. This g in Mao Tse-tung garb, is presenting a concert in Shanghai. With traditional instruments, joined by a Western violin, they play folk and modified tradi music.

A Shanghai newspaper billboard. The poster at left stresses vigilance against tendencies toward capitalist thinking, a theme echoed in the newspaper articles. The poster itself was produced by the revolutionary committee of the Shanghai transportation workers' training school.

Henri Brugmans: The West as a World Catalyst

WESTERN CIVILIZATION AND THE WORLD

Western Europe ranked after North America and Soviet Russia as one of the three greatest concentrations of industrial power in the world in the decades following the Second World War. Westerners were prosperous and self-confident. They were, however, faced with a very sensitive and complex situation as more than sixty new nations were established in these years out of former colonial empires. Caught in a tide of nationalism and pushed by population pressures, the peoples of the developing nations wished as soon as possible to enjoy the comforts and power of Western industrial technology. With the knowledge that the capacity to deliver nuclear weapons was spreading and that the decisions of today would be portentous for the shape of tomorrow, the Western nations tried to come to terms with the states they had spawned.

Dutch-born Henri Brugmans (1906–   ) became rector of the College of Europe in 1950. This Belgium-based institution strove to strengthen the European idea by providing a postgraduate center for study of the problems presented by the union of Europe. In this selection Dr. Brugmans attempts to pin down major contribution of Western civilization to the world. From Henri Brugmans, "Historical Considerations" in *Basic Values of the Atlantic Community,* L. Cerych, ed. Pall Mall Press, London (for the Conference on Atlantic Community, 1962), pp. 13–15, 18–20, 32. Granted by permission of Fredrick A. Praeger, Inc.

In earlier centuries, while the West was exploring, occupying and colonizing large parts of the globe, we often spoke of "civilized" countries as opposed to those others which were inhabited by men called, somewhat scornfully, "natives."

It goes without saying that not all Europeans thought in such elementary terms. Our scholars in particular studied the old African and Asian civilizations and the pre-Columbian civilizations of America. Often they knew them better than the Asians, Africans and American Indians themselves.

But the image of the West, as it appeared overseas, was not principally determined by linguists or archaeologists, ethnologists or cultural sociologists. On the contrary, the least civilized Westerners too often enjoyed the limelight and it was they who showed the least understanding of the "natives." For many "average" colonizers, "civilization" meant their own civilization, and this notion was sometimes limited to the least original of the West's achievements, especially a certain technique of comfort reserved for the Westerners themselves.

Now that "imperialism" is being liquidated and the West finds itself thrown back on its own resources, it is taking the opportunity to question and rediscover itself. It sees that it is not "civilization" incarnate, but that it represents, in a human family which must become united, *one* type of culture, different from the score of others which the world has known and which Toynbee lists in his *Study of History.*

This is for us a lesson in humility. But at the same time we observe that the great majority of civilizations catalogued by science belongs to the past. For societies, as for individuals and peoples, the dead are much more numerous than the living. The European and Western civilization is indeed one of the very few on the planet to survive and continue its career. What is more, it alone has become truly universal. . . .

Undoubtedly there is no guarantee that this situation will remain for ever. God knows what new creative forces are to mould the future. But today we must start with the existing reality which, to a very large extent, results from Western efforts. In particular, the technology which is today accepted, welcomed and demanded by all the world is an inseparable part of the West's development. It is, even more, a product of Western society as a whole and not only of a few specialists which it would be enough to buy or imitate.

Finally, the globe, as it appears now at the beginning of the second half of the twentieth century, has not lost its Western look because the West has lost a series of political holds. Quite the opposite: it seems much more Westernized than the world of 1900. Our adversaries—like ourselves—will do well to ponder this fact and wonder how the West has managed to perform this kind of miracle, and above all what the consequences of this will be. . . .

The Western world has always been *rerum novarum cupidi,* eager to see and create something new. In our bookshops the "just published" advertisement can count on a favourable response, and any chairman of a society can be sure of success and will be considered dynamic and courageous when announcing to the members that "now we are going to start afresh, break with the past. . . ."

The West, which has known the Romanesque, the Gothic, the Renaissance, the Reformation and the Counter-Reformation, the Baroque, the Rococo, the Romantic Movement, Realism and the modern styles, which has found its inspiration in the Greeks and Romans, Israel and the pre-Columbian cultures, which has lived in feudal and dynastic, republican and monarchical, agrarian and capitalist frameworks, and which sees living side by side countries and regions governed variously by Conservatives, Christian Democrats or Socialists—the West owes this universality to its flexibility. . . .

The very essence of our culture commands our humility. We have no panaceas to sell. In an anguished world we can reassure no one, since we offer no ready-made solution. The free society which we mean to promote is not that of flapping flags and endless processions. It is a society where the dissatisfied can speak their mind—and who is not dissatisfied in a free society? It is a society in which the majority expects its government to do more and the minority forecasts disasters. The West does not promise joyful tomorrows but a tolerable today. For it the true life is not that of tomorrow, after the miracle of the revolution. It is situated in the here and now, where men toil to mitigate a few cases of real injustice, abolish some glaring anomalies, or improve the working of some new institutions. These men know that they are not working for eternity, since everything in history always remains to be done again. But they know also that, but for their efforts, stagnation would bring about decadence. . . .

Decline and Triumph of the West

L. S. Stavrianos, *The World Since 1500: A Global History,* © 1966. Reprinted by permission of Prentice-Hall, Inc., Englewood Cliffs, New Jersey.

A major difference between World War I and World War II lay in their colonial aftermaths. Europe's hold over the colonial empires was weakened but not broken by World War I; indeed, the colonial holdings were expanded by the acquisition of Arab lands as mandates. After World War II, by contrast, an irrepressible revolutionary wave swept the colonial empires and ended European domination with dramatic dispatch. In 1939, the only independent states in sub-Saharan Africa were Liberia and South Africa, and they owed their independence to their atypical historical backgrounds. The one had been settled in the early nineteenth century by freed slaves, and the other was controlled by a resident European minority. Twenty-five years later, the only significant colonies left in sub-Saharan Africa were Portuguese Angola and Mozambique, and the cluster under South Africa's shadow: Southern Rhodesia, South-West Africa, Bechuanaland, Swaziland, and Basutoland. Just as most of Europe's colonies had been swiftly acquired in the last two decades of the nineteenth century, so most of them now were lost in an equally short period of time in the two decades following World War II. Between 1944 and 1964, a total of 53 countries had won their independence. These included in mid-1963 a little over one billion people, or 31 per cent of the world's 3.18 billion at that date (see Table 1). After so many epoch-making triumphs and achievements overseas, the Europeans appeared in the mid-twentieth century to be retreating back to the small Eurasian peninsula whence they had set forth half a millennium earlier. . . .

An unprecedented weakening of the foremost colonial powers took place during the Second World War: France and Holland were overrun and occupied, while Britain was debilitated economically and militarily. Equally important was the growth of democratic, anti-imperialist sentiment within the imperial countries themselves. Gone were the days when white men in the colonies confidently asserted, "We are here because we are superior." Now their presence was questioned, not only by their subjects but also by their own fellow countrymen. Mussolini's attack on Ethiopia in 1935 was widely regarded in Western Europe as a deplorable throwback, while the Anglo-French assault on the Suez in 1956 aroused vehement popular opposition in both Britain and France. The end of the West's global hegemony was due as much to the lack of will to rule as it was to lack of strength.

In addition, the colonial revolution was helped along by the fact that the two dominant postwar powers, the United States and the Soviet Union, were not interested in acquiring overseas possessions at the expense of their defeated enemies or their weakened allies. They did gain control, directly or indirectly, over strategic islands and satellite states in the Pacific Ocean and in Eastern Europe, but they did not follow the example of Britain and France who eagerly divided German and Turkish colonies following World War I. Instead, by a curious paradox, the opposite occurred: The colonials exploited the Cold War to play off the Soviet Union against the United States and to use both powers in winning their independence and in obtaining economic assistance.

The short-lived Japanese Empire in Asia also contributed substantially to the colonial revolution. Western military prestige was shattered by the ease with which the Japanese drove the British out of Malaya and Burma, the French out of Indochina, the Dutch out of Indonesia, and the Americans out of the Philippines. The political foundations of Western imperialism were undermined by Japanese propaganda based on the slogan "Asia for the Asians." When the Japanese were at last forced to surrender their conquests, they deliberately made the restoration of Western rule as difficult as possible by leaving arms with local nationalist organizations and by recognizing these organizations

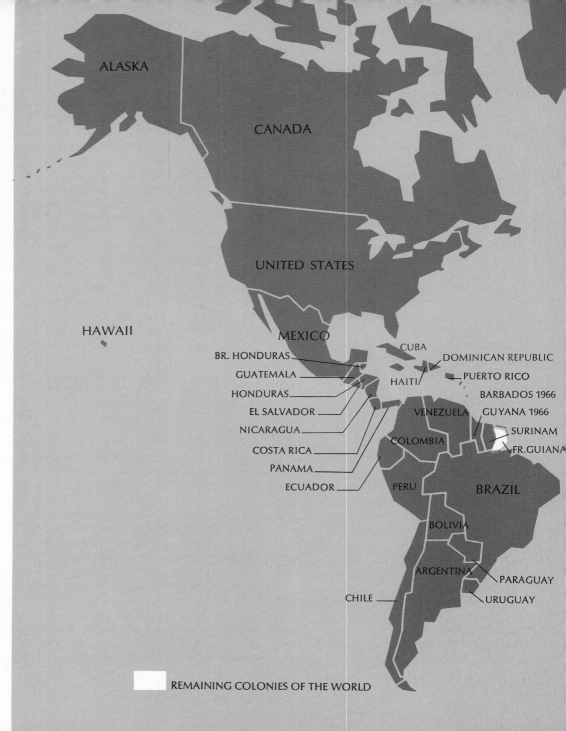

REMAINING COLONIES OF THE WORLD

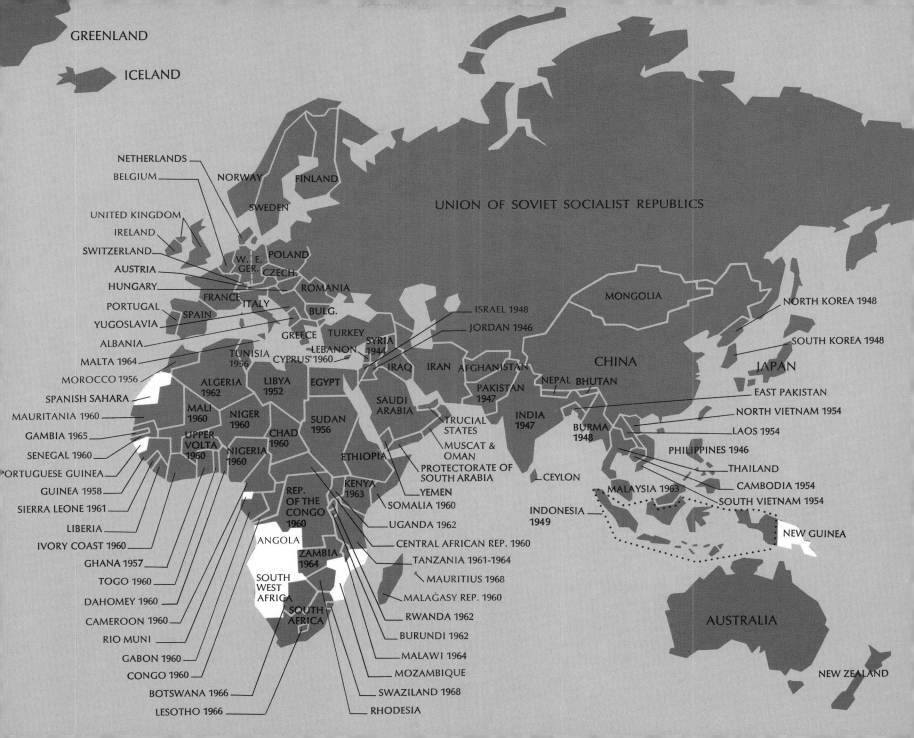

GREENLAND

ICELAND

NETHERLANDS
BELGIUM
NORWAY
FINLAND
SWEDEN

UNION OF SOVIET SOCIALIST REPUBLICS

UNITED KINGDOM
IRELAND
SWITZERLAND
AUSTRIA
HUNGARY
PORTUGAL
YUGOSLAVIA
ALBANIA
MALTA 1964
MOROCCO 1956
SPANISH SAHARA
MAURITANIA 1960
GAMBIA 1965
SENEGAL 1960
PORTUGUESE GUINEA
GUINEA 1958
SIERRA LEONE 1961
LIBERIA
IVORY COAST 1960
GHANA 1957
TOGO 1960
DAHOMEY 1960
CAMEROON 1960
RIO MUNI
GABON 1960
CONGO 1960
BOTSWANA 1966
LESOTHO 1966

W.   E.
GER.
CZECH.
POLAND
FRANCE
ITALY
SPAIN
ROMANIA
BULG.
GREECE
TURKEY
TUNISIA
1956
LEBANON
CYPRUS 1960
SYRIA
1944
ALGERIA
1962
LIBYA
1952
EGYPT
IRAQ
IRAN
AFGHANISTAN
ISRAEL 1948
JORDAN 1946
MONGOLIA

NORTH KOREA 1948
SOUTH KOREA 1948
JAPAN
CHINA

NEPAL BHUTAN
PAKISTAN
1947
INDIA
1947
EAST PAKISTAN
NORTH VIETNAM 1954
BURMA
1948
LAOS 1954
PHILIPPINES 1946
THAILAND
CAMBODIA 1954
SOUTH VIETNAM 1954

MALI
1960
NIGER
1960
CHAD
1960
SUDAN
1956
SAUDI
ARABIA
TRUCIAL
STATES
MUSCAT &
OMAN
PROTECTORATE OF
SOUTH ARABIA
YEMEN
CEYLON
MALAYSIA 1963

UPPER
VOLTA
1960
NIGERIA
1960
ETHIOPIA
KENYA
1963
SOMALIA 1960
UGANDA 1962
CENTRAL AFRICAN REP. 1960
TANZANIA 1961-1964
MAURITIUS 1968
INDONESIA
1949
NEW GUINEA

REP.
OF THE
CONGO
1960
ANGOLA
ZAMBIA
1964
SOUTH
WEST
AFRICA
SOUTH
AFRICA
MALAGASY REP. 1960
RWANDA 1962
BURUNDI 1962
MALAWI 1964
MOZAMBIQUE
SWAZILAND 1968
RHODESIA

AUSTRALIA

NEW ZEALAND

TABLE 1 AFRICAN-ASIAN MARCH TO INDEPENDENCE

	BECAME INDEPENDENT OF	YEAR	ESTIMATED POPULATION MID-1963 (MILLIONS)		BECAME INDEPENDENT OF	YEAR	ESTIMATED POPULATION MID-1963 (MILLIONS)
Syria	France	1944	5.0	Mali	France	1960	4.4
Lebanon	France	1944	1.8	Senegal	France	1960	3.0
Jordan	Britain	1946	1.8	Malagasy	France	1960	5.9
Philippines	United States	1946	30.6	Togo	France	1960	1.5
India	Britain	1947	461.3	Cyprus	Britain	1960	0.5
Pakistan	Britain	1947	98.6	Ivory Coast	France	1960	3.4
Burma	Britain	1948	22.8	Upper Volta	France	1960	4.5
N. Korea	Japan	1948	8.9	Niger	France	1960	3.1
S. Korea	Japan	1948	26.9	Dahomey	France	1960	2.2
Israel	Britain	1948	2.3	Congo Republic	France	1960	0.9
Ceylon	Britain	1948	10.8	Central African Republic	France	1960	1.3
Indonesia	Netherlands	1949	100.1	Chad	France	1960	2.8
Libya	Italy	1952	1.3	Gabon	France	1960	0.5
Cambodia	France	1954	5.9	Mauritania	France	1960	0.8
Laos	France	1954	2.0	Sierra Leone	Britain	1961	2.6
N. Vietnam	France	1954	17.0	Tanganyika**	Britain	1961	9.7
S. Vietnam	France	1954	15.5	Algeria	France	1962	12.0
Sudan	Britain-Egypt	1956	12.8	Burundi	Belgium	1962	2.6
Morocco	France	1956	12.6	Rwanda	Belgium	1962	2.9
Tunisia	France	1956	4.4	Uganda	Britain	1962	7.2
Ghana	Britain	1957	7.3	Kenya	Britain	1963	8.8
Malaya*	Britain	1957	7.6	Zanzibar**	Britain	1963	0.7
Guinea	France	1958	3.3	Malta	Britain	1964	0.3
Republic of the Congo	Belgium	1960	15.2	Malawi	Britain	1964	3.0
Somalia	Italy	1960	2.0	Zambia	Britain	1964	2.5
Nigeria	Britain	1960	37.2	Gambia	Britain	1965	0.3
Cameroon	France	1960	4.4	**TOTAL**			**1,006.8**

*Combined in 1963 with Singapore, Sarawak, and Sabah (British North Borneo), to form the state of Malaysia with a population of 10 million.

**Tanganyika and Zanzibar combined in 1964 to form the United Republic of Tanganyika and Zanzibar, or Tanzania.

as independent governments—as in the case of Ho Chi Minh's Viet Minh in Indochina, and Sukarno's Putera in Indonesia.

It should be noted, however, that the Africans who escaped Japanese invasion also won freedom along with the Asians, thus pointing up the fact that, important as the Japanese impact was, it merely intensified the great unrest and awakening that had been gathering momentum since the beginning of the century. The series of colonial uprisings following World War I reflected this burgeoning movement. . . . In the intervening years it had gained strength and purpose, with the growth of a Western-educated native intelligentsia. It was not accidental that the successful nationalist leaders were not unreconstructed Malayan sultans or Nigerian chiefs or Indian princes, but rather men who had studied in Western universities and observed Western institutions in operation—men like Gandhi, Nehru, Sukarno, Nkrumah, Azikwe, and Bourguiba.

This worldwide colonial awakening was further stimulated during World War II with the services of millions of colonials in both Allied and Japanese armies and labor battalions. Many Africans fought under the British, French, and Italian flags, while over two million Indians volunteered for the British forces, and an additional 40,000 Indian prisoners captured in Hong Kong, Singapore, and Burma signed up for the Japanese-sponsored Indian National army. When all these men returned to their homes, they inevitably regarded in a new light the local colonial officials and native leaders. The civilian populations were affected at this time, as during World War I, by the Allied propaganda regarding freedom and self-determination, as well as by the privation and suffering brought on by the war in certain regions. . . .

In one sense, the course of twentieth century history represented the decline of Europe. London, Paris, and Berlin no longer dominated world news. No longer did they control world empires. Their armies and navies and alliance systems had ceased to dominate the globe. In 1860, for example, Western Europe was responsible for 72 per cent of the world's total industrial output; by 1913 the percentage had dropped to 42; by the eve of World War II, to 30; and by 1960, to 25. It was self-evident that Europe's nineteenth century global hegemony had ended, and ended forever: there is no possibility of Europe's regaining her colonial empires or reestablishing her former military and political predominance. On the other hand, Europe

had not fallen from primacy to subservience, as had appeared likely to happen immediately following World War II. To the contrary, although Europe was suffering relative decline in her military, economic, and political power, her culture was sweeping the world as never before.

Europe was entering a period of triumph as well as decline: her ideas, techniques, and institutions were spreading throughout the globe more rapidly than at any time in the past. Fundamentally, this represented the diffusion of Europe's three great revolutions— the Industrial, the scientific, and the political— which earlier had given her the power, the drive, and the knowledge to expand all over the world and to conquer the great colonial empires. . . . But Europe's epochal success had boomeranged: for the colonial empires, by their very existence, facilitated the diffusion of the three revolutions. The subject peoples, profoundly affected by these revolutions, had reacted by selectively adopting some of their features in order better to resist the intruding West.

The Industrial Revolution spread in the nineteenth century from England to Europe and the United States, and in the first half of the twentieth century to Japan and the British Dominions. Following World War II, this diffusion accelerated rapidly. As each new country became independent, its first and foremost task was to promote economic development. All over the world a wide assortment of economic plans was being formulated and implemented, with varying degrees of success. . . .

Science also spread rapidly from Europe, and, indeed, has become the one body of knowledge that all peoples have been anxious to acquire. Its objective methodology has

made it acceptable to non-Western peoples who, by contrast, may not be interested in European art or religion or philosophy. Science has been eagerly sought after also because it constitutes the basis for advance in technology and general economic development. Thus, Europe has lost its monopoly on science; in the mid-sixties, more scientific work was being done in the United States and the Soviet Union than in any Western European country. By 1964, the United States had won 64 Nobel Prizes in science, as against 5 each for the closest competitors, Germany and Britain. The scientific revolution also has begun to make itself felt in non-Western countries, though the obstacles here have been formidable because of the interrelatedness of science and industry. While it is true that research in pure science can be undertaken independently of industry, the *development* of scientific discoveries depends upon a considerable industrial base. Even if a scientist has mastered the theory of breaking up the atom and has evolved a technical process for doing so, the production of atomic energy could only be undertaken by a society with large financial and industrial resources. Consequently, advanced scientific work is possible only in an advanced industrial country.

Many of the new Afro-Asian states have been trapped in this vicious circle, so that the most modest scientific progress has been virtually impossible in the poorer and least developed of the new countries. Others of them, however, have had the requisite material and human resources, and have utilized them to the utmost. This is especially true of the two giant states, India and China, which by 1964 had won one and two Nobel Prizes respectively in science. India began with the

At a construction site in India, poor women carry away baskets of earth. Mechanization has left many areas still untouched despite India's great strides in science and technology.

A contrasting view of the Indian economy shows the use of modern equipment in the construction of the Nagarjunasagar Dam.

strongest base in science, for the British had established certain technical institutes, and, more important, the industrial magnate Jamshedji Tata had founded the Indian Institute of Science in 1905. The scale of operations has been expanded since the winning of independence, so that Indian science has begun to make significant contributions in various fields. This is also true of China, where the government, like most Communist regimes, has allocated an extraordinary percentage of the national income to scientific research. In 1955 it adopted a Twelve Year Science Plan, calling for the graduation by 1967 of two million engineers and 10,500 scientists with doctoral degrees. The stated objective of China's Plan was to catch up with the world "in those branches of science and technology which are essential to our national economy. . . ."

Europe's third revolution, the political, also has been sweeping the entire globe. The most obvious manifestation of this political awakening has been the burgeoning nationalism expressed in the colonial revolutions and the end of empires. But nationalism has by no means been the only wind blowing from the West. A variety of other isms have been enveloping the globe, including constitutionalism, communism, socialism, and military authoritarianism. The first of these enjoyed a brief vogue with the wave of democratic enthusiasm immediately after World War II. In country after country, however, the parliamentary regimes succumbed to military dictatorships or to Marxist, one-party rule. This trend, it should be noted, also had ample precedent in Europe. With the exception of Czechoslovakia, every country in Central and Eastern Europe was by 1939 under one form or another of authoritarian government. . . . In both cases, corrupt and ineffective parliamentary systems together with the lack of the necessary economic and social foundations led to the imposition of dictatorial rule.

Despite the variety of institutional forms, all the new countries have had one common political characteristic: the gradual awakening and activization of the masses regardless of whether they were participating formally in their governments. This is the essence of the political revolution—the passing of the age-old concept of a divinely ordained division of humanity into rulers and ruled. In more general terms, it means replacing the isolation, ignorance, and acquiescence of traditionalism with the participation, knowledge, and initiative of modernism. . . .

A British-educated lawyer wears his court wig and robe. He is also the King of Akure, West Nigeria.

Two tribal chiefs in Ghana.

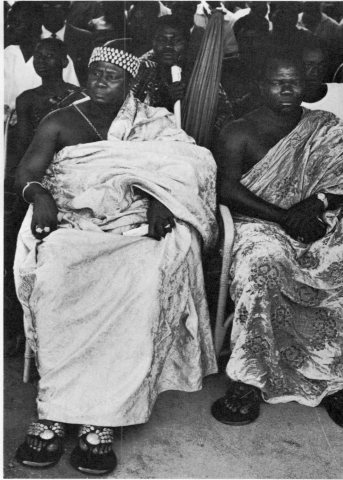

We may conclude that behind Europe's decline has been Europe's triumph. The one led naturally and inevitably to the other. If Europe has lost its place as the dominant force in the world, the basic reason has been the diffusion throughout the world of Europe's three great revolutions. Furthermore, this diffusion has continually been gaining in momentum, because for the first time it has affected the masses of the people. Until the twentieth century only an insignificant leisure class was participating in the process of westernization. Only this handful comprehended the meaning of the West from their knowledge of European languages and literatures, and their travels in European lands. In the postwar years, by contrast, a growing

A modern African city. Independence Avenue and traffic circle in Dar-Es-Salaam, Tanzania, East Africa. Cars drive on the left as in Great Britain.

proportion of the masses were being involved actively and consciously.

The explanation is to be found partly in the factories where they have found employment and the highways that have been ending their isolation. But equally important have been the new mass media of tabloids, radio, and movies which have overshadowed the old class media of books and travel. Westernization has gained its tremendous impetus by becoming dependent not on Oxford colleges and Paris salons, but on loudspeakers blaring out on illiterate yet responsive multitudes in village squares. New regimes and leaders have begun purposefully to exploit the mass media to the utmost in order to mobilize popular support for their revolutionary programs. "It is true," stated President Nasser, "that most of our people are still illiterate. But politically that counts far less than it did twenty years ago. . . . Radio has changed everything. . . . Today people in the most remote villages hear of what is happening everywhere and form their opinions. Leaders cannot govern as they once did. We live in a new world."

Nasser's "new world" now has been taking form all over the globe. This is evident in the following headlines from *The New York Times*—which could be multiplied indefinitely, for they appear daily in the world's press:

Students to Brush Up. Egypt to Give Toothbrush and Paste Free to Schools. (April, 1960)

Indonesia Fights Cha-Cha Culture. "Crazy" Music and Dances Assailed by Sukarno as "Subversive" Influence. (Feb. 1960)

Nudity Forbidden by Guinea Regime. Dresses of Young Women Now Cover Torso, as do Those of Ghanaians. (May 1959)

Folk Music is Fading in Kenya. Official's Research Shows Art Losing to Western Ways. (Nov. 1959)

Cairo TV Invaded by Cowboys and the Children Just Love It. But Parents Fret at Programs' Effect. (Nov. 1962)

Young Love vs. Japan's Old Code. Boy Now Has the Constitutional Right to Meet (and Get) Girl. (March 1958)

Industry Denting India's Folkways. Weakening Family and Caste Systems. (Jan. 1955)

Africans Evolve New Middle Class. Sons of Rural Tribesmen Run Businesses in Rhodesia—Some Achieve Wealth. (Aug. 1959)

The significance of these headlines becomes apparent if it is recalled that only a century ago virtually all Moslems looked down with contempt upon the infidel Christian world, convinced that nothing in that world could be worthy of their attention. In 1793, likewise, the emperor of China flatly refused to consider closer relations with England because "there is nothing we lack . . . we have never set much store on strange or ingenious objects. . . ." Today, by contrast, all people everywhere hanker not only for such "strange or ingenious objects," but also, as the headlines quoted above indicate, for

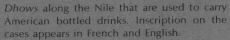

Dhows along the Nile that are used to carry American bottled drinks. Inscription on the cases appears in French and English.

Italian and American films with an international cast are billed on a wall in Cairo. A father and son in traditional dress glance at the signs in passing.

Kikuyu tribesmen inspect a British-made double-decker bus in Nairobi, Kenya.

African and Western dress appear in this Ghanaian street scene. Signs overhead advertise American soft drinks and a British automobile.

the other attributes of what is now commonly referred to as "civilization." This is indicative of the scope and depth of Europe's triumph, or, of what is commonly called the process of modernization. The latter term is preferable to *Europeanization* or *westernization* because the impulse for change, despite its ultimate European origins, may come today from the United States, or the Soviet Union, or even China, as well as from Europe.

Whatever term is used, the essential point is that societies everywhere are now being affected to a greater or lesser degree by this inexorable march of change. The question naturally arises whether the regional autonomy now developing in the political sphere will be nullified by a global homogenization process, as indicated by the headlines quoted above. Some maintain that homogenization will never become complete and all-embracing because of the residual effect of very different indigenous civilizations. It is pointed out that although industrialization is spreading rapidly, the social organization of a Japanese factory today differs basically from that of a Soviet or American factory. Likewise, modernization is proceeding apace in agriculture, but the organizational forms differ drastically from an American family farm to an Israeli kibbutz and to a Soviet state farm. . . .

It may be concluded that homogeneity indeed is taking place, though with regional variations reflecting the heterogeneity of cultural backgrounds. The global diffusion of Europe's three revolutions, though proceeding today under varying auspices, seems nevertheless to be creating at accelerating speed a world culture that will be uniform in basic characteristics, though diverse in detail.

Sukarno Urges That a New Asia and Africa Be Born (1955)

President Sukarno of Indonesia (1902–   ), who led the fight to liberate the peoples of the East Indies from Dutch rule, invited the leaders of the other Asian and African nations to a conference at Bandung in Indonesia in April 1955 to impress the reality of Asian-African solidarity upon the Western world. The interplay of Eastern and Western ideas are noticeable in his welcoming address to the delegates. From Republic of Indonesia, Ministry of Foreign Affairs, "Let a New Asia and a New Africa Be Born!" (Bandung, 1955). Reprinted from George M. Kahin: *The Asian-African Conference*. © 1956 by Cornell University. Used by permission of Cornell University Press.

Sisters and Brothers, how terrificly dynamic is our time! I recall that, several years ago, I had occasion to make a public analysis of colonialism, and that I then drew attention to what I called the "Life-line of imperialism." This line runs from the Straits of Gibraltar, through the Mediterranean, the Suez Canal, the Red Sea, the Indian Ocean, the South China Sea and the Sea of Japan. For most of that enormous distance, the territories on both sides of this life-line were colonies, the peoples were unfree, their futures mortgaged to an alien system. Along that life-line, that main artery of imperialism, there was pumped the life-blood of colonialism.

And today in this hall are gathered together the leaders of those same peoples. They are no longer the victims of colonialism. They are no longer the tools of others and the playthings of forces they cannot influence. Today, you are representatives of free peoples, peoples of a different stature and standing in the world.

Yes, there had indeed been a "Sturm über Asien"—and over Africa too. The last few years have seen enormous changes. Nations, States, have awoken from a sleep of centuries. The passive peoples have gone, the outward tranquility has made place for struggle and activity. Irresistible forces have swept the two continents. The mental, spiritual and political face of the whole world has been changed, and the process is still not complete. There are new conditions, new concepts, new problems, new ideals abroad in the world. Hurricanes of national awakening and reawakening have swept over the land, shaking it, changing it, changing it for the better.

This twentieth century has been a period of terrific dynamism. Perhaps the last fifty years have seen more developments and more material progress than the previous five hundred years. Man has learned to control many of the scourges which once threatened him. He has learned to consume distance. He has learned to project his voice and his picture across oceans and continents. He has probed deep into the secrets of nature and learned how to make the desert bloom and the plants of the earth increase their bounty. He has learned how to release the immense forces locked in the smallest particles of matter.

But has man's political skill marched hand-in-hand with his technical and scientific skill? Man can chain lightning to his command—can he control the society in which he lives? The answer is No! The political skill of man has been far outstripped by his technical skill, and what he has made he cannot be sure of controlling.

The result of this is fear. And man gasps for safety and morality.

Perhaps now more than at any other moment in the history of the world, society, government and statesmanship need to be based upon the highest code of morality and ethics. And in political terms, what is the highest code of morality? It is the subordination of everything to the well-being of mankind. But today we are faced with a situation where the well-being of mankind is not always the primary consideration. Many who are in places of high power think, rather, of controlling the world.

Yes, we are living in a world of fear. The life of man today is corroded and made bitter by fear. Fear of the future, fear of the hydrogen bomb, fear of ideologies. Perhaps this fear is a greater danger than the danger itself, because it is fear which drives men to act foolishly, to act thoughtlessly, to act dangerously.

In your deliberations, Sisters and Brothers, I beg of you, do not be guided by these fears, because fear is an acid which etches man's actions into curious patterns. Be guided by hopes and determination, be guided by ideals, and, yes, be guided by dreams!

We are of many different nations, we are of many different social backgrounds and cultural patterns. Our ways of life are different. Our national characters, or colours or motifs—call it what you will—are different. Our racial stock is different, and even the colour of our skin is different. But what does that matter? Mankind is united or divided by considerations other than these. Conflict comes not from variety of skins, nor from variety of religion, but from variety of desires.

All of us, I am certain, are united by more important things than those which superficially divide us. We are united, for instance, by a common detestation of colonialism in whatever form it appears. We are united by a common detestation of racialism. And we are united by a common determination to preserve and stabilise peace in the world. . . .

The battle against colonialism has been a long one, and do you know that today is a famous anniversary in that battle? On the eighteenth day of April, 1775, just one hundred and eighty years ago, Paul Revere rode at midnight through the New England countryside, warning of the approach of British troops and of the opening of the American War of Independence, the first successful anti-colonial war in history. About this midnight ride the poet Longfellow wrote:

A cry of defiance and not of fear,
A voice in the darkness, a knock at the door,
And a word that shall echo for evermore. . . .

Yes, it shall echo for evermore, just as the other anti-colonial words which gave us comfort and reassurance during the darkest days of our struggle shall echo for evermore. But remember, that battle which began 180 years ago is not yet completely won, and it will not have been completely won until we can survey this our own world, and can say that colonialism is dead. . . .

Not so very long ago we argued that peace was necessary for us because an outbreak of fighting in our part of the world would imperil our precious independence, so recently won at such great cost.

Today, the picture is more black. War would not only mean a threat to our independence, it may mean the end of civilization and even of human life. There is a force loose in the world whose potentiality for evil no man truly knows. Even in practice and rehearsal for war the effects may well be building up into something of unknown horror.

Not so long ago it was possible to take some little comfort from the idea that the clash, if it came, could perhaps be settled by what were called "conventional weapons"—bombs, tanks, cannon and men. Today that little grain of comfort is denied us, for it has been made clear that the weapons of ultimate horror will certainly be used, and the military planning of nations is on that basis. The unconventional has become the conventional, and who knows what other examples of misguided and diabolical scientific skill have been discovered as a plague on humanity.

And do not think that the oceans and the seas will protect us. The food that we eat, the water that we drink, yes, even the very air that we breathe can be contaminated by poisons originating from thousands of miles away. And it could be that, even if we ourselves escaped lightly, the unborn generations of our children would bear on their distorted bodies the marks of our failure to control the forces which have been released on the world.

No task is more urgent than that of preserving peace. Without peace our independence means little. The rehabilitation and upbuilding of our countries will have little meaning. Our revolutions will not be allowed to run their course.

What can we do? The peoples of Asia and Africa wield little physical power. Even their economic strength is dispersed and slight. We cannot indulge in power politics. Diplomacy for us is not a matter of the big stick. Our statesmen, by and large, are not backed up with serried ranks of jet bombers.

What can we do? We can do much! We can inject the voice of reason into world affairs. We can mobilise all the spiritual, all the moral, all the political strength of Asia and Africa on the side of peace. Yes, we! We, the peoples of Asia and Africa, 1,400,000,000 strong, far more than half the human population of the world, we can mobilise what I have called the *Moral Violence of Nations* in favour of peace. We can demonstrate to the minority of the world which lives on the other continents that we, the majority, are for peace, not for war, and that whatever strength we have will always be thrown on to the side of peace. . . .

So, let this Asian-African Conference be a great success! Make the "Live and let live" principle and the "Unity in Diversity" motto the unifying force which brings us all together—to seek in friendly, uninhibited discussion, ways and means by which each of us can live his own life, and let others live

Asian masses at Anantnag, Kashmir, waiting for a festival to begin.

their own lives, in their own way, in harmony, and in peace.

If we succeed in doing so, the effect of it for the freedom, independence and welfare of man will be great on the world at large. The Light of Understanding has again been lit, the Pillar of Cooperation again erected. The likelihood of success of this Conference is proved already by the very presence of you all here today. It is for us to give it strength, to give it the power of inspiration—to spread its message all over the World. . . .

Relatively speaking, all of us gathered here today are neighbours. Almost all of us have ties of common experience, the experience of colonialism. Many of us have a common religion. Many of us have common cultural roots. Many of us, the so-called "underdeveloped" nations, have more or less similar economic problems, so that each can profit from the others' experience and help. And I think I may say that we all hold dear the ideals of national independence and freedom. Yes, we have so much in common. And yet we know so little of each other. . . .

Let us not be bitter about the past, but let us keep our eyes firmly on the future. Let us remember that no blessing of God is so sweet as life and liberty. Let us remember that the stature of all mankind is diminished so long as nations or parts of nations are still unfree. Let us remember that the highest purpose of man is the liberation of man from his bonds of fear, his bonds of human degradation, his bonds of poverty—the liberation of man from the physical, spiritual and intellectual bonds which have for too long stunted the development of humanity's majority.

And let us remember, Sisters and Brothers, that for the sake of all that, we Asians and Africans must be united.

B. K. Nehru: History Points to a Remedy for World Discontent (1961)

Braj Kumar Nehru (1909–   ) was educated at Oxford and the London School of Economics and had a long career as an Indian civil servant and diplomatic official before becoming Indian Ambassador to the United States in 1961. Appointed Commissioner General for Economic Affairs in 1958, he gained the reputation as India's greatest fundraiser, obtaining in the next three years billions of dollars in international loans to implement India's Five Year Plan for economic progress. The fruit of his experience is distilled in the following article. From *The New York Times Magazine,* April 16, 1961, pp. 22, 116–117. © 1961 by the New York Times Company. Reprinted by permission.

. . . Complex and bewildering as the crises of our times appear to us, however, they are not without a parallel in human history—and comparatively recent history at that. And the gratifying part about the historical experience I have in mind is that it points to the only permanent remedy for our present-day ferment of discontent.

I venture to suggest that the violent upheavals in many parts of the world today are but an international version of the conflicts that raged within the nation-states of Europe in the eighteenth and nineteenth centuries. If the nation-states of Europe have not collapsed under the pressure of internal conflicts, among different classes, but have emerged instead as dynamic and harmonious societies, it is as a result of certain definite policies adopted to bridge the difference between group and group. It is precisely the kind of measures which saved the nations of Europe from erosion from within that are required today, on an international level, for the preservation and strengthening of international society.

The American people have long considered, and rightly, that their own revolution found a natural echo in many lands for many years to come. "The shot heard round the world" was followed a few years later by the storming of the Bastille. For a hundred years thereafter and more the states of Europe, when they were not at war with each other, were engaged in dealing with revolution at home, opposing to it sometimes the organized force of the state, and attempting at other times to deal in a more sophisticated manner with the causes of the revolutionary outbreaks from which they suffered.

Why was it that the people of France revolted in 1789? Why were there revolutions, uprisings, and widespread national unrest in 1830 and in 1848 in France, Germany, Italy, Austria, Hungary and Poland? Why was even the mature and stable society of Great Britain rocked to its foundations by popular agitation? What was the genesis of Nihilism in Russia, the St. Petersburg uprising in 1905, the bread riots which followed, and, finally, the holocaust of the October Revolution?

The human race is not prone to indulge in disorder for its own sake; if there is a history of continuous disorder, it is obvious that the people occupied with it lack something which they regard as more valuable than the maintenance of the regime, of the law under which they live. All the European revolutions, and the disorders which did not reach the stage of revolutionary violence, can be traced to the frustration of two of the most fundamental desires of man: the desire for liberty and the desire for bread.

The European system of the time concentrated political power in the hands of a hereditary monarchy tempered sometimes by a hereditary nobility. As almost invariably happens, this political power was exercised for the benefit of those who wielded it, while those outside the pale suffered the consequences. One of the consequences was an extreme inequality in the distribution of wealth; so much so that in countries not lacking in production there were large segments in society which could not earn enough to live a life that could by any standards be regarded as human.

The system was unjust; but it had prevailed with little change for centuries. Why was it that at this particular period of history large masses of people in Europe became so dissatisfied with it that they were willing to shatter to bits old institutions hallowed by tradition at great material cost to themselves?

There was, of course, the force of ideas, for it is ideas that guide the action of those who wield the arms. The philosophers and the men of the Age of Reason had preached the virtues of liberty and equality. And it was these ideas, born of the meditations of secluded philosophers, that filtered down ultimately to the illiterate and "swinish multitude," "the great unwashed," and made them resolve to rebuild the system under which they lived.

But the intellectual acceptance of ideas does not provide a sufficient motive force for those great earthquakes of humanity which are known as revolutions. Nor does emptiness of the human stomach—a very powerful force indeed—explain why revolutionary forces erupted at the time they did in Europe. The poor had, of course, always been poor since the dawn of history. But the poor had been in good company for, apart from a very small handful of those who lived somewhat better, the entire mass of humanity had been poor.

It was during the late eighteenth and nineteenth centuries, when the winds of technical change began to sweep across Europe, that this began to be no longer true. The wealth created by trade and commerce, and later by the Industrial Revolution, had been substantial. The rich had become very much richer and were using their wealth for luxury and ostentation and display. The poor had had no benefit at all from this accumulation of wealth to the nation; they were as poor as they ever had been before, if not, on occasion, poorer. And it was this new spectacle of poverty in the midst of plenty and the growing realization that poverty was no longer inevitable that essentially sparked the revolutions of the time.

The remarkable thing about the nation-states of Western Europe, however, is that despite the trials and tribulations to which they were subject throughout the nineteenth century, and contrary to the dire prophesies of Karl Marx, they have managed to survive. And they have survived not as weak and feeble organisms, but as vital, dynamic, growing societies, integrated within themselves. What was it that effected this change?

What effected this change was that the nation-state took steps to see throughout the nineteenth century that the causes of discontent were removed. Political power was gradually transferred from those who held a monopoly of it to the entire mass of the adult population. Economic inequality was reduced so that the benefits of the new productive powers which humanity had discovered were not restricted to any one group but were shared by the community as a whole. Combinations of working men were permitted in order that the bargaining power of the poor should be increased.

Laws regulating factories insured that those working in them were not reduced to the level of animals. Acts governing education insured that the children of the poor, not only those of the rich, were given access to knowledge. Medical care was continuously made cheaper and more easily accessible.

In essence, all these reforms meant a reduction in the inequality of real incomes. And the great over-all instrument which enabled all these reforms to be financed was the progressive income tax.

It is the policy of all nation-states today, whether they are governed by parties of the Right or by those of the Left, to insure that there are transferences of wealth from the rich to the poor; not only from rich individuals to poor individuals, but also from the richer areas within the community to the poorer areas within that same community. With growing evidence of sufficiency for all and the development of a sense of responsibility on the part of those who have more, the discontents of yesterday and the scars of hurt pride they produced have all but disappeared.

Few people in the nineteenth century could have analyzed clearly the basic causes of the discontents of their times. To them the times were merely out of joint. It is only the hindsight of history that enables us to get a glimpse of what really was then happening.

Equally understandably, the basic causes responsible for the turmoil in the international world today are not always apparent to those who are living through them. But if we look around today at conditions in the world, can we really escape the conclusion that much of the contemporary stresses and strains in international society are the exact counterparts of the stresses and strains with which the nation-states of the nineteenth century were faced?

At the same time, are not the methods of restoring stability to, and of strengthening, international society today exactly those which were applied during the nineteenth century within the nation-state? The difference, of course, is that whereas the discontent within the nation-state was that of individuals, the discontents within international society are those of nations.

I said earlier that the two fundamental causes of the revolutions and disorders of the nineteenth century were the desire for liberty and the desire for bread. Internationally, the twentieth century started off with an equilibrium which though manifestly unjust, seemed so stable as to be able to endure for eternity.

The colonial system which had deprived the majority of the human race of political liberty caused, by the very act of that deprivation, a great intensification of the desire for liberty. One consequence of that deprivation of liberty was the growth of nationalism, for nationalism never develops so fast nor grows so strongly as in opposition to an alien power.

The rationalist movements of Asia and Africa were a constant threat to the maintenance of the status quo in the earlier half of this century. The demand for freedom could, at last, no longer be resisted and the internal strength which the colonies developed, together with changes in the ideas of the majority of the colonial powers themselves, has led to the rapid liquidation of colonial empires since the end of the last world war.

While the desire for liberty is thus in the process of being satisfied, the desire for bread is not. There are, internationally speaking, the same inequalities of wealth between nations that were prevalent between individuals within the nation-states of the nineteenth century. Also, as happened in those states before they took themselves in hand, these inequalities are growing.

The average per capita income of the developed parts of the world (Europe, North America, Australia and Japan) is $1,200 per annum. The same figure for the under-developed world is $125 per annum. These averages conceal the true contrast, which is better illustrated by comparing the two ends of the scale.

At one end is the United States, with a per capita income of $2,700 per annum; near the other end of the scale is India, with one-third of the population of the non-Communist under-developed world, with a per capita income of $70 per annum. The existing discrepancies are so great that even if the under-developed societies develop at a much faster rate than the developed ones the difference between them would still continue to grow.

A 3 per cent rate of growth in the American economy would increase per capita incomes by $81 per annum—the increase being more than the total income of the Indian. An increase at the presently unimaginable rate of 10 per cent would increase the Indian income by only $7 per annum, so that at the end of twelve months the difference between the American's income and the Indian's income would be even greater than it is today.

The people in the under-developed world are not content with this situation any more than the under-privileged European in the nineteenth century was with his. Once again, poverty is nothing new and its continuance would not have aroused discontent had it continued to be regarded as inevitable. But, like the have-not rioters of Paris or the have-not Chartists of England, the have-not nations of the world see today that poverty is not the will of God and that there are nations in which it has been removed by the hand of man.

Unfortunately, the analogy between the nation-state of the nineteenth century and international society today breaks down in one vital respect. In the case of the nation-state, the gradual spread of political power among the masses of the people, combined with the growing accumulation of capital and technical know-how within the nation-state

THE GROWTH OF WORLD POPULATION (*in millions*)

	1800	1850	1900	1950	2000 (est)
Europe	187	266	401	559	1000
N. America	16	39	106	217	330
S. America	9	20	38	111	650
Asia	602	749	937	1302	4300
Africa	90	95	120	198	660
Oceania	2	2	6	13	30
Total	906	1171	1608	2400	6970

itself, provided the natural means for eradicating the contrast between the "haves" and the "have-nots."

In the case of the international society of today, however, the achievement of political independence among the "have-nots" provides no automatic means of harnessing the growing wealth of the "haves" for the betterment of the "have-nots."

The great reforms within the nation-state of the nineteenth century consisted in essence in raising the standard of living of the mass of the citizenry by taking a part of the annual growth in the already large incomes of the rich and devoting it, through public expenditures, to ends which helped the under-privileged to increase their incomes.

In international society today there is no such mechanism. The United Nations is very far from a world government. The means through which it operates are not the organized force of the state, but moral persuasion. It cannot abolish colonialism by force, as slavery was abolished by force. It cannot tax rich nations for the benefit of poor nations, as the nation-state taxed the rich for the benefit of the poor.

And yet it would appear to me that what is required today is . . . to fashion ways and means which would enable the have-not nations to share in the prosperity that is technically available to the whole human race. . . .

The factors restricting the growth of the economies of the under-developed countries—or in other words, the factors which keep them poor—are many and they vary from country to country. For the removal of some, no help can come from the outside. People must by themselves develop the strength to face the sacrifices necessary for economic development and must by themselves learn how to organize so that they can work together for the attainment of their national aspirations. What can be supplied from the outside is technical assistance—in its widest sense—and development capital.

There are societies which require teachers, doctors, administrators, lawyers and the like. The outside world can surely provide the means by which personnel of this kind can be trained in large numbers. There are others which are short of technicians in certain branches of industrial or agricultural practice; these can be supplied from abroad. But what all under-developed countries are short of is developmental capital—a poor society, like a poor man, cannot save enough and, therefore, invest enough, to enable its income to grow at a rapid enough rate.

Many of the under-developed countries are at a stage of development where large amounts of capital cannot be usefully absorbed; in those countries conditions have first to be created which will enable investment to be usefully carried out. There are, however, some countries which have reached a stage where the only shortage is that of capital; and the absolute amounts required are so large and in such fields that they are wholly beyond the capabilities of the private investor to supply.

It is for this reason that government-to-government and international programs of foreign aid have come into being. No firm estimates have ever been really made as to what it would cost either the developed or the under-developed world to pursue a program of rapid economic development in the under-developed countries. But the general consensus seems to be that the figure involved for external aid is somewhere around $7 billion a year, matched by several times this amount from the under-developed world itself. . . .

The U.N. General Assembly at its last session adopted a resolution recommending that there should be a transfer of capital from the developed countries to the under-developed equal to 1 per cent of the national income of the former. It would appear that the Kennedy administration is in sympathy with this proposal, for there are welcome indications that it wishes to urge that the burden of financing the external needs of the under-developed world should be shared by the richer countries on some such basis.

The essence of the argument that I have endeavored to develop is that the roots of the threat with which national societies were faced in the nineteenth century lay in the maldistribution of political power and economic well-being; that the roots of the present international discontents are exactly the same, except that the maldistribution is between nations and not individuals; that the nation-states stabilized themselves by correcting this maldistribution, first through broadening the base of political power, and next through using the authority of government to reduce inequalities of income; that international society should endeavor to achieve the same ends by ending colonialism as soon as practicable and transferring wealth to the poorer nations; that the sacrifices involved in the task are by no means great; but that, whereas in the case of national governments this was done compulsorily, in the case of international society this will have to be done on a voluntary basis, since we do not as yet have a government of the world.

India's March to Independence

The passage of the Independence Act on August 15, 1947 brought to a close almost two centuries of British rule in India. Recognizing that her material resources had been greatly diminished in the World War II and faced by continuing rioting in India, the British were persuaded that an end to empire offered the best assurance of internal peace in India and the clearest protection for Britain's own commercial interests.

The Indian National Congress, founded in 1885, played a critical role in the move to independence. Its leadership in the early years, strongly influenced by Western ideas of government, nationhood and education, sought autonomy within the framework of the British Empire. Radical nationalists first emerged openly at the Congress session in 1905, demanding that India's government be "autonomous and absolutely free of British control." For its part, the British government, compelled to draw heavily on Indian resources during World War I, responded to the demand for self-government by a commitment to "the progressive realization of responsible government in India as an integral part of the British Empire."

Discontented with the pace of reform, Mohandas K. Gandhi (1869–1948), called Mahatma, or Holy Man, by his followers, took over the leadership of the Congress in 1920. He brought to it his successful experience with non-violent non-cooperation and civil disobedience gained in defending the rights of Indians in South Africa, where he had long lived, and after his return to his homeland

Civil disobedience on the eve of independence (1945–1946). A scene from the film *Bhowani Junction* (1956).

Pandit Nehru at Harrow, where he was sent at 15 to pursue his education in the company of Britain's future elites. From Harrow he went to Trinity College, Cambridge where he majored in the natural sciences.

Nehru and Gandhi at a meeting of the All-India Conference Committee in Bombay on July 8, 1940, where a campaign of civil disobedience was launched. Both men were arrested shortly afterwards.

Prime Minister Indira Gandhi campaigns amongst villagers in the spring of 1971.

in 1914, the interests of mill-hands and plantation laborers in India. In the 1920s and 1930s Gandhi repeatedly put non-cooperation into action and frequently landed in jail. The policy of passive resistance gave way in 1940 to a call for "individual civil disobedience" and two years later to a massive and popular "quit India" movement.

As the reality of independence neared, Gandhi, committed spiritually to nonviolence, tried to reduce tension between the Hindus and large Moslem minority. His personal intervention in the civil disturbances between the hostile religious groups eventually cost him his life. Gandhi was assassinated in 1948 by Hindu extremists; India had previously been divided into a separate Moslem Pakistan and a secular (but largely Hindu) India.

Pandit Jawaharlal Nehru, who had worked closely with the Mahatma since the end of World War I, became the first prime minister (1948–1964) of an independent India and quickly gained prestige for his country by his programs of social development and ardent internationalism. Two years after his death, his daughter Srimati Indira Gandhi succeeded him in office.

India's march to independence was concerned, however, with more than political freedom. The accelerating needs of her hungry millions, still predominantly part of a traditional society, demanded a crash program of economic development. Technical know-how had to be built up, capital acquired, industry constructed. India had to catch up with the developed world to avoid catastrophe. The accompanying illustrations attempt to provide an overview of India's route toward self-realization.

Power lines pass overhead as young Indians walk along a muddy path. Rural electrification proceeds slowly in a country covering more than one million square miles.

(Bottom) Despite the availability of motorized transport, nine men prove the least expensive way to move this piano in the city of Calcutta.

Women wash clothing in a traditional pattern opposite the Bokaro power station and dam on the bank of the Konar River. The project of which this is part includes seven multi-purpose dams, each with an attached power station, designed to provide flood control, power generation, and irrigation with navigation.

STUDY QUESTIONS

1. What, according to Brugmans, is the central component of Western civilization? How did he evaluate the Western role in the world?

2. What conclusions would you draw from the table "African-Asian March to Independence"? What explains the rapid success of the postwar colonial revolution? How did the war affect the movement to independence?

3. What was the effect on the world of the Western industrial, scientific, and political revolutions? Why does the author of Reading 250 write of both the "decline" and the "triumph" of the West?

4. What are the advantages and disadvantages of modernization (Westernization) on a world scale?

5. What are the aspirations of the non-Western world? To what degree are they Western in source? What are the limitations of a broad concept such as the "non-West"?

6. What problems, according to Sukarno, are faced by the non-Western world? To what extent are they common to all men? What did Sukarno propose that the men invited to Bandung do about their problems?

7. Evaluate Nehru's analogy between the way Western problems of modernization were "solved" and how those of contemporary non-Western society should be attacked. Do you agree that inequities of income are among the most serious problems faced by the world today? How likely is it that Nehru's proposal will be adopted?

Kenneth Boulding: The Great Transition

TOPIC 49

TOWARD THE YEAR 2000

The present is fraught with both promise and peril. The advances of Western science and technology have brought the prospect of longer life, better health, and greater security and prosperity to the developing nations of the world. At the same time the advanced industrial powers, earlier beneficiaries of the evolution of the West, sense themselves at a new threshold, enjoying a control over their environment never before known in human history. Achievement of the mastery of nature and of the just ordering of society that has long been sought by Western thought is threatened, however, by the persistence of lurking disaster. Burgeoning population, intensified power of destruction, human aggressiveness and acquisitiveness, and the limits of man's rationality and ability to plan, all menace the world he has created. The readings deal with some of contemporary man's major problems and pose the question whether the greatest obstacle to the evolution of mankind and to the progress of world civilization may not lie in the use man chooses to make of his knowledge and resources.

Professor Kenneth E. Boulding (1910–   ), economic theorist and author of several books concerned with economic change and society, is a provocative spokesman for the belief that the contemporary world is in the midst of a sweeping transition between what we call civilization and an even more developed society. This fully industrialized society, "postcivilization" as Boulding terms it, organically follows civilization as civilization itself grew out of precivilization. Such major shifts in the history of mankind, he attributes to changes in human knowledge. In this reading the author considers the directions the transition may take and postulates possible traps that may rob it of its potential. Abridgement of pp. 1–2, 5–9, 21–26, *The Meaning of the Twentieth Century* by Kenneth E. Boulding. Copyright © 1964 by Kenneth Ewart Boulding. By permission of Harper & Row, Publishers.

The twentieth century marks the middle period of a great transition in the state of the human race. It may properly be called the second great transition in the history of mankind.

The first transition was that from precivilized to civilized society which began to take place about five thousand years ago. This is a transition that is still going on in some parts of the world, although it can be regarded as almost complete. Precivilized society can now be found only in small and rapidly diminishing pockets in remote areas. It is doubtful whether more than 5 per cent of the world's population could now be classified as living in a genuinely precivilized society.

Even as the first great transition is approaching completion, however, a second great transition is treading on its heels. It may be called the transition from civilized to post-civilized society. We are so accustomed to giving the word civilization a favorable over-tone that the words postcivilized or postcivilization may strike us as implying something unfavorable. If, therefore, the word techno-logical or the term developed society is pre-ferred I would have no objection. The word postcivilized, however, does bring out the fact that civilization is an intermediate state of man dividing the million or so years of pre-civilized society from an equally long or longer period which we may expect to extend into the future postcivilization. . . .

The origins of the second great transition are perhaps not so obscure as the origins of the first but there are many puzzling and unresolved questions connected with them. All through the history of civilization, indeed, one can detect a slowly rising stream of knowledge and organization that has a differ-ent quality from that of the civilized society around it. The astronomy of Babylonia, the geometry of the Greeks, and the algebra of the Arabs represent as it were foretastes of the great flood of knowledge and techno-logical change to come. Some of the ancient empires, even the Roman Empire, seem to have been technologically stagnant and scien-tifically backward. If one is looking for the beginning of a continuous process of scien-tific and technological development this might be traced to the monastic movement in the West of the sixth century A.D., espe-cially the Benedictines. Here for almost the first time in history we had intellectuals who worked with their hands, and who belonged to a religion which regarded the physical world as in some sense sacred and capable of enshrining goodness. It is not surprising therefore that an interest in the economizing of labor and in extending its productive pow-ers began in the monasteries, however slowly. From the sixth century on we can trace a slowly expanding technology. The water wheel comes in the sixth century, the stirrup in the eighth, the horse collar and the rudder in the ninth, the windmill in the twelfth, and so on. For Europe the invention of printing in the fifteenth century represents an irre-versible take-off, because from this point on the dissemination of information increased with great rapidity. The seventeenth century saw the beginning of science, the eighteenth century an acceleration of technological change so great that it has been called, per-haps misleadingly, the Industrial Revolution. The nineteenth century saw the development of science as an ongoing social organization, and the twentieth century has seen research and development heavily institutionalized with an enormous increase in the rate of change both of knowledge and of technology as a result. It must be emphasized that the rate of change still seems to be accelerating. We may not even have reached the middle of whatever process we are passing through, and there are certainly no signs that the rate of change is slowing down. It seems clear for instance that we are now on the edge of a biological revolution which may have results for mankind just as dramatic as the nuclear revolution of a generation ago.

A few symptoms will indicate the magni-tude of the change through which we are now passing. Consider for instance the posi-tion of agriculture in the most developed societies today. In all societies of classical civilization, as we have seen, at least 75 per cent of the population, and often a larger percentage, were engaged in agriculture and would merely produce enough to support themselves and the remaining urban 25 per cent. Even in the United States at the time of the American Revolution, it has been esti-mated that about 90 per cent of the people were in agriculture. Today in the United States only about 10 per cent of the population are so engaged, and if present trends continue it will not be long before we can produce all the food that we need with 5 per cent, or even less, of the population. This is be-cause with modern techniques, a single farmer and his family can produce enough food to feed ten, twenty, or even thirty fami-lies. This releases more than 90 per cent of the population to work on other things, and to produce automobiles, houses, clothing, all the luxuries and conveniences of life as well as missiles and nuclear weapons.

Another indication of the magnitude of the present transition is the fact that, as far as many statistical series related to activities of mankind are concerned, the date that divides human history into two equal parts is well within living memory. For the volume and number of chemical publications, for in-stance, this date is now (*i.e.* 1964) about 1950. For many statistical series of quantities of metal or other materials extracted, this date is about 1910. That is, man took about as much out of mines before 1910 as he did after 1910. Another startling fact is that about 25 per cent of the human beings who have ever lived are now alive, and what is even more astonishing, something like 90 per cent of all the scientists who have ever lived are now alive. My eight-year-old son asked me the other day, "Daddy, were you born in the olden days?" It is the sort of question that makes a parent feel suddenly middle-aged. There is perhaps more truth in his remark than he knew. In a very real sense the changes in the state of mankind since the date of my birth have been greater than the changes that took place in many thousands of years before this date.

Another indication of the magnitude of the transition is the extraordinary ability of modern societies to recover from disaster. In 1945, for instance, many of the cities of Germany and Japan lay in almost total ruin. Today it is hard to tell that they were ever destroyed, for they have been completely rebuilt in a space of less than twenty years. It took Western Europe almost three hundred years to recover from the fall of the Roman Empire, and it took Germany decades to recover from the Thirty Years War (1618–1648). It is perhaps an optimistic feature of the present time that as well as great powers of destruction, we also have greatly increased powers of recuperation and recovery.

The great transition is not only something that takes place in science, technology, the physical machinery of society, and in the utilization of physical energy. It is also a transition in social institutions. Changes in technology produce change in social institutions, and changes in institutions produce change in technology. In the enormously complex world of social interrelations we cannot say in any simple way that one change produces the other, only that they are enormously interrelated and both aspects of human life change together. . . .

The great question as to whether the transition from civilization to postcivilization is a "good" change is one that cannot be an-swered completely until we know the nature and quality of different postcivilized societies. We might well argue in contemplating the first great transition from precivilized to civilized societies that in many cases this was a transition from a better state of man to a worse. As we contemplate the innumerable wars of civilized societies, as we contemplate the hideous religion of human sacrifice and the bloody backs of innumerable slaves on which the great monuments of civilization have been built, it is sometimes hard to refrain from a certain romantic nostalgia for the "noble savage." Indeed, the *philosophes* of the eighteenth century indulged in this feeling at great length. Anthropologists have somewhat dispelled the romantic view of precivilized society, which was in many cases not only poor but cruel and disagreeable beyond even the excesses of civilization. Nevertheless it will not be difficult to contrast the best of precivilized societies and the worst of civilized societies and come out much in favor of the precivilized. Similarly a type of postcivilized society is possible as portrayed, for instance, in the anti-Utopias of George Orwell, and Aldous Huxley in the middle of the twentieth century, in which the quality of human life and the dignity of man seem to be much inferior to that in the best of civilized societies.

There is clearly here a problem to be solved. We do not make men automatically good and virtuous by making them rich and powerful; indeed the truth frequently seems to be the opposite. Nevertheless we must not fall into the other trap of equating innocence with ignorance or of thinking that impotence is the same thing as virtue. An increase in power increases the potential both for good and for evil. A postcivilized society of unshakable tyranny, resting upon all the knowledge which we are going to gain in social sciences, and of unspeakable corruption resting on man's enormous power over nature, especially biological nature, is by no means inconceivable. On the other hand the techniques of postcivilization also offer us the possibility of a society in which the major sources of human misery have been eliminated, a society in which there will be no war, poverty, or disease, and in which a large majority of human beings will be able to live out their lives in relative freedom from most of the ills which now oppress a major part of mankind. This is a prize worth driving for even at the risk of tyranny and corruption. There is no real virtue in impotence, and the virtue to strive for is surely the combination of power with goodness.

In any case there is probably no way back. The growth of knowledge is one of the most irreversible forces known to mankind. It takes a catastrophe of very large dimensions to diminish the total stock of knowledge in the possession of man. Even in the rise and fall of great civilizations surprisingly little has been permanently lost, and much that was lost for a short time was easily regained. Hence there is no hope for ignorance or for a morality based on it. Once we have tasted the fruit of the tree of knowledge, as the Biblical story illustrates so well, Eden is closed to us. We cannot go back to our own childhood without disaster. Eden has been lost to us forever and an angel with a flaming sword stands guard at its gates. Therefore either we must wander hopelessly in the world or we must press forward to Zion. We must learn to master ourselves as we are learning to master nature. There is no reason in the nature of things which says that ethical development is impossible, and indeed one would expect that the process of development, whether economic, political, or social, will go hand in hand with a similar process of ethical development which will enable us to use wisely the power that we have gained. This ethical development may take forms which will seem strange to us now, but just as we can trace development in the values and ethical standards of mankind as his economic and physical powers increased from precivilized society, so it is reasonable that new ethical standards will arise appropriate to the new technology of postcivilization.

We must emphasize that there is no inevitability and no determination in making this great transition. As we shall see in subsequent chapters, there are a number of traps which lie along the way and which may either prevent man and his planet earth from making the transition altogether or delay it for many generations or even thousands of years. The first most obvious and immediate trap is the war trap. It is now theoretically possible for man to build a device which will eliminate all life from the earth. Even if this extreme event is highly improbable, less extreme disasters are at least within a range of probability that makes them a matter of serious concern. A major nuclear war would unquestionably set back the transition to a postcivilized world by many generations, and it might indeed eliminate the possibility of making this transition altogether. The effect of such war on the whole ecological system of the planet is so unpredictable that we cannot tell how large a disaster it will be, although we know it will be very large. It is possible that such a disaster will be irretrievable. It is also possible that even if we had a retrievable disaster we might not learn enough from it to retrieve ourselves. It is clear that what is desperately needed at the present time is to diminish the probability of such a disaster to the vanishing point.

Another possible trap which might delay the attainment of the transition for a long time is the population trap. This is perhaps the main reason for believing that the impact of a few postcivilized techniques on existing civilized societies might easily be disastrous in the next hundred years or so. One of the first impacts of postcivilized medicine and medical knowledge on civilized society is a large and immediate reduction in the death rate, especially in infant mortality. This is seldom if ever accompanied by a similar decrease in birth rate, and hence the first impact of postcivilized techniques on a previously stable civilized society is a tremendous upsurge in the rate of population increase. This increase may be so large that the society is incapable of adapting itself to it, and incapable in particular of devoting sufficient resources to the education of its unusually large cohorts of young people. We therefore have the tragic situation that the alleviation of much human misery and suffering in the short run may result in enormous insoluble problems in a longer period.

A third possible trap is the technological trap itself: that we may not be able to develop a genuinely stable high-level technology which is independent of exhaustible resources. Technology at the present time, even the highest technology, is largely dependent for its sources of energy and materials on accumulations in the earth which date from its geological past. In a few centuries, or at most a few thousand years, these are likely to be exhausted, and either man will fall back on a more primitive technology or he will have to advance to knowledge well beyond what he has now. Fortunately there are signs that this transition to a stable high-level technology may be accomplished, but we certainly cannot claim that it has been accomplished up to date.

A fourth possible trap may lie in the very nature of man itself. If the dangers and difficulties which now beset man are eliminated in postcivilized society and if he has no longer anything to fear but death itself, will not his creativity be diminished and may he not dissipate his energies in a vast ennui and boredom? This is a question which cannot be answered. But it lurks uneasily at the back of all optimistic statements about the long-run future of man. . . .

The Threat of Nuclear War (1962)

In October, 1962 American reconnaissance uncovered Russian plans to establish offensive rocket bases in Cuba. Alleged to be "defensive" by Soviet leaders, the launching sites nonetheless had within their potential target area an extensive segment of the North American continent. In the end, the Russians chose to back down and disarmed their installations. The tension of that moment is recalled, however, in this article, written in a news magazine a year after the confrontation. "The Cuba Crisis: Nuclear War Was Hours Away," *Newsweek* (October 28, 1963), pp. 24–25. Copyright Newsweek, Inc. October 1963.

Far down in the gray concrete vitals of the Pentagon, in the U.S. Air Force's "War Room," a handful of red-eyed, weary, uniformed men sat on a balcony, stared down into a plastic-trimmed nightmare of electronics, and pondered the fate of the world. Panoramic screens scanned U.S. outposts around the globe, bulb-clustered boxes showed troop movements, lighted maps flashed with blobs of color, each indicating a nuclear warplane or missile aimed and "cocked" at millions of human beings who lived on in ignorance of their peril.

The target: the Soviet Union. Detonation: hours away.

That was just one year ago this week. The U.S. and the U.S.S.R. stood frighteningly close to war, the world terrifyingly close to destruction. It was the first all-out nuclear confrontation in history. From the perspective of a year later, it appears to have brought the world from deathbed to plausible hope for a peaceful future. And a year later, the handful of men who had their forefingers pointed at the ultimate buttons could relive—in hitherto undisclosed detail—the critical week when Russia mounted the missiles on Cuba, when President Kennedy ordered that island sealed off from the world, when Russia's Premier Nikita Khrushchev was told to order the rockets out—or else.

"When I went down to the command post, I had a feeling I never had before," an Air Force captain recalled. "I wondered if I would see my wife and kids again. I felt we were near to war."

The captain, in that dread week of Oct. 22, 1962, descended the escalator to the Pentagon's lowest level, walked down concrete steps, and wound through deep corridors to Room BD 927. He pushed a buzzer, spoke into the microphone in a two-way mirror, and, identified, pushed through the green door that leads to the War Room.

There, he found himself on the balcony overlooking the controls and five translucent screens. Each of them showed major commands in a state of DEFCON 2—the symbol for the last combat step short of DEFCON 1, or Defense Condition 1, which is war. Among the officers who sat in the eighteen softly upholstered, beige cloth-covered chairs was Gen. Curtis E. LeMay, Air Force Chief of Staff, who usually stays in touch from a fourth-floor office. The captain's apprehensions, in short, were well based.

For the 30-odd officers, a general's star was the only sure ticket to a seat. They could see a small box which relayed radar readings of BMEWS (Ballistic Missile Early Warning System) from stations across the top of North America; flashing numbers would count Russian missiles fired at the U.S. and predict their toll. Nearby hung a U.S. map, where NUDETS (Nuclear Detection System) would show in red dots wherever a nuclear weapon might strike.

Down on the floor of the room itself, a team of seven officers and sergeants had control of the push buttons—the lines that carried the word from these world-wide detectors to the President, the Secretary of Defense, and the Joint Chiefs of Staff. They dressed the part.

One officer and one sergeant carried holstered .38-caliber pistols, bonehandled, snub-nosed weapons intended only to shoot any member of the team who might crumble under pressure and threaten to set off war on his own panicky impulse. Two officers wore keys around their necks, each affixed to plastic tags.

Should President Kennedy himself sound the Klaxon signal for DEFCON 1, they would remove the keys, unlock separate padlocks on a red box, 2 feet by 6 inches, take out 5-inch-square plastic bags, tear them open, and pull out the same typewritten message to all Strategic Air Commands from Alaska to Guam, Spain to England. The coded message: go to war.

"We came mighty near hearing the Klaxon horn," an officer caught up in the War Room nightmare said last week. "If Khrushchev had made the wrong move and fired any of his MRBM's [medium-range ballistic missiles] at this country, SAC would have gone in."

The controls in the War Room that week showed that 90 B-52s packed with 25- and 50-megaton bombs were constantly criss-crossing the Atlantic, awaiting the order to go. On the ground, 550 more loaded B-52s, 800 lighter B-47s, and 70 faster and newer B-58 Hustlers were standing by. Eight Polaris submarines in the North Atlantic had their 128 missiles trained on Russia. In the Mediterranean and China seas, Sixth and Seventh Fleet aircraft carriers had nuclear bombers poised for take-off. Across the U.S., 102 Atlas, 54 Titan, and twelve Minuteman ICBM's [intercontinental ballistic missiles] sat on their launching pads.

SAC bombers, while circling the seas, also watched for Soviet ships heading for Cuba. "We surprised hell out of the Navy by furnishing not only the longitude and latitude but the course and speed and the name of the ships," said an Air Force officer.

While this awesome nuclear air armada assembled, other services too were one step short of war at DEFCON 2. The Army had put

Strategic Air Command planes refueling in air. Jet-to-jet refueling means that a 650-mph heavy bomber with nuclear bombs can remain on course and at operational speeds and altitudes longer.

together the biggest invasion force since World War II, rushing about 100,000 men to the Southeast, principally Florida, where they could be ferried the 90 miles to Cuba. Besides those 100,000, said Gen. Earle G. Wheeler, Army Chief of Staff, he had 10,000 to 20,000 more for backup support. The Florida buildup included the First Armored Division, rushed from Fort Hood, Texas, by rail and air; and the Peninsula Base Command collected from the Second Logistical Command; the 82nd and 101st Airborne Divisions, and two infantry divisions.

Even before President Kennedy spoke on Oct. 22, proclaiming the quarantine of Cuba, the Army had put on air defense the Hawk missile battalion and its launchers in Key West. The First Armored began moving the next day.

The Navy broke off exercises at sea, stationing 183 warships manned by 85,000 men along a 2,100-mile quarantine line to watch for Soviet ships. Marines, thousands-strong, also moved into Florida and the Fifth Marine Brigade, plus a battalion landing team, hastened to the defense of Guantanamo, the U.S. naval base on the flank of Cuba herself.

Nor was the Soviet Union unarmed. The medium-range (1,200 miles) missiles on Cuba were all but ready to go. The intermediate-range (2,200) missiles probably would have been ready in early December. U.S. military experts fully expected the Russian threat from Cuba before Christmas.

And then Khrushchev flinched. The drooping but still vigilant men in the War Room could draw a deep, shuddering breath; the world could live for yet a while. . . .

As McNamara [Secretary of Defense] put it: "We confronted the Soviet Union with nuclear war over the issue of the offensive weapons and forced them to remove the offensive weapons rather than engage in nuclear war. This was our purpose, it was our objective, we accomplished it."

Philip Hauser: The Population Explosion

Philip M. Hauser (1909–), American sociologist and demographer, is well-known for his work on the problems of population and urbanization. Here he reviews population growth in the past, examines recent trends in world population, and suggests the prospects for the future. From "The Population of the World: Recent Trends and Prospects" by Philip Hauser, copyright 1964 by Philip M. Hauser. From *Population: The Vital Revolution* edited by Ronald Freeman. Reprinted by permission of Doubleday & Company, Inc.

Knowledge about population in the past, the present, and the future enables a person to see himself as an element in world population. It provides perspective of one's self in relation to fellow men in the same manner as astronomy provides one with perspective about this earth as an element in the solar system, the galaxy, and the universe. . . .

Although the first complete census of mankind has yet to be taken, it is possible to reconstruct, within reasonable error limits, the estimated population of the world from the end of the neolithic period (the new stone age) in Europe, 8000 to 7000 B.C. World population at that time is estimated to have been some ten million; and perhaps was as low as

five million. At the beginning of the Christian era, the population of the world probably numbered between 200 and 300 million. At the beginning of the modern era, 1650, world population had reached about 500 million. In 1962, world population totaled three billion. A relatively simple analysis of these numbers discloses that an enormous increase in the rate of world population growth has occurred, especially during the past three centuries. . . .

The present rate of world population growth cannot possibly persist for very long into the future. As a matter of fact, in the long run, given a finite globe and excluding the possibilities of exporting human population to outer space, any rate of population growth would in time saturate the globe and exhaust space itself. In the long run, man will necessarily be faced with the problem of restricting his rate of increase to maintain some balance between his numbers and the finite dimensions of this planet.

It is possible to quickly summarize the remarkable acceleration of his growth rate which man has experienced. It took most of the millennia of man's habitation of this planet to produce a population as great as one billion persons, which was not achieved until about 1850. To produce a population of two billion persons required only an additional 75 years which was achieved by 1925. To reach a population of three billion persons, which was the total in 1962, required only an additional 37 years. Continuation of the trend would produce a fourth billion in about 15 years and a fifth billion in less than an additional ten years.

Analyses of this type have led the student of population to use emotional and unscientific language on occasion to describe popula-

tion developments. Such a phrase as "the population explosion" is admittedly non-scientific language, but it serves to emphasize the dramatic increase in man's rate of growth and to call attention to its many implications. . . .

This spectacular acceleration in growth rate may be traced to the impact of the many technological, economic, and social changes which are summarized by the phrases "agricultural revolution," "technological revolution," "commercial revolution," and "industrial revolution," climaxed by "scientific revolution." The profound changes in man's way of life generated by these developments produced the "demographic revolution." More specifically, the combination of developments accelerated the rate of population growth because it brought about a sharp and unprecedented decline in death rates, with a corresponding great increase in average length of life.

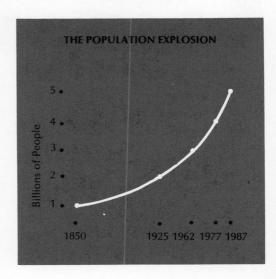

THE POPULATION EXPLOSION

Two Tanzanian doctors offer free medical services at the side of the main road near Bunju, twenty miles north of Dar-Es-Salaam.

first was the general increase in level of living resulting both from technological advances and from comparatively long periods of peace and tranquility by reason of the emergence of relatively powerful, stable central governments. The second major factor accounting for the decrease in mortality was the achievement of environmental sanitation and improved personal hygiene. During the nineteenth century great strides were made in purifying food and water and improving personal cleanliness, which contributed materially to the elimination of parasitic and infectious diseases. The third major factor is of course to be found in the great and growing contribution of modern medicine, enhanced by the recent progress in chemotherapy and the insecticides. . . .

At the present time, a number of the industrialized countries of the world, largely European nations and Japan, are growing relatively slowly at rates which would double their populations in from 50 to 100 years. Some of the industrialized countries, including the United States, the Soviet Union, Australia, New Zealand, Canada, and Argentina are growing somewhat more rapidly, at rates which would double their populations in about 30 to 40 years, about the average for the world.

The less developed areas of the world, containing two-thirds of the total population, are now the most rapidly growing regions of the world. They are increasing at rates which would double their population in 20 to 40 years. . . .

By the end of the century, Latin America will have the most rapidly growing population, more than trebling to reach a total of 650 million from a level of about 200 million. Asia and Africa will each increase by 2.5-fold.

Precise information is not available, but in all probability the expectation of life at birth in Egypt, Greece, and Rome around the beginning of the Christian era was probably not above 30 years. During the first half century of the modern era (1650 to 1700), life expectation at birth in Western Europe and North America was at a level of about 33 years. . . . By 1900, life expectation at birth in Western Europe and North America had reached a level of 45 to 50 years. By 1960, another 20 years of life had been gained, and life expectation in Western Europe and North America reached a level of about 70 years.

Although some changes in birth rates were also involved, it is clear that the major factor in the great acceleration of population growth first evident in Europe and areas of European settlement, was the decline in the death rate. Three factors contributed to this decline. The

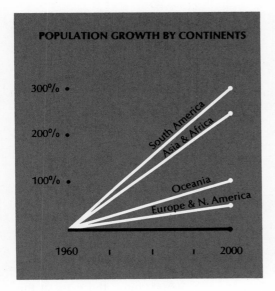

POPULATION GROWTH BY CONTINENTS

300% •

200% •

100% •

South America
Asia & Africa

Oceania

Europe & N. America

1960 | | | 2000

Africa's population will rise from 250 million in 1960 to 660 million by 2000. Asia's population will increase from 1.7 billion to 4.3 billion. The slowest growing regions of the world between now and the end of this century will be the industrialized areas. North America and Europe will each increase by about 50 per cent while Oceania will less than double during the remainder of this century. The population of Europe will total about one billion in 2000, compared with 640 million in 1960; that of North America will number 330 million in 2000, as compared with 200 million in 1960. Oceania will have about 30 million persons in 2000 as compared with 17 million in 1960. . . .

The world's population is unevenly distributed over the surface of the globe. About two-thirds of the people on the earth live on about seven per cent of the land area. There are four areas of great population concentration—eastern Asia, south central Asia, Europe, and northeastern United States. This distribution of the world's peoples is, of course, the result of the adjustment of population to world resources that has taken place over the millennia.

Differences in rates of population growth, past and projected, alter the distribution of the world's population by regions. In 1650, Asia contained 61 per cent of the world's people. Africa and Europe each had 18 per cent, and the remaining continents, North America, Latin America, and Oceania combined, had less than three per cent of the world's total population. By 1950, the effects

DISTRIBUTION OF WORLD POPULATION

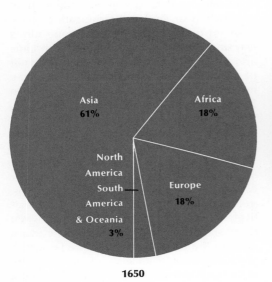

1650

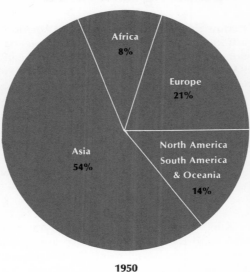

1950

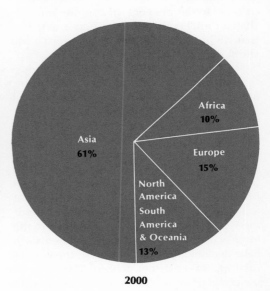

2000

of the demographic transition in Europe and the areas colonized by Europe were clearly visible. Asia's share of the world's total population had shrunk to 54 per cent and Africa's to only eight per cent of the total. Europe's share had increased 23 per cent, and the areas of European colonization (North America, South America, and Oceania) had increased their share of the world's total to over 14 per cent.

Differential growth rates during the remainder of the century, reflecting the demographic transition in the less developed areas, will reverse the previous pattern of change in population distribution. The economically less developed continents—Asia, Africa, and Latin America—will increase their share of the world's total population at the expense of North America and Europe. Asia's share of the world's total will increase about 62 per cent, Latin America's to over nine per cent, Africa's to close to ten per cent. In contrast Europe's share of total population will decrease to less than 15 per cent, while North America's will shrink to less than five per cent.

At mid-twentieth century, the industrialized continents—North America, Europe, and Oceania—contained over 30 per cent of the world's total population. The less developed continents—Asia, Africa, and Latin America—contained the remainder. In the course of the twentieth century, the proportion of the world's population in the less developed continents will have increased from less than two-thirds in 1900 to about four-fifths by 2000. Conversely, the share of the world's total population contained in the more economically developed continents will have declined from 36 per cent of the world's total in 1900 to 21 per cent in 2000.

Acceleration in the rate of the world's population growth is still under way. But it is clear that even present rates of world population growth cannot continue for very long into the future. Man is the only culture-building animal on the face of the earth. He not only adapts to environment but creates environment in which to adapt. In developing his culture and precipitating the technological, industrial, and scientific revolutions, man has profoundly altered the rhythm of his own reproduction. He has destroyed the equilibrium between the birth rate and the death rate which existed for most of the millennia he has been on this globe. . . .

Harlow Shapley: The Human Response to an Expanding Universe

Harlow Shapley (1885–   ), famed American astronomer who has received numerous national and international prizes for his scientific discoveries and was for long years professor of astronomy at Harvard, reveals the modesty of the discerning scientist as in this article he reflects on what man has learned over the centuries and what role he plays in the universe. Pp. 7–9, 33–35, 71–81, of *The View from a Distant Star* by Harlow Shapley, © 1963 by Basic Books, Inc., Publishers, New York.

I

From where we stand our Milky Way is a mess, with dense star clouds, dust clouds, and aggregations of gas all confusing the picture. Also, these various objects are in motions which are both smooth and turbulent. Further, we on the rotating earth are in motion around the sun, which is in motion with respect to the neighboring stars, which are participating with us in a long circulatory motion about the center of the galaxy. Confronted with these complicated motions, we cannot give a clear and conclusive description of the central nucleus, or a value of its distance that is correct within 5 per cent. There is an uncertainty of 10 per cent or more in the measurement of our speed around the galactic center, and similar error in our value of the duration of one revolution. For the time being we settle on a speed of some 200 miles a second (for us and the neighboring stars), and a revolution time of 200 million years. Finally, we put the total mass of our great spiral galaxy at something like 200 billion times the mass of our sun, which in turn is more than 300,000 times the mass of the earth.

All these superlatives are inserted without explanation or apology to indicate that we have, in studies of the universe, gone a long way since 1917 when we first gazed with some astonishment at the evidence that the center of our "universe"—our galaxy among the myriads of galaxies—is apparently more than 30,000 light-years from our little local abode. When someone asks me now, "What are you doing for the good of the world?", I ask, "What do you mean by 'world'?". . .

After seven years of work with large instruments on questions concerning the globular star clusters—their structure, relationships, stellar content—I realized that we were relatively more ignorant about them than when I had started my investigation. I had added more to the unknown than to the known. A score of technical papers had been written, but I could not catch up with the unfolding scheme. I found problems we had not known were in existence. Even now, many years later, I remain chagrined that we are still ignorant, without even good leading hypotheses, concerning the origin, dynamics, and destiny of these great stellar systems. It was something of a jolt to discover "how much the unknown transcends the what we know" (in Longfellow's words) and to realize that it will ever be so, unless there should come favorable mutations in the human intellect toward greater wisdom and comprehension. With our present neural equipment we are not able to know everything about anything, and doubtless there are vast fields of the partly knowable that we do not even understand well enough to realize that we are ignorant about them. . . .

Two or three millennia ago, when early man began to explore and grope for answers to astronomical puzzles, the primeval human vanity and anthropocentric philosophy had to give way to geocentrism. That earth-center theory was a bit complicated, and eventually the simpler sun-centered concept (heliocentrism) took over. It was simpler for the sincere scholar, though perhaps not simple for the unthinking man, wrapped up in self-esteem. There was even a bit of resistance on the part of the thoughtful, because change naturally incites resistance. For example, in its early days Harvard College stood by the geocentric interpretation for more than a century after the appearance of *De Revolutionibus Orbium Coelestium*.

The Copernican heliocentric cosmogony, as a successor of geocentrism, prevailed for more than three centuries and widened its range. The sun came to be considered central not only in its own planetary family but also in the whole world of stars. Central, but scarcely a ruling body, for the early telescopes had revealed millions of stars, and there was no good evidence that they were relatively small, or weak, or easily manageable. Admittedly the sun might not control the stellar universe, but the presumed central position of the sun and its planets supported man's claim to some vague cosmic pre-eminence.

The heliocentric hypothesis still stands firm so far as the local planets are concerned. But in 1917 the place of the sun with respect to the trillions of stars in the Milky Way and outside came under closer scrutiny. The powerful photographic telescopes were rapidly piling up revelations about this overall system of stars and nebulae. In the preceding decades, researches had suggested to a few that the sun was not exactly dead-center, but still it seemed to occupy the central position in the Milky Way, for its millions of stars formed a continuous circular band of light around us. Moreover, the numbers of stars were found to fall off with distance in nearly all directions, thus further supporting the suggestion of a central position for the sun and its planets.

Then came suspicions. When we learned how to estimate their distances, we found that the globular star clusters were concentrated in and around the southern Milky Way star clouds; novae (exploding stars) were likewise more frequent in southern Sagittarius, and so were bright nebulosities, super-luminous variable stars, and star clouds.

These researches ended, after a few brief struggles with a few cautious conservatives. . . . The sun is no longer thought to be in a central position. Rather, the center of the Milky Way galaxy is now known to be some 30,000 light-years distant.

The displacement of the sun and earth from positional importance, the sudden relegating of man to the edge of one ordinary galaxy in an explorable universe of billions of galaxies—that humiliating (or inspiring) development is or should be the death knell of anthropocentrism. It should incite orienting thoughts by modern philosophers and theologians, and perhaps it has and will. . . .

II

Fish or *Homo*—that is the question. Which animal type will be here 10,000 years from now; which will more likely fall the victim of fate or folly? The answer, of course, is too obvious, painfully obvious. The fish have been here several hundred million years; man, but a few hundred thousand. The oceans are stable enough in their salinity, temperature, and food supplies to suit indefinitely a thousand species of fish. It is difficult to imagine a way of curtailing the life of that class of animals without complete disruption of the planet, or the poisoning of the plankton food in all the seven seas. But 10,000 years is a pretty long time for *Homo*. His structure and social manners do not make him a good insurance risk. How will he eventually be dispossessed?

What Opposes Man's Survival?

About three-fourths of the earth's crust is under the oceans; the remainder protrudes above the water level to various heights. There is some advance and recession of the shore lines. The mountains rise up through the wrinkling of the earth's crust, and are worn down by the winds and rains. In general, however, the continents seem to be pretty stable over geological eras. Extrapolating into the future, we should say that it is extremely unlikely that man will be drowned out of existence by the rising sea or desiccated by lack of water. A man-eliminating deluge is not in the cards, nor is a worldwide, totally lethal drought.

Human ignorance of the universe was lessened by an infinitesimal degree when two American astronauts set foot on the moon on July 20, 1969. The moon landing is, nonetheless, witness to modern man's never-ending quest for the unknown and to the high level of his scientific achievement in the twentieth century. In this scene, recorded by television camera, Edwin Aldrin walks on the dusty surface of the moon in his white space suit. The Lunar Exploration Module, in which he and his colleague Neil Armstrong landed, is reflected in his face visor, as are Armstrong, the American flag, and the television camera itself.

Let us take a wider view and consider sketchily the project of a complete extermination of the human race. In what manner might we, as agents of Nature (or the devil), devise the elimination of *Homo sapiens*? First we set a time limit for the operation—not too short, not too long. Let us examine the probability of man not being on the earth's surface 10,000 years from now.

We begin with macrocosmic instruments for eradication. What is the possibility or probability of a collision of the earth with a star? If the earth or even the sun were struck by one of those stellar masses, our goal would be achieved: terrestrial biology would be finished. But the stars are so widely separated that collisions are out of the question in our chosen short time interval of 10,000 years. The probabilities are overwhelmingly against trouble with stars.

Appreciating that escape, let us then ask about the sun cooling down enough to freeze us out, or blowing up into a nova and incinerating the planet. No likelihood at all, or at least highly improbable, for the sun appears to be a relatively stable type of star; its radiation has been steady for many hundreds of millions of years. Its hydrogen content is ample to supply energy, produced by atomic fusion, for a million times 10,000 years.

Safe from annihilation by stars and sun, should we fear some misbehavior of the earth, such as its abandoning orbital regularity and getting too near the sun or too far away? The answer is No. Our observations and mathematical analyses show that the planetary orbits are completely stable over time intervals such as we are here considering. The earth moves in what is practically a vacuum, in a nearly circular path around the sun, and neither its daily rotation nor its yearly revolution will change perceptibly in the allotted hundred centuries. (We can of course adapt ourselves to the coming and going of the ice sheets, such as those that occurred in the northern hemisphere during the past hundred thousand years.)

Already we have mentioned the relative constancy in the height of continents and depths of oceans. Terrestrial life has readily adjusted itself to the ups and downs of land and sea in the past million years, and in the next 10,000 years the slow-moving mountains and shore lines will present little danger.

Poison the atmosphere with an over-abundance of volcanic gases and make it unbreathable by land animals, including man? Well, such has not happened in the past 500 million years and it is certainly unlikely in the next 10,000; the earth is gradually getting over its eruptive birth-pangs.

Outer space presents some dangers—noxious gases, meteors, and cosmic rays. But the poisoning of our atmosphere by interstellar gas and dust is a very long chance. The gas in space is mostly non-poisonous hydrogen and helium, and its distribution is so thin that our own nitrogen-oxygen atmosphere shields us completely. It protects us also from the tiny, high-speed interplanetary meteors and from lethal radiations.

To summarize the progress so far in this project of eliminating man (and other animals) from the earth's surface, we get no likely help from the stars, from interstellar dust, from the sun's radiation or its lack, from the deviation of the earth from its present orbit, from deadly climates, or from the chemistry of the earth's land, air, and water.

We turn to the biological sciences. The large beasts are no longer a threat, nor, in fact, are any of the plant and animal forms. We are now competent also to cope with bacteria, viruses, and the like, at least sufficiently well to keep our species going, even if millions perished in some wild epidemic.

Of course some worldwide disaster could happen, coming to us anywhere from star crash to infective protein, but the chances are heavily against it—less than one chance in a million, I would surmise, for trouble with astronomical bodies, less than one in a thousand for serious difficulties with climate, volcanoes, worldwide floods, or desiccation, and perhaps less than one chance in a hundred for planet-wide incurable diseases.

(Even if 99 per cent of the world's population of Homo sapiens should fall foul of sudden disaster, there would yet be left more than 25 million humans rapidly reseeding the earth; therefore the total-elimination effort would have been a failure. Spoiling a culture or civilization is one thing, and perhaps not too arduous; complete eradication of a widespread organic species is quite another, and vastly more difficult.)

In other words, man seems to have a healthy prospect, a long security from stars, climate, and terminating germs. But wait! I have not named the real danger, and it is bleakly ominous, as everyone in these days agrees. The danger is man himself. He is his own worst enemy. He is acquiring tools and studying techniques which might solve the problem of attaining complete elimination of Homo from the planet Earth.

STUDY QUESTIONS

1. What marks off the present as a new stage in history according to Boulding? What problems (traps) does he see as influencing the shape of postcivilization?

2. In what sense was the Cuban missile crisis a turning-point in postwar history? Was the success of the showdown predictable? How dangerous is what Boulding calls the "war trap"?

3. What has been responsible for the acceleration of the birth rate? How has it affected the position of the West in the world? What does it portend for the future?

4. How has science altered man's sense of his place in the universe? To what extent does nature threaten him with disaster?